STAFF LIBRARY
RAMPTON HOSPITAL

Butterworths New Law Guide Mental Capacity Act 2005

Personal Welfare Decisions

KV-314-734

Aswini Weereratne
Doughty Street Chambers, London

Sally Hatfield
Doughty Street Chambers, London (and Byrom Chambers, Manchester)

Ulele Burnham
Doughty Street Chambers, London

Alison Gerry
Doughty Street Chambers, London

WITHDRAWN
FROM
DMH STAFF LIBRARY

WITHDRAWN
FROM
DMH STAFF LIBRARY

Members of the LexisNexis Group worldwide

United Kingdom	LexisNexis, a Division of Reed Elsevier (UK) Ltd, Halsbury House, 35 Chancery Lane, London, WC2A 1EL, and London House, 20–22 East London Street, Edinburgh EH7 4BQ
Austria	LexisNexis Verlag ARD Orac GmbH & Co KG, Vienna
Benelux	LexisNexis Benelux, Amsterdam
Canada	LexisNexis Canada, Markham, Ontario
China	LexisNexis China, Beijing and Shanghai
France	LexisNexis SA, Paris
Germany	LexisNexis Deutschland GmbH, Munster
Hong Kong	LexisNexis Hong Kong, Hong Kong
India	LexisNexis India, New Delhi
Italy	Giuffrè Editore, Milan
Japan	LexisNexis Japan, Tokyo
Malaysia	Malayan Law Journal Sdn Bhd, Kuala Lumpur
New Zealand	LexisNexis NZ Ltd, Wellington
Poland	Wydawnictwo Prawnicze LexisNexis Sp, Warsaw
Singapore	LexisNexis Singapore, Singapore
South Africa	LexisNexis Butterworths, Durban
USA	LexisNexis, Dayton, Ohio

© Reed Elsevier (UK) Ltd 2008

Published by LexisNexis

All rights reserved. No part of this publication may be reproduced in any material form (including photocopying or storing it in any medium by electronic means and whether or not transiently or incidentally to some other use of this publication) without the written permission of the copyright owner except in accordance with the provisions of the Copyright, Designs and Patents Act 1988 or under the terms of a licence issued by the Copyright Licensing Agency Ltd, Saffron House, 6–10 Kirby Street, London EC1N 8TS. Applications for the copyright owner's written permission to reproduce any part of this publication should be addressed to the publisher.

Warning: The doing of an unauthorised act in relation to a copyright work may result in both a civil claim for damages and criminal prosecution.

Crown copyright material is reproduced with the permission of the Controller of HMSO and the Queen's Printer for Scotland. Parliamentary copyright material is reproduced with the permission of the Controller of Her Majesty's Stationery Office on behalf of Parliament. Any European material in this work which has been reproduced from EUR-lex, the official European Communities legislation website, is European Communities copyright.

A CIP Catalogue record for this book is available from the British Library.

ISBN: 9781405725422

Typeset by Letterpart Ltd, Reigate, Surrey

Printed in the UK by CPI William Clowes Beccles NR34 7TL

Visit LexisNexis at www.lexisnexis.co.uk

Foreword

In 1991 the Law Commission embarked upon a review of the law relating to 'mentally incapacitated adults' the main thrust of which withstood the vagaries of the legislative process to become the Mental Capacity Act 2005. Thus England and Wales at last acquired a specific legislative framework to provide for decision making on behalf of adults who lack capacity. The passing of the 2005 Act marked a significant step towards the protection of a highly vulnerable section of the population. However, even as it was evolving the Mental Capacity Bill was over taken by events. The judgment of the European Court of Human Rights in *HL v United Kingdom* made it abundantly clear that the new legislative structure would fail to meet the UK's Convention obligations with regard to the deprivation of liberty. Caught inexplicably unprepared the government's response has been to use the Mental Health Act 2007 to introduce amendments to the 2005 Act in order to provide a structure for the deprivation of liberty using Mental Capacity Act powers. Thus, in addition to the Mental Capacity Act and its still to be completed Code of Practice, we now have the amendments introduced by the Mental Health Act 2007 to both the Mental Capacity Act 2005 and the Mental Health Act 1983, the new draft Mental Health Act Code of Practice, and a draft Addendum to the Mental Capacity Act Code of Practice.

Against such a baffling array of legislation a comprehensive guide to the 2005 Act explaining the recent amendments and setting them in context was desperately needed. With this book Aswini Weereratne and colleagues have more than filled that gap. They have brought extensive practical experience and impressive analytical skills to the task of understanding and explaining the workings of the 2005 Act and its complex set of relationships with the Mental Health Act, the common law and the European Convention on Human Rights. It is a wonderfully authoritative yet accessible resource.

The book largely follows the structure of the Act and provides lucid explanation accompanied by frequent reference to the Code of Practice and illustrative case studies. Some aspects of the Act may present particular difficulties for health care practitioners and the book is full of useful clarification, as in relation to the obligations of clinicians with regard to advance decisions and the precise scope of the protections provided for acts in connection with care of treatment. It also tackles some of the more conceptual issues raised by the Act. There is a particularly interesting discussion of the role of the diagnostic threshold and Chapters 2 and 8 provide a comprehensive analysis of the elements of capacity and their application to particular patient groups.

But the book is not limited to a discussion of the 2005 Act in isolation. Its greatest strength lies in the authors' wide knowledge and experience of the broader context within which the Act must operate. Most notably perhaps Chapter 17 presents a clear and very thoughtful account of the requirements of the Human Rights Act and the European Convention, together with other international instruments. One question of particular relevance to those operating the Mental Capacity Act must be the extent to which private nursing homes are directly bound by the obligations contained within the European Convention. To some extent the case law is still developing here but Chapter 17 provides an excellent analysis of current judicial thinking. Also of considerable practical assistance is the discussion of welfare decisions in Chapter 7. The relationship between the welfare powers in the 2005 Act and the powers contained within both the Mental Health Act and community care legislation is described with great clarity. The chapters on personal information and general litigation also stray beyond the confines of the 2005 Act and present relevant principles from other areas of the law which might not be so familiar to health care professionals.

Finally, the book has to grapple with the aftermath of *HL v United Kingdom*, the question of the deprivation of liberty and the relationship between the Mental Capacity Act and the Mental Health Act. Here it is outstanding. With exceptional rigour Chapter 9 analyses the evolving case law on deprivation of liberty and draws out what principles it can to guide the practitioners who have to operate the scheme. Chapter 16 then follows up with a comprehensive explanation of the fraught relationship between Mental Health Act and Mental Capacity Act powers. Between them these two chapters both lay bare the fundamental conceptual difficulties that underlie the relationship between the two legislative schemes and do the best possible job to explain how that relationship is intended to work in practice. It is a formidable achievement.

In short this book is an essential text for all those who hope to understand the 2005 Act and its complex context. It is fascinating reading and I strongly recommend it.

Genevra Richardson
Professor of Law, King's College London

March 2008

Preface

This book is about personal welfare decision-making for incapacitated adults under the Mental Capacity Act 2005 which came into force on 1 October 2007. The Act's protracted legislative history is described in Chapter 1. However, it is has already been amended in an important respect by the Mental Health Act 2007 which introduces deprivation of liberty powers for the Court of Protection, and an authorisation process for responsible authorities designed to fill the legislative gap for compliant, but incapacitated people who need to be detained for treatment and care. This gap was identified as an article 5(1)(e) and (4) violation in *HL v United Kingdom* (2005) 40 EHRR 32, the so called 'Bournewood gap'. The implementation of these provisions of the MHA 2007 has been delayed amidst concerns about their unwieldy and impractical nature, and they are now due to come into force in April 2009. The subordinate legislation supporting them remains in draft form, but the extended consultation process ended on 24 January 2008.

The MCA draws together two separate jurisdictions providing one coherent set of principles which enable decision-making for incapacitated adults. It also creates a new Court of Protection the functions of which are tailored to secure that purpose. The first of the two jurisdictions it combines is the inherent jurisdiction of the High Court. The inherent jurisdiction has historically stepped in to the breach where there was no specific provision relating to health and welfare decisions and has developed apace over the last 20 years since it was effectively rediscovered for this purpose by the House of Lords in *Re F* [1990]. More recently it has been used to fill a gap in the legislation prior to the MCA coming into force, by authorising deprivations of liberty in welfare cases (see paras 1.4 and 7.8 in particular). However, the role of the inherent jurisdiction would appear to be far from usurped, and the Court of Appeal has recently and robustly confirmed that it is not ousted by the MCA and will still be relevant where any gap in the legislation may exist: *KC and NNC v City of Westminster Social and Community Services Department and IC (protected party by his litigation friend the OS)* [2008] EWCA Civ 198. There remain difficult areas of decision-making, for example, for capacitated but vulnerable adults, which have drawn upon its protective orders: *Re SA (Vulnerable Adults with Capacity: Marriage)* [2006] 1 FLR 867. Its use in this fashion is pragmatic and ultimately beneficent. Declaratory relief has developed as a flexible remedy and so its use in this context seems untramelled, but this development has not been wholly embraced and needs to be approached with some care and principle.

The second jurisdiction absorbed by the MCA is that of the old Court of Protection under part VII of the Mental Health Act 1983 (now repealed). Also repealed is the Enduring Powers of Attorney Act 1985. This jurisdiction encompassed decisions regarding finances and property and affairs. This book does not cover this aspect of the new jurisdiction save where it overlaps with welfare decisions, such as for lasting powers of attorney which can now be used in respect of welfare and financial decisions (Chapter 5).

This is a book intended for legal practitioners in the fields of social welfare, health and mental health predominantly, whether acting on behalf of social services or health authorities or private individuals, but it is hoped that it will also be of use to all professionals and carers responsible for incapacitated adults. It aims therefore to set the MCA into the context of welfare and health decision-making as broadly as possible and includes for that purpose detailed consideration of the overlap with the MHA 1983 (as amended) at Chapter 16. It also aims to contextualise the reach of the MCA in chapters covering human rights, general civil and criminal litigation, and specific practice areas such as discrimination, prisons and crime.

We are delighted to have the honour of a recommendation from Professor Genevra Richardson whose eminence in public law, mental health and capacity is without parallel.

We are pleased to be able to include the entire MCA Code of Practice and the Court of Protection Rules in the appendices as these are essential to the understanding of the MCA and the new Court of Protection. We also recommend the website of the Public Guardian: www.publicguardian.gov.uk for all the latest forms and Practice Directions.

We apologise for any mistakes in the text for which we alone must take complete responsibility.

Aswini Weereratne

Sally Hatfield

Ulele Burnham

Alison Gerry

April 2008

Authors

Aswini Weereratne
Aswini Weereratne has been in practice at Doughty Street Chambers in London since 1991. Her practice encompasses private and public law cases in the areas of mental health, health and social welfare including mental capacity, institutional abuse, prisons, and community care. She is a part-time Mental Health Review Tribunal chair and consultant editor to Halsbury's Laws, Mental Health volume.

Ulele Burnham
Ulele Burnham's practice cuts across the areas of mental health/mental capacity law, actions related to a wide range of detaining authorities and employment/discrimination law. Before becoming a barrister she was a graduate teaching student in politics at Queen Mary and Westfield College, London and has more recently been an occasional tutor at the London School of Economics in labour law. She is an Executive Committee member of the Discrimination Law Association and takes an active interest in the formulation of policy and legislation related to all aspects of equality provision including in relation to mental disability.

Alison Gerry
Alison Gerry has been in practice at Doughty Street Chambers since 2004. Prior to coming to the bar she worked at the Human Rights Centre at the Essex University and as the Human Rights Adviser to the Consulate Directorate at the Foreign and Commonwealth Office. Her practice encompasses private and public law cases in the areas of mental health, health and social welfare, community care, prisons and actions against the police. She is an Executive Committee member of the Human Rights Lawyers Association.

Sally Hatfield
Sally Hatfield joined Doughty Street in 1990. She now lives in Manchester where she practises in addition from Byrom Street Chambers. Sally has a civil law practice with a specialism in medical law, involving clinical and psychiatric issues arising in the community, hospital or in custody. She sits as a Recorder and is a member of an NHS research ethics committee.

Contents

Chapter 4 – Acts Connected with Care or Treatment and Restraint: Limitations on Civil and Criminal Liability

Chapter 8 – Medical Care

Chapter 9 – Deprivation of Liberty: the Bournewood Safeguards

Chapter 10 – The Court of Protection

Chapter 11 – Court Deputies

Chapter 12 – Public Guardian; Court of Protection Visitors

Chapter 13 – Medical research

Chapter 14 – Personal information: access and disclosure

Chapter 15 – General Litigation

Chapter 16 – The relationship between the MCA 2005 and the MHA 1983

Chapter 17 – Human Rights Standards: Domestic and International

Chapter 18 – Mental Capacity and Specific Practice Areas

Appendices

Table of Statutes

Paragraph references printed in **bold** type indicate where the Statute is set out in part or in full.

Table of Statutory Instruments

References in **bold** type indicate that the Statutory Instrument is set out in part or in full.

Table of Codes of Practice

References in **bold** type indicate that the Code of Practice is set out in part or in full.

Table of European and International Legislation

References in **bold** type indicate that the Legislation is set out in part or in full.

PARA

SECONDARY LEGISLATION

DIRECTIVES

Table of Cases

A

PARA

B

PARA

D

E

F

PARA

F, Re [1990] 2 AC 1, [1989] 2 WLR 1025, [1989] 2 FLR 376, [1989] Fam Law 390, 133 Sol Jo 785, [1989] NLJR 789, sub nom F v West Berkshire Health Authority (Mental Health Act Commission intervening) [1989] 2 All ER 545, 4 BMLR 1, HL 1.11, 3.6, 4.2, 4.4, 5.25, 7.4, 7.16, 7.25, 8.39, 8.51, 10.15, 10.63

F (adult: court's jurisdiction), Re [2001] Fam 38, [2000] 3 WLR 1740, [2000] 3 FCR 30, [2000] 2 FLR 512, [2000] Fam Law 709, 55 BMLR 81, 3 CCL Rep 210, [2000] Lloyd's Rep Med 381, [2000] UKHRR 712, [2000] All ER (D) 870, CA 7.13, 7.26

F (Mental Health Act guardianship), Re [2000] 1 FCR 11, [2000] 1 FLR 192, [2000] Fam Law 18, 51 BMLR 128, [1999] 39 LS Gaz R 38, [1999] All ER (D) 1043, CA 7.37, 7.45

F (adult: court's jurisdiction), Re [2001] Fam 38, [2000] 3 WLR 1740, [2000] 3 FCR 30, [2000] 2 FLR 512, [2000] Fam Law 709, 55 BMLR 81, 3 CCL Rep 210, [2000] All ER (D) 870, [2000] Lloyd's Rep Med 381, [2000] UKHRR 712, CA 7.15, 7.20

F v F (1993) 7 BMLR 135. See GF, Re

F v West Berkshire Health Authority (Mental Health Act Commission intervening). See F, Re [1990] 2 AC 1

Folks v Faizey [2006] EWCA Civ 381, [2006] All ER (D) 83 (Apr) 15.4

G

G (adult patient: publicity), Re [1996] 1 FCR 413, [1995] 2 FLR 528, [1995] Fam Law 677 .... 10.18

G (an adult) (mental capacity: court's jurisdiction), Re [2004] EWHC 2222 (Fam), [2004] All ER (D) 33 (Oct) 7.53, 10.19

GF (mental patient: medical treatment), Re [1991] FCR 786, [1992] 1 FLR 293, [1992] Fam Law 63, [1993] 4 Med LR 77, sub nom F v F 7 BMLR 135 .... 8.38, 10.17

GF (Adult patient: sterilisation: patient's best interest), Re [1992] 2 FLR 389 .... 8.38

Gaskin v United Kingdom (Application 10454/83) (1989) 12 EHRR 36, [1990] 1 FLR 167, ECtHR 14.9, 14.15, 14.24, 14.39, 17.45

Gillick v West Norfolk and Wisbech Area Health Authority [1986] AC 112, [1985] 3 All ER 402, [1985] 3 WLR 830, [1986] 1 FLR 224, [1986] Crim LR 113, 129 Sol Jo 738, 2 BMLR 11, [1985] LS Gaz R 3551, [1985] NLJ Rep 1055, HL 8.15

Glass v United Kingdom (Application 61827/00) (2004) 39 EHRR 15, [2004] 1 FCR 553, [2004] 1 FLR 1019, [2004] Fam Law 410, 77 BMLR 120, (2004) Times, 11 March, [2004] All ER (D) 166 (Mar), ECtHR 2.47, 5.14, 8.21, 17.5, 17.45, 17.55

Guzzardi v Italy (Application 7367/76) (1980) 3 EHRR 333, ECtHR 9.4, 17.28, 18.5

H

H (minors) (sexual abuse: standard of proof), Re [1996] AC 563, [1996] 1 All ER 1, [1996] 2 WLR 8, [1996] 1 FCR 509, [1996] 1 FLR 80, [1996] Fam Law 74, 140 Sol Jo LB 24, HL 6.34, 7.22, 7.50

HE v A Hospital NHS Trust [2003] EWHC 1017 (Fam), [2003] 2 FLR 408, [2003] Fam Law 733 .... 3.1, 3.18

HL v United Kingdom (Application 45508/99) (2005) 40 EHRR 32, 81 BMLR 131, (2004) Times, 19 October, 17 BHRC 418, [2004] All ER (D) 39 (Oct), [2004] ECHR 45508/99, ECtHR 1.4, 6.1, 7.46, 9.2, 9.6, 9.8, 9.9, 9.13, 9.15, 9.75, 10.9

HM v Switzerland (39187/98) (2004) 38 EHRR 17 .... 9.5, 9.6, 9.8

Handyside v United Kingdom (Application 5493/72) (1976) 1 EHRR 737, [1976] ECHR 5493/72, ECtHR 14.43, 17.42

Harwood v Baker (1840) 3 Moo PCC 282 .... 15.1

Henaf v France (2005) 40 EHRR 44 .... 17.26

Herczegfalvy v Austria (Applications 10533/83) (1992) 15 EHRR 437, 18 BMLR 48, ECtHR 4.35, 4.36, 8.20, 17.21, 17.24

R

PARA

PARA

S

T

PARA

Y

Z

Chapter 1

INTRODUCTION

WHAT IS THE MENTAL CAPACITY ACT 2005?

1.1 The Mental Capacity Act 2005 (MCA 2005) gained Royal Assent on 7 April 2005. The preamble states that it is 'an Act to make new provision relating to persons who lack capacity; to establish a superior court of record called the Court of Protection in place of the office of the Supreme Court called by that name; to make provision in connection with the Convention on the International Protection of Adults signed at the Hague on 13 January 2000 and for connected purposes'[1].

The MCA 2005 offers a new and integrated statutory framework for all decision-making on behalf of incapacitated adults relating to their welfare (including health) and property and financial affairs. The scheme it provides applies to all acts of care and treatment, whether by family and friends, or by professional carers or clinicians. The MCA 2005 will apply whether people are being cared for at home or, in residential or other care, or in hospital.

The MCA 2005's provisions supplant the ever expanding inherent jurisdiction of the High Court in so far as it relates to treatment and welfare decisions for incapacitated adults. Part VII of the Mental Health Act 1983 (MHA 1983), which dealt with the old Court of Protection and the Enduring Powers of Attorney Act 1985, both of which were confined to decisions about property and affairs are now repealed. The inherent jurisdiction remains relevant for the protection of vulnerable but capable adults and for detaining incapacitated adults pursuant to their assessed care needs. The latter aspect of the inherent jurisdiction will remain of particular significance until the coming into force of amendments to the MCA 2005 by the Mental Health Act 2007 (MHA 2007) which will permit deprivations of liberty by the Court of Protection or by the Bournewood Safeguards authorisation process (see below).

The MCA 2005 is an important piece of new legislation. It effectively codifies the existing common law in relation to decisions concerning the capacity and best interests of incapacitated adults (over the age of 16). Personal welfare is widely defined to include all aspects of daily care, accommodation, contact, and medical treatment, including serious medical treatment, for example, organ donation, sterilisation and life-sustaining treatment. Advance decisions to refuse medical treatment are now regulated under the MCA 2005, which also creates for the first time a power of attorney empowering the donee to make welfare and health decisions, and establishes a statutory advocacy scheme which must be deployed in certain circumstances on behalf of the incapacitated adult. Powers designed to enable medical research on conditions causing or relating to incapacity are also new. A Code of Practice provides guidance and information for those responsible for the daily care of incapacitated adults.

1 Implementation of the MCA 2005 is dealt with at 1.14.

WHO IS THIS BOOK FOR?

1.2 This book is a guide to the MCA 2005 for health care, mental health and social welfare practitioners. It is primarily aimed at assisting legal practitioners, whether acting for decision-makers or for those who are incapacitated, but it is hoped that it offers assistance to all professionals and carers involved in taking care and treatment decisions for incapacitated people. It outlines the new law and draws on pre-existing law where appropriate to aid interpretation and highlight practice issues. It does not, however, provide any detailed consideration of property and affairs decisions, which are outside its scope.

HOW DOES THE MCA 2005 FIT WITH THE MENTAL HEALTH ACT 1983?

1.3 The MCA 2005 is entirely separate to the MHA 1983 and uses different medical and legal concepts to achieve its ends. It does not deal with the medical treatment of mental disorder for those under the MHA 1983, or the deprivation of liberty of those with mental disorder requiring in-patient treatment. This book does not provide detailed guidance on the MHA 1983[1] for which practitioners should look to other specialised texts.

1 Or as soon to be amended by the Mental Health Act 2007, the majority of which is expected to come into force in October 2008.

Deprivation of liberty[1]

1.4 The MCA 2005 has already been amended by the MHA 2007 which received Royal Assent on 19 July 2007. These amendments are predominantly concerned with providing powers and procedures for authorising the deprivation of liberty of unresisting incapacitated people in response to the judgment of the European Court of Human Rights in *HL v United Kingdom*[2] in which the UK was held to be in violation of Article 5(1) (the right to liberty) of the European Convention on Human Rights (ECHR). The broad basis for this decision was that HL, an incapacitated and compliant man was being effectively deprived of his liberty by a procedure that was not sufficiently certain in law, and which did not offer any of the required safeguards under Article 5(4) ECHR in terms of regular reviews. The amendments made to the MCA 2005 aim, therefore, to close the so-called 'Bournewood gap' in the existing UK legislative scheme. The implementation of these amendments is, at the time of writing, still being consulted upon. They have not been well received, largely by reason of being unwieldy, cumbersome and difficult to understand and to apply. The proposed implementation date for the amendments has been delayed until April 2009[3]. As a result much of the ancillary provision is still in draft form and liable to alteration. Until it is implemented, the MCA 2005 contains no express power enabling deprivation of liberty and no safeguards should a deprivation of liberty result from a welfare order (s 16). It is debatable whether, in the mean time, therefore, authorisations of care plans requiring the detention of an incapacitated person not subject to the MHA 1983 must be sought from the High Court in the exercise of its inherent jurisdiction, or are available under s 16.

1 The legislative history of the MCA 2005 demonstrates that it was not intended to permit deprivations of liberty. It was acknowledged that no Bournewood safeguards existed within it: JCHR 23rd report of session 2003–2004 para 2.12, 2.34–42; 4th report of 2004–2005 paras 4.8 and 4.10, HC Official Report, SC A (Mental Capacity Bill), 21 Oct 2004, cols 121–24, 28 October 2004, cols 249–54, and Joint Scrutiny Report at para 223. The debate took place in the context of ss 5 and 6 and there is no evidence that detention was contemplated under s 16 by order of the court: HC Official Report, SC A (Mental Capacity Bill), 26 October 2004, col 187; 668 HL Official Report (5th series), cols 1250–51, 25 January 2005 (where it was stated that the new MCA 2005 does not change the need to use the doctrine of necessity for Bournewood patients). By new s 4A and 16A, it is now acknowledged that a s 16 welfare order of the Court of Protection may well include a deprivation of liberty. Purists may find it unsatisfactory that by this route it is likely that the Court of Protection will, in advance of amendment, be capable of sanctioning a deprivation of liberty under s 16. This is considered further at Chapter 7 on welfare decisions at 7.8, Chapter 9 and at 10.9 in connection with the court's powers.

2 (2005) 40 EHRR 32.

3 Announced by the Department of Health on 21 November 2007, gateway ref 9114 and briefing sheet gateway ref 8965.

BACKGROUND TO THE MCA 2005

1.5 The MCA 2005 is the culmination of an extensive consultation process initiated by the Law Commission in 1989 (no 185, Cm 800). The Law

Commission's final report is entitled 'Mental Incapacity' and was published in 1995 (Cm 231). The Law Commission consultation papers are:

- Mentally Incapacitated Adults and Decision-Making: An Overview (CP 119);
- Mentally Incapacitated Adults and Decision-Making: A New Jurisdiction (CP 128);
- Mentally Incapacitated Adults and Decision-Making: Medical Treatment and Research (CP 129);
- Mentally Incapacitated Adults and Decision-Making: Public law Protection (CP 130).

The concern of the Law Commission was that specific legislation was needed to aid decision-making on behalf of incapacitated persons which was otherwise dependent on the common law. Case law was felt to be unsystematic and full of gaps and often not reflecting changing societal *mores*.

DRAFTING AND CONSULTATION HISTORY OF THE MCA 2005

1.6 Summary of key events:

- Draft Incapacity Bill attached to Law Commission report of 1995 above.
- 'Who Decides? Making Decisions on Behalf of Mentally Incapacitated Adults', Consultation paper, Cmnd 3803, (1997).
- Government's response: 'Making Decisions: The Government's proposals for making decisions on behalf of mentally incapacitated adults': Cmnd 4465, (1999).
- Draft Mental Incapacity Bill: Cm 5859–1 June 2003.
- Joint Committee on the Draft Mental Incapacity Bill, report published on 28 November 2003, HL Paper 189–1, HC 1083–1, session 2002–03. Largely accepted by the Government. Title changed to 'Mental Capacity Act' as a result.
- Government's response published in February 2004 (Cm 6121).
- June 2004 new Mental Capacity Bill introduced in the Commons.
- Joint Committee on Human Rights reports: session 2002–03, 15th report (HL 149/HC1005); session 2003–04, 23rd report, session 2004–05, 4th report (HL 26/HC 224), session 2007–08, 16th report.
- Mental Health Amendment Bill introduced into Parliament: 16 November 2006.
- Mental Health Act 2007 received Royal Assent: 19 July 2007.

The Joint Committee on the Draft Mental Incapacity Bill (referred to throughout this book as the 'Joint Scrutiny Committee' or the Report as the 'Joint Scrutiny Report') drew attention to numerous shortcomings in the Bill which resulted in its being re-drafted and re-presented to the House of Commons in June 2004 as the 'Mental Capacity Bill'. It endorsed the foundation of the legislative proposals, namely the well-established common law doctrine of necessity and the presumption of capacity, and the aim of replacing common law uncertainties with a comprehensive statutory framework. Amongst its 99 recommendations it recommended that there should be a set of principles on the face of the MCA 2005 (now s 1)[1] and that there should be an independent advocacy service to safeguard against exploitation and abuse. It is probably right to say that the resulting IMCA service does not in fact go as far as the Committee envisaged. It agreed that 'no list of "best interest" factors can ever be comprehensive or applicable in all situations'[2]. What the MCA 2005 provides therefore is a 'checklist of common factors' to be considered in all cases.

On introducing the re-worked Mental Capacity Bill to the House of Commons in October 2004 the Minister said:

> 'The Bill will affect everyone in this country. Nearly 750,000 people have dementia. At some point, 1 per cent of the population will suffer from schizophrenia and 5 per cent from depression or serious bipolar disease. More than 5 million people in England and Wales are carers for people who lack mental capacity. All those people, and many others, may need decisions to be made on their behalf, or need to make decisions on behalf of someone else.'[3]

Other conditions giving rise to incapacity, or potentially doing so, discussed in Parliament included: autism, neurone disease, learning difficulties, persistent vegetative state, Alzheimer's disease, brain injury (including those injured as a result of a road traffic accident)[4].

The Government accepted the majority of the recommendations made by the Joint Scrutiny Committee (see above). Significantly, the name was changed from 'incapacity' to 'capacity' in order to emphasise the focus on enablement, a set of key principles was included within the MCA 2005 (s 1), and the protection of those caring for and treating incapacitated persons on a daily basis was clarified (ss 5 and 6). Emphasis was placed by the Government on the fact that individuals should be assumed to be capable of making decisions and helped to make them wherever possible. The Code of Practice provides extensive guidance on how this might be achieved. Thus reference was made to 'empowerment and personal autonomy, and the key obligation of all carers to support and maximise the decision-making capacity of the person who lacks capacity'[5]. If a person cannot make a decision, then each act or decision taken on their behalf must be based on the 'best interests' of the individual.

The new law is not intended to change practice with regard to day-to-day life, but to support it and enable it to take place so far as possible without interference, especially from the court. It also enables people to plan ahead for a time when they might lose capacity. In that event they now have available the possibility of an advance decision refusing specified treatment, including life-sustaining treatment if they so desire and a welfare donee under a Lasting Power of Attorney, who might also be empowered specifically to take life-sustaining treatment decisions.

These provisions inspired much heated Parliamentary debate on issues such as euthanasia, the provision of artificial nutrition and hydration, assisted suicide and suicide. Concerns were expressed about the extent of power granted to doctors or welfare donees with regard to life-sustaining treatment and the potential for the abuse of such power[6]. The Government's response is contained in s 62 of the MCA 2005 which declares specifically that nothing in the Act is to be taken to affect the law on murder, manslaughter, and assisted suicide. This was in response to a recommendation made by the Joint Scrutiny Committee which also said that in its view the fears over 'euthanasia by the back door' were misplaced[7].

1 See paras 43 and 44.
2 At para 85.
3 425 HC Official Report (6th series), col 22, 11 October 2004.
4 HC Official Report SC A (Mental Capacity Bill), 19 October 2004 and Committee Stage generally.
5 HC Official Report SC A (Mental Capacity Bill), 21 October 2004, cols 105–107.
6 See eg 425 HC Official Report (6th series), cols 43, 61, 11 October 2004; 432 HC Official Report (6th series) col 1373, 5 April 2005.
7 At para 204.

WHAT THE MCA 2005 DOES

1.7 The MCA 2005 provides a decision-making framework for incapacitated adults. In summary it:

- Codifies the common law in relation to capacity (functional test) and best interests for adults over the age of 16. It thus ensures that *all decisions* taken for incapacitated adults are made in their *best interests* and allows incapacitated adults to take as many decisions as they can for themselves. This it does by a set of principles on the face of the MCA 2005 at s 1. The test of capacity and the application of 'best interests' are considered in Chapter 2.
- Applies to decisions relating to *personal welfare* and *property and affairs*, thereby repealing Part VII of the MHA 1983 and the whole of the Enduring Powers of Attorney Act 1985. This book deals only with the former, including healthcare. Welfare and health decisions are considered in Chapters 7 and 8. Other specific areas including, deprivation of liberty, MHA 1983 cross over, discrimination, prisons and crime are at Chapters 9, 16, and 18.
- Currently it does not permit the deprivation of liberty of any person (see above at 1.4). But amendments not yet in force propose a new system for authorising *deprivation of liberty*, by PCTs and local authorities or the Court of Protection for detaining incapacitated but unresisting patients in need of treatment or care in hospital or a care home. See Chapter 9[1].
- Codifies the common law defence of necessity to provide protection from criminal and civil liability for those carers and professionals who have honestly and reasonably sought to act in the best interests of the person for whom they have cared, including paying for goods and services: ss 5–8. It limits protection in relation to acts intended to restrain an incapacitated person. However, liability for civil and criminal acts founded on negligence is preserved. See Chapter 4.
- Provides clarity in relation to the carrying out of research involving people who lack capacity. See Chapter 13.

- Creates a criminal offence of ill-treatment and wilful neglect: s 44. See Chapters 4 and 18.
- Makes a specific declaration regarding the law on murder, manslaughter and assisted suicide which is not affected by the MCA 2005 (s 62).
- Gives effect to the Hague Convention on the Protection of Adults in order to avoid conflicts in respect of jurisdiction, applicable law, recognition and enforcement of measures for the protection of adults (s 63 and Sch 3). See Chapter 17.

NEW DECISION-MAKERS AND STRUCTURES

1.8 The MCA 2005 provides radical new decision-making tools for health and welfare decisions:

1 Regulation of advance decisions for medical treatment: ss 24–26.
2 Lasting powers of attorney (LPA): ss 9–14.
3 A new Court of Protection jurisdiction is empowered to:
   (a) supervise decisions through declaratory relief: s 15;
   (b) make decisions: substituted decision-making: s 16;
   (c) appoint court deputies;
   (d) supervise LPAs: ss 22 and 23;
   (e) be the decision-maker of last resort;
   (f) authorise and review a deprivation of liberty (not yet in force).
4 New statutory individuals called Independent Mental Capacity Advocates (IMCA), are created to *support and represent* individuals who have no family or friends to do so in relation to serious medical treatment and long term accommodation (and in due course in relation to the authorisation of any deprivation of liberty).
5 There is also a brand new Office of the Public Guardian. Court of Protection Visitors are a familiar part of the old Court of Protection system and are re-vamped to cover welfare decision-making (ss 57–61).

1 As mentioned above these proposals are introduced by the MHA 2007 and are not yet in force. Implementation has been delayed until April 2009.

CODE OF PRACTICE: SS 42–43

1.9 The final Code of Practice was issued on 23 April 2007 (draft laid before Parliament in February). It is referred to as the 'Main Code' throughout this work because a draft addendum Code dealing with the proposed deprivation of liberty provisions has been published and will come into effect when finalised. The Main Code offers guidance and information to those who will use the MCA 2005 on a daily basis to care for incapacitated people. It uses scenarios and simple language to elucidate the concepts and procedures in the MCA 2005. Unfortunately it is a large and unwieldy document comprising 16 chapters and running to over 300 pages[1].

Section 42(4) provides that 'it is the *duty of a person to have regard to* any relevant code if he is acting in relation to a person who lacks capacity …' Thus whether the person is acting:

- as a donee of an LPA, or
- a court deputy, or
- a person carrying out research, or
- an IMCA, or
- in a professional capacity, or
- in a paid, or remunerated, capacity,

they do not have a legal duty to comply with the Main Code, but must have a good reason for not doing so[2]. What might amount to good reason not to follow the Code is not clear.

The last two categories above specifically include all health and social care professionals, including therapists, dentists, psychologists, nurses, radiologists, ambulance staff, and other carers or care or healthcare assistants who are paid to look after a person. A question which is considered in the context of ordinary civil litigation is how wide is the obligation to comply with the Main Code (see Chapter 15).

Although family and other informal carers are not subject to the duty above, they are equally subject to the provisions of the MCA 2005 and should use the Code for guidance. Also donees of existing enduring powers of attorney are not listed, but would be expected to be aware of the Code and use it for guidance.

Section 42(5) makes the Main Code, or a failure to comply with it, a relevant question for a court or tribunal to take into account in conducting criminal or civil proceedings. Thus although there are no explicit sanctions for a failure to use the Code, this may be a relevant factor for the purpose of proceedings. Professionals and other carers should be advised to ensure they are aware of contents the Main Code, and in applying or taking them into account are able to justify decisions by reference to what the Code requires. This may require recording the use of the Main Code in relevant clinical or other notes.

The Main Code is an essential part of the operation of the MCA 2005 and is available at www.publicguardian.gov.uk[1].

1 See also Appendix 3.
2 *R (on the application of Munjaz) v MerseyCare NHS Trust* [2003] EWCA Civ 1036, [2004] QB 395.

PERSONAL WELFARE

1.10 'Personal welfare' includes healthcare and medical treatment decisions and s 17 (court's powers) and the Main Code, para 7.21 (LPAs) suggest the following:

(a) determining place of residence and with whom;
(b) day-to-day care, including diet and dress;
(c) who the person may have contact with;
(d) consenting to or refusing medical examination and treatment;
(e) arrangements for medical, dental or optical treatment;

(f) assessments for and provision of community care services;
(g) social, leisure activities, education or training;
(h) rights of access to personal information;
(i) complaints about care and treatment.

PROPERTY AND AFFAIRS

1.11 'Property and affairs' means 'business matters, legal transactions and other dealings of a similar kind'[1]. Section 18 (court's powers) and the Main Code, Chapter 7 (LPAs) suggest that the following are included:

(a) buying or selling property;
(b) opening, closing or operating any bank, building society or other account;
(c) giving access to the donor's financial information;
(d) claiming, receiving and using (on person's behalf) all benefits, pensions, allowances;
(e) receiving income, inheritance etc;
(f) dealing with tax;
(g) paying mortgage, rent, household expenses;
(h) insuring, maintaining and repairing property;
(i) investing savings;
(j) making gifts (limited);
(k) paying for private medical care and residential or nursing care home fees;
(l) applying for any entitlement to funding for NHS care, social care or adaptations;
(m) buying motor vehicle or other equipment;
(n) repaying interest and capital on any loan.

1 *Re F* [1990] 2 AC 1 per Lord Brandon at 59H.

WHAT THE MCA 2005 DOES NOT DO

1.12

1 It does *not* apply to the treatment of *mental disorder* of a patient detained under the MHA 1983 and subject to the consent to treatment provisions of Part IV of that Act. Advance decisions do not apply to such treatment and nor do LPAs: s 28.

2 Other excluded matters:

(a) family relationships: s 27 (eg consenting to marriage or civil partnership, sexual relations, divorce, dissolution of marriage or civil partnership, placing child for adoption, parental responsibilities, consent under the Human Fertilisation and Embryology Act 1990);

(b) voting rights: s 29 (at an election for any public office or referendum).

3 The MCA 2005 does not apply to vulnerable, capacitated adults. Such individuals are protected by protection of vulnerable adults (POVA) arrangements and the inherent jurisdiction of the High Court will continue to apply.

4 Sections 27 to 29 disapply the MCA 2005 so that no one, including the court, may *consent* to decisions on behalf of incapacitated patients. It is contended that the MCA 2005 does apply, therefore, to the determination of issues of capacity in relation to such decisions by the Court of Protection. This is considered further at Chapter 7 in the context of decisions to marry.

HUMAN RIGHTS

1.13 In its report on the Mental Capacity Bill as introduced into the Commons in June 2004 the Joint Committee on Human Rights (JCHR) outlined the various fundamental rights engaged: the right to dignity and personal autonomy protected by Articles 3 and 8 ECHR the right to life under Article 2; the right to liberty under Article 5 and the right under Article 14 not to be discriminated against in the enjoyment of any of these rights on grounds of mental instability. It stated that on initial consideration the Bill was to be 'broadly welcomed from a human rights perspective because it enhances the ability of people who lack capacity to make their own decisions where they can, and makes it more likely that sound decisions will be made on their behalf where they cannot make those decisions for themselves'. This was repeated in the report of January 2005 by which time the Government had responded to previous concerns, for example clarifying that the MCA 2005 does not authorise deprivation of liberty under Article 5. This was prior to the proposals now contained in the MHA 2007. Other issues discussed were life sustaining treatment and advance decisions and research. Reference should be made to individual chapters for more on these issues and also Chapter 17 on human rights more broadly.

IMPLEMENTATION

1.14 There are four Commencement Orders:

1 Mental Capacity Act 2005 (Commencement No 1) Order 2006, SI 2006/2814 (as amended by SI 2006/3473).

2 Mental Capacity Act 2005 (Commencement) (Wales) Order 2006, SI 2007/856 (W.79).

3 Mental Capacity Act 2005 (Commencement No 1) (England and Wales) Order 2007, SI 2007/563.

4 Mental Capacity Act 2005 (Commencement No 2) Order 2007, SI 2007/1897.

Table 1: Implementation[1]

Provision	*Date of commencement England*	*Date of commencement Wales*
ss 30–34 (in respect of any research carried out as part of a project begun on or after 1 October 2007).	1 October 2007	1 October 2007
ss 30–34 (for the purpose of enabling research applications to be made to, and determined by, an appropriate body).	1 October 2007	1 July 2007
ss 30–34 (where a research project has begun before 1 October 2007 and was approved before that date).	1 October 2008	1 October 2008
ss 35–41 (to enable the Secretary of State for Health to make arrangements to make IMCAs available and to enable local authorities to approve IMCAs).	1 November 2006	
ss 35–41 (and regulations) (fully into force).	1 April 2007	1 October 2007

Table 2: Provisions coming into force on 1 April 2007[2]

ss 1–4: principles, capacity, inability to make decisions and best interests, for purposes relating to IMCAs and s 44 (neglect and ill-treatment). England only.
s 42 (1), (2), (3), (6), (7) (Codes of practice). England and Wales.
s 42(4) and (5) for purposes relating to IMCAs and s 44. England only.
ss 43 (Main Code) and 44. England and Wales. (Issued on 23 April 2007.)
s 54 (interpretation) for ss 42, 44 and 1–4.

The implementation date of all other provisions was 1 October 2007: ss 5–29, 45–63, 65–69, Schs 1–7 and ss 1–4, 42(4) and (5) (Codes of Practice) and s 64 (interpretation) for all purposes[3].

A table of minor and consequential amendments pursuant to Sch 6 and 7 is at Appendix 2.

MHA 2007, ss 49 and 51 (ie IMCA service exceptions and amendments to s 20(11) came into force on 1 October 2007[4]. Section 50(5) and part of Sch 7 on 1 April 2008.

1 Mental Capacity Act 2005 (Commencement No 1) Order, SI 2006/2814 (as amended by SI 2006/3473) and Mental Capacity Act 2005 (Commencement) (Wales) Order, SI 2007/856 (W.79).

2 Mental Capacity Act 2005 (Commencement No 1) (England and Wales) Order 2007, SI 2007/563.

3 See Mental Capacity Act 2005 (Commencement No 2) Order 2007, SI 2007/1897.

4 Mental Health Act 2007 (Commencement No 3) Order 2007, SI 2007/2798; Mental Health Act 2007 (Commencement No 2) Order 2007, SI 2007/2635. Also SI 2008/745.

Chapter 2

CAPACITY AND BEST INTERESTS

- **MCA 2005, ss 1–4**
- **Main Code, Chapters 1–5**

INTRODUCTION

2.1 The capacity and best interests elements of the MCA 2005 result from a process of consultation which began in 1989 and led to a final Law Commission Report in 1995[1]. The Law Commission recommended that in place of the existing ad hoc development of common law principles, 'there should be a single comprehensive piece of legislation to make new provision for people who lack mental capacity'[2].

The proposal was widely welcomed by commentators, both to replace with one codified scheme the existing regime which derived from a series of individual decisions, and also to promote a policy of empowerment to assist those lacking capacity to make as many decisions as possible[3].

Accordingly, the MCA 2005:

- explicitly seeks to maximise as far as possible the autonomy and independence of incapacitated adults;
- provides a statutory definition of incapacity;
- provides that decisions or actions in respect of treatment, care or financial affairs may be taken on behalf of an incapacitated adult where they are in the person's best interests.

The MCA 2005 aims to achieve these ends by:

- an overarching set of principles at the outset of the statute;
- reiteration of the importance of communication with the person both:
  (a) to assess capacity, and
  (b) even where capacity is lost, to assist in an assessment of what is in the person's best interests;

- the immensely detailed Main Code[4], explicitly intended by the government to reinforce the Act's message of maximising capacity and promoting people's rights to make as many of their own decisions as possible[5], whilst protecting them from harm if they do lack capacity to make decisions themselves[6].

This chapter sets out the detail of those overarching principles, the assessment of capacity and the practical meaning of best interests. These provisions apply to every decision taken under the MCA 2005.

1 Law Commission Report 231, Mental Incapacity, HMSO, 28 February 1995.
2 Law Commission Report 231, Mental Incapacity, HMSO, 28 February 1995, Summary, para 1.2.
3 See for example the Report of the Joint Scrutiny Committee on the draft Mental Incapacity Bill (as it was originally named), HL Paper 189 HC 1083, published on 17 November 2003 (hereinafter 'The Scrutiny Report'): 'We concur with the widely-held view that a new Bill is needed to provide a comprehensive statutory framework for assisting those lacking capacity to make decisions for themselves wherever possible and for proper decisions to be made by others on their behalf where that is not possible'; para 30.
4 Issued on 23 April 2007, and referred to as the 'Main Code', in the light of the draft addendum Code issued to deal with the Bournewood situation and deprivation of liberty: see Chapter 9 below.
5 See for example the government's response to the Joint Committee on the Draft Mental Incapacity Bill, February 2004.
6 See para 1.4 of the Main Code.

SECTION 1: THE OVERARCHING PRINCIPLES

2.2 The MCA 2005 begins with a set of principles which 'apply for the purposes of this Act'[1], ie to be deployed throughout the analysis and interpretation of the Act. This is unusual in legislation for England and Wales, and was not part of the originally published Bill. Opening principles were, however, included in the Adults with Incapacity (Scotland) Act 2000, one of the first statutes enacted by the Scottish Parliament. This practice impressed the Joint Scrutiny Committee, who felt an opening statement of principles could give valuable guidance to the courts, as well as help non-lawyers to weigh up difficult decisions[2]. The Scrutiny Committee's recommendation to include a similar statement of principles was accepted by the government and now forms s 1 of the MCA 2005.

The principles do not break new ground. Essentially they codify the existing common law, but as intended, they provide a clear statement of overarching principle in considering issues of capacity. They are as follows:

- there is a presumption of capacity;
- incapacity is not to be established unless all practicable steps to help the person have been taken, without success;
- incapacity is not established merely by the person making a rash decision;
- an act or decision made under this Act on behalf of a person lacking capacity must be in his best interests;
- before making a decision on behalf of an incapacitated person, the decision-maker must consider the least restrictive form appropriate.

2.2 *Capacity and Best Interests*

1 Section 1(1)
2 Scrutiny Committee Report, para 43.

1st principle – the presumption of capacity

2.3

> 'A person must be assumed to have capacity unless it is established that he lacks capacity.'[1]

The opening principle is thus that capacity must be assumed unless the contrary is established. This is in line with the expressed aim of the statute to improve the abilities of people to take their own decisions rather than restricting them.

The section refers to incapacity having to be 'established' to defeat the presumption. How is this to be done, who is to establish it and when is it to be established?

1 Section 1(2).

Standard of proof in establishing capacity

2.4 Section 2(4) provides that the evidential burden is the ordinary civil standard of the balance of probabilities. The question will thus be: is it more likely than not that the person lacks capacity[1]?

1 Rather than the criminal standard of beyond reasonable doubt.

Who decides whether incapacity is established?

2.5 In any case where a decision is proposed to be taken, or an act done for an incapacitated adult, it is the person who is proposing to make the decision or to take the act who has to satisfy themselves of that other's incapacity – and who also, as is discussed below, has the burden of promoting the person's capacity and deciding upon their best interests if capacity is lacking. This will cover a very wide range of people and actions, from care workers making routine decisions to do with the activities of daily living, to clinicians making treatment decisions, to donees or others making financial or property decisions. For each, whilst the nature of the enquiry as to capacity and best interests will clearly vary with the magnitude or import of the decision, the process will be the same, and applies across the board.

The obligation to assess capacity thus rests upon the person proposing to make the decision. This may be straightforward. Where it is not, and where particularly weighty or difficult decisions are involved, advice might be sought from an appropriate expert, such as a consultant psychiatrist. In cases on this issue decided both before and after the enactment of the MCA 2005 the courts have held that the decision-maker is not, however, bound to accept even expert opinion, and will retain responsibility for making the final decision[1].

The Court of Appeal has said that 'Expert assistance is of course of considerable assistance ... , but the expert's opinion, however authoritative, is not conclusive. The judge decides.'

1 *Bailey v Warren* [2006] EWCA Civ 51 at para 87, [2006] All ER (D) 78 (Feb). And see *Saulle v Nouvet* [2007] EWHC 2902, QB: 'Incapacity is a matter of legal classifcation, based on medical and factual evidence. It is not a matter of diagnosis.' (at para 53).

When is the decision as to capacity made?

2.6 As will be seen, capacity is a fact-specific concept; in other words, the question on each occasion when someone proposes to make a decision or do an act on behalf of another, is whether that other lacks the capacity to make that particular decision or do that particular act. The Act does not permit a blanket judgement about a person's incapacity. Whilst it may be apparent for example, that a severely learning disabled adult will lack capacity to do very much, the Act requires the assessment to be made in respect of each act or decision proposed to be made on behalf of another, at the time it has to be made[1].

1 See 15.2 below on the possible tension between this principle and situations requiring extended periods of decision making, such as civil litigation.

2nd principle: Incapacity not to be established unless all practicable steps have been taken to help the person make their own decision

2.7

> 'A person is not to be treated as unable to make decision unless all practicable steps to help him to do so have been taken without success.'[1]

This is demanding. It requires the would-be decision maker to do more than take all 'reasonably practicable' steps; before incapacity can be established 'all practicable steps' must have been taken to help the patient make the decision for him or herself. What does this mean? The Main Code covers the topic extensively, beginning with a statement of principle:

> 'It is important to do everything practical ... to help a person make a decision for themselves before concluding that they lack capacity to do so. People with an illness or disability affecting their ability to make a decision should receive support to help them make as many decisions as they can. This principle aims to stop people being automatically labelled as lacking capacity to make particular decisions. Because it encourages individuals to play as big a role as possible in decision-making, it also helps prevent unnecessary interventions in their lives.'[2]

The Code acknowledges that the kind of support people might need to make a decision will vary, according to personal circumstances, the kind of decision that has to be made, and the time available to make the decision. It may include:

- using a different form of communication – eg non-verbal;
- providing information in more accessible form – eg photos, drawings;

- treating a medical condition which may be affecting the person's capacity;
- having a structured programme to improve a person's capacity to make particular decisions – eg helping a person with learning disabilities to learn new skills[3].

In addition, there is a whole chapter of the Code, Chapter 3, dedicated to helping people make their own decisions:

1 Section 1(3).
2 Main Code, para 2.6.
3 Main Code, para 2.7.

Helping people make their own decisions: Chapter 3 of the Code

2.8 Chapter 3 of the Code recommends a number of techniques for maximising a person's decision-making ability. It acknowledges that in most cases only some of the steps will be relevant or appropriate; clearly significant one-off decisions will require a different approach to daily decisions about care and welfare. However, the same general process should apply to each, and in each case the aim is to 'find the most effective way of communicating with the person concerned'[1]. The techniques cover the following:

- provision of information;
- methods of communication;
- location and timing;
- support from other people or sources.

1 Main Code, para 3.4.

PROVISION OF INFORMATION

2.9 Clearly, a person requires appropriate information in order to be able to make a decision. The type of information relevant to a particular decision will of course relate specifically to that decision and neither the Code nor the Act can cater for any given situation; judgement will be required[1]. The Code however suggests that anyone trying to help someone to make a decision for him or herself should follow these steps:

1 Take time to explain anything that might help the person make a decision. It is important that they have access to all the information they need to make an informed decision.
2 Try not to give more detail than the person needs – this might confuse them. In some cases, a simple, broad explanation will be enough. But it must not miss out important information.
3 What are the risks and benefits? Describe any foreseeable consequences of making the decision, and of not making any decision at all.
4 Explain the effects that the decision might have on the person and those close to them – including the people involved in their care.
5 If there is a choice, give the person the same information in a balanced way for all the options.

6 For some types of decisions, it may be important to give access to advice from elsewhere. This may be independent or specialist advice (for example, from a medical practitioner or a financial or legal adviser). But it might simply be advice from trusted friends or relatives[2].

1 The issue of the provision of information with a view to obtaining consent for medical treatment is considered at Chapter 8.
2 Main Code, para 3.9.

METHODS OF COMMUNICATION

2.10 The Code emphasises the importance of addressing communication skills, using appropriate language, volume, speed, diagrams or pictures as appropriate. It also suggests that advice might be sought about the best method of communication from people who know the person.

The person's family and friends might also be approached to help communicate, but confidentiality needs to be respected. Family members might be used as interpreters if there is a language barrier, but again one should be alert to any conflict here and it may be more appropriate to use a professional interpreter.

Cultural issues need to be borne in mind. Consideration may have to be given to engaging an advocate to improve communication[1].

Alternatively, the Code asks whether there may be communication aids or devices which the person might use to communicate, or if time permitted, skills the person might be taught to use themselves[2]?

1 See Chapter 6 on advocates.
2 Main Code, para 2.11.

LOCATION AND TIMING

2.11 The Code then considers the issues of location and timing which, if optimised, can assist the person to make their own decision. Those providing information should therefore consider:

- the location where the person feels most at ease, where it is quiet and likely to be uninterrupted; alternatively, if appropriate, a visit to a location relevant to the decision to assist in decision-making;
- the time of day when the person is likely to be most alert, bearing in mind sleeping habits or medication side effects if relevant;
- whether to stage the decisions to be made, one at a time, and not rushing the person, particularly if there is no pressing urgency for the decision to be made.

SUPPORT FROM OTHER PEOPLE OR SOURCES

2.12 The Code recognises that it may be helpful to the person to have some other person present or involved to support them in this process. This must be approached with care, however; it is possible that the person might find it intrusive or anxiety-provoking. Care must be taken to ensure that the person does want and need another involved, and to respect confidentiality.

Assistance alternatively might be found in a support group, in discussion groups or in published materials, or via appropriate technology which the person can either use now or be helped to use in the future.

EMERGENCY SITUATIONS

2.13 The Code does acknowledge that in an emergency situation urgent decisions may have to be made and immediate action taken in a person's best interests. In these circumstances it may not be possible to delay action whilst trying to help the person make their own decision. However, 'even in emergency situations [decision-makers] should try to communicate with the person and keep them informed of what is happening'[1].

1 Main Code, para 3.6.

3rd principle: Incapacity not established by the making of a rash decision

2.14

> 'A person is not to be treated as unable to make a decision merely because he makes an unwise decision.'[1]

The third principle of s 1 focuses on one of the long-established, but cardinal features of the notion of capacity, namely that it cannot be found to be lost merely by reason of a rash decision taken by the person. As Lord Donaldsdon MR stated in a case involving the refusal of a blood transfusion by a young woman whose parents were Jehovah's witnesses:

> '[A patient's] right of choice is not limited to decisions which others might regard as sensible. It exists notwithstanding that the reasons for making the choice are rational, irrational, unknown or even non-existent.'[2]

This is of course wholly in keeping with the ostensible aim of the Act, namely to promote the ability of people generally to make their own decisions, whether or not they seem to observers to be rash or unwise. It is likely that the inclusion of this proposition as one of the guiding principles of the Act is intended to keep awareness of this at the forefront of carers' and clinicians' minds. It is a laudable statement of principle. The difficulty of course, for the carer/decision-maker, which runs through the assessment of both incapacity and best interests, lies in its practical application, in laying aside one's own value systems when making appraisals under the Act. This difficulty must be addressed – although in truth the Main Code does little really to acknowledge its complexities beyond the bland exhortation that:

> 'everybody has their own values, beliefs, preferences and attitudes. A person should not be assumed to lack the capacity to make a decision just because other people think their decision is unwise.'[3]

Accordingly where, for example, a patient declines a life-saving and relatively risk-free medical treatment, the clinician is very likely to find it to be unwise. To comply with s 1(4) the doctor must, however, endeavour to look outside their own value system as a clinician and assess the position from the standpoint of the patient; how this is to be done and whether, in fact, the exhortation at s 1(4) leads to different outcomes in practice, remains to be seen.

Nevertheless, it is important to remember that s 1(4) requires the decision maker not to assume incapacity 'merely' by reason of an unwise decision. Both the Joint Scrutiny Committee on the Mental Incapacity Bill and the Government were anxious that carers and clinicians respected patient autonomy, but equally, did not fail to act to protect a person where necessary. Accordingly, a very unwise decision, or a series of unwise decisions may – and may rightly – trigger suspicions or concerns that the person in fact is losing or has lost capacity. The Main Code picks this up, stating that there may be cause for concern:

> 'if somebody repeatedly makes unwise decisions that put them at significant risk of harm or exploitation, or makes a particular unwise decision that is obviously irrational or out of character.'[4]

Such concern, says the Code, does not necessarily lead to a conclusion of incapacity. But it may legitimately trigger further investigation:

> 'taking into account the person's past decisions and choices. For example, have they developed a medical condition or disorder that is affecting their capacity to make particular decisions? Are they easily influenced by undue pressure? Or do they need more information to help them understand the consequences of the decision they are making?'[5]

1 Section 1(4).
2 *Re T (adult: refusal of treatment)* [1992] 4 All ER 649 (CA).
3 Main Code para 2.10.
4 Main Code, para 2.11.
5 Main Code, para 2.11.

4th principle: An act or decision under the MCA 2005 for the incapacitated must be in their best interests

2.15

> 'An act done, or decision made, under this Act for or on behalf of a person who lacks capacity must be done, or made, in his best interests.'[1]

1 Section 1(5).

Decisions 'under this Act' – decisions not covered by the Act

2.16 The best interests principle applies to decisions made under the Act. Some decisions are outside its scope, as set out below. Where this is the case, the Act cannot confer authority on anyone – including a donee of a power of attorney or the Court of Protection – to make these decisions on behalf of an incapacitated adult.

Decisions outside the Act comprise:

- specific intimate family decisions;
- treatment decisions under the Mental Health Act 1983;
- voting decisions;
- decisions in relation to children under 16 (save for 2 exceptions).

FAMILY DECISIONS

2.17 By s 27 the MCA 2005 cannot be used to authorise intimate family decisions such as consent to:

- marriage or civil partnership;
- sexual relations;
- divorce or civil partnership dissolution on the basis of two years' separation;
- placement of a child for adoption or the making of an adoption order;
- discharge of parental responsibilities not relating to a child's property;
- matters under the Human Fertilisation and Embryology Act 1990.

TREATMENT UNDER THE MENTAL HEALTH ACT 1983

2.18 Further, by s 28, the MCA 2005 cannot be used in relation to treatment which is being provided under Part IV of the Mental Health Act 1983, to give a patient medical treatment for mental disorder' or to give consent to a patient being given medical treatment for mental disorder.

What this means is that the treatment of detained patients to whom Part IV of the Mental Health Act 1983 applies remains unaffected by the MCA 2005 – see further Chapter 9 on the deprivation of liberty.

VOTING

By s 29 the MCA 2005 cannot be used to permit a decision on voting at an election or referendum to be made on behalf of a person.

DECISIONS IN RELATION TO CHILDREN

2.19 By s 2(5), with two exceptions, no powers under the MCA 2005 may be exercised in relation to a child under 16. The exceptions are that:

– By s 18, the Court of Protection's decision-making powers at s 16 of the MCA 2005 in relation to a person's property and affairs extend to cover a child if it seems likely that the child will lack capacity in relation to their property and affairs on reaching the age of 18.
– The offences of ill-treatment and neglect created by s 44 apply to protect those lacking capacity, without age restriction.

Best interests

2.20 The core of decision-making under the MCA 2005 for those without capacity is that decisions made or acts done must be in their best interests. The use of the concept of best interests in relation to the incapacitated is not new[1]. What, however, does it mean under the MCA 2005? This, the heart of this part of the statute, remains undefined. The omission is deliberate and considered[2]. The Law Commission in its report on mental incapacity acknowledged that no statutory guidance could offer an exhaustive account of what is in a person's best interests[3]. The Law Commission was anxious also to ensure that the individual patient and their individual circumstances remained centre stage and determined the result. It recommended therefore that statute set out a checklist of common factors which needed always to be taken into account in assessing best interests. This is how the Act has reached the statute-book, the procedural steps being set out at s 4[4].

There is then no further definition or explanation of the term 'best interests'. The Joint Scrutiny Committee wondered whether there should, however, be this gloss, that there be a notion of benefit resulting to the person. It rejected even this however, and the Government agreed:

> 'as to do so would potentially be too prescriptive. There may be instances where the concept of "benefit", especially if interpreted as requiring "positive benefit" could act as a unjustifiable barrier to a course of action which was indeed in an incapacitated person's overall best interests. We would be concerned about it being interpreted as imposing a "starting-point" of inaction.'[5]

1 See for example decisions such as *Re T (Adult – refusal of medical treatment)* [1992] 4 All ER 649, CA, *Re MB (Medical treatment)* [1997] 2 FLR 426, CA, *Re W (Adult: refusal of medical treatment)* [2002] EWHC 901 (Fam).

2 As indeed it has been at common law: see for example the decision of the Court of Appeal in *R (on the application of Burke) v General Medical Council* [2005] EWCA Civ 1003, [2006] QB 273: 'We do not think it possible to attempt to define what is in the best interests of a patient by a single test, applicable in all the circumstances' at para 63.

3 Law Commission Report 231, Mental Incapacity, HMSO, 28 February 1995. The Joint Scrutiny Committee agreed: Joiny Scrutiny Report, para 85.

4 See below 2.40ff.

5 Government's response, February 2004 to para 86 of the Joint Scrutiny Report.

5th Principle: Take the least restrictive alternative in making a decision on behalf of an incapacitated adult

2.21

> 'Before the act is done, or the decision is made, regard must be had to whether the purpose for which it is needed can be as effectively achieved in a way that is less restrictive of the person's rights and freedom of action.'[1]

The task of the decision-maker is to make a decision which is in the incapacitated person's best interests – the aim being to strive for **the** decision which is in his best interests. Clearly, however, there may be more than one decision which might be felt to be in the person's best interests, and where there are, this, the final principle of s 1, requires the decision-maker to opt for the least restrictive alternative. The Code reminds us that this principle 'includes considering whether there is a need to act or make a decision at all'[2].

The Code gives an example of the learning disabled adult who also suffers from severe and unpredictable epilepsy; medical advice is that, to avoid serious injury from one of these attacks, he needs either close observation or a protective helmet. It is plain however that the patient dislikes close observation, making the least restrictive option clearly the helmet – to protect his head but maximise his freedom from observation.[3]

1 Section 1(6).
2 Main Code, para 2.14.
3 Main Code, scenario at para 2.16.

SECTIONS 2 AND 3: THE CONCEPT OF INCAPACITY

2.22

> 'A person lacks capacity in relation to a matter if, at the material time he is unable to make a decision for himself in relation to the matter because of an impairment of, or a disturbance in the functioning of the mind or brain.'[1]

1 Section 2(1).

A functional test

2.23 The opening words of s 2 define the core concept of capacity, confirming that it is a test of function: a person will lack capacity if he is unable to make a decision about a matter at the material time, and the reason for that inability is an impairment of or disturbance to the functioning of the mind or brain.

The words 'at the material time' and 'in relation to the matter' confirm that this is a time- and situation-specific test; does the person have the capacity to make a particular decision at the time it needs to be made? Section 2 does not permit a general determination of incapacity, nor was this sought by the majority of commentators on the legislation during its parliamentary passage[1]. Whilst it may be, for example, that the severity of the learning disability or medical condition make it inevitable that the person can make no decisions at all, s 2 requires the decision-maker nevertheless to consider the question, and may find that the person is in fact able to make a decision for himself about, for example, a daily activity or minor medical intervention. Section 2 enjoins carers and clinicians to remember this[2].

1 See for example the Report of the Joint Scrutiny Committee on the draft Mental Incapacity Bill, HL Paper 189 HC 1083, 17 November 2003, para 67, with the interesting exception of the Master of the Court of Protection, para 68.

2 See further 2.32 below on fluctuating capacity and 15.2 for a further discussion of the implications of the transaction-specific concept of incapacity in the arena of civil litigation.

Temporary incapacity

2.24 Clearly, if capacity is a time- and situation-specific test, it can be something which may be lost temporarily. The serious road traffic accident victim, the person heavily under the influence of alcohol or drugs, the person recovering from a stroke, are all likely to lack capacity, even if they are equally likely to be expected to regain it. Section 2(3) provides that 'it does not matter whether the impairment or disturbance is permanent or temporary'.

Capacity to be established and not assumed

2.25 The first general principle must be borne in mind here: a person must be assumed to have capacity unless the contrary is established.[1]

Further, in assessing capacity, s 2(3) warns carers and decision-makers against stereotypical or formulaic thinking:

> 'A lack of capacity cannot be established merely by reference to:
> (a) a person's age or appearance; or
> (b) a condition of his, or an aspect of his behaviour, which might lead others to make unjustified assumptions about his capacity.'

As a final preliminary, s 2 also establishes the evidential standard necessary for the question of capacity:

> 'In proceedings under this Act, or any other enactment, any question whether a person lacks capacity within the meaning of this Act must be decided *on the balance of probabilities*.'[2]

1 Section 1(2), discussed at 2.3 above.
2 Section 2(4); emphasis added.

The elements of incapacity

2.26 Turning now to the test of capacity, it will be seen that it comprises two stages, a diagnostic threshold and an impairment of decision-making function:

- Has the person an impairment of mind or brain, or some disturbance which affects the way their mind or brain works?
- If so, does that impairment or disturbance mean that the person is unable to make the decision in question at the time it needs to be made?

Stage 1: The diagnostic threshold

2.27 An impairment of, or disturbance in the functioning of the mind or brain must be established. This may be temporary or permanent, applying thus to a victim of a serious road traffic accident rendered unconscious, or a severely learning disabled adult. Unless, however, there is such an impairment or disturbance of the mind or brain, there will be no lack of capacity under the Act.

The diagnostic threshold may be obviously satisfied, as in the two examples above. The Main Code gives further examples:

- conditions associated with some forms of mental illness;
- dementia;
- significant learning disabilities;
- the long term effects of brain damage;
- physical or medical conditions that cause confusion, drowsiness or loss of consciousness;
- delirium;
- concussion following a head injury;
- the symptoms of alcohol or drug use.[1]

It may however be a far more subtle question. What for example of the pregnant woman who needs an emergency caesarean section to save her much-wanted baby, but whose needle phobia renders her unable to agree to the operation? Or the anorexic who articulately resists attempts to cajole him into eating? Might they have an impairment of, or disturbance in the functioning of the mind or brain sufficient to pass the diagnostic threshold? Clearly much will depend on the particular facts of any given question (and in the medical context, this is considered more fully at Chapter 8 below[2]). However, in particular cases, courts have held that:

- A pregnant woman needing a caesarean, but unable to consent to the injection needed to commence the anaesthetic, lacked capacity because her fear dominated her completely and rendered her incapable of making any decision, which was sufficient to amount to a disabling 'impairment of her mental functioning'[3].
- An anorexic refusing to eat crossed the diagnostic threshold as she had a deluded image of her own body; she considered she was fat when, objectively, this was far from the case. This fixed idea enabled the court to find that this was a deranged thought process, and the product of a mental disorder[4].

Consider also the comments of Lord Donaldson in *Re T (adult: refusal of treatment)*[5]:

> '[Those] who would normally have … capacity may be deprived of it or have it reduced by reason of temporary factors, such as unconsciousness or confusion or other *effects of shock, severe fatigue, pain or drugs* being used in their treatment.'

The decision in *Re T* predates the MCA 2005 of course, but there is no reason to think that this, or other authorities on this point will not be relevant in the interpretation of the new Act. If then the effects of even severe fatigue may satisfy the diagnostic threshold, it may in practice not be a particularly difficult hurdle to cross for decision-makers. Note, however, that if it is not crossed, then there can be no question of the patient lacking capacity – the Main Code gives an illustration:

> 'Mrs Collins is 82 and has had a stroke. This has weakened the left-hand side of her body. She is living in a house that has been the family home for years. Her son wants her to sell her house and live with him.
>
> Mrs Collins likes the idea, but her daughter does not. She thinks her mother will lose independence and her condition will get worse. She talks to her mother's consultant to get information that will help stop the sale. But he says that although Mrs Collins is anxious about the physical effects the stroke has had on her body, it has not caused any mental impairment or affected her brain, so she still has capacity to make her own decision about selling her house.'[6]

This is an interesting example, in reminding us that if the diagnostic threshold is not crossed then it will not be possible for another person to intervene to make decisions on behalf of another, however unwisely it seems that that person is acting. Does it however really illustrate the more difficult questions which might arise on this issue? How for example would the scenario result were there grounds to suspect that Mrs Collins' son was intent on financial exploitation of his mother? Might the consultant look somewhat differently at the question of cerebral impairment following the stroke? As ever throughout this subject, issues are complex and multi-layered. The MCA 2005 will assist in demonstrating the procedural questions to be asked and steps in which those questions must be answered; it cannot render any easier the judgement involved in answering the questions.

1 Main Code, para 4.12.
2 See further Chapter 18 below on discrimination, for the further issues which may arise in this context.
3 *Re MB (an adult: medical treatment)* (1997) 38 BMLR 175 (CA), per Butler Sloss LJ.
4 *Re KB (adult) (mental patient: medical treatment)* (1994) 19 BMLR 144. Clearly the extent of the condition will again be relevant at the second, decision making stage – see below.
5 [1992] 4 All ER 649, emphasis added.
6 Main Code, para 4.12.

Stage 2: Inability to make a decision

2.28 It is not enough merely to be satisfied that the diagnostic threshold is established. The decision-maker must further be satisfied that the impairment or disturbance has the effect of rendering the person unable to make the decision him or herself.

What this means is addressed by s 3 of the Act:

> ' … A person is unable to make a decision for himself if he is unable:
> (a) to understand the information relevant to a decision;
> (b) to retain that information;
> (c) to use or weigh that information as part of the process of making the decision; or
> (d) to communicate his decision (whether by talking, using sign language or any other means).'[1]

Having set out the definition of inability to decide at s 3(1), the Act immediately proceeds at s 3(2) to remind decision-makers of the second of the overarching principles of s 1:

> 'A person is not to be regarded as unable to understand the information relevant to a decision if he is able to understand an explanation of it given to him in a way that is appropriate to his circumstances (using simple language, visual aids or any other means).'[1]

It is explicit then that the assessment of ability, or inability, to decide cannot be made unless all practicable steps to be taken to assist the person to make the decision himself have been taken. This takes us back to the detailed steps advocated at Chapter 3 of the Main Code and summarised above.[3] In this context the Code at Chapter 4 also offers a further illustration:

> 'Mr Leslie has learning disabilities and has developed an irregular heartbeat. He has been prescribed medication for this, but is anxious about having regular blood tests to check his medication levels. His doctor gives him a leaflet to explain:
> - the reason for the tests;
> - what a blood test involves;
> - the risks in having or not having the tests; and
> - that he has the right to decide whether or not to have the test.
>
> The leaflet uses simple language and photographs to explain these things. Mr Leslie's carer helps him read the leaflet over the next few days, and checks that he understands it.
>
> Mr Leslie goes back to tell the doctor that, even though he is scared of needles, he will agree to the blood tests so that he can get the right medication. He is able to pick out the equipment needed to do the blood test. So the doctor concludes that Mr Leslie can understand, retain and use the relevant information and therefore has the capacity to make the decision to have the test.'[4]

Again, it may be felt that the example is of interest more for the straightforward case rather than the complex. It is relatively simple as long as the patient agrees with the doctor's advice. But what if the hypothetical Mr Leslie decides against medical advice and refuses the blood test? In such a case, if there were significant medical risks in taking the cardiac medication without regular review by blood test, might his refusal not tempt the doctor to look more critically at the issue of capacity? The doctor would have to remember that a decision s/he regarded as unwise did not necessarily imply incapacity, but would perhaps be forgiven for asking whether or not such a refusal did indeed suggest incapacity. The doctor would then have to make the difficult assessment alone, and exhortations to provide information in simple and accessible form may be of little practical assistance. Again, the Act and the Code can clearly set out the steps to be taken by the carer or clinician; they cannot provide the judgement.

1 Section 3(1).
2 Section 3(2).
3 See above, 2.8.
4 Main Code, para 4.19.

Whose assessment?

2.29 Who makes the assessment? As the Mr Leslie example reminds us, this role is placed on the person who is seeking a decision from the patient – in this case, the doctor advising him to have blood tests[1]. As ever, other opinion may be needed in the appropriate case – either from a clinician, or from a multi-disciplinary discussion, or from family or friends as appropriate.

1 If Mr Leslie had created a lasting power of attorney which covered health decisions such as this, the primary decision maker would be the donee of the power – see further on this Chapter 5 below.

Inability to decide: understanding, retaining, using information and communicating

2.30 Under the MCA 2005, as at common law[1], ability to make a decision is gauged by reference to the person's capability to deal with information relevant to that decision.

What information is relevant? This is a complex subject in its own right, particularly in the medical setting, as is considered at Chapter 8. However, as the Main Code sets out, relevant information includes information about the nature of the decision, the reason why it is needed, and the likely effects of deciding one way or another, or making no decision at all[2]. Much will depend upon the nature or gravity of the decision in issue. It may be enough to give a broad explanation using simple language; alternatively, the person may need more detailed information or access to advice, particularly if the decision could have serious or grave consequences[3].

How should the person with memory difficulties be approached? Throughout the Act as has been seen, the intention is to assist as many people as possible to make their own decisions, whilst protecting those who cannot. On the issue of memory, the balance between support and protection becomes very fine: Section 3(1) requires the person to be able to retain information relevant to the decision, and the Main Code states that:

> 'the person must be able to hold the information in their mind long enough to use it to make an effective decision.'[4]

However, s 3(3) provides that memory problems will not necessarily render the person unable to make a decision:

> 'The fact that a person is able to retain the information relevant to a decision for a short period only does not prevent him from being regarded as able to make the decision.'

The application of these principles will call for some fine judgement and careful work. The Main Code reminds decision-makers to consider the use of visual aids to assist memory such as notebooks, photographs, posters, videos and voice recorders. This is useful. What the Code does not explore are the boundaries of the principle: the point where the gravity or long term implications of the decision would render one concerned were a person with fluctuating memory problems to be making it. The Code gives this example:

'Walter, an elderly man, is diagnosed with dementia and has problems remembering things in the short term. He can't always remember his great-grandchildren's names, but he recognises them when they come to visit. He can also pick them out on photographs.

Walter would like to buy premium bonds (a type of financial investment) for each of his great-grandchildren. He asks his solicitor to make the arrangements. After assessing his capacity to make financial decisions, the solicitor is satisfied that Walter has capacity to make this decision, despite his short-term memory problems.'[5]

What the Code does not grapple with are those who can retain the information about a major decision whilst it is being explained, but would shortly afterwards forget it – and be distressed by the situation in which they then found themselves. The Walter example is fairly straightforward, and is considerably assisted by the benign nature of the decision Walter seeks to make. Matters are likely to be more difficult if, for example, the financial gifts he wanted to make would make a major inroad on his income or if it were a decision with long-term ramifications, the complexities of which he will only be able to retain for a very short period.

Section 3 requires the person to be able to understand, use and weigh the relevant information in order to have capacity to make a decision. This is where further very difficult questions of evaluation and assessment come to the fore and where the very real tension between benevolent paternalism and individual autonomy may be exposed. This is because, although the definition of incapacity is phrased in the MCA in terms of an inability to make a decision by reason of mental impairment, the really difficult cases are likely to be those where a patient has actually made a decision but it is one which the carer or clinician find difficult to accept – for example, the anorexic refusing food, the pregnant woman declining a caesarean, the patient seeking to give all their property to a very new friend. Here the enquiry, in truth, becomes one of assessment of whether the decision which the patient seeks to make is binding on the carer or clinician, or can actually be dismissed as one which their incapacity renders invalid[6].

The Main Code does not offer more than this:

'4.21: For someone to have capacity, they must have the ability to weigh up information and use it to arrive at a decision. Sometimes people can understand information but an impairment or disturbance stops them using it. In other cases, the impairment or disturbance leads to a person making a specific decision without understanding or using the information they have been given

4.22: For example, a person with the eating disorder anorexia nervosa may understand information about the consequences of not eating. But their compulsion not to eat may be too strong for them to ignore. Some people who have serious brain damage might make impulsive decisions regardless of the information they have been given or their understanding of it.'

The Code does not spell out what is actually being assessed in some of these cases, namely whether there is a disturbance of brain functioning sufficient to render the person's purported decision invalid so that their autonomy can in fact be overruled. It offers no further guidance.

How then have the courts approached this question?

In short, with anxiety, as Butler Sloss P explained in the case of *Re C (Adult: refusal of medical treatment)*[7]:

> 'The general law on mental capacity is, in my judgement, clear and easily to be understood by lawyers. Its application to individual cases in the context of a general practitioner's surgery, a hospital ward and especially in an intensive care unit is infinitely more difficult to achieve.'

What the courts have looked for is evidence about the requirements now cited in the MCA 2005, namely comprehension of information, ability to use and weigh it. They have tended also to look for a further facet, namely the patient's ability to *believe* the information being given, for without believing advice, i e accepting that it is true, the patient will be unable to use or weigh it. For example, consider the well-known case of *Re C*[8]. In this case C, a patient at Broadmoor with a diagnosis of paranoid schizophrenia and well-established grandiose ideas (including that he had had a distinguished medical career), developed a gangrenous ulcer of the foot. He was advised to undergo amputation, and advised of the likelihood of death without surgery. He was adamant in his refusal of an amputation and sought a declaration in the High Court prohibiting his clinicians from operating. The court heard evidence as to C's capacity from C himself, from expert psychiatrists and from C's clinicians, and concluded in favour of the patient: Thorpe J concluded:

> 'I am completely satisfied that the presumption that C has the right of self-determination has not been displaced. Although his general capacity is impaired by schizophrenia, it has not been established that he does not sufficiently understand the nature, purpose and effects of the treatment he refuses. Indeed, I am satisfied that he has understood and retained the relevant treatment information, that *in his own way he believes it*, and that in the same fashion he has arrived at a clear choice.'[9]

From the judgment of Thorpe J it is plain that he had been concerned about the issue of belief in the information. He was careful to emphasise the absence of evidence that C's attitude resulted from persecutory beliefs; C did not believe that the condition of his foot was caused by his clinicians. Further, he found that C accepted the advice he had been given, namely that without surgery there was a risk of death. It is perhaps likely then that, but for these elements of belief, C's capacity would have been found to have been eroded, and his refusal to consent to amputation liable to be overridden.

Thus, it will be under this part of the test of capacity that the anorexic or needle-phobic patient may be found to be incapable of making a competent decision, or rather that their decision to refuse treatment may be found to be invalid by reason of incapacity: as has been seen, the courts have found that the anorexia or phobia can constitute an impairment or disturbance of the functioning of the mind or brain; they have further found that conditions such as this can suffice to render the sufferer incapable of making a valid decision:

– The needle-phobic patient may be unable to weigh or use the information due to the temporary paralysis in mental functioning caused by her fear:

> 'She could not bring herself to undergo the caesarian section she desired because, as the evidence established, "a fear of needles ... has got in the way of proceeding with the operation ... At the moment of panic ... her fear dominated all ... at the actual point she was not capable of making a decision at all ... at that moment the needle or mask dominated her thinking and made her quite unable to consider anything else.". On that evidence she was incapable of making a decision at all. She was at that moment suffering an impairment of her mental functioning which disabled her. She was temporarily incompetent.'[10]

– The anorexic may be unable to understand, use or weigh the advice as to the necessity of eating given the dominance in her thinking of the very disorder of anorexia from which she is suffering:

> 'It is a feature of anorexia nervosa that it is capable of destroying the ability to make an informed choice. It creates a compulsion to refuse treatment or only to accept treatment which is likely to be ineffective. This attitude is part and parcel of the disease and the more advanced the illness, the more compelling it may become.'[11]

1 *Re MB (Medical treatment)* [1997] 2 FLR 426.
2 Main Code, para 4.16.
3 Main Code, para 4.19.
4 Main Code, para 4.20.
5 Main Code, para 4.20
6 See the case of the tetraplegic patient seeking to have ventilation withdrawn, discussed at Chapter 8: *Re B (adult: refusal of medical treatment)* [2002] 2 All ER 449.
7 [2002] 2 All ER 449.
8 [1994] 1 All ER 819 Fam.
9 [1994] 1 All ER 819 Fam at p 824, emphasis added.
10 *Re MB (an adult: medical treatment* (1997) 38 BMLR 175 (CA) Butler Sloss LJ.
11 *Re W: (a minor) (medical treatment)* [1992] 4 All ER 627.

Inability to communicate

2.31 The final requirement of the test of inability to make a decision is whether the person has the ability to communicate it. If such ability is lacking, then the person will lack capacity under the MCA 2005[1]. Understandably, the Main Code asserts that this inability must be total before an assessment of incapacity can be made, and that all practical and appropriate efforts are used to help the person communicate before this conclusion can be reached, including consideration of the need for speech and language therapists, specialists in non-verbal communication or other professionals[2]. To reinforce the point, the totality of the inability to communicate required is illustrated by giving examples of those affected: people who are unconscious or in a coma, or those who suffer from 'locked in syndrome', ie are conscious but cannot speak or move at all[3].

1 Section 3(1)(d).
2 Main Code, para 4.24.
3 Main Code, para 4.23.

Fluctuating capacity

2.32 It is explicit in the MCA 2005 that capacity can be lost on a temporary or long-term basis[1]. This is plainly correct, given that it is an issue-specific function: if, for example, the unconscious victim of an accident requires immediate life-saving surgery, they will not be able at that time to make a decision about the operation by reason of a disturbance in the functioning of their brain, and the incapacity requirements of s 3 will be satisfied, even if it is perfectly apparent that, should they recover consciousness, capacity will be regained. Alternatively, the patient with bipolar disorder may for long periods of time be perfectly capable of making decisions about their finances, but will be likely to lose this ability during manic phases.

What is important then in cases of temporary or fluctuating incapacity is to be alert to the nature of the decision or action being proposed. Is it needed now? If so, are there means by which the person's ability to decide can be promoted, such as those set out at Chapter 3 of the Code[2]? Alternatively, are there means by which the person may be helped to regain capacity, and can the decision or action wait until then? The Main Code requires would-be decision makers to bear these issues in mind. Also, it reminds them to undertake a periodic review of capacity of those in their care with long-term problems, as it may always be possible to support them further[3].

1 Section 2(2).
2 And summarised above at 2.8.
3 Main Code, para 2.9.

Consulting others about capacity

2.33 The person who has to make a decision about another's capacity is the person who is involved in the relevant decision or action, for example the carers considering accommodation issues, or the clinician deciding on medical treatment[1]. As can be seen from the general principles of s 1 of the MCA 2005, however, capacity must be assumed unless the contrary is established and all practicable steps to assist a person to make their own decision must be taken[2]. Further, as is discussed at Chapter 4 below, to be protected from liability if making treatment or welfare decisions on behalf of another, carers must take reasonable steps to establish capacity, and reasonably believe that the person lacks capacity[3].

This may be straightforward and plain. Frequently, however, the decision maker will be assisted by the input from others, and the Main Code recommends that consideration be given to whether others, such as a family member or advocate, could help the person make a decision or express a view[4]. However, at all times confidentiality needs to be respected, and the decision-maker will need to be alert to the appropriateness of suggesting the involvement of family members or others.

In some cases it may be appropriate to seek professional opinions from, for example, a psychiatrist, a psychologist, an old-age physician, a speech and language therapist, an occupational therapist or a social worker. Remember that the opinion obtained is just that, an opinion, and the decision-maker retains ultimate responsibility for making the decision[5]. Clearly, however, professional opinion is likely to be very important in an appropriate case.

What would be an appropriate case? The Main Code gives helpful illustrations: where for instance:

- the decision that needs to be made is complicated or has serious consequences;
- the assessor's belief that the person lacks capacity is challenged by the person;
- family members, carers and/or professionals disagree about a person's capacity;
- the person being assessed is expressing different views to different people – he may be trying to please everyone or telling people what he thinks they want to hear;
- somebody might challenge the person's capacity to make the decision, either at the time or later (eg a family member might challenge a will after a person has died, claiming incapacity);
- somebody has been accused of abusing a vulnerable adult who may lack capacity to make decisions that protect him;
- a person repeatedly makes decisions that puts him at risk or could result in suffering or damage[6].

1 See above, 2.29.
2 Section 1(2) and (3), discussed above at 2.3 and 2.7.
3 Section 5(1).
4 Main Code, paras 3.15, 4.36.
5 See 2.29 above.
6 Main Code, para 4.53.

The non-compliant person

2.34 The Main Code considers the position of the person whose capacity is in doubt but who refuses to be examined[1]. This can be difficult, and the carer's tools are limited. The first action must clearly be discussion and attempts at persuasion, telling the person why an assessment is needed and what is at stake. It is possible that the provisions of the Mental Health Act 1983 might be invoked in a serious case – where there are worries about the person's mental health and the conditions for assessment in hospital under the 1983 Act are met. However, the Code reminds us that simple refusal of an assessment is 'in no way sufficient grounds' for an assessment under the Mental Health Act 1983, and that threats or attempts to force the person to agree to an assessment are not acceptable.

How then can a carer deal with a person suspected of lacking capacity but who refuses a capacity assessment and does not meet the criteria for hospital assessment under the Mental Health Act? The Main Code does not assist further. However, application of the principles of the MCA 2005 would suggest that if a carer believes an action or decision needs to be made by or on behalf of the person which cannot be postponed, and where the person has refused to participate in all attempts to secure his co-operation, the carer simply has to use the information available; ie to ask, judging from all the sources of information the carer does have (past history, present behaviour etc), is it reasonable to conclude that the person lacks capacity within the meaning of s 2 – ie is s/he unable to make a decision for him/herself by reason of an impairment of, or a disturbance in the functioning of the mind or brain?

1 Main Code, paras 4.57–4.59.

Challenging a decision

2.35 As set out above, the assessment that a person lacks – or retains – capacity will be made by the person proposing to make a decision or take an action on their behalf. There will inevitably be occasions when others disagree with that assessment. The Main Code suggests informal methods of resolution of the disagreement initially – raising it with the person who made the assessment and asking for reasons and evidence[1]. If the challenge comes from the person said to lack capacity, they may need support from family, friends or an advocate.

In the event of continued disagreement the Code suggests recourse to a second opinion, mediation or local complaints procedures[2]. The ultimate arbiter will however be the Court of Protection which can be asked to rule on whether the person has capacity to make the relevant decision.[3]

1 Main Code, para 4.63.
2 Developed in detail at Chapter 15 of the Main Code.
3 See further Chapter 10 below.

Practical application

2.36 The Code sets out two checklists of practical action and steps in the approach to an assessment of capacity. The first concentrates on the approach to the person and maximising his ability to have capacity, the second on the issue of information:

Practical steps in the approach to the person:

- Start by assuming the person has capacity to make the specific decision. Is there anything to prove otherwise?
- Does the person have a previous diagnosis of disability or mental disorder? Does that condition now affect their capacity to make this decision? If there has been no previous diagnosis, it may be best to get a medical opinion.
- Make every effort to communicate with the person to explain what is happening.
- See if there is a way to explain or present information about the decision in a way that makes it easier to understand. If the person has a choice, do they have information about all the options?

- Can the decision be delayed to take time to help the person make the decision, or to give them time to regain the capacity to make the decision for themselves?
- Does the person understand what decision they need to make and why they need to make it?
- Can they understand information about the decision? Can they retain it, use it and weigh it to make the decision?
- Be aware that the fact that a person agrees with you or assents to what is proposed does not necessarily mean that they have capacity to make the decision[1].

Practical steps in the approach to the question of information: would-be decision makers need to consider which of the following are relevant:

- They should make sure that they understand the nature and effect of the decision to be made themselves. They may need access to relevant documents and background information (for example, details of the person's finances if assessing capacity to manage affairs).
- They may need other relevant information to support the assessment (for example, healthcare records or the views of staff involved in the person's care).
- Family members and close friends may be able to provide valuable background information (for example, the person's past behaviour and abilities and the types of decisions he can currently make). But their personal views and wishes about what they would want for the person must not influence the assessment.
- They should again explain to the person all the information relevant to the decision. The explanation must be in the most appropriate and effective form of communication for that person.
- Check the person's understanding after a few minutes. They should be able to give a rough explanation of the information that was explained. There are different methods for people who use non-verbal means of communication (for example, observing behaviour or their ability to recognise objects or pictures).
- Avoid questions that need only a 'yes' or 'no' answer (for example, did you understand what I just said?). They are not enough to asses the person's capacity to make a decision. But there may be no alternative in cases where there are major communication difficulties. In these cases, check the response by asking questions again in a different way.
- Skills and behaviour do not necessarily reflect the person's capacity to make specific decisions. The fact that someone has good social or language skills, polite behaviour or good manners does not necessarily mean he understands the information or is able to weigh it up.
- Repeating these steps can help confirm the result.[2]

1 Main Code, para 4.45.
2 Main Code, para 4.49.

Best interests

2.37 Where a person lacks capacity then an act done or decision made on their behalf must be done or made in their best interests[1].

1 Section 1(4) of the Act, the fourth of the general principles of s 1, applicable unless there is a valid advance decision covering the issue at hand – see Chapter 3 below, or in specified circumstances of medical research – see Chapter 13 below.

The best interests decision, not a decision within a range

2.38 Note that the MCA 2005 requires the decision-maker to make a decision which is in the person's best interests, rather than a decision which might reasonably be thought to be *amongst those* which are in their best interests. Whilst a decision maker will not be liable for a decision made on behalf of an incapacitated patient if s/he takes reasonable steps to establish incapacity and reasonably believes that the decision is in the patient's best interests[1], the task of the decision maker is nevertheless to find *the* best interests decision, not merely one amongst an acceptable range.

1 Section 5, developed at Chapter 4 below.

Who makes the decision?

2.39 As with the assessment of incapacity, the burden falls on the person proposing to make the decision or do the act. Thus, it will apply to anyone making decisions or acting under the Act, including family or paid carers, clinicians, social care staff, donees under powers of attorney, deputies appointed by the Court of Protection, and the Court of Protection itself. On occasion it may require a joint or multi-disciplinary approach.

The making of the best interests decision

2.40 How is the assessment made? As set out above (2.20) that the MCA 2005 does not create a definition of best interests. What the Act does is to set out a procedural code. Section 4 states what must not be used in the assessment, and then sets out the required steps. The latter comprise a checklist of factors to be taken into account in reaching the best interests decision.

There is no weighting given to any one of the factors over any other. Some commentators during the passage of the legislation urged the weighting of the incapacitated person's wishes, where they could be ascertained, in order to ensure that their voice was heard; others suggested giving preference to outcomes which maximised independence, and others to preferring the views of family carers over professional carers. The Joint Scrutiny Committee did not endorse these recommendations, concluding that flexibility was the best method of achieving the appropriate best interests response:

> 'We acknowledge that consideration of best interests requires flexibility, by allowing and encouraging the person to be involved to the fullest possible extent but also enabling the decision-maker to take account of a variety of circumstances, views and attitudes which may have a bearing on the decision in question. This flexibility is particularly important in cases of partial or fluctuating capacity. Determining best interests is a judgement, requiring

consideration of what will often be conflicting or competing concerns, while seeking to achieve a consensus approach to decision-making. We do not recommend any weighting or giving priority to the factors involved in determining best interests.'[1]

The Government agreed. Thus there is no one factor in the statutory checklist which takes priority over any other in reaching an assessment of best interests. In particular, the MCA 2005 does not include any requirement that the preservation of life be incorporated within the best interests test. This reflects the common law position, where there is certainly a presumption in favour of life-sustaining treatment, but it is a rebuttable presumption, for it may not be in the best interests of a person to continue to receive life sustaining treatment[2].

1 Scrutiny Report, para 81.
2 See for example *Airedale NHS Trust v Bland* [1993] AC 789, Main Code, paras 5.31–5.33 and Chapter 8 below on medical treatment.

The prohibited step

2.41 In determining what is in the incapacitated person's best interests, the decision-maker must not make a decision:

> 'merely on the basis of:
> (a) the person's age or appearance, or
> (b) a condition of his, or an aspect of his behaviour, which might lead others to make unjustified assumptions about what might be in his best interests.'[1]

What this requires is that in the best interests assessment, the decision-maker must start with a blank slate, and undertake a full and objective evaluation, rather than, for example ruling out life-sustaining treatment for an elderly stroke victim *merely* because of their age.

1 Section 4(1).

The required steps

2.42

> 'The person making the determination must consider all the relevant circumstances ...'[1]

What comprise 'all the relevant circumstances'? Section 4(11) provides that they are those:

> '(a) of which the person making the determination is aware, and
> (b) which it would be reasonable to regard as relevant.'

The Code recognises that these will vary with each case, but gives helpful examples:

- In a medical context when making a decision about major medical treatment, a doctor would need to consider the clinical needs of the patient, the potential benefits and burdens of the treatment on the person's health and life expectancy and any other factors relevant to making a professional judgement. But it would not be reasonable to consider issues such as life expectancy when working out whether it would be in someone's best interests to be given medication for a minor problem.
- In a financial context, if a person had received a substantial sum of money as compensation for an accident resulting in brain injury the decision-maker would have to consider a wide range of circumstances when making decisions about how the money is spent or invested, such as whether the person's condition is likely to change; whether the person needs professional care, and whether the person needs to live somewhere else to make it easier for him[2].

Section 4(2) continues:

> '… and, in particular, take the following steps'.

The remainder of s 4 sets out a series of procedural steps the decision-maker must consider. Note that the extent to which they are considered will vary with the circumstances, and with the gravity of the decision in issue, but the decision-maker must consider them with the following aim:

> 'the decision-maker should try to identify all the issues that would be most relevant to the individual who lacks capacity and to the particular decision'.[3]

The steps are, in summary as follows:

- to consider the likelihood of the person regaining capacity;
- to promote and encourage participation of the person so far as possible;
- with regard to life sustaining treatment, not be motivated by a desire to bring about death;
- to consider the person's wishes, beliefs and other factors the person would be likely to consider were they able to do so;
- take account as appropriate of the views of named others.

1 Section 4(2).
2 Main Code, paras 5.19–5.20.
3 Main Code, para 5.18.

Likelihood of recovery of capacity

2.43 The decision-maker:

> 'must consider
> (a) whether it is likely that the person will at some time have capacity in relation to the matter in question, and
> (b) if it appears likely that he will, when that is likely to be.'[1]

Implicit in this subsection, and explicit in the Code[2], is the requirement that, if the decision can be postponed to a time when the person is likely to have regained capacity, it should be. The prospect of recovery from stroke, or from the effects of medication, alcohol or shock should be borne in mind if the decision can wait. Further, again if time permits, any steps which could reasonably be taken to encourage the person to regain capacity so that they can make the decision themselves, should be taken.

1 Section 4(3).
2 Main Code, paras 5.25–5.27.

Promotion of participation by the incapacitated person

2.44 The decision-maker:

> 'must, so far as reasonably practicable, permit and encourage the person to participate, or to improve his ability to participate, as fully as possible in any act done for him and any decision affecting him.'[1]

Section 4(4) repeats the recurrent theme in this part of the Act, namely the obligation on carers and clinicians to maximise the opportunities of those in their care to make their own decisions. So, even where capacity is clearly lost, the patient must still – where practicable – be encouraged to participate as far as possible in the decision-making process. The Main Code states:

> 'Wherever possible, the person who lacks capacity to make a decision should still be involved in the decision-making process.
>
> Even if the person lacks capacity to make the decision, they may have views on matters affecting the decision, and on what outcome would be preferred. Their involvement can help work out what would be in their best interests.'[1]

1 Section 4(4).
2 Main Code, paras 5.21–5.22.

Not be motivated by a desire to bring about death in the context of life sustaining treatment

2.45 Section 4(5) provides that:

> 'Where the determination relates to life-sustaining treatment he must not, in considering whether the treatment is in the best interests of the person concerned, be motivated by a desire to bring about his death.'

This subsection was inserted at the Committee stage of the Bill's passage in the House of Lords to respond to concerns that decisions about life-sustaining treatment could lead to euthanasia, and it makes the position which already exists in law absolutely clear. Equally however, the subsection does not establish that decisions can never be made which have the result of bringing about a person's death, as the Main Code explains:

> 'All reasonable steps which are in the person's best interests should be taken to prolong their life. There will be a limited number of cases where treatment is futile, overly burdensome to the patient or where there is no prospect of recovery. In circumstances such as these, it may be that an assessment of best interests leads to the conclusion that it would be in the best interests of the

> patient to withdraw or withhold life-sustaining treatment, even if this may result in the person's death. The decision-maker must make a decision based on the best interests of the person who lacks capacity. They must not be motivated by a desire to bring about the person's death for whatever reason, even if this is from a sense of compassion.'[1]

Note that under s 4(10) life sustaining treatment is defined as 'treatment which in the view of a person providing health care for the person concerned is necessary to sustain life'. The original drafting of this subsection included the word 'his' before 'life'. It was amended during the passage of the Bill with the aim of ensuring that, in the case of a pregnant woman, the life of the baby as well as her own life must in appropriate cases be considered.

Whether or not a treatment is life-sustaining will depend on the circumstances of the case. As the Main Code explains, giving antibiotics may or may not be life-sustaining depending upon the nature of the person's illness and general condition[2].

Even if a treatment is life sustaining, the same best interests checklist must be used as in all other situations involving an incapacitated person. Further, as developed in Chapter 8 on medical treatment, s 4(5) does not oblige doctors to provide life-sustaining treatment where that would not be in the best interests of the person, even where death is likely to result; the doctor must apply the checklist and make a judgement as to whether they consider life-sustaining treatment is in the person's best interests. If they decide that it is, it will only be in the case of a valid and applicable advance directive refusing life-sustaining treatment that will 'trump' the contrary opinion of a clinician, donee of a lasting power of attorney, or even the Court of Protection[3].

Of course, save in the case of the valid and applicable advance directive, the Court of Protection can be asked to rule upon whether life-sustaining treatment is in the person's best interests. In these circumstances, s 6(7) of the Act provides that the clinician can provide life-sustaining treatment, or act in a way s/he believes necessary to prevent a serious deterioration in the patient's health, whilst a ruling is sought from the Court of Protection.

1 Main Code, para 5.31, essentially reflecting the common law position with regard to the cessation of life-sustaining treatment – see Chapter 8.
2 Main Code, para 5.30.
3 See Chapter 3 below.

Consideration of the incapacitated person's wishes, feelings, beliefs and values

2.46 Section 4(6) requires the decision maker, when making a best interests assessment, to consider:

> 'so far as is reasonably ascertainable—
> (a) the person's past and present wishes and feelings (and, in particular, any relevant written statement made by him when he had capacity);
> (b) the beliefs and values that would be likely to influence his decision if he had capacity, and

(c) the other factors that he would be likely to consider if he were able to do so.'

The Main Code states that this subsection 'puts the person who lacks capacity at the centre of the decision to be made', so that the question is considered from their perspective[1]. The person's wishes, feelings, beliefs and values should be taken fully into account, whether expressed in the past or present, even though they cannot dictate the outcome or decision, which will depend on the entirety of the best interests assessment.

What is 'reasonably ascertainable' will depend upon the circumstances, and particularly on how much time is available to make the enquiry: emergency situations will clearly differ, although even here the Code recommends communication as far as possible with the person or their family.

Accordingly, all reasonably practicable steps should be taken to find out as much about the person as possible to inform the best interests decision. The expression of past wishes, and particularly anything written by the person before losing capacity, is relevant. Similarly, clearly held beliefs and values must be considered. The Main Code gives an example in this context:

> 'Anita, a young woman, suffers serious brain damage during a car accident. The court appoints her father as deputy to invest the compensation she received. As the decision-maker he must think about her wishes, beliefs and values before deciding how to invest the money.
>
> Anita had worked for an overseas charity. Her father talks to her former colleagues. They tell him how Anita's political beliefs shaped her work and personal beliefs, so he decides not to invest in the bonds that a financial adviser had recommended, because they are from companies Anita would not have approved of. Instead, he employs an ethical investment adviser to choose appropriate companies in line with her beliefs.'[2]

This example is interesting so far as it goes, but how would, or should, Anita's father have reacted if advised that the ethical investments carried a lower rate of return, and would barely meet the cost of Anita's care and equipment? This would make the best interests decision much more challenging.

The Code does however make clear that the wishes or beliefs of the incapacitated person are not, in the last analysis, conclusive. They are very important factors to be used in the decision-making process, but it must be for decision-makers ultimately to make their own decision as to what is in the best interests of the incapacitated person. This is the case whether or not the source of the person's expression of wishes is oral or written (unless the latter constitutes a valid, and therefore binding, advance directive[3]). The Act requires the decision-maker explicitly to heed anything relevant written by the person before capacity was lost; if not a valid advance directive however, even this cannot be determinative if the decision-maker forms the view, having followed all of the steps in the checklist, that the written request does not accord with the best interests test.

Under this subsection, having considered the person's wishes and feelings, beliefs and values, the decision-maker must also consider as far as ascertainable, 'the other factors that he would be likely to consider if he were able to do so'[4]. This is an enormously wide notion, but mirrors the common law understanding of best interests, which was well established to be a very broad test. It is considered in the context of medical treatment at Chapter 8 below, but note that in relation to medical treatment, best interests were described by Butler Sloss P in *Re A (Male sterilisation)*[5] as encompassing 'medical, emotional and all other welfare issues'.

The breadth of the concept is echoed in the Main Code which says this:

> 'The Act allows actions that benefit other people, as long as they are in the best interests of the person who lacks capacity to make the decision. For example, having considered all the circumstances of the particular case, a decision might be to take a blood sample from a person who lacks capacity to consent, to check for a genetic link for cancer within the family, because this might benefit someone else in the family. But it might still be in the best interests of the person who lacks capacity. …
>
> For example, courts have previously ruled that possible wider benefits to a person who lacks capacity to consent, such as providing or gaining emotional support from close relationships, are important factors in working out the person's own best interests. If it is likely that the person who lacks capacity would have considered these factors themselves, they can be seen as part of the person's best interests.'[6]

On that latter point, it has been held to be appropriate to act here on the assumption that the incapacitated person would be 'a normal decent person, acting in accordance with contemporary standards of morality'[7].

1 Main Code, para 5.38.
2 Main Code, para 5.46.
3 See Chapter 3 below.
4 Section 4(6)(c).
5 [2000] 1 FLR 549, CA.
6 Main Code, para 5.48.
7 *Re C (Spinster and mental patient)* [1991] 3 All ER 866.

Account to be taken, if appropriate, of the views of others

2.47 By s 4(7) the decision-maker:

> 'must take into account, if it is practicable and appropriate to consult them, the views of:
> (a) anyone named by the person as someone to be consulted on the matter in question or on matters of that kind,
> (b) anyone engaged in caring for the person or interested in his welfare,
> (c) any donee of a lasting power of attorney granted by the person, and
> (d) any deputy appointed for the person by the court,
> as to what would be in the person's best interests and, in particular, as to the matters mentioned in subsection (6).'

Note that this does not impose an obligation to consult in all cases, but to consider firstly whether it is 'practicable and appropriate' to consult, and then to take into account, the consultees' views. It may not be appropriate to consult a particular family member or carer for example, where credible allegations of abuse have been made. However, the Main Code advises the decision maker to show they have thought carefully about who to speak to, must consult if practical and appropriate to do so, and must take the responses into account, and must be able to explain why they did not consult a particular person. It adds:

> 'It is also good practice to give careful consideration to the views of family carers, if it is possible to do so.'[1]

It is important to note the purpose of the consultation. It is not to find out what the consultee believes should be done, but to assist the decision-maker to find out what is in the incapacitated person's best interests, a rather different question. The consultee can help particularly with the inquiry required at s 4(6), namely the investigation of the person's wishes and feelings, beliefs and values. The consultee cannot determine the decision; that task remains with the carer or clinician proposing to act. The Main Code acknowledges this, but seeks to encourage collaboration, as indeed it must if it is to respect the rights to privacy and family life of both the incapacitated person and their family under Article 8 ECHR[2]. Accordingly, says the Main Code, the decision maker:

> 'will need to find a way of balancing [differing or opposing] concerns or deciding between them. The first approach should be to review all elements of the best interests check list with everyone involved. They should include the person who lacks capacity (as much as they are able to take part) and anyone who has been involved in earlier discussions. It may be possible to reach an agreement at a meeting to air everyone's concerns. But an agreement in itself might not be in the person's best interests. Ultimate responsibility for working out best interests lies with the decision-maker.'[3]

The Main Code reminds decision-makers of the different perspectives which can be brought by a range of consultees. Sometimes the decision-maker will find that carers have an insight into how to interpret a person's wishes and feelings that can help them reach a decision. On the other hand, non-family carers may have specialist knowledge about up-to-date care options or treatments. Some may also have known the person for many years[4]. Further, people with conflicting interests should not necessarily be cut out of the process (for example, those who stand to inherit from the person's will may still have a right to be consulted about the person's care or medical treatment). But decision-makers must always ensure that the interests of those consulted do not overly influence the process of working out a person's best interests. In weighing up different contributions the decision-maker should consider how long an individual has known the person who lacks capacity, and what their relationship is[5].

Finally on this topic, decision-makers need to balance their statutory obligation to consider consultation with their duties of confidentiality. The Main Code advises healthcare and social care staff who are trying to determine a person's best interests to follow their professional guidance about confidentiality[6].

1 Main Code, para 5.52.

2 See *Glass v United Kingdom* [2004] 1 FLR 1019.
3 Main Code para 5.64.
4 Main Code, para 5.65–5.66.
5 Main Code, para 5.67.
6 Main Code, para 5.57.

Compliance with the best interests checklist

2.48 Section 4(9) provides:

> 'In the case of an act done, or a decision made, by a person other than the court, there is sufficient compliance with this section if (having complied with the requirements of subsections (1) to (7)) he reasonably believes that what he does or decides is in the best interests of the person concerned.'

In other words, if having followed the best interests checklist, the decision-maker comes to hold a reasonable belief that the decision proposed to be made is in the best interests of the person concerned, they will be found to have complied with this section[1].

Thus, the decision-maker will need both to hold that belief, and be able to identify objective reasons in support, to establish it to be reasonable.

1 See further Chapter 4 on acts in connection with care or treatment.

Conflict in the assessment of best interests

2.49 Here, as in the assessment of incapacity, there are may well be strongly held but opposing views. The Main Code recommends a series of steps to tackle persisting conflict:

- Involve an advocate on behalf of the incapacitated person[1];
- Seek a second opinion;
- Hold a formal or 'best interests' case conference;
- attempt mediation;
- Ultimately, if all else has failed, consider taking the matter to the Court of Protection[2], remembering that whilst seeking a ruling the clinician can continue to provide life sustaining treatment and can act where s/he reasonably believes it to be necessary to prevent a serious deterioration in the patient's condition[3].

1 See Chapter 6 below.
2 See Chapter 10 below.
3 Section 6(7).

PRACTICE POINTS

2.50 It is suggested that, questions of judgement aside, one of the most important issues for carers and clinicians to have in the forefront of their assessment are the appropriate decision pathways. When faced with a person whose capacity is in doubt in relation to a particular issue, it is necessary to ask the correct questions in the right order. The following are suggested:

Where an issue of capacity arises:

- What is the decision or action about which the question of capacity has arisen?

  Is it for example a medical treatment which is recommended, a decision about appropriate accommodation, or something which is being done by the person which is giving cause for concern for his welfare (eg rash financial actions, self neglect etc)?
- Is the decision or action one covered by the MCA 2005?
- Who is it who is seeking to explore the person's capacity with regard to that decision, and who bears responsibility for making the assessment of capacity and best interests?

  Remember that both of these roles will fall upon the person seeking to act or decide on behalf of the person, unless there is a valid and applicable lasting power of attorney, in which case the best interests decision will fall upon the donee to take.
- Is the diagnostic threshold crossed?

  ie does the person have an impairment of, or disturbance in the functioning of the brain?

  In considering this question do not make assumptions merely by reference to the person's age, appearance, condition or behaviour.
- If the person has an impairment or disturbance in the functioning of the brain is this causing them to be unable to make a decision?

  Remember that this question will cover the person genuinely unable to make a decision, and the person who has made an apparent decision but which is one which has caused others to question their capacity.
- In assessing inability to make a decision, or the validity of a worrying decision purportedly made, consider whether the person is able:
  (a) to understand the information relevant to the decision, given in a manner appropriate to their condition and circumstances, and covering the consequences of deciding one way or the other, or of failing to make any decision;
  (b) to retain that information (for a period sufficient to be satisfied that they can make the decision);
  (c) to use or weigh that information as part of the process of making the decision;
  (d) to communicate that decision by whatever means?
- Remember that at every stage of this enquiry all practicable steps are to be taken to help the person make their own decision before concluding that they lack capacity.

Where it is concluded that the person lacks capacity with regard to the relevant decision or action:

- Is there a valid and applicable advance decision which covers the present circumstances?[1]
- Can the decision be postponed pending a foreseeable or possible recovery of capacity?

- If not, upon whom does the best interests decision fall?
- What is in the best interests of the person? In making this assessment:
  - (a) do not make it merely on the basis of his age, appearance, condition or behaviour;
  - (b) consider all the relevant circumstances of which the decision-maker is aware;
  - (c) permit the person so far as reasonably practicable to participate, or improve their ability to participate in the decision-making;
  - (d) where the decision relates to life-sustaining treatment, do not be motivated by a desire to bring about the person's death;
  - (e) consider so far as reasonably practicable in assessing best interests:
    - (i) the person's past and present wishes and feelings (in particular anything written by them);
    - (ii) the beliefs and values likely to influence the person if they had capacity;
    - (iii) the other factors the person would be likely to consider if able to do so;
    - (iv) the views of anyone named by the person, those caring for them, the donee of a lasting power of attorney, any deputy appointed by the courts.
- Having made a decision as to the person's best interests, consider whether it can be achieved as effectively in a manner less restrictive of the person's rights and freedom of action?

1 See Chapter 3 below.

Chapter 3

ADVANCE DECISIONS TO REFUSE TREATMENT

- **MCA 2005, ss 24–26**
- **Main Code, Chapter 9**

INTRODUCTION

3.1 The advance decision is a logical extension of the principle of patient autonomy which recognises the right of a competent patient to decline medical treatment. It is a tool which provides patients with a means of extending their entitlement to refuse medical treatment, even where life-saving, to a time when they have lost capacity.

If valid, it has the same force as the contemporaneous refusal of treatment by a patient with capacity. In other words, neither a clinician, a donee of a power of attorney, nor the Court of Protection will be able to invoke the best interests doctrine and, should a doctor give medical treatment validly declined under an advance decision s/he will be liable to prosecution for assault or civil claim for damages[1].

It is not clear to what extent advance decisions will be taken up under the MCA 2005, the Main Code acknowledging that many people will prefer to leave it to healthcare professionals to make that best interests decision on their behalf[2]. However, a valid advance decision is a means whereby a person can retain some control over what happens to them should they lose capacity in the future[3].

The advance decision does not only bind the clinician: the Court of Protection can be asked to rule upon whether an advance decision is applicable to the situation in hand and is valid, but if the court finds that it is both valid and applicable, it has no power to override it.

The only circumstance where an otherwise valid and applicable advance decision can be overridden is where the patient is detained under the Mental Health Act 1983 and liable to compulsory treatment for mental illness (but see Chapter 16 at 16.6 for an exception and 16.38).

The MCA 2005 does not create the concept of advance decisions. They have been recognised for some years[4]. However, as with the definition of capacity and best interests, the MCA 2005 is intended to codify and clarify the existing common law on the subject.

In its deliberations on the Mental Incapacity Bill, as it then was, the Joint Scrutiny Committee[5] received a considerable amount of evidence expressing grave concern about advance decisions, the concerns being in summary as follows:

- that it was morally wrong to introduce a statute that could enable decisions to be taken which would effectively shorten life;
- that it was unacceptable to require a doctor not to give treatment that the doctor believed was in the patient's best interests;
- that the provisions were introducing euthanasia by the back door;
- that the notion of 'treatment' did not exclude artificial nutrition and hydration ('ANH'); it was argued that this was unacceptable as it would result in a patient refusing ANH suffering a very painful and undignified death;

- that people when capable are unable accurately to foresee how they might wish to act if incapable, and should not commit themselves to a course of action from which they could not withdraw; further the advance decision will not be able to take into account the effects of progress in medical treatment, or the fact that putting the refusal into practice might in fact increase rather than relieve suffering[6].

The Joint Scrutiny Committee did hear evidence in support of the advance decision as the logical extension of the principle of patient autonomy, and it was of course aware that such decisions had been recognised in the High Court already. It was concerned that were the Bill to omit reference to advance decisions, an opportunity to codify and clarify would be lost, as would the ability of the new Court of Protection to be the arbiter of issues of applicability and validity[7]. Accordingly, it endorsed the Bill's proposals about advance decisions, but made a number of recommendations designed to strengthen the safeguards protecting patients in this field.

The Joint Committee on Human Rights (JCHR) also took care to scrutinise the advance decisions sections of the Bill. It did not consider that the provisions themselves raised issues of compatibility with the ECHR, in particular Article 2, as 'it is well established in current law that, important though the principle of the sanctity of life is in human rights law, it may have to yield where it comes into conflict with the rights to dignity and personal autonomy protected by Articles 3 and 8 ECHR.'[8]

The issue for the JCHR was whether the safeguards surrounding such advance directives were adequate. It was generally satisfied that they were, save in two respects – it was concerned that an advance decision might be made orally, and that the public in general may not know that artificial nutrition and hydration might be covered by an advance decision. These issues are considered further at 3.7 and 3.6 below[9].

1 Note also that the protections provided under s 5 are expressly inapplicable to advance decisions: s 5(4).
2 Main Code, para 9.4.
3 An alternative would be to create a lasting power of attorney, allowing a trusted friend or relative to make the best interests decision on his behalf on personal welfare decisions should he lose capacity: see below Chapter 5.
4 See *Re T (Adult: refusal of medical treatment)* [1993] Fam 95, [1992] 3 WLR 782, *Re C (Adult: refusal of medical treatment)* [1994] 1 All ER 819, *Re AK (Adult patient) (Medical treatment: consent)* [2001] 1 FLR 129, *HE v A Hospital NHS Trust* [2003] EWHC 1017 (Fam [2003] 2 FLR 408).
5 The Report of the Joint Scrutiny Committee on the draft Mental Incapacity Bill (as it was originally named), HL Paper 189/HC 1083, published on 17 November 2003 (hereinafter 'The Joint Scrutiny Report').
6 See Joint Scrutiny Report, paras 195–198.
7 Joint Scrutiny Report, paras 199–202.
8 Joint Committee on Human Rights, Final Progress Report, HL Paper 210/HC 1282, published 29 November 2004, para 2.44.
9 See also Chapter 17 below.

GENERAL POINTS ABOUT ADVANCE DECISIONS

Negative not positive decisions

3.2 Advance decisions are decisions to refuse medical treatment, and are only valid in this negative sense. They do not operate to compel a clinician to provide care which runs against the clinician's professional recommendation. Chapter 8 considers this issue in more detail, but in summary, the patient cannot insist upon being provided with a course of treatment which his doctor cannot professionally recommend[1]. This position is unaffected by ss 24–26 of the MCA 2005.

Accordingly, as set out in Chapter 2 above, whilst an incapacitated patient's earlier written expression of preference is a matter a clinician is bound to consider when assessing his best interests[1], unless that expression amounts to a valid, applicable – and negative – advance decision, it will not be binding upon the clinician.

1 See the decision of the Court of Appeal in *R (on the application of Burke) v General Medical Council* [2005] EWCA Civ 1003, paras 51–55, [2006] QB 273: 'In truth the right to choose is no more than a reflection of the fact that it is the doctor's duty to provide a treatment that he considers to be in the best interests of the patient and that the patient is prepared to accept' at para 51.

2 Section 4(6)(a).

Format

3.3 To be valid, an advance decision does not have to be in any particular form, unless it relates to life-sustaining treatment, in which case it must be in writing and witnessed[1].

The difficulty with this may be that casually expressed comment might later be elevated into a binding advance decision contrary to the real wishes of the patient. Both the JCHR[2] and the Joint Scrutiny Committee recommended that advance decisions should generally have to be in writing[3]. On this point the government disagreed, but for this reason – if the advance decision had to be in writing, there would be a risk that revoking the decision would also require a formal process, which may have the effect of discouraging people, or making it very difficult for them, from making clear that they had changed their decision[4]. Accordingly under the MCA 2005, an advance decision may be made, save with regard to life sustaining treatment, wholly orally, and any advance decision can be revoked or altered wholly orally[5].

Clearly, the applicability and validity, and indeed the very existence of an advance decision, are likely to be more easily established if contained in wholly written and precise form. However, s 24(2) provides that it may validly specify a treatment or circumstances 'even though expressed in layman's terms'. The practicalities of making or assessing the validity and applicability of an advance decision are considered further at 3.13 below.

1 See 3.10 below.

2 23rd report, HL Paper 210 (2003–2004), HC 1282, para 2.46.

3 Joint Scrutiny Report, para 205.

4 Government's response to the Joint Scrutiny Committee Report, February 2004, re Recommendation 58.

5 Unless the alteration in itself seeks to create an advance decision to refuse life-sustaining treatment, in which case the alteration will require to be in writing and be witnessed: s 24(4) and (5).

Requirements

3.4 The principle requirements of an advance decision (subject to the more rigorous demands of one relating to life-sustaining treatment) are that:

- the maker is over 18;
- the maker has capacity to make the decision at the time he makes it;
- at the time in question:
  - (a) the patient lacks capacity to decide; and
  - (b) the advance decision remains valid and is applicable to the particular treatment in issue.

THE DEFINITION AND SCOPE OF AN ADVANCE DECISION

3.5 An advance decision means a decision made by an adult with capacity:

> 'that if
> (a) at a later time and in such circumstances as he may specify, a specified treatment is proposed to be carried out or continued by a person providing healthcare for him, and
> (b) at that time he lacks capacity to consent to the carrying out or continuation of the treatment,
> the specified treatment is not to be carried out or continued.'[1]

1 Section 24(1).

Treatment and basic care

3.6 The decision must relate to 'a specified treatment'; expression of a general desire not to be treated is not enough, although as noted above, it does not need to be expressed in technical or medical language[1]. Equally, the Main Code provides that a refusal of all treatment in any given situation may be valid and applicable[2].

Treatment is defined non-exhaustively (and perhaps unhelpfully) at s 64(1): ' "treatment" includes a diagnostic or other procedure'[3]; unhelpful in that it is not immediately apparent that a diagnostic procedure would count as 'treatment'. Clearly, the majority of medical treatments will be readily identifiable as such, for example, surgery or a course of drugs.

Consider however the incidentals to medical treatment, namely keeping the patient adequately hydrated, nourished, warm and comfortable, whilst such treatment takes effect, or even whilst awaiting the terminal event in a fatal condition – should they be classed as treatment?

It is in fact now well established that the provision of nutrition and hydration by artificial means, where the patient is unable orally to ingest food or fluid, falls within the concept of medical treatment[4]. The consequence of this is that an advance decision could validly refuse consent for artificial nutrition and hydration. The result of such a decision would in all likelihood be exceptionally painful for carers and clinicians to witness. Whilst not seeking to remove artificial nutrition and hydration from the concept of treatment, it is perhaps unsurprising that policy makers and commentators have been anxious that there be a limit to what can be validly declined by way of advance decision:

- The Law Commission recommended that an advance decision should not be able to preclude the provision of basic care – namely care to maintain bodily cleanliness and to alleviate severe pain, or the provision of direct oral nutrition and hydration:

  > 'On consultation there was general agreement to the proposition that a patient's right to self-determination could properly be limited by considerations based on public policy. ... Our proposed definition of "basic care" reflects a level of care which it would be contrary to public policy to withhold from a patient without capacity.'[5]

- The Joint Scrutiny Committee agreed, concluding that basic care, in which it included the giving of normal methods of nutrition and hydration (as opposed to artificial methods, such as via drips or naso-gastric tubes) fell outside what was normally considered to be treatment and should always be available to people[6].

The MCA 2005 accordingly provides at s 24 that advance decisions apply to 'treatment' within the healthcare context. This is certainly the area within which the decided cases have examined advance decisions – the courts have been called upon to assess the validity of decisions relating to the refusal of blood transfusions, or of ANH, or of ventilation, where it is clear that the refusal would lead to death.

Consider, however, the patient with capacity who seeks to make an advance refusal of nursing care, or of treatment provided in a particular fashion (or by a type of person): for example:

1. a statement, made on religious grounds, refusing any medical treatment which involved the cutting or loss of the patient's facial or head hair;
2. a statement, made on no discernible ground of principle, that were the patient to become ill, he would not want his hair cut;
3. a statement, made by a female survivor of sexual abuse, refusing any medical treatment which was delivered by a man;
4. a statement made by an elderly patient unable to provide himself with basic nursing care, refusing to consent to his admission to a nursing home for such care.

It is suggested that these scenarios raise difficult questions. The first step would be to assess whether they fell within the meaning of an advance decision under the MCA 2005, in the sense of whether they related to 'a specified treatment' within the meaning of s 24(1)(a):

- Number 1, although broad, may be felt to come within the definition in much the same way as a Jehovah's Witness' refusal of all treatment by way of blood transfusion.
- Number 3 appears to relate to medical treatment, but actually only purports to raise objections to the manner of delivery of the treatment: would the Court of Protection find that to be a 'specified treatment'?
- Numbers 2 and 4 do not relate to medical treatment, and thus it would seem that the MCA 2005 cannot apply. Does that mean, however, that the patient with capacity cannot validly refuse basic nursing care or non-therapeutic adjuncts of medical care?

As noted above, the Law Commission and Joint Scrutiny Committee certainly wanted to limit advance decisions to those refusing medical care, considering it to be contrary to public policy for the law to permit the withholding of basic care. The Main Code takes the same approach:

> 'An advance decision cannot refuse actions that are needed to keep a person comfortable (sometimes called basic care). Examples include warmth, shelter, actions to keep a person clean and the offer of food and water by mouth. Section 5 of the Act allows healthcare professionals to carry out these actions in the best interests of a person who lacks capacity to consent.'[7]

This is perfectly understandable. It is suggested however that it does not wholly answer the questions posed above, given the principle of patient autonomy. If it is right that a patient with capacity can validly refuse medical treatment for a future time when he has lost capacity, so that to provide it would be an assault, why would it not also constitute an assault to contravene the wishes of the patients in examples 2, 3 and 4, ie:

- for a man to provide treatment to patient 3 who had refused male clinicians;
- to cut the hair of patient 2 who expressly wanted its length preserved;
- to provide basic nursing care to patient 4 who had expressly rejected it?

Even though points such as these may be thought to be unlikely to arise, should they in fact do so in practice, then a further difficulty may present itself in that the Court of Protection may find that it is outside the scope of ss 24–26 of the MCA 2005 because the advance decision would not be valid and applicable within the meaning of the Act. It is perhaps likely that the Court of Protection would want to approach the issue as one of an non-valid or inapplicable advance decision, giving it full discretion to make a best interests decision under s 16 of the MCA 2005. But does that actually answer the question of the status of an advance decision to refuse, for example, basic nursing care, which does not fall within the MCA 2005 but was made deliberately and after consideration by a person with full capacity at the time it was made? Would the High Court here retain its inherent jurisdiction? If so, how would it approach the issue? Would it find that, for reasons of public policy, such basic treatment could not constitute an assault, as it formed part of the physical contact generally acceptable in the ordiniary conduct of everyday life? The difficulty with that is that Lord Goff in the case of *Re F (Mental Patient: sterilisation)*[8] expressly found that this exception to liability in assault did not apply to medical treatment, and that the general rule remained that consent was necessary to render such treatment lawful. This is an area which may require examination of previous common law principles, and further case law to elucidate.

1 Section 24(2).
2 Main Code, para 9.13.
3 Contrast this with the wider definition of medical treatment under the Mental Health Act 1983: ' "Medical treatment" includes nursing, and also includes care, habilitation and rehabilitation under medical supervision' – s 145(1).
4 *Airedale NHS Trust v Bland* [1993] AC 789, HL, on the basis that it is a medically controlled and unnatural procedure. Note, however, that the JCHR in 2004 remained concerned that this may not be well known to lay people: para 2.46.
5 Law Commission Report, Mental Incapacity, Report No 231, 1995, para 9.34.
6 Joint Scrutiny Report, para 211.
7 Main Code, para 9.28.
8 [1990] 2 AC 1, at 73.

MAKING AN ADVANCE DECISION

Advice in the Main Code

3.7 As noted above, an advance decision may be made wholly informally and orally (save with regard to life sustaining treatment). The Main Code acknowledges nevertheless that the processes of proof and validity will be eased with a certain amount of formality, and gives some general guidance at paras 9.10–9.17.

It advises those considering making an advance decision to take advice from healthcare professionals or organisations which can advise on specific conditions or situations. It suggests that legal advice may assist in achieving clarity of expression of the decision, and indeed in establishing the existence of the decision in the future.

The Main Code advises giving as much precision as possible about the circumstances when the refusal should apply, with reasons, and with consideration to future circumstances – for example a woman may want to state in an advance decision whether it should still apply were she to be pregnant.

It suggests that people consider how they are going to let family or carers know of the existence of an advance decision, or how it should be communicated to hospital clinicians in the event of an emergency – some will opt to carry a card or bracelet for example.

A written advance decision

3.8 The Main Code acknowledges that a written advance decision can help in establishing the existence and scope of an advance decision, and offers further advice, albeit acknowledging that there are no set requirements (save with regard to life-sustaining treatment). Nevertheless, if a person is going to write an advance decision, the Main Code suggests that it would be helpful to include the following information[1]:

- full details of the person, including date of birth, home address, any distinguishing features (in case of emergency need for identification);
- name and address of GP and whether s/he has a copy of the document;
- a statement that the document should be used if the person ever lacks capacity to make treatment decisions;
- a clear statement of the decision, the treatment to be refused and the circumstances in which the decision will apply;
- the date the document was written (or reviewed);
- the person's signature (or the signature of someone the person has asked to sign on their behalf and in their presence);
- the signature of the person witnessing the signature if there is one (or a statement directing somebody to sign on the person's behalf) – albeit that witnessing is not essential, merely a further aid in clarifying the extent and scope of the advance decision.

1 Main Code, para 9.19.

Oral advance decisions

3.9 The orally expressed advance decision may well pose difficult questions in practice. Accordingly the Main Code advises healthcare professionals to take care to document verbal refusals in the patient's records, suggesting that the record include[1]:

- a note that the decision should apply if the person lacks capacity to make treatment decisions in future;
- a clear note of the decision, the treatment to be refused and the circumstances in which the decision will apply;
- details of someone who was present when the oral advance decision was recorded and the role in which they were was present (eg healthcare professional or family member); and
- whether they heard the decision, took part in it or were just aware that it exists.

1 Main Code, para 9.23.

Making an advance decision with regard to life-sustaining treatment

3.10 As might be expected, more rigour attaches to the creation of an advance decision which seeks to refuse life-sustaining treatment[1]. Under s 25(5) and (6), an advance decision which aims so to do is only valid if:

- it is verified by a statement by the maker to the effect that it is to apply to that treatment even if life is at risk;
- it is in writing – note that it must be in writing, not that it must be written by the maker. Accordingly, it could be written by a clinician at the request of the patient in his clinical records;
- it is signed, by the maker, or by another person in the maker's presence and by the maker's direction;
- the signature is made or acknowledged by the maker in the presence of a witness;

– the witness signs it, or acknowledges his signature in the presence of the maker.

The Main Code advises the patient proposing to make such an advance decision to talk it over with a healthcare professional[2].

Note that regulations have been made which protect the validity of an advance decision to refuse life-sustaining treatment which is not signed and witnessed, and is not verified by the maker to the effect that it is to apply even where life is at risk, if it was made before 1 October 2007 and the maker has not regained capacity since that time, and where the other requirements for validity and applicability are met[3].

1 Which has the definition provided at s 4(10), the best interests section – see 2.45 above, namely 'treatment which in the view of a person providing healthcare for the person concerned is necessary to sustain life'.
2 Main Code, para 9.27.
3 Mental Capacity Act 2005 (Transitional and Consequential Provisions) Order 2007, SI 2007/1898.

Review of or updating an advance decision

3.11 As will be seen below, at the time an advance decision is to be called into effect, clinicians will have to assess whether it remains valid and applicable to the issue in hand. An advance decision made some time before, or in different circumstances, may be found not to be valid or applicable. Accordingly, the Main Code advises anyone who has made an advance decision regularly to review and update it; in that way it is more likely to – and to be found to – have taken into account relevant changes in the person's situation and circumstances[1].

1 Main Code, para 9.29.

Withdrawal or alteration of an advance decision

3.12 The maker of an advance decision can withdraw or alter it at any time, provided s/he has capacity to do so at that time[1].

With one exception, withdrawal or alteration does not need to be in any particular format[2]. It may then be constituted by a very last-minute change of heart orally expressed.

This applies to any advance decision, even one refusing life sustaining treatment: whilst the making of such a decision must be in writing, its revocation or alteration can be wholly informal or oral, save for one situation: where a withdrawal or alteration of an advance decision results itself in the creation of an advance decision refusing life-sustaining treatment, that withdrawal or alteration itself must be in writing and satisfy the requirements of s 25(6)[3].

Again the Main Code advises healthcare professionals to take care to record any alteration or cancellation of advance decisions in the patient's records[4].

1 Section 24(3).
2 Section 24(4).
3 Section 24(5).
4 Main Code, para 9.31.

THE VALIDITY AND APPLICABILITY OF AN ADVANCE DECISION

3.13 An advance decision constitutes a binding refusal of treatment, as effective as one made contemporaneously by a competent person. Accordingly healthcare professionals will render themselves liable in assault if they act in contravention of an advance directive[1].

However, to be binding, it must be valid and applicable.

1 See further 3.23 below.

Validity

Capacity

3.14 The first requirements for validity are as set out above, namely that the maker of the advance decision was aged 18 or over at the time it was made and had capacity at that time to make it[1].

As to capacity, the first of the overarching principles of s 1 of the MCA 2005 needs to be remembered here, namely the presumption of capacity unless the contrary is shown[2]. Accordingly, unless the clinician or carer has reason to believe that at the time it was made, the patient lacked capacity, capacity must be presumed.

The Main Code gives helpful guidance on this issue in the case of patients with a history of suicidal thoughts or attempts, where clinicians may have particular concerns about capacity and advance decisions:

> 'It is important to remember that making an advance decision which, if followed, may result in death does not necessarily mean a person is or feels suicidal. Nor does it necessarily mean the person lacks capacity to make the advance decision.'[3]

1 Section 24(1).
2 Section 1(2).
3 Main Code, para 9.9.

Change of mind

3.15 The issue of validity is further addressed at s 25 of the MCA 2005, but in negative terms, i e when an advance decision will *not* be valid or applicable. Under s 25(2) an advance decision will not be valid if the maker:

> '(a) has withdrawn the decision at a time when he had capacity to do so,
> (b) has, under a lasting power of attorney created after the advance decision was made, conferred authority on the donee (or, if more than one, any of them) to give or refuse consent to the treatment to which the advance decision relates, or
> (c) has done anything else clearly inconsistent with the advance decision remaining his fixed decision.'

This subsection acknowledges the very real possibility that the maker may, as circumstances change, change their mind about the advance decision, and further acknowledges that a change of heart may be real even if not explicitly articulated.

Withdrawal

3.16 Accordingly, as noted above, the maker of an advance decision can withdraw or resile from it at any time provided that at that time s/he has capacity to do so. An advance decision will not be valid if it has been withdrawn or amended[1].

1 Section 25(2)(a).

Subsequent creation of lasting power of attorney

3.17 The MCA 2005 also provides that an advance decision can be invalidated by the subsequent grant to the donee of a power of attorney covering the same treatment[1].

1 Section 25(2)(b). Note that only a power of attorney which addresses the question of the medical care covered in a previous advance decision will supersede the advance decision. The advance decision will remain valid in the presence of any other power of attorney, confirmed at s 25(7). See further on this, Chapter 5.

Inconsistent behaviour

3.18 Further, the MCA 2005 provides that an advance decision can be invalidated by inference from behaviour – by the maker doing anything else 'clearly inconsistent with the advance decision remaining his fixed decision'[1].

Behaviour apparently inconsistent with a prior advance decision has been found sufficient to invalidate the decision in a number of cases at common law[2], and is further illustrated in the Main Code:

> 'A young man, Angus, sees a friend die after prolonged hospital treatment. Angus makes a signed and witnessed advance decision to refuse treatment to keep him alive if he is ever injured in this way. The advance decision includes a statement that this will apply even if his life is at risk.
>
> A few years later Angus is seriously injured in a road traffic accident. He is paralysed from the neck down and cannot breathe without the aid of a

machine. At first he stays conscious and gives permission to be treated. He takes part in a rehabilitation programme. Some months later he loses consciousness.

At this point somebody finds his written advance decision, even though Angus has not mentioned it during his treatment. His actions before his lack of capacity obviously go against the advance decision. Anyone assessing the advance decision needs to consider very carefully the doubt this has created about the validity of the advance decision, and whether the advance decision is valid and applicable as a result.'

1 Section 25(2(c).

2 See for example, *Re T (Adult: refusal of medical treatment)* [1993] Fam 95, [1992] 3 WLR 782, *HE v A Hospital NHS Trust* [2003] EWHC 1017 (Fam), [2003] 2 FLR 408.

Applicability

3.19 In addition to validity, the advance decision must also be found to be applicable to the treatment in question. The issue of applicability is addressed at s 25(3) and (4) of the MCA 2005:

'(3) An advance decision is not applicable to the treatment in question if at the material time [the maker] has capacity to give or refuse consent to it.

(4) An advance decision is not applicable to the treatment in question if:

(a) that treatment is not the treatment specified in the advance decision;

(b) any circumstances specified in the advance decision are absent, or

(c) there are reasonable grounds for believing that circumstances exist which [the maker] did not anticipate at the time of the advance decision and which would have affected his decision had he anticipated them.'

Retention of capacity

3.20 The point at subs (3) is self explanatory: if at the time of the treatment in question the decision maker retains capacity, the advance decision cannot apply; it only applies to situations once the decision-maker has lost capacity.

Assessment of applicability

3.21 Subsection (4) seeks to give clear guidance in a situation which is likely to be fraught. The clinicians will doubtless be anxious to administer the treatment, and concerned about the fate of the patient without treatment; the advance decision seeks to stop them. They will accordingly want to ensure that it really does cover the situation in hand, and s 25(4) provides the steps to take here:

– Specified treatment

Firstly, is the treatment that specified in the advance decision?[1]

Remember however that the advance decision may validly be phrased in lay terms[2]. Therefore the clinician cannot deny applicability merely because the decision is not couched in precisely the correct medical terms. The implication of s 24(2) must be that, provided the decision adequately conveys the meaning of a treatment, it will be applicable even if not wholly precisely phrased.

– Absent circumstances

Secondly, are there any circumstances specified in the advance decision which are absent?

Note on this point that the Main Code curiously misphrases this requirement thus: the advance decision will not be applicable if 'the circumstances are different from those that may have been set out in the advance decision'[3].

– Altered circumstances

Thirdly, are there reasonable grounds for believing that circumstances exist which the decision-maker did not anticipate at the time of the advance decision and which would have affected their decision had they been anticipated?

It is suggested that this will be the more useful of the applicability tests. It can clearly cover changes in the personal circumstances of the decision-maker, who may for example have become pregnant, or in the medical treatment available, which the decision-maker may not have appreciated at the time he made the decision.

The Main Code illustrates the latter point[4]:

> 'Mr Moss is HIV positive. Several years ago he began to have AIDS-related symptoms. He has accepted general treatment, but made an advance decision to refuse specific retro-viral treatments, saying he didn't want to be a "guinea pig" for the medical profession. Five years later, he is admitted to hospital seriously ill, and keeps falling unconscious.
>
> The doctors treating Mr Moss examine his advance decision. They are aware that there have been major developments in retro-viral treatment recently. They discuss this with Mr Moss' partner and both agree that there are reasonable grounds to believe that Mr Moss may have changed his advance decision if he had known about newer treatment options. So the doctors decide the advance decision does not apply to the new retro-virals and give him treatment.
>
> If Mr Moss regains his capacity, he can change his advance decision and accept or refuse future treatment.'

1 And does it in fact relate to medical treatment? See 3.6 above.
2 Section 24(2).
3 Main Code, para 9.42
4 Main Code, para 9.44.

Effect of invalidity or non-applicability

3.22 It follows that if an advance decision is not valid or applicable to the current circumstances, the onus of decision-making falls back upon the clinician, to treat the patient in their best interests. Clearly in making that assessment the advance decision is not wholly to be disregarded, but must be weighed up with all of the other statutory factors in the assessment of best interests under s 4[1].

[1] See Chapter 2 above.

THE OBLIGATIONS AND RESPONSIBILITIES OF CLINICIANS

3.23 Section 26(1) makes the effect of a valid and applicable advance decision absolutely explicit:

> 'If [the decision maker] has made an advance decision which is—
> (a) valid, and
> (b) applicable to a treatment,
> the decision has effect as if he had made it, and had had capacity to make it, at the time when the question arises whether the treatment should be carried out or continued.'

It is in short, binding, and treatment given in contravention of its terms is not lawful; the clinician will be exposed to liability for the criminal and civil wrong of assault or battery.

Section 26 proceeds, however, to elucidate the circumstances in which a clinician will escape liability either for not following an advance decision, or for following it.

Liability for not following an advance decision

3.24 Section 26(2) provides that:

> 'A person does not incur liability for carrying out or continuing the treatment unless, at the time, he is satisfied that an advance decision exists which is valid and applicable to the treatment.'[1]

This subsection provides that a clinician must actually be satisfied of the existence of a valid and applicable advance decision before incurring liability for acting in contravention of it. What does 'being satisfied' mean? It is suggested that this will mean on the balance of probabilities. Accordingly, a doctor will not be liable for not following a patient's wishes as expressed in an apparent advance decision unless s/he concludes, on the balance of probabilities, that the advance decision exists, is valid, and is applicable to the treatment in question. In other words, if the doctor accepts that the advance decision exists, is valid and applicable, but disregards it s/he will be exposed to liability in assault, even if the intention is to treat the patient in the doctor's assessment of their best interests.

This subsection clearly should not be seen as licensing a clinician to turn a blind eye to an advance decision in order to assert that s/he was not satisfied of its qualifying criteria. It is contended that the clinician's duty of care to the patient, and the patient's right to respect for their private and family life under Article 8 ECHR ensure that the clinician is bound to take at least reasonable steps to explore the existence, validity and applicability of an advance decision of which s/he is informed or has reason to be aware.

1 Using the tests for validity and applicability set out at s 25, see 3.23ff above.

Liability for following an advance decision

3.25 Thus, the clinician will not be liable for *not following* an advance decision if not satisfied of its existence, validity or applicability. The converse is not the case however: s 26(3) provides that the clinician will not be liable for the injurious consequences of *following* an advance decision if he 'reasonably believes' that an advance decision exists, is valid and applicable to the treatment in question. This phraseology assists the clinician – if deciding to follow an advance decision he does not have to be 'satisfied' of its existence, validity and applicability, rather he must reasonably believe those features to exist, a somewhat lower threshold test than that for continuing to provide treatment in apparent contravention of an advance decision.

The Main Code however reminds clinicians that 'they must be able to demonstrate that their belief was reasonable, and point to reasonable grounds showing why they believe this'[1].

Should the situation be very unclear, or disputed, and a declaration is sought from the Court of Protection, s 26(5) of the MCA 2005 provides that the clinician may provide life-sustaining treatment or act as he reasonably considers to be necessary to prevent a serious deterioration in the patient's condition pending the court's decision.

1 Main Code, para 9.59.

Ethical objections to following an advance decision

3.26 The Main Code recognises that a clinician may disagree in principle with a patient's right to refuse life-sustaining treatment. The clinician cannot be compelled to act against their beliefs – either to provide or withhold treatment – but the Main Code reminds the practitioner of the obligation not to abandon the patient or cause their care to suffer by arranging for the transfer of care to another professional or body[1]. Note also that the Court of Protection is empowered by s 17(1)(e) to make a direction transferring the responsibility for a patient's healthcare from one person to another.

1 Main Code, para 9.61–9.63.

DISAGREEMENT ABOUT AN ADVANCE DECISION

3.27 It is worth remembering the identity of the primary decision-maker in situations which may be covered by an advance decision – it will be where the patient has lost capacity, and thus, unless there is a donee of a relevant power of attorney, the decision about treatment will lie with the clinician. The clinician's role will be to decide upon the treatment s/he considers to be in the patient's best interests, following the steps under the MCA 2005[1], and then to provide it – unless prohibited by a valid and applicable advance decision. It remains then the primary decision of the clinician as to whether there is indeed a valid and applicable advance decision.

Nevertheless, in the event of disagreement about the scope of an advance decision between clinicians or between clinicians and family members, it will clearly be important for the clinician (and the Main Code recommends that this should be a senior clinician) to review all of the available evidence and consult as widely as possible with colleagues and those close to or familiar with the patient, including the patient's GP[2].

The Main Code reminds the clinician that the point of such consultation 'should not be to try to overrule the person's advance decision but rather to seek evidence concerning its validity and to confirm its scope and applicability to the current circumstances.' Details of these discussions should be recorded in the person's healthcare records. Where the senior clinician has a reasonable belief that an advance decision to refuse medical treatment is both valid and applicable, the advance decision should be complied with[3].

In the case of genuine doubt or irreconcilable difference the Court of Protection can be asked to make a declaration as to whether an advance decision exists, is valid or is applicable to a treatment[1]. Note that the court's power is limited to those defined areas; it does not have the power to overturn a valid and applicable advance decision.

Should a decision be sought from the Court of Protection about an advance decision, s 26(5) provides that life-sustaining treatment, or treatment which is necessary to prevent a serious deterioration in the patient's condition may be provided pending the court's ruling.

1 See above, Chapter 2.
2 Main Code, para 9.64.
3 Main Code, para 9.66.

PRACTICE POINTS

3.28 It is suggested that the following points will be important to bear in mind in practice:

Making an advance decision:

- If the patient is proposing to make – or has made – an advance decision to refuse all life sustaining treatment in a particular scenario, consider or ask whether the patient has:
  (a) considered why s/he wishes to do so, and understands what it would be likely to entail;
  (b) taken into account the possibilities of advances in medical science which might alleviate their condition;

(c) appreciated that s/he is aware that artificial nutrition and hydration would rank as treatment; is it clear that this was intentionally included?

Scope of an advance decision: is it clear that the advance decision relates to medical treatment? If not, consider how and whether it might take effect.

Evidence about an advance decision: if an oral advance decision (not relating to life-sustaining treatment) is made, consider how this can most effectively be established, stored and used.

Validity and applicability of an advance decision: the steps to follow are these:

- Did the patient have capacity to make the decision at the time it was made? (remembering the statutory presumption of capacity)
- Was s/he over 18 at the time?
- Is the decision still valid:
  - (a) Has the maker withdrawn it (at a time when s/he had capacity)?
  - (b) Has the maker made a subsequently lasting power of attorney covering the same treatment?
  - (c) Has the maker done anything else clearly inconsistent with the advance decision remaining his fixed decision?
- Is the decision applicable:
  - (a) Is it applicable to the treatment in question?
  - (b) Are any circumstances specified in the advance decision absent?
  - (c) Are there reasonable grounds for believing that circumstances exist which the maker did not anticipate at the time the advance decision was made and which would have affected the decision had they been anticipated?

Steps to take in the event of a dispute:

- Engage senior clinician and conduct as wide ranging an enquiry as possible.
- Seek the ruling of the Court of Protection, taking steps to treat the patient in the meantime if life-sustaining treatment or treatment necessary to prevent a serious deterioration in the patient's condition is necessary.

1 Section 26(5).

Chapter 4

ACTS CONNECTED WITH CARE OR TREATMENT AND RESTRAINT: LIMITATIONS ON CIVIL AND CRIMINAL LIABILITY

- **MCA 2005, ss 5, 6**
- **Main Code, Chapter 6**

INTRODUCTION

4.1 Section 5 of the MCA 2005 creates a general defence in respect of acts which are done 'in connection with the care or treatment' of those who are reasonably believed to lack capacity. Section 6 delimits, with some precision, the boundaries of the s 5 defence where the act or acts in question amount to 'restraint'[1].

It has been widely asserted that the rationale underlying these provisions is to clarify the common law principle of 'necessity' and to immunise those responsible for the care and treatment of incapacitated persons from civil or criminal liability provided that the acts done or decisions made in that connection are done in the incapacitated person's best interests[2].

No formal authorisation is required for acts which fall within the aegis of s 5. There are no general recording or documenting requirements and s 5 acts are not restricted to particular sites, settings or premises. The absence of a requirement for formalities of this kind reflects the broad reach of the new provision. It covers day-to-day activities, planned medical intervention and emergency situations. Since the s 5 protection was intended to provide a clear legal basis for ordinary acts undertaken by lay carers, as well as healthcare professionals, for the personal welfare or health of people lacking capacity, it does not expressly require detailed capacity assessments and best interest determinations to be made in respect of every decision which may fall within its ambit. Nonetheless, adherence to the capacity and best interests principles central to the steer of the MCA 2005, and discussed in detail in Chapter 2, is critical to successful reliance on the defence afforded by s 5.

1 'Restraint' is defined in s 6(4) and is discussed in detail below.

2 See statement of David Lammy, Under Secretary of State for Constitutional Affairs, in425 HC Official Report (6th series), col 29, 11 October 2004. David Lammy specifically stated that: 'important clarification of the law surrounding what someone can do to or for a person lacking mental capacity who is unable to give consent. The current law is based on the poorly understood and obscure "doctrine of necessity" …'

Limitations on the scope of section 5

4.2 There are, however, limits to the protection from liability offered by s 5. Neither s 5 nor the associated provisions which restrict legal liability for the use of restraint contained in s 6 are intended to create a general exclusion from liability for tortious or criminal conduct.

The performance of acts connected with care and treatment in respect of a non-consenting person *with* capacity would usually amount to a trespass to the person (assault/battery). Whereas s 5 justifies the performance of such acts where they are in the best interests of a person *without* capacity (non-consenting or otherwise), neither civil nor criminal liability for negligent acts is excluded by the s 5 protection[1]. The elements of the tort of negligence are reasonably well known[2] and it is clear that acts which are done in breach of the requisite duty of care will not be saved by these provisions. Similarly, where negligence is a component of a criminal offence (eg gross negligence manslaughter) neither s 5 nor 6 can operate as an effective defence if the conduct in question could properly be described as negligent and the other elements of the crime are made out[3].

There are, also, other important limitations on the reach of s 5 which are consistent with the capacity principles set out in s 1. The first of those is that s 5 does not create any power or right to make decisions on behalf of the incapacitated person[4]. Second, s 5 does not permit any person to act in defiance of a valid and applicable advance decision made in accordance with the provisions of ss 24–26[5].

As alluded to above, s 6 further circumscribes the protective ambit of s 5. It places specific limitations on the circumstances in which 'restraint' (that is, the threat or use of force against an incapacitated person) may be authorised by reference to s 5. Section 6 also excludes from the category of s 5 protected acts, acts which conflict with decisions made either by a donee under a lasting power of attorney or a court-appointed deputy[6]. The restriction of the scope of s 5 to matters which do not conflict with P's competent decisions as to treatment (an advance decision) or P's competent delegation of his decision-making capacity (via an LPA) is likely to operate as a very important safeguard against any attempts at erosion of patient autonomy.

1 See s 5(3); see also the Main Code, para 6.36.

2 See *Caparo Industries plc v Dickman* [1990] 2 AC 605.

3 Archbold, *Criminal Pleading, Evidence and Practice* (2007) Sweet & Maxwell, para 19–108. See also s 44 which creates a specific offence of ill-treatment or neglect for carers including donees of LPAs, attorneys acting under EPAs and court deputies.

4 In this sense the law, as set out in *F v West Berkshire Health Authority* [1989] 2 All ER 545, HL, remains applicable. Section 5 creates no separate power of substituted decision-making.

5 This is so because an advance decision has the same effect as a competent and contemporaneous refusal of treatment and the MCA 2005 preserves the common law position that a capacitated person is entitled to refuse treatment. A clinician would be liable in assault/battery for treating a patient who validly refused treatment: see *Airedale NHS Trust v Bland* [1993] AC 789, HL at 882 per Lord Browne-Wilkinson; *Re T (Adult: Refusal of Treatment)* [1993] Fam 95, CA at 102 per Lord Donaldson MR; *Re MB (Medical Treatment)* [1997] 2 FLR 426, CA at 432 per Butler-Sloss LJ; *R (on the application of Burke) v GMC* [2005] 2 WLR 431 at paras 31 and 57 per Lord Phillips MR; *Re AK (Medical Treatment: Consent)* [2001] 1 FLR 129.

6 See s 6(6).

Relationship between sections 5 and 6 and the deprivation of liberty

4.3 In the version of the MCA 2005 which received Royal Assent on 7 April 2005, s 6(5) expressly excluded anything which amounted to a 'deprivation of liberty' within the meaning of Article 5(1) ECHR from the definition of permissible 'restraint'[1]. Section 6(5) has since been repealed and replaced with new ss 4A, 4B and 16A by the MHA 2007[2]. These new sections will make it lawful to deprive a person of his liberty only in circumstances prescribed by Sch A1 to the MCA 2005 or where the deprivation of liberty is a consequence of giving effect to an order of the Court of Protection on a personal welfare matter. The Sch A1 scheme, described as the 'Deprivation of Liberty Safeguards' or the 'Bournewood Safeguards', is considered in detail in Chapter 9.

It is instructive to note that the amended provisions (ss 4A, 4B, 16A and Schedule A1) are not intended to come into force until April 2009. Until the amendments take effect, the exclusion in the unamended s 6(5) of the MCA 2005 represents the position at law. Even after the amendments come into force, it will remain the case that neither s 5 nor s 6 can be taken to authorise any act or circumstance which amounts to a deprivation of liberty[3]. Deprivations of liberty will only be lawful under the MCA 2005 where specifically permitted by its provisions[4].

1 In its *Twenty-third Report of Session 2003–04*, HL Paper 210, HC 1282, at paras 2.12–2.33, the Joint Committee on Human Rights (JCHR) expressed concern that the provisions now contained in ss 5 and 6 appeared to permit deprivations of liberty in the absence of the requisite convention safeguards as set out in *Winterwerp v Netherlands* (1979–80) 2 EHRR 387. Section 6(5) was inserted by the House of Lords at the report stage in response to the JCHR's further suggestion at para 49 of the *Fourth Report of Session 2004–05*, HL Paper 26, HC 224, that the statutory definition of 'restraint' should expressly exclude deprivations of liberty.

2 MHA 2007, ss 50(1), (4)(a), 55, Sch 11, Pt 10.

3 Subsections 4A(2)–(5) specifically set out the circumstances in which the MCA 2005 can be taken to authorise deprivations of liberty. Acts/circumstances which are not covered by these provisions are caught by the general words of s 4A(1) which state that 'This Act does not authorise any person ("D") to deprive any other person ("P") of his liberty'.

4 See Chapter 9.

WHAT DOES SECTION 5 MEAN?

The common law

4.4 The doctrine of 'necessity' has, at least since 1989, developed apace in the context of the medical treatment of incapacitated persons. In a line of cases beginning with the case of *Re F (Mental Patient: Sterilisation)*[1], the non-consensual treatment of incapacitated patients in their best interests has been held to be lawful. Of course, the doctrine of necessity, extended to cover the medical treatment (contraceptive sterilisation) in *Re F*, had previously been used to justify the reasonable use of measures of restraint, including detention, in order to prevent a breach of peace[2] and harm to person or property[3]. Sections 5 and 6 seek to place these principles on a statutory footing.

1 [1990] 2 AC 1, [1989] 2 WLR 1025.

2 See *Albert v Lavin* [1981] 3 ALL ER 878.
3 See *R v Howell* [1981] 3 All ER 383; *Black v Forsey* 1987 SLT 681.

Section 5

4.5 Section 5 provides a defence or exclusion from liability in respect of an act done by a person D 'in connection with the care or treatment of another person ("P")'[1]. However, in order to benefit from the protection afforded by s 5, the person D, who may be a personal carer or a member of healthcare or social staff of a hospital or care home[2], must take reasonable steps to ascertain whether P lacks capacity in relation to the act in question[3]. When performing the act, D must also *reasonably believe* that P lacks capacity in relation to it and that it is in P's best interests[4]. In those circumstances, D will not incur any further liability (that is no liability other than that which he would otherwise have incurred as a matter of criminal or civil law) which would not have arisen if P had capacity and had consented[5].

In summary, the prerequisites for s 5 protection are:

- The act must be related to the care or treatment of P[6].
- D must take *reasonable steps* to establish P's lack of capacity[7].
- 'Reasonable steps' must always include taking all practical and appropriate steps to help people make a decision about an action themselves, and applying the two-stage capacity test[8].
- The two-stage test is:
  - Stage 1: Does the person have an impairment of, or disturbance in the functioning of, their mind or brain?
  - Stage 2: Does the impairment or disturbance mean that the person is unable to make a specific decision when they need to?
- D must *reasonably believe* that P lacks capacity at the time the act needs to be taken[9].
- D must *reasonably believe* that the act is in P's best interests. D should apply all the elements of the best interests checklist[10]

1 Section 5(1).
2 See Chapter 6 of the Main Code.
3 Section 5(1)(a).
4 Section 5(1)(b). Note that The Main Code, in effect, repeats the requirement in s 5(1)(b) for D to *reasonably* believe both that P lacks capacity and that the act proposed to be done is in P's best interests.
5 Section 5(2).
6 See Main Code, para 6.22.
7 Section 5(1)(a).
8 See Main Code, para 6.27.
9 Section 5(1)(b)(i) and Main Code, para 6.27.
9 Section 5(1)(b)(i) and Main Code, para 6.27.
10 Section 5(1)(b)(ii) and Main Code, para 6.28.

What is reasonable?

4.6 The first requirement for D to take *reasonable steps* to establish capacity prefigures the second (and third) requirement to *reasonably believe* that P lacks capacity and that the act is in P's best interests. The starting point is a presumption of capacity and an understanding of the fact that it is 'issue-specific'[1]. D must therefore focus on whether P has the capacity to make a specific decision at the time it needs to be made (eg a decision about whether P ought to be bathed will entail a different sort of capacity assessment as compared with a decision about change of residence). Examples of the persons expected to assess specific types of capacity are found at paras 4.38–4.43 of the the Main Code.

1 See *Masterman-Lister v Brutton & Co*, [2002] EWCA Civ 1889, [2003] 3 All ER 162.

Reasonable steps

4.7 In light of the subjectivity and contextual nature of any capacity assessment, the question of what constitutes '*reasonable steps*' will depend upon the 'individual circumstances and the urgency of the decision'[1]. Carers are not expected to be expert assessors but assessments by professionals will be expected to be fuller and commensurate with their higher degree of knowledge and experience. Paragraph 4.45 of the Main Code gives guidance on matters which ought to be considered in assessing capacity.

1 See Main Code, para 4.45.

Reasonable belief

4.8

It follows then that a '*reasonable belief*' in a lack of capacity must be preceded by the '*reasonable steps*' assessment. Paragraph 6.31 of the Main Code provides that carers and professionals will be protected from liability as long as they are able to provide *objective reasons* for their belief in a lack of capacity and to show that that belief was founded upon the taking of reasonable steps to determine capacity. In order to demonstrate a reasonable belief that the act is in P's best interests, D must be able to show that he considered all relevant circumstances and applied the best interests checklist[1].

Where there is a care plan in existence which involved an assessment of capacity, it will be reasonable for healthcare and social care staff to assume that the care planning process assessed best interests. As might be expected, what is 'reasonable' in an emergency context will differ from what might be considered to be so in a non-urgent situation[2].

1 See Main Code, para 6.32.
2 See Main Code, para.6.35.

Civil and criminal liability

4.9 The issue of the standards of conduct of informal decision-makers and the consequences for them if they make poor decisions was raised in the report of the Joint Scrutiny Committee in the 2002–03 session during the MCA 2005's passage through parliament[1]. The Committee recommended that there be clear guidance on standards of conduct and a statutory duty of care on the face of the MCA 2005. However, the course adopted in the MCA 2005 was simply to make clear that negligent conduct was not protected by s 5.

The consequence of the legislative approach adopted in s 5 is that all relevant s 5 decision-makers/actors are subject to:

(a) a common law duty of care[2]; and
(b) liability to conviction for the criminal offence of ill-treatment or wilful neglect (punishable by a maximum of 12 months' imprisonment if dealt with summarily and five years on indictment)[3].

1 *Joint Committee Report on the Draft Mental Incapacity Bill*, Session 2002–03, HL,189–1/HC 1083–1, paras 97–99.
2 See *R (on the application of Munjaz) v Mersey Care NHS Trust* [2005] UKHL 58, [2006] 2 AC 148 at 182A, para 4.
3 Section 44, which also extends to donees of LPAs, attorneys acting under EPAs and court deputies. A single act might be sufficient to constitute 'ill-treatment': *R v Holmes* [1979] Crim LR 52.

The section 44 offence of ill-treatment and wilful neglect

4.10 Section 44 creates the criminal offence of ill-treatment or wilful neglect of an incapacitated person. The offence augments the common law duty of care owed by those responsible for care and treatment of incapacitated patients and is designed to impose criminal penalties in respect of acts of deliberate maltreatment of such persons. The s 44 offence can be committed by anyone who has care of a person reasonably believed to lack capacity, a donee of an LPA or an EPA, or a court-appointed deputy. The offence is punishable with a maximum sentence of 12 months imprisonment on summary conviction and five years on indictment.

The s 44 offence is not entirely without precedent in the context of the treatment and care of those who may suffer a mental disorder. In this sense the statutory precursor to s 44 is s 127 of the MHA 1983 which introduced three specific offences of ill-treatment and neglect of mentally disordered patients. The s 127 offences can be committed against those in receipt of treatment under the MHA 2007 as in-patients or out-patients, those subject to guardianship or otherwise in the custody or care of the alleged offender, and those subject to supervised after-care under that Act[1]. The s 44 offence does not have the apparent rigidity of the s 127 offences and can be committed by a carer, donee or deputy in any context. In addition, unlike prosecutions for alleged offences contrary to s 127, there is no requirement for s 44 prosecutions to be instigated by or consented to by the Director of Public Prosecutions.

Neither care, nor ill-treatment nor wilful neglect is defined on the face of the MCA 2005. It is clear that the definitions of ill-treatment and wilful neglect for the purposes of s 44 mirror those used in respect of s 127. The Main Code describes 'ill-treatment' and 'wilful neglect' as separate offences[2]. Whether characterised as a single offence which may be committed in two distinct ways or as two different offences, the Court of Appeal has stated that 'ill-treatment' and 'wilful neglect' are not to be conflated and ought to form separate counts on an indictment where both offences (or forms of the offence) are sought to be prosecuted[3].

1 The MHA 1983, s 127(1) offences of ill-treatment or wilful neglect of an inpatient or an out-patient can only be committed by an officer, employee or manager of a hospital or care home. The s 127(2) and (2A) offences of wilfully neglecting or ill-treating mentally disordered persons subject to guardianship, supervised aftercare or otherwise in the care or custody of the alleged offender can be committed by any individual.

2 See Main Code, paras 14.25–14.26.

3 See *R v Newington* (1990) 91 Cr App Rep 247 at p.242 per Watkins LJ.

The relevance of capacity

4.11 Section 44(1)(a) and (2) provide that an offence is committed where someone (D) who has care of a person (P) 'who lacks or whom D reasonably believes to lack capacity', ill-treats or wilfully neglects P. As a matter of pure statutory construction, these provisions indicate that the offence may be committed where *either* P *actually* lacks capacity *or* D *reasonably believes* that to be the case. It would appear, therefore, that if D believes P to have capacity when s/he actually does not, the offence may still be committed.

What is ill-treatment

4.12 The working definition of ill-treatment to be used for the purposes of this offence is the ordinary dictionary definition: 'to treat badly, ill-use, maltreat'[1]. The elements of the offence of ill-treatment involve:

- Deliberate conduct by the alleged, including a single act, which could properly be described as ill-treatment.
- An appreciation by the alleged that s/he was inexcusably ill-treating the incapacitated person *or* recklessness as to whether s/he was acting in that way[2].

The elements of 'ill-treatment' may be satisfied in the absence of a course of conduct (ie a single act will be sufficient) and in the absence of any threatened or actual injury or damage to the incapacitated person[3]. In the circumstances, a single act of violence, for example a slap or a punch, is capable of amounting to an offence under this part of s 44. In the case of offences which could also amount to criminal assaults, the point of instigating a prosecution under s 44 would be to specifically penalise (stigmatise) such treatment by those in a position of trust or care in respect of vulnerable persons. Such a course of action would also be necessary to comply with the State's positive obligations under article 3 ECHR (see Chapter 17 on human rights).

1 Note that this was the Oxford Concise Dictionary definition relied upon by the Bodmin Crown Court in *R v Holmes* [1979] Crim LR 52.

2 See *R v Newington* (1990) 91 Cr App Rep 247 at 252.

3 *R v Newington* (1990) 91 Cr App Rep 247 at 254.

What is wilful neglect?

4.13 The definition of wilful neglect found in the Main Code broadly replicates that found in domestic case law interpretations of this term in a number of statutory contexts[1]. It is described as occurring where 'a person has deliberately failed to carry out an act they knew they had a duty to do.' Acts of wilful neglect can include a conscious decision not to provide or call for necessary medical care. This aspect of the offence may be committed where there is subjective recklessness[2] but cannot be committed where the alleged offender genuinely fails, through ignorance or stupidity, to appreciate the duty in question.

1 See *R v Sheppard* [1981] AC 394 at 418 per Lord Keith and see also *Robert de Maroussem v The Comr for Income Tax* [2004] UKPC 43, [2004] 1 WLR 2865.

2 The guidance given by Lord Keith in *R v Sheppard* clearly suggests that only subjective recklessness will suffice for this offence.

Who to alert in relation to potential offences

4.14 Paragraphs 14.27–14.38 of the Main Code make clear reference to a number of multi-disciplinary agencies and steps which may be taken where there are concerns about potential abuse or offences under s 44.

WHAT 'ACTS' ARE COVERED BY SECTION 5?

4.15 As described above, s 5 applies to acts 'in connection with … care or treatment'. 'Care' is not defined in either the MCA 2005 or the Main Code despite the suggestion by the Joint Scrutiny Committee that the meaning of that term be clarified[1]. 'Treatment' is said, in the interpretation provisions of the MCA 2005[2], to 'include a diagnostic or other procedure'. The Main Code does, however, issue specific guidance on the sorts of actions that will attract the protection of s 5. In particular, Chapter 6 of the Main Code provides a non-exhaustive list of actions which *might* be afforded protection by s 5. The list of permissible actions, categorised under the headings of 'Personal care' and 'Healthcare and treatment', are as follows:

Personal care

- helping with washing, dressing or personal hygiene
- helping with eating and drinking
- helping with communication
- helping with mobility (moving around)
- helping someone take part in education, social or leisure activities
- going into a person's home to drop off shopping or to see if they are alright
- doing the shopping or buying necessary goods with the person's money
- arranging household services (for example, arranging repairs or maintenance for gas and electricity supplies)

- providing services that help around the home (such as homecare or meals on wheels)
- undertaking actions related to community care services (for example, day care, residential accommodation or nursing care)
- helping someone to move home (including moving property and clearing the former home).

HEALTHCARE AND TREATMENT

- carrying out diagnostic examinations and tests (to identify an illness, condition or other problem)
- providing professional medical, dental and similar treatment
- giving medication
- taking someone to hospital for assessment or treatment
- providing nursing care (whether in hospital or in the community)
- carrying out any other necessary medical procedures (for example, taking a blood sample) or therapies (for example, physiotherapy or chiropody)
- providing care in an emergency.

The Main Code reiterates the need for s 5 acts to be accompanied by a reasonable belief in P's lack of capacity and stresses that all decisions must be taken in accordance with the guiding principles, capacity and best interests tests[3].

Chapter 6 of the Main Code gives specific consideration to the approach to be taken to acts which involve healthcare or treatment decisions[4] and those which involve a change of residence[5].

1 *Joint Committee Report on the Draft Mental Incapacity Bill*, Session 2002–03, HL,189–1/HC 1083–1, paras 97–99.
2 Section 64(1).
3 See Main Code, paras 6.6 and 6.26 onwards.
4 See Main Code, paras 6.15–6.19.
5 See Main Code, paras 6–8–6.14. Note also that care should be taken, before reliance is placed upon the sections of the Main Code which deal with deprivations of liberty. Where a deprivation of liberty appears likely or is being considered, the appropriate guidance (subject of course to such changes as might occur after the end of the consultation process) is contained in the draft Addendum Code. See Chapter 9 for more on this.

Healthcare and treatment decisions

4.16 The Main Code suggests that acts coincidental to treatment such as conveying a person to hospital or arranging admission will be covered by s 5 even if the person objects[1]. However, conveyance to hospital can involve a deprivation of liberty[2] and such deprivations are not authorised by s 5 of the unamended MCA 2005. The JCHR in its 4th Report of Session 2006–2007 was particularly insistent that extreme care should therefore be taken before reliance is placed upon this aspect of the Main Code's guidance. Rather, it is suggested that the authorisation of the Court of Protection[3] should be sought where a deprivation of liberty may result from the transportation of a person to a care home or hospital. Nonetheless, it is clear the requirements for s 5 protection will be significantly affected by:

- the enormity of the decision in question; and
- the professional or other role of the decision-maker.

1 See para 6.15 of the Main Code.
2 See in particular the JCHR 4th Report of Session 2006–2007, HL 40/HC 288 at para 89 where the JCHR states: 'We consider that if it is known that a person will be taken from their home to a place where they will be prevented from leaving, and complete and effective control will be exercised over their movements, that person is deprived of liberty from the point of removal from their home.'
3 Chapter 7 at 7.8.

Major healthcare decisions

4.17 Special consideration is required in respect of major healthcare and treatment decisions. The example of such a decision given in the Main Code is a 'do not resuscitate' (DNR) instruction. In these circumstances healthcare staff *cannot* act contrary to a valid and applicable advance decision. In the absence of such restriction, the Main Code indicates that healthcare staff must carefully work out:

- what would be in the person's best interests by reference to s 4 and the guidance in the Main Code on the determination of best interests (note that if there is no one appropriate to consult an IMCA must be appointed)[1].
- whether there are alternative less restrictive or intrusive treatment options[2].

Paragraph 6.17 of the Main Code advises that multi-disciplinary meetings are the best way to determine best interests. However, the following steps are instructive in relation to major healthcare decisions:

- Final responsibility for determining best interests rests with the member of healthcare staff responsible for treatment.
- The decision as to best interests and the objective reasons for that decision must be recorded in the person's clinical notes.

Therefore, if the decision relates to invasive surgery to excise a cancerous tumour, it is likely that the best interests determination will need to be carried out by the clinicians responsible for the proposed surgery. The treating clinicians may expose themselves to liability in tort (assault or negligence) if they fail to carry out a proper best interests determination and/or to record the reasons for their conclusions in the clinical notes.

1 See Chapter 6 re the appointment of IMCAs.
2 Specific considerations attach to decisions about the provision or withdrawal of life-sustaining treatment; see Main Code, para 6.16.

Less serious decisions about daily living care

4.18 By contrast with major treatment decisions made by clinicians, carers do not need to follow formal processes in order to satisfy the '*reasonable steps*' and '*reasonable belief*' criteria which would exclude liability for their acts. So the carer and/or the district nurse who need to decide whether the person requires to be bathed and/or dressed will not have to conduct rigorous best interests and capacity assessments of the kind demanded of a surgeon proposing to amputate a gangrenous leg[1].

1 See, in particular, Main Code, paras 4.44, 6.22.

Change of residence

4.19 Acts which involve a change of residence may cause great distress to elderly and/or incapacitated persons. A move from a prior home can involve dislocation from all that is familiar or stable. The Main Code therefore demands that the decision-making process in respect of a putative change of residence, like that for major healthcare matters, must involve consideration of the least restrictive option and a thorough best interests determination including the appointment of an IMCA where appropriate[1].

Two further matters are of some consequence in proposals to alter a person's place of residence:

- Facilitating the move of an incapacitated person may involve the use of 'restraint' as defined in s 6. Where force is used or threatened, it must be reasonably believed to be necessary to avoid harm and must be proportionate to the risk of harm anticipated[2].
- Very careful consideration ought to be given to whether the proposed move will lead to a deprivation of liberty. If the circumstances of the new accommodation for treatment amount to a detention, the relevant representatives of the hospital or care home in question will be required to apply for authorisation via the Bournewood Safeguards procedure[3] when those procedures come into effect. Until such time authorisation by the Court of Protection or the High Court should be sought. A deprivation of liberty cannot be authorised by s 5 or 6. Again, in this connection the decision-maker is enjoined to look at a range of alternative and less restrictive options[4].

1 This includes requirements to encourage participation, identify all relevant circumstances, find out the person's views, avoid discrimination, assess whether the person might regain capacity, consider specific matters relating to life-sustaining treatment, consult others, avoid restricting the person's rights and to weigh up all of these factors to work out what is in the person's best interests. Note also that an IMCA is only required to be appointed in relation to a change of residence if there is no one else appropriate to consult.

2 Section 6(3).

3 Note that paras 6.13 and 6.49–6.53 of the main Code, which refer to deprivations of liberty, were written before the Bournewood Safeguards procedure was enacted. The draft Addendum Code give fuller guidance on deprivations of liberty but is only a draft.

4 It is worth emphasising that compliance with the Bournewood Safeguards procedure in relation to prospective or actual deprivations of liberty will only be Convention compatible if 'less severe measures have been considered and found to be insufficient to safeguard the individual or public interests which might require the person concerned to be detained'. (*Litwa v Poland* (2001) 33 EHRR 53 at para 78).

Objections of incapacitated person

4.20 The objection of the incapacitated patient is a factor which *must* be taken account of as part of the pre-requisite assessment of best interests if the s 5 protection is to operate[1]. Nonetheless, an act which may in principle be protected by s 5 will *not* be unlawful merely because of the patient's objection. In keeping with the rule of thumb identified at 4.16 above – that the enormity of the decision and the professional status of the decision-maker will be major determinants of whether the s 5 requirements are satisfied in relation to a particular act – the more serious the decision, and the more strenuous the patient's objection, the more exacting the capacity and best interests determinations are required to be.

The objection of the incapacitated patient may also turn a s 5 act into an act of *restraint* (the threat or use of force where P resists or which restricts P's movement) within the meaning of s 6. Simply put, the administration of an injection may not usually require any actual or threatened force but, where P refuses to consent, some force may be used to hold P's arm. Where s 6 restraint is used, the requirements of s 6 (described below) must be satisfied in addition to the s 5 criteria.

1 Section 4(6) specifically requires regard to be had to the incapacitated persons wishes, feelings, beliefs and values.

Disagreements

4.21 Major disagreements may arise between the healthcare staff themselves, the healthcare staff and the patient, and/or any number of the persons who are likely to be involved in the patient's care and treatment. They may arise because the patient objects and the views of the relevant people differ as to the assessment of his best interests. Difficult decisions with considerable potential consequences for the patient are better resolved consensually. However, those are precisely the kinds of decision about which there are likely to be a range of disparate views. A helpful approach may be as follows:

- Potential changes of residence, major treatment decisions (eg DNR and major surgery) and decisions of similar magnitude are best taken at a multi-disciplinary level. Clinicians should consider seeking the views of other clinicians with relevant expertise before making such challenging decisions. In any event, the decision-making process ought to involve thorough consideration of the principle issues of capacity and best interests.
- Where there is still serious disagreement about what is in the patient's best interests (whether by reason of the patient's objection to a proposed course or a lack of consenus on the part of relevantly qualified experts) an application may be made to the Court of Protection.[1]

1 See Main Code, paras 6.12 and 6.18.

When should the Court of Protection's assistance be sought?

4.22 Some forms of medical intervention have, as a matter of common law, been regarded as so serious as to require the sanction of the Court of Protection (the court) before they are undertaken, and, even if all parties are in agreement. The MCA 2005 has preserved these aspects of the common law. In consequence, decisions pertaining to:

(a) the proposed withholding or withdrawal of artificial nutrition and hydration (ANH) from a patient in a permanent vegetative state (PVS);
(b) cases where it is proposed that a person who lacks capacity to consent should donate an organ or bone marrow to another person;
(c) the proposed non-therapeutic sterilisation of a person who lacks capacity to consent (for example, for contraceptive purposes); or
(d) cases where there is a dispute about whether a particular treatment will be in a person's best interests

should be reserved for the court[1].

The jurisdiction of the court as regards the lawfulness of acts which may fall within s 5 or 6 is wide[2]. The court has the power to make declarations as to a person's capacity and has an express power to declare 'the lawfulness or otherwise of any act done or yet to be done, in relation to that person'[3]. This does not of course mean that routine applications ought to be made to the court about minor issues of care[4]. The following list provides a guide to the kinds of cases which may be appropriate to refer to the court in relation to ss 5 and 6:

(a) serious disagreements between professionals and/or professionals and carers and/or family members etc about:
   (i) P's capacity to make a serious decision;
   (ii) whether a particular treatment (usually a major healthcare decision) or a proposed change of residence is in P's best interests;
(b) whether a specific act relating to a person's care or treatment is lawful (It is suggested that acts with serious consequences or to which P raises serious objections are the kind likely to give rise to an application under this head).

It is anticipated that the determination of the legality of any act connected with care or treatment will necessarily require the court to adjudicate upon the question of the *reasonableness* of (a) the steps taken to assess capacity; and (b) the belief in lack of capacity and best interests. The lawfulness of any s 5 act (including restraint) is likely to be determined by reference to the actor's (D) ability to establish that s/he complied with the requirements of s 5 where there is no restraint involved and ss 5 and 6 where there is restraint.

1 See Main Code, para 6.18.
2 See Chapter 10 for details of the jurisdiction of the court.
3 See s 15(1)(c). Note also that an 'act' for the purposes of s 15 includes omissions and a course of conduct.
4 Paragraph 8.18 of the Main Code suggests that other cases 'where there is a doubt or dispute about whether a particular treatment will be in a person's best interests' should be referred to the court.

WHO IS PROTECTED BY SECTION 5?

4.23 The Main Code makes clear that a range of people may act under the protection of s 5. They include:

- family carers and other kinds of carers
- care workers
- healthcare and social care staff
- others who may occasionally be involved in the care or treatment of a person who lacks capacity to consent, such as ambulance staff, housing workers, police officers and volunteer support workers

The Main Code specifically underscores the present legal position, referred to above, that s 5 does not authorise others to consent on behalf of or take decisions on behalf of an incapacitated person. Paragraph 6.21 of the Main Code also makes clear that s 5 does not identify specific personnel as authorised to do specific acts; nor does it privilege any or any category of actor/decision-maker.

SECTION 6: RESTRAINT

4.24 Section 6 places two major limitations on the protective operation of s 5. The first limitation relates to acts intended to 'restrain' a person. The second relates to acts which may conflict with a valid decision made by a donee of a Lasting Power of Attorney or a court-appointed deputy. Where s 5 acts amount to 'restraint', s 6 restricts the s 5 protection/defence to acts which are:

- necessary to prevent harm to P and are proportionate to the assessed level and risk of harm;
- not in conflict with a decision made by either the donee of an LPA or a court-appointed deputy.

Restraint

4.25 '*Restraint*' occurs where D:

> 'uses or threatens to use force to secure the doing of an act which P resists, or restricts P's liberty of movement, whether or not P resists.'[1]

Any act intended to restrain an incapacitated person will only be a s 5 protected act where the following two conditions are met:

- D *reasonably believes* that it is necessary to do the act in order to prevent *harm* to P; and
- the act is a *proportionate* response to the likelihood of the person lacking capacity suffering harm and to the seriousness of the harm.

The Main Code suggests at para 6.42 that healthcare and social care staff should refer to professional and other guidance and national standards in relation to the use of restraint. Since neither the statute nor the Main Code makes provision for the adherence to specific policies or procedures on restraint, other guidance will be crucial to insuring that restraint is only used in appropriate circumstances.

1 Section 6(4).

A reasonable belief

4.26 The Main Code does not give clear guidance on the circumstances in which a belief can be construed to be *reasonable*[1]. This may lead to the use of ss 5 and 6 as a defence where many others might regard the use of restraint as inappropriate. In particular, a lay carer may misunderstand what a '*reasonable belief*' is and an incapacitated person may be subject to restraint without adequate safeguards.

1 See the comments made by the Joint Scrutiny Committee at para 117 of their Report on the Draft Bill HL 189–1/HC 1083–1.

Harm

4.27 *Harm* is not defined in the MCA 2005. The Main Code states that it will depend on the situation and gives the following examples of circumstances which are indicative of a risk of harm:

- a person with learning disabilities might run into a busy road without warning, if they do not understand the dangers of cars;
- a person with dementia may wander away from home and get lost if they cannot remember where they live;
- a person with manic depression might engage in excessive spending during a manic phase, causing them to get into debt;
- a person may also be at risk of harm if they behave in a way that encourages others to assault or exploit them (for example, by behaving in a dangerously provocative way)[1].

1 See Main Code, para 6.45.

Risk assessment

4.28 Often, the effective assessment of the risk of harm and the way in which it may be obviated will be best achieved by prior planning. For example, where a person has a history of wandering off and engaging in risky behaviour it may be useful for the care plan to note this risk, provide guidance to staff and/or carers about how to avoid the associated risks and issue instructions on steps to be taken where the risk does materialise.

The assessment of the risk of *harm* and the calibration of a *proportionate response* throw up a number of knotty issues for the relevant healthcare professionals. It may frequently be unclear whether the appropriate regime to be used should be the MCA 2005 or the MHA 2007. Where, for example, risky behaviour may lead to a risk of harm to self and others, and the proportionate response is likely to involve a deprivation of liberty, the relevant hospital or care home will need to consider seeking an authorisation pursuant to the Bournewood Safeguards scheme and/or detention pursuant to the MHA 2007. Practitioners will need to weigh the benefit of one regime or another carefully, possibly with the help of expert evidence. Specific guidance on decision-making in relation to the correct choice of regime is given at Chapter 16.

A proportionate response

4.29 The concept of 'proportionality' is now reasonably well entrenched in both domestic and Convention law. It is often the basis for the justified interference with rights under the Convention. Many measures adopted by the state which pursue a legitimate aim, but which interfere with qualified rights such as the right to respect for privacy for example, will be justified only if the manner in which or the means by which they are adopted is 'proportionate' to the aim sought to be achieved[1]. Inherent in the obligation to act 'proportionately' is the obligation to adopt the measure which will least restrict the person concerned or least limit the right in question.

The '*proportionate response*' requirement in s 6 mirrors the requirements of the Convention concept of proportionality. The following table gives illustrative examples, taken in part from the Main Code's guidance, of what a proportionate response is:

Risk	*Proportionate Response*	*Disproportionate Response*
1. P harming himself by blithely wandering onto busy road because he does not understand the dangers.	Holding P's hand or securing lock on door facing busy road.	Refusing to let P outdoors at all or locking him in a very confined space (bedroom) to prevent him going outdoors.
2. P injuring herself by falling out of bed at night.	Requiring P to use a bed which has a rail to prevent her from falling.	Strapping P to her bed every night.

Risk	*Proportionate Response*	*Disproportionate Response*
3. P, with learning disabilities, occasionally punching the wall at college when frustrated.	Physical restraint when it is clear P is about to hit the wall may be appropriate depending on how much force is used. A less restrictive and appropriate response may be achieved by consultation with P's community team to assist in understanding triggers for P's behaviour and managing it without physical restraint.	Removing P from the college course altogether.

If the 'disproportionate responses' in the table above were to be adopted by a member of the health or social care team responsible for P, that member of staff would be unlikely to be able to rely on the protection offered by s 5. In other words, they, or their employers, might be exposed to liability for their acts. For example, in all three scenarios there may be liability in assault or potential breaches of the Article 8 right to respect for private life.

1 See in particular, in the mental health context, the judgment of Newman J in *R (on the application of N) v Ashworth Special Hospital and the Secretary of State for Health* [2001] MHLR 77, at para 9.

The common law

4.30 According to the Main Code, the common law may be used to assist in situations where there may be harm to others and a person is restrained to prevent harm to another person[1]. This must be so in an emergency situation, but where a person is known to have a history of causing harm or attempting to do so to others, then it is conceivable that there will be situations in which recourse to the common law will not be adequate in the face of other existing statutory regimes enabling a person to be dealt with safely.

When the common law is used, there remains a requirement to use the least restrictive measure available to achieve the desired ends in the best interests of the person who lacks capacity[2]. Similarly, the least force possible must be used when force is judged necessary to prevent harm. The proper response will depend on individual situations and is largely a matter of common sense. If it is practicable to achieve the same ends by less restrictive means then that must done. If a person's capacity is known to fluctuate and the act in question is not urgently needed, then the least restrictive response would be to allow time for the person to be capable of taking the decision themselves.

1 Main Code, para 6.43.
2 Main Code, para 6.47.

Acts contrary to a decision by an LPA or court deputy

4.31 Section 5 protection does not extend to acts that are contrary to the decision of someone authorised under an LPA or a court deputy. This assumes that the decision is within the scope of the relevant authority[1]. If there is a disagreement between carers and donees/deputies that cannot be resolved by informal means, then an application to the court might become necessary. If this dispute concerns life sustaining treatment, or treatment that is intended to prevent a serious deterioration in the person's condition, the relevant treatment may be given pending an application to the court[2].

1 The powers of the LPA are considered in detail at Chapter 5.
2 Section 6(6).

PAYMENT FOR NECESSARY GOODS AND SERVICES

4.32 Sections 7 and 8 deal with the payment for goods and services which are regarded as '*necessary*' for a person who lacks capacity. If '*necessary*' goods or services are supplied to a person who lacks capacity to contract for the supply, the incapacitated person must pay for them[1]. The pre-MCA 2005 position at law was governed by s 3(2) of the Sale of Goods Act 1979 (SGA 1979). SGA 1979, s 3(2) had the effect of rendering a contract between an incapacitated person and another void and unenforceable where that other person could be imputed with knowledge of P's lack of capacity. Section 7(1) modifies this rule so as to ensure that an incapacitated person pays for '*necessary*' services supplied under such a contract.

1 Section 7(1).

Necessary

4.33 Section 7(2) defines 'necessary' as 'suitable to a person's condition in life and to his actual requirements at the time when the goods or services are supplied'. 'Condition in Iife' is said by the Main Code to mean a person's place in society rather than their mental or physical condition[1]. When determining whether the relevant goods or services are necessary, regard must be had to the person's lifestyle before s/he lost capacity. The Main Code explains that, in this sense, designer clothing would be 'necessary' if P would have chosen to buy and wear designer clothes prior to his loss of capacity.

Goods which are surplus to requirements, ie which the incapacitated person already has a sufficient supply of, will not be construed to be necessary[2].

1 See Main Code, para 6.58.
2 See Main Code, para 6.59.

Expenditure on behalf of an incapacitated person

4.34 Sections 5 and 8 permit a carer or other person to arrange for payment for necessary goods and services from funds belonging to, or credit attributable to, P. Of course, s 8 only empowers a carer or other person to take these steps where the expenditure is for an act connected with care or treatment. It should, however, be noted that s 8 does not affect the powers and duties of those who have lawful control over P's funds (eg a donee or a deputy). In addition, a carer could not use s 8 to justify expenditure which conflicts with the lawful decision of a donee or deputy[1].

1 Section 6(6).

INTERNATIONAL INSTRUMENTS RELATING TO RESTRAINT

4.35 Many of the international instruments concerned with securing the rights of incapacitated and/or mentally disordered persons give express guidance on the permissible use of restraint. The CPT Standards[1] require restraint to be used only where 'necessary'[2]. The UN 'Principles for the Protection of Persons with Mental Illness'[3] appear to set a higher threshold for the use of physical restraint which they state is only justified where 'it is the only means available to prevent immediate or imminent harm to the patient or to others'. Both instruments require the use of restraint to accord with an approved policy or procedure and to be recorded. The CPT Standards refer to the following additional important principles:

- Restraint should, as far as possible, be non-physical and where physical, should, in principle, be limited to manual control[4].
- Staff in psychiatric establishments should receive training in both non-physical and manual control techniques with the aim of equipping staff to respond appropriately to difficult situations and to reduce the risk of injury to patients[5].
- The use of instruments of physical restraint will rarely be justified and must always be ordered or approved by a doctor. Such instruments should be removed at the earliest opportunity and should never be applied as a punishment[6].
- The use of instruments of physical restraint for more than a period of days must be therapeutically justified[7].

CPT country reports indicate that the Committee regards routine handcuffing and use of caged and/or net-beds to be outwith the CPT Standards[8].

It is an established principle of ECHR (and domestic) jurisprudence that the use of restraint in the case of incapacitated patients can only be justified by reference to a 'convincing medical necessity'[9]. The forcible administration of food or neuroleptics and/or the prolonged use of physical restraint or seclusion in the absence of therapeutic necessity can amount to a breach of Articles 3 and/or 5 and 8 ECHR[10].

A reading of the CPT Standards alongside the relevant Convention jurisprudence indicates that conduct connected with the care or treatment of an incapacitated patient, including restraint as defined, must also be therapeutically necessary. It is also widely believed that the common law provides authority for restraint to prevent harm to the person concerned or to others as long as the force used was necessary and proportionate[11]. In this sense there is little discrepancy, in theory, between the relevant international standards, Convention principles, the common law and the new ss 5 and 6.

1 The Standards of the European Committee for the Prevention of Torture and Inhuman or Degrading Treatment or Punishment, CPT/Inf/E(2002) – Rev 2006.

2 Paragraph 47 of the CPT Standards provides that 'In any psychiatric establishment, the restraint of agitated and/or violent patients may on occasion be necessary ... The restraint of patients should be the subject of a clearly defined policy. That policy should make clear that initial attempts to restrain agitated or violent patients should, as far as possible, be non-physical (eg verbal instruction) and that where physical restraint is necessary, it should in principle be limited to manual control.'

3 Adopted by General Assembly resolution 46/119 of 17 December 1991.

4 CPT, para 47.

5 CPT para 47.

6 CPT, para 48.

7 CPT, para 48.

8 For more on this see Bartlett, Lewis and Thorold, *Mental Disability and the European Convention on Human Rights*, pp.98–100.

9 See *Herczegfalvy v Austria* (1993) 15 EHRR 437 at paras 79–84.

10 *Herczegfalvy v Austria* (1993) 15 EHRR 437 at paras 82 and 86. See also *R (on the application of Wilkinson) v Broadmoor Hospital Authority* [2001] EWCA Civ 1545, [2002] 1 WLR 419 at 446, paras 79–82. Note also that an individual may not be able to assert a breach of these Convention rights against persons or bodies who are not 'public authorities' within the meaning of the Human Rights Act 1998. See Chapter 17 for more on this.

11 See *Black v Forsey* 1987 SLT 681. See also Hoggett, B, *Mental Health Law* (1996),at pp 140, 141.

PROBLEM AREAS AND PRACTICE POINTS

Concerns about inappropriate detention

4.36 Many of the features of ss 5 and 6 which exercised consultees during the MCA 2005's passage through Parliament have been resolved by, or at any rate transferred to, the Bournewood Safeguards. The JCHR, in its Twenty-Third Report of Session 2003–04, was concerned that ss 5 and 6 could be used to secure the admission into hospital of an incapacitated person, whether resistant or not, without any provision to ensure that the concomitant deprivation of liberty was accompanied by the necessary procedural safeguards[1].

The JCHR believed that the failure to confine the use or threat of force or other restriction of liberty to emergency situations could lead to unlawful deprivations of liberty of the kind found to exist in *HL v United Kingdom*. However, the final amendment of the MCA 2005 to include ss 4A, 4B and 16A has in large part removed these fears by requiring detention to be justified by reference to those provisions rather than by reference to ss 5 and/or 6.There would appear to be merit to the Government's stated position that the restriction of the use or threat of force, outside of the context of a putative deprivation of liberty, to urgent situations could have the effect of exacerbating the harm which might eventually be caused to an individual[2].

However, it remains important to ensure that the proportionality analysis required by s 6, and implicit in s 5, is respectfully adhered to. Any departure from that analysis may risk contravention of Articles 3 and/or 8 ECHR[3].

1 See in particular para 2.23 of the JCHR's Report, HL/210, HC/1282. Note also that these concerns were echoed by JUSTICE in their 'Revised Justice Briefing for Commons Second Reading' on the Mental Capacity Bill, October 2004 at paras 18–21.

2 The Government's response, in a letter from the Parliamentary-Under Secretary of State to the Chair of the JCHR dated 16 December 2004 was that: 'Sometimes it is not always in a person's best interests for matters to be left until it is an urgent situation. For example, restraint may be necessary in order to undertake a diagnostic procedure. If such a procedure is left until there is an urgent need or an emergency, then the resulting harm to the person may be worse. If a person needs treatment for a bad tooth, it will generally be in that person's best interests to be restrained, and to have the tooth treated, rather than wait until it is so bad as to count as an emergency requiring intervention'.

3 See in particular *Herczegfalvy v Austria* (1993) 15 EHRR 437 and *Stork v Germany*, Judgment of 16 June 2005.

Inadequate clarity about the standards of 'reasonableness'

4.37 As alluded to above, neither the Main Code nor the MCA 2005 provides adequate guidance on the '*reasonable belief*' required to justify restraint under s 6. Some guidance is given by the Main Code on the '*reasonable steps*' which must be taken to determine capacity, and the '*reasonable belief*' in lack of capacity and best interests, which are required to justify a s 5 act[1]. It may be presumed that the *reasonable belief* required to justify restraint under s 6 must in principle satisfy the thrust of the Main Code's guidance in relation to the *reasonable belief* in lack of capacity for s 5 (ie showing that all relevant circumstances were considered, some consideration of best interests, obtaining the views of the incapacitated person and other relevant persons). However, the absence of specific guidance remains a worrying omission since s 6 can be used to authorise intrusive physical contact, chemical restraints such as sedation and restrictions of movement which fall just short of deprivations of liberty. The absence of an explanation of what is meant by *reasonable belief* may lead to interferences with the physical or psychological autonomy of the incapacitated person (many of significant magnitude) without objective justification. This may well give rise to potential contravention of Articles 3 and 8 ECHR.

1 See Main Code, paras 6.26–6.34.

Other potential human rights issues

4.38 The following matters may give rise to difficulties in terms of Convention compliance:

- There are no general recording requirements in relation to s 6 acts despite clear guidance to that effect in the UN Mental Health Principles and the CPT Standards. There is a requirement under the Main Code (para 6.17) for healthcare and treatment decisions to be recorded. There is, however, a danger that a number of acts of restraint which might be assumed not to be healthcare or treatment decisions may sufficiently interfere with a person's physical and psychological integrity as to engage Article 8. The absence of a system of recording such restraint may create significant hurdles for a carer or healthcare professional who seeks to justify such an interference. It can also be argued that a requirement for recording in cases of restraint ought to be construed as part of a state's positive obligation under Article 8. The Main Code does not place sufficient emphasis or give clear enough prescription in respect of these important safeguards.
- There is no provision in the primary legislation or the Main Code which refers to the importance of staff training. Again, the absence of proper provision for training may give rise to potential breaches of the positive obligation under Article 8[1].
- The use of restraint under the MHA 1983 is governed by para 19 of the MHA 1983 Code of Practice. The MHA Code requires there to be a clear written policy and obliges the relevant authorities to record and review every episode of restraint. This desiderata of obligations is not replicated in the Main Code in respect of the use of s 6. This does not appear to accord with the requirements of either the Convention or the international instruments referred to above.

1 This is the suggestion made in Bartlett et al at p 98.

Particular problem areas

4.39 The following are situations or circumstances which may present practical difficulties for the operation of ss 5 and 6:

- *Chemical restraint*: It may sometimes be difficult to determine whether the use of medication is less restrictive than another form of restraint. This may complicate the picture for clinicians in the absence of specific guidance on the circumstances in which:
  - the administration of neuroleptics, for example, may itself amount to or be used as a restraint; or
  - medication may justifiably be used under s 6.
- *Seclusion*: Technically, there is no reason why s 6 could not be used to authorise seclusion. However, as indicated above, there is no specific guidance on how these provisions will operate in relation to seclusions[1].
- *Boundary between deprivation of liberty and restraint*: If restraint – by way of seclusion for example – is used regularly, there would appear to be a clear risk that the situation may amount to a deprivation of liberty. It is not clear whether in such circumstances it would be appropriate to seek a Bournewood Safeguards authorisation.
  - Take for example the scenario in which a young learning disabled woman living in a specialist facility is periodically placed in a padded room to manage bouts of serious but episodic

violent behaviour. Does regular seclusion in the padded room tip the circumstances of her accommodation in the facility into a deprivation of liberty? What would best practice be in relation to ensuring that the removal to the padded room was used only when necessary and that her rights were secured?

– In this sort of situation, a careful record of the reasons for all seclusions is crucial. Similarly it would be important to document the reasons in the care plan together with an analysis of all of the less restrictive options. In the circumstances described, it is likely that there would already be an authorisation for detention in place. However, if it was not, it is not clear whether it would be required and serious consideration ought to be given to the need for it.

1 In *R (on the application of Munjaz) v Mersey Care NHS Trust* [2005] UKHL 58, [2006] 2 AC 148 the House of Lords specifically stated that any departure from the MHA Code of Practice on seclusion would require cogent justification. As there is no guidance on seclusion for MCA 2005 purposes, incapacitated persons would appear to be offered a lower level of protection from arbitrary or unjustified seclusion/restraint than MHA 2003 patients.

Chapter 5

LASTING POWER OF ATTORNEY (LPA)

- **MCA 2005, ss 9–14, Schedule 1**
- **Main Code chapter 7**
- **Lasting Powers of Attorney, Enduring Powers of Attorney and Public Guardian Regulations 2007, SI 2007/1253**

INTRODUCTION

5.1 Lasting Powers of Attorney (LPA) are powers granted by a person with capacity, the donor, to another or others known as 'donees', to make decisions on their behalf when they have lost the capacity to do so themselves. They replace Enduring Powers of Attorney (EPA) created under the Enduring Powers of Attorney Act 1985 (EPAA 1985). A major innovation of the MCA 2005 is that LPA's extend beyond financial and property decisions to include welfare decisions, which cover healthcare and medical needs.

During the passage of the MCA 2005 through Parliament there was much concern expressed about financial abuse occurring under LPAs, as under existing EPAs, and the potential power of a donee in relation to withdrawal of life-sustaining treatment, particularly where a conflict of interests may exist, for example, because a close relative acting as donee is also the beneficiary under the donor's Will.

These concerns have been addressed in large part by the requirement that an LPA must be registered by the Public Guardian before it can be used, whether or not the donor has lost capacity, thereby subjecting the power to the scrutiny of the new Public Guardian. There are specific provisions regulating decisions about life-sustaining treatment. The Public Guardian is responsible for maintaining registers of LPAs and responding to representations and complaints made about LPAs (see Chapter 12). The Court of Protection has express powers in relation to LPAs (ss 22 and 23).

Once registered, financial LPA's may be used even before the donor has lost capacity; welfare LPA's may only be used on the incapacity of the donor. The MCA 2005 allows for more than one person to undertake these tasks if the donor so desires. It was emphasised in Parliament that donor choice is a key principle behind the appointment of donees. The Main Code draws the donor's attention to the need to appoint someone they trust to the position of donee.

The creation and registration of LPAs is governed by s 10 of and Sch 1 to the MCA 2005 and the Lasting Powers of Attorney, Enduring Powers of Attorney and Public Guardian Regulations 2007 as amended[1] ('LPA Regulations').

5.1 *Lasting Power of Attorney (LPA)*

Chapter 7 of the Main Code deals with LPAs.

It is worth remembering that the MCA 2005 allows there to be more than one decision-maker for a person without capacity. Where there are issues of welfare, for example, there are likely to be many in relation to different types of decisions ranging from daily care to medical treatment and within a multi-disciplinary team. Furthermore, s 4(7) creates a list of people to be consulted, including the donee of an LPA, by a decision-maker determining the best interests of a person.

1 SI 2007/1253 amended by SI 2007/2161.

IMPORTANT FEATURES OF AN LPA

5.2 An LPA:

- may only be granted by a person with capacity over 18 years of age[1];
- must comply with s 10, be contained in a legal document[2] and be registered in accordance with Sch 1 before it may be used[3];
- empowers a donee, or donees, to make decisions about (a) the *personal welfare* or specified matters concerning the personal welfare of a person, and (b) the *property and affairs* or specified matters concerning the property and affairs of a person. Donees must act jointly where there is no other specification as to how they should act[4];
- can operate as an 'ordinary' power of attorney in relation to financial and property matters when the donor has full mental capacity, but it will also continue to operate after the donor has lost capacity (ss 9(1); 11(7)(a));
- a donee must only act within the scope of the LPA. Any acts outside its scope may be protected by ss 5 and 6 of the MCA 2005,
- a welfare LPA is only effective on the incapacity of the donor[5];
- is expressly subject to the provisions of the MCA 2005 and in particular s 1 (principles) and s 4 (best interests) and any conditions or restrictions specified in the instrument by the donor (s 9(4));
- may be subject to conditions and restrictions on areas a donor would not wish a donee to act. Conditions or restrictions imposed by the donor are not required to be in the donor's best interests;
- may extend to the giving or refusing of consent to carrying out or continuing life sustaining treatment *only* if expressly authorised (s 11(8)(a));
- is subject to any relevant advance decision made by the donor and relevant to the decision to be taken (s 11(7)). However, if the LPA was made after the advance decision a donee may be able to act[6].

1 Section 9(2)(c).
2 Prescribed forms and guidance are contained in Sch 1 of the Lasting Powers of Attorney, Enduring Powers of Attorney and Public Guardian Regulations 2007, SI 2007/1253 coming into force on 1 October 2007. There are separate forms for the creation of welfare LPAs and property and affairs LPAs. See table of forms at Appendix 5.
3 Section 9(2)(a) and (b).
4 Main Code, para 7.12.
5 Section 11(7)(a).
6 See s 25(2)(b).

ENDURING POWERS OF ATTORNEY ACT 1985

5.3 The LPA provisions of the MCA 2005 came into force on 1 October 2007. The EPAA 1985 has from that date been repealed in its entirety[1]. Prior to the EPAA 1985 a power of attorney automatically terminated as soon as the donor lost mental capacity. The EPAA 1985 allowed for powers of attorney to continue post incapacity subject to registration with the Public Guardian.[2] The operation of unregistered EPAs created prior to the MCA 2005 coming into force is now governed by Sch 4 and transitional provisions are in Sch 5, Part 2[3].

1 Section 67(2) and Sch 7. By s 66, Part 7 of the Mental Health Act 1983 and the EPAA 1985 cease to have effect. No new EPA may be created after the commencement of this provision (1 October 2007). Schedule 4 has effect in relation to existing EPAs and provides for registration upon supervening incapacity and effectively preserves the previous regime under the EPAA 1985 for this purpose only. The new Court of Protection will continue to have powers to deal with a registered power: MCA 2005, Sch 4, Pt 5, para 16.

2 EPAA 1985 came into force on 10 March 1986. Further regulations relating to the powers of the Court of Protection were contained in the Court of Protection (Enduring Powers of Attorney) Rules 2001, SI 2001/825, now superseded.

3 See s 66(3) and (4).

EPAs made prior to 1 October 2007

5.4 The legal effect of an existing EPA is preserved and incorporated into the new Act[1]. During Committee Stage in the House of Lords it was confirmed that there is to be no retrospective application of ss 1–4 of the MCA 2005 in relation to existing EPAs. Thus if a person has an unregistered EPA and retains the capacity to do so, they should be encouraged to tear up their old EPAs and make a new LPA. However, the principles under the MCA 2005 will be still considered good practice for all concerned with incapacitated adults[2]. Other protections in relation to old EPA's will exist under the common law because a donee will continue to owe fiduciary and other duties to a donor[3] (see below at 5.29).

1 It is beyond the scope of this book to explain the detail of EPAs which are concerned only with decisions about financial affairs. Refer to chapters 6 and 7 of Heywood and Massey, *Court of Protection Practice* (Sweet and Maxwell, looseleaf) for details of the creation and registration of EPAs and Court of Protection powers.

2 See Main Code, para 7.79.

3 669 HL Official Report (5th series), col 783, 8 February 2005.

Differences between EPA and LPA

5.5 There are a number of differences between LPAs and EPAs and these are listed in the Main Code[1]. Attorneys acting under an LPA have a legal duty to have regard to the guidance in the Main Code[2]. EPAs do not have such a duty, but the Code will still offer assistance[3].

Two key differences between an LPA and an EPA are:

1 EPAs are only capable of covering a person's property and affairs. An LPA may extend to personal welfare decisions in addition. A person

may have separate donees under an LPA to cover welfare and property and affairs, or may have one to cover both. The choice is likely to depend upon the relevant skills of the individuals concerned.

2 An LPA *must* be registered before a donee may act under it, regardless of whether or not the donor has lost capacity. This is a safeguard intended to prevent abuse by a donee of an LPA and to reduce the incidence of financial impropriety and criminal activity that was brought to the attention of the Joint Scrutiny Committee. Registration enables the Public Guardian to institute investigations about the donee if called upon to do so (see 5.63below). A personal welfare LPA may only be used once the donor has, or may reasonably be believed to have, lost capacity[4]. A financial LPA may enable a donee to act whether or not the donor has lost capacity. However, the donor may stipulate that the donee may only act under the LPA following his or her loss of capacity[5].

1 Main Code, para 7.5, Table. See also para 140 of the Joint Scrutiny Report.
2 Section 42(4)(a).
3 Main Code, Chapter 7, para 7.5.
4 Section 11(7).
5 See Forms attached to the LPA Regulations at http://www.publicguardian.gov.uk/forms/forms.htm.

SCOPE OF AN LPA

Source of authority

5.6 An LPA is contained in a legal document[1] and confers authority on the appointed donee(s), to make decisions about (a) the personal welfare or specified matters concerning the personal welfare of a person, and/or (b) the property and affairs or specified matters concerning the property and affairs of a person.

Importantly a welfare donee may only make those personal welfare decisions authorised by the LPA and cannot also make decisions about other welfare matters or financial affairs. Similarly a financial and property donee has no power over welfare matters. It is clear that the same person may, however, be appointed to fulfil both types of function in which case they may take both personal welfare and financial and property decisions insofar as provided for by the instrument creating the LPA and subject to conditions and restrictions (s 9(4)).

As a matter of good practice decision-makers should consult with donees about decisions or actions whether or not they are expressly covered by the terms of the LPA. This is especially if the donee is likely to have known the donor for some time and may have information about their wishes and feelings[2]. This applies also to different donees appointed under personal welfare or financial powers.

1 Prescribed forms and guidance are contained in Sch 1 of The Lasting Powers of Attorney, Enduring Powers of Attorney and Public Guardian Regulations 2007, SI 2007/1253 coming into force on 1 October 2007. There are separate forms for the creation of welfare LPAs and property and affairs LPAs. See table at Appendix 5.
2 Main Code, para 7.57.

Donees' powers insufficient

5.7 If a donee requires more powers than provided in the LPA, s/he must apply to the Court of Protection which may expand the donees' authority or appoint the donee as a court deputy with the requested powers[1].

1 Main Code, para 7.56 and chapter 8.

Statutory principles and best interests

5.8 The exercise of the authority conferred by an LPA is expressly governed by the provisions of the MCA 2005 and in particular s 1 (principles) and s 4 (best interests) and any conditions or restrictions specified in the instrument by the donor[1]. Conditions or restrictions imposed by the donor are not required to be in the donor's best interests. Making decisions includes where appropriate acting on them[2].

A donee must have regard to the Main Code[3] which addresses the scope of an LPA in detail. It reiterates the duty to follow the scheme of the MCA 2005, have regard to the Main Code (in particular Chapters 2–6, 8, 9 and 15) and make only those decisions that the LPA gives them authority to make[4].

1 Section 9(4).
2 Section 64(2).
3 Section 42(4)(a).
4 Main Code, paras 7.18, 7.52–68.

Welfare decisions

5.9 A donee may only make a welfare decision that is authorised by the instrument creating the LPA and, in addition:

1 the instrument is is registered with the Public Guardian,
2 the donor lacks capacity, or the donee reasonably believes that s/he does,
3 is subject to any applicable advance decisions[1], and
4 is subject to any conditions or restrictions (see below).

1 Section 11(7)(a), (b).

Meaning of 'welfare'

5.10 The term 'welfare' includes healthcare and medical treatment decisions and might also include a wide range of social care and accommodation issues, such as:

- where the donor should live and who they should live with;
- day-to-day care, including diet and dress;
- who the donor may have contact with;
- consenting to or refusing medical examination and treatment on the donor's behalf;
- arrangements needed for the donor to be given medical, dental or optical treatment;
- assessments for and provision for community care services;
- whether the donor should take part in social activities, leisure activities, education or training;
- the donor's personal correspondence and papers;
- rights of access to personal information about the donor; or
- complaints about the donor's care and treatment[1].

This list is not exhaustive and broadly coincides with the definition of 'personal welfare' for the purposes of decisions taken by the court and court-appointed deputies[2].

1 See Main Code, para 7.21.
2 Sections 16(1) and 17. Welfare decisions under the MCA 2005 are dealt with in more detail in Chapter 7.

Medical treatment and healthcare[1]

5.11 The authority extends to the giving or refusing of consent to the carrying out or continuation of a treatment[2] by a person providing healthcare. The MCA 2005 restricts the giving or refusing of consent by a donee to the carrying out or continuation of life-sustaining treatment, unless the instrument expressly allows it and subject to any other conditions or restrictions imposed by the donor[3]. Thus a donee is not permitted to demand any specific treatment, simply to refuse a treatment or to give consent to a proposed treatment. This introduces a proxy into health (and welfare) decision-making for incapacitated adults for the first time.

These are controversial provisions the implementation of which will require great care. They allow a person to influence treatment decisions about them even after they have lost capacity, through a donee. This means that such decisions should become less doctor-driven but they will always be underpinned by the requirement that they be in the donor's best interests.

1 See also Chapter 8 on medical decision-making.
2 Defined in s 64(1) as a 'diagnostic or other procedure'.
3 Section 11(7)(c) and (8).

Life-sustaining treatments

5.12 'Life-sustaining treatment' is defined as 'treatment which in the view of a person providing health care for the person concerned is necessary to sustain life'[1]. It is for the doctor or healthcare professional in each individual situation to determine whether or not a treatment falls within this definition[2].

As stated above, a donor must specify in the LPA if s/he wants a donee to be able to make decisions regarding life-sustaining treatments. A donee may not make decisions regarding life-sustaining treatment in the absence of such an express authority. It will be seen that these requirements are not as stringent as those for an advance decision because the donor is not required to specify the treatment to which it applies, although they may do so – See Chapter 3. Nevertheless, when exercising such a power a donee must act within the scope of the authority and in the best interests of the donee, and must not be motivated by a desire to bring about the donor's death (see below).

1 Section 4(10).
2 Main Code, para 5.30. And see Chapter 8 on medical decision-making.

LPA MUST NOT BE MOTIVATED BY A DESIRE TO BRING ABOUT DEATH: S 4(5)

5.13 The donee must act in the donor's best interests and must consult carers, family and others who may be interested in the donor's welfare[1]. Section 4(5) states specifically that where a decision relates to life sustaining treatment, the person taking the decision in the donor's best interests must not 'be motivated by a desire to bring about his death'. This applies to a donee empowered to take such decisions. A difficulty may arise for a donee where a donor has stipulated elsewhere that they would not wish to be kept alive artificially. A donee might feel bound to refuse treatment in accordance with the donor's wish, knowing that it will have the result of, or with the aim of, bringing about their death.

A valid advance decision to that effect would trump any decision of a donee to permit treatment whether or not it was in the donor's best interests (but see 5.21 below and s 25(2)). Anything short of a clear advance decision refusing life-saving treatment would leave the donee in a position of having to take account of the donor's wishes expressed when he or she had sufficient capacity to do so.

A donee faced with an LPA granting such a power may be well advised to insist that the donor make a valid advance decision relating to life sustaining treatment at the time of creating the LPA, in order not to be faced with such a conundrum, or that the power be cast in more specific terms.

There was discussion concerning the difficulty in detecting a motivation to bring about death because it could be wrapped up in a plausible best interests argument[2]. The Joint Committee on Human Rights (JCHR)[3] welcomed the insertion of s 4(5) to attempt to meet concerns regarding abusive decisions being taken for vulnerable people, but in terms of practical value deemed it more declaratory of the intention behind the MCA 2005 than a substantive safeguard. See Chapter 17 in relation to the human rights implications of life-sustaining treatment decisions. Thus while criminal sanctions for contravening s 4(5) are a possibility, this suggests that they are unlikely to be a reality.

Furthermore, the MCA 2005 accepts that a doctor cannot be expected by virtue of s 4(5) to provide or continue to provide a person with life-sustaining treatment that is not in their best interests, even if death is foreseen. This must apply equally to a donee, offering some protection as long as the decision is in the donor's best interests. If the doctor's (donee's) opinion or decision is disputed and no resolution is achieved, ultimately the court may be asked to decide the issue[4].

The Main Code makes it clear that all reasonable steps which are in the person's best interests must be taken to prolong their life. In a limited number of cases such steps will be futile and burdensome to the patient with little prospect of recovery. In such circumstances decisions to withdraw or withhold life-sustaining treatment (including artificial nutrition and hydration (ANH)) may be taken[5]. Such decisions must accord with the person's best interests[6].

In Parliament the Government explained that sometimes 'it is in a person's best interests for treatment to be withheld because it would confer no real benefit ... In some end of life situations, it cannot be assumed that all or any treatments should be given just because they are available'[7].

1 Main Code, paras 7.30–7.31.
2 670 HL Official Report (5th series), col 1484, 17 March 2005.
3 JCHR Fourth Report of Session 2004–2005, published 24 January 2005 at paras 4.39–4.43 which discuss safeguards in relation to withdrawal of life-sustaining treatment and the declaratory nature of the provision made.
4 Main Code, para 5.33.
5 Main Code, para 5.31.
6 Unless they are taken in response to a valid advance decision.
7 670 HL Official Report (5th series), col 1467, 17 March 2005; Main Code, para 5.32.

Fettering clinical judgement

5.14 Concern has been expressed that giving a donee power over life-sustaining treatments puts doctors in a difficult position placing an onus on them to make applications to the court, or be 'browbeaten' into a position that runs contrary to their clinical judgement – see Chapter 8 on medical decisions

Parliamentary debates highlighted an apparent contradiction where the Bill was careful in other respects not to fetter the clinical freedom and professional judgement of doctors except where a person has expressed a valid advance decision. The argument is that at least an advance decision is the decision of the person concerned unlike a donee's decision, which is one step removed from that person and endeavouring to convey/interpret their wishes. The Government's response relied upon the fact that a power over life sustaining decisions cannot be created accidentally: it must be explicit. Further if there is a doubt, the MCA 2005 is skewed towards treatment and doctors can seek court clarification regarding decisions which will protect them from a negligence action or criminal prosecution[1]. Section 6(7) enables them to treat while they do so without fear of liability[2].

Other reasons given by the Government for opposing an amendment to withdraw life-sustaining treatment from the remit of donees included:

(a) that it would weaken the ability of families to speak up for their loved ones;
(b) that it would place a donee in a weaker position than a court deputy if they could not approve or refuse such treatment;
(c) healthcare bodies had welcomed this explicit role for donees;
(d) donees do not make clinical decisions about medical best interests;
(e) a donee has only the same power as a patient with capacity, he can only give or refuse consent, he cannot make medical decisions;
(f) a doctor continues to have a professional duty of care for his or her patient and can be sued for breaching that duty.

An important caveat to (e) above is that a donee must act in the donor's best interests and cannot take unwise decisions, as a donor might do when capacitous.

1 670 HL Official Report (5th series), cols 1485 and 1489–1490, 17 March 2005. See also JCHR Fourth Report of Session 2004–2005, published 24 January 2005, as above at 5.13.
2 670 HL Official Report (5th series), cols 433–438, 24 March 2005, citing *Glass v United Kingdom* [2004] IFCR 553 where the ECtHR criticised doctors for failing to go to court when they disagreed with a mother's refusal of consent to treat on behalf of her son resulting in an Article 8 ECHR violation.

Withdrawal of artificial nutrition and hydration

5.15 The JCHR raised concerns about the failure to require a specific authority in relation to the withdrawal of ANH, as with life-sustaining treatments[1]. The question was whether an LPA which expressly extended to life-sustaining treatments also authorised the donee to refuse ANH in the absence of specific authorisation of such a refusal? This is a similar concern to that expressed in relation to advance decisions covering life-sustaining treatment in the same report. The JCHR was concerned about confusions arising because the donor may not have appreciated that ANH counts as treatment, thereby conferring power to refuse food and drink on their behalf.

Safeguards in the Main Code were considered insufficiently strong to deal with this concern. The opinion of the JCHR was that the legal framework required there to be a duty to provide ANH, if it is in the person's best interests, in order to be compatible with Articles 2, 3 and 8 ECHR.

In the early stages of debate a harrowing example was given of a woman in Florida whose brother held her power of attorney and reported that she had wanted nutrition withdrawn, but nursing staff said she had been able to indicate that she wanted food and fluids: she had been restrained from raiding other patients' food trays[2].

When drafting welfare LPAs it will be important to draw this point concerning the extent of life-sustaining treatment to the attention of the donor.

1 JCHR, Fourth Report of Session 2004–5 at paras 4.44–4.50. See also JCHR 23rd report of Session 2003–4, para 2.51.
2 425 HC Official Report (6th series), cols 59–60, 11 October 2004.

Difference of opinion between healthcare team, doctor and donee

5.16 A clinical team and an LPA are both mandated to act in the person's best interests. If there is a difference of opinion between a clinician or healthcare team and a donee the healthcare team should in the first instance discuss the case with other medical experts and/or get a formal second opinion and further discuss the case with the donee[1]. An application to the Court of Protection by the treating hospital would become necessary if they fail to resolve the issue.

1 Main Code, para 7.29.

GROUNDS OF APPLICATION TO COURT OF PROTECTION

5.17 An application to the court may be made by healthcare staff or health authority, or the donee.

A dispute might arise on grounds of disagreement over:

(a) the validity and scope of the LPA instrument (ss 22 and 23);
(b) the provision of medical treatment (whether life-sustaining or not) , and the best interests of the donor; and/or
(c) a donor's wishes and feelings as expressed to or known by the donee or contained in a written statement not amounting to an advance decision[1], or indeed an advance decision.

1 See Main Code, para 5.33 for more on the effect of written statements ie not advance decisions.

EVIDENCE

5.18 In (b) above, a court will require expert medical evidence to support the donee's position. In situations (a) and (c) above, the court will require cogent evidence of the donor's wishes and intentions when making the LPA and/or other statement or decision. It remains to be seen, particularly, in relation to life-sustaining treatments whether the court will import safeguards akin to those applied to advance decisions, namely, that the wish is expressed in writing, or has been expressed verbally on more than one occasion to more than one person and is precise in nature, ie relates to a specified treatment.

REMEDIES

5.19 In addition to its powers to determine questions relating to validity and scope of an LPA under ss 22 and 23, the court may give declaratory relief as to whether the serious medical treatment or withdrawal of treatment proposed was lawful and in the person's best interests[1], or make a substituted decision under s 16. A donee's challenge might in addition seek interim injunctive relief to prevent treatment pending the court application (except in relation to life-sustaining treatment). Alternatively, the agreement of the clinician to abstain from treatment pending a court decision may be achieved. In a situation where treatment has proceeded, tortious damages may be available for any trespass and resulting injury.

A clinician cannot have s 5 protection if s/he were to treat a donor in conflict with a valid donee's decision made within the scope of the authority granted by an LPA[2]. However, a clinician could provide life-sustaining treatment that s/he 'reasonably believes to be necessary to prevent a serious deterioration in P's condition, while a decision as respects any relevant issue is sought from the court'[3].

If a donee (or doctor) acquiesces and allows treatment which results in damage to the person, the possibility of a civil negligence claim arises – see Chapter 4 on s 5 protections and liabilities and Chapter 15 on civil litigation generally.

1 Section 15(1)(c). See Chapter 10 for the powers of the Court of Protection and also the Main Code, paras 7.45–7.49.
2 Section 6(6)(a).
3 Section 6(7).

Welfare and care plans

5.20 Health or social care staff preparing a care plan for a person without capacity must assess whether the person has the capacity to agree to the plan or parts of it. If not, they must consult any donee and obtain their permission to the care plan. They must also consult the donee as to the person's best interests[1]. It is suggested that consultation with the donee would be good practice even if the person is deemed to have sufficient capacity to agree and that doing so would accord with the spirit of the Main Code.

1 Main Code, para 7.25 and see Chapter 7 at 7.73–7.74.

EFFECT OF AN ADVANCE DECISION

5.21 If a donor has made an advance decision to refuse a proposed treatment, then the donee's power does not allow a different decision to be taken in relation to that decision[1]. However, if the LPA was made after the advance decision and relates to the same treatment a donee may be able to act[2].

1 Section 11(7)(b).
2 See s 25(2)(b) and Chapter 3 on advance decisions.

Decisions excluded from welfare LPAs

5.22 A donee under a welfare LPA that includes healthcare decisions has no power to make decisions if:

- the donor retains capacity in relation to the particular health care decision[1];
- there is an advance decision in relation to that decision[2], unless a later LPA covers the same treatment[3];
- the decision relates to life-sustaining treatment, unless it is expressly authorised by the LPA[4];
- they are decisions relating to medical treatment for mental disorder if the donor is subject to Part IV of the Mental Health Act 1983[5];
- an LPA cannot authorise a donee to demand a specific form of treatment.

1 Section 11(7)(a).
2 Section 11(7)(b).
3 Section 25(2)(b).
4 Section 11(7)(c).
5 Section 28. But see 5.76, fn 2 below for an exception regarding Community Treatment Orders to be introduced in October 2008 and ECT.

Decisions falling outside LPA authority and section 5 protection

5.23 Decisions to be taken that fall outside the authorised power must be referred to the court, or be protected by ss 5 and 6 of the MCA 2005 – see Chapter 4.

Section 5 does not authorise a person to act in conflict with a decision within the scope of a valid LPA[1]. But there is an exception relating to providing life-sustaining treatment pending the decision of the court[2].

1 Section 6(6)(a).
2 See above and s 6(7).

Property and affairs decisions[1]

5.24 A financial LPA is effective from the moment of registration unless the donor stipulates otherwise so that the power is only effective upon the donor's incapacity to make the relevant decisions. It is for the donor to decide how their capacity should be assessed if the LPA is only to take effect on their incapacity[2].

A financial LPA does not prevent a donor from taking decisions on their own behalf where they have capacity to do so. They may have fluctuating capacity in relation to their financial affairs. A donee must encourage and enable a donor to do as much as possible and only act when requested to do so, or upon the donor's incapacity[3].

1 Main Code, paras 7.32–7.42.
2 Eg by medical certificate; Main Code, para 7.33.
3 Main Code, para 7.34.

Meaning of 'property and affairs'

5.25 This means 'business matters, legal transactions and other dealings of a similar kind'[1]. If a donor does not restrict the LPA or impose conditions, the donee will be able to decide on any or all of the person's property and financial affairs. This might include:

- buying or selling property;
- opening, closing or operating any bank, building society or other account;
- giving access to the donor's financial information;
- receiving any income, inheritance or other entitlement on behalf of the donor;
- claiming, receiving and using (on the donor's behalf) all benefits, pensions, allowances and rebates (unless the Department for Work and Pensions has already appointed someone and everyone is happy for this to continue);
- dealing with the donor's tax affairs;
- paying the donor's mortgage, rent and household expenses;
- insuring, maintaining and repairing the donor's property;
- investing the donor's savings[2].

The provisions for the appointment of an attorney jointly and/or severally above apply.

1 *Re F* [1990] 2 AC 1 per Lord Brandon at 59H.
2 See long list in Main Code, para 7.36.

Gifts

5.26 Where an LPA concerns property and affairs there is a restriction on the gifts that a donee can make out of the donor's property (s 12)[1]. A donee may make gifts on 'customary occasions' to others (including him or herself) who are connected with the donor. These are anniversaries, birthdays and so on; or to any charity that the donor supported or might have been expected to support. This is subject to any specific conditions or restrictions contained in the instrument. Of course a donee may only act in the best interests of the donor. The court has authority to authorise more substantial gifts if satisfied it is in the donor's best interests (s 23(4))[2].

1 This is similar to s 3(5) of the EPAA 1985: Explanatory note, para 59.
2 For example for tax planning reasons if the donor has substantial assets. Explanatory note para 59, above; Main Code, paras 7.40–7.42.

Conditions and restrictions: welfare and property and affairs

5.27 A donor can add restrictions or conditions to areas where they would not wish the attorney to have the power to act. For example, restricting the power granted to social care and not healthcare decisions, or to particular kinds of health decisions.

5.27 *Lasting Power of Attorney (LPA)*

An LPA may be quite a subtle instrument as explained in the Main Code. For example, a person may appoint their daughter to act as a personal welfare donee, but stipulate that she have no power to determine contact with other members of the family because the donor is aware that the daughter does not have a good relationship with wider family members. If the daughter then wishes to prevent contact with any other family she would have to make an application to the court[1].

Decisions regarding life-sustaining treatments are provided for explicitly[2].

Decisions to be taken that fall outside the authorised power must be referred to the court, or be protected by sections 5 and 6 of the MCA 2005 (care and treatment only) – see above at 5.7 and Chapter 4.

1 See scenario set out at Main Code, para 7.23.
2 Section 11 and 5.12 above; Main Code, para 7.22.

DUTIES OF DONEES

5.28 Donees are required to act to a reasonable standard in law or potentially face criminal or civil action – see Chapter 4 on protections and liabilities.

Donees' duties under the common law: agency[1]

5.29 A donee acts as the agent of the person granting the authority. Common law duties arising include a duty:

- to act with due care and skill, to act in good faith;
- to carry out the donor's instructions;
- not to take advantage of their position and not benefit themselves, but benefit the donor (fiduciary duty);
- not to delegate a function or decision to another, unless authorised;
- to keep the donor's affairs confidential;
- to comply with directions of the Court of Protection;
- not to give up the role without telling the donor and the court;
- financial LPAs must also keep accounts and keep the donor's money and property separate from their own[2];
- to keep accounts of moneys received or paid on the donor's behalf[3].

Further guidance on the 'duty of care' owed is set out in the Main Code. A donee owes a duty of care to carry out their functions to a certain standard of care which will depend upon whether they are paid or have relevant professional qualifications. A person who is unpaid must exercise the same care and skill as they would for decisions they take about their own lives. If they are being paid, a higher standard of skill is expected. Professionals must display professional skill and competence according to the standards of their profession eg solicitors or accountants[4].

1 An account of the law of agency is beyond the scope of this book. Please refer to Bowstead and Reynolds on Agency (18th edn) Sweet and Maxwell, Common Law Library series. See also 668 HL Official Report (5th series), col 1426, 27 January 2005.

2 Main Code, para 7.58.
3 See the Main Code, para 7.58; also paras 7.60–7.68.
4 Main Code, para 7.59.

FORMALITIES

Creating a valid LPA

5.30 There are three requirements for creating a valid authority under an LPA:

1 the appointment of donees must be achieved in conformity with s 10 formalities (see Table 1 below);
2 The instrument must be *created* and *registered* in accordance with Sch 1[1] (see Tables 2a and b and 3 below); and
3 the person making the instrument must have capacity at the time and be at least 18 years old[2].

1 The prescribed form of instrument is contained in the Lasting Powers of Attorney, Enduring Powers of Attorney and Public Guardian Regulations 2007, SI 2007/1253, coming into force on 1 October 2007. See http://www.publicguardian.gov.uk/forms/forms.htm.
2 Sections 2 and 3.

Capacity to create an LPA

5.31 This is to be judged and determined as provided for in the MCA 2005, which replaces the common law arising from the creation of EPAs. The determination of capacity to make all types of welfare, treatment and financial decisions is dealt with elsewhere in this book – see Chapter 2.

Common law test

5.32 Nevertheless, the common law continues to carry interpretative value in relation to the MCA 2005, always bearing in mind that EPAs conferred powers in relation to property and finance only. The donor should have understood:

> 'First, (if such be the terms of the power) that the attorney will be able to assume complete authority over the donor's affairs. Secondly, (if such be the terms of the power) that the attorney will in general be able to do anything with the donor's property which he himself could have done. Thirdly, that the authority will continue if the donor should be or become mentally incapable. Fourthly, that if he should be or become mentally incapable, the power will be irrevocable without confirmation by the court.'[1]

1 *Re K, Re F (Enduring Power of Attorney)* [1988] Ch 310, *Re W (Enduring Power of Attorney)* [2001] Ch 609 at 614.

Proof of capacity when instrument made

5.33 The requisite capacity must be in relation to the specific powers granted to the donee(s) by the instrument, or the general power if that is what is granted. The creation and registration of an LPA requires at least one certificate from a person declaring that at the time of execution of the instrument the donor understood the purpose of the instrument and the scope of its authority, amongst other things[1]. There is a list of those who are disqualified to act here, which includes family members and donees[2]. This offers some reassurance that, save for a situation of outright fraud, it is unlikely that an LPA will be created by a person lacking sufficient capacity to do so. There is no penalty for signing an LPA certificate in bad faith. Bad faith would be difficult to establish where what is in issue is the opinion of an individual[3].

1 Lasting Powers of Attorney, Enduring Powers of Attorney and Public Guardian Regulations 2007, SI 2007/1253, Part 2, reg 7; MCA 2005, Sch 1, Part 1, para 2(1)(e); see Table 2a below at 5.86.
2 See Table 2a below at 5.86.
3 668 HL Official Report (5th series), cols 1430–1432, 27 January 2005. Response to consultation on forms and guidance attracted strongest opinion in relation to the certification process – Department of Constitutional Affairs publication dated 17 July 2006.

Objections and invalid instrument

5.34 The lack of capacity of the donor at the time of creating the LPA is a ground of objection for registration of the power[1]. There is specific protection for those acting in pursuance of an invalid LPA[2].

1 By s 13(6)(d) the power is terminated.
2 Section 14.

Appointment of donees by donor

Free choice

5.35 Enabling a donor to choose his or her own attorney free from restrictions is intended to pursue the principle of autonomy and empowerment that underpins the MCA 2005 and as a safeguard against abuse. There is thus no prescribed 'type' of person deemed as suitable to act as a donee, who must simply be an individual over the age of 18 for a welfare LPA, and in addition for a financial LPA, not bankrupt, nor a trust corporation.

Potential conflict and trustworthy donees

5.36 The Joint Scrutiny Committee was concerned that donors should be notified of potential conflicts arising if donees had a vested interest in either welfare or financial decisions[1]. Examples of conflict include situations where close family acting as donees were also beneficiaries under insurance policies, or would be interested to preserve the donor's estate where they stood to inherit all or part of it.

Notification to donors of the need to exercise care in choosing donees is contained in the Main Code which states that:

> 'Attorneys [donees] are in a position of trust, so there is always a risk of them abusing their position. Donors can help prevent abuse by carefully choosing a suitable and trustworthy attorney. But others have a role in looking out for possible signs of abuse or exploitation, and reporting any concerns to the Office of the Public Guardian. The OPG will then follow this up in co-operation with relevant agencies.'[2]

The Main Code also states that 'A donor should think carefully before choosing someone to be their attorney. A donee should be someone who is trustworthy, competent and reliable. They should have the skill and ability to carry out the necessary tasks'[3].

1 Scrutiny Report, paras 145–150.
2 Main Code, para 7.69.
3 Main Code, para 7.8.

Unsuitable donees

5.37 Under the EPAA 1985 there was provision for objecting to the registration of an instrument on the basis that, amongst other things, the donee was 'unsuitable'[1]. This was not to be taken as an opportunity to replace a donee merely because he or she was not the sort of person a particular relative might have chosen. The donor's wish carried considerable weight under this provision. So a mother may desire to appoint her son her donee, despite being aware of his conviction for theft[2].

This ground of objection is not repeated in the current legislation, being replaced instead with the provision relating to the behaviour of the donee in a way that contravenes his authority, or is not in the donor's best interests, or proposes to behave in such a way[3]. The question then as now is essentially whether a donee is capable of acting in the donor's best interests and so little difference is likely to result by this change. This question becomes pertinent not only in relation to the acts of an individual donee, but when there is more than one donee and they are refusing to act jointly, and yet are unwilling to allow the other to act separately, whereupon an instrument would become unworkable, with arguably none of the donees able to act in the donor's best interests.

For example, if a person appoints his second wife to act jointly with his daughter from his first marriage, and they are unable to and refuse to agree or work together, this is likely to make the instrument unworkable. If the donees refuse to work together then they are not acting in the donor's best interests.

1 Section 6(5)(e).

2 Law Commission: *The Incapacitated Principal* (Law Com no 122, 1983) para 4.49(e), and Heywood and Massey at 6–052.
3 Section 22(2), (3) and Sch 1, para 13(4).

Forms

5.38 The forms creating LPAs refer to the need to appoint someone trusted and that the donee's duties are contained in the Main Code[1].

1 These and other extensive documentation are now available at http://www.publicguardian.gov.uk/forms/forms.htm.

Acceptance by a donee of appointment

5.39 A donee cannot be forced to act as such and may refuse appointment. Signing the LPA form is confirmation of their willingness to act upon registration. A donee may withdraw if they become incapable or unwilling to act. Where an LPA has been registered this must follow the procedure provided. In particular the donor and the OPG must be notified[1].

1 Main Code, paras 7.66 and 7.50.

Termination of appointment

5.40 Whether an instrument has been registered or not, s 13(6) provides four grounds which terminate a doneeship. These grounds also apply to revoke the power or instrument[1] unless a donee is replaced under the terms of the instrument or he is one of two or more persons appointed to act jointly and severally in respect of any matter, and there is at least one remaining donee[2].

Bankruptcy of the donor or donee does not terminate a personal welfare doneeship or revoke that power[3]. Interim bankruptcy of the donee or donor suspends an individual's doneeship for the duration of the order in relation to financial LPAs only. It does not revoke the power[4].

Divorce or annulment of marriage or civil partnership between the donor and donee does not terminate the appointment of a donee nor revoke the power if the instrument provides that it should not do so[5].

1 See Table 1 and 5.70 below for revocation.
2 Section 13(6)(b), (7).
3 Section 13(3), (8).
4 Section 13(4), (9).
5 Section 13(11).

More than one attorney

5.41 A donor may wish to appoint more than one welfare attorney to act jointly or jointly and severally[1], and specify that they must act jointly in relation to specified matters, for example consenting to surgery or other serious medical procedures. Attorneys must act jointly where there is no other specification as to how they should act[2].

1 'Jointly' means that they must act together in any decision. 'Jointly and severally' means that may act together or independently of each other.
2 Section 10(4) and (5) and Main Code, para 7.12.

Forms for creating LPA[1]

5.42 An LPA is not created under Sch 1 to the MCA 2005 unless it is in the prescribed form in accordance with Sch 1, Part 1, para 2 and includes:

- prescribed information about the purpose and effect of a LPA;
- a statement by the donor to the effect that he has read the prescribed information or has had it read to him and intends the authority conferred to include authority to make decisions on his behalf in circumstances where he no longer has capacity;
- a statement by the donor naming a person or person to be notified of any application for registration of the instrument, or stating that there are no such persons in the event of any such application;
- a statement by the donee (or each of them if there is more than one) to the effect that s/he has read the prescribed information or has had it read to him/her and understands the duties imposed on a donee of an LPA under ss 1 and 4; and
- a certificate by a person of a prescribed description that in their opinion, at the time the LPA is executed, the donor understands the purpose of the instrument and the scope of the authority under it, no fraud or undue pressure was used to induce the donor to create the LPA and there is nothing else which could prevent a LPA from being created by the instrument.

The forms are set out in LPA Regulations (see Table 2a below). They refer also to a 'Guide for people who want to make a personal welfare [finance and property] LPA'[2].

The steps prescribed in LPA Regulations for the creation and execution of an instrument are set out in table 2b below.

1 See Appendix 5 for a table of forms and http://www.publicguardian.gov.uk/forms/forms.htm.
2 Available from the OPG; guidance available in the Main Code, copies available from Her Majesty's Stationary Office. Notes for completion of the forms are available on: http://www.dca.gov.uk/menincap/legis.htm.

Creating and executing an LPA

5.43 The requirements for creating an LPA are set out in Table 2a below at 5.86.

Safeguards

5.44 Two key safeguards against the abuse of LPAs are firstly, the 'named persons' to be notified of any application to register an LPA, and secondly, the LPA certificate, which offers reassurance in relation to the circumstances prevailing at the time that the instrument is made. The latter is a new safeguard not previously available under the EPAA 1985[1]. There are two types of people prescribed as enabled to provide certificates; one must have been personally known to the donor for at least two years and the other must have suitable professional skills and expertise.

1 See 5.33 regarding the lack of any penalty for signing a certificate in bad faith.

Prescribed forms and content of authority

5.45 The basic steps required to execute an LPA are set out in Table 2b below. This demonstrates that reg 9 of the LPA Regulations requires the donor to have read, or have read to him or her, 'prescribed information' which is the information contained in the form used for the instrument which appears under the heading 'prescribed information'[1].

The previous position under the EPAA 1985 and relevant regulations was that the information accompanying the prescribed form and the marginal notes to it were an essential part of the form itself and required if the instrument was to be capable of taking effect as an enduring power[2]. This is replicated under the MCA 2005. Schedule 1 contains the requirements as to the contents of the instrument which includes reference to the prescribed information about the purposes and effect of the LPA that it must include[3]. Failure to comply with these requirements in an immaterial respect will not be treated as invalid by the PG on registration. The court may also declare that an instrument not in the prescribed form is to be treated as if it were if it is satisfied that the person creating it intended to create an LPA[4].

1 LPA Regulations, reg 2.
2 See EPAA 1985, s 2(6) and EPA (Prescribed Form) Regulations 1990, SI 1990/1376, reg 2, as amended in 2005 (SI 2005/3116) and 2007 (SI 2007/548) also *Heywood and Massey* para 6–007.
3 MCA 2005, Sch 1, Part 1, para 2(1); 'prescribed information' is also defined as the information contained in the form used for the instrument which appears under that heading: Lasting Powers of Attorney, Enduring Powers of Attorney and Public Guardian Regulations 2007, SI 2007/1253, reg 2.
4 MCA 2005, Sch 1, Part 1, para 3. By s 23(1) the court may determine any question as to the meaning or effect of 'an instrument purporting to create' an LPA.

Registration of an LPA with the Office of the Public Guardian (see Table 3)

5.46 An LPA must be registered with the Office of the Public Guardian (OPG) before it can be used. An unregistered LPA will not confer any power on the donee to make decisions on behalf of the donor. This is one of the main safeguards intended against the abuse of LPAs and especially financial abuse. Registration allows complaints about donees and the operation of the LPA to be investigated by the OPG. The donor can also register the LPA while they still have capacity to do so, or the donee may do so at any time.[1]

1 Main Code, chapter 7, para 7.14.

When should LPA be registered?

5.47 The Main Code advises registration of an LPA soon after it is made so that there is no delay when it needs to be used. If it has been registered but not used for some time, then the donee should notify the OPG when they begin to act under it. This will enable the OPG to send the donee up-to-date and relevant information about the use of the LPA[1]. This requirement appears as guidance in the Main Code only and so potentially raises a question about the effectiveness of the monitoring of registered LPAs by the OPG if they are unaware that they are being used because the donee has failed to notify them. Of more concern is the fact that if registered while the donor has capacity, there is no requirement on the donee to provide a certificate of incapacity to the Public Guardian (PG) in order to commence using the power (see 5.49 below).

1 Main Code, para 7.16. See Chapter 12 at 12.30 for fees payable.

Proof of the contents of the instrument and of registration

5.48 On registration the PG will give notice to the donor and donee(s) in a prescribed form and retain a copy of the instrument returning the original to the applicant; each page will be stamped by the OPG. In the UK proof of the instrument by an office copy of a registered instrument is sufficient evidence of the contents of the instrument and the fact that it has been registered[1].

1 See Table 3 below.

No need to notify PG of use or provide a certification of the donor's incapacity

5.49 A requirement to notify the OPG before use and on the incapacity of the donor was considered overly restrictive because of the existence of a registered document (see above) that could be presented to, for example, a bank official. Personal welfare LPAs may need to be used in an emergency situation where, for example, a person has been in an accident, and before notification of incapacity could be given[1].

During the Bill's passage through Parliament the Government stressed the need for flexibility in the procedures and reliance on the donor's choice of donee. The intention is not to make the task of a donee too onerous and to strike a balance between safeguards and fairness. There was a concern not to make the process over bureaucratic. Capacity is usually not lost in an instant, or in one event, but is a process that can take time and affect different decision-making skills. Hence the difficulty in requiring notification to the

OPG of use. It was also questioned whether in cases where an LPA is used infrequently, or during the period of an accident and then not again for many years, notifying the OPG would serve any purpose[2]. See 5.47 above.

1 668 HL Official Report (5th series), col 1409, 27 January 2005.
2 668 HL Official Report (5th series), cols 1402–1412, 27 January 2005.

Notification of material changes

5.50 There is an obligation imposed on the donor and donee to keep the OPG informed of changes in relevant information such as changes in address and circumstances of the donee in order to keep the OPGs records up to date[1]. There are no sanctions if the donee fails to notify relevant changes. Again the Government view was that flexibility is needed so as not to make the task too onerous for the donee. It asked the rhetorical question 'What end would be served by invalidating an LPA for failure to notify of a change of address?'

The registration steps are explained in Table 3 below. The basic steps are:

1 application;
2 notification of named person(s);
3 registration by the PG after six weeks if there is no objection or defect;
4 notice of registration.

1 Main Code, para 7.17.

Registration of EPAs

5.51 The registration of an EPA created prior to 1 October 2007 is provided for in Parts 4 and 5 of Sch 4 and Part 3 of the LPA Regulations, which contain relevant forms at Schs 7 and 8.

Property and affairs LPA: supplementary provisions

5.52 There are provisions relating to s 18 (execution of a Will) in Sch 2.

Defects

5.53 An LPA may differ in an immaterial respect of form or mode of expression from the prescribed forms and be treated by the Public Guardian as sufficient on registration. Also a court may declare that an instrument that is not in the prescribed form is to be treated as if it were if it is satisfied that the person making it intended to create an LPA[1].

1 Schedule 1, Part 1, para 3(1) and (2), and see 5.45 above.

Non-registration of an instrument by the PG

5.54 The grounds on which the PG must not register an instrument are set out in Table 3. In each case the court may direct the PG to register on the application of the PG or the person applying to register the instrument. The grounds are:

(a) the instrument is not created in accordance with the requirements of Sch 1 to the MCA 2005 as to form and content (see above)[1];
(b) there is an existing court deputy with conflicting powers[2];
(c) a named person or donee receiving notification of registration[3] gives notice of *objection* before the end of the prescribed period[4] on the ground that an event in s 13(3) (donor's bankruptcy) or (6)(a)–(d) has occurred and the instrument has been revoked[5];
(d) a named person or donee receives notice of registration as above and notifies the PG in writing of an *objection* to the court on a *prescribed ground*[6]: see s 22(2) and (3) (below at 5.59) for the prescribed grounds.;
(e) a donor on receipt of notification of registration under Sch 1, para 8 gives notice of objection to the PG, unless the court on application of the donee or any of them, is satisfied that the donor lacks capacity to object to the registration[7];
(f) the instrument provided is neither an original nor a certified copy of it, unless the court directs[8].

Notification to the PG may be given by any named person notified of an application to register an LPA in respect of both personal welfare and financial LPAs.

1 Schedule 1, Pt 2, para 11(1).
2 Schedule 1, Pt 2, para 12(2).
3 Schedule 1, Pt 2, paras 6, 7, 8, and 13(1), (2).
4 Five weeks beginning with the date on which notice given: LPA Regulations, reg 14(2), (3).
5 Schedule 1, Pt 2, para 13(1), (2).
6 Schedule 1, Pt 2, para 13(4).
7 Schedule 1, Pt 2, para 14.
8 LPA Regulations, reg 11(2).

Objections to the registration of an LPA under section 13

5.55 Section 13 relates to the termination and revocation of an instrument intended to create an LPA before or after it is registered and is relevant here (see 5.40 and 5.70). A person notified of the impending registration of an LPA may object in writing to the PG, and the PG must cancel registration if satisfied of[1]:

1 the donor's bankruptcy[2];
2 the donee's disclaimer of the appointment[3];
3 the death or bankruptcy of the donee (not for personal LPA), or if the donee is a trust corporation, its winding-up or dissolution[4];
4 The dissolution or annulment of a marriage or civil partnership between the donor and donee, unless the instrument provides expressly for the power to continue if either of these events occur[5];

5 The lack of capacity of the donee[6].

1 Form LPA 7 available from OPG on 0845 330 2900 and at http://www.publicguardian.gov.uk/forms/forms.htm; Sch 1, para 17.
2 Section 13(3).
3 Section 13(6)(a).
4 Section 13(6)(b). Interim bankruptcy order only has the effect of suspending a power in relation to the particular donee (if there is more than one) for the period the order has effect: (9), (10).
5 Section 13(6)(c).
6 Section 13(6)(d).

Proof of section 13 objection

5.56 Objections 1–4 above are based on facts which should be readily capable of proof through documentation. Proof of the donee's lack of capacity will require medical evidence which may be difficult for an objector to obtain. The PG may have to obtain the necessary evidence through the use of a Court Visitor[1].

1 Section 58(1)(d). See Chapter 12

Effect of section 13 objection

Unregistered power

5.57 The PG must not register the LPA on receipt of notice of an objection under this section unless directed to do so by the court. The court may so direct on the application of the person objecting if satisfied that the ground is not established[1].

1 Schedule 1, Pt 2, para 13(2).

Registered power

5.58 The PG must cancel registration of an LPA on being satisfied of revocation under s 13[1].

1 Schedule 1, Pt 3, para 17.

Objections to the court on prescribed grounds (s 22)

5.59 An objection to the court may only be made on s 22 prescribed grounds before or after registration of the LPA:

1 the power purported to be created by the instrument is not valid because one or more of the requirements for creation have not been met, ie s 9(2), (3), and for example, the donor did not have capacity at the time of its creation[1];
2 the power has been revoked or otherwise come to an end[2];

3 that fraud or undue pressure was used to induce the donor to create the LPA[3];

4 that the donee (or if more than one, any of them) has behaved, or is behaving, in a way that contravenes their authority, or is not in the donor's best interests, or proposes to behave in such a way[4].

1 Section 22(2)(a).
2 Section 22(2)(b).
3 Section 22(3)(a).
4 Section 22(3)(b).

Effect of s 22 objection: cancellation of the LPA by the court

Registered power

5.60 If satisfied that the power is not valid or has been revoked under paras 1 or 2 above, the court must direct the PG to cancel its registration.

If satisfied as to any of the matters in s 22(3), then the court must revoke the instrument or power if the donor lacks capacity to do so[1].

The court must also notify the PG of any determination under s 23(1) that an LPA is either ineffective or contains a provision which prevents the instrument from operating as a valid LPA. The notification must either be to sever the provision, or direct the PG to cancel the registration of that LPA.

1 Schedule 1, Pt 3, para 18.

Unregistered power

5.61 The court may also direct that an instrument not be registered on grounds in s 22(3)(a) and (b)[1].

1 Section 22(4)(a).

Proof of s 22 prescribed grounds

5.62 Grounds 1 and 3 below are familiar to the previous Court of Protection jurisdiction. Ground (d) is new and replaces the old category of 'unsuitability'[1].

1 capacity of donor at the time of creating the instrument;
2 LPA revoked (see 5.55 above under s 13 grounds);
3 fraud or undue pressure;
4 donee not acting within terms of authority or in donor's best interests, or proposes to do so.

An objection must be in writing.[2]

1 EPAA 1985, s 6(5)(e) see 5.37 above.
2 See fn 4 at 5.54 above.

Role of PG

5.63 As to the scrutiny of donees by the PG see 5.77 below.

In general the PG has powers to direct Court Visitors to visit a donee, or to request a report or information from a donee. The latter arises where it appears to the PG that a donee is behaving or may be behaving in way that contravenes their authority or is not in the best interests of the donor, or is proposing to behave in such a way. These powers support the PG (and the court) when investigating objections on these prescribed grounds[1].

1 Section 58 and Chapter 12 on PGs powers.

Capacity

5.64 The LPA certificate(s) required for the creation of an LPA will help to establish the circumstances pertaining at the relevant time. The person assessing may, however, not have any professional skill in assessing capacity. Nevertheless a certificate that the donor understands the purpose and scope of the LPA and that there is nothing else which would prevent the LPA being created will be persuasive evidence against this ground of objection.

Burden of proof

5.65 Under the EPAA 1985 it was for the objector(s) to prove that the person did not have capacity at the time the instrument was created. Thus the court did not have to be satisfied that the person did have capacity at the relevant time, but that they did not[1].

This makes it difficult to establish lack of capacity retrospectively[2]. The court will usually prefer contemporaneous and reliable evidence especially from people in contact with the donor around the time the LPA was made[3] to retrospective expert evidence (see below).

1 *Re W(Enduring Power of Attorney)* [2000] Ch 343 at 345H–346B. Confirmed by the CA: [2001] Ch 609.
2 This approach was applied in the case of John Neville Smale, decision of Master Lush (unreported, 5 December 2006), in which the instrument was not in fact registered because there was sufficient contemporaneous evidence that Major Smale did not have sufficient capacity at the relevant time.
3 *Heywood and Massey* para 6–036.

Expert evidence

5.66 Medical evidence will assist, particularly if it is contemporaneous. An opinion from a consultant psychiatrist with relevant experience may otherwise be persuasive if there is other documentation to rely upon. A face to face assessment of capacity retrospectively is unlikely to overcome the burden of proof.

Evidence from a solicitor or other legal practitioner in relation to capacity to create financial LPAs may be preferred[1].

1 *Heywood and Massey* at 6–036 states that there is a strong body of opinion in support of the view that a solicitor is in a better position to judge whether a person has capacity to perform a 'juristic' act than a medical practitioner. This is the course taken in Scotland in the Adults with Incapacity (Scotland) Act 2000.

Special Court Visitor

5.67 The PG or the court can direct a medical practitioner who is a Special Court Visitor to visit a donor or donee of an LPA and prepare a report on capacity[1].

1 Section 58(1)(d) and s 49. See Chapter 12 and also 5.63 and 5.80 for their role in supervising and investigating donees.

Fraud and undue pressure

5.68 This was aground of objection under the EPAA 1985[1]. There has been no reported decision on this ground of objection. As with capacity, the existence of an LPA certificate will be probative, if not determinative, of this issue, unless it can be proved that the certificate itself was provided fraudulently[2].

The right to revoke an instrument is relevant where a donor has had time to do so after registration but has not done so. The court may be less likely to uphold an objection on these grounds unless it can also be shown that the donor did not exercise the right to revoke through continued fear or undue pressure[3].

The objector must prove: 'fraud' *or* 'undue pressure' and that it has 'induced' the creation of the power.

Fraud or the tort of deceit occurs when it is proved that:

> 'a false representation has been made (i) knowingly, (ii) without belief in its truth, or (iii) recklessly, careless whether it be true or false. Although I have treated the second and third as distinct cases, I think the third is but an instance of the second, for one who makes a statement under such circumstances can have no real belief in the truth of what he states. To prevent a false statement from being fraudulent, there must, I think, always be an honest belief in its truth.'[4]

Undue pressure is not the same as 'undue influence'. Master Lush has held that:

> 'The burden of proof is on the objectors to prove to the satisfaction of the Court that:
> 2. [The donor] was "induced" to create the power;
> 3. "Pressure' was used to induce [the donor] to create it; and
> 4. The pressure was "undue".

The word "induce" should be construed in its ordinary meaning, that is "to persuade or to prevail upon to bring about": *Commission of Racial Equality v Imperial Society of Teachers of Dancing* [1983] ICR 473. So, where, for example, the impetus or initiative to create an enduring power of attorney comes from the donor personally, it can hardly be said that he or she had been induced to create the power.

To use "pressure" means to behave in a manner whereby the will of the donor is overborne by the will of another person, so that in creating the power the donor is not acting of his or her own free will.

Pressure can assume various forms. It can be physical, psychological, emotional, financial, and even pharmacological, though I would not venture to suggest that this list is exhaustive. Physical pressure constitutes any act or rough treatment directed towards the donor, whether or not actual physical injury results, and includes hitting, slapping and the misuse of restraints.

Psychological or emotional pressure includes any behaviour that may diminish the donor's sense of identity, dignity and self-worth, including humiliation, intimidation, verbal abuse, threats, infantilisation and isolation. For example "sign here, or I will put you in an old folks' home", or "sign this, or I won't let you see your grandchildren".

Financial pressure includes the deliberate denial of the donor's access to his or her money or property. Excessive medication or the intentional withholding of medication would constitute pharmacological pressure.

The meaning of "undue" has been considered judicially in the context of hardship and delay. For example in *Liberian Shipping Corporation v A. King and Sons Ltd* [1967] 1 All ER 934, 938, CA, Lord Denning M.R. said; "'Undue' simply means excessive. It means greater hardship than the circumstances warrant."

In other words, the means should be proportionate to the end: the end being, in this instance the creation of a form of agency which will enable the donor's property and financial affairs to be managed lawfully and effectively whilst she is mentally incapacitated.

It may come as a surprise to note that by implication the Enduring Powers of Attorney Act assumes that some donors will be put under pressure to sign an instrument, but the Act is only concerned to invalidate those powers that have been created under pressure which can be qualified by the adjective "undue".

This principle of proportionality leaves a great deal to the discretion of the court, and generally speaking the court will not intervene unless there has been a clear and obvious infringement of the principle and it is satisfied that the creation of the power was not ultimately for the benefit of the donor.'[5]

1 Section 6(5)(d).

2 668 HL Official Report (5th series), col 1431, 27 January 2005.

3 *Heywood and Massey* (above) at para 6–051.

4 *Derry v Peek* (1889) 14 App Cas 337 per Lord Herschell at 374. See also Clerk and Lindsell 19th edn, para 18–17.

5 Unreported decision of Master Lush, 11 October 2001, no. 5059932, in *Re G* cited in *Heywood and Massey* at para 6–50. In the context of medical treatment see Lord Donaldson in *Re T (Adult:Refusal of Medical Treatment)* [1992] 4 All ER 649 in which the the court took a not dissimilar approach albeit based on 'undue influence'. It approved persuasion and even strong persuasion, but not such as to 'overbear the independence of the patient's decision.'

Acting within the authority and best interests

5.69 An objection might be taken on these grounds at the time of the registration of an LPA or later.

Evidence of the failure of a donee to act within the terms of the authority may of itself be evidence of an inability to act in the donor's best interests. For example, the donee might make gifts falling outside of what is stipulated. It seems unlikely that an objection on such grounds would be sustained on the grounds of a single error, or one caused through a lack of proper guidance or information. This might form an appropriate ground for application to the court if a doctor takes issue with the decision of a donee of a LPA.

Revocation

5.70 The following applies to an unregistered instrument intended to create an LPA and to a registered LPA[1]:

(i) P may revoke at any time when he has capacity to do so[2];
(ii) P's bankruptcy revokes a property and affairs LPA[3], (but an interim bankruptcy order only suspends the power[4];
(iii) disclaimer of the appointment by the donee[5];
(iv) death or bankruptcy (not insofar as authority for welfare is within the LPA[6] and not in the event of interim bankruptcy restrictions order[7]) of the donee, or if a trust corporation its winding up or dissolution[8];
(v) annulment or dissolution of a marriage or civil partnership between the donor and donee[9]. This can be expressly excluded by the instrument[10];
(vi) Lack of capacity of the donee[11].

Exceptions (iii)–(vii) above relate to the termination of the appointment of the donee as well as revocation of the LPA. Exceptions (iv) to (vii) above occur where the donee is replaced under the terms of the instrument or s/he is one of two or more persons appointed to act joist and severally and, there remains at least one donee[12].

Temporary capacity of a person allows them to make those decisions which they have capacity to make. As far as the donee is concerned, during Parliamentary debate the Government suggested that:

> 'in the case of a donee with fluctuating capacity, or indeed with a long period of incapacity, it is better for the revocation of the power of attorney to be final, and for the ex attorney to apply to the court for appointment as deputy if the court considers that to be in the person's best interests.'[13]

1 Section 13(1).
2 Section 13(2).
3 Section 13(3).
4 Section 13(4).
5 Section 13(6)(a).
6 Section 13(8).
7 Section 13(9).
8 Section 13(6)(b).
9 Section 13(6)(c).

10 Section 13(11).
11 Section 13(6)(d).
12 Section 13(7).
13 668 HL Official Report (5th series), col 1426, 27 January 2005.

Protection of the donee and others if no power is created or it is revoked (s 14)

5.71 A donee is protected from liability to the donor or other person where an instrument has been registered but no valid LPA created, unless s/he knows that the power was not created or is aware of circumstances whereby if the LPA had been created, then it would have terminated the authority to act as donee[1].

This provision protects attorneys and third parties from liability if they were unaware that the LPA was invalid or had come to an end.

Thus any transaction between the donee and another is valid, including in relation to property, in favour of that person unless they had knowledge as described above[2].

1 Section 14(2).
2 Section 14(4) and (5).

Restraint: welfare LPAs under s 11[1]

5.72–5.73 Restraint includes a threat to restrict or use force, or restrict liberty of movement whether or not the person is resisting and includes authorising another to do any of those things[2].

Three conditions apply if restraint is to be used:

1 P must lack, or donee must reasonably believe that P lacks, capacity in relation to the matter in question;
2 the donee must reasonably believe that it is 'necessary to do the act in order to prevent harm to P'; and
3 the act is proportionate to the likelihood of P's suffering harm, and the seriousness of that harm[3].

1 and 2 require objective reasons to be identified to justify the proposed course of action. 'Harm' is not defined but see para 6.45 of the Main Code for examples including financial and psychological harm.

A donee restrains the person if he '(a) uses, or threatens to use, force to secure the doing of an act which P resists, or (b) restricts liberty of movement, whether or not P resists, or if he authorises another person to do any of those things'[4].

These restrictions mirror those in ss 5 and 6(1)–(3) relating to 'acts in connection with care or treatment' and to court deputies[5]. See Chapter 4 for an explanation of restrictions on restraint generally within the MCA 2005.

These provisions sanction the use of minimum force or restraint within the principle of least restriction. It enables a person to be transported to hospital forcibly in a manner that results in a restriction though not deprivation of liberty, or to be held steady for an injection.

1 See Main Code, Chapter 7, para 7.43 (the Code is to be updated on this point) and Chapter 6.
2 Section 11(5).
3 Section 11(1)–(4).
4 Section 11(5).
5 Section 20.

Deprivation of liberty

5.74 At the time of Royal Assent the MCA 2005 also specifically excluded acts going beyond restraint by way of a deprivation of liberty falling within the meaning of Article 5(1) ECHR[1]. This is to be repealed by the Mental Health Act 2007[2]. The MCA 2005 will not in due course authorise any person to deprive another of liberty unless they are doing so to give effect to a welfare order of the court, for the purposes of giving life-sustaining treatment or doing any vital act, or under a Sch A1 authorisation[3]. See Chapter 9.

1 In relation to donees at s 11(6) now omitted by virtue of the MHA 2007, s 50(4)(b).
2 The relevant repeals are to take effect in April 2009. Announced by the Department of Health on 21 November 2007, gateway ref 9114 and briefing sheet gateway ref 8965.
3 See ss 4A, 4B and Sch A1 as inserted by s 50(2) and Sch 7 of the Mental Health Act 2007. Not yet in force and due for implementation in April 2009 as fn above. See Chapter 7 at 7.8 and Chapter 10 at 10.34 for the position regarding authorisation of deprivations of liberty pre-April 2009.

Role of donee in authorisation process and deprivation of liberty

5.75 A valid decision of a donee may constitute a 'refusal' within para 20 of Sch A1 meaning that the 'no refusals' requirement is not met[1]. There is a refusal if to require the person to be accommodated in a relevant hospital or care home in circumstances amounting to a deprivation of liberty or at all, conflicts with a valid decision of a donee. In other words a donee can prevent a person being deprived of their liberty under the MCA 2005 by a valid decision within the terms of his or her authority. Conversely there is no refusal if a decision accords with a decision of, or is supported by, a donee of an LPA[2].

The appointment and functions of a personal representative under Part 10 (see Chapter 9 on deprivation of liberty) are additional to those of any donee or deputy[3]. There is no express requirement for consultation with a donee for the purposes of a standard authorisation under Sch A1; however, a donee is an appropriate person to be consulted in determining best interests under s 4(7)[4]. The availability of a donee means that the appointment of an Independent

Mental Capacity Advocate is unnecessary (see Chapter 9 at 9.85). It would appear, therefore, that a personal representative and a donee are to work side by side under Sch A1.

1 See 'qualifying requirements' under Part 3 of Sch A1. See also Part 4 for standard authorisations and para 33(2)(f). Not yet in force see fn to 5.74 above. See Chapter 9, at 9.45.
2 Schedule A1, para 18. See Chapter 9 for more detail. See also 'eligibility criteria' under Sch 1A inserted by the MHA 2007 at 9.42 Case D, scenario 2 and at 16.18.
3 Schedule A1, Part 10, para 141.
4 See Chapter 9 at 9.35 for more on best interests assessments under Sch A1.

Donee and detention under the Mental Health Act 1983

5.76 If the donor becomes detained[1] under the MHA 1983, a donee cannot consent to or refuse treatment for a mental disorder[2] for the donor whose treatment is then governed by the provisions of the MHA 1983[3]. Treatment of a physical disorder for a patient detained under the MHA 1983, however, will fall within the MCA 2005.

1 This does not apply to patients subject to emergency or short term provisions under MHA 1983, ss 4(4)(a), 5(2), (4), 35, 135, or 136, or conditional discharge under ss 42(2) or 73 or 74 or to guardianship (or community treatment orders, s 37(4) or 45A(5)) (as amended).
2 The definition of 'mental disorder' under the MHA 1983 will be widened once the provisions of the MHA 2007 come into effect. The MHA 2007, s 32 introduces community treatment orders (CTOs) by inserting new ss 17A–17G into the MHA 1983. Patients under CTO are not exempted from Part IV but are to be recalled to hospital for treatment or mental disorder in hospital. MHA 1983, s 56 is amended accordingly and a new s 62A applies (inserted by MHA 2007, s 34). MHA 2007, s 35 inserts a new Part 4A and ss 64B–64D relating to treatment in the community of those under CTO, which allow a welfare donee or the Court of Protection to consent to s 58 (or new s 58A as inserted by MHA 2007, s 27) treatments ie those requiring consent or a second opinion. See Chapter 16 at 16.5 and for an amendment relating to ECT see 16.6 and also 16.39.
3 Section 28 thus (subject to fn 2 above) excludes from the MCA 2005 those patients subject to the 'consent to treatment' provisions under Part IV of the MHA 1983.

SCRUTINY OF DONEES

Financial abuse and conflicts of interest

5.77 The Joint Scrutiny Report noted the prevalence of the abuse of financial powers under EPAs[1]. This has been addressed by the requirement that an LPA has to be registered with the Public Guardian prior to becoming effective. This means that a donee is subject to the supervisory jurisdiction of the Public Guardian, although in practice this will only be exercised if someone makes a complaint.

It is not difficult to see how conflicts may arise between a donor and donee. When close family act as donees there may be issues around benefiting from insurance policies, or preserving the value of an estate for inheritance purposes. In the latter situation the conflict might arise in a welfare context if the donor's best interests require nursing or other care in a residential setting which must be paid for out of the donor's funds or a relevant life insurance policy that expires at a certain age.

1 Scrutiny Report, para 138. Statistics presented suggested that financial abuse occurred in 15–20% of cases involving EPAs, although the figure is imprecise as the number of EPAs in existence is not known; there is no requirement for them to be registered prior to the loss or impending loss of capacity of the donor. The evidence was presented by Master Lush, Master of the Court of Protection.

Joint Scrutiny Committee

5.78 The Joint Scrutiny Committee recommended that there be an obligation on the donee to notify the PG and the donor when a donor was losing capacity so as to open up the possibility of a challenge[1], but as discussed above this was rejected so as to prevent the role from becoming over bureaucratic.

The principle is that a donor should be able to choose his or her own donee free from restriction, but the Joint Scrutiny Report suggested that they should be notified of potential conflicts arising if donees had a vested interest in either welfare or financial decisions. The Main Code states that 'a donor should think carefully before choosing someone to be their attorney'[2], but offers no examples of situations in which difficulties might arise. In addition the Scrutiny Committee recommended that the Main Code should contain additional safeguards whereby the Court of Protection and Public Guardian can monitor LPAs with a view to preventing abuse and exploitation of a donee's powers[3].

Donors must appoint attorneys with care, but others have a role to play in looking out for possible signs of abuse or exploitation and reporting concerns to the PG. The PG may then follow this up in co-operation with other agencies.

1 Scrutiny Report, para 157.
2 Main Code, para 7.8.
3 Scrutiny Report, para 150.

Main Code

5.79 The Main Code lists signs that are sufficient to raise concerns that a donee may be exploiting the donor or failing to act in the donor's best interests[1].

1 stopping relatives or friends contacting the donor;
2 sudden unexplained changes in living arrangements (for example someone moves in to care for a donor that they have had little contact with);
3 not allowing healthcare or social care staff to see the donor;
4 taking the donor out of the hospital against medical advice, while the donor is having necessary medical treatment;
5 unpaid bills (for example residential care or nursing home fees);

6 a donee opening a credit card account for the donor;
7 spending money on things that are not obviously related to the donor's needs;
8 the attorney spending money in an unusual or extravagant way;
9 transferring financial assets to another country.

1 Main Code, para 7.70.

What can be done and by whom?

5.80 If a person suspects abuse by a donee they should contact the OPG in the first instance. The PG may direct a Court Visitor to visit a donee and investigate. In cases of suspected physical or sexual abuse, theft or serious fraud, the person should contact the police. They might also be able to refer the matter to the relevant local adult protection authorities[1].

1 Main Code 7.71.

Public Guardian and Court of Protection Visitors

5.81 The provisions relating to the Public Guardian and Court of Protection Visitors are set out at ss 57–61 and discussed at Chapter 12.

Court of Protection (ss 22 and 23)

5.82 There are three categories of supervisory power vested in the court and these have been discussed above at 5.59 and are relevant to the scrutiny of LPAs:

A Where an LPA has been executed or registered, the court has power to determine any question relating to (1) whether the requirements for creating the LPOA have been met, and (2) whether it has been revoked or come to an end[1].

B If the court is satisfied that fraud or undue pressure was used to induce P to execute an instrument for an LPA or to create and LPA, or that the donee of the LPA has behaved or is behaving in a way that contravenes his or her authority or against the P's best interests, or proposes to behave in such a way, the court may direct that the LPA is not registered or, if P lacks capacity to do so, revoke the instrument of LPA. If there is more than one donee, then the court may act in relation only to one of them. Donee includes an intended donee[2].

C The court may determine any question as to the meaning or effect of an LPA or an instrument purporting to create one. It may give directions with respect to decisions which the donee has power to make as agent for the person who lacks capacity to make the decision. An example of this is where the donee would like to purchase the person's property but the power provides that the donor must give consent, or where a doctor or other healthcare professional is of the opinion that the donee is not acting within the authority of the power granted to them. It may give consent or authorisation to act which the donee would have to obtain from the person if he or she had capacity to give the same[3].

The court may give directions to the donee with respect to the rendering of accounts or reports and the production of records kept by the donee for that purpose, or to supply information or documents or things in his possession as donee, or with a view to remuneration or expenses, or relieve the donee entirely from any liability s/he has or may incur on account of a breach of his or duties as donee[4]. This is a very broad power.

The court also has powers in relation to the making of gifts and where there is more than one donee.

The court's supervisory powers will need to be triggered by someone concerned to do so and in close contact with P.

See Chapter 10 on the operation of the court.

1 Section 22(1), (2).
2 Section 22(3), (4) and (5).
3 Section 23(1), (2).
4 Section 23(3).

Ill-treatment or neglect: section 44

5.83 A donee, attorney under an EPA or court deputy, or other person who has care of a person lacking in capacity, is guilty of an offence if s/he ill-treats or wilfully neglects[1] the person concerned. On summary conviction imprisonment for a term not exceeding 12 months or a fine not exceeding the statutory maximum, or both, apply. On conviction on indictment, the maximum term of imprisonment is five years or a fine or both[2].

Theft or misappropriation of property or funds will be dealt with under the existing criminal law of theft.

1 Creates two separate offences.
2 See Chapters 4 and 18 for more on s 44.

Protected act in connection with care and treatment: sections 5 and 6

5.84 Sections 5 and 6 apply to protect all those performing acts in connection with care and treatment in prescribed circumstances. A welfare donee may act only within the terms of the LPA instrument and in the donor's best interests. By s 6(6) no one is authorised under s 5 to do an act which conflicts with a donee's valid decision which will, therefore, take precedence over any act under this provision by a carer or professional. Chapter 4 discusses these provisions in detail.

Duties owed by the donee

5.85 See above at 5.28. The donee could be liable at common law for damages in negligence or for breaches of duty as agent.

PRACTICE POINTS

5.86 *Safeguards against abuse.* A donee under an LPA is a powerful character. It remains to be seen whether the new safeguards are sufficient to prevent the abuses of the past. Vigilance of all those around an incapacitated person will be important in bringing any untoward behaviour to the attention of the PG and the court.

Donor changing views. A person's views about medical treatment are not fixed. This is true of a person making an advance decision also. It is difficult to predict how one will actually feel when faced with the prospect of dying. Evidence to the Joint Scrutiny Committee suggests that people change their minds even in situations where an advance directive was made, and accept treatment they previously thought they would refuse. This needs to be taken into account when making an LPA as well and a person needs to be advised of this very real possibility. Another example where minds could change is where new treatments are developed.

Fluctuating capacity. The Joint Scrutiny Committee aired concerns expressed to it that there was a lack of clarity surrounding when a donee could act under the LPA and the difficulty of taking decisions regarding the loss of capacity. In particular, it was concernd that it needed to be emphasised to donees and professional and other carers that before the donor lost capacity completely they would be capable of taking relevant welfare and treatment decisions. Where a person has fluctuating capacity decision-making will move to and fro between the person and the donee. Alternatively, the person may be capable of making simple decisions but not more complex decisions leading to real practical difficulties.

Access to information. A donee needs information on which to make a decision on behalf of a person. This information must be the same as the incapacitated person would have had to make the decision had they had sufficient capacity to do so. In many but not all cases the donee, if they are family or close friend may know all the information that is needed to make a decision. But there is no express provision made by the MCA 2005 with regard to accessing records by donees. Chapter 14 deals with access to information including by donees.

Life-sustaining treatment. A donee faced with an LPA granting power to refuse life-sustaining treatment may be well advised to insist that the donor make a valid advance decision relating to life-sustaining treatment in order not to be faced with the conundrum of bringing about the donor's death and potentially acting in contravention of s 4(5).

Locus of decision-making. It is important to remember that a donee is exercising delegated decision-making powers on behalf of a donor exercisable only in the best interests of the donor. This is in contrast with an advance decision which need not satisfy a best interests test. Clinicians will be responsible for decisions regarding medical best interests which need not accord with a best interests analysis based simply on the wishes and beliefs of the person. Any lingering disputes may have to be referred to the court.

Best interests. Most concerns about the activities of a donee are likely to be capable of falling within the heading 'not acting in the donor's best interests' and may be brought to the attention of the PG or the court by any person.

Financial powers of attorney were and are instruments of the wealthy. It remains to be seen whether welfare LPA's will fall into the same category. If they do, in most situations issues of daily treatment and care will fall to be made by family and professional carers without any specific input from a specially instructed donee.

Table 1

APPOINTMENT OF DONEES Section 10 requirements	
APPOINTMENT	DETAILS
Individual (aged 18 or more): s 10(1)(a)(b)	Not if bankrupt: for property and affairs only: s 10(2)
Trust Corporation[1]: s 10(1)(b)	Property and affairs only
Two or more donees:	May act: (a) jointly, (b) jointly and severally (c) jointly in respect of some matters and jointly and severally in respect of others: s 10(4) If unspecified then jointly: s 10(5)
Acting jointly	Instrument fails if one fails to comply with sub-s (1) or (2) or Part 1 (creating an instrument) or Part 2 (registration of LPA) of Sch 1: s 10(6)
Acting jointly and severally	A failure as above by one of the donees prevents appointment taking effect in her case, but not in the case of the other(s): s 10(7)
Substitute or successor donee(s)	1 A donee may not make an appointment: s 10(8)(a)[2] 2 Donor may make provision for the appointment of a replacement if an event in s 13(6)(a)–(d) takes place: s 10(8)(b) Section 13(6) relates to the termination of an appointment of a donee in the event of his or her: (a) disclaimer of the appointment; (LPA reg 20 and form 'LPA 005'); (b) death or bankruptcy (but not in relation to a welfare LPA) and, upon an interim bankruptcy order, the authority is merely suspended for the duration of the order (s 13(8) and (9)); (c) dissolution or annulment of marriage or civil partnership[3] between donor and donee, subject to the instrument specifying that it will not terminate on such an event taking place; (d) lack of capacity.

1 See Trustee Act 1925, s 68(1): 'Public Trustee or a corporation either appointed by the court in any particular case to be a trustee, or entitled by rules made under s 4(3) of the Public Trustee Act 1906 to act a custodian trustee.' See MCA 2005 explanatory notes, para 53.

2 This would be inconsistent with the core principle that the donor is giving authority to a chosen attorney: explanatory notes, para 56.

3 A civil partnership is a registered relationship between two people of the same sex which ends only on death, dissolution or annulment, as provided for in the Civil Partnership Act 2004: explanatory notes, para 56.

Table 2a

CREATING LPA INSTRUMENT MCA 2005 Sch 1 and the Lasting Powers of Attorney, Enduring Powers of Attorney and Public Guardian Regulations 2007, SI 2007/1253, Part 1	
REQUIREMENTS	DETAILS
Forms	MCA 2005, Sch 1, Part1, paras 1, 2 Sch 1, LPA Regulations, Parts 1 and 2: finance and property and welfare respectively: reg 5
Notification of 'named persons' of any application for registration of the instrument[1]	Maximum of five named persons: reg 6
LPA certificate by a person declaring that at the time of execution of the instrument: (i) the donor understands the purpose of the instrument and the scope of its authority, (ii) no fraud, undue pressure is used to induce the donor to create the instrument, and (iii) there is nothing else which would prevent the LPA being created by the instrument[2]	Two required where there are no named persons. Each by a separate person (reg 7)[3]: (a) A person chosen by the donor as being someone who has known him/her personally for the period of at least two years which ends immediately before the date on which that person signs the LPA certificate; (b) a person chosen by the donor who, on account of his professional skills and expertise, reasonably considers that s/he is competent to make the judgments necessary to certify the matters set out in Sch 1, para 2(1)(e): reg 8 The following are examples of persons within para (b) (above): – a registered health care professional[4]; – a barrister, solicitor or advocate called or admitted in any part of the United Kingdom; – a registered social worker[5]; or – an independent mental capacity advocate[6]. A person is disqualified from giving an LPA certificate under (a) above in respect of any instrument intended to create a lasting power of attorney if that person is: – a family member of the donor; – a donee of that power; – a donee of: (i) any other lasting power of attorney, or (ii) an enduring power of attorney, which has been executed by the donor (whether or not it has been revoked); – a family member of a donee of that power; – a director or employee of a trust corporation acting as a donee of that power; – a business partner or employee of: (i) the donor, or (ii) a donee of that power; – an owner, director, manager or employee of any care home[7] in which the donor is living when the instrument is executed; or – a family member of an owner etc of any care home in which the donor is living when the instrument is executed: reg 8(1)–(3)

1 MCA 2005, Sch 1, Part 1, para 2(1)(c), 2(2).
2 MCA 2005, Sch 1, Part 1, para 2(1)(e).
3 MCA 2005, Sch 1, Part 1, para 2(1)(e).
4 A 'registered health care professional' means a person who is a member of a profession regulated by a body mentioned in s 25(3) of the National Health Service Reform and Health Care Professions Act 2002: LPA Regulations, Part 2, reg 8(4).

5 A 'registered social worker' means a person registered as a social worker in a register maintained by – (a) the General Social Care Council; (b) the Care Council for Wales; (c) the Scottish Social Services Council; or (d) the Northern Ireland Social Care Council: LPA Regulations, Part 1, reg 8(4).

6 'Care home' has the meaning given in s 3 of the Care Standards Act 2000: LPA Regulations, reg 8(4).

Table 2b

EXECUTION OF AN INSTRUMENT Lasting Powers of Attorney, Enduring Powers of Attorney and Public Guardian Regulations 2007 SI 2007/1253, Part 1, reg 9	
STEP ONE	Donor must read, (or have read to him/her), the prescribed information: reg 9(2) ('prescribed information', in relation to any instrument intended to create a lasting power of attorney, means the information contained in the form used for the instrument which appears under the heading 'prescribed information': reg 2) As soon as reasonably practicable thereafter:
STEP TWO	Donor must complete the provisions of Part A of the instrument that apply to him/her (or direct another person to do so) Subject to reg 9(7) (LPA certificates), sign Part A of the instrument in the presence of a witness: reg 9(3) As soon as reasonably practicable thereafter:
STEP THREE	The person giving an LPA certificate, or if reg 7 applies (two LPA certificates required), each of the persons giving a certificate, must complete the LPA certificate at Part B of the instrument and sign it: reg 9(4) As soon as reasonably practicable thereafter:
STEP FOUR	The donee, or if more than one, each of the donees, must read (or have read to him/her) all the prescribed information: reg 9(5) As soon as reasonably practicable thereafter:
STEP FIVE	The donee or, if more than one, each of them: (a) must complete the provisions of Part C of the instrument that apply to him (or direct another person to do so); and (b) subject to reg 9(7) (below), must sign Part C of the instrument in the presence of a witness: reg 9(6)
WITNESSES AND SIGNATURES	If the instrument is to be signed by any person at the direction of the donor, or at the direction of any donee, the signature must be done in the presence of two witnesses: reg 9(7): 9(8) For the purposes of this regulation— (a) the donor may not witness any signature required for the power; (b) a donee may not witness any signature required for the power apart from that of another donee. 9(9) A person witnessing a signature must— (a) sign the instrument; and (b) give his full name and address. 9(10) Any reference in this regulation to a person signing an instrument (however expressed) includes his signing it by means of a mark made on the instrument at the appropriate place.

Table 3

REGISTRATION OF LPA with OFFICE OF THE PUBLIC GUARDIAN
MCA 2005, Sch 1, Part 2 and Lasting Powers of Attorney, Enduring Powers of Attorney and Public Guardian Regulations 2007 SI 2007/1253, Part 2

Application forms	Schedule 1, Part 2, para 4(1). LPA Regulations, Sch 3 form LPA 002. There is a fee payable. See Chapter 12 at 12.30 for fees.
Applicant	Donor, donee(s), or any of them appointed jointly and severally: Sch 1, para 4(2)
False information	Criminal offence punishable on summary conviction to a maximum of 12 months imprisonment or fine not exceeding statutory maximum or both; on indictment to maximum of 2 years imprisonment or fine or both: Sch 1 para 4(4)
Notification of named person	Donor and donee(s) must notify of impending registration: Sch 1, para 6. See LPA Regulations, Sch 2, form LPA 001. Court may dispense with notification if satisfied that no useful purpose would be served by the notice: Sch 1, para 10 eg the donor chose not to name any one
Notification of donee	By Public Guardian as soon as is practicable after receiving an application by the donor: Sch 1, para 7[1]
Notification of donor and any other donee(s)	By the PG as soon as is practicable after receiving an application by the donee(s): Sch 1, para 8[2]. The PG must offer an explanation of the notice to the donor in appropriate terms: reg 13(2)
PG must register in the absence of objection or defect	At the end of six weeks from the time of giving notification under Sch 1, paras 7 and 8 (above) or if notification is on more than one date, within six weeks of the latest date: Sch 1, para 5; reg 12
PG must not register instrument See also 'Applications to the court' below	– If instrument accompanying application is not made in accordance with Sch 1 *unless* court directs PG to do so: Sch 1, para 11(1) – if the instrument appears to contain a provision which would be ineffective as part of an LPA or would prevent the instrument from operating as a valid LPA and has referred the matter to the court under s 23(1): Sch 1, para 11(2)(3) – as above and the court orders the instrument not to be registered: Sch 1, para 11(4)(5) – If the powers of an existing court deputy would conflict with those of the donee *unless* directed by the court to do so: Sch 1, para 12(2) – If a named person or donee receiving notification of registration gives notice of *objection* before the end of the prescribed period[3] on ground that an event in s 13(3) (donor's bankruptcy) or (6)(a)–(d) (see Table 1)has occurred and the instrument has been revoked, *unless* the court directs registration on application by the applicant because it is satisfied that the ground is not established: Sch 1, para 13(1)(2) – If a named person or donee notifies the PG of an *objection* to the court on a *prescribed ground*, *unless* the court directs PG to register it: Sch 1, para 13(4). See s 22(2) and (3) for the prescribed grounds: invalid, revoked, fraud or under pressure to induce the creation of the instrument, or donee or any of them has behaved, or is behaving, in a way that contravenes his authority or is not in the donor's best interests, or proposes to behave in such a way. –If a donor on receipt of notification under Sch 1, para 8 gives notice of objection to the PG[4], *unless* the court on application of the donee or any of them, is satisfied that the donor lacks capacity to object to the registration: Sch 1, para 14 – If the instrument provided is neither an original nor a certified copy of it, *unless* the court directs: reg 11(2)

Notice of registration	PG must give notice in prescribed form to the donor and donee or each of them: Sch 1, para 15; reg 17; form LPA 004 PG must retain a copy of the instrument while returning original to applicant: reg 17(1) (PG is to establish register of LPAs registered) PG must give donor understandable explanation of notice of registration where there is 'good reason to do so': reg 17(3)(4).
Applications to court	Whether the LPA is registered or not (s 22(1)): (i) By PG or other, if instrument not created in accordance with Sch 1 to determine whether valid or revoked: s 22(2) (ii) By named person or donee or other person including where appropriate, the donor, if undue pressure to execute or create LPA or the donee(s) are or propose to act in contravention of the donor's best interests: s 22(3) (prescribed grounds): Court may direct no registration: s 22(4)(a), or revocation: s 22(4)(b), against any one of the donee(s), if more than one: s 22(5) (iii) By PG under s 23(1) if it appears that the instrument contains a provision which would be ineffective or prevent the instrument from operating as a valid LPA: Sch 1, para 11(2)(3). The court will notify the PG that the provision has been severed, or direct him not to register it: Sch 1, para 11(5) Sch 1. (iv) By an applicant that s 13(3) and (6) grounds are not made out: see 'PG must not register instrument'. (v) The court may determine any question as to meaning or effect of an LPA under s 23(1). If court severs a provision PG must register with a note[5] to that that effect attached to it: Sch 1, para 11(6). See reg 18.
Proof of instrument	In the UK a copy purporting to be an office copy of a registered LPA is evidence of the contents of the instrument and the fact that it has been registered: Sch 1, para 16.
PG must cancel registration on revocation	– Bankruptcy of donor – Section 13(6)(a) to (d) events: Sch 1, Part 3, para 17 And notify donor and donee and each of them
Court must direct PG to cancel	– if under s 22(2) it determines that a requirement for creating the power was not met or it has been revoked or otherwise come to an end or revokes the power under s 22(4)(b) (fraud etc): Sch 1, para 18 – if under s 23(1) the court makes a determination as in Sch 1, para 11(5) above: Sch 1, para 19.
Notification of non-registration	Regulation 16
Effect of cancellation	Instrument and any office copies must be delivered up the PC to be cancelled: Sch 1, para 20
Records of alterations in registered powers	Schedule 1, Part 4.
Loss or destruction of registered LPA	Regulation 19
Revocation by donor	Regulation 21
Revocation on death of donor	Regulation 22

1 LPA Regulations, reg 13, Sch 4, Part 1; form LPA 003A.

2 LPA Regulations, reg 13, Sch 4, Part 2; form LPA 003B.

3 5 weeks beginning with the date on which notice given: LPA Regulations, reg 14(2) as amended by reg 3(3) of the Lasting Powers of Attorney, Enduring Powers of Attorney and Public Guardian Amendment Regulations 2007, SI 2007/2161.

4 LPA Regulations, reg 14A(2) as inserted by SI 2007/2161, reg 4.

5 This 'note' could be electronic: 668 HL Official Report (5th series), col 1419, 27 January 2005.

Chapter 6

INDEPENDENT MENTAL CAPACITY ADVOCATES (IMCA)

- **MCA 2005, ss 35–41 (as amended)**
- **Main Code, Chapter 10**
- **Mental Capacity Act 2005 (Independent Mental Capacity Advocates) (General) Regulations 2006, SI 2006/1832**
- **Mental Capacity Act 2005 (Independent Mental Capacity Advocates) (Expansion of Role) Regulations 2006, SI 2006/2883**[1]

1 For Wales see the Mental Capacity Act 2005 (Independent Mental Capacity Advocates)(Wales) Regulations 2006, SI 2006/852 (W.77).

INTRODUCTION

6.1 Sections 35–41 introduce a new statutory function: Independent Mental Capacity Advocate (IMCA), a national statutory advocacy service. The scope of the service outlined by these provisions has been defined and extended by regulations[1] and amendments inserted by the MHA 2007[2]. The instruction of IMCAs will be carried out by NHS bodies and local authorities[3].

The original clauses on the IMCA service were introduced into the Mental Capacity Bill in June 2004 in response to concerns about a lack of safeguards for particularly serious health and welfare decisions for the most vulnerable people in the draft Mental Incapacity Bill published in June 2003[4]. Concerns were expressed by the Parliamentary Joint Scrutiny Committee[5] about the need for independent advocacy services as a safeguard against a misuse of powers under the MCA 2005 by carers and as a means of enabling people without capacity to participate as fully as possible in hearings concerning their rights and entitlements[6].

These provisions were initially a partial response to the lacuna in due process safeguards when unresisting incapacitated persons requiring long term care were effectively deprived of liberty in hospitals or care homes[7] (ie 'Bournewood' patients). The Joint Scrutiny Committee clearly envisaged a broader role for independent advocacy than has been provided for, but it recognised the significant resource implications restricting the same[8]. The government has promised to expand the service further to ensure that those with no family and friends will receive the services of an IMCA in relation to serious medical treatment and long term accommodation decisions even where they have appointed an LPA or there is a court deputy appointed solely in relation to their property and affairs[9].

Prior to the MHA 2007 the IMCA service was focused solely on supporting specific types of decisions set out in the MCA 2005, namely those concerning serious medical treatment, long term accommodation and expanded in Regulations[10] to cover care reviews and adult protection. Except for adult protection purposes they are to be appointed only where there is no other 'appropriate' person for the decision-maker to consult on behalf of the person concerned. The MHA 2007 has introduced further functions for the IMCA where a person is or is to become subject to a deprivation of liberty under the provisions of Sch A1[11], inserted into the MCA 2005. Schedule A1 is intended to satisfy the due process safeguards identified as lacking by the ECtHR in the Bournewood case[12]. The new provisions for depriving a person of their liberty under s 4A and Sch A1 of the MCA 2005 are dealt with in Chapter 9.

IMCAs appointed to act for Sch A1 persons[13] have additional prescribed functions[14]. They are to be appointed in three different sets of circumstances and are referred to as section 39A, 39C and 39D IMCAs. In this chapter they will be referred to collectively as 'A1 IMCAs', in addition. Also of relevance to this role is the 'relevant person's representative' (RPR) of the person, a role subject to appointment under Sch A1[15]. An A1 IMCA's role applies in the absence of a PR. The role of the A1 IMCA and the PR is covered in summary only in this chapter. The relevant provisions of the MHA 2007 are not yet in force. For more detail see Chapter 9.

Importantly IMCAs are not decision-makers. They are empowered to support and represent an incapacitated person only. The IMCA has access to records and may make unfettered inquiries. Once an IMCA is instructed, their report or submissions must be taken into account by the decision maker. This is an extended advocacy role referred to as 'advocacy plus' by the Minister in the Commons[16].

The IMCA service is distinct from the advocacy services that already exist[17]. It does not preclude the use of such advocacy services in appropriate circumstances. The IMCA service is to work in combination with existing advocacy services. Nothing in these provisions prevents the use or appointment of an IMCA in other situations subject to appropriate funding. The Secretary of State's powers in this regard are confined to prescribed circumstances[18].

This service is not to be confused with the Independent Mental Health Advocate (IMHA) being introduced by the Mental Health Act 2007[19] (see para 6.67).

An evaluative study of a pilot IMCA service was commissioned by the Department of Health and published its report in December 2006[20]. Its summary findings are referred to in this chapter. The study found shortcomings in the pilot service.

The Main Code deals with IMCAs in Chapter 10[21].

1 Mental Capacity Act 2005 (Independent Mental Capacity Advocates) (General) Regulations 2006, SI 2006/1832 ('IMCA General Regulations'); Mental Capacity Act 2005 (Independent Mental Capacity Advocates) (Expansion of Role) Regulations 2006, SI 2006/2883 ('Expansion Regulations').
2 Schedule A1, Part 11 (inserted by MHA 2007, s 50(5), Sch 7; amendments are also made to the MCA 2005 by s 50(7) and Sch 9). Not yet in force.
3 The 'supervisory body' for A1 IMCAs.
4 Explanatory notes impact assessment 3.2.
5 Scrutiny Report, November 2003, Chapter 16.
6 See Scrutiny Report, paras 127 and 170.
7 Ie patients falling into the so-called 'Bournewood gap' now provided for in Sch A1 as inserted by the MHA 2007 and due to come into force in April 2009. See Chapter 1 at 1.4.
8 Scrutiny Report, para 302.
9 Main Code, 10.71.
10 The Expansion Regulations (above).
11 Inserted by MHA 2007, s 50(5), Sch 7. Not yet in force.
12 See *HL v United Kingdom* (2005) EHRR 32.
13 See MHA 2007, s 50(7), Sch 9. Not yet in force.
14 Schedule A1, Part 11. Not yet in force.
15 Schedule A1, Part 10. Not in force.
16 HC Official Report SC A (Mental Capacity Bill), 2 November 2004, cols 317 and 332, and subject to a duty of confidentiality.
17 For example, the Independent Complaints Advocacy Service (ICAS) which was set up under the Health and Social Care Act 2001 by the DoH in 2003 to enable and support people to access NHS complaints procedures. See also Scrutiny Report paras 298, 299.
18 Expansion Regulations, explanatory memorandum, para 4.12.
19 MHA 1983, ss 130A–130D as inserted by MHA 2007, s 30. Not yet in force.
20 'The Evaluation of the Pilot Independent Mental Advocacy (IMCA) Service', conducted by Cambridge University for the DoH. Gateway ref 7564.
21 Reference must be made to the draft addendum Code of Practice in relation to A1 IMCAs.

INSTRUCTING AN IMCA: SUMMARY

6.2

1 An IMCA must or may be instructed in the following circumstances if the person in question lacks capacity and there is no one 'whom it

would be appropriate to consult in determining what would be in [their] best interests' save for a paid carer or professional[1].

2 An IMCA *must* be instructed, and consulted

- by an NHS body proposing to provide serious medical treatment[2]; or
- by an NHS body or local authority proposing to arrange accommodation (or change accommodation) in hospital for over 28 days or a care home for over eight weeks[3].

3 An IMCA *may* be instructed to support a person lacking capacity make decisions about:

- care reviews where there are no family and friends to consult;
- adult protection cases, whether or not family, friends or others are involved.

[4 A section 39A IMCA *must* be instructed to represent the person:

- by a supervisory body if that person becomes subject to Sch A1[4].

5 A section 39C IMCA *must* be instructed to represent the person:

- by a supervisory body on notification by the relevant managing authority, if an authorisation under Sch A1 is in force[5];
- the appointment of a personal representative ends in accordance with Sch A1, Part 10.

6 A section 39D IMCA *must* be instructed to represent a person, including for specified purposes:

- by a supervisory body if an authorisation under Sch A1 is in force and there is no paid personal representative;
- upon request by (i) a the person, (ii) the unpaid representative or (iii) where the supervisory body has reason to believe that the person and the unpaid representative would be unable to, or have failed to or are unlikely to, exercise the right to apply to a court (MCA 2005, s 21A) or for a review (MCA 2005, Sch A1, Part 8).[6]]

1 Sections 37(1)(b), 38(1)(b) and 39(1)(b). For the purposes of ss 38, 39, 39A and 39C a personal representative appointed under Sch A1, Part 10 is not a paid carer: ss 38(10), 39(10), 39A(6) and 39C(6) (as inserted by MHA 2007, s 50(7), Sch 9, paras 4(3), 6) and so there is no duty to appoint an IMCA under those provisions where a PR has been appointed for a person deprived of their liberty. This does not apply under s 37 and an IMCA must be appointed for decisions about serious medical treatment whether or not a PR has been appointed. Thus subject to the above, a PR does not exclude appointment of an IMCA, but where a PR is not a paid carer, there is no duty to appoint an IMCA. A PR is not the same as a 'nominated' person: s 40(2) (as inserted by MHA 2007, s 50(7), Sch 9, para 7(4)). These provisions are not yet in force. MHA 2007 (Commencement No 3) Order 2007, SI 2007/2798 only brings MHA 2007, s 49 into force on 1 October 2007. This amends s 40(1) only.

2 This applies whether or not a person deprived of their liberty has an A1 IMCA or PR appointed (see above fn) and provides an additional safeguard in these circumstances.

3 This requirement will not apply if there is an A1 IMCA under s 39A or 39C or a personal representative appointed: ss 38(2A) and 39(3A) as amended by MHA 2007, s 50(7), Sch 9, paras 4(2) and 5(2).

4 Section 39A(1)(a), (b). See s 39B(2)–(7) for the meaning of 'becomes subject to Schedule A' (inserted by MHA 2007, Sch 9, para 6). Not yet in force.

5 Section 39C(1), (3) (inserted by MHA 2007, Sch 9). Not in force.

6 Section 39D (inserted by MHA 2007, Sch 9). Not in force.

SUMMARY FUNCTIONS OF AN IMCA: GENERAL

6.3

1 IMCAs are not empowered to take decisions themselves[1]. They will work with and *support* those who lack capacity and *represent* their views to those who will make the best interests decisions. Decisions will be taken by an NHS body, local authority, appropriate professional or multi-disciplinary team or supervisory body under Sch A1. They may also be taken by a welfare donee or court deputy.

2 The NHS body or other decision-maker must take account of the submissions or report of an instructed IMCA[2].

3 An IMCA (and a PR) has a duty to act in accordance with the statutory principles and in the person's best interests[3].

4 An IMCA is intended to represent a person's wishes, feelings, beliefs and values and not their own.

5 IMCAs may interview the person in private and may have access to his or her health record, any record held by a local authority in connection with a social services function and any record held by a person registered under Part II of the Care Standards Act 2000.

6 The functions of a non-A1 IMCA are set out in s 36 and supported by regulations: MCA 2005 (IMCA) (General) Regulations 2006 ('IMCA General Regulations')[4].

7 The specific functions of Sch A1 IMCAs are provided for by Sch A1[5].

1 Section 35(1).
2 Sections 37(5), 38(5) and 39(6), Expansion Regulations, reg 5(2)(b) and by Sch A1, para 132 this applies to all A1 IMCAs and PR for the purposes of assessments for standard authorisations. Also see the Main Code at paragraph 10.4 and 10.13.
3 Section 1(5) and Main Code, para 10.2.
4 SI 2006/1832. These are discussed at 6.10 below. The IMCA General Regulations do not currently apply to A1 IMCAs.
5 See Chapter 9.

GENERAL PROVISIONS: NON-A1 IMCAS

Appointment

6.4 The Secretary of State for Health is the 'appropriate authority' empowered to fund the IMCA service and make regulations for their appointment (or National Assembly for Wales)[1]. Regulation 5 of the IMCA General Regulations provides that an IMCA must be approved by the local authority because s/he satisfies the appointment requirements, or belongs to a class of persons approved by a local authority, satisfying requirements for that class. These are minimum requirements that currently apply to all except A1 IMCAs[2]. The appointment requirements are:

1 *Qualifications* Appropriate experience or training or an appropriate combination of the two[3]. There are as yet no specific qualifications demanded. While these are awaited IMCAs will be provided with induction training[4];

2 *Character* Integrity and good character. An enhanced criminal record certificate issued pursuant to s 113B or 113A of the Police Act 1997 is

required. The purposes for which such a certificate may be issued have been extended to include the suitability of a person to work in care services or provide advocacy for vulnerable adults[5]. Enhanced disclosure is not confined to checks with the Police National Computer. It extends to local police records. During 2008 IMCAs will become subject to the scheme under the Safeguarding of Vulnerable Groups Act 2006[6].

3 *Independence* The ability to act independently of any person who instructs him or her[7].

1 See s 35(1) and regulations under s 35(3); IMCA General Regulations, reg 5; s 35(7).

2 IMCA General Regulations explanatory memorandum, para 4.11. Expansion Regulations explanatory memorandum, para 4.9; reg 2 applies arrangements under s 35 to these regulations. The IMCA General Regulations specifically refer to IMCAs appointed under ss 37–39 and 41 (reg 5(1)) and do not currently extend to A1 IMCAs.

3 On 1 November 2006 the Department of Health issued circular guidance on the setting up and funding of an IMCA service by Councils with Social Services Responsibility (CSSR) and for the necessary staff training. Standardised training materials have been prepared for staff. LAC 2006 (15): *The MCA and Independent Mental Capacity Advocate (IMCA) Service.*

4 IMCA General Regulations explanatory memorandum, para 7.6.

5 Police Act 1997 (Criminal Records) Regulations 2002, SI 2002/233 as amended by Police Act 1997 (Criminal Records) (Amendment No 2) Regulations 2006, SI 2006/2181.

6 Main Code, para 10.18.

7 Discussed further below at 6.6.

Commissioning of the service

6.5 Local authorities are responsible for the approval and appointment of IMCAs, although services will usually be jointly commissioned by local authorities in partnership with NHS bodies[1].

The service is to be commissioned by Councils with Social Services Responsibility (CSSR)[2]. It must be independent of both CSSRs and health providers. These services will be commissioned from other bodies, usually advocacy organisations[3]. There is not intended to be an automatic transfer into this service for existing advocates[4]. This is to be a professional and specialised role regarding the most difficult decisions. Guidance has been issued to local health boards and local authorities involved in commissioning IMCA services for their area[5]. The service is to be delivered by the Secretary of State for Health through local authorities in partnership with NHS organisations.

Local authorities have financial responsibility for the service. They are responsible together with NHS organisations for instructing an IMCA and in these circumstances are known as 'responsible bodies'[6].

Training and other materials are available on the Department of Health website.

1 IMCA General Regulations , explanatory memorandum, para 4.11.

2 LAC 2006 (15): The Mental Capacity Act and the Independent Mental Capacity Advocate (IMCA) Service. This deals with training for IMCAs as well.

3 Main Code, para 10.7. The DoH website contains of list of IMCA providers as at 1 April 2007.

4 HC Official Report SC A (Mental Capacity Bill), 2 November 2004, col 326.
5 Main Code, para 10.6.
6 See 6.21 below.

Independence

6.6 Section 35(4) states that in making arrangements the authority 'must have regard to the principle ... *so far as practicable*' (emphasis added) that the person is 'independent of any person who will be responsible for the act or decision.' The need for independence was emphasised through the consultation process leading to the setting up of the service.

A person *cannot act* as IMCA if they either act as carer for or treat the person (paid or professional), or have *links* to the person instructing them, decision-maker or other individuals involved in the person's care or treatment that may affect their independence[1]. A PR is not a 'paid carer' for these purposes[2].

This does not prevent an ex-employee of local services or groups funded by social services from acting, or it might become impossible to make any appointments. The intention was not to be overly prescriptive regarding eligibility for appointment and a provision for payment has been made[3]. Independence is to be maintained by the introduction of national standards and contracts[4].

1 Main Code, para 10.19.
2 Schedule A1 and 6.2, fn 1 above.
3 HC Official Report SC A (Mental Capacity Bill), 2 November 2004, col 329. See 6.66 below 'remuneration'.
4 Response to IMCA consultation.

Access to information (s 35(6))

6.7 This provision applies to all IMCAs.

Private interview

6.8 An IMCA may interview the person in private. This is unlikely to cause any problems in practice but may be important if for some reason access to the person is difficult, eg they are living in a neighbour's house and the neighbour is unco-operative.

Records

6.9 The first question will always be 'can the person consent to the release of his records?'

IMCAs may have access to (ie examine and take copies of) records of health, social services and under the Care Standards Act (Part II)[1], if the record holder considers they 'may be relevant to the IMCA's investigation'[2].

This is not a carte blanche right of access to records. It remains subject to the Data Protection Act 1998, Article 8 ECHR and to a common law duty of confidentiality in relation to any records received or examined.

The record holder must determine the relevance of records to be disclosed to the issue in hand. In order to do so they must review the documents to make a decision as to what should reasonably be disclosed. The disclosure of irrelevant material to an IMCA would breach the person's rights under Article 8 ECHR, his confidentiality and may also be unlawful under the DPA. An IMCA receives and holds any such information in confidence.

Staff training should enable them to know when and how to give disclosure of relevant information without delay and provide access to the person for private interview, provide information regarding changes that may affect the IMCA's role, inform all relevant people that an IMCA has been instructed and inform the IMCA of the final decision taken and the reasons for it[3].

There is general guidance on access to information in Chapter 16 of the Main Code and see Chapter 14.

1 Eg independent hospital or care home.
2 HC Official Report SC A (Mental Capacity Bill), 2 November 2004, col 332; it was noted that it was important for IMCAs (and others) to have access to 'all the information that they need to carry out their functions'. This included health and social care records, including from private homes and records that may not be health related.
3 Main Code, para 10.14. The Pilot Evaluation suggests that access to records did not present a problem.

GENERAL FUNCTIONS OF IMCAS: NON-A1 IMCAS[1]

6.10 IMCAs will work with and *support* those who lack capacity and *represent* their views to those who will make the best interests decisions. This may be a difficult and subtle task in some circumstances. Section 36(2) sets out the functions that are further elaborated upon in the IMCA General Regulations and in para 10.20 of the Main Code:

(a) providing support to enable the person (P) to participate as fully as possible in the decision being made. An IMCA must first confirm that the person instructing him has the authority to do so[2];
(b) obtaining and evaluating relevant information;
(c) ascertaining what P's wishes and feelings would be likely to be, and the beliefs and values that would be likely to influence P, if he had capacity;
(d) ascertaining what alternative courses of action are available in relation to P;
(e) obtaining a further medical opinion where treatment is proposed and the advocate thinks that one should be obtained;
(f) challenging any relevant decision.[3]

1 Section 36; IMCA General Regulations, reg 6; Main Code, paras 10.20–10.39: currently extend to all except A1 IMCAs (ie IMCAs under the Expansion Regulations are included). See Regulation 2 of the General Regulations.
2 IMCA General Regulations, reg 6(4)(a) and Main Code, para 10.20.
3 IMCA General Regulations, reg 7.

Code of Practice: the Main Code

6.11 An IMCA must:

A Act in accordance with s 1 principles[1].
B Have regard to the guidance in the relevant Code of Practice[2]. This means the Code as a whole and not simply Chapter 10.

1 Main Code, para 10.20.
2 Section 42(4)(d). In due course this will include for A1 IMCAs the Addendum to the Main Code of Practice, currently available only in draft.

Support and represent

6.12 It is for the IMCA to determine how best to do this[1]. The process is broadly comprised of three steps.

Step 1: Gathering information. In particular, to the 'extent that it is practicable and appropriate' to do so, this *must* involve:

- interviewing the person in private[2];
- examining the records available under s 35(6)[3];
- consulting with paid or professional carers[4];
- consulting with others who could comment on person's wishes, feelings and beliefs;
- obtaining such other information as the IMCA considers necessary about the person or the relevant act or decision[5].

Step 2: Evaluating the information[6] for the purposes of:

- ascertaining the extent to which the person has been helped to participate in making the decision[7];
- ascertaining the person's wishes and feelings, beliefs and values[8];
- considering alternative courses of action available. This might include questions about the proposed course in addition to suggesting alternatives[9];
- determining, if medical treatment is proposed, the need for a second opinion.

Step 3: Preparing a report for the decision-maker. This may include submissions on the person's behalf in relation to the act or decision proposed[10].

1 IMCA General Regulations, reg 6(3).
2 Main Code, para 10.26.
3 Main Code, para 10.26

4 Main Code, para 10.27: these people may help assess the information in case records or other sources. They can comment on alternative courses of action amongst other things. It is intended that the ultimate decision in the person's best interests be taken through discussion involving all the relevant people who are providing care and treatment, as well as the IMCA.

5 IMCA General Regulations, reg 6(4)(a)–(d).

6 IMCA General Regulations, reg 6(5).

7 The guidance in Chapter 5 of the Main Code relating to best interests is relevant to these functions and should be referred to. Chapter 3 contains more guidance on helping someone make their own decision. See also Main Code, paras 10.23–10.25 and 10.28.

8 Main Code, para 10.21. The guidance in Chapter 5 of the Main Code relating to best interests is relevant and should be referred to. See also Main Code, para 10.23.

9 Main Code, paras 10.21, 10.29–10.30. The IMCA must check that the decision-maker has considered all possible options. Subject to the person's confidentiality, they may also consider discuss possible options with professional and paid carers.

10 IMCA General Regulations, reg 6(6), (7).

Practicable and appropriate

6.13 The Step 1 tasks are imbued with a high degree of common sense and practicality. It is not intended that the IMCA will conduct extensive searches for elusive information or people to consult. Factors relevant to the extent of searches might be the urgency or nature of the decision and whether they would represent a proportionate use of time. This is not a task of perfection. It is recognised that in some situations not all the information will be accessed. It is for the IMCA to exercise his or her judgement about what can be achieved in the time available to support and represent the person[1].

An IMCA must be in a position to justify the steps taken to access relevant information and to justify the failure to do so. It is suggested that this is best dealt with in the body of the report provided to the decision-maker under Step 3. Where it has not been possible to access information or get a good picture of what the person might want, the IMCA should still present the relevant information gathered to the decision-maker, raising any questions and issues[2] and expressing any appropriate caveats.

It should be recalled that the primary decision-maker has duties under s 4 to consult with prescribed persons and obtain and evaluate information in relation to a particular decision and whether or not it is in the person's best interests.[3]

1 Main Code, para 10.24. See the meaning of 'practicable' as elaborated by Scarman LJ in *Dedman v British Building and Engineering Appliances Ltd* [1974] 1 All ER 520, [1974] 1 WLR 171 at 179G–H in the context of presenting a complaint for unfair dismissal in time.

2 Main Code, para 10.25.

3 See ss 4(6) and (7).

Obtaining a second medical opinion

6.14 The MCA 2005 aims to give people lacking capacity the same rights as those with capacity and no more. Thus the IMCA has the possibility of accessing a second medical opinion from a doctor with appropriate expertise[1].

6.14 *Independent Mental Capacity Advocates (IMCA)*

Whether an IMCA will be capable of knowing when to instruct a second opinion was an issue raised in Parliament[2]. Regulations do not provide for the funding for such an opinion. Extra funds for disputed cases should be available within the budgets of commissioning authorities[3].

1 Main Code, para 10.31.
2 HC Official Report SC A (Mental Capacity Bill), 2 November 2004, col 336.
3 'Consultation on the IMCA service', July 2005: Chapter 3, para 27. See www.dh.gov.uk.

IMCA pilot

6.15 This found that IMCA case workers requested a second medical opinion in a few cases only[1] and suggests that this is a task that needs to be reinforced in instructions given to an IMCA, if appropriate, and also in training.

1 Redley et al, *Evaluation of Pilot IMCA service* published December 2006, Cambridge University. DoH Gateway ref: 7564 at 6.7.2. Available at http://www.dh.gov.uk/en/Publicationsandstatistics/Publications/PublicationsPolicyAndGuidance/DH_063676.

Challenging decisions

6.16 An IMCA may disagree with the decision taken on behalf of the person by the decision-maker. If they are particular concerned about a decision, the use of the information provided or the use of powers generally, the IMCA may challenge the decision[1]. The Main Code deals with the resolution of disagreements generally in Chapter 15.

An IMCA has the same rights to challenge a decision as any other interested person or person engaged in caring for the person. The challenge may be a decision regarding capacity and/or best interests[2].

1 Main Code, paras 10.32–10.39, 10.15 and 10.16.
2 IMCA General Regulations, reg 7(2); Main Code, para 10.33.

Informal resolution

6.17 Disputes do not have to end up in court. The Main Code advocates the use of informal methods of discussion prior to the use of formal complaints procedures[1].

1 Main Code, para 10.34–10.36.

Court of Protection

6.18 If the matter is particularly serious or urgent, an IMCA may seek permission to refer a case to the Court of Protection with the assistance of the Official Solicitor or may seek permission him or herself[1]. Applications to the court may be in respect of capacity and/or best interests decisions which the Court of Protection may make.

1 Main Code, para 10.38.

JUDICIAL REVIEW PROCEEDINGS[1]

6.19 Applications may be made under CPR Pt 54 where issues of public law arise: errors or law, procedural irregularities, irrationality, or under the HRA 1998. See Chapter 15 for more on judicial review.

1 Main Code, para 10.39.

IMCA PILOT SCHEME

6.20 This found that case workers challenged very few of the 'best interests' decisions made by practitioners. Any challenges made were through informal channels e.g. telephone or letter. Responses from the practitioners involved were rare[1].

The report suggests that IMCAs found it difficult to know when to challenge decisions that were progressing slowly, or how to respond to the discovery of care below the expected standard, short of abuse, or the discovery of 'do not resuscitate' notices in a persons file or a decision that family and friends were not appropriate to consult[2].

1 IMCA Pilot Report above, at para 6.7.1. It was suggested that this was due to the pilot nature of the work which did not at that stage carry statutory authority. In *Making decisions: The Independent Mental Capacity Advocate (IMCA) Service* published on 17 April 2007 and available on www.dh.gov.uk, it is suggested that an IMCA's role includes monitoring the best interests decision-making. This is implicit in the power to challenge a decision, but it would probably have helped if it was more explicitly stated in s 36 or the IMCA General Regulations.

2 One reason canvassed for this was the failure of decision makers to explain their decisions to IMCAs so that a challenge could properly be made. See IMCA Pilot report at para 6.7.3.

INSTRUCTING AN IMCA (NON-A1)

Responsible body

6.21 IMCAs will be instructed by local authorities and NHS organisations. It is important to be able to know precisely which authority or organisation carries that responsibility for a particular person. The Main Code offers guidance:

1 For decisions about serious medical treatment the responsible body will be the NHS organisation providing the person's healthcare or treatment[1].

2 For decisions about admission to accommodation in hospital for 28 days or more, the responsible body will be the NHS body that manages the hospital[2].

3 For decisions about moves into long term accommodation (eight weeks or longer), the responsible body will be either: the NHS body that proposes the move or change of accommodation or the local authority that has carried out an assessment of the person under the NHS and CCA 1990 and decided that that move may be necessary[3].

6.21 *Independent Mental Capacity Advocates (IMCA)*

More problematic is likely to be the situation where NHS organisations and local authorities make decisions together about moving a person into long-term care. Guidance states vaguely that the instructing body must be the one that is 'ultimately responsible for the decision to move the person'. The IMCA to be instructed is the one who works wherever the person is at the time that the person needs support and accommodation[4].

1 Main Code, para 10.9.
2 Main Code, para 10.10.
3 Main Code, para 10.11.
4 Main Code, para 10.12.

Independent or voluntary sector hospital

6.22 The responsible body will be the NHS organisation arranging and funding the person's care, and which should have in place arrangements with the hospital to ensure the prompt appointment of an IMCA[1]. A person is entitled to an IMCA even if they are being treated or cared for in the private sector[2].

1 Main Code, paras. 10.9 and 10.10.
2 HC Official Report, SC A (Mental Capacity Bill), 2 November 2004, col 333. Main Code, para 10.56.

NHS body

6.23 An NHS body is defined in reg 3 of the IMCA General Regulations as a Strategic Health Authority, NHS Foundation Trust, PCT, NHS Trust or Care Trust. These terms are further defined in reg 3(2). The regulations are reproduced at Appendix 4.

Procedures, training and awareness programmes[1]

6.24 The Main Code requires responsible bodies to have procedures, training and awareness programmes to enable staff to know when they need to instruct an IMCA and to be able to do so without delay.

Procedures should cover the method of instructing an IMCA.

Procedures must enable the IMCA to communicate their findings easily and effectively.

1 Main Code, para 10.14.

Record keeping

6.25 Procedures should cover the recording of the IMCA's involvement and any decision provided to aid decision-making. There should be a record of how the information provided by an IMCA has been taken account of by the responsible body.

WHEN *MUST* AN IMCA BE INSTRUCTED (NON-A1)

6.26 The relevant provisions at contained in IMCA General Regulations, sections 37–39, and Main Code, paras 10.40–10.80.

A responsible body has a duty to instruct an IMCA on behalf of an incapacitated person for decisions concerning:

1 Serious medical treatment: s 37.
2 Long term accommodation: ss 38 and 39.
3 A change in long term accommodation: ss 38 and 39.

Lack of capacity

6.27 It is a given that in all cases the person concerned must lack capacity which is to be determined in accordance with the provisions of the MCA.

No appropriate person to consult

6.28 The IMCA's role is to safeguard those who lack capacity in relation to serious decisions, because they have no one close to them who could otherwise be consulted. In other words, those without friends and family who take an interest in their welfare or who are willing to do so[1]. This criterion does not apply in relation to adult protection decisions (see below). The issue in those cases is not so much whether or not the person has family and friends, but rather whether it is appropriate to consult them.

The instructing body must be satisfied that there is no person 'appropriate to consult in determining what would be in [the person's] best interests'[2]. Paid carers and professionals are not 'appropriate' for these purposes. The Main Code introduces the concept of 'practical' into this determination so that an IMCA must be instructed if it is not 'practical or appropriate' to consult with anyone. It provides the examples of an elderly person with dementia with adult children now living in Australia, or who rarely visit or who refuse to be consulted. In such situations an IMCA must be instructed and the decision should be documented[3].

If a relative or friend is unwilling to be involved in a formal role or is too frail or too distant to be effective, then unless they fall into category 1, 2 or 3 below, then it is for the IMCA to attempt to involve them to the extent possible in a more informal way[4].

It is for the responsible body to determine whether or not any 'appropriate' person exists who might qualify as an IMCA alternative. A person would not be 'appropriate' for consultation if s/he:

1 has a history of abusing or ill-treating the person;
2 is likely to cause distress to the person if s/he was aware of the consultation;

3 is not available to be consulted because their whereabouts are unknown;
4 could only be consulted with the use of disproportionate time and effort to contact him/her;
5 has very limited knowledge of the person;
6 is unwilling to be a consultee[5];
7 is unlikely to be available for effective consultation, for example, if s/he lives in a remote location.

These provisions do not sanction the removal of family and friends who are considered difficult to deal with or who disagree with the decision-maker[6]. To do so would clearly be contrary to the intention behind this provision and is likely to lead to the displaced person lodging a formal complaint or making an application for judicial review.

Any available s 40 individual (see 6.30 below) would preclude the appointment of an IMCA and the responsible body must take steps to determine whether or not any such persons are available. The Main Code states that if it is not 'possible, practical and appropriate to consult anyone, an IMCA should be instructed'[7].

1 Main Code, para 10.74.
2 Sections 37(1)(b), 38(1) and 39(1).
3 Main Code, paras 10.76, 10.77.
4 Main Code, para 10.78.
5 Jones R, *Mental Capacity Act Manual* (2nd edn) Sweet and Maxwell, para 1–270.
6 Main Code, para 10.79.
7 Main Code, para 10.76.

Pilot scheme

6.29 The IMCA pilot foreshadowing the introduction of the service found that decision-makers in responsible bodies found it difficult to establish when an IMCA was required and there were many ineligible referrals (40%)[1]. This was partly due to the perceived conflict with s 4(7) which requires that there shall be consultation about a person's best interests with, among others, any nominated person, anyone caring for them, or interested in their welfare[2], and guidance given as to when it may not be practicable or appropriate to consult family (see above). The majority of IMCA clients in the pilot had family or friends but it was judged not 'practicable and appropriate to consult them' (63%). The study reports the tension in the application of this provision, and that the IMCAs did not seek or feel able to challenge these decisions[3].

Except in limited circumstances an IMCA should consult with any available family members. See 6.28 above for a discussion of this issue.

1 Pilot IMCA Report, para 4.1.
2 Main Code, para 10.75.
3 Pilot IMCA Report , para 4.6.

No duty to instruct an IMCA: section 40

6.30 The IMCA provisions do not apply if any of those persons listed in s 40[1] are available: a nominated person, a donee of an LPA or a court deputy, empowered in relation to the decision in issue.

1 As amended by MHA 2007, s 49 and Sch 9, para 7. Mental Health Act 2007 (Commencement No 3) Order 2007, SI 2007/2798.

Mental Health Act 1983

6.31 If the person is detained under the MHA 1983 and is subject to Part IV of the MHA, no IMCA is necessary for any decision regarding serious medical treatment[1]. Similarly no IMCA is necessary for issues of accommodation arising as an obligation imposed by the MHA[2].

1 Section 37(2).
2 Sections 38(2) and 39(3). See 6.61, fn 1 below.

Relevant person's representative (RPR) under Sch A1, Part 10

6.32 A RPR appointed under Sch A1 is not a paid or professional carer for long term accommodation decisions (ss 38 and 39)[1] and no duty to appoint an IMCA arises under those provisions if an RPR is available. This does not apply to serious medical treatment (s 37) and an IMCA must be appointed even if there is an RPR. Subject to the foregoing, an RPR is not a 'nominated person' under s 40(1)(a) (see 6.30 above)[2] whose appointment excludes an IMCA.

1 MCA 2005, ss 38(10) and 39(7). See 6.1, fn 1 above.
2 MHA 2007, Sch 9, para 7(4) and s 50(7). This provision appears currently to be in conflict with draft appointment regulations for RPRs: reg 2 which provides that an RPR is 'nominated person'. See also 6.1, fn 1 above.

Serious medical treatment: s 37

6.33 An NHS body[1] is the responsible body with a duty to instruct an IMCA where it is proposing 'serious medical treatment'[2]. 'Serious medical treatment' is defined in reg 4 of the IMCA General Regulations as providing, withdrawing or withholding treatment in circumstances where:

- a single treatment is proposed with finely balanced risks/benefits;
- a choice of treatments is available, a decision as to which one to use is finely balanced, or
- what is proposed is *likely* to involve serious consequences for the patient.

The definition is wide and affords considerable discretion to the decision-maker. This provision applies not only to new proposed treatments but also to those already being provided but to be stopped or changed.

Finely balanced decisions may include those treatments which are relatively minor in nature. Such treatments would appear to need the instruction of an IMCA. The guidance in the Main Code (see 6.36 below) assists in relation to what kinds of treatments may be considered 'serious'. But an appendectomy might be serious due to the risk of peritonitis, or due to anaesthetic risks, depending on the individual circumstances.

'*Serious consequences*' is not defined in the MCA 2005. The Main Code[3] states that they are treatments that have a 'serious impact on the patient, either from the effects of the treatment itself or its wider implications.' They may include:

- serious and prolonged pain, distress or side effects;
- potentially major consequences eg stopping life sustaining treatment or major surgery;
- serious impact on future life choices such as fertility.

1 IMCA General Regulations, reg 3 (reproduced at Appendix 4).
2 MCA 2005, s 37(6).
3 At para 10.44.

Threshold for appointing an IMCA

6.34 'Likely' with regard to serious consequences means that the consequence must be 'more likely than not' or 'on balance'. In this situation it is suggested that no higher degree of evidential cogency is required simply because 'serious consequences' are under contemplation[1] and responsible bodies and practitioners should not become overly restrictive in appointing IMCAs on this ground. The threshold for instructing an IMCA for a person who qualifies in other respects should not be set too high.

1 In *Re H (Minors)(Sexual Abuse: Standard of Proof)* [1996] AC 563, the need for more cogent evidence was expressed in the context of allegations of sexual abuse for the proof of which a court would require more cogent evidence when applying a 'balance of probabilities' test. It is suggested that the appointment of IMCAs falls into a wholly different and more benign category for which such exacting standards are unnecessary.

Clinical judgement

6.35 The standard of what a responsible body of practitioners of similar skill would do, or should have done, in the same circumstances[1] will apply and there is always the possibility that an opposing medical view, as to how finely balanced or serious the consequences of a medical treatment are, can be found. These decisions will inevitably rest on clinical judgements.

1 *Bolam v Friern Hospital Management Committee,* [1957] 2 All ER 118, [1957] 1 WLR 582; *Bolitho v City and Hackney Health Authority* [1997] 4 All ER 771.

The Main Code

6.36 This endeavours to provide a list of non-exhaustive examples of treatments that may amount to 'serious medical treatments'[1] They are:

- chemotherapy and surgery for cancer;
- ECT;
- therapeutic sterilisation;
- major surgery;
- major amputation;
- permanent loss of sight or hearing;
- withholding or stopping ANH;
- termination of pregnancy.

1 Main Code, para 10.45.

Timescales

6.37 The duty arises before the treatment is provided and must await the outcome of the IMCAs investigations because the NHS body must take into account any information given, or submissions made by the IMCA[1]. There is no stipulated timescale for an IMCA's investigations. It would clearly be beneficial to the process of treatment to instruct an IMCA without delay and as soon as it is known that a serious medical treatment is being considered.

In some IMCA pilot areas the inclusion of the question 'Need to instruct an IMCA?' on patient or service user forms allowed staff to identify the need for an IMCA as early as possible, and to discuss the timetable for the decision to be made. IMCA involvement led to better informed discharge planning, with a clearer focus on the person's best interests[2]. Such user forms can be used to good effect to keep the need for an IMCA under review. It is suggested that forms should record the names of relatives, friends and others who might be consulted in the care of a person at the first opportunity. This process will identify also the lack of any such appropriate persons for consultation and the likely need for an IMCA should the circumstances arise.

1 Section 37(3) and (5). The decision-maker must continue to act in the person's best interests while awaiting the IMCA's report: Main Code, para 10.47.
2 Main Code, para 10.22.

Record keeping

6.38 Proper records should be kept by a responsible body of how an IMCA's submissions and information were taken into account and the reasons for any disagreement with the IMCA, if any. If disagreements cannot be resolved informally, an IMCA may resort to complaints procedures or the court[1].

1 See 6.16 above and Chapter 10 on the Court of Protection.

Mental or physical disorder

6.39 The proposed treatment may be for either mental or physical disorder, although if it is for mental disorder under Part IV of the MHA 1983 (as amended), then it is excluded from this provision and no IMCA is necessary[1].

6.39 *Independent Mental Capacity Advocates (IMCA)*

Part IV allows treatment for mental disorder to be given without the patient's consent in prescribed circumstances and subject to procedural safeguards.

If the patient detained under the MHA requires serious treatment for a physical disorder, for example treatment for a cancer, then an IMCA must be instructed if the criteria are satisfied.

1 Sections 28 and 37(2).

Urgent decisions

6.40 When an urgent decision is required, an IMCA does not need to be instructed[1]. The Main Code states that the decision must be recorded and an IMCA instructed for any following serious treatment[2].

1 Section 37(4).
2 Main code, para 10.46.

Role of the court: serious treatment

6.41 The Main Code states that some decisions about treatment will be so serious that the courts will be required to make them. An IMCA should still be instructed and the OS may become involved as litigation friend for the person concerned[1]. See Chapter 8 on medical decisions and Chapter 10 on the Court of Protection. Where the IMCA disagrees with the decision-maker and informal and other resolution mechanisms have failed, he or she may apply to the court. The IMCA has the 'same rights to challenge the decision as he would have if he were a person (other than the IMCA) engaged in caring for [the person] or interested in his welfare'[2]. The challenge may also relate to the decision regarding lack of capacity.

1 Main Code, para 10.48.
2 IMCA General Regulations, reg 7.

Long term accommodation: ss 38 and 39

Responsible body

6.42 NHS body[1] or local authority[2] must instruct an IMCA where they are proposing to provide *accommodation* or a change of such accommodation. The duty on the NHS body arises in relation to accommodation in a hospital or care home for a minimum period of 28 days or eight weeks[3]. The duty on the local authority arises in relation to residential accommodation of eight weeks or more[4].

1 Section 39 and see 6.23 above for definition.
2 Section 38 and defined in s 64(1) as amended by MHA 2007, Sch 9, para 10(2). Except in Sch A1 a local authority is: in England, county council where there are no district councils, district council; in Wales: council of county or county borough; City of London: common council; Scilly Isles: council.
3 Section 38(3) and (9).
4 Section 39(4)(a).

Care home

6.43 This is as defined in s 3 of the Care Standards Act 2000[1] ie the provision of accommodation with nursing or personal care to a defined group of persons including those who have or have had a mental disorder, or are disabled and infirm. A hospital, independent clinic or children's home is not a 'care home', nor an institution excepted from the definition by regulations.

1 Section 38(6).

Hospital

6.44 This means a health service hospital[1] or an independent hospital within s 2 of the Care Standards Act 2000, ie where the main purpose is to provide medical or psychiatric treatment for illness, mental disorder or palliative care or where procedures under anaesthesia, or listed specialist services are provided, and any other establishment where treatment or nursing is provided for those liable to be detained under the MHA 1983.

1 Section 38(7): NHS Act 2006, s 275 or NHS (Wales) Act 2006, s 206.

Residential accommodation

6.45 A local authority's duty arises in relation to 'accommodation' within s 21 or 29 of the National Assistance Act 1948, or the MHA 1983, s 117, as a result of a decision under s 47 of the NHS and Community Care Act 1990.

The meaning of 'accommodation' under the 1948 Act is wide and flexible; it includes care homes, ordinary and sheltered housing, housing association and other registered social housing, hostel and private sector housing[1]. It may be provided directly by the local authority or via a third party.

People who are self funding still have a right to an IMCA where the assessment has been carried out by the local authority and it has decided that a duty is owed to the person[2].

1 *R (Batantu) v Islington London Borough Council* [2000] All ER (D) 1744.
2 Main Code, para 10.56.

Preferred accommodation

6.46 A local authority must endeavour to provide a person with their preferred accommodation[1]. An advocate, carer or legal guardian should be considered if the person has insufficient capacity to express a preference to do so in substitution[2]. An IMCA falls within these provisions and must in any event be instructed if the duration of the accommodation is likely to be eight weeks or more.

1 National Assistance Act (Choice of Accommodation) Directions 1992 which were issued annexed to the Department of Health Circular no. LAC (92)27 available at http://www.dh.gov.uk/en/Publicationsandstatistics/Lettersandcirculars/LocalAuthorityCirculars/

AllLocalAuthority/DH_4004615 and amended by the National Assistance Act 1948 (Choice of Accommodation)(Amendment) (England) Directions published by the DoH on 3 October 2001 and available as above on dh.gov.uk.

2 Department of Health Circular LAC (2004) 20 Guidance on Choice of Accommodation Directions above at para 5.1. Available as above.

Threshold for appointing an IMCA

6.47 The decision to appoint an IMCA is an active process and should not be left as a secondary matter. When to instruct an IMCA in this assessment process may be difficult if it is not known at the outset that long term residential accommodation is an option. It is suggested that an IMCA must be instructed as soon as long term residential accommodation becomes a likely, as opposed to a possible, option, assuming all other criteria are satisfied. The local authority must demonstrate that it has actively considered the duration of the accommodation in order to be 'satisfied' that it was likely to be for a shorter period than eight weeks. The threshold for instructing an IMCA should not be set too high.

Section 47 community care assessments

6.48 In this regard the guidance in the Main Code appears to be anomalous because it states that an IMCA must be appointed once it has been decided under s 47 of the National Health Service and Community Care Act 1990 Act to provide long term accommodation[1]. This would rather defeat the purpose of instructing an IMCA because it would come after the decision had been made.

If satisfied that the period of accommodation will be less than eight weeks or it is urgent, then the exceptions in s 39(4)(a) and (b) will apply and an IMCA must be subsequently instructed if the local authority has reason to believe that the accommodation will exceed eight weeks[2]. See 6.52 below.

1 Main Code, para 10.53. See also Chapter 7 on welfare decisions which considers community care provisions.

2 Section 39(5).

Section 117 Mental Health Act

6.49 A duty falls on the relevant NHS and local authority to provide after-care services to patients who have been discharged from detention under the Act. These services may include long term accommodation. The duty does not apply to patients detained under emergency provisions. The duty bites after actual discharge[1] but planning usually begins beforehand and it is at this stage that an IMCA should be instructed if appropriate[2].

1 See MHA 1983, s 117(1) and *R (on the application of B) v Camden London Borough Council* [2005] MHLR 258.

2 Main Code, para 10.58.

Long term accommodation

6.50 The applicable periods are 28 days or longer in a hospital and eight weeks or longer in a care home or other residential accommodation[1].

1 Section 38(3)(a) and (9); s 39(4)(a).

Timescales and urgent decisions

6.51 The duty arises before the arrangements are made, unless the accommodation is for less than the minimum period stipulated (see 6.37 above), or is needed as a matter of urgency[1].

As with serious medical treatment the decision-maker must await the outcome of the IMCA's investigations because the responsible body must take into account any information given, or submissions made by the IMCA[2]. There is no stipulated timescale for an IMCA investigation. It would clearly be beneficial to the process of treatment to instruct an IMCA without delay and as soon as it is known that a serious medical treatment is being considered.

The comments in 6.37 above also apply in relation to the use of forms.

1 Sections 38(3)(b) and 39(4)(b).
2 Sections 38(3), (5) and 39(4) and (6). The decision-maker must continue to act in the person's best interests while awaiting the IMCA's report: Main Code, para 10.47.

Subsequent instruction of IMCA

6.52 If no IMCA was instructed because the duration of the accommodation was less than the periods prescribed, or the matter was urgent, and it subsequently becomes apparent that the accommodation will last for longer than the prescribed periods then an IMCA must be instructed[1].

1 Sections 38(4) and 39(5); Main Code, para 10.55.

Care review

6.53 A responsible authority has a discretion to instruct an IMCA where a review of the accommodation is to take place[1].

1 Mental Capacity Act 2005 (Independent Mental Capacity Advocates) (Expansion of Role) Regulations 2006, SI 2006/2883, reg 3. See 6.61 below.

Record keeping

6.54 Proper records should be kept by a responsible body of how an IMCA's submissions and information were taken into account and the reasons for any disagreement with the IMCA, if any. If disagreements cannot be resolved informally, an IMCA may resort to complaints procedures or the court.

Court

6.55 Where disagreement arises and neither informal resolution nor formal complaints mechanisms have succeeded, then under reg 7 of the IMCA General Regulations, an IMCA may apply to the Court of Protection. The IMCA has the 'same rights to challenge the decision as he would have if he were a person (other than the IMCA) engaged in caring for [the person] or interested in his welfare'[1]. The challenge may also relate to the decision regarding lack of capacity.

1 IMCA General Regulations, reg 7.

USING AN IMCA: MAIN CODE CASE STUDIES

6.56 The following concerns long-term accommodation and is based on the scenario at para 10.30 of the Main Code.

Mrs Nolan has dementia. She is being discharged from hospital. She has no family or friends willing to be consulted or involved in her care living, nor has she nominated anyone to consult on her behalf. Her only close relative lives in New Zealand. She also lacks the capacity to decide whether she should return home or move to a care home. The local authority instructs an IMCA to assist with the assessment of her long term accommodation needs.

Mrs Nolan tells the IMCA that she wants to go back to her own home, which she can remember and describe. But the hospital care team thinks she needs additional support, which can only be provided in a care home.

The IMCA applied for and obtained all the relevant records from the hospital and local authority, reviewed all the assessments of Mrs Nolan's needs, spoke to people involved in her care and her relative in New Zealand and wrote a report stating that Mrs Nolan had strong and clear wishes. The IMCA also suggested that a care package could be provided to support Mrs Nolan if she were allowed to return home. The care manager now has to decide what is in Mrs Nolan's best interests. He must consider the views of the hospital care team and the IMCA's report. The care manager should notify the IMCA of his decision.

6.57 The following concerns serious medical treatment and is based on para 10.47 of the Main Code.

Mr Jones had a fall and suffered serious head injuries. Hospital staff could not find any family or friends. He needed urgent brain surgery, but afterwards still lacked capacity to accept or refuse medical treatment.

The hospital did not involve an IMCA in the decision to operate, because it needed to make an emergency decision. But it did instruct an IMCA when it needed to carry out further serious medical treatment.

The IMCA obtained Mr Jones' case notes, met with him, reviewed the options with the consultant and wrote a report. The decision-maker then made the clinical decision about Mr Jones' best interests taking into account the IMCA's report and notified the IMCA of his decision.[1]

If the IMCA in either of the cases above is unhappy with the decision taken, s/he can challenge it, and in the case of the medical treatment, also obtain a second medical opinion. There is no provision for obtaining a second opinion regarding accommodation.

1 At p 27 of *Making decisions: The Independent Mental Capacity Advocate (IMCA) Service* published on 17 April 2007 and available on www.dh.gov.uk, the DoH, DCA and OPG suggest that the role of an IMCA ends when he becomes aware that the proposed action has been taken. This guidance is unclear and it is suggested that an IMCA may only know this once a decision-taker has notified him of the decision and provided brief reasons if the IMCAs recommendation has not been accepted.

6.58 Further action by the IMCA after her formal role had ended:

While reading Mr Jones' case notes the IMCA had found references to physical and verbal abuse of Mr Jones by another patient in the care home where he resided. It seemed possible from something Mr Jones had told her that Mr Jones had been pushed down the stairs by this patient. The IMCA noted these matters in her final report and then took steps to notify the hospital and care home managers of this evidence and ensure that the protection of vulnerable adults policy was implemented and the police notified. The IMCA considered the use of a local advocacy service for ongoing support for Mr Jones.

EXCEPTIONS

6.59 In summary, no IMCA is necessary:

1 where accommodation is for less than 28 days in a hospital or 8 weeks in a care home[1];
2 for urgent treatment/accommodation[2] eg life saving[3];
3 for accommodation of persons deprived of liberty under Sch A1 where a s 39A or 39C IMCA has been appointed[4].
4 for treatment for mental disorder regulated under Part IV of the MHA 1983[5]. This means that an IMCA may be appropriate for medical treatment for mental disorder for those under emergency admission powers, guardianship, [leave of absence] conditional discharge, supervised discharge or community treatment orders[6].
5 in relation to accommodation that is provided as a result of an obligation on the person under the MHA 1983 ie assessment or treatment under s 2 or 3, guardianship, leave of absence, conditional discharge, supervised discharge or community treatment orders.
6 in relation to persons who have an LPA, court deputy, or other person nominated in whatever manner to be consulted, empowered in relation to the matter in hand[7].

7 in relation to accommodation if there is an RPR under Sch A1, Part 10 to consult.

1 Sections 38(9); 39(4)(a).
2 Section 37(4), 38(3)(b) or 39(4)(b)
3 Main Code, para 10.46.
4 Section 38(2A) and 39(3A) as amended and inserted by MHA 2007, Sch 9, Part 1, para 4(2) and s 50(7).
5 Sections 28 and 37(2).
6 MHA 1983 as amended by MHA 2007.
7 Section 40 as amended.

WHEN *MAY* AN IMCA BE INSTRUCTED? EXPANDED ROLE

6.60 The Expansion Regulations, pursuant to s 41, permit the Secretary of State to make arrangements under s 35 to allow for the purposes of this expanded role[1]. An NHS body or LA is not prevented from appointing an IMCA in other circumstances, the Secretary of State is simply not required or empowered to make arrangements beyond those prescribed[2].

The appointment provisions under reg 5 of the IMCA General Regulations (see 6.4 above) apply[3].

The IMCA's functions are those set out in s 36 and reg 6 of the IMCA General Regulations (see 6.10 above).

An NHS body or local authority has (i) a discretion to instruct an IMCA if it is satisfied that it would 'be of particular benefit' to the person, and (ii) then *must* take into account information or submissions made by the IMCA[4], in two prescribed situations, as follows.

1 IMCA General Regulations, reg 2.
2 IMCA General Regulations, explanatory memorandum para 4.12. The policy intention is to put the instruction of IMCA in relation to some important decisions on a statutory footing: para 7.10.
3 IMCA General Regulations, explanatory memorandum, para 4.9.
4 IMCA General Regulations, reg 5(1) and (2).

Review of accommodation: reg 3

6.61 The information or submissions made by the IMCA must be taken into account where accommodation has been provided for a continuous period of 12 weeks or longer, and not as an obligation imposed under MHA 1983[1], by an NHS body or local authority for a person lacking in capacity to agree to such arrangements, and a review of the arrangements is proposed or in progress[2]. The explanatory note makes it clear that this means that the person must lack the capacity to participate in the review.

'Accommodation' must be in a 'care home' or 'hospital' as defined under s 38, or pursuant to the National Assistance Act 1948, ss 21 and 29 or the MHA

1983, s 117 by virtue of a decision of a local authority under s 47 of the National Health Service and Community Care Act 1990[3]. See above at 6.43–6.45 and 6.48.

The proposed review may be under a care plan or otherwise, but where this includes a proposed change of accommodation then ss 38 and 39 will apply a duty to instruct an IMCA.

1 Eg if a person is detained in hospital, or subject to guardianship (s 8), conditions of residence under leave of absence (s 17), conditional discharge (s 73) or community treatment order (s 17A, as amended), MHA 1983 contains its own safeguards and appeal process: explanatory memorandum para 4.7.

2 IMCA General Regulations, reg 3. Local Authority Social Services Act 1970, s 7 sets out the current requirements for care reviews. There should be a review within three months of help being provided or major changes made to services. There should then be a review annually, or more often if needed.

3 IMCA General Regulations, reg 3(2).

Adult protection: reg 4

6.62 The second situation where the information or submissions made by the IMCA must be taken into account is where protective measures are proposed or have been taken in relation to a person lacking the capacity to agree to such measures, following receipt of an allegation or evidence of abuse, neglect by another person or the person lacking capacity, and in accordance with vulnerable adult arrangements[1].

This includes steps to minimise the risk that any abuse will continue[2]. An IMCA may be appointed even if there is another appropriate person to consult, including an LPA or court deputy, family or friends[3].

Once these steps have been taken and it becomes apparent that a person needs to be moved to different accommodation in their best interests, then an IMCA must be instructed if there is no other appropriate person to consult[4].

1 Under Local Authority Social Services Act 1970, s 7. Guidance on the creation of relevant multi-agency policies is contained in *No secrets: guidance on developing and implementing multi-agency policies and procedures to protect vulnerable adults from abuse*, available on the Department of Health website at http://www.dh.gov.uk/PublicationsAndStatistics/Publications/PublicationsPolicyAndGuidance/. See explanatory note to reg 4 and explanatory memorandum to Expansion Regulations, para 4.6.

2 IMCA General Regulations, reg 4(2).

3 Main Code, para 10.67.

4 Main Code, para 10.68.

Other qualifying criteria

6.63 These are:

– Sections 37, 38 and 39 do not apply.

- For care reviews only: there is no other appropriate person to consult in determining the person's best interests (this does not include a paid carer or professional) and no nominated person, LPA, attorney under an EPA or court deputy[1].
- For adult protection only: reg 3 does not apply.

Where the qualifying criteria are met, it would be unlawful for the LA or NHS not to consider the exercise of their power to instruct IMCAs for accommodation reviews or in relation to adult protection[2].

1 IMCA General Regulations, reg 3(1)(c) and (d).
2 *Adult protection, care reviews and IMCAs: Guidance on Interpreting the Regulations Extending the IMCA Role*, available at www.dh.gov.uk.

Policy and guidance

6.64 DoH guidance recommends the adoption of a written local policy in relation to eligibility for the IMCA service to be made widely available[1]. The Main Code states that responsible bodies are expected to take a strategic approach in deciding when they will use IMCAs in these additional situations. A local policy should be established which should include consideration of the particular factors to be taken into account when assessing the benefit to the person concerned. Each must be considered separately however[2].

1 Adult protection, care reviews and IMCAs: *Guidance on Interpreting the Regulations Extending the IMCA Role* avaliable at www.dh.gov.uk.
2 Main Code, para 10.61.

Prison

6.65 IMCA provisions extend into prison[1].

1 Main Code, para 10.73.

COST AND REMUNERATION: NON-A1 IMCA SERVICE

6.66 The DoH estimated annual costs at £6.5 million in the first phase of non-A1 IMCAs, reducing to about £3.4 million for an estimated 16,000 decisions each year in England, 6,000 relating to serious treatment and 10,000 to accommodation ie an estimate that 20 per cent of incapacitated adults are unbefriended[1].

An IMCA may be remunerated[2]. A fee of £100 per IMCA decision at an average of four hours per decision was initially mooted. This was increased to eight hours following consultation within the existing budget[3]. There are additional funds for disputed cases of £500,000 which will presumably cover obtaining second medical opinions and court action where appropriate. The estimated requirement is for 144 advocates and 18 managers[4]. The IMCA pilot evaluation reported that IMCAs spent on average seven hours per decision.

The poor levels of remuneration available are unlikely to improve the quality of this service. The IMCA pilot evaluation study has reported a number of areas in which the service is likely to be strained and require improvement or focused training, if it is to achieve its somewhat ambitious aims. The IMCA pilot findings are summarised at 6.71 below under 'Practice Points'.

1 669 HL Official Report (5th series), col 212, 1 February 2005. See also regulatory impact assessment, para 7. Available on http://www.dca.gov.uk/menincap/.
2 Section 35(5).
3 Regulatory impact assessment para 6.1 and 7.4 (above). £200 for an eight hour assessment.
4 'Consultation on the IMCA service', July 2005: Chapter 3, paras 26 and 27. See www.dh.gov.uk.

INDEPENDENT MENTAL HEALTH ADVOCATE: MENTAL HEALTH ACT 2007

6.67 Section 30 of the MHA 2007 introduces new ss 130A–130D into the MHA 1983 which provide for Independent Mental Health Advocates (IMHA).

Qualifying patient

6.68 A patient qualifies for an IMHA if he or she is liable to be detained under the MHA 1983 (except under ss 4, 5(2) or (4), 135 or 136), subject to guardianship, or a community patient[1].

A patient may also qualify for an IMHA if they are not detained or subject to the Act as set out above, but the possibility of treatment under s 57 is being discussed with a registered medical practitioner or approved clinician[2], or they are under 18 and the possibility of treatment under s 58A is being discussed[3].

1 Section 130C(2). These provisions come into force in October 2008.
2 Definitions: s 57 applies to psycosurgery or hormone implantation and requires the patient's consent and a SOAD and two MHAC certificates.
3 Section 130C(3)(a), (b).

Overlap with IMCA

6.69 A person appointed as IMHA must so far as practicable be independent of any person professionally concerned with the patient's medical treatment. An IMCA appointed under s 35 is not regarded as a person professionally concerned with a person's treatment and so may double up as an IMHA[1]. Once a person is detained under the MHA 1983 and subject to Part IV of that Act, the occasions for instruction of a non-A1 IMCA are restricted (see 6.39 and 6.49 above). A1 IMCAs are only appropriate if a person is subject to a deprivation of liberty or likely to be so, under Sch A1 and not the MHA.

1 Section 130A(4) and (5).

Role of IMHA: treatment safeguard

6.70 An IMHA will help a qualifying patient (above) in a number of respects including, obtaining information about and understanding the provisions of the MHA 1983, any conditions or restrictions to which s/he is subject under that Act, what (if any) medical treatment is proposed and why, the authority under which it would be given, the treatment provisions of the Act[1].

An IMHA is to have access to records which relate to the patient subject to the patient's capacity and ability to consent and any decision of an LPA donee or court deputy[2].

1 Section 130B(1).
2 Section 130B(3), (4).

PRACTICE POINTS

6.71 The IMCA pilot evaluation study has helpfully noted practical issues and concerns which will be instructive for the appointment of IMCAs and the effective running of the service. In summary they are as follows:

1 *Time:* IMCA decisions took on average seven hours (plus travelling time) over an average of 65 days. Thus the process may add to the time taken in making best interests determinations. The study noted that there were no reports of IMCAs impeding the decision-making process.
2 *Remit:* The decision-specific nature of an IMCAs instruction may create a lack of clarity over whether action may be taken if other matters come to the notice of an IMCA on perusal of notes or following investigation eg sub standard care, or on one occasion locating a 'do not resuscitate' (DNR) notice on the person's medical file which had not been the conclusion of a 'best interests' process, nor involved an IMCA. It is worth remembering that all IMCAs are bound to act in the person's best interests and in accordance with the Main Code and must bring such matters to the attention of the proper body. It is suggested that all such findings are noted in the final report under a heading such as 'other matters'.
3 *End of a case:* Allied to the point above is the lack of clarity around the point at which an IMCA's involvement with a person ceases. It is suggested that the case is closed when the final decision has been taken by the best interests decision-maker and not before. The study has recommended that the Department of Health offers further guidance to decision-makers as to the requirement to formally acknowledge receipt of final reports and how they have been used in the decision taken.
4 *DNR notices*: the study found instances of these being used without a formal decision-making process. It is suggested that decisions regarding DNR ('do not resuscitate') notices fulfil the definition of 'serious medical treatment' within s 37, mandating an IMCA if the other qualifying criteria are met.
5 *Challenging decisions:* the instruction of IMCAs should make it clear that this is an important part of their role which they should consider exercising if they are at all concerned about the decisions being made,

including whether or not there are family and friends who are appropriate to consult. There must be clear training regarding the types of challenge that may be made falling short of an application to the court.

6 *Second opinions:* this point is allied to the ability to challenge decisions. As already stated above, this part of an IMCA's role must be reinforced in their instructions. It is an important function.

7 *Consulting with family or friends:* an IMCA should seek to consult with any family and friends available to the extent possible. See 6.28 above for discussion of the circumstances when it may not be possible to consult with a family member. The appointment of an IMCA does not preclude such consultation. It is not difficult to see, however, that the provision may be sought to be used by a responsible body like a nearest relative displacement process under the MHA 1983[1], for example, if the family and friends are objecting to a treatment or accommodation proposal. This would be improper and should be challenged by the IMCA.

8 *Accountability:* In addition the quality of the service and individual case-working will require close monitoring. It is not clear how this will be achieved nor to what extent an individual IMCA may be held accountable for his practice. Unless an IMCA's report is to be used for court purposes there will be no independent check on quality or usefulness. There will be no one to raise issues of competence or challenge the working of a particular IMCA[2].

1 MHA 1983, s 29.

2 The DoH, DCA and OPG suggest that any dissatisfaction with an IMCA be dealt with via the IMCA, his manager, the complaints policy and the commissioning authority of the relevant service respectively: Chapter 6 of *Making decisions: The Independent Mental Capacity Advocate (IMCA) Service* published on 17 April 2007 and available on www.dh.gov.uk.

Chapter 7

SOCIAL WELFARE DECISIONS INCLUDING GUARDIANSHIP AND COMMUNITY CARE

INTRODUCTION

7.1 The capacity and best interests regime contained in the MCA 2005, ss 1–4 and described in Chapter 2 covers all areas of decision-making for incapacitated adults. These are usefully summarised as decisions regarding health, welfare and property and affairs. Sections 5 and 6 provide protection for those concerned with care and treatment, ie health and welfare, of those without capacity on a day to day basis[1]. There are other potential decision-makers in relation to welfare (including health), namely donees of welfare lasting powers of attorney (LPAs) (welfare donees) and deputies, subject to specific authority and independent mental capacity advocates (IMCAs), who are not decision-makers but support and represent incapacitated persons on specific issues to do with health or welfare[2]. The Court of Protection has declaratory or decision-making powers as a last resort for serious, intractable decisions that cannot be resolved by consensus or other means. Chapter 8 deals specifically with health and medical treatment decisions. Some particularly serious treatment decisions must be referred to the court[3].

This chapter is concerned with decision-making under the MCA 2005 for what is broadly termed 'social welfare,' (ie welfare excluding health), and the related area of guardianship for adults under the Mental Health Act 1983 (MHA 1983), both of which are devoted to the delivery of care in the community and provide mechanisms for safeguarding incapacitated adults from abuse. It will also outline the entitlement of a person to the provision of community care services by local authorities and other agencies, under the NHS and CCA 1990[4]. The potential for deprivation of liberty while providing care under the MCA 2005 or MHA 1983 is also relevant to the consideration of welfare provision and community care. This is a 'deprivation of liberty' as determined by reference to ECHR case law and Article 5, a right to liberty[5].

There are other measures available for the protection of vulnerable adults (POVA). These are contained in:

(a) the Care Standards Act 2000 which provides controls aimed at preventing unsuitable people from working in institutions with vulnerable people and for a list of such unsuitable people to be maintain (POVA list); and
(b) Safeguarding Vulnerable Groups Act 2006 which will come into force in the autumn of 2008 provides a new POVA scheme.

Relevant guidance is contained in 'No secrets' and 'In Safe Hands'[6]. They are, of course, relevant to the protection of incapacitated adults also, but will not be considered in any detail in this chapter.

The broad definition of a 'vulnerable adult' referred to in the 1997 Consultation Paper *Who decides?*[7], is a person:

> 'who is or may be in need of community care services by reason of mental or other disability, age or illness; and who is or may be unable to take care of him or herself, or unable to protect him or herself against significant harm or exploitation'.

'No secrets' identifies 'abuse as: physical, sexual, psychological, financial or material, neglect or 'acts or omission' and discriminatory abuse.

Protective measures include the inherent jurisdiction of the High Court, the Court of Protection and the MHA 1983 and these are considered in Chapters 10 and 16 and below.

1 See Chapter 4.
2 See Chapters 5, 6 and 11.
3 See also Chapter 10 on the Court of Protection.
4 This chapter is not intended to provide a detailed analysis of guardianship or community care law and the reader is referred to other texts devoted to these subjects and in particular Jones, *Mental Health Act Manual* (10th edn (with supplement)) Sweet and Maxwell and Clements and Thompson, *Community Care and the Law* (4th edn) LAG.
5 This is discussed in detail in Chapter 9.
6 *No secrets: guidance on developing and implementing multi-agency policies and procedures to protect vulnerable adults from abuse* (Department of Health at www.dh.gov.uk); *In safe hands: implementing adult protection procedures in Wales* (Welsh Assembly, July 2000, available at www.new.wales.gov.uk/docrepos).
7 Issued by the Lord Chancellor's Department.

WHAT IS SOCIAL WELFARE?

7.2 There is no overarching definition of 'welfare' for the purposes of the MCA 2005. What provision there is derives from the subject-matter of decisions of the High Court made under its inherent jurisdiction prior to the MCA 2005 coming into force. Thus, s 17 provides a list of 'welfare' issues for the purposes of decisions that the court and deputies may be charged with taking under s 16. This list is augmented by the Main Code. In combination they provide as follows[1]:

Section 17: section 16 powers and personal welfare	*Main Code para 6.5: personal care protected under s 5*	*Main Code para 7.21: personal welfare donees*
• deciding where the person should live	• helping with washing, dressing or personal hygiene	• where the donor should live and who they should live with
• deciding what contact, if any, the person should have with any specified person(s)	• helping with eating and drinking	• the donor's day-to-day care, including diet and dress
• [giving or refusing consent to medical treatment and directions regarding responsibility for health care.]	• helping with communication	• who the donor may have contact with

Section 17: section 16 powers and personal welfare	*Main Code para 6.5: personal care protected under s 5*	*Main Code para 7.21: personal welfare donees*
	• helping with mobility (moving around)	• [consenting to or refusing medical examination and treatment on the donor's behalf]
	• helping someone take part in education, social or leisure activities	• [arrangements needed for the donor to be given medical, dental or optical treatment]
	• going into a person's home to drop off shopping or to see if they are alright	• assessments for and provision of community care services
	• doing the shopping or buying necessary goods with the person's money	• whether the donor should take part in social activities, leisure activities, education or training
	• arranging household services (for example, arranging repairs or maintenance for gas and electricity supplies)	• the donor's personal correspondence and papers
	• providing services that help around the home (such as homecare or meals on wheels)	• rights of access to personal information about the donor, or
	• undertaking actions related to community care services (for example, day care, residential accommodation or nursing care)	• complaints about the donor's care or treatment.
	• helping someone to move home (including moving property and clearing the former home).	

The breadth of issues falling under this heading will be immediately apparent from the table above. Under the inherent jurisdiction of the High Court, the wide scope of welfare issues was reinforced relatively early in the development of that jurisdiction as protective of incapacitated adults in *Re S (Hospital Patient: Court's jurisdiction)*[2], when Sir Thomas Bingham, MR (as he then was), referred to the future care and residence of an elderly man struck down by a stroke as being 'a serious justiciable issue, involving as it potentially does the happiness and welfare of a helpless human being'[3].

It will also be apparent that there is not a perfectly contained categorisation of 'social welfare' issues. Instead, there is considerable overlap with healthcare issues, eg where a person may have particular residential needs for medical reasons, or medical assessment or the arrangement of routine medical or dental care. This overlap is now reflected in the way in which services are provided by the integration of social and health care services in the community (see below). For the purposes of any application to the court, welfare and healthcare issues referred to as 'personal welfare', may be raised in the same application as property and affairs decisions.

1 The entries in square brackets [ ] refer to healthcare matters which are dealt with in Chapter 8.
2 [1996] Fam 1.
3 At 19A. See also Dame Elizabeth Butler-Sloss P in Re A (Male Sterilisation) [2000] 1 FLR 549 at 555, where she said that best interests embrace medical, emotional and all other welfare issues.

SOCIAL WELFARE DECISIONS UNDER THE MCA 2005

Daily care

7.3 The cement binding all daily decisions will be the scheme provided by the MCA 2005 of capacity and best interests which has been elucidated elsewhere in this book (see Chapter 2). It includes acting in accordance with the principles set out in s 1. Thus the MCA 2005 provides a mechanism by which care may be provided for an incapacitated adult either within their own home, in a care home or hospital.

Protected acts

7.4 The table above demonstrates that daily welfare and care is intended to be performed by carers, family and professionals under the auspices of the s 5 protection. Section 5 codifies the common law doctrine of necessity that was previously used to fill the gap in protection for incapacitated adults under the inherent jurisdiction[1]. Thus the majority of an incapacitated person's care, whether at home, in hospital or residential care, will be conducted without the intervention of the court. Any disagreements are intended to be resolved through informal methods, or with the help of an IMCA in appropriate circumstances. Section 5 does not provide a substituted decision-making power. The basic position at common law promoted by the High Court under its inherent jurisdiction[2] is therefore not altered by this provision. It is a power for a person to act in a way that s/he 'reasonably believes' is in the best interests of the incapacitated person (s 5(1)). This applies also to most medical treatments that a person may need. Substitute decision-making powers reside with donees, and the court and court deputies under s 16.

1 *Re F (Mental Patient:Sterilisation)* [1990] 2 AC 1.
2 *Re F (Mental Patient:Sterilisation)* [1990] 2 AC 1.

Limits on section 5 protection

7.5 The protection offered by s 5 is removed if a carer or professional acts in a way that is contrary to a valid decision of a welfare donee or court deputy (s 6(6)). A person who detains the incapacitated person or restrains them in a manner not falling within s 6 will not be protected[1]. The operation of ss 5 and 6 is considered in detail in Chapter 4.

Case study 1

J is an 82 year old man who suffered a debilitating stroke in November 2007 and is incapacitated in relation to most aspects of his daily life. He is wheelchair bound and has lost the power of speech. His wife of the last ten years, S, arranges medical and nursing care for him, firstly in hospital and then at home where she is now caring for him herself. She is able to do this by virtue of the protection afforded by s 5 and appears to be managing well with the input of social and health services. She has help to bathe him, but otherwise does everything for him, including feeding him, brushing his teeth and changing his incontinence pads. He is uncomplaining.

1 Amendments to be made by the MHA 2007 and due for implementation in April 2009, will enable a deprivation of liberty to be authorised under the MCA 2005 but only by the Court of Protection, or under the procedure in Sch A1. See 7.46 and Chapter 9. Section 6(5), which prevents acts of restraint amounting to a deprivation of liberty under Article 5 ECHR is to be repealed: MHA 2007, s 50(4) and Sch 10, Pt 9.

Welfare donee

7.6 A welfare donee (LPA) may, if appropriately authorised by the appointing instrument, also take these decisions or assist in decision-making by other carers or professionals. The power conferred on a welfare donee is one that allows him to make decisions on behalf of the incapacitated person. See Chapter 5.

Independent Mental Capacity Advocate service (IMCA)

7.7 The IMCA provisions are dealt with in detail in Chapter 6. Their role is to support and represent an incapacitated person in cases where there is no one else appropriate to do so, for example, no family or close friends, or none that are willing or able to get involved. IMCAs *must* be instructed for specific decisions either related to serious medical treatment, long term accommodation or change of accommodation. They *may* be instructed in relation to care reviews and the protection of vulnerable adults.

A local authority's duty in relation to the provision of 'accommodation' falling within the IMCA provisions, arises under s 21 or 29 of the National Assistance Act 1948, or s 117 of the MHA 1983, as a result of a decision under s 47 of the NHS and Community Care Act 1990 (see below). So consideration should be given to the need for an IMCA at a time when accommodation is being provided or changed under these enactments.

Once an IMCA is instructed, their report or submissions must be taken into account by the decision maker. Thus they are well placed to influence decisions, including welfare decisions, taken by the relevant decision-maker.

Their functions include ascertaining what alternative courses of action are available in relation to P; obtaining a further medical opinion where treatment/care is proposed and the advocate thinks that one should be obtained; *and* challenging any relevant decision, which includes making an application to the court[1]. An IMCA's challenge may also lie to the Administrative Court for judicial review of an authority's failure to provide services to which the person is entitled (see below and Chapter 15).

1 MCA 2005 (IMCA) General Regulations 2006, SI 2006/1832, reg 7; MCA 2005, s 36(2); Main Code, para 10.20.

Deprivation of liberty

7.8 The provision of community care (see below) for some incapacitated persons, usually in residential care homes, may involve questions of deprivation of liberty for their own care and safety. This may occur, for example, if an elderly person with Alzheimer's disease is incapable of negotiating the street safely because, they may be prevented from leaving the care home without an escort or other person accompanying them in circumstances which objectively amount to a detention; or where a family member is threatening to remove a person from a care home, and in order to prevent this from happening, the person would have to be stopped from leaving the institution[1]. Similarly, the provision of health care, eg an operation under anaesthetic, or in patient care, may require prolonged restraint amounting to a detention. Any reasonable restraint not amounting to a deprivation of liberty is currently protected by s 6 (see Chapter 4)[2]. Whether or not a person is being deprived of their liberty is matter of fact which is discussed in detail in Chapter 9.

The MCA 2005 presently carries no express power allowing detention of persons in the circumstances described above. This point is reinforced by the legislative history and raises the question of how any deprivation of liberty arising in cases, such as those above, is to be authorised pending the amendments to be introduced by the MHA 2007 in April 2009: is it necessary to rely on the doctrine of necessity and the inherent jurisdiction of the High Court, or can a welfare order under MCA 2005, s 16 be utilised?

It was acknowledged during Parliamentary debates on the Bournewood issue that the MCA 2005 as currently drafted did not satisfy the Article 5 ECHR procedural safeguards as required by *HL v United Kingdom*. This left open the possibility that the inherent jurisdiction may still be relevant for such cases . A welfare order under s 16 of the MCA 2005 is certainly *capable* of including an authorisation for deprivation of liberty in such cases. By the new ss 4A and 16A (not yet in force), it is now acknowledged that a s 16 welfare order of the Court of Protection may well authorise a deprivation of liberty. In addition insofar as welfare orders are intended to reflect prior decisions of the High Court, the decision of the High Court in *Re PS* (fn 1 above) and other similar cases extending the use of the inherent jurisdiction prior to the MCA 2005, reinforce the argument that a s 16 order could include orders permitting a deprivation of liberty. Thus the Court of Protection exercising its welfare jurisdiction may feel able to make a detention order. However, assuming that a

High Court judge will always be necessary for such an order, the practical effect whether made under s 16 or the inherent jurisdiction will be the same, thus rendering the distinction insignificant for practical purposes[3]. If the person concerned satisfies the criteria for an MHA detention, this should always be considered in light of the more formal safeguards available (see Chapter 16 generally which deals with the overlap between the MCA 2005 and the MHA 1983 amended, and 16.42 and also Chapter 10 at 10.34).

The court's order must be sought in advance and seek to comply with the requirements of Article 5 ECHR (see Chapter 9 and and 7.46 and practice points below at 7.80)[4].

1 The summary facts of *Re PS (incapacitated vulnerable adult)* [2007] EWHC 623 (Fam), [2007] 2 FLR 1083.

2 Section 6(5) is due to be removed by amendments under the MHA 2007 due to come into force in April 2009.

3 This point does not appear to have been debated during the Bill's passage through Parliament save to acknowledge the lack of Bournewood safeguards in the MCA 2005 as passed. The Main Code says nothing about this aspect of the Court of Protection's functions either. Purists may well feel aggrieved at the lack of coherence in the situation which now arises, but as stated, for practical purposes it makes no difference. See HC Official Report, SC A (Mental Capacity Bill), 21 October 2004, cols 121–124, 26 October 2004, col 187 and 28 October 2004, cols 249–54; 668 HL Official Report (5th series), col 101, 10 January 2005, 25 January 2005, cols 1250–51 and 17 March 2005, cols 1468, 1544–1550.

4 *Re PS* above.

RESOLVING DISPUTES

7.9 The process of following the steps at s 4 for making a best interests decision may expose conflicting opinions as to the best interests of the person. The Main Code exhorts decision-makers to strive to achieve consensus.

Informal resolution

7.10 The Main Code devotes a chapter to processes designed to assist in the resolution of conflict[1], expressing the view that it is usually preferable to settle such conflict informally. It suggests the following:

- setting out the different options in a way that is easy to understand;
- inviting a colleague to talk to the family and offer a second opinion;
- offering to get independent expert advice;
- using an advocate to support and represent the person who lacks capacity;
- arranging a case conference or meeting to discuss matters in detail;
- listening to, acknowledging and addressing worries;
- where the situation is not urgent, allowing the family to think it over;
- arranging mediation[2].

Nevertheless, irreconcilable differences of opinion may emerge between carers and family or welfare donees. Should the dispute remain seriously unresolved, an application to the Court of Protection will be the only option, the court being asked to make a declaration or decision as to best interests. Chapter 10 discusses in more detail the process of application to the Court of Protection. The issues relevant to welfare decisions are also considered below.

1 Main Code, ch 15.
2 Main Code, paras 15.3–15.17.

The Court of Protection

7.11 This is a new court and jurisdiction created by MCA 2005, ss 45–56. The court's powers are contained in ss 15 and 16. The court is now given a statutory declaratory jurisdiction by s 15. Section 16 provides the core substituted decision-making power which can be exercised by the court or a court-appointed deputy. The principles developed under the High Court's inherent jurisdiction are likely to remain relevant and inform the approach of the new court and what follows draws upon existing practice where it is considered that it may remain helpful. Chapters 10 and 11 consider the powers of the court and court deputies in more detail. Other powers of the court in ss 19–23 relate to court deputies and LPAs. The court has powers over existing enduring powers of attorney (EPAs) set out in Sch 4.

Capacity

7.12 The statutory capacity test under s 3 applies to all personal welfare decisions and, as previously stated, draws on common law foundations. Where there are areas of decision-making falling outside the jurisdiction of the Court of Protection and MCA 2005, and still subject to resolution by the High Court under its inherent jurisdiction (see below), then it would be unfortunate if that court were to adopt a significantly different approach than that adopted by the same judge sitting in the Court of Protection[1]. It is suggested, therefore, that in those cases also capacity should be determined by reference to the MCA 2005.

1 *Local Authority X v MM (by her litigation friend the Official Solicitor) and KM* [2007] EWHC 2003 (Fam), [2007] Fam Law 1132 at 78–80. Attention is drawn in that case to para 4.33 of the Main Code which refers to the variety of tests of capacity developed under the common law. Reference is made to the correct approach when issues of capacity arise before other courts, i e other than the Court of Protection, and whether the MCA 2005 test should still apply. It is suggested that the common law may now be shaped by the MCA 2005. See below at 7.47–7.49 regarding capacity to marry. See also Chapter 15 for capacity to litigate and the CPR Pt 21 at 15.4

Serious justiciable issue

7.13 The court's previous jurisdiction was confined to disputes over serious welfare and healthcare issues. Knowing when to go to court will be crucial, not all disputes will be entertained by the court. In the past welfare decisions have been largely residence and contact issues, driven by deep seated family conflicts[1], sexual abuse/neglect[2], or the effects of publishing inquiry reports/ broadcasting a film[3] or a deprivation of liberty[4]. Whether or not there is a serious issue will depend upon the facts of any particular case. The test of a 'serious justiciable issue' as developed under the inherent jurisdiction of the court has been applied in a wide variety of, apparently disparate, cases permitting the court's intervention. See, for example, *Re S*[5] in which Lord Justice Bingham MR (as he then was) also said that in 'cases of controversy and cases involving momentous and irrevocable decisions, the courts have treated as justiciable any genuine question as to what the best interests of a patient require or justify'.

Strictly speaking the issue determined by the court in that case does not appear to fall within this formulation; it concerned the issue of the residence of the elderly stroke victim with his family in Norway or with his common law partner in the UK. This was a decision which may not have been momentous or serious even had he been in a permanently vegetative state, because he would undoubtedly have received healthcare comparable to that available in the UK in Norway. But as he was not immune from pain and emotion, it was considered unsafe to assume that he did not have preferences about his future care and residence, even though he could not express them, thus giving rise to a serious justiciable issue.

It is suggested that most intractable disputes over residence and contact of an incapacitated person will be treated as serious issues justifying the courts' intervention as before[6]. This approach is reinforced by the terms of s 17 which, in elucidating the meaning of 'welfare' for these purposes, plumps for residence and contact, though not intending to be exhaustive by doing so. See Chapter 10, at 10.32.

1 *Re S (Hospital Patient: Courts Jurisdiction)* [1996] Fam 1; *Re D-R (Contact mentally incapacitated adult)* [1999] 1 FLR 1161; *Re S (Adult Patient) (Inherent Jurisdiction: Family Life)* [2002] EWCH 2278 (Fam), [2003] 1 FLR 292; *Re S (Adult's Lack of Capacity)(Carer and Residence)* [2003] 2 FLR 1235.

2 *Re F (Adult:Court's Jurisdiction)* [2001] Fam 38, [2000] 2 FLR 512.

3 *In Local Authority v Health Authority (Inquiry: Restraint on publication)* [2004] 2 WLR 926; *E (by her litigation friend, the Official Solicitor) v Channel 4; News International Ltd and St Helen's Borough Council* [2005] 2 FLR 913.

4 *Re PS (incapacitated or vulnerable adult)* above. A deprivation of liberty will always need the authorisation of the court.

5 [1996] Fam 1 at 18 (see also above at 7.2).

6 See Chapter 10 at 10.13 for the allocation of judges by the Court of Protection. Many welfare cases may now be dealt with by District Judges sitting in Archway. The applicant may need to identify clearly at the outset if the case merits determination by a High Court judge.

Article 8 ECHR

7.14 This is highly relevant to issues of welfare affecting as they do the realms of personal autonomy, family relationships and connections between the incapacitated person and the wider community. Article 8 is a qualified right protecting respect for private and family life. 'Private' life has at least two components: it protects the 'inner life' of a person ie the way a person lives his own life and 'outer life' ie relationships with the wider world. This includes a person's psychological and physical integrity[1]. Thus Article 8 is engaged in relation to all care and welfare issues so far as it removes the autonomy of the individual to live his own life, as well as when family relationships are under threat, as they are when a change of carer/residence is proposed.

1 *Niemetz v Germany* (1993) 16 EHRR 97 and *Botta v Italy* (1998) 26 EHRR 241,

Contact and residence

7.15 Relationships between people, even family members, cannot be forced or imposed. A father or mother alleged to cause detriment to an incapacitated adult son or daughter cannot use their own Article 8 rights to trump those of the son or daughter. Article 8 includes the right to form relationships as well as to exclude them. Their rights may compete and a careful balance must be struck between their respective rights. However, the courts' approach to date has been to make the welfare of the incapacitated person a paramount concern[1]. In striking the balance the focus will lie with the incapacitated person.

1 *Re S (Adult Patient) (Inherent Jurisdiction: Family Life)* [2002] EWCH 2278 (Fam), [2003] 1 FLR 292 at 30–39; *Re F (Adult:Court's jurisdiction)* [2000] 2 FLR 512 per Sedley LJ at 531; *Re D-R* [1999] 1 FLR 1161. Most recently these issues have been considered in detail in *Local Authority X v MM (by her litigation friend, the Official Solicitor) and KM* [2007] EWHC 2003 (Fam) from para 100 onwards.

Who may apply to the court

7.16 The applicant will vary depending on the circumstances. Subject to the requirement of permission (see 7.19), there is a long list of potential applicants: the incapacitated person, the Official Solicitor, the Public Guardian, donee, deputy, IMCA, doctor, family member, friend or carer. For decisions about serious or major medical treatment, the NHS Trust proposing treatment should apply. For serious welfare decisions, the organisation responsible for the persons' care will normally make the application[1].

1 Main Code, paras 8.7–8.8. This reflects the decision in *Re F (sterilisation)* [1990] 2 AC 1 at 65E.

Duty of local authority and ECHR

7.17 The engagement of Article 8 in issues of welfare (see above) places a particular onus on a local authority to take positive measures to protect the incapacitated person where necessary[1]. This might include interfering with a family or caring relationship through implementation of an adult protection policy, or making an application to the court to determine residence and contact. The practical and evidential burden of establishing that it is the more appropriate body to look after the person lies with the local authority[2]. The positive obligations inherent in Article 8 are well-established. As the court put it in *Botta v Italy* at para 33:

> 'While the essential object of Art 8 is to protect the individual against arbitrary interference by the public authorities, it does not merely compel the State to abstain from such interference: in addition to this negative undertaking, there

may be positive obligations inherent in effective respect for private or family life. These obligations may involve the adoption of measures designed to secure respect for private life even in the sphere of the relations of individuals between themselves ... In order to determine whether such obligations exist, regard must be had to the fair balance that has to be struck between the general interest and the interests of the individual.'[3]

1 There is a separate and additional positive obligation to intervene and investigate in cases where there are allegations or suspicions of abuse or neglect on grounds of Article 3 – also, protection against torture, inhuman or degrading treatment. See *Z v United Kingdom* (2002) 34 EHRR 3; *Assenov v Bulgaria* (1997) 28 EHRR 652.

2 *Local Authority X v MM (by her litigation friend the Official Solicitor) and KM* [2007] EWHC 2003 (Fam).

3 (1998) 26 EHRR 241.

Duty of the local authority and vulnerable adults

7.18 In *Re Z (local authority: duty)*[1], a local authority obtained an interim injunction under the court's inherent jurisdiction to prevent a husband from taking his disabled wife to Switzerland, in accordance with her wishes, so that she could be helped to die. The court issued guidance on the duty of a local authority in relation to vulnerable adults under the Local Government Act 1972, s 222[2]:

'(i) to investigate the position of the vulnerable adult to consider what was her true position and intention;
(ii) to consider whether she was legally competent to make and carry out her decision and intention;
(iii) to consider whether any other (and, if so, what) influence could be operating on her position and intention and to ensure that she had all relevant information and knew all the available options;
(iv) to consider whether she was legally competent to make and carry out her decision and intention;
(v) to consider whether to invoke the inherent jurisdiction of the High Court [or now Court of Protection], so that the question of competence could be judicially investigated and determined;
(vi) in the event of the adult not being competent, to provide all such assistance as might be reasonably required both to determine and give effect to her best interests;
(vii) in the event of the adult being competent, to allow her in any lawful way to give effect to her decision although that should not preclude the giving of advice or assistance in accordance with what were perceived to be her best interests;
(viii) where there were reasonable grounds to suspect that the commission of a criminal offence might be involved, to draw that to the attention of the police; and
(ix) in very exceptional circumstances, to invoke the jurisdiction of the court under section 222 of the 1972 Act.'

Case study 2

In Case study 1 above, J's 42-year-old son by his first marriage, M, is unhappy with the care arranged for his father, and also the arrangements for contact between him and his father. Previously he saw his father only very rarely as there had been a long standing disagreement between them. M now accuses S of deliberately isolating his father from his family and of physically abusing him and neglecting his care. He has brought this to the attention of the local authority which is reluctant to interfere with what appears to them to be a family feud. One of the care assistants notes some bruising on J. S is adamant that it was caused accidentally, but she is unable to say how. She is also adamant that in restricting access of M to his father she is following his father's previously stated wishes. S has not permitted social services to do an assessment of her ability to care for J. The local authority is unable to satisfy itself that S is acting in J's best interests. It makes an application to the court to decide the issue of J's residence and contact on his behalf.

1 [2005] 3 All ER 280.

2 Section 222 provides, so far as material: '(1) Where a local authority consider it expedient for the promotion or protection of the interests of the inhabitants of their area—(a) they may prosecute or defend or appear in any legal proceedings and, in the case of civil proceedings, may institute them in their own name ...'.

Permission

7.19 There is a requirement to obtain permission to make an application to the Court of Protection. There is a long list of those who will not need permission which includes the incapacitated person himself, the Official Solicitor, the Public Guardian, a donee or deputy[1]. This increases the burden on a local authority or healthcare trust who must apply in appropriate cases because they will have to obtain the court's permission to make an application. Family members, or other carers, and any IMCA will also have to apply for permission.

In deciding whether to grant permission the court must have regard to:

(a) the applicant's connection with the person to whom the application relates,
(b) the reasons for the application,
(c) the benefit to the person to whom the application relates of a proposed order or directions, and
(d) whether the benefit can be achieved in any other way[2].

Thus any application for permission should focus on these factors.

An applicant does not have to demonstrate any specific legal right to make an application to the court. Under the inherent jurisdiction the Court of Appeal held that[3]:

> 'it cannot be suggested that any stranger or officious busybody, however remotely connected with a patient or with the subject matter of proceedings, can properly seek or obtain declaratory or any other relief (in private law any more than public law proceedings). But it can be suggested that where a serious justiciable issue is brought before the court by a party with a genuine and legitimate interest in obtaining a decision ... the court will not impose nice tests to determine the precise legal standing of that claimant.'

It is likely to be highly unusual for an application by a local authority to be refused permission, but it will add an element of delay to the resolution of a serious issue. If an urgent application is made and interim relief granted, it is suggested that permission will still be required as with judicial review (see Chapter 10).

1 See chapter on the Court of Protection at 10.57 for a full list of those not requiring permission to apply to the court.
2 Section 50(3).
3 *Re S (Hospital Patient: Court's jurisdiction)* [1996] Fam 1 at 18). Also in *A (A Patient) v A Health Authority* [2002] EWHC 18 (Fam/Admin), [2002] Fam 213.

Welfare test

7.20 The incremental development of the High Court's jurisdiction to encompass non-medical cases extended the common law doctrine of necessity, the backbone of the declaratory jurisdiction, to a benefit or welfare test. Thus the issue of the incapacitated person's welfare, a wide and pragmatic concept not intended to be different from that of 'best interests' formed the focus of the court's inquiry[1].

There are four essential questions for the court which are likely to continue to be relevant:

1 is mental capacity established?
2 is there a serious justiciable issue relating to welfare?
3 what is it?
4 with the welfare of the incapable person as the paramount concern, what are the balance sheet factors that may be drawn up to assist in deciding which course of action is in their best interests?[2]

1 *Re A (Medical Treatment Male Sterilisation)* [2000] 1 FLR 549; *Re F* [2000] 1 FLR 512; *Local Authority v Health Authority* [2003] EWHC 2476 (Fam), [2004] Fam 96, [2004] 2 WLR 926.
2 *Re S (Adult's lack of capacity: carer and residence)* [2003] 2 FLR 1235, per Wall J at 21. See Chapter 10 at 10.18.

Balance sheet approach

7.21 There is court guidance on how to determine the serious justiciable issues arising[1]:

> 'The first entry should be of any factor or factors of actual benefit ... Then on the other sheet the judge should write any counter-balancing disbenefits to the applicant ... Then the judge should enter on each sheet the potential gains and losses in each instance making some estimate of the extent of the possibility that the gain or loss might accrue. At the end of that exercise the judge should be better placed to strike a balance between the sum of the certain and possible gains against the sum of the certain and possible losses. Obviously only if the account is in relatively significant credit will the judge conclude that the application is likely to advance the best interests of the claimant.'

This guidance is useful in the instruction of experts on the issue of best interests.

1 *Re S (Adult's lack of capacity: carer and residence)* [2003] 2 FLR 1235 per Wall J at 14, citing Thorpe LJ in *Re A (Male Sterilisation)* [2000] 1 FLR 549 at 560F–560H. See *A Local Authority v E and D and A (by her litigation friend the Official Solicitor)* [2007] EWHC 2396 (Fam), [2007] All ER (D) 291 (Oct) for a case in which it was difficult to apply the balance sheet approach (at 73).

Findings of fact

7.22 Cases involving disputes between family and local authorities may necessitate the resolution of facts around allegations of neglect, assault and so on. These can often be historic and incapable of resolution or prosecution because of the lack of independent witnesses and the inability of the incapacitated person to give reliable evidence. Some cases will be fact specific, but there are others in which the principle concern will be the future, the suitability of plans which each party can put forward in the short and long term for the care of the incapacitated adult. The court should only seek to make findings of fact in such circumstances if they are required to determine the identification of the incapable person's best interests[1]. This approach is a natural consequence of the focus being placed on the incapacitated person's welfare. However, the need to identify precisely the issues and relevant facts for the resolution of the court is an essential ingredient of any such case, and particularly where injunctive relief is being sought[2]. The standard of proof is the 'balance of probabilities', ie 'more likely than not', and the burden of proof will lie on the applicant. In cases involving allegations of sexual and other abuse, the applicant must prove a 'real possibility' of harm[3].

1 *Re S (Adult's lack of capacity: carer and residence)* [2003] 2 FLR 1235 per Wall J at para 18.
2 *Surrey County Council v MB, SB and A PCT* [2007] EWHC 2290 (Fam) per Charles J at paras 4–11.
3 In *Re H (Minors) (Sexual abuse: standard of proof)* [1996] AC 563.

Remedies

7.23 The court's powers now combine interim remedies, declarations and orders to provide maximum flexibility with regard to what may be required to protect an incapacitated person. The power to make orders in relation to decisions under s 16 is new.

Interim remedies

7.24 The court has express powers in relation to interim declarations, orders and other relief, including injunctive relief: ss 47 and 48. See Chapter 10 for procedure.

Declaratory relief[1]

7.25 The court has express jurisdiction to give discretionary declaratory relief by virtue of s 15 and is no longer dependent upon the inherent jurisdiction of the High Court (save in particular circumstances, see below). There are unlikely, therefore, to be any challenges to the court's jurisdiction in relation to those lacking capacity.

- As described above, application for such relief will only be permitted for serious cases and reference to the previous case law will be of assistance.
- Declarations of the lawfulness of any act (or omission) done or to be done, do not carry the force of court approval which is vested in a decision under s 16, whereby the court may make a decision on behalf of the incapacitated person. This jurisdiction has been extended to welfare decisions so that the court's role has been described as 'a surrogate decision-maker on behalf of the [adult]'[2]. In other words decisions will be taken on behalf of the incapacitated person based on their best interests as assessed by the court.
- A declaration is not necessary to establish lawfulness of a medical procedure, but it has become practice (promoted by the courts) to seek one when serious medical treatment is proposed. The desirability of doing so to inform those involved whether a proposed course of conduct will render them civilly or criminally liable, as a safeguard against malpractice, abuse and unjustified action, and upon the determination of an impartial court has been recognised[3].
- Declarations were developed under the inherent jurisdiction as a 'flexible remedy' which could be tailor-made by a judge according to the facts of any particular case, and subsequently varied if necessary. Often the making of a non-coercive declaration is sufficient to bring about a resolution. In principle there is nothing to inhibit the making of declarations, and they may be used to safeguard a clearly defined and reasonably anticipated future dispute[4]. However, in essence, based as they are on the facts of an individual's case, they are not designed to provide general guidance as to the resolution of future cases[5].

1 Main Code, paras 8.15–8.24.

2 *Re S (Adult Patient) (Inherent Jurisdiction: Family Life)* [2002] EWHC 2278 (Fam), [2003] 1 FLR 292.

3 *Re F* [1990] 2 AC 1per Lord Brandon and Lord Goff at 79G; *Re S (Hospital Patient: Court's Jurisdiction)* [1996] Fam 1 per Bingham at 18 above. In *Re S (Hospital Patient: court jurisdiction)*, Hale J, at first instance, said that a declaration is a 'binding statement of the legal position'.

4 *Re Wyatt* [2005] EWHC 2293 (Fam), [2005] 4 All ER 1325 and *Wyatt v Portsmouth Hospital NHS Trust* [2005] EWCA Civ 1181 at 118, [2005] 3 FCR 263. *Re R (Adult: Medical Treatment)* [1996] 2 FLR 99 at 108C and 109D in relation to the future prospect of administering antibiotics, the court decided that 'it was appropriate for the court to make a declaration in terms which would not require a further future application to the court …'.

5 *Re F (Adult: Court's jurisdiction)* [2000] 2 FLR 512 at 524. See also Butler Sloss LJ in *Local Authority v Health Authority (Inquiry: Restraint on publication)* [2004] 2 WLR 926 and Munby J in *Re S (Adult Patient) (Inherent Jurisdiction: Family Life)* [2003] 1 FLR 292 at [50].

Injunctions

7.26 Where necessary the court can, as before, grant injunctive relief[1]. This might be necessary to make a declaration effective. For example a court may declare that it is not in the best interests of an incapacitated person to be taken abroad, or out of their place of residence. In some cases such a declaration may need an injunction, or at least an undertaking to ensure that this does not happen contrary to the court's declaration.

1 Section 47.

Orders and decisions of the court under section 16[1]

7.27–7.28 These will flow from the core substitute decision-making jurisdiction of the court. This attaches largely to decisions regarding residence, contact and health[2]. The court may make an order or directions in the person's best interests regardless of whether or not a specific application has been made in that regard[3].

- When making such orders or decisions, the court will endeavour to stand in the shoes of the incapacitated person in order to try and take the decision as they might have done for themselves. In spite of the guidance in the Main Code as to how to assess a person's best interests[4], a difficulty with this approach arises where there is nothing available to guide the court as to what the person may have done, ie their wishes and feelings, had they had capacity. This may happen, for example, where someone has always lacked capacity, so that there is no prior history to draw upon[5]. In those circumstances, it is suggested that declaratory relief of what is lawful in their best interests is the more appropriate remedy.
- The Main Code advises that a decision of the court may be required
  (a) if there is a serious dispute eg about the residence of an incapacitated person;
  (b) if the disclosure of personal information is sought by a family carer or solicitor eg to investigate allegations of abuse;
  (c) if there is a risk of harm or abuse from an identified person so that the court can by order or interim order, prevent contact with that person until the matter is resolved.

Other specific decisions might include entering into a tenancy agreement in respect of housing provision[6], or interpretation of the powers of a welfare donee[7].

1 Main Code para 8.25–29 and see Chapter 10 at 10.31.
2 Section 17(1)(a)–(c).
3 Section 16(5).
4 Main Code paras 5.37–5.48.
5 See Law Commission Consultation Paper no 119 at paras. 4.22–4.27 for a discussion of the merits of a substituted decision making approach vs the 'best interests' test.
6 *Heywood and Massey* at paras 2–015 and 2–016 deal with contracts that are void and voidable. Section 18(1)(f) gives the court power to enter into contracts. Contracts entered into by deputies under the court's authority do not mean that they will incur personal liability. Any debts incurred are the responsibility of the incapacitated person's estate. In

relation to a tenancy agreement, any breach of it by misconduct or other prohibited behaviour is likely to lead to a termination of the agreement.

7 See ss 22 and 23.

Appointment of a court deputy

7.29 This will occur in relation to welfare matters only in exceptional circumstances – see Chapter 11.

Case study 3

Mrs W has Alzheimer's disease. Her son and daughter cannot agree over which care home their mother should move to. Mrs W has sufficient money to pay the fees of a care home. Her solicitor holds a registered EPA, but has no power, nor desire to become involved in the family dispute. He makes an application to the court which decides which care home is in Mrs W's best interests. There is no need to appoint a deputy as the matter is now resolved. (Main Code, Chapter 8).

Sections 15 and 16: what is the difference?

7.30 There is a conceptual difference underlying the making and effect of declaratory relief under s 15, as against the substituted decision-making under s 16, as described above. Yet both require that decisions are taken in the best interests of the person as set out in s 4, and the person's past wishes and beliefs are relevant to both. Given the difficulties of making an accurate or true substituted decision, the difference between the two approaches may be more theoretical than real in terms of the way in which the declaration or decision is actually made. Furthermore, a court may well be asked to exercise both in one case. Ultimately, the difference may lie in the subject matter before the court and whether there is sufficient evidence upon which a court can make substituted decision. Section 15 is likely to be confined to decisions about serious medical treatment with irreversible consequences, and those conditions set out in the Main Code, or where the lawfulness of an act or omission is required retrospectively. In those, and other, cases where a court is unable to make a substituted decision, a declaration will be available as an alternative. The quality of the decision is intended to be different, and the result is that: a carer or professional will be authorised to act if a substituted decision is made, or be entitled to act (or not), if a proposed act is declared to be lawful.

The court application form (COP1) (see 7.32 below) makes no distinction between decisions of the court and declarations. This tends to reinforce the point above that there may be a blurring of approach between the two provisions.

Case study 4

Ms V, aged 23, is severely learning disabled and has been incapacitated since birth with cerebral palsy. There is a dispute between her parents and social services as to her place of residence. Her parents argue that the home identified for her does not adequately fulfil her needs as set out in her care plan. The court has been asked to decide where she should live. The expert evidence of an independent social worker was equivocal. The court decided that it did not have sufficient information about the wishes and beliefs of Ms V to make a substituted decision on her behalf. It, therefore, declared that her placement as identified by social services was not in her best interests and therefore not lawful. Social services complied with the declaration and moved Ms V.

Preparing to make an application to the court

7.31 The required supporting information (form COP1B) includes accommodation arrangements, whether or not the person is subject to guardianship under the MHA 1983 (see 7.35) and whether or not there is a welfare or other donee in place. At section 4 of the form a chronology of key dates and facts is requested. Other supportive information will have to be supplied in the form of witness statements. This will include elucidating the dispute upon which the court is being asked to decide with supporting evidence – see Chapter 10 at 10.39 onwards.).

Court forms

7.32 The following will be required:

- COP1: application form;
- COP1B Annex B: supporting information for personal welfare applications[1];
- [COP2: permission form (if applicable)];
- COP3: assessment of capacity;
- COP4: deputy's declaration (if applicable);
- Copy of LPA or EPA (if applicable);
- Fee[2].

1 COP1A will be required if a financial or property decision is required in addition.
2 Currently £400: Court of Protection Fees Order (SI 2007/1745, arts 3 and 4 and Sch.

Urgent applications

7.33 The procedure for making urgent applications is set out in the Court of Protection Rules 2007 (CoP Rules) Practice Direction (PD) 10B. See Chapter 10 at 10.46.

Litigation friend

7.34 At the first directions hearing the court will consider the issue of the appointment of a litigation friend to act on behalf of the incapacitated person. Part 17 of the CoP Rules and PD 17A set out this procedure. More often than not it is the Official Solicitor who will be invited to act by the court as a litigation friend, although technically a litigation friend of last resort[1].

1 See www.officialsolicitor.gov.uk; see also the Practice Note (official solicitors: declaratory proceedings: medical and welfare decisions for adults who lack capacity) at [2006] 2 FLR 373.

GUARDIANSHIP UNDER THE MHA 1983[1]

7.35 The separate statutory regimes of the MHA 1983, namely detention in hospital for assessment and/or treatment, supervised discharge, guardianship, and the MCA 2005[2] will now exist side by side. Guardianship does not provide legal authority to detain a person[3], although it has been advocated as a suitable vehicle for filling the so-called 'Bournewood gap', offering certainty and safeguards for those unresisting incapacitated adults in need of residential care who are *de facto* detained[4]. This proposal was rejected by the Government as being too stigmatising. The MCA 2005 cannot be used to contradict the decision or power of a guardian. Thus a guardian's decisions will carry authority over carers, welfare donees and deputies in matters covered by the MHA 1983. Issues such as life-sustaining treatment would not come under the authority of the MHA 1983, and so may, if appropriate, be left to a welfare donee, or doctor and the court. It is important to note that guardianship does not provide any additional entitlement to services. The entitlement to services arises under other enactments (see 7.56).

1 Main Code, paras 13.16–13.21. This chapter of the Main Code is shortly to be revised to reflect the changes made to the MCA 2005 by the MHA 2007 in relation to deprivation of liberty.
2 The relationship between guardianship and the deprivation of liberty regime to be introduced by amendments introduced into the MCA 2005 by the MHA 2007 are discussed in Chapter 16 at 16.7 and 16.45.
3 Main Code, para 13.8. Main Code is always the MCA.
4 Robinson, R, 'Amending the Mental Capacity Act 2005 to provide for deprivation of liberty', (2007) J. Mental Health Law 25. See also Jones, *Mental Health Act Manual* (10th edn), para 1–099. See 7.43 and 7.46 for problems with this approach. Chapter 9 deals with the 'Bournewood gap' and deprivation of liberty.

Guardianship powers

7.36 A guardian (usually the local authority) appointed under s 7 of the MHA 1983 has powers limited to requiring the person to reside at a specified place, to attend for medical treatment, occupation or training, and to give access at any place where the person is living to people such as doctors and social workers[1]. The direction lasts a period of six months in the first instance and is renewable thereafter for periods of six months and then 12 months[2]. A guardian's powers must be exercised in accordance with the provisions of the MCA 2005 where it applies, i e in the best interests of an incapacitated person should still prevail when making decisions regarding residence and other daily care.

1 MHA 1983, s 8(1). The criminal courts have power to make a guardianship order under powers in MHA 1983, Pt III.
2 MHA 1983, s 20.

Criteria for guardianship

7.37 The person must have either a mental disorder within the meaning of the MHA 1983 (whether or not he also lacks capacity), or a mental illness, severe mental impairment, a psychopathic disorder or mental impairment and his mental disorder must be of a nature or degree which warrants reception into guardianship; it must also be necessary in the interests of the welfare of the person or for the protection of others that he be so received[1]. Severe mental impairment, mental impairment and psychopathic disorder are defined in MHA 1983, s 1(2)[2]. Each of these categories must additionally be associated with abnormally aggressive and socially irresponsible conduct. It is clear, therefore, that these requirements will operate to restrict the type of person who will be eligible for guardianship[3]. Not all incapacitated persons will be eligible. Equally eligibility for guardianship does not depend on the person being incapacitated. Thus a person who is incapacitated by reason of a physical disorder such as a stroke cannot be subject to guardianship.

1 MHA 1983, s 7(2).
2 Provisions of the MHA 2007 which will come into force in October 2008 amend the definition of 'mental disorder'. A new s 1(2A) (inserted by s 2), states that a learning disability is not a mental disorder, including for s 7 purposes, unless it is associated with abnormally aggressive or socially irresponsible conduct. A new s 1(4) defines 'learning disability' as 'a state of arrested or incomplete development'. See also MHA 2007, Sch 1, para 3.Thus there will be little material difference in the application of guardianship powers as a result of amendments in the MHA 2007.
3 See *Re F (Mental Health Act Guardianship)* [2000] 1 FLR 192 in which a restrictive construction was placed on these words.

Application

7.38 The application is to be made by an approved social worker or nearest relative, supported by two medical recommendations[1]. In the event of a disagreement with the nearest relative, proceedings may be required to displace the nearest relative under MHA 1983, s 29, if he is objecting unreasonably or has exercised his right to discharge the person without due regard to the welfare of the person concerned, or the interests of the public. This is by way of an application to the county court. There is no requirement that a social services department apply to the High Court for a best interests declaration (or now a substituted decision) when the statutory criteria for guardianship are fulfilled. Of course, if matters of contact need to be resolved, then such an application may additionally be required[2].

1 MHA 1983, s 7(3).
2 *Lewis v Gibson* [2005] EWCA Civ 587, [2005] 2 FCR 241.

Purpose of guardianship

7.39 The MHA Code of Practice, para 13.1 (1999) states that the:

> 'purpose of guardianship is to enable patients to receive care in the community where it cannot be provided without the use of compulsory powers. It provides an authoritative framework for working with a patient, with a minimum of

constraint, to achieve as independent a life as possible within the community. Where it is used it must be part of the patient's overall care and treatment plan.'

As already stated it is not intended to provide a power of detention and a guardian does not have legal power to detain.

Daily care

7.40 Guardianship offers little in addition to the MCA 2005 in relation to acts of daily care of an incapacitated person. Section 7 contains an implied statutory duty to act to promote the welfare of the patient. An example given has been that of a person being provided with a sexually provocative magazine. The guardian would be under a duty to monitor the effects of the magazine and to remove it if necessary[1]. It may now not be necessary to rely on an implied duty because the MCA 2005 would step in for welfare: so that if the magazine was not promoting the best interests of the person, it could be removed from them. This would equally apply to matters of daily care. Presumably a guardian would also owe a person a common law duty to take reasonable care of them so as not to cause any foreseeable harm.

1 *R v Kent County Council ex p. Marston* (CO 18/19/96) (9 July 1997, unreported).

Consent to treatment

7.41 A person under guardianship is not 'liable to be detained' for the purposes of MHA 1983, Pt IV and so is not subject to the consent to treatment provisions. They cannot be compulsorily medicated for their mental disorde. By section 28 treatment for mental disorder is excluded from the MCA 2005 where provided under part IV (see 7.52). Those under guardianship are therefore potentially subject to the provisions of the MCA for treatment of their mental disorder (see Chapter 16 at 16.18, 16.19 and 16.45, Chapter 9 at 9.41). Treatment for other illnesses or disorders will fall within the MCA 2005 even if the person is subject to part IV of the MHA 1983[1].

1 See 7.52 and Chapter 16 for more on treatment of mental disorders and amendments made by the MHA 2007. The definition of 'medical treatment' under MHA 1983 s 145 is wide and will be widened by MHA 2007, s 7 to include 'psychological intervention and special mental health habilitation, rehabilitation and care'.

Enforcement

7.42 There is no method of enforcement under guardianship. Therefore, the co-operation of the person is an important element in ensuring the success of guardianship. This suggests that the person must be capable of consenting to the conditions of the guardianship or be compliant if incapacitated. If the person absconds from the specified place of residence under the direction he may be brought back to it. There is, however, no power to convey a resisting person to the specified place of residence in the first instance. Local authorities may turn to MHA 1983, s 135 which allows a constable, accompanied by a doctor and a social worker to remove a person, pursuant to a warrant issued by a magistrate, to a place of safety pending an application under the MHA 1983 or other arrangements for treatment and care. Alternatively, an application to the Court of Protection for a declaration that removing the person would be lawful and in his best interests should be considered.

Mental Health Review Tribunal

7.43 There is a right of access exercisable by the person, to a Mental Health Review Tribunal (MHRT) to review the ongoing guardianship[1]. This is exercisable once in the first six months and thereafter during each period of renewal[2]. There is no automatic reference procedure, and a nearest relative cannot make an application because they have an unfettered power to discharge the order[3]. There is a question mark over the efficacy of this system as a safeguard, for someone who is incapacitated and may not be able to make an application. There is an obligation on the managers of the care home to make every effort to inform and assist the person by providing information[4]. The powers of the MHRT are limited to those prescribed under the MHA 1983[5]. Thus it has no power to determine the legality of the application process. Nor, it is suggested, would it have the power to determine or rule on issues of deprivation of liberty should they arise for a person under guardianship[6].

1 MHA 1983, s 66(1)(c).
2 MHA 1983, s 66(2)(c).
3 MHA 1983, s 23(2)(b). There is no barring order power under s 25. The Secretary of State may refer an application to the MHRT if requested to do so: s 67(1).
4 See *R (on the application of H) v Secretary of State for Health* [2005] UKHL 60; [2005] 4 All ER 1311 which dealt with the issue in the context of an incapacitated patient detained under s 2 and held that their inability to make an application to the MHRT themselves was not incompatible with Article 5(4) ECHR.
5 MHA 1983, s 72(4).
6 Amendments to be introduced in April 2009 will include a new authorisation process under Sch A1 and powers of court in s 16A. See Chapter 9 and also Chapter 16 at 16.45 for more on the overlap between the MCA and guardianship under the MHA 1983.

After care under supervision, leave of absence, after-care and community treatment orders

7.44 There are other community care regimes under the MHA 1983 which are accessed via hospital detention. These are after care under supervision (s 25A); leave of absence from hospital (s 17) and after-care following discharge from hospital (s 117). From October 2008 community treatment orders (s 17A) will replace after-care under supervision which is to be abolished[1]. For the position of a person subject to guardianship or detention in hospital, whether granted leave of absence or not, community treatment order and after-care under supervision, and whether or not they will be eligible for care involving a deprivation of liberty authorised under the new MCA 2005 regime once it is in force, see Chapter 9 at 9.41–9.44. A person under s 117 may be so eligible, so long as it is also in his best interests and fulfils all the assessment requirements under that regime. The MCA is not intended to provide, and should not be used as, a default detention power once a person is discharged from the MHA 1983. Section 117 is considered below.

1 MHA 2007, s 32 introduces a new s 17A which deals with community treatment orders. See Chapter 16 at 16.8.

Benefits of guardianship

7.45 It will be apparent that where the provision of community care for an incapacitated person requires residence at a particular place, this may be achieved by the use of powers under the MCA 2005 or under MHA 1983 guardianship, subject to differing qualifying criteria. Under the MCA 2005 such decisions may be taken by family or carers, in an informal manner, if the person is compliant and no unreasonable force or coercion is required. As such they would be protected by MCA 2005, ss 5 and 6. They may also be taken by a welfare donee under proper authority, or in the event of a dispute, by the court or a court deputy. In the majority of cases, therefore, guardianship is unlikely to add anything significant.

The Main Code makes the following points in connection with deciding between guardianship and MCA 2005:

> '[The local authority] may conclude that guardianship is the best option for a person with a mental disorder who lacks capacity to make those decisions if, for example:
>
> - they think it is important that one person or authority should be in charge of making decisions about where the person should live (for example, where there have been long-running or difficult disagreements about where the person should live)
> - they think the person will probably respond well to the authority and attention of a guardian, and so be more prepared to accept treatment for the mental disorder (whether they are able to consent to it or it is being provided for them under the MCA), or
> - they need authority to return the person to the place they are to live (for example, a care home) if they were to go absent. Decision-makers must never consider guardianship as a way to avoid applying the MCA.' (para 13.20)

In addition it is worth remembering that there is no power to regulate contact[1] with others under guardianship apart from the blunt situation in which a person is removed from the care of a particular person. If more measured or monitored contact arrangements are to be adjudicated upon the Court of Protection must be asked to make that decision, in the absence of informal resolution.

1 *Re F (Mental Health Act: Guardianship)* [2000] 1 FLR 192 per Thorpe LJ.

Deprivation of liberty

7.46 Although guardianship is not intended to involve a deprivation of liberty[1], in reality many, whether under guardianship or not, find themselves in institutions in which they are effectively deprived of their liberty, for example, because their care home operates a locked door policy, or because individuals are prevented from leaving for their own protection. Even though guardianship offers some of the safeguards that a deprivation of liberty process demands, namely, a defined procedure of application involving medical recommendation and a speedy and regular review by a MHRT[2], there are clear shortcomings in this procedure for patients under guardianship who may be deprived of their liberty, as discussed above. The simple point, however, is that guardianship is not designed, nor lawful, for this purpose.

Whether or not a person is detained is a question of fact[3]. The proper approach to a person deprived of their liberty prior to the coming into force of the MHA 2007 and amendments to the MCA 2005, is discussed at 7.8 above. See also Chapter 9.

1 Main Code, para 13.16.
2 *HL v United Kingdom* (2005) 40 EHRR 32.
3 See Chapter 9.
4 *R v Bournewood Community and Mental Health NHS Trust, ex p L* [1999] 1 AC 458.

EXCLUDED DECISIONS

Family relationships: excluded by MCA 2005, s 27

7.47 The following personal decisions are expressly excluded from the scheme of the MCA 2005 so that decisions cannot be made on behalf of incapacitated adults by others in respect of them. This would include by welfare donees, court deputies, carers and family or the Court of Protection. This reflects the position at common law. The decisions are the following:

- consenting to marriage or civil partnership;
- consenting to have sexual relations;
- consenting to a decree of divorce after two years separation;
- consenting to a dissolution order in relation to a civil partnership on the basis of a two year separation;
- consenting to a child's being placed for adoption by an adoption agency;
- consenting to the making of an adoption order;
- discharging parental responsibilities in matters not relating to a child's property;
- giving consent under the Human Fertilisation and Embryology Act 1990 eg egg and sperm donation and storage.

It is suggested that s 27 does not prevent the Court of Protection deciding issues of capacity in relation to the excluded categories, nor from preventing or restraining marriage for a particular person – see 7.50) in accordance with the principles of the MCA. Capacity decisions in relation to some of the above may arise in the context of other welfare decision-making, eg the issue of marriage, or forced or arranged marriage, or sexual relations, for an incapacitated adult may well impact on other arrangements such as residence and contact.

The test of capacity to marry and have sexual relations in common law has been approached on a different basis from that for other welfare decisions, such as medical treatment (see below). Therefore, it does not easily translate into the definition under MCA 2005, s 3. The Main Code does offer some assistance and has been considered by the High Court. It adverts to the variety of different common law tests of capacity (including for marriage) that are not replaced by the MCA 2005, noting that judges in other courts can choose whether to adopt the s 3 definition if appropriate. Thus it is suggested that the Court of Protection exercising its statutory jurisdiction under the MCA 2005 is not entitled to disregard the capacity test in s 3 in any type of case, but judges determining issues of capacity in other courts can adopt the new definition if appropriate, having regard to the existing common law[1].

1 Main Code, para 4.33 and *Local Authority X v MM (by her litigation friend the Official Solicitor) and KM* [2007] EWHC 2003 (Fam), [2007] Fam Law 1132 at 80. See also 7.12 above, 7.49, fn 1 and Chapter 15 on civil litigation at 15.1 and 15.4.

Consenting to marriage and to sexual relations[1]

7.48 The basic proposition is that no one, not even the Court of Protection, may consent to marriage, or sexual relations, on behalf of an incapacitated person. The doctrine of necessity has no application in this context.

1 *Sheffield County Council v E* [2004] EWCH 2808 (Fam), [2005] 2 WLR 953 per Munby J; *X City Council v MB, NB and MAB (by his litigation friend the Official Solicitor)* [2006] EWCH 168 (Fam), [2006] 2 FLR 968.

Capacity to marry and have sexual relations under common law

7.49 The role of the court with regard to marriage (or sexual relations) at common law is simply to declare whether a person has capacity to understand the nature of the marriage contract and the duties and responsibilities that are involved, or the nature and character of the sexual act. The court has held that a person does not require a high degree of capacity for either. The marriage contract is a relatively simple one. The court does not have jurisdiction to decide whether or not, if the person lacks the requisite capacity, it is in their best interests to get married ie the court cannot consent to a marriage. If a person purports to marry, the 'marriage' may be challenged and is voidable. There can be no valid marriage in the absence of consent and the appropriate form of declaration is that 'any marriage entered into by [ ] would not be recognised under English law'[1].

The common law test of capacity to consent to sexual relations is essentially that required by the criminal law. The question is 'Does the person have sufficient knowledge and understanding of the nature and character – the *sexual* nature and character – of the act of sexual intercourse, and of the reasonably foreseeable consequences of sexual intercourse, to have the capacity to choose whether or not to engage in it, the capacity to decide whether to give or withhold consent to sexual intercourse (and, where relevant, to communicate their choice to their spouse)?' This question is not the same as whether the person has capacity to marry, although a sexual relationship is 'generally speaking' implicit in a marriage and so 'someone who lacks capacity to consent to sexual relations will for that very reason necessarily lack capacity to marry'. The converse may not be true. As with capacity to marry, no expert guidance is required to aid the person's understanding. The issues are not so complex as to require the refined analysis of the case law relating to capacity for medical treatment, although it remains relevant[2].

The questions of capacity to marry or have sexual relations are not considered by reference to any particular individual ie prospective partner, but instead more generally: 'it is difficult to see how it can sensibly be said that [she] has capacity to consent to a particular sexual act with Y whilst at the same time lacking capacity to consent to precisely the same sexual act with Z'[3].

The threshold for capacity to consent to sexual relations is such as to be sensitive to the fact that it is necessary not to forbid sexual expression to those of low intelligence. Similarly for marriage, that it is capable of enriching the lives of those of limited or borderline capacity.

The determination of capacity to consent to marriage or sexual relations is now arguably affected by the provisions of the MCA 2005 and one which may be decided by the Court of Protection.

1 *X City Council v MB, NB and MAB (by his litigation friend the Official Solicitor)* [2006] 2 FLR 968. Approved by the Court of Appeal in *City of Westminster Social and Community Services Department v C* [2008] EWCA Civ 198, [2008] All ER (D) 276 (Mar).

2 *Local Authority X v MM (by her litigation friend the Official Solicitor) and KM* [2007] EWHC 2003 (Fam).

3 *Local Authority X v MM (by her litigation friend the Official Solicitor) and KM* [2007] EWHC 2003 (Fam) at [87].

Injunctive relief and marriage at common law

7.50 In appropriate circumstances, the High Court has restrained the person responsible for an adult incapacitated in relation to marriage from arranging a marriage if required to do so to protect the best interests of that person[1]. A 'welfare' appraisal and a balance sheet approach as outlined above is appropriate. Intervention is justified if there is a real possibility of harm as set out in *Re H (Minors) (Sexual abuse: standard of proof)*[2]. The approach taken is that 'prevention is better than cure'[3]. See also below and *Re SK (Proposed Plaintiff) (An Adult by her litigation friend)*[4]. As stated above at 7.47 it is suggested that the exclusions in s 27 would not appear to stop the court from preventing or restraining marriage in the best interests of the person.

1 *M v B, A and S (by the Official Solicitor)* [2005] EWCH 1681 (Fam), [2006] 1 FLR 117 per Sumner J. The Forced Marriage (Civil Protection) Act 2007 gained Royal Assent on 26 July 2007 and is not yet in force. It amends the Family Law Act 1996 to introduce 'forced marriage protection orders' to protect any person faced with forced marriage, or a victim of one. A forced marriage is one not entered into with full and free consent. An order may contain prohibitions, restrictions and requirement or other terms. This Act makes no reference to the 'best interests' principle, the MCA, or the Court of Protection but is clearly of relevance in protecting those who are incapacitated and enter into

marriage. An order is not dependent on there being 'family proceedings' underway and does not require the person to be incapacitated. This Act would appear to provide another route to protecting a person from being subjected to a forced marriage.

2 [1996] AC 563.

3 *X City Council v MB, NB and MAB (by his litigation friend the Official Solicitor)* [2006] EWCH 168 (Fam), [2006] 2 FLR 968 at para 27.

4 [2005] 2 FLR 230.

Vulnerable adults with capacity (and marriage)

7.51 The inherent jurisdiction has recently been extended to protect a vulnerable adult not lacking in capacity, but subjected to constraint, coercion and undue influence from her parents, such that she was held to be unable to make a free choice or express her genuine consent to any marriage and was thereby incapacitated. The young woman in question was not mentally incapacitated but was profoundly deaf, had no speech, or oral communication skills and had visual loss in one eye. She could not lip read her family's mother tongue which was Punjabi, and they were unable to use British Sign Language. Accepting evidence that there was a real possibility that the parents would remove their daughter to Pakistan for marriage and that she was unable to protect herself, the court granted an injunction restraining the parents from removing her from the jurisdiction. In doing so the judge underlined the flexible nature of declaratory relief[1]. The court has granted relief in circumstances where the vulnerable adult was not within the jurisdiction but in Pakistan. In the face of evidence that the young woman was being detained there against her will, it was considered appropriate to grant relief even if it should turn out later that she was consenting[2].

1 *Re SA (Vulnerable Adults with capacity: marriage)* [2006] 1 FLR 867.

2 *Re SK (Proposed Plaintiff) (An Adult by her litigation friend)* [2005] 2 FLR 230 per Singer J. See fn 1 to 7.50 above in relation to the Force Marriage (Civil Protection) Act 2007 and Chapter 10 at 10.19.

Medical treatment for mental disorder

7.52 Authorising the giving of, or consent to, medical treatment for mental disorder is expressly excluded from the MCA 2005 where it is being provided under Pt IV of the MHA 1983. 'Medical treatment', 'mental disorder' and 'patient', have the same meaning as in the MHA 1983. 'Medical treatment' is defined widely (see 7.41 fn).

If a compliant incapacitated person with a mental illness within the definition contained in the MHA 1983 requires medical treatment for their mental illness, e.g. ECT, then they do not need to be detained under the MHA 1983 in order to be treated. If they are within the scope of the MHA 1983, and are objecting to the proposed treatment or part of it, then they must be treated under the MHA 1983 and will be ineligible for treatment under the MCA 2005 under the forthcoming amendments made by the MHA 2007.[1] If they are not within the scope of the MHA 1983 and are objecting to admission to hospital for assessment or treatment of their mental disorder, then the forthcoming provisions of the MCA 2005 are unlikely to assist (see Chapter 9 at 9.41 for the relevant eligibility criteria). This latter type of case must be referred to the High Court for an authorisation under its inherent jurisdiction [2].

1 MCA 2005, Sch 1A as inserted by MHA 2007, Sch 8. See also amendments to the consent to treatment provisions regarding ECT which will in future involve advance decisions, welfare donee or court deputy if appropriate. See Chapter 16 at 16.6. For exceptions regarding the Court and donees in relation to Community Treatment Orders see Chapter 5 at 5.76 and 5.22.

2 See Chapter 16, case study 3 and *Surrey County Council v MB, SB and A PCT* [2007] EWHC 2290 (Fam) for an example of a case in which the MHA did not apply and 16.19 for a consideration of when the MCA or MHA might apply for treatment for mental disorder.

WHAT REMAINS OF THE INHERENT JURISDICTION

7.53 The inherent jurisdiction will remain relevant for vulnerable adults with capacity, for example, those who are deemed incapacitated through an inability to exercise free choice, and some cases of treatment for mental disorder (see 7.51 and 7.52 above). The Court of Appeal has held that the MCA 2005 does not in any event oust the inherent jurisdiction of the High Court and remains to fill any gap that may exist in the MCA for the protection of incapacitated adults also[1]. Cases heard by the appropriate level of judge, namely, a judge of the High Court, should not be hindered by any lack of jurisdiction under the MCA 2005.

In a case of fluctuating capacity the Court of Protection will be seized of the matter at the time of incapacity and may exercise its powers to protect the future position even once capacity has been regained[2].

This point is also considered in the medical treatment context in Chapter 8 at 8.11.

1 *City of Westminster Social and Community Services Department v C* [2008] EWCA Civ 198, [2008] All ER (D) 276 (Mar).

2 *Re G (An Adult) (Mental Capacity: court's jurisdiction)* [2004] EWHC 2222 (Fam), [2004] All ER (D) 33 (Oct). As to future medical treatment see also *D v A NHS Trust (by her Litigation Friend the Official Solicitor)* [2003] EWHC 2793, [2004] 1 FLR 1110 and *Re Wyatt* [2005] EWHC 2293 (Fam), [2005] 4 All ER 1325 and *Wyatt v Portsmouth NHS Trust* [2005] EWCA Civ 1181, [2005] 3 FCR 263. See also Chapter 10 at 10.3.

COMMUNITY CARE REGIME

7.54 The term 'community care services' embraces primarily residential care and the provision of home helps, adaptations, day centres and meals on wheels. These are largely the responsibility of local social services departments, but are often provided by the NHS which also now carries community care responsibilities. This is an extensive area of law contained in statutes, guidance and case law. It is not intended, nor possible to provide a detailed exposition of its features in this chapter[1]. Instead the intention is to provide an overview of the entitlement to and provision of community care services that may be of relevance to decision-makers under the MCA 2005, ie day-to-day carers and professionals, welfare donees and IMCAs in particular.

The National Health Service and Community Care Act 1990 (NHSCCA 1990) defines 'community care services'. It sets out a common framework for the assessment of needs, and the provision of all services falling under its umbrella, which is at the heart of the provision of community care services. This is a two stage process whereby a local authority first has a duty to carry out an assessment of needs and, secondly, decides whether the provision of any services on its part is required.

1 See Clements and Thompson, *Community Care and the Law* (4th edn) LAG.

Public law

7.55 In carrying out obligations under this statutory regime, a local (and other) authority is required to comply with the requirements of proper and fair decision-making under public law principles. In order to be lawful all decisions must comply with the requirements of:

1 legality;
2 rationality (the standard of *Wednesbury* unreasonableness applies);
3 procedural propriety (this includes proper consultation and compliance with directions, guidance and policy); and
4 compatibility with the person's rights under the ECHR.

Public law challenges by way of judicial review are considered further at Chapter 15.

Community care services

7.56 A local authority[1] may provide or arrange to be provided services under any of the following provisions:

(a) National Assistance Act 1948 (NAA 1948), Pt III;
(b) Health Services and Public Health Act 1968 (HSPHA 1968), s 45;
(c) National Health Service Act 2006[2] (NHSA 2006), s 254 and Sch 20; and
(d) Mental Health Act 1983 (MHA 1983), s 117.

1 Defined in NHSCCA 1990, s 46(3).
2 National Health Service Act (Wales) 2006, s 192 and Sch 15.

NAA 1948, Part III

7.57 Of relevance under the MCA 2005 is:

- the duty on local authorities to provide residential accommodation for those aged 18 or over, or who *by reason of age, illness, disability or any other circumstances* are in need of care and attention which is not otherwise available to them (s 21(1)(a));
- the duty to make arrangements promoting the welfare of those over 18, or who are blind, deaf, dumb or suffer from a mental disorder of any

description and other person who are substantially and permanently handicapped by illness, injury or congenital deformity or other prescribed disabilities (s 29(1)). This covers the provision by the local authority or voluntary agency or other person, of:

- educational training about an individual's disabilities at home or elsewhere;
- occupational workshops and hostels;
- work at home or elsewhere;
- recreational facilities at home or elsewhere (s 29(4) and s 30);

- the s 29 duty encompasses the duty to make provision of welfare services under s 2 of the Chronically Sick and Disabled Persons Act 1970 (CSDPA 1970):
  - practical assistance in the home;
  - provision of or assistance obtaining radio, television, library or other similar recreational facilities;
  - provision of lectures, games, outings or other recreational facilities outside home, or assistance in taking advantage of available educational facilities;
  - travel for the purposes of taking advantage of arrangements under s 29 or similar;
  - assistance in carrying out home adaptations or similar;
  - holidays;
  - meals at home or elsewhere;
  - provision of, or assistance obtaining a telephone and any special equipment necessary to enable the use of a telephone.

HSPHA 1968, s 45

7.58 This concerns the promotion of the welfare of the elderly by local authorities or voluntary organisation.

NHSA 2006, s 254 and Sch 20

7.59 Authorities have a duty to provide for:

- care of mothers;
- prevention of illness, care and after-care;
- home help and laundry facilities.

MHA 1983, s 117

7.60 There is a duty placed on social services and health authorities to provide after-care for mentally disordered people discharged from compulsory hospital treatment under the MHA 1983. It also applies to those on s 17[1] leave from hospital, and restricted patients detained under ss 37 and 41 who are conditionally discharged under MHA 1983, s 73(2). This duty accounts for only a small number of those entitled to community care services. The majority of those with mental health problems requiring community services will receive them under other enactments (see above). Section 117 creates an entitlement to a wide range of services including accommodation. There is no power to charge for any of these services. The duty arises once discharge has taken place. The duty on the relevant authority is to 'use its best endeavours to procure' services which it deems necessary, or which have been directed by a Mental Health Review Tribunal[2].

1 And s 17A from October 2008 which relates to those under a community treatment order. MHA 2007, Sch 3, para 24 amends s 117 to include all 'community patients'.

2 See *R (on the application of K) v Camden and Islington Health Authority* [2001] 3 WLR 553; *R (on the application of B) v Camden London Borough Council* [2005] EWHC (Admin) 1366, 85 BMLR 28; *R (on the application of H) Secretary of State for the Home Department* [2003] UKHL 59, [2004] 2 AC 253 [2003] 3 WLR 1278; *R v Ealing District Health Authority, ex p Fox* [1993] 3 All ER 170, [1993] 1 WLR 373; *R v Mental Health Review Tribunal ex p Hall* [1999] 4 All ER 883, [2000] 1 WLR 1323; *R v Manchester City Council ex p Stennett* [2002] UKHL 34, [2002] 3 WLR 584 (no charging).

Duty to assess needs

7.61 By NHSCCA 1990, s 47(1)(a) there is a *duty* on a local authority to assess a person's needs for community care services as defined above. This duty arises 'where it appears to a local authority that any person for whom they may provide or arrange for the provision of community care may be in need of such services'. The identification of a potential need is a matter of professional judgement normally carried out by social workers.

- This duty is applicable to all and not only to those lacking in mental capacity.
- The threshold for triggering this duty is low[1].
- There is no need to request an assessment.
- It is not resource dependent.
- The duty not displaced by entitlement to continuing NHS care[2].
- Financial circumstances are irrelevant to this duty[3].

1 *R v Bristol City Council ex p Penfold* [1998] 1 CCLR 315.

2 Clements and Thompson at 3.76.

3 Local authority circular LAC (98)19 available on www.dh.gov.uk.

Disabled person[1]

7.62 If at any time during the assessment of needs it appears to the local authority that the person being assessed is disabled, there is a duty to proceed to make a decision as to the services required under s 4 of the Disabled Persons (Services, Consultation and Representation) Act 1986 without any request under that provision[2].

1 As defined by the Disabled Persons (Services, Consultation and Representation) Act 1986.

2 Discrimination in the provisions of services under the Disability Discrimination Act 1995 is considered in Chapter 18.

Involvement of other services/agencies

7.63 There is a duty to notify a relevant Primary Care Trust, Health Authority or local housing authority, and to invite them to assist in the assessment of needs and the decision to provide services, to such extent as is reasonable, if during the assessment of needs it appears to the local authority that there may be need for health or housing provision[1].

[1] NHSCCA 1990, s 47(3).

Temporary or urgent provision prior to assessment

7.64 A local authority is not prevented from providing community care services on a temporary basis without a prior assessment, if in its opinion the person's condition is such that they are required as a matter of urgency. An assessment of needs must be done as soon as practicable thereafter, however[1].

[1] NHSCCA 1990, s 47(5), (6).

Scope of an assessment

7.65 This will be determined by the complexity of the person's presenting needs. It may involve a multi-disciplinary approach with assessments by other disciplines, for example, occupational speech and language and other therapists, as required.

Assessments of incapacitated adults

7.66 The Secretary of State has issued directions as to the form an assessment should take under NHSCCA 1990, s 47(4)[1]. This is of importance when assessing a person without mental capacity to participate fully in the assessment process. The directions require consultation with the person, including with appropriate carers. The performance of such an assessment is now to be carried out in accordance with the principles of the MCA 2005 and in the person's best interests. A formal decision regarding the person's capacity should be made and, it is suggested, recorded. Once that is done ss 1 and 4 will be relevant in terms of guiding the assessment in the person's best interests[2].

Additionally, it will be necessary to identify the existence of any MCA 2005 decision-makers such as a welfare donee or court appointed deputy for consultation in decision-making. Donees or deputies with solely financial powers are also relevant for consultation if the person is likely to have sufficient funds to pay for their care.

If the assessment concerns the provision of long term accommodation or the change of such accommodation, the instruction of an IMCA may be mandated if the person has no other appropriate person to consult (see Chapter 6).

There is a discretion to instruct an IMCA in relation to a care review or if action is being taken under a protection of vulnerable adults policy. In the absence of strict eligibility for an IMCA, the instruction of an independent advocate should in any event be considered to support and represent a person lacking capacity during the assessment process.

1 In England these are Community Care Assessments Directions 2004 available at www.dh-.gov.uk. No directions exist in relation to Wales, but proper public law principles apply.
2 An assessor should pay close regard to the Main Code in this regard. Policy and other guidance accompanying the NHSCCA 1990 also highlights the need for proper communication with those lacking capacity: *Community Care in the Next Decade and Beyond: policy guidance* HMSO 1990. See also Clements and Thompson at 3.111.

Provision of assessed needs or service provision decision

7.67 NHSCCA 1990, s 47(1)(b) contains a separate stage of the process at which the local authority must decide which of a person's identified needs call for the provision of community care services. In making that decision the local authority must have regard to the prior assessment of needs. There is no obligation to provide all of the assessed needs. This is the crucial decision by which the actual provision of services for an individual is determined. Resources are relevant to the exercise of this discretion.[1]

1 See the Court of Appeal in *R v Gloucestershire CC ex p Barry* [1996] 4 All ER 421; 1 CCLR 19. This part of the decision of the CA was not reversed in the HL.

Individual financial circumstances

7.68 These are not relevant to the exercise of the discretion but are relevant insofar as the person may be required to contribute to the cost of the service to be provided. NAA 1948, s 21 permits a local authority to treat a person with sufficient assets as not being in need of care and attention which is 'not otherwise available' ie they can afford to pay for and arrange their own care. This assumes also that the person is able to, or has someone who is willing and able to make suitable alternative arrangements.

Eligibility criteria and guidance

7.69 The desirability of eligibility criteria by which local authorities could standardise provision of services has been recognised. Detailed policy guidance has been issued by the Department of Health and the Welsh Assembly that standardises individual local authority eligibility criteria for community care services. These are known as FACS 2002 in England, and UFSAMC 2002 in Wales.

The relationship between eligibility criteria and resources is a knotty one. In general local authorities are entitled to take into account available resources when drawing up such criteria. This is subject to:

(a) an obligation to re-assess if the authority wishes to re-draw the criteria due to resources;
(b) resources are relevant to the criteria and not the assessment of needs;
(c) resources cannot be the sole criterion; and
(d) resources cannot justify a violation of human rights[1].

1 Clements and Thompson at 3.166.

Care planning

7.70 Once an authority has decided under NHSCCA 1990, s 47(1)(b) that services are required then it must provide those services. The process of providing services is called 'care planning' and good practice requires that a written care plan of the services an individual is entitled to receive and associated information should be prepared. See 7.73.

Documentation

Written assessments

7.71 There is no requirement that assessments be recorded in writing. There is no express right vested in a person to receive a copy of an assessment. Most local authorities provide a copy of a care plan (see 7.73) to the assessed person. A copy of the assessment may be obtained by an application under the Data Protection Act 1998 (see Chapter 14).

Reviews and reassessments

7.72 Guidance underpins the need for periodic review and reassessment. An initial review should be held at three months and thereafter annually, or more often depending on circumstances.

Care plans

7.73 These are the cornerstone of the provision of community care services but are not provided for by statute. There is extensive policy and guidance dealing with (a) format and content and (b) principles and aims underpinning the content[1]. Following the appropriate guidance can be unwieldy because it consists of the 1990 policy guidance to the NHSCCA 1990 (now out of print), FACS 2002, FACS practice guidance and 1991 practice guidance[2]. The role of welfare donees in the making of care plans is discussed in Chapter 5 at 5.20.

1 See in particular *Caring for People: Community Care in the next decade and beyond* (Cmd 849, HMSO 1989) which states that 'promoting choice and independence underlies all the Government's proposals'.
2 *Clements and Thompson* at 4.3 ff.

Challenging care plans

7.74 The proper procedure will usually be the local authority complaints procedure which may be a better vehicle for disputing the actual content of the plan, because judicial review does not normally permit a review of the merits of a decision.

Care plans must satisfy the demands of the various policy and practice guidance that is applicable in any particular case. In addition they must comply with public law and good administrative practice. This is aimed at providing clarity for the person concerned in terms of detail and the process by which the decision was reached.

If they do not satisfy these demands they may become the subject of judicial review. A care plan cannot be quashed, but the court may make a mandatory order requiring the authority to provide a care plan that complies with specified guidance, a declaratory order that the authority has acted unlawfully and in breach of policy and/or guidance in failing to make service provision decision under NHSCCA 1990, s 47(1)(b) and a declaration that the authority has acted unlawfully and contrary to policy guidance in failing to produce a lawful care plan[1].

1 *R v Islington LBC ex p Rixon* [1998] CCLR 119; *R v Sutton London Borough Council ex p Tucker* [1998] CCLR 251.

Guidance for specific groups of people

Learning disabled

7.75 People with learning disabilities fall within the definition of 'disabled person' for the purposes of all the main community care statutes (see 7.56). Additionally, the Disability Discrimination Act 1995 applies to this group which therefore has an equal right of access to these services (see Chapter 18). There is much specific guidance that is relevant including HSG (92)43 and LAC (92)17 in relation to NHS continuing health care. The overarching approach to learning disability is provided for in *Valuing People: A New Strategy for Learning Disability for the 21st Century*[1]. The guiding principles are 'Rights, independence, choice and inclusion'. This is intended to be a 'person-centred' approach to planning[2].

1 Published on 28 January 2002 and available at http://www.dh.gov.uk/en/Publicationsandstatistics/Publications/PublicationsPolicyAndGuidance/DH_4006564. See also the implementation guidance HSC2001/016: LAC(2001)23. The policy in Wales is still under development. A 1983 Welsh Office Strategy for Services for Mentally Handicapped People updated in 1994 is unavailable on the internet. In 2004 the Welsh Assembly issued a policy document: *Guidance on Service Principles and Service Responses for Adults and Older Persons with a Learning Disability*.

2 See also *Planning with People Towards Person Centred Approaches – Guidance for Partnership Boards* (Department of Health, 2001). See also guidance of January 2002 on http://www.dh.gov.uk/en/Publicationsandstatistics/Publications/PublicationsPolicyAndGuidance/DH_4006564.

Older people (over 60)

7.76 The 2001 *National Service Framework for Older People*[1] contains eight key service standards: anti-discrimination, person-centred care, intermediate care, general hospital care, stroke, falls, mental health and promotion of active life in older age. This includes a single assessment process so that a person does not have to retell their story on numerous occasions[2].

1 *The Strategy for Older People in Wales* (2003) in Wales.
2 HSC 2002/001 and LAC (2002)1.

Mentally disordered

7.77 The definition of 'mental disorder' is contained in MHA 1983, s 1 (as amended, though not yet in force)[1]. Entitlement to services is not based on the use of compulsory powers under the MHA 1983). There is a 1999 'National Service Framework for Mental Health'[2]. There are seven standards. Central to the assessment process is the 'Care Programme Approach' (CPA)[3] which is intended to apply to all those in contact with specialist psychiatric services and provides for a 'standard' or 'enhanced' care plan depending on the complexity of the needs of the individual. This is a health-led assessment process although the obligation falls jointly upon health and social services. The most recent update to the CPA was in 1999[4]. Also relevant here is the MHA Code of Practice (1999) which contains guidance on the application of the CPA in Chapter 27. The overlap between the CPA, care planning under NHSCCA 1990, s 47, and after-care under MHA 1983, s 117 has caused some service confusion. An ineligibility under CPA does not preclude assessment under NHSCCA 1990, s 47[5].

1 MHA 2007 introduces amendments to the MHA 1983 some of which will come into force in October 2008.
2 2002 and 2005 in Wales.
3 HC(90)23:LASSL(90)11; WC19/96 for Wales.
4 See *Guidance on the Discharge of Mentally Disordered People and their Continuing Care in the Community* (HSG (94)27: LASSL(94)4); *Effective care co-ordination in mental health services: modernising the care programme approach – a policy booklet* (1999). *Mental Health Policy Wales Implementation Guidance: The Care Programme Approach for Mental Health Service Users* (Welsh Assembly, 2003).
5 *R (on the application of HP and KP) v Islington London Borough Council* (2004) 82 BMLR 113.

PRACTICE POINTS

Care plans

7.78 Most of the daily care of incapacitated persons will be handled under the protection of ss 5 and 6 whether at home or in residential care. In either situation a care planning process should be carried out, ie an assessment of needs, a decision regarding service provision followed by a care plan. The care plan should identify:

1 the functional capacity of the person in relation to various daily and other tasks;
2 the ability of and the method by which the person communicates, and how daily and other tasks may be best explained to them in order to achieve the fullest possible participation and understanding of what is to be done;
3 family, friends, donees of LPAs etc who are available and willing and able to be consulted in relation to the care of the person;
4 if family or friends are unwilling or unable to act as consultees, then the need for an IMCA for appropriate decisions should be highlighted;
5 if any restraint may be required in relation to the person's care; and detailed instructions as to its use and limits;
6 if any restraint or other measures in place, eg locked doors, mean that the person is deprived of their liberty, in which case the court's authorisation should be sought.

Applications to the court

7.79 Whether to the Administrative Court for judicial review or the Court of Protection, applications to the court will be a matter of last resort. Most applications concerning welfare disputes are likely to be initiated by social services departments. Public law challenges to service provision and care plans are likely to be made by the person through a litigation friend.

Once an application to the Court of Protection for a best interests decision is made, and permission granted, the procedure to be followed is likely to mirror that which pertained under the inherent jurisdiction. A directions hearing will be required at which the court will appoint the Official Solicitor[1] (or other litigation friend) to represent the incapacitated person, determine the need for expert evidence, what investigations are required, make any necessary orders, including interim relief, and a date for a final hearing.

Orders sought may relate to: contact, disclosure of records, reasonable access to the person for the purposes of assessment and reporting. Records are likely to include: health, including hospital, GP and community records if held separately, social care records, housing, bank and building society and police.

Thereafter the facts of the case will determine the frequency with which the matter comes before the court for the purposes of directions and further order prior to a final hearing.

It will be apparent that some cases involving the welfare of incapacitated adults may only involve issues of public law, in which case they should only be pursued in the Administrative Court in an application for judicial review (see Chapter 15). If the decision is not amenable to judicial review, the court, in determining a person's best interests, must choose between the services that are available, but 'an endless pursuit for the perfect is certainly not a result that the court can dictate'[2].

1 See Official Solicitor's practice note in relation to medical and welfare cases issued on 28 July 2006 which still contains useful guidance: [2006] 2 FLR 373.

2 *Surrey County Council v MB, SB and A PCT* [2007] EWHC 2290 (Fam) at 30.

Deprivation of liberty

7.80 Until April 2009, or the date on which the MCA amendments permitting a deprivation of liberty are implemented, the court must exercise special care if asked to do something which would amount to authorising a deprivation of liberty. Care must be taken to ensure that the Article 5 ECHR requirements in relation to medical evidence of 'unsound mind', and regular reviews, if the deprivation is to be for more than a short and defined period, are complied with (see 7.8 above, Chapter 9 at 9.15 and Chapter 10 at 10.34). It is suggested that the period in question should be no more than 28 days in the first instance – that being the assessment period under MHA 1983, s 2. Court authorisation should be obtained in advance of any actual deprivation of liberty taking place.

The following are suggested as being necessary in cases of detention under the inherent jurisdiction:

- any order the court makes must be based upon and justified by convincing evidence from appropriate experts that the treatment regime proposed:
  (a) accords with expert medical opinion, and
  (b) is therapeutically necessary;
- any order the court makes should direct or authorise the minimum degree of force or restraint, and in the case of an order directing or authorising the detention of the a child the minimum period of detention, consistent with the welfare principle;
- any order directing or authorising detention should:
  (a) specify the place where the person is to be detained;
  (b) specify:
    (i) the maximum period for which the detention is authorised and, if thought appropriate;
    (ii) a date on which the matter is to be reviewed by the court; and
- any order directing or authorising detention should contain an express liberty to any party (including the incapacitated person) to apply to the court for further directions on the shortest reasonable notice[1].

There are currently likely to be many incapacitated people in care homes whether under guardianship of the MHA 1983 or not who are effectively deprived of their liberty as a result of the care planning process. This must be seen as distinct from those who are detained in hospital under the MHA 1983 whose detention is not the product of care planning. Responsible local authorities and NHS Trusts must now review such patients to ensure that they are not being deprived of their liberty without court authorisation and make applications to the court where necessary.

After April 2009 the procedures described in Chapter 9 will apply.

[1] Per Munby J in *Re PS (incapacitated or vulnerable adult)* [2007] EWHC 623 at paras 26 and 27, [2007] FLR 1083.

Chapter 8

MEDICAL CARE

INTRODUCTION

8.1 The basic principle underpinning the need for the development of the best interests jurisdiction, and now the MCA 2005 itself, is that of individual autonomy. Every individual has autonomy to make their own decisions, and, thus, to perform physically invasive medical treatment upon a patient without their consent or other authority will constitute an assault. This presupposes, however, that the patient is capable of providing consent. Where the patient lacks capacity to do so, the development of the best interests principle and common law doctrine of necessity under the High Court's declaratory jurisdiction have enabled clinicians to act without the need to obtain the express consent of the patient. Accordingly, where the patient lacks capacity to decide, it is the duty of their doctor to treat them in the way they consider, in the exercise of their clinical judgment, to be in the patient's best interests. The capacity and best interests regime is contained in ss 1–4 of the MCA 2005 and described in Chapter 2. The doctrine of necessity is now within ss 5 and 6 which is considered in Chapter 4 and is intended to allow daily acts of healthcare without recourse to the courts.

As we have seen, the MCA 2005 enshrines that development in statutory form and adds a series of requirements designed to ensure that the decision-maker, the clinician in this chapter, uses the best available evidence about the patient's best interests, and consults widely. Further, the consultation must be real, and will be more demanding than at common law. This is not simply in order to ensure that the terms of s 4 are applied, but in particular cases where the holder of a lasting power of attorney (LPA) is enabled to consent to or veto particular healthcare decisions, where the MCA 2005 requires consultation of an independent mental capacity advocate (IMCA), or where the Court of Protection has appointed a deputy in relation to healthcare issues, albeit the latter is likely to occur only in exceptional circumstances. A clinician must additionally be alive to the existence of any relevant advance decision, its terms and applicability to any proposed procedure.

In most respects these changes are unlikely to alter the reality of a clinician's daily practice. The welfare LPA and advance decision are the most radical alterations to the pre-existing position, the true effect of which must yet be observed. In theory, however, (and a point raised during Parliamentary debates on the MCA 2005) there is the prospect of clinicians being placed in a position of bearing the onus to make applications to the court to challenge or determine the validity of an advance decision or the act of welfare donee. These points have been dealt with in detail in Chapters 3 and 5 and will not be considered at length here.

Clearly, the MCA 2005 applies to much more than medical treatment. 'Welfare' within the Act is a term that encompasses healthcare and personal welfare decisions such as residential care and contact with family. The reader is referred to Chapter 7 for a detailed analysis of the MCA 2005 on social welfare decisions, which in terms of principle applies also to medical treatment. In this chapter, however, the focus is on health and medical decision-making. It starts with a discussion of the type of difficult issue that may confront the clinician or patient in medical cases where capacity is in doubt or absent, and the way in which those issues may be resolved. It will be crucial for legal and other practitioners to understand what the law requires in connection with informed consent so as to know how to approach the issue of best interests and the information required for medical decision-making under the MCA 2005. It is then followed by an outline of decision-making in healthcare situations under the Act.

THE MEANING OF 'HEALTHCARE' UNDER THE MCA 2005

8.2 There is no magic test for this; it is largely a matter of common sense. The MCA 2005 is intended to apply to all acts of personal care without the need for fine distinctions of terminology such as health or other welfare. In many respects there will be overlap in terms of any strict categorisation of acts of care. There is a common application system for health and welfare decisions to the Court of Protection (see Chapter 10). If it assists, the Main Code and s 17 provide the following which are illustrative and should not by any means be treated as exhaustive:

Main Code para 6.5: personal care protected under s 5	*Main Code para 7.21: personal welfare donees*	*Section 17: section 16 powers*	*Section 15: declaratory relief. Main code 8.18–8.24*
'Healthcare and treatment			Reserved for serious healthcare and treatment decisions:
• carrying out diagnostic examinations and tests (to identify an illness, condition or other problem)	• consenting to or refusing medical examination and treatment on the donor's behalf	• giving or refusing consent to medical treatment and directions regarding responsibility for health care	• proposed withholding or withdrawal of ANH from persons in PVS
• providing professional medical, dental and similar treatment	• arrangements needed for the donor to be given medical, dental or optical treatment		• organ or bone marrow donation
• giving medication			• non-therapeutic sterilisation
• taking someone to hospital for assessment or treatment			• any other case where there is a doubt as to whether it is in the patient's best interests eg ethical dilemmas or other irresolvable disputes between healthcare staff or staff and family
• providing nursing care (whether in hospital or in the community)			
• carrying out any other necessary medical procedures (for example, taking a blood sample) or therapies (for example, physiotherapy or chiropody)			
• providing care in an emergency.' (Main Code, para 6.5)			

DIFFICULT CAPACITY ISSUES AND MEDICAL TREATMENT

8.3 Difficult issues of capacity with respect to medical treatment are likely to arise most commonly in two broad settings:

- the patient who refuses treatment which the clinician strongly recommends to prevent serious harm, and where the refusal causes the clinician to wonder about the patient's capacity; and
- the patient who clearly lacks capacity and where the question as to what treatment should be provided is a matter of contention between clinician and the patient's family.

The refusing patient

8.4 To recap the fundamentals:

- Every adult with capacity has the right to decide whether or not they will accept medical treatment;.
- Enforced treatment (outside the ambit of compulsory treatment for mental disorder under the MHA 1983) constitutes an assault, however well-intentioned.

The MCA 2005 does not alter this position. It seeks in fact to reinforce the premise of patient autonomy in its opening principles and its reiteration of the requirement to assist the patient to make their own decisions as far as possible[1].

This principle may cause the clinician considerable concern. It means that an adult with capacity — unless suffering from mental illness justifying compulsory treatment for their own protection or that of others under the MHA 1983 — may conclusively decline medical treatment, even if the refusal may risk serious injury or even lead to premature death. This applies to all, including a pregnant woman the life of whose foetus may be jeopardised by her decision[2]. Thus, for example:

- a person who has taken a life-threatening overdose, who does not qualify for compulsory treatment under the MHA 1983, may not be forcibly medically treated if they have capacity and decline; or
- a gravely disabled patient dependent upon ventilation but who retained full capacity, may require discontinuance of all treatment, even if to do so would precipitate his death, and his request must be honoured[3].

The clinicians' role in such a case will be difficult. Unless satisfied that the patient lacks capacity, all they can, and indeed should, do is to attempt to persuade the patient to accept treatment, in as many ways as possible — providing information about the implications of refusal, exploring the reasoning underpinning the patient's refusal, suggesting consultation with others, etc. In the last analysis, however, the patient's refusal is binding, and the clinician is powerless to act.

It is not surprising in those circumstances that the issue of capacity may be raised. Whilst the MCA 2005 describes incapacity as an *inability* to make a decision, the most difficult cases are likely in fact to be those where the patient has very clearly made a decision, but it is a decision which appears so abnormal or rash that it raises a suspicion as to whether it is a decision made in fact with capacity — for example the pregnant woman who needs an emergency caesarean section, and who wants her baby, but who cannot consent to the induction of anaesthesia due to an overwhelming needle phobia.

1 Sections 1–4.
2 See eg *Re MB (an adult: medical treatment)* (1997) 38 BMLR 175 (CA).
3 See eg *Re B (adult: refusal of medicinal treatment)* [2002] EWHC 429 (Fam), [2002] 2 All ER 449.

THE ASSESSMENT OF CAPACITY IN THE MEDICAL SETTING

Capacity

8.5 When faced with a patient such as described in the preceding paragraph, the MCA 2005 sets out a clear line of reasoning: remembering that one must presume capacity unless the contrary is shown, and that an unwise decision does not by itself prove incapacity[1], the clinician needs to ask whether the patient is:

- suffering from an impairment of, or disturbance in the functioning of the mind or brain[2], albeit possibly only temporarily;
- and thereby unable to
  - understand information relevant to a decision;
  - retain that information;
  - use or weigh that information as part of the process of making a decision; or
  - communicate that decision[3].

The detail of this chain of reasoning is considered at Chapter 2. If it is followed then resolution of the issue should become clearer. Certainly the clinician can, and in serious cases often should, seek advice from psychiatrists, psychologists or gerontologists as appropriate. But it is important to ask them the correct question and to provide them with appropriate information: what the consultee is being asked about is the diagnostic threshold, and, with reference to the particular situation in hand, the issues of comprehension, retention and use of information. The question of detainability under the MHA 1983 is logically wholly separate, and must remain so. The clarity of the MCA 2005 will, it is hoped, help to clarify the steps to be taken in these difficult cases.

1 Sections 1(2) and (4).
2 Section 2(1).
3 Section 3(1).

Information relevant to treatment decisions: informed consent

8.6 Clearly, even if the reasoning algorithm is clarified by the MCA 2005, the exercise of judgement in a decision as to capacity will remain difficult. However, before being able to decide whether the patient can understand, retain and use information sufficiently to be able to make a decision, one must consider the question of the amount of information the patient needs to have about the issue. This is not defined by the MCA 2005, and existing principles on the issue will remain relevant.

To be able to consent to a treatment decision, the patient does not need to understand everything about its technicalities or implications[1]. Indeed, to give sufficient consent to absolve the clinician from liability in assault, the patient merely needs to understand '*in broad terms*' the nature of the procedure proposed[2]. Nevertheless, it is a recognised part of the clinician's duty of care (and thus his or her potential liability in negligence) to inform the patient appropriately of the risks and benefits of treatment proposed. What is the test of appropriate information? The House of Lords was clear that the test derived from clinical judgement which accorded with a body of responsible opinion among the medical profession:

> 'To decide what risks the existence of which a patient should be voluntarily warned and the terms in which such warning, if any, should be given, having regard to the effect that the warning may have, is as much an exercise of professional skill and judgement as any other part of the doctor's comprehensive duty of care to the individual patient. ... The *Bolam* test should be applied.'[3]

Certainly in that case Lords Bridge and Harwich suggested that a court may conclude that disclosure of a particular risk was so obviously necessary to a real choice on the part of the patient that no reasonably prudent doctor would fail to give it (and would be liable in negligence should they fail). Lord Bridge suggested by way of example an operation involving a substantial risk of grave consequences, such as a 10% risk of stroke, saying that in such a case:

> 'in the absence of some cogent clinical reason why the patient should not be informed, a doctor, recognising and respecting his patient's right of decision, could hardly fail to appreciate the necessity for an appropriate warning.'[4]

Nevertheless, the circumstances in which a court would find that a practice widely held to be acceptable amongst the medical profession was not in fact reasonable or responsible, will be rare. The issue of the amount of information to provide to a patient about a proposed procedure is thus essentially self-policed amongst clinicians. That is not to say, however, that the medical profession has not given the issue of consent and information considerable thought. On the contrary, the GMC has published guidance entitled *Seeking Patients' consent: the ethical issues*[5]. This is a long and detailed document which addresses carefully the issues involved in consent. It is beyond the scope of this book to set out those issues in detail, but by way of example on the issue of the information necessary to give consent, the guidance states, in part, the following, before going on to give much more detail:

'Patients have a right to information about their condition and the treatment options available to them. The amount of information you give each patient will vary, according to factors such as the nature of the condition, the complexity of the treatment, the risks associated with the treatment or procedure, and the patient's own wishes. For example, patients may need more information to make an informed decision about a procedure which carries a high risk of failure or adverse side effects; or about an investigation for a condition which, if present, could have serious implications for the patient's employment, social or personal life.'[6]

Additionally, the Main Code considers the issue of provision of information in detail, described above at Chapter 2[7].

1 *R v Mental Health Commission ex p X* (1998) 9 BMLR 77.
2 *Chatterton v Gerson* [1981] QB 432.
3 *Sidaway v Bethlem Royal Hospital Governors* [1985] 1 AC 871, per Lord Diplock at 895.
4 *Sidaway v Bethlem Royal Hospital Governors* [1985] 1 AC 871at 900, the court's reserve power to adjudicate upon the medical profession's assessment of responsible and reasonable standards being reiterated in *Bolitho v City and Hackney HA* [1998] AC 232.
5 November 1998, see the GMC website at www.gmc-uk.org/guidance. The Department of Health has also published a document entitled *Reference Guide to Consent for Examination or Treatment*, April 2001, obtainable from www.dh.gov.uk.
6 *Seeking patients' consent: the ethical issues*, para 4.
7 Main Code, para 3.9.

Specific patient groups

8.7 The assessment of capacity may be straightforward — the unconscious patient following a head injury, for example. There are groups of patients where it is unlikely to be so easy, such as the following.

Those under the influence of drink or drugs

8.8 If the effect of the intoxicant is profound then, at the time of the assessment, the patient will be likely both to satisfy the diagnostic threshold (disturbance in the functioning of the mind), and to be unable to understand, retain or use information sufficiently to make a valid decision. Clearly the intoxication is likely to be temporary, but the scheme of the MCA 2005 is clear — capacity may be lost temporarily, and the crucial issue is whether it is absent at the time a decision needs to be made.

Accordingly, the clinician can, in such circumstances, must make the treatment decision s/he believes to be the best interests decision for the patient. The clinician must however bear in mind the further requirements of s 4 of the MCA 2005, namely:

- to consider whether or not the decision can be deferred until the patient regains capacity[1];
- to promote the patient's participation in the decision so far as possible, even though capacity is lost[2].

1 Section 4(3).
2 Section 4(4).

Those with limited comprehension

8.9 In truth, almost all non-doctors are likely to have limited comprehension of the real nature of the medical issues at stake in any treatment decision. That will not rob them of capacity. Those, however, whose cognition is particularly limited will present an assessment challenge in terms of capacity, and it is here that the detailed guidance in the Main Code as to methods of information provision will be crucial: see above Chapter 2, from 2.8. The role of the clinician will be to take all practicable steps to facilitate communication with the patient and then ask themselves whether they believe that the patient does in fact have the capacity to make the treatment decision in issue. As ever, the decision is taken by the clinician proposing treatment. Advice may be sought as appropriate, but the burden of decision-making lies upon the person proposing treatment.

The frail, timid or deferential

8.10 What about those whose response is '*What would you do, doctor?*' This may not be an uncommon patient group, and it will be a group from whom it is likely to be difficult to extract a decision. That difficulty does not however deprive the patient of capacity. The doctor's role will be to assist the patient here to make a decision. Certainly it is not inappropriate to recommend a particular treatment. It does, however, remain important for the doctor to point out reasonably available alternatives which s/he would be prepared to offer, and to explain the likely consequences of taking no action.

Those whose decision may not be voluntary

8.11 To be valid, the consent, or refusal, of a patient to treatment must be voluntary. The GMC and the Department of Health[1] exhort clinicians to satisfy themselves that the patient's will is not being unduly influenced by others. The Court of Appeal considered the issue in *Re T (adult: refusal of treatment)*[2], where a young woman, seriously injured following a road traffic accident (which had resulted in the stillbirth of her baby born by caesarean section), critically needed a blood transfusion. She had been brought up by her mother who was a fervent Jehovah's witness, but T was not, as an adult, a member of that faith. Nevertheless, in a conversation with her mother shortly before her collapse, T said that she did not want treatment by way of blood transfusion. Following her deterioration the hospital sought an urgent declaration that it would not be unlawful to treat her by way of blood transfusion. The declaration was granted, and the matter was further considered on appeal, when the declaration was upheld. The decision was on the basis that at the time of the refusal, T's decision was in fact the subject of undue influence, and thus invalid. Lord Donaldson MR considered the issue of family influence:

> 'A special problem may arise if at the time the decision is made the patient has been subjected to the influence of some third party. This is by no means to say that the patient is not entitled to receive and indeed invite advice and assistance

> from others in reaching a decision, particularly from members of the family. But the doctors have to consider whether the decision is really that of the patient. It is wholly acceptable that the patient should have been persuaded by others of the merits of such a decision and have decided accordingly. It matters not how strong the persuasion was, so long as it did not overbear the independence of the patient's decision. The real question in each case is: "Does the patient really mean what he says, or is he merely saying it for a quiet life, to satisfy someone else or because the advice and persuasion to which he has been subjected is such that he can no longer think and decide for himself?" ' In other words "Is it a decision expressed in form only, not reality?" '

Lord Donaldson suggested that two aspects were of crucial importance in considering the effect of outside influence:

- The strength and will of the patient: 'one who is very tired, in pain or depressed will be much less able to resist to having his will overborne than one who is rested, free from pain and cheerful'.
- The relationship of the 'persuader', whether a family member, whether deploying arguments based upon religious faith, 'and the fact that arguments based upon religious beliefs are being deployed by someone in a very close relationship with the patient will give them added force and should alert the doctors to the possibility — no more — that the patient's capacity or will to decide has been overborne. In other words, that the patient may not mean what he says'.

It should be noted that the issue is addressed in terms of undue influence, whether the apparent consent/refusal is in fact invalid by reason of undue pressure. It was not suggested in *Re T*, for example, or elsewhere, that the effect of undue influence is to deprive the patient of capacity. It is not classed in the same way as a disorder of cognition as in the cases of needle-phobic's terror or the anorexic's desperation to refuse food discussed below. The result must then be that patients in this category do not fall within the MCA 2005, and, should serious issues arise such as in *Re T*, the High Court's inherent jurisdiction developed in relation to vulnerable adults ought to be invoked. See further Chapters 7 and 10 on this.

1 *Seeking patients' consent: the ethical issues*; *Reference Guide to Consent*; see 8.6.
2 [1992] 4 All ER 649.

The patient who is refusing, but whose refusal appears to be the result of a mental condition rather than a real choice

8.12 An example here is the anorexic or needle-phobic patient. It is likely that such patients will be perfectly capable of making decisions about many aspects of their lives, and will appear wholly lucid and rational in general terms. At first blush they will not appear to lack capacity. The recommendation of food, or of urgently needed invasive treatment is likely however to trigger an unequivocal refusal. This is touched on in Chapter 2 above, at 2.27; the courts have suggested the following:

- Of the anorexic:

> 'It is a feature of anorexia nervosa that it is capable of destroying the ability to make an informed choice. It creates a compulsion to refuse treatment or only to accept treatment which is likely to be ineffective. This attitude is part and parcel of the disease and the more advanced the illness, the more compelling it may become.'[1]

- Where the anorexic patient was quite capable of taking in, understanding and believing information given to her about the necessary amount of food needed to maintain weight:

> 'the problem lies in her capacity to use that information, when necessary to balance risks and needs. It is my view that [the patient] is easily able to selectively ignore what she knows, or to twist or distort such information so that it suits her immediate purposes without heed for the long-term consequences. I believe that it is likely that these distorting processes happen largely unconsciously and she is not always able to control them. It is a feature of anorexia nervosa and related eating disorders that information is distorted in this way. The immediate gratification involved in being able to override the pangs of hunger, and to feel in control, is such that worries about the effects on the body, and eventually threats to life itself, are ignored.'[2]

- Of the needle-phobic:

> 'She could not bring herself to undergo the caesarian section she desired because, as the evidence established, "a fear of needles ... has got in the way of proceeding with the operation ... At the moment of panic ... her fear dominated all ... at the actual point she was not capable of making a decision at all ... at that moment the needle or mask dominated her thinking and made her quite unable to consider anything else." On that evidence she was incapable of making a decision at all. She was at that moment suffering an impairment of her mental functioning which disabled her. She was temporarily incompetent.'[3]

1 *Re W: (a minor) (medical treatment)* [1992] 4 All ER 627.

2 *ReC (a minor) (detention for medical treatment)* [1997] 2 FLR 180 (Fam Div); see also *R v Collins and Ashworth Hospital Authority ex parte Ian Brady* [2000] MHLR 17, at para 65 where Maurice Kay J held (obiter) that Ian Brady lacked capacity regarding his decision to refuse food because of his paranoid psychopathic disorder: 'notwithstanding the fact that he is a man of well above average intelligence, he has engaged in his battle of wills in such a way that, as a result of his severe personality disorder, he has eschewed the weighing of information and the balancing of the risks and needs to such an extent that, from that time until this, his decisions on food refusal and force feeding have been incapacitated. As a result, the doctors have been legally empowered to supply medical treatment in his best interests.'

3 *Re MB (an adult: medical treatment* (1997) 38 BMLR 175 (CA) Butler-Sloss LJ.

Children and young people

8.13 The MCA 2005 applies to those aged 16 and over. It sits alongside the existing regime governing consent to medical treatment by and on behalf of children and young people. The result is, it is suggested, as follows.

A person does not attain the age of majority until 18[1]. Until that time they are, for most legal purposes, under a disability, as is considered in relation to civil litigation at Chapter 15. Accordingly, the best interests test is the touchstone for medical treatment. Whilst not explicitly applicable to children under 16 it is most likely that the best interests principle of s 4 of the MCA 2005 will underpin best interests assessments in the case of children.

An important difference between treatment for the incapacitated adult and the child lies in the fact that consent to medical treatment can, for the latter, be provided on their behalf by a person with parental responsibility. Save as provided by the MCA 2005 there is no proxy facility available in the case of incapacitated adults[2].

In relation to those under 18, the person with parental responsibility will be as follows:

- in the case of parents married at the time of the child's birth, either parent;
- in the case of unmarried parents, the mother alone, unless the father has specifically acquired parental responsibility under the Children Act 1989[3].

The consent of only one person with parental responsibility is strictly required for medical treatment[4], although the courts have said that for major treatment where parental opinion is divided, a ruling should be sought[5].

Note that no one other than a person with parental responsibility can give consent on behalf of a child. Accordingly, in an emergency situation, if it is not possible to contact a person with parental responsibility, the clinician is entitled and bound to treat the child in accordance with their best interests and without obtaining consent. Certainly one should consult as widely as possible, and views of the carer or teacher for example, who carries a document signed by the parent authorising medical treatment, will be relevant. They are not, however, binding or determinative.

Further, the test of medical treatment being that which is in the child's best interests, the court retains the power to make a ruling as to what this entails. This is likely to be invoked in cases of serious medical treatment, and/or where there is clinical or family dispute. Parental views can be overridden by the court. This has been seen in cases such as the refusal of consent to a blood transfusion by Jehovah's Witness parents[6], or the decision as to the fate of the conjoined twins[7]. The relevant court will remain the High Court in relation to children under 16, the Court of Protection only having jurisdiction under the MCA 2005 for those over 16[8].

1 Family Law Reform Act 1969, s 1.
2 Deputies or donees of lasting powers of attorney authorised under the MCA 2005 – see Chapters 5 and 11 .
3 Children Act 1989, s 2.
4 Children Act 1989, s 2(7).
5 *Re J (Specific Issue Orders: Child's Religious Upbringing and Circumcision)* [2000] 1 FLR 571, CA.
6 eg *Re S (A minor) (Medical Treatment)* [1993] 1 FLR 376: 'The court … should be very slow to allow an infant to martyr himself', per Ward J at 394.
7 *Re A (Conjoined Twins: surgical separation)* [2000] 4 All ER 961, CA.
8 Section 2(5).

Young people aged 16–17

8.14 Section 8 of the Family Law Reform Act 1969 provides that a young person aged 16 or 17 can give a valid consent to medical treatment, and that where this is done, there is no need for further consent to be given by the person with parental responsibility, and the young person's *consent* cannot be overridden by the person with parental responsibility for them. This of course presupposes that the young person has capacity, but the effect of s 8 is to create a presumption of capacity in people of this age. The same test for assessing capacity will apply as it does to the incapacitated adult, namely that under the MCA 2005.

The fact that the person aged 16–17 remains a minor means that the person with parental responsibility in their case can, strictly, overrule a *refusal* they seek to make with respect to medical treatment. The courts have, however, indicated that it should be wholly exceptional for a parent to override a young person's clear and informed refusal of consent to treatment. The refusal should be a very important consideration for those making clinical judgements, and for the court, should it be asked to make a best interests ruling[1].

1 See eg *Re W (A minor) (Medical treatment)* [1992] 4 All ER 627, CA.

Adolescents under 16

8.15 An older child can also give a valid consent to medical treatment, which can then be performed without the need to obtain parental consent. The requirement here is simply that the child has capacity. This has long been described as 'Gillick competence', following the decision of the House of Lords in *Gillick v West Norfolk and Wisbech Area Health Authority*[1]. It was described there as applying to a child who had reached an age where they had sufficient understanding and intelligence to enable them to understand fully what was proposed, and to be capable of making up their mind on the matter. It is, in fact, the identical test for capacity as applies to adults.

Again, whilst a Gillick competent child can give a valid *consent* to medical treatment, the person with parental responsibility retains the right to override the child's *refusal*. Again, however, the court will be wary of overruling a competent child's clear and sustained refusal.

1 [1986] AC 112, [1986] 1 FLR 224.

MEDICAL TREATMENT UNDER THE MCA 2005 OF THOSE LACKING CAPACITY

8.16 Where an adult patient lacks capacity, and unless there is a valid and applicable advance decision, the clinician's role is to provide the medical treatment which the clinician considers to be in the patient's best interests[1]. As has been seen throughout the discussion of the MCA 2005, the primary decision-maker is the clinician. There are, however, important exceptions to the clinician's power to decide:

- A major innovation of the MCA 2005 is to introduce for the first time the possibility of proxies in relation to consent, in the form of the donee of a lasting power of attorney or court deputy. These are touched on below and considered in detail at Chapters 5 and 11. Their existence in any given case will be very important as it is they who will make the decision to refuse or give consent to medical treatment recommended by the clinician.
- Further, the clinician is bound by any valid and applicable advance decision made by the patient before capacity was lost. Advance decisions are examined at Chapter 3, but where valid and applicable, they bind the clinician to withhold the medical treatment they specify.

1 Section 1(5), ss 24–26, and see Chapter 3 relating to advance decisions. For the treatment of mental disorder see Chapter 7 at 7.52 and Chapter 16 at 16.17–16.19.

Assessment of best interests under the MCA 2005

8.17 Even in the presence of an LPA or deputy, the clinician will need to make the best interests assessment (consulting the donee, deputy and others as required by the MCA 2005), in order to make an assessment of what the best interests of the patient require. This will require exactly the same process of assessment as in any decision affecting the incapacitated adult. See Chapter 2 which sets the process out in detail. However, in summary:

- the decision-maker will be the clinician proposing the treatment, and formal consent need not be obtained, save where there is a valid LPA or deputy with authorisation covering the medical treatment in issue;
- the patient's ability to participate in the treatment decision must be promoted as far as possible, and the decision deferred if it is likely that the patient will regain capacity within a period before which the decision needs to be made[1];
- the least restrictive alternative must be adopted[2];
- the best interest decision must be made as follows:
  - not on the basis merely of age, appearance or condition;
  - taking into account all relevant circumstances;
  - not, in relation to life-sustaining treatment, motivated by a desire to bring about the patient's death;
  - taking into account, so far as reasonably ascertainable:
    - the patient's past and present wishes and feelings (including any written statement made before capacity was lost);
    - the beliefs and values that would be likely to influence the patient if they had capacity; and
    - the other factors that the patient would be likely to consider were they able to do so.
  - taking into account if appropriate and practicable, the views of:
    - anyone named by the patient as someone to be consulted on matters of this kind;
    - anyone engaged in caring for the patient or interested in their welfare;
    - any donee of a lasting power of attorney;
    - any deputy appointed by the court[3].

1 Section 4(4) and 4(3).
2 Section 1(6).
3 Section 4.

Obligations under the European Convention on Human Rights

8.18 Clinicians working in the NHS are working for a public authority within the meaning of the Human Rights Act 1998 and are thus bound to adhere to the requirements of the European Convention on Human Rights (ECHR) in their dealings with their patients.

The extent of those requirements is fully considered at Chapter 17, but in summary, they are likely to apply in the healthcare context most frequently as follows.

Article 2: the right to life

8.19 This enjoins the state to have a suitable system of regulation of healthcare, and an effective investigatory system in relation to deaths in state institutions[1]. Article 2 is not inconsistent with decisions to discontinue life support treatment in appropriate cases – the presumption of the continuance of life is not irrebuttable, as discussed below[2]. However, where a person wishes to end their own life because it has become or will become intolerable through the course of a degenerative disease, there is no enforceable 'right to die'[3]. This situation is probably not ameliorated for the person concerned by the making of an advance decision refusing life-sustaining treatment if the illness is of a kind that involves gradual degeneration.

1 In some cases an inquest will be the means by which the state discharges its obligation to have an independent and effective investigation into a death which may involve a violation of Article 2. The case law concerning when Article 2 is engaged and when an inquest must fulfil the investigatory obligation is currently in a state of flux, the cases of *Savage v. South Essex Partnership NHS Foundation Trust* [2007] EWCA Civ 1375, [2007] All ER (D) 316 (Dec); *Smith v Chief Constable of Sussex Police* [2008] EWCA Civ 39, [2008] All ER (D) 48 (Feb), and *Van Colle v Chief Constable of Hertfordshire Police* [2007] EWCA Civ 325, [2007] 3 All ER 122, [2007] 1 WLR 1827 which all deal with the relevant test and obligations are all due to be heard by the House of Lords in 2008.
2 *Pretty v United Kingdom* [2002] 2 FCR 97, 12 BHRC 149.

Article 3: the prohibition on torture or inhuman and degrading treatment

8.20 The European Court of Human Rights considered this in the case of *Pretty v United Kingdom*[1]:

> 'As regards the types of 'treatment' which fall within the scope of art 3 of the convention, the court's case law refers to 'ill-treatment' that attains a minimum level of severity and involves actual bodily injury or intense physical or mental suffering (see *Ireland v UK* [1979–80] 2 EHRR 25 at para 167 and *V v UK* [2000] 30 EHRR 121 para 71). Where treatment humiliates or debases an individual showing a lack of respect for, or diminishing, his or her human dignity or arouses feelings of fear, anguish or inferiority capable of breaking an

> individual's moral and physical resistance, it may be characterised as degrading and also fall within the prohibition of art 3 (see amongst recent authorities, *Price v UK* [2002] 34 EHRR 53, at paras 24–30 and *Valasinas v Lithuania* (2001) 12 BHRC 266 at para 117). The suffering which flows from naturally occurring illness, physical or mental, may be covered by art 3, where it is, or risks being, exacerbated by treatment, whether flowing from conditions of detention, expulsion or other measures, for which the authorities can be held responsible (see *D v UK [1997] 24 EHRR 423*(1997) 2 BHRC 273 and *Keenan v UK* [2001] 33 EHRR 38 and also *Bensaid v UK* [2001] 33 EHRR 205).'

Thus, treatment which attains a minimum level of severity and involves actual bodily injury or intense physical or mental suffering may be found to be inhuman or degrading, even if not maliciously intended. It will not be found to be so if a 'therapeutic necessity'[2]. That apart, it is absolutely prohibited. It does not however permit another to end a life found by the sufferer to be intolerable[3].

1 [2002] 35 EHRR 1 at para 52.
2 *R (on the application of Wilkinson) v. Responsible Medical Officer Broadmoor Hospital* [2001] EWCA Civ 1545, [2002] 1 WLR 419; *Herczegfalvy v Austria* (1992) 15 EHRR 437.
3 *Pretty v United Kingdom* [2002] 35 EHRR 1 and see also *Re Z (Local Authority: Duty)* [2004] EWCH 2817 (Fam), [2005] 3 All ER 280.

Article 8: the right to respect for private and family life

8.21 This right will require the clinician to afford respect to their patient's private and family life. Whilst the clinician's primary duty will remain towards the patient rather than their family[1], nevertheless the family's interest does need to be borne in mind. In the case, for example, of a serious conflict over medical treatment for an incapacitated family member or child, it may amount to a breach of the Article 8 rights of both patient and family to fail to deploy the procedures available for seeking a declaration as appropriate from the court[2].

1 See *D v East Berkshire Community NHS Trust* [2005] UKHL 23, [2005] 2 AC 373.
2 See *Glass v United Kingdom* (2004) 39 EHRR 15.

Healthcare decisions under the MCA 2005: general

Application of the best interests principle in relation to medical treatment

8.22 There is no statutory definition of best interests. The decision as to what is in a patient's best interests must be made by following the procedures set out at ss 1 and 4 of the MCA 2005, summarised above and developed in full in Chapter 2. These decisions are now made at several levels and consideration must include the actions of proxy decision-makers under the MCA 2005. Every case will depend upon its own particular facts, but there is a general approach provided for by the MCA 2005.

Daily care and section 5 protection

8.23 The best interests doctrine of course applies as much to routine daily healthcare as to major treatment decisions. Chapter 4 describes the protection offered by s 5 to acts in connection with care or treatment, but in summary, the clinician or carer is protected if s/he:

- takes reasonable steps to establish a lack of capacity; and
- reasonably believes that the patient lacks capacity and that it is in the patient's best interests for the act to be done.

This section codifies the common law doctrine of necessity, and is likely to be the mechanism by which the majority of healthcare treatments are given to incapacitated adults.

Unprotected acts, welfare donees and deputies

8.24 As in welfare cases however, s 5 affords no protection if the clinician acts in a way that is contrary to a valid decision of a welfare donee or court deputy[1]. A person who detains the incapacitated person or restrains them in a manner not falling within s 6 will not be protected (see also below).

1 Section 6(6).

Lasting powers of attorney: welfare donees

8.25 These are discussed in full at Chapter 5. In brief, however, a lasting power of attorney in the healthcare context may:

- be made by an adult with capacity (ie aged 18 or over);
- confer on a donee the authority to make decisions about the patient's personal welfare (including healthcare) or specified matters concerning the patient's welfare at a time when the patient has lost capacity (examples may be consenting or refusing consent to medical examination and treatment on the donor's behalf);
- empower the donee to make decisions relating to life-sustaining treatment about the patient, but this requires express provision in the creating instrument.

As stated above, the introduction of a person authorised to make a treatment decision on behalf of an incapacitated adult is new. Clinicians under the common law doctrine of necessity, and now under the best interests doctrine, have always needed to consult widely to inform themselves as to the patient's best interests. Whilst nothing alters the principle that a clinician cannot be compelled to provide medical treatment contrary to their clinical judgement[1], nevertheless the power of consent or veto vested in an appropriately authorised donee will require a change of thinking on the part of the clinician. The issues arising for clinicians, the powers of welfare donees over life-sustaining treatment, including artificial nutrition and hydration (ANH), and the need to make applications to the court are fully discussed in Chapter 5.

1 See below 8.31, and the *Burke* judgment.

Court deputies

8.26 These are discussed at Chapter 11. Again, in summary, they may be appointed by the Court of Protection to make specified decisions within the scope of their appointment. Those decisions may relate to welfare or medical decisions. The power of consent or veto to proposed medical treatment will be vested in a validly appointed deputy in the same way as for a validly created LPA. However, the Main Code suggests that court appointed deputies will primarily be appointed to deal with patients' property and affairs, and that those appointed to take medical or welfare decisions will be most uncommon:

> 'Deputies for personal welfare decisions [which includes healthcare] will only be required in the most difficult cases where:
> - important and necessary actions cannot be carried out without the court's authority; or
> - there is no other way of settling the matter in the best interests of the [patient].'[1]

Note that the donee of an LPA and court deputy are obliged to apply the best interests test in the same way as the clinician. In the event of a serious dispute between a donee or deputy and the clinician, the Court of Protection may be asked to make a decision as to the best interests of the patient, this is considered in further detail below.

1 Main Code, para 8.36.

Independent mental capacity advocate

8.27 It may also be appropriate for an independent mental capacity advocate (IMCA) to be instructed and appointed. It must be remembered, however, that an IMCA is not a decision-maker, but represents and supports a person in relation to specific issues. IMCAs are considered in detail at Chapter 6. However, in very brief summary in the healthcare setting:

- an IMCA must be instructed and then consulted for incapacitated adults who have no one else to support them, other than paid staff, whenever:
  - an NHS body is proposing to provide serious medical treatment;
  - an NHS body is proposing to arrange accommodation or a change of accommodation in hospital or a care home, and the person will stay in hospital longer than 28 days, or in a care home for more than eight weeks;
- an IMCA may be instructed to support someone who lacks capacity to make decisions concerning:
  - care reviews, where no one else is available to be consulted;

  - adult protection cases, whether or not family, friends or others are involved;
- information or reports provided by an IMCA must be taken into account as part of the process of working out the best interests of the incapacitated adult.

An NHS body[1] is the responsible body with a duty to instruct an IMCA where it is proposing 'serious medical treatment'[2]. 'Serious medical treatment' is defined in reg 4 of the IMCA General Regulations as providing, withdrawing or withholding treatment in circumstances where:

- a single treatment is proposed with finely balanced risks/benefits;
- a choice of treatments is available, a decision as to which one to use is finely balanced, or
- what is proposed is *likely* to involve serious consequences for the patient.

The definition is wide and affords considerable discretion to the decision-maker. This provision applies not only to new proposed treatments but also to those already being provided but are to be stopped or changed[3].

1 The Mental Capacity Act 2005 (Independent Mental Capacity Advocate) (General) Regulations 2006, SI 2006/1832, reg 3: see regulations at Appendix 4.
2 Section 37(6).
3 See Chapter 6.

Healthcare decisions under the MCA 2005: specific

8.28 This section considers specific principles arising out of existing case law which will continue to have relevance to clinicians taking decisions under the MCA 2005, and to decisions of the Court of Protection.

The sanctity or prolongation of life

8.29 This is a fundamental principle, and there will be a very strong presumption in favour of a course of action which will prolong life as being determinative of the best interests question. That presumption is not, however, irrebuttable. See, for example, Lord Goff in *Airedale NHS Trust v Bland*[1]:

> 'But this principle, fundamental though it is, is not absolute … We are concerned with circumstances in which it may be lawful to withhold from a patient medical treatment or care by means of which his life may be prolonged. But here too there is no absolute rule that the patient's life must be prolonged by such treatment or care, if available, regardless of the circumstances.'

Thus, in a situation where treatment to preserve the continuance of life at all costs is found to be likely to be excessively painful or futile, it is possible that a declaration may be granted that discontinuance of the treatment (as opposed to the administration of a lethal injection which is, and remains, unlawful) is in the patient's best interests. The court will draw up a balance sheet in order to assess all the relevant factors[2].

This process has been found by the domestic courts to be compatible with Articles 2 and 8 ECHR: in the case of *NHS Trust A v M, NHS Trust B v H*[3], Dame Elizabeth Butler-Sloss, then President of the Family Division, found that if it was no longer in the best interests of a patient to continue to be provided with treatment (in this case the continuance of artificial nutrition and hydration to patients in a persistent vegetative state), continued treatment would in fact violate the patients' autonomy, even though discontinuance would shorten their lives.

Decisions regarding life-sustaining treatment may be referred to the Court of Protection (see below). Advance decisions and welfare donees may also be of relevance to these decisions[4].

1 [1993] AC 789, [1993] 1 All ER 821.
2 See *Re A (Medical Treatment: Male Sterilisation)* [2000] 1 FLR 549, orthe case of the brain injured baby Charlotte Wyatt, *Darren Wyatt v Portsmouth NHS Trust and Charlotte Wyatt*, considered by the Court of Appeal at [2005] EWCA Civ 1181, para 87; [2005] 3 FCR 263.
3 [2001] 1 All ER 801, [2001] 2 WLR 942.
4 See Chapters 3 and 5.

Best interests not restricted to medical best interests

8.30 The breadth of the notion of best interests has been considered in Chapter 2. That breadth extends to the medical setting, and does not embrace merely medical considerations. Thus, in assessing the best interests of the incapacitated adult the clinician must look widely at all aspects of the patient's life and wellbeing, covering 'medical, emotional and all other welfare issues'[1]. It has been held, for example, to be in the best interests of an incapacitated patient to provide bone marrow for her sister who was suffering from leukaemia, as the sister's death would be such a blow to the patient's mother that it would threaten the bond between them, to the patient's detriment[2].

1 *Re A (Male sterilisation)* [2000] 1 FLR 549, per Butler-Sloss P.
2 *Re Y (Mental Incapacity: Bone marrow transplant)* [1996] 2 FLR 787.

Compulsion of a doctor?

8.31 The involvement of an LPA donee, deputy, or order by the Court of Protection under s 16 raises the issue of compulsion of clinicians. It has, however, been settled for the present by the Court of Appeal in the case of *R (on the application of Burke) v General Medical Council*[1].

The role of the doctor in assessing the treatment needs of an incapacitated patient is to assess what is in the patient's best interests. This does not, however, require the doctor to offer or perform treatment which is contrary to his or her clinical judgement. Certainly, a doctor must have regard to the wishes of the patient, but Lord Phillips MR said that 'ultimately however a patient cannot demand that a doctor administer a treatment which the doctor considers is adverse to the patient's clinical needs'. The proper analysis should be as follows:

- the doctor, exercising his or her professional clinical judgement, decides what treatment options are clinically indicated (ie will provide overall clinical benefit) for the patient;
- the doctor then offers those treatment options to the patient, explaining to the patient the risks, benefits, side effects etc involved in each of the treatment options;
- the patient then decides whether to accept any of those treatment options and, if so, which one;
- if the patient chooses one of the treatment options offered, the doctor will then proceed to provide it;
- if, however, the patient refuses all of the treatment options offered, and instead informs the doctor that s/he wants a form of treatment which the doctor has not offered, the doctor will, no doubt, discuss that form of treatment with the patient, but if the doctor concludes that this treatment is not clinically indicated, the doctor is not required (ie is under no legal obligation) to provide it to the patient (although a second opinion should be offered).

In this context, said Lord Phillips, the patient's 'right to choose' treatment was in truth 'no more than a reflection of the fact that it is the doctor's duty to provide a treatment that he considers to be in the interests of the patient and that the patient is prepared to accept'[2].

The MCA 2005 does not alter this. It does, however, explicitly provide that one of the powers of the Court of Protection in relation to medical care is to give a direction that 'a person responsible for P's healthcare allow a different person to take over that responsibility'[3]. Thus, the court will not seek to compel a doctor to act contrary to his or her clinical judgement, but may require the doctor to transfer the care of the patient to another clinician in an appropriate case.

1 [2005] EWCA Civ 1003, [2006] QB 273; see also *National Health Service Trust v D* [2000] 2 FLR 677 at 686.
2 [2006] QB 273, at para 51.
3 Section 17(1)(e).

Emergencies

8.32 Section 5 protection will enable a doctor lawfully to provide medical treatment if a patient needs immediate emergency treatment. A doctor will need to consider whether the treatment may be delayed until the person regains capacity. A clinician will be bound by any applicable advance decision or a decision of a welfare donee. This pre-supposes that the clinician is aware of the advance decision or the existence and identity of a welfare donee. If they are not, it is suggested that the s 5 protection will still apply to protect the acts of the doctor, so long as the treatment is in the best interests of the person. If an irresolvable dispute develops the matter may be referred to the court for resolution under s 15 (see 8.37 below). Another conundrum presents itself where the clinician is made aware of an advance decision or welfare LPA but does not have sufficient time, or is unable to obtain a copy or proof of the same to see its precise terms, due to the emergency. It is still suggested that s 5 will protect a clinician who chooses to act in those circumstances as above.

Pioneering treatment

8.33 An incapacitated adult should not be deprived of the possibility of receiving pioneering treatment, in the absence of other orthodox treatment, if it is likely that they would have consented if able to do so. The view of the family will be important[1].

1 *Simms v Simms* [2002] EWHC 2734 (Fam), [2003] 1 All ER 669, per Butler-Sloss P.

Restraint or deprivation of liberty

8.34 It may be necessary to restrain a person to administer treatment, eg an injection, taking blood, or other transient treatment measure. This might include anaesthesia for a surgical procedure. The provisions of ss 5 and 6 will apply to permit such restraint in defined circumstances (see Chapter 4). Any uncertainties or disputes may require resolution by the court under its powers in ss 15 or 16 (below). If an incapacitated and resisting person needs to be hospitalised for treatment and follow up of a physical disorder, in circumstances likely to amount to a deprivation of liberty within the meaning of Article 5 ECHR ie they would not be free to leave the hospital if they tried to do so, then this is not presently protected by the MCA 2005 at all[1]. Similarly where hospital treatment is necessary, if an incapacitated person is resisting being taken to hospital for treatment for a physical disorder, then consideration must be given to the use of reasonable force under the provisions of ss 5 and 6, or to the court as above. If treatment was required for a mental disorder, then use of the provisions of the MHA 1983 would have to be considered.

1 See Chapter 9 on Deprivation of Liberty and 9.107. New provisions inserted into the MCA 2005 by the MHA 2007 will not come into force until April 2009 at the earliest. And see Chapter 7 at 7.8, Chapter 10 at 10.34 for how this is to be managed in the meantime.

DISPUTE RESOLUTION AND SERIOUS CASES

8.35 The process of making the best interests assessment may expose conflicting opinions. The Main Code at Chapter 15 exhorts clinicians to strive to achieve consensus. Nevertheless, irreconcilable differences of opinion may emerge between doctor and family, donee or deputy. We have seen above that a clinician cannot be compelled to provide treatment contrary to his or her professional judgement. How should such disputes be resolved?

Resolution of dispute

8.36 The Main Code devotes a chapter to processes designed to assist in the resolution of conflict[1], expressing the view that it is usually preferable to settle such conflict informally. It suggests the following:

- setting out the different options in a way that is easy to understand;
- inviting a colleague to talk to the family and offer a second opinion;
- offering to get independent expert advice;
- using an advocate to support and represent the person who lacks capacity;
- arranging a case conference or meeting to discuss matters in detail;
- listening to, acknowledging and addressing worries;
- where the situation is not urgent, allowing the family to think it over;
- arranging mediation[2].

1 Main Code, Chapter 15.
2 Main Code, paras 15.3–15.17.

Application to the Court of Protection

8.37 Should the dispute remain seriously unresolved an application to the Court of Protection (or High Court in the case of a child under 16) will be the only option, the court being asked to make the decision as to best interests. Chapters 7 and 10 discuss in detail the process of application to the Court of Protection, but in summary and with relevance to medical treatment, this section touches on the following:

- Upon what kind of issue will the Court of Protection adjudicate?
- Application and permission.
- How will it approach its role, ie a substituted decision maker or as a maker of declarations?
- How will it make its decisions?
- Is there any remaining role for the exercise of the High Court's inherent jurisdiction?

Issues upon which the Court of Protection will adjudicate: serious medical treatment

8.38 The High Court, in the exercise of its inherent jurisdiction, has asserted that declarations are appropriate in the following type of cases:

- sterilisation[1];
- PVS withdrawal of artificial feeding;
- where force might have to be used to administer anaesthetic;
- patient requiring CT scan;
- harvesting bone marrow;
- sterilisation of incompetent adult[2];
- termination of pregnancy[3];
- late termination[4];
- future treatment[5];
- cases of momentous and irrevocable decisions and controversy[6].

This is likely to remain the case under the MCA 2005. At para 8.18 of the Main Code appears a very similar list of types of case that should be brought to court:

- decisions about the proposed withholding or withdrawal of ANH from patients in a permanent vegetative state (PVS);
- cases involving organ or bone marrow donation by a person who lacks capacity to consent;
- cases involving the proposed non-therapeutic sterilisation of a person who lacks capacity to consent to this (eg for contraceptive purposes);
- all other cases where there is a doubt or dispute about whether a particular treatment will be in a person's best interests.

Practice Direction 9E to Part 9 of the Court of Protection Rules ('CoP Rules') defines 'serious medical treatment' by reference to the consequences of the treatment:

> '3. Serious medical treatment means treatment which involves providing, withdrawing or withholding treatment in circumstances where:
> (a) in a case where a single treatment is being proposed, there is a fine balance between its benefits to P and the burdens and risks it is likely to entail for him;
> (b) in a case where there is a choice of treatments, a decision as to which one to use is finely balanced; or
> (c) the treatment, procedure or investigation proposed would be likely to involve serious consequences for P.
>
> 4. "Serious consequences" are those which could have a serious impact on P, either from the effects of the treatment, procedure or investigation itself or its wider implications. This may include treatments, procedures or investigations which:
> (a) cause, or may cause, serious and prolonged pain, distress or side effects;
> (b) have potentially major consequences for P; or
> (c) have a serious impact on P's future life choices.'

Practice Direction 9E reiterates the list of cases that should go to the court and are contained in the Main Code (above). It also points out that there is no exhaustive list of medical treatments that are suitable for the court. Each case depends on its own circumstances and the consequences for the person[7].

1 *Re S (Adult Patient: Sterilisation: Patient's Best Interests)* [2000] 2 FLR 389.

2 *Re GF (mental patient: medical treatment)* [1992] 1 FLR 293; *Re LC (medical treatment: sterilisation)* [1997] 2 FLR 258; *Re SS (An Adult: Medical treatment)* [2001] 1 FLR 445.

3 *D v An NHS Trust* [2003] EWCH 2793 (Fam), [2004] 1 FLR 1110.

4 *Re SS (Medical Treatment: Late termination)* [1996] Fam 118.

5 *NHS Trust v T(adult patient: refusal of medical treatment)* [2004] EWHC 1279 (Fam), [2005] 1 All ER 387.

6 *Re S (Hospital Patient: Court's Jurisdiction)* [1996] Fam 1, [1995] 3 All ER 290, [1995] 3 WLR 78, where Sir Thomas Bingham said:

> 'In cases of controversy and cases involving momentous and irrevocable decisions, the courts have treated as justiciable any genuine question as to what the best interests of a patient require or justify. In making these decisions the courts have recognised the desirability of informing those involved whether a proposed course of conduct will render them criminally or civilly liable; they have acknowledged their duty to act as a safeguard against malpractice, abuse and unjustified action; and they have recognised the desirability, in the last resort, of decisions being made by an impartial, independent tribunal'.

7 PD 9E paras 5, 6, and 7.

Who may apply to the Court of Protection?

8.39 Applications to the Court of Protection may be made without permission by the patient[1], a donor of an LPA or a deputy with authority over the issue to which the application relates[2]. All other applications require permission. This will cover family members, clinicians, NHS Trusts and local authorities. For decisions about serious or major medical treatment, the NHS Trust proposing treatment should apply[3].

1 Or the person with parental responsibility for them if aged 16–18.
2 Section 50.
3 Main Code, paras 8.7–8.8. This reflects the decision in *Re F (sterilisation)* [1990] 2 AC 1 at 65E.

When should an application be made?

8.40 The following guidance as to when an application should be made has been given by the court:

- where there is a dispute as to capacity, or where there is a realistic prospect that the patient will regain capacity following treatment;
- where there is a lack of unanimity amongst the medical professionals as to the patient's best interests;
- where the patient or his immediate family (one might now add a welfare donee or advance decision) opposes or expresses views inconsistent with the proposed treatment; or
- where there are other exceptional circumstances[1].

Where there is any doubt as to any of these matters, it is suggested that an application should be made.

1 *D v An NHS Trust* [2003] EWHC 2793 (Fam), [2004] 1 FLR 1110 in the context of termination of pregnancy.

Application and permission

8.41 The application and permission process is dealt with in Chapter 10. Applications are made under the CoP Rules, Part 9 and Practice Direction (PD) 9E defines 'serious medical treatment' for those purposes (see above).

An urgent application may be necessary for injunctive or other interim relief to preserve the status quo pending a final decision. Part 10 of the CoP Rules and PD 10E apply.

In deciding whether to grant permission the court must have regard to:

(a) the applicant's connection with the person to whom the application relates;
(b) the reasons for the application;
(c) the benefit to the person to whom the application relates of a proposed order or directions; and

(d) whether the benefit can be achieved in any other way[1].

Thus any application for permission should focus on these factors.

An applicant does not have to demonstrate any specific legal right to make an application to the court. Under the inherent jurisdiction the Court of Appeal held that:

> 'it cannot be suggested that any stranger or officious busybody, however remotely connected with a patient or with the subject matter of proceedings, can properly seek or obtain declaratory or any other relief (in private law any more than public law proceedings). But it can be suggested that where a serious justiciable issue is brought before the court by a party with a genuine and legitimate interest in obtaining a decision … the court will not impose nice tests to determine the precise legal standing of that claimant.'[2]

It is likely to be highly unusual for an application by a Trust to be refused permission, but it will add an element of delay to the resolution of a serious issue. If an urgent application is made and interim relief granted, it is suggested that permission will still be required as with judicial review (see Chapter 10).

1 Section 50(3).
2 *Re S* [1995] 3 WLR 78. Also in *A (A Patient) v A Health Authority* [2002] EWHC 18 (Fam/Admin), [2002] Fam 213.

Preparing to make an application to the court

8.42 The required supporting information (form COP1B) includes accommodation arrangements, whether or not the person is subject to guardianship under the MHA 1983 and whether or not there is a welfare LPA or other donee in place. At s 4 a chronology of key dates and facts is requested. Other supportive information will have to be supplied in the form of witness statements. This will include elucidating the dispute upon which the court is being asked to decide with supporting evidence[1].

1 See further Chapter 10.

Court forms

8.43 The following will be required:

- COP1: application form;
- COP1B Annex B: supporting information for personal welfare applications[1];
- COP2: permission form (if applicable);
- COP3: assessment of capacity;
- COP4: deputy's declaration (if applicable);
- Copy of LPA or EPA (if applicable);
- Fee[2].

1 COP1A will be required if a financial or property decision is required in addition.
2 Currently £400: Court of Protection Fees Order, SI 2007/1745, arts 3 and 4 and Schedule.

Urgent applications

8.44 The procedure for making urgent applications is set out in Chapter 10 and the CoP Rules; PD 10B applies.

Litigation friend

8.45 At the first directions hearing the court will consider the issue of the appointment of a litigation friend to act on behalf of the incapacitated person. Part 17 of the CoP Rules and PD 17A set out this procedure. More often than not it is the Official Solicitor who will be invited to act by the court as a litigation friend, although technically a litigation friend of last resort[1].

1 See www.officialsolicitor.gov.uk and Practice Note at [2006] 2 FLR 373.

Approach of the court

8.46 The Court of Protection has two powers in relation to healthcare issues:

- Under s 15 to make declarations:
  - as to whether a person has or lacks capacity to make a decision or decisions specified or described in the declaration;
  - as to the lawfulness or otherwise of any act done or yet to be done in relation to the person.
- Under s 16 to make decisions in relation to the person's personal welfare, including the giving or refusing of consent to medical treatment and directions regarding responsibility for health care, based upon its assessment of the patient's best interests.

These sections enshrine two different approaches, that of giving declaratory relief and that of substituted decision-making. The difference between the two is that the former is a form of approval (or otherwise) of the decision of another and the latter is an active and involved decision taken by the court. Chapter 10 sets out the history of the development of the High Court's inherent jurisdiction and its gradual shift from the paternalism at the heart of the declaratory approach towards an attitude closer to that of substituted decision-making. The new Court of Protection will have to consider the same best interests test of s 4 in its approach to both ss 15 and 16. The result may thus be that there is little difference between the approaches. This is an area on which however the court's attitude will need to be observed[1].

It is likely that the court's approach will reflect case law developed by the High Court in the exercise of its inherent jurisdiction.

The court will ask the following questions:

1 is mental capacity established?
2 is there an issue regarding serious medical treatment?

3 applying the best interests test as set out in s 4, what are the balance sheet factors that may be drawn up to assist in deciding where the person's best interests lie[2]?

1 See also Chapter 10.
2 See *Re A*, discussed at 8.29 above.

'Bolam' standards

8.47 The test established in *Bolam* and *Bolitho*[1] will be relevant only at the outset of the court's decision-making so that the proposed treatment is one that falls within the standard of the 'responsible body of medical opinion'. It is a professional standard that is not apt to determine an individual's best interests.

1 *Bolam v Friern Hospital Management Committee* [1957] 2 All ER 118; *Bolitho v City and Hackney Health Authority* [1998] AC 232. See also *Simms v Simms* [2002] EWHC 2734 (Fam), [2003] 1 All ER 229.

Evidence

8.48 The court can make declarations or decisions itself. It may also appoint a deputy to make decisions. Upon what basis will it do so? Chapters 7 and 10 consider the procedural and evidential aspects of applications to the Court of Protection, and the appropriate level of judge to hear a decision. It is uncontroversial that in a healthcare decision, supportive medical evidence, and almost inevitably, expert medical evidence, will be crucial for those seeking to challenge prevailing clinical opinion, which experience has shown to be highly influential in cases heard under the High Court's inherent jurisdiction.

Remedies

8.49 The Court of Protection's powers now combine interim remedies, declarations and orders to provide maximum flexibility with regard to what may be required to protect an incapacitated person. The power to make orders in relation to decisions under s 16 is new.

Interim remedies

8.50 The court has express powers in relation to interim declarations, orders and other relief, including injunctive relief: ss 47 and 48. See Chapter 10 for procedure.

Declaratory relief[1]

8.51 The court has express jurisdiction to give discretionary declaratory relief by virtue of s 15 and is no longer dependent upon the inherent jurisdiction of the High Court (save in particular circumstances, see below). There are unlikely, therefore, to be any challenges to the court's jurisdiction in relation to those lacking capacity.

As described above, application for such relief will only be permitted for serious cases and reference to the previous case law may be of assistance.

A declaration is not necessary to establish lawfulness of a medical procedure, but it has become practice (promoted by the courts) to seek one when serious medical treatment is proposed. The desirability of doing so has been recognised, to inform those involved whether a proposed course of conduct will render them civilly or criminally liable, as a safeguard against malpractice, abuse and unjustified action, and upon the determination of an impartial court[2].

1 Main Code, paras 8.15–8.24.

2 *Re F* [1990] 2 AC 1 at 55per Lord Brandon and Lord Goff at 79G; *Re S (Hospital Patient: Court's Jurisdiction)* [1995] 3 WLR 78 per Bingham at 18 above. In the *Re S* case, Hale J, at first instance said that a declaration is a 'binding statement of the legal position'.

Orders and decisions of the court under section 16[1]

8.52 These will flow from the core substitute decision-making jurisdiction of the court. This attaches largely to decisions regarding residence, contact and health[2]. The court may make an order or directions in the person's best interests regardless of whether or not a specific application has been made in that regard[3].

When making such orders or decisions, the court will endeavour to stand in the shoes of the incapacitated person in order to try and take the decision as they might have done for themselves. A difficulty with this approach arises where there is nothing available to guide the court as to what the person may have done had they had capacity. This may happen, for example, where someone has always lacked capacity, so that there is no prior history to draw upon[4]. In those circumstances, it is suggested that declaratory relief is the more appropriate remedy. It is likely that declaratory relief will remain appropriate for most court decisions regarding serious medical treatment. The application process does not, however, require a distinction to be drawn between applications under ss 15 and 16.

1 Main Code, paras 8.25–8.29.

2 Section 17(1)(a)–(c).

3 Section 16(6).

4 See Law Commission Consultation Paper no 119 at paras 4.22–4.27 for a discussion of the merits of a substituted decision making approach vs the 'best interests' test.

Remaining role for the High Court's inherent jurisdiction?

8.53 The Court of Protection is only empowered to act under the auspices of the MCA 2005. Medical treatment decisions involving those under 16 will remain within the ambit of the High Court's inherent jurisdiction. In relation to incapacitated adults (over 16) the MCA 2005 will have authority to determine healthcare decisions. It is suggested that it may only be in the case of vulnerable adults who nevertheless retain capacity, such as those liable to have their consent vitiated by undue influence[1], that the High Court will retain any jurisdiction in relation to healthcare decisions involving adults.

1 See above, the discussion of *Re T* [1992] 4 All ER 649 at 8.53, and Chapter 7.

CASE STUDY

8.54 The following aims to elucidate some of the interplay between the provisions of the MCA 2005 and medical decisions.

The case of Mr Leslie has already been referred to (see 2.28). He has learning disabilities and an irregular heartbeat for which he has been prescribed medication. He is anxious about the regular blood checks to monitor his medication levels and has been assessed to lack capacity to consent. His son, Jack, has been appointed a donee under an LPA to take welfare decisions. There is no specific authority to take life-sustaining decisions. The donee has refused to allow the blood checks to take place. The reason he gives for this is that he knows that Mr Leslie's anxiety is based on his needle-phobia. Therefore, taking his known feelings and beliefs into account, Jack says that his father's best interests lie in refusing the blood tests. He is not persuaded by arguments as to his father's medical best interests, namely, that without the blood checks the heartbeat medication might be ineffective and lead his father to have a heart attack. Jack says his father, at 83, has had a 'good innings' and would not want this intrusive measure to be taken.

1 The hospital cannot act against Jack's validly taken decision as donee. If it did so, its clinical staff would not have protection under s 5 and would face potential civil or criminal liability if they go ahead and take blood from Mr Leslie. This might also result from the use of any restraint in taking the blood.
2 The hospital makes an application to the court seeking a decision (a) that the blood tests are in fact life sustaining treatment within s 4(10) and Jack is acting outside the scope of his authority in refusing consent; and (b) treatment would in any event be lawful and in Mr Leslie's best interests.
3 Just before the first hearing, Jack uncovers an advance decision made by his father stating his refusal to any treatment involving the use of needles to withdraw blood. If valid this advance decision will trump the hospital's application to the court and prevent blood tests: an advance decision need not meet a best interests test.
4 The hospital discovers that Jack is the sole beneficiary under his father's Will and stands to inherit £50,000 on his death. It amends its application to the court to challenge the advance decision on the basis that it is a fake and Jack is not acting in his father's best interests and not an appropriate person to act as donee (s 22).
5 The court does not accept Jack's evidence as to his father's needle-phobia. It finds that he is not acting in his father's best interests and terminates his doneeship. It declares that the blood tests are lawful and

in Mr Leslie's best interests and that the use of some minimal restraint on these occasions is proportionate. It also feels able to take a substituted decision on behalf of Mr Leslie and order that the blood tests are carried out.

PRACTICE POINTS

Decision-making

8.55 This is an area infused by clinical judgement, and so practice points for clinicians are minimal, and where they occur, are largely referred to in the text above.

It bears repeating, however, that the MCA 2005 should make little difference to the daily care and treatment of incapacitated adults. The main change will be in the emphasis on and level of consultation required when exercising judgement in a person's best interests, and to that end clinicians responsible for incapacitated patients must be alive to the possibility of an advance decision or welfare donee. These are radical new provisions, the development of which is only just beginning. Practice and protocols should be developed to highlight these changes.

In addition, the existence or otherwise of family willing or able to participate in a person's healthcare decision-making should be noted. Where there are no such family or friends or they are unwilling so to act, the possible need to instruct an IMCA for a serious medical treatment decision should be prominently noted in their records.

Applications to court

8.56 Legal advisers must be conscious of the need to obtain permission for any application to the court by an NHS Trust and the ensuing delay. Of course where the issue is life-sustaining treatment, the treatment may continue pending resolution of any dispute by the court.

PD 9E refers explicitly to cases dealing with 'serious medical treatment' and usefully sets out the matters to be considered at the first directions hearing in such a case:

> '13. Unless the matter is one which needs to be disposed of urgently, the court will list it for a first directions hearing.
>
> (Practice direction B accompanying Part 10 sets out the procedure to be followed for urgent applications.)
>
> 14. The court may give such directions as it considers appropriate. If the court has not already done so, it should in particular consider whether to do any or all of the following at the first directions hearing:
> (a) decide whether P should be joined as party to the proceedings, and give directions to that effect;

(b) if P is to be joined as a party to the proceedings, decide whether the Official Solicitor should be invited to act as a litigation friend or whether some other person should be appointed as a litigation friend;

(c) identify anyone else who has been notified of the proceedings and who has filed an acknowledgement and applied to be joined as a party to proceedings, and consider that application; and

(d) set a timetable for the proceedings including, where possible, a date for the final hearing.

15. The court should also consider whether to give any of the other directions listed in rule 85(2). [These include a report under section 49 MCA, disclosure, witness statements, expert evidence, cross-examination etc, see chapter 8].

16. The court will ordinarily make an order pursuant to rule 92 that any hearing shall be held in public, with restrictions to be imposed in relation to publication of information about the proceedings.

Declarations

17. Where a declaration is needed, the order sought should be in the following or similar terms:

- That P lacks capacity to make a decision in relation to the (proposed medical treatment or procedure).

E.g. 'That P lacks capacity to make a decision in relation to sterilisation by vasectomy'; and

- That, having regard to the best interests of P, it is lawful for the (proposed medical treatment or procedure) to be carried out by (proposed healthcare provider).

18. Where the application is for the withdrawal of life-sustaining treatment, the order sought should be in the following or similar terms:

- That P lacks capacity to consent to continued life-sustaining treatment measures (and specify what these are); and
- That, having regard to the best interests of P, it is lawful for (name of healthcare provider) to withdraw the life-sustaining treatment from P.'

Chapter 9

DEPRIVATION OF LIBERTY: THE BOURNEWOOD SAFEGUARDS

INTRODUCTION

9.1 As we saw in Chapter 4, the MCA 2005 as currently enacted does not authorise any act connected with care or treatment, or any act of restraint, which amounts to a deprivation of liberty[1]. Similarly, neither an LPA nor a deputy can at present deprive a person of his liberty under authority of the MCA 2005[2]. There is also no express power conferred by the unamended MCA 2005 on the Court of Protection to order such deprivations of liberty[3]. However, the MCA 2005 has since been amended by the Mental Health Act 2007 (MHA 2007). The relevant amendments, not yet in force, insert new ss 4A, 4B, 16A of and Sch A1 to the MCA 2005.The amended provisions expressly confer on the Court of Protection the power to include an authorisation for a deprivation of liberty in a welfare order once specified conditions are met[4] and identify the circumstances in which detention/deprivation can otherwise be lawful[5].

Apart from the powers conferred upon the Court of Protection, s 4A(5) will make deprivations of liberty under the MCA 2005 lawful if authorised by Sch A1. Schedule A1 creates a regime described as the 'Bournewood Safeguards' or the 'Deprivation of Liberty Safeguards'[6]. These terms are used interchangeably throughout this chapter and are also referred to as the 'Bournewood Safeguards Procedures'.

The new powers in the Court of Protection and the Bournewood Safeguards were introduced in order to provide appropriate legal protection for incapacitated individuals who are or may be deprived of their liberty outside of the framework of the MHA 1983. The new s 4A makes provision for the lawful deprivation of liberty by two distinct methods, either (i) as the consequence of an order of the Court of Protection relating to personal welfare[7], or (ii) where it is authorised by the provisions of Sch A1. Section 4B makes provision for a deprivation of liberty to occur where it is, or consists wholly or partly of the giving of, life-sustaining treatment or performing a vital act while the court is deciding any relevant issue and there is a question about whether there is authority to detain under s 4A. The powers of the court are dealt with separately below.

Schedule A1 has been supplemented by a draft addendum to the MCA Code of Practice[8] (The draft Addendum Code) and two sets of draft Regulations[9]. Both the draft Addendum Code and the draft Regulations were the subject of a consultation exercise which was scheduled to have closed on 2 December 2007[10]. There is, as yet, no indication of the date at which these provisions are likely to be in final form. It is however clear that the scheme will run alongside the MHA 1983 regime. This chapter therefore outlines the proposed scheme as it is currently understood and on the basis that it is very likely to be subject to revision before the anticipated enforcement date of April 2009. The relationship of the Bournewood Safeguards scheme with the provisions of the MHA 1983 is considered in Chapter 16.

In essence, the proposed Bournewood Safeguards scheme is one which requires the body responsible for administering the hospital or care home in which such persons may be detained, the 'managing authority', to seek authorisation for any deprivation of liberty. Such authorisation must be sought from the 'supervisory body' which will usually be the relevant Primary Care Trust in the case of a hospital or the relevant local authority in the case of a care home[11]. Schedule A1 and the accompanying draft Addendum Code and draft Regulations set out the procedures for and responsibilities in relation to the operation of the authorisation process and its review. All of the principal constitutive elements of the scheme are detailed and analysed in this chapter. The specific powers of the Court of Protection in relation to deprivations of liberty are also considered.

1 See MCA 2005, s 6(5).
2 See MCA 2005, ss 11(6) and 20(3).
3 See Chapter 10 for more on this.
4 See in particular MCA 2005, s 4A(3)–(4) and ss 16A(1) and (4) and 16(2)(a).
5 For example, MCA 2005, s 4B makes it lawful for a deprivation of liberty to occur whilst a decision on the lawfulness of that course of action is pending before the Court of Protection in respect of giving life saving treatment or performing a vital act and the deprivation of liberty is necessary for those purposes.
6 See DOH Briefing Sheet, November 2006 'Mental Health Bill: Bournewood Safeguards'.
7 See MCA 2005, ss 4A(3), (4) and 16(2)(a).
8 The Mental Capacity Act 2005 Code of Practice issued on 23 April 2007 is referred to in this work, as it is in the draft addendum, as 'The Main Code'.
9 The Mental Capacity (Deprivation of Liberty: Appointment of Relevant Person's Representative) Regulations 2008 and the Mental Capacity (Deprivation of Liberty: Eligibility, Selection of Assessors, Assessments, Request for Standard Authorisations and Disputes about the Place of Ordinary Residence) Regulations 2008. These Regulations were published in September 2007.
10 Joint Consultation Paper published by the Ministry of Justice and the Department of Health on 10 September 2007, 'Mental Capacity Act 2005 Deprivation of Liberty Safeguards', CP23/07. At the time of writing the outcome of the consultation process is not known.
11 'Managing Authority' and 'Supervisory Body' are defined at MCA 2005, Sch A1, Pt 7, paras 176 and 180 respectively. The Addendum Code provides guidance for proper identification of these bodies at paras. 3.1–3.2.

Impetus for legislative change

9.2 The absence of effective domestic legal regulation of the detention of this class of vulnerable persons was highlighted in the judgment of the European Court of Human Rights (ECtHR) in *HL v United Kingdom*[1], the 'Bournewood' case, as far back as 2004. HL lacked the capacity to consent to his admission to Bournewood Hospital for treatment. He was a compliant patient, who was required to remain in hospital and was subject to intensive supervision and control by the relevant healthcare professionals. The ECtHR determined that *HL* had been deprived of his liberty in contravention of both his entitlement to be detained only in accordance with a procedure prescribed by law and his right to a speedy review of the lawfulness of his detention[2].

As the Joint Committee on Human Rights (JCHR) noted in its Fourth Report of Session 2006–07[3], the ECtHR was struck by the ' "lack of any fixed procedural rules by which the admission and detention of compliant incapacitated persons is conducted" and noted the significant contrast between the lack of regulation of admissions of compliant incapable patients and the extensive network of safeguards applicable to psychiatric committals covered by the 1983 Act'[4].

The Bournewood Safeguards represent the long-awaited statutory scheme for affording persons in HL's position the legal protection required by the Convention and found to be absent in that case.

1 (2005) 40 EHRR 32.
2 (2005) 40 EHRR 32 at paras 124 and 142. These rights are guaranteed by Articles 5(1) and 5(4) ECHR.
3 JCHR, Fourth Report of Session 2006–07, HL/40, HC/288.
4 HL/40, HC/288, para 81.

LAWFUL DEPRIVATION OF LIBERTY: ARTICLE 5 ECHR

What is a deprivation of liberty

9.3 Article 5 ECHR contains an express prohibition against depriving a person of his liberty unless a legally prescribed procedure is followed in order to achieve a limited number of aims specifically set out at sub-paragraphs (a)–(f) of Article 5(1)[1]. The MCA 2005, as amended by the MHA 2007, specifically defines the term 'deprivation of liberty' by reference to Article 5(1)[2]. A 'deprivation of liberty' is to be given an autonomous Convention meaning and ought not to be equated with the domestic tort of false imprisonment. The circumstances in which a deprivation of liberty may lawfully occur are, therefore, entirely circumscribed by the provisions of Article 5. Deprivations of liberty which do not fall within the exceptions to Article 5(1) will *not* accord with the Convention[3].

The bases on which a person may be legally subject to a deprivation of liberty in accordance with Article 5 are those which typify the powers of detention associated with a liberal democratic state. They include, for example, detention after arrest but before trial, detention following conviction and, important for these purposes, Article 5(1)(e) which permits 'the lawful detention of persons … of unsound mind, alcoholics, drug addicts or vagrants'[4]. The deprivations of liberty authorised, or sought to be authorised, under the Bournewood Safeguards procedure will invariably fall to be scrutinised or justified by reference to Article 5(1)(e).

In order to comply with the provisions of Article 5(1)(e), three minimum conditions, known as the *Winterwerp* criteria, must be satisfied: The individual must be reliably shown to be suffering from a mental disorder on objective medical evidence; the disorder must be of a kind or degree to warrant compulsory confinement; and the validity/lawfulness of continued confinement will depend upon the persistence of that disorder[5].

The proper characterisation of a 'deprivation of liberty' is therefore a crucial first step in the process of determining whether a public body, empowered to detain, is acting in accordance with the Convention. There is much guidance provided by Strasbourg and domestic jurisprudence and by both the Main and draft Addendum Codes on how a deprivation of liberty might be identified. Unfortunately, there are subtle differences of interpretation as between Strasbourg and domestic jurisprudence and as between the case law and the Codes as currently drafted. What follows, therefore, is a discussion of the varying interpretations of the autonomous convention term 'deprivation of liberty' and an attempt to provide useful and accurate guidance on how the term ought to be applied in the context of the detention of incapacitated persons.

1 See Chapter 17 for the text of Article 5.
2 See MHA 2007, Sch 9, para 10(4) which amends MCA 2005, s 64 to include new sub-ss (5) and (6) which state that deprivations of liberty have the same meaning as in Article 5.
3 In order to be lawful, a deprivation of liberty must, in addition to falling within sub-paras (a)–(f) of Article 5(1)(a)–(f), accord with national law and procedure.
4 Article 5(1)(e).
5 See *Winterwerp v Netherlands* (1979) 2 EHRR 387.

The starting point or the scope of the enquiry

9.4 It is reasonably clear, as a matter of Convention principle, that the concept of deprivation of liberty is not limited to cases in which physical compulsion is deployed to ensure confinement. In *Guzzardi v Italy*[1] the ECtHR stated that the question of whether there was a deprivation of liberty required consideration, not merely of the presence or absence of physical barriers, but 'the starting point must be [his] concrete situation and account must be taken of a whole range of criteria such as the type, duration, effects and manner of implementation of the measures in question'[2]. Nonetheless, the ECtHR was careful to stress two further points of fundamental importance to the exercise. The first was that a distinction must be drawn between a deprivation of liberty and restriction on liberty of movement[3] since the latter does not fall within the protective ambit of Article 5. The second, underlined by the court in recognition of the difficulty attached to any practical attempt to fix, for all time, a boundary between restriction and deprivation, was that the distinction was 'merely one of degree or intensity, and not one of nature or substance'[4]. Despite there being much dispute about what factors are *relevant to* or *decisive of* the question of whether a person has been deprived of liberty, there is a clear consensus both in Strasbourg and in the UK that the focus must be the range of criteria referred to in *Guzzardi*[5].

1 (1980) 3 EHRR 333.
2 *Guzzardi* above at para 92.
3 Protected by Article 2 of Protocol 4 to the Convention and not by Article 5.
4 *Guzzardi v Italy* [1980] 3 EHRR 333 at paras 92–93. This formulation of the starting point for determining whether there is a deprivation of liberty was adopted in *Ashingdane v United Kingdom* (1985) 7 EHRR 528 at para 41.

5 There has been no dissent from the scope of the enquiry delineated in *Guzzardi* in more recent Strasbourg jurisprudence including *HL v United Kingdom*. Similarly, the formulation has been widely adopted in the UK including in the relevant cases of *JE v DE (by his litigation friend, the Official Solicitor) Surrey County Council and EW* [2007] MHLR 39 and *Secretary of State for the Home Department v JJ* [2007] UKHL 45, [2007] 3 WLR 642.

The State must be accountable for the deprivation

9.5 There have been, in particular, two subsequent judgments of the ECtHR which have made the Strasbourg guidance on how deprivation of liberty may be identified less than clear: *Nielsen v Denmark*[1] and *HM v Switzerland*[2]. In *Nielson,* the 'concrete situation' was that a boy of 12 was admitted to a psychiatric hospital for several months at the request of his mother and in the context of an acrimonious custody battle between his parents. The boy was not adjudged to have a mental disorder justifying confinement but the ECtHR recorded that he did receive treatment for neurosis during the admission[3]. The ECtHR concluded that there was no deprivation of liberty since:

(a) the decision to hospitalise the boy was taken by his mother in the proper exercise of her parental capacity. The assistance rendered by the authorities was of a limited and subsidiary nature and was insufficient to render the state accountable under Article 5[4];
(b) the restrictions placed on him whilst admitted were not of a nature or degree analogous to cases of deprivations of liberty specified in any of the sub-paragraphs of Article 5(1) and were no more than normal requirements for the care of a child of that age receiving treatment in hospital[5]; and
(c) it was permissible for a child of that age to be admitted to hospital at the behest of the holder of parental rights, against his wishes without Article 5(1) being engaged or contravened[6].

The majority judgment in *Neilson* did appear to imply that the reason for the putative deprivation of liberty (in that case the exercise of proper parental authority) was relevant to, and determinative of, whether there was an actual deprivation of liberty[7]. The question of whether 'beneficence of purpose'[8] can or ought to prevent a particular state of affairs from amounting to a deprivation of liberty is discussed below. However, one of the less problematic principles which can be deduced from *Nielsen* is the principle that the deprivation *must* be imputable to the state and not to a non-state organ (the mother in that case).

1 (1989) 11 EHRR 175.
2 (2004) 38 EHRR 17.
3 (1989) 11 EHRR 175 at para 70.
4 (1989) 11 EHRR 175 at paras 63–64.
5 (1989) 11 EHRR 175 at para 72
6 (1989) 11 EHRR 175 at para 72.
7 It is worthwhile to note that the seven dissenting judges concluded that the placement of the boy in a psychiatric institution when not mentally unwell for several months was in fact a deprivation of liberty which could not be justified with reference to the stipulated exceptions to Article 5(1).

8 An expression used by Munby J in his exegesis of the relevant convention case law in *JE v DE (by his litigation friend, the Official Solicitor) Surrey County Council and EW* [2007] MHLR 39 at paras 46–47.

Is the aim or purpose of the putative deprivation relevant?

9.6 The notion, at least incipient in *Nielsen,* that a philanthropic purpose could prevent what was otherwise a deprivation of liberty from being so characterised, emerged as an express proposition in *HM v Switzerland*[1]. In *HM* an 84 year old woman with leg sores and cataract was placed in a nursing home for an unlimited period by order of the court on the basis that her living conditions, in the flat she had shared with her son, were untenable. Whilst she initially objected to the placement, after some time she appeared to agree to stay there[2]. Later decisions of the ECtHR appear to confirm that the applicant in *HM* was legally capable of consenting to the placement[3]. Before arriving at its conclusion that there had been no deprivation of liberty, the court found that:

(a) the applicant's non-cooperation with the authorities capable of assisting with her care whilst living with her son, and the deterioration in her living conditions, hygiene and medical care, had led to the order placing her in a foster home;
(b) she was not placed on a closed ward and had freedom of movement and the ability to entertain social contacts with the outside world;
(c) the domestic body which reviewed the applicant's circumstances had concluded that she hardly felt the effects of her stay in the home and was undecided about which option she preferred;
(d) the applicant's agreement to stay in the home had led to the lifting of the order requiring her to stay there[4].

The majority of the ECtHR in *HM v Switzerland* placed specific reliance upon the fact that the applicant had been placed in the home 'in her own interests in order to provide her with the necessary medical care …' and what it described as 'the comparable circumstances' of the case of *Nielson v Denmark*[5] in reaching its conclusion that the placement was not a deprivation of liberty. Rather, in its view, it was 'a responsible measure taken by the competent authorities in the applicant's interests'[6].

As highlighted by Munby J in his exegesis of the relevant Strasbourg jurisprudence in *JE v DE (by his litigation friend, the Official Solicitor) Surrey County Council and EW*[7], the majority view in *HM* is flawed in two important, if linked, respects.

First, it appears to equate the circumstances of a case involving the exercise of parental authority vis-à-vis a child with the circumstances of serious restrictions placed upon an apparently capable adult. One of the aims of the introduction of the MCA 2005 was to underline the importance of respecting the express wishes of a capable, even if vulnerable, adult. The comparison with the circumstances of *Nielson* is inapposite precisely because it could operate to infantilise potentially competent non-consenting adults.

Second, it conflates the question of whether there has been a deprivation of liberty with the necessarily distinct question of whether the alleged deprivation may be justified. There is a clear suggestion, in *HM*, that a finding that there has been a 'deprivation of liberty' can be avoided where the measure is adopted in the best interests of the person concerned. Since this interpretation has appeared to find some favour in domestic courts, it is important to analyse it with care.

In *R (on the application of the Secretary of State for the Home Department) v Mental Health Review Tribunal (PH, Interested Party)*[8], the Court of Appeal considered the question of whether a conditional discharge package which required a patient to reside in specialist accommodation, and to be accompanied by an escort whenever he left the premises, amounted to a deprivation of liberty. *PH,* whose aim was to preserve the discharge package which would see him out of detention in hospital, argued that the conditions of residence and escort were put in place to protect him. He argued that the fact that they were designed, in large part, to facilitate his contact with the outside world, robbed them of the quality of a deprivation. In finding for *PH,* the court cited both *Nielsen* and *HM* as authority for the proposition that the purpose sought to be achieved by the measures under scrutiny is relevant to the determination[9]. On the other hand, in *R (on the application of G) v Mental Health Review Tribunal*[10], a case not entirely factually dissimilar from *PH,* Collins J expressed healthy scepticism about whether the motivation to act in the bests interests of the individual in question could save a detention from being characterised as a deprivation of liberty.

However, in *Secretary of State for the Home Department v JJ*[11], in the context of considering whether the control orders imposed upon suspected terrorists by the Secretary of State deprived the suspects of their liberty in breach of Article 5, Baroness Hale, albeit obiter, endorsed the view that restrictions 'designed, at least in part, for the benefit of the person concerned are less likely to be considered a deprivation of liberty than are restrictions designed for the protection of society'[12]. The purpose of a detention was crucial to the recent decision of the Court of Appeal in *Austin and Saxby v Commissioner of Police for the Metropolis*[13]. The court concluded in that case that the confinement of 'May Day' protesters in Oxford Circus by the police for seven hours in 2001 did not amount to a deprivation. Basing itself upon *HM v Switzerland*, the court in *Austin* assented to the proposition that the officers' motivation to protect both the confined individuals and others from the risk of crime, violence and disorder prevented the restriction from conflicting with the true aim of Article 5(1); to 'avoid arbitrary detention'[14]. In this sense *Austin* seems to narrow the definition of a deprivation of liberty yet further to exclude restrictions undertaken not merely for reasons of paternalism (i.e. if one is detained in one's best interests then one is not detained) but also for reasons of social protection.

Despite Baroness Hale's comments in *JJ* (in which the contested issue was the objective circumstances of the suspects rather than any question of motive) and the Court of Appeal's extension of the 'best interests' approach in *Austin,* there must be doubt about whether this line of reasoning can stand the test of time or rigour. It is of note that the judgment in *JE,* in which Munby J eschewed the approach to *HM* approved by their Lordships in *Austin,* does not appear to have been considered by their Lordships in either *JJ* or *Austin.* It is suggested that Munby J's analysis in *JE* represents the most compelling distillation of the relevant case law. His analysis, and the reasons that it ought still to be regarded as the most accurate statement of the law, can be summarised as follows:

- The question of whether a measure amounts to a deprivation of liberty does not depend on whether it is intended to serve or actually serves the interests of the person concerned[15]. Any other view would lead inexorably to the unattractive conclusion that all detentions declared to be for 'useful' or 'beneficient' purposes could evade Article 5 scrutiny. That which ought to be tested by reference to Article 5 would be thereby be confirmed without inquiry.
- HM and Nielson can no longer be seen as authority for the proposition that beneficial restrictions may turn what would otherwise be a deprivation of liberty into something less than that. This is because the ECtHR failed to adopt this as a criterion for determining the issues in the subsequent important cases of *HL v United Kingdom*[16] and *Storck v Germany*[17]. In both of those cases, the ECtHR indicated that the decision in HM turned substantially on the applicant's apparently capable consent to the restrictive measures.
- Insofar as *PH* appears to support the 'best interests' or 'beneficent purpose' test, it should be viewed with some caution as having been decided before *HL v United Kingdom* and *Storck*. A useful approach to the decision in *PH*, which would be consistent with the approach taken by Munby J in *JE*, may be that *PH* was also a marginal decision in which the claimant's consent to the conditions negated a finding of a deprivation of liberty on those particular facts.
- Insofar as Austin appears to extend the 'beneficient purpose' test to include purposes which detaining authorities regard as 'necessary', it ought to be seen as confined to the rare circumstances in which (a) restrictions on liberty are required to be used as forms of responsible crowd control; and (b) such restrictions do not easily lend themselves to justification by reference to any of the sub-paragraphs of Article 5(1).

1 (2004) 38 EHRR 17.
2 See (2004) 38 EHRR 17 at 323 for the court's findings of fact.
3 See *Storck v Germany* [2005] MHLR 211 at para 77.
4 (2004) 38 EHRR 17 at 323.
5 (1989) 11 EHRR 175.
6 (2004) 38 EHRR 17 at 323–324.
7 [2007] MHLR 39.
8 [2002] EWCA Civ 1868, [2002] All ER (D) 07 (Dec).
9 [2002] EWCA Civ 1868 paras 14–17 and 24.
10 [2004] EWHC 2193 (Admin), [2004] All ER (D) 86 (Oct).
11 [2007] UKHL 45, [2007] All ER (D) 489 (Oct).
12 [2007] UKHL 45 at para 58.
13 [2007] EWCA Civ 989; promulgated some two weeks before judgment was handed down in *JJ*.
14 [2007] EWCA Civ 989 at paras 95–107.

15 Support for this proposition is found in *De Wilde, Ooms and Versyp v Belgium* (1971) 1 EHRR 373; *R(on the application of G) v Mental Health Review Tribunal* [2004] EWHC 2193 (Admin) [2004] All ER (D) 86 (Oct), the dissenting opinion of Judge Loucaides in *HM v Switzerland* at paras 0-II11 to 0-II13, and paras 46–47 of Munby's judgment in *JE*.

16 (2005) 40 EHRR 32.

17 (2005) 43 EHRR 96 at para 77.

What is the role of consent?

9.7 The case of *Storck v Germany* saw the (formal) addition of a subjective element – the question of whether the individual *validly* consented to the confinement – to the test for deprivation of liberty[1]. The applicant in *Storck* was placed in a locked ward in a clinic in Bremen under the continuous supervision and control of the clinical personnel and was not free to leave the clinic during her entire stay of some 20 months. Whereas she presented herself voluntarily to the clinic, she did not sign the relevant admission documents and later behaved in a manner inconsistent with agreement to stay. She was shackled on one occasion when she attempted to leave and was returned to the clinic by the police on another.

The ECtHR's starting point was the principle, adumbrated in *De Wilde, Ooms and Versyp*, that 'the right to liberty is too important in a 'democratic society ... for a person to lose the benefit of the protection of the Convention for the single reason that he gives himself up to be taken into detention. Detention might violate Art 5 even although the person concerned might have agreed to it'[2]. However, the ECtHR, in effect, qualified the *De Wilde* principle by stating that, in addition to the objective element of confinement, a 'person can only be considered to have been deprived of his or her liberty if, as an additional subjective element, he or she has not validly consented to the confinement in question'[3]. It was the applicant's absence of consent to continued detention in the clinic which, the ECtHR opined, distinguished her case from that of *HM* who was legally capable of consenting to, if equivocal about, her stay in the nursing home. By contrast to the situation in *HM*, the behaviour of the applicant in *Storck* was inconsistent with valid consent and, in any event, she was possibly incapable of validly consenting by reason of the administration of strong medication[4].

The ECtHR in *Storck* regarded the judgment in *HL v United Kingdom* as entirely supportive of its conclusions on the importance of valid consent. It reasoned that if there was a deprivation of liberty in *HL v United Kingdom*, where the applicant lacked capacity to consent but did not attempt to leave, there must exist a deprivation of liberty on the facts of *Storck* where the applicant repeatedly displayed resistance to her confinement[5].

1 It can certainly be argued that the ECtHR's introduction of this subjective element was perhaps, in part, inspired by the need to distinguish *HM*.

2 See para 65 of *De Wilde, Ooms and Versyp v Belgium* (A12): (1979–80) 1 EHHR 373 at para 65. The judgment in De Wilde would seem, at first blush, to conflict with the suggestion it is possible to 'waive' one's right to have objective detention treated as a deprivation of liberty. In particular, para 65 goes on to state that: 'Insofar as the wishes of the applicants were taken into account, they cannot in any event remove or disguise the mandatory, as opposed to contractual, character of the decisions complained of ...'.

3 (2005) 43 EHRR 96 at para 74.

4 (2005) 43 EHRR 96 at para 76.
5 (2005) 43 EHRR 96 at para 77.

The relevance of freedom of movement within the restrictive regime

9.8 The judgment in *HM v Switzerland* introduced the notion that the level of freedom within the conditions of confinement could determine whether there was a deprivation. One of the facts which appeared to lead the court in *HM* to the view that there was no detention was that the applicant was 'not placed in the closed ward of the foster home' and 'had freedom of movement and was able to entertain social contacts with the outside world'[1]. The point made by the dissenting judges in *HM,* and reiterated by Munby in *JE,* was that Strasbourg jurisprudence had not previously contemplated that latitude of movement within typical places of detention could convert a detention into a mere restriction of movement[2]. It was recognised in *Ashingdane* and in *HL v United Kingdom* for example, that prisoners who benefited from low security regimes, and could avail themselves of day release, were no less detained because of these circumstances[3].

It is worth noting that both the applicant and the court in *HL* did concede that the freedom enjoyed by *HM* within the nursing home did distinguish *HM's* objective situation from that of *HL*[4]. However, the notion that the conditions of the restrictive regime under scrutiny can generally be regarded as decisive is not easy to reconcile with certain of the key passages in the ECtHR's judgment in *HL*. Properly interpreted, the *HL* judgment provides that there are two matters determinative of whether *HL's* 'concrete situation' was a deprivation: the fact that he 'was under continuous supervision and control' and the fact that he 'was not free to leave'[5]. As discussed below, it is difficult to envisage a circumstance in which a person is found not to be free to leave but is, simultaneously, found not to be deprived of his liberty by reason of a degree of freedom of movement within the establishment. Once again, therefore, Munby J's analysis in *JE* that a permissive internal regime is *relevant* but cannot be seen to be *determinative* of whether the 'concrete situation' amounts to a deprivation of liberty[6] would appear to hold true.

1 (2004) 38 EHRR 17 at para 48.
2 (2004) 38 EHRR 17; see in particular the dissenting judgments of Judges Jorundsson and Loucaides at paras 0–16 and 0–115 and *Ashingdane v United Kingdom* (1985) 7 EHRR 528 at para 42.
3 See in particular para 92 of the judgment in *HL v United Kingdom* (2004) 40 EHRR 761.
4 It is the view of some commentators that a close reading of *HL* demonstrates that the ECtHR distinguished *HM* from *HL* not merely because of the role of consent but also because of the difference of intensity and degree of respective regimes. See, in particular, 'Deprivation of Liberty: the Bournewood proposals, the Mental Capacity Act 2005 and the decision in *JE v DE and Surrey County Council*', Seminar Paper by Fenella Morris and Alex Ruck-Keene accessible at http://www.39essex.com/index.php?art_id=477.
5 See *HL v United Kingdom* (2005) 40 EHRR 32 at para 91.
6 *JE v DE (by his litigation friend, the Official Solicitor) Surrey County Council and EW* [2007] MHLR 39 at para 57 citing judgment in *HL v United Kingdom* (2004) 40 EHRR 761 at para 92.

Is the key factor 'whether the person is free to leave'?

9.9 So if both freedom of movement within the institution under scrutiny, and more controversially, the motive of the detaining authority, are relevant but not necessarily determinative considerations, are there any decisive factors relevant to the objective element of the test? The crux, in Munby J's view, *is* in fact whether a person is free to leave. This conclusion is attractive not merely because of its logical simplicity but because it appears the only way of reconciling important, but at times incoherent, convention jurisprudence. Most people would perhaps agree that the quintessential indicator of whether they were dispossessed of their liberty would be whether the choice to leave was, ultimately, and effectively, theirs. Few would say that it was dependent upon how many phone calls they were allowed to make from within the confines of the place they could not choose to leave.

Similarly, Munby J's review of the *Strasbourg* case law reveals this question as the key, simple and instructive factor, particularly in marginal cases.[1] There is a very important reason why Munby J's identification of this aspect as a crucial determinant should be considered correct. The rationale lies in the logical impossibility of conceiving of a circumstance in which someone is *not* free to leave confinement for a non-negligble length of time but is, yet, *not* detained. Where there is a great degree of freedom of movement within the circumstances of putative confinement, it would be wholly irrational, as a matter of common sense and of precedent (*Ashingdane*) to determine the deprivation of liberty issue on the basis only of how restrictive the internal regime was found to be. In other words, the beneficiary of a liberal internal regime may be found not to be detained only if he is also free to leave. Conversely, someone who is subject to particularly restrictive internal measures cannot be regarded as dispossessed of his liberty if he has real choice about where he can live. The best characterisation of an objective test in such cases would appear to be whether the person can, in a practical and effective sense, leave.

Freedom to leave is not therefore predicated upon an expression of desire to leave or an attempt to leave. What is central is whether there is, in practical terms, freedom to live where and with whom, and to go where and with whom, one chooses. In *HL* this question was regarded as decisive despite the fact that HL made no attempt to leave. His freedom to leave was the relevant question because the control exercised over him did, in a real sense, dispossess him of his liberty[2]. In the case of *JE* itself, Munby J was careful to point out that the claimant in that case was deprived of his liberty in circumstances where he was led, erroneously, to believe that the police could lawfully prevent him from being removed from the care home in which he was detained[3]. He too was not therefore free to leave.

1 See *JE v DE (by his litigation friend, the Official Solicitor) Surrey County Council and EW* [2007] MHLR 39 at para 44.
2 *HL v United Kingdom* (2005) 40 EHRR 32 at para 91.
3 See *JE v DE (by his litigation friend, the Official Solicitor) Surrey County Council and EW* [2007] MHLR 39 at para 125.

The 'JE' test for the deprivation of liberty

9.10 The claimant in *JE* was blind, had significant impairment to his short-term memory and was thought to lack capacity to decide where he should live. He married DE, a co-defendant in the proceedings, in June 2005. In September 2005, DE was unable to cope with caring for JE and he was placed in X home at the behest of Surrey County Council. In November 2005, JE moved to Y home and Surrey County Council formed the view that it was in his best interests to remain there. It was accepted by all parties that JE repeatedly indicated his wish to return to live with DE. Munby J also found as a fact that DE, reasonably, concluded that the police would be called to prevent her from removing JE from Y home had she so attempted.

Munby J determined that there had been a deprivation of liberty and reduced the test for deprivation of liberty to three elements. His formulation does, as far as is possible, mirror the issues identified as relevant by the ECtHR:

- An *objective* element of a person's confinement in a particular restricted space for a non-negligible length of time. The key factor is whether the person is free to leave. This may be tested by determining whether those treating and managing the person exercise complete and effective control over the person's care and movements. The question of physical barriers is relevant but not determinative.
- A *subjective* element, namely the absence of valid consent to the confinement. For a capacitated individual, this element *may* be taken to be satisfied by the absence of objection. An express refusal to consent by a individual with capacity *will* satisfy this element. In respect of the incapacitated individual, consent *may not* be inferred from the absence of objection. Irrespective of capacity, consent ought not to be unproblematically assumed from the mere fact that a person may have acquiesced into detention.
- The deprivation must be imputable to the State[1].

[1] See *JE v DE (by his litigation friend, the Official Solicitor) Surrey County Council and EW* [2007] MHLR 39 at paras 77–78.

How does the 'JE' test compare with the Guidance in the Main and draft Addendum Codes?

9.11 As indicated in the introduction to this chapter, it is perhaps best to assume for present purposes that the guidance in the Main Code is to be superseded by that in the draft Addendum Code. The focus here will therefore be on the compatibility of the provisions in the draft Addendum Code with the relevant law as best expressed in *JE*.

The draft Addendum Code begins by giving guidance consistent with the scope of the inquiry as set out in *HL and Guzzardi* and correctly identifies the kinds of factors which may lead to a finding of a deprivation of liberty. Paragraph 2.2 of the draft Addendum Code states that the following may be seen as contributing to a deprivation of liberty:

- Restraint was used, including sedation, to admit a person who was resisting.
- Staff exercised complete and effective control over care and movement for a significant period.
- Staff exercised control over assessments, treatment, contacts and residence.
- A decision has been taken that the person would be prevented from leaving if they made a meaningful attempt to do so.
- A request by carers for the person to be discharged to their care was refused.
- The person was unable to maintain social contacts because of restrictions placed on access to other people.
- The person lost autonomy because they were under continuous supervision and control.

Similarly, para 2.4 highlights the importance of considering the duration of the restrictive measures in issue and para 2.6 places due emphasis on the fact that the presence or absence of physical barriers may well be neutral to an assessment, which must necessarily take account of the combined effect of all factors, in any given case. Interestingly, para 2.5 of the draft Addendum Code suggests that a deprivation of liberty may still result from restrictions necessary in the interests of the person's safety. This does appear more consistent with Munby J's proposition that coincidence with best interests cannot save a restriction from being a deprivation than with the contrary view associated with *HM*.

However, the potential divergence as between the draft Addendum Code and the *JE* guidance is apparent in paras 2.8–2.16 of the draft Addendum Code. Paragraph 2.8 points to three factors likely to be considered by the courts as relevant to the question of deprivation:

- The person is not allowed to leave the facility.
- The person has no, or very limited, choice about their life within the care home or hospital.
- The person is prevented from maintaining contact with the world outside the care home or hospital.

The main points of distinction between the draft Addendum Code and the *JE* guidance relate to the role of consent and the lack of prominence afforded by the Code to the question of whether the person is free to leave the facility.

The issue of consent, which is specifically identified in *Storck*, and in *JE*, as a determining feature, does not appear at all in the draft Addendum Code's discussion of relevant factors. This is a particularly significant omission in the context of guidance which accompanies an instrument which has the 'capacity principles' at its core. As Munby J stated in *JE*, consent is supremely relevant since it can negative a deprivation of liberty if given by a capacitated person but cannot be assumed to have that effect if given by an incapacitated person. Detaining authorities will be well advised therefore to consider the issue of consent together with the issue of capacity in addition to the factors identified in the draft Addendum Code.

The second point of distinction is the fact that the question of 'freedom to leave' is not accorded the 'key' status it is expressly given by Munby J in *JE*. Rather it is simply identified as one of the three relevant matters for the court's consideration. Whereas the draft Addendum Code uses the facts of *JE* to demonstrate how a deprivation of liberty may be found to exist where a person is not free to leave, it does not, for example, venture to try to explain how a deprivation could ever be found *not* to exist in those circumstances, however extensive the other freedoms afforded the person concerned might be. This failure to highlight the centrality of the question 'whether or not the person is free to leave' was criticised by the JCHR in its Fourth Report of Session 2006–07[1]. The JCHR stated that the draft guidance tended to present the concept of a deprivation of liberty as 'less flexible and elusive' than it actually is. The JCHR expressly approved Munby J's judgment in *JE* and stated of the factors outlined in the draft Addendum Code[2] that:

> 'It is not necessary for all the elements identified in the list of factors contributing to a deprivation of liberty to be present. There will be a deprivation of liberty if it is known that a person is to be prevented from leaving the place where they are being taken to reside.'[3]

1 HL Paper 40 HC 288, para 86, p 30.
2 It should be noted that the JCHR was at that time commenting on an earlier draft Illustrative Code but the provision under scrutiny are the same.
3 HL Paper 40 HC 288, para 86, p 30.

The best guidance on deprivations of liberty at present?

9.12 It follows from the discussion above that health and social care professionals, hospital managers and proprietors of residential care homes would be best advised to be guided by the *JE* formulation which breaks the question of whether there is a deprivation of liberty down into three constitutive elements set out at 9.10 above. All three elements ought to be satisfied in order for there to be a deprivation but paramountcy must be given to the question, as part of the objective element, of 'whether or not the person is free to leave'.

HL v United Kingdom: Procedural requirements and doctrine of necessity

9.13 In *R v Bournewood Community and Mental Health Trust, ex p L*[1], the judgment of the House of Lords which preceded *HL v United Kingdom*, the House of Lords concluded that patients in HL's position – i e patients who lack competence to consent to treatment and were informally admitted to hospital without recourse to the formal detention provisions of the MHA 1983[2] – could lawfully be treated, and detained, on the basis of the common law doctrine of necessity. This doctrine empowers hospitals to detain, treat and care for persons who are incapable of consenting but only where the relevant measures are consonant with the relevant person's best interests[2]. The House of Lords unanimously determined that HL was lawfully admitted to Bournewood Hospital and treated in accordance with the doctrine of necessity. It remains lawful, in principle, to detain and treat incapacitated patients in their best interests. However, the judgment in *HL v United Kingdom* did, unlike the House of Lords, go on to conclude that HL was deprived of his liberty without adequate procedural safeguards[3]. The court's concern was less that the doctrine of necessity was 'imprecise' or 'unforeseeable' (as had been argued by HL) and more that the further element of lawfulness, 'the aim of avoiding arbitrariness'[4] had not been satisfied in HL's case[5]. The ECtHR stated that:

> 'In this latter respect, the Court finds striking the lack of any fixed procedural rules by which the admission and detention of compliant incapacitated persons is conducted. The dearth of regulation and the extensive network of safeguards applicable to psychiatric committals covered by the 1983 Act ... is in the Court's view significant.
>
> In particular, and most obviously, the Court notes the lack of any formalised admission procedures which indicate who can propose admission, for what reasons, and on the basis of what kind of medical and other assessments and conclusions. There is no requirement to fix the exact purpose of admission (for example, for assessment or for treatment) and consistently, no limits in terms of time, treatment or care attach to that admission. Nor is there any specific provision requiring a continuing clinical assessment of the persistence of a disorder warranting detention. The nomination of a representative of a patient who could make certain objections and applications on his or her behalf is a procedural protection accorded to those committed involuntarily under the 1983 Act and which would be of equal importance for patients who are legally incapacitated and have, as in the present case, extremely limited communication abilities.'[6]

There are indications from other extracts from the court's judgment in *HL* that it did not intend its criticisms to be treated as edict. It acknowledged that there were good reasons to avoid the formality and inflexibility of the 1983 Act in any scheme aimed at regulating the detention of incapacitated persons[7]. The court's criticisms should therefore be treated as a broad indication of the sort of protection that might avoid arbitrariness. It should be used as guidance, rather than prescription, on compliance with Article 5.

1 [1999] 1 AC 458.

1 That is patients who are not formally detained by reference to either the civil sections of the MHA 1983 (ss 2, 3, 4 or 5 for example) or the provisions for detention under the MHA 1983 after the commission of a criminal offence (ss 37 and 41 for example).

2 See [1999] 1 AC 458, per Goff L at 485–486; per Steyn L at 495–497. See also Chapter 10 for a full explication of the requirements of the doctrine of necessity.

3 The House of Lords found, by a majority of three to two, that HL was not detained or deprived of his liberty. Its attention would not therefore have been focussed on procedural compliance with the requirements of Article 5.

4 At para 119.

5 See Robinson, R 'Amending the Mental Capacity Act 2005 to provide for deprivation of liberty', *J Mental Health L* 25 2007, at pp 29–31 for more on this.

6 At para 120.

7 See *HL v United Kingdom* (2004) 40 EHRR 761 at para 122. See also Robinson, R, at pp 39–40 where he expresses the view that the government has misinterpreted the court's criticism and adopted too rigid a response via the Bournewood Safeguards Procedure.

The Bournewood Safeguards under the MCA 2005

9.14 These are aimed solely at ensuring that there is a proper process in place for dealing with deprivations of liberty which are necessary for the provision of care and treatment in the best interests of incapacitated persons. They do not include any new powers to decide that a person who lacks capacity should be accommodated in a care home or hospital[1].

1 DH Briefing Sheet – Bournewood – November 2006, 'Mental Health Bill Bournewood Safeguards'.

Summary of important points of principle in relation to the legality of deprivations of liberty

9.15 The following is a guide to considering the lawfulness of actual and proposed deprivations of liberty. These general points of principle do not at this stage make reference to the Bournewood Safeguards but amount to the yardstick against which the Safeguards ought to be measured:

- **Has there been or is there imminently going to be a deprivation of liberty?** This question ought to be determined by reference to the three elements referred to at 9.10 above. The key factor is whether or not the person is free to leave. In so far as the draft Addendum Code does not highlight this key factor, the approach adopted by Munby J in *JE* is to be preferred. The ECtHR case law discussed above should be relied upon as guidance.
- **If there is or is to be a deprivation of liberty, it will only comply with Article 5(1)(e) if it satisfies the *Winterwerp* criteria.** It must therefore be:
  - founded upon objective medical evidence of mental disorder;
  - the mental disorder must be such as to justify compulsory confinement; and
  - justified by reference to the persistence of that disorder.
- **The common law doctrine of necessity can be used to justify the admission and treatment of an incapacitated patient. However, mere compliance with the doctrine's elements will not satisfy the procedural elements of Article 5. The elements of that doctrine are:**
  - there must be a necessity to act when it is not practicable to communicate with the person concerned; and
  - the action taken must be such as a reasonable person would in all circumstances take, acting in the best interest of the assisted person.
- **In determining whether a deprivation of liberty satisfies the procedural requirements of Article 5(1) and Article 5(4), regard should be had to whether there is provision for the following:**
  - formalised admission procedures which indicate who can propose admission, for what reasons, and on the basis of what kind of medical and other assessments and conclusions;
  - requirements as to the exact purpose of the admission; ie whether for treatment or for assessment;
  - limits in terms of time, treatment or care attached;
  - specific provisions requiring a continuing clinical assessment of the persistence of a disorder warranting detention;

  - provisions for the nomination of a representative of the individual concerned who could make certain objections and applications on his behalf;
  - the right to a speedy review by a court which is wide enough to bear on those conditions which are essential for the lawful detention of a person on the ground of unsoundness of mind[1].

- **Deprivations of liberty will need to be authorised/declared lawful by the High Court or Court of Protection.** It should be noted that it remains something of a live issue as to whether the use of the High Court's inherent jurisdiction will be sufficient to satisfy the procedural requirements set out in *HL*[2]. The best guidance to date is to be found in *Re PS*[3].

1 See (2005) 40 EHRR 32 at para 135.

2 See (2005) 40 EHRR 32 at para 141–142. The ECtHR suggested that there was no evidence at the time that the declaratory jurisdiction of the High Court had been extended to consider the legality of deprivations of liberty in HL's circumstances. On this basis the ECtHR concluded that the requirements of Article 5 had not been satisfied. However, the case of *Re PS (incapacitated or vulnerable adult)* [2007] EWHC 623 (Fam) is an example of the declaratory jurisdiction being used for precisely this purpose. See Chapter 7 at 7.8, Chapter 10 at 10.34 and Chapter 16 at 16.42–16.43. These considerations apply also to orders of the Court of Protection, so that any order must be made specifically Article 5 compliant. See 9.107 below.

3 [2007] EWHC 623 (Fam), [2007] 2 FLR 1083. See also Chapter 7 at 7.8 and 7.80 where *Re PS* is considered in the context of welfare decision-making.

DEPRIVATIONS OF LIBERTY UNDER THE MCA 2005[1]

The Bournewood Safeguards

9.16 As stated before this refers to depriving a person of their liberty under the MCA 2005 authorisation under Sch A1[2].

1 The 'Scheme' is here used to describe Sch A1, the draft Addendum Code and the draft Regulations referred to above.

2 Section 4A 4) and (5) as inserted by MHA 2007, s 50(2).

To whom do the Safeguards apply?

9.17 The Safeguards apply to persons in England and Wales who are deprived or are likely to be deprived of their liberty for the purpose of being given care or treatment in a hospital or care home[1]. Despite calls from JUSTICE and the JCHR for 'deprivation of liberty' to be defined in primary legislation, only 'guidance' on the meaning of the concept has so far been provided at in the draft Addendum Code at Chapter 2. A clear understanding of the circumstances which may amount to a deprivation of liberty is a crucial first step as outlined above, both for those who may be required to act, or make assessments, in accordance with the Safeguards, and interested persons who may wish to challenge or review authorisations made. A failure to appreciate the circumstances in which such a deprivation may be held to exist could result in unauthorised, and therefore unlawful, detentions.

Importantly, the Safeguards are principally directed at those who are not or ought not to be subject to the provisions of the MHA 1983. Nonetheless persons who have previously been subject to MHA detention, and whose obligations under the MHA permit, may come to be dealt with under the MCA 2005. It is anticipated that the Safeguards will protect a significant number of persons, like HL, who lack capacity to consent to the arrangements made for their care and treatment. The use of the Sch A1 authorisation process is likely to be triggered where a care assessment identifies a need for detention amounting to a deprivation of liberty[2]. Detention will only be lawful under the Sch A1 regime where the proposed or actual detention is in a hospital or care home. Detention in other settings has to be ordered by the Court of Protection.

1 See draft Addendum Code, para 1.12. 'Care' is not defined in the MCA 2005 and MCA 2005, s 64(1) provides that 'treatment' 'includes a diagnostic or other procedure'.
2 See draft Addendum Code, para 1.22.

Schedule A1 authorisations: general

Terminology

9.18 Schedule A1, and the accompanying draft Addendum Code and draft Regulations, use a number of new definitions relating to bodies/persons with rights or responsibilities under the resultant scheme and/or to specific procedures/requirements which must be satisfied. The terms with which it is necessary to be conversant are set out and abbreviated as follows:

- Managing Authority (MA)[1]:
  - In the case of an NHS Hospital, the NHS body responsible for the running of the hospital in which a person (P) may be deprived of his liberty.
  - In the case of a care home or a private hospital, the person registered.
- Supervisory Body (SB)[2]:
  - In the case of a hospital, usually the relevant PCT or the National Assembly for Wales.
  - In the case of a care home, either the local authority in which P is ordinarily resident or in which the care home is situated.
- Detained Resident (DR)[3]:
  - 'a person detained in a hospital or care home – for the purpose of being given care or treatment-in circumstances which amount to a deprivation of liberty.'
- Qualifying Requirements (QR)[4]:
  - Six requirements which must be met after assessment in order for a standard authorisation to be given.
- Standard Authorisation (SA)[5]:
  - Authorisation which may be given by the SB in accordance with Sch A1, Pt 4.
- Urgent Authorisation (UA)[6]:
  - Authorisation which may be given by the MA in accordance with Sch A1, Pt 5.

1 See Sch A1, Pt 13 and draft Addendum Code, para 3.1.
2 See Sch A1, Pt 13 and draft Addendum Code, para 3.2.
3 See Sch A1, Pt 2.
4 See Sch A1, Pt 3.
5 Schedule A1, Pt 4; see also paras 11(1) and 55(1)(d).
6 Schedule A1, Pt 5; see also paras 11(2) and 80(d).

The qualifying requirements

9.19 There are six QRs all of which *must* be met, or be likely to be met within 28 days of the request[1], before an SA is given by the SB upon a request being made by the MA. The satisfaction, or the apparent satisfaction, of all six QRs is thus pivotal to the scheme and forms the focus of the assessment process under Sch A1, Pt 4 described below.

The relevant QRs are as follows:

- **The age requirement:** The relevant person must have reached the age of 18[2].
- **The mental health requirement:** The relevant person must be suffering from a mental disorder within the meaning of the MHA 1983 *or* from a learning disability which need not meet the MHA 1983 detention criteria[3].
- **The mental capacity requirement:** The relevant person must lack capacity in relation to the question of whether or not he should be accommodated in the relevant hospital or care home for relevant care or treatment[4].
- **The best interests requirement**[5]: There are four conditions to be satisfied:
  - The relevant person is or is about to be a detained resident.
  - It must be in the best interests of the relevant person to be a DR.
  - It is necessary for the relevant person to be a DR in order to prevent harm to him.
  - It is a proportionate response to the likelihood of P suffering harm, and the seriousness of that harm, for him to be a DR.
- **The eligibility requirement:** The relevant person is ineligible by reason of the provisions of Sch 1A (see below)[6]. In very broad terms P will be ineligible if he is either detained under the MHA 1983, subject to a regime under the MHA 1983 the terms of which would be inconsistent with detention under the safeguards procedure or objects to treatment/detention for mental disorder[7].
- **The 'no refusals' requirement:** This requirement is met where either a valid advance decision is applicable to some or all of the relevant treatment or the proposed accommodation for care/treatment conflicts with a valid decision of a welfare donee or a court appointed deputy[8].

1 Schedule A1, Pt 4, para 24.
2 Schedule A1, Pt 3, para 13.
3 Schedule A1, Pt 3, para 14. Note that, in relation to learning disability, that the relevant person can meet this requirement whether or not that disability is associated with abnormally aggressive or seriously irresponsible behaviour. See amendment under MHA 2007, ss 1 and 2, and Sch 11.

4 Schedule A1, Pt 3, para 15. The draft Addendum Code, para 3.40 makes clear that the capacity assessment for these purposes must conform to the capacity principles in the MCA 2005 and the guidance set out in the Main Code, Chapter 4.

5 Schedule A1, Pt 3, para 16.

6 Schedule A1, Pt 3, para 17; see also Sch 1A, paras 2 and 5.

7 See discussion of eligibility at 9.41–9.44 below. This QR applies also to court orders under s 16(2)(a) MCA 2005. See s 16A as inserted by MHA 2007, s 50(2).

8 Schedule A1, Pt 3, paras 18–20.

Standard Authorisation

The request for an SA

9.20 The Managing Authority is required to seek standard authorisation for a deprivation of liberty in the following circumstances:

- **Basic Cases:** In general terms, these are cases in which the relevant person is or is about to become a detained resident and is likely to meet the qualifying requirements within 28 days[1]. Therefore, an authorisation must be sought if the patient/person is about to be accommodated in circumstances amounting to a deprivation of liberty or is already being so accommodated. This procedure permits the MA to seek an authorisation for a deprivation of liberty *after* the detention has commenced. In this regard it has been criticised by the JCHR as being incompatible with the Article 5 requirement to provide for an authorisation procedure which precedes detention in all cases[2].
- **Change of residence:** Where the relevant person is already subject to a standard authorisation and it is proposed that the place of detention ought to be changed[3]. Since authorisations are specific to a particular hospital or care home, a change of residence requires a new authorisation.
- **Renewal:** To ensure that a previous authority for detention does not expire without renewal. An example of this sort of situation is provided for in Sch A1, paras 27 and 29. It applies where a deprivation of liberty has been authorised by the Court of Protection under MCA 2005, s 4A(3) or by the supervisory body under Sch A1, Pt 4 and would only take effect after the existing authorisation for detention expires and it would be unreasonable to delay the making of a further request[4]. The making of requests of this kind is likely to occur when it is considered that the relevant person ought to continue to be detained after the relevant court order or standard authorisation expires. It is not unlike the procedure for renewal contained in MHA 1983, s 20.
- **Prior refusal:** Sch A1, para 28 requires a new request for standard authorisation to be made where one has previously been refused by the SB *and* a change in the relevant person's case is likely to lead to the SB to alter its decision and grant the request[5].

The MA authority has a discretion to request an SA in the following case:

- **Review of existing authorisation:** The MA *may* seek a new standard authorisation to take effect after the expiry of the existing authorisation where the existing authorisation is the subject of a review under Sch A1, Pt 8[6].

1 Schedule A1, Pt 4, para 24.
2 See JCHR, *Fourth Report of Session 2006–07*, HL 40/HC 288, para 83 and JCHR. *7th Progress Report, 15th Report of Session 2006–07*, HL 112/HC 555, paras 1.28–1.29. It may be that the use of an urgent authorisation can ameliorate this problem as it has the effect of speeding up the assessment process. However, the absence of a requirement to satisfy the *Winterwerp* criteria before detention commences in an ordinary case remains unsatisfactory.
3 Schedule A1, Pt 4, para 25.
4 Schedule A1, Pt 4, para 27.
5 Schedule A1, Pt 4, para 28.
6 Schedule A1, Pt 4, para 30.

Formalities relating to requests for Standard Authorisation by the Managing Authority

9.21 The draft Addendum Code suggests that MAs ought to have a procedure/protocol in place to determine whether authorisation ought to be sought, how to request such authorisation, the review of matters pertaining to the application process and the personnel required to act[1]. Before the request is made, consideration must be given to whether the qualifying requirements are met and it must be apparent to the MA that they will be met within 28 days of any request.

A request for standard authorisation by a MA must be made in writing to the relevant SB. The draft Mental Capacity (Deprivation of Liberty: Eligibility, Selection of Assessors, Assessments, Request for Standard Authorisations and Disputes about the Place of Ordinary Residence) Regulations 2008 (the draft Eligibility Regulations) require the written request (at least insofar as the MA is subject to the Regulations for England) to specify the formal requirements which include:

- the details of the care home or hospital;
- details of the person's mental disorder;
- the purpose of the proposed deprivation of liberty, including relevant care plans and needs assessments;
- a summary of the restrictions considered to amount to deprivation of liberty (ie why the application is needed);
- the date from which the deprivation of liberty authorisation is sought;
- whether there is anyone to consult who is not paid to provide care for the person (in order to inform the SB whether an independent mental capacity advocates (IMCA) is needed);
- whether an urgent authorisation has been issued and, if so, the date of expiry.

Information which ought to be included if available, such as the relevant person's address, their age, gender and ethnic group, contact details of relevant professionals, carers, friends and family, IMCAs, donees and/or deputies, is also set out in the draft Eligibility Regulations[2].

Requests must be sent to the relevant SB which is likely to be either a PCT or a local authority. Applications sent to the wrong SB may be sent to the correct one without the need for reapplication. The MA should inform the relevant person's friends, relatives and carers that an authorisation for a deprivation of liberty has been applied for. It must consult with any named consultees for the relevant person and must notify the SB if there is no such appropriate person. In these circumstances the SB must instruct an IMCA to support and represent the relevant person[3].

The MA must keep a written record of every request made for standard authorisation together with reasons for making such requests[4].

1 Draft Addendum Code, para 3.4.
2 Draft Eligibility /regulations, reg 12(2).
3 See draft Addendum Code, paras 3.8–3.10.
4 Schedule A1, Pt 4, para.32.

Duties of the supervisory body after receipt of request for SA

9.22 The draft Addendum Code states that the SB should have a procedure/ protocol for dealing with requests for deprivations of liberty to be authorised. The SB should consider whether the request is appropriate and ought to be pursued. It ought to seek any information that may assist in this decision-making process from the MA. A request may be made by the MA well in advance of the time at which it is intended to take effect. However, the SB may invite the MA to withdraw requests made too far ahead on the basis that accurate assessments may not be capable of being made of the relevant person's circumstances by the time the authorisation is intended to be in force.

Duties in relation to assessments

9.23 Save in the limited circumstances referred to below, the SB is then required to ensure that assessments are carried out in relation to each of the six qualifying requirements by appropriate assessors. The SB is exempt from the requirement to carry out one or more particular assessments if it has a copy of an 'equivalent assessment'. An 'equivalent assessment' is an assessment which:

(a) has been carried out in the preceding 12 months although not necessarily for the purpose of authorising a deprivation of liberty[1];
(b) meets all of the requirements for an assessment of that kind as provided for in Sch A1;
(c) the SB has no reason to believe it is no longer accurate.

1 This is not required in the case of an age assessment: Sch A1, para 49(4).

The assessment process

9.24 The assessment process is the process by which the SB must ascertain, by appointment of relevantly qualified assessors, whether all of the QRs are met. If one or more of the QRs is not met, the SA cannot be given. The duty to ensure that appropriate assessments in relation to each QR are carried out, or have been carried out[1], falls to the SB[2].

1 The SB is permitted, by Sch A1, para 49, to treat a prior assessment, of which they have a copy and which complies with the requirements as would attach to an assessment performed after the request for SA, equivalent to a fresh assessment provided that it was carried out in the previous 12 months and there is no reason to conclude that it may no longer be accurate.

2 See Sch A1, para 33(2).

TIME LIMITS FOR ASSESSMENTS TO BE CARRIED OUT

9.25 All assessments are to be carried out within 21 days of receipt of a request for standard authorisation. However, where an urgent authorisation is in force (see below), the assessment must be completed before the expiry of the urgent authorisation (ie within seven days)[1].

1 Draft Eligibility Regulations, reg 9(1).

General provisions relating to assessors

INSURANCE

9.26 All assessors must be insured to carry out assessments. The SB must be satisfied that they have relevant qualifications, skills and experience[1].

1 See draft Eligibility Regulations, reg 3.

MINIMUM OF TWO ASSESSORS

9.27 There must be at least two assessors in relation to any application for authorisation. This is because there is a requirement that the mental health and best interest assessors are different people[1].

1 See draft Addendum Code, para 3.18.

INDEPENDENCE

9.28 The assessor selected by the SB in any individual case may not be a close relative of the relevant person, financially interested in the care of the relevant person or a close relative of someone who is financially interested in the care of the relevant person[1].

1 'Close relative' is defined in reg 7(2) of the draft Eligibility Regulations and includes civil partners and same or opposite sex partners living together in an enduring family relationship.

Specific provisions in relation to specific assessors

9.29 A person is only eligible to conduct a 'mental health assessment' if s/he is approved under s 12 of the MHA 1983 or is a registered medical practitioner whom the SB is satisfied has special experience in the diagnosis and treatment of mental disorder.

The 'best interests assessment' can only be carried out by one of the following persons:

(a) an approved mental health professional[1];
(b) a registered social worker;
(c) a first level nurse;
(d) a registered occupational therapist; or
(e) a registered chartered psychologist[2].

In addition, the SB must be satisfied that the putative best interests assessor has the ability to take account of diverse views and weigh them appropriately in decision-making.

The 'mental capacity assessment' can be carried out by a person eligible to carry out either the mental health or best interests assessments. However, as stated above, the mental health and the best interests assessors must be different people. This, it would seem, is intended to ensure that the crucial 'best interests' determination is truly independent.

Any person generally eligible to be an assessor can be an eligibility assessor. However, where the eligibility assessor is different from the best interests assessor, s/he must consult that assessor to glean information about the relevant person's attitude to the arrangements being made for care and treatment. Her/his task is to determine whether the relevant person is eligible for detention under the Bournewood Safeguards or, conversely, ought to be dealt with pursuant to a mental health regime.

1 This is new terminology inserted by MHA 2007, s 18.
2 Regulation 5 of the draft Eligibility Regulations sets out the precise nature of registration/qualification required in each case.

The contents of the assessments

AGE

9.30 The 'age assessment' will be satisfied by confirmation that the relevant person has reached the age of 18. The draft Addendum Code suggests that this can be verified by a birth certificate or other reliable means. Since there are no specific requirements applying to age assessors, any assessor who meets the general criteria for assessors can be an age assessor.

MENTAL HEALTH

9.31 The main aim of the mental health assessment is to ascertain whether the mental health QR is met. In other words, it is to establish whether the person is suffering from a MHA 1983 mental disorder or a learning disability which need not result in 'abnormally aggressive or seriously irresponsible conduct'[1]. One of the other duties of the mental health assessor is to consider how, if at all, the relevant person's mental health is likely to be affected by being a detained resident. The mental health assessor must also notify the best interests assessor of his/her conclusions.

1 A person can only be detained under the MHA 1983 on the basis of a mental impairment if it does result in such conduct. By contrast, a person can be detained under the MCA 2005 in the absence of such conduct. See MHA 2007, ss 1 and 2 which reflect this provision but which are not yet in force.

Mental capacity

9.32 The 'capacity assessment' is intended to determine whether the relevant person lacks capacity to decide whether s/he should be accommodated in the relevant hospital or care home for relevant care or treatment. This assessment ought to be made according to the capacity principles, the definition of lack of capacity and the test for adjudging capacity set out at MCA 2005, ss 1–3.

Best interests

9.33 The 'best interests assessment' is by far the most complex and, possibly, the most central to the question of whether a deprivation of liberty ought to be authorised. What is required to be determined is, firstly whether there is or is to be a deprivation of liberty or not (see above), and then whether the four conditions of the best interests requirement are met (see above).

Deciding whether there is a deprivation of liberty

9.34 Careful regard must be had by the best interests assessor to the nuances of the test for a deprivation of liberty discussed above. If the assessor concludes that there is in fact no deprivation of liberty there is no need for any authorisation and the SB should be notified accordingly.

Conducting a full best interests assessment

9.35 If, on the other hand the best interests assessor concludes that there is or will be a deprivation, s/he is required to conduct a full best interests assessment, and in line with MCA 2005, s 4(7) this includes consulting with and recording the details of consultees[1]. The draft Addendum Code provides helpful illustrations of the utility of consulting on best interests issues[2].

Particular regard should be had to the relevant principles contained in the MCA 2005 (s 1) and the Main Code (Chapter 5). Given the specific conditions (above) required to be satisfied for the best interest requirement to be met in the context of a proposed detention, the following factors must be considered:

(a) whether it is in the best interests of the relevant person to be a detained resident;
(b) the nature of the possible harm that may arise if the relevant person is not deprived of his/her liberty;

(c) the likelihood/risk of such harm materialising and whether it is justifiable to take the step of detaining the relevant person so as to avoid the risk of harm identified;

(d) an evaluation of other care options and/or the proposals for avoiding a deprivation of liberty in the future if it is found to be unavoidable.

It is instructive to recall that the proportionality analysis referred to in Sch A1, para 16(5) — ie whether the proposed detention is a proportionate response to the likelihood and seriousness of the harm — is, ultimately, the touchstone. Moreover, any such analysis must accord with the Convention jurisprudence on proportionality in these circumstances[3].

1 See the draft Addendum Code, paras 3.50–3.58.

2 See the draft Addendum Code, pp 38–40.

3 See for example *Litwa v Poland* (2001) 33 EHRR 53 at para 78.

Consultation with the mental health assessor and the MA

9.36 The best interests assessor has a duty to have regard to the conclusions of the mental health assessor in relation to the mental health requirement and any relevant needs assessment or care plan. Such needs assessments and care plans as the SB and the MA have carried out or had drawn up must be provided to the best interests assessor[1]. The best interests assessor must also consult the MA of the relevant hospital or care home.

1 A relevant care plan and a relevant needs assessment are defined at Sch A1, para 39(4), (5).

Setting the maximum authorisation period

9.37 If the best interests assessor concludes that the best interests requirement is met, he must state in his assessment the maximum period he considers appropriate for the relevant person to be a detained resident up to 12 months[1]. It is important that the assessor has regard to the requirement that the authorisation should be for the minimum period necessary. This accords with the principle of least restriction in MCA 2005, s 1. Whatever period is specified, whether 12 months or less, it ought to be justified by reference to the likelihood of any change in the relevant person's circumstances.

1 Schedule A1, para 42(2) provides for a default maximum of one year or such shorter period as may be prescribed in Regulations.

Recommending conditions

9.38 The best interests assessor may also include a recommendation as to conditions which ought to be attached to the standard authorisation[1]. The kinds of conditions anticipated by the draft Addendum Code are issues relating to contact, culturally specific matters or other issues which were crucial to the determination that the deprivation *was* in the person's best interests. Again, in relation to conditions, the principle of the least restrictive measure necessary is instrumental. As the draft Addendum Code provides, the best interests assessor should seek to 'impose the minimum necessary constraints, so that they do not unnecessarily prevent or inhibit the staff of the hospital or care home from responding appropriately to the person's needs …'[2].

1 The SB is required by Sch A1, para 53 to have regard to the recommendations of the best interests assessor before deciding whether to impose conditions.
2 Draft Addendum Code, para 3.57.

Reporting on unauthorised deprivations of liberty

9.39 If the best interests assessor concludes that there is an unauthorised deprivation of liberty, in other words a deprivation of liberty by the MA without authorisation or other lawful authority provided by MCA 2005, s 4A, he must so state in his assessment. The SB must notify the MA, relevant person or any interested person and any IMCA instructed under MCA 2005, s 39A ('s 39A IMCA') so that they may take appropriate action[1].

1 Schedule A1, para 136(3)(c). An application to the Court of Protection for authorisation or determination of liability pending finalisation of the SA may be appropriate.

Recommending a 'relevant person's representative'

9.40 The role of the 'relevant person's representative' (RPR) is discussed in greater detail at 9.77–9.84 below. The best interests assessor ought to recommend a suitable RPR where it is appropriate to do so[1].

1 Draft Addendum Code, para 3.58.

ELIGIBILITY

9.41 As indicated above, the eligibility assessor does not need to possess any qualifications over and above what is required for all assessors under Sch A1. The draft Addendum Code suggests that the eligibility assessment will often be carried out by the best interests' assessor. This may expedite what could otherwise be a protracted process and is a particularly useful time saver where meaningful consultation between those two assessors would be required to decide what ought to be done about a person who is assessed to be ineligible for Bournewood detention[1]. The eligibility criteria reflect the exclusion under MCA 2005, s 28 of treatment for mental disorder of patients detained under the MHA 1983 and subject to the consent to treatment provisions[2]. There may be cases in which it will be difficult to disentangle the circumstances relevant to the MCA 2005 from those applicable to the MHA 1983 (see below and Chapter 16 on the overlap with MHA 1983).

The question of eligibility/ineligibility is to be determined by reference to Sch 1A (not to be confused with Sch A1) of the MCA 2005[3]. The way in which the eligibility criteria are described in Sch 1A is cumbersome. Paragraph 2 of Sch 1A sets out a table of five cases (Cases A–E) in which a person will be deemed to be ineligible if the relevant corresponding provisions of the table and Schedule are satisfied. The following paragraph sets out a narrative explanation of how a person, P, might be found to be ineligible in any of cases A–E. Some of the cases identified can give rise to ineligibility in more than one regard. Where appropriate, the distinct scenarios are set out below. A summary is provided at 9.44.

1 For example, if the best interests and/or eligibility assessor conclude that the person is ineligible under Sch 1A, but the best interests assessment concludes a deprivation of liberty is necessary in the person's best interests, the draft Addendum Code suggests that the eligibility assessor should take immediate steps to arrange appropriate action under the MHA 1983: draft Addendum Code, para 3.66. This might involve arranging an MHA 1983 assessment or contacting any existing responsible medical officer or clinician or local social services authority. This course might be appropriate on the grounds of an anticipated objection by the person to treatment for mental disorder.

2 These are in Part IV of the MHA 1983 and considered in more detail in Chapter 16. In this way the MCA 2005 indicates that non-consensual treatment for mental disorder ought properly to be authorised under the MHA 1983.

3 Inserted by MHA 2007, s 50 and Sch 8. As stated earlier Sch 1A applies by virtue of s 16A to detentions by the Court of Protection.

Circumstances of ineligibility

9.42 A person is *not* eligible for a Bournewood Safeguards deprivation of liberty in the following circumstances:

- **Case A: S/he is detained pursuant to a hospital treatment regime**: A 'hospital treatment regime' is defined in Sch 1A. In essence it means a person who is subject to a 'hospital treatment obligation' (such as an application for admission or treatment under s 2 or 3 or a hospital order pursuant to s 37 of the MHA 1983) under the MHA 1983. In order for a person to be ineligible in this case s/he must be subject to a hospital treatment obligation *and* must also be detained pursuant to that obligation. This case therefore excludes persons subject to in-patient detention under the MHA 1983[1] from Bournewood Safeguards detention.
- **Case B, Scenario 1**: P is subject to a hospital treatment regime, is not detained under that regime, but detention for care and treatment under the Bournewood Safeguards procedure conflicts with a requirement imposed by that hospital treatment regime[2].

  This kind of ineligibility may arise where, for example, a person is liable to detention under MHA 1983, s 3 but has been granted MHA 1983, s 17 leave of absence which requires him to reside at a particular address. If the proposed Bournewood Safeguards detention would require him to live elsewhere, that would not be 'in accordance with a requirement which the relevant [hospital treatment] regime imposes'[3]. He would therefore be ineligible for detention under the Bournewood Safeguards procedure.
- **Case B, Scenario 2**: P is subject to a hospital treatment regime, is not detained under that regime but the care and treatment proposed under the Bournewood Safeguards detention is, in whole or in part, medical treatment for mental disorder in hospital[4]. A person would be ineligible by reference to this Case B scenario where, for example, he was granted MHA 1983, s 17 leave of absence and the medical treatment[5] proposed to be given would overlap with treatment he could/would be given if actually detained under MHA 1983, s 3. It would appear that this particular instance of ineligibility is intended to ensure that persons who are liable to detention for mental disorder under the MHA 1983 ought to be detained under the MHA 1983 and not under the Bournewood provisions for the same or similar treatment. In other

words, 'a[n] authorisation cannot be used as an alternative to the procedures for recall in the 1983 Act'[6].

- **Case C, Scenario 1:** P is subject to a community treatment regime[7] and detention for care and treatment under the Bournewood Safeguards procedure conflicts with a requirement imposed by that community treatment regime. A community treatment regime is, in essence, a community treatment order (CTO) made under MHA 1983, s 17A as inserted by MHA 2007[8]. The provisions relating to CTOs are not scheduled to come into force until October 2008. Under MHA 1983, s 17B, the clinician responsible for the person concerned may attach conditions to the CTO. These conditions could involve, for example, weekly attendance at a hospital in London for the administration of medication. If the place of detention specified in the request for an SA is elsewhere or prevents such attendance, detention is unlikely to be found to be in accord with the relevant CTO[9].
- **Case C, Scenario 2:** P is subject to a community treatment regime and the proposed detention for care and treatment under the Bournewood Safeguards is, in whole or in part, medical treatment for mental disorder in hospital[10]. This kind of case is analogous to the situation in Case B, Scenario 2 discussed above. Again it is believed that the legislative intention was to ensure that persons who are subject to a mental health regime ought to be detained under the MHA 1983 for medical treatment for mental disorder, if appropriate.
- **Case D, Scenario 1:** P is subject to the guardianship regime and detention for care and treatment under the Bournewood Safeguards procedure conflicts with a requirement imposed by that guardianship regime[11]. P is subject to the guardianship regime if he is subject to a guardianship application/order under the MHA 1983. This basis of ineligibility is analogous to those discussed in relation to Scenario 1 of Cases B and C above.

  An accepted guardianship application made under MHA 1983, s 7 gives the guardian, usually the local social services authority, the authority to require a person to reside at a particular place. If the proposed MCA 2005 detention would not accord with such a requirement, for example by requiring P to live elsewhere, and the guardian objects to it, P would be ineligible. If on the other hand the guardianship required P to live at home in normal circumstances, but P needed respite in a care home necessitating a brief deprivation of liberty, an MCA 2005 authorisation could be granted so as to accommodate P in the relevant respite/care home[12]. So long as the guardian does not object there is no conflict between the two regimes.
- **Case D, Scenario 2:** There are three conditions which must be met for P, subject to a guardianship regime, to be ineligible in this scenario:
  - *The relevant instrument authorises P to be a mental health patient.* This means that the relevant standard authorisation specifically proposes[13] to authorise P's accommodation in hospital for medical treatment for mental disorder[14].
  - *P objects to being a mental health patient or being given some or all of the mental health treatment.* For this condition to be met P must object to admission to hospital for medical treatment for

mental disorder or must object to being given some of the medical treatment for which, it is proposed, he ought to be detained.

- *Neither a donee nor a deputy has validly consented to each matter to which P objects.* Donees and deputies are empowered by the MCA 2005 to make decisions in relation to an incapacitated person in prescribed circumstances[15]. If a properly appointed donee or deputy validly consents to treatment for mental disorder to which P objects, this particular condition will not be satisfied.

- **Case E:** P is within the scope of the MHA 1983 but is not subject to any mental health regime and the three conditions outlined above in relation to Case D, Scenario 2 are met. P will be within the scope of the MHA 1983 if he could be lawfully detained pursuant to s 2 or 3. In other words, if the medical and risk criteria for detention under either s 2 or 3 are met, on the assumption that the appropriate medical recommendations were also made, P will be within the scope of the MHA 1983. Note, however, that, in relation to s 3, it must be assumed for these purposes that treatment which is necessary in the interests of the heath or safety of the patient or for public protection cannot be given under the MCA 2005.

The implications of this for determining whether the MCA 2005 or MHA 1983 regime is appropriate in any given case under Case D or E are considered further at Chapter 16.

1 See Case A at Sch 1A, Pt 1, para 2.

2 Schedule 1A, Pt 1, para 3(2)–(3) provides, insofar as is relevant to Case B, that 'P is ineligible if the authorised course of action is not in accordance with a requirement which the relevant regime imposes' and that a requirement imposed by the relevant regime 'includes any requirement as to where P is, or is not, to reside'. The 'relevant regime' in relation to case B is a 'hospital treatment regime' as defined at Sch 1A, para 8.

3 See Case B at para 2 and in particular Sch 1A, Pt 1, para 3(2).

4 See Case B at para 2 and in particular Sch 1A, Pt 1, para 4.

5 Schedule 1A, para 17(2), provides that 'medical treatment' has the same meaning as in the MHA 1983. This means that it 'includes nursing, and also includes care, habilitation and rehabilitation' as defined in MHA 1983, s 145.

6 See Explanatory Notes to MHA 2007, p 36, para 201.

7 Defined at Sch 1A, Pt 2, para 9.

8 CTOs will replace supervised discharge under MHA 1983, s 25A–25G.

9 Schedule 1A, Pt 1, para 3(2), as it applies to Case C provides that 'P is ineligible if the authorised course of action is not in accordance with a requirement which the relevant regime imposes'.

10 See Case C at para 2 and Sch 1A, Pt 1, para 4.

11 See Case D at para 2 and Sch 1A, Pt 1, para 3.

12 Note also that this is the example given in the Explanatory Notes to the MHA 2007, p 36, para 201. These issues are also discussed on Chapter 16. Guardianship is also discussed in Chapter 7.

13 A standard authorisation cannot be given if a person is ineligible. Sch 1A, para 15 makes it clear that where ineligibility is relevant to the decision about whether or not to grant a standard authorisation, all references in Sch 1A to a standard authorisation should be read as if the standard authorisation were, in fact, given.

14 See Case D at para 2 and Sch 1A, Pt 1, para 5(2). 'Mental health patient' is defined at Sch 1A, para 16(1).

15 See MCA 2005, s 9 and Chapter 5 and ss 19–20 and Chapter 11.

Determining whether P objects to mental health treatment

9.43 In those categories of case in which ineligibility may be the result of P's valid objection to detention or treatment of a mental disorder (Cases D, Scenario 2 and Case E above), specific guidance is provided on how to ascertain whether P does, in fact, object. In any determination of whether P objects, all of the circumstances, including in particular P's past and present behaviour, wishes, feelings, views, beliefs and values, insofar as they are reasonably ascertainable, must be examined[1]. Since a number of persons who may find themselves vulnerable to detention under the Bournewood Safeguards may have difficulty communicating or understanding what is being proposed, careful attempts to enable either an objection, or elicit a willingness to consent, will be vital[2].

Paragraph 5(7) of Sch 1A contains the requirement that 'regard is to be had to circumstances from the past only so far as it is appropriate to have regard to them'. It is likely that this specific adjuration was intended to ensure that only past beliefs, values and views which remain relevant, and which it may be assumed that the incapacitated person would still wish to inform their care and treatment, are acted upon. This requirement ought not, however, to be regarded as a dispensation to ignore the incapacitated person's past expressed views. Often the most proximate assumption of what an incapacitated person's wishes might be in relation to the proposed treatment/detention will be garnered from evidence of the values, beliefs and convictions they had held or expressed in the past. It may be said that past views are more likely than present views, in this context, to be the manifestation of a competent outlook consonant with that person's cultural, religious, political, philosophical or ethnographical instincts or beliefs.

Whatever the balance struck between past views and present views in determining whether the person concerned should be taken to be objecting in any particular case, the draft Addendum Code offers the following important advice:

- If there is a reason to think that a patient would object if able, the patient should be assumed to be objecting.
- The eligibility assessor's job is to establish whether there is an objection, not to establish the reasonableness of such an objection.

1 Schedule 1A, para 5(6).
2 Draft Addendum Code, paras 3.63–3.65 and Main Code, paras 5.37–5.48 offer some instruction on what this process should entail.

Summary guidance on ineligibility

9.44 In summary, a person will *not* be eligible if they are:

- detained under the MHA 1983;
- subject to a mental health regime (ie on leave of absence from detention under the MHA 1983, subject to guardianship, community treatment, or conditional discharge under the MHA 1983) *and* are subject to a measure in connection with the relevant mental health regime which would be inconsistent with a Bournewood authorisation;

- subject to a mental health regime, other than a guardianship regime, *and* the proposed authorisation would be, at least in part, for medical treatment for mental disorder in hospital;
- subject to guardianship, or would otherwise meet the criteria for detention under MHA 1983, Part II, *and* validly object to some or all of the treatment at which the proposed authorisation is directed.

NO REFUSALS

9.45 This assessment can be undertaken by any qualified assessor and is aimed at determining whether there is a conflict with an existing authority for decision making for the relevant person[1]. Paragraph 3.72 of the draft Addendum Code gives the following examples of circumstances in which the 'no refusals' assessment would lead to a standard authorisation not being granted:

- If the relevant person has made an advance decision that remains valid and is applicable to some or all of the treatment that the person would receive if authorisation were granted. Advance decisions specifically relate to the refusal of treatment.
- If any part of the proposal to deprive the person of their liberty (including any element of the care plan) would be in conflict with a valid decision of an LPA or a deputy.

Take the example of a person who made an advance decision in relation to specific treatment by the administration of the anti-psychotic medication haloperidol. If treatment using haloperidol was central to the treatment proposed to be given under the SA, the authorisation could not be granted because the 'no refusals' requirement would not be met. Similarly, if that person were subject to a guardianship regime, the eligibility criteria would not be met either since there would be a valid objection to some or all of the mental health treatment (medical treatment for mental disorder for which description haloperidol would qualify). In this example, both the no refusals and the eligibility assessors must have the aim of the MCA 2005, as distinct from the role of the MHA 1983, clearly in mind.

1 See draft Addendum Code, paras 3.71–3.74.

Recording, access to records, and other provisions relating to the work of assessors

9.46 Assessors must keep written records of all assessments performed and give copies to the SB as soon as practicable after carrying out an assessment[1]. They are entitled to inspect and copy medical and social care records which may be relevant to an assessment[2] and must take account of information provided either by the relevant person's representative (see below) or any relevant IMCA[3]. Assessors are not required to carry out assessments if the SB gives notice that another assessment in connection with the SA has reached a negative conclusion[4].

1 See Sch A1, para 134.
2 See Sch A1, para 131.
3 See Sch A1, para 132.
4 See Sch A1, para 133.

Duties of the Supervisory Body upon receipt of assessments

9.47 The SB *must* give an SA if (i) *all* of the six required assessments are positive (ie the QR's are met) and (ii) it has copies of all of them. The SB cannot give a standard authorisation unless these two essential pre-conditions are satisfied[1]. Once any QR assessment comes to a negative conclusion (ie that the QR is not met) the SB is required to give notice to the *other* assessors to stop any assessment process in relation to that particular request[2].

1 See Sch A1, Pt 4, para 50.
2 Note that Sch A1, Pt 9, para 133(4) specifically relieves any assessor of an obligation to perform an assessment under the Schedule if directed to cease by the SB.

Granting a standard authorisation

9.48 When granting a standard authorisation, the SB must set out the period for which it should remain in force. This period must be no longer than the maximum authorised by the best interests assessment and can, in any event, be no longer than the current statutory maximum of 12 months. The standard authorisation can provide for detention to begin at a date which is later than the date on which the authorisation is granted. The SB may attach conditions but must have regard to the recommendations of the best interests assessor in so doing. The MA of the relevant hospital or care home must ensure that any conditions to which the authorisation is subject are complied with. In light of the fact that the safeguards were intended to animate convention rights, the draft Addendum Code correctly stresses the importance of ensuring that authorisations ought to be granted for the shortest period possible[1].

Notably, nothing other than a deprivation of liberty can be authorised by the provisions of Sch A1. As far as treatment and care is concerned, such matters can only lawfully be given in pursuance of primary provisions of the MCA 2005 itself. However, once a standard authorisation is in force, any person who does an act for the purposes of detaining the person concerned is protected from civil or criminal liability in much the same way as is a person who acts in accordance with MCA 2005, s 5 or 6[2].

1 See draft Addendum Code, para 3.80.
2 See Sch A1, Pt 1, paras 2–4. See also Chapter 4 on the protection from liability for acts connected with care and treatment contained in MCA 2005, s 5. At the time of writing the MCA 2005 expressly excludes any deprivation of liberty within the meaning of Article 5 ECHR: ss 6(5), 11(6) and 20(13). These provisions are to be repealed when the MHA 2007 comes into force: s 50(4) and Sch 11, Pt 10.

Formalities in relation to the grant of a standard authorisation

9.49 A standard authorisation is required to be in writing and to state the following:

(a) the name of the relevant person;
(b) the name of the relevant hospital or care home;
(c) the period during which the authorisation is to be in force;
(d) the purpose for which the authorisation is given;
(e) any conditions subject to which the authorisation is given;
(f) the reason why each QR is met.

The draft Addendum Code suggests that conditions should be 'as recommended by the best interests assessor'. This tends to suggest that there is no expectation that the SB will impose conditions which were not recommended by the best interests assessor.

Copies of the written authorisation and the assessments upon which it is based[1] must be provided to the following persons as soon as practicable after it is given[2]:

(a) the relevant person's representative (discussed below);
(b) the MA;
(c) the relevant person;
(d) any s 39A IMCA;
(e) every interested person consulted by the best interests assessor.

1 See Sch A1, Pt 4, para 57 and Pt 9, para 135(3).
2 Schedule A1, Pt 4, para 57.

Duties of Managing Authority on receipt of Standard Authorisation: information and right to review

9.50 The MA must take steps, as soon as practicable, to provide information about, and to ensure that the relevant person understands, the effect of the authorisation and the right to a review by the court under MCA 2005, s 21A, and under Pt 8, the right have a s 39A IMCA and how to appoint an IMCA under s 39D.[1]

1 Schedule A1, Pt 4, para 59.

No power to convey persons to detaining units

9.51 There is no express power to transport or convey a person to a hospital or care home contained under the Bournewood Safeguards[1]. The Government considered that such powers were not necessary 'because it is unlikely that such transportation alone would amount to a deprivation of liberty under Article 5'[2]. The Government also stated that in the rare cases where it was only possible to transport a patient to hospital by detaining them, legal authority, such as an order from the Court of Protection, would be required[3].

Where conveyance or transportation does not involve a deprivation of liberty, it can lawfully be carried out if it satisfies the requirements of s 5 and 6 of the MCA 2005. The requirements of s 6 will be satisfied where necessary and proportionate force is either used or threatened to prevent harm to the person concerned. In addition, the act of conveyance must be an act 'carried out in connection with care or treatment' and must be in the person's best interests[4].

1 DH Briefing Sheet – Bournewood – November 2006, 'Mental Health Bill Bournewood Safeguards'.
2 See HL Paper 40 HC 288, para 88, p 30 where the Government's response to the JCHR's questions is quoted. In its Fifteenth Report of Session 2006–07, HL 97/HC 496, the JCHR was again very critical of the absence of any provision under the Bournewood Safeguards Procedure for a person to be taken and conveyed to the place of detention and concluded that the omission was incompatible with Article 5.
3 See HL Paper 40 HC 288, para 88, p.30. See Chapter 7 at 7.8, Chapter 10 at 10.34, Chapter 16 at 16.42–16.43 and at 9.107 below.
4 See Chapter 4 and MCA 2005, s 5; Main Code, paras 6.6, 6.8–6.14.

Formalities in relation to the refusal to grant a Standard Authorisation

9.52 If the SB is prohibited from granting an SA because one or more of the QRs is not met[1], the SB must give notice of the prohibition to the MA, the relevant person, any s 39A IMCA and every interested person consulted by the best interests assessor. Notice of a prohibition must be given as soon as practicable after it becomes apparent. The SB is also obliged to provide the relevant parties (MA, any IMCA, the RPR and the relevant person) with copies of the assessments which were actually carried out by the time that the authorisation process was terminated[2].

1 Schedule A1, Pt 4, para 50(2).
2 See Sch A1, Pt 4, para 58 and Pt 9, para 135(4).

Other considerations following a refusal to grant a Standard Authorisation: civil/criminal liability

9.53 If the Supervisory Body refuses to grant an SA, important questions arise as to what duties fall to that body and to the MA. It is clear from Sch A1, Pt 1 that the MA will incur civil and/or criminal liability in consequence of detention which occurs in the absence of an SA or UA.[1] If, as the draft Addendum Code indicates, the SB is also responsible for the commissioning of care, it must ensure that any care package does not conflict with the decision not to authorise detention. In short, neither the commissioners of care nor the MA ought to facilitate or perpetuate an unlawful deprivation of liberty. If they do so, they will be vulnerable to habeas corpus applications, actions for damages under the HRA 1998 and in tort[2].

But what are some of the positive actions that the SB or MA ought to take if the authorisation has been refused? The following steps will be pertinent to almost every refusal of an authorisation:

- Immediate review of care provision and care plan to attempt to exclude factors which have lead or will lead to deprivation.
- Recording of steps taken to end/avoid deprivation.

Paragraph 3.95 of the draft Addendum Code provides further helpful guidance in relation to specific grounds for refusal and is paraphrased below:

- **Best interests assessors finds no actual or likely deprivation of liberty:** No action on the part of either the SB or MA is required.
- **Best interests assessor concludes that proposed deprivation of liberty would not be in P's best interests:** MA and commissioners of care, in consultation with the relevant assessor and family and carers, need to ensure that care plan *precludes* a deprivation of liberty. This process will need to focus on involving all interested persons since the outcome could range from a decision not to admit the person to the care home or hospital or alterations in the care plan on the basis that the person will still be admitted. A clear understanding of the best interests assessor's reasons for ruling out a deprivation will aid the decision-making process. Similarly, the participation of all persons interested in P's care will be important to achieving an optimal outcome.
- **Capacity assessor determines that P has capacity to make decisions about care:** MA and commissioners of care need to provide support and assistance to P in making his decision.
- **P ineligible:** Consideration should be given to mental health detention in consultation with the best interests assessor and any relevant responsible clinicians under the MHA 1983.
- **P does not have a mental disorder:** P cannot be detained under the Bournewood procedure but care can be provided under a care plan which excludes a deprivation.
- **Valid refusal by donee or deputy or by advance decision:** Alternative care arrangements will need to be made. If there is a question of the validity of the refusal, an application should be made to the Court of Protection.
- **P under 18:** Consider using the Children Act 1989 (see Chapter 16).

1 Schedule A1, Pt 1, paras 1–4.

2 It is assumed that damages for detention in these circumstances are likely to be awarded in accordance with *R (on the application of KB) v Mental Health Review Tribunal* [2003] EWHC 193 (Admin), [2004] QB 936, [2003] 3 WLR 185.

Possible action by third parties in cases of a suspected unauthorised deprivation of liberty

9.54 An unauthorised deprivation occurs where a person is *already* detained in a hospital or care home and that detention is *not* authorised by any of the following means:

(a) the Court of Protection in the exercise of its powers to make a welfare order[1] (see below);

(b) a Sch A1 authorisation[2];

(c) if while the person/body detaining P, 'D', is awaiting a decision of the court on any relevant issue and (i) there is a question about whether D is authorised to deprive P of his liberty under MCA 2005, s 4A, (ii) the deprivation of liberty is wholly or partly in order to administer life-sustaining treatment or do a vital act for which that deprivation is necessary[3].

1 See Sch A1, Pt 1, para 67 and MCA 2005, s 4A(3), (4).

2 See Sch A1, Pt 1, para 67 and MCA 2005, s 4A(5).

3 See Sch A1, Pt 1, para 67 and MCA 2005, s 4B. Section 4B(5) defines a 'vital act' as an act which D reasonably believes to be necessary to prevent a serious deterioration in P's condition. 'Life-sustaining treatment' is defined at MCA 2005, s 4(10).

What are the first steps to be taken by someone concerned about an unauthorised deprivation?

9.55 If any person other than the MA, an 'eligible person', (for example a carer, friend, relative, advocate or member of a relevant existing inspectorate) believes that P is being subjected to an unauthorised deprivation of liberty, s/he should first inform the MA and then invite them to request an SA. It is hoped that this will lead to swift action by the MA to apply for an SA within 24 hours[1]. If the MA then fails to apply for an authorisation within a reasonable period, the eligible person is entitled to make a request to the SB to determine whether or not there is an unauthorised deprivation of liberty[2]. For clarity, the eligible person cannot make a such a request of the SB unless the three following conditions are satisfied:

1 The MA has been informed of suspected deprivation of liberty.
2 The MA has been invited to request an SA.
3 The MA has failed to request an SA within a reasonable period (ie within 24 hrs).

1 Paragraph 6.1 of the draft Addendum Code suggests that this is the time period in which the MA would be expected to respond.
2 See Sch A1, Pt 1, para 68.

The Supervisory Body must appoint an assessor to determine whether there is a deprivation of liberty

9.56 Subject to the exception below, the SB is required to select and appoint a person who is suitable and eligible to decide whether there is an unauthorised deprivation upon a proper request being made as outlined above. For this purpose a best interests assessor will qualify under the draft Eligibility Regulations[1].

1 Regulation 5 of the draft Eligibility Regulations sets out the precise nature of registration/qualification required of each eligible professional.

When is the appointment of an assessor not required in relation to potential unlawful deprivation?

9.57 The SB is *not* required to select and appoint an appropriate assessor in the following circumstances:

(a) Where the request appears frivolous or vexatious. The draft Addendum Code suggests this may occur where there is very obviously no deprivation or where repeated requests are received even though there have been very recent assessments.

(b) Where the question of whether there is or is not an unauthorised deprivation of liberty has already been considered *and* there is no change of circumstances to warrant reconsideration[1].

1 See the draft Addendum Code, para 6.4 and Sch A1, Pt 1, para 69(4)–(5).

Notification requirements

9.58 The SB *must* notify (a) the person who made the request; (b) the person subject to the putative unlawful deprivation; (c) the MA; and (d) any s 39A IMCA of the following matters:

- the fact that a request to decide whether there is an unauthorised deprivation of liberty has been made;
- the SB's decision as to whether or not to appoint an appropriate assessor; and if that decision was positive
- the name of the appointed assessor.

Time limit within which the unlawful deprivation assessment must be complete

9.59 Except in circumstances in which the SB properly decides that it need not appoint an assessor (ie the request is frivolous or vexatious and/or there is no merit to reconsidering a recent decision in this regard) the assessment of whether there has been an unauthorised deprivation *must be completed within seven days of receipt of the request.*

Duties of the unlawful deprivation assessor

9.60 The assessor is required to consult with the MA and has the same duties in relation to the examination of records (ie health records, care plans and needs assessments) as do assessors performing assessments as part of the standard authorisation process. The assessor will speak to the person who made the request for a determination and should consult as widely as possible with interested persons including, of course, the person subject to the putative unauthorised detention. If there is no one appropriate to consult amongst family and friends, the SB should be informed and arrangements made for the instruction of an IMCA[1].

1 See draft Addendum Code para 6.5.

What happens after the unlawful deprivation assessment is completed?

9.61 There are three possible conclusions which may be arrived at in consequence an assessment of whether there is an unauthorised deprivation of liberty:

- The relevant person is *not* being deprived of his liberty.

- The relevant person is *being lawfully* deprived of his liberty since an authorisation exists.
- The relevant person is being *unlawfully* deprived of his liberty.

If the person is being unlawfully deprived of his liberty, the SB and MA must consider the same options as they would in relation to the refusal to grant an SA (see above) so as to ensure that the unlawful deprivation is not prolonged.

Suspension of a Standard Authorisation: eligibility requirement not satisfied

9.62 An SA becomes suspended only where the relevant person becomes ineligible, ie the eligibility QR ceases to be satisfied for a short period of time (save if this occurs under Sch A1, para 5, see below). The purpose of a suspension, and the pre-requisites for triggering it, are very different from those which relate to a Part 8 review.

Where the MA is satisfied that the relevant person ceases to meet the eligibility requirement and gives the SB notice to that effect, the SA becomes suspended with immediate effect. The SB must then give notice to the relevant person, his or her representative and the MA that the SA has been suspended[1].

The effect of a suspension is that there will be no authorisation for detention/deprivation of liberty and no protection from liability for acts done for the purpose of depriving a person of his liberty under Pt 1 of Sch A1. In addition, no review under Pt 8 of Sch A1 (see below) may be requested or carried out whilst the suspension is in force[2].

A suspension is likely to be used where the relevant person has been detained under the MHA 1983, or where, for example, the guardian of a person subject to a guardianship order is no longer satisfied that a deprivation of liberty is appropriate and objects to it. Care must be taken in such a case to ensure that the deprivation ceases even if the person remains resident in the care home in which detention was authorised. Particular attention would then have to be paid to what it is that caused the relevant person's objective circumstances to amount to a deprivation of liberty so as to ensure that a deprivation is avoided.

1 Schedule A1, Pt 5, paras 91–93.
2 Schedule A1, Pt 5, para 122.

Revival of Standard Authorisation

9.63 If during the suspension the relevant person meets the eligibility requirement again, the MA must give notice of this fact to the SB. The suspension ceases as soon as this is done. The SB must give notice that the SA is re-instated to the relevant person, the relevant person's representative, any s 39D IMCA and the MA as soon as practicable after notice is given by the MA[1]. If the MA does not give the SB notice that the eligibility requirement is again met within a period of 28 days beginning with the date of suspension, the SA will come to an end at the end of that 28-day period.

1 Schedule A1, Pt 5, para 95.

No suspension of Standard Authorisation for ineligibility under Sch 1A, para 5

9.64 Suspension will not be appropriate where the 'ineligibility' arises for by reason of Sch A1, para 5 (Case D, Scenario 2 and Case E above) ie where a person is ineligible because he objects either to being a mental health patient or to being given medical treatment for mental disorder. The appropriate procedure will be a Part 8 review (see 9.87–9.102 below).

Change in supervisory responsibility

9.65 Following a change in SB, the new SB stands in the shoes of the old SB. Any acts done by or in relation to the old body in connection with the authorisation will have effect as if done by or in relation to the new SB 'in so far as is necessary for continuing its effect after the change'[1]. This suggests that the restriction of the deemed responsibility of the new body to acts which *need* to have continuing effect means that new body will not, for example, be deemed to have granted authorisations which had come to an end before the new body took over.

In addition the new body may continue anything which was being done by the old body in relation to the authorisation. However, the new SB does not, by virtue of these provisions, assume liability for the conduct of the old body.[1]

1 Schedule A1, Pt 7, para 100(2).
2 Schedule A1, Pt 7, para 100(4).

Urgent authorisations

9.66 The urgent authorisation process is, in essence, a process which permits the MA itself to authorise a deprivation of liberty where the need for detention is too urgent to await the disposal of a request made via the SA process[1] or too urgent to allow time for the making of such a request[2]. An urgent authorisation (UA) is one which is granted by the MA to itself but, unless extended by the SB, can only last for up to seven days. It is not, however, intended to be used to side-step the SA process. The grant of UA must be accompanied by a request for an SA or, at least, a stated intention to make such a request imminently[3].

The draft Code suggests that UAs should normally be used in response to sudden and unforeseen needs but may also be used in care planning, for example, to avoid any delay in a transfer to a care home where the accommodation in the home would involve a deprivation of liberty.

Having granted itself a UA in any case, the MA cannot itself authorise further detention by the use of a further UA. Any extension of a UA can only be granted upon application to the SB. Only one extension request may be made in relation to the original UA[4].

1 See Sch A1, Pt 5, para 76(3).
2 See Sch A1, Pt 5, para 76(2).
3 The draft Addendum Code suggests that 'an urgent authorisation can never be issued without a request for a standard authorisation being made'. This is not a statutory requirement but is the implication which can be drawn from Sch A1, para 76 and the draft Addendum Code's guidance.
4 See Sch A1, Pt 5, para 77.

Pre-requisites for urgent authorisations

9.67 The following apply:

- The MA has made a request for an SA or is required to do so by Sch A1, paras 24 or 25 (in other words the relevant person is or is about to be deprived of his liberty and all of QRs have or will be met within 28 days *or* an SA is already in force and there is a need for a change of residence)[1].
- The MA believes that the need for detention is too urgent to await either the making or the determination of a request for an SA[2].
- No UA has previously been given in relation to the particular or 'existing' detention[3].
- The MA has decided upon a period no greater than seven days for which the UA will be in force[4].

The draft Addendum Code suggests that both SB and MA ought to have a procedure or protocol in respect of the UA process[5]. It reiterates the importance of taking account of the views of others with caring roles and the centrality of the best interests analysis in all decision-making under the MCA 2005[6]. In particular it invites MAs to give careful consideration to the merits of using of the UA process for moving a person to a new type of care where a change of location may have such a detrimental affect on their mental health as to outweigh the benefits of the move[7].

1 Schedule A1, Pt 5, paras 76(2)–(3).
2 Schedule A1, Pt 5, paras 76(2)–(3).
3 Schedule A1, Pt 5, para 77(2).
4 Schedule A1, Pt 5, para 78.
5 Draft Addendum Code, para 3.102.
6 Draft Addendum Code, para 3.105.
7 Draft Addendum Code, para 3.110. An example is also given on p 52 of the draft Addendum Code of a circumstance in which a much more accurate mental health assessment was obtained in relation to a learning disabled man precisely because it was determined, after consultation, that assessment at home rather than admission to hospital was in his best interests.

Formalities in respect of Urgent Authorisations

9.68 A UA must be in writing and must state:

- the name of the relevant person;
- the name of the relevant hospital or care home;
- the period during which the authorisation is to be in force;
- the purpose for which the authorisation is given.

Recording, copying and information requirements

9.69 A record of the reason for the grant of a UA must be kept by the MA and a copy of that record must be given to the relevant person and any s 39A IMCA[1]. The MA must take 'practicable' steps, both orally and in writing, 'as soon as practicable' after the UA is granted to ensure that the relevant person understands the effect of the authorisation and the right to challenge it by application to the Court of Protection[2]. Records should also be kept, according to the draft Addendum Code, of all steps taken to consult with family, friends, staff and carers about the decision to grant a UA. Such records should also include a record of the views of these consultees and the reasons for the decision to give the authorisation.

1 Schedule A1, Pt 5, para 82. The role and relevance of a s 39A IMCA is dealt with at 9.86–9.88 below.
2 Schedule A1, Pt 5, para 83.

Extending an urgent authorisation

9.70 As indicated above, only the supervisory body is empowered to extend an urgent authorisation beyond the maximum of seven days which the managing authority may grant itself. If the managing authority wishes to extend an urgent authorisation, it must make a request to the supervisory body. Only one such request may be made in relation to any urgent authorisation which the managing authority grants itself[1] and the extension may only be for a maximum of a further seven days[2].

1 Schedule A1, Pt 5, para 77(3)–(4).
2 Schedule A1, Pt 5, para 85.

Pre-requisites for the grant of an extension

9.71 The SB may only grant an extension of a UA if it appears to them that:

(a) the MA has made the required request for an SA;
(b) there are exceptional reasons why that request has not yet been disposed of/determined; and
(c) it is essential for the existing detention to continue until the request is disposed of.

The draft addendum Code indicates that extensions should be truly exceptional rather than routine. The example given of an appropriate request for an extension is where the best interests assessor would be unable to contact a person whose input would be crucial to his or her assessment without an extension for a specified period[1].

1 Draft Addendum Code, para 3.113.

Granting an extension

9.72 Where the SB decides to grant an extension it must:

(a) decide on the period of extension which can be no longer than seven days; and
(b) give the MA notice of the period of extension[1].

There is a corresponding obligation on the MA to vary the original authorisation so that the stated duration includes the extension.

1 Schedule A1, Pt 5, paras 85(2), (3).

Refusal to grant an extension

9.73 If the supervisory body rejects a request for an extension, it must give notice of both the decision and the reasons for it to the MA.

Recording, copying and informing requirements in respect of extensions

9.74 The MA must record the reasons for a request for an extension and must give notice of the request to the relevant person[1]. The SB must also keep a written record of any request made to them.

Where the request leads to a refusal the SB, in addition to giving notice to the MA as described above, must keep a written record of the outcome[2]. The MA must give a copy of the SB's decision and reasons to the relevant person and to any s 39A IMCA[3].

Where the SB decides to grant an extension, the SB is required to keep a record of the outcome of the request and the period of extension. The MA is required to record the variation and fulfil the same recording, copying and informing obligations as it would have had to have done when the UA was originally granted[4].

1 Schedule A1, Pt 5, para 84(2), (3).
2 Schedule A1, Pt 5, para 86(4).
3 Schedule A1, Pt 5, para 86(3).
4 Schedule A1, Pt 5, para 85(6).

THE RELEVANT PERSON'S REPRESENTATIVE

9.75 One of the reasons for the ECtHR's conclusion in *HL v United Kingdom* that there were inadequate procedural safeguards applicable to HL's detention was that there was no provision for the appointment of a representative of the patient who could make objections and applications on his or her behalf[1]. The court placed some emphasis on the unfavourable comparison of Bournewood patients with MHA 1983 detainees whose 'nearest relatives' played a crucial role in securing their rights[2]. The role of 'relevant person's representative' (RPR), defined in Pt 10 of Sch A1, is intended to provide a potential Bournewood patient with a representative who would support and represent him or her in relation to any putative detention under Sch A1.

Every person who becomes subject to an SA is entitled to have an RPR appointed for him by the SB as soon as practicable after the authorisation is given[3] and as recommended by the best interests assessor if appropriate. The SB may also be required to appoint such a representative where this role becomes vacant whilst the authorisation is in force. There is provision for an RPR to be paid[4].

1 (2005) 40 EHRR 32 at para 120.
2 See *R (M) v Secretary of State for Health* [2003] MHLR 348 at paras 4, 5 for a useful summary of the role of the nearest relative in the scheme of the MHA 1983.
3 Schedule A1, Pt 10, para 139.
4 Schedule A1, Pt 10, para 151.

Role of RPR

9.76 The role of the RPR is to:

- maintain contact with the relevant person; and
- represent and support the relevant person in matters relating to or connected with Sch A1[1].

The draft Addendum Code provides that this role includes triggering a review, using the complaints procedure or making an application to the Court of Protection. This role is, correctly, intended to be independent of commissioners and providers of services and the draft Addendum Code is careful to point out that the RPR ought not to be chosen on the basis that he supports or will support the deprivation of liberty[1].

1 Schedule A1, Pt 10, para 140(1).
2 Draft Addendum Code, para 4.16.

Eligibility to act as RPR: regulation 5 of the Appointment Regulations

9.77 The RPR must be 18 or over, willing to act as RPR, able to keep in contact and must be independent of the relevant MA and SB.

It should not be assumed that the RPR will be the same individual as the nearest relative for the purposes of the MHA 1983. Further, the role is distinct from that of an LPA or a deputy and operates alongside those roles.

When should the relevant person's representative be appointed?

9.78 Since the role of the representative might include raising objections to the proposed detention, it is clearly important for the appointment to occur as early as possible after the request for an SA is made. The procedure for appointment must commence as soon as:

(a) a best interests assessor is identified; or
(b) an RPR's appointment terminates or is to be terminated in accordance with reg 14 of the draft Appointment Regulations (detailed below)[1].

The best interests assessor should identify a person who he might recommend to act as the RPR and discuss this with the appropriate consultees during the best interests assessment.

1 See the draft Mental Capacity (Deprivation of Liberty: Appointment of Relevant Person's Representative) Regulations 2008 (the draft Appointment Regulations) applicable to England only.

Selection process for RPR in a particular case

9.79 It is anticipated that the best interests assessor will play a pivotal role in this process. Where the relevant person has the capacity to chose an RPR, he can choose a family member, friend or carer[1]. The determination of the relevant person's capacity to make this decision will be performed by the best interests assessor with whom ultimate responsibility rests for the recommendation of the person to act as RPR. The SB cannot appoint a family member, friend or carer who has not been recommended by the best interests assessor. It is assumed that the reason for this is a legislative imperative to ensure that a person who was not considered appropriate by the arbiter of the relevant person's best interests is not chosen by the SB. The SB should pay particular attention to the communication and cultural needs of the relevant person when making its choice of RPR.

The RPR will only be selected by the SB where the best interests assessor does not make a recommendation based upon the capacitous wishes of the relevant person, the selection by a donee or deputy or by the best interests assessor him or herself[2]. If the best interests assessor does not make any recommendation, the SB should invite the person it has identified to be the RPR. If the person identified by the SB is willing, he will be appointed. If, on the other hand he refuses, the SB must identify another eligible person and must repeat the process until an RPR is appointed[3].

1 Draft Appointment Regulations, reg 7.
2 Draft Appointment Regulations, reg 11.
3 Draft Addendum Code, para 4.21.

Formalities of appointment

9.80 The appointment must be in writing and must state the duration of the relevant SA. The prospective RPR must express willingness to act and a copy of the written appointment must be sent by the SB to all concerned[1].

1 See draft Appointment Regulations, Part 3, paras 12, 13. The persons to whom the appointment must be sent are the appointed person (RPR), the relevant person, the MA, any donee or deputy, any IMCA involved in the relevant person's case and any person consulted by the best interests assessor.

Supporting and monitoring the RPR

9.81 There is provision for regulations to require the MA to monitor and report to the SB on the extent to which the RPR is maintaining contact with the relevant person[1]. However, there are no express monitoring and reporting obligations upon the MA. There is guidance as follows:

- It is important for the RPR to maintain contact and to have face-to face contact with the relevant person. Visits at reasonable times must be facilitated and details of the RPR should be recorded in the relevant person's health and social care records.
- MAs and SBs should provide the RPR with information about sources of support including IMCAs.
- Any review of the relevant person's care plan by the MA should include consideration of whether the RPR is in sufficient contact to be effective. Records should be kept of the frequency of contact.
- If the RPR ceases to maintain contact, the MA will need to consider whether to inform the SB. The MA may consider it appropriate to raise the matter with the RPR before informing the SB[2].

1 Schedule A1, Pt 10, para 147.
2 Draft Addendum Code, paras 4.24–4.27.

Termination of the appointment of RPR

9.82 Termination of the appointment as RPR can occur in a number of ways. The appointment terminates in consequence of any of the following circumstances[1]:

(a) on death of the RPR;
(b) if the RPR informs the SB that he is no longer willing to act;
(c) where the period of appointment comes to an end (ie the SA comes to an end and there is no new SA);
(d) where the RPR was selected by the relevant person and the relevant person informs the SB that he objects to the RPR continuing in that role;
(e) where the RPR was selected by a donee or deputy who informs the SB that he objects to the RPR continuing in that role;
(f) the SB terminates the appointment because the RPR is not maintaining sufficient contact;
(g) the SB terminates the appointment because the RPR no longer meets the eligibility criteria.

The draft Addendum Code suggests that if the SB is considering termination on the grounds of ineligibility or insufficient contact, it should contact the RPR before deciding to terminate.

1 See draft Appointment Regulations, reg 14 and draft Addendum Code, para 4.28.

Formalities in respect of termination

9.83 Where termination does not result from the death of the RPR or his unwillingness to continue acting, the SB must inform the RPR of the pending termination, the reasons for it and the date on which the appointment will end[1]. Copies of the termination must be sent to:

- the relevant person;
- the MA.
- any donee or deputy;
- any IMCA; and
- any person consulted by the best interests assessor[2].

1 Draft Appointment Regulations, reg 15(1).
2 Draft Appointment Regulations, reg 15(2).

Appointing a new RPR or IMCA following a termination

9.84 Where the SA continues after termination of the RPR role (ie where the termination is not the result of the period of lawful deprivation of liberty coming to an end), the SB must identify a suitable representative as soon as possible. The best interests assessor should, in the first instance, determine the views of the outgoing representative on a potential replacement. The person identified as most suitable ought to be recommended to the SB. If that person declines or is ineligible, the process ought to be repeated until an eligible person is willing to accept appointment[1].

An IMCA appointed under Sch A1 (see below) may also be appointed and act in the absence of an RPR.

1 Draft Addendum Code, para 4.31.

THE INSTRUCTION OF AN IMCA

9.85 Schedule 9 of the Mental Health Act 2007 inserts a clutch of new provisions into the MCA 2005 which apply to the instruction of IMCAs in relation to the A1 authorisations (A1 IMCAs).[1]

There are three kinds of A1 IMCAs:

(a) a s 39A IMCA;
(b) a s 39C IMCA; and
(c) a s 39D IMCA[2].

1 Non-A1 IMCAs are dealt with in Chapter 6.
2 See Sch A1, Pt 11, paras 155–157.

Section 39A IMCA: no RPR appointed

9.86 A s 39A IMCA must be appointed by the SB where an incapacitated person (a) 'becomes subject to Schedule A1' and (b) there is no other appropriate person to be consulted in determining that person's best interests[1].

1 MCA 2005, s 39A(1), (3), as amended by MHA 2007, Sch 9, para 6 and inserted by MHA 2007, s 50(7). Chapter 6 considers the meaning of 'no other appropriate person to be consulted'.

'Becomes subject to Schedule A1'

9.87 An incapacitated person, 'P', 'becomes subject to schedule A1' in three potential ways[1]:

(a) an urgent authorisation is given under Sch A1, para 76(2); or
(b) all of the following three conditions exist:
- an SA has been requested;
- no UA was given before that request was made;
- the requested SA will not be in force on or before, or immediately after, the expiry of an existing SA; or

(c) the SB appoints a person to assess whether or not person is detained, pursuant to a request by a third party to consider whether an authorisation for a detention is necessary[2].

1 MCA 2005, s 39B supplementary provisions.
2 Schedule A1, Pt 4, para 69(2).

RPR and limits on a s 39A IMCA

9.88 If an RPR has been appointed in accordance with Part 10, there will be no need for a s 39A IMCA to perform the role of the RPR as the RPR will be an appropriate consultee[1].

If following the appointment of a s 39A IMCA, an RPR is appointed, then the duties and powers to be exercised by the s 39A IMCA, or towards the s 39A IMCA by others, no longer apply[2]. In other words, once the RPR is appointed, the s 39A IMCA ceases to be required to fulfil his role.

There is one function retained by a s 39A IMCA notwithstanding the appointment of an RPR. That function is the s 39A IMCA's power to make an application to the court to exercise its jurisdiction under s 21A in connection with the giving of an SA[3]. A s 39A IMCA retains this 'power of challenge' even if an RPR is appointed but must consult the RPR in relation to the challenge[4].

1 MCA 2005, s 39A(1), (6).
2 Schedule A1, Pt 11, para 161(1)–(3).

3 Schedule A1, Pt 11, para 161(7).
4 Schedule A1, Pt 11, para 161(6); draft Addendum Code, para 4.35.

Section 39C IMCA: RPR appointment ends

9.89 Section 39C(3) provides that the SB must instruct a s 39C IMCA on notification by the MA that s 39C applies. According to s 39C(1), s 39C applies if:

(a) an authorisation under Sch A1 is in force[1],
(b) the appointment of a RPR ends in accordance with Regulations under Part 10; and
(c) there is no other appropriate person to consult about the person's best interests (as above)[2].

As with a s 39A IMCA, the s 39C IMCA stands in the shoes of the RPR. The appointment of a s 39C IMCA ends when a new RPR is appointed under Part 10 of Sch A1. Where a function (see below) has been exercised by or towards the s 39C IMCA, it does not need to be repeated in relation to the new RPR[3]. A RPR is an appropriate person to consult under s 39C(1) precluding the instruction of the IMCA[4].

1 Standard or urgent authorisation.
2 MCA 2005, s 39C(1).
3 Schedule A1, Pt 11, para 160(2).
4 MCA 2005, s 39C(6).

Functions

9.90 As 39C IMCA will carry out certain functions stipulated for a RPR as long as that function is not suspended under Pt 10 of Sch A1. As indicated above, the draft Appointment Regulations applicable to England do not make any provision for:

- request for a review under Part 8 (Sch A1, Pt 10, para 102(3)(b));
- notice of review under Part 8 (Sch A1, Pt 10, para 108(1)(b));
- notice of outcome of review under Part 8 (Sch A1, Pt 10, para 120(1)(c))[1].

1 Schedule A1, Pt 11, para 159(4).

Section 39D IMCA: unpaid RPR

9.91 The SB must instruct a s 39D IMCA if (a) an authorisation under Sch A1 is in force[1], (b) an RPR is appointed under Part 10 and (c) the RPR is not paid under regulations under that Part for so acting[2].

Instruction must take place in any one of three situations:

1 where the person requests an advocate;
2 where the RPR requests an advocate;

3 where the SB has reason to believe that without an IMCA, neither the person nor the RPR would be able to exercise relevant rights (see below), or have failed to exercise them or are unlikely to exercise them when it would be reasonable to do so[3].

1 Standard or urgent authorisation.
2 MCA 2005, s 39D(1), (2).
3 MCA 2005, s 39D(5).

Limitations on instructing s 39D IMCA

9.92 If a s 39D IMCA is already instructed pursuant to 2 or 3 above, then no additional IMCA is to be instructed by virtue of a request made by the person under 1 above[1].

1 MCA 2005, s 39E.

Functions

9.93 In particular, to 'take such steps as are practicable' to help the person and the RPR to understand:

(a) the effect of the authorisation;
(b) the purpose of the authorisation;
(c) the duration of the authorisation;
(d) any conditions to which the authorisation is subject;
(e) the reasons why each assessor who carried out an assessment in connection with the request for the authorisation, or a review of the same decide that the person met the qualifying requirement in question;
(f) the relevant rights;
(g) how to exercise the relevant rights[1].

1 MCA 2005, s 39D(7).

Relevant rights

9.94 The IMCA is particularly to 'take such steps as are practicable' to help the person or the RPR to (a) exercise the right to apply to court under s 21A if it appears to them that the person or the RPR wishes to exercise that right, or (b) to exercise the right to request a review under Part 8 of Sch A1 in similar circumstances[1].

If the IMCA is assisting with (b) above, then he or she may make submissions to the SB on whether a QR is reviewable and may give information or make submissions to any assessor carrying out a review assessment[2].

1 MCA 2005, s 39D(8), (10).
2 MCA 2005, s 39D(9).

Access to records

9.95 The right under MCA 2005, s 35(6) to interview the relevant person in private and access records applies to A1 IMCAs[1].

1 See Chapters 6 and 14 for more on this.

A1 IMCA/RPR functions

9.96

Provision of Sch A1	*Action*	*Which IMCA or RPR*
Standard authorisation		
para 49(6)(a)–(c)	Accuracy of equivalent assessments	ss 36C IMCA, 36D IMCA and RPR
para 57(2)(a)	Receive copy of SA	s 39A IMCA and RPR
para 58(2)(c)	Receive notification of prohibition re SA	s 39A IMCA
para 59(2)(c), (e), (7), (8)	Information about right to s 39D	Relevant person
para 65(3)(c)	Notification of cessation of SA	RPR
para 68(5)	Right to require SA by 'eligible person'	All
para 69(8)	Notification of assessment under para 68	All
para 71(4), 73(2)	Notification of outcome	All
Urgent authorisation		
para 82(3)		s 39A IMCA
para 86(3)(b)	Extension of UA	s 39A IMCA
para 90(3)(b)	Extension of UA	s 39A IMCA
Suspension of SA: eligibility requirement not met		
para 95(3)(c)(b)	Notice of suspension	s 39D IMCA and RPR
Request review of SA		
para 102(3)(b)		RPR or s 39C IMCA
para 108(1)(b), (c)		RPR or s 39C IMCA
para 120(1)(c), (d)		RPR or s 39C IMCA
Assessment: part 4 or 8		
para 132(a)–(d)	Notice of outcome of review	All
para 135(2)(c), (d)	Copy of assessment	s 39A IMCA and RPR

Provision of Sch A1	*Action*	*Which IMCA or RPR*
para 136(3)(c)	Notification of unauthorised deprivation of liberty	s 39A IMCA and any interested person

PART 8 REVIEW OF STANDARD AUTHORISATIONS

9.97 The Part 8 review is essentially a process of re-assessing the validity of the QRs assessed on initial grant of the SA. The incapacitated person's interests in the process will be protected by the requirement of consultation with the RPR and others as before under Sch A1, Pt 4 (above).

The SB is mandated to carry out a review if requested to do so by an 'eligible person'[1]:

- the relevant person;
- the RPR (or a s 39C IMCA if there is one)[2], or
- the relevant MA.

The SB (a) *must* conduct a review if invited to do so by any of the persons referred to above, and (b) *may* carry out a review of an SA at any time[3].

The MA *must* invite the SB to carry out a review if it appears that any of the six QRs are not met[4]. The scheme of Sch A1 does not prevent persons other than those described as 'eligible' above from requesting a review. This suggests that others including friends, welfare donees or court deputies may request the SB to review an SA, but the SB would not be required to conduct a review upon to request of anyone other than an eligible person. Moreover, the SB would not be required to give notice of the carrying out of a review to any other person even if that person had, in fact, requested the review[5].

1 See Sch A1, Pt 8, para 102(3).
2 See Sch A1, Pt 11, para 159(1)–(4) which provide that if there is a s 39C IMCA, that person may request a Part 8 Review.
3 See Sch A1, Pt 8, para 102(1).
4 See Sch A1, Pt 8, paras 103(2) and 105.
5 See Sch A1, Pt 8, para 108(3).

What are the grounds on which a Standard Authorisation may be reviewed?

9.98 There are three permissible grounds of review which are intended to be exhaustive[1]:

- the 'non-qualification' ground (NQ);
- the 'change of reason' ground (COR); and
- the 'variation of conditions' (VOC)ground.

The NQ and COR grounds will entail a review of *all* QR's. For NQ the eligibility requirement may only be reviewed by reference to MCA 2005, Sch 1A, para 5 (see 9.42 above, Case D, Scenario 2 and Case E) That is, it is only reviewable if it arises on the ground that the person is ineligible by reason of an objection to some or all of the medical treatment for mental disorder proposed to be given under the SA.

An age assessment review is not required under COR.

The VOC ground applies *only* to the 'best interests' QR and arises where there has been a change in the relevant person's case making it appropriate to vary or amend or recast the condition(s) attached to the SA in question, as recommended by the best interests assessor following the initial assessment under Sch A1, Pt 4. To be clear the best interests QR is reviewable on NQ and COR grounds as well.

1 See Sch A1, Pt 8, para 104.

Steps to be taken by the Supervisory Body upon receipt of a Part 8 review request

9.99

1. SB must decide whether any of the six QRs appear to be reviewable: Sch A1, para 109.
2. *If none of the QR's appear reviewable*: no further action by the SB is necessary and review is complete: Sch A1, paras 110 and 118(2).
3. *If one or more of the QR's appears reviewable*: SB must proceed to conduct separate review assessments of each of those QR's following Part 4 assessment duties as before (but see below for special provisions relating to the best interests review) : Sch A1, paras 111(2), 112 and 113.
4. *If one or more of the review assessments is negative* (ie QR is not met): SB must terminate the SA with immediate effect, the review is complete and no further action by the SB in this regard is required : Sch A1, paras 117 and 118.
5. *If each of the review assessments carried out (save for best interests (below) and age) is positive*: SB must then decide whether any of those assessments is reviewable under COR. If yes, SB *must* vary the SA to reflect the reason why the requirement is now satisfied. If no, SB needs take no further action. The review is now complete: Sch A1, paras 116 and 118.

Best interests review: special considerations

9.100

- If the SB concludes that the best interests QR appears reviewable, the review assessment *must* include recommendations as to whether, and if so how, the conditions attached to the SA should be varied. This is a departure from the duty under Sch A1, Pt 4, para 43 (above) (Sch A1, para 113(2)(3)).

- No best interests review assessment is necessary where the SB concludes that it appears to be 'non-assessable' ie it appears reviewable only on the VOC ground and the change is not significant (Sch A1, para 111(3)–(5)). The SB *may* then vary the conditions attached to the SA in such ways as it thinks appropriate in the circumstances and without any consultation. The review is complete (Sch A1, paras 114, 118(4)).
- If the best interests review assessment is positive (ie QR is met), the SB must still consider whether or not it is reviewable under the COR or VOC grounds, and if so whether the change in the case is significant (Sch A1, para 115):
  - if reviewable on COR grounds only, then the SB *must* vary the SA accordingly;
  - if reviewable on VOC grounds and the change is not significant, the SB *may* vary the SA condition(s) as it considers appropriate;
  - if reviewable on VOC grounds and the change is significant, the SB *must* vary (by adding, deleting or altering) the condition(s) attached to the SA as it considers appropriate.
  - the review is complete (Sch A1, para 118(3), (4)).
- If SB conclude that the best interests requirement in not reviewable for COR or VOC, then no action is needed in relation to that aspect of the SA (Sch A1, para 115(6)).
- If the best interests review is negative the SA will terminate as above and the assessor is not required to make a statement regarding any unauthorised deprivation of liberty (Sch A1, para 113(3)).

Best interests review: is there a significant change in the relevant person's case?

9.101 In making this decision regard must be had to the:

(a) nature of the change, and
(b) period that the change is likely to last for (Sch A1, para 111(5)).

It can be seen from the summary above that where a best interests review is positive and reviewable on VOC grounds and there has been a significant change in the person's case, the extent of any variation of a relevant condition remains at the SB's discretion. A mandatory variation of a condition may make an SA unworkable. These provisions maintains sufficient flexibility to enable a significant change to be recorded without any alteration to a condition where the change can still be accommodated. The residual discretion in the SB even where the change is 'significant' may make the provisions potentially difficult to apply. The following case study is taken from the draft Addendum Code and illustrates a situation where a significant change does not lead to a variation of the original conditions:

Case study

Louise is 28 and has autism and a learning disability. Louise's residential home has been granted an authorisation to deprive her of her liberty. One of the conditions of the authorisation was that Louise goes back to stay with her family once a week.

This arrangement worked well, until Louise started to become very upset when she returned to her care home, The distress lasted for a few days each time and neither the care home nor Louise's family were able to identify the reason. The home became concerned about her behaviour and decided that the contact with her family was causing distress to Louise.

The care home requested a review from the supervisory body, suggesting a change to the conditions attached to the authorisation, so that Louise would go home every week but for a day visit rather than an overnight stay, to reduce the disruption to her routine. The supervisory body decided that this was a significant enough change to the conditions to require a best interests assessment.

The best interests assessor consulted the appointed representative – Louise's mother Francine – and other people who knew Louise.

The best interests assessor wanted to communicate with Louise to see if she could find out what was upsetting her. She spoke to Francine and the care home, and considered the written information that the care home had submitted during the initial request for authorisation, which included Louise's communication and language needs. Because Louise doesn't communicate using speech, she had in the past worked with a speech and language therapist. The best interests assessor arranged for this therapist to meet Louise and use a visual communication system with her, to which Louise had previously responded well. Using this system, and her experience that Louise was more comfortable communicating where she felt relaxed, for example in the garden of the care home, the therapist was able to find out the reasons for the increase in Louise's anxiety.

It became clear that Louise was upset because her brother normally drove her home at the end of the visit but had not been doing so for the past three weeks. Following consultation with Francine, the best interests assessor discovered that the reason for this was that Louise's brother had hurt his ankle. It was the change of routine at the end of the weekend that had been upsetting Louise, so it was explained to Louise why her brother wasn't driving the car and the family agreed that Louise's brother would accompany her back to the care home until he was able to drive again.

The outcome of the best interests review assessment was that the authorisation and the conditions originally attached should remain unchanged.

Formalities and procedure in respect of standard authorisation reviews

9.102 The supervisory body is required to give notice of a decision to carry out a review to the relevant person, his or her representative and the MA. Such notice must be given, if practicable, before the review begins and, if not, as soon as practicable thereafter.[1] The SB must give notice of the completion of the review to the MA, the relevant person and his representative and any s 39D IMCA[2]. The notice must state the outcome of the review and what, if any, variation has been made to the SA. Variations must themselves be in writing. Records of the following must be kept by the SB:

- each request for a review made to the SB;
- the outcome of each request;
- each review carried out;
- the outcome of each review;
- any variation of an authorisation made in consequence of a review.

1 See Sch A1, Pt 8, para 108.
2 See Sch A1, Pt 8, para 120(1).

Relationship between Part 8 Review, suspension and new requests for standard authorisation

Suspension

9.103 A standard authorisation may be suspended, as discussed at 9.62 above. This procedure applies only to the eligibility QR, where it ceases to be met for a short period of time for a reason which does not relate to resistance to treatment, or detention for treatment, for mental disorder (see below). According to the draft Addendum Code, it can be used if the relevant person is detained in hospital pursuant to the MHA 1983.[1] If the MA does not give notice that such a person is again eligible within 28 days of the suspension, the SA will cease to have effect at the end of the 28-day period.

1 See draft Addendum Code, para 5.12.

Review

9.104 The eligibility QR will only be reviewable under the Part 8 procedure if the potential ineligibility arises by virtue of MHA 1983, Sch 1A, para 5 (Case D scenario 2; Case E above) ie the reason it appears reviewable is the relevant person's resistance to treatment or detention for treatment for mental disorder. If this is the case the Part 8 review procedure should be commenced immediately by the MA, the RPR or s 39C IMCA or the relevant person himself.

A Part 8 review may not otherwise be requested during the currency of a suspension. If a review has already been requested when the SA is suspended, no action may be taken on the review during the suspension period[1]. It will be important for practitioners to be conversant with the precise circumstances in which each of these two procedures is applicable.

1 See Sch A1, Pt 8, para 122.

Request for new authorisation

9.105 If a request has already been made for a new authorisation to begin after the expiry of the existing authorisation (ie for the purposes of a renewal), a Part 8 review cannot be requested until the new authorisation request has been determined. If, however, the review had already been requested, or is being carried out, before the request for the new authorisation was made, the review must be stayed until the new request is disposed of[1].

1 See Sch A1, Pt 4, para 30, Pt 8, para 124.

THE ROLE OF THE COURT OF PROTECTION

Jurisdiction of the court in relation to deprivations of liberty

9.106 Amendments to the MCA 2005 will give the Court of Protection two roles concerning deprivations of liberty: (a) authorising by court welfare order a deprivation of liberty[1] ('welfare order') and (b) reviewing specific matters pertaining to standard and urgent authorisations under Sch A1 (see above)[2] ('A1 review')[3].

1 MCA 2005, ss 4A(4) (inserted by MHA 2007, s 50(2), s 50(2)), 16(2)(a) and 16A (inserted by MHA 2007, s 50(3)).
2 MCA 2005, s 21A (as inserted by MHA 2007, Sch 9, para 2).
3 It is important to note that these powers are as yet unavailable since the jurisdiction to deal with deprivations of liberty, conferred by the amendments referred to is not now expected to come into force until in April 2009.

Authorisation of a deprivation of liberty under a welfare order: sections 16 and 16A

9.107 Once the above-mentioned amendments to the MCA 2005 come into force the Court of Protection will be empowered to make welfare orders under MCA 2005, s 16(2)(a), authorising or approving care plans or other arrangements requiring a deprivation of the person's liberty, if it is in their best interests. Until these provisions come into force the MCA 2005 does not contain any express authority to detain a person. Pre-amendment, the intention and purpose of the MCA 2005 specifically excludes acts amounting to a deprivation of liberty under Article 5 ECHR[1]. Until the relevant amendments are in force, therefore, there is does exist a real question as to whether the High Court, under the exercise of its inherent jurisdiction, or the Court of Protection is the appropriate forum for authorising deprivations. What is clear is that either way the court must fill in the Article 5 ECHR requirements that would otherwise be missing prior to the introduction of the Bournewood Safeguards. As far as the Court of Protection is concerned, it is suggested that a deprivation order *may* be made under s 16 of the MCA 2005. However, such an order will not be Article 5 compliant unless the court specifically adheres to the conditions required to be satisfied in order to achieve that end. Those conditions were identified in the pre-MCA 2005 case of *Re PS*,[2] in which specific guidance was given in respect of the convention compliant exercise of the High Court's inherent jurisdiction in these circumstances. In essence, it is suggested that if the MCA, s 16 route is adopted before the amendments to the MCA 2005 take effect, the *R*(*PS*) guidance remains instructive. This is discussed in greater detail at Chapter 7 at 7.8 and 7.80 and Chapter 10 at 10.9, 10.20 and 10.34. Article 5 compliance must also be secured by any welfare order of the Court of Protection post amendment. See 9.119 below regarding the need for reviews.

1 MCA 2005, ss 6(5), 11(6) and 20(13) which prevent any deprivation of liberty within the meaning of Article 5 ECHR under the MCA 2005, are to be repealed in concert with the new Bournewood safeguards allowing a deprivation of liberty under the MCA 2005: MHA 2007, s 50(4) and Sch 11. The power to detain is, however, confined to the court and authorisations under Sch A1 (s 4A(4) and (5)). No other person may detain a person under this Act: s 4A(1).

2 [2007] EWHC 623 (Fam), [2007] 2 FLR 1083.

Eligibility requirements and the court

9.108 MCA 2005, s 16A (not yet in force), specifically provides that the court may *not* authorise a deprivation of liberty within the context of a welfare order if a person is 'ineligible' by virtue of MHA 1983, Sch 1A[1]. Section 16A(1) and (4) expressly prevent the court from authorising detention without determining eligibility by reference to Sch 1A. This achieves consistency with the Sch A1 Bournewood authorisation process as discussed above at 9.42.

In summary a person will be ineligible to be subject to a welfare order depriving him of his liberty where he is:

- detained under the MHA 1983;
- subject to a mental health regime (i e on leave of absence from detention under the MHA 1983, subject to guardianship, community treatment or conditional discharge under the MHA 1983) *and* is subject to a measure in connection with the relevant mental health regime (i e hospital treatment, guardianship or community treatment) which would be inconsistent with detention under the Bournewood provisions;
- subject to a mental health regime, other than a guardianship regime, *and* the proposed authorisation would be, at least in part, for medical treatment for mental disorder in hospital;
- subject to guardianship, or would otherwise meet the criteria for detention under Part II MHA 1983, *and* validly objects to some or all of the treatment at which the proposed authorisation is directed.

1 To be inserted by MHA 2007, Sch 8.

Section 21A and Sch A1 reviews: the powers of the court relating to standard and urgent authorisations

9.109 The court has the power to determine specific questions relating to existing standard and urgent authorisations and has a consequential power to vary or terminate the relevant order or to direct that the SB or MA does so. Permission will not be required for an application by the relevant person, welfare donee, court deputy[1] or RPR to the court to review a standard or urgent authorisation[2]. The CoP Rules[3] do not currently make specific provision for applications to the court pertaining to deprivations of liberty.

1 MCA 2005, s 50(1).

2 See MHA 2007, Sch 9, para 9 which inserts a new s 50(1A) into the MCA 2005. See also Chapter 10 for more on the court's procedures.

3 SI 2007/1744.

Section 21A powers in relation to standard authorisations

9.110 The questions which the court may determine in respect of an SA which has been given may *relate* to any of the following matters:

- whether the relevant person meets one or more of the qualifying requirements;
- the period during which the SA is to be in force;
- the purpose for which the SA is to be given;
- the conditions subject to which the SA is given[1].

The draft Addendum Code states that both the relevant person and the RPR have the right to apply to the court to determine any question *relating* to these four matters and not merely the matters themselves. This indicates that the court's power to consider important details in relation to SAs is wide. The court then has the right to vary or terminate the SA itself or to direct the SB to do so[2].

1 See MCA 2005, s 21A(2), inserted by MHA 2007, s 50, Sch 9.

2 MCA 2007, s 21A(3) , inserted by MHA 2007, Sch 9, para 2.

Section 21A powers in relation to urgent authorisations

9.111 As far as urgent authorisations are concerned, the court has the power to determine questions relating to:

- whether the UA should have been given;
- the period during which the UA is to be in force;
- the purpose for which the UA was given[1].

The court has the same power to vary or to direct variation as it does in relation to SAs[2].

1 See new MCA 2005, s 21A(4), inserted by MHA 2007, Sch 9, para 2.

2 MCA 2005, s 21A(5), inserted by MHA 2007, Sch 9, para 2.

Power to make orders about liability

9.112 The court does have the power under MCA 2005, s 21A to make orders which determine a person's liability 'for any act done in connection with the standard or urgent authorisation before its variation or termination'. What this means is that where the court varies or terminates an SA or UA it can also determine liability in relation to any related act and not just an unlawful deprivation of liberty.

CONCLUSION AND PRACTICAL CONSIDERATIONS: IS THE MCA 2005 SCHEME FOR DEPRIVATION OF LIBERTY CONVENTION COMPLIANT?

9.113 Since the Bournewood Safeguards were intended to be a panacea for lack of safeguards found to exist in *HL v United Kingdom* , the question of compliance of the MCA 2005 scheme with the ECHR is of primary concern. However, the commentary below must be seen as provisional in light of the fact that all of the supporting and subordinate legislation is still in draft form. It is natural to make direct comparisons with the more familiar processes under the MHA 1983, especially given the body of domestic case law now available. Care must be taken in making such comparisons because the underlying purpose of each regime is different. As discussed in Chapter 16, detention does not form the core of the MCA 2005. Indeed, at the time of writing, the statute does not contain any provisions which expressly authorise it. Even when the Sch A1 scheme comes into effect, detention will be provided for only as a necessary consequential feature of a care package based on a best interests assessment. The MHA 1983, on the other hand,does have detention of mentally disordered persons at its core. It is based on coercive treatment for mental disorder where necessary and is concerned with the prevention of harm to the relevant person or to others.

There are also likely to be differences in the patient population subject to each regime though as noted above there will be overlaps too. MCA 2005 patients requiring Sch A1 authorisation as part of their care package are those likely to be compliant and in long term residential care. Of course proper safeguards are no less important for such persons, but its beneficent purpose may well inform the approach of the court to any challenges or disputes brought before it. Authorisation of detention by order of the Court of Protection is likely to be useful for short term needs such as conveying a person or hospital treatment for defined physical disorders.

The following matters are worth highlighting in an attempt to consider whether the scheme does or will address the points arising out of *HL v United Kingdom* as summarised in 9.12–9.13 above.

Deprivation of liberty

9.114 This was noted above to be the crucial first step and an important one for assessors, MAs and healthcare professionals if unlawful detention is to be avoided. The law provides a nuanced approach to what is essentially a factual issue. The MCA 2005 fails to provide either a definition or clear guidance as to what amounts to a deprivation of liberty, save by referring to Article 5 ECHR. The Strasbourg and domestic case law set out in some detail at 9.2–9.12 above. The draft Addendum Code appears deficient on this issue at present but is still the subject of public consultation which may lead to a revision.

Objective medical evidence

9.115 There must be objective medical evidence of a true mental disorder of a kind or degree requiring compulsory confinement and, except in emergency situations, this is a requirement of lawfulness under Article 5(1)(e) ECHR[1]. This appears to be satisfied under the Sch A1 scheme by the multitude of assessments which must be provided including mental capacity, mental health and best interests assessors. There is no express requirement for presentation of such evidence to the court when seeking a welfare order including a deprivation of liberty. The court and practitioners will have to be alive to the need for such evidence.

1 *Winterwerp v Netherlands* (1979–80) 2 EHRR 387.

Formalised admission procedures

9.116 These undoubtedly now exist and Sch A1 and Sch 1A are, at their heart, directed at providing the same. There is clarity about who will detain and the elucidation of reasons for a detention, whether for treatment or care. However, it will be apparent from the text above that the accompanying processes are highly complex. This must impact on their clarity for the purposes of the requirement of certainty and practicability. A primary criticism of the scheme made by many commentators including the JCHR is that it may be so complex and technical in its processes as to negate the benefits of its procedural safeguards: 'the proposals … are detailed and complex, and we question whether they will be readily understood by proprietors of residential care homes, even with the benefit of professional advice'[1]. A question remains, therefore, as to the compliance of the Sch A1 scheme as a whole with Article 5.

Concerns have also been expressed by the JCHR about the fact that the Sch A1 scheme permits detention to be authorised *after* the relevant person has been detained, rather than before detention commences. It has been suggested above that the use of an urgent authorisation may offer a partial/practical solution to this problem, but a lack of precision about timing in the current provisions (see below) must raise some doubt about whether there the Sch A1 Scheme leaves too much scope for prolonged unauthorised detentions.

1 JCHR 4th Report of Sesssion 2006–07, p 31, para 90. It should be noted that the Council on tribunals also commented on the 'staggering complexity' of the Bournewood proposals (now MHA 2007) at paras 17–19 in their Memorandum to the JCHR on on the MH Bill which can be found at http://www.council-on-tribunals.gov.uk/docs/memorandum_to_the_joint_committee_on_human_rights_re_mh_bill.pdf The Council also lamented the apparent lack of independence inherent in a review process in which the Supervisory Body (ie the PCT in most cases) is both initial decision-maker and reviewer.

Limits in terms of time

9.117 The ECHR prescribes no time limits for the duration of a detention in these circumstances. There is a requirement to have regard to the principle that it should be for the minimum period necessary[1]. A maximum period of 12 months for a Sch A1 authorisation may seem long, but the main concern in this regard is that there is no automatic right of review (see below).

There is at present no guidance on how long the Sch A1 process ought to take. The draft Assessment Regulations suggest that the assessment process should be completed within 21 days of receipt of a request for an SA and within seven days of a UA. As far as SAs are concerned, if it does take 21 days to perform the assessments, it can be assumed that the process of authorisation could take at least one month in any given case. This is significantly longer than the process under the MHA 1983 which normally takes place over a few days.

1 See draft Addendum Code, para 3.54.

Right to a speedy review by a court

9.118 The Part 8 review process is also time-consuming and does not provide an oral hearing before a court-like body with any judicial character[1]. It is suggested that it cannot, therefore, fulfil the requirements under Article 5(4) and a person must rely on the reviews before the court under s 21A. Case law pertaining to delays in hearings under the MHA 1983 states that it should be practicable for tribunals to hear s 3 cases within eight weeks of application[2]. There are, at present, no specific rules available regarding access to the court under the MCA 2005 scheme for these purposes. A simple point, however, is that this court, unlike Mental Heath Review Tribunals which are peripatetic and sit in whichever hospital the patient is detained in, will only sit in prescribed locations. This raises questions in relation to physical access in addition to speed.

A real concern is that there is no automatic periodic review at reasonable intervals[3] either under Part 8 or before the court. A review must be initiated by the person or his representative. There is also no default position whereby the MA or SB refer the case for review[4]. But as set out below the MA has a duty to monitor cases on an ongoing basis to see whether there is a change in circumstances regarding the need for a deprivation of liberty. There must be some doubt as to the efficacy of a system of review based on nothing stronger.

1 *X v United Kingdom* (1981) 4 EHRR 181.
2 See *R (KB) v MHRT* [2003] MHLR 28.
3 *X v United Kingdom* (1981) 4 EHRR 181.
4 See of course *R (H) v Secretary of State for Health* [2006] 1 AC 441 at 455, paras 20–27 in which Baroness Hale stated that the right to 'take proceedings' under Article 5(4) ECHR did not require a right of referral in every case.

Reviews of welfare orders

9.119 A deprivation of liberty arising out of a court order is sanctioned by the court in the first instance, but there are no statutory or other safeguards provided in relation to subsequent reviews should the detention be ongoing. The court and practitioners must be alive to this issue and provide for reviews in the court order. The guidance in *R (PS)*[1] set out in Chapter 7 may remain relevant for that purpose.

Continuing clinical assessment

9.120 Only the draft Addendum Codes places the onus on the MA to facilitate the termination of any deprivation of liberty if it is no longer justified[1]. There does not appear to be a statutory duty expressed in these terms but the government indicated, during the parliamentary passage of the MHA 2007, that the MA will be under a duty to keep deprivations of liberty under review[2]. It is difficult to see how the MA could be in a position to request a review of authorisations, in other words to be in a position to detect that one or more of the qualifying requirements was reviewable, if there was no concomitant and continuing obligation to monitor each case.

It is envisaged that Regulations will create a new inspectorate with responsibility for monitoring and reporting on the Bournewood Safeguards procedure in 2008[3]. However, it would appear that this body's functions will essentially be to ensure that the provisions are generally being applied correctly. It will not revisit individual assessments. Much of the responsibility for monitoring and reviewing individual cases will rest with the SB and the MA.

1 See draft Addendum Code, Chapter 5, p 63.
2 See Letter dated 17 November 2006, from the Rt Hon Rosie Winterton MP, Minister of State, Department of Health, Appendix 1 to the JCHR's 4th Report of Session 2006–07, HL 40/HC 288, p 46.
3 See draft Addendum Code, paras 8.1–8.8.

Provisions for nomination of a representative

9.121 This is provided for in much detail and this requirement now seems to be satisfied. These provisions too are cumbersome, and are essentially based on patient choice where this is possible, or otherwise upon consultation including with any welfare donee or deputy[1].

1 This requirement would appear to comply with the decisions in *JT v United Kingdom* [2000] 1 FLR 909 and *R (on the application of M) Secretary of State for Health* [2003] EWHC 1094 (Admin), [2003] 3 All ER 672.

Chapter 10

THE COURT OF PROTECTION

- **MCA 2005, ss 15 and 16, 45–56**
- **Main Code, Chapter 8**
- **Court of Protection Rules**

INTRODUCTION AND OVERVIEW

10.1 This chapter will focus on the new Court of Protection's role in welfare and healthcare (but not deprivation of liberty) decisions. The first section will provide a brief overview of the court's powers, jurisdiction and operation. The rest of the chapter will then go on to set out in more detail the powers of the new court, including a summary of how the High Court developed the common law and the inherent jurisdiction to protect incapacitated and vulnerable adults, give an overview of the role of court deputies (for a more detailed guide see Chapter 11), and highlight the key features of the new Rules and procedures. There is much useful guidance, together with forms and application packs available on the website of the Office of the Public Guardian on www.publicguardian.gov.uk.

Jurisdiction of the new Court of Protection

10.2 The MCA 2005 has abolished the existing Court of Protection; s 45(6) states that the office of the Supreme Court called the Court of Protection will cease to exist. The 'old' Court of Protection dealt only with financial affairs; the old court had the power to 'do or secure the doing of all such things as appear necessary and expedient', but only over a person's property and affairs.

Under the MCA 2005 a new court has been established, also called the Court of Protection (the court). This is an upgraded superior court of record[1] with statutory jurisdiction that straddles, and aims to combine, the functions of both previous jurisdictions over welfare, healthcare and financial affairs of people who lack mental capacity. It has the same powers, rights, privileges and authority as the High Court[2] (although it is not part of the High Court), so it is able to establish precedent by its decisions[3], and it has an official seal[4].

1 Section 45(1).
2 Section 47(1).
3 Main Code, para 8.2.
4 Section 45(2).

The inherent jurisdiction

10.3 The inherent jurisdiction of the High Court and the new powers of the Court of Protection exist side by side, but the inherent jurisdiction is only available where the proceedings do not fall within the MCA 2005.

In recent years the inherent jurisdiction has been developed in relation to decisions involving serious medical treatment and welfare decisions concerning those who are vulnerable and/or incapacitated. As such it has provided a complementary jurisdiction to that of the old Court of Protection in order to protect incapacitated adults. Declaratory relief under the inherent jurisdiction of the High Court will remain relevant to those who do not fall within the MCA 2005, eg for vulnerable, capable adults. It will be exercisable by judges of the High Court in tandem with the MCA 2005 jurisdiction. In the case of fluctuating capacity, a High Court judge sitting in the Court of Protection will be able to use both the powers under the MCA 2005 and the inherent jurisdiction in order to provide seamless protection, she or he will be able to grant the necessary orders to provide for both the times when the vulnerable adult has and does not have capacity. Otherwise the new Court of Protection will be the court with the power to determine all welfare and health matters concerning those who lack capacity.

Powers of the court and court deputies

10.4 Sections 15 and 16 of the MCA 2005 provide the court with both declaratory and substituted decision-making powers respectively, the latter providing its core jurisdiction under the MCA whereby the court may take the decision on behalf of the incapacitated person. It is anticipated that the majority of daily decisions will however fall to be made by carers and professionals under the protection provided in ss 5 and 6 of the MCA 2005 (see Chapter 4), which is the codification of the common law defence of necessity developed under the inherent jurisdiction and thus not a substituted decision-making power. The court will only be concerned with serious issues of welfare and health.

Section 15: declaratory powers

10.5 By MCA 2005, s 15 the court may make declarations regarding capacity and the lawfulness of acts (or omissions) done or to be done to a person. The case law developed under the inherent jurisdiction will remain relevant, although with the advent of a statutory declaratory jurisdiction in relation to serious health and welfare decisions (but not currently for deprivation of liberty), the value of the previous case law is likely to be limited because it is heavily fact dependent. Much of the principle of the previous case law has however been absorbed into the Main Code.

Section 16: substituted decision-making

10.6 The court's core substituted decision-making power is contained in MCA 2005, s 16[1] and may be exercised on behalf of incapacitated adults primarily by the court, but also by a court appointed deputy. The kinds of decisions, whether about personal welfare, healthcare or property and affairs, which could arise under this jurisdiction are set out non-exhaustively in MCA 2005, ss 17 and 18, they have been taken from previous decisions of the High Court. In making financial and property decisions (and appointing deputies) the court is likely to look to the past practice and expertise of the old Court of Protection where relevant.

1 MCA 2005, Explanatory Notes, para 66.

Making decisions

10.7 In every case the court (and any deputy) must act in accordance with the statutory principles and the person's best interests (ss 1 and 4). The principle of least restrictive intervention (s 1(6)) is reinforced. Additionally, it is preferable that the court should take decisions rather than delegate them to a deputy[1].

The Government has stated that court deputies should be appointed to make personal welfare and healthcare decisions in only the most extreme cases. The vast majority of deputies are expected to be financial deputies[2]. The protection for acts in connection with care and treatment under ss 5 and 6 are likely to be sufficient for most day-to-day welfare and healthcare decisions, making the appointment of a deputy for such a role unnecessary. (See Chapter 11 for a detailed review of deputies.)

1 Section 16(4); Explanatory Notes, paras 67 and 68.
2 HC Official Report, SC A (Mental Capacity Bill), 26 October 2004, col 194.

LPAs and PG

10.8 The role of the Public Guardian (PG) has changed under the MCA 2005. It is now purely regulatory and no longer carries investment powers. Investment will be carried out by deputies within the scope of their appointment and with applications to the court as necessary to update or vary powers (see Chapter 11). The court has other powers in relation to Lasting Powers of Attorney (LPA), which are described in Chapter 5.

Authorising deprivation of liberty

10.9 It is important to note that amendments made by the MHA 2007 (not yet in force) will extend the jurisdiction of the court to expressly encompass authorising the deprivation of liberty of an incapacitated adult. In addition the court is to have powers of review in relation to standard or urgent authorisations made under the new Sch A1[1]. Until these provisions come into force, which at the time of writing is scheduled for April 2009, there is no express provision in the MCA 2005 authorising deprivation of liberty to be carried out by any person, or by the court. Its legislative history suggests that the use of the Court of Protection to authorise deprivations of liberty was not contemplated by Parliament. While this indicates that the MCA 2005 cannot be used for these purposes, it is likely that s 16 will be used to do so because a welfare order is capable of containing a deprivation of liberty. Any such order should take care to provide for regular reviews and persist only over a definite period of time so that the requirements of Article 5(4) ECHR are not violated[2].

1 The decision of the court permitting a person to deprive an incapacitated adult of their liberty, may be made under its personal welfare powers contained in s 16(2)(a): s 4A(4) (inserted by MHA 2007, s 50(2)). The court's powers in this regard are limited by s 16A (as inserted by MHA 2007, s 50(3)). A deprivation of liberty may also be authorised by standard or urgent authorisation under Sch A1 to the MCA 2005 (inserted by MHA 2007, Sch 7). Section 21A (as inserted by MHA 2007, Sch 9, Part 1) gives the new court a review power over authorisations made under Sch A1. The operation of these new provisions is considered in Chapter 9.

2 As per *HL v United Kingdom* (2005) 40 EHRR 32. See 10.20 and 10.34 below and Chapter 7 at 7.8 and 7.80.

Court of Protection Rules

10.10 There is an extensive new set of Rules to govern the new court (CoP Rules). The existing Court of Protection and Court of Protection (Enduring Powers of Attorney) Rules are revoked[1]. There are 202 new rules, 35 Practice Directions (PDs) and 37 forms[2]. This chapter will seek only to highlight some of those that may be relevant to welfare (including health) decisions and applications.

1 See Court of Protection Rules 2007, SI 2007/1744, r 2.

2 See the website of the Office of the Public Guardian available at www.publicguardian.gov.uk.

Main Code

10.11 Chapter 8 of the Main Code deals with the court and court-appointed deputies. The latter are to have regard to whole of the Main Code.

Location

10.12 The court may sit at any place. It has a central office and registry at Archway Tower, Archway, London, which is to be the hearing centre for London and the South East of England. Some cases will, however, be heard at the Royal Courts of Justice, Strand, London or at Brent Magistrates' Court, should a larger court be needed for London and the South East. Regional offices are at Birmingham, Bristol, Cardiff, Manchester, Newcastle and Preston. However, all applications and communications are to be dealt with by the central registry in Archway.

Judges

10.13 The President of the new Court of Protection is Sir Mark Potter, President of the Family Division. Sir Andrew Morritt, Chancellor of the Chancery Division, is the Vice-President[1]. Day-to-day running of the court will be by Denzil Lush, previously the Master of the old Court of Protection and now the Senior Judge[2]. He and two full-time District Judges will hear cases at Archway. The President has nominated High Court, Circuit Court and District Judges to hear cases where they sit across the country on a part-time basis[3]. Practice Direction (PD) 12A, which supplements r 86 of the CoP Rules, sets out how the court's jurisdiction is to be exercised by certain judges. Cases about artificial nutrition and hydration (ANH) or involving an untested ethical dilemma will be heard by the President or his nominee. Cases about serious medical treatment (see also PD 9E) or involving a declaration of incompatibility under the Human Rights Act 1998 (HRA 1998) are to be heard by the President, Vice-President or puisne judge of the High Court[4]. The senior judge or his nominee may decide whether this PD applies to any particular case, but the allocated judge may re-allocate the case if in his view it may properly be dealt with by another judge.

1 Section 46(3).
2 Section 46(4).
3 See s 46 and www.publicguardian.gov.uk for details.
4 That is, a judge nominated under s 46(2)(a)–(c). It is suggested that the listing of a case that may involve declaratory relief concerning a deprivation of liberty should be before a High Court judge with suitable experience.

THE DEVELOPMENT OF THE INHERENT JURISDICTION

10.14 The new Court of Protection, as a new statutory court, has no inherent jurisdiction of its own. However, the development of the common law and the use of the inherent jurisdiction of the High Court in relation to decisions regarding medical treatment and the welfare of those who lack capacity is likely to remain of relevance to the new Court of Protection exercising its declaratory powers under s 15, and its decision-making powers under s 16.

The inherent jurisdiction is not a straightforward jurisdiction to describe, but in summary it provides to the court powers which are necessary to enable it to act effectively and which the court must have in order to 'enforce its rules of practice and to suppress any abuse of its process and to defeat any attempted thwarting of its processes'[1]. It is part of the procedural law, both civil and criminal, and is not part of substantive law.

For those who do not lack capacity, but who are vulnerable, the best interests jurisdiction of the High Court will remain the means by which their welfare (including health) can be protected. This leads to the slightly anomalous situation whereby the case law of the High Court's inherent jurisdiction will carry on developing in that regard. It is anticipated, however, that this will now be brought into line, to the extent that it is not already, with the best interests test contained in the MCA 2005.

Set out below is a brief summary of the principles that have developed under common law and the manner in which the High Court has used its powers within its inherent jurisdiction in order to provide protection to those who either lack capacity or who are vulnerable. The case law is also considered in Chapters 7 and 8 which deal with welfare and medical treatment decisions respectively.

1 See Civil Procedure, The White Book Service 2007, vol 2, para 9A-59.

Use of declaratory relief

10.15 It was the case of *Re F (Mental Patient: Sterilisation)*[1] that highlighted the lack of a statutory jurisdiction to make medical treatment decisions on behalf of incapacitated adults. All the existing statutory powers contained limitations: the MHA 1983 applies only to treatment for mental disorder; the old Court of Protection (Part VII of the MHA 1983) concerned only property and affairs decisions; the High Court's prior *parens patriae* jurisdiction in relation to incapacitated adults had been revoked, and now resides in the court's wardship jurisdiction only in relation to those under 18 years of age. The court in *Re F* accepted that the lack of a *parens patriae* jurisdiction meant that it could not approve[2] the proposed sterilisation of F (who was about to turn 18), so the court turned instead to its inherent jurisdiction to fill the gap in provision for incapacitated adults and to declare that the proposed course of action was lawful. As a procedural infill, however, the inherent jurisdiction could not confer a substantive jurisdiction on the court that it did not already have, hence it remained purely declaratory of the lawfulness of the proposed course of conduct[3].

1 [1990] 2 AC 1.
2 At 63C and Lord Goff at 81D.
3 Lord Brandon at 63 generally. CPR 40.20(2) (and its precursor RSC Ord 15, r 16) allows a court to make binding declarations whether or not other remedies are claimed. Declaratory relief is discretionary and is an important procedural device for ascertaining and determining the rights of parties and for the determination of points of law.

Development of the common law

10.16 It was the common law doctrine of necessity that permitted intervention in serious cases where the person was unable to consent to a proposed course of action or treatment; the common law justified what would otherwise be tortious and sought to act in the persons' 'best interest'. The use of best interests in this context was somewhat paternalistic; as used in *Re F* the best interests jurisdiction was used to make a decision that the decision-maker thought best for the individual. This is to be contrasted with the 'substituted judgement' approach whereby an attempt is made to make the decision that the person would have made for himself. In the MCA 2005, the best interests approach has shifted its focus to the wishes and beliefs of the person (see s 4). A substituted decision-making power has generally been considered to be preferable to a strict best interests approach, but it has its own difficulties[1].

1 See Law Commission, Consultation paper no 119, 'Mentally Incapacitated Adults and Decision-Making: An Overview', HMSO (1991) at paras 2.23, 4.22–23.

Treatment issues

10.17 The best interests jurisdiction of the High Court was first developed in the context of serious medical treatment, so for example it involved decisions concerning withdrawal of artificial feeding, the sterilisation of incompetent adult[1], and cases of momentous and irrevocable decisions and controversy[2]. For a consideration of medical decisions under the MCA 2005 see Chapter 8.

1 *Re GF (mental patient medical treatment)* [1992] 1 FLR 293, *Re LC (medical treatment: sterilisation)* [1997] 2 FLR 258; *Re S (Medical Treatment: Adult Sterilisation)* [1998] 1 FLR 944.

2 *Re S (Hospital Patient: Court's Jurisdiction)* [1996] Fam 1, [1995] 3 All ER 290, where Sir Thomas Bingham said:

> 'In cases of controversy and cases involving momentous and irrevocable decisions, the courts have treated as justiciable any genuine question as to what the best interests of a patient require or justify. In making these decisions the courts have recognised the desirability of informing those involved whether a proposed course of conduct will render them criminally or civilly liable; they have acknowledged their duty to act as a safeguard against malpractice, abuse and unjustified action; and they have recognised the desirability, in the last resort, of decisions being made by an impartial, independent tribunal.'

Welfare decisions

10.18 From the relatively narrow beginning of the use of the best interests jurisdiction for only serious medical decisions the power began to be extended to cover much wider welfare issues, including, for example issues such as contact, residence, marriage and publicity. The case law developed to the point at which it became acknowledged that 'the court exercises in substance and reality, a jurisdiction in relation to incompetent adults which is for all purposes indistinguishable from well-established *parens patriae* or wardship jurisdictions in relation to children'[1]. For a consideration of welfare (excluding health) decisions under the MCA 2005, see Chapter 7.

[1] *Re SA (vulnerable adult with capacity: marriage)* [2005] EWHC 2942 (Fam), para 37 [2007] 2 FCR 563; see also *Re G (Adult Patient: Publicity)* [1995] 2 FLR 528 at p.530; *In re S (Adult patient: Sterilisation)* [2001] Fam 15 at pp 29–30; *A v A Health Authority, In Re J (A child), R(on the application of S) v Secretary of State for the Home Department* [2002] EWHC 18 (Fam/Admin), [2002] Fam 213 at paras 38 45, and *E (By her Litigation Friend the Official Solicitor) v Channel Four, News International Ltd and St Helen's Borough Council* [2005] EWHC 1144 (Fam), [2005] FLR 913.

Vulnerable but capacitous adults

10.19 In addition to extending the scope of the use of the inherent jurisdiction to cover all manner of welfare issues, the ambit of the jurisdiction was also extended to cover not just those who lacked capacity or who were unable to communicate, but also those who had capacity but nevertheless required the protection of the courts due to their vulnerability[1].

[1] *Re G (an adult) (mental capacity: court's jurisdiction)* [2004] EWHC 2222 (Fam), [2004] All ER (D) 33 (Oct). See also Chapter 7 at 7.51.

Deprivation of liberty

10.20 Finally, more recently the inherent jurisdiction has been used to authorise a deprivation of liberty[1]. This is likely to influence the way in which s 16 welfare orders will be made by the Court of Protection, so that deprivations of liberty may now be authorised under that provision. However, in strict statutory terms the position is not clear. This is discussed further at 10.34 below and Chapter 7 at 7.8.

[1] See *JE v DE (by his litigation friend, the Official Solicitor) Surrey County Cpuncil and EW* [2007] MHLR 39 and *Re PS (incapacitated and vulnerable adult)* [2007] EWHC 623 Fam, [2007] 2 FLR 1083.

Flexible remedy

10.21 The inherent jurisdiction and the common law have been utilised in a very flexible manner. As noted above the scope and ambit of the inherent jurisdiction has been extended in order to provide a remedy for many different health and welfare situations and for different types of vulnerable adults. It has also allowed for flexibility in the type of remedy available, including the use of interim declarations and injunctions. In *Sheffield City Council v E* it was stated by Munby J that the court's inherent jurisdiction extends not merely to declaratory relief but also to the granting of injunctive relief, and it also extends not only to the grant of interlocutory injunctions but also to the granting of final injunctions[1].

The fact that the courts have viewed the inherent jurisdiction as being such a flexible and adaptable remedy has enabled the courts to look at and deal with issues such as future care, choice of carer, who should have contact and under what circumstances, powers of staff and the use of restraint and detention[2]. This means that it can be a very useful remedy in cases, for example, where the equivalent of a guardianship order under the MHA 1983 is needed to provide for and protect the welfare of a vulnerable adult, but where such a person does not suffer from a mental illness as defined by MHA 1983, s 1(2).

1 [2004] EWHC 2808 (Fam), [2005] Fam 326 at para 108.
2 See Bingham MR in *Re S (Hospital Patient: Courts' Jurisdiction) (No 1)* [1996] Fam 1, CA.

Serious justiciable issue

10.22 One of the principles developed within the inherent jurisdiction is that the court will have jurisdiction to intervene when there is a 'serious justiciable issue' to be determined. In *Re S*[1] it was said that in 'cases of controversy and cases involving momentous and irrevocable decisions, the courts have treated as justiciable any genuine question as to what the best interests of a patient require or justify'.

1 *Re S (Hospital Patient: Court's Jurisdiction)* [1995] 1 FLR 1075 at 1087.

Standing

10.23 Under the inherent jurisdiction the issue also arose as to what standing an applicant had to have in order to bring a case. It was decided that there was no requirement for the applicant to have a legal right that was in dispute, or that would be affected by the outcome of the proceedings before they had standing. What was required was a 'genuine and legitimate interest'. In *Re S* Sir Thomas Bingham (as he was then), after reviewing the previous cases, said that:

> 'It cannot of course be suggested that any stranger or officious busybody, however remotely connected with a patient or with the subject matter of proceedings, can properly seek or obtain declaratory or any other relief (in private law any more than public law proceedings). But it can be suggested that where a serious justiciable issue is brought before the court by a party with a genuine and legitimate interest in obtaining a decision against an adverse party the court will not impose nice tests to determine the precise legal standing of that claimant.'[1]

It is likely that the principles and rulings under the inherent jurisdiction concerning the flexibility of remedies, serious justiciable issues and standing will continue to be relevant to the Court of Protection when deciding when, if and how it can and should intervene.

1 *Re S (Hospital Patient: Court's Jurisdiction)* [1995] 1 FLR 1075 at 1087.

THE SCOPE AND POWERS OF THE COURT OF PROTECTION

10.24 In summary the new Court may:

1 make declarations on specific issues, eg:
   (a) whether a person has or lacks capacity to make a decision specified or described in the declaration;

(b) the lawfulness of any act (or omission) done, or yet to be done to that person (s 15(1), (2)). This is the classic declaratory jurisdiction of the High Court that is discussed above;

2 make decisions, and appoint deputies to make decisions, on personal welfare and/or property and affairs (s 16(1), (2)(a) and (b)). This is the core substituted decision-making power of the Court;

3 revoke the appointment of a deputy if satisfied that s/he has behaved in contravention of their authority or against the best interests of the person concerned, or vary the powers conferred (s 16(8));

4 make decisions with regard to LPAs and EPAs (ss 22 and 23, Sch 4);

5 make interim orders and directions pending the determination of any application, if:

(a) it reasonably believes the person lacks capacity in relation to the matter;

(ii) it has power to deal with it; and

(iii) it is in the person's best interests to make the order, or give the directions, without delay (s 48);

6 call for reports to be made to it by the Public Guardian or a Court of Protection Visitor (s 49).

Dual jurisdiction

10.25 The new Court is essentially the merger of two different cultures, one relatively new dealing with welfare and health, and the other a more mature one dealing historically with the property and affairs of a 'patient'. This merger brings together two distinct styles of resolving issues, the former being more trial orientated and the latter more informal. How the new Court will manage this merger in practice remains to be seen. The structure of the Court and the CoP Rules (below) allow sufficient flexibility to enable both to be pursued in the right case. One thing that is clear is that the new Court is not to be seen as an adversarial forum, it is to be a forum that promotes and resolves issues concerning the 'best interests' of the person[1]. Adversarial disputes should be pursued in the ordinary forms of litigation available, as to which see Chapter 15.

1 Ashton, G, 'Will the New Court of Protection Damage Your Mental Health?' May 2007, *Journal of Mental Health Law*, 19.

Declaratory relief and substituted decision making

10.26 Conceptually there is a distinction to be drawn between declaratory relief and substituted decision-making in terms of outcome; a declaration is not approval of an intervention, nor of an approach, but merely a declaration of lawfulness. It is to be contrasted with substituted decision-making where an attempt is made to make the decision that the person would make for themselves. Although there has been a blurring of the approaches within the inherent jurisdiction of the High Court, the Court's power under s 16 now explicitly seeks to take the latter approach, ie standing in the shoes of the incapacitated person. This is obviously difficult to achieve, particularly where the person has always been incapacitated and has never been in a position to express their wishes and beliefs. In those cases the decisions are, inevitably, likely to be more paternalistic[1].

1 Law Commission, Consultation paper no 119 at 4.23.

Human rights

10.27 As a 'public body' within the meaning of HRA 1998, s 6, the Court of Protection will have to respect and protect the human rights of those for whom, and on whose behalf, decisions or declarations are made. For example if a declaration is to be about the contact with and between family members the Article 8 rights of all those involved will have to be taken into consideration. For a more detailed discussion of the relevant Convention rights (under the European Convention on Human Rights), see Chapter 17.

Declarations: section 15

10.28 The power to make declarations is contained in s 15 of the MCA 2005. The court can make declarations in relation to whether a person lacks capacity to make a specific decision as either specified or described in the declaration, and can declare the lawfulness or otherwise of an act done, being done, or to be done. This also includes an omission or failure to act, including the provision of treatment or care. The types of decisions falling under this power are those where there are 'serious justiciable issues' concerning welfare and healthcare, and are the types of issues that were previously dealt with by the High Court under its inherent jurisdiction (see further above at 10.17 and 10.18.)

Declaration of incapacity

10.29 The Main Code suggests that applications for a declaration that a person lacks capacity will be rare as this should usually be resolved informally[1]. However, the Code suggests that in the following circumstances an application may be relevant:

- where a person wishes to challenge a decision that they lack capacity;
- where professionals disagree about a person's capacity to make a specific (usually serious) decision;
- where there is a dispute over whether a person has capacity (for example, between family members).

1 Main Code, para 8.16.

Serious or life threatening treatment decisions

10.30 The Main Code suggests the following types of treatment are ones which the court should be asked to decide upon:

- decisions about the proposed withdrawal of ANH from patients in a permanent vegetative state;
- cases involving organ or bone marrow donation by a person who lacks capacity;
- cases involving the proposed non-therapeutic sterilisation of a person who lacks capacity;
- all other cases where there is a doubt or dispute about whether a particular treatment will be in a person's best interest.

With regard to withdrawal of ANH, reference is specifically made in the Main Code to the case of *Bland*[1] which is unaffected by the MCA 2005. Also specifically referred to is the case law on organ and bone marrow donation and on non-therapeutic sterilisation. This body of case law is again said to be unaffected by the MCA 2005 and decisions should be referred to the court of Protection for approval.

1 *Airedale NHS Trust v Bland* [1993] AC 789; see Main Code, para 8.19.

Decisions and appointment of deputies: section 16[1]

10.31 The court can either make a decision itself, or will appoint a deputy if there is a need for on-going decision-making powers and there is no relevant Enduring Power of Attorney (EPA) or LPA. The Court will also decide whether a deputy has suitable skills to act depending on the decisions to be taken and whether s/he is reliable and trustworthy[2]. When appointing a deputy the court will state what decisions the deputy has power to make. An appointment may take place upon application by a person wishing to act as a deputy or as part of extant proceedings before the court.

When exercising its power under s 16, the court must apply the two following principles: (a) that a decision by the court is to be preferred and (b) that the powers conferred on a deputy are to be as limited in scope and duration as is reasonably practicable in the circumstances[3]. The court has a wide discretion as to further orders, and powers or duties, which may be conferred, or imposed, on a deputy[4].

The court may make whatever order, directions, or make the appointment of the deputy on whatever terms it considers are in the person's best interests, and can do so even if no application is before it in relation to the same[5].

1 Again the website of the OPG contains much useful information for deputies, including a newsletter called 'Reaching Out'. The autumn 2007 edition comes with a CD of relevant forms.
2 Main Code, para 8.32.
3 Section 16(4).
4 Section 16(5).
5 Section 16(6).

What decisions will the court take?

10.32 The court will make a decision where there is a 'serious dispute'. The Main Code suggests that a 'serious dispute' is one where there is 'no other way of finding a solution, or when the authority of the court is needed in order to make a particular decision or take a particular action'[1]. This might occur, for example, when there is no EPA or property and affairs donee to take financial decisions for a person, or a will needs to be made[2]. Other examples given in the Main Code are where there is a genuine doubt or disagreement about the existence, validity or applicability of an advance decision, where there is a major disagreement regarding a serious decision (for example, about where a person who lacks capacity to decide should reside), where a family carer or solicitor asks for personal information about someone who lacks capacity and to consent to that information being revealed is requested (for example where there have been allegations of abuse of a person living in a care home) and where someone suspects that a person who lacks capacity to make decisions to protect himself is at risk of harm or abuse from a named individual (the court could stop that individual contacting the person who lacks capacity).

Sections 17 and 18 offer examples of the types of matters that may come before the court for decisions under s 16 (see below).

1 Main Code, para 8.25.
2 Main Code, para 8.27.

Deputies

10.33 The role of a deputy can be summarised as follows. A deputy:

- acts only on appointment by the court;
- may take decisions on behalf of an incapacitated person;
- must act only under the direction of the court;
- must act in accordance with the statutory principles, the best interests of the person and take account of the Main Code;
- must apply to the court for any extra or varied powers;
- may be appointed jointly, or jointly and severally, to act in relation to welfare, healthcare and financial decisions;
- will only exceptionally be appointed for welfare or healthcare decisions;
- has no power to deprive a person of their liberty[1];
- may restrain the person subject to certain conditions;
- may not prohibit contact or direct a change of healthcare provider;
- must not act contrary to a donee of an LPA;
- may not refuse consent to life-sustaining treatment;
- carries all the investment powers without the assistance of the OPG;
- may be required to provide security against misconduct;
- must be supervised by the PG;
- may claim remuneration and expenses;
- may only be removed by the court.

For a detailed review of the appointment, powers and duties of court deputies, see Chapter 11.

1 This may change post-1 October 2008 when amendments to the MCA 2005 will enable the court to make orders depriving a person of their liberty under s 16(2)(a).

Decision making: personal welfare, section 17

10.34 Personal welfare is defined in s 17, which sets out the types of personal welfare matters that, under s 16, the court may either determine itself or for which it may appoint a deputy to make decisions on behalf of the patient (P). The list is not exhaustive but includes deciding issues of residence, contact and medical treatment. The power of deputies is restricted (s 20, see above at at 10.33). A deputy can refuse treatment for P (as long as it is not life sustaining), but cannot direct treatment against clinical judgment. The list is based on the decisions already dealt with under the High Court's inherent jurisdiction, i.e. the common law (see above at 10.16–10.18). These are examples of decisions that may go to court for a decision, they do not have to be taken to the court.

Until the new amendments come into force (see Chapter 9) the court does not have the express power to authorise a person's detention or to deprive a person of their liberty[1]. Any such detention would fall foul of Article 5(4) ECHR because of the lack of a speedy or regular review. This has given rise to a conundrum as to whether the inherent jurisdiction is still relevant to authorise a deprivation of liberty in the interim. The legislative history of the MCA 2005 suggests that it was not contemplated for authorising deprivations of liberty as it stands. The Main Code offers no guidance on this issue. However, it must be recognised that the making of a welfare order may well include authorising a care plan that involves depriving a person of their liberty in their best interests and so s 16 is *capable* of authorising deprivations of liberty. This possibility has become more real since the recent cases under the inherent jurisdiction (at 10.20 above) authorising deprivations of liberty and the non-exhaustive list under s 17 based on High Court decisions at the time of drafting, may be supplemented in this respect. By the forthcoming s 4A and 16A it is now acknowledged that a s 16 welfare order may well authorise a deprivation of liberty. It would seem, therefore, that s 16 can be utilised in this regard pending the forthcoming amendments. This point is also discussed at Chapter 7 para 7.8 (and see footnotes thereto). Any order made by the Court of Protection must be made Article 5 compliant so far as possible. This may be achieved in the way described in *Re PS* (above) and set out at Chapter 7 at 7.80. Until the amendments are in force consideration should also be given to the use of the MHA 1983 if the admission criteria are fulfilled due to the availability of in built Article 5 and treatment safeguards (see Chapter 16 at 16.42).

1 Although a High Court judge sitting in the court could exercise the inherent jurisdiction of the High Court in order to authorise a detention.

Residence decisions

10.35 In deciding where P is to live the court cannot override the provision of the National Health Service and Community Care Act 1990 or the National Assistance Act (Choice of Accommodation) Directions 1992. Disputes under these Acts are likely to be resolved by way of Judicial Review (see Chapter 15 on judicial review proceedings and Chapter 7 on Community Care).

Decision making: property and affairs, section 18

10.36 Section 18 sets out the list of matters which can be undertaken and is supplemented by Sch 2. These relate to property and financial affairs, including carrying on a trade, profession or business on behalf of P, discharging debts or obligations, and the carrying out of any contract entered into by P. The detail is beyond the scope of this book, but of relevance is the ability to conduct legal proceedings in P's name or on P's behalf[1]. This is not restricted just to proceedings under the MCA 2005. Again the deputy's powers are restricted by s 20. This list reflects that previously provided under MHA 1983, s 96. The definition of property is wide and is contained in s 64; 'property' includes any thing in action and any interest in real or personal property.

1 Section 18(1)(k). It is not clear whether the court or deputy has the authority to enter into a tenancy agreement for an incapacitated person, but the reality must be that if they did it is unlikely that anyone would seek to argue that such a contract would be unenforceable as it would be in no-one's interests to do so. Therefore even if such a contract was technically voidable, it is very unlikely a court would ever be asked to consider the matter.

Sections 15 and 16, what is the difference?

10.37 The conceptual difference underlying the making and effect of declaratory relief under s 15, as against the substituted decision-making under s 16, has been referred to above (see 10.26). Both, however, require that decisions are taken in the best interests of the person as set out in s 4, and so the person's past wishes and beliefs are relevant to both. Given the difficulties of making an accurate or true substituted decision, the difference between the two approaches may, however, be more theoretical than real in terms of the way in which the declaration or decision is actually made. Ultimately, the difference may lie in the subject matter before the court and whether there is sufficient evidence upon which the court can make a substituted decision.

Section 15 is likely to be confined to decisions about serious medical treatment with irreversible consequences, and those conditions set out in the Main Code, or where a declaration of the lawfulness of an act or omission is required retrospectively. In those, and other, cases where the court is unable to make a substituted decision, a declaration will be available as an alternative. The quality of the decision is different, but the result, however, is unlikely to be so: a carer or professional will be authorised to act if a substituted decision is made, or feel themselves entitled to act (or not), if it is not.

Supervision of LPAs: sections 22 and 23[1]

10.38 There are three categories of supervisory power vested in the court:

1 Where an LPA has been executed or registered, the court has power to determine any question relating to (a) whether the requirements for creating the LPA have been met, and (b) whether it has been revoked or come to an end[2].

If the court is satisfied that fraud or undue pressure was used to induce P to execute an instrument for an LPA or to create an LPA, or that the donee of the LPA has behaved or is behaving in a way that contravenes his or her authority or against the P's best interests, or proposes to behave in such a way[3], the court may direct that the LPA is not registered or, if P lacks capacity to do so, revoke the instrument of LPA[4]. If there is more than one donee, then the court may act in relation only to one of them[5]. Donee includes an intended donee.

2 The court may determine any question as to the meaning or effect of a LPA or an instrument purporting to create one. It may give directions with respect to decisions which the donee has power to make and which P lacks capacity to make. The donee is the agent of P. An example of this is where the donee would like to purchase the P's property but the power provides that the donor must give consent. It may give consent or authorisation to act which the donee would have to obtain from P if he or she had capacity to give the same[6].

3 The court may give directions to the donee with respect to the rendering of accounts or reports and the production of records kept by him for that purpose, or to supply information or documents or things in his possession as donee, or with a view to remuneration or expenses, or relieve the donee entirely from any liability he has or may incur on account of a breach of his duties as donee[7]. This is a very broad power.

The court also has powers in relation to the making of gifts and where there is more than one donee. The court's supervisory powers will need to be triggered by someone concerned to do so and in close contact with P.

1 See also Chapter 5 on LPAs.
2 Section 22(1), (2).
3 Section 21(3).
4 Section 21(4).
5 Section 21(5).
6 Section 23(1), (2).
7 Section 23(3).

PROCEDURE AND RULES

Introduction

10.39 Very detailed rules[1] have been drafted for the new Court of Protection. The CoP Rules are divided into 23 Parts, and in total there are just over 200 rules. The Explanatory Note states that one of the main policy aims of the CoP Rules is to provide a 'human rights-compliant process'. Reference must also be made to the relevant Practice Directions (PDs) under each part. These are too extensive to refer to in any detail in this chapter, but where particularly relevant have been referenced.

For the most part the CoP Rules are very similar to the CPR and much is a direct copy across, however there are some important differences both with regard to particular rules and with regard to the overall approach towards case management and the roles of the parties and the court. In general the court has been given a much more active and direct role in case management and the proceedings, and is often granted much more discretion and power as to how matters will proceed than the CPR provides.

There are some processes that are unique to the new court, examples of which are:

- a requirement that the person who lacks capacity who is the subject of the proceedings is to be personally informed of the proceedings in a meaningful way (Part 7);
- a range of ways for involving the person who lacks capacity in the proceedings, to enable the new court to decide on the best approach in each individual case (Parts 7, 9 and 14);
- provision for serving the application form and supporting documents on named respondents (who have or may have a direct interest) and also notifying others who might have an interest in the proceedings (Part 9);
- a general rule that hearings are to be held in private to ensure that the privacy of the person who lacks capacity is safeguarded, while enabling the court to admit the media and members of the public where it considers it is appropriate to do so (Part 13);
- two different starting points in relation to costs which reflect the status quo; in property and financial affairs cases the starting point is that the costs of the proceedings will be paid from the estate of the person who lacks capacity, and in personal welfare cases the starting point is that each party will bear their own costs – with judicial discretion to depart from these starting points where appropriate (Part 19); and
- transitory provisions for cases pending in the old Court of Protection at the time of commencement (cases pending in the High Court will remain in the High Court until finalisation and will not be transferred to the new Court) (Part 22)[2].

1 SI 2007/1744.
2 See Explanatory Note and see the Mental Capacity Act 2005 (Transitional and Consequential Provisions) Order 2007, SI 2007/1898, art 3.

Overriding objective

10.40 The CoP Rules set out the overriding objective in r 3. It is in identical terms to the CPR, except it is stated in terms that the court will have regard to the principles contained in the MCA 2005, and that dealing with a case justly includes:

> '(b) ensuring that P's best interests and position are properly considered'.

Application of CPR to Court proceedings

10.41 The CPR has been amended[1] following the coming into force of the CoP Rules. There are two main changes. First, in CPR 2.2(1) reference to Part VII of the MHA 1983 proceedings has been substituted for MCA 2005 proceedings. This amendment reflects that fact that the CPR does not apply to proceedings before the court except to the extent that the MCA 2005 and CoP Rules specify they apply.

CoP Rules, r 9 states:

> 'In any case not expressly provided for by these Rules or the practice directions made under them, the Civil Procedure Rules (1998) (including any practice directions made under them) may be applied with any necessary modifications as is necessary to further the overriding objective.'

Therefore the CPR will be relevant and should be followed where no specific provision has been made in the CoP Rules.

The other significant change to the CPR is that wherever the CPR referred to 'patients' it now refers to 'protected parties'. A protected party is defined in the CoP Rules[2] as a person who lacks capacity to conduct proceedings but is neither a child nor 'P'[3].

The Explanatory Notes set out all the changes to the CPR made by the CoP Rules. These are:

- CPR 19.9 is amended and new rr 19.9A–19.9F are inserted as a result of new procedures for derivative claims under the Companies Act 2006;
- Part 21 is amended as a consequence of the Mental Capacity Act 2005 to include provisions about 'protected parties' and 'protected beneficiaries', the appointment of a litigation friend for a protected party and the settlement or compromise of proceedings on behalf of a protected party;
- CPR 2.1(2), 2.3(1), 6.6(1) and (2), 12.10(a)(i), 12.11(3), 14.1(4), 30.7, 32.13(3)(e), 36.9(2), 39.2(3)(d), 45.10(2)(c), 46.2(1)(c), 47.3(1)(c) and 48.5 are amended to reflect the amendments to Part 21;
- CPR 46.2 and 46.3 are amended to make provision for the increase to the amount of fast track trial costs which the court may award where the fast track trial commences on or after 1 October 2007;
- CPR 47.22 is amended to increase the time within which an appeal of a decision of an authorised court officer relating to detailed assessment of costs may be filed from 14 days to 21 days;
- a new CPR 52.12A is inserted to make provision for third parties to apply for permission to file evidence or make representations at an appeal hearing in relation to statutory appeals;
- a new CPR 52.18 is inserted to provide that an appeal from a decision of the Secretary of State under the Law of Property Act 1922, Sch 15, para 16 lies to the High Court;
- a new CPRR 52.19 is inserted to provide that an appeal from a decision of a tribunal referred to in s 11(1) of the Tribunals and Inquiries Act 1992 lies to the High Court and that the tribunal may of its own initiative or at the request of a party to the proceedings state a case for the decision of the High Court;
- a new CPR 52.20 is inserted to provide that an appeal from certain decisions of the Secretary of State under the Town and Country

Planning Act 1990 or under the Planning (Listed Buildings and Conservation Areas) Act 1990 lies to the High Court;

- CPR 65.1, 65.8, 65.9 and 65.10 have been amended and new CPR 65.37–65.41 inserted as a consequence of the Police and Justice Act 2006, ss 24 and 27;
- RSC Ord 93, rr 4, 5, 9, 10, 16, 17, 18 and 19, Ord 94, rr 4, 5, 8, 9, 12 and 13 and Ord 95, rr 1, 4, 5 and 6 are revoked, because they have been incorporated into either the main body of the CPR or a Practice Direction supplementing the CPR or because they are no longer relevant, as the case may be; and
- CCR Ord 45 is revoked.

1 SI 2007/2204.
2 Rule 6.
3 See 10.64 on litigation friends.

Pending proceedings as at 1 October 2007

Part VII of the Mental Health Act 1983

10.42 All orders and appointments or any other thing done and deemed to have effect immediately before the commencement of the MCA 2005 will continue to have effect. If the orders or appointments could have been made under ss 15–20 they will be treated as if those provisions had been in force at the relevant time. Pending proceedings will be dealt with as if under ss 16–20, so far as a corresponding power is available. Part VII and relevant rules will apply to appeals brought under s 105 of the MHA 1983 which have not been determined prior to the commencement of the MCA 2005. If no judge has begun to hear the appeal, it is be heard by a puisne Judge of the High Court nominated under s 46. All fees and other payments due but not paid to the former Court of Protection are to be paid to the new court[1].

1 Section 66(4), Sch 5, Part 1 paras 2–5. See also CoP Rules, Part 22 and PD 22B, and see also Chapter 11 'Existing Receivers' above.

Enduring Powers of Attorney Act 1985

10.43 Anything done under this Act and which took effect prior to the commencement of the MCA 2005 remains in effect and the provisions of Sch 4 apply as if they had been in force. A pending application for registration, objection to registration and proceedings under s 5 of the Enduring Powers of Attorney Act 1985 are to be treated under the appropriate provisions of Sch 4 to the MCA 2005. Previous legislation and rules continue to apply to any undetermined appeals. The provision relating to the appropriate judge above is replicated[1].

1 Section 66(4), Sch 5, Part 2, paras 11–13.

Generally

10.44 Any step in proceedings (as above) on or after commencement is to be in accordance with the new CoP Rules, subject to any contrary provision in PD 22A or any directions given by the court. Any step taken prior to commencement will remain valid. There will be no need to repeat any prior steps, eg evidence already given in accordance with the former rules. There will be no need for permission. Any service of documents or notification given after commencement of pending proceedings in accordance with the former rules, may be treated by the court as valid. Prior orders must be complied with. Costs on or after commencement will be dealt with in accordance with Part 19 of the CoP Rules.[1]

1 PD 22A.

Under the inherent jurisdiction of the High Court

10.45 The transitional provisions in relation to existing health or welfare cases in the High Court that have not been finally determined by 1 October 2007, may continue to be dealt with under the previous jurisdiction and do not have to be transferred to the new court[1].

1 See the Mental Capacity Act 2005 (Transitional and Consequential Provisions) Order 2007, SI 2007/1898, art 3.

Making an application

Urgent and interim applications: PD 10B

10.46 Urgent and interim applications are likely to relate to health and welfare decisions and be necessary, as where an urgent decision of the court is required, in relation to life-sustaining or other serious medical treatment, or when an interim order or injunctive relief is required to maintain the status quo pending a determination by the court. The procedure for such applications is contained in Part 10 of the CoP Rules, which applies to application notices within proceedings, and in PD 10B. The applicant may indicate in the application notice that the application is urgent, requires a particular level of judge, or hearing[1]. The court may grant an interim remedy before an application form has been issued, but only if the matter is urgent or it is otherwise necessary in the interest of justice[2].

Applicants are encouraged to make urgent applications during court hours and they will normally be dealt with at court.

1 PD 10B, para 13.
2 Rule 11(2)(b) and (3)(a), (b).

Telephone applications: PD 10B, paras 2, 3, 11 and 12

10.47 In cases of extreme urgency applications may be dealt with by telephone. The PD provides the relevant telephone numbers: 084 5330 2900 during business hours and 020 7947 6000 outside business hours. The latter is the number for the security office at the Royal Courts of Justice in the Strand. The security officer should be informed of the nature of the case. A tape-recorded conference call is preferred, and should be arranged (and paid for) by the applicant. The applicant should order a transcript of the hearing. Any concerns regarding the inappropriate use of the urgent application system may be dealt with separately by the judge.

The need for an urgent or interim application may arise in one of two situations: (a) the application form has already been issued, or (b) no application form has been issued, and in both cases no notice has been given to the respondent(s).

Applications without notice: PD 10B, paras 5 and 6

10.48 Efforts must be made to notify any respondent(s) by telephone or in writing, unless justice would be defeated by doing so. Any order made without notice will usually require an undertaking by the applicant to serve the application notice, evidence in support and any order made, on the respondent, and any other person directed by the Court either as soon as possible or as ordered by the Court, and a return date for a further hearing at which all the parties can be present: PD 10B, para 6(a). This replicates prior practice in the High Court.

In *Re S (Ex Parte Orders)*[1] Munby J gave detailed guidance about applications without notice in the Family Division. It is suggested that this guidance should be followed where applications without notice are made in the Court of Protection. Munby J summarised the guidance as being:

1 that there is a requirement of full, frank and candid disclosure;
2 those who obtain injunctive relief without notice are under an obligation to bring to the attention of the respondent, and at the earliest practicable opportunity, the evidential and other persuasive materials on the basis of which the injunction without notice was granted;
3 generally speaking it is appropriate when granting injunctive relief without notice for the court to require the applicant (and, where appropriate, the applicant's solicitors) to give the following undertakings:
   (a) where proceedings have not yet been issued, to issue and serve on the respondent either by some specified time or as soon as practicable, proceedings either in the form of the draft produced to the court or otherwise as may be appropriate;
   (b) where the application has been made otherwise than on sworn evidence, to cause to be sworn, filed and served on the respondent as soon as practicable an affidavit or affidavits substantially in the terms of the draft affidavit(s) produced to the court or, as the case may be, confirming the substance of what was said to the court by the applicant's counsel or solicitors; and
   (c) subject to (a) and (b) above, to serve on the respondent as soon as practicable:

(i) the proceedings;
(ii) a sealed copy of the order;
(iii) copies of the affidavit(s) and exhibit(s) containing the evidence relied on by the applicant; and
(iv) notice of the return date including details of the application to be made on the return date;

4 a person who has given an undertaking to the court is under a plain and unqualified obligation to comply to the letter with his undertaking. Where the undertaking is to do something by a specified time, then time is of the essence. A person who finds himself unable to comply timeously with his undertaking should either:
(a) apply for an extension of time before the time for compliance has expired; or
(b) pass the task to someone who has available the time in which to do it;

5 whether or not express undertakings to this effect have been given, but subject to any order to the contrary, an applicant who obtains injunctive relief without notice is under an obligation to the Court, and the solicitor acting for the applicant is under an obligation both to the Court and to his lay client, to carry out the various steps referred to above;

6 any order without notice containing injunctions should set out on its face, either by way of recital or in a schedule, a list of all affidavits, witness statements and other evidential materials read by the judge. The applicant's legal representatives should, whenever possible, liaise with the associate with a view to ensuring that the order as drawn contains this information. On receipt of the order from the court the applicant's legal representatives should satisfy themselves that the order as drawn correctly sets out the relevant information and, if it does not, take urgent steps to have the order amended under the slip rule;

6 persons injuncted without notice are entitled to be given, if they ask, proper information as to what happened at the hearing and to be told, if they ask:
(a) exactly what documents, bundles or other evidential materials were lodged with the Court either before or during the course of the hearing; and
(ii) what legal authorities were cited to the judge;

7 the applicant's legal representatives should respond forthwith to any reasonable request from the respondent or his legal representatives either for copies of the materials read by the judge or for information about what took place at the hearing; and

8 given this, it would be prudent for those acting for the applicant in such a case to keep a proper note of the proceedings, lest they otherwise find themselves embarrassed by a proper request for information which they are unable to provide.

1 [2001] 1 FLR 308.

Applications where proceedings already issued: PD 10B, paras 7 and 8

10.49 An application notice (form COP9), evidence in support and a draft order must be filed with the court in advance of the hearing wherever possible. The PD makes provision for any unusually long or complex draft order to be made available on disc in a format compatible with that used by the court (see the provisions about application notices generally under Part 10). If an application is made before the notice is filed, a draft order should be provided at the hearing with the evidence in support and the notice to be filed the next day or as directed by the court.

Applications prior to the issue of an application form: PD 10B, para 9

10.50 An application prior to the issue of an application form is permitted in cases of exceptional urgency only. The application will be made orally to the court. An undertaking must be given that an application in the terms of the oral application will be filed on the next working day or as directed by the court. Where time permits the PD urges that an application in writing must be made.

Serious medical treatment

10.51 With regard to serious medical treatment, in addition to the above see PDs 9E and 12A. Such decisions as defined in the Main Code must be brought to the court. PD 9E defines 'serious medical treatment' and both PDs offer guidance on allocation of an appropriate level of judge. Unless the matter is urgent the matter will be listed for a directions hearing.

Interim injunctions

10.52 Rule 82(1)(a) of the CoP Rules enables the court to grant an interim injunction. The order must set out clearly what the respondent or other person must or must not do. The order may contain an undertaking by the applicant to pay any damages which the respondent(s) sustains which in the court's consideration s/he should pay[1].

1 PD 10B, para 16.

Interim orders or declarations

10.53 Rule 82(1)(b) and (c) of the CoP Rules empower the court to make an interim declaration or other order, if it considers it appropriate to do so. A person on whom an application form under Part 9 (see 10.63–10.71 below) is served may not apply for an interim remedy before filing an acknowledgment of service, unless the court orders otherwise (r 82(2)). The criteria for making interim orders and declarations are contained in s 48:

(a) there must be reason to believe that the person lacks capacity in relation to the relevant matter;
(b) the matter must be one to which the court's powers extend under the MCA 2005; and
(c) it must be in the person's best interests to make the order, or give the directions without delay.

The granting of an interim order or directions will not negate the need to obtain permission (if it is a case where permission is required). The test for granting an interim order/directions is not the same as that for permission. It is likely to be the case that any interim orders will remain in place until permission is decided, at which point they will be reconsidered.

Commencing proceedings

10.54 Parts 8 and 9 of the CoP Rules and PDs 8A and 9A–9H apply.

Listings

10.55 Before filing an application or permission form consideration should be given as to what level of judge the case should go before. A request should then be made in either a covering letter, or by telephone, for the case to be listed in front of the appropriate judge (for details of judges see above at 10.13).

Official Solicitor[1]

10.56 Before any proceedings are commenced, consideration should be given as to whether the Official Solicitor needs to become involved, and if so he should be contacted. The Official Solicitor acts for people who lack mental capacity, or who cannot properly manage their own affairs, or who are unable to represent themselves and no other suitable person or agency is able and willing to act. He usually becomes formally involved when appointed by the court, and he may act as his own solicitor, or instruct a private firm of solicitors to act for him.

1 For information on the Official Solicitor see http://www.officialsolicitor.gov.uk/os/offsol.htm.

Permission: Part 8

10.57 Part 8 deals with permission to make an application to the court. Part 9 of the CoP Rules deal with making an application to commence proceedings. In order to start proceedings an application form must be filed with the court. The appropriate forms *must* be used, although variations are permitted so long as no required information is omitted and the guidance is followed (r 61(2)).

The proceedings actually start once the court issues the application form. The court will not issue the form unless and until permission is granted. Set out below are the forms required for different applications.

Application type	*Forms*[1]
Application relating to property and affairs only	COP1: Application form COP1A annex A: Supporting information [COP2: Permission form (if applicable)] COP3: Assessment of capacity form COP4: Deputy's declaration (if applying to be a deputy) Copy of LPA or EPA (if applicable) Fee
Application relation to personal welfare only	COP1 COP1B Annex B: supporting information for personal welfare applications [COP2: permission form (if applicable)] COP3 COP4 Copy of LPA or EPA (if applicable) Fee
Application relating to property and affairs and personal welfare	COP1 COP1A and 1B [COP2: permission form (if applicable)] COP3 COP4 Copy of LPA or EPA (if applicable) Fee

As a general rule permission is required for all applications to the court. No permission is however required where the application is made by, or concerns, the following[2]:

(a) the person lacking or alleged to lack capacity
(b) anyone with parental responsibility[3] for a person lacking or alleged to lack capacity who is under 18 years of age;
(c) the Official Solicitor;
(d) the Public Guardian;
(e) it concerns an LPA, which is or purports to be, created under the MCA 2005, or is made by the donor or donee to which the application relates;
(f) it is by a deputy appointed by the court for a person to whom the application relates;
(g) it is by a person named in an existing order of the court, if the application relates to the order;
(h) it concerns an EPA which is, or purports to be, an enduring power of attorney under the MCA 2005;
(i) in most applications relating solely to the exercise of the court's powers in relation to P's property and affairs (unless it is an application specified in r 52, see further below);
(j) the application is made within existing proceedings, which includes within appeal proceedings (see Part 10);

(k) it concerns a different order than that applied for by the applicant and is contained in an acknowledgment of service within the same proceedings;
(l) in connection with declarations relating to private international law under Sch 3, para 20(2);
(m) it is an application to the court under s 21A by the relevant person's representative. (See s 50(1), (1A) of the MCA 2005 as amended by the MHA 2007, not yet in force)

As stated above, no permission is required for applications relating to property and financial affairs except for particular applications specified in r 52 (see r 52(1)(a)). The exceptions relate to various applications for the court to exercise its jurisdiction under the Trustees Act 1925 and the Trusts of Land and Appointment of Trustees Act 1996.

Clearly therefore a family member will need permission, as will an NHS or local authority body, unless the matter relates solely to property and affairs. Thus questions over life-sustaining or other medical treatment and welfare issues will require permission if the applicant is the NHS Trust or family member. But if the application is made by a donee of an LPA, or deputy empowered to make welfare decisions, then no permission is required.

Applications objecting to the registration of an LPA or EPA do not require permission, and neither do applications seeking the exercise of the court's powers under ss 22 and 23 in relation to donees.

1 Taken from COP42: Making an application to the Court of Protection, published by the OPG and available on www.publicguardian.gsi.gov.uk.
2 See s 50 and r 51(1) and (2).
3 'Parental responsibility' has the same meaning as in the Children Act 1989: s 50(4).

Test for permission

10.58 The MCA 2005 sets out no specific criteria for the granting of permission. The Main Code at para 8.12 says that when deciding whether to give permission the court must consider the applicant's connection to the person the application is about, the reasons for the application, whether a proposed order or direction of the court will benefit the person the application is about and whether it is possible to get that benefit another way[1].

The scheme of the MCA 2005 allows for welfare decisions to be taken by carers and professionals in many circumstances without the need to apply to the court. These occur in the daily routine of caring for a person and ss 5 and 6 apply to protect acts in connection with care and treatment (see Chapters 4 and 7). Consequently, personal welfare issues should only be brought to court when they cannot be resolved by any other means, or where the matter is so serious that the court needs to decide the matter. The MCA 2005 therefore contains provisions concerning the need for permission in order to provide a 'check' to ensure that an application is well founded.

The need for permission is not only, however, to ensure an application is well founded but also so that any proceedings are designed to promote the benefit of the person concerned[2]. Thus it is likely that the court will ask itself two preliminary questions:

1 how serious is the matter that it is being asked to determine? In considering this it may look to the previous case law and apply a 'serious justiciable issue' test as before in relation to declaratory relief; and
2 what will be the benefit to the person lacking capacity?

This looks similar to a best interests question, which of course has no statutory definition. At the permission stage it is difficult to prescribe how to establish 'benefit' save by simple assertion, or where it is obvious because the treatment proposed is life sustaining, or there are allegations of abuse by a carer or at a residential establishment and the proposal is to move the person.

1 See also s 50(3).
2 See Explanatory Notes, para 136.

Documents to be filed with the permission form

10.59 Permission must be applied for by filing a permission form (see table at 10.57) and it must be filed together with a draft application form, an assessment of capacity form (where required by the relevant PD) and any other document that any relevant PD specifies[1]. It is not mandatory for the information in annexes to the application form to be filed at this time, nor the information in r 64 (see 10.66 below). If the applicant is unable to complete an assessment of capacity form either because the person does not live with them, or they are unable to take the person to a doctor or they refuse to undergo an assessment, the applicant must file a witness statement explaining:

(a) why he has not been able to complete the form;
(b) what steps have been taken to try and do so; and
(c) why he knows or believes the person to lack capacity in relation to the decision or decisions in relation to the proposed subject matter of the court[2].

Where part of an application requires permission and part does not, permission need only be sought for that part requiring it. This may be done in one application whereby the part not needing permission must await permission being granted (or not) in the other part, before proceeding. Alternatively, two applications (and fees) may be issued so that the part not requiring permission may proceed without waiting. If permission is subsequently granted the two applications may be consolidated[3].

1 See r 54 and PD 8A.
2 PD 8A.
3 Rule 53(2) and PD 8A.

Determination of the permission application

10.60 Determination of permission will be done by the court on the papers or alternatively a hearing date may be fixed. Within 14 days of the permission form being filed the court will issue the form and either grant permission in full or in part, or fix a date for the hearing of the application for permission (see r 55). Part 20 of the Rules deals with appeals against the granting or refusal of permission (see below at 10.87).

Oral hearing fixed

10.61 If an oral hearing for permission is to be held the court will notify the applicant and any other person(s) as it thinks fit and will provide them with copies of the documents filed at court, and a form for acknowledging notification (r 56). The court may direct that any forms to be provided under this rule are to be edited. Any person who has been notified of an application for permission and who wishes to take part in the permission hearing must file an acknowledgment of notification (COP5) not more than 21 days later (r 57).

Acknowledgment of notification

10.62 The acknowledgment of notification must state:

(a) whether the person consents to the application;
(b) opposes the application and the grounds for doing so;
c) whether he proposes that permission should be granted for a different order, and if so, set out the order;
(d) provide an address for service; and
(e) be signed by him or his legal representative.

This document may be accompanied by an application for directions (Part 10). Subject to rules restricting the filing of expert's report and evidence[1], where a person opposes an application or proposes a different order, the acknowledgment must be accompanied by a witness statement containing any evidence that person intends to rely on.

1 Rules 120 and 123.

Application: Part 9

Who can make an application?

10.63 The applicant will usually be a local authority, or NHS Trust, or the parent or guardian of P, ie the person with responsibility for the care of P, or who is proposing treatment or intervention (see Main Code at paras 8.8, and the comments of Lord Brandon in *Re F (Mental Patient: Sterilisation)*[1]. This is reflected in the rules concerning who does not need permission to bring a claim (see 10.56 above). However, as noted above at 10.23, it is likely that the same principles with regard to standing as applied under the inherent jurisdiction will continue to be relevant to the question of standing in the court . So in order to make an application to the court there will be no requirement for the applicant to have a legal right that is in dispute, or that would be affected by the outcome of the proceedings, but what will be required is a 'genuine and legitimate interest'.

1 [1990] 2 AC 1, at 65.

Litigation friends

10.64 Part 17 of the CoP Rules sets out the provisions concerning litigation friends. It is these provisions that apply in the Court of Protection[1]. Practice Direction 17A provides a further explanation and guidance with regard to litigation friends.

A litigation friend *may* be appointed to act for P, a child or a 'protected party'[2]. A protected party is a person who lacks capacity to conduct proceedings but is neither a child nor P[3]. A litigation friend *must* be appointed for a protected party if they are a party to the proceedings, and for a child if they are a party to the proceedings, unless, in the case of a child, the court orders otherwise.

The criteria that must be satisfied before a person can be appointed as a litigation friend are that they must be able to conduct proceedings fairly and competently and have no interests adverse to the person on whose behalf they intend to act[4]. The court can, on its own initiative or following an application, appoint or substitute a litigation friend, or terminate a litigation friend's appointment[5]. Any application for a court to use its powers with regard to the appointment or removal of a litigation friend must be supported by evidence and must be served on all other parties and on the proposed or concerned litigation friend[6]. An application for an order appointing a litigation friend must be made by filing a COP9 application notice, in accordance with the Part 10 procedure. These provisions reflect what is set out in the CPR, but as stated above it is the CoP Rules that apply in the court.

When a child reaches the age of 18 the litigation friend's appointment comes to an end without the need for a court order, unless s/he is P or a protected party[7]. Such a child must serve notice on every other party informing them that the litigation friend's appointment has come to an end and provide an address for service.

A Court Order is required to bring to an end the appointment of a litigation friend who is acting on behalf of either P or a protected party. An application for such an order must be made using an application notice and must be served on all other parties to the proceedings.

Where P ceases to lack capacity both for conducting proceedings and in relation to the matters to which the application relates, the litigation friend or any other person who is a party to the proceedings may make an application to end the proceedings[8].

1 In addition changes have been made to Part 21 of CPR concerning children and what were referred to as 'patients' and are now 'protected parties': SI 2007/2204 Sch 2 amends CPR Pt 21.

2 Rule 140(2).
3 Protected party is defined in r 6 'interpretation'.
4 Rule 140(1).
5 Rule 144(1).
6 Rules 144 and 145.
7 Rule 146(1)(a) and (2).
8 Rule 148.

What must be included in the application form

10.65 The application form must state the question the court must decide, the order that is being sought, who is making the application, in what capacity the applicant is making the application (if it is not on their own behalf), that permission is requested (if it is necessary) and contain any other information required in any practice direction (see r 63).

Documents to be filed with the application form

10.66 The application form must be supported by evidence set out in either: (a) a witness statement; or (b) the application form, provided it is verified by a statement of truth. The evidence must set out the facts on which the applicant relies, and all material facts known to the applicant of which the court should be made aware. The documents or instruments, as the case may be, specified in the table below must be filed with the court along with the application form, unless this is impractical or the court has directed otherwise[1].

Type of document or instrument	*When document is to be filed*
Any order granting permission	If permission is required.
Assessment of capacity form (COP3)	Unless already filed with the permission form.
Annex A: Supporting information for property and affairs applications (COP1A)	Where an order relating to P's property and affairs is sought.
Annex B: Supporting information for personal welfare applications (COP1B)	Where an order relating to P's personal welfare is sought.
Lasting power of attorney or enduring power of attorney	Where the application concerns the court's power under s 22 or 23 of, or Sch 4 to, the Act (where available).
Deputy's declaration (COP4)	Where the application is for the appointment of a deputy.
Order appointing a deputy	Where the application relates to or is made by a deputy.
Order appointing a litigation friend	Where the application is made by, or where the application relates to the appointment of, a litigation friend.
Order of the Court of Protection	Where the application relates to the order.

Type of document or instrument	*When document is to be filed*
Order of another court (and where the judgment is not in English, a translation of it into English: (i) certified by a notary public or other qualified person; or (ii) accompanied by written evidence confirming that the translation is accurate)	Where the application relates to an order made by another court.

1 See PD 9A.

Filing and issuing the application form

10.67 When an application is filed with the court the applicant must also file any written evidence upon which s/he relies and any other documents referred to in the application form, an assessment of capacity form (where required), and any other document as directed by any Practice Direction (see Table above). For welfare decisions Form CO1B is required to be served; this form asks for information about P's accommodation, marital status, GP details, visitors, guardianship, LPAs/EPA and Wills. In addition, as set out above, if permission was required the court's order granting permission must also be filed (see r 64).

The court will then issue the application as soon as practicable. This will only be done in cases where either permission is not required, or where permission has been granted.

Notification

10.68 In accordance with r 70, Practice Direction 9B (notification of other persons that an application form has been issued) sets out who should be notified of an application. The applicant must seek to identify at least three persons who are likely to have an interest in being notified that an application form has been issued. The applicant should notify them:

(a) that an application form has been issued;
(b) whether it relates to the exercise of the court's jurisdiction in relation to P's property and affairs, or his personal welfare, or both; and
(c) of the order or orders sought.

Members of P's close family are, by virtue of their relationship to P, likely to have an interest in being notified that an application has been made to the court concerning P. It should be presumed, for example that a spouse or civil partner, any other partner, parents and children are likely to have an interest in the application (see paras 4 and 5 of PD 9B).

Where a decision is taken not to notify a category of person who it is said to be presumed to require notification because, for example, they have had little or no involvement in P's life and have shown no inclination to do so, then the Practice Direction states that the evidence in support of the application form must also set out why that person was not notified.

Unless the applicant is P or is the donor of an LPA, the applicant also has to provide P personally with information concerning the application. P must be told personally what the application concerns, who has made it, that it raises the question of capacity, what will happen if the order or direction sought is made, what steps P can take, and, where the application proposes that a person be appointed to make decisions on behalf of P, who that person is. P must also be provided with an acknowledgment of service and a form applying for joinder. Once the information has been provided to P the applicant must file a certificate confirming that this has happened within seven days (see Part 7 of the CoP Rules, and r 69). An application can be made to the court to dispense with this requirement or to ask that some other person be responsible for notification to P (see r 49.)

Service

10.69 Once the application has been issued or as soon as practicable thereafter, and in any event within 21 days, the applicant must serve on all named respondents copies of the application form together with all related documents and an acknowledgment of service form. A certificate of service must be filed within seven days of service.

In addition to named respondents the applicant must also serve a copy of the application form together with an acknowledgment of service on the person with parental responsibility if P is under 18, any appointed attorney or deputy, and any relatives of P. Where the applicant is a relative s/he need only serve the form on any relative that has the same or a nearer degree of relationship to P than the applicant.

Rule 67 requires that if the application concerns an LPA the form must also be served, together with an acknowledgment of service, on the donor and all donees. Anyone served with a form under this rule will also be named as a respondent to the proceedings. Similarly where the application relates to an EPA, copies of the application form and related documents, plus an acknowledgment of service form must be served on the donor and donees (see r 68). Service on donors and donees must again be completed within 21 days and certificates of service filed within seven days of service.

Acknowledgment of service

10.70 The acknowledgment of service must be filed within 21 days of service of the application form; the court will then serve the acknowledgment of service on all relevant parties. The acknowledgement of service should include, as well as stating whether the person acknowledging service consents to or opposes the application, any alternative order sought. If the application is to be opposed, or if a different order is sought, then a witness statement must also be served which states what evidence[1] is to be relied upon (see r 72).

Where the person on whom a document must be served is a child or a protected party then r 32 sets out who should be served, as follows:

Type of document	*Nature of party*	*Person to be served*
Application form	Child	– A person who has parental responsibility for the child within the meaning of the Children Act 1989; or – if there is no such person, a person with whom the child resides or in whose care the child is.
Application form	Protected party	– The person who is authorised to conduct the proceedings in the protected party's name or on his behalf; or – a person who is a duly appointed attorney, donee or deputy of the protected party; or – if there is no such person, a person with whom the protected party lives or in whose care the latter is.
Application for an order appointing a litigation friend, where a child or protected party has no litigation friend	Child or protected party	– See r 145 (appointment of litigation friend by court order – supplementary).
Any other document	Child or protected party	– The litigation friend or other duly authorised person who is conducting the proceedings on behalf of the child or protected party.

The above does not apply if the court has granted an application that a child does not require a litigation friend (see above at 10.64. The court may grant an order that documents can be served on a person other than that specified, and also can deem there to have been good service even if not on the person specified or ordered[2]. An application to serve documents on a person other than that specified can be made without notice.

1 Subject to restrictions on the filing of expert evidence contained in rr 120 and 123, see below at 10.81.

2 Rule 32.

Parties

10.71 The applicant and any named respondent will, clearly, be parties to the proceedings. In addition the court will consider whether anyone not already a party should be joined as a party to the proceedings. Other persons with sufficient interest may apply to be joined as parties to the proceedings[1]. In respect of cases involving issues concerning 'serious medical treatment', an organisation which is, or will be, responsible for providing clinical or caring services to P should usually be named as a respondent in the application form[2]. It is suggested that although it is not mandatory that P be joined as a party to the proceedings, in order to comply with P's Article 6 and Article 8 rights they should be joined in any case that will involve a determination of their civil rights and obligations, or where the decision will affect an important aspect of their right to respect for their family life[3]. The court may also direct that any party be removed. P cannot be named as a respondent (unless the court orders otherwise); however, P will be bound by any orders made or directions given by the court (see rr 73 and 74).

Any party with sufficient interest can apply to become a party by completing an application notice. The application notice must be accompanied by a witness statement setting out the parties interest, any proposed order and any evidence which will be relied upon. Again the restrictions on expert evidence apply (see below at 10.81). The court will serve the notice and documents on all other parties and so sufficient copies must be provided to the Court. The Court will then decide whether to join the party. In an earlier draft of the rules provision was made for other parties to make representations before the court decided whether to join a party and could also have had an oral hearing to determine the matter. These provisions are not contained in the final version of the rules.

1 Rule 75.
2 See PD 9E, para 9.
3 See Chapter 17, in particular at 17.48.

Application within proceedings: Part 10

10.72 Part 10 of the CoP Rules sets out the procedure for making applications within the proceedings; for example an application to be joined as a party.

Interim remedies

10.73 The court can grant an interim remedy if the matter is urgent, or if it is in the interests of justice to do so[1]. The court has the power to grant an interim injunction, declaration or any other appropriate order. In addition the CoP Rules do not limit any other power the court may have to grant interim relief. Interim remedies cannot be sought by any person served with an application form or given notice of an application until they have filed an acknowledgment of service or notification[2].

1 Rule 77.
2 Rule 82.

Application without notice

10.74 An application can be made without notice, but once the court has dealt with the application the applicant must serve on all parties and named respondents, and other persons as directed by the court, a copy of the application notice, a copy of the order of the court and any evidence filed in support of the application (see r 81).

The core procedure

Dealing with the application

10.75 Once the court has issued the application it will consider how to deal with it, including whether it is necessary to hold a hearing.

Hearings[1]

10.76 When considering whether to hold a hearing the court shall have regard to the following:

(a) the nature of the proceedings and the orders sought;
(b) whether the application is opposed by a person who appears to have an interest in matters relating to P's best interests;
(c) whether the application involves a substantial dispute of fact;
(d) the complexity of the facts and law;
(e) any wider public interest;
(f) the circumstances of P and of any other party, in particular as to whether their rights would be adequately protected if a hearing were not held;
(g) whether the parties agree that the court should dispose of the matter without a hearing; and
(h) any other matter specified in the relevant practice direction[2].

The CoP Rules do not set out any particular procedure for making representations concerning the need for a hearing. Any such representations should therefore be made within either the application form or the acknowledgment of service and should address which of the above considerations applies and why.

1 Part 13.
2 Rule 84(3).

Directions hearings

10.77 The court also has the power to order a directions hearing, but is not required to do so. If the court decides to hold a hearing it will give notice to the parties and state whether it is for the disposal of the matter or for directions. A party who wishes to apply to vary the date fixed for a hearing, or the period within which a final hearing is to take place, must do so in writing[1], the CoP Rules do not state that this must be by way of a Part 10 application. Any other direction that a person do an act within a specified time may (subject to any practice directions saying otherwise or the court saying otherwise) be varied by agreement between the parties, so long as it does not affect the date set by the court for the final hearing or the time within which the final hearing is to take place[2].

1 Rule 85(5).
2 Rule 85(5) and (6).

Public or private hearing?

10.78 When the court decides to hold an oral hearing, generally the hearing will be in private, but the court can order a public hearing[1]. An earlier draft of the CoP Rules stated that generally hearings were to be held in public except where to hold it in public hearing would defeat the object of the hearing, where matters of national security are involved, where there is confidential information and publication would destroy the confidentiality, and where it was in the interests of P to have the hearing in private. In the final version of the CoP Rules however, the presumption has clearly been reversed and the court has now been given the power to determine whether a public hearing should be held.

Private hearings are defined as those at which only the parties, P, any litigation friend, any associated legal representatives, and court officers may attend. The court has the power in a private hearing to order that any other person or class of person can attend, and also has the power to exclude any person from attending, presumably including those specified as allowed to attend private hearings[2]. Information about the proceedings can be published for the purposes of the law relating to contempt of court, and the court may impose restrictions on the identification of any person[3].

If a public hearing is ordered the court also has the power to exclude any person or class of person and impose restrictions on publicising the identity of any person and on any information relating to the proceedings as the Court sees fit.

The only requirement in the CoP Rules for deciding whether to order a hearing to take place in private or in public, or whether to impose reporting restrictions, is that there must 'appear to the court' to be a 'good reason' for the order[4]. Clearly however this will be subject to the right contained in Article 6 ECHR to a public hearing; any restrictions imposed on the right to a public hearing must be in accordance with any Article 6 rights that are engaged by the proceedings.

1 See Rule 92.
2 Rule 90.
3 Rule 91.
4 Rule 93.

Evidence

Witness evidence

10.79 Witness evidence can be contained in a witness statement with a signed statement of truth, unless the court orders that an affidavit is required or some other rule or practice direction requires affidavit evidence.

Where there is a final hearing any fact that needs to be proved by the evidence of a witness will require the witness to give oral evidence, although their witness statement will stand as evidence in chief. The court can permit, however, that the witness statement or witness summary (see below) can be varied or added to in oral evidence if there is good reason to do so.

If a party is not in a position to file a full witness statement for use in a final hearing it can file a 'witness summary' without notice. The summary must set out, where known, the evidence which would otherwise be contained in a witness statement, or if the evidence is not known the matters about which the party filing the summary proposes to question the witness about at the final hearing. The witness' name and address must be included (unless the court directs otherwise) and the summary must be filed within the same timeframe as the court directs that witness statements must be filed[1].

The court has the power to issue witness summons. Any party can make an application to the court for a witness summons using an application notice. A witness summons is binding if served more than seven days before the final hearing, or where there is less than seven days if the court orders that it is binding. An application for a witness summons must include the grounds on which it is being made. Once issued the party requesting the summons must serve it, unless the court directs otherwise[2].

A party may apply to the court for a deposition to be taken from a person before the hearing takes place. The procedure and rules surrounding the taking of the deposition are contained in rr 108 to 113, and are the same as those in CPR 34.8–34.13. The party who requested the order for a deposition must pay the associated costs.

1 Rule 101.
2 Rule 106.

Section 49 reports and visitors

10.80 The court has the power to and may call for reports (s 49). This may be called for from the Public Guardian or Court of Protection Visitor, or the local authority or an NHS body, by one of its officers or employees, or such other person as considered appropriate[1]. The reports of the Visitor should be disclosed to P and the court office will send a copy of the report to such persons as the court may direct[2].

The report writer must seek to interview any relevant persons and where possible ascertain what P's wishes are, and what beliefs and values would be likely to influence P if he had capacity. A copy of the report will be sent to all parties[3].

The parties to the proceedings are permitted to request that written questions are put to the writer of any section 49 report. The request must be made to the court. The court may amend any of the questions put. All replies will be sent to the court who will then send a copy of the replies to all the parties and any other person as the court may direct[4].

The writer of a section 49 report is not treated as an 'expert'[5], see 10.81 below.

1 Rule 5.
2 Rule 42(5).
3 Rule 117.
4 Rule 118.
5 Rule 119(b).

Expert evidence

10.81 Experts are defined in r 119 as any expert who has been instructed to give or prepare evidence for the purpose of court proceedings, but does not include the writer of a section 49 report.

As with the CPR the CoP Rules stipulate that expert evidence cannot be filed without the permission of the court, although additionally the CoP Rules do allow for a practice direction to permit a party to adduce expert evidence. An important exception to this rule is evidence concerning P's capacity and best interests filed with the application form or permission form[1], so no permission for this is required. However, the evidence can only be used for the purpose, and to the extent the court allows and so the court does retain control over its use.

Unlike the CPR, when applying for permission to adduce expert evidence in addition to providing details of the expert and his/her field of expertise, a party must provide a copy of a draft letter of instruction. When granting an application, the court shall specify the field/s in respect of which the expert evidence is to be provided. Again this differs slightly from the CPR which states that when permission is granted it is only in respect of the field/s that have been specified in the application[2]. The CoP Rules therefore appear at least to give the court more discretion and power in relation to the field/s of expertise any expert evidence can cover. The court may also specify the person who is to provide the expert evidence, which again seems to give the court more power and control over expert evidence than the CPR does.

Expert evidence is to be given in writing unless the court directs otherwise and the court will give directions for the service of the report on the parties and any other person the court directs.

Any party can put written questions to an expert instructed by any other party. The procedure and rules for doing so are set out in r 125 and are essentially the same as those contained in CPR 35.6. However, it should be noted that under r 125(7) the instructing party is responsible for the payment of the expert's fees and expenses including the expert's costs of answering questions put by another party.

Another notable difference between the CPR and the CoP Rules concerning experts is that the instructions to the expert shall not be privileged against disclosure. Under the CPR while the same applies, it is qualified by the rule that the court will not order disclosure or permit any questions to be put by a non-instructing party concerning instructions, unless it is satisfied that the instructions were either inaccurate or incomplete.

Discussion between experts can be directed as would be expected and the experts can be directed to provide a report of their discussions. There is a change of emphasis in the CoP Rules, however, as regards the ability of parties to refer to any discussions between experts in that parties are allowed to do so unless the court directs otherwise. In the CPR parties can only refer to such discussions if all parties agree[3]. Missing from the CoP Rules is an equivalent of CPR 35.12(5), which states that 'Where experts reach agreement on an issue during their discussions, the agreement shall not bind the parties unless the parties expressly agree to be bound by the agreement.'

The rules concerning the use and instruction of a single joint expert are the same as those in the CPR[4].

1 Rule 120.
2 See CPR 35.4(3).
3 CPR 35.12(4).
4 CPR 35.7 and 35.8; CoP Rules, rr 130 and 131.

Disclosure

10.82 The disclosure provisions are similar but not identical to those in the CPR. The CoP Rules refer to 'general and specific disclosure' rather than standard disclosure and in the CoP Rules there is no reference to any proportionality test.

The court may order general or specific disclosure at the request of a party or on its own initiative. General disclosure is the same as standard disclosure and so requires a party to disclose the documents on which he relies and the documents that adversely affect his case, another party's case, or supports another party's case. Specific disclosure requires a party to disclose documents or classes of documents, and/or to carry out a search for documents and disclose anything found as a result[1].

The time limit for allowing inspection of documents and providing copies of documents differs from the CPR. In the CPR parties are only given seven days in which to comply with a request. In the CoP Rules the parties are given 14 days[2].

Disclosure can be problematic in cases concerning best interests as there will often be issues of confidentiality. Rule 138 sets out that where a party wishes to claim that he has a right or a duty not to disclose a document that is disclosable then he must state in writing that this is the case and the grounds on which he claims that right or duty. This statement should be included in the list of documents to be disclosed. An application may be made to the court (using the Part 10 procedure) requesting the court to make a decision as to whether the document should be disclosed. If a party therefore seeks to rely on any duty or right not to disclose a document and another party disagrees that party can apply to the court for the matter to be determined.

Guidance on disclosure where the material is confidential was provided in the case of *R (on the application of Stevens) v Plymouth City Council*[3]. The court in that case stated that medical reports and recommendations and information which would usually be held by a local or health authority in relation to guardianship/detention under the MHA 1983 would, by its very nature, be confidential to the person in question[4]. However, the obligation of confidence is liable to be overridden in circumstances in which there is a stronger public interest. The court stated that there is a balance to be struck, both in terms of the common law and the ECHR, and set out that the interests to be balanced were the confidentiality of the information to be sought, the administration of justice, any Article 8 rights to respect for family life, and the protection against any risk to the safety and health of the person(s) concerned.

Example case

J is an 82-year-old man who suffered a debilitating stroke in November 2007 and is incapacitated in relation to most aspects of his daily life. His wife of the last ten years, S, arranges medical and nursing care for him, firstly in hospital and then at home where she is now caring for him herself. She is able to do this by virtue of the protection afforded by s 5 and appears to be managing well with the input of social and health services. She has help to bathe him, but otherwise does everything for him, including feeding him, brushing his teeth and changing his incontinence pads. He is uncomplaining. J's 42-year-old son by his first marriage, M, is unhappy with the care arranged for his father, and also the arrangements for contact between him and his father. Previously he saw his father only very rarely as there had been a long standing disagreement between them. M now accuses S of deliberately isolating his father from his family and of physically abusing him and neglecting his care. He has brought this to the attention of the local authority which is reluctant to interfere with what appears to them to be a family feud. One of the care assistants notes some bruising on J. S is adamant that it was caused accidentally, but she is unable to say how. She is also adamant that in restricting access of M to his father she is following his father's previously stated wishes. S has not permitted social services to do an assessment of her ability to care for J. The local authority is unable to satisfy itself that S is acting in J's best interests. It makes an application to the court to decide the issue of his residence and contact on his behalf.

What applications should be made to the court?

Urgency: Is there a need for any urgent interim relief? Permission is likely to take two weeks, after which a hearing date will be set. If there is evidence that

J should be removed immediately an urgent application should be made, if possible on notice to S and M. In cases of exceptional urgency an application may be started without filing an application form and can be made to the court orally, but if time permits an application should be made in writing. The court will require an undertaking that the application form in the terms of the oral application be filed on the next working day, or as ordered by the court. A draft order should, where possible, be provided to the court, and any order made should state in the title after the names of the applicant and the respondent, 'the Applicant and Respondent in an Intended Application' (see PD 10B). The draft order should include an invitation to the Official Solicitor to act as litigation friend; at the next hearing an order can then be made appointing him as litigation friend.

***The Official Solicitor*:** If the urgent procedure set out above is not followed then the Official Solicitor should be contacted and invited to act on behalf of J. He should be asked to attend the first hearing. If this is not possible then at the very least a letter from the Official Solicitor stating that he does not object to being appointed as litigation friend should be obtained.

Filing the Application and Permission form: An application form, a COP1, and a permission form, COP2, must be filed with the central office in Archway. This must contain the question the court must decide, the order(s) that are being sought, who is making the application and in what capacity. A form COP3 should also be completed, which is the assessment of capacity form. Although at this stage there may not have been a full capacity assessment, such information as is available should be included so that the court can be asked to make at least an interim decision on capacity.

What evidence must be supplied? A witness statement from the carer setting out his concerns and any evidence of bruising etc and a witness statement covering the reluctance of S for assessment should be filed (or alternatively a statement of truth signed in the application form). This is likely to be an application to the court under its powers in s 16 for a welfare decision to be taken in accordance with s 17. Thus the evidence presented must so far as possible enable the Court to make the decision on behalf of J. Clearly evidence independent of S and M is desirable. If neither of them are considered appropriate to consult on this issue because they are in dispute then it may be advisable to instruct an IMCA in addition, as this is potentially an issue of long term accommodation.

Permission: An application in these circumstances is most likely to be brought by the local authority as they have a duty under Article 8 ECHR to protect J, and it is also a serious issue, permission therefore is unlikely to be contentious (see r 54 and PD 8A) and a first Directions hearing will be listed.

***Directions hearing*:** At the Directions hearing interim orders should be sought:

- as to lack of capacity, residence and contact;
- disclosure: of social services records, health records (to the Official Solicitor in the first instance if there are concerns about S and M having access to them);

- timetable for further evidence: witness evidence of all parties, expert evidence. The latter is likely to be required from a consultant psychiatrist in relation to capacity and best interests, and for an independent social worker in relation to the same and should be by joint instruction led by the Official Solicitor;
- date for further directions or final hearing;
- timetable for position statements (see below) from parties to be served and lodged with the Court in time for the hearing and the lodging of a court bundle by the applicant.

1 Rule 133.
2 Rule 137.
3 [2002] EWCH Civ 388, [2002] 1 WLR 2583.
4 At 2594G–H, para 33.

Position statements

10.83 Position statements drafted by the parties set out the issues for the court. The CoP Rules do not specify that position statements are required. However, it has been the practice of the Family Division to require such statements, and it is suggested this practice should be continued in the Court of Protection, at least where welfare decisions are concerned. They provide a useful tool for the parties to clearly set out the issues for the court prior to a hearing.

Appeals

Who to appeal to?

10.84 The MCA 2005 provides in s 53 that, subject to any rules made, an appeal direct to the Court of Appeal lies from any decision of the court[1]. The Act provides that the Rules can stipulate that where a decision of the court is made by a district judge, a circuit judge or by a person exercising the jurisdiction of the court by virtue of any rule[2] then an appeal from that decision lies to a prescribed higher judge of the court and not the Court of Appeal.

The relevant Rules are set out in Part 20. Rule 180 states that, except in accordance with the relevant practice direction:

(a) an appeal from a first instance decision of a circuit judge shall be heard by a judge of the court nominated by virtue of s 46(2)(a)–(c) of the MCA 2005; and
(b) an appeal from a decision of a district judge shall be heard by a circuit judge.

To be nominated a judge must be either:

(a) the President of the Family Division;
(b) the Vice-Chancellor;
(c) a puisine judge of the High Court;

(d) a circuit judge; or
(e) a district judge.

When the first instance decision has not been taken by a nominated judge then an appeal will lie to a higher judge of the court, and thereafter an appeal lies to the Court of Appeal. In this case only the Court of Appeal can grant permission to appeal. Where a nominated judge has taken the decision at first instance then an appeal will only lie to the Court of Appeal. Where this is the case the nominated judge may also grant permission to appeal to the Court of Appeal (for permission see further below)[1].

1 Section 53(1).
2 Section 53(2).
3 Rule 181.

Application to appeal

10.85 In order to appeal against a decision of the court an appellant's notice must be filed within 21 days of the decision to be appealed, or within such time as directed by the court making the decision. The court will then issue the appellant's notice and the appellant must serve it, as soon as practicable and in any event within 21 days, on each respondent and on anyone else the court directs. A certificate of service must be filed within seven days.

In addition P must be notified that an appeal notice has been issued by the court and of the date on which a hearing is to be heard. It must be explained to P who the appellant is, the issues the appeal raises and what will happen if the court grants the appeal. If the appeal is subsequently withdrawn P must be informed and the consequences explained. P must also be informed of his/her right to seek advice and assistance concerning any matter s/he has been notified of[1].

A respondent's notice must be filed if the respondent is seeking permission to appeal, or if he is seeking that the decision be upheld for different reasons to those given by the first instance judge. The respondent's notice must be filed within 21 days of service of the appellant's notice, where permission has already been granted or where no permission is required, or within 21 days of being given notification that permission being granted, or within 21 days of notification that permission and the appeal itself are to be heard together. The court will then issue the respondent's notices and this must be served on the appellant and any other party as the court may direct as soon as practicable, or in any event within 21 days. A certificate of service must be filed within seven days thereafter[2].

An application to vary the time limits imposed by the CoP Rules must be made to the appeal judge, no variation can be agreed between the parties.

1 Rule 43.
2 Rule 176.

Who can appeal?

10.86 In addition to the parties any person bound by an order by virtue of r 74 (persons to be bound as if parties) may seek permission to appeal.

Permission

10.87 Permission is required for all appeals (except against an order for committal to prison). Permission to appeal a first instance decision may be made either to the first instance judge or to the appeal judge[1]. If permission is refused by a district judge then an appeal against that decision can be made to:

- the President
- the Vice-President;
- one of the other judges nominated by virtue of s 46(2)(a)–(c);
- a circuit judge[2].

If permission was refused by a circuit judge then permission can only be granted by either the President, the Vice President or one of the other nominated judges[3].

The test for permission is whether there is a real prospect of success or there is some other compelling reason why the appeal should be heard. Permission can be granted on a limited basis or with conditions[4].

Where a party wishes to appeal a decision of an appeal judge then only the Court of Appeal can grant permission. In this case the Court of Appeal will only grant permission if the appeal would raise an important point of principle or practice, or there is some other compelling reason why the Court of Appeal ought to hear the appeal[1].

1 Rule 172(4).
2 Rule 172(6).
3 Rule 172(7).
4 Rule 173.
5 Rule 182.

PUBLIC FUNDING

10.88 No public funding was available for proceedings before the old Court of Protection at all[1]. For applications concerning purely property and affairs it remains the case that they fall outside of the scope of legal aid. Full legal aid, subject to a means and merits test was (and is) available for proceedings in the High Court heard under the court's inherent jurisdiction.

The new Court of Protection is not part of the High Court and therefore advocacy brought before it is excluded by Sch 2 to the Access to Justice Act 1999. However a Direction has been issued under s 6(8) of that Act which brings certain cases before the Court of Protection within the scope of Community Legal Services ('CLS') funding. Legal aid will therefore be available for those cases for which it would have been available previously in best interests cases before the High Court[2].

Where legal services are required for eligible clients in relation to issues under the MCA 2005, which do not need to be taken to court, Legal Help will be the normal vehicle for funding advice and assistance. Under the new fee schemes which apply to Controlled Work in the Mental Health category from 1 January 2008, Legal Help in relation to the MCA 2005 is funded as Level 1 Non-MHRT work under the rules contained in the Unified Contract Civil Specification.

Legal Representation at a formal hearing will be available for cases before the court which raise fundamental issues, for example cases concerning decisions over the giving or withholding of medical treatment.

The text of the authorisation is:

'1. This is an authorisation by the Lord Chancellor under section 6(8) of the Access to Justice Act 1999 ("the Act"). It authorizes the Legal Services Commission ("the Commission") to fund, in the circumstances specified below, services generally excluded from the scope of the Community Legal Service Fund by Schedule 2 to the Act.

2. References in this authorisation to which services the Commission may fund are to the levels of service defined in those terms in the Commission's Funding Code ("the Code").

3. All applications under this authorisation remain subject to the relevant regulations under the Act and all relevant criteria in the Code.

4. The Lord Chancellor authorizes the Commission to fund Legal Help, Help at Court and Legal Representation in relation to proceedings or potential proceedings before the Court of Protection in the circumstances specified below.

5. The circumstances are where:
   (i) the proceedings fall within paragraph 6 below AND
   (ii)the Court has ordered or is likely to order an oral hearing at which it will be
necessary for the applicant for funding to be legally represented.

6. The proceedings specified in paragraph 5 above are those which, in relation to the person whose personal welfare is the subject of the proceedings, concern that person's:
   - Life
   - Liberty
   - Physical safety
   - Medical treatment (including psychological treatment)
   - Capacity to marry or enter into a civil partnership
   - Capacity to enter into sexual relations OR
   - Right to family life

7. The Lord Chancellor authorises the Commission to fund Legal Help in relation to the making of Lasting Powers of Attorney and advance decisions where the client is:
   (a) aged 70 or over; or
   (b) a disabled person within the meaning of section 1 of the Disability Discrimination Act 1995.'

The above therefore sets out two substantive tests for bringing a case before the court within the scope of CLS funding. The first test is whether the case concerns one or more of the issues listed in paragraph 6 in relation to 'P' whose personal welfare is the subject of the proceedings. The second test is whether it is necessary for the applicant for funding to be represented at an oral hearing. The wording of the authorisation makes it clear that funding can extend not just to 'P' himself or herself but sometimes for other parties, such as 'P's' immediate family, provided all other relevant criteria are satisfied.

Since the authorisation is intended to capture the serious health and welfare cases, which would previously have been considered by the High Court under its inherent jurisdiction, the Commission is said to take into account case law on that jurisdiction in deciding whether a case comes within the authorisation.

Examples of medical treatment cases which would fall within the authorisation are said to include:

(a) Where it is proposed to withdraw artificial nutrition and hydration from a patient in a permanent vegetative state — see, for example, *Airedale NHS Trust v Bland*[3].
(b) Where the issue is withdrawal or withholding of life sustaining treatment, where the legality of so doing is in doubt — see *R (on the application of Burke) v General Medical Council*[4].
(c) Where the issue is whether to sterilise a person for contraceptive purposes when they cannot give consent — see *Re S (Sterilisation)*[5].
(d) Certain termination of pregnancy cases — see *D v An NHS Trust*[6].

The guidance of the Official Solicitor, in the Official Solicitor Practice Note of 28 July 2006 on Declaratory Proceedings: *Medical & Welfare Decisions for Adults Who Lack Capacity*[7], says in general, any serious treatment decision where there is a disagreement between those involved and those close to P, where the treatment proposed may involve the use of force to restrain P or otherwise may be resisted by P or where there are doubts and difficulties over the assessment of either the person's capacity or best interests, should be referred to the court. The guidance on the authorisation says that many, but not all, cases within that guidance will also come within the terms of the authorisation.

The authorisation is not limited to cases concerning medical treatment. Proceedings concerning the deprivation of liberty will also fall within the authorisation, so applications that involve decisions that have the effect of depriving a person who lacks capacity of their liberty will come within the scope of the authorisation.

Many welfare cases will concern accommodation issues, but these will not as such fall within the scope of the authorisation. However, accommodation cases will be within scope where they concern P's family life. This is likely to be the case where either the issue is whether or not P should remain with his or her family or where a change of accommodation would have a serious impact on contact between P and his or her family. Cost benefit criteria may also be an important consideration in such applications. As there will be no quantifiable benefit, the cost benefit analysis will in this case be the private client test, so funding will be refused 'unless the likely benefits to be gained from the proceedings justify the likely cost, such that a reasonable private paying client would be prepared to litigate, having regard to the prospects of success and all other circumstances'.

The second limb of the authorisation requires that the applicant will need to be represented at an oral hearing. Under the CoP Rules, the court has the discretion as to whether to hold an oral hearing to decide the application before it and will give directions on whether an oral hearing is required during proceedings. In the most urgent and important cases legal representation may be granted before the court has made any determination on whether to direct an oral hearing, whilst in other cases it may appropriate to await what directions the court makes before a decision on the need for representation is made.

However, in practice, many cases within paragraph 6 of the authorisation will be those for which an oral hearing is likely to be directed by the court. If Legal Representation is granted but the court subsequently directs that an oral hearing is not required, consideration will be given by the Commission to the discharge of the certificate.

In considering whether it is necessary for the applicant to be represented at an oral hearing it will often be necessary for P to be legally represented as well as represented by a litigation friend where the court has directed that P should be a party, but this is less likely to be true of any other parties. Typically applicants will include close family members of P or others with an LPA or EPA or those who have been appointed as deputies under the MCA 2005. In deciding whether it is necessary for parties to be represented the Commission will take into account all the circumstances, in particular:

(a) the applicant's connection with 'P' and hence their interest in the proceedings;
(b) the submissions that the applicant proposes to make, and whether oral advocacy as opposed to written submissions is the best means of putting that case to the Court;
(c) all other parties that are likely to be before the court and the submissions they are expected to make;
(d) any directions or indications given by the court;
(e) whether or not the proceedings are being brought by a local authority or NHS body and whether or not they are being heard by a High Court Judge.

In general the Commission will only grant Legal Representation if the applicant wishes to put forward a new and significant argument which would not otherwise be advanced. As a general rule there should not be more parties separately represented before the court than there are either cases to put or desired outcomes.

Cases which come within the authorisation must still satisfy all relevant merits criteria in the Funding Code. Cases before the Court of Protection are likely to be considered under the general Funding Code. The most important criteria will often be prospects of success. Many (but not all) of the cases which come within paragraph 6 of the authorisation will also fall within the test of 'Overwhelming Importance to the Client' as defined in section 2.4 of the Funding Code. For cases of overwhelming importance to the client the requirement is to have at least borderline prospects of achieving the outcome desired by the applicant. For this purpose in relation to applications on behalf of the family of P the issues will be treated as of overwhelming importance to the applicant if they are of overwhelming importance to P.

Cost benefit will be an important consideration in many cases before the Court of Protection. All costs will be subject to the Private Client Test at Code Criterion 5.7.4. Cost benefit is unlikely to be an issue in medical treatment cases, especially for P. It is recognised that parties other than P may well have no direct and tangible interest or benefit other than the desire to secure the best outcome for P. This interest will be taken into account under the private client test but in all cases the likely costs must be proportionate to the importance of the issues to the applicant.

With regard to LPAs and advance decisions, Legal Help may be appropriate in some circumstances in relation to an application or proposed application to the Court of Protection under s 22 or 23 of the MCA 2005 concerning questions about the validity or operation of lasting powers of attorney. Similarly, it may in some cases be appropriate to provide Legal Help concerning questions under s 25 of the Act about the validity and applicability of Advance Decisions.

Further, under paragraph 7 of the Lord Chancellor's Authorisation, Legal Help in relation to the making of an LPA or an Advance Decision is brought into scope of funding where the client is aged 70 or is a disabled person within the meaning of s 1 of the Disability Discrimination Act 1995. Legal Help can only be provided, however, where there is sufficient benefit to the client in terms of their financial circumstances or potential decisions concerning medical treatment or other welfare matters.

1 See also www.dca.gov.uk/consult/court-protection-cases/cp2606.htm.
2 See www.legalservices.gov.uk/docs/civil_contracting/guidance_mental_capacity_0607.pdf for guidance and the authorisation.
3 [1993] AC 789.
4 [2005] EWCA Civ 1003, [2006] QB 273.
5 [2000] 2 FLR 389.
6 [2003] EWHC 2793 (Fam), [2004] 1 FLR 1110.
7 [2006] 2 FLR 373.

COSTS: PART 19

10.89 Section 55 states that the costs of, and incidental to, all proceedings in the court are in the court's discretion and subject to CoP Rules. The general rules prevailing under each of the previous jurisdictions, namely the old Court of Protection and the inherent jurisdiction of the High Court, are now replicated by rr 156 and 157. Part 19 of the CoP Rules sets out in detail the rules on costs and how they and the CPR on costs apply.

In summary CPR Pts 44, 47, and 48 and the related Practice Directions apply with the modifications as set out in CoP Rules, r 160 and the COP Practice Direction (PD 19A). In addition the definitions contained in CPR Pt 43, that are relevant to Pts 44, 47 and 48, apply, except where they differ from the definitions in CoP Rules, r 155. Where this happens the CoP Rules prevail.

Property and affairs: rule 156

10.90 The general rule is that the costs of the proceedings or that part of the proceedings relating to property and affairs of the person concerned shall be paid by the person or charged to his estate.[1] This recognises that welfare issues may now be determined in the same proceedings and a different general rule applies to those costs.

1 This Rule essentially replicates the position in the old Court of Protection Rules whereby the normal rule that costs should follow the event did not apply. Costs were entirely in the discretion of the Court. A successful party could apply for its costs out of the estate of the donor of the EPA. Court of Protection Rules 2001, rr 84 and 89 (now revoked).

Personal welfare: rule 157

10.91 The general rule is that there will be no order as to costs of the proceedings or that part of the proceedings that concerns welfare. The courts have interpreted the 'normal' rule that 'costs follow the event' in the context of applications relating to children, so that the usual order is that there be 'no order as to costs'. This will depend on the reasonableness of the parties' conduct in the litigation.

Apportionment of costs: rule 158

10.92 The general rule is that where proceedings in court are about both property and affairs and welfare, costs will be apportioned, so far as possible between the respective issues.

Departing from the general rules above: rule 159

10.93 The court has a discretion to depart from the general rules above where such a course of action is justified by all the circumstances. The court may look at the conduct of the parties, whether a party has succeeded on part of his case, and the role of any public body.

The consideration of 'conduct' is further explained at r 159(2), where it is said to include:

- conduct before and during the proceedings;
- the reasonableness with which any particular issue was raised or pursued or contested;

- the manner in which a party has made or responded to an application or particular issue;
- whether the successful party exaggerated any matter contained in his application or response.

The above appears to incorporate the principles in *Re Cathcart*[1] whereby a party that refuses to abandon its application to register a power of attorney unreasonably may have to bear its own costs and possibly that of other parties also.

The principles in *Re Cathcart* have been considered in Heywood and Massey, para 19–003. In particular it is said that:

(a) Where an application is made in good faith, supported by medical evidence where appropriate, in the best interests of the patient or donor and without any personal motive, the applicant is generally entitled to his costs from the patient's or donor's estate, even where he is unsuccessful,

(b) The court has an unlimited discretion to make whatever order for costs it considers that the justice of the case requires.

(c) In exercising its discretion the Court must have regard to all the circumstances of the case, including, though not limited to, the relationship between the parties, their conduct, and the amount of costs involved.

Where a person places himself in a hostile position to a patient or donor, or where his conduct results in the costs of the proceedings being more expensive than they would otherwise have been, or where the Court considers an application or objection to have been frivolous, malicious, vexatious or motivated by self interest, it may consider it appropriate to penalise that person in costs.

1 [1893] 1 Ch 466.

Fixed costs: rule 159(3)

10.94 These are to be recovered in accordance with the relevant CPR Practice Directions (see CPR Cost Practice Direction 43 to 48).

Detailed assessment of costs: rule 161

10.95 If ordered by the court, detailed assessment must take place in the High Court and the amount payable is that certified by the court as payable. A fee is payable. The venue is the Supreme Court Costs Office, Clifford's Inn, Fetter Lane, London EC4A 1DQ.

Duplication of representation: rule 162

10.96 Only one set of costs will be allowed where two or more persons have the same interests in relation to one set of proceedings, unless and to the extent that the Court certifies that the circumstances justify separate representation. In practice this is an important rule but its application will depend on the type of case being pursued and so it is not possible to provide definitive guidance on its scope. In a medical treatment case in which family and/or a donee of an LPA are challenging a decision, then the family and donee should consider joint representation. In a case challenging the actions of a donee or donees, then there are may be separate interests between the donees and between donees and those challenging them such that separate representation will be necessary.

The point may also arise, for example, where a local authority has objected to the registration of a lasting power of attorney and the Official Solicitor is appointed to act for the donor, if they both pursue the same objections. Why are duplicate costs potentially payable out of the estate of the donor? In such a case a decision should be made between the parties as to who should take the lead role. It is preferable, especially where the relationship between the donee and the local authority has broken down, for whatever reason, that the Official Solicitor should take the lead role. This may require a shift of culture on the part of the Official Solicitor. If there are welfare issues at stake, in addition, then the local authority may justifiably be separately represented and take an active role in relation to those issues.

Remuneration of a deputy, donee or attorney: rule 167

10.97 The court may make an order remunerating a deputy, donee or attorney out of P's estate. The order may be for a fixed amount, a specified rate, or to be determined in accordance with a fee schedule in a relevant practice direction. The amount ordered will constitute a debt owed by P's estate. The court may also order that there be a detailed assessment of the remuneration by a costs officers in accordance with r 164.

Official Solicitor's costs: rule 163

10.98 Costs incurred in relation to proceedings under the CoP Rules or in carrying out directions of the court and not provided for by remuneration under r 167 (deputies, donees or attorneys), are to be paid by such persons, or out of such funds as the Court may direct.

Procedure for assessing costs: rule 164

10.99 The rules provide for summary or detailed assessment of costs by a costs officer subject to any rule, practice direction or provision of any other enactment.

Order for costs following death of P: rule 165

10.100 The court may order that costs incurred during P's life time be paid out of or charged on his estate within six years after P's death.

Costs orders in favour of or against non-parties: rule 166

10.101 A non-party against or in favour of whom an order for costs is being considered by the Court must be added as a party to the proceedings for the purposes of costs only, and must be given a reasonable opportunity to attend a hearing at which the court will consider the matter further. This does not apply where the court is considering making an order against the Legal Services Commission (LSC).

Costs against the Legal Services Commission

10.102 CPR 44.17 deals with the provisions concerning LSC funded clients. CoP r 160(5) has modified CPR 44.17, to the extent that references to Pt 45 (fixed costs) and Pt 46 (fast track trial costs) do not apply. CPR 44.17, with regard to proceedings in the Court of Protection, therefore provides that CPR Pts 44, 47 and 48 do not apply to the assessment of costs in proceedings to the extent that the Access to Justice Act 1999, s 11 or Regulations made under the Legal Aid Act 1988 make different provision.

Section 11 of the Access to Justice Act 1999 provides special protection against liability for costs for parties who receive LSC funding. Any costs ordered to be paid by a LSC funded party must not exceed the amount which is reasonable for him to pay having regard to all the circumstances. This includes the financial resources of the all the parties to the proceedings and their conduct in connection with the dispute to which the proceedings relate.

Costs protection only applies to certain levels of service; it does not apply for example where the party has received only 'help at Court' or 'Legal Help'. Costs protection will apply to any work done under a certificate for Full Legal Representation.

Regulation 5 of the Community Legal Service (Cost Protection) Regulations 2000[1] governs when costs can be awarded against the LSC. This provision applies where (i) the costs protection applies and (ii) where the costs ordered to be paid by the LSC funded party do not fully meet the costs that would have been paid but for the costs protection. Before the LSC can be ordered to pay the whole or part of any non-LSC funded party's costs, the following criteria must be met:

1 the proceedings are finally decided in favour of a non-funded party;
2 unless there is good reason for delay, the non-funded party provides written notice of intention to seek an order against the LSC within three months of the making of a section 11(1) costs order;

3 the court is satisfied that it is just and equitable in the circumstances that provision for the costs should be made out of public funds; and
4 where the costs were incurred in a court of first instance, the following additional criteria must be met:
 (a) the proceedings were instituted by the LSC funded party;
 (b) the non-funded party is an individual; and
 (c) the non-funded party will suffer financial hardship unless the order is made.

An order for costs against the LSC can only be made when the proceedings (including any appeal) have been finally decided. Therefore, where a court of fist instance decides in favour of a non-funded party and an appeal lies, any order made against the LSC cannot be enforced until any time limit for permission to appeal has passed, or where permission is not needed or has been granted, the time limit to appeal expires without an appeal being brought. This means that if the LSC funded party appeals, any earlier order against the LSC for costs can never take effect. If the appeal is unsuccessful an application can be made to the appeal court for a fresh order.

The Costs Practice Direction applies to proceedings in the Court of Protection and section 21 sets out the procedure to be followed where a party is wholly or partially funded by the Legal Services Commission.

1 SI 2000/824.

Wasted costs

10.103 The CoP Rules have not modified CPR 48.8, and so the provisions concerning wasted costs orders remain in tact. Such orders can be made at any stage in the proceedings up to and including the proceedings relating to the detailed assessment of costs. In general, applications for wasted costs are best left until after the end of the trial.

The court can make a wasted costs order against a legal representative only if:

1 the legal representative has acted improperly, unreasonably or negligently;
2 his conduct has caused a party to incur unnecessary costs, and
3 it is just in all the circumstances to order him to compensate that party for the whole or part of those costs.

Section 53 of the Cost Practice Direction deals with wasted costs orders in detail.

FEES

10.104 The Court of Protection Fees are contained in the Court of Protection Fees Order 2007. There are flat fees for an application and for the substantive hearing. There is no fee applicable for a directions hearing. The application fee (payable on initial application and every subsequent variation) is set at £400 as is the fee for an appeal. Hearing fees are set at £500 and are payable on completion of the hearing.

1 SI 2007/1745.

Chapter 11

COURT DEPUTIES

- **MCA 2005, ss 16, 19–20**
- **Main Code, Chapter 8**

INTRODUCTION

11.1 This chapter should be read in conjunction with Chapter 10 which sets out the jurisdiction and powers of the new Court of Protection (the court). This chapter deals with the details of the appointment and supervision of court deputies. Chapter 8 of the Main Code also provides useful guidance.

Powers of the court and court deputies

11.2 The powers of the new Court of Protection, over welfare, healthcare and financial decisions, are contained in MCA 2005, ss 15 and 16. Section 16 gives the court power to appoint a court deputy.

Section 16 'substituted decision making'

11.3 The court's core substituted decision-making power is contained in s 16[1] and may be exercised on behalf of incapacitated adults primarily by the court, but also by a court appointed deputy. The kinds of decisions, whether about personal welfare, healthcare or property and affairs, which could arise under this jurisdiction are set out non-exhaustively in ss 17 and 18. They have been taken from previous decisions of the High Court. In making financial and property decisions (and appointing deputies) the court is likely to look to the past practice and expertise of the old Court of Protection where relevant.

1 Explanatory Notes, para 66.

Making decisions

11.4 In every case the court, and any deputy, must act in accordance with the statutory principles and the person's best interests (ss 1 and 4). The principle of least restrictive intervention (s 1(6)) is reinforced. Additionally, it is preferable that the court should take decisions rather than delegate them to a deputy[1].

The Government has stated that court deputies would be appointed to make personal welfare and healthcare decisions in only the most extreme cases. The vast majority of deputies are expected to be financial deputies[2]. The protection for acts in connection with care and treatment under ss 5 and 6 are likely to be sufficient for most day-to-day welfare and healthcare decisions, making the appointment of a deputy for such a role unnecessary.

1 Section 16(4); Explanatory Notes paras 67 and 68.
2 HC Official Report, SC A (Mental Capacity Bill), 26 October 2004, col 194.

COURT'S POWERS TO MAKE DECISIONS AND TO APPOINT DEPUTIES[1]

11.5 The court can either make a decision itself, or will appoint a deputy if there is a need for on-going decision making powers and there is no relevant enduring power of attorney (EPA) or lasting power of attorney (LPA). The court will also decide whether a deputy has suitable skills to act depending on the decisions to be taken and whether s/he is reliable and trustworthy[2]. When appointing a deputy the court will state what decisions the deputy has power to make. An appointment may take place upon application by a person wishing to act as a deputy[3] or part of extant proceedings before the court[4].

1 Again the website of the OPG contains much useful information for deputies, including a newsletter called 'Reaching Out'. The autumn 2007 edition comes with a CD of relevant forms.
2 Main Code, para 8.32.
3 Form COP 004 is a form of declaration to be completed and submitted to the court by a person applying to become a deputy. It also contains a section requiring personal undertakings to be given in accordance with a deputy's duties. Most applications are likely to be dealt with on the papers.
4 Part 10 of the CoP Rules and COP 009 will apply to such applications. Evidence in support of the application will be necessary (COP 024 – witness statement). It may be more convenient to use a form COP 004 in any event. If there is doubt over which form should be used the central registry in Archway should be contacted for advice.

Summary of role of deputy

11.6 The deputy:

- acts on appointment by the court only;
- may take decisions on behalf of an incapacitated person (P);
- must act only at the direction of the court;
- must act in accordance with the statutory principles and in the best interests of P and take account of the Main Code
- must apply to the court for any extra or varied powers;
- may be appointed jointly, or jointly and severally, to act in relation to welfare, healthcare and financial decisions;
- will only exceptionally be appointed for welfare or healthcare decisions;
- has no power to deprive P of his liberty[1];
- may restrain P subject to certain conditions;
- may not prohibit contact or direct a change of healthcare provider;
- must not act contrary to a donee of an LPA;
- may not refuse consent to life-sustaining treatment;
- carries all the investment powers without the assistance of the Office of the Public Guardian (OPG);
- may be required to provide security against misconduct;

- must be supervised by the Public Guardian (PG);
- may claim remuneration and expenses;
- may be removed by the court only.

1 This may depend on what view is taken of the power under s 16(2)(a) pending amendments contained in the MHA 2007 to take effect in April 2009. This is discussed further in Chapters 7, 9 and 10. See also amendments to be made by the MHA 2007 in relation to Community Treatment Orders which are noted at 16.5, fn 2.

How is a deputy appointed and who can be a deputy?

Appointing a deputy: section 19

11.7 The provision setting out criteria for the appointment of a deputy is s 19(1). All deputies must consent to their appointment and be at least 18 years of age[1].

1 Section 19(3), (1)(a).

What is a deputy?

11.8 A deputy is P's agent in relation to anything done or decided by him within the scope of his appointment in accordance with this Part of the MCA 2005. This puts on a statutory footing the prior position at common law[1].

1 *Re EG* [1914] 1 Ch 927. The Main Code at para 8.55 onwards sets out the duties of an agent under common law.

Who can be a deputy?

11.9 A deputy must be an individual who has reached the age of 18. Property and affairs deputies may be a trust corporation[1]. An individual may also be appointed by the current holder of a specified office or position[2] eg the Director of Adult Services in England (Director of Social Services in Wales)[3].

The Main Code suggests that in the majority of cases a member of the family is likely to be appointed, or someone who knows P well[4]. Presumably this is subject to the stipulation that the court will appoint only someone with the requisite skills to act in relation to particular decisions. It makes good sense in the context of welfare decisions to appoint a family member. During Parliamentary debates the Government made it clear that in the rare cases where health and welfare are in issue, then the court is unlikely to appoint someone unknown to the person[5]. This reassurance was provided because in some situations a deputy may have the power to refuse medical treatment. In other cases an independent deputy might be necessary, either because P has complex financial needs, or there is some conflict with family members.

Under the old receivership system the court developed an order of preference for the appointment of receivers: spouse, family member, independent person or friend, professional adviser (usually not an accountant) and as a last resort a receiver on the PG's panel[6]. The factors to be taken into account in deciding who to appoint as a receiver were said to include: size and complexity of the estate, patient's own wishes, the ability of the receiver to interact with the patient, where the receiver resides, love, devotion and affection between the receiver and the patient, the care regime of the patient and the remuneration required by the receiver[7]. This may remain useful guidance to aid the choice of an appropriate deputy. The OPG has a panel of professional deputies specialising in this function who may be appointed to deal with P's property and affairs if the court decides that this would be in his best interests.

1 Section 19(1)(b).
2 Section 19(2).
3 See Main Code, para 8.60.
4 Main Code, para 8.33.
5 HC Official Report, SC A (Mental Capacity Bill), 26 October 2004, col 194.
6 Heywood and Massey, para 4–005.
7 Heywood and Massey, para 4–006.

Conflict of interests

11.10 A conflict of interests would not appear to be an absolute bar to the appointment of a family member as long as s/he is able to act in accordance with his or her fiduciary duty[1]. Similar considerations apply when the person appointed holds office as the Director of Adult Services and there are costs implications to care services being provided. The court must be satisfied that there are proper arrangements in place to avoid possible conflicts[2]. In the event that a suitable deputy cannot be found a panel deputy may be appointed. The Official Solicitor may also act as a deputy of last resort.

1 Main Code, para 8.59.
2 Main Code, para 8.60.

More than one deputy?

11.11 Two or more deputies may act jointly[1], jointly and severally, or jointly with respect to some matters and jointly and severally with respect to others. The court may appoint successor(s) in circumstances specified by the court[2]. The latter may be useful if the deputy is elderly and wants to ensure that there will be somebody to take over their duties in the future, if necessary[3].

1 Joint receivership was not favoured under the previous system because it was not considered to promote convenience or the smooth running of affairs: Heywood and Massey, para 4–007.
2 Section 19(5).
3 Main Code, para 8.44.

Interim orders

11.12 By s 48 and CoP Rules, r 82(1)(c)[1], the court may make an interim order appointing a deputy pending the determination of any application to it in respect of P. The exercise of this power is subject to:

(a) there being evidence of incapacity in relation to the relevant matter for which the deputy is to be appointed;

(b) the matter being one which falls within the jurisdiction of the court under the MCA 2005; and

(c) it being in P's best interests for the order to be made.

Such an application is likely to be made within existing, or at the commencement of, proceedings before the court.

1 The procedure in Part 10 of the CoP Rules apply. See 11.5 above in relation to the need for evidence and/or a form COP 004.

Deputies and welfare decisions

11.13 As already stated, the appointment of deputies regarding welfare decisions will be rare and this is said to be reinforced by the terms of s 5[1]. The Main Code suggests they will only be required in the most difficult cases where the important and necessary actions cannot be carried out without the court's authority, or there is no other way of settling the matter in the best interests of the person who lacks capacity to make a particular welfare decision[2].

1 See the Government's response to Joint Scrutiny Report, published in February 2004 (Cm 6121).

2 Main Code, para 8.38. See also HC Official Report, SC A (Mental Capacity Bill), 26 October 2004, col 194 onwards.

Deputies and property and finance decisions

11.14 The appointment of deputies to make decisions concerning property and affairs is likely to arise in circumstances similar to that of the receiver under the MHA 1983 Part VII (now repealed)[1]. If a person who lacks capacity has not made an EPA or an LPA, then applications to the court for a deputy to be appointed will be necessary for dealing with cash assets over a certain amount, for selling P's property or where P has a level of income or capital, eg from a court award of compensation, that the court thinks a deputy needs to manage. Where P's only income is from social security and s/he has no other savings or assets there will usually be no need for a deputy to be appointed[2].

1 See *Re EG* [1914] Ch 927; *Bell v Todd* [2001] All ER (D) 348 (Jun); *Cassel v Riverside HA* [1992] PIQR Q 168.

2 See Main Code, para 8.36.

Fees and expenses of deputies

Expenses and fees

11.15 A deputy is entitled to reasonable expenses in discharging his or her functions out of P's property and, if the court so directs at the time of appointment, to remuneration also out of P's estate[1]. Rule 167 applies and enables the court to order remuneration at a fixed amount, a specified rate or according to the 'schedule of fees in the Practice Direction'. At the time of writing there is no applicable PD or schedule. The amount allowed is to constitute a debt from P's estate and may be subject to detailed assessment by a costs officer[2] in accordance with r 164(b).

1 Section 19(7). If the deputy is an officer of a local authority, s 49 of the National Assistance Act 1948 (as amended) provides that the local authority may defray expenses, if not recoverable from any other service.

2 The Supreme Court Costs Office, Cliffords Inn, Fetter Lane, London EC4A 1DQ.

Appointment fees

11.16 The OPG provides information on appointing deputies and the appropriate fees at www.publicguardian.gov.uk[1]. Currently the fee for appointing a deputy is £125. All fees are payable by P, ie out of his estate.

1 Fees are published in the Public Guardian (Fees etc) Regulations 2007, SI 2007/2051. See also guidance on fees remission and exemption in OPG 506 and application form OPG506A at www.publicguardian.gov.uk.

Supervision fees

11.17 Supervision is dealt with below. Fees payable by P to the PG will be subject to the level of supervision that the PG determines is appropriate under s 58(1)(c). The highest level of supervision is Type I (£800.00 per annum), the lower level is Type II (£175.00 per annum) and the minimal is Type III (no charge)[1]. Fees are payable within 30 days of invoice annually in arrears on 31 March. If there has been more than one type of supervision in one year then the fees are calculated on a *pro rata* basis. Where the period is less than one year the fee payable is the relevant proportion of the full fee. There is an exemption from fees for a person in receipt of a qualifying benefit, unless the person has received an award of damages of over £16,000 which has been disregarded for the purposes of determining eligibility for that benefit[2]. There is also provision for reduction or remission in exceptional circumstances. This will depend on gross annual income. There is no fee if income is below £11,500 and a full fee if income is over £16,000. There are bands in between at 25% intervals[3]. The PG retains a discretion to make further exemptions or remission on application.

1 The level of support and supervision the OPG allocates to a deputy is decided after carrying out an assessment of the individual circumstances of the case.

2 Public Guardian (Fees Etc) Regulations 2007, reg 9.

3 See OPG 506 published by the Court of Protection and OPG available at www.publicguardian.co.uk.

POWERS OF A DEPUTY

Powers of a deputy

11.18 The court may empower the deputy to take possession or control of all or any specified part of P's property and to exercise specified powers including power of investment as the court may determine[1]. The court may require a deputy to give to the PG a security against misconduct in the discharge of his or her functions, and to submit to the PG such reports as the court may direct.

1 Section 19(8).
2 Section 19(9).

Restrictions on deputies: section 20

11.19 There are certain restrictions on what deputies can do. The key principle is that they cannot do more than P himself could do if s/he had capacity[1]. The general restriction is that deputies' authority is conferred subject to ss 1 and 4. There are also specific restrictions and these are set out in s 20.

1 HC Official Report, SC A (Mental Capacity Bill), 26 October 2004, cols 190–192.

Capacity and fluctuating capacity

11.20 A deputy cannot act where s/he believes, or has reasonable grounds to believe, that the person s/he acts for, has capacity. This is about fluctuating capacity and suggests that the deputy must regularly appraise themself as to the person's ongoing incapacity before making any specific decisions on his or her behalf, taking professional advice if necessary[1]

1 Section 20(1) and Explanatory Notes at para 75.

Welfare restrictions

11.21 A deputy cannot prohibit a named person from having contact with P, nor direct that a different person take over P's healthcare[1]. Deputies cannot refuse consent to life sustaining treatment[2]. Such decisions must be taken by the court.

1 Section 20(2)(a), (b).
2 Section 20(5). See also 16.5, fn 2 in relation to treatment for mental disorder under the MHA 1983 as amended.'

Financial restrictions

11.22 Restrictions with regard to property are at s 20(3).

LPAs

11.23 A deputy cannot make a decision, nor be given the power to make a decision that is inconsistent with that made by a donee(s) under an LPA within the scope of his or her authority in accordance with the MCA 2005[1].

1 Section 20(4).

Acts of restraint

11.24 In addition a deputy may not do an act intended to restrain P unless four conditions are satisfied:

1. he or she is acting within express authority conferred by the court[1];
2. P lacks, or the deputy reasonably believes s/he lacks capacity in relation to the matter[2];
3. the deputy reasonably believes it is necessary to prevent harm to P[3];
4. the act is proportionate to the likelihood of harm by P *and* the seriousness of that harm[4].

'Restrain' means to use or threaten force to secure the doing of an act which P resists, or restricting P's liberty, whether or not P resists. There is no definition of 'harm'. There are similar restrictions applying to restraining incapacitated persons that apply to ordinary carers and professionals and donees of an LPA under ss 6 and 11[5]. Section 20(13), which prevents any restraint that amounts to a deprivation of liberty is due to be repealed[6].

1 Section 20(8).
2 Section 20(9).
3 Section 20(10).
4 Section 20(11) as amended by MHA 2007, s 51 and in force since 1 October 2007 (MHA 2007 (Commencement No 2) Order, SI 2007/2635). This corrects a drafting error.
5 See particularly Chapter 4.
6 This will happen when MHA 2007, s 50(4) comes into force. See also MHA 2007, Sch 11, Pt 10.

DUTIES OF THE DEPUTY

General

11.25 A deputy must only act in accordance with the powers and duties afforded to them by the court under s 16(5). If other powers or duties become necessary for the fulfilment of an appointment then the deputy must apply to the court for such powers or duties. A deputy must follow the statutory principles of the MCA 2005 and only make decisions or act in the person's best interests. The deputy must have regard to the guidance in the Main Code and can only make decisions the court has authorised them to make[1].

The Main Code sets out the other duties of a deputy:

> '8.55 Section 19(6) states that a deputy is to be treated as "the agent" of the person who lacks capacity when they act on their behalf. Being an agent means that the deputy has legal duties (under the law of agency) to the person they are representing. It also means that when they carry out tasks within their powers, they are not personally liable to third parties.
>
> 8.56 Deputies must carry out their duties carefully and responsibly. They have a duty to:
>
> - act with due care and skill (duty of care)
> - not take advantage of their situation (fiduciary duty)
> - indemnify the person against liability to third parties caused by the deputy's negligence

- not delegate duties unless authorised to do so
- act in good faith
- respect the person's confidentiality, and
- comply with the directions of the Court of Protection.

Property and affairs deputies also have a duty to:

- keep accounts, and
- keep the person's money and property separate from own finances.'

Deputies are allowed to seek advice from third parties, for example experts, but they are not able to give their powers to someone else. However, in some circumstances the court will authorise the delegation of the decision-making power in relation to a specific decision, the example given in the Main Code is the appointment of an investment manager for the conduct of investment business[2]. In an emergency, or where there are unforeseen circumstances a deputy can delegate their power concerning a specific decision, but only if that decision does not rely on the exercise of their discretion.

1 Main Code, paras 8.50–8.54. See also other duties in paras 8.55–8.67.
2 Main Code, para 8.61.

Applications to the court by a deputy

11.26 As stated above a deputy may make such an application for extended or varied powers or duties, or the determination of any serious welfare or healthcare issues on behalf of the person, if this is outside their remit[1]. A deputy does not need the permission of the court to make such an application[2].

1 The court's power to make further orders is in s 16(5).
2 Section 50(1)(d). See also rr 51 and 52. The latter stipulates that permission is required in relation to some property and affairs matters. PD 9D provides the procedure for applications relating to property and affairs decisions. See Chapter 10 at 10.57.

Litigation friend

11.27 A deputy empowered by the order appointing him to conduct legal proceedings in the name of the incapacitated or protected person, is entitled to act as litigation friend in any proceedings to which their power relates[1]. This must include best interests or other proceedings before the court on behalf of the protected person.

1 Rule 142(2).

Variation of powers

11.28 A deputy must apply to the court to vary powers of appointment should they find that they are insufficient to carry out their duties towards P[1]. The OPG no longer has a role to play in this regard. The court may also grant a power on condition that the PG consents to certain actions: it would be 'disproportionately burdensome and costly to require them to apply to the court all the time for authority to act. That supervisory role should properly be undertaken by the public guardian'[2].

1 Section 16(5), (7).
2 670 HL Official Report (5th series), col 1474, 17 March 2005.

Termination of deputyship

11.29 The court may vary or discharge the order appointing a deputy by a subsequent order[1], or the order may be revoked if the deputy has behaved, or proposes to behave, in a way that contravenes their authority or is not in P's best interests[2].

1 Section 16(7).
2 Section 16(8).

SUPERVISION AND MONITORING OF DEPUTIES

Security

11.30 This may be provided by bond or other means ordered by the court. The bond must be endorsed by an authorised insurance company or deposit-taker. The PG will monitor the security eg the payment of any monthly premiums. The court may enforce or discharge a security[1]. The security must be given before the deputy may act or discharge his functions, unless the court permits it to be given subsequently. The CoP Rules make provision for the payment of the security when it is required to be given before any action is taken[2].

As stated above a deputy may be asked to give a security to safeguard the performance of their duties. The court may revoke or vary powers conferred on a deputy if it is satisfied of the matters in s 16(8)(a) and (b), that is that the deputy has behaved, or proposes to behave, outside their powers or in contravention of P's best interests. This power is similar to that in relation to donees[3].

The PG is responsible for maintaining a register of orders appointing deputies, supervising deputies, receiving any security required by the court, receiving reports, dealing with complaints about deputies[4]. It is through investigations by the PG that the court may revoke or discharge an order. Others can be involved in supervising these functions with the PG. If any person has concerns about a deputy's conduct then these should be brought to the attention of the PG[5].

To assist the PG in its supervisory functions the PG is entitled to receive court documents that it considers reasonably necessary for the discharge of its functions. This is subject to court approval; the court may act on its own initiative or on the application of the PG, either at the same time that the court appoints the deputy, or subsequently. The relevant documents are those filed in connection with the proceedings in which the court appoints the deputy and are relevant to the decision to make that appointment, any powers conferred, duties imposed or any other terms applying to those powers or duties as contained in the order. The court may direct that any document provided to the PG be edited[6].

The level of supervision to be accorded to any deputy has been divided into three categories: Type I is for the highest level of supervision, Type II is next followed by Type III which is for cases demanding minimal supervision. The appropriate level will be decided upon by the PG and will depend upon on:

- the complexity of the affairs of P;
- the types of decisions that need to be made;
- the care requirements of P; and
- the relationship between the deputy and P[7].

1 Section 58(1)(e), (4)(a); Lasting Powers of Attorney, Enduring Powers of Attorney and Public Guardian Regulations 2007, SI 2007/1253, regs 33–37. See also Chapter 12 at 12.28.
2 Rule 200.
3 Section 22(3), (4)
4 Section 58(1)(b), (h)) and (4). See also regs 38–42 of the Lasting Powers of Attorney, Enduring Powers of Attorney and Public Guardian Regulations 2007 and Chapter 12.
5 See Chapter 12 for more on this point.
6 CoP Rules, r 20.
7 See COP43, published by the Court of Protection, and the Autumn 2007 edition of the newsletter for deputies 'Reaching out', both available on www.publicguardian.gov.uk.

APPOINTEES AND EXISTING RECEIVERS

Appointees

11.31 If P is only in receipt of social security benefits and has no property or savings, his benefits can be managed by an 'appointee' appointed by the Department of Work and Pensions[1]. Appointees are not covered by the MCA 2005, a point which disgruntled many in Parliament[2]. They will nevertheless be expected to act in P's best interests, and must do so if they are involved in his care[3].

An appointee is appointed by the Secretary of State and may exercise the person's rights and duties under social security legislation, receive benefits and deal with money received on P's behalf. Concerns about the quality of this service were raised in Parliament during the passage of the MCA 2005. In particular there is no system of monitoring and supervision.

1 Social Security (Claims and Payment) Regulations 1987, SI 1987/1968, reg 33.
2 HC Official Report, SC A (Mental Capacity Bill), 26 October 2004, cols 183–185.
3 See Main Code, para 8.36.

Existing receivers

11.32 Schedule 5 deals with existing receivers appointed under the MHA 1983, Part VII prior to the commencement of the MCA 2005. A receiver now becomes a deputy but with the same functions as when s/he was appointed. All references to a deputy include a receiver appointed previously. Part 22 of the CoP Rules and PD 22B provide a special procedure for existing receivers to apply for a court order which is operational only until 30 June 2008. After that date the procedure in Parts 9 and 10 will apply. In the months leading up to the implementation of the MCA 2005 the OPG reviewed existing receiverships and issued one of two orders to bring them more into line with modern deputyships and to cover the period of transition: (a) an extended general order allows a deputy access to all of the client's assets and (b) a restricted general order allows access to a specified sum only[1]. It should be remembered that if any deputy should need additional powers to carry out his duty, then this can now only be achieved by application to the court. The OPG has no function to serve in this connection.

1 See the newsletter 'Reaching Out' for Autumn 2007, published for deputies by the OPG. It is available on www.publicguardian.gov.uk.

DECISION MAKING UNDER MCA 2005, SECTION 16: PERSONAL WELFARE, SECTION 17

11.33 Personal welfare is defined at s 17, which sets out the types of personal welfare matters that, under s 16, the court may either determine itself or appoint a deputy to make decisions about on P's behalf. The list is not exhaustive but includes deciding issues of residence, contact and medical treatment. The power of deputies is restricted (s 20, see 11.19). A deputy can refuse treatment for P (as long as it is not life sustaining), but cannot direct treatment against clinical judgement. The list is based on the decisions already made under the court's inherent jurisdiction ie the common law (see Chapter 10). These are examples of decisions that may go to court for a decision; they do not have to be taken to the court. Neither the court nor any deputy has the power to detain or deprive a person of his or her liberty[1].

1 This is due to change in April 2009 when new provisions introduced by the MHA 2007 come into force. See Chapter 9. And in relation to treatment for mental disorder for the those under Community Treatment Orders see Chapter 16 at 16.5, fn 2.

DECISION MAKING: PROPERTY AND AFFAIRS, SECTION 18

11.34 Section 18 sets out the list of matters which can be undertaken and is supplemented by Sch 2. These relate to property and financial affairs, including carrying on a trade, profession or business on behalf of P, discharging debts or obligations, carrying out of any contract entered into by P. The detail is beyond the scope of this book, but of relevance is the ability to conduct legal proceedings in P's name on P's behalf[1]. This is not restricted only to proceedings under the MCA 2005. Again the deputy's powers are restricted by s 20. This list reflects that previously provided under MHA 1983, s 96. The definition of property is wide and is contained in s 64; 'property' includes any thing in action and any interest in real or personal property.

1 Section 18(1)(k).

Chapter 12

PUBLIC GUARDIAN; COURT OF PROTECTION VISITORS

- **MCA 2005, ss 57–61**
- **Main Code, Chapter 14**
- **Lasting Powers of Attorney, Enduring Powers of Attorney and Public Guardian Regulations 2007, SI 2007/1253**
- **Public Guardian Board Regulations 2007, SI 2007/1770**

INTRODUCTION

12.1 The MCA 2005 introduces a new public official, the Public Guardian (PG)[1], to be appointed by the Lord Chancellor who may provide officers and staff directly or under him to assist in the proper discharge of functions under the MCA 2005. The PG may delegate his functions to be performed by any of his officers[2] and must provide an annual report to the Lord Chancellor which will be laid before Parliament[3].

Court of Protection Visitors (Court Visitors) are appointed to carry out visits and produce reports, as directed by the court[4] or the PG[5] in relation to those who lack capacity. Their functions and powers are similar to those of Lord Chancellor's Visitors appointed under the now repealed Part VII of the Mental Health Act 1983[6].

The PG will have administrative and supervisory functions as set out in s 58 and regulations, and will be subject to the scrutiny of the Public Guardianship Board (PGB)[7]. He will be supported by the new Office of the Public Guardian (OPG), an executive agency of the Department of Constitutional Affairs, which replaces the existing Public Guardianship Office[8]. The new PG will have none of the receivership functions of old[9].

By way of summary the PG is to have three functions:

1 as a registration body he will have an important role in maintaining registers of LPAs ('donees') and court deputies;
2 as a supervisory body, over court deputies, reporting to the Court of Protection (the court); and
3 as an investigatory body, responding to complaints about the performance of donees, existing attorneys under Enduring Powers of Attorney (EPAs) and court appointed deputies[10].

These provide scrutiny of any abuse of the powers granted to such persons although sanctions rest with the court. The PG also may direct visits by the Court Visitor to the relevant person and receive security for the discharge of his functions. The PG may publish any information he thinks appropriate about the discharge of his functions. The PG has access to specified records for the purpose of discharging these functions.

The PG and Court Visitors have a pivotal role in the protection of vulnerable, incapacitated adults from abuse. This role is described in Chapter 14 of the Main Code.

This chapter sets out the functions of the PG as expanded by the Lasting Powers of Attorney, Enduring Powers of Attorney and Public Guardian Regulations (LPA Regulations)[11]. It is expressly provided that the PG may discharge his function in co-operation with others who have functions in relation to the care and treatment of the incapacitated person. It is intended that the PG will work closely with other organisations such as local authorities and NHS bodies[12].

There is extensive information and documentation now available about the OPG on http://www.publicguardian.gov.uk.

1 Richard Brook, the chief executive of the outgoing Public Guardianship Office, has been appointed as Public Guardian.
2 Section 57.
3 Section 60.
4 Section 49(2)
5 Section 58(1)(d)
6 Explanatory notes to MCA 2005, para 153.
7 Section 59.
8 The PGO was governed by a framework document laid before Parliament on 29 March 2001. Its stated aim was to promote and protect the financial and social well-being of people with mental incapacity by providing a seamless service responsive to their needs. *Heywood and Massey*, para 1–023.
9 These functions together with deficiencies in its operation were described in Parliament: The chief executive of the PGO was to act as receiver of last resort. A case worker from the receivership department then took over the client's affairs, acting under the delegated authority of the court. The difficulties in these arrangements and the extent to which the PGO was failing in its handling of its clients' moneys have previously been raised in Parliament and referred to the Parliamentary Ombudsman. The Ombudsman's report was published in November 2004 and made findings of gross negligence. Deficient financial systems were identified. 669 HL Official Report (5th series), cols 765–770, 8 February 2005. See also the report of the comptroller and auditor general '*Public Guardianship Office: Protecting and promoting the financial affairs of people who lose mental capacity*' National Audit Office (2005). HC Session 2005–06, 8 June 2005.
10 669 HL Official Report (5th series), col 770, 8 February 2005.
11 SI 2007/1253. Section 58(3) gives the Lord Chancellor a regulation making power in relation to the functions of the public guardian including conferring 'other functions in connection with this Act'.
12 Explanatory notes to MCA 2005, para 146.

APPOINTMENT OF THE PUBLIC GUARDIAN

12.2 The Public Guardian is appointed by the Lord Chancellor[1]. Remuneration will be set by the Lord Chancellor and provided by Parliament. The Lord Chancellor may also provide other officers and staff as appropriate for the discharge of the PG's functions.

1 Section 57(2).

DELEGATION OF FUNCTIONS

12.3 The PG's functions (below) may be performed by any of his officers to the extent authorised by the PG[1].

1 Section 57(5).

FUNCTIONS OF THE PUBLIC GUARDIAN: S 58

12.4 The details of the PG's functions are set out below. In headline they are:

- Establishing and maintaining registers – donees and deputies: s 58(1)(a), (b) and EPAs.
- Supervising deputies: s 58(1)(c).
- Directing visits and reports from Court Visitors: s 58(1)(d).
- Receiving reports: s 58(1)(f).
- Reporting to court: s 58(1)(g).
- Dealing with complaints and representations: s 58(1)(h).
- Receiving security: s 58(1)(e).
- Publishing information: s 58(1)(h).

ESTABLISHING AND MAINTAINING REGISTERS – LPAS, DEPUTIES AND EPAS

Registers

12.5 The PG must establish and maintain registers of LPAs and deputies[1]. The LPA Regulations provide that this must be done in relation to EPAs also[2]. The information in the registers describing instruments and orders, including those that have been cancelled, is at the discretion of the PG[3].

The Main Code recommends that if a donee proposes to use a registered LPA that has not been used for some time he should notify the OPG so that the PG can send up to date information to donees about rules governing donees[4]. Further, the PG must make sure that an LPA meets the MCA 2005's requirements. Documentation must be checked before registration. Bankruptcy status is relevant to financial LPAs and must also be checked. Once an LPA is registered the PG will not normally become involved unless concerns are raised about a donee's performance (see 12.22–12.23 below)[5].

The PG has a wide range of functions in relation to the registration of an LPA and these are set out in table 3 in Chapter 5 which deals with LPAs[6]. In summary the PG must register an LPA in the absence of an objection or defect in the instrument. If an objection is made because the power has been terminated or revoked (s 13 grounds), on prescribed grounds (s 22), or there is a defect in the instrument, then the PG must not register the LPA unless directed to do so by the court[7].

1 Section 58(1)(a), (b). For relevant fees see 12.30 below.
2 Regulation 30(1).
3 Regulation 30(2).

4 Main Code, para 7.16.
5 Main Code, paras 14.12–14.14.
6 See Sch 4 for powers relating to EPAs.
7 See MCA 2005, Sch 1 and LPA Regulations 2007.

Disclosure of information on the register(s)

12.6 This may be achieved on application to the PG who will carry out the search. It must state which register(s) is to be searched, the name of the person whom the application concerns, and other information as the PG may require to carry out the search[1]. The application must be accompanied by the appropriate fee. The PG may require further information eg documentation to assist in the search as he 'reasonably considers necessary to enable him to carry out the search'.

The PG must 'as soon as reasonably practicable' provide the result of the search including if there has been more than one entry on the register.

1 LPA Regulations, reg 31. For fees see 12.30 below.

Disclosure of additional information

12.7 If the PGs search above identifies the existence of a registered instrument (LPA or EPA) or order appointing a deputy and conferring decision-making powers in relation to any person[1], then a further application may be made for additional information which the PG may disclose if he considers there is 'good reason' to do so. This is for additional information obtained by the PG in the course of his duties, but not appearing on the register[2].

The application must state the name of the person concerned, ie the subject of the doneeship, attorneyship or order, reasons for it, and the steps taken to obtain the information from P. In exercising this power the PG must, in particular, have regard to:

'(a) the connection between the person concerned and the applicant;
(b) the reasons for requesting the information (in particular, why the information cannot or should not be obtained directly from the person concerned);
(c) the benefit to the person concerned, or any detriment he may suffer, if a disclosure is made; and
(d) any detriment that another person may suffer if a disclosure is made.'[3]

These provisions allow *any* person to apply for information from the PG. This will enable a carer or other interested person to determine the existence of a relevant decision-maker in the event of any doubt. It will also enable checks to be run on the number of doneeships any particular LPA holds, or appointments as court deputies, in case of concerns over the behaviour of any attorney or deputy. There is no guidance as to what the additional information might be except that it would have been obtained by the PG in the course of his duties, as to which see below. Any disclosure made must be in accordance with the person's rights under Article 8 ECHR (see Chapters 14 and 17).

1 This would apply to welfare or financial decisions.
2 LPA Regulations, reg 32.
3 LPA Regulations, reg 32(6).

SUPERVISING DEPUTIES

12.8 This function[1] is expressly to be discharged in co-operation with any person who is responsible for the care and treatment of the person to whom the appointment of the deputy relates[2]. As already noted it is intended that the PG will work closely with organisations such as local authorities and NHS bodies[3]. This reinforces the protective role to be played by the PG. There must be a channel of communication open between the relevant bodies and the PG if this relationship is to be successful.

This function is also intended to be supportive of a deputy (Chapter 11 deals with deputies). Deputies are most likely to be needed for financial decisions where a continued authority to act is necessary. It is envisaged that most welfare decisions will be made on a one-off basis by the court. In either situation the PG will run checks on the potential deputy and carry out a risk assessment to determine what kind of supervision the deputy will need once appointed. The deputy is accountable to the court and is supervised by the PG on the court's behalf[4].

Any concerns about the behaviour of a deputy must be notified to the PG immediately. The PG may then instruct a Court Visitor to visit the deputy and/or the incapacitated person and report back on matters of concern (see 12.9 below). The PG may apply to the court to cancel the deputy's appointment[5] or to request a report from the deputy (below). The PG is to act on representations or complaints made by others. He has other functions relevant to this function, as to which see other sections in this chapter (below). Any serious concerns over sexual or physical abuse or fraud should also be notified immediately to the police and relevant social services[6].

1 Section 58(1)(c).
2 Section 58(2)
3 Explanatory notes to MCA 2005, para 146.
4 Main Code, paras 14.15–14.18.
5 See Main Code 8.70 and see table 3 Chapter 5 at 5.86.
6 Main Code, para 8.71 and Chapter 18 at 18.18.

DIRECTING VISITS AND REPORTS FROM COURT VISITORS

12.9 Section 58(1)(d) stipulates that a PG may direct visits and reports from Court Visitors relating to LPAs, deputies and the incapacitated person who has granted the LPA or for whom the deputy has been appointed. Section 58(6) permits the PG to interview the incapacitated person in order to discharge his functions (see 12.26). This power assists the PG in his supervisory and investigatory roles. LPA Regs Regulation 44 covers visits by the PG or the Court Visitors at the PG's direction as follows.

Visits by Public Guardian

12.10 There should be prior notification of a visit to include the date or dates proposed, any specific matters likely to be covered during the visit (if it is practicable to do so), and any proposal to inform any other person that the visit it to take place[1].

1 Section 44(2).

Visit by Court Visitor

12.11 The PG may in his discretion give such directions and provide such information concerning the person to be visited as he considers necessary for the purpose of preparing a report[1].

The Visitor 'must seek to carry out the visit and take all reasonable steps to obtain such other information as he considers necessary for the purpose of preparing a report'[2]. 'Other information' must relate to information not provided by the PG or available in the records to which the Visitor has access or by interviewing the person (see below)[3]. The Court Visitor is not limited to the information considered necessary by the PG.

A Court Visitor must comply with the timetable specified by the PG.

The PG may direct a Court Visitor to visit an attorney under a registered EPA or its' donor and to report to him[4].

1 Section 44(3)(a).
2 Section 44(3)(b).
3 Section 61(5), (6).
4 LPA Regulations, reg 48(a).

Final report

12.12 The PG may, if he considers it appropriate to do so, disclose the report or invite comment on it from any person interviewed in the course of preparing a report[1].

1 Section 44(5). Under the MHA 1983 it was for the Judge to authorise any disclosure of a Visitor's report (MHA 1983, s 103(8)). Unauthorised disclosure was previously subject to criminal sanction (MHA 1983, s 103(9)). In *Re WLW* [1972] Ch 456, the court said that a judge should lean towards disclosure of the report and refuse it only if the best interests of the patient would be better served. Alternatively disclosure should be directed if there was an advantage to the patient or the judge in the exercise of his functions, in doing so. Furthermore, 'save in exceptional circumstances' a judge should allow attendance and cross examination in relation to a disclosed report [at 461B–462F].

RECEIVING REPORTS

12.13 The provision[1] simply states that the PG has the function of receiving reports from LPAs and deputies appointed by the court. It assists the PG in his supervisory and investigatory roles.

1 Section 58(1)(f).

LPAs

12.14 An LPA may report abuse or exploitation of an incapacitated person by another and ask the PG for advice. The LPA may also seek to notify the police or adult protection authorities[1].

1 Main Code, paras 7.73–7.74. See Chapter 5 on LPAs.

Deputies

12.15 The LPA Regulations provide in relation to deputies that reports to the PG are to be at the request of the court[1], and allow the PG to vary the time limits for submission of the same set by the court[2]. The PG cannot then take any steps to secure performance of the deputy's duty to submit the report, as long as it is submitted on or before such later date as the PG may specify.

The content of the reports is to be directed by the court, but the PG may specify further information or documents of a 'specified description' as may be reasonably required by the PG in the exercise of his functions under the MCA 2005[3] and which the PG specifies[4].

In relation to powers concerning financial affairs given to the deputy by the court under s 16, the information which the PG specifies may include accounts dealing with specified matters in a specified form, including verification of information or documentation in such manner as the PG may reasonably require[5].

1 See section 19(9)(b) and section on 'security' below.
2 LPA Regulations, reg 38.
3 LPA Regulations, reg 39.
4 LPA Regulations, reg 39(6).
5 LPA Regulations, reg 39.

Deputies' final report

12.16 The PG may require a final report where:

1 the person on whose behalf the deputy was appointed has died; or
2 the deputy has died or the court has made an order discharging the deputy; or
3 the deputy otherwise ceases to be under a duty to discharge the functions appointed to him.

Where the deputy has died the final report requirement may fall on his or her personal representatives. If the PG is not satisfied with any aspect of the final report he may apply to the court for an appropriate remedy including enforcement of security given by the deputy[1]. The PG has a duty to consider the final report and any other information he may have relating to the discharge of functions by the deputy.

1 LPA Regulations, reg 40(5).

REPORTING TO COURT

12.17 The PG may report to the court on such matters 'relating to proceedings under this Act' as the court requires[1] (see Chapter 10) As already noted above this will include matters relating to the non-registration of LPAs on receipt of an objection or notification of a defect in the instrument. These matters are dealt with in more detail in Chapter 5.

1 Section 58(1)(g). Also s 49(2).

DEALING WITH COMPLAINTS AND REPRESENTATIONS

12.18 The PG deals with complaints and representations[1]. He has power to safeguard against the abuse of their power by LPAs and deputies[2]. The General Regulations add a power for the PG to seek accountability from EPAs.

1 Section 58(1)(h).
2 Main Code, Chapter 14 provides guidance about what constitutes 'abuse' and how to deal with it. See paras 14.1–14.3, 14.8, 14.19.

Co-operating with others

12.19 As when supervising deputies (see 12.8 above), this function[1] is expressly to be discharged in co-operation with any person who is responsible for the care and treatment of the person to whom the LPA or appointment of the deputy relates[2]. Again this will require an effective channel of communication between carers etc and the PG.

1 Section 58(2).
2 Explanatory notes to MCA 2005, para 146.

Deputies

12.20 The LPA Regulations refer to representations (including complaints) to the PG about the way in which a deputy is exercising his powers or any failure to exercise them[1]. Once received, the PG has the power to require information specified in a written notice or documents from the deputy if it appears to him that there are 'other circumstances' giving rise to concerns or dissatisfaction with the conduct of the deputy or which constitute good reason to seek information about the deputy's discharge of his functions.

1 LPA Regulations, reg 41.

Right of review

12.21 The deputy may require the PG to reconsider any decision he has taken in relation to him, on providing a notice of appeal within 14 days of the decision of the PG. Such a notice must state the grounds on which reconsideration is required or be accompanied by any relevant information or documents. The PG may seek further information from the deputy and must provide written notice of any decision including a statement of reasons if he upholds his previous decision[1].

1 LPA Regulations, reg 42. The requirement to provide reasons is a fundamental aspect of good public administration and focuses a decision-maker's mind on what it is that has to be decided. There is a considerable body of case law now available dealing with adequacy of reasons. At its most basic level there is a duty to identify and explain the resolution of issues that were vital to the decision. See generally *R v Solihull Metropolitan Borough Council Housing Benefits Review Board ex parte Simpson* (1993) 26 HLR 370 at 377and *R (on the application of Ashworth Hospital Authority) v MHRT* [2002] MHLR 314 per Dyson LJ.

LPAs

12.22 There is a similar power to require information from an LPA as from a court deputy (see above)[1]. It does not refer to 'representations' or 'complaints', but applies where:

> 'it appears to the PG that there are circumstances suggesting that the donee of a lasting power of attorney may—
> (a) have behaved, or may be behaving, in a way that contravenes his authority or is not in the best interests of the donor of the power,
> (b) be proposing to behave in a way that would contravene that authority or would not be in the donor's best interests, or
> (c) have failed to comply with the requirements of an order made, or direction given, by the court.'[2]

The PG may require any specified information (or information of a specified description), or documents within a reasonable period and verified in such manner as the PG may reasonably require.

This function supports the PG and the court in an investigation of an objection or complaint regarding a donee of an LPA on this ground which is a prescribed ground for objecting to the registration of an LPA contained in s 22(3)(b) and Sch 1, para 18 to the MCA 2005[3].

There is no express right of review of a PG's decisions by a donee; presumably this is because any disgruntled donee will have recourse to the court which has the final power to cancel an LPA or terminate or revoke it, on this ground (see 12.25 below).

1 LPA Regulations, reg 46.
2 LPA Regulations, reg 46(1).
3 See Chapter 5 LPA at 5.59.

Making a complaint

12.23 Any person can notify the PG of suspected abuse, whether of physical or sexual abuse or fraud. They might also involve the police and adult protection authorities[1]; or other relevant agencies[2].

In serious cases the PG will refer the matter to the court which may revoke the LPA or, where it has yet to be registered, ask the PG not to register it[3]. The court may then have to consider making any relevant decisions or appointing a deputy to do so in the absence of an LPA.

1 Main Code, paras 7.69–7.72.
2 Main Code, paras 14.19–14.22. See Main Code, Chapter 14 generally.
3 Main Code, para 7.72.

EPAs

12.24 The PG has an identical power to require information from the donee of an EPA to that relating to an LPA (see above)[1]. This function is triggered if it appears to the PG that there are circumstances suggesting that 'having regard to all the circumstances (and in particular the attorney's relationship to or connection with the donor) the attorney under a registered enduring power of attorney may be unsuitable to be the donor's attorney'. The reference to 'unsuitable' is to one of the grounds for objecting to the registration of an EPA[2].

The PG may also direct a Court Visitor to visit the donee or donor of an EPA and report to the PG, and deal more generally with representations or complaints about the way in which an attorney under a registered EPA is exercising his powers[3].

1 LPA Regulations, reg 47.
2 Schedule 4, para 13(9)(e) of the MCA 2005 (formerly Enduring Powers of Attorney Act 1985, s 6(5)(e)).
3 LPA Regulations, reg 48.

Outcome of investigation

12.25 Depending on the decision made by the PG it may be appropriate to take further action in relation to any complaints or representations received. For example, a PG might consider referring any issue arising to a formal complaints procedure, whether to a health or social care authority or financial institution. Any potential criminal activity should be notified to the police. The PG should in those circumstances also consider steps to either terminate the authority under which an attorney acts or notify the court in order to terminate the appointment of a court deputy (see 5.57–5.63 and 11.29).

Save for his powers as set out above, the PG has no power to investigate any allegations of abuse himself.

ACCESS TO RECORDS AND INTERVIEW WITH THE PATIENT[1]

12.26 For the purposes of carrying out the functions of the office of PG, the PG may:

> 'at all reasonable times, examine and take copies of—
> (a) any health record,
> (b) any record of, or held by a local authority and compiled in connection with a social services function, and
> (c) any record held by a person registered under Part 2 of the Care Standards Act 2000...'[2]

Access to records is limited 'so far as records relate to P', thus reinforcing the confidentiality of third parties identified in the records, although it must be the case that such information may also 'relate to P' eg an abusive relationship with another, a significant or important relationship with another who may be a carer, friend or relative, or an LPA or deputy.

The PG may also interview the incapacitated person in private for the purposes of discharging his statutory functions.

1 Section 58(5), (6).
2 For definitions see s 64(1)

Court of Protection: s 49 reports

12.27 The PG is provided with a specific power to access records and interview the patient in identical terms to the above when acting under the direction of the court to prepare a report: s 49(2), (7) (8).

OTHER

Security

12.28 The provision of a security[1] protects against misbehaviour by a deputy who may also be required by the court to submit reports to the PG[2].

The PG may receive and supervise a security required from any person by the court. This function is expanded in LPA Regulations which set out the form in which security may be given, the requirement for endorsement, enforcement by the court and discharge of endorsed security.

The court may require a security to be given to the PG by a deputy for the 'due discharge of his functions'[3].

1 Section 58(1)(e), (4)(a); LPA Regulations, regs 33 – 37. A security is defined as a bond endorsed by an authorised insurance company or deposit taker: reg 34.

2 Section 19(9). See 12.15 above and Main Code, para 8.45.
3 Section 19(9).

Public information

12.29 The PG may publish any information about the exercise of his functions, in any manner he considers appropriate[1].

1 Section 58(1)(i).

Fees

12.30 Section 58(4)(b)–(e) provides for regulations under s 58(3)(b) to make provision for fees to be charged by the PG. The Public Guardian (Fees etc) Regulations 2007[1]provide a Schedule[2] of fees for the PG to claim in the following situations:

- Upon application to register an EPA under the LPA Regulations, reg 24[3]. This is payable by the donor[4].
- Upon application to register an LPA under the LPA Regulations, reg 11[5]. This is payable by the donor[6].
- Upon application to search the registers under the LPA Regulations, reg 31[7]. This is payable by the person making the application[8].
- Upon the appoint of a deputy by the court under s 16, or if an existing Receiver is treated as if they were a deputy appoint under Sch 5, para 1(2)(a) to the MCA 2005. The fee shall be payable by the incapacitated person on whose behalf the deputy or Receiver is appointed[9].
- Supervision fees for court deputies. These will depend upon the PG's assessment of the level of supervision that will be required: type I, II, or III[10]. This is payable by the incapacitated person on whose behalf the deputy is appointed. Type III will attract no fee.
- In response to consultation, there will be no fee for objecting to the registration of EPAs or LPAs, or for a court report produced by the PG reporting service[11].

1 SI 2007/2051.
2 Public Guardian (Fees etc) Regulations 2007, reg 3.
3 Public Guardian (Fees etc) Regulations 2007, reg 4.
4 Public Guardian (Fees etc) Regulations 2007, reg 9(3).
5 Public Guardian (Fees etc) Regulations 2007, reg 5.
6 Public Guardian (Fees etc) Regulations 2007, reg 9(4).
7 Public Guardian (Fees etc) Regulations 2007, reg 6 and see 12.5 above.
8 Public Guardian (Fees etc) Regulations 2007, reg 9(5).
9 Public Guardian (Fees etc) Regulations 2007, reg 7.
10 Public Guardian (Fees etc) Regulations 2007, reg 8.
11 See Explanatory Memorandum to Public Guardian (Fees etc) Regulations 2007 and Court of Protection Fees Order 2007 at para 7.9. The full response is at http://www.dca.gov.uk/consult/court-protection-rules/response2306.pdf.

Exemptions, reductions and remissions

12.31 These are in Public Guardian (Fees etc) Regulations 2007, regs 9 and 10. A person in receipt of a qualifying benefit is exempt from a fee unless they are in receipt of damages in excess of £16,000 which has been disregarded for the purposes of determining the eligibility for that benefit. 'Qualifying benefits' are defined in reg 9(7): income support under the Social Security Contributions and Benefits Act 1992; working tax credit, subject to provisos regarding child tax credit; income-based job seeker's allowance under the Jobseekers Act 1995; guarantee credit under the State Pensions Credit Act 2002; council tax benefit under the Social Security Contributions and Benefits Act 1992; housing benefit under the Social Security Contributions and Benefits Act 1992.

The PG retains a discretion to reduce or remit fees 'owing to the exceptional circumstances of the particular case'[1].

1 Public Guardian (Fees etc) Regulations 2007, reg 10. 'The OPG will publish widely an exemptions and remissions policy, which will provide greater clarity as to when a fee is incurred, and help to ensure that applicants are not deterred from using the services of the court and the Public Guardian.' See para 7.3 of the Explanatory Memorandum to the Regulations.

Transitional provisions

12.32 The appropriate proportion of fees that would have been payable under rule 78 of the Court of Protection Rules 2001 on 31 March 2008 shall now be due on 30 September 2007[1].

1 Public Guardian (Fees etc) Regulations 2007, reg 11(1), (2).

SCRUTINY AND REVIEW OF THE PG

12.33 The Public Guardianship Board (PGB) has a duty to scrutinise and review the way in which the PG discharges his functions and to make such recommendations as appropriate to the Lord Chancellor.

Provision for the Lord Chancellor to appoint the PGB has been repealed[1]. At least one member must be a judge of the court, and at least four must appear to the Lord Chancellor to have appropriate knowledge or experience of the work of the PG. The Lord Chancellor will make payments to or in respect of the reimbursement of expenses, allowances and remuneration as he may determine.

Regulations provide for the appointment of a chair of the PGB, term of office of members, resignation and suspension of members, board procedures and public access[2].

1 SI 2006/1016, art 2, Sch. 1 para 36, pursuant to the Constitutional Reform Act 2005.

2 Public Guardian Board Regulations 2007, SI 2007/1770. The first board was appointed on 21 July 2007; see http://www.justice.gov.uk/news/newsrelease200607b.htm.

PUBLIC GUARDIAN'S ANNUAL REPORT

12.34 The PG must make an annual report to the Lord Chancellor about the discharge of his functions. This may be laid before Parliament within a month of receipt[1].

1 The last annual report of the old PGO for 2006–07 is available on http://www.mca2005.co.uk/access/pdf_files/PGO_Annual_Report_2006–07.pdf.

COURT OF PROTECTION VISITORS

12.35 Section 61 provides for the appointment and remuneration of Court of Protection Visitors. They will fulfil similar functions to the Lord Chancellor's Visitors under Part VII of the MHA 1983 (now repealed)[1]. They are to provide independent advice to the court and the PG and have an important role to play in investigating possible abuse. They may also be used to check on the well being of an incapacitated person generally and support donees and deputies in carrying out their role[2]. If a deputy or donee fails to co-operate with a Court Visitor, the court may terminate their appointment if it considers that they are not acting in the person's best interests[3].

1 Explanatory notes to MCA 2005, para 153.
2 Main Code, para 14.11.
3 Main Code, para 14.10.

Types of Court Visitor

12.36 The Lord Chancellor will appoint a panel of (a) Special Visitors and (b) General Visitors[1]. The cost of and responsibility for instructing a Court Visitor will be borne by the court.

1 Section 61(1).

Special visitors

12.37 These will be registered medical practitioners, or appear to the Lord Chancellor to have 'other suitable qualifications or training' and have special knowledge or and experience in cases of 'impairment of or disturbance in the functioning of the mind or brain'[1]. The latter suggests that a Special Visitor does not have to be a medical practitioner and an appropriate skilled clinical psychologist, or other healthcare professional, may well fit the requirement. The Main Code, however, suggests that a Special Visitor must be a medical practitioner[2].

1 Section 61(2).
2 See Main Code, para 14.10.

General Visitors

12.38 General Visitors need not have a medical qualification, however, this does not preclude the appointment of someone with a medical qualification to the role.

Functions of Court of Protection Visitors

12.39 The relevant functions are as follows:

1. Upon request to provide a report to the court. For this purpose a specific right of access to records and to interview the patient is repeated as above[1].
2. If required to make a report as above, a Special Visitor may upon the direction of the court carry out a medical, psychiatric or psychological examination of the person's capacity and condition[2].
3. Under the direction of the PG, to visit an LPA, deputy or incapacitated person and report to the PG[3]. See 12.9 above.

The Court Visitor is an important part of the system for protecting vulnerable, incapacitated adults from abuse. See Chapter 14 of the Main Code and below. This they do by supporting the role of the PG and the court by providing reports on specific issues as instructed.

1 Section 49(2), (7), (8).
2 Section 49(9), (11).
3 Section 58(1)(d) supplemented by LPA Regulations, reg 44.

Access to records and interview with the patient[1]

12.40–12.41 A Court of Protection Visitor has similar rights of access to information as the Public Guardian (see 12.26 above) for the purpose of fulfilling functions under the MCA 2005, and so may:

> 'at all reasonable times, examine and take copies of—
> (a) any health record,
> (b) any record of, or held by a local authority and compiled in connection with a social services function,
> (c) any record held by a person registered under Part 2 of the Care Standards Act 2000.'[2]

This access to records is limited 'so far as records relate to P', thus reinforcing the confidentiality of third parties identified in the records, although it must be the case that such information may also 'relate to P' eg an abusive relationship with another, a significant or important relationship with another who may be a carer, friend or relative, or an LPA or deputy. Any or all of such persons may be relevant for the purposes of any decision under the MCA 2005. Disclosure must accord with the person's Article 8 ECHR rights (see Chapters 14 and 17).

A Court Visitor may also interview the incapacitated person in private for the purposes of discharging his statutory functions[3].

1 Sections 61(5) and (6).
2 Section 61(5). See s 64(1) for definitions.
3 Previously anyone who without reasonable cause refused to allow a Visitor to conduct his or her business or obstructed the same was liable to criminal sanction: s 129(1).

MAIN CODE: CHAPTER 14

12.42 Chapter 14 describes the way in which vulnerable incapacitated adults are protected from abuse by the MCA 2005 and various other agencies. It describes the wide range of acts that could constitute 'abuse' encompassing financial and welfare matters[1]. If anyone suspects that abuse is taking place then they should contact the OPG in addition to instituting any local protection procedures[2].

The role of the OPG and Court Visitors in overseeing the activities of attorneys (LPAs and EPAs) and deputies is set out in the Main Code at paras 14.8–14.22. The PG fulfils this role through its functions as set out in s 58 and the LPA Regulations and discussed above and in Chapter 5. The PG's role is supported by the Court Visitors.

The following is an example based on one in the Main Code of how the PG might act on receipt of a report from a General Visitor[3]:

Mrs Quinn made an LPA appointing her nephew, Ian, as her financial attorney. She recently lost capacity to make her own financial decisions, and Ian has registered the LPA. He has taken control of Mrs Quinn's financial affairs.

But Mrs Quinn's niece suspects that Ian is using Mrs Quinn's money to pay off his own debts. She contacts the OPG, which sends a General Visitor to visit Mrs Quinn and Ian. The visitor's report will assess the facts. It might suggest the case go to court to consider whether Ian has behaved in a way which:

- goes against his authority under the LPA, or
- is not in Mrs Quinn's best interests.

The Public Guardian will decide whether the court should be involved in the matter. The court will then decide if it requires further evidence. If it thinks that Ian is abusing his position, the court may cancel the LPA. Additionally, and before he decides whether the court should be involved, the PG may require information from the donee under the LPA Regulations, reg 46.

1 See Main Code, paras 14.1–14.4. Local adult protection procedures will be important.
2 Main Code, paras 14.5 and 14.6.
3 Main Code, para 14.10 scenario.

12.43 The Main Code offers another example about an abusive welfare donee:

Norma is 95 and has Alzheimer's disease. Her son, Brendan, is her personal welfare attorney under an LPA. A district nurse has noticed that Norma has bruises and other injuries. She suspects Brendan may be assaulting his mother when he is drunk. She alerts the police and the local Adult Protection Committee.

Following a criminal investigation, Brendan is charged with ill-treating his mother. The Public Guardian applies to the court to cancel the LPA. Social services start to make alternative arrangements for Norma's care[1].

Steps will be required to assess Norma's needs and ensure that Brendan does not have the care of her in the future. Once the LPA is cancelled this path is made easier and the local authority can assess her best interests.

1 Main Code, para 14.26.

Chapter 13

MEDICAL RESEARCH

- **MCA 2005, ss 30–34**
- **Main Code, Chapter 11**

INTRODUCTION

13.1 The original draft Bill which led to the MCA 2005[1] did not include provisions relating to research involving incapacitated adults. These provisions were introduced following recommendations by the parliamentary Joint Scrutiny Committee on the Government's draft Bill[2].

At common law there is no provision for research involving incapacitated adults. Thus, strictly, research on such patients should not have been carried out unless it was, in the opinion of their treating clinician, in their particular best interests.

The Joint Scrutiny Committee recognised this area as raising very difficult ethical issues, having heard evidence from proponents of research involving incapacitated adults and their opponents. It concluded, however, that there was potential advantage in endorsing properly regulated research involving such patients:

> 'We understand that properly constituted medical research is the process whereby knowledge about a specific disorder or problem is obtained in order to inform the development of new treatments or support strategies that can then be demonstrated to be effective or not, through the use of controlled trials. Such information is essential if new treatments are to be developed and if the National Institute of Clinical Excellence is to advise whether those treatments should be freely available. If properly regulated research involving people who may lack capacity is not possible then treatments for incapacitating disorders will not be developed.'[3]

The Joint Scrutiny Committee therefore recommended that the Bill set out key principles which should govern research involving incapacitated adults. The Government accepted this recommendation, with clauses which have now become ss 30 – 34 of the MCA 2005. In this process the Government also sought to give effect to the key international standards relevant to the area, namely the Oviedo Convention and the Clinical Trials Directive[4].

The Joint Committee on Human Rights (JCHR) was concerned that these clauses did not replicate the very stringent requirements protecting incapacitated adults in relation to research which appeared in the Oviedo Convention[5]. The Government disagreed. It considered that the clauses made adequate provision for safeguarding the incapacitated adult and provided clear tests for research ethics committees, who would have to approve the projects, to apply[6].

The best interests test is not mentioned in the sections governing research under the MCA 2005 nor in the Main Code. This is considered further below, following a description of the provisions relating to research under the Act.

1 The Mental Incapacity Bill.

2 House of Commons and House of Lords Joint Committee on the draft Mental Incapacity Bill, HL paper 189–1, HC 1083–1, November 2003.

3 Joint Scrutiny Committee report above, at para 276.

4 The Convention for the Protection of Human Rights and Dignity of the Human Being with regard to the Application of Biology and Medicine: Convention on Human Rights and Biomedicine, CETS no. 164, 4 April 1997, chapter V, Articles 15–17, known as 'The Orviedo Convention'; and the European Clinical Trials Directive 2001/20 EC which resulted domestically in the Medicines for Human Use (Clinical Trials) Regulations 2004 ('the Clinical Trials Regulations') – see further below.

5 JCHR, *23rd Report*, HL Paper 210, HC 1282, 17 November 2004, paras 2.56–2.62.

6 Paragraph 53 onwards of the Government's response to the JHRC's letter of November 2004.

RESEARCH REGULATED BY THE MCA 2005

13.2 The type of research which is regulated by the MCA 2005 constitutes research upon people over the age of 16:

- which is 'intrusive';
- which is not part of research governed by the clinical trials regulations;
- which is proposed to be performed on a patient unable to provide consent by reason of incapacity.

Definition of research

13.3 The MCA 2005 does not define 'research'. The Research Governance Framework for Health and Social Care[1] describes it thus: 'research can be defined as the attempt to derive generalisable new knowledge by addressing clearly defined questions with systematic and rigorous methods'.

The Main Code to the MCA 2005 says:

> 'Research may
> – provide information that can be applied generally to an illness, disorder or condition
> – demonstrate how effective and safe a new treatment is
> – add to evidence that one form of treatment works better than another
> – add to evidence that one form of treatment is safer than another, or
> – examine wider issues (for example, the factors that affect someone's capacity to make a decision.'[2]

It is important to differentiate research in this sense from experimental treatment. Novel or experimental treatments may be found to be in the best interests of a patient[3], but if proposed as treatment, ie with a view to improving the patient's condition as opposed to contributing towards a body of knowledge, will not amount to research governed by these sections of the MCA 2005.

1 Published by the Department of Health in England, and the National Assembly for Wales.

2 Main Code, para 11.2.

3 See for example the authorisation of experimental and untested treatments on two sufferers of CJD: *Simms v Simms* [2002] EWHC 2734 (Fam), [2003] Fam 83.

Intrusive research

13.4 Intrusive research is defined at s 30(2) as research which would be unlawful if it were carried out in relation to someone who had capacity to consent to it but had not consented. This will clearly apply to conduct which involves any touching of a patient, which would, without their consent, constitute assault. Many research projects do not, however, involve bodily invasion in the sense described here, but involve interview or observation. It is not wholly clear that these projects would be caught by the MCA 2005. It was certainly, however, the Government's intention that this type of research should be regulated by the Act[1], and in any event, no Research Ethics Committee would approve a research study involving observation or interview without being satisfied of adequate processes for obtaining the participant's consent.

The MCA 2005 will not apply, however, to certain types of research where no consent would be needed (even where the participants had capacity), namely research involving wholly anonymised data, or human tissue that has been anonymised[2] or collected before 31 August 2006[3], or research pursuant to s 251 of the National Health Service Act 2006 permitting the use of confidential patient information[4].

1 See for example para 59 of the Government's Response to the JCHR's letter of November 2004.
2 Under the Human Tissue Act 2004, where the research has ethical approval, and the tissue comes from a living person.
3 But ethical approval will usually be required.
4 Applications considered by the Patient Information Advisory Group on behalf of the Secretary of State. See further www.advisorybodies.doh.gov.uk/PIAG.

Research covered by the clinical trials regulations

13.5 Research involving incapacitated adults governed by the clinical trials regulations is not governed by the MCA 2005. The clinical trials regulations comprise the Medicines for Human Use (Clinical Trials) Regulations 2004[1] (the 2004 Regulations) and essentially involve pharmaceutical trials. Clinical trials under these regulations are defined as:

> 'any investigation in human subjects, other than a non-interventional trial, intended—
> (a) to discover or verify the clinical, pharmacological or other pharmacodynamic effects of one or more medicinal products,
> (b) to identify any adverse reactions to one or more such products, or
> (c) to study absorption, distribution, metabolism and excretion of one or more such products,
> with the object of ascertaining the safety or efficacy of those products.'[2]

Pharmaceutical trials under these regulations are outside the scope of the MCA 2005 as the 2004 Regulations provide their own mechanism for regulating the involvement of incapacitated adults[3]. This mechanism is, however, somewhat different from that set out under the MCA 2005. The 2004 Regulations, in summary, provide that an incapacitated adult may participate in a clinical trial where:

- their 'legal representative'[4] has been fully informed about the proposed trial, of the right to withdraw from the trial at any time, and has given consent to the patient's participation;
- the patient has received information, appropriate to their level of capacity, about the trial, its risks and benefits;
- the expression of an 'explicit wish' by the patient to withdraw from the trial at any time 'is considered by the investigator';
- no incentive or financial inducement is given to the legal representative or patient;
- there are grounds for expecting that administering the medicinal product to be tested in the trial will produce a benefit to the subject outweighing the risks or produce no risk at all;
- the trial is 'essential' to validate data obtained in other trials involving adults with capacity or by other research methods;
- the trial relates directly to a life-threatening or debilitating clinical condition from which the patient suffers;
- the clinical trial has been designed to minimise pain, discomfort, fear and any other foreseeable risk in relation to the disease and the cognitive abilities of the patient.
- the risk threshold and the degree of distress have to be specially defined and constantly monitored;
- the interests of the patient always prevail over those of science and society.

1 SI 2004/1031. Section 30(5) empowers the Secretary of State so to designate other regulations relating to clinical trials. There are none at present.
2 SI 2004/1031, reg 2(1).
3 At SI 2004/1031, Sch 1, Part 5.
4 Someone who, by virtue with their relationship with the patient, is suitable to act as their legal representative for the purposes of the trial, and is able and willing to do so; or in the absence of such a person, the doctor primarily responsible for the patient's treatment: SI 2004/1031, Sch 1, Part 1, para 2.

Patients without capacity

13.6 The research sections of the MCA 2005 apply to patients whose inclusion in a research project is proposed but who lack the capacity to make a decision for themselves about participation in the project. Exactly the same process of assessing capacity and of assisting the patient to make their own decisions will apply here: see generally Chapter 2 above.

AUTHORISATION OF A RESEARCH PROJECT

13.7 Section 30 provides that intrusive research carried out in relation to a patient without capacity is unlawful unless it is carried out as part of a research project approved by an 'appropriate body' in accordance with s 31 of the MCA 2005, and in accordance with the consultation provisions of s 32, and further safeguards of s 33.

Approval by an appropriate body – the requirements of s 31

13.8 The 'appropriate body' for these purposes is a Research Ethics Committee recognised by the Secretary of State for Health in England, or by the Welsh Assembly Government[1].

The appropriate body may not approve a research project under the MCA 2005 unless satisfied that the requirements of s 31 will be met. They are considered below, but are in summary that:

- the research is in connection with an 'impairing condition' suffered by the patient;
- there are reasonable grounds for believing that comparable research cannot be carried out if confined to those with capacity;
- the research either:
  - (a) has a potential to benefit the patient without imposing a disproportionate burden; or
  - (b) is intended to provide knowledge about the condition suffered by the patient with only a negligible risk;
- there are reasonable arrangements in place for ensuring that the consultation provisions of s 32 and the further protections of s 33 will be met.

1 Section 30(6); MCA (Appropriate Body) (England) Regulations 2006, SI 2006/2810; MCA (Appropriate Body) (England) (Amendment) Regulations 2006, SI 2006/3474; MCA (Appropriate Body) (Wales) Regulations 2007, SI 2007/833.

Research in connection with an 'impairing condition'

13.9 The research must be connected to an impairing condition which affects the patient, or its treatment[1].

'Impairing condition' means, essentially, a condition which is, or may be connected with the patient's lack of capacity:

> ' "Impairing condition" means a condition which is (or may be) attributable to, or which causes or contributes to (or may cause or contribute to), the impairment of, or disturbance in the functioning of, the mind or brain.'[2]

Accordingly, the incapacitated patient cannot be involved under the MCA 2005 in research into subjects not connected with their incapacity. This will not necessarily be confined to cognitive issues per se: if for example a patient was in a coma by reason of a particular organ failure, a research project looking into that organ failure or its treatment may in fact be relevant to the patient's coma, and thus their impaired mental functioning. What the MCA 2005 does do, however, is prohibit any involvement of an incapacitated adult into research wholly unrelated to their incapacity.

1 Section 31(2).
2 Section 31(3).

Research which cannot effectively be performed using those with capacity

13.10 Section 31(4) provides that there must be reasonable grounds for believing that the research project would be less effective if confined to those with capacity. This again serves to limit the research projects to which the incapacitated can be exposed, as it must be established to be likely that the research would be inhibited were it not to involve the incapacitated.

Potential benefit to the patient or to knowledge base

13.11 Research projects under the MCA 2005 must meet one of two requirements:

- that there is a potential to benefit the patient without imposing a burden disproportionate to the potential benefit[1]; alternatively
- that the project is:
  - (a) intended to increase the knowledge base of the causes, treatment or care of those affected by the same or a similar condition to that suffered by the patient; *and*
  - (b) there are reasonable grounds for believing that:
    - (i) the risks of participation to the patient 'are likely to be negligible';
    - (ii) the project will not interfere with the patient's freedom of action or privacy in a significant way or be unduly invasive or restrictive[2].

1 Section 31(5)(a).
2 Section 31(5)(b) and (6).

Potential benefit to the patient

13.12 Note the requirement of the section that the research project anticipates only a 'potential' benefit; if an actual benefit were anticipated, the ethics committee would be anxious to ask why it was not classed as treatment, and provided in any event as being in the patient's best interests[1].

The MCA 2005 does not address the boundary between a project with the potential to benefit the patient, and a project intended to provide knowledge of the causes, treatment or care of those with similar conditions to the patient. The Main Code, however, suggests a fairly wide interpretation of the former category, a category with a lower threshold for approval than the latter:

> 'Potential benefits of research for a person who lacks capacity [ie under s 31(5)(a)] could include
> – developing more effective ways of treating a person or managing their condition;
> – improving the quality of healthcare, social care or other services that they have access to
> – discovering the cause of their condition, if they would benefit from that knowledge;

- reducing the risk of the person being harmed, excluded or disadvantaged.'[2]

The Main Code further suggests that potential benefit under s 31(5)(a) could include indirect benefit, for example if policies or care packages affecting them were changed as a result of the research, or if the research involved interviews, and the patient had the opportunity to express their view, this could be considered of real benefit to them[3].

A further requirement of projects considered to be of potential benefit under s 31(5)(a) is that they must be considered not to impose a disproportionate burden upon the patient relative to that potential benefit. This will involve an assessment of the risks entailed in the research and what it will involve for the patient. For example, repeated venepuncture for patients with psychosis may be felt to be too distressing and intrusive, in relation to the potential benefits of the treatment.

1 See 13.3 above, although note that this is in fact a requirement of the provisions relating to research involving incapacitated adults in Scotland: Adults with Incapacity (Scotland) Act 2000.
2 Main code, para 11.14.
3 Main Code, para 11.13.

Increase in the knowledge base

13.13 Research projects aiming to increase general understanding of an incapacitated adult's condition or its treatment or care are permissible under the MCA 2005, but require more rigorous assessment than those with the potential to benefit the patient personally.

The knowledge base in question need not be confined to a condition identical to that suffered by the patient, but may be similar to it[1]. The Main Code gives this example:

> 'Research into ways of supporting people with learning disabilities to live more independently might involve a person with a learning disability caused by a head trauma. But its findings might help people with similar learning disabilities that have different causes.'[2]

In such a project, however, the ethics committee must be satisfied that the risks of participation to the patients are 'likely to be negligible'[3], and unlikely to interfere substantially with the patient's freedom of action or privacy, or be unduly invasive or restrictive[4]. The Main Code says that 'this means that a person should suffer no harm or distress by taking part', adding that this relates to psychological as well as physical wellbeing[5].

1 Section 31(5)(b).
2 Main Code, para 11.17.
3 Section 31(6)(a).
4 Section 31(6)(b).
5 Main Code, para 11.18.

Mixed projects

13.14 The Main Code, in a case scenario, anticipates that some projects may carry potential benefit to some, but not all, of the anticipated participants. In such a case the ethics committee would need to be satisfied that in relation to both groups of patients, the qualifying criteria of s 31(5) would be fulfilled[1].

1 Main Code, para 11.19.

Arrangements for compliance with ss 32 and 33

13.15 The research ethics committee which approves the project is not only concerned with the nature of the project under s 31. It must also be satisfied that there are reasonable arrangements in place for consultation and for the additional protection to the patient under s 33. These issues will need to be addressed in the researcher's application for approval.

RECRUITING PATIENTS INTO THE PROJECT

13.16 Obtaining ethics committee approval under s 31 of the MCA 2005 is necessary but not sufficient for compliance with these sections of the Act. Once the project has been approved, the researcher needs to consult with appropriate carers under s 32, and heed the further safeguards of s 33 before being able to recruit an incapacitated person into the project.

Consultation

Identification of a consultee

13.17 Where a researcher wishes to recruit an incapacitated adult into an approved project, s/he must first 'take reasonable steps' to find an appropriate person to consult[1]. The Department of Health in its draft guidance (see below) suggests that the use of the term 'reasonable steps' means that the researcher will have a degree of flexibility about the extent to which it is necessary to approach distant or remote relatives or friends:

> 'In some circumstances, it will be possible to establish that the person who lacks capacity has no close relatives in regular contact and that it would be more appropriate to identify a nominated consultee who has more regular contact with the person who lacks capacity.'[2]

The first type of consultee sought should be a person who is engaged in caring for the patient, or interested in the patient's welfare, although not on a remunerated basis. Thus, non-professional donees of lasting powers of attorney or deputies may be appropriate consultees[3]. The person must also be prepared to be consulted by the researcher[4].

If the researcher is unable to find such a consultee s/he must 'in accordance with guidance issued by the appropriate authority' nominate a person who is prepared to be consulted but has no connection with the research project[5]. The Department of Health and National Assembly for Wales on 22 June 2007 issued a draft guidance document entitled '*Guidance on nominating a consultee for research involving adults who lack capacity to consent*'. The Department has sought responses on the guidance, and has not yet published final guidance. However, the document sets out clearly the types of nominated consultee who may be appropriate, independence from the research project or its implications being the key: thus carers in a care home with close knowledge of the patient may well be appropriate consultees, provided that the research project was not sponsored by the home, or did not seek to research aspects of care in the home.

The draft guidance suggests that, at the application for approval stage by the research ethics committee, the researcher address the arrangements for nominating a consultee. This will enable the committee to consider the variety of circumstances where a readily identifiable personal consultee might not be available.

1 Section 32(2).
2 Guidance on nominating a consultee for research involving adults who lack capacity to consent. Issued by the Department of Health and National Assembly for Wales in accordance with MCA 2005, s 32(5), 22 June 2007.
3 Section 32(7).
4 Section 32(2)(b).
5 Section 32(3).

Role of the consultee

13.18 The role of the consultee is as follows: having been provided with information about the research project, to advise the researcher as to whether the patient should take part, and what, in the consultee's opinion, would be the patient's wishes and feelings about participation if they had capacity in relation to the matter[1]. Note that the consultee is not explicitly required, at s 32, to make a best interests decision. However, the consultee must be bound, as are all those dealing with incapacitated adults under the MCA 2005 to apply the overriding principles of s 1, the fourth of which demands that decisions taken on behalf of the incapacitated must be those which are in their best interests[2]. This is considered further below[3].

The draft guidance document suggests that it may be helpful to remind the consultee that they are not being asked for advice on their personal views on participation in the specific project or research in general. The consultee will need to set aside any views they may have about the research and consider only what the patient's views and interests are. A consultee should be asked to consider the broad aims of the research and the practicalities of what taking part will mean for the person who lacks capacity. The consultee should consider the patient's past views on the overall nature of the research. It is also essential to consider their present views and wishes. The draft guidance gives the example of a study which involves activities in the afternoon when the person who lacks capacity is most tired so would find it a strain, or conversely that it involves an activity that the person who lacks capacity particularly enjoys.

The guidance further suggests that it may be helpful to provide the consultee with independent advice about their role.

A professional or nominated consultee has the same role as a personal consultee. They may, however, not know the patient particularly well, and should take steps to consult family or friends as appropriate, respecting always issues of confidentiality. The draft guidance suggests that research ethics committees will want to be satisfied about arrangements for confidentiality when granting approval to the project.

If the consultee advises the researcher that 'in his opinion [the patient's] wishes and feelings would be likely to lead him to decline to take part in the project' the researcher must ensure that the patient is not recruited into the project[4].

The consultee's role extends into the research project itself: if they come to believe during the project that the patient would wish to withdraw from it, the researcher is obliged to remove the patient from the project. The researcher may only continue the patient's participation in the project if there are reasonable grounds to believe that there would be a 'significant risk' to the patient's health to discontinue the research treatment[5].

1 Section 32(4).
2 Section 1(5), discussed at Chapter 2 above. Further, any person acting in relation to a person without capacity within the meaning of s 42 needs to have regard to the Main Code – see 1.9 above.
3 See 13.27 below.
4 Section 32(5).
5 Section 32(5)(b) and (6).

Emergency treatment and consultation

13.19 The consultation process is mandatory in order to recruit a patient onto an approved research project save with one exception: where the patient needs urgent medical treatment but a researcher wants to include them in a research project. The provisions of s 32(8) and (9) permit a patient to be recruited onto a research study which has already been approved under s 31 without following the detailed consultation requirements of s 32(4) where:

- an incapacitated patient requires medical treatment as a matter of urgency;
- the researcher, 'having regard to the nature of the research and of the particular circumstances of the case', considers that it is necessary 'to take action for the purposes of the research as a matter of urgency', but that it is not reasonably practicable to follow the consultation procedure; and
- the researcher either:
  - (a) obtains the agreement of a medical practitioner unconnected with the project, to the patient's inclusion in the project; or
  - (b) where it is not reasonably practicable even to obtain a medical practitioner's agreement, follows a procedure that has been approved in advance by the ethics committee which approved the project.

This process only permits the researcher to proceed without following the detailed consultation process whilst it remains necessary to take urgent action with regard to the patient or the research project[1]. As soon as the emergency is over the Guidance document (see 13.17 above) exhorts the researcher to consult in the standard manner.

Accordingly, in research which might be anticipated to involve such emergencies (such as research into trauma, or intensive care practices), the researcher needs, at the time of seeking ethics committee approval, to address the manner in which emergency situations will be dealt with. The draft guidance suggests that the researcher should identify doctors ready to be contacted in emergency situations.

1 Section 32(10).

ADDITIONAL SAFEGUARDS

13.20 Once the researcher has obtained approval from the appropriate body for the research project, and following appropriate consultation has recruited an incapacitated adult into the project, the research may commence. However, during the currency of the project additional principles and safeguards serve to protect the patient. They are considered below, but in summary are as follows:

- there is a prohibition of action to which the patient appears to object;
- there is a prohibition of action covered by an advance decision or advance statement;
- the interests of the patient outweigh those of science and society;
- the patient must be withdrawn from the project if such a wish is expressed;
- particular steps to be taken if the s 31 requirements are no longer met.

Prohibition of action to which the patient appears to object

13.21 If the patient expresses objection to something being done in the project, it must be stopped. The terms of s 33(2) are robust: 'Nothing may be done to, or in relation to the patient in the course of the research' to which he appears to object. The only exception to this is where the action being done is intended to protect the patient from harm or reduce or prevent harm or discomfort[1].

The researcher needs here to bear in mind that an incapacitated patient may express objection in a variety of ways, which may be indirect. The researcher should be alert for subtle methods of communication of distress.

1 Section 33(2).

Prohibition of action covered by an advance decision or other statement

13.22 The prohibition at s 33 extends to advance decisions and other statements: the patient may not be subjected to research processes which are contrary to:

- a valid and applicable advance decision previously made;
- any other form of statement made by the patient and not previously withdrawn[1].

Chapter 3 considers the topic of advance decisions. Where valid and applicable they remain as binding in the research setting as they are in the treatment context. In the treatment context in the assessment of best interests, statements which do not constitute valid and applicable advance decisions are not binding, merely one of the factors which the decision-maker needs to take into account in the assessment of best interests[2]. In the research setting, however, such statements are binding on the researcher.

1 Section 33(2)(b).
2 Section 4(6), considered at Chapter 2 above.

The interests of the patient outweigh those of science and society

13.23 This declaration, found at s 33(3) is an important safeguard to the patient, and needs to be borne in mind by researchers throughout their dealings with the incapacitated patient.

Withdrawal from the project if such a wish is expressed

13.24 Section 33(2) prohibits actions within the project to which the patient appears to object. Section 33(4) requires the researcher to remove the patient completely from the project if the patient indicates such a desire. Again the researcher will need to be alert to the expression of such a wish as the patient's ability to communicate may be limited.

If the request is made, the researcher must remove the patient from the project 'without delay'. Again the only exception to this requirement is where the researcher has reasonable grounds to believe that there would be a significant risk to the patient's health were the research project discontinued in the patient's case[1].

1 Section 33(4) and (6).

Loss of the s 31 requirements

13.25 One final circumstance requires the researcher to remove the patient from the project without delay, unless there are reasonable grounds to believe this would cause a significant risk to the patient's health: this is where the researcher acquires reasonable grounds to believe that one or more of the s 31 requirements is no longer met in relation to the patient.

Those requirements are set out above, but in summary comprise the requirements that:

- the research is connected with an impairing condition affecting the patient, or its treatment;
- there are reasonable grounds for believing that research of comparable effectiveness cannot be carried out if confined to those with capacity;
- the research has the potential to benefit the patient without imposing a disproportionate burden; or
- the research is intended to improve knowledge of the causes, treatment or care of those with similar conditions to that suffered by the patient, the risks of participation are negligible and the research will not interfere significantly with the patient's freedom of action or privacy, or be unduly invasive or restrictive.

Use of data where there has been a loss of capacity during a project commenced before October 2007

13.26 The final part the MCA 2005 which covers research projects is s 34. This concerns projects commenced before 1 October 2007[1] in which a patient with capacity had consented to participate, but who has lost capacity prior to the completion of the research. Ordinarily, such loss of capacity would vitiate the patient's earlier expression of consent. Under s 34, however, regulations have been issued by which data obtained before the loss of capacity can continue to be used in the research project[2]. The regulations, in summary, are as follows:

- They apply to projects commenced before 1 October 2007 and where a person has, prior to 31 March 2008, consented to take part, but who subsequently loses capacity to continue to consent.
- They provide that research under such a project may be continued using information collected prior to the patient's loss of capacity, provided the information or material consists of data within the meaning of the Data Protection Act 1998, or material which consists of human cells or DNA. Note that the regulations do not permit the continuance of further active steps in the research process in relation to an adult who has lost capacity. For those purposes the provisions of ss 30–33 need to be complied with.
- They require a protocol to be established by the research ethics committee to cover the eventuality of a participant losing capacity.
- They reiterate in this context the consultation requirements and additional safeguards of ss 33 and 34 of the MCA 2005.

1 When these provisions of the MCA 2005 came into force.

2 Mental Capacity Act 2005 (Loss of Capacity During Research Project) (England) Regulations 2007, SI 2007/679; Mental Capacity Act 2005 (Loss of Capacity During Research Project) (Wales) Regulations 2007, SI 2007/837.

DISPUTES AND BEST INTERESTS

13.27 The inclusion of research projects involving incapacitated adults represents a welcome advance of regulation and scrutiny into what has hitherto been an unregulated and uncertain area. Clearly, however, many difficult ethical issues remain to be worked out in individual cases. How for example should the consultee actually decide whether the patient should participate in a project? Given that by definition, research projects are primarily designed to test a hypothesis or research question rather than provide care, it may be very difficult to be satisfied of the overriding principles of s 1, namely that a decision taken on behalf of an incapacitated person must be that which is in his or her best interests, and the least restrictive alternative should be taken[1]. As has been discussed at Chapters 2 and 8 'best interests' has long been recognised as comprising a very broad notion. However, it will, it is suggested, present a challenging question for the consultee.

Are issues requiring dispute resolution likely to emerge? Given the consultee's absolute power of veto, dispute between the consultee and researcher about the wisdom of a patient's involvement will perhaps be unlikely, although there may be issues requiring challenge, probably by way of judicial review if there is a dispute about the researcher's adherence to the procedural requirements of ss 30–34[2].

It is however possible that different family members or carers will have different views about a patient's inclusion in a research project. In such a case how should the dispute be resolved? It is suggested that the Court of Protection should have jurisdiction. Its power at s 16 of the MCA 2005 permits it to make decisions about an incapacitated person's personal welfare, and this must include jurisdiction to consider research inclusion. In approaching the issue the court also will be bound to apply the best interests and least restrictive option requirements of ss 1 and 4. As there is no developed body of common law consideration of research, the approach of the Court of Protection in such a case would offer valuable insight into the practical parameters of the best interests test.

1 Sections 1(5) and (6), s 4.
2 See the judicial review section of Chapter 15.

Chapter 14

PERSONAL INFORMATION: ACCESS AND DISCLOSURE

INTRODUCTION

14.1 The assessment of a person's mental capacity and best interests, whether to do with welfare or finances and property, will in most cases require access to, and the sharing of, personal information relating to the person being assessed. Most obviously this information will be contained in health and social care records, bank and other financial statements and is likely also to be confidential information. Sharing and disclosure of information will take place between carers, agencies, family and decision-makers (including LPA's and court deputies).[1,2,3] This could occur on a daily basis or specifically on occasion for more formal decision-making. Consultation between different types of individuals is a requirement in the assessment of best interests under the s 4(7) of the MCA 2005 and will often involve information sharing.

On a practical level the sharing of specific welfare information between carers, family and decision-makers is unlikely to pose any problems. It is more than likely that it was obtained for the purposes of care and treatment and is to be used for those purposes. More problematic is the use of information for different purposes, for example, the use of health information for obtaining social security benefits or of financial information in relation to suitable accommodation.

The MCA 2005 makes specific but limited provision for disclosure of records to independent mental capacity advocates (IMCAs), the Public Guardian and any Court of Protection Visitor[4]. LPA's and court deputies may be authorised to access specific information by the terms of their appointment but otherwise access to records is not provided for by the MCA 2005. It is an implicit requirement of the Act that a donee or deputy or other decision-maker needs information on which to make a decision on behalf of a person. This information must be the same as the person him or herself would have had to make the decision in question had they had sufficient capacity to do so. In the case of a dispute arising the court must be asked to determine the issue.

Access to and disclosure of personal information relating to incapacitated adults is not specifically regulated by law and remains subject to the Data

Protection Act 1998 (DPA 1998), the common law of confidentiality, Article 8 ECHR, and any specific statutory provisions allowing access[5]. Chapter 16 of the Main Code provides general guidance on access to information. Professional codes of conduct are also a useful guide to the practice within different professions, but must not be taken as a statement of the law. The Joint Scrutiny Report commented on the lack of specific provision for access to information within the Bill which it thought might lead to delayed decision-making if applications to the court became necessary to authorise access or disclosure. This difficulty was acknowledged by the government who said they would be dealt with by consequential amendments and guidance and in consultation with the Information Commissioner[6].

Disclosure of information may be available in the context of legal proceedings to determine capacity and best interests and litigation more generally and subject to court order. The CoP Rules 2007 or CPR 1998 respectively will apply. This is dealt with in Chapter 10 with respect to the Court of Protection.

This chapter will consider the general principles that apply when access to or disclosure of information classified as personal or confidential is sought from a local authority or a court. This is not intended to be an exhaustive analysis of this complex area of law[7]. For these purposes the terms 'personal', 'private' and 'confidential' are used interchangeably to refer to information sharing similar characteristics including the additional quality of confidentiality. It will be seen that protection of such information is not absolute and disclosure is not solely dependent upon the consent of the subject. This means that the personal information of those lacking capacity to consent may still be accessed or disclosed. There is a broad overlap in the circumstances allowing for disclosure whether in pursuance of a public or private interest under the DPA, common law of confidentiality or Article 8.

This chapter will also outline the relevant issues surrounding restraining the publication of personal and confidential information.

1 Main Code, Chapter 4, paras 4.49, 4.52, 4.55–4.56.
2 MCA 2005, s 4(7).
3 Main Code, Chapter 5; Main Code, paras 5.56–5.57.
4 Subsections 35(6), 49(7), 58(5) and 61(5). See Chapters 6 and 12.
5 Such as those pertaining to IMCAs, PGs and Court of Protection Visitors. Footnote 4 above.
6 See Joint Scrutiny Report, Chapter 18, paras 351–356.
7 Please see R Toulson and C Phipp *Confidentiality* (2nd edn) Sweet and Maxwell. There is also much helpful guidance on www.ico.gov.uk, the website of the Information Commissioner who is responsible for operation of the Data Protection Act 1998.

LEGAL FRAMEWORK

Generally

14.2 The use of sensitive and confidential personal information is governed by:

1 the Data Protection Act 1998;

2 the common law of confidentiality;
3 European Convention on Human Rights[1], Article 8, as incorporated into UK law by the Human Rights Act 1998;
4 any specific statutory provisions, such as those within the MCA 2005[2]; and
5 codes of conduct of professional bodies.

Guidance and procedures relating to access to information should also be made available by local authorities, NHS bodies and others, in local policies available to all.

Other points to consider include whether a person has a legitimate expectation in relation to disclosure arising out of the policy and conduct of a relevant public body, and whether any local policy on sharing of information has been applied fairly and lawfully.

Access must be determined on a case-by-case basis.

1 Rome, 4 November 1950; TS 71 (1953); Cmd 8969.
2 See 14.1 above at fn 4.

Capacity to consent

14.3 Most uses or disclosures of personal information will be justified if the consent of the individual has been obtained. It will be necessary to determine whether a person has the capacity to consent to a particular disclosure of information in accordance with the scheme of the MCA 2005. A valid consent for these purposes must be (a) informed, (b) freely given and, may be, (c) explicitly or impliedly given[1].

The first question is, therefore, whether the person lacks capacity to consent to disclosure of the information sought or needed. The functional test of capacity means that even if a person is incapable of making some decisions, they may retain the ability to give consent to disclosure of their medical records to someone else or otherwise participate in the process of disclosure[2].

1 See Chapter 8 in the context of medical procedures.
2 Main Code, para 16.5 and see 14.21 below in relation to the requirement of 'fairness' under the DPA 1998.

Nature of confidential information/personal data

14.4 All information relevant to welfare or financial decision-making for incapacitated adults is likely to fall into the category of personal data within the DPA 1998. The majority of it is likely also to be sensitive personal data within the DPA 1998 or confidential and private information within the common law and Article 8 protection:

1 Welfare
- health records
- social care records

- residential care records

2 Financial and property
- bank statements
- benefits records
- assets
- wills

Data Protection Act 1998

Personal data

14.5 Under the DPA 1998 'personal data' is data (written and held manually or electronically) which relate to a living individual who can be identified from that data or that data plus other information[1]. Thus the DPA 1998 does not apply to information identifying a dead person, nor to sufficiently anonymised information. It includes expressions of opinion and statements of intent about the individual.

1 DPA 1998, s 1(1).

Sensitive personal data

14.6 'Sensitive personal data' is defined to include additionally information as to 'physical or mental health or condition'[1]. All welfare information is likely to fall within this category but financial information will not.

1 DPA 1998, s 2(e).

Health records

14.7 Health records are defined as information relating to the physical or mental health of an individual, made by a health professional[1]. A 'health professional' includes doctors, nurses, dentists, opticians, pharmacists, osteopath, chiropractor, clinical psychologist, speech therapist, music therapist, scientific head of department of an NHS body.

1 Defined in DPA 1998, s 68(2).
2 DPA 1998, s 69.

Common law: confidential information

14.8 Confidential information at common law has the additional quality of confidentiality that depends on (1) the circumstances in which the information is provided and (2) the nature of the information itself.

The circumstances are usually derived from contract or equity and are such as to place the confidant in a position of trust eg doctor, social worker, bank manager, lawyer, counsellor or priest. Information provided to doctors working in the NHS gives rise to an equitable relationship of confidence because there is no contractual relationship between doctor and patient. Reports written by experts on behalf of individuals who instruct them are also subject to a duty of confidence on the basis of the contractual relationship between the doctor and the individual. A bank or other financial institution owes a duty of confidentiality to its customers through principles of contract law.

The confidential nature of information is largely a question of common sense. If the information is plainly confidential then it is not necessary that it must be expressly imparted in confidence.

If the information disclosed is common knowledge then disclosure will not be a betrayal of a confidence. It is only when the information is private or confidential and which a person wishes to keep away from being public knowledge that a breach of confidence may arise[1]. Private has been described as 'personal to the person who possesses it and that he does not intend shall be imparted to the general public. The nature of the information, or the form in which it is kept, may suffice to make it plain that the information satisfies these criteria.'[2]

1 *Douglas v Hello!* [2005] EWCA Civ 595, [2006] QB 125 paras 55 and 56. See *Campbell v MGN* [2004] 2 AC 457 at paras 91–100 for a gloss on this approach in cases of uncertainty. This case considered the publication in a newspaper in text and pictures of private information relating to the treatment for narcotics addiction of Naomi Campbell, the model. It was decided in her favour, in a majority decision, on the issue of the correct balance to be struck between Articles 8 and 10 ECHR.

2 *Campbell v Mirror Group Newspapers Ltd* [2004] UKHL 22, [2004] 2 AC 457 at para 83.

Article 8 ECHR

14.9 'Private life' is not exhaustively defined in Strasbourg case law but is unlikely to exclude any of the categories of information relevant to decision-making under the MCA 2005. In *Pretty v United Kingdom* the court said that 'the concept of 'private life' is a broad term not susceptible to exhaustive definition[1]. The ECtHR has recognised the need to protect information contained in health and social care records[2].

Specifically in relation to medical records, the court in Strasbourg has held that:

> '... the protection of personal data, not least medical data, is of fundamental importance to a person's enjoyment of his or her right to respect for private and family life as guaranteed by Article 8 of the Convention. Respecting the confidentiality of health data is a vital principle in the legal systems of all Contracting Parties to the Convention. It is crucial not only to respect the sense of privacy of a patient but also to preserve his or her confidence in the medical profession and in the health service in general.'[3]

Information falling under a duty of confidentiality, such as banking information, is also likely to come within the Article 8(1) (protection from unwarranted disclosure)[4].

1 [2002] 35 EHRR 1 at para 61.

2 *Z v Finland* (1997) 25 EHRR 371; *Gaskin v United Kingdom* [1990] 1 FLR 167 at para 37.
3 *Z v Finland* (1997) 25 EHRR 371.
4 Dr Robert Stokes, 'The Banker's Duty of Confidentiality, Money Laundering and the Human Rights Act', (2007) JBL 502–526.

RIGHTS OF ACCESS TO OR DISCLOSURE OF INFORMATION

Generally

14.10 The DPA 1998 provides a complex scheme for permitting access to and for 'processing' personal and sensitive personal data. Even in the absence of a person's consent it permits access to or disclosure subject to compliance with specific data principles. This is of assistance in the ordinary course of daily activity when information needs to be shared between carers or with decision-makers so long as it is fair and lawful ie not a breach of confidence or violation of Article 8. The real crunch, however, is that while the DPA 1998 does not prevent disclosure in appropriate circumstances, neither does it require disclosure[1]. If a disagreement over disclosure arises, therefore, it will be necessary to look to the wider law of confidentiality and Article 8 in particular, to demonstrate a public or private interest authorising disclosure.

1 *R (on the application of S) v Plymouth City Council* [2002] MHLR 118 at 27 per Hale LJ (as she then was).

Data Protection Act 1998

14.11 The DPA 1998 gives effect to EC Directive 95/46/EC in the UK, and sets out the standards for information handling through eight data protection principles. The DPA 1998 protects the processing of data: this includes a variety of activities such as obtaining, holding, recording, altering, erasing, using and disclosing by 'transmission, dissemination or otherwise making it available'.

A data controller must comply with the data protection principles[2]. There is detailed and useful guidance on the operation of the DPA 1998 on the website of the Information Commissioner: www.ico.gov.uk[3].

The DPA gives an individual a wide range of rights including of access, compensation, correction and the prevention of processing of personal information held about him or herself.

1 DPA 1998, s 1(1).
2 DPA 1998, s 4(4).
3 See 'Legal Guidance' by the Commissioner published in or around 2001 the exact date is not stated.

Subject's right of access to information

14.12 Subject to specific exemptions (see below), a person has a right of access to their own personal data upon written request and payment of a fee and, if required, must supply information reasonably sought as to their identity and the location of the information sought[1]. There is nothing to limit the purpose for which a subject access request may be made, nor for requiring a statement of the purpose for which the information is to be used. It is the opinion of the Information Commissioner that a data controller may not refuse to comply with an access request where legal proceedings are contemplated or have begun[2].

The disclosure of personal information apart from under the subject's right of access is subject to the non-disclosure principles which are set out below.

1 Section 7(2) and (3).
2 *Data Protection Technical Guidance: Subject access requests and legal proceedings*, dated 29 April 2005 available on www.ico.gov.uk.

Failure to comply with request for access

14.13 If a data controller fails or refuses to comply with a proper subject access request, then a complaint may be made to the Information Commissioner who has a discretion to serve an enforcement notice requiring the data controller to comply with the request under s 40 or an application made to the court for an Order under DPA 1998, s 7(9).

Content of the right of access

14.14 The DPA 1998, s 7 right includes the right:

1 To be told if personal data is being processed by or on behalf of that data controller.
2 If so, to be given a description of the personal data, the purposes for which it is being processed and those to whom it may be disclosed.
3 To have communicated in an intelligible form the information constituting the personal data and any information available to the data controller as to the source of that information. This obligation includes providing a copy of the information unless that would require disproportionate effort, or is not required.[1]
4 To be informed of the reasoning behind decisions relying on automatic evaluation of personal information[2] eg cognitive and other psychological or psychometric testing relying on automatic means of evaluation.
5 A request for access must be complied with promptly and, in any event, within 40 days[3] (ss 7–9).

1 DPA 1998, ss 7(1)(c)(i) and 8(2).
2 DPA 1998, s 7(1)(d).
3 DPA 1998, ss 7–9. Credit files must be supplied within seven days. See also amendment to s 7 in Freedom of Information Act 2001 Sch 6, para 1 which deals with the identity of the person making the request.

Third party information

14.15 If responding to an access request involves providing personal information relating to another individual (a third party) this may lead to a conflict of interests between the requesting person's rights and those of the third party. For example, records may identify persons providing information and contributing to the records in confidence, or where it is considered that disclosure of their identity may cause distress or harm to the person seeking access or the third party. Section 7(4) of the DPA 1998 provides that the data controller does not need to comply with that request unless:

- the third party has consented to it;
- it is reasonable in all the circumstances to comply with the request without the consent of the third party.

The Information Commissioner has provided technical guidance for this situation[1]:

1 Does the request require the disclosure of information which identifies a third party individual? Section 7(4) applies only if disclosure of the third parties information is *necessary* as part of the information being requested. Any indirect method of identifying the third party, eg a job title, must be taken into account. It may be possible to comply with the request without disclosing the third party information by redaction or deletion/editing or disclosing so much of the information as may be disclosed without identifying the third party[2] (but see below). The obligation is to provide the information and not the actual documents. If it is not possible to comply with the request in this way then s 7(4) applies ie the disclosure is necessary.

2 Third party consent. There is no obligation to try and get the consent of the third party. If the information from the third party is known to the requesting individual then it would be reasonable to disclose it without the third party's consent. It may not be appropriate to obtain consent if to do so would inevitably disclose personal information relating to the requesting person to the third party. More likely, however, is that the third party will be hard to locate, or will refuse consent or it may be impractical or costly to get consent. In these circumstances it is necessary to consider whether or not it is 'reasonable' to disclose the information anyway.

3 Disclosure without third party consent. A non-exhaustive list of factors to be taken into account is provided in s 7(6):
   - any duty of confidentiality owed to the third party individual (see above);
   - any steps taken to try and get consent;
   - whether the third party is capable of giving consent;
   - any express refusal of consent by the third party.

There are specific exemptions from non-disclosure dealing with the disclosure of information relating to health, social services and education professionals (see below).

Where there has been an express refusal by the third party to comply with a request, the data controller must still weigh the public interest in preserving confidentiality against the individual's right to access information about his life[3].

1 'Dealing with subject access requests involving other people's information', dated 10 August 2007.
2 DPA 1998, s 7(5).
3 See *Gaskin v United Kingdom* [1990] 1 FLR 167 at para 49. These provisions of the DPA reflect the decision in *Gaskin*. If a contributor is not available or withholds consent, then a system conforms with the principle of proportionality only if it provides an independent authority to finally decide whether access has to be granted.

Right of access to information by an incapacitated person

14.16 There is no specific provision for the right of access to be exercised by incapacitated adults under the DPA 1998. Under the Human Rights Act 1998 (HRA 1998) its provisions must be interpreted so as to be compatible with an individual's Convention rights, and Article 8 requires there to be fair procedures in place to secure a proper protection of this right and to enable full participation from those affected.[1] Unless there is a donee of an Enduring or Lasting Power of Attorney, or Court Deputy, then access may only be achieved by means of an application to the court.

1 See Chapter 17.

ENDURING OR LASTING POWER OF ATTORNEY

14.17 Prior to the MCA 2005, a person holding an enduring power of attorney acting as agent could make an access request. Such a course of action would fall within the scope of a general power of attorney limited to the 'management of the property and affairs' of the donor[1]. Such an attorney would only have had authority to access financial and similar information and not welfare information unless it was demonstrably relevant to a decision authorised under the power. By the same analysis under the MCA 2005 this capability should now reside with an LPA within the terms of the individual power granting authority whether in relation to finance or welfare decisions and subject to clarification by the court as necessary. Such an approach would promote compatibility with Article 8 rights[2].

1 DPA legal guidance, published by the ICO; see www.ico.gov.uk downloaded July 2007.
2 See Joint Scrutiny Report at Chapter 18 where the Government stated that the guidance of the Information Commissioner would be updated in this regard. See Chapter 5 for LPAs generally.

RECEIVER OR COURT DEPUTY

14.18 On the same grounds a receiver[1], or now a deputy appointed by the court, would have the right to make a request for personal data on behalf of an incapacitated adult.

If there is a doubt in any case over the extent of the authority of the attorney, deputy or receiver, it will be necessary to apply to the court for disclosure. The court will take account of the common law and Article 8 rights (see 14.32 and 14.38 below).

1 Appointed under Part VII of the MHA 1983, now repealed.

Use and disclosure: non-disclosure – data principles

14.19 The use and disclosure of personal information (or 'processing') outside the subject access provisions is governed by the 'non-disclosure' principles. Subject to specific exemptions from the data principles, a data controller has a duty to comply with the data protection principles in relation to all data which s/he controls[1]. DPA 1998, Sch 1, Part I sets out eight principles. The 'non-disclosure' principles are the first principle, subject to Schs 2 and 3, second to fifth principles, ss 10 and 14. Principles 1 and 2 are most relevant in the present context.[2]

1 DPA 1998, s 4(4). Exemptions are in Part IV. See s 27(1).
2 The Information Commissioner has provided further useful guidance on the operation of these provisions in the context of health data: 'Use and Disclosure of Health Data' published in May 2002 available on www.ico.gov.uk.

THE FIRST PRINCIPLE

14.20 This provides that personal data:

> 'shall be processed *fairly* and *lawfully* and, in particular, shall not be processed unless—
> (a) at least one of the conditions of schedule 2 is met, and
> (b) in the case of sensitive personal data, at least one of the conditions in Schedule 3 is also met.' (emphasis added).

The Sch 2 and 3 conditions that are likely to apply and be satisfied so as to enable disclosure in this context are set out at 14.24–14.25 below.

Fair processing

14.21 Schedule 1, Part II provides some interpretation of the principles contained in Part I. In relation to principle 1 fair processing essentials may be summarised as follows:

- How was the information obtained? There must be no deceiving or misleading the person from whom the information was obtained as to the purposes of the processing[1].
- The information must be obtained from someone who is authorised or required to provide it by any enactment or convention or other international obligation on the UK.
- The following information must also be provided to the subject of the information so far as practicable, unless it would involve disproportionate[2] effort or the data controller is acting under a legal obligation:
  (a) the identity of the data controller,

(b) the identity of any nominated representative,
(c) the purpose(s) for which the data is to be processed[3].

If a person has insufficient capacity then it may not be 'practicable' to provide them with this information. However, an effort must be made to provide this information to a person lacking capacity in a manner and form that is understandable by them. How precisely this is to be achieved will vary from person to person, depending on their level of understanding. If an appropriate LPA or court deputy is available then it is suggested that the information should be provided to them.

In the event that it is not possible to provide a person lacking capacity with all the necessary fair processing information that person will be unable to exercise their rights under the DPA 1998 eg of access, rectification and so on. It is suggested that if a welfare attorney or court deputy is available, it may be appropriate to supply the information to them.

1 The importance of the identification of the purpose(s) of processing is reinforced by principle 2.

2 This is not defined. The IC suggests that it includes, but is not dependent on, the nature of the data, the length of time and the cost involved in providing the data. See also the Data Protection (Conditions under Paragraph 3 of Part II of Schedule 1) Order 2000, SI 2000/185 which provides that any data controller who does not supply fair processing information must still provide it to any individual who requests it. If it is not provided because it involves disproportionate effort then the reasons for this must be recorded.

3 DPA 1998, Sch 1, Part II, paras 2 and 3.

Exceptions to fair processing

14.22 These are disclosures:

- for the prevention or detection of crime (s 29);
- for protecting members of the public against 'dishonesty, malpractice or other seriously improper conduct by, or the unfitness or incompetence of, persons authorised to carry on any profession or activity.' This allows personal information to be provided to professional bodies for the purpose of investigating malpractice (s 31(2)(a)(iii));
- to the Health Service Ombudsman (s 31(4)(iii));
- pursuant to a requirement of law or for the purpose of establishing, exercising or defending legal rights (s 35).

Lawfully

14.23 The DPA 1998 provides no guidance on the meaning of 'lawfully' within principle 1. The effect of this provision is to require compliance with all relevant rules of law whether in common law or statute relating to the use and disclosure of personal information. In the context of decisions under the MCA 2005, the DPA 1998 therefore requires that the common law of confidentiality, the HRA 1998 and MCA 2005 are complied with. Any unjustified disclosure in breach of confidence, or Article 8 or under the MCA 2005 will be unlawful processing under the DPA 1998.

SCHEDULE 2 CONDITIONS

14.24 The most relevant Sch 2 conditions are likely to be:

- consent of the subject (para 1), or where it is *necessary*;
- for the performance of a contract to which the person is a party (para 2);
- to protect the vital interests of the person ie relevant to life and health and not just life and death situations[1]. This would apply to the disclosure of medical information in an emergency or the disclosure of other medical information for the treatment of an individual even if he were refusing his consent (para 4);
- for the administration of justice (para 5(a));
- for the exercise of functions under any enactment. This could apply to functions under the MCA 2005 (para 5(b));
- for the exercise of any other functions of a public nature exercised in the public interest by any person (para 5(d)). For example a local or health authority or other public authority;
- for the purposes of legitimate interests pursued by the data controller or by the third parties or parties to whom the data are disclosed, except where the processing is prejudicial to the rights and freedoms or legitimate interests of the data subject eg research, financial accounting, management, defending a legal action in relation to the data controller or third parties (para 6).

1 IC Legal Guidance at para 3.1.1 says it must involve life and death. But Kennedy and Grubb, *Medical Law* (3rd edn) Butterworths, disagree. In *Gaskin v United Kingdom* the ECtHR said that 'receiving the information necessary to know and to understand their childhood and early development' was a 'vital interest' (at para 49). This suggests that the IC's interpretation is open to challenge. It was *Gaskin* after all that identified the need for a procedure enabling individual's to access their personal information.

SCHEDULE 3 CONDITIONS[1]

14.25 The most relevant Sch 3 conditions include:

- the explicit consent of the person (para 1), or where it is necessary:
- for the vital interests[2] of the person or another person, where consent cannot be given by or on behalf of the data subject or his consent cannot reasonably be expected to be obtained (ie to protect a third party's vital interests probably in situations where a person poses a danger to another identifiable person such as dangerous psychiatric patients, child abusers or the transmission of infectious disease) (para 3);
- for the purpose of, or in connection with, any legal proceedings (including prospective legal proceedings), for obtaining legal advice or otherwise establishing or defending legal rights. (para 6);
- for the administration of justice (para 7(a));
- exercise of functions under any enactment (as above) (para 7(b));
- for medical purposes by a health professional or similar (para 8).

'Medical purposes' include 'preventative medicine, medical diagnosis, medical research, the provision of care and treatment and the management of healthcare services' (para 8(2))[3].

'Necessary' means that a data controller must be able to demonstrate that their purposes could not reasonably be achieved in any other way or that processing was proportionate to the aim pursued. This might include the use of privacy enhancing technology such as encryption, anonymisation[4]. This aspect of the first principle is reinforced by the third principle: 'Personal data shall be adequate, relevant and not excessive in relation to the purpose or purposes for which they are processed.'

1 See also Data Protection (Processing of Sensitive Personal Data) Order 2000 (SI 2000/417) pursuant to Sch 3, para 10 which sets out 10 supplemental conditions for processing of sensitive personal information.
2 See 14.24 at fn 1 above.
3 For a definition of 'health professional' see DPA 1998, s 69.
4 See also Principle 3 and 'Use and Disclosure of Health Data', published by the IC in May 2002 and available on www.ica.gov.uk.

THE SECOND PRINCIPLE

14.26 This provides that 'personal data shall be obtained only for one or more specified and lawful[1] purposes, and shall not be further processed in any manner incompatible with that purpose or those purposes.'

Notification of purposes is required in accordance with fair processing requirements above. This principle reinforces the first principle and limits further processing for purposes not notified to those that are 'compatible' with the original purposes.

1 See DPA 1998, Sch 1, Part II for interpretation.

Disclosure of personal/sensitive data relating to incapacitated adults

14.27 So long as it is done fairly and lawfully (see 14.21 and 14.23 above), disclosure is likely to be permissible by virtue of Sch 2 and 3 conditions being satisfied[1]. Furthermore, for daily activities the information shared will be that stored and intended to be used for the purposes of care and treatment and unlikely to be controversial.

1 DPA 1998, Sch 3, paras 3–7.

Remedies

14.28 A person may

(a) apply to the IC or the court to enforce a subject access request[1];
(b) claim compensation for any contravention of the requirements of this Act[2];
(c) seek rectification, erasure of inaccurate details[3].

The jurisdiction under DPA 1998, ss 7–14 is exercisable by the High Court and the county court[4].

1 DPA 1998, s 7(9).
2 DPA 1998, s 13(1).
3 DPA 1998, s 14.
4 DPA 1998, s 15.

Exemptions

14.29 There are a number of exemptions from, and modifications to, provisions of the DPA 1998 which are contained in Part IV (ss 28–39), Sch 7 and various statutory instruments. Of relevance here are the modifications to the right of access under s 7, and the exemptions from non-disclosure provisions:

1 There are two relevant subject access modification orders:
   - Data Protection (Subject Access Modification) (Health) Order 2000[1];
   - Data Protection (Subject Access Modification) (Social Work) Order 2000[2].

   These Orders are in similar terms as summarised below.

2 Information relating to physical or mental health or the condition of the person is exempt from disclosure under DPA 1998, s 7 if it would be 'likely to cause serious harm to the physical or mental health or condition' of the person or any other person. If the data controller is not a health professional, the information may only be withheld if an appropriate health professional has been consulted as to the effect of disclosure. This requirement does not apply if the data controller already has a written opinion, within the previous six months, from the health professional that disclosure is likely to cause serious harm.[3] This should be someone with knowledge of the person. 'Serious harm' is not defined.

3 Information cannot be refused on the grounds that it may identify a health professional who has compiled or contributed to the record or has been involved in the care or the person, unless serious harm is likely to be caused to the health professional's physical or mental health or condition.[4] A similar provision exists in relation to social work information and access cannot be refused on the grounds that the information identifies a third party, defined to include employees of the bodies identified in the schedule or a guardian ad litem[5].

4 Information in a court report or other evidence to a court given by a local authority, health trust, probation office and others, may be withheld from disclosure by order of the court[6]. This exemption applies to information disclosable under s 7 and the first data principle.

5 Information relating to social work is defined in the schedule to the social work exemption order[7]. This order does not apply to personal data within the health order above.

6 The exemptions apply to a person authorised by court order to make a request on behalf of someone who is incapable of managing their own affairs. Information must not be disclosed if the incapacitated person

provided the information in the clear or express expectation that it would not be disclosed to the person making the request, unless there has subsequently been an express indication to the contrary. This provision would probably now apply to a court appointed deputy with powers over an incapacitated person's financial affairs, but would require amendment if it is to apply to welfare decisions by a court deputy[8].

1 SI 2000/413.
2 SI 2000/415, as amended by SI 2005/467.
3 See Data Protection (Subject Access Modification) (Health) Order 2000, SI 2000/413, arts 5, 6 and 7 for more details; art 5 of the Data Protection (Subject Access Modification) (Social Work) Order 2000, SI 2000/415 adds a gloss in situations where the harm caused by disclosure of information to which that Order applies (see Schedule) is likely to prejudice the 'carrying out of social work' which is defined in the accompanying schedule.
4 SI 2000/413, art 8.
5 SI 2000/415, art 7 and Schedule.
6 SI 2000/413, art 4; SI 2000/415, art 4 and Sch, para 2.
7 See above. SI 2000/415. In summary it relates to data processed by a local authority in connection with social services functions within the Local Authority Social Services Act 1970, Health and Social Services and Social Security Adjudications Act 1983, Children Act 1989 or Part VI of the Education Act 1996.
8 See SI 2000/413, SI 2000/415, art 5 respectively for details. These provisions clearly pre-date the MCA 2005 but contemplate a request being made by a court appointed person. This would now apply to a court deputy appointed to manage the person's affairs ie not welfare. The Joint ScrutinyReport refers to this at Chapter 18. The government has stated that the Information Commissioner is looking into updating the 2000 Orders in light of the changes in the MCA 2005.

Other exemptions

14.30

1 Processing of personal data for the purposes of preventing or detecting crime, apprehending or prosecuting offenders, or assessing or collecting tax are exempt from the non-disclosure provisions of the DPA 1998[1].
2 There is a research exemption for personal data processed for the purposes of research[2]. The exemption if from the second data principle, namely, that personal data obtained for one or more lawful purposes shall not be further processed in a way that is incompatible with that purpose (see 14.26 above). It may be so processed if the research is not about a particular individual and no substantial damage or distress is likely to be caused to any data subject[3]. Research under the MCA 2005 is dealt with in Chapter 13.
3 Disclosure is a requirement of law, statute or court order or in connection with legal proceedings or seeking legal advice or for the purpose of establishing or defending legal rights[4]. Schedules 2 and 3 still have to be complied with.

1 DPA 1998, s 29(1).
2 DPA 1998, s 33.
3 See the Information Commissioner's health data guidance at www.ico.gov.uk for more details.
4 DPA 1998, s 35.

Other individual rights under the DPA

14.31

1 Prevent processing likely to cause damage or distress (s 10).
2 Prevent processing for the purposes of direct marketing (s 11).
3 In relation to automated decision-making (s 12).
4 Compensation for damage or distress (s 13).
5 Rectification, erasure or destruction of inaccurate information (s 14).

The above may be exercised by the data subject only. As for the right of access, in the absence of an appropriate attorney (EPA or LPA), it is possible for the Court of Protection to appoint a court deputy with specific power to exercise these rights on behalf of an incapacitated adult.

Common law of confidentiality

The duty of confidentiality

14.32 This depends on (1) the circumstances in which the information is gathered and (2) the nature of the information. A breach occurs when the confidential information is or will be misused.

The duty of confidence applies to priests, doctors, social workers, lawyers, accountants and bankers alike[1]. The common law recognises an important public interest in maintaining professional duties of confidence, but these are not absolute and are liable to be overridden where there is a stronger public interest in disclosure, under compulsion of law or by consent.

If the information has been brought into existence for certain authorised purposes, then it can be disclosed for those purposes. Medical reports and recommendations are intended for disclosure to other professionals acting in the care of an individual and so can be disclosed to them[2]. This principle applies to health and social care records enabling members of a clinical, community or other care team to disclose records and share information with other practitioners relevant to the care of the person concerned.

1 *W v Egdell* [1990] Ch 359 at 419 per Bingham LJ (as he then was).
2 *W v Egdell* [1990] Ch 359.

Compulsion of law

14.33 This includes by express statutory provision enabling disclosure, or by court order. For example under the Health and Social Care Act 2001, s 60 or under the provisions of the MCA 2005 applying to IMCAs, Public Guardian or Court Visitor, although these are qualified (see 14.44 and 14.45 below). Where statute provides a discretion to disclose information the exercise of that discretion will be guided by the common law and ECHR.

Consent

14.34 As before most uses or disclosures of confidential information will be justified if the consent of the individual has been obtained. It will be necessary to determine in accordance with the scheme of the MCA 2005 whether a person has the capacity to consent to a particular disclosure of information. A valid consent for these purposes must be (a) informed, (b) freely given and may be (c) explicitly or impliedly given.

Balancing exercise

14.35 Prior to any disclosure taking place there is a balancing exercise to be conducted weighing up the interest in maintaining a confidence against a countervailing interest in favour of disclosure. The burden of proving that the interest supports disclosure falls on the person disclosing the information[1]. Proper policies and procedures are necessary to safeguard the exercise of judgement in this regard.

1 *W v Egdell* [1990] Ch 359.

Public interests

14.36 There is a strong public interest in keeping medical (and other) records confidential that must be weighed against the public interest in keeping the public safe. The court in *Egdell* found that disclosure by an expert of his report to relevant authorities was lawful in the interests of public safety in view of the serious offences committed by the patient (with capacity).

When it comes to weighing the public interests in relation to disclosure by a public body, for example of findings of abuse or criminality by police, social services or following care proceedings[1] to the public[2], police[3], housing authorities, or employers[4], then further factors and an element of 'pressing need' have been identified by the courts to countermand the strong public interest in preserving the confidentiality of proceedings and information in relation to the protection of children or vulnerable adults, even if the information is already in the public domain.

1 *Re V and Re L (Sexual Abuse: Disclosure)* [1999] 1 FLR 267; *Brent Borough Council v SK and HK (a Minor)* [2007] EWHC 1250 (Fam).
2 *R v Chief Constable of North Wales Police, ex p Thorpe* [1998] 2 FLR 571.
3 *Re C (A Minor) (Care Proceedings: Disclosure)* [1997] Fam 76; *R v Local Authority and Police Authority in the Midlands ex parte LM* [2000] 1 FLR 612, a case in which a decision not to give an assurance as to non-disclosure of allegations of indecent assault on a seven-year-old girl was quashed.
4 *Brent Borough Council v SK and HK (a Minor)* [2007] EWHC 1250 (Fam).

Private interests

14.37 There are also private interests to be weighed, namely, the private interest in maintaining an individual confidence that may be outweighed by the private interests in disclosing the information, for example, for medical treatment or other best interests of the person, including obtaining benefits or insurance[1].

1 *R (on the application of S) v Plymouth City Council* [2002] MHLR 118 at para 32

Article 8 ECHR

Human Rights Act 1998

14.38 As a result of s 6(1) of the HRA 1998, any decision by a public authority must comply with an individual's ECHR rights. A public authority for these purposes will include health and social services and housing authorities. For a summary of the operation of the HRA in this context see Chapter 17.

Interference – access and disclosure

14.39 Personal information contained in health and social care records is without doubt within the scope of the Article 8 'private life' protection as stated above. Access to personal information requires an adequate independent procedure especially for enabling access to records when a contributor to the records is either unavailable or unreasonably objecting to disclosure[1]. This is a positive obligation falling on the state. These procedures are now contained in the DPA 1998.

Similarly the disclosure of personal information contained in health or social security records to third parties (including other government agencies) has also been found to be a breach of Article 8(1)[2]. In *MS v Sweden* it was also important to the final determination that the information had been disclosed for a different reason to that for which it had been gathered. This reflects the position under common law and in the DPA. The information had been gathered in connection with medical treatment and disclosed in relation to an application for compensation. These purposes were held to be unconnected[3].

1 *Gaskin v United Kingdom* (1989) 12 EHRR 36; *McMichael v United Kingdom* (1995) 20 EHRR 205.
2 *Z v Finland* (1997) 25 EHRR 371 at 71; *MS v Sweden* (1997) 45 BMLR 133.
3 *MS v Sweden* (1997) 45 BMLR 133 at para 35.

Justification

14.40 The crucial area of dispute when it comes to disclosure will normally lie within Article 8(2). An interference with Article 8 is justified if it (a) is in accordance with the law, (b) pursues a legitimate aim and (c) is necessary in a democratic society. Once again what is involved is a balancing exercise between the right to have one's personal or confidential information protected and the countervailing considerations in favour of disclosure.

Lawfulness

14.41 The requirement of lawfulness is satisfied by statute or common law as long as it is 'adequately accessible' and 'formulated with sufficient precision to enable the citizen to regulate his conduct'[1]. This will be easily fulfilled by the DPA 1998, MCA 2005 and common law of confidentiality.

1 *Sunday Times v United Kingdom* (1979) 2 EHRR 245 at para 49.

Legitimate aim

14.42 The scope of the legitimate aim is set out in Article 8(2) itself, namely: national security, public safety, the economic well-being of the country, for the prevention of disorder or crime, for the protection of health or morals, or for the protection of the rights and freedoms of others. Again disclosure in the context of the MCA 2005 is more than likely to satisfy the aim of the 'protection of health' in connection with treatment and care.

Proportionality

14.43 'Necessary in democratic society' means that the measure being challenged must fulfil a pressing social need and be 'proportionate to the legitimate aim pursued'[1]. Proportionality is at the heart of the balancing exercise and is essentially about striking a fair balance between the individual and the community, and in some situations third parties. This will be struck in circumstances where only relevant information is disclosed. Relevance will of course be determined by the particular issues arising in any particular case. For example, concerns about a person's capacity and needs in or around 2004, are unlikely to justify disclosure of records arising between the 1930s and 2000. Also under domestic law a person who receives confidential information is not permitted to disclose it further unless it is necessary and relevant to do so and this restriction is important in achieving compliance with the principle of proportionality. Further, information about third parties can be redacted out to prevent unnecessary disclosure.

There is much UK case law on the principle of proportionality. A three stage test has emerged:

1 Is the stated objective sufficiently important to justify limiting a fundamental right?
2 Are the measures designed to meet the objective rationally connected to it?
3 Are the means used to impair the right no more than is necessary to achieve the objective?[2]

The object of Article 8 is to protect an individual against arbitrary interference by a public authority. It includes positive obligations on the state to take measures to secure respect for family and private life even as between private individuals[3].

1 *Handyside v United Kingdom* (1976) 1 EHRR 737 at para 49.
2 *R (on the application of Daly) v Secretary of State for the Home Department* [2001] UKHL 26, [2001] 2 WLR 1622.
3 *X and Y v Netherlands* (1986) 8 EHRR 235.

Relevant provisions of the MCA 2005

Independent Mental Capacity Advocates: s 35(6)

14.44 An Independent Mental Capacity Advocate (IMCA) may:

> '(b) ... at all reasonable times, examine and take copies of—
> (i) any health record,
> (ii) any record of, or held by, a local authority and compiled in connection with a social services function, and
> (iii) any record held by a person registered under Part 2 of the Care Standards Act 2000,
>
> which the person holding the record considers may be relevant to the independent mental capacity advocates investigation.'

This is a limited right of access confined to 'relevant' information in the opinion of the record holder. This accords with the common law and is a restriction that is probably compatible with Article 8. An IMCA can challenge the withholding of records deemed to have been conducted unfairly or unreasonably or otherwise unlawfully.

Public Guardian and Court of Protection Visitor: ss 49(7), 58(5) and 61(5)

14.45 The provisions relating to a Public Guardian or Court of Protection Visitor are in similar, though not identical terms as for an IMCA:

> '... may at all reasonable times, examine and take copies of—
> (a) any health record,
> (b) any record of, or held by, a local authority and compiled in connection with a social services function, and
> c) any record held by a person registered under Part 2 of the Care Standards Act 2000,
>
> so far as the record relates to P.'

This is in different terms to that applying to IMCAs. It appears to be less restricted because it refers to records relating to P as opposed to a particular task in hand, ie relevant to an investigation. Further, disclosure to these public officials is not subject to the opinion of the record-holder. The omission of such a reference may mean that the PG or CV can see all records. They would do so subject to a duty of confidentiality themselves and must consider carefully the disclosure of information within the body of any report to the court which may be disclosable more widely. See Chapter 12.

Professional codes

14.46 These are helpful in establishing the purposes for which any profession obtains, stores and uses personal information that it receives. The General Medical Council (GMC), Nursing and Midwifery Council and British Association of Social Workers all publish codes of conduct for their members[1].

1 For GMC see http://www.gmc-uk.org/guidance/current/library/confidentiality.asp#Principles published in April 2004. For the Nursing and Midwifery Council, see http://www.nmc-uk.org/aFrameDisplay.aspx?DocumentID=1560. Downloaded July 07. For BASW http://www.basw.co.uk/Default.aspx?tabid=64, section 11, para 4.1.7, published March 2005. The banking code is at http://www.bankingcode.org.uk/pdfdocs/BANKING%20CODE.pdf.

Restraint on publication

14.47 If there has been unwanted publication of confidential information, or such publication is threatened the Court of Protection has jurisdiction to prevent such publication if it is in the individual's best interests to do so using the scheme of the MCA 2005. Existing case law arose under the court's inherent jurisdiction[1]. However, the House of Lords has said that the jurisdiction to restrain publication arises now under the ECHR and not the inherent jurisdiction although the approach remains similar.[2]

The balancing exercise must weigh the public interest in preserving a person's Article 8 right to a private life against the Article 10 rights of the media to freedom of expression. This exercise begins when the 'person publishing the information knows or ought to know that there is a reasonable expectation that the information in question will be kept confidential'[3].

1 *In Local Authority v Health Authority* [2003] EWHC 2746 (Fam), [2004] (Fam) 96, [2004] 2 WLR 926.
2 *In Re S (A child) (Identification: Restrictions on Publication)* [2004] UKHL 47, [2005] 1 AC 593, [2004] 3 WLR 1129 per Lord Steyn at para 23, a case concerned with revealing the identity of a child following criminal proceedings against his mother for the murder of his brother.
3 *Campbell v Mirror Group Newspapers Ltd* [2004] 2 AC 457 per Lady Hale at para 134; see also *Re Roddy (A child) (Identification: Restriction on Publication)* [2003] EWCH 2927 (Fam), [2004] 2 FLR 949, for a treatment of the balancing exercise by Munby J.

Injunctions

14.48 The court has the same rights, privileges and authority as the High Court and, therefore, has jurisdiction to grant injunctions. It also has jurisdiction to grant interim relief 'pending the determination of an application to it'[1].

Interim injunctions are to be granted in exceptional cases only and a full and proper record of the information before the court and the time taken for the hearing must be kept so that a transcript may be obtained or a note of the hearing provided to the other parties. The following guidance has been provided under the inherent jurisdiction:

'Inevitably on a without notice application the court hears from only the applicant. Good practice, fairness and indeed common sense demand that on any such application the applicant should provide the court with:

i) a balanced, fair and particularised account of the events leading up to the application and thus of the matters upon which it is based. In many cases this should include a brief account of what the applicant thinks the respondent's case is, or is likely to be,

ii) where available and appropriate, independent evidence,

iii) a clear and particularised explanation of the reasons why the application is made without notice and the reasons why the permission to apply to vary or discharge the injunction granted should be on notice (rather than immediately or forthwith as in the standard collection and location orders) and why the return date should not be within a short period of time. As to that I accept and acknowledge that a reference to notice being given if practicable, or for a short period of notice (say 2 working hours or just two hours if a week end or holiday period is imminent), may often provide an appropriate balance to avoid a sequence of effectively without notice applications, and that in some cases a longer period of notice may be appropriate, and

iv) in many cases an account of the steps the applicant proposes concerning service, the giving of an explanation of the order and the implementation of an order. This is likely to be of particular importance in cases such as this one where emotional issues are involved and family members of a person who lacks capacity are the subject of the injunctions and orders. In such cases, as here, information as to those intentions are likely to inform issues as to the need for, and the proportionality of, the relief sought and granted.'[2]

1 MCA 2005, ss 47(1) and 48.

2 *B Borough Council v S (by the Official Solicitor)* [2006] EWHC 2584 (Fam), [2007] 1 FCR 574, Charles J, at paras 38–43 and 158.

Interim injunctions against the media

14.49 These are available against the media but HRA 1998, s 12(3) is relevant because it protects freedom of speech as contained in ECHR, Article 10 so that injunctions without notice are discouraged unless there are exceptional reasons, or all practicable steps to notify have been taken: HRA 1998, s 12(2)[1]. The 'court is not to make an interim restraint order unless it is satisfied the applicant's prospects of success at the trial are sufficiently favourable to justify such an order being made in the particular circumstances of the case'[2].

1 Test before grant of any interlocutory relief is in DPA 1998, s 12(3). *Cream Holdings Ltd v Banerjee* [2004] UKHL 44, [2005] 1 AC 253, HL is the leading case.

2 *Cream Holdings Ltd v Banerjee* [2005] 1 AC 253 at para 22 per Lord Nicholl; *E (By her litigation friend the Official Solicitor) v Channel Four; News International* [2005] 2 FLR 913, a case concerning a woman with dissociative identity disorder and the broadcast of a film about her.

PRACTICE POINTS

14.50 An application for disclosure of personal information should:

1 Identify clearly who is making the application. If it is being made on behalf of someone else, it must contain their written consent, or that of a donee or court deputy if available, providing proof of their authority.
2 The purpose for which disclosure is sought should be clearly set out, including the extent of any further disclosure intended eg to experts and family and if so to whom. This should identify, so far as possible, the data protection principles relied upon to permit disclosure eg for the purposes of a capacity/best interests decision under the MCA 2005 (Sch 2, para 5(b)) and for medical purposes (Sch 3, para 8), or other public interest considerations. In most cases under the MCA 2005 the protection of the health and welfare of the individual will probably suffice.
3 The extent of the disclosure sought must be identified, if possible. A court will not allow 'fishing expeditions'. For example, in relation to health or social care records the time span that it is relevant to the inquiry.

Responding to an application, a body should:

1 Make available any relevant policy or guidance.
2 Make it clear that a decision will be made on the facts of the individual case.
3 Consider the extent of necessary disclosure for the purposes sought.
4 Consider whether there is any third party information that is contained in the information: is there a conflict of interests between the third party and the person requesting the information? Is that information *necessary* to satisfy the application? May the information be disclosed in a format that does not involve disclosing the identity of the third party? Can consent of the third party obtained? Would it be reasonable to disclose the information without their consent? (See above at 14.15.)
5 Consider whether there is any other reason to limit the extent of disclosure eg under an applicable Modification Order (see 'Exemptions' above at 14.29), or on the contrary, any reason why the fair processing requirements do not apply (14.22 above).
6 Record the reasons for disclosing or not disclosing any or any part of the information sought.

Chapter 15

GENERAL LITIGATION

- **CPR Pt 21 and Practice Direction**
- **CPR Pa 54 and Practice Direction**
- **Criminal proceedings**

CIVIL LITIGATION AND MENTAL INCAPACITY

15.1 This chapter is concerned with the conduct of civil litigation involving those lacking capacity. It considers the mechanics of general civil litigation where one of the parties lacks capacity, where those mechanics have been altered as a result of the MCA 2005. Litigation where the status or best interests of the incapacitated person are the focus of the proceedings is covered in Chapter 10.

The opening sections of the MCA 2005 are principally concerned with the promotion of individual autonomy, to ensure, so far as possible, that individuals retain power to make decisions for themselves. Thus, a person with capacity can decide upon a course of action with regard to their welfare, property and affairs, which others would regard as rash or unwise. The corollary of course is that those who do lack capacity require protection in their dealings with others[1]. Thus, as has long been established at common law, to make a legally effective decision (including one in the course of litigation) a person must have mental capacity to make it[2]. In the absence of capacity, actions taken will be either void, or liable to being declared void.

These principles are not disturbed by the MCA 2005. Indeed, the MCA 2005 itself does not affect the process of civil litigation involving those without capacity; this is achieved by amendments to Part 21 of the Civil Procedure Rules (CPR) which came into force on 1 October 2007. The new Part 21 in turn does not substantially alter the long established rules which deal with civil litigation involving those lacking mental capacity. Those rules were streamlined and simplified with the introduction of the CPR 1998[3] and remain largely intact. Both CPR Part 21 and the Practice Direction have been amended in the wake of the MCA 2005[4] but there are no major changes of substance in the rules, the amendments being largely terminological or clarificatory. In those circumstances this chapter does not seek to reiterate all of the provisions relating to litigation by and on behalf of those who lack capacity. It does, however, summarise those amendments to the rules which have been made and offer an overview of alterations in practitioners' thinking which the MCA 2005 will require in this field.

This chapter is not concerned with issues of capacity arising before the courts generally, for example in relation to disputes over contracts or wills. In such cases judges have the option to choose whether to apply any pre-existing common law test of capacity or the MCA 2005 as appropriate. This is not to supplant the capacity test in s 3 in cases before the Court of Protection: It would be sensible for judges now to strive to apply the s 3 test wherever possible, so that the common law now develops in concert with it, particularly as the s 3 test essentially encapsulates the common law test of capacity epitomised by *Re MB*[5].

1 As indeed may those who need to have dealings with them

2 For requirement for capacity to make a will, see *Harwood v Baker* (1840) 3 Moo PCC 282, *Banks v Goodfellow* [1870] LR 5 QB 549; execution of deeds: *Ball v Mannin* (1829) 3 Bligh NS 1, *In Re Beaney, deceased* [1978] 1 WLR 770; marriage: *Durham v Durham* (1885) 10 PD 80, *Re Park's Estate, Park v Park* [1954] P 89; consent to divorce: *Mason v Mason* [1972] Fam 302; consent to medical treatment, see generally Chapter 8.

3 CPR Pt 21, supplemented by a Practice Direction, PD 21, covering children and those lacking capacity.

4 Forty-fifth set of amendments, in force from 1 October 2007.

5 See Main Code, para 4.33 and *Local Authority X v MM (by her litigation friend the Official Solicitor) and KM* [2007] EWHC 2003 Fam at 80, *Re MB (medical treatment)* [1997] 2 FLR 426.

Lack of capacity with regard to litigation — assessment

Incapacity

15.2 Part 21 of the CPR continues to govern civil litigation by and on behalf of children and those without capacity. Formerly, the definition of the latter was a person 'who by reason of mental disorder within the meaning of the MHA 1983 is incapable of managing and administering his property and affairs'. This test thus incorporated the MHA 1983's diagnostic threshold[1], coupled with a requirement that the patient be incapable of managing his or her property and affairs.

The amended Part 21 replaces that test with the general test for incapacity under the MCA 2005; accordingly, a person will lack capacity for the purposes of civil litigation where they are unable to make a decision for themselves in the litigation by reason of an impairment in, or disturbance, of the functioning of their mind or brain[2]. It was held by William Edis QC, sitting as a deputy High Court Judge in *Saulle v Nouvet*[3] that the MCA 2005 definition was introduced into civil litigation only via the new CPR; the MCA 2005 did not itself affect civil litigation, its definition of incapacity applying only 'for the purposes of this Act[4].' It was also held in *Saulle* that if the MCA 2005 definition of incapacity was introduced into civil litigation, so also were the opening principles of s 1. Accordingly, all of the steps and questions required by ss 1–3 of the MCA 2005 will apply here and the question will be situation, or transaction, specific. Thus, for example, a person is not to be deprived of his or her autonomy to litigate unless all practical steps to help them to do so have been taken without success, and a blanket assertion of incapacity will not be tenable – the decision-maker must be satisfied that the person lacks capacity to conduct the specific piece of litigation in which they are involved before bringing in a litigation friend.

Interesting questions arise here: what is the breadth of the situation or transaction which the litigant must grasp in order to have capacity, and to what extent is the full ethos of the MCA 2005 introduced into civil litigation to inform this question? In a decision in 2006, prior to the MCA 2005 coming into force, the Court of Appeal decided by a majority, that capacity in the context of civil litigation, connoted capacity to 'conduct the proceedings', namely the ability to understand and give instructions, assisted where appropriate, about the litigation in general, rather than with regard to any particular element[5]. Ward LJ stated, at para 178 of the judgment:

> 'If, as it seems to me, the relevant capacity is capacity to conduct proceedings, then the client must be able to understand all aspects of those proceedings and take an informed decision, with the help of such explanation as he is given, which bears upon them. It cannot be judged piecemeal. If he has the ability to understand what is meant by a 50–50 split of liability, but lacks the capacity to understand the concept of damages which results from that division of liability, then he lacks true capacity to conduct the proceedings.'

This may seem sensible in terms of the practical conduct of litigation. However, it perhaps sits uneasily with the issue-specific nature of the MCA 2005 test and exhortations in the Main Code: An assessment of capacity must be based on the person's 'ability to make a specific decision at the time it needs to be made, and not on their ability to make decisions in general.' This was echoed in *Saulle v Nouvet*, at para 51 of the judgment: where capacity was contested, it being held that the court 'must focus on matters which arise for decision now, and on the claimant's capacity to deal with them'. If it is correct that the full ethos of the MCA 2005 is now enshrined in civil litigation involving the incapacitated, this is likely to be correct. Whether it proves to be manageable in practice needs to be observed. It is interesting to note that in Saulle itself the court did look more broadly at the claimant's capacity over time: in that case the claimant was found to have periods when he would lapse into a state of incapacity, but the judge considered it important that there was no evidence that he had ever attempted to make major decisions during those periods, and had enough control to postpone making such decisions until he was able to do so. However time-specific the MCA 2005 and the Main Code encourage us to be, it is clear that it will be difficult to confine the assessment of capacity to conduct legal proceedings solely to the decision in hand at the precise moment of assessment.

1 ' "Mental disorder" means mental illness, arrested or incomplete development of mind, psychopathic disorder and any other disorder or disability of mind' MHA 1983, s 1(2) (before amendment by the Mental Health Act 2007).

2 Section 2(1).

3 [2007] EWHC 2902 (QB).

4 MCA 2005, s 2(1).

5 *Bailey v Warren* [2006] EWCA Civ 51.

Medical and other evidence

15.3 In the assessment of capacity expert medical opinion will generally be necessary, particularly in cases of difficulty or uncertainty. It is not however obligatory[1], and the duty to make the decision about capacity lies ultimately with the person proposing to make decisions on behalf of another. Thus, as the Court of Appeal noted in the case of *Masterman Lister v Brutton & Co*[2] it is part of the duty of a solicitor with conduct of litigation to assess the capacity of their client, and to make a decision about it. Usually of course medical opinion will be determinative, but it is important to appreciate that a conclusion of incapacity is a matter of legal classification rather than medical diagnosis[3]. It is accordingly possible to envisage a situation where a solicitor, with close and extensive knowledge of the litigant and of the complexities involved in a piece of litigation, may be better placed to make a decision about capacity than a medical practitioner who has not seen the patient for some time or has not fully appreciated what the litigation will involve. Clearly, much can and should be done with careful instruction of the medical practitioner, but ultimately, it is contended that in such a situation the lawyer will need to make (and of course be able to justify) their own decision.

Also, in cases of dispute, whilst medical evidence will be important, witness evidence about the practical living skills of the person will also be of the utmost significance. It is noteworthy that in *Lindsay v Wood*[4] the court ultimately preferred the evidence of the claimant's wife over the medical experts.

1 The terms of CPR Pt 21 and the Practice Direction in relation to medical terms are couched in terms such as '*if* his belief is based upon medical opinion or the opinion of another suitably qualified expert ...' PD21, para 2.2(d) (emphasis added).
2 [2002] EWCA Civ 1889, [2003] All ER 162, [2003] 1 WLR 1511, CA.
3 See *Bailey v Warren* [2006] EWCA Civ 51, (2006) Times, 20 February, [2006] All ER (D) 78 (Feb), *Saulle v Nouvet* [2007] EWHC 2902 (QB), para 53.
4 [2006] EWHC 2895 (QB).

Dispute about lack of capacity

15.4 It is possible to envisage a situation where the issue of capacity is disputed. For example:

- where the litigant asserts that they retain capacity contrary to legal and medical consensus;
- where the litigant's family or friends assert that the litigant lacks capacity;
- where the opposing party resists the argument that the litigant lacks capacity. This may be in circumstances where, if the litigant had capacity, his or her claim would be statute barred, and it is only the assertion of incapacity which prevents the claim being out of time[1]; alternatively, a defendant may consider a claimant to have capacity, and thus to assert that damages representing a Court of Protection Deputy's costs are inappropriate;

- where years after a negotiated settlement in an action a party seeks to set it aside on the basis that they lacked capacity at the time and thus that the settlement is void[2].

The Main Code suggests that such disputes are likely to be rare, confident that 'people can usually settle doubts and disagreements informally'[3]. In the context of litigation that may be so, at least historically; Kennedy LJ noted in *Masterman Lister* that there was no reported English decision directly concerned with capacity to litigate[4], even though data from the Official Solicitor suggested that the Official Solicitor generally acted at any one time as litigation friend for about 1,700 incapacitated adults in civil and family proceedings[5]. It may thus be correct that issues about capacity to litigate will continue to be rare and/or informally resolved. However, this cannot be guaranteed given the increased focus upon these questions by the publicity surrounding the MCA 2005. It is perhaps noteworthy that four such cases required adjudication in 2006–07[6].

If a dispute about capacity did develop and could not be informally settled[7], how should it be resolved? Certainly the Court of Protection would have jurisdiction under s 15 to make a declaration that the person did or did not have capacity to conduct the litigation (then or at an earlier time). Judges of the Court of Protection will become versed and experienced in the issues. This will, however, involve satellite litigation, and will not be without cost. Moreover, the Court of Protection would have no jurisdiction to make any other order in the litigation. The court, however, in which the existing proceedings was ongoing (or were concluded) has and retains the power to resolve the point on application – either by way of preliminary issue, or to reopen apparently concluded proceedings. The advantage of making an application in this way would be that the court hearing the application would be seized of those existing proceedings (or apparently concluded earlier proceedings) and be able to take action within the case. This was the procedure adopted in the recent cases noted above, and is the likely means by which the issue should be resolved.

Where there is uncertainty about the capacity of a litigant in civil proceedings, the courts have had to consider the issue of the burden of proof: In *Lindsay v Wood* there was doubt amongst the medical experts as to whether the claimant had capacity. The issue had arisen and required resolution, but the claimant did not assert that he lacked (or indeed had) capacity; he was neutral; the defendant asserted that the claimant had capacity. The burden of proof, however, lies on the party asserting a lack of capacity; as no party made that assertion, there was a 'forensic imbalance'. In those circumstances Stanley Burnton J suggested that consideration should be given to seeking an order of the court to direct the Official Solicitor to become involved, instruct experts and make representations as appropriate. In *Saulle v Nouvet* the judge found that the parties had given consideration to seeking the involvement of the Official Solicitor but had decided that it would not be proportionate to make such an application. The judge agreed, finding that with seven medical reports before him and the opportunity to hear the experts give evidence on the preliminary issue, he did not lack evidence; there remained the lack of an advocate pressing for a finding of incapacity, but the judge felt that in the light of the evidence it was unlikely that the Official Solicitor would have made such an argument in any event. The judge accordingly felt able to determine the matter without intervention from the Official Solicitor.

Where a court finds that a party lacked capacity at the time a case was settled, albeit no one had cause to suspect it at the time, the Court of Appeal in *Bailey v Warren*[8] held that the settlement required court approval and was not binding without it. It also held that the test for approval should be whether the settlement was in the interests of the party, judged as at the time of the late approval. However, whilst expressing disapproval of the test suggested in Masterman Lister, namely whether the settlement was at a 'manifest disadvantage' to the party, the practical effect of the majority's approach in *Bailey* may be little different: Arden and Ward LJJ both found that a number of factors were relevant to the assessment – that both the claimant and his family had approved the settlement at the time, that a number of years had passed, the interest in promoting settlement, the interests of the defendant and the promotion of stability in litigation were all of relevance to the question.

Cases which have had to consider the issue of capacity have so far involved issues arising as between the parties. What would be the position where a solicitor doubted the capacity of the client, but the client resisted any such suggestion and refused to be medically examined for the purpose? This will not be an easy situation to resolve. However, it is suggested that the solicitor cannot be deflected from an investigation of capacity if they have serious doubts; their warranty of authority assumes a client with capacity; further, their duty of care to the client requires, it is suggested, full investigation. Should then the client persist in a refusal to co-operate with investigation, the solicitor will need to bring the matter before the court.

1 Limitation periods under the Limitation Act 1980 being inapplicable to those lacking capacity. Note now that the MCA 2005 definition of incapacity is incorporated into the Limitation Act 1980 by Sch 6, para 25, which amends s 38(2) of the 1980 Act.
2 This, and the previous example above comprised the subject matter in *Masterman Lister v Brutton & Co* [2003] 1 WLR 1511, CA.
3 Main Code, para 8.16.
4 Main Code, para 22.
5 Together with any number of non-official litigation friends – see the judgment at para 15.
6 *Bailey v Warren* [2006] EWCA Civ 51, (2006) Times, 20 February, [2006] All ER (D) 78 (Feb); *Folks v Faizey* [2006] EWCA Civ 381, [2006] All ER (D) 83 (Apr), *Lindsay v Wood* [2006] EWHC 2895 (QB), (2006) Times, 8 December, [2006] All ER (D) 204 (Nov); *Saulle v Nouvet* [2007] EWHC 2902 (QB).
7 Note the decision in *Folks v Faizey*, where the Court of Appeal was highly critical of the conduct of the defendant who had opposed the claimant's solicitor's assertion of incapacity and sought a lengthy trial of a preliminary issue on the point.
8 [2006] EWCA Civ 51, (2006) Times, 20 February, [2006] All ER (D) 78 (Feb)

Terminology in the civil courts

Protected parties

15.5 Hitherto, litigants without capacity have been termed 'patients'. Under the amended CPR, those lacking capacity to conduct litigation are to be called 'protected parties'[1]. Proceedings involving them are to be entitled 'AB (A protected party, by CD his litigation friend)'.[2]

1 CPR 21.1(2)(d) ' "Protected party" means a party, or an intended party, who lacks capacity to conduct the proceedings'.
2 CPR PD 21 para 1.1.

Protected beneficiaries

15.6 A person may lack capacity to make complex decisions about the conduct of litigation, but may be capable of managing modest sums of money, particularly if the enabling principles under the MCA 2005 are observed. By contrast, liability issues in a road traffic negligence claim may be fairly simple and straightforward but, if the injury and resulting award of damages were substantial, the claimant might not be able to make investment decisions once the claim was concluded. The common law recognised this distinction: in the case of *Masterman Lister v Brutton & Co*[1] Kennedy and Chadwick LJJ respectively made the following observations:

> 'It is not difficult to envisage claimants in personal injury actions with capacity to deal with all matters and take all 'lay client' decisions related to their actions up to and including a decision whether or not to settle, but lacking capacity to decide (even with advice) how to administer a large award. I see no justification for the assertion that the claimant is to be regarded as a patient from the commencement of proceedings.'[2]

> 'I reject the submission that a person would be incapable of taking investment decisions in relation to a large sum received as compensation is to be held, for that reason, to be incapable of pursuing a claim for that compensation. I accept that capacity to pursue a claim requires capacity to take a decision to compromise that claim; and that capacity to compromise requires an understanding of what the effects of a compromise will be – in particular, an understanding that will be necessary to deal with the compensation monies in a way which will provide for the future. But that does not, as it seems to me, require an understanding as to how that will be done ... There is no logical reason why a person who understands that something needs to be done, but who does not have the requisite understanding to do it for himself, should not confer on another the power to do what needs to be done.'[1]

The requirement to give separate consideration to capacity to conduct litigation and capacity to manage a sum of damages is now explicit in the amended CPR Pt 21: those who lack capacity to manage and control money received in litigation are termed 'protected beneficiaries'[4], and CPR 21.11(3) requires the issue of capacity to manage compensation explicitly to be considered upon settlement of a claim involving a protected party[5].

1 See *Masterman Lister v Brutton & Co* [2002] EWCA Civ 1889, [2003] 1 WLR 1511, CA.
2 Per Kennedy LJ at para 27.
3 Per Chadwick LJ at para 83.
4 CPR 21.1(2)(e) ' "Protected beneficiary" means a party who lacks capacity to manage and control any money recovered by him or on his behalf or for his benefit in the proceedings'.
5 See further 15.10 below.

The litigation friend

15.7 Under CPR 21.1 a person without capacity to conduct litigation (whether as claimant or defendant) must have a litigation friend to do so on their behalf.

Apart from changing the terminology, and streamlining the process to some extent, the new Part 21 does not effect any substantial alteration in the procedure for appointing a litigation friend. Thus, in very brief summary:

- A litigation friend is needed before any substantive step can be taken in the litigation, and a step taken without a litigation friend being in place is invalid unless the court orders otherwise[1].
- The role of litigation friend can be taken by:
  - (a) a deputy appointed by the court if it is within the scope of the deputy's authority; or
  - (b) any suitable person who can fairly and competently conduct the proceedings on behalf of the person who lacks capacity, has no interest adverse to that person, and undertakes to pay any ordered costs[2].
- A litigation friend can be appointed either with or without court order, upon the service of evidence or a certificate of suitability which sets out the grounds for belief that the party lacks capacity and the suitability of the proposed litigation friend[3].
- Should the protected party regain capacity, the court can be asked to terminate the appointment of the litigation friend[4].
- The court may direct that an existing litigation friend cease to act, and appoint a replacement[5].

What is the role of the litigation friend? Neither the MCA 2005 nor the newly amended Part 21 of the CPR explicitly require the litigation friend to act in the best interests of the protected party. The only requirement is that s/he can 'fairly and competently conduct proceedings on behalf of the … protected party', has 'no interest adverse to that of … the protected party' and undertakes, where the protected party is a claimant, to repay any costs the protected party may be ordered to pay (subject to any right of repayment by the protected party)[6]. This terminology does not differ from the previous Part 21. It is inconceivable, however, that the role of the litigation friend would be (or ever have been) interpreted as anything other than to act in the best interests of the protected party. Nevertheless, if that is right, then surely the process of assessing what is in the best interests of the protected party set out at s 4[7] will require adherence. Whilst s 4 may only make explicit what was hitherto implicit, it may lead to a perception at least, that the role of litigation friend has become more onerous.

1 CPR 21.2–21.3.
2 CPR 21.4. The Official Solicitor may also act as litigation friend in specific litigation: see the Official Solicitor website on this: www.officialsolicitor.gov.uk. See also the Practice Note (official solicitor: declaratory proceedings: medical and welfare decisions for adults who lack capacity) at [2006] 2 FLR 373.
3 CPR 21.5–21.6.
4 CPR 21.9.
5 CPR 21.7.

6 CPR 21.4(3).
7 See Chapter 2.

Children and young people

15.8 At common law the rules relating to the mentally incapacitated apply as well to children; both are 'under a disability', the former by virtue of mental disorder, the latter due to their immaturity. CPR Pt 21 thus applies both to children and to adults with incapacity.

The MCA 2005, however, does not apply to decisions made on behalf of children aged under 16[1]. Further, Part 21, even in its newly amended form, retains the existing definition of child as 'a person under 18'[2]. Accordingly, the child must generally act by a litigation friend and, as with an incapacitated adult, any settlement or compromise involving a person under 18 is invalid unless approved by the court[3]. There is no formal alteration of the rules of civil procedure involving children as a result of the MCA 2005.

In practice, however, whilst court approval will remain mandatory in settlement of cases involving young people under 18, it is suggested that a more careful evaluation of their practical involvement within litigation in their name ought to develop, particularly in the case of young people aged 16 and 17. CPR 21.2(2) provides initially that, as with protected parties, those under 18 require litigation to be conducted by a litigation friend. There is however a proviso in the case of children — a child must have a litigation friend to conduct proceedings on his/her behalf unless the court makes an order permitting him/her to conduct the litigation alone[1].

This provision is not new; it existed in the CPR prior to the amendments resulting from the MCA 2005. It has then always been possible for a young person under 18 to seek to conduct litigation without a litigation friend. It is suggested, however, that it should be more frequently considered, at the very least, by reason of the cultural shift sought by the MCA 2005 and the likelihood that many young people under 18 are very likely to have capacity to make decisions within litigation themselves.

1 Section 2(5).
2 CPR 21.1(2)(b).
3 CPR 21.10.
4 CPR 21.2(3).

Settlement or compromise involving a protected party

Approval of the settlement

15.9 A litigant without capacity requires assistance in order to conduct their litigation and instruct their legal team – hence the requirement of a litigation friend. The opponent of a litigant without capacity needs assurance that any settlement or compromise will be a binding and final resolution of the issues in the case – hence the requirement for court approval. The provisions of the

CPR requiring court approval of settlements are essentially unchanged: no settlement involving a protected party shall be valid without the approval of the court[1]. Again, it is beyond the scope of this book to reiterate the procedural requirements of the CPR where unchanged by the MCA 2005. However, in brief summary, what the CPR requires is court approval of the proposed settlement, approval to be based upon the filing of the consent of the litigation friend and (usually) advice from counsel or solicitor.

What is the test to be deployed by the court on an approval hearing? The CPR is silent. It is likely to be a best interests test. However, is there a tension between the tortious principles of recovery of damages, and the best interests test? Might one have to cede to the other? Note that MCA 2005, s 42(4), requires those having dealings with an incapacitated person to have regard to the Main Code. Is this to be incorporated into civil litigation? Should it affect those, such as care experts, instructed to assess a personal injury claimant's future needs, and if, so, will that affect the assessment of those needs? How should the litigation friend – and indeed the court – approach these issues? Questions such as these were touched on in the pre-MCA 2005 first instance decision of *Ashan v University Hospitals NHS Trust*[2].

Note that the former practice of seeking the approval of the Court of Protection of settlement of litigation on behalf of a patient does not survive with the new Court of Protection. The only court needing to approve the settlement is the court in which the proceedings are ongoing.

1 CPR 21.10, including now explicitly acceptance of an interim payment and a Fatal Accidents Act 1976 settlement involving children.

2 [2006] EWHC 2624 (QB), [2006] All ER (D) 451 (Jul).

Management of damages awarded to protected parties

15.10 The amended rules and practice direction do signal an alteration in the management of damages sums awarded to protected parties.

The first step is that, having approved a settlement involving a protected party claimant, the court must assess whether or not the person is a protected beneficiary, i e is someone incapable of handling the damages. It is possible, as noted above, that someone who lacked capacity to conduct the litigation, may be able, with support, to make decisions with regard to the management of their damages[1].

In the case of a protected beneficiary, decisions need to be made about the fate of the sum of damages. As set out in Chapter 12, the investment role of the Public Guardian has been abolished and the new Practice Direction to Part 21 provides that:

- where the sum is in excess of £30,000 the court approving settlement must, unless there is an attorney under a lasting power of attorney (LPA)[2] or a deputy appointed under the Court of Protection authorised to administer or deal with the party's financial affairs, make a direction that the litigation friend apply to the Court of Protection for the appointment of a deputy, after which the fund will be dealt with by the Court of Protection[3];

- where the sum is less than £30,000, the sum may be retained in court (not the Court of Protection) and invested in the same way as the fund of a child[4]: ie, unless a very small amount, it will be paid into court and placed into the special investment account until further investment directions have been given by the court[5].

Consideration of financial management in relation to the funds of incapacitated adults is beyond the scope of this work. The Office of the Public Guardian however has a very informative website which considers this issue in depth: see www.publicguardian.gov.uk.

1 CPR 21.11(3), and see 15.6 above.
2 Or attorney under a registered enduring power of attorney (EPA).
3 PD 21 para 10.2(1).
4 PD 21 para 10.2(2).
5 PD 21 para 9.3.

JUDICIAL REVIEW

Introduction

15.11 Judicial review is the means by which the legality of acts, omissions and decisions taken by public bodies, inferior courts and tribunals can be scrutinised by the High Court (the Administrative Court in the Queen's Bench Division). It is a jurisdiction that is concerned with the decision-making process, rather than the substance or merits of the decision itself. It is not therefore a forum in which disputes over facts are usually settled, and it is rare for the Administrative Court to substitute its own decisions for that of the public body, court or tribunal. Rather the challenge will most likely be based on known and/or agreed facts and the Administrative Court will analyse whether a decision has been taken lawfully, fairly and reasonably, and if it has not it will quash the decision and most likely remit it back to the original decision making body. In cases where there has been a failure to act, the Administrative Court can order that an act be done.

Where there is an unlawful act or omission by a public body that affects a person who lacks capacity, a remedy in judicial review may arise. The act or omission may or may not be directly connected to issue of capacity, so for example a person who lacks capacity may have a claim in judicial review against a planning body that has failed to act lawfully when considering a planning application and the issue of capacity could be irrelevant or incidental to the claim itself. A person who lacks capacity will require a litigation friend to pursue their claim (see above). Other challenges may, however, arise that are more directly or indirectly connected to the person's lack of capacity, for example where an authority has failed to provide services that an incapacitated adult is entitled to, or where it is alleged that a decision or omission has violated the Convention rights of the incapacitated person and the fact of capacity is relevant to the claim.

Most challenges to treatment, contact or residence decisions will be brought by way of proceedings in the Court of Protection. This will enable the lawfulness of the decision in terms of the person's best interests, a largely factual dispute, to be determined, and provide relief by way of substituted decision-making or declaration if appropriate.

Some treatment decisions, however, may be more appropriately challenged by way of judicial review if they do not involve a best interests assessment. For example, if a Primary Care Trust (PCT) refused to pay for drugs and the decision was not in line with the relevant funding guidance or policy (irrespective of lack of capacity), the more appropriate remedy would be by way of judicial review. The remedy sought would simply be an order quashing the decision and a mandatory order requiring the PCT to take the decision lawfully.

For challenges to decisions concerning research involving those who lack capacity, whether or not the appropriate remedy is judicial review, or an application to the Court of Protection, will again likely turn on whether there is a need for a best interests decision. If for example the complaint is that the incorrect procedure was used[1], or the decision was ultra vires, then the most appropriate remedy is likely to be judicial review. If, however, a potential claimant believes the wrong decision has been made, as it is not in the best interests for the incapacitated person to be part of a research programme, then an application to the Court of Protection for a best interests decision under (probably) s 16 would be the appropriate claim to bring.

The following section sets out a brief overview of the principles of judicial review, including the remedies available, who is amenable to judicial review, the grounds of review and the procedural rules[2].

1 For details of the procedure that must be followed see Chapter 13 on research.
2 For a detailed and authoritative text on judicial review, readers should see Michael Fordham, *The Judicial Review Handbook* (4th edn) Hart Publishing.

Remedies

15.12 The Administrative Court has the power to quash decisions, make mandatory orders, and make prohibiting orders; it can also make declarations, injunctions and award damages (although damages can only be sought alongside other remedies, judicial review cannot be used if all that is being sought is damages)[1]. The granting of any remedy is, however, discretionary, and so even if the Administrative Court finds a decision or a failure to act to be unlawful it does not have to grant any remedy.

1 CPR 54.3(2).

Public bodies

15.13 Which bodies are amenable to judicial review has been the subject of much debate and case law, but in essence a decision by an individual or public body involving a public duty, power or function can be challenged by way of judicial review. In the context of this book the decisions of local authorities, hospitals, doctors, social workers and carers, where they concern a public duty owed or the exercise of a statutory power are likely to be amenable to judicial review. In addition as an inferior court the legality and fairness of any decision made by the Court of Protection, but not the merits, could be amenable to judicial review.

Remedy of last resort

15.14 If there is an alternative remedy that has not been exhausted then the Administrative Court is likely to refuse permission to judicially review a decision. Any internal and alternative dispute resolution mechanisms should therefore be exhausted prior to issuing judicial review proceedings.

Standing

15.15 A claimant in judicial review proceedings must be able to show at the permission stage and at the substantive hearing that they have a 'sufficient interest' in the matter to which the application relates[1]. The test has been found to be one that concerns both fact and law and will depend on the relationship between the claimant and the matter in question, and on all the circumstances of the case. The approach to standing by the courts may be summarised in the following way[2]:

- the general approach by the courts is a liberal one;
- financial interest may be sufficient but will seldom be necessary;
- the public interest considerations favour the testing of the legality of executive action;
- it would operate against the public interest if there were a areas of 'vacuum' of unchecked illegality for want of a challenger with standing;
- the courts seek to strike a balance, distinguishing broadly between busybodies and those with a legitimate grievance or interest; and
- one factor which may in some situations count against a claimant is if there is an obviously better-placed challenger who is not complaining.

1 See Supreme Court Act 1981, s 31(3).
2 Michael Fordham, *Judicial Review Handbook* (4th edn) Hart Publishing, p 730, para 38.2.

Time limit

15.16 An application for permission to judicially review an act or omission must be made promptly, and in any event within three months of the act or failure to act[1].

1 CPR 54.5.

Grounds of review

15.17 The grounds of review can be summarised as follows:

1 *ultra vires* — the decision was not one that the body had the power to make;
2 *illegality* — the decision-maker misinterpreted or misapplied the law, failed to consider all relevant factors, or considered irrelevant factors, fettered its discretion, unlawfully delegated a power or duty, or failed to follow policies or guidance;
3 *irrationality* — the decision made was perverse in that no body could have reasonably made the decision;
4 *procedural impropriety* — lack of fairness;
5 *breach of fundamental rights* — breach of Convention rights as contained in the Human Rights Act 1998.

Grounds of review will often overlap. In the context of the MCA 2005 the most likely grounds of review will be that the decision made failed to comply with the decision-making process as set out and required in the MCA 2005, or was procedurally unfair, or was in breach of a Convention right.

Procedure[1]

Pre-action protocol

15.18 Before issuing a claim for judicial review the pre-action protocol must be complied with, unless it is not possible to do so. A letter before claim should be sent to the proposed defendant setting out the decision (or omission) being challenged, the grounds of challenge, and the remedy sought. In addition any interested parties should be identified. The defendant should be given 14 days to reply to the letter before claim.

1 CPR Pt 54 and related Practice Directions.

Three-month time limit

15.19 As noted above there is a strict three-month time limit during which a claim must be issued, and in some cases even if a claim is brought within the three months the court can refuse permission if the claim is not brought 'promptly'. The court will not accept as a reason for delay compliance with the pre action protocol, therefore a claim should be issued if the three months will expire while the protocol is being complied with.

Litigation friend

15.20 A person who lacks capacity to litigate must bring a claim through a litigation friend (see 15.7).

Claim form

15.21 An application for permission to judicially review a decision, or failure to act, must be made by completing the N461 form, and if the matter is urgent an N463 form must also be completed. The claim form requires that details are provided of the decision, act or failure to act, under challenge, the facts relied upon, the grounds of review, and the remedies sought[1].

The claim form must be served on the defendant (and any interested parties) and filed with the Administrative Court by the applicant.

1 CPR 54.6.

Interim relief and urgent applications

15.22 Requests for interim remedies should be included in the N461 claim form (section 6). If the matter is urgent however the N463 form should also be used to set out any interim orders or injunctions being sought (section 3), these can then be considered prior to a decision on permission. The N463 form allows the claimant to set down a proposed timetable, including by when the decision on permission should be taken, and by when a substantive hearing should be heard[1].

In cases of exceptional urgency arising outside of court hours a telephone application can be made for interim relief. In cases of emergency all reasonable steps must be made to alert the proposed defendant to the application and in making the application the claimant must give full and frank disclosure and put forward any observations or submissions requested by the proposed defendant. Such emergency orders are usually time limited to the decision on permission, at which time the judge deciding permission will also consider whether any orders made should remain in place until the substantive hearing.

1 See CPR Pt 25.

Permission

15.23 Permission is required for all judicial review claims. A decision on permission will first usually be taken on the papers, although in some cases the court will direct that there is a 'rolled up hearing' at which both permission and the substantive claim will be considered. In considering permission the court will consider delay, the availability of alternative remedies and whether the case is 'arguable'. If permission is refused it can be renewed at an oral hearing[1].

If permission is granted a date will be set for the substantive hearing.

1 CPR 54.4.

Habeas corpus

15.24 The writ of habeas corpus is a prerogative remedy that requires the release of an applicant from detention where the detention is unlawful. Although such proceedings can be brought against a public body where it is said they are unlawfully detaining a person, such claims are now more usually, and more appropriately, dealt with by way of judicial review. For example if a person is being detained under the MHA 1983 where the necessary criteria are not met then an application for their release could be brought by applying for a writ of habeas corpus, but more usually the procedure would be to make an urgent judicial review claim.

A writ of habeas corpus is more likely to be the appropriate remedy in cases where an incapacitated adult's freedom is being curtailed or otherwise restrained, not by a public body (and so Article 5 is not engaged and judicial review is not available), but by, for example, family members. This could extend to lack of access to an incapacitated adult as well as confinement within a house. In *Re SA (Vulnerable Adult With Capacity: Marriage)*[1], Mr Justice Mumby referred with approval to Mr Justice Eastham's judgment in *Re C (Mental Patient: Contact)*[2].

Eastham J in *Re C* said that although in the normal habeas corpus case the applicant is totally incarcerated, the cases reveal that it is not limited to such cases. It was argued in that case that the interference by a custodial parent with the other parent's access to a child was capable of being remedied by habeas corpus. This was accepted by Eastham J, who said that if it were the case that, either contrary to the will of C if she is able to express her will, or, if contrary to her best interests as found by the court she is not being allowed to see her mother and not being allowed to have access and is otherwise being restrained, then habeas corpus would definitely be available[3].

Applications for a writ of habeas corpus are governed by CPR Sch 1 and RSC Ord 54 together with its Practice Direction, RSC PD 54. The rules are essentially those of the old Order 54 procedure applicable prior to CPR Part 54 coming into force. The forms to be used are set out in the practice direction and vary according to the type of case.

An application may be made without notice being served on any other party and must be supported by a witness statement or affidavit by the detained person and must set out the nature of the restraint. If the person lacks capacity then the witness statement or affidavit may be made by some other person on his behalf and it must state that the person detained or restrained is unable to make the witness statement or affidavit himself and for what reason.

It should be noted that an application by a parent or guardian of a child for a writ of habeas corpus relative to the custody, care or control of the child must be made in the Family Division.

1 [2005] EWHC 2942 (Fam), [2006] 1 FLR 867.
2 [1993] 1 FLR 940.
3 At p 944.

CRIMINAL PROCEEDINGS

Introduction

15.25 It is beyond the scope of this book to provide detailed guidance and analysis of the criminal law and how those who may lack capacity can be affected by, and are treated by it. This chapter will therefore just provide a brief overview of some of the issues those who lack capacity may face within criminal proceedings, including attendance at a police station and interview by police, CPS decisions of whether or not to prosecute, fitness to plead and stand trial, and the giving of evidence in court.

At the police station

15.26 When a person is brought to a police station for questioning, whether under arrest or not, their treatment is subject to the Police and Criminal Evidence Act 1984 (PACE). Code C of PACE sets out the requirements for the detention, treatment and questioning of suspects in police custody by police officers. Under Code C para 1.7, the police have to involve an 'appropriate adult' whenever they suspect, or are told in good faith, that a person they have detained or arrested is 'mentally vulnerable'.

Mentally vulnerable

15.27 A detainee, who, because of their mental state or capacity, may not understand the significance of what is said, or of questions or of their replies, will be considered 'mentally vulnerable'. Code C states that when a custody officer has any doubt about the mental state or capacity of a detainee, that detainee should be treated as mentally vulnerable and an appropriate adult called.

An appropriate adult

15.28 An appropriate adult may be:

1. a relative, guardian or other person responsible for their care or custody;
2. someone experienced in dealing with mentally disordered or mentally vulnerable people but who is not a police officer or employed by the police;
3. failing these, some other responsible adult aged 18 or over who is not a police officer or employed by the police[1].

In the case of people who are mentally disordered or otherwise mentally vulnerable, Code C says that it may be more satisfactory if the appropriate adult is someone experienced or trained in their care rather than a relative. If, however, the detained person prefers a relative to a better qualified stranger or objects to a particular person their wishes should, if practicable, be respected.

The role of the appropriate adult is to aid communication and assist the vulnerable adult; s/he is not there to provide any legal advice, and no professional privilege attaches to the communication between an appropriate adult and the detained person. A person who lacks capacity should be given the opportunity, if they wish, to consult with a solicitor in the absence of an appropriate adult.

An important decision for someone arrested for an offence and who is to be questioned, is whether they wish to exercise their right to have a solicitor present. If a person lacks, or may lack capacity, to make this decision then an appropriate adult should again be utilised and should, it is suggested, make the decision in accordance with the principles of the MCA 2005. In particular they should consider whether it is in the best interests of the person arrested to have a solicitor present during questioning. If a mentally disordered or otherwise mentally vulnerable adult is to be cautioned for an offence this must be done in the presence of the appropriate adult.

1 Code C para 1.7(b).

Interviews

15.29 A person who is mentally vulnerable must not be interviewed regarding their involvement or suspected involvement in a criminal offence, or asked to provide or sign a written statement under caution, in the absence of the appropriate adult, except in limited circumstances. The role of the appropriate adult in an interview is to aid communication; they are not there to provide any legal advice. If an appropriate adult is present at an interview, s/he must be informed that s/he is not expected to act simply as an observer; and that the purpose of their presence is to (i) advise the person being interviewed; (ii) observe whether the interview is being conducted properly and fairly; and (iii) to facilitate communication with the person being interviewed.

Reliable evidence

15.30 In Code C it states that care should be taken when questioning someone who is mentally vulnerable. The guidance given is that although people who are mentally disordered or otherwise mentally vulnerable:

> 'are often capable of providing reliable evidence, they may, without knowing or wishing to do so, be particularly prone in certain circumstances to provide information that may be unreliable, misleading or self-incriminating. Special care should always be taken when questioning such a person, and the appropriate adult should be involved if there is any doubt about a person's age, mental state or capacity.'[1]

1 Code C, Guidance notes, para 11C.

Cautions

15.31 An appropriate adult will be particularly important when the police propose to caution (rather than charge) a person who may lack capacity. A caution can only be administered when a person is able to understand the allegation and is able to admit to committing the offence. If a person lacks capacity to make such an assessment and decision then they cannot be cautioned. An appropriate adult may therefore need to advocate on behalf of the person who lacks capacity that they should not be cautioned.

The decision to prosecute

Crown Prosecution Service decisions of whether or not to prosecute

15.32 There are two tests for the Crown Prosecution Service (CPS) to apply when deciding whether to prosecute for an offence; the first is the 'evidential test', which is whether there is sufficient evidence to provide a 'realistic prospect of conviction' and the second is the 'public interest test'. The evidential test must be considered first, and if, but only it, it is passed then the second test, the public interest test, must be applied. Capacity may be a relevant factor when applying both tests.

Where the victim of an alleged offence may or does lack capacity the crucial question is likely to be whether the evidential test is met. Where the case depends to a large degree on the evidence of someone who lacks capacity the prosecutor will need to consider how reliable and how credible his or her evidence is, and indeed whether it will be admissible (see further below). If this test is satisfied, however, it is very likely the public interest test will be met. In the Code for Crown Prosecutors, one of the public interest factors in favour of a prosecution is that the victim was vulnerable. If the alleged offender is a carer, then another of the factors in favour of a prosecution will be present, namely that the defendant was in a position of authority or trust.

Where the alleged offender is a person who lacks capacity then (assuming they are fit to stand trial) the relevant public interest factor against prosecution is whether a prosecution is likely to have an adverse effect on the victim's mental health.

Pre-trial issues

Fitness to plead and stand trial

15.33 In the Crown Court the question of whether or not a person is fit to be tried in the Crown Court is decided by the court and not by the jury[1]. Before a determination can be made that a defendant is not fit to plead and stand trial it is necessary to obtain the written or oral evidence of two or more registered medical practitioners, at least one of whom is approved under MHA 1983, s 12[2]. If it is the defence that contends that the defendant is unfit to plead and stand trial then the burden of proof falls on the defence and the standard of proof is on the balance of probabilities. If the matter is raised by the court or the prosecution then the burden is on the prosecution and the standard of proof is beyond reasonable doubt.

The test applied is that set down in *R v Pritchard*[3], which concerned a defendant who appeared to be 'deaf, dumb and also of non-sane mind'. When considering whether a defendant is fit to plead there are essentially four considerations:

1 whether they are able to instruct their solicitor and/or counsel;
2 whether they are fit to plead to the indictment;
3 whether they are able to challenge a juror; and
4 whether they are able to understand the evidence and give evidence.

The mere fact that someone is unable to act in their own best interests had been found not to be sufficient to find a person unfit to stand trial[4].

It is suggested that medical practitioners asked to provide evidence to the court on a person's fitness to plead and stand trial, should be instructed to approach each of the considerations above by applying the capacity test contained in the MCA 2005. In essence the test of fitness to plead and stand trial will be whether the person has the capacity to understand the charges made, the capacity to understand the evidence against them, whether they have the capacity to provide instructions to their legal team and whether they can challenge a juror.

1 Prior to the coming into force of s 59 of the Domestic Violence, Crime and Victims Act 2004 it was a matter for the jury.
2 See Criminal Procedure (Insanity) Act 1964, s 5.
3 (1836) 7 C. & P. 303.
4 *R v Robertson* 52 Cr App R 690 CA.

Disposal

15.34 If a defendant is found unfit to plead and stand trial then there will be a determination by the jury of whether the defendant did the act charged against him[1]. If the jury find that the act charged was done by the defendant then the court has the power to either make a hospital order under MHA 1983, s 37 (with or without a restriction order under s 41), a supervision order or an order for his absolute discharge[2]. If the jury find that the defendant did not do the act then s/he will of course be acquitted.

1 Criminal Procedure (Insanity) Act 1964, s 4A.
2 Criminal Procedure (Insanity) Act 1964, s 5.

In the magistrates' and youth court

15.35 The procedure for those who are unfit, or may be unfit, to plead and stand trial in the magistrates' and youth court differs to that in the Crown Court. The provisions of the Criminal Procedure (Insanity) Act 1964 do not apply. Instead where the issue of fitness to plead and stand trial is raised in the magistrates' or youth court the court will first determine whether the defendant did the act charged. If so, then the court will adjourn to consider the defendant's mental condition[1]. The magistrates' and youth court have the power to impose a hospital order under MHA 1983, s 37(3), or a guardianship order, but cannot impose a restriction order under s 41.

1 See Powers of the Criminal Courts (Sentencing) Act 2000, s 11(1).

Evidence in court

Capability to make a statement and give evidence

15.36 The test of whether a person is capable of making a statement, and therefore whether a statement is admissible, is set down in s 123(3) of the Criminal Justice Act 2003. There are two requirements: first the person must be capable of understanding questions put and secondly the person must be able to give answers to such questions which can be understood. Where there is a dispute as to the witness' capability to give a statement the matter will be determined by the judge in the absence of the jury. Expert evidence can be called, and again it is suggested that experts called to give evidence in relation to the capability of a person to make a statement will approach the issue using the capacity test contained in the MCA 2005.

Likewise, where a witness is to give oral evidence and it is contended that they are not a 'competent witness' due to mental illness, it will be a matter for the judge as to whether or not the person has sufficient understanding in order to give evidence. If the judge is satisfied that s/he has, then it will be a matter for the jury to decide on the weight and reliability of the evidence given[1].

1 See *R v Hill* (1851) 2 Den 254 and *R v Dunning* [1965] Crim LR 372.

Special measures

15.37 If a witness suffers from a mental illness within the meaning of MHA 1983, or otherwise has 'a significant impairment of intelligence and social functioning' they are eligible for special assistance when giving evidence if not doing so will diminish the quality of their evidence[1].

The types of special measures available are those contained in ss 23–30 of the Youth Justice Criminal Evidence Act 1999. They include the use of screens, live video link, video recorded evidence in chief, and the giving of evidence in private. A special measures direction can also provide that wigs and gowns are not worn in the Crown Court.

1 See Youth Justice and Criminal Evidence Act 1999, s 16.

Chapter 16

THE RELATIONSHIP BETWEEN THE MCA 2005 AND THE MHA 1983

INTRODUCTION

16.1 The primary provisions of the MCA 2005[1], the Main and draft Addendum Codes and other departmental guidance[2] indicate that the MCA 2005 and the MHA 1983 are to be regarded as giving rise to distinct regimes for the care, treatment and detention of those who suffer mental disorder: The MHA 1983 is relevant only to the treatment of mental disorder and permits the compulsory confinement and treatment of mentally disordered persons where the same is justified by reference to statutorily defined diagnostic and risk criteria that contain no components relating to capacity or best interests[3]. On the other hand, the key determinants in relation to treatment in accordance with the MCA 2005, even where a deprivation of liberty is involved, will be the competence and best interests of the person concerned. Furthermore, the MCA 2005 applies to decision-making in connection with all acts of care and treatment of an incapacitated person, including for mental disorder, except where treatment is governed by Part IV of the MHA 1983[4].

It would be misleading, however, to suggest that the two regimes will not, in a very practical sense, be interconnected. For example, those who make decisions about potential formal admission under the MHA 1983 regime are enjoined to consider carefully whether the aims sought to be achieved could be met safely and effectively within the framework of the MCA 2005[5]. This may, in many circumstances, involve consideration of whether the range of permissible options afforded by MCA 2005, ss 5 and 6 for acts done in connection with the care and treatment of mentally incapacitated persons obviate the need for formal admission under the MHA 1983[6]. Similarly, a deprivation of liberty under the forthcoming Bournewood Safeguards Procedure[7] cannot be authorised in respect of a person who, in terms prescribed by the new Sch 1A to the MCA 2005 inserted by the MHA 2007[8], falls to be dealt with under the aegis of the MHA 1983. Knowledge of the benefits, burdens and purpose of each regime in a given situation will be vital for those charged with the care of incapacitated persons.

Unfortunately the boundary between the two co-existing regimes will not be easy to identify in many instances and there may be an active choice to be made about which of the two schemes is the most appropriate. The boundary between the two regimes may be easier to articulate than it will be to demarcate in practice. The aim of this chapter is therefore to set out the differences in aim and effect as between the relevant schemes and to provide legal and practical guidance in respect of the circumstances in which a particular scheme must be or may be used. In doing so it should be stressed that definitive answers are often not possible and so the guidance offered should be treated as illustrative of problems rather than fixed solutions.

The MHA 2007 has introduced amendments into the MHA 1983 and the MCA 2005 which are not yet in force but are of relevance to this chapter and will be referred to as they arise. As a consequence Chapter 13 of the Main Code, which currently deals with the overlap between the MHA 1983 (unamended) and the MCA 2005, is awaiting revision[9].

1 The principle provision in the MCA 2005 is s 28.
2 See Department of Health Briefing Sheet, Bournewood, November 2006.
3 See *R v Mental Health Review Tribunal ex p Pickering* [1986] 1 All ER 99 per Forbes J where the provisions of MHA 1983, s 72(1)(b)(i)–(ii) are so described.
4 See Robinson, R, 'Amending the Mental Capacity Act 2005 to provide for deprivation of liberty', *J Mental Health L* May 2007, pp 25–40 at p 38 for a comparison of the two regimes.
5 See 'Quick Summary', Main Code, Chapter 13.
6 These provisions are considered in Chapter 4.
7 Intended to be effective from April 2009 and discussed in detail in Chapter 9.
8 See MHA 2007, Sch 8 which inserts Sch 1A into the MCA 2005.
9 See Main Code, paras 13.46–13.55.

WHAT ARE THE PRIMARY FEATURES OF THE MHA 1983 TREATMENT AND DETENTION REGIME RELEVANT FOR COMPARATIVE PURPOSES?

Admission for treatment

16.2 Save in limited circumstances, such as cases of emergency[1], formal admission to hospital under the MHA 1983 will only be lawful where the person concerned is said to be suffering from a mental disorder of a nature or degree which warrants liability to detention for medical treatment (the diagnostic question) and such detention for treatment is necessary for his own health, safety or for the protection of the public (the risk question)[2]. An application for admission must generally be supported by two medical recommendations by suitably qualified medical practitioners[3].

1 MHA 1983, s 4, for example, permits compulsory admission for up to 72 hours in urgent cases in the absence of the formalities required in relation to admissions for assessment under MHA 1983, s 2 and for treatment under s 3.
2 See MHA 1983, s 3.
3 See MHA 1983, ss 2(3) and 3(3). Part 2 of the MHA 2007 introduces new terminology to describe the clinicians who will be responsible for admitting patients to hospital for treatment under Part 2 of the MHA 1983 and including Part IV thereof.

Nearest relative

16.3 A patient's nearest relative can prevent admission by objecting and may discharge a patient from hospital. However, he may find himself 'displaced' from so acting, usually by an approved social worker upon application to the county court, if the court finds him incapacitated by mental disorder, insufficiently concerned with the welfare of the patient or the public and/or finds his objection to the patient's admission unreasonable[1].

1 See MHA 2007, s 29(3). Approved social workers are to be replaced by a broader category of professionals to be known as 'approved mental health professionals': MHA 2007. Further amendments to the nearest relative provisions are in MHA 2007, ss 23–25.

Treatment under the MHA 1983

16.4 The definition of treatment for the purposes of the MHA 1983 is wide. It includes nursing, [psychological intervention, and specialist mental health habilitation] rehabilitation and care under medical supervision[1] and also:

> 'includes all manner of treatment under medical supervision of those suffering from mental disorders from cure to containment. It includes treatment under medical supervision which is designed to alleviate or prevent the deterioration of the patient's condition, even if it will have no effect on the disorder itself.'[2]

1 See MHA 2007, s 145(1). The words in square brackets are to be introduced by MHA 2007, s 7(2).
2 *R (on the application of Munjaz) v Mersey Care National Health Service Trust* [2005] UKHL 58, [2006] 2 AC 148 per Lord Hope at 204A–B, para 66. See also *Reid v Secretary of State for Scotland* [1999] 2 AC 512, per Lord Hope at 529–531. By MHA 2007, s 7(2), s 145(1) MHA 1983 is amended to define medical treatment as including "nursing psychological intervention and specialist mental health habilitation, rehabilitation and care". In addition MHA 2007, s 7(3) inserts a new sub-s (4) into MHA 1983, s 145 so that 'medical treatment, in relation to mental disorder, shall be construed as a reference to medical treatment the purpose of which is to alleviate, or prevent a worsening of, the disorder or one or more of its symptoms or manifestations'.

Treatment without consent under MHA 1983

16.5 Part IV of MHA 1983, commonly known as the 'consent to treatment' provisions, applies to most patients liable to be detained. This category of persons includes those detained under MHA 1983, s 2 or 3 for assessment or treatment[1]. These provisions do not apply to those under guardianship or supervised discharge (see below) because they are not 'liable to be detained'[2].

MHA 1983, s 63 authorises the imposition of medical treatment, excluding surgical treatment which is destructive of brain tissue or other serious medical treatment[3], on a detained patient in the absence of his consent. The administration of treatment by way of medication for more than three months to a non-consenting patient requires the approval of a second opinion doctor[4]. However, the second opinion doctor may authorise medication by any means, and against the wishes of the patient, as long as s/he is able to conclude that, 'having regard to the likelihood of its alleviating or preventing the deterioration of his condition, it should be given'[5]. Serious medical treatment and surgical treatment destructive of brain tissue require both the certified consent of the patient *and* approval by a second opinion appointed doctor[6].

However, in determining these issues neither the responsible medical officer nor the independent second opinion doctor is required to accord the question of the patient's capacity particular weight. Significantly, despite appointment to use his own independent clinical judgment, the second opinion doctor is not required to be satisfied that the medication to which the patient objects is in his or her best interests before authorising it. However, a patient's capacity may be relevant to the question of whether a given treatment can be found to be therapeutically necessary[7]. On the other hand as adverted to above, the presence or absence of capacity can never be determinative of the issue of whether *detention* for treatment for mental disorder is justified.

1 The exceptions are those admitted under emergency procedures (s 4); informal patients detained up to 72 hours to enable proper applications for admission under s 2 or 3 to be made (s 5(2)); those detained for a short period by a nurse using a holding power pursuant to s 5(4)); those remanded to hospital by a court for the production of a report on mental condition (s 35); those suffering mental disorder removed under warrant to a place of safety (ss 135–136); patients discharged from hospital but subject to conditions (ss 73–74).

2 MHA 2007, s 32 introduces community treatment orders (CTOs) by inserting new ss 17A–17G into the MHA 1983. Patients under CTO are not exempted from Part IV but are to be recalled to hospital for treatment or mental disorder in hospital. MHA 1983, s 56 is amended accordingly and a new s 62A applies (inserted by MHA 2007, s 34). MHA 2007, s 35 inserts a new Part 4A and ss 64B–64D relating to treatment in the community of those under CTO, which allow a welfare donee or the Court of Protection to consent to s 58 (or new s 58A as inserted by MHA 2007, s 27) treatments i e those requiring consent or a second opinion. Supervised discharge provisions are repealed: s 36(2). See Chapter 5 at 5.76 and Chapter 7 at 7.44 and 7.52.

3 See MHA 1983, ss 57, 58. Note that the new s 58A inserted by s.27 MHA 2007 adds a clutch of new safeguards in respect of the administration of ECT (see 16.6 below). In particular, where a patient over 18 lacks capacity, a valid and applicable advance decision refusing ECT can prevent such treatment from being administered (MHA, s 58A(5)). Special safeguards apply to serious medical treatment (MHA, s 57).

4 See MHA 1983, s 58(1)(b).

5 See MHA 1983, s 58(3)(b).

6 See MHA 1983, s 57(2)–(3).

7 See *R (on the application of Wilkinson) v Responsible Medical Officer Broadmoor Hospital* [2002] 1 WLR 419; *R (B) v Dr SS, Dr G and the Secretary of State for the Department of Health* [2005] EWHC 1936 (Admin), [2005] All ER (D) 38 (Sep).

ECT and consent to treatment

16.6 An amendment introduced by the MHA 2007 now makes it clear that ECT (and other specified forms of treatment) will require a patient's consent before it may be administered when the relevant provisions of the MHA 2007 take effect. A second opinion doctor (referred to as a registered medical practitioner not being the 'responsible' or 'approved clinician' in the terminology of the new provisions) must certify (a) that the person is not capable of consenting (ie understanding the nature, purpose and likely effects of the treatment), (b) that it is 'appropriate' and (c) that it does not conflict with a valid and applicable advance decision or decision of a welfare donee or court deputy[1]. This would appear to introduce an exception to the exclusion in MCA 2005, s 28 regarding the application of the provisions of the MCA 2005 to those to whom MHA 1983, Part IV applies (see below). Thus advance decisions, and decisions of welfare donees and deputies are exceptionally applicable to decisions regarding ECT (and specified treatments).

1 MHA 1983, s 58A(5) as inserted by MHA 2007, s 27. See 16.5 above fn 2 and 16.39 below for more about donees and the MHA.

Guardianship

16.7 The MHA 1983 scheme also includes an adult guardianship regime under which patients may receive care in the community with 'a minimum constraint to achieve as independent a life as possible within the community'[1]. Guardianship is also considered in Chapter 7 at 7.35–7.46. In summary, successful guardianship applications must satisfy diagnostic and risk criteria analogous to those required for detention under the MHA 1983 and similar formalities are attached to the application procedure[2]. The guardian, usually the local social services authority, has exclusive power to require the patient to reside at a particular place, to attend specific places at specified times for the purposes of treatment, occupation, education or training and to direct the patient to give access to a doctor, approved social worker or other such person[3]. As stated in Chapter 7, the powers of a guardian do not extend to authorising deprivations of liberty[4]. The effect of an existing guardianship on a proposed authorisation of detention under the MCA 2005 is specifically reflected in the eligibility criteria for the same[5] and is considered at 16.45 below. As in respect of detention under s 3 of the MHA 1983, a nearest relative may discharge a patient from guardianship.

1 See Mental Health Act 1983, Code of Practice, para 13.1.
2 See MHA 1983, s 7. See also Chapter 7 in which the precise statutory criteria are set out.
3 See MHA 1983, s 8.
4 See 7.46. See Main Code, para 13.16 and 7th Progress Report of the Joint Committee on Human Rights on the Mental Health Bill, HL112/HC 555, p 13, para 1.30.
5 See new MCA 2005, Sch 1A, paras 2, 3 and 5 inserted by MHA 2007, Sch 8, due to come into force in April 2009.

After-care under supervised discharge

16.8 The MHA also permits a responsible medical officer to make an application for 'supervised discharge' in respect of a patient who has been subject to detention under the MHA 1983. The supervised discharge regime is governed by MHA 1983, ss 25A–25G. The responsible medical officer may make such an application where the patient in question is over 16, liable to detention for treatment, meets the applicable diagnostic and risk criteria and is likely to be helped in obtaining the requisite after-care by provision under supervision[1]. Supervised discharge takes effect only after the person leaves hospital and is subject to after care under MHA 1983, s 117. This arrangement is available for patients suffering from any of the four forms of mental disorder but is primarily directed at those with severe mental illness[2]. Requirements analogous to those applicable under the guardianship regime (residence, attendance and access) may be imposed.

Supervised discharge will cease to be available once the amendments to the MHA 2007 come into force. It will be replaced by community treatment orders[3].

1 See MHA 1983, s 25A(4).

2 See *Mental Health (Patients in the Community) Act 1995 – Guidance on Supervised Discharge (After-Care Under Supervision) and Related Provisions*, (August 1993, supplement to MHA Code of Practice), para 3. The categories of mental disorder in MHA 1983, s 1(2) are amended by MHA 2007, ss 1–3 so that it covers 'any disorder or disability of mind'. The categories of mental impairment, severe mental impairment and psychopathic disorder are removed. 'Learning disability' is included only when it is associated with 'abnormally aggressive or seriously irresponsible conduct'.

3 See 16.5 fn 3 above.

Review and challenge to detention

16.9 The three schemes described above are not the only circumstances in which persons may fall to be dealt with under the aegis of the MHA 1983. However, they are the ones referred to here since they are the most relevant for the purposes of considering the overlap between the MHA 1983 and the MCA 2005. Patients who are detained or subject to guardianship or supervised discharge (or their nearest relatives) may apply to the Mental Health Review Tribunal (MHRT) at regular intervals in order to challenge the lawfulness of the application of the relevant regime to them. The MHRT is required, in each case, to consider whether the statutory medical and risk criteria are met and must determine the lawfulness of the continued application of the particular regime by balancing the risk of discharge against the risk to the patient or the public[1]. The usual aim of any application for discharge from one of these regimes is to regain such liberty as has been eroded or restricted.

1 Robinson, R, 'Amending the Mental Capacity Act 2005 to provide for deprivation of liberty', *J Mental Health L*, May 2007, pp 25–40 states at p 38 that this is the exercise that ought to be conducted in relation to release from detention but similar principles apply to the exercise in relation to discharge from guardianship or after-care under supervision.

Discharge and after care: section 117

16.10 There is a statutory duty placed on PCTs/health authorities and local social services authorities to provide after care services for those who cease to be detained under the MHA 1983 and leave hospital[1]. The principles of the MCA 2005, namely capacity and best interests, will apply to decisions and care planning under this provision. They will also be relevant during the planning for any conditional discharge of a restricted patient under MHA 1983, s 73(2). Where long term accommodation is being planned, an independent mental capacity advocate (IMCA) may be appropriate if there is no other person to be consulted on behalf of an incapacitated person. Any restrictions on a person's freedom of movement should be justified by reference to the 'best interests' principle. This is a complex area and is discussed in detail at Chapter 9 in the context of deprivation of liberty and Article 5 ECHR. It would be inappropriate, and a step to be taken only in exceptional cases, effectively to re-detain a person for the purposes of giving care or treatment under the MCA 2005 in these circumstances, unless such a course of action was justified by reference to the principle of best interests as dictated by the person's strict care needs, and permissible by reference to the relevant eligibility criteria (see below).

1 See MHA 1983, s 117(1), (2).

Capacity and the MHA 1983

16.11 Despite the suggestion made by a specially appointed Expert Committee as far back as 1999[1] that the focus of the MHA 1983 regime should be shifted to a capacity-based rather than a risk-based framework, there has been no political enthusiasm for making patient autonomy a key determinant. In consequence 'capacity' and 'best interests' do not form a part of the formal rationale for detention and treatment under the MHA 1983. The prevailing rationale for detention and treatment under the MHA 1983, which has been subject to rigorous criticism by expert commentators[2], is a combination of medical paternalism and social protection[3]. The MCA 2005, designed to codify a network of protective safeguards for vulnerable persons who are unable to make decisions for themselves, leaves the MHA 1983 regime virtually intact.

As will be seen further below, the exclusions from the MCA 2005 apply only to those treatments for mental disorder falling within Part IV[4]. This leaves all other care and treatment decisions, for example treatment for physical disorders and after-care provision under MHA 1983, s 117, within the purview of the MCA 2005.

1 Richardson, G, *Review of the Mental Health Act 1983: Report of the Expert Committee* (1999, London: Department of Health).
2 See Szmukler G and Holloway, F, 'Maudsley Discussion Paper No. 10, Mental Health Law: Discrimination or Protection'; Dawson, J and Szmukler, G, 'Fusion of Mental Health and Incapacity Legislation', *British Journal of Psychiatry* (2006), 188, 504–509; Richardson, G, above.
3 See Richardson, G, above, pp 10–12 for a more detailed analysis of the way in which these concepts are reflected in the current MHA 1983 framework.
4 Treatments under the forthcoming Part IV A are not excluded.

WHAT ARE THE PRIMARY FEATURES OF THE MCA 2005 TREATMENT AND DETENTION REGIME RELEVANT FOR COMPARATIVE PURPOSES?

16.12 The two concepts which both underpin and animate the MCA 2005 framework are the concepts of capacity and best interests. The areas of decision-making with which this text is concerned are personal welfare and healthcare. The five key capacity principles, set out in MCA 2005, s 1, and discussed in detail in Chapter 2, must guide all decision-making under the MCA 2005. The Act contains specific provision for substitute decision-making via advance decisions to refuse treatment and the facility for health and welfare decision-making to be delegated to a donee of a lasting power of attorney (LPA)[1] or undertaken by the Court of Protection or a court appointed deputy[2].

The precise nature of the capacity and best interests tests are examined in Chapter 2. Incapacity is defined as the inability to make decisions in relation to a specific matter because of an impairment of, or a disturbance in the functioning of the mind or brain. The test for determining capacity in MCA 2005, s 3 replicates the previous position at common law: the inability to understand the information relevant to the decision, retain that information, use or weigh the information as part of the decision making process or communicate the decision[3]. This is a function specific test. All acts done or decisions made under the MCA 2005 in respect of an incapacitated person must be in that person's best interests. The question of best interests is to be determined by reference to a number of factors including whether the person may regain capacity and his past and present wishes and feelings. Where practicable there must be consultation with as wide as possible a range of consultees including carers, donees, deputies, IMCAs and personal representatives, as appropriate[4].

1 See MCA 2005, ss 9–14 and Chapter 5.
2 See MCA 2005, ss 16–20 and Chapter 10.
3 See *Masterman-Lister v Brutton & Co Ltd* [2002] EWCA Civ 1889, [2003] 3 All ER 163.
4 MCA 2005, s 4.

Treatment under the MCA 2005

16.13 Treatment is not specifically defined in the MCA 2005 but, according to the interpretation provisions, it includes 'a diagnostic or other procedure'. Whereas the MHA 1983 definition of treatment encompasses 'care'[1], 'care' and 'treatment' are set apart on the face of the MCA 2005[2] and are distinguished from each other in the Main Code's guidance on MCA 2005, ss 5 and 6.

1 See MHA 1983, s 145(1) and *R (on the application of Munjaz) v Mersey Care National Health Service Trust* [2005] UKHL 58, [2006] 2 AC 148 per Lord Hope at 204A–204B, para 66. Note the amendments made to ss 145(1) and 145(4) referred to in fn 2 above.
2 MCA 2005, s 5(1) refers to acts done in connection with 'care or treatment'. The de-coupling of care and treatment in the MCA 2005 context is also apparent in the provisions of the Act which relate to advance decisions. It is clear that an advance decision to refuse specific treatment can only be made in relation to 'treatment' rather than care. Paragraph 6.5 of the Main Code also distinguishes between acts of care, such as help with washing and dressing, and acts of treatment which include diagnostic examinations, medication or the carrying out of any other medical procedures.

Protected acts in connection with care and treatment

16.14 The MCA 2005 does not specifically authorise care or treatment but s 5 affords carers, healthcare professionals and others protection from liability for acts carried out in connection with care and treatment of incapacitated persons. Section 6 sets the parameters of 'restraint' which may be used in respect of a person lacking capacity without falling outside of the range of acts which will not give rise to civil or criminal liability. In order for liability to be avoided, the person performing an act connected with the care and treatment of an incapacitated person, P, must reasonably believe both that P lacks capacity and that the intended act is in P's best interests. In similar vein, acts of restraint – ie the use or threat of force to overcome P's resistance or to restrict his liberty of movement – must be reasonably believed to be necessary to prevent harm to P and must be a proportionate response to both the likelihood and seriousness of harm anticipated. See Chapter 4 for a more detailed consideration of these issues.

Account must be taken of any resistance or objection by the person as part of the requisite best interests determination. It is perhaps unsurprising that the MCA 2005 permits treatment to be given in spite of the relevant person's objection. It might be expected that a statute intended to ensure the effective care and treatment of those who have lost important decision-making competence would include a facility to provide treatment and care in such persons' best interests even if they objected. In this way it is contemplated that acts of daily care and treatment will not be impeded. As a matter of principle it is perhaps less easy to reconcile why capacitous consent can be so easily be overridden under Part IV of the MHA 1983. This difference may be explained by the focus on the risks associated with mental disorder under the MHA 1983.

Effect of advance decisions, welfare LPA or court appointed deputy

16.15 Worthy of note in relation to the regime under MCA 2005, ss 5 and 6 is the fact that the exclusion from liability does not extend to acts contrary to a valid advance decision or a decision taken within the scope of the proper authority of a donee or deputy. In this sense, the s 5 protection does not authorise the performance of acts connected with care or treatment which go against P's capacitous wishes (as expressed either through a valid advance decision or the valid delegation of decision-making authority).

Life-sustaining treatment and disputes

16.16 However, where the treatment in question can properly be described as 'life-sustaining' it may be given despite objections — either by a donee or contained in a valid advance decision — whilst determination by the Court of Protection is sought[1]. Disagreements between professionals or between professionals, carers and relatives etc may be resolved by application to the Court of Protection as well[2].

1 See MCA 2005, s 6(7).

2 See Chapters 3 and 5 on advance decisions and LPAs respectively and Chapter 7 on the role of the court in welfare decisions.

Treatment for mental disorder and the MCA 2005: emergency treatment

16.17 Section 28 of the MCA 2005 expressly states that the MCA 2005 regime does not authorise either the giving of treatment for mental disorder or the consent to a patient being given treatment for mental disorder where the consent to treatment provisions of Part IV of the MHA 1983 apply. Part IV of the MHA 1983 is discussed above and applies only to the defined category of patients who are 'liable to be detained'. An exception relating to the administration of ECT is introduced by the new MHA 1983, s 58A(5) (see 16.6) and in relation to forthcoming CTOs (see 16.5, fn 2). This still leaves a category of others who may fall within the aegis of the MHA 1983 but for whom the provisions of the MCA 2005 are relevant even in relation to treatment for mental disorder. An important category of such patients is those for whom emergency or urgent treatment is required.

Treatment for mental disorder and eligibility criteria for MCA 2005 deprivation of liberty: Schedule 1A

16.18 The rationale of the MCA 2005, s 28 exclusion is reflected in the Bournewood Safeguards Procedure. Persons who are detained under the MHA 1983 cannot be detained under the Sch A1 scheme. Similarly, persons who are subject to a 'mental heath regimes'[1] — these include those who are not actually detained but are subject to a hospital treatment regime[2], those who are subject to a 'community treatment regime'[3] and those subject to guardianship — are not eligible for detention where the proposed authorisation conflicts with a requirement of the relevant regime. If a person is subject to guardianship or 'within the scope of the Mental Health Act'[4] they are unlikely to be detainable for treatment for mental disorder under the MCA 2005 where certain conditions are fulfilled[5]. Those conditions, all three of which *must* be fulfilled in order to preclude detention under the Safeguards Procedure, are as follows:

- that the authorisation for detention under the Bournewood Safeguards Procedure grants authority for P to be accommodated in hospital for medical treatment for mental disorder;
- P objects either to being accommodated for the purposes of treatment for mental disorder or to some or all of the medical treatment for mental disorder that is to be given in the context of such accommodation; and
- a donee or deputy has not validly consented to any of the matters to which P objects.

The detention for treatment of a mental disorder of a person, who is within the scope of the MHA 1983, under the Safeguards Procedure is only excluded where he objects *and* a properly appointed donee or deputy has not validly consented on his behalf. This appears to be confirmed by the Explanatory Notes to the MHA 2007 which amends the MCA 2005 to include Sch 1A[6]. By necessary implication, treatment for mental disorder *can* be given to such a person under the MCA 2005 regime if he does *not* validly object (see 16.46 below).

As far as the guardianship patient is concerned, detention for mental health treatment under the Bournewood Procedure is permissible as long as it does not conflict with the terms of the guardianship regime *and* as long as P does not validly object.

1 See MCA 2005, Sch 1A, paras 7–10 for the definition of a mental health regime.
2 MCA 2005, Sch 1A, para 8(1) defines a hospital treatment regime as one in which the relevant person is subject to a 'hospital treatment obligation'. That obligation includes persons who are liable to detention under MHA 1983, ss 2–4, 35–38, 44, 45A, 47–48 and 51. It includes those subject to MHA 1983, s 17 leave.
3 MCA 2005, Sch 1A, para 9 defines a community treatment regime as one in which a person is subject to a community treatment order under MHA 1983, s 17A (as amended) or other obligation of similar effect.
4 This phrase is defined at MCA 2005, Sch 1A, para 12. In essence it means that category of person who would meet the admission criteria for MHA 1983, s 2 or 3.
5 See MCA 2005, Sch 1A, paras 2 and 5 and see para 202 of the Explanatory Notes to the Mental Health Act 2007. The eligibility criteria are considered in detail in Chapter 9.
6 See para 202 of the Explanatory Notes to the Mental Health Act 2007.

Treatment for mental disorder: MCA 2005 or MHA 1983?

16.19 So where does this leave us in terms of the proper interpretation of s 28 of the MCA 2005? Read alongside the other relevant provisions of the MCA 2005 and the yet to be enforced provisions of Schs A1 and 1A, we can be clear about the fact that treatment for mental disorder cannot be *authorised or given under* the MCA 2005 except where the person concerned cannot be taken to be validly objecting.

If a patient is subject to the consent to treatment provisions of the MHA 1983, treatment for mental disorder will be governed by that statute rather than the principles of the MCA 2005. In consequence, the administration of psychotropic medication to a patient who is subject to s 17 leave of absence from hospital under the MHA 1983 cannot be lawfully authorised by reference to the MCA 2005. Treatment by medication in such a case must be given in accordance with the provisions of MHA 1983, ss 63 and 58 as described above. Where the consent to treatment provisions apply, they will regulate any treatment for mental disorder and treatment for mental disorder in such circumstances cannot be avoided or impeded by the use of advance decisions or other forms of substitute decision-making which *do* have an impact on the administration of treatment under the MCA 2005 (except in the circumstances specifically provided for in the new MHA 1983, s 58A described at 16.6, and also 16.5, fn 2, which will not be in force until October 2008). Conversely, where the consent to treatment provisions do *not* apply – or the person does not need to be deprived of their liberty to be treated, or treatment is for a person under MHA 1983 guardianship (excluding resisting patients), supervised discharge or for emergency/urgent treatment – then treatment for mental disorder may be given by reference to the principles of the MCA 2005[1]. This means that any applicable advance decisions and appropriate welfare LPAs will apply. In the case of a person who is subject to guardianship or merely falls within the scope of the MHA 1983, treatment for mental disorder may be given to person detained under the MCA 2005 as long as he is not resisting.

Whilst the MCA 2005 may be used instead of the MHA 1983 where both schemes could potentially be used for the treatment of mental disorder in incapacitated persons, the precise circumstances in which the MCA 2005 *ought* to be used when available remain far from clear. Indeed, the picture is further complicated by the MCA 2005, Sch 1A eligibility provisions (discussed below)[2].

1 The Government confirmed to the Joint Scrutiny Committee that MCA 2005, s 28 was not to be interpreted as excluding the use of MCA 2005 provisions in any case in which MHA 1983 powers could *potentially* be applied. The Joint Scrutiny Report, HL189/HC 1083 was published on 28 November 2003 (see para 219). This reflected similar concerns expressed by Professor Genevra Richardson in her written Memorandum to the Joint Committee on Human Rights (JCHR) (MIB 556).The Government's Response to the Report can be found at http://www.dca.gov.uk/pubs/reports/mental-incapacity.htm#part2. The Committee and Professor Richardson were concerned to ensure that s 28 did not lead to the use of the coercive powers of the MHA 1983 instead of the MCA 2005 in every case in which it was possible to use the MHA 1983. The result they feared would be that persons who might already be receiving care under the MCA 2005 would have to go through a potentially cumbersome process of admission under the MHA 1983 in order to receive treatment for mental disorder simply because such treatment could potentially be given under the MHA 1983. If s 28 were interpreted as widely as they feared, the use of the MHA 1983 would be required even if there were every incentive to administer that treatment without recourse to the MHA 1983. Such a case would be, for example, where the patient was non-resistant, the mental health treatment was in his best interests, and it could be safely and effectively administered without disruption of the MCA 2005 care regime to which he was already subject. See para 9 of Professor Richardson's written Memorandum to the Joint Committee (MIB 556).

2 Without clear statement to the contrary effect, these provisions may be open to the wide interpretation feared by the Joint Scrutiny Committee. See for more on this Robinson, R, *J Mental Health L* 37 2007, pp 35–37.

Detention under the MCA 2005

16.20 As described in detail in Chapter 9, a deprivation of liberty may be authorised under the Bournewood Safeguards Procedure in Sch A1 to the MCA 2005 or by the Court of Protection under MCA 2005, ss 4A, 15, 16 and 16A when those provisions come into effect. Implementation of these provisions has been delayed until April 2009; there is a draft Code of Practice (the draft Addendum code), draft secondary legislation and as stated previously, Chapter 13 of the Main Code which deals with the overlap between the MHA 1983 and the MCA 2005 is subject to revision. What follows should therefore be regarded as provisional. The position pending implementation of the new MCA 2005 provisions is dealt with specifically below.

Deprivation of liberty

16.21 The question of what amounts to a deprivation of liberty[1] is important in a context in which care is determined by the best interests of an individual as opposed to being designed primarily for the detention of those with mental disorder under the MHA 1983. Thus a care plan or treatment plan may contain elements pertaining to physical or mental health which require the person concerned to be restrained or indeed deprived of their liberty even for a short period. The task in relation to the MCA 2005 Scheme is for such potential deprivations to be recognised and properly authorised.

1 This question is addressed in detail in Chapter 9. See also MCA 2005, Sch A1, para 24.

Standard authorisation

16.22 Detention under the Bournewood Safeguards Procedure (or by the Court of Protection), unlike the MHA 1983, can occur in either a hospital or a care home. There is a wholly separate procedure for seeking a standard authorisation. What follows is a summary of that procedure. When a person is, or is likely to be deprived of his liberty:

A The 'managing authority' (the managers of the hospital or registered owner of the care home) of the hospital or care home must apply to the 'supervisory body' (the relevant PCT in respect of a hospital or the relevant local authority in respect of a care home) to have that deprivation of liberty authorised.

B In order to make such an application, it must appear to the managing authority that the six qualifying requirements[1] — age, mental health, mental capacity, best interests, eligibility and no refusals — are either met or are likely to be met within 28 days.

C The supervisory body is then required to commission assessments in relation to each of the qualifying requirements.

D If any of these assessments is negative, the supervisory body cannot authorise detention.

E If all of the assessments are positive the supervisory body must grant the authorisation and inform the managing authority, the person concerned and other personnel specified in Sch A1.

F The supervisory body is required to specify the period for which the authorisation will last, any conditions to be attached and the purpose for which the authorisation is given. The maximum period of a standard authorisation is 12 months but the period specified in the authorisation will usually be set by the best interests assessor who must set only the minimum period necessary in the circumstances.

1 See Chapter 9 and MCA 2005, Sch A1, Part 3 for the content of the six qualifying requirements.

Urgent authorisation

16.23 There is provision in Sch A1 for detention to be authorised by the managing authority for an initial seven day period in urgent cases (an urgent authorisation) but any extension of this seven day period may only be granted by the supervisory body.

Court of Protection

16.24 When the provisions of MCA 2005, ss 4A, 4B and 16A come into force, the Court of Protection will be empowered to authorise a deprivation of liberty as part of a welfare order made under the MCA 2005 or in the context of the administration of life-sustaining treatment. The eligibility criteria for detentions under a welfare order mirror those applicable to the Bournewood Safeguards Procedure. The Court of Protection will also act as the reviewing court in relation to standard and urgent authorisations and can determine liability in relation to these matters.

Contrast with the MHA 1983

Capacity

16.25 With respect to the standard authorisation, four of the assessments mentioned above are particularly relevant. In order for the mental capacity assessment to be met, the mental capacity assessor must conclude that the relevant person lacks the capacity to decide whether he should be accommodated in the relevant care home or hospital for care or treatment. In contradistinction to the MHA 1983 regime therefore, the absence of capacity is essential for detention under the MCA 2005.

Best interests

16.26 The best interests assessment is similarly crucial. The best interests assessor must decide whether there is or will be a deprivation of liberty in consequence of the proposed accommodation. If there is, or will be, he must conduct a full assessment in accordance with MCA 2005, s 4(7) to determine whether it is in the best interests of the relevant person to be detained. If detention is not in the relevant person's best interests, the deprivation of liberty cannot be authorised. Again, this requirement is in sharp contrast with the provisions which authorise detention under the MHA 1983.

Eligibility

16.27 As stated above, this is determined solely by reference to the application or putative application of the MHA 1983 to the person concerned. A person will, broadly speaking, be ineligible for detention under the MCA 2005 if adherence to a MHA 1983 regime to which he is subject rules it out. The eligibility criteria are difficult to distil but, in summary, a person will *not* be eligible if he is:

- detained under the MHA 1983;
- subject to a mental health regime (i e on leave of absence from detention under the MHA 1983, subject to guardianship, community treatment order or conditional discharge under the MHA 1983) *and* is subject to a measure in connection with the relevant mental health regime (i e hospital treatment, guardianship or community treatment) which would be inconsistent with detention under the Bournewood provisions;

- subject to a mental health regime, other than a guardianship regime, *and* the proposed authorisation would be, at least in part, for medical treatment for mental disorder in hospital;
- subject to guardianship, or would otherwise meet the criteria for detention under Part II MHA, *and* validly objects to some or all of the treatment at which the proposed authorisation is directed.

The eligibility criteria attempt to steer a path between the use of the MCA 2005 or MHA 1983 to achieve treatment in circumstances involving a deprivation of liberty. However, where there is a choice, none of the legislative provisions give healthcare professionals clear direction as to which regime ought to be used and, if so, in what circumstances. The varied ethical and practical difficulties thrown up by this lack of clarity are discussed in some detail below.

No refusals

16.28 The requirement for there to have been 'no refusals' means that a standard authorisation for detention under the Bournewood Safeguards Procedure cannot be given where there is either (a) a valid advance decision refusing some or all of the treatment envisaged or (b) a valid decision of a donee or deputy which would be flouted by the proposed accommodation for treatment or deprivation of liberty[1]. In this way, and again in contradistinction to detention under the MHA 1983, the autonomy of the person concerned is respected. Detention cannot be authorised if it is contrary to his express capacitous wishes or to the decision of a person to whom his decision-making power was validly delegated.

1 See MCA 2005, Sch A1, paras 18–20.

Relevant person's representatives

16.29 Schedule A1 makes specific provision for the appointment of a representative of the person concerned whose role it will be to represent and support him in all matters relating to the operation of the Bournewood Procedure. This will include the instigation of a review, the use of the complaints mechanism or the making of applications to the Court of Protection where appropriate[1]. This person will not necessarily be the same as the relevant person's nearest relative in the MHA 1983 context[2]. The role of the relevant person's representative (RPR) is additional to the role of any welfare donee or court deputy, but she may be recommended by the donee or deputy to the best interests assessor who may then make a recommendation to the supervisory body. The RPR must be selected by the supervisory body if all else fails. If for any reason there is no RPR, an IMCA must be appointed to perform that role. A crucial distinction between the RPR and a nearest relative under the MHA 1983 is that the RPR does not have the power to discharge the relevant person from detention.

1 See MCA 2005, Sch A1, Part 10 and the draft Addendum Code, para 4.2.

[2] Independent Mental Health Advocates (IMHA), specific to the MHA 1983 only, are now to be introduced when the MHA 2007 comes into force. They will provide an additional safeguard in relation to specific treatment decisions. See Chapter 6 on IMCAs at 6.33.

Unauthorised deprivation of liberty

16.30 A request for the supervisory body to determine whether there is an unauthorised deprivation of liberty may be triggered by any person via the managing authority. Once seized of a request for such a determination, the supervisory body is duty bound to appoint a person to carry out an assessment to determine whether the relevant person is being deprived of his liberty unless the request is frivolous or the issue has been recently and adequately decided. The assessment must otherwise be completed within seven days.

Reviews and challenge to detention

16.31 Reviews of a standard authorisation may be carried out by the supervisory body at any time but must be carried out if requested by the relevant person, his representative or the managing authority unless this is exempted by the provisions of Sch A1. Reviews may only be based on three grounds: non-qualification, change of reason and variation of conditions[1]. If after the review the supervisory body concludes that one of the qualifying requirements is not met, it must terminate the authorisation immediately. If the reason that a particular qualifying requirement was initially found to be met has changed, the supervisory must vary the authorisation to reflect the change. If there is a significant change in the relevant person's case, the supervisory body may vary the conditions attached to the authorisation in such a way as it thinks appropriate.

As stated above the Court of Protection will also act as a reviewing court in relation to standard and urgent authorisations and can determine liability in relation to these matters, namely, whether or not there has been an unlawful deprivation of liberty.

There is no review mechanism for orders authorising a deprivation of liberty made by the court as opposed to those made under Sch A1. Such orders must be subject to the control of the court making them.

[1] See Chapter 9, 9.97–9.104 for more on this.

Principle of least restriction

16.32 Section 1(6) of the MCA 2005 contains an express requirement for regard to be had to whether there is a less restrictive option whenever any act is done or decision made under the Act. This is not matched by any such statement in the primary MHA 1983 legislation, albeit that adherence to the principle is referred to in the MHA 1983 Code of Practice.

Children and young people: MCA 2005

16.33 The assessment of capacity of children and young people is discussed in Chapter 8 in the context of medical treatment. The provisions of the MCA 2005, with three exceptions, apply to young people over 16: s 2(5).[1] Those exceptions are that only those over 18 can make:

- a lasting power of attorney: s 9(2);
- an advance decision to refuse treatment: s 24(1);
- a will: s 18(2).

The MCA 2005 will apply to those over 16 who lack capacity (ie those who satisfy the diagnostic threshold). In relation to this category, there is however a potential overlap here with the Children Act 1989, and with the High Court's inherent jurisdiction in relation to children and young people. As the Main Code points out, there are currently no specific rules for deciding which regime should be utilised in respect of a young person in this category[2].

In cases where neither the MCA 2005 nor the Children Act 1989 supplies a solution, then recourse to the MHA 1983 or the High Court's inherent jurisdiction may be appropriate.

1 Chapter 12 of the Main Code applies and see also Chapter 13 herein for the relevant provisions regarding research.
2 Paragraph 12.7 sets out some examples of when recourse to the MCA 2005 might be appropriate.

Children under 16

16.34 With two exceptions under the MCA 2005, the care and treatment of children and young people under 16 is governed by the Children Acts, MHA 1983 and the common law.

The exceptions are as follows:

- the Court of Protection can make a decision about a child's property or finances if the child lacks capacity (within the meaning of the MCA 2005, not simply by virtue of age) and is likely to do so when reaching 18 (s 18(3));
- the offences of ill-treatment or neglect of a person lacking capacity apply to those under as well as over 16 (s 44).

Children and young people: MHA 1983

16.35 The MHA 1983 Code of Practice makes it clear that there is no minimum age limit for admission to hospital under the MHA 1983. However, for guardianship under the MHA 1983, or supervised after care, a person must have attained the age of 16[1]. The relevant legal framework is complicated and there is an overlap with the Children Act 1989. It is safe to say that the use of the MHA 1983 is likely to be appropriate where the predominant issue is a discrete need for treatment for a mental disorder[2].

MHA 1983, s 131(2) provides that anyone 16 or over 'capable of expressing his own wishes' can admit him or herself as an informal patient irrespective of the wishes of a parent or guardian[3].

The consent to treatment provisions of MHA 1983, Part IV apply to a child admitted to hospital for treatment under that Act[4].

1 See Chapter 31.1.

2 See Jones, R. *Mental Health Act Manual* (10th edn) para 4–272; general note to MHA 1983 Code of Practice para 31.2.

3 MHA 2007, s 43 amends and expands s 131(2) to reinforce the principle of autonomy for those aged 16 or over who may not be admitted to hospital informally under the MHA 1983 without their consent.

4 MHA 2007, s 27 inserts a new MHA 1983, s 58A to deal specifically with the administration of ECT and other specified forms of treatment in respect of which consent is required if the patient has capacity. An added safeguard is introduced where the patient is under 18 whereby a second opinion doctor must certify that the treatment is 'appropriate': s 58A(4). The best interests test does not apply.

Children under 16

16.36 As is the case for adults, admission will not be dependent upon incapacity. Parents, or those with parental responsibility, may arrange for informal admission of a child to hospital. However a 'Gillick' competent child may decide for himself (see Chapter 8 for more on children's competence), albeit that a resisting child's wishes may be overborne by parental consent. If a child's wish to be admitted is objected to by a parent, or similar, then the parents views should be seriously considered, but their objections will not necessarily prevail[1].

1 MHA 1983 Code of Practice, paras 31.6 and 31.7.

WHAT ARE THE IMPORTANT DISTINCTIONS BETWEEN THE TWO REGIMES?

16.37 The following table highlights the important distinctions between the MHA 1983 and the MCA 2005 regimes, many of which are evident from the preceding outline of the features of both schemes[1].

1 Specific acknowledgement is made of the reliance placed on Professor Richardson's Memorandum to the JCHR referred to at fn 1 to 16.19 above for the content of much of the comparison made in this table.

	MHA 1983	**MCA 2005**
Role of capacity	A person meets the criteria for detention, guardianship, supervised discharge etc, under the MHA irrespective of capacity	MCA 2005 applies only to those who lack capacity on a function specific basis

	MHA 1983	**MCA 2005**
Role of consent	MHA regime is a coercive regime specifically designed to provide compulsory treatment to patients who may actively resist. Medical and risk criteria govern the detention regime	MCA 2005 regime promotes patient autonomy and restricts treatment of resisting patients to a limited set of circumstances
Role of best interests	There is no requirement for decisions to be taken, or treatment authorised under the Act to be administered, in P's best interests	All decisions in respect of care, treatment and detention, taken under the MCA 2005 must be taken in P's best interests
Principle of least restriction	Is consigned to the MHA Code of Practice, para.1.1	Is contained on the face of the Act in s 1(6) and applies to all acts of care and treatment
Definition of treatment	Restricted to treatment for mental disorder even though it may include treatment ancilliary to the core mental health treatment and includes care: s 145(1)	Includes diagnostic and other procedures. Encompasses all medical treatment and care, including for physical disorders
Treatment for mental disorder	Must be dealt with under this regime if P has capacity and is resistant. Except for guardianship, if P requires detention in hospital, regardless of capacity	Can only be given in circumstances not excluded by s 28 e g emergency and guardianship and, if detained, as permitted by Sch 1A. Resistant persons cannot be detained for treatment for mental disorder under this regime
Treatment for physical disorder	Cannot be authorised under this regime	Can be given under this regime once P lacks capacity and can be given even if P is resisting or in emergencies, once capacity and best interest principles respected. If P has capacity recourse is to the common law only
Place of detention	Must be in a hospital	Can be in either a hospital or care home
Advance decisions	Not referred to in the MHA and are trumped by the consent to treatment provisions of Part IV save in limited circumstances.	Permit P make a decision, at a time when he had capacity to do so, to refuse specific treatment if incapacitated. P can neither be treated nor detained contrary to a valid advance decision save in very limited circumstances

	MHA 1983	MCA 2005
Safeguards	Panoply of safeguards to avoid arbitrary detention	Sch A1 now provides an array of similar safeguards but some differences in procedural protections highlighted below
1	Approval of Second Opinion Appointed Doctor required for involuntary medication and other serious medical treatment. Independent Mental Health Advocate to be introduced.	Approval of SOAD not required in any case but scheme underpinned by notion of best interests (see Chapter 15)
2	Nearest relative (NR) has power to discharge from detention under s 3 and wealth of other powers.	RPR cannot discharge from detention and powers not as extensive as NR
3	IMCAs are not required to be involved in decisions about serious medical treatment or accommodation (unless under MHA, s 117 as after care upon discharge from hospital)	IMCAs are required to be involved in the making of these decisions and may be instructed in other circumstances also
4	Detention under most common treatment section, s 3, subject to initial maximum period of 6 months	Detention pursuant to standard authorisation can, at present, last for up to 12 months
After-care upon discharge from detention	Section 117 provides specifically for this and is operable by reference to MCA 2005 principles	There is no express provision. MCA 2005 principles continue to apply
Children and young people	There is no age limit for admission to hospital. See s 131(2) in relation to those aged 16 and 17	MCA 2005 applies to those over the age of 16 with some exceptions
Offence of ill-treatment	Section 127. Maximum penalty is increased from 2 to 5 years: MHA 2007, s 42	Section 44 etc

THE EFFECT OF THE MCA 2005 ON THOSE SUBJECT TO MHA REGIMES

Advance decisions

16.38 The MHA 1983, Part IV consent to treatment provisions will trump any conflicting advance decision, donee of an LPA or a deputy. However, the MCA 2005 is not wholly irrelevant to the MHA 1983 context (16.6 above).

In relation to advance decisions, the Main Code advises that healthcare staff should still take account of an advance decision and consider whether the detained patient can be safely treated using a form of treatment which he has not refused in advance. The issue of capacity has been held to be relevant to the question of whether treatment to which a detained patient objects is therapeutically necessary within the meaning of Articles 3 and 8 ECHR and to the test under MHA 1983, s 58 which must be satisfied before a patient can be involuntarily medicated[1]. It can be assumed that the existence of an advance decision will now also be taken account of in these determinations.

Further, advance decisions will come to play a role in certain forms of treatment when the amendments to the MHA 1983 by the MHA 2007 come into force. ECT and other treatments which may be specified by the Secretary of State, and treatment of incapable patients can only be given if such treatment is not in conflict with a valid advance decision.

1 See *R (on the application of B) v S* [2005] EWHC 1936 (Admin), [2005] All ER (D) 38 (Sep).

Donees and deputies

16.39 As far as donees and deputies are concerned, they can neither consent to treatment under the MHA 1983 nor make decisions which conflict with the requirements of a guardianship regime on behalf of a patient under the MHA 1983. Detained patients can create LPAs and the Court of Protection can still appoint deputies in respect of such patients. However, if donees take decisions which conflict with the requirements of a particular mental health regime, such as a condition to maintain contact with health services in respect of a patient on s 17 leave, this will be treated as if it were the decision of the patient and could lead to the potentially adverse consequence of recall to hospital[1].

Attorneys and deputies are able to exercise the patient's rights under the MHA 1983 on behalf of patients provided that they have the requisite authority. They cannot, however, exercise the powers of the nearest relative unless they are in fact the patient's nearest relative.

1 See Main Code, paras 13.38–13.45. But see 16.5, fn 2 and 16.6 above for exceptions.

IMCAs

16.40 The instruction of an IMCA is not required for serious medical treatment for mental disorder given under MHA 1983, Part IV and is not required for a change of residence if the requirement to reside in a particular place arises out of an obligation under the MHA 1983 (eg the guardianship regime or supervised discharge regime). However, if the serious medical treatment does not fall under Part IV, the rules in relation to the instruction of

IMCAs are the same as for any other patient[1]. As stated above, patients under MHA 1983, s 117 after care if eligible, will be entitled to an IMCA for long term accommodation decisions.

1 See Main Code, paras 13.46–13.48. See chapter 6 generally.

WHICH REGIME?

16.41 The Main Code does provide some guidance on which regime ought to be used in what circumstances. However, some of the guidance has been superseded by the passage of the MHA 2007 which amended the MCA 2005 to include Schs A1 and 1A. Indeed, as stated before, Chapter 13 of the Main Code specifically indicates that the guidance therein on the relationship between the MHA 1983 and MCA 2005, and that in relation to protection from liability for persons providing care and treatment (Chapter 6), will need to be fully revised to take account of the Bournewood Provisions.

Having regard to the provisions enacted after the Main Code was drafted, and the foregoing analysis, it can safely be said that professionals ought to consider using the MHA 1983 to detain and treat and incapacitated persons in the following circumstances:

- Where the person needs treatment for mental disorder which cannot be given under the MCA 2005 (eg because the person has made a valid and applicable advance decision to refuse an essential part of the treatment intended to be given whether proposed to be administered under a Bournewood authorisation or not).
- Where it is not possible to assess or treat the person safely or effectively for mental disorder without the treatment being compulsory. This is because treatment for mental disorder cannot occur under any MCA 2005 detention regime if the person validly objects to it.
- Where there is good reason to believe that the person may not get the required treatment for mental disorder without recourse to the MHA 1983 and a member of the public may suffer harm in consequence. This is precisely the sort of situation in which detention for treatment for mental disorder might be justified by reference to the risk to the public.
- Where the person lacks capacity to decide on some elements of the treatment for mental disorder but has the capacity to refuse a vital element of it and does do so. If a person is known to have capacity in relation to a particular matter, treatment for that cannot be given under the MCA 2005.

In the Quick Summary provided at the beginning of Chapter 13 of the Main Code, it is also suggested that consideration ought to be given to use of the MHA 1983 where:

- it is not possible to give the person the care or treatment they need without doing something that might deprive them of their liberty; or
- the person may need to be restrained in a way that is not allowed under the MCA 2005.

These two circumstances will not necessarily point towards the use of the MHA 1983 when the Bournewood Safeguards Procedure is in force. At the time that the Main Code was drafted, there were no enacted provisions permitting the lawful deprivation of liberty under the MCA 2005. It is correct that, until those provisions come into force, consideration should be given to the use of the MHA 1983 if a deprivation of liberty is required, or if the proposed restraint will exceed that permitted by MCA 2005, s 6. However, two additional points ought to be noted:

- The MHA 1983 *can only* be used to effect detention for compulsory treatment if the admission criteria (the diagnostic and risk questions) for that Act are met.
- The MHA 1983 *cannot* be used where the person concerned requires treatment for a physical disorder.

The position before the MCA 2005 deprivation of liberty provisions come into force

16.42 Prior to the MCA 2005 a deprivation of liberty in this context was achieved via the MHA 1983 or the inherent jurisdiction of the High Court. The position now, and prior to the amendments of the MCA 2005 coming into effect, is less clear. For practical purposes it is suggested that what follows below is what is discernible about the position at law as currently understood.

If the treatment sought to be given in conditions which may amount to a deprivation of liberty is treatment for mental disorder, and it is believed that the MHA 1983 criteria will be met, serious consideration ought to be given to the use of the MHA 1983. This will provide the person with the panoply of safeguards available under the MHA 1983, including access to the MHRT. As far as the carers or professionals are concerned, the use of the MHA 1983 in these circumstances will also avoid any suggestion that the person is being unlawfully deprived of his liberty.

If the treatment proposed is treatment for physical disorder, or if the MHA 1983 admission criteria will not be met, it will be possible to turn to the Court of Protection for a welfare order under s 16 to obtain an authorisation of a deprivation of liberty as a necessary part of a care plan or other assessed need. As discussed elsewhere in this book, the provisions of the MCA 2005 are not currently Article 5 compliant for this purpose[1]. The court should, therefore, be invited to adapt its approach to comply in the manner set out in *Re PS (incapacitated or vulnerable adult)*[2]. Any authority for detention given by the court must be adapted to comply with the requirements of Article 5 ECHR. The minimum requirements according to Munby J are:

(i) The detention must be authorised by the court on application made by the local authority and *before* detention commences.
(ii) Subject to the exigencies of urgency or emergency the evidence must establish unsoundness of mind of a kind or degree warranting compulsory confinement. In other words there must be evidence establishing at

least a prima facie case that the individual lacks capacity and that confinement of the nature proposed is appropriate.

(iii) Any order authorising detention must contain provision for adequate review at reasonable intervals, in particular with a view to ascertaining whether there still persists unsoundness of mind warranting compulsory confinement[3].

1 The precise foundation of the Court of Protection's jurisdiction in this regard is discussed in Chapter 7 at 7.8 and Chapter 10 at 10.34.
2 [2007] EWHC 623 (Fam), [2007] 2 FLR 1083.
3 [2007] EWHC 623 (Fam), [2007] 2 FLR 1083 at para 23.

The position after the MCA 2005 deprivation of liberty provisions come into force

16.43 The Bournewood Safeguards and new powers of the Court of Protection are intended to provide a scheme for authorising the detention of incapacitated persons. It will not therefore be necessary to use the MHA 1983 if the Bournewood Safeguards Procedure applies or where the Court of Protection is empowered to authorise a deprivation of liberty. It must however be remembered that the ineligibility criteria contained in MCA 2005, Sch 1A will prevent the court and the Safeguards Procedure from authorising the detention and treatment for mental disorder of a resistant patient. Care must therefore be taken to ascertain whether the person concerned is objecting to mental health treatment, in accordance with the provisions of the draft Addendum Code at paras 5.37–5.48, before a decision is made about whether the MCA 2005 route is the appropriate one.

Special considerations applying to those who are subject to guardianship and those 'within the scope of the Mental Health Act'

16.44 These apply after the new MCA 2005 provisions come into force only. According to the provisions of MCA 2005, Sch 1A, those who are subject to guardianship and those who fall within the scope of the MHA 1983 cannot be detained for treatment for mental disorder under the MCA 2005 if they validly object to such treatment. It is anticipated that the decision as to eligibility/ineligibility of these categories of person for MCA 2005 detention will prove the most difficult to determine and a closer examination is therefore required.

Guardianship

16.45 The Main Code suggests that guardianship may be the best option for a person who lacks capacity to make relevant decisions in the following circumstances[1]:

(a) it is important that one person or authority should be in charge of making decisions about where the person should live (for example where there have been long-running or difficult disagreements about where the person should live);

(b) it is thought that the person will probably respond well to the authority and attention of a guardian, and so be more prepared to accept treatment for the mental disorder (whether they are able to consent to it or it is being provided for them under the MCA 2005), or
(c) authority is needed to return the person to the place they are to live (for example a care home) if they were absent.

A patient who is subject to the guardianship regime may be detained under the MCA 2005 if two conditions are met:

- It does not conflict with a requirement imposed by the guardianship regime[2]. For example, a guardian's right to impose residence at a specified place cannot be countermanded under the MCA 2005. However, as suggested in Chapter 9, if the guardian does not object to the patient being accommodated in the care home or hospital in which the proposed Bournewood detention would occur, that patient would not be ineligible for the Bournewood detention on this ground.
- It is for the purpose of being given medical treatment for mental disorder, but only if (a) she does not object to the relevant accommodation and/or treatment for mental disorder; and (b) if a validly appointed donee or deputy has not consented to the matters to which he objects.

What these particular ineligibility provisions indicate is that the adult guardianship regime and MCA 2005 detention are not intended to be entirely mutually exclusive. What the adult guardianship regime under the MHA *cannot* do, however, is authorise a deprivation of liberty[3]. In consequence, the guidance given in the Main Code on the circumstances in which guardianship may be the best option hold true but guardianship alone will not suffice where it is envisaged that detention will be necessary to effect appropriate care and treatment.

Where detention is thought to be appropriate in respect of a person subject to guardianship questions do arise as to the correct choice of regime. The answers are not clear cut, but the following is intended to elucidate the issues.

Case study 1

Mr H, aged 25, has a learning disability with a psychotic depression and is subject to guardianship with a requirement that he reside in a care home. The clinical team decides that he would benefit from a course of psychotropic medication for his depression with monitoring and supervision which could only be safely and effectively managed in hospital. If there is no objection from the guardian to his residence being temporarily changed for this purpose, and Mr H is unresisting, then this treatment could in theory be given in hospital under the MCA 2005 with an appropriate authorisation for detention if necessary[4]. Such a decision should properly weigh up the benefits, or otherwise, of using the MHA 1983 as an alternative. For the patient the MHA 1983 contains important added safeguards under Part IV eg the need for a second opinion in the event that the treatment were to continue beyond three months (see above) if he cannot consent to the treatment. A practical solution might involve obtaining a second opinion even if the MCA 2005 were to be used. This might be an option urged by any IMCA or other family and friends consulted. The deciding factor, however, is likely to be the need to detain Mr H should he resist being in hospital. If that were necessary, the MHA 1983 may be preferable (assuming all the admission criteria were met) and less cumbersome than applying to the court for an authorisation under the MCA 2005. The guardianship must then, however, be discharged, which adds another layer of complication to the case.

This is precisely the kind of case in which commentators have suggested that the guidance contained in the legislation and accompanying Codes provides little assistance[5]. It is currently understood that the decision will be left to the relevant healthcare professionals and whilst the government has made clear that MCA 2005 treatment will not be precluded in such cases, there has been no official statement from the Government to date which encourages the use of the MCA 2005 in these circumstances[6].

In practical and welfare terms, when the Bournewood provisions come into force, there will be sufficient safeguards in place to make MCA 2005 detention in this case the preferred option. However, until that stage, it may be thought that the MHA provides better automatic safeguards than might be obtained via s 16 of the Court of Protection or the use of the inherent jurisdiction of the High Court.

In other cases determining factors may include:

(a) Whether the proposed treatment is treatment to which special regulations as to administration without consent apply under the MHA 1983, eg psychosurgery. This treatment can *only* be given under the MHA 1983 having regard to the provisions of MHA 1983, s 57 and MCA 2005, s 28 since consent is always required.
(b) Whether the treatment for mental disorder can be properly monitored and supervised outside of the MHA 1983 regime (eg it involves the administration of psychotropic medication and it is considered that the care plan would be most effective under the MHA 1983 if the patient later resisted).

1 See Main Code, para 13.20.
2 See Case D, Scenario 2, Chapter 9 and MCA 2005, Sch 1A, para 3.
3 This was specifically acknowledged by the JCHR in its 7th Progress Report, *15th Report of Session 2006–07*, HL 112/HC 555 at para 1.30. It is also stated in clear terms at para 13.16 of the Main Code.
4 See MHA 1983 Code of Practice para 13.10(a), but there is nothing to suggest that a temporary informal admission to hospital even for treatment for mental disorder is not permissible in such circumstances. Where the guardian is the local authority, they must comply with the welfare provisions under MHA 1983, s 116.
5 See in particular Robinson, R, 'Amending the Mental Capacity Act 2005 to provide for deprivation of liberty', *J Mental Health L*, May 2007, pp 25–40 at p 37.
6 The Department of Health's 'Briefing Sheet – Deprivation of Liberty Safeguards' published in November 2007 merely reiterates the statement made in the DOH's November 2006 Briefing Sheet. It states that: 'The new procedure cannot be used to detain people in hospital for treatment of mental disorder in situations where the Mental Health Act 1983 could be used instead if they are thought to object to being in hospital or treatment. This will mean that people who object will be treated in broadly the same way as people with capacity who are refusing treatment for mental disorder and who need to be detained as a

result. People who need to be covered by the deprivation of liberty safeguards will be mainly those with significant learning disabilities or elderly people suffering from dementia, but will include a minority of others who have suffered significant injury.'

Those 'within the scope of the Mental Health Act'

16.46 The uncertainties for this category of patient are similar to those affecting guardianship patients in the sense that the dilemmas as to choice of regime where the patient is not resisting exist in both cases. In many cases the decision taken as to whether a person should be dealt with under a regime in which risk is central (MHA) or one in which best interests is central (MCA) may be arbitrary.

Case study 2

Mrs S suffers from Alzheimers disease. She needs treatment for her mental disorder in hospital but objects to it. She later agrees to treatment[1]. Mrs S satisfies the MHA 1983 criteria and must be detained under the MHA 1983 for such treatment in hospital to be given initially. When she stops resisting the treatment, it might be considered that she could be discharged to a residential care home. Whereas the treatment regime will remain entirely the same in the care home setting, she cannot be detained under the MHA 1983 in that setting since MHA 1983 detention can only take place in hospital. On her move to the care home, therefore, a Bournewood authorisation will need to be sought if it is thought that the regime in the home deprives her of her liberty. This patient will therefore have been subject to two distinct regimes for the same treatment (though not simultaneously), primarily because the MHA 1983 does not facilitate detention in care homes[2].

Case Study 3

Mrs P is suffering from a learning disability which is not 'associated with abnormally aggressive or seriously irresponsible conduct' and objects to treatment for mental disorder under the MCA 2005. Mrs P would appear to fall between two stools. She cannot be detained under the MHA 1983 (other than for assessment under s 2) because her mental disorder does not bring her within the MHA 1983[1]. On the other hand she is objecting to treatment for mental disorder within the meaning of MCA 2005, Sch 1A and therefore cannot be detained for treatment under the Bournewood Safeguards Procedure. The only recourse in this circumstance would be to the common law (see Chapter 7 at 7.52).

1 This example is in part based on an example given by Robinson, R , 'Amending the Mental Capacity Act 2005 to provide for deprivation of liberty', *J Mental Health L*, May 2007, pp 25–40 at p 37. *Surrey County Council v MB, SB and a PCT* [2007] EWHC 2290 (Fam) is a case in which the MHA 1983 criteria were not met and the person was resistant to treatment.

2 Robinson, R, above, at p 37 is particularly critical of this inflexibility. He states that: 'It is difficult to identify any principled reason why a different regime, with different legal criteria and procedural safeguards should apply according only to the place of detention.'

3 The four categories of mental disorder set out in MHA 1983, s 1 are to be replaced by the simple definition of mental disorder, 'any disorder or disability of the mind' after amendment by MHA 2007, s 1. MHA 2007, s 2 does, however, stipulate that for all of the

relevant treatment sections of the MHA 1983, a person suffering from a learning disability will still not be detainable unless that disability is associated with abnormally aggressive or serious irresponsible conduct.

CONCLUSION

16.47 Many anomalies and uncertainties may therefore result from the problematic boundaries between the two regimes. The complexity of determining which regime ought to be used, and indeed the difficulty involved in discerning the principles on which such a decision should be based in some cases, is undesirable. There is much to be said for the suggestion that it would have been much cleaner, clearer and principled to have one scheme for those who object to a care regime which deprives them of their liberty and another for those who do not object to such a regime[1]. This would avoid anachronistic and arbitrary decisions about whether the MHA 1983 or the MCA 2005 ought to be used. More importantly, if the legislative aim was for the MCA 2005 to be used in preference to the MHA 1983 where possible, it would have been helpful for this to have been set out by way of legislative provision.

The points about the relationship between the two regimes which are at this stage clear are:

- Only treatment for mental disorder can be given under authority of the MHA 1983. Treatment for physical disorders (and in some circumstances mental disorders) can be given under the MCA 2005.
- Where the consent to treatment provisions apply, ie where a person is liable to detention under the MHA 1983, the MHA 1983 will govern the administration of treatment.
- Advance decision and LPAs will have only limited impact on the consent to treatment provisions of the MHA 1983 (ie can be trumped by those provisions except where the contrary is provided, eg the new MHA 1983, s 58(A))
- Decision-making under the MCA 2005 is governed by the twin principles of best interests and capacity/autonomy whereas under the MHA 1983, decision-making (both in relation to treatment and detention) continues to be driven by a 'clinical model'[2] with a significant focus on risk.
- Capacity and best interests are not irrelevant to MHA 1983 detention and treatment. Capacity will be relevant to issues of consent to treatment since it will always be relevant to the validity of consent. It is also relevant to questions of therapeutic necessity. The MCA 2005 principles should still be used, as far as possible, in relation to treatment and care plans. Chapter 13 of the Main Code and Chapter 15 of the MHA 1983 Code reflect this.
- The MCA 2005 will apply to those entitled to MHA 1983, s 117 after care services.
- Detention for treatment for mental disorder under the MCA 2005 is restricted, in relation to those subject to guardianship and those who would meet the MHA 1983 admission criteria, to non-resisting patients (Sch 1A, paras.2, 3 and 5).

- Detention/treatment under the MCA 2005 cannot take place in defiance of a valid advance decision or a decision of a donee (MCA 2005, s 26(1); Sch A1, paras 18–20).
- Detention/ treatment for mental disorder under the MCA 2005 of those who are not subject to mental health regimes or do not fall within the scope of the MHA 1983 is regulated by the capacity and best interests principles of the MCA 2005.

1 This is the suggestion made by Robinson, R, 'Amending the Mental Capacity Act 2005 to provide for deprivation of liberty', *J Mental Health L*, May 2007, pp 25–40 at p.39.

2 See Dawson, J and Szmukler, G, 'Fusion of Mental Health and Incapacity Legislation', *British Journal of Psychiatry* (2006), 188, 504-509 at p 505.

Chapter 17

HUMAN RIGHTS STANDARDS: DOMESTIC AND INTERNATIONAL

INTRODUCTION

17.1 This chapter will set out the human rights standards under domestic law that may be relevant under the MCA 2005, and will touch on some of those under international law. In particular it should be noted that Schedule 3 to the MCA 2005 gives effect to the Hague Convention on the International Protection of Adults (s 63). It will also consider some of the situations where issues concerning human rights are most likely to arise when dealing with the issue of capacity and with those who lack capacity. It is beyond the scope of this book to provide a comprehensive analysis of these complex issues and reference should also be made to specialist texts.

In particular the following areas will be discussed:

- Advance decisions.
- Research.
- Medical treatment.
- Residential placements and care.
- Access to information.
- Compulsory detention.

- Religious beliefs.
- Right to marry.
- Discrimination.

THE HUMAN RIGHTS ACT 1998

17.2 There are two ways in which the Human Rights Act 1998 (HRA 1998) secures and protects human rights, first it requires that legislation be compatible with the rights set out in the European Convention on Human Rights 1950 (the Convention) and second it requires public authorities to act compatibly with Convention rights. These two requirements will be considered further below, following which the Convention rights themselves will be considered.

Compatibility of the MCA 2005 with Convention rights

17.3 The Mental Capacity Bill was scrutinised by the Joint Committee on Human Rights (JCHR) for its compatibility with the Convention, as well as with other international instruments relevant to the care and treatment of those who lack capacity[1]. The Bill was initially considered in November 2004 and a number of questions were raised. Following the Government's response and amendments to the Bill the JCHR provided a final report in January 2005[2]. Some concerns still remained, in particular with regard to advance decisions, withdrawal of life-sustaining treatment and research (these will be considered further below at 17.16, 17.18 and 17.46 respectively). However, the JCHR expressed the view that 'the Bill should be broadly welcomed from a human rights perspective, because it enhances the ability of people who lack capacity to make their own decisions where they can and makes it more likely that sound decisions will be made on their behalf where they cannot make those decisions for themselves.'[3]

A statement of compatibility with the Convention, under HRA 1998, s 19, was made by the government.

1 See further below 17.53–17.58.
2 Scrutiny: First Progress Report, Fourth Report of Session 2004–2005 (Scrutiny Report).
3 Scrutiny Report, para 4.5.

Primary Legislation

17.4 The HRA 1998 carefully preserves the balance and separation of power between the legislature, the executive and the judiciary in the manner in which it protects and secures human rights. The courts have a duty to read all legislation as far as it is possible to do so compatibly with Convention rights (see HRA 1998, s 3); however, if they are not able to read primary legislation compatibly then they do not have the power to strike it down. In addition under s 6(2) a public body has a defence to a claim under HRA 1998, s 7 if primary legislation prevented it from acting in any other way.

Where the courts find primary legislation to be incompatible with Convention rights then the only likely remedy (save possibly from compensation) would be a declaration of incompatibility under HRA 1998, s 4. Only the High Court and above can make a declaration of incompatibility. Such a declaration will lead to remedial action under HRA 1998, s 9.

Therefore if a case raises an incompatibility between provisions within the MCA 2005 and Convention rights in the future, the only remedy, unless the MCA 2005 can be read compatibly under HRA 1998, s 3, is likely to be a declaration under HRA 1998, s 4 and possibly compensation.

Public authorities must act compatibly

17.5 The HRA 1998 makes it unlawful for a 'public body' to act incompatibly with the Convention rights that are set out in Sch 1 to the Act[1].

What constitutes a 'public authority' was not fully defined by Parliament in the HRA 1998, save that it includes a court or tribunal, and 'any person certain of whose functions are functions of a public nature'[2]. In addition it stipulates that in relation to a particular act, a person is not a public authority if the nature of the act is private[3].

Importantly therefore the HRA 1998 requires not only core public bodies to act compatibly with Convention rights, but also 'hybrid' bodies, so those bodies which, while private, carry out a function that is 'public in nature'. The question of whether the function being performed is a public function is to be widely interpreted, and is wider than the amenability test in public law. In *Aston Cantlow & Wilmcote with Billesley Parochial Church Council v Wallbank*[4] it was stated that 'a generously wide scope' should be given to the expression 'public function' in HRA 1998, s 6(3)(b) and that there is no one single test of universal application to determine what a public authority is for the purposes of HRA 1998, s 6; a number of factors will be relevant but no one factor is likely to be determinative.

Doctors and other healthcare professionals within the NHS will clearly be 'public authorities' under HRA 1998, s 6 and so they must ensure that they act compatibly with patients Convention rights[5]. The same will be true of those providing social care under the provisions of community care legislation[6].

1 HRA 1998, s 6(1).
2 HRA 1998, s 6(3).
3 HRA 1998, s 6(5).
4 [2003] UKHL 37; [2004] 1 AC 546.
5 For example see *Razzel v Snowball* [1954] 3 All ER 429, [1954] 1 WLR 1382; *R (on the application of Wilkinson) v Broadmoor Special Hospital Authority* [2001] EWCA Civ 1545, [2002] 1 WLR 419. In *Glass v United Kingdom* (2004) EHRR 15, para 71 it is noted that the UK Government did not contest this issue.
6 For example under the National Assistance Act 1948, ss 21 and 29; Children Act 1989; Chronically Sick and Disabled Persons Act 1970; National Health Service Act 1977, ss 1–3; National Health Service and Community Care Act 1990; Local Authority Social Services Act 1970; and the MHA 1983, s 117. See Chapter 7.

Private care homes

17.6 There have however been cases involving private care homes where, despite this 'generously wide scope' being given to the meaning of 'public function', the courts have found that the homes were not public authorities for the purposes of HRA 1998.

The case of *YL (By Her Litigation Friend The Official Solicitor) v Birmingham City Council*[1] (*YL*) concerned an 84-year-old woman who suffered from Alzheimer's and who had been living in a nursing home owned and run by a private limited company. She had been given a notice to quit by the nursing home. The contract between the local authority and the nursing home was that the home would provide accommodation and care in line with the care plan devised by the local authority. In addition the home also agreed to provide nursing care assessed as needed by the local NHS primary care trust ('PCT'). The local authority funded the place at the home and the PCT paid for the nursing care.

The House of Lords, by a majority of three to two, upheld the decision of the lower court that the private nursing home was not a 'public authority' and dismissed the appeal. Lord Bingham and Baroness Hale dissented. The JCHR disagree with the majority decision and have stated that they agree with the minority view, broadly for the reasons given in their speeches[2]. The opinions are helpful, however, as they set out the approach that should be taken when assessing whether a function falls within HRA 1998, s 6.

All members of the House agreed that the determination of whether a body is a 'public authority' is reached not by looking at the body in question, but by looking at the function involved. What is clear from the HRA 1998 is that if the function is a private one then HRA 1998, s 6 will not apply[3]; the important consideration is therefore the function and not the body.

1 [2007] UKHL 27, [2007] 3 All ER 957.
2 Eighteenth Report of Session 2006–2007 'The Human Rights of Older People in Healthcare', 14 August 2007, para 159. See also *Ninth Report of session 2006–2007, The Meaning of Public Authority under the Human Rights Act*, HL Paper 7/HC 410.
3 HRA 1998, s 6(5).

Identifying a 'public function'

17.7 The approach that should be taken when deciding whether a function is a public one is first to identify the nature of the body performing it, so is it a private or public body? And then to go on and consider other relevant factors that include:

- the role and responsibility of the state;
- the nature and extent of any public interest;
- the nature and extent of any statutory power or duty;
- whether the state directly or indirectly regulates, supervises and/or inspects the performance of the function in question; and

– whether, and to what extent, the state directly or indirectly funds the function.

It is important not to assume that just because of the decisions in *YL*, and the earlier decision in *R (on the application of Heather) v Leornard Cheshire Foundation*[1] where the private care homes were found not to be 'public authorities', that it will always be the case that private homes can never be bound by HRA 1998, s 6. Each case will depend on its own facts.

It is suggested that in any event the primary duty to protect the Convention rights of those in private care homes will rest and remain with the local authority and/or PCT, and they will have to ensure that when contracting with private providers of care that Convention rights are fully respected and protected. The decisions to date are unfortunate, however, because they impede the development of a culture of protecting human rights at all levels, from the grass-roots to top of government.

Clearly those detained under the MHA in private hospitals will however be protected by the HRA 1998, and those looking after and treating such patients must therefore act compatibly with their Convention rights.

1 [2002] EWCA Civ 366; [2002] 2 All ER 936.

Remedies

17.8 If a public body has acted, or failed to act, in a way that violates one of the Convention rights, then a cause of action exists under HRA 1998, s 7[1]. The public body can be required to act compatibly, and/or pay the victim of the violation 'just satisfaction'. In some cases 'just satisfaction' will require the public body to pay compensation, but in others the declaration of a violation will be sufficient. Levels of compensatory awards under the HRA 1998 are to be in line with those awarded by the European Court of Human Rights[2], and are often less than those that the domestic courts award in other damages claims.

In some cases there will be no measurable damage as such, but the European Court of Human Rights does sometimes in these cases award a sum for 'anxiety and frustration'. In *R (on the application of Greenfield) v Secretary of State for the Home Department*[3], it was said that where damages were awarded by the European Court for anxiety and frustration, they tended to be for modest sums and that although judges in England and Wales were not bound by awards of the European Court, they should not aim to be significantly more or less generous than the European Court might be expected to be if it was willing to make an award at all on the facts.

In cases where the damage caused is akin to tortious damage then the level of award is likely to be more in line with domestic levels. In *R (on the application of Bernard) v Enfield London Borough Council*[4] where damages were awarded under HRA 1998, s 8 for a breach of Article 8, Sullivan J took the view that awards made under s 8 should be comparable with tortious awards where there was no justification for a reduction.

1 As noted above (17.4) there is a defence to a s 7 claim where the public body could not have acted differently due to primary legislation (s 6(2)). In these circumstances the only remedy would be a declaration of incompatibility under HRA 1998, s 4.
2 See HRA 1998, s 8(4).
3 [2005] UKHL 14, [2005] 2 All ER 240.
4 [2002] EWHC 2282 (Admin), [2003] LGR 423, (2003) HRLR 4, (2003) UKHRR 148, (2003) HLR 27, (2003) BLGR 423, (2003) ACD 26, (2002) Times, 8 November.

Limitation period

17.9 A claim under the HRA 1998 must be brought within a year of the act complained of, although the court retains a discretion to allow a claim outside the limitation period if it is equitable to do so having regard to all the circumstances[1].

1 See HRA 1998, s 7(5).

CONVENTION RIGHTS

17.10 Many of the functions performed under the MCA 2005 and by those caring for those who lack capacity are likely to engage Convention rights. The rights most likely to be engaged are Article 2, the right to life, Article 3, freedom from torture, inhuman and degrading treatment, Article 5, right to liberty, Article 6, right to a fair and public hearing, Article 8, right to respect for family life, Article 9, the right to freedom of religion, Article 12, the right to marry, and Article 14, right not to be discriminated against in the protection of rights. As stated earlier it is beyond the scope of this book to provide an in depth analysis of these issues for which reference to other specialist texts should be made.

Article 2: the right to life

17.11 Article 2 imposes both a negative duty on the state not to arbitrarily deprive a person of their right to life[1], and a positive obligation to protect the right to life[2]. There is also a duty on the state to have an effective investigation into the death of a person where the state may have violated either the negative duty or the positive obligation[3]. In addition Article 2 imposes an obligation on the state to provide proper healthcare to those it detains[4].

1 For example, see *McCann v United Kingdom* (1996) 21 EHRR 97.
2 For example, see *Osman v United Kingdom* (1998) 29 EHRR 245; *W v Ireland* App No 9360/81, (1983) 5 EHRR 506; *Ergi v Turkey* (2001) 32 EHRR 18. See also *R (on the application of Hurst) v HM Coroner for Northern District of London* [2003] EWHC 1721 (Admin), [2003] All ER (D) 80 (Jul).
3 For what constitutes an 'effective investigation' see *Jordan v United Kingdom* (2003) 37 EHRR 2. See also with regard to domestic cases *R (on the application of Middleton) v West Somerset Coroner* [2004] UKHL 10, [2004] 2 AC 182.
4 See *McFeeley v United Kingdom* (1981) 3 EHRR 161, *McGlinchey v United Kingdom* (2003) 37 EHRR 41.

Negative duty

17.12 In relation to those covered by the MCA 2005, Article 2 will potentially be engaged by any negligent act on behalf of a medical professional or carer that leads to a death, and issues concerning the continuance of withdrawal of life-sustaining treatments.

Positive obligation

17.13 The positive obligation would be engaged where, for example, the state failed to put in place a proper regulatory system to ensure professional levels of care or, where the state has failed to ensure the provision of sufficient training and equipment for resuscitation where patients in a ward are, for example, at risk of suicide attempts (see 17.14 below).

Suicide risk

17.14 In addition Article 2 may be engaged where a person in the care of the state commits suicide. The positive obligation to protect life will be engaged where a state actor 'knew or ought to have known' that there was a 'real and immediate risk to life' and failed to take measures reasonably available to protect life. An example would be where a detained patient took their own life in circumstances where there was an obvious suicide risk and the authority failed to provide a safe environment[1].

1 *Keenan v United Kingdom* (2001) 33 EHRR 38. See also *Anna Savage v South Essex Partnership NHS Foundation Trust & Mind (Intervener)* [2007] EWCA Civ 1375, [2007] All ER (D) 316 (Dec).

Foreseeable risks

17.15 The European and domestic case law makes clear that Article 2 creates an obligation to prevent not only risks created by third parties or the individual themselves, but also other foreseeable risks to life. An example in a care home or hospital situation would be where a person with dementia is left in a room unattended with an obvious risk to life.

In *R (on the application of Longfield Care Homes Ltd) v HM Coroner for Blackburn*[1] an elderly resident of the care home who suffered from dementia was left unattended in a room with a window open. The lady subsequently fell out of the window and sustained injuries (fractures). The lady died soon after from bronchopneumonia. Although the death itself was not due to the injuries sustained it was found by the inquest jury that they contributed to the death by inducing further stress and immobility, which could have further exacerbated the pneumonic process. The case did not raise Article 2 issues directly, but it can be seen as an example of a case where Article 2 may be engaged in cases of vulnerable adults being exposed to foreseeable risks.

1 [2004] EWHC 2467 (Admin), 14 October 2004.

Advance decisions[1]

17.16 During the passage of the bill a real concern that was raised involved advance decisions and the question of legalised euthanasia. There were fears expressed that the MCA 2005 would open the door to wider acceptability to euthanasia and that the provisions concerning advance decisions did not properly protect the right to life[2]. Specifically the JCHR raised concerns about the adequacy of the safeguards provided to ensure that advance decisions to refuse treatment were correctly interpreted and complied with.

Amendments were made to the Bill to require that decisions concerning life-sustaining treatments be recorded in writing and witnessed. The JCHR also wanted there to be a requirement that those making advance decisions had to have had the benefit of medical advice explaining the consequences of such decisions. This requirement was, however, not included, although in Chapter 9 of the Main Code it is recommended that people thinking about making an advance decision get advice from healthcare professionals, but that it is up to the person whether they do this or not[3].

1 See Chapter 3 for detailed discussion on Advance Decisions.
2 JUSTICE took the view that the provisions of the MCA 2005 with regard to Advance decisions adequately protected Article 2 (and Article 3) rights. See Revised JUSTICE Briefing for Commons and Second Reading, October 2004, para22.
3 Main Code, para 9.14.

Artificial nutrition and hydration

17.17 The JCHR was also concerned that the MCA 2005 did not specify in terms that artificial nutrition and hydration (ANH) was 'treatment' and that there was therefore a risk that an advance decision refusing life sustaining treatment in general might be construed as including ANH when this was not intended. Reference was made to the case of *W Healthcare NHS Trust v KH*[1], as an example of a case where confusion had arisen as to whether an advance directive under the common law refusing life sustaining treatment extended to include ANH. The court found it did not. In the end the Government decided against including a specific reference to ANH in the MCA 2005 as it was of the view that the requirement to specify precisely the treatment being refused was sufficient to meet this concern[2].

1 [2004] EWCA Civ 1324, [2005] All ER (D) 94 (Jan).
2 Scrutiny Report, paras 4.25–4.33.

Withdrawal of life-sustaining treatment

17.18 The domestic courts have found that the withdrawal of life-sustaining treatment from terminally ill patients will not violate Article 2[1] (the European Court has yet to rule on the matter). Article 2 does not impose an obligation to prolong life at all costs. If responsible medical professionals take the view that treatment is no longer in the patient's best interests there can be no violation of Article 2.

The common law however recognised that an advance directive requiring the provision of ANH is, in certain circumstances, determinative of whether ANH should be continued. In *R (on the application of Burke) v GMC and Disability Rights Commission*[2] the court found that where a competent patient indicated his/her wish to be kept alive by the provision of artificial nutrition and hydration, any doctor who deliberately brought that patient's life to an end by discontinuing the supply of artificial nutrition and hydration would not merely be in breach of duty but would be guilty of murder. The JCHR wanted there to be a provision in the MCA 2005 allowing for an advance decision to not only specify the refusal of treatment but also requiring ANH[3]. This was rejected by the government. A patient can include such a request in an advance statement, but not in an advance decision.

With regard to decisions of a donee, MCA 2005, s 11(7)(c) and (8) expressly refer to the giving and refusing of consent to the carrying out or continuation of treatment or life sustaining treatment. If a donee refuses consent to a treatment then a clinician cannot proceed with treatment, and likewise if a donee gives consent a clinician may proceed. However, this does not include demanding any particular treatment. A donee is therefore in the same position as someone who has made an advance decision and so cannot demand that ANH continues.

The positive obligation under Article 2 is likely not only to cover the provision of ANH but also other treatment that, while not usually life sustaining, can be so in certain circumstances. For example, giving antibiotics to a patient whose life would be at risk were they to contract a usually harmless infection.

It should be noted that under the MCA 2005 a person will not be found to be liable for withdrawing or withholding treatment if he reasonably believes that an advance decision exists that is valid and applicable[4].

1 *Airedale NHS Trust v Bland* [1993] AC 789, *Re A (Children) (Conjoined twins: Surgical Separation)* [2001] Fam 147.
2 [2005] EWCA Civ 1003, [2006] QB 273, [2005] 3 WLR 1132.
3 Scrutiny Report, paras 4.34–4.38.
4 See s 26(3).

Article 3: torture, inhuman and degrading treatment or punishment

17.19 Article 3 protects against 'torture, inhuman and degrading treatment or punishment'. It absolutely prohibits any treatment that falls within its scope. As with Article 2, Article 3 contains both a negative obligation not to inflict treatment that amounts to torture, or inhuman and degrading treatment, and a positive obligation to protect against such treatment[1]. There is also a procedural obligation to investigate any treatment that may amount to a violation of Article 3[2].

In order for treatment or punishment to fall within the scope of Article 3 the level of ill treatment must reach a minimum level. The test was first stated in *Ireland v United Kingdom*[3], and has been re-iterated in many cases since. It is that:

'Ill-treatment must attain a minimum of severity if it is to fall within the scope of article 3. The assessment of this minimum is in the nature of things relative: it depends on all the circumstances of the case, such as the duration of the treatment, its physical or mental effects and, in some cases, the sex, age and state of health of the victim.'

1 *A v United Kingdom* (1998) 27 EHRR 611; *Z v United Kingdom* (2002) 34 EHRR 3.
2 *Assenov v Bulgaria* (1998) 28 EHRR 652.
3 (1978) 2 EHRR 25.

What is inhuman and degrading treatment?

17.20 The European Court had differentiated between treatment that amounts to 'torture' and that which is 'inhuman and degrading', although all such treatment is prohibited absolutely. In *Pretty v United Kingdom*[1] at para 52 it was said:

> 'As regards the types of 'treatment' which fall within the scope of Article 3 of the Convention, the Court's case-law refers to 'ill-treatment' that attains a minimum level of severity and involves actual bodily injury or intense physical or mental suffering (see *Ireland v. the United Kingdom*, cited above, p. 66, § 167; *V. v. the United Kingdom* [GC], no. 24888/94, § 71, ECHR 1999-IX). Where treatment humiliates or debases an individual, showing a lack of respect for, or diminishing, his or her human dignity, or arouses feelings of fear, anguish or inferiority capable of breaking an individual's moral and physical resistance, it may be characterised as degrading and also fall within the prohibition of Article 3 (see amongst recent authorities, *Price v. the United Kingdom*, no. 33394/96, §§ 24–30, ECHR 2001-VII, and *Valašinas v. Lithuania*, no. 44558/98, § 117, ECHR 2001-VIII). The suffering which flows from naturally occurring illness, physical or mental, may be covered by Article 3, where it is, or risks being, exacerbated by treatment, whether flowing from conditions of detention, expulsion or other measures, for which the authorities can be held responsible (see *D. v. the United Kingdom* and *Keenan*, both cited above, and *Bensaid v. the United Kingdom*, no. 44599/98, ECHR 2000-I).'

It is clear therefore that where treatment does, or could, exacerbate suffering arising from an illness or injury, then it could fall within the scope of Article 3. It is also clear that there is no requirement for there to be an intention to treat someone in an inhuman or degrading way before a violation of Article 3 is found.

In *Price v United Kingdom*[2] a violation of Article 3 was found where the conditions in which the applicant, who was confined to a wheelchair and also suffered from recurrent kidney problems, was detained in prison. While there was no evidence of any positive intention to humiliate or debase her, the European Court found a violation of Article 3. Ms Price spent three days in cold conditions, with inadequate sleeping arrangements (she had to sleep in her wheelchair as she was unable to use the bed), and without appropriate toilet arrangements; male officers had been required to assist in lifting her on to and off the toilet, and by the time of her release she had to be catheterised because the lack of fluid intake and problems in getting to the toilet had caused her to retain urine.

There is conflicting case law in relation to the question of whether there can be an Article 3 violation where a person is unaware of the treatment they are receiving. In *NHS Trust A v M and NHS Trust B v H*[3], Butler-Sloss found that in order for there to be a violation of Article 3 the 'victim had to be aware of the inhuman and degrading treatment which he or she is experiencing or at least in a state of physical or mental suffering'. It is suggested however that the correct view is that expressed by Mumby J in *R (on the application of Burke) v General Medical Council*, Mumby J said that:

> 'In my judgement treatment is capable of being 'degrading' within the meaning of Article 3, whether or not is arouses feelings of fear, anguish and inferiority in the victim. It is enough if judged by the standard of right thinking bystanders – human rights violations obviously cannot be judged by the standards of the perpetrators – it would be viewed as humiliating or debasing the victim, showing a lack of respect for, or diminishing, his or her human dignity.'[4]

1 [2002] 2 FCR 97.
2 (2002) 34 EHRR 53.
3 [2001] 1 All ER 801.
4 [2005] EWCA Civ 1003, [2005] 3 WLR 1132 at [149].

Therapeutic necessity

17.21 Medical treatment will not fall within the scope of Article 3 if it can be 'convincingly shown' that it is a 'therapeutic necessity'. It must be noted that this does not amount to a justification for the treatment, but it prevents the treatment reaching the required level to cross the threshold into Article 3. As stated above Article 3 prohibits absolutely ill treatment that meets the threshold[1].

1 *R (on the application of Wilkinson) v Responsible Medical Officer Broadmoor Hospital* [2001] EWCA Civ 1545, [2002] 1 WLR 419, *Herczegfalvy v Austria* (1992) 15 EHRR 437.

Acts of individuals

17.22 Convention rights protect individuals from acts of the state that violate their rights, and require the state to protect their rights. There is no direct responsibility on the part of the state for acts of private individuals. In this way they have a 'vertical' rather than 'horizontal' effect. However, the state is under an obligation to have in place regulatory provisions and a legislative framework to protect individuals from the acts of others, and so the state has an obligation to protect individuals from ill treatment[1].

1 See or example *E v United Kingdom* App No. 33218/96, Judgment of 26 November 2006.

Ending life to prevent suffering

17.23 Article 3 does not allow a person to end another's life in order to prevent them from suffering ill-treatment. Article 3 has to be read in light of Article 2. In *Pretty v United Kingdom* the court rejected an argument that the failure of the State to give an undertaking that it would not prosecute the applicant's husband were he to assist in her suicide was a violation of Article 3[1].

1 (2002) 35 EHRR 1 at [56].

Forced treating and forcefeeding

17.24 Treating a person who has capacity against their will is very likely to constitute inhuman or degrading treatment. Whether the same is true with regard to those who lack capacity is more difficult to decide.

Forced treatment, including force-feeding will not reach the minimum threshold if it is a 'therapeutic necessity from the point of view of established principles of medicine'[1]. It should be noted that those detained will be seen to be particularly vulnerable and so great care needs to be taken when deciding whether to give medical treatment. In *Herczegfalvy* the applicant was a psychiatric in-patient detained under the Austrian equivalent of the Mental Health Act. He went on hunger strike and was forcibly administered food and neuroleptics; in addition he was kept in seclusion and handcuffed to a security bed for several weeks. The European Court stated:

> '82. The Court considers that the position of inferiority and powerlessness which is typical of patients confined in psychiatric hospitals calls for increased vigilance in reviewing whether the Convention has been complied with. While it is for the medical authorities to decide, on the basis of the recognised rules of medical science, on the therapeutic methods to be used, if necessary by force, to preserve the physical and mental health of patients who are entirely incapable of deciding for themselves and for whom they are therefore responsible, such patients nevertheless remain under the protection of Article 3 (art. 3), whose requirements permit of no derogation.'

The established principles of medicine are admittedly in principle decisive in such cases; as a general rule, a measure which is a therapeutic necessity cannot be regarded as inhuman or degrading. The court must nevertheless satisfy itself that the medical necessity has been convincingly shown to exist.

1 *Herczegfalvy v Austria* (1992) 15 EHRR 437 and *Nevmerzhitsky v Ukraine*, 5 April 2005, unreported.

Living conditions

17.25 Article 3 issues could also be raised in relation to the conditions in which a person is living, although it is more likely that such conditions will raise issues under Article 8 (see further 17.44 below). If a person were to be detained in an inappropriate environment then the minimum level of severity threshold may be crossed, so for example detaining a psychiatric patient in a non-therapeutic environment or one which exacerbated their mental health problems may amount to a violation of Article 3[1]. In *Kudla v Poland*[2] the European Court said that under Article 3 the state must ensure that a person is detained in conditions that are compatible with respect for human dignity.

If a person were to be living in conditions of destitution then Article 3 is likely to be violated. In *R (on the application of Limbuela) v Secretary of State for the Home Department*[3] (which concerned a destitute asylum seeker), Lord Bingham said:

> '... if there were persuasive evidence that a [person] was obliged to sleep in the street, save perhaps for a short and foreseeably finite period, or was seriously hungry, or unable to satisfy the most basic requirements of hygiene, the threshold would, in the ordinary way, be crossed.'

In cases where the person concerned was in the actual care of the state (for example detained under the Mental Health Act or under the Bournewood provisions) the threshold is more likely to be crossed.

1 *Aerts v Belgium* (2000) 29 EHRR 50.
2 (2002) 35 EHRR 11, at para 94.
3 [2005] UKHL 66, [2006] 1 AC 396.

Use of restraints

17.26 The use of restraints may in some circumstances amount to a violation of Article 3. For example in *Henaf v France*[1] the use of handcuffs on a 75-year-old prisoner in order to shackle him to his bed the night before an operation was found to be a violation of Article 3 and in *Mouisel v France*[2], handcuffing together with the continued detention of a seriously ill prisoner was also found to be a violation of Article 3.

1 (2005) 40 EHRR 44.
2 App No 29462/95, judgment of 28 November 2000, unreported.

Article 5: the right to liberty

17.27 Article 5 protects the right to liberty and guards against arbitrary and unlawful detention. Article 5(1) sets out in what circumstances it is lawful for the state to deprive a person of their right to liberty, including in Article 5(1)(e) the detention of persons of 'unsound mind'.

In order for a person to be lawfully detained on the grounds of 'unsound mind' (except in emergencies) they must be shown by objective medical evidence to be suffering from a mental disorder of a nature or degree to warrant compulsory confinement and it must persist throughout the period of detention[1].

1 *Winterwerp v Netherlands* (1979) 2 EHRR 387, para 42.

Scope of Article 5[1]

17.28 Article 5 is concerned with the deprivation of liberty. It is not engaged by mere restrictions on liberty[2] (*Engels v Netherlands*[3]). In determining whether the level of restraint or restriction amounts to a detention under

Article 5, regard should be had to a whole range of criteria, including the type of detention, its duration, its effects and the manner of implementation (*Guzzardi v Italy*[4]).

Guardianship under the MHA 1983 should not amount to a deprivation of liberty, although in reality if accompanied by a condition of residence it may well cross the line into a deprivation of liberty. A locked door at night in a care home or hospital would be very unlikely to amount to a deprivation of liberty, but on the other hand the fact that a ward is not locked will not necessarily mean that there is no detention. In *Ashingdane v United Kingdom*[5] a patient residing in a psychiatric hospital was found to be detained even though he was not always on a locked ward and was on occasion free to leave unaccompanied.

A one off emergency measure of locking a person in a room for a short duration in order to keep him safe would be unlikely to amount to a detention. However, the duration of a detention will not be decisive, for example detaining someone just to carry out a compulsory blood test could amount to a detention[6].

In *R (on the application of Munjaz) v Mersey Care NHS Trust*[7] it was held that the seclusion of a detained patient does not engage Article 5 as is concerns the conditions of detention and not the detention itself.

It should be noted that it has been made clear that nothing in MCA 2005, ss 5 and 6 can amount to a deprivation of liberty under Article 5 of the convention (see Chapter 9)[8]. Article 5 will not be engaged where a person consents to a detention, as long as the consent is clearly established, is unequivocal, and the person has capacity to give consent.

1 For a more detailed discussion about what amounts to a deprivation of liberty see Chapter 9.
2 Lesser restrictions on liberty are governed by Article 2 of the 4th Protocol to the Convention, but the UK is not a party to that Protocol.
3 (1976) 1 EHRR 647.
4 (1980) 3 EHRR 333.
5 (1985) 7 EHRR 528.
6 *X v Austria* App No 8278/78 18 D.R. 154, the applicant alleged that compulsory submitting him to a blood test would violate Article 5. The Commission found that enforcing a blood test on a person is a deprivation of liberty even if this deprivation is of very short length. However, the Commission found in this case that it did not violate Article 5 as there was a court order in place and so it was justified under Article 5(1)(b), which permits detention of a person for non-compliance with the lawful order of a court or in order to secure the fulfilment of any obligation prescribed by law .
7 [2006] 2 AC 148.
8 See MHA 2007 for amendments and Chapter 7 at 7.8, Chapter 10 at 10.34 and Chapter 16 at 16.42 for more on deprivation of liberty.

Conditions of detention

17.29 In *Ashingdane* it was found that in order for a detention to be lawful under Article 5(1)(e), detention had to be in a hospital, clinic, or other appropriate institution authorised for the detention of such persons. However, the Convention does not allow a person to choose where they should be detained and in what conditions or what treatment they should receive (see also *Valle v Finland*[1], *Aerts v Belgium*[2].)

1 [2000] MHLR 255, (2000) 30 EHRR CD 59.
2 (2000) 29 EHRR 50.

Procedural safeguards

17.30 In order to further protect against arbitrary detention Article 5(4) provides the procedural safeguard of the right to have the lawfulness of a detention to be decided speedily by a court. The right is to a 'speedy' review[1], but this is determined by the facts of each case[2]. A state must set up its' legal system to ensure that Article 5(4) is complied with and delays on the grounds of work load or administrative convenience will not prevent a breach of Article 5(4). It will be imperative therefore that if the Court of Protection is called upon to determine whether a person is being lawfully detained it does so 'speedily'. Another key question will be the availability of legal aid; in order to comply with Article 5(4) there must be the provision of legal aid to enable applications to the Court of Protection to be made.

1 *E v Norway* (1990) 17 EHRR 30.
2 *Sanchez-Reisse v Switzerland* (1987) 9 EHRR 71.

Compensation for Breach of Article 5

17.31 Article 5(5) provides the right to compensation for a violation of Article 5. For an exposition of likely levels of awards see *R (on the application of KB and others) v Mental Health Review Tribunal and another*[1]. For many of the claimants in KB, where no significant levels of distress could be shown, the finding of a violation was found to be an adequate remedy ('just satisfaction'). In cases where significant distress was found (so could be shown by for example reference to medical records), damages in the region of £1,000 were awarded. The highest award was £4,000 where it was shown that not only was there significant distress caused, but also deterioration in mental state and a loss of opportunity for release.

1 [2003] EWCH 193 (Admin), [2003] 2 All ER 209.

Article 6: the right to a fair trial

17.32 Article 6(1) guarantees the right to a fair and to a public hearing within a reasonable time by an independent and impartial tribunal in determination of civil rights and obligations and of any criminal charge.

Public hearing

17.33 The right to a public hearing is intended to protect litigants from secret hearings without public scrutiny. However Article 6(1) does not prevent private hearings in some cases, and the exceptions include for 'the protection of the private life of the parties'.

As a general rule hearings before the Court of Protection are to be held in private[1] to ensure that the privacy of the person who lacks capacity is safeguarded, but the rules do allow the court to admit the media and members of the public where it considers it is appropriate to do so. Judges of the Court of Protection must be careful to ensure that the correct balance is struck between the right to a public hearing and the right to privacy of those involved in order to comply with Article 6(1).

The right to a public hearing also includes a right to an oral hearing, but again this right can be limited in cases where the law and facts are straightforward and not in dispute. Again the judges of the Court of Protection will have to ensure that they strike the right balance between administrative and economical convenience and the right to a public hearing[2]. The CoP Rules set out the factors to be considered when deciding whether or not to have an oral hearing[3], an additional factor will have to be whether in order to satisfy Article 6(1) an oral hearing needs to take place.

1 See CoP Rules, Part 13. See also Chapter 10 at 10.78.
2 *Scarth v United Kingdom* App No ADD, Judgment of 22 July 1999; *Varela Assalino v Portugal*, App No 64336/01, *Dory v Sweden* App No 28394/95, Judgment of 12 November 2002 and *Salomonsson v Sweden* App No. 38978/97; *Miller v Sweden* App No 55853/00 Judgment of 8 February 2005.
3 CoP Rules, r 84(3).

Within a reasonable time

17.34 The right to a hearing within a reasonable time reflects the 'importance of rendering justice without delays which might jeopardise its effectiveness and credibility'[1]. What constitutes a reasonable time will depend on the case; factors that will be relevant are the complexity of the case, what is at stake for the applicant, the conduct of the relevant authorities, including the courts, and the conduct of the applicant. Certain types of cases call for particular diligence, which will include cases concerning the elderly and incapacitated.

1 *Pelissier v France* (2000) 30 EHRR 715, for domestic cases see *Porter v Magill* [2001] UKHL 67, [2002] 2 AC 357; *Prosecutor Fiscal v Watson and Burrows* [2002] 1 AC 379.

Determination of a civil right or obligation

17.35 For Article 6 to be engaged there must be a 'determination of a civil right or obligation'. In *Winterwerp* the European Court found that depriving the applicant of his ability to deal with his property automatically when he was admitted to hospital amounted to a determination of his civil rights and therefore the guarantees in Article 6(1) applied.

In *R (on the application of Wilkinson) v The Responsible Medical Officer of Broadmoor Hospital*[1] it was found the decision to forcibly treat a patient inevitably determined civil rights (see para 35). The decision to detain will also be a determination of a civil right and obligation and so rights arise under Article 6(1), although in reality this right is likely to be sufficiently protected by the requirements of Article 5.

1 [2001] EWCA Civ 1545, [2002] 1 WLR 419.

Right of access to a court

17.36 The right of access to a court has been read into the notion of a fair trial. Access to court is not however an absolute right[1]; restrictions are permitted but only in so far as they pursue a legitimate aim and are proportionate. Reasonable limitation periods and time limits can be lawful[2], as can restrictions on vexatious litigants. Security of costs can operate as a restriction on access to court and therefore they need to be treated with caution, it may be appropriate to make such an order on appeal, but it is less likely to be appropriate at first instance[3]. Court fees can also amount to an unjustified restriction on access to court, whether they do will depend on the circumstances of the case, in particular on the ability of the applicant to pay, and the phase of the proceedings in which they are imposed[4].

Immunities which prevent access to court under limited circumstances can be lawful. The immunity from liability, save where there has been bad faith or lack of reasonable care, and the requirement for leave in MHA 1983, s 139 has been found to be compatible with Article 6(1)[5].

1 Although the right to a fair trial is.
2 *Stubbings v United Kingdom* (1997) 23 EHRR 213.
3 *Tolstoy Miloslavsky v United Kingdom* (1995) 20 EHRR 442.
4 *Kreuz v Poland* App. No. 28249/95 (2001) 11 BHRC 456.
5 *Ashingdane v United Kingdom* (1985) 7 EHRR 528.

Legal aid

17.37 Article 6 does not require legal aid to be made available for all civil proceedings; however, under certain circumstances the lack of state provision of legal assistance can interfere with the right of access to court depending upon the nature and complexity of the case[1].

It is permissible to restrict the provision of legal aid on the ground that the cost of the litigation is disproportionate to likely damages[2], and, as long as a decision is not arbitrary, on the grounds that the claim has no reasonable prospects of success[3].

1 *Airey v Ireland* (1979) 2 EHRR 305.
2 *Stewart-Brady v United Kingdom* (1997) 24 EHRR CD 38, App Nos 27436/95 and 28406/95.
3 *X v United Kingdom* App No. 8158/78 21 DR 95.

Procedural safeguards

17.38 The requirements of fairness in civil proceedings contained in Article 6(1) are not as exacting as those in criminal matters in Article 6(3). Although as a minimum requirement, each party must be afforded a reasonable opportunity to present his or her case, including his or her evidence, under conditions that do not place him/her at a substantial disadvantage vis-à-vis his or her opponent[1]. This will also include the right to disclosure in order to be able to properly prepare for the case and meet any arguments made against you.

In addition, procedural fairness places a duty on the tribunal/court to 'conduct a proper examination of the submissions, arguments and evidence adduced by the parties'[2].

1 *Dombo Beheer BV v Netherlands* (1994) 18 EHRR 213.
2 *Kraska v Switzerland* App no 13942/88 (1993) 18 EHRR 188s, para 30.

Article 8: protection of private life, family and correspondence

17.39 Article 8 protects the right to respect for private and family life, home and correspondence and so is likely to be engaged in a variety of different ways in respect of those who lack capacity, for example the giving or refusing of medical treatment, the right to have contact with family members, issues concerning residency, access to information, and participation in decision making processes. In full it provides:

> '(1) Everyone has the right to respect for his private and family life, his home and his correspondence.
>
> (2) There shall be no interference by a public authority with the exercise of this right except such as is in accordance with the law and is necessary in a democratic society in the interests of national security, public safety or the economic well-being of the country, for the prevention of disorder or crime, for the protection of health or morals, or for the protection of the rights and freedoms of others.'

Unlike Articles 2, 3 and 6, Article 8 is a qualified right and so an interference with respect for family life may be justified. But to be a lawful interference the requirements in Article 8(2) must be complied with, so the interference must be prescribed by law, serve a legitimate aim, be necessary and proportionate and non-discriminatory.

Article 8 not only prohibits states from interfering with the right to respect for family life, but also creates a positive obligation on the state to take appropriate measures to ensure that the right to family life is enjoyed[2].

1 *Markx v Belgium* (1979) 2 EHRR 330.

Scope of Article 8

17.40 As stated above, Article 8(1) guarantees the right to respect for private and family life, home and correspondence. The concept of 'private life' includes both the physical and psychological integrity of a person and is capable of encompassing many things, as the European Court explained in *Pretty v United Kingdom*[1]:

> 'the concept of 'private life' is a broad term not susceptible to exhaustive definition. It covers the physical and psychological integrity of a person.'

And at para 65 that:

> 'The very essence of the Convention is respect for human dignity and human freedom.'

The scope of Article 8(1) also extends to include the right to develop as an individual, to 'establish and develop relationships with other human beings' and the right of the disabled to participate in the life of the community and to have 'access to essential economic and social activities and an appropriate range of recreational and cultural activities'[2].

Additionally Article 8 creates positive obligations on the state to take appropriate measures designed to ensure, to the greatest extent feasible, that a disabled person is not 'so circumscribed and so isolated as to be deprived of the possibility of developing his personality'[3].

1 (2002) 35 EHRR 1, at 35–36, para 61.
2 *Niemietz v Germany* (1992) 16 EHRR 97 at para 29.
3 *Botta v Italy* (1998) 26 EHRR 241 and *A v East Sussex County Council* [2003] EWHC 167 (Admin) at para 99, [2003] All ER (D) 233 (Feb).

Acts of individuals

17.41 In theory, as stated above, Convention rights are only designed to regulate conduct between the individual and the state. The reality is, however, that the European Court has intervened on a number of occasions in relation to disputes and violations of Convention rights between private parties. The mere fact that a public authority is not directly responsible for a breach of an individual's Convention right does not render Convention rights inapplicable[1]. In certain circumstances public authorities come under a duty to protect private individuals from breaches of the ECHR by other private individuals[2].

Furthermore, a breach of a Convention right can be established where a court makes an order in litigation between private parties or fails to provide a remedy[3]. Under the HRA 1998 public authorities specifically include courts and tribunals and so in making decisions and providing judgments courts and tribunals must respect the Convention rights of the parties before it.

1 *X & Y v Netherlands* (1985) 8 EHRR 235; *Costello-Roberts v United Kingdom* (1993) 19 EHRR 112; *Rommelfanger v Germany* (1989) 62 DR 151.
2 *A v United Kingdom* (1998) 27 EHRR 611.
3 *Hoffmann v Austria* (1993) 17 EHRR 293; *Casodo Coca v Spain* (1994) 18 EHRR 1.

Qualifications

17.42 Article 8(2) allows for restrictions and interferences with Article 8(1) rights as long as they are lawful, pursue a legitimate aim, are necessary and proportionate and non-discriminatory. Once a measure or decision falls within Article 8(1) it is for the person wishing to limit or interfere with the right to justify the action taken, or failure to act.

The test of proportionality and necessity is much stricter then the test of reasonableness. While it may be reasonable to interfere with a right, it may not be necessary or proportionate.

'Necessary' does not mean indispensable, but neither does it mean 'reasonable' or 'desirable' (*Sunday Times v United Kingdom*[1]). What it implies is a pressing social need and that pressing social need must accord with the requirements of a democratic society, the essential hallmarks of which are tolerance and broad-mindedness (*Handyside v United Kingdom*[2]).

What 'proportionality' requires is that there is a reasonable relationship between the means employed and the aims sought to be achieved. Essentially what the Court is required to do is determine whether a measure of interference which is aimed at promoting a legitimate public policy is either unacceptably broad in its application or has imposed an excessive or unreasonable burden on certain individuals (*Sporrong & Lonroth v Sweden*[3]).

It has been recognised by the domestic courts that where measures, acts or decisions of public authorities engage Convention rights, the correct approach to assessing the lawfulness of the act or decision in question is not the traditional *Wednesbury* unreasonableness test, but the test of proportionality[4].

1 (1979) 2 EHRR 245.
2 (1976) 1 EHRR 737.
3 (1982) 5 EHRR 35.
4 *R (on the application of Daly) v Secretary of State for the Home Department* [2001] 2 AC 532.

Accommodation and contact

17.43 Article 8 is wide enough to encompass lack of association with others and seclusion as well as the right to have contact with family members. When making best interest decisions the right to respect for family life will be of some significance. It will affect decisions about residence as consideration will need to be given to proximity to family and friends and availability of recreational activities; it will also be highly relevant to decisions concerning contact.

Living conditions

17.44 Article 8 will also be engaged in relation to living conditions. If a person is living in very poor conditions, but they are conditions that do not cross the threshold for Article 3, they may nevertheless amount to a violation of Article 8.

In *R (on the application of Bernard) v Enfield London Borough Council*[1] the court did not find that the threshold for Article 3 had been crossed but did find a violation of Article 8. The case concerned a severely disabled woman with limited mobility (she was dependent on an electronic wheelchair) and who suffered from incontinence and diabetes. She was cared for at home by her husband, who also looked after their six children who lived with them. Due to mortgage arrears the family had to move out of their specially adapted house and they fell to be assisted with finding suitable accommodation by the local authority under the National Assistance Act 1948, s 21(1)(a). The authority failed to provide suitably adapted accommodation. The court found that the authority was under an obligation to take positive steps to enable the claimants and their children to lead as normal a family life as possible, which would have secured the claimant's physical and psychological integrity and restored her dignity as a human being. The failure to act was said to show a lack of respect for the claimants' private and family life and was a breach of Article 8.

1 [2002] EWHC 2282 (Admin), [2003] LGR 423, [2002] All ER (D) 383 (Oct).

Medical treatment

17.45 Even a minor interference with the physical integrity of an individual is an interference with the right to respect for private life under Article 8(1), if it is carried out against the individual's will (*Storck v Germany*[1]).

Again medical treatment may raise issues under Article 8 where the minimum level threshold of Article 3 has not been reached. Although the overriding of an individual's right of autonomy may pursue a legitimate aim under Article 8(2), namely the 'protection of health' and 'the protection of the rights and freedoms of others' it must, however, be shown to be 'necessary', that is to say it must correspond with a pressing social need and be proportionate to that aim. This is, essentially, the same approach as required under Article 3: is the treatment a 'therapeutic necessity from the point of view of established principles of medicine' (*R (on the application of B) v Ashworth Hospital Authority*[2])?

In *Glass v United Kingdom*[3], the European Court had to consider whether force-treating a severely handicapped child with diamorphine in a life threatening situation against her mother's wishes amounted to a violation of Article 8(1). In particular it was argued by the child's mother that the treating doctors should have sought a decision of the High Court as to 'best interests' before administering the treatment. The court found that the decision to impose treatment in defiance of the mother's objections gave rise to an interference with the child's right to respect for his private life, and in particular his right to physical integrity. This interference was found not be justified as the doctors should have had recourse to the courts in order to decide on that course was in the 'best interests' of the child.

1 (2005) 43 EHRR 96, para 168.
2 [2005] UKHL 20, [2005] 2 AC 278, [2005] 2 WLR 695 at [36].
3 [2004] 1 FCR 553, [2004] 1 FLR 1019, (2004) 39 EHRR 15.

Research

17.46 The provisions in the MCA 2005 concerning research on those who lack capacity could raise issues under Article 8[1]. The JCHR in its first progress review raised real concerns about the lack of safeguards provided[2]. In particular the JCHR was concerned about the use of the phrase 'reasonable grounds for believing' in s 31(4) with regard to the need to include those who lack capacity within a research project in order to ensure its effectiveness. The JCHR was of the view that the wording should be 'no alternative' so as to reflect the internationally recognised standards. Likewise the JCHR were concerned that the requirement for there to be a benefit to the patient is weaker in the MCA 2005 than is required by international standards.

For a full discussion of research under the MCA 2005 see Chapter 13.

1 Sections 30–34.
2 Fourth Report of session 2004–2005, para 4.51–4.47.

Personal data

17.47 Article 8 also protects personal data, both its collection and retention, access to it and disclosure of it without consent. This aspect of Article is dealt with in detail in Chapter 14.

Article 8 provides for the right to have access to public records in certain circumstances. For example in *Gaskin v United Kingdom*[1] the applicant had been in foster care all his life and wanted access to information held concerning his foster placements as he believed he had been ill treated. The access was denied as some of those who had contributed to the data refused consent to its disclosure. The European Court found that the applicant had a vital interest in receiving the information and that the domestic procedures for access violated his rights under Article 8. While it could be compatible with Article 8 for access to information to be dependent on the consent of others, this has to be balanced against the interest of the individual seeking disclosure.

However, the disclosure of personal information without the consent of the person concerned will amount to a violation of Article 8, unless it can be justified on the basis of some overriding public interest[2]. Safeguards must be in place to protect access to and disclosure of such information[3].

1 (1990) 12 EHRR 36.

2 See *MS v Sweden* (1997) 28 EHRR 313.
3 See *Z v Finland* (1997) 25 EHRR 371.

Procedural safeguards

17.48 It is now well established that Article 8 incorporates procedural safeguards where decisions concerning family life are concerned. In *TP and KM v United Kingdom*[1] the court said:

> 'while there are no explicit procedural requirements contained in Art. 8, the case law establishes that where decisions may have a drastic effect on the relations between a parent and a child and may become irreversible, there is a particular need for protection against arbitrary interference.'

In *McMichael v United Kingdom*[2] the court said:

> '... not only does the procedural requirement inherent in Article 8 cover administrative proceedings as well as judicial proceedings, but it is ancillary to the wider purpose of ensuring proper respect for, *inter alia*, family life. The difference between the purpose pursued by the respective safeguards afforded by Articles 6(1) and Article 8 may, in the light of the particular circumstances, justify the examination of the same set of facts under both Articles.'

It is likely that most, if not all, decisions taken on behalf of a person who lacks capacity will engage Article 8, and it will therefore be necessary to ensure that that person concerned is involved and able to participate to the greatest extent possible with decisions made. A failure to do so may result in a violation of the procedural rights under Article 8.

1 [2001] 2 FCR 289 at [72].
2 (1995) 20 EHRR 205 at paras 91–92.

Intimate relationships

17.49 The right to private life also includes sexual life, and sexual identity[1]. In *Bruggemann and Scheuten v Germany* the European Commission said:

> 'The right to respect for private life is of such scope as to secure to the individual a sphere within which he can freely pursue the development and fulfilment of his personality. To this effect, he must also have the possibility of establishing relationships of various kinds, including sexual, with other persons'[2].

Decisions concerning marriage and sexual partners are excluded from the MCA 2005, s 27, but clearly in order to protect an incapacitated person's right to such relationships under Article 8 consideration must be given to this aspect of a person's private life when making best interests decisions.

1 *Dudgeon v United Kingdom* (1981) 4 EHRR 149; *Norris v Ireland* (1991) 13 EHRR 186.
2 (1997) 3 EHRR 244, para 55.

Article 9: the right to freedom of religion

17.50 Article 9 protects the right to freedom of thought, conscience and religion. Like Article 8 it is a qualified right and so may be limited in accordance with Article 9(1).

The qualified nature of the right arises in relation to the manifestation of religion and belief. It is for a person to prove that their right to manifest religion and belief has been interfered with, and it is then for the state to justify their actions on the basis of legality, necessity, proportionality and non-discrimination

Article 9 will raise additional considerations for those assessing best interests; a person's religion and beliefs must be taken into account. So for example, where it is known that a person is a vegetarian, or his religion prescribes a certain diet, this must be respected once he loses capacity.

Article 12: the right to marry and found a family

17.51 Article 12 gives 'men and woman' of marriageable age the right to marry and found a family. Although the right is expressed in absolute terms limitations are permitted and the right is subject to national laws. For example the European Court has found that restrictions on the right of prisoners to 'found a family' do not breach Article 12.

Decisions concerning marriage, divorce, civil partnerships, sexual relationships, adoption and consent to fertility treatment are all excluded from the MCA 2005, s 27 (see Chapter 7 in particular 7.47 on excluded decisions). Decisions made under the MCA 2005 are unlikely therefore to engage Article 12.

Article 14: the right not to be discriminated against in the protection of rights

17.52 Article 14 protects against discrimination in the enjoyment of the rights set out in the Convention. It is not a 'free standing' right to be free from discriminatory acts or treatment, but requires that everyone's rights set out in the Convention are protected equally. Article 14 is therefore only engaged when one of the other rights in the Convention is engaged. The treatment or act in question must fall with the ambit of another right, although it need not itself be a violation of that right.

An act or treatment that differs on the grounds of 'sex, race, colour, language, religion, political or other opinion, national or social origin, association with a national minority, property, birth or other status' will violate Article 14 where the act or treatment falls within the ambit of another right and it cannot be justified. 'Other status' could include physical and mental capacity[1].

For a full discussion on discrimination see Chapter 18.

1 For example see *R (on the application of Pretty) v DPP* [2001] UKHL 61, [2002] 1 AC 800 (per Lord Hops at para 105) and *B v Secretary of State for Work and Pensions* [2005] EWCA Civ 929, per Sedley LJ at para 25, [2005 1 WLR 3796.

INTERNATIONAL STANDARDS

The relevance of international obligations

17.53 International human rights standards and obligations are not binding on the domestic courts, unless they have become part of customary international law, or have been specifically incorporated into domestic law (as in the case of the European Convention on Human Rights). However, they will be relevant where there is an ambiguity in relation to how to interpret or implement domestic law.

Ambiguous in this context is where the law is capable of either a meaning that conforms to international obligations or one that conflicts. In such circumstances the courts will presume that the legislature intended to legislate in conformity with treaty obligations, and not in conflict with them[1] and will therefore prefer the meaning which is consonant with a treaty obligation[2].

1 *R v Secretary of State for the Home Department, ex p Brind* [1991] 1 AC 696 per Lord Bridge pp 747–748.
2 *Salomon v Customs and Excise Comrs* [1967] 2 QB 116 at pp 143F–144A.

The Hague Convention on the International Protection of Adults, January 2000

17.54 The MCA 2005 makes specific reference in s 63 to the Convention on the International Protection of Adults. The section sets out that Sch 3 'gives effect to' the Convention on the Protection of Adults. The aim of the Convention is to avoid conflicts between signatory parties in their legal systems in respect of jurisdiction, applicable law, recognition and enforcement of measures for the protection of adults. It is intended to improve the protection of incapacitated adults involved in cross-border proceedings that are determining the need for care and/or detention (referred to as 'protective measures'), for example by clarifying which law applies and which court has jurisdiction in such matters.

Article 1 of the Convention sets out that the Convention is 'to provide for the protection in international situations of adults who, by reason of impairment or insufficiency in their personal faculties, are not in a position to defend their interests'. It establishes rules on jurisdiction, applicable in law, international recognition and enforcement measures in order to protect those who, due to impairment or insufficiency, cannot protect their own interests.

The Convention applies in particular to:

(a) the determination of incapacity and the institution of a protective regime;
(b) the placing of the adult under the protection of a judicial or administrative authority;
(c) guardianship, curatorship and analogous institutions;
(d) the designation and functions of any person or body having charge of the adult's person or property, representing or assisting the adult;
(e) the placement of the adult in an establishment or other place where protection can be provided;
(f) the administration, conservation or disposal of the adult's property;
(g) the authorisation of a specific intervention for the protection of the person or property of the adult[1].

It does not apply to:

(a) maintenance obligations;
(b) the formation, annulment and dissolution of marriage or any similar relationship, as well as legal separation;
(c) property regimes in respect of marriage or any similar relationship;
(d) trusts or succession;
(e) social security;
(f) public measures of a general nature in matters of health;
(g) measures taken in respect of a person as a result of penal offences committed by that person;
(h) decisions on the right of asylum and on immigration;
(i) measures directed solely to public safety[2].

An example of when and how it may work is given on German Ministry of Justice Website:

A Scottish man marries a German woman. The couple resides in Germany. As the Scottish man begins to suffer from age-related dementia, the question arises as to which courts have jurisdiction to designate a person to assume care and/or custody of the husband. In addition, it must be clarified whether such protective measures will be governed by German or Scottish law. Pursuant to the Convention, jurisdiction lies with the German courts because the affected adult is habitually resident in Germany. In this way, the court located nearest the affected adult decides. The decision-making process is accelerated by the fact that the court is required to apply German, and not Scottish, law governing protective measures for incapacitated adults, since determining foreign law can be time-consuming and costly. The fact that the Convention also applies in Scotland ensures that the person designated to assume care and/or custody in Germany will also be recognised in Scotland. The German court issues the caregiver/custodian a special certification for this purpose, which also possesses evidentiary value in Scotland. This is important, for example, if the incapacitated adult still has property or assets in Scotland (such as real estate or a bank account) over which the caregiver/custodian must have power of disposition in the affected adult's interest[3].

The Convention was signed at The Hague on 13 January 2000. An equivalent provision can be found in Sch 3 to the Adults with Incapacity (Scotland) Act 2000.

1 Article 3.
2 Article 4.
3 www.bmj.bund.de/.../Press_Office/Press_Releases_zg.html.

COUNCIL OF EUROPE

The European Biomedicine Convention

17.55 The full title of the convention is the Council of Europe's Convention for the Protection of Human Rights and Dignity of the Human Being with regard to the Application of Biology and Medicine: Convention on Human Rights and Biomedicine. It was open to signature at Oviedo on 4 April 1997[1]. Parties to this Convention must protect the dignity and identity of all persons and guarantee everyone, without discrimination, respect for their integrity and other rights with regard to the application of biology and medicine. The interests and welfare of the human being are stated to prevail over the sole interest of society or science[2].

Article 5 of the Convention lays down the general rule that treatment may only be given where the person concerned has given free and informed consent. Article 6 provides protection for persons who are incapable of giving consent, and Article 7 makes specific provision for persons with mental disorder.

The Convention was applied by the European Court of Human Rights in *Glass v United Kingdom*[3], when determining the ambit of the rights contained in Article 8.

1 Signed by 32 members of the Council of Europe, but not signed by the United Kingdom.
2 Article 2.
3 (2004) 39 EHRR 15 [2004] 1 FCR 553.

The European Committee for the Prevention of Torture

17.56 The European Committee for the Prevention of Torture and Inhuman or Degrading Treatment or Punishment has a mandate, by means of visits, to examine the treatment of all persons deprived of their liberty with a view to strengthening the protection of such persons from torture and from inhuman or degrading treatment or punishment.

The Committee produces reports and makes recommendations about the treatment of all those in detention.

For more information on the Committee see : http://www.cpt.coe.int/en/about.htm.

THE UNITED NATIONS

The Convention on the Rights of Persons with Disabilities

17.57 The Convention on the Rights of Persons with Disabilities was adopted on 13 December 2006 by the UN General Assembly[1]. The Convention and its Optional Protocol was opened for signature on 30 March 2007.

The purpose of the convention is set out in Article 1 and is to 'promote, protect and ensure the full and equal enjoyment of all human rights and fundamental freedoms by all persons with disabilities, and to promote respect for their inherent dignity'.

Persons with disabilities include those who have long-term physical, mental, intellectual or sensory impairments which may hinder their full and effective participation in society on an equal basis with others.

For more information on the Convention see http://www.un.org/disabilities/convention/index.shtml

1 By resolution A/RES/61/106.

The UN Mental Illness Principles

17.58 United Nations General Assembly Resolution 46/119 of 17 December 1991 'Principles for the Protection of Persons with Mental Illness' contains the important principles concerning the protection of those with mental illness. The principles have been recognised as 'the most complete standards for the protection of the rights of persons with mental disability at the international level ... [these] principles serve as a guide to States in the design or reform of mental health systems and are of utmost utility in evaluating the practice of existing systems'[1].

The principles have been used by international oversight and enforcement bodies as an authoritative interpretation of the requirements of the International Covenant on Economic Social and Cultural Rights 1966 and the American Convention on Human Rights[2].

1 *Case of Victor Rosario Congo*, Inter-American Commission on Human Rights, Report 29/99Case 11,427, Ecuador, adopted in Sess 1424, OEA/Ser/L.V/II.
2 'The Role of International Human Rights in National Mental Health Legislation', Department of Mental Health, WHO (2004), p 21.

Chapter 18

MENTAL CAPACITY AND SPECIFIC PRACTICE AREAS

- **Discrimination**
- **Prisons**
- **Criminal Offences**

SUMMARY

18.1 This chapter will consider lack of capacity and specific practice areas, namely discrimination, prison law, substantive criminal offences[1] and Anti Social Behaviour Orders ('ASBOs'). This chapter is not intended to give a detailed analysis of these practise areas, but will just highlight some of the specific issues and situations that may arise when dealing with those who lack capacity within these fields.

1 For issues concerning criminal procedure see Chapter 15.

DISCRIMINATION

Introduction

18.2 Stigmatisation, it is said, is one of the defining, and debilitating, experiences of those who suffer or have suffered mental disorder[1]. That much is well recognised and easily observable. It has been argued by several expert commentators that mental health legislation has served to reinforce the commonly held erroneous belief that mental disorder is to be equated with a loss of judgment and decision-making capacity and a tendency towards violent criminality[2]. Such critics of the MHA 1983 regime would say that the regime is itself discriminatory in at least two important respects. In the first instance it accords less weight to the autonomy of mentally disordered patients than it does to those suffering from physical illness in relation to treatment decisions. Secondly, it places people with mental disorders in the uniquely disadvantageous position of being liable to detention in hospital in the absence of the commission of any criminal offence.

The picture is further complicated by the fact that the disadvantage experienced by those who suffer mental disorder may be compounded by other forms of inequality. It is often stated, for example, that black people are more likely to be compulsorily admitted than their white counterparts[3], that Afro-Caribbean men face a disproportionate risk of diagnostic misattribution, over-medication and the use of excessive restraint whilst in psychiatric care[4], that women are more likely to suffer or be diagnosed with depressive illnesses than men and that harassment and bullying of gay men and lesbians could be linked to statistically significant levels of mental disorder[5]. Indeed, none of these classes or groups of potential service users is mutually exclusive. The disadvantage therefore experienced by many may be the result of discrimination on grounds of mental disorder *and* one or more grounds of discrimination proscribed by law.

As a piece of legislation aimed at securing the rights of vulnerable persons, it is important that the MCA 2005 operates in accordance with fundamental principles of equality and dignity. On the one hand it is important to touch briefly on the extent to which the MCA 2005 regime will ameliorate the discrimination perceived to attach to the care and treatment of mentally disordered persons. On the other, this section is intended to provide very basic guidance to those using the MCA 2005 on how other forms of prohibited discrimination (on grounds of race, sex, disability, sexual orientation, religion or belief and age) may be avoided/challenged within the MCA 2005 context.

1 For a review of personal accounts of this experience, see Thornicroft, G, *Shunned: discrimination against people with mental illness* (OUP, 2006).

2 See for example the views expressed by Professor Genevra Richardson in 'Autonomy, Guardianship and Mental Disorder: One Problem, Two Solutions', pp 6–12; Szmukler, G and Dawson, J 'Fusion of mental health and incapacity legislation', *British Journal of Psychiatry* (2006), 188, 504–509 at p 504; Szmukler, G and Holloway, F, 'Maudsley Discussion Paper No. 10: Mental Health Law: Discrimination or Protection?' pp 7–10.

3 See Szmukler, G and Holloway, F; 'Maudsley Discussion Paper No 10: Mental Health Law: Discrimination or Protection?'.

4 See Burnham, U and Hill, H, 'Big, Black and Dangerous?', *Briefings*, June 2005, pp 3–8 citing *Report on Independent Inquiry into the Death of David Bennett*, December 2003 and Sashidharan, SP 'Institutional Racism in British Psychiatry', Psychiatric Bulletin (2001) 25: 244–247.

5 See www.imperial.ac.uk/medicine/news/p40112.

Discrimination on grounds of mental disorder

18.3 The comparison of the MHA 1983 and the MCA 2005 regimes undertaken in Chapter 16 demonstrates that the two regimes will operate in parallel. Though interconnected, the principles and purpose of the two schemes are different and the criticised discriminatory aspect of the MHA 1983 is not significantly ameliorated by the passage of the MCA 2005. The distinctions between the two regimes are considered in some detail in Chapter 16 and are not therefore repeated here. However, the following indicate the extent to which the discriminatory features alluded to above are preserved:

- By MCA 2005, s 28, the consent to treatment provisions will trump any of the MCA 2005's principles in respect of any patient to whom they apply. This means that many of the procedures for respecting the wishes of an incapacitated person (ie the provisions in respect of advance decisions and LPAs) will be dissapplied where that person is 'liable to be detained' under the MHA 1983 except in limited circumstances[1].
- Medical and risk criteria will continue to govern the MHA 1983 detention regime. Capacity and best interests, the concepts which drive the MCA 2005, will not have formal relevance to the detention criteria or the provision of treatment under the MHA 1983. The new 'appropriateness' criteria for detention under the MHA 1983[2] scheduled to come into effect in October 2008 is less explicitly concerned with 'best interests' than the current 'treatability' test[3].
- Those liable to be treated for physical disorders will continue to have their capacitated wishes respected (whether detained or treated under the MCA 2005 or as a matter of common law) whereas those liable to be detained under the MHA 1983 for mental disorders can be treated/ detained without consent irrespective of capacity.

1 The circumstances in which an LPA or advance decision will be determinative under the MHA 1983 are set out in the new MHA 1983, s 58A(5) as inserted by MHA 2007, s 27. This provision is due to come into effect in October 2008. Where the treatment proposed is ECT or other treatments as may be specified by the Secretary of State, it cannot be given to a patient who is not capable of understanding its nature, purpose and likely effects if it conflicts with a valid advance decision or decision of a donee or deputy.

2 This amendment to the MHA 1983 is introduced by the MHA 2007, s 4.

3 This is because it is shifts the focus further away from therapeutic benefit and towards a regime of social control. In their Memorandum to theJoint Committee on Human Rights (JCHR), at p 71 of the JCHR's *4th Report of Session 2006–07*, HL40/HC 288, the Mental Health Alliance suggested that the new definition would operate 'to change health

legislation into legislation of social control, even if that is not the intention. This would be profoundly discriminatory towards a particular group of people who are already unfairly stigmatised within society and who are therefore easy, even popular, targets for further discrimination.'

Domestic case law

18.4 The potential discriminatory aspects of the MHA regime alluded to above have been unsuccessfully challenged in the domestic courts. In the case of *R (on the application of B) v SOAD and the Secretary of State for Health*[1] the Court of Appeal confirmed that:

- The issue of whether a patient detained under the MHA 1983 had capacity to consent to/refuse treatment was not critical to the issue of whether such treatment could be administered without consent.
- International instruments which suggested that capacity could be determinative of the issue of the administration of treatment without consent[2] were not binding on the court[3].
- The principles contained in such international instruments were not decisive of whether the treatment of a capacitated patient without consent violated Articles 3 and/or 8 ECHR (ie they were not determinative of whether a convincing medical necessity for treatment was shown to exist)[4].
- The requirement for imposing certain kinds of treatment against a detained patient's will (ie that the Second Opinion Appointed Doctor concluded that it should be given having regard to the likelihood of its alleviation or preventing the deterioration of the condition) was not to be equated with a requirement that the treatment be in the patient's best interests[5].

The decision in *R (B)*, and the will of Parliament as expressed in MCA 2005, s 28, means that there will be limited scope at present for challenging the consent to treatment provisions of Part IV of the MHA 1983 on the basis that they are discriminatory as against those who suffer mental disorder.

1 [2005] MHLR 347 (Admin), [2006] MHLR 131 (CA). Some support was given by Simon Brown LJ, as he then was, to the proposition that there was an emerging international consensus that the refusal of treatment by competent patients ought to be regarded differently from the refusal by incompetent patients within an involuntary treatment regime in *R (on the application of Wilkinson) v Responsible Medical Officer Broadmoor Hospital* [2001] EWCA Civ 1545, [2002] 1 WLR 419 at 433, paras 28–30. However, in paras 80–81 of her judgment, Hale LJ did not agree that the stage had yet been reached where there was widespread agreement that capacitated patients could only be treated against their will for the protection of others or for their own safety as was argued for by counsel for *Wilkinson*. The view adopted in *R (B)* was consonant with that adopted by Hale LJ in *R (Wilkinson)*.

2 Relevant international instruments/material cited to the court were: the 8th General Report of European Committee for the Prevention of Torture and Inhuman or Degrading Treatment or Punishment in August 2000, (CPT/Inf (98) 12); the Council of Europe 'White Paper' on the Protection of the Human Rights and Dignity of People Suffering from Mental Disorder, 3 January 2000; the United Nations General Assembly Resolution 46/119 of 17 December 1991 'Principles for the Protection of Persons with Mental Illness; Council of Europe's Convention for the Protection of Human Rights and Dignity of the Human Being with regard to the Application of Biology and Medicine (1997).

3 See *R (B)* at para 56.

4 See *R (B)* at paras 58–62.
5 See Richardson, G, above, pp 16–17.

The Convention

18.5 It also appears clear that there is no real support to be garnered from Convention case law at this stage as far as the MHA 1983 regime is concerned.

Article 14 ECHR, as described in Chapter 17, prohibits discrimination in relation to the enjoyment of other Convention rights. A breach of Article 14 may be occasioned where the following criteria are satisfied:

(a) The facts fall within the ambit of one or more convention rights.
(b) There is a difference in treatment, in respect of the relevant Convention rights, as between the complainant and other comparators.
(c) The complainant and the persons put forward for comparison are in an analogous situation.
(d) The difference in treatment is not justified (ie it either does not have a legitimate aim and/or the measure in question does not bear a reasonable relationship of proportionality to that aim).

In principle it would be logically possible to argue that the MHA 1983 permitted unjustified discrimination as between mentally disordered and physically disordered persons in relation to non-consensual treatment and/or detention. The other Convention rights ostensibly engaged would be Articles 5 and 8. However the Article 5(1)(e) *Winterwerp*[1] criteria do not require a capacity-based justification for compulsory detention/treatment for mental disorder. In this sense, the relevant Convention case law already permits mentally disordered persons to be treated differently from others and it is very likely that a Convention challenge on this basis would lead to the European Court of Human Rights ('ECtHR') concluding that the difference in treatment was justified by reference to risk[2].

It would appear that further challenges to the discriminatory effect of the mental health legislation may have to await future developments in the medico-ethical field at an international level which would cause both the government and the ECtHR to revisit their current positions. Many of the international instruments which support a less discriminatory approach to the treatment/detention of those suffering mental disorder do not afford an individual right of petition unless the instrument has been signed and ratified by the relevant member state. This is also true of the fairly recently adopted UN Convention on the Rights of Persons with Disabilities (adopted 13 December 2006) (the Disability Convention)[3]. The Disability Convention is wide-ranging and a full review is beyond the scope of this section. Whilst it is not at present binding on domestic courts or the ECtHR, its provisions will provide persuasive authority for any interpretation of the scope of the rights of disabled persons. Importantly, it contains specific provisions in relation to capacity, liberty of the person and the rights of disabled persons to the highest attainable standards of health. It also places a series of positive duties on countries to combat stereotypes and prejudices and to guarantee that persons with disabilities enjoy equal protection before the law. Given that the ECHR is intended to be evolutive (and as a consequence the Human Rights Act 1998 must be similarly interpreted) there may be some scope in the future for challenges to the entrenched forms of discrimination described above when there is a clearer international consensus on the role of capacity in involuntary treatment regimes.

As far as detention/treatment under the MCA 2005 regime itself is concerned, there is no readily apparent discrimination as between mentally disordered person and others.

1 *Winterwerp v Netherlands* (1979) 2 EHRR 387.
2 This is borne out by the fact that in *Guzzardi v Italy* (1980) 3 EHRR 333, the ECtHR indicated that detention could be justified by reference to public safety under Article 5(1)(e).
3 The Disability Convention can be found at www.un.org/disabilities/default.asp?navid=17&pid=150.

OTHER FORMS OF PROHIBITED DISCRIMINATION WHICH MAY BE RELEVANT TO THE MCA 2005

18.6 The Sex Discrimination Act 1975 (SDA 1975) Part III, the Race Relations Act 1976 (RRA 1976) Pt III, the Disability Discrimination Act 1995 (DDA 1995) Part III, the Equality Act 2006 Pt II and the Equality Act (Sexual Orientation) Regulations 2007 prohibit discrimination on grounds of sex, race, disability, religion and sexual orientation both by public authorities and in connection with the provision of goods, facilities and services (gfs). These provisions also prohibit discrimination by public authorities (the definition being the same as that under the Human Rights Act 1998 (HRA 1998)) and the RRA 1976, SDA 1975 and DDA 1995 place general duties on public authorities to have regard to the need to eliminate discrimination and promote equality. The role of the 'legacy' commissions created to regulate matters which fell within the scope of the respective legislative provisions (the Commission for Racial Equality, the Equal Opportunities Commission and the Disability Rights Commission) has been taken over by the Equality and Human Rights Commission (EHRC)[1]. Statutory codes of practice on gfs provision and public duties in relation to race, sex and disability can be found on the EHRC's website[2].

The statutory provisions referred to above may be relevant to treatment, care and detention under the MCA 2005 and brief descriptions of the forms of prohibited discrimination are therefore set out below. Age discrimination is not currently subject to express statutory regulation (apart, of course, from the HRA 1998) outside of the employment field.

1 The new statutory regulator of matters pertaining to human rights and the 'equality enactments' created by the Equality Act 2006.
2 www.equalityhumanrights.com.

Disability Discrimination

18.7 The DDA 1995 prohibits discrimination against 'disabled' persons in prescribed areas of social and public life. 'Disability' is defined as:

> 'a physical or mental impairment which has a substantial and long-term adverse effect on his ability to carry out normal day-to day activities'

The requirement for a mental illness to be 'clinically well recognised' in order to qualify as a disability has now been removed[1]. It is anticipated that almost all persons subject to the treatment and detention provisions of the MCA 2005 will meet the definition of disability within the meaning of the DDA 1995[2].

The DDA 1995 outlaws discrimination by providers of gfs. DDA 1995, s 19 provides that it is unlawful for a service provider to discriminate against a disabled person by:

(a) refusing to provide or deliberately not providing, to the disabled person any service which he provides, or is prepared to provide, to members of the public;
(b) failing to comply with any duty imposed on him by DDA 1995, s 21 (duty to make reasonable adjustments) in circumstances in which the effect of that failure is to make it impossible or unreasonably difficult for the disabled persons to make use of such service;
(c) in the standard of service which he provides to the disabled person or the manner in which he provides it to him; or
(d) in the terms on which he provides a service to the disabled person.

The duty imposed by DDA 1995, s 21 — the reasonable adjustments duty — is distinct from any other existing statutory duties under the other equality enactments. The distinction resides in the fact that it places a positive obligation upon the service provider (unlike the merely negative prohibition contained in the older race and sex legislation) to take reasonable steps to change any practice, policy or procedure which has the effect of making it impossible or unreasonably difficult for disabled persons to make use of the service provided. The reasonable adjustment duty is a duty to take reasonable steps to ameliorate the identified effect which makes it impossible/ unreasonably difficult for the disabled person to have access to the service in question.

There are three forms of discrimination applicable to this provision:

- a failure to make reasonable adjustments;
- disability-related discrimination; and
- victimisation.

Disability-related discrimination occurs where a provider of services, without justification, 'for a reason which relates to the disabled person's disability, ... treats him less favourably than he treats or would treat others to whom that reason does not or would not apply'[3]. Both discrimination by way of a failure to make reasonable adjustments and disability-related discrimination can be justified on specific grounds[4].

The victimisation provisions of the DDA 1995, broadly analogous to those contained in all of the other equality enactments, protect persons, whether disabled or not, who seek to enforce the DDA 1995 either as complainants or witnesses. As with all of the victimisation provisions contained in domestic equality enactments, the claimant in a victimisation case does not need to have been the person at whom the discriminatory treatment was directed. The victimisation provisions protect all of those who are treated less favourably for taking steps (eg by giving evidence) to enforce the protections afforded by the legislation.

Many of the facilities in which incapacitated persons are cared for, treated or detained will be 'public authorities' within the meaning of the DDA 1995 . The DDA 1995 now, by s 21B, prohibits discrimination by such authorities. In this context, the forms of discrimination outlawed are disability-related discrimination (see above) and the failure to comply with a reasonable adjustment duty.

The DDA 1995, s 49A also places a fairly new statutory duty on public authorities, when carrying out their functions, to have due regard to:

- the need to eliminate discrimination and harassment against disabled people;
- the need to promote equality of opportunity between disabled and non-disabled people;
- the need to take steps to take account of disabled persons' disabilities, even where that involves treating disabled persons more favourably than other persons;
- the need to promote positive attitudes towards disabled persons;
- the need to encourage participation by disabled persons in public life.

The public duty comprises a general public duty applicable to all public authorities as defined by the HRA 1998 and a specific duty which may be imposed by the Secretary of State by regulation upon specific public bodies to enable them to meet their general duty[5]. The DDA 1995 general duty is potentially wider than the corresponding duties under the RRA 1976 and SDA 1975. The specific duties under the DDA 1995 are also distinct from those under the RRA 1976. The distinctions between the DDA 1995 on the one hand, and the RRA 1976 and SDA 1975 on the other, are intended in this regard to the reflect the fact that the DDA 1995 permits more favourable treatment of disabled persons whereas the SDA 1975 and RRA 1976 are more concerned with achieving parity of treatment as between different sexes and racial groups.

1 By amendment of DDA 1995, ss 1, 2 by the Disability Discrimination Act 2005 (DDA 2005).

2 Although it should be noted that in *McDougall v Richmond Adult Community Centre* [2007] IRLR 771 at para 19, the Employment Appeal Tribunal held that the satisfaction of the conditions for admission under the MHA 1983 did not necessarily mean that the

definition of disability under the DDA 1995 would be satisfied. However, the fact that incapacity is required for care and treatment under the MCA 2005 is very likely to mean that persons subject to the MCA 2005 are very likely to meet the DDA 1995 criteria in practice.

3 DDA 1995, s 19.

4 See DDA 1995, s 20(3), (4).

5 *R (on the application of (1) Priti Hansraj Chavda (2) Margaret Fitzpatrick (by her daughter and litigation friend Pamela Fitzpatrick) (3) Milton George Maos v Harrow London Borough Council* [2007] EWHC 3064 (Admin), [2007] All ER (D) 337 (Dec). This is one of the early cases since the introduction of the disability duty. The Administrative Court held that the local authority's failure to alert its decision-makers to the terms of the duty when they were making a decision which had an adverse impact on a significant number of disabled service users amounted to a breach of the duty.

Sex discrimination and race discrimination

18.8 Both of these statutory provisions contain prohibitions against direct discrimination, harassment, indirect discrimination and victimisation[1]. They prohibit such discrimination in connection with the provision of goods facilities and services[2]. They both contains provision specific to public authorities[3] which render it unlawful for a public authority to do an act which constitutes discrimination in the carrying out of its public functions. The RRA 1976 also confers a general duty on all public authorities to 'have due regard to the need to eliminate unlawful racial discrimination and to promote equality of opportunity and good relations between persons of different racial groups'[4]. The SDA now also includes a comparable general duty to have 'due regard to the need to eliminate unlawful discrimination and harassment and to promote equality of opportunity between men and women'[5].'. Specific duties directed at designated public authorities attach to the general public authority duties in respect of both the RRA 1976 and SDA 1975.

1 These concepts are defined in the relevant statutes.

2 RRA 1976, s 20 and SDA 1975, s 29.

3 RRA 1976, s 19B and SDA 1975, s 21A.

4 RRA 1976, s 71.

5 SDA 1975, s 76A.

Sexual orientation and religion

18.9 Discrimination on these grounds has only recently come to be statutorily prohibited. The Equality Act (Sexual Orientation) Regulations 2007 (EASOR)[1] prohibit direct discrimination (less favourable treatment on the grounds of the sexual orientation of anyone other than the discriminator), indirect discrimination and victimisation in the non-employment field.

Similar protections in relation to discrimination on the grounds of religion or belief are to be found in the Equality Act 2006, ss 45, 46. The new definition of 'belief' for these purposes is an expansive one. There is no longer a requirement for the belief to be similar to a philosophical belief and non-believers are expressly protected[2]. This may mean that beliefs not usually associated with, or analogous to, the doctrine of organised religions may be covered.

Both of the EASOR and the religion provisions of the Equality Act 2006 will apply to the provision of care and treatment services under the MCA 2005. They both also outlaw discrimination by public authorities but, unlike the RRA 1976, SDA 1975 or DDA 1995, neither contains a general public duty to eliminate discrimination or promote equality on those grounds.

1 SI 2007/1263.
2 See Equality Act 2006, s 44.

Age

18.10 Less favourable treatment on the grounds of age is likely to be a live issue in the context of detention and treatment under the MCA 2005 as many of the persons who will fall to be dealt with under the MCA 2005 will be elderly. Although the Main Code specifically prohibits the making of decisions as to capacity or best interests on the grounds of age, it is not improbable that some age-related prejudice may creep into decision-making processes under the MCA 2005. As stated above, however, there are no domestic statutory provisions directed specifically at the prohibition of age discrimination outside of the employment context. Unless and until this is remedied by legislation, consideration will have to be given to the HRA 1998 in relation to challenges focussed specifically on age discrimination.

Enforcement

18.11 In many of the cases in which potential discriminatory treatment may occur, these matters may be raised and dealt with informally. However, if litigation is advised, claims by individuals under the equality provisions described above will usually be justiciable in the county court in England and Wales or in the Sheriff Court in Scotland. The primary time limit for such claims will be six months subject to extension by the court in prescribed circumstances[1]. Since the relevant claimant in such cases will be incapacitated (unless the claim is brought by a friend or carer etc who is complaining about their own treatment) a litigation friend is likely to be required. Remedies include a declaration that there has been unlawful discrimination, damages for injury to feelings[2] and aggravated and exemplary damages. As also alluded to below, a breach of the equality duties will be justiciable in the Administrative Court.

1 See for example RRA 1976, s 68 which permits time to be extended where it is 'just and equitable' to do so. There is also provision for continuing discrimination under s 68 and the associated provisions of the other equality enactments described above. Time limits in these claims may also be extended where the conciliation services of the Equality and Human Rights Commission are sought by a claimant (RRA 1976, s 68(3C)).
2 The leading authority on the level of awards to be made under this head of damage is *Vento v Chief Constable of West Yorkshire Police (No 2)* [2002] EWCA Civ 1871, [2003] IRLR 102.

How might these issues arise in the MCA 2005 context?

18.12 Since the full panoply of equality enactments described above will apply to the provision of care and other services under the MCA 2005, it will be important for those responsible for the provision of care and treatment to ensure that no unlawful discrimination occurs in that context. It will be important to ensure that neither intended nor unintended discriminatory conduct creeps into any of the MCA 2005 decision-making processes. Examples of how this may occur are:

- A decision that a man with cerebral palsy who has a speech impediment does not have capacity to make a decision about where he should reside simply because of his communication difficulties (potential disability-related discrimination; potential failure to make reasonable adjustments to enable an assessment of capacity to be appropriately determined in respect of a person who has difficulty communicating).
- A decision to ignore the past wishes and feelings of a woman in the context of a best interests determination because they were based on her religious beliefs (potential direct religious discrimination).
- An inclination on the part of a particular residential home to use powerful sedatives with noticeable side effects on black male patients with behavioural difficulties whereas white and female patients with similar behavioural difficulties are habitually provided with psychological therapies (potential direct race/sex discrimination).

Sections 2(3) and 4(1) of the MCA 2005 prevent a lack of capacity or a best interests determination from being founded merely on a person's age, appearance, assumptions about their condition or any aspect of his behaviour. This is reiterated in the Main Code's guidance at paras 4.7–4.9 and 5.16–5.17. Quite apart from the statutory anti-discrimination provisions, it will be extremely important for decision-makers to be sensitive to the varied cultural, ethnic, political and religious contexts from which the persons cared for come. That diversity will make careful communication with carers and others vital if these determinations are to be truly reflective of, and responsive to, the matters which are of great import to a particular individual. Carelessness or insensitivity in respect of the specificity of the decision-making process in any one case may well lead to potential discrimination complaints.

Mention is made above of the general statutory duties applying to public authorities under the RRA 1976, SDA 1975 and DDA 1995. The failure of a public authority to comply with its statutory duties is justiciable in the Administrative Court by way of judicial review[1]. Where there is concern about persistent discriminatory treatment by a particular PCT or local authority in relation to the provision of care or treatment it will be very important to remind that body of the existence of their general promotional duties. Specific public authorities, like the Department of Health, will be subject to a specific public authority duty which require them to conduct equality impact assessments in order to comply with their general duties[2]. If there are concerns about widespread discriminatory treatment, and the responsible body is a public authority to whom the specific duties apply, it will often be a useful tool to invite that body to consider conducting an equality impact assessment so that the true impact on a minority/disadvantaged group may be appreciated. The product of such an exercise may be valuable in terms of persuading the relevant body to act to prevent discrimination. In addition a failure to undertake an assessment where the specific duty applies will be justiciable in the High Court and will provide the sound basis for a private law claim in unlawful discrimination against the relevant body[3].

1 See *R(on the application of Elias) v Secretary of State for Defence, CRE intervening* [2005] EWHC 1435 (Admin), [2005] IRLR 788, [2006] EWCA Civ 1293, [2006] 1 WLR 3213, CA.

2 See *R (o the application of BAPIO) v Secretary of State for the Home Department* [2007] EWHC 199 (QB), [2007] All ER (D) 127 (Feb) for more on the importance of conducting race equality impact assessments in order to demonstrate compliance with the general equality duty under RRA 1976, s 71.

3 Ie contrary to RRA 1976, s 19B; SDA 1975, s 21D and DDA 1995, s 21B.

PRISONS

Introduction

18.13 The MCA 2005 applies equally to those in prison as it does to those in the community. Prison officers and healthcare staff working in prisons will have to, as with any other carers, abide by the principles contained within the MCA 2005 when dealing with prisoners who lack capacity. Healthcare in prisons in now provided by the NHS, and the treatment that is received inside a prison should be of the same standard as that received in the community. For decisions about serious medical treatment or long-term accommodation the Main Code explicitly states that the services of an independent mental capacity advocate (IMCA) should be available to those in prison[1].

It is likely to be those cases where a prisoner loses capacity while in prison that the MCA 2005 will be most relevant. Those who lack capacity at the time of conviction or sentence are unlikely to be sent to prison in the first place, but instead will either have been dealt with by way of a discharge or hospital order. However, many prisoners suffer from learning disabilities and/or mental illness[2] which may prevent them from having capacity for particular decisions, but which did not prevent the imposition of a sentence of imprisonment.

1 See Main Code, para 10.73.

2 Around 70% of sentenced prisoners suffer two or more mental health problems and 20% of male and 15% of female prisoners have previously experienced a psychiatric acute admission to hospital – The Sainsbury Centre of Mental Health, 25 June 2007.

Transfer under the Mental Health Act

18.14 For those who lack capacity through mental illness, if they become detainable under the MHA 1983 and require hospital treatment, consideration should be given to transferring them out of the prison estate to a secure mental health hospital under MHA 1983, s 47 (if sentenced) or 48 (if on remand or awaiting sentence).

A prisoner may be transferred to hospital by warrant under the direction of the Secretary of State for Justice if he is of the opinion that, having regard to the public interest and all the circumstances, it is expedient to do so and if he is satisfied on the evidence of at least two medical practitioners that the prisoner is suffering from a mental illness, psychopathic disorder, or severe mental impairment and that that disorder is of a nature of degree which requires his detention in hospital for medical treatment, and that the treatment is likely to alleviate or prevent a deterioration of his condition[1]. At least one of the medical practitioners must be approved under MHA 1983, s 12.

The procedure to be followed is set out in detail in Prison Service Instruction 03/2006. Essentially the process is that a General Practitioner, or possibly a psychiatrist, visiting or working in the prison undertakes an initial assessment of a prisoner who has been identified as possibly requiring treatment in a psychiatric hospital. If following this initial assessment transfer to hospital is thought necessary then the prison healthcare staff contact the responsible PCT[2] and the Mental Health Unit within the Ministry of Justice to inform them, and they (the prison healthcare staff) arrange for a second medical assessment to be done, ideally by a doctor from an appropriate secure unit able to provide a bed to the prisoner. The medical reports together with the prisoner's details (on a form HI003) are then sent to the Mental Health Unit at the Ministry of Justice who will then determine whether to issue a warrant for transfer.

In cases of extreme emergency the Secretary of State for Justice can direct the removal of a prisoner immediately from prison to a hospital under s 22(2)(b) of the Prison Act 1952. This power is generally used for those suffering from physical illness but can be used for those suffering from mental disorder. If this power is used the prisoner must be escorted at all times. If a prisoner appears to be suffering from a mental disorder and, for example is refusing food or fluid, then he could be transferred to hospital immediately for treatment. If the assessment of the prisoner in such a case indicates a lack of capacity, an application must be made for a court order before he can be forcibly treated or given food or fluid. The relevant court for such an application used to be to the magistrates' court but is now likely to be to the Court of Protection.

1 Note that both the definition of mental disorder and the statutory detention criteria are to be altered by the MHA 2007 which is scheduled to come into force in October 2008.

2 This will be the PCT for the area in which the prisoner last resided or was registered with a GP.

Early release on compassionate grounds

18.15 Early release on compassionate grounds for medical reasons[1] may apply to someone who has lost capacity. However, unless the prisoner is also suffering form a terminal illness he would more likely be transferred to the secure mental health estate rather than be released early on compassionate grounds.

The criteria for release under ss 30 and s 31 of the Criminal Justice Act 1991 require that a prisoner is suffering from a terminal illness and that death is likely to occur soon, or that the prisoner is bedridden or similarly incapacitated[2]. These criteria are very strictly applied, and it is unlikely that a prisoner will be released on compassionate grounds unless their life expectancy is only a matter of months[3].

In the first instance a request for early release on compassionate grounds is made to the prison governor, and it is then for him/her to assess whether the prisoner meets the criteria for early release. Alternatively the governor of his own volition could decide that a prisoner ought to be considered for early release on compassionate grounds.

The full procedure to be followed is set out in Chapter 12 of Prison Service Order 6000. In summary if the governor supports a prisoner's application then a Form 210 must be completed by the prison, with a registered doctor completing section 4 with full details of the medical condition, and sent to the Early Release and Recall Section of the Ministry of Justice. In addition any other reports that are available, for example from hospital consultants, must also be forwarded. Section 5 must be completed by the seconded probation officer, who should comment on the care available to the prisoner in the community and any relevant issues that go to risk. All reports must be disclosed to the prisoner, unless there are good reasons for withholding the information.

On receipt of an application, the Early Release and Recall Section will, as necessary, obtain the opinion of the Medical Director, Prison Health (at the Department of Health), on the merits of the application. A final decision to release may only be made by Ministers, but senior officers in the Early Release and Recall Section have delegated authority to refuse applications.

The decisions of the prison governor, the Early Release and Recall Section, and ultimately the Minister of Justice will all be amenable to judicial review. Should any of these bodies fail to exercise their discretion lawfully it would be open to a prisoner to apply to the Administrative Court to challenge their decision by way of judicial review[4].

1 It is also possible to be released early on compassionate grounds where there are tragic family circumstances.
2 See Prison Service Order 6000, Chapter 12, Appendix A.
3 See for example *R (on the application of Spinks) v Secretary of State for the Home Department* [2005] EWCA Civ 275, [2005] All ER (D) 297 (Jan) and PSO6000 which suggests a life expectancy in the region of three months.
4 See Chapter 15 (at 15.11–15.24) for summary of judicial review procedure.

Discrimination in the prison context

18.16 The DDA 2005 applies in prisons[1] and requires that those prisoners suffering from a mental disability are not discriminated against, and have access to education, and work opportunities etc. The prison is required to make 'reasonable adjustments' in order to meet the needs of those who are disabled; this could include, for example, assisting someone with learning disabilities understand what is said to them and to able to participate in prison life. The other statutory provisions referred to in the discrimination section above (at 18.8–8.10) in relation to race, sex, sexual orientation and religion will also apply. The DDA is specifically referred to here because it may be the most immediately relevant discrimination provision in relation to capacity.

Suggested adjustments for those with learning disabilities are given in PSO 2855 as being the provision of documents/posters in pictorial format, access to learning support in offending Behaviour Programmes (also see further below), simplification of forms used, easy to understand language when giving explanations and instructions, and the giving of prior warning of events and changes wherever possible with clear explanations. A failure to make reasonable adjustments, or discriminating against a prisoner who is disabled, will amount to a breach of the DDA 2005 unless it can be justified.

1 PSO2855 sets out how the DDA 2005 applies in prisons.

Offender behaviour courses

18.17 There are already available specially adapted offender behaviour courses for those who have learning disabilities and/or a low IQ, for example the adapted sex offender treatment programme (for those with an IQ of below 80) and the adapted enhanced thinking skills course. It is anticipated that more will become available. As noted above, additional consideration should be given to providing a prisoner with learning disabilities access to learning support when undertaking offender behaviour courses. Again failure to do this could be a breach of the DDA 1995.

It is extremely important that those with learning disabilities who have been sentenced to any form of indeterminate sentence are able to participate in such courses, as they will need to be able to demonstrate to the Parole Board a reduction in risk before they can be released. The Board is very unlikely to find that there has been a reduction in risk without evidence of the successful completion of offending behaviour work. In addition when considering security classification the prison will consider the risk posed by a prisoner of escape and further offending, and again the successful completion of offending behaviour work will be critical in enabling a prisoner to progress from high security (Category A and B) through to low security (Category C and D).

CRIMINAL OFFENCES

Specific offences under the MCA 2005

18.18 The MCA 2005 has created two new offences under s 44: ill-treatment and wilful neglect of a person who lacks capacity to make relevant decisions[1]. The offences apply to a person who cares for, is the donee of an LPA (or EPA) or who is a deputy of the person who lacks capacity. The offence carries a maximum penalty (if tried in the Crown Court) of five years' imprisonment.

Section 44 states:

'44 Ill-treatment or neglect

(1) Subsection (2) applies if a person ('D')—

(a) has the care of a person ('P') who lacks, or whom D reasonably believes to lack, capacity,

(b) is the donee of a lasting power of attorney, or an enduring power of attorney (within the meaning of Schedule 4), created by P, or

(c) is a deputy appointed by the court for P.

(2) D is guilty of an offence if he ill-treats or wilfully neglects P.

(3) A person guilty of an offence under this section is liable—

(a) on summary conviction, to imprisonment for a term not exceeding 12 months or a fine not exceeding the statutory maximum or both;

(b) on conviction on indictment, to imprisonment for a term not exceeding 5 years or a fine or both.'

The test for capacity is that contained in s 2 of the MCA 2005, so a person will lack capacity if at the material time, he is unable to make a decision for himself because of an impairment of, or a disturbance in the functioning of, the mind or brain. It is immaterial if the impairment or disturbance is permanent or temporary (see MCA 2005, s 2(2)). A lack of capacity cannot be established merely by reference to a person's age or appearance, or by a condition, or an aspect of behaviour, which might lead others to make unjustified assumptions about capacity (s 2(3)).

The question of whether a person lacks capacity within the meaning of the MCA 2005 is to be decided on the balance of probabilities (s 2(4)). Accordingly, there must be evidence to support the fact that the person lacked mental capacity at the time the offence was committed.

In the guidance provided by the Crown Prosecution Service (CPS), prosecutors are advised that if the defence challenge the evidence on capacity, they should have a conference with the expert and ensure that he has sight of all relevant material, including the defence's statements or reports. He should comment upon the defence contentions. Further prosecutors are advised that prior to trial, the prosecution and defence expert should discuss the issues and agree common ground[2].

It is important to note however that even if the victim has capacity, it will still be an offence if the person who had the care of him reasonably believed he lacked capacity and ill-treated or neglected him. 'Reasonable belief' means that in all the circumstances, a reasonable person would believe that the victim lacked capacity.

As the MCA 2005 applies to everyone who looks after or cares for someone who lacks mental capacity, it therefore includes both those who have regular day-to-day care as well as those who only have very short term care, whether they are family carers, professional carers or other carers.

The MCA 2005 does not define 'ill-treatment' and 'wilful neglect', and so these concepts are to be given their ordinary meaning[3]. In the Main Code at para 14.25 it is said that ill treatment and neglect are separate offences and that for a person to be found guilty of ill treatment they must *either* have deliberately ill treated the person *or* have been reckless in the way they were ill-treating the person. It does not matter whether the behaviour was likely to cause, or actually caused, harm or damage to the victim's health. The meaning of 'wilful neglect' is said in the Main Code to vary depending on the circumstances, but that it usually means that a person has deliberately failed to carry out an act they knew they had a duty to do.

The CPS guidance says, with regard to the decision on whether to charge or not, that if the evidential test is met (ie that the prosecutor is satisfied that there is enough evidence to provide a realistic prospect of conviction), then 'the public interest will nearly always demand that a prosecution occurs due to the position of trust that the suspect held in relation to the victim, as well as the extreme vulnerability of the victim'.

With regard to witness care issues prosecutors are advised to 'carefully consider whether the offence can be proved without the victim having to give evidence. If the victim is able to give evidence, and it is necessary for him to give evidence, then special measures must be considered as the person is a 'vulnerable witness' for the purposes of the Youth Justice and Criminal Evidence Act 1999'[4] (see further below).

1 These offences are also described at Chapter 4, at 4.9–4.14.
2 http://www.cps.gov.uk/legal/section5/chapter_c.html.
3 For 'willful neglect' see Archbold 2007 17–47–17–48, 19–300–19–303 which deals with the offence of 'willful neglect' and 'ill treatment' of children. On what constitutes 'ill-treatment', reference should be made to Archbold 19–282, which deals with 'ill-treatment' of persons of unsound mind. Offences of ill-treatment and wilful neglect are continuing offences (*R v Hayles* [1969] 1 QB 364, 53 Cr App Rep 36, CA).
4 http://www.cps.gov.uk/legal/section5/chapter_c.html.

Specific Offences under Sexual Offences Act 2003

18.19 Those who lack capcaity and/or who suffer from a mental disorder are especially vulnerable to sexual exploitation. Parliament has clearly recognised the need to provide specific protection for this vulnerable group and the Sexual Offences Act 2003 creates particular offences concerning those who lack capacity and/or suffer with a mental disorder.

There are three categories of offences: first offences committed against persons with a mental disorder impeding choice, second offences where a person with a mental disorder, by means of inducement, threat or deception, is engaged in various sexual activites, and third offences committed by care workers on those with a mental disorder.

The various offences covered are:

- intentional sexual touching of a person with a mental disorder impeding choice (s 30);
- causing or inciting a mental disorder impeding choice to engage in sexual activity (s 31);
- engaging in sexual activity in the presence of a person with a mental disorder impeding choice (s 32);

- causing a person with a mental disorder impeding choice to watch a sexual act (s 33);
- inducement, threat or deception to procure sexual activity with a person with a mental disorder (s 34);
- causing a person with a mental disorder to engage in or agree to engage in sexual activity by inducement, threat or deception (s 35);
- engaging in sexual activity in the presence, procured by inducement, threat or deception, of a person with a mental disorder (s 36);
- causing a person with a mental disorder to watch a sexual act by inducement, threat or deception (s 37);
- care workers engaging in sexual activity with a person with a mental disorder (s 38);
- care workers causing or inciting sexual activity (s 39);
- care workers engaging in sexual activity in the presence of a person with a mental disorder (s 40);
- care workers causing a person with a mental disorder to watch a sexual act (s 41).

For the first category of offences the necessary elements of the offences to be proved are that (i) the victim is unable to refuse because of or for a reason related to a mental disorder, (ii) the offender knows or could reasonably be expected to know of the disorder and therefore the victim is likely to be unable to refuse. The victim will be found to be unable to refuse if he lacks the capacity to choose to agree to the activity, eg lacks sufficient understanding of the nature of the activity, or he is unable to communicate such a choice to the offender.

For the second category of offences, what is required (in addition to to the sexual elements of the offence) is that the offender obtains the victom's agreement by means of an inducement, a threat made or a deception practised by the offender for that purpose and that the vicitm has a mental disorder, and the offender knows or could reasonably be expected to know that the victim has a mental disorder.

For the third category of offences, what is required in addition to the sexual elements being proven, is that the victim was suffering from a mental disorder and the offender knew or could be reasonably expected to know that they suffered with a mental disorder and that the offender was a 'care worker'. A care worker is defined in s 42 by the application of a two-stage test, the first is whether or not the vicitm is accomodated and cared for in a home, a community home, voluntary home or childrens' home, and the second is whether the alleged offender has functions to perform in the home in the course of employment which have brought him, or are likely to bring him, into regular face-to-face contact with the victim.

Also covered are the situations where the victim is a patient for whom services are provided by a NHS body or by an independent medical agency, or in an independent clinic or in an independent hospital, and the alleged offender has functions to perform in the course of employment which have brought him or are likely to bring him into regular face to face contact with the patient.

It is in the first category of offence that the question of capacity (rather than the question of mental illness), is of critical importance. The case of *Hulme v DPP*[1] provides an example of how the test of capacity applies to these types of offences. The victim in that case suffered from cerebral palsy and had a mental age below her actual age of 27 years. It was alleged that the defendant had touched the victim over her clothing in the area of her vagina and pressed down hard with his hand. He had his trouser zip open and placed her hand on his soft penis. The defendant was charged under s 30 of the Sexual Offences Act 2003. At trial the victim gave evidence that the defendant had touched her 'private parts', that she did not know what to do or say but that the touching made her feel sad, hurt and upset. The defendant accepted that the victim suffered from a mental disorder but contended that the prosecution had failed to show that she lacked the capacity to choose whether to agree to the touching. The question for the court was whether at the time of the alleged assaults, the victim was able to understand that she could agree or not to the sexual activity. If the the court was of the view that she did not have the capacity to do that, then they had to consider whether the incapacity was for a reason related to her mental disorder[2].

The magistrates' court found that the victim understood the nature of sexual relations but did not have the capacity to understand that she could refuse to be touched sexually. Accordingly, she was not capable of stopping the defendant from carrying out sexual activity with her due to her mental disorder although she was clearly upset by his actions. The defendant was found guilty. The defendant appealed (by way of case stated) on the grounds that the magistrates had not been advised to consider the victim's ability to communicate any refusal, but his appeal was unsuccessful. The Divisional Court found that the magistrates' reasoning made clear that they had considered whether the vicitm had been able to communicate her lack of consent and concluded that she could not.

1 [2006] EWHC 1347 (Admin), 170 JP 598.
2 Sexual Offences Act 2003, s 30(2)(a).

ASBOS[1]

18.20 Anti-Social Behaviour Order's (ASBOs) were introduced to prohibit behaviour that is anti-social. There are two conditions that need to be met before an ASBO can be imposed: first is that there has been or is likely to be anti-social behaviour and the second is that an order is necessary to protect persons from that behaviour. There are also two ways in which an ASBO can be imposed, first an authority can apply to the court for an ASBO, if it appears to that authority that a person has acted in an anti-social manner and, second, following a conviction for a criminal offence.

Anti-social behaviour is defined as behaviour that usually causes 'harassment, alarm or distress'. The Home Office in a 2002 publication entitled 'A guide to Anti-Social Behaviour Orders and Acceptable Behaviour Contracts' gave examples of the types of behaviour which the Home Office considered could be tackled by ASBOs. The list (which does not purport to be exhaustive) comprises: harassment of residents or passers by, verbal abuse, criminal damage, vandalism, noise nuisance, writing graffiti, engaging in threatening behaviour in large groups, racial abuse, smoking or drinking alcohol while under age, substance misuse, joyriding, begging, prostitution, kerb-crawling, throwing missiles, assault and vehicle crime.

Of course, those who lack capacity are just as likely, and possibly more so where such a person also has a mental health disorder, as those who have capacity to behave in an anti-social manner. The fact of capacity is therefore unlikely to be of any relevance to the first condition. However, with regard to the second condition, that of necessity for the order, the lack of capacity may be of significant relevance.

Obtaining an ASBO against someone who has behavioural or learning disabilities is very unlikely to prevent them from behaving in anti-social manner in the future. As noted above, ASBOs are meant to be preventative and not punitive; if they are unlikely to prevent future anti-social behaviour they are unlikely to be found by the courts to be 'necessary'. In the case of *R v Werner*[2] an ASBO imposed following conviction was quashed by the Court of Appeal on the basis that it did not fulfil the test of necessity. The appellant in that case suffered from a schizo-affective disorder.

In addition the terms of an ASBO must be understood by the person on whom it is imposed, clearly therefore an assessment of capacity will have to be made in cases where the person may not have the capacity to understand the terms and/or the significance of the Order. Even if the test of necessity is made out, the court does have a discretion as to whether to impose an ASBO, and it is suggested that where a person does not have the capacity to understand the terms or significance of an order one should not be made.

1 A detailed discussion on ASBOs is beyond the scope of this book. For a comprehensive guide to ASBOs see Sikand, M, *ASBOs: a practitioner's guide to defending anti-social behaviour orders* (2006) LAG.

2 [2004] EWCA Crim 2931, [2004] All ER (D) 137 (Nov).

Appendix 1

THE MENTAL CAPACITY ACT 2005

MENTAL CAPACITY ACT 2005

2005 CHAPTER 9

An Act to make new provision relating to persons who lack capacity; to establish a superior court of record called the Court of Protection in place of the office of the Supreme Court called by that name; to make provision in connection with the Convention on the International Protection of Adults signed at the Hague on 13th January 2000; and for connected purposes.

[7th April 2005]

Be it enacted by the Queen's most Excellent Majesty, by and with the advice and consent of the Lords Spiritual and Temporal, and Commons, in this present Parliament assembled, and by the authority of the same, as follows:—

PART 1
PERSONS WHO LACK CAPACITY

The principles

A1.1

1 The principles

(1) The following principles apply for the purposes of this Act.

(2) A person must be assumed to have capacity unless it is established that he lacks capacity.

(3) A person is not to be treated as unable to make a decision unless all practicable steps to help him to do so have been taken without success.

(4) A person is not to be treated as unable to make a decision merely because he makes an unwise decision.

(5) An act done, or decision made, under this Act for or on behalf of a person who lacks capacity must be done, or made, in his best interests.

(6) Before the act is done, or the decision is made, regard must be had to whether the purpose for which it is needed can be as effectively achieved in a way that is less restrictive of the person's rights and freedom of action.

NOTES

Initial Commencement

To be appointed: see s 68(1).

Appointment

Appointment (in relation to England for certain purposes): 1 April 2007: see SI 2007/563, art 2(2)(a).
Appointment (for certain purposes): 1 April 2007: see SI 2007/563, art 2(2)(a), (3).
Appointment (for remaining purposes): 1 October 2007: see SI 2007/1897, art 2(2)(a).

Preliminary

A1.2

2 People who lack capacity

(1) For the purposes of this Act, a person lacks capacity in relation to a matter if at the material time he is unable to make a decision for himself in relation to the matter because of an impairment of, or a disturbance in the functioning of, the mind or brain.

(2) It does not matter whether the impairment or disturbance is permanent or temporary.

(3) A lack of capacity cannot be established merely by reference to—

- (a) a person's age or appearance, or
- (b) a condition of his, or an aspect of his behaviour, which might lead others to make unjustified assumptions about his capacity.

(4) In proceedings under this Act or any other enactment, any question whether a person lacks capacity within the meaning of this Act must be decided on the balance of probabilities.

(5) No power which a person ("D") may exercise under this Act—

- (a) in relation to a person who lacks capacity, or
- (b) where D reasonably thinks that a person lacks capacity,

is exercisable in relation to a person under 16.

(6) Subsection (5) is subject to section 18(3).

NOTES

Initial Commencement

To be appointed: see s 68(1).

Appointment

Appointment (in relation to England for certain purposes): 1 April 2007: see SI 2007/563, art 2(2)(b).
Appointment (for certain purposes): 1 April 2007: see SI 2007/563, art 2(2)(b), (3).
Appointment (for remaining purposes): 1 October 2007: see SI 2007/1897, art 2(2)(b).

A1.3

3 Inability to make decisions

(1) For the purposes of section 2, a person is unable to make a decision for himself if he is unable—

- (a) to understand the information relevant to the decision,
- (b) to retain that information,
- (c) to use or weigh that information as part of the process of making the decision, or
- (d) to communicate his decision (whether by talking, using sign language or any other means).

(2) A person is not to be regarded as unable to understand the information relevant to a decision if he is able to understand an explanation of it given to him in a way that is appropriate to his circumstances (using simple language, visual aids or any other means).

(3) The fact that a person is able to retain the information relevant to a decision for a short period only does not prevent him from being regarded as able to make the decision.

(4) The information relevant to a decision includes information about the reasonably foreseeable consequences of—

- (a) deciding one way or another, or

(b) failing to make the decision.

NOTES

Initial Commencement

To be appointed: see s 68(1).

Appointment

Appointment (in relation to England for certain purposes): 1 April 2007: see SI 2007/563, art 2(2)(c).
Appointment (for certain purposes): 1 April 2007: see SI 2007/563, art 2(2)(c), (3).
Appointment (for remaining purposes): 1 October 2007: see SI 2007/1897, art 2(2)(c).

A1.4

4 Best interests

(1) In determining for the purposes of this Act what is in a person's best interests, the person making the determination must not make it merely on the basis of—

(a) the person's age or appearance, or
(b) a condition of his, or an aspect of his behaviour, which might lead others to make unjustified assumptions about what might be in his best interests.

(2) The person making the determination must consider all the relevant circumstances and, in particular, take the following steps.

(3) He must consider—

(a) whether it is likely that the person will at some time have capacity in relation to the matter in question, and
(b) if it appears likely that he will, when that is likely to be.

(4) He must, so far as reasonably practicable, permit and encourage the person to participate, or to improve his ability to participate, as fully as possible in any act done for him and any decision affecting him.

(5) Where the determination relates to life-sustaining treatment he must not, in considering whether the treatment is in the best interests of the person concerned, be motivated by a desire to bring about his death.

(6) He must consider, so far as is reasonably ascertainable—

(a) the person's past and present wishes and feelings (and, in particular, any relevant written statement made by him when he had capacity),
(b) the beliefs and values that would be likely to influence his decision if he had capacity, and
(c) the other factors that he would be likely to consider if he were able to do so.

(7) He must take into account, if it is practicable and appropriate to consult them, the views of—

(a) anyone named by the person as someone to be consulted on the matter in question or on matters of that kind,
(b) anyone engaged in caring for the person or interested in his welfare,
(c) any donee of a lasting power of attorney granted by the person, and
(d) any deputy appointed for the person by the court,

as to what would be in the person's best interests and, in particular, as to the matters mentioned in subsection (6).

(8) The duties imposed by subsections (1) to (7) also apply in relation to the exercise of any powers which—

(a) are exercisable under a lasting power of attorney, or
(b) are exercisable by a person under this Act where he reasonably believes that another person lacks capacity.

(9) In the case of an act done, or a decision made, by a person other than the court, there is sufficient compliance with this section if (having complied with the requirements of subsections (1) to (7)) he reasonably believes that what he does or decides is in the best interests of the person concerned.

(10) "Life-sustaining treatment" means treatment which in the view of a person providing health care for the person concerned is necessary to sustain life.

(11) "Relevant circumstances" are those—

(a) of which the person making the determination is aware, and
(b) which it would be reasonable to regard as relevant.

NOTES

Initial Commencement
To be appointed: see s 68(1).

Appointment
Appointment (in relation to England for certain purposes): 1 April 2007: see SI 2007/563, art 2(2)(d).
Appointment (for certain purposes): 1 April 2007: see SI 2007/563, art 2(2)(d), (3).
Appointment (for remaining purposes): 1 October 2007: see SI 2007/1897, art 2(2)(d).

A1.5

[4A Restriction on deprivation of liberty]

[(1) This Act does not authorise any person ("D") to deprive any other person ("P") of his liberty.

(2) But that is subject to—

(a) the following provisions of this section, and
(b) section 4B.

(3) D may deprive P of his liberty if, by doing so, D is giving effect to a relevant decision of the court.

(4) A relevant decision of the court is a decision made by an order under section 16(2)(a) in relation to a matter concerning P's personal welfare.

(5) D may deprive P of his liberty if the deprivation is authorised by Schedule A1 (hospital and care home residents: deprivation of liberty).]

NOTES

Amendment
Inserted by the Mental Health Act 2007, s 50(1), (2). Date in force: to be appointed: see the Mental Health Act 2007, s 56(1).

A1.6

[4B Deprivation of liberty necessary for life-sustaining treatment etc]

[(1) If the following conditions are met, D is authorised to deprive P of his liberty while a decision as respects any relevant issue is sought from the court.

(2) The first condition is that there is a question about whether D is authorised to deprive P of his liberty under section 4A.

(3) The second condition is that the deprivation of liberty—

(a) is wholly or partly for the purpose of—
  (i) giving P life-sustaining treatment, or
  (ii) doing any vital act, or
(b) consists wholly or partly of—
  (i) giving P life-sustaining treatment, or
  (ii) doing any vital act.

(4) The third condition is that the deprivation of liberty is necessary in order to—

- (a) give the life-sustaining treatment, or
- (b) do the vital act.

(5) A vital act is any act which the person doing it reasonably believes to be necessary to prevent a serious deterioration in P's condition.]

NOTES

Amendment

Inserted by the Mental Health Act 2007, s 50(1), (2). Date in force: to be appointed: see the Mental Health Act 2007, s 56(1).

A1.7

5 Acts in connection with care or treatment

(1) If a person ("D") does an act in connection with the care or treatment of another person ("P"), the act is one to which this section applies if—

- (a) before doing the act, D takes reasonable steps to establish whether P lacks capacity in relation to the matter in question, and
- (b) when doing the act, D reasonably believes—
  - (i) that P lacks capacity in relation to the matter, and
  - (ii) that it will be in P's best interests for the act to be done.

(2) D does not incur any liability in relation to the act that he would not have incurred if P—

- (a) had had capacity to consent in relation to the matter, and
- (b) had consented to D's doing the act.

(3) Nothing in this section excludes a person's civil liability for loss or damage, or his criminal liability, resulting from his negligence in doing the act.

(4) Nothing in this section affects the operation of sections 24 to 26 (advance decisions to refuse treatment).

Initial Commencement

To be appointed: see s 68(1).

Appointment

Appointment: 1 October 2007: see SI 2007/1897, art 2(1)(a).

A1.8

6 Section 5 acts: limitations

(1) If D does an act that is intended to restrain P, it is not an act to which section 5 applies unless two further conditions are satisfied.

(2) The first condition is that D reasonably believes that it is necessary to do the act in order to prevent harm to P.

(3) The second is that the act is a proportionate response to—

- (a) the likelihood of P's suffering harm, and
- (b) the seriousness of that harm.

(4) For the purposes of this section D restrains P if he—

- (a) uses, or threatens to use, force to secure the doing of an act which P resists, or
- (b) restricts P's liberty of movement, whether or not P resists.

(5) *But D does more than merely restrain P if he deprives P of his liberty within the meaning of Article 5(1) of the Human Rights Convention (whether or not D is a public authority).*

(6) Section 5 does not authorise a person to do an act which conflicts with a decision made, within the scope of his authority and in accordance with this Part, by—

- (a) a donee of a lasting power of attorney granted by P, or

(b) a deputy appointed for P by the court.

(7) But nothing in subsection (6) stops a person—

(a) providing life-sustaining treatment, or
(b) doing any act which he reasonably believes to be necessary to prevent a serious deterioration in P's condition,

while a decision as respects any relevant issue is sought from the court.

NOTES

Initial Commencement
To be appointed: see s 68(1).

Appointment
Appointment: 1 October 2007: see SI 2007/1897, art 2(1)(a).

Amendment
Sub-s (5): repealed by the Mental Health Act 2007, ss 50(1), (4)(a), 55, Sch 11, Pt 10. Date in force: to be appointed: see the Mental Health Act 2007, s 56(1).

A1.9

7 Payment for necessary goods and services

(1) If necessary goods or services are supplied to a person who lacks capacity to contract for the supply, he must pay a reasonable price for them.

(2) "Necessary" means suitable to a person's condition in life and to his actual requirements at the time when the goods or services are supplied.

NOTES

Initial Commencement
To be appointed: see s 68(1).

Appointment
Appointment: 1 October 2007: see SI 2007/1897, art 2(1)(a).

A1.10

8 Expenditure

(1) If an act to which section 5 applies involves expenditure, it is lawful for D—

(a) to pledge P's credit for the purpose of the expenditure, and
(b) to apply money in P's possession for meeting the expenditure.

(2) If the expenditure is borne for P by D, it is lawful for D—

(a) to reimburse himself out of money in P's possession, or
(b) to be otherwise indemnified by P.

(3) Subsections (1) and (2) do not affect any power under which (apart from those subsections) a person—

(a) has lawful control of P's money or other property, and
(b) has power to spend money for P's benefit.

NOTES

Initial Commencement
To be appointed: see s 68(1).

Appointment
Appointment: 1 October 2007: see SI 2007/1897, art 2(1)(a).

Lasting powers of attorney

A1.11

9 Lasting powers of attorney

(1) A lasting power of attorney is a power of attorney under which the donor ("P") confers on the donee (or donees) authority to make decisions about all or any of the following—

(a) P's personal welfare or specified matters concerning P's personal welfare, and
(b) P's property and affairs or specified matters concerning P's property and affairs,

and which includes authority to make such decisions in circumstances where P no longer has capacity.

(2) A lasting power of attorney is not created unless—

(a) section 10 is complied with,
(b) an instrument conferring authority of the kind mentioned in subsection (1) is made and registered in accordance with Schedule 1, and
(c) at the time when P executes the instrument, P has reached 18 and has capacity to execute it.

(3) An instrument which—

(a) purports to create a lasting power of attorney, but
(b) does not comply with this section, section 10 or Schedule 1,

confers no authority.

(4) The authority conferred by a lasting power of attorney is subject to—

(a) the provisions of this Act and, in particular, sections 1 (the principles) and 4 (best interests), and
(b) any conditions or restrictions specified in the instrument.

NOTES

Initial Commencement
To be appointed: see s 68(1).

Appointment
Appointment: 1 October 2007: see SI 2007/1897, art 2(1)(a).

A1.12

10 Appointment of donees

(1) A donee of a lasting power of attorney must be—

(a) an individual who has reached 18, or
(b) if the power relates only to P's property and affairs, either such an individual or a trust corporation.

(2) An individual who is bankrupt may not be appointed as donee of a lasting power of attorney in relation to P's property and affairs.

(3) Subsections (4) to (7) apply in relation to an instrument under which two or more persons are to act as donees of a lasting power of attorney.

(4) The instrument may appoint them to act—

(a) jointly,
(b) jointly and severally, or
(c) jointly in respect of some matters and jointly and severally in respect of others.

(5) To the extent to which it does not specify whether they are to act jointly or jointly and severally, the instrument is to be assumed to appoint them to act jointly.

(6) If they are to act jointly, a failure, as respects one of them, to comply with the requirements of subsection (1) or (2) or Part 1 or 2 of Schedule 1 prevents a lasting power of attorney from being created.

(7) If they are to act jointly and severally, a failure, as respects one of them, to comply with the requirements of subsection (1) or (2) or Part 1 or 2 of Schedule 1—

- (a) prevents the appointment taking effect in his case, but
- (b) does not prevent a lasting power of attorney from being created in the case of the other or others.

(8) An instrument used to create a lasting power of attorney—

- (a) cannot give the donee (or, if more than one, any of them) power to appoint a substitute or successor, but
- (b) may itself appoint a person to replace the donee (or, if more than one, any of them) on the occurrence of an event mentioned in section 13(6)(a) to (d) which has the effect of terminating the donee's appointment.

NOTES

Initial Commencement

To be appointed: see s 68(1).

Appointment

Appointment: 1 October 2007: see SI 2007/1897, art 2(1)(a).

A1.13

11 Lasting powers of attorney: restrictions

(1) A lasting power of attorney does not authorise the donee (or, if more than one, any of them) to do an act that is intended to restrain P, unless three conditions are satisfied.

(2) The first condition is that P lacks, or the donee reasonably believes that P lacks, capacity in relation to the matter in question.

(3) The second is that the donee reasonably believes that it is necessary to do the act in order to prevent harm to P.

(4) The third is that the act is a proportionate response to—

- (a) the likelihood of P's suffering harm, and
- (b) the seriousness of that harm.

(5) For the purposes of this section, the donee restrains P if he—

- (a) uses, or threatens to use, force to secure the doing of an act which P resists, or
- (b) restricts P's liberty of movement, whether or not P resists,

or if he authorises another person to do any of those things.

(6) *But the donee does more than merely restrain P if he deprives P of his liberty within the meaning of Article 5(1) of the Human Rights Convention.*

(7) Where a lasting power of attorney authorises the donee (or, if more than one, any of them) to make decisions about P's personal welfare, the authority—

- (a) does not extend to making such decisions in circumstances other than those where P lacks, or the donee reasonably believes that P lacks, capacity,
- (b) is subject to sections 24 to 26 (advance decisions to refuse treatment), and
- (c) extends to giving or refusing consent to the carrying out or continuation of a treatment by a person providing health care for P.

(8) But subsection (7)(c)—

- (a) does not authorise the giving or refusing of consent to the carrying out or continuation of life-sustaining treatment, unless the instrument contains express provision to that effect, and
- (b) is subject to any conditions or restrictions in the instrument.

NOTES

Initial Commencement

To be appointed: see s 68(1).

Appointment

Appointment: 1 October 2007: see SI 2007/1897, art 2(1)(a).

Amendment

Sub-s (6): repealed by the Mental Health Act 2007, ss 50(1), (4)(b), 55, Sch 11, Pt 10. Date in force: to be appointed: see the Mental Health Act 2007, s 56(1).

A1.14

12 Scope of lasting powers of attorney: gifts

(1) Where a lasting power of attorney confers authority to make decisions about P's property and affairs, it does not authorise a donee (or, if more than one, any of them) to dispose of the donor's property by making gifts except to the extent permitted by subsection (2).

(2) The donee may make gifts—

(a) on customary occasions to persons (including himself) who are related to or connected with the donor, or
(b) to any charity to whom the donor made or might have been expected to make gifts,

if the value of each such gift is not unreasonable having regard to all the circumstances and, in particular, the size of the donor's estate.

(3) "Customary occasion" means—

(a) the occasion or anniversary of a birth, a marriage or the formation of a civil partnership, or
(b) any other occasion on which presents are customarily given within families or among friends or associates.

(4) Subsection (2) is subject to any conditions or restrictions in the instrument.

NOTES

Initial Commencement

To be appointed: see s 68(1).

Appointment

Appointment: 1 October 2007: see SI 2007/1897, art 2(1)(a).

A1.15

13 Revocation of lasting powers of attorney etc

(1) This section applies if—

(a) P has executed an instrument with a view to creating a lasting power of attorney, or
(b) a lasting power of attorney is registered as having been conferred by P,

and in this section references to revoking the power include revoking the instrument.

(2) P may, at any time when he has capacity to do so, revoke the power.

(3) P's bankruptcy revokes the power so far as it relates to P's property and affairs.

(4) But where P is bankrupt merely because an interim bankruptcy restrictions order has effect in respect of him, the power is suspended, so far as it relates to P's property and affairs, for so long as the order has effect.

(5) The occurrence in relation to a donee of an event mentioned in subsection (6)—

(a) terminates his appointment, and
(b) except in the cases given in subsection (7), revokes the power.

(6) The events are—

(a) the disclaimer of the appointment by the donee in accordance with such requirements as may be prescribed for the purposes of this section in regulations made by the Lord Chancellor,
(b) subject to subsections (8) and (9), the death or bankruptcy of the donee or, if the donee is a trust corporation, its winding-up or dissolution,
(c) subject to subsection (11), the dissolution or annulment of a marriage or civil partnership between the donor and the donee,
(d) the lack of capacity of the donee.

(7) The cases are—

(a) the donee is replaced under the terms of the instrument,
(b) he is one of two or more persons appointed to act as donees jointly and severally in respect of any matter and, after the event, there is at least one remaining donee.

(8) The bankruptcy of a donee does not terminate his appointment, or revoke the power, in so far as his authority relates to P's personal welfare.

(9) Where the donee is bankrupt merely because an interim bankruptcy restrictions order has effect in respect of him, his appointment and the power are suspended, so far as they relate to P's property and affairs, for so long as the order has effect.

(10) Where the donee is one of two or more appointed to act jointly and severally under the power in respect of any matter, the reference in subsection (9) to the suspension of the power is to its suspension in so far as it relates to that donee.

(11) The dissolution or annulment of a marriage or civil partnership does not terminate the appointment of a donee, or revoke the power, if the instrument provided that it was not to do so.

NOTES

Initial Commencement
To be appointed see s 68(1).

Appointment
Appointment: 1 October 2007: see SI 2007/1897, art 2(1)(a).

Subordinate Legislation
Lasting Powers of Attorney, Enduring Powers of Attorney and Public Guardian Regulations 2007, SI 2007/1253 (made under sub-s (6)(a)).

A1.16

14 Protection of donee and others if no power created or power revoked

(1) Subsections (2) and (3) apply if—

(a) an instrument has been registered under Schedule 1 as a lasting power of attorney, but
(b) a lasting power of attorney was not created,

whether or not the registration has been cancelled at the time of the act or transaction in question.

(2) A donee who acts in purported exercise of the power does not incur any liability (to P or any other person) because of the non-existence of the power unless at the time of acting he—

(a) knows that a lasting power of attorney was not created, or
(b) is aware of circumstances which, if a lasting power of attorney had been created, would have terminated his authority to act as a donee.

(3) Any transaction between the donee and another person is, in favour of that person, as valid as if the power had been in existence, unless at the time of the transaction that person has knowledge of a matter referred to in subsection (2).

(4) If the interest of a purchaser depends on whether a transaction between the donee and the other person was valid by virtue of subsection (3), it is conclusively presumed in favour of the purchaser that the transaction was valid if—

(a) the transaction was completed within 12 months of the date on which the instrument was registered, or

(b) the other person makes a statutory declaration, before or within 3 months after the completion of the purchase, that he had no reason at the time of the transaction to doubt that the donee had authority to dispose of the property which was the subject of the transaction.

(5) In its application to a lasting power of attorney which relates to matters in addition to P's property and affairs, section 5 of the Powers of Attorney Act 1971 (c 27) (protection where power is revoked) has effect as if references to revocation included the cessation of the power in relation to P's property and affairs.

(6) Where two or more donees are appointed under a lasting power of attorney, this section applies as if references to the donee were to all or any of them.

NOTES

Initial Commencement

To be appointed: see s 68(1).

Appointment

Appointment: 1 October 2007: see SI 2007/1897, art 2(1)(a).

General powers of the court and appointment of deputies

A1.17

15 Power to make declarations

(1) The court may make declarations as to—

(a) whether a person has or lacks capacity to make a decision specified in the declaration;
(b) whether a person has or lacks capacity to make decisions on such matters as are described in the declaration;
(c) the lawfulness or otherwise of any act done, or yet to be done, in relation to that person.

(2) "Act" includes an omission and a course of conduct.

NOTES

Initial Commencement

To be appointed: see s 68(1).

Appointment

Appointment: 1 October 2007: see SI 2007/1897, art 2(1)(a).

A1.18

16 Powers to make decisions and appoint deputies: general

(1) This section applies if a person ("P") lacks capacity in relation to a matter or matters concerning—

(a) P's personal welfare, or
(b) P's property and affairs.

(2) The court may—

(a) by making an order, make the decision or decisions on P's behalf in relation to the matter or matters, or
(b) appoint a person (a "deputy") to make decisions on P's behalf in relation to the matter or matters.

(3) The powers of the court under this section are subject to the provisions of this Act and, in particular, to sections 1 (the principles) and 4 (best interests).

(4) When deciding whether it is in P's best interests to appoint a deputy, the court must have regard (in addition to the matters mentioned in section 4) to the principles that—

(a) a decision by the court is to be preferred to the appointment of a deputy to make a decision, and
(b) the powers conferred on a deputy should be as limited in scope and duration as is reasonably practicable in the circumstances.

(5) The court may make such further orders or give such directions, and confer on a deputy such powers or impose on him such duties, as it thinks necessary or expedient for giving effect to, or otherwise in connection with, an order or appointment made by it under subsection (2).

(6) Without prejudice to section 4, the court may make the order, give the directions or make the appointment on such terms as it considers are in P's best interests, even though no application is before the court for an order, directions or an appointment on those terms.

(7) An order of the court may be varied or discharged by a subsequent order.

(8) The court may, in particular, revoke the appointment of a deputy or vary the powers conferred on him if it is satisfied that the deputy—

(a) has behaved, or is behaving, in a way that contravenes the authority conferred on him by the court or is not in P's best interests, or
(b) proposes to behave in a way that would contravene that authority or would not be in P's best interests.

NOTES

Initial Commencement

To be appointed: see s 68(1).

Appointment

Appointment: 1 October 2007: see SI 2007/1897, art 2(1)(a).

A1.19

[16A Section 16 powers: Mental Health Act patients etc]

[(1) If a person is ineligible to be deprived of liberty by this Act, the court may not include in a welfare order provision which authorises the person to be deprived of his liberty.

(2) If—

(a) a welfare order includes provision which authorises a person to be deprived of his liberty, and
(b) that person becomes ineligible to be deprived of liberty by this Act,

the provision ceases to have effect for as long as the person remains ineligible.

(3) Nothing in subsection (2) affects the power of the court under section 16(7) to vary or discharge the welfare order.

(4) For the purposes of this section—

(a) Schedule 1A applies for determining whether or not P is ineligible to be deprived of liberty by this Act;
(b) "welfare order" means an order under section 16(2)(a).]

NOTES

Amendment

Inserted by the Mental Health Act 2007, s 50(1), (3). Date in force: to be appointed: see the Mental Health Act 2007, s 56(1).

A1.20

17 Section 16 powers: personal welfare

(1) The powers under section 16 as respects P's personal welfare extend in particular to—

(a) deciding where P is to live;
(b) deciding what contact, if any, P is to have with any specified persons;

- (c) making an order prohibiting a named person from having contact with P;
- (d) giving or refusing consent to the carrying out or continuation of a treatment by a person providing health care for P;
- (e) giving a direction that a person responsible for P's health care allow a different person to take over that responsibility.

(2) Subsection (1) is subject to section 20 (restrictions on deputies).

NOTES

Initial Commencement

To be appointed: see s 68(1).

Appointment

Appointment: 1 October 2007: see SI 2007/1897, art 2(1)(a).

A1.21

18 Section 16 powers: property and affairs

(1) The powers under section 16 as respects P's property and affairs extend in particular to—

- (a) the control and management of P's property;
- (b) the sale, exchange, charging, gift or other disposition of P's property;
- (c) the acquisition of property in P's name or on P's behalf;
- (d) the carrying on, on P's behalf, of any profession, trade or business;
- (e) the taking of a decision which will have the effect of dissolving a partnership of which P is a member;
- (f) the carrying out of any contract entered into by P;
- (g) the discharge of P's debts and of any of P's obligations, whether legally enforceable or not;
- (h) the settlement of any of P's property, whether for P's benefit or for the benefit of others;
- (i) the execution for P of a will;
- (j) the exercise of any power (including a power to consent) vested in P whether beneficially or as trustee or otherwise;
- (k) the conduct of legal proceedings in P's name or on P's behalf.

(2) No will may be made under subsection (1)(i) at a time when P has not reached 18.

(3) The powers under section 16 as respects any other matter relating to P's property and affairs may be exercised even though P has not reached 16, if the court considers it likely that P will still lack capacity to make decisions in respect of that matter when he reaches 18.

(4) Schedule 2 supplements the provisions of this section.

(5) Section 16(7) (variation and discharge of court orders) is subject to paragraph 6 of Schedule 2.

(6) Subsection (1) is subject to section 20 (restrictions on deputies).

NOTES

Initial Commencement

To be appointed: see s 68(1).

Appointment

Appointment: 1 October 2007: see SI 2007/1897, art 2(1)(a).

A1.22

19 Appointment of deputies

(1) A deputy appointed by the court must be—

- (a) an individual who has reached 18, or
- (b) as respects powers in relation to property and affairs, an individual who has reached 18 or a trust corporation.

(2) The court may appoint an individual by appointing the holder for the time being of a specified office or position.

(3) A person may not be appointed as a deputy without his consent.

(4) The court may appoint two or more deputies to act—

(a) jointly,
(b) jointly and severally, or
(c) jointly in respect of some matters and jointly and severally in respect of others.

(5) When appointing a deputy or deputies, the court may at the same time appoint one or more other persons to succeed the existing deputy or those deputies—

(a) in such circumstances, or on the happening of such events, as may be specified by the court;
(b) for such period as may be so specified.

(6) A deputy is to be treated as P's agent in relation to anything done or decided by him within the scope of his appointment and in accordance with this Part.

(7) The deputy is entitled—

(a) to be reimbursed out of P's property for his reasonable expenses in discharging his functions, and
(b) if the court so directs when appointing him, to remuneration out of P's property for discharging them.

(8) The court may confer on a deputy powers to—

(a) take possession or control of all or any specified part of P's property;
(b) exercise all or any specified powers in respect of it, including such powers of investment as the court may determine.

(9) The court may require a deputy—

(a) to give to the Public Guardian such security as the court thinks fit for the due discharge of his functions, and
(b) to submit to the Public Guardian such reports at such times or at such intervals as the court may direct.

NOTES

Initial Commencement
To be appointed: see s 68(1).

Appointment
Appointment: 1 October 2007: see SI 2007/1897, art 2(1)(a).

A1.23

20 Restrictions on deputies

(1) A deputy does not have power to make a decision on behalf of P in relation to a matter if he knows or has reasonable grounds for believing that P has capacity in relation to the matter.

(2) Nothing in section 16(5) or 17 permits a deputy to be given power—

(a) to prohibit a named person from having contact with P;
(b) to direct a person responsible for P's health care to allow a different person to take over that responsibility.

(3) A deputy may not be given powers with respect to—

(a) the settlement of any of P's property, whether for P's benefit or for the benefit of others,
(b) the execution for P of a will, or
(c) the exercise of any power (including a power to consent) vested in P whether beneficially or as trustee or otherwise.

(4) A deputy may not be given power to make a decision on behalf of P which is inconsistent with a decision made, within the scope of his authority and in accordance with this Act, by the donee of a lasting power of attorney granted by P (or, if there is more than one donee, by any of them).

(5) A deputy may not refuse consent to the carrying out or continuation of life-sustaining treatment in relation to P.

(6) The authority conferred on a deputy is subject to the provisions of this Act and, in particular, sections 1 (the principles) and 4 (best interests).

(7) A deputy may not do an act that is intended to restrain P unless four conditions are satisfied.

(8) The first condition is that, in doing the act, the deputy is acting within the scope of an authority expressly conferred on him by the court.

(9) The second is that P lacks, or the deputy reasonably believes that P lacks, capacity in relation to the matter in question.

(10) The third is that the deputy reasonably believes that it is necessary to do the act in order to prevent harm to P.

(11) The fourth is that the act is a proportionate response to—

- (a) the likelihood of P's suffering harm, [and]
- (b) the seriousness of that harm.

(12) For the purposes of this section, a deputy restrains P if he—

- (a) uses, or threatens to use, force to secure the doing of an act which P resists, or
- (b) restricts P's liberty of movement, whether or not P resists,

or if he authorises another person to do any of those things.

(13) *But a deputy does more than merely restrain P if he deprives P of his liberty within the meaning of Article 5(1) of the Human Rights Convention (whether or not the deputy is a public authority).*

NOTES

Initial Commencement
To be appointed: see s 68(1).

Appointment
Appointment: 1 October 2007: see SI 2007/1897, art 2(1)(a).

Amendment
Sub-s (11): in para (a) word "and" in square brackets substituted by the Mental Health Act 2007, s 51. Date in force: 1 October 2007: see SI 2007/2635, art 2.
Sub-s (13): repealed by the Mental Health Act 2007, ss 50(1), (4)(c), 55, Sch 11, Pt 10. Date in force: to be appointed: see the Mental Health Act 2007, s 56(1).

A1.24

21 Transfer of proceedings relating to people under 18

[(1)] The [Lord Chief Justice, with the concurrence of the Lord Chancellor,] may by order make provision as to the transfer of proceedings relating to a person under 18, in such circumstances as are specified in the order—

- (a) from the Court of Protection to a court having jurisdiction under the Children Act 1989 (c 41), or
- (b) from a court having jurisdiction under that Act to the Court of Protection.

[(2) The Lord Chief Justice may nominate any of the following to exercise his functions under this section—

- (a) the President of the Court of Protection;
- (b) a judicial office holder (as defined in section 109(4) of the Constitutional Reform Act 2005).]

NOTES

Initial Commencement
To be appointed: see s 68(1).

Appointment
Appointment: 1 October 2007: see SI 2007/1897, art 2(1)(a).

Amendment
Sub-s (1): numbered as such by SI 2006/1016, art 2, Sch 1, paras 30, 31(1), (2). Date in force: 3 April 2006: see SI 2006/1016, art 1.
Sub-s (1): words "Lord Chief Justice, with the concurrence of the Lord Chancellor," in square brackets substituted by SI 2006/1016, art 2, Sch 1, paras 30, 31(1), (3). Date in force: 3 April 2006: see SI 2006/1016, art 1.
Sub-s (2): inserted by SI 2006/1016, art 2, Sch 1, paras 30, 31(1), (4). Date in force: 3 April 2006: see SI 2006/1016, art 1.

Subordinate Legislation
Mental Capacity Act 2005 (Transfer Of Proceedings) Order 2007, SI 2007/1899.

[Powers of the court in relation to Schedule A1]

NOTES

Amendment
Inserted by the Mental Health Act 2007, s 50(7), Sch 9, Pt 1, paras 1, 2. Date in force: to be appointed: see the Mental Health Act 2007, s 56(1).

A1.25

[21A Powers of court in relation to Schedule A1]

[(1) This section applies if either of the following has been given under Schedule A1—

(a) a standard authorisation;
(b) an urgent authorisation.

(2) Where a standard authorisation has been given, the court may determine any question relating to any of the following matters—

(a) whether the relevant person meets one or more of the qualifying requirements;
(b) the period during which the standard authorisation is to be in force;
(c) the purpose for which the standard authorisation is given;
(d) the conditions subject to which the standard authorisation is given.

(3) If the court determines any question under subsection (2), the court may make an order—

(a) varying or terminating the standard authorisation, or
(b) directing the supervisory body to vary or terminate the standard authorisation.

(4) Where an urgent authorisation has been given, the court may determine any question relating to any of the following matters—

(a) whether the urgent authorisation should have been given;
(b) the period during which the urgent authorisation is to be in force;
(c) the purpose for which the urgent authorisation is given.

(5) Where the court determines any question under subsection (4), the court may make an order—

(a) varying or terminating the urgent authorisation, or
(b) directing the managing authority of the relevant hospital or care home to vary or terminate the urgent authorisation.

(6) Where the court makes an order under subsection (3) or (5), the court may make an order about a person's liability for any act done in connection with the standard or urgent authorisation before its variation or termination.

(7) An order under subsection (6) may, in particular, exclude a person from liability.]

NOTES

Amendment

Inserted by the Mental Health Act 2007, s 50(7), Sch 9, Pt 1, paras 1, 2. Date in force: to be appointed: see the Mental Health Act 2007, s 56(1).

Powers of the court in relation to lasting powers of attorney

A1.26

22 Powers of court in relation to validity of lasting powers of attorney

(1) This section and section 23 apply if—

- (a) a person ("P") has executed or purported to execute an instrument with a view to creating a lasting power of attorney, or
- (b) an instrument has been registered as a lasting power of attorney conferred by P.

(2) The court may determine any question relating to—

- (a) whether one or more of the requirements for the creation of a lasting power of attorney have been met;
- (b) whether the power has been revoked or has otherwise come to an end.

(3) Subsection (4) applies if the court is satisfied—

- (a) that fraud or undue pressure was used to induce P—
  - (i) to execute an instrument for the purpose of creating a lasting power of attorney, or
  - (ii) to create a lasting power of attorney, or
- (b) that the donee (or, if more than one, any of them) of a lasting power of attorney—
  - (i) has behaved, or is behaving, in a way that contravenes his authority or is not in P's best interests, or
  - (ii) proposes to behave in a way that would contravene his authority or would not be in P's best interests.

(4) The court may—

- (a) direct that an instrument purporting to create the lasting power of attorney is not to be registered, or
- (b) if P lacks capacity to do so, revoke the instrument or the lasting power of attorney.

(5) If there is more than one donee, the court may under subsection (4)(b) revoke the instrument or the lasting power of attorney so far as it relates to any of them.

(6) "Donee" includes an intended donee.

NOTES

Initial Commencement

To be appointed: see s 68(1).

Appointment

Appointment: 1 October 2007: see SI 2007/1897, art 2(1)(a).

A1.27

23 Powers of court in relation to operation of lasting powers of attorney

(1) The court may determine any question as to the meaning or effect of a lasting power of attorney or an instrument purporting to create one.

(2) The court may—

- (a) give directions with respect to decisions—
  - (i) which the donee of a lasting power of attorney has authority to make, and
  - (ii) which P lacks capacity to make;

(b) give any consent or authorisation to act which the donee would have to obtain from P if P had capacity to give it.

(3) The court may, if P lacks capacity to do so—

(a) give directions to the donee with respect to the rendering by him of reports or accounts and the production of records kept by him for that purpose;
(b) require the donee to supply information or produce documents or things in his possession as donee;
(c) give directions with respect to the remuneration or expenses of the donee;
(d) relieve the donee wholly or partly from any liability which he has or may have incurred on account of a breach of his duties as donee.

(4) The court may authorise the making of gifts which are not within section 12(2) (permitted gifts).

(5) Where two or more donees are appointed under a lasting power of attorney, this section applies as if references to the donee were to all or any of them.

NOTES

Initial Commencement

To be appointed: see s 68(1).

Appointment

Appointment: 1 October 2007: see SI 2007/1897, art 2(1)(a).

Advance decisions to refuse treatment

A1.28

24 Advance decisions to refuse treatment: general

(1) "Advance decision" means a decision made by a person ("P"), after he has reached 18 and when he has capacity to do so, that if—

(a) at a later time and in such circumstances as he may specify, a specified treatment is proposed to be carried out or continued by a person providing health care for him, and
(b) at that time he lacks capacity to consent to the carrying out or continuation of the treatment,

the specified treatment is not to be carried out or continued.

(2) For the purposes of subsection (1)(a), a decision may be regarded as specifying a treatment or circumstances even though expressed in layman's terms.

(3) P may withdraw or alter an advance decision at any time when he has capacity to do so.

(4) A withdrawal (including a partial withdrawal) need not be in writing.

(5) An alteration of an advance decision need not be in writing (unless section 25(5) applies in relation to the decision resulting from the alteration).

NOTES

Initial Commencement

To be appointed: see s 68(1).

Appointment

Appointment: 1 October 2007: see SI 2007/1897, art 2(1)(a).

A1.29

25 Validity and applicability of advance decisions

(1) An advance decision does not affect the liability which a person may incur for carrying out or continuing a treatment in relation to P unless the decision is at the material time—

(a) valid, and

(b) applicable to the treatment.

(2) An advance decision is not valid if P—

(a) has withdrawn the decision at a time when he had capacity to do so,
(b) has, under a lasting power of attorney created after the advance decision was made, conferred authority on the donee (or, if more than one, any of them) to give or refuse consent to the treatment to which the advance decision relates, or
(c) has done anything else clearly inconsistent with the advance decision remaining his fixed decision.

(3) An advance decision is not applicable to the treatment in question if at the material time P has capacity to give or refuse consent to it.

(4) An advance decision is not applicable to the treatment in question if—

(a) that treatment is not the treatment specified in the advance decision,
(b) any circumstances specified in the advance decision are absent, or
(c) there are reasonable grounds for believing that circumstances exist which P did not anticipate at the time of the advance decision and which would have affected his decision had he anticipated them.

(5) An advance decision is not applicable to life-sustaining treatment unless—

(a) the decision is verified by a statement by P to the effect that it is to apply to that treatment even if life is at risk, and
(b) the decision and statement comply with subsection (6).

(6) A decision or statement complies with this subsection only if—

(a) it is in writing,
(b) it is signed by P or by another person in P's presence and by P's direction,
(c) the signature is made or acknowledged by P in the presence of a witness, and
(d) the witness signs it, or acknowledges his signature, in P's presence.

(7) The existence of any lasting power of attorney other than one of a description mentioned in subsection (2)(b) does not prevent the advance decision from being regarded as valid and applicable.

NOTES

Initial Commencement

To be appointed: see s 68(1).

Appointment

Appointment: 1 October 2007: see SI 2007/1897, art 2(1)(a).

A1.30

26 Effect of advance decisions

(1) If P has made an advance decision which is—

(a) valid, and
(b) applicable to a treatment,

the decision has effect as if he had made it, and had had capacity to make it, at the time when the question arises whether the treatment should be carried out or continued.

(2) A person does not incur liability for carrying out or continuing the treatment unless, at the time, he is satisfied that an advance decision exists which is valid and applicable to the treatment.

(3) A person does not incur liability for the consequences of withholding or withdrawing a treatment from P if, at the time, he reasonably believes that an advance decision exists which is valid and applicable to the treatment.

(4) The court may make a declaration as to whether an advance decision—

(a) exists;
(b) is valid;
(c) is applicable to a treatment.

(5) Nothing in an apparent advance decision stops a person—

(a) providing life-sustaining treatment, or
(b) doing any act he reasonably believes to be necessary to prevent a serious deterioration in P's condition,

while a decision as respects any relevant issue is sought from the court.

NOTES

Initial Commencement
To be appointed: see s 68(1).

Appointment
Appointment: 1 October 2007: see SI 2007/1897, art 2(1)(a).

Excluded decisions

A1.31

27 Family relationships etc

(1) Nothing in this Act permits a decision on any of the following matters to be made on behalf of a person—

(a) consenting to marriage or a civil partnership,
(b) consenting to have sexual relations,
(c) consenting to a decree of divorce being granted on the basis of two years' separation,
(d) consenting to a dissolution order being made in relation to a civil partnership on the basis of two years' separation,
(e) consenting to a child's being placed for adoption by an adoption agency,
(f) consenting to the making of an adoption order,
(g) discharging parental responsibilities in matters not relating to a child's property,
(h) giving a consent under the Human Fertilisation and Embryology Act 1990 (c 37).

(2) "Adoption order" means—

(a) an adoption order within the meaning of the Adoption and Children Act 2002 (c 38) (including a future adoption order), and
(b) an order under section 84 of that Act (parental responsibility prior to adoption abroad).

NOTES

Initial Commencement
To be appointed: see s 68(1).

Appointment
Appointment: 1 October 2007: see SI 2007/1897, art 2(1)(a).

A1.32

28 Mental Health Act matters

(1) Nothing in this Act authorises anyone—

(a) to give a patient medical treatment for mental disorder, or
(b) to consent to a patient's being given medical treatment for mental disorder,

if, at the time when it is proposed to treat the patient, his treatment is regulated by Part 4 of the Mental Health Act.

[(1A) Subsection (1) does not apply in relation to any form of treatment to which section 58A of that Act (electro-convulsive therapy, etc) applies if the patient comes within subsection (7) of that section (informal patient under 18 who cannot give consent).]

[(1B) Section 5 does not apply to an act to which section 64B of the Mental Health Act applies (treatment of community patients not recalled to hospital).]

(2) "Medical treatment", "mental disorder" and "patient" have the same meaning as in that Act.

NOTES

Initial Commencement

To be appointed: see s 68(1).

Appointment

Appointment: 1 October 2007: see SI 2007/1897, art 2(1)(a).

Amendment

Sub-s (1A): inserted by the Mental Health Act 2007, s 28(10); for transitional provisions and savings see s 53, Sch 10, paras 1, 3(2), (3) thereto. Date in force: to be appointed: see the Mental Health Act 2007, s 56(1).
Sub-s (1B): inserted by the Mental Health Act 2007, s 35(4), (5). Date in force: to be appointed: see the Mental Health Act 2007, s 56(1).

A1.33

29 Voting rights

(1) Nothing in this Act permits a decision on voting at an election for any public office, or at a referendum, to be made on behalf of a person.

(2) "Referendum" has the same meaning as in section 101 of the Political Parties, Elections and Referendums Act 2000 (c 41).

NOTES

Initial Commencement

To be appointed: see s 68(1).

Appointment

Appointment: 1 October 2007: see SI 2007/1897, art 2(1)(a).

Research

A1.34

30 Research

(1) Intrusive research carried out on, or in relation to, a person who lacks capacity to consent to it is unlawful unless it is carried out—

- (a) as part of a research project which is for the time being approved by the appropriate body for the purposes of this Act in accordance with section 31, and
- (b) in accordance with sections 32 and 33.

(2) Research is intrusive if it is of a kind that would be unlawful if it was carried out—

- (a) on or in relation to a person who had capacity to consent to it, but
- (b) without his consent.

(3) A clinical trial which is subject to the provisions of clinical trials regulations is not to be treated as research for the purposes of this section.

(4) "Appropriate body", in relation to a research project, means the person, committee or other body specified in regulations made by the appropriate authority as the appropriate body in relation to a project of the kind in question.

(5) "Clinical trials regulations" means—

- (a) the Medicines for Human Use (Clinical Trials) Regulations 2004 (SI 2004/1031) and any other regulations replacing those regulations or amending them, and
- (b) any other regulations relating to clinical trials and designated by the Secretary of State as clinical trials regulations for the purposes of this section.

(6) In this section, section 32 and section 34, "appropriate authority" means—

(a) in relation to the carrying out of research in England, the Secretary of State, and
(b) in relation to the carrying out of research in Wales, the National Assembly for Wales.

NOTES

Initial Commencement
To be appointed: see s 68(1), (2).

Appointment
Appointment (in relation to England for the purpose of enabling research applications to be made to, and determined by, an appropriate body): 1 July 2007: see SI 2006/2814, art 3 (as amended by SI 2006/3473, art 2(b)).
Appointment (in relation to England in respect of any research carried out as part of a project begun on or after 1 October 2007): 1 October 2007: see SI 2006/2814, art 2 (as amended by SI 2006/3473, art 2(a)).
Appointment (in relation to England for the purposes of research projects begun and approved before 1 October 2007): 1 October 2008: see SI 2006/2814, art 4 (as amended by SI 2006/3473, art 2(c)–(e)).
Appointment (in relation to Wales for the purpose of enabling research applications to be made to, and determined by, an appropriate body): 1 July 2007: see SI 2007/856, art 3.
Appointment (in relation to Wales in respect of any research carried out as part of a project begun on or after 1 October 2007): 1 October 2007: see SI 2007/856, art 2.
Appointment (in relation to Wales for the purposes of research projects begun and approved before 1 October 2007): 1 October 2008: see SI 2007/856, art 4.

Subordinate Legislation
Mental Capacity Act 2005 (Appropriate Body) (England) Regulations 2006, SI 2006/2810 (made under sub-ss (4), (6)(a))
Mental Capacity Act 2005 (Appropriate Body) (England) (Amendment) Regulations 2006, SI 2006/3474 (made under sub-s (4), (6)(a)).
Mental Capacity Act 2005 (Appropriate Body) (Wales) Regulations 2007, SI 2007/833 (made under sub-ss (4), (6)).

A1.35

31 Requirements for approval

(1) The appropriate body may not approve a research project for the purposes of this Act unless satisfied that the following requirements will be met in relation to research carried out as part of the project on, or in relation to, a person who lacks capacity to consent to taking part in the project ("P").

(2) The research must be connected with—

(a) an impairing condition affecting P, or
(b) its treatment.

(3) "Impairing condition" means a condition which is (or may be) attributable to, or which causes or contributes to (or may cause or contribute to), the impairment of, or disturbance in the functioning of, the mind or brain.

(4) There must be reasonable grounds for believing that research of comparable effectiveness cannot be carried out if the project has to be confined to, or relate only to, persons who have capacity to consent to taking part in it.

(5) The research must—

(a) have the potential to benefit P without imposing on P a burden that is disproportionate to the potential benefit to P, or
(b) be intended to provide knowledge of the causes or treatment of, or of the care of persons affected by, the same or a similar condition.

(6) If the research falls within paragraph (b) of subsection (5) but not within paragraph (a), there must be reasonable grounds for believing—

(a) that the risk to P from taking part in the project is likely to be negligible, and
(b) that anything done to, or in relation to, P will not—
  (i) interfere with P's freedom of action or privacy in a significant way, or
  (ii) be unduly invasive or restrictive.

(7) There must be reasonable arrangements in place for ensuring that the requirements of sections 32 and 33 will be met.

NOTES

Initial Commencement

To be appointed: see s 68(1), (2).

Appointment

Appointment (in relation to England for the purpose of enabling research applications to be made to, and determined by, an appropriate body): 1 July 2007: see SI 2006/2814, art 3 (as amended by SI 2006/3473, art 2(b)).

Appointment (in relation to England in respect of any research carried out as part of a project begun on or after 1 October 2007): 1 October 2007: see SI 2006/2814, art 2 (as amended by SI 2006/3473, art 2(a)).

Appointment (in relation to England for the purposes of research projects begun and approved before 1 October 2007): 1 October 2008: see SI 2006/2814, art 4 (as amended by SI 2006/3473, art 2(c)–(e)).

Appointment (in relation to Wales for the purpose of enabling research applications to be made to, and determined by, an appropriate body): 1 July 2007: see SI 2007/856, art 3.

Appointment (in relation to Wales in respect of any research carried out as part of a project begun on or after 1 October 2007): 1 October 2007: see SI 2007/856, art 2.

Appointment (in relation to Wales for the purposes of research projects begun and approved before 1 October 2007): 1 October 2008: see SI 2007/856, art 4.

A1.36

32 Consulting carers etc

(1) This section applies if a person ("R")—

(a) is conducting an approved research project, and
(b) wishes to carry out research, as part of the project, on or in relation to a person ("P") who lacks capacity to consent to taking part in the project.

(2) R must take reasonable steps to identify a person who—

(a) otherwise than in a professional capacity or for remuneration, is engaged in caring for P or is interested in P's welfare, and
(b) is prepared to be consulted by R under this section.

(3) If R is unable to identify such a person he must, in accordance with guidance issued by the appropriate authority, nominate a person who—

(a) is prepared to be consulted by R under this section, but
(b) has no connection with the project.

(4) R must provide the person identified under subsection (2), or nominated under subsection (3), with information about the project and ask him—

(a) for advice as to whether P should take part in the project, and
(b) what, in his opinion, P's wishes and feelings about taking part in the project would be likely to be if P had capacity in relation to the matter.

(5) If, at any time, the person consulted advises R that in his opinion P's wishes and feelings would be likely to lead him to decline to take part in the project (or to wish to withdraw from it) if he had capacity in relation to the matter, R must ensure—

(a) if P is not already taking part in the project, that he does not take part in it;
(b) if P is taking part in the project, that he is withdrawn from it.

(6) But subsection (5)(b) does not require treatment that P has been receiving as part of the project to be discontinued if R has reasonable grounds for believing that there would be a significant risk to P's health if it were discontinued.

(7) The fact that a person is the donee of a lasting power of attorney given by P, or is P's deputy, does not prevent him from being the person consulted under this section.

(8) Subsection (9) applies if treatment is being, or is about to be, provided for P as a matter of urgency and R considers that, having regard to the nature of the research and of the particular circumstances of the case—

(a) it is also necessary to take action for the purposes of the research as a matter of urgency, but

(b) it is not reasonably practicable to consult under the previous provisions of this section.

(9) R may take the action if—

(a) he has the agreement of a registered medical practitioner who is not involved in the organisation or conduct of the research project, or

(b) where it is not reasonably practicable in the time available to obtain that agreement, he acts in accordance with a procedure approved by the appropriate body at the time when the research project was approved under section 31.

(10) But R may not continue to act in reliance on subsection (9) if he has reasonable grounds for believing that it is no longer necessary to take the action as a matter of urgency.

NOTES

Initial Commencement

To be appointed: see s 68(1), (2).

Appointment

Appointment (in relation to England for the purpose of enabling research applications to be made to, and determined by, an appropriate body): 1 July 2007: see SI 2006/2814, art 3 (as amended by SI 2006/3473, art 2(b)).
Appointment (in relation to England in respect of any research carried out as part of a project begun on or after 1 October 2007): 1 October 2007: see SI 2006/2814, art 2 (as amended by SI 2006/3473, art 2(a)).
Appointment (in relation to England for the purposes of research projects begun and approved before 1 October 2007): 1 October 2008: see SI 2006/2814, art 4 (as amended by SI 2006/3473, art 2(c)–(e)).
Appointment (in relation to Wales for the purpose of enabling research applications to be made to, and determined by, an appropriate body): 1 July 2007: see SI 2007/856, art 3.
Appointment (in relation to Wales in respect of any research carried out as part of a project begun on or after 1 October 2007): 1 October 2007: see SI 2007/856, art 2.
Appointment (in relation to Wales for the purposes of research projects begun and approved before 1 October 2007): 1 October 2008: see SI 2007/856, art 4.

A1.37

33 Additional safeguards

(1) This section applies in relation to a person who is taking part in an approved research project even though he lacks capacity to consent to taking part.

(2) Nothing may be done to, or in relation to, him in the course of the research—

(a) to which he appears to object (whether by showing signs of resistance or otherwise) except where what is being done is intended to protect him from harm or to reduce or prevent pain or discomfort, or

(b) which would be contrary to—

 (i) an advance decision of his which has effect, or

 (ii) any other form of statement made by him and not subsequently withdrawn,

of which R is aware.

(3) The interests of the person must be assumed to outweigh those of science and society.

(4) If he indicates (in any way) that he wishes to be withdrawn from the project he must be withdrawn without delay.

(5) P must be withdrawn from the project, without delay, if at any time the person conducting the research has reasonable grounds for believing that one or more of the requirements set out in section 31(2) to (7) is no longer met in relation to research being carried out on, or in relation to, P.

(6) But neither subsection (4) nor subsection (5) requires treatment that P has been receiving as part of the project to be discontinued if R has reasonable grounds for believing that there would be a significant risk to P's health if it were discontinued.

NOTES

Initial Commencement

To be appointed: see s 68(1), (2).

Appointment

Appointment (in relation to England for the purpose of enabling research applications to be made to, and determined by, an appropriate body): 1 July 2007: see SI 2006/2814, art 3 (as amended by SI 2006/3473, art 2(b)).

Appointment (in relation to England in respect of any research carried out as part of a project begun on or after 1 October 2007): 1 October 2007: see SI 2006/2814, art 2 (as amended by SI 2006/3473, art 2(a)).

Appointment (in relation to England for the purposes of research projects begun and approved before 1 October 2007): 1 October 2008: see SI 2006/2814, art 4 (as amended by SI 2006/3473, art 2(c)–(e)).

Appointment (in relation to Wales for the purpose of enabling research applications to be made to, and determined by, an appropriate body): 1 July 2007: see SI 2007/856, art 3.

Appointment (in relation to Wales in respect of any research carried out as part of a project begun on or after 1 October 2007): 1 October 2007: see SI 2007/856, art 2.

Appointment (in relation to Wales for the purposes of research projects begun and approved before 1 October 2007): 1 October 2008: see SI 2007/856, art 4.

A1.38

34 Loss of capacity during research project

(1) This section applies where a person ("P")—

(a) has consented to take part in a research project begun before the commencement of section 30, but
(b) before the conclusion of the project, loses capacity to consent to continue to take part in it.

(2) The appropriate authority may by regulations provide that, despite P's loss of capacity, research of a prescribed kind may be carried out on, or in relation to, P if—

(a) the project satisfies prescribed requirements,
(b) any information or material relating to P which is used in the research is of a prescribed description and was obtained before P's loss of capacity, and
(c) the person conducting the project takes in relation to P such steps as may be prescribed for the purpose of protecting him.

(3) The regulations may, in particular,—

(a) make provision about when, for the purposes of the regulations, a project is to be treated as having begun;
(b) include provision similar to any made by section 31, 32 or 33.

NOTES

Initial Commencement

To be appointed: see s 68(1), (2).

Appointment

Appointment (in relation to England for the purpose of enabling research applications to be made to, and determined by, an appropriate body): 1 July 2007: see SI 2006/2814, art 3 (as amended by SI 2006/3473, art 2(b)).

Appointment (in relation to England in respect of any research carried out as part of a project begun on or after 1 October 2007): 1 October 2007: see SI 2006/2814, art 2 (as amended by SI 2006/3473, art 2(a)).

Appointment (in relation to England for the purposes of research projects begun and approved before 1 October 2007): 1 October 2008: see SI 2006/2814, art 4 (as amended by SI 2006/3473, art 2(c)–(e)).

Appointment (in relation to Wales for the purpose of enabling research applications to be made to, and determined by, an appropriate body): 1 July 2007: see SI 2007/856, art 3.

Appointment (in relation to Wales in respect of any research carried out as part of a project begun on or after 1 October 2007): 1 October 2007: see SI 2007/856, art 2.

Appointment (in relation to Wales for the purposes of research projects begun and approved before 1 October 2007): 1 October 2008: see SI 2007/856, art 4.

Subordinate Legislation
Mental Capacity Act 2005 (Loss of Capacity during Research Project) (England) Regulations 2007, SI 2007/679 (made under sub-ss (1), (2), (3)(b)).
Mental Capacity Act 2005 (Loss of Capacity during Research Project) (Wales) Regulations 2007, SI 2007/837.

Independent mental capacity advocate service

A1.39

35 Appointment of independent mental capacity advocates

(1) The appropriate authority must make such arrangements as it considers reasonable to enable persons ("independent mental capacity advocates") to be available to represent and support persons to whom acts or decisions proposed under sections 37, 38 and 39 relate [or persons who fall within section 39A, 39C or 39D].

(2) The appropriate authority may make regulations as to the appointment of independent mental capacity advocates.

(3) The regulations may, in particular, provide—

- (a) that a person may act as an independent mental capacity advocate only in such circumstances, or only subject to such conditions, as may be prescribed;
- (b) for the appointment of a person as an independent mental capacity advocate to be subject to approval in accordance with the regulations.

(4) In making arrangements under subsection (1), the appropriate authority must have regard to the principle that a person to whom a proposed act or decision relates should, so far as practicable, be represented and supported by a person who is independent of any person who will be responsible for the act or decision.

(5) The arrangements may include provision for payments to be made to, or in relation to, persons carrying out functions in accordance with the arrangements.

(6) For the purpose of enabling him to carry out his functions, an independent mental capacity advocate—

- (a) may interview in private the person whom he has been instructed to represent, and
- (b) may, at all reasonable times, examine and take copies of—
  - (i) any health record,
  - (ii) any record of, or held by, a local authority and compiled in connection with a social services function, and
  - (iii) any record held by a person registered under Part 2 of the Care Standards Act 2000 (c 14),

which the person holding the record considers may be relevant to the independent mental capacity advocate's investigation.

(7) In this section, section 36 and section 37, "the appropriate authority" means—

- (a) in relation to the provision of the services of independent mental capacity advocates in England, the Secretary of State, and
- (b) in relation to the provision of the services of independent mental capacity advocates in Wales, the National Assembly for Wales.

NOTES

Initial Commencement
To be appointed: see s 68(1), (2).

Appointment
Appointment (in relation to England for certain purposes): 1 November 2006: see SI 2006/2814, art 5(a).
Appointment (in relation to England for remaining purposes): 1 April 2007: see SI 2006/2814, art 5(b).
Appointment (in relation to Wales): 1 October 2007: see SI 2007/856, art 5.

Amendment

Sub-s (1): words "or persons who fall within section 39A, 39C or 39D" in square brackets inserted by the Mental Health Act 2007, s 50(7), Sch 9, Pt 1, paras 1, 3. Date in force: to be appointed: see the Mental Health Act 2007, s 56(1).

Subordinate Legislation

Mental Capacity Act 2005 (Independent Mental Capacity Advocates) (General) Regulations 2006, SI 2006/1832 (made under sub-ss (2), (3)).
Mental Capacity Act 2005 (Independent Mental Capacity Advocates) (Wales) Regulations 2007, SI 2007/852 (made under sub-ss (2), (3)).

A1.40

36 Functions of independent mental capacity advocates

(1) The appropriate authority may make regulations as to the functions of independent mental capacity advocates.

(2) The regulations may, in particular, make provision requiring an advocate to take such steps as may be prescribed for the purpose of—

- (a) providing support to the person whom he has been instructed to represent ("P") so that P may participate as fully as possible in any relevant decision;
- (b) obtaining and evaluating relevant information;
- (c) ascertaining what P's wishes and feelings would be likely to be, and the beliefs and values that would be likely to influence P, if he had capacity;
- (d) ascertaining what alternative courses of action are available in relation to P;
- (e) obtaining a further medical opinion where treatment is proposed and the advocate thinks that one should be obtained.

(3) The regulations may also make provision as to circumstances in which the advocate may challenge, or provide assistance for the purpose of challenging, any relevant decision.

NOTES

Initial Commencement

To be appointed: see s 68(1), (2).

Appointment

Appointment (in relation to England for certain purposes): 1 November 2006: see SI 2006/2814, art 5(a).
Appointment (in relation to England for remaining purposes): 1 April 2007: see SI 2006/2814, art 5(b).
Appointment (in relation to Wales): 1 October 2007: see SI 2007/856, art 5.

Subordinate Legislation

Mental Capacity Act 2005 (Independent Mental Capacity Advocates) (General) Regulations 2006, SI 2006/1832.
Mental Capacity Act 2005 (Independent Mental Capacity Advocates) (Wales) Regulations 2007, SI 2007/852.

A1.41

37 Provision of serious medical treatment by NHS body

(1) This section applies if an NHS body—

- (a) is proposing to provide, or secure the provision of, serious medical treatment for a person ("P") who lacks capacity to consent to the treatment, and
- (b) is satisfied that there is no person, other than one engaged in providing care or treatment for P in a professional capacity or for remuneration, whom it would be appropriate to consult in determining what would be in P's best interests.

(2) But this section does not apply if P's treatment is regulated by Part 4 [or 4A] of the Mental Health Act.

(3) Before the treatment is provided, the NHS body must instruct an independent mental capacity advocate to represent P.

(4) If the treatment needs to be provided as a matter of urgency, it may be provided even though the NHS body has not been able to comply with subsection (3).

(5) The NHS body must, in providing or securing the provision of treatment for P, take into account any information given, or submissions made, by the independent mental capacity advocate.

(6) "Serious medical treatment" means treatment which involves providing, withholding or withdrawing treatment of a kind prescribed by regulations made by the appropriate authority.

(7) "NHS body" has such meaning as may be prescribed by regulations made for the purposes of this section by—

(a) the Secretary of State, in relation to bodies in England, or
(b) the National Assembly for Wales, in relation to bodies in Wales.

NOTES

Initial Commencement

To be appointed: see s 68(1), (2).

Appointment

Appointment (in relation to England for certain purposes): 1 November 2006: see SI 2006/2814, art 5(a).
Appointment (in relation to England for remaining purposes): 1 April 2007: see SI 2006/2814, art 5(b).
Appointment (in relation to Wales): 1 October 2007: see SI 2007/856, art 5.

Amendment

Sub-s (2): words "or 4A" in square brackets inserted by the Mental Health Act 2007, s 35(4), (6). Date in force: to be appointed: see the Mental Health Act 2007, s 56(1).

Subordinate Legislation

Mental Capacity Act 2005 (Independent Mental Capacity Advocates) (Wales) Regulations 2007, SI 2007/852 (made under sub-ss (6), (7)).

A1.42

38 Provision of accommodation by NHS body

(1) This section applies if an NHS body proposes to make arrangements—

(a) for the provision of accommodation in a hospital or care home for a person ("P") who lacks capacity to agree to the arrangements, or
(b) for a change in P's accommodation to another hospital or care home,

and is satisfied that there is no person, other than one engaged in providing care or treatment for P in a professional capacity or for remuneration, whom it would be appropriate for it to consult in determining what would be in P's best interests.

(2) But this section does not apply if P is accommodated as a result of an obligation imposed on him under the Mental Health Act.

[(2A) And this section does not apply if—

(a) an independent mental capacity advocate must be appointed under section 39A or 39C (whether or not by the NHS body) to represent P, and
(b) the hospital or care home in which P is to be accommodated under the arrangements referred to in this section is the relevant hospital or care home under the authorisation referred to in that section.]

(3) Before making the arrangements, the NHS body must instruct an independent mental capacity advocate to represent P unless it is satisfied that—

(a) the accommodation is likely to be provided for a continuous period which is less than the applicable period, or
(b) the arrangements need to be made as a matter of urgency.

(4) If the NHS body—

(a) did not instruct an independent mental capacity advocate to represent P before making the arrangements because it was satisfied that subsection (3)(a) or (b) applied, but

(b) subsequently has reason to believe that the accommodation is likely to be provided for a continuous period—
  (i) beginning with the day on which accommodation was first provided in accordance with the arrangements, and
  (ii) ending on or after the expiry of the applicable period,

it must instruct an independent mental capacity advocate to represent P.

(5) The NHS body must, in deciding what arrangements to make for P, take into account any information given, or submissions made, by the independent mental capacity advocate.

(6) "Care home" has the meaning given in section 3 of the Care Standards Act 2000 (c 14).

(7) "Hospital" means—

(a) a health service hospital as defined by [section 275 of the National Health Service Act 2006 or section 206 of the National Health Service (Wales) Act 2006], or
(b) an independent hospital as defined by section 2 of the Care Standards Act 2000.

(8) "NHS body" has such meaning as may be prescribed by regulations made for the purposes of this section by—

(a) the Secretary of State, in relation to bodies in England, or
(b) the National Assembly for Wales, in relation to bodies in Wales.

(9) "Applicable period" means—

(a) in relation to accommodation in a hospital, 28 days, and
(b) in relation to accommodation in a care home, 8 weeks.

[(10) For the purposes of subsection (1), a person appointed under Part 10 of Schedule A1 to be P's representative is not, by virtue of that appointment, engaged in providing care or treatment for P in a professional capacity or for remuneration.]

NOTES

Initial Commencement

To be appointed: see s 68(1), (2).

Appointment

Appointment (in relation to England for certain purposes): 1 November 2006: see SI 2006/2814, art 5(a).
Appointment (in relation to England for remaining purposes): 1 April 2007: see SI 2006/2814, art 5(b).
Appointment (in relation to Wales): 1 October 2007: see SI 2007/856, art 5.

Amendment

Sub-s (2A): inserted by the Mental Health Act 2007, s 50(7), Sch 9, Pt 1, paras 1, 4(1), (2). Date in force: to be appointed: see the Mental Health Act 2007, s 56(1).
Sub-s (7): in para (a) words from "section 275 of" to "National Health Service (Wales) Act 2006" in square brackets substituted by the National Health Service (Consequential Provisions) Act 2006, s 2, Sch 1, paras 277, 278. Date in force: 1 March 2007: see the National Health Service (Consequential Provisions) Act 2006, s 8(2).
Sub-s (10): inserted by the Mental Health Act 2007, s 50(7), Sch 9, Pt 1, paras 1, 4(1), (3). Date in force: to be appointed: see the Mental Health Act 2007, s 56(1).

Subordinate Legislation

Mental Capacity Act 2005 (Independent Mental Capacity Advocates) (Wales) Regulations 2007, SI 2007/852 (made under sub-s (8)).

A1.43

39 Provision of accommodation by local authority

(1) This section applies if a local authority propose to make arrangements—

(a) for the provision of residential accommodation for a person ("P") who lacks capacity to agree to the arrangements, or
(b) for a change in P's residential accommodation,

and are satisfied that there is no person, other than one engaged in providing care or treatment for P in a professional capacity or for remuneration, whom it would be appropriate for them to consult in determining what would be in P's best interests.

(2) But this section applies only if the accommodation is to be provided in accordance with—

(a) section 21 or 29 of the National Assistance Act 1948 (c 29), or
(b) section 117 of the Mental Health Act,

as the result of a decision taken by the local authority under section 47 of the National Health Service and Community Care Act 1990 (c 19).

(3) This section does not apply if P is accommodated as a result of an obligation imposed on him under the Mental Health Act.

[(3A) And this section does not apply if—

(a) an independent mental capacity advocate must be appointed under section 39A or 39C (whether or not by the local authority) to represent P, and
(b) the place in which P is to be accommodated under the arrangements referred to in this section is the relevant hospital or care home under the authorisation referred to in that section.]

(4) Before making the arrangements, the local authority must instruct an independent mental capacity advocate to represent P unless they are satisfied that—

(a) the accommodation is likely to be provided for a continuous period of less than 8 weeks, or
(b) the arrangements need to be made as a matter of urgency.

(5) If the local authority—

(a) did not instruct an independent mental capacity advocate to represent P before making the arrangements because they were satisfied that subsection (4)(a) or (b) applied, but
(b) subsequently have reason to believe that the accommodation is likely to be provided for a continuous period that will end 8 weeks or more after the day on which accommodation was first provided in accordance with the arrangements,

they must instruct an independent mental capacity advocate to represent P.

(6) The local authority must, in deciding what arrangements to make for P, take into account any information given, or submissions made, by the independent mental capacity advocate.

[(7) For the purposes of subsection (1), a person appointed under Part 10 of Schedule A1 to be P's representative is not, by virtue of that appointment, engaged in providing care or treatment for P in a professional capacity or for remuneration.]

NOTES

Initial Commencement
To be appointed: see s 68(1), (2).

Appointment
Appointment (in relation to England for certain purposes): 1 November 2006: see SI 2006/2814, art 5(a).
Appointment (in relation to England for remaining purposes): 1 April 2007: see SI 2006/2814, art 5(b).
Appointment (in relation to Wales): 1 October 2007: see SI 2007/856, art 5.

Amendment
Sub-s (3A): inserted by the Mental Health Act 2007, s 50(7), Sch 9, Pt 1, paras 1, 5(1), (2). Date in force: to be appointed: see the Mental Health Act 2007, s 56(1).
Sub-s (7): inserted by the Mental Health Act 2007, s 50(7), Sch 9, Pt 1, paras 1, 5(1), (3). Date in force: to be appointed: see the Mental Health Act 2007, s 56(1).

A1.44

[39A Person becomes subject to Schedule A1]

[(1) This section applies if—

(a) a person ("P") becomes subject to Schedule A1, and
(b) the managing authority of the relevant hospital or care home are satisfied that there is no person, other than one engaged in providing care or treatment for P in a professional capacity or for remuneration, whom it would be appropriate to consult in determining what would be in P's best interests.

(2) The managing authority must notify the supervisory body that this section applies.

(3) The supervisory body must instruct an independent mental capacity advocate to represent P.

(4) Schedule A1 makes provision about the role of an independent mental capacity advocate appointed under this section.

(5) This section is subject to paragraph 161 of Schedule A1.

(6) For the purposes of subsection (1), a person appointed under Part 10 of Schedule A1 to be P's representative is not, by virtue of that appointment, engaged in providing care or treatment for P in a professional capacity or for remuneration.]

NOTES

Amendment

Inserted by the Mental Health Act 2007, s 50(7), Sch 9, Pt 1, paras 1, 6. Date in force: to be appointed: see the Mental Health Act 2007, s 56(1).

A1.45

[39B Section 39A: supplementary provision]

[(1) This section applies for the purposes of section 39A.

(2) P becomes subject to Schedule A1 in any of the following cases.

(3) The first case is where an urgent authorisation is given in relation to P under paragraph 76(2) of Schedule A1 (urgent authorisation given before request made for standard authorisation).

(4) The second case is where the following conditions are met.

(5) The first condition is that a request is made under Schedule A1 for a standard authorisation to be given in relation to P ("the requested authorisation").

(6) The second condition is that no urgent authorisation was given under paragraph 76(2) of Schedule A1 before that request was made.

(7) The third condition is that the requested authorisation will not be in force on or before, or immediately after, the expiry of an existing standard authorisation.

(8) The expiry of a standard authorisation is the date when the authorisation is expected to cease to be in force.

(9) The third case is where, under paragraph 69 of Schedule A1, the supervisory body select a person to carry out an assessment of whether or not the relevant person is a detained resident.]

NOTES

Amendment

Inserted by the Mental Health Act 2007, s 50(7), Sch 9, Pt 1, paras 1, 6. Date in force: to be appointed: see the Mental Health Act 2007, s 56(1).

A1.46

[39C Person unrepresented whilst subject to Schedule A1]

[(1) This section applies if—

- (a) an authorisation under Schedule A1 is in force in relation to a person ("P"),
- (b) the appointment of a person as P's representative ends in accordance with regulations made under Part 10 of Schedule A1, and
- (c) the managing authority of the relevant hospital or care home are satisfied that there is no person, other than one engaged in providing care or treatment for P in a professional capacity or for remuneration, whom it would be appropriate to consult in determining what would be in P's best interests.

(2) The managing authority must notify the supervisory body that this section applies.

(3) The supervisory body must instruct an independent mental capacity advocate to represent P.

(4) Paragraph 159 of Schedule A1 makes provision about the role of an independent mental capacity advocate appointed under this section.

(5) The appointment of an independent mental capacity advocate under this section ends when a new appointment of a person as P's representative is made in accordance with Part 10 of Schedule A1.

(6) For the purposes of subsection (1), a person appointed under Part 10 of Schedule A1 to be P's representative is not, by virtue of that appointment, engaged in providing care or treatment for P in a professional capacity or for remuneration.]

NOTES

Amendment

Inserted by the Mental Health Act 2007, s 50(7), Sch 9, Pt 1, paras 1, 6. Date in force: to be appointed: see the Mental Health Act 2007, s 56(1).

A1.47

[39D Person subject to Schedule A1 without paid representative]

[(1) This section applies if—

- (a) an authorisation under Schedule A1 is in force in relation to a person ("P"),
- (b) P has a representative ("R") appointed under Part 10 of Schedule A1, and
- (c) R is not being paid under regulations under Part 10 of Schedule A1 for acting as P's representative.

(2) The supervisory body must instruct an independent mental capacity advocate to represent P in any of the following cases.

(3) The first case is where P makes a request to the supervisory body to instruct an advocate.

(4) The second case is where R makes a request to the supervisory body to instruct an advocate.

(5) The third case is where the supervisory body have reason to believe one or more of the following—

- (a) that, without the help of an advocate, P and R would be unable to exercise one or both of the relevant rights;
- (b) that P and R have each failed to exercise a relevant right when it would have been reasonable to exercise it;
- (c) that P and R are each unlikely to exercise a relevant right when it would be reasonable to exercise it.

(6) The duty in subsection (2) is subject to section 39E.

(7) If an advocate is appointed under this section, the advocate is, in particular, to take such steps as are practicable to help P and R to understand the following matters—

- (a) the effect of the authorisation;
- (b) the purpose of the authorisation;
- (c) the duration of the authorisation;
- (d) any conditions to which the authorisation is subject;
- (e) the reasons why each assessor who carried out an assessment in connection with the request for the authorisation, or in connection with a review of the authorisation, decided that P met the qualifying requirement in question;
- (f) the relevant rights;
- (g) how to exercise the relevant rights.

(8) The advocate is, in particular, to take such steps as are practicable to help P or R—

- (a) to exercise the right to apply to court, if it appears to the advocate that P or R wishes to exercise that right, or
- (b) to exercise the right of review, if it appears to the advocate that P or R wishes to exercise that right.

(9) If the advocate helps P or R to exercise the right of review—

(a) the advocate may make submissions to the supervisory body on the question of whether a qualifying requirement is reviewable;
(b) the advocate may give information, or make submissions, to any assessor carrying out a review assessment.

(10) In this section—

"relevant rights" means—
(a) the right to apply to court, and
(b) the right of review;
"right to apply to court" means the right to make an application to the court to exercise its jurisdiction under section 21A;
"right of review" means the right under Part 8 of Schedule A1 to request a review.]

NOTES

Amendment

Inserted by the Mental Health Act 2007, s 50(7), Sch 9, Pt 1, paras 1, 6. Date in force: to be appointed: see the Mental Health Act 2007, s 56(1).

A1.48

[39E Limitation on duty to instruct advocate under section 39D]

[(1) This section applies if an advocate is already representing P in accordance with an instruction under section 39D.

(2) Section 39D(2) does not require another advocate to be instructed, unless the following conditions are met.

(3) The first condition is that the existing advocate was instructed—

(a) because of a request by R, or
(b) because the supervisory body had reason to believe one or more of the things in section 39D(5).

(4) The second condition is that the other advocate would be instructed because of a request by P.]

NOTES

Amendment

Inserted by the Mental Health Act 2007, s 50(7), Sch 9, Pt 1, paras 1, 6. Date in force: to be appointed: see the Mental Health Act 2007, s 56(1).

A1.49

[40 **Exceptions**]

[[(1)] The duty imposed by section 37(3), 38(3) or (4) *or 39(4) or (5)* [, 39(4) or (5), 39A(3), 39C(3) or 39D(2)] does not apply where there is—

(a) a person nominated by P (in whatever manner) as a person to be consulted on matters to which that duty relates,
(b) a donee of a lasting power of attorney created by P who is authorised to make decisions in relation to those matters, or
(c) a deputy appointed by the court for P with power to make decisions in relation to those matters.

[(2) A person appointed under Part 10 of Schedule A1 to be P's representative is not, by virtue of that appointment, a person nominated by P as a person to be consulted in matters to which a duty mentioned in subsection (1) relates.]]

NOTES

Amendment

Substituted by the Mental Health Act 2007, s 49. Date in force: 1 October 2007: see SI 2007/2798, art 2(h).

Sub-s (1): numbered as such by the Mental Health Act 2007, s 50(7), Sch 9, Pt 1, paras 1, 7(1), (2). Date in force: to be appointed: see the Mental Health Act 2007, s 56(1).
Sub-s (1): words "or 39(4) or (5)" in italics repealed and subsequent words in square brackets substituted by the Mental Health Act 2007, s 50(7), Sch 9, Pt 1, paras 1, 7(1), (3). Date in force: to be appointed: see the Mental Health Act 2007, s 56(1).
Sub-s (2): inserted by the Mental Health Act 2007, s 50(7), Sch 9, Pt 1, paras 1, 7(1), (4). Date in force: to be appointed: see the Mental Health Act 2007, s 56(1).

A1.50

41 Power to adjust role of independent mental capacity advocate

(1) The appropriate authority may make regulations—

- (a) expanding the role of independent mental capacity advocates in relation to persons who lack capacity, and
- (b) adjusting the obligation to make arrangements imposed by section 35.

(2) The regulations may, in particular—

- (a) prescribe circumstances (different to those set out in sections 37, 38 and 39) in which an independent mental capacity advocate must, or circumstances in which one may, be instructed by a person of a prescribed description to represent a person who lacks capacity, and
- (b) include provision similar to any made by section 37, 38, 39 or 40.

(3) "Appropriate authority" has the same meaning as in section 35.

NOTES

Initial Commencement

To be appointed: see s 68(1), (2).

Appointment

Appointment (in relation to England for certain purposes): 1 November 2006: see SI 2006/2814, art 5(a).
Appointment (in relation to England for remaining purposes): 1 April 2007: see SI 2006/2814, art 5(b).
Appointment (in relation to Wales): 1 October 2007: see SI 2007/856, art 5.

Subordinate Legislation

Mental Capacity Act 2005 (Independent Mental Capacity Advocates) (Expansion of Role) Regulations 2006, SI 2006/2883 (made under sub-ss (1), (2)).
Mental Capacity Act 2005 (Independent Mental Capacity Advocates) (Wales) Regulations 2007, SI 2007/852.

Miscellaneous and supplementary

A1.51

42 Codes of practice

(1) The Lord Chancellor must prepare and issue one or more codes of practice—

- (a) for the guidance of persons assessing whether a person has capacity in relation to any matter,
- (b) for the guidance of persons acting in connection with the care or treatment of another person (see section 5),
- (c) for the guidance of donees of lasting powers of attorney,
- (d) for the guidance of deputies appointed by the court,
- (e) for the guidance of persons carrying out research in reliance on any provision made by or under this Act (and otherwise with respect to sections 30 to 34),
- (f) for the guidance of independent mental capacity advocates,
- [(fa) for the guidance of persons exercising functions under Schedule A1,
- (fb) for the guidance of representatives appointed under Part 10 of Schedule A1,]
- (g) with respect to the provisions of sections 24 to 26 (advance decisions and apparent advance decisions), and
- (h) with respect to such other matters concerned with this Act as he thinks fit.

(2) The Lord Chancellor may from time to time revise a code.

(3) The Lord Chancellor may delegate the preparation or revision of the whole or any part of a code so far as he considers expedient.

(4) It is the duty of a person to have regard to any relevant code if he is acting in relation to a person who lacks capacity and is doing so in one or more of the following ways—

(a) as the donee of a lasting power of attorney,
(b) as a deputy appointed by the court,
(c) as a person carrying out research in reliance on any provision made by or under this Act (see sections 30 to 34),
(d) as an independent mental capacity advocate,
[(da) in the exercise of functions under Schedule A1,
(db) as a representative appointed under Part 10 of Schedule A1,]
(e) in a professional capacity,
(f) for remuneration.

(5) If it appears to a court or tribunal conducting any criminal or civil proceedings that—

(a) a provision of a code, or
(b) a failure to comply with a code,

is relevant to a question arising in the proceedings, the provision or failure must be taken into account in deciding the question.

(6) A code under subsection (1)(d) may contain separate guidance for deputies appointed by virtue of paragraph 1(2) of Schedule 5 (functions of deputy conferred on receiver appointed under the Mental Health Act).

(7) In this section and in section 43, "code" means a code prepared or revised under this section.

NOTES

Initial Commencement

To be appointed: see s 68(1).

Appointment

Sub-ss (1)–(3), (6), (7): Appointment: 1 April 2007: see SI 2007/563, art 2(1)(a).

Sub-ss (4), (5): Appointment (in relation to England for certain purposes): 1 April 2007: see SI 2007/563, art 2(2)(e).

Sub-ss (4), (5): Appointment (for certain purposes): 1 April 2007: see SI 2007/563, art 2(2)(e), (3).

Sub-ss (4), (5): Appointment (for remaining purposes): 1 October 2007: see SI 2007/1897, art 2(2)(e).

Amendment

Sub-s (1): paras (fa), (fb) inserted by the Mental Health Act 2007, s 50(7), Sch 9, Pt 1, paras 1, 8(1), (2). Date in force: to be appointed: see the Mental Health Act 2007, s 56(1).

Sub-s (4): paras (da), (db) inserted by the Mental Health Act 2007, s 50(7), Sch 9, Pt 1, paras 1, 8(1), (3). Date in force:1 April 2008: see SI 2008/745, art 4(b).

A1.52

43 Codes of practice: procedure

(1) Before preparing or revising a code, the Lord Chancellor must consult—

(a) the National Assembly for Wales, and
(b) such other persons as he considers appropriate.

(2) The Lord Chancellor may not issue a code unless—

(a) a draft of the code has been laid by him before both Houses of Parliament, and
(b) the 40 day period has elapsed without either House resolving not to approve the draft.

(3) The Lord Chancellor must arrange for any code that he has issued to be published in such a way as he considers appropriate for bringing it to the attention of persons likely to be concerned with its provisions.

(4) "40 day period", in relation to the draft of a proposed code, means—

(a) if the draft is laid before one House on a day later than the day on which it is laid before the other House, the period of 40 days beginning with the later of the two days;
(b) in any other case, the period of 40 days beginning with the day on which it is laid before each House.

(5) In calculating the period of 40 days, no account is to be taken of any period during which Parliament is dissolved or prorogued or during which both Houses are adjourned for more than 4 days.

NOTES

Initial Commencement
To be appointed: see s 68(1).

Appointment
Appointment: 1 April 2007: see SI 2007/563, art 2(1)(a).

A1.53

44 Ill-treatment or neglect

(1) Subsection (2) applies if a person ("D")—

(a) has the care of a person ("P") who lacks, or whom D reasonably believes to lack, capacity,
(b) is the donee of a lasting power of attorney, or an enduring power of attorney (within the meaning of Schedule 4), created by P, or
(c) is a deputy appointed by the court for P.

(2) D is guilty of an offence if he ill-treats or wilfully neglects P.

(3) A person guilty of an offence under this section is liable—

(a) on summary conviction, to imprisonment for a term not exceeding 12 months or a fine not exceeding the statutory maximum or both;
(b) on conviction on indictment, to imprisonment for a term not exceeding 5 years or a fine or both.

NOTES

Initial Commencement
To be appointed: see s 68(1).

Appointment
Appointment: 1 April 2007: see SI 2007/563, art 2(1)(b).

PART 2
THE COURT OF PROTECTION AND THE PUBLIC GUARDIAN

The Court of Protection

A1.54

45 The Court of Protection

(1) There is to be a superior court of record known as the Court of Protection.

(2) The court is to have an official seal.

(3) The court may sit at any place in England and Wales, on any day and at any time.

(4) The court is to have a central office and registry at a place appointed by the Lord Chancellor[, after consulting the Lord Chief Justice].

(5) The Lord Chancellor may[, after consulting the Lord Chief Justice,] designate as additional registries of the court any district registry of the High Court and any county court office.

[(5A) The Lord Chief Justice may nominate any of the following to exercise his functions under this section—

(a) the President of the Court of Protection;
(b) a judicial office holder (as defined in section 109(4) of the Constitutional Reform Act 2005).]

(6) The office of the Supreme Court called the Court of Protection ceases to exist.

NOTES

Initial Commencement

To be appointed: see s 68(1).

Appointment

Appointment: 1 October 2007: see SI 2007/1897, art 2(1)(b).

Amendment

Sub-s (4): words ", after consulting the Lord Chief Justice" in square brackets inserted by SI 2006/1016, art 2, Sch 1, paras 30, 32(1), (2). Date in force: 3 April 2006: see SI 2006/1016, art 1.

Sub-s (5) words ", after consulting the Lord Chief Justice," in square brackets inserted by SI 2006/1016, art 2, Sch 1, paras 30, 32(1), (3). Date in force: 3 April 2006: see SI 2006/1016, art 1.

Sub-s (5A): inserted by SI 2006/1016, art 2, Sch 1, paras 30, 32(1), (4). Date in force: 3 April 2006: see SI 2006/1016, art 1.

A1.55

46 The judges of the Court of Protection

(1) Subject to Court of Protection Rules under section 51(2)(d), the jurisdiction of the court is exercisable by a judge nominated for that purpose by—

(a) the [Lord Chief Justice], or
[(b) where nominated by the Lord Chief Justice to act on his behalf under this subsection—
  (i) the President of the Court of Protection; or
  (ii) a judicial office holder (as defined in section 109(4) of the Constitutional Reform Act 2005)].

(2) To be nominated, a judge must be—

(a) the President of the Family Division,
(b) the Vice-Chancellor,
(c) a puisne judge of the High Court,
(d) a circuit judge, or
(e) a district judge.

(3) The [Lord Chief Justice, after consulting the Lord Chancellor,] must—

(a) appoint one of the judges nominated by virtue of subsection (2)(a) to (c) to be President of the Court of Protection, and
(b) appoint another of those judges to be Vice-President of the Court of Protection.

(4) The [Lord Chief Justice, after consulting the Lord Chancellor,] must appoint one of the judges nominated by virtue of subsection (2)(d) or (e) to be Senior Judge of the Court of Protection, having such administrative functions in relation to the court as the Lord Chancellor[, after consulting the Lord Chief Justice,] may direct.

NOTES

Initial Commencement

To be appointed: see s 68(1).

Appointment

Appointment: 1 October 2007: see SI 2007/1897, art 2(1)(b).

Amendment

Sub-s (1): in para (a) words "Lord Chief Justice" in square brackets substituted by SI 2006/1016, art 2, Sch 1, paras 30, 33(1), (2). Date in force: 3 April 2006: see SI 2006/1016, art 1.

Sub-s (1): para (b) substituted by SI 2006/1016, art 2, Sch 1, paras 30, 33(1), (3). Date in force: 3 April 2006: see SI 2006/1016, art 1.

Sub-s (3): words "Lord Chief Justice, after consulting the Lord Chancellor," in square brackets substituted by SI 2006/1016, art 2, Sch 1, paras 30, 33(1), (4). Date in force: 3 April 2006: see SI 2006/1016, art 1.
Sub-s (4): words "Lord Chief Justice, after consulting the Lord Chancellor," in square brackets substituted by SI 2006/1016, art 2, Sch 1, paras 30, 33(1), (5)(a). Date in force: 3 April 2006: see SI 2006/1016, art 1.
Sub-s (4): words ", after consulting the Lord Chief Justice," in square brackets inserted by SI 2006/1016, art 2, Sch 1, paras 30, 33(1), (5)(b). Date in force: 3 April 2006: see SI 2006/1016, art 1.

Supplementary powers

A1.56

47 General powers and effect of orders etc

(1) The court has in connection with its jurisdiction the same powers, rights, privileges and authority as the High Court.

(2) Section 204 of the Law of Property Act 1925 (c 20) (orders of High Court conclusive in favour of purchasers) applies in relation to orders and directions of the court as it applies to orders of the High Court.

(3) Office copies of orders made, directions given or other instruments issued by the court and sealed with its official seal are admissible in all legal proceedings as evidence of the originals without any further proof.

NOTES

Initial Commencement
To be appointed: see s 68(1).

Appointment
Appointment: 1 October 2007: see SI 2007/1897, art 2(1)(b).

A1.57

48 Interim orders and directions

The court may, pending the determination of an application to it in relation to a person ("P"), make an order or give directions in respect of any matter if—

(a) there is reason to believe that P lacks capacity in relation to the matter,
(b) the matter is one to which its powers under this Act extend, and
(c) it is in P's best interests to make the order, or give the directions, without delay.

NOTES

Initial Commencement
To be appointed: see s 68(1).

Appointment
Appointment: 1 October 2007: see SI 2007/1897, art 2(1)(b).

A1.58

49 Power to call for reports

(1) This section applies where, in proceedings brought in respect of a person ("P") under Part 1, the court is considering a question relating to P.

(2) The court may require a report to be made to it by the Public Guardian or by a Court of Protection Visitor.

(3) The court may require a local authority, or an NHS body, to arrange for a report to be made—

(a) by one of its officers or employees, or

(b) by such other person (other than the Public Guardian or a Court of Protection Visitor) as the authority, or the NHS body, considers appropriate.

(4) The report must deal with such matters relating to P as the court may direct.

(5) Court of Protection Rules may specify matters which, unless the court directs otherwise, must also be dealt with in the report.

(6) The report may be made in writing or orally, as the court may direct.

(7) In complying with a requirement, the Public Guardian or a Court of Protection Visitor may, at all reasonable times, examine and take copies of—

(a) any health record,
(b) any record of, or held by, a local authority and compiled in connection with a social services function, and
(c) any record held by a person registered under Part 2 of the Care Standards Act 2000 (c 14),

so far as the record relates to P.

(8) If the Public Guardian or a Court of Protection Visitor is making a visit in the course of complying with a requirement, he may interview P in private.

(9) If a Court of Protection Visitor who is a Special Visitor is making a visit in the course of complying with a requirement, he may if the court so directs carry out in private a medical, psychiatric or psychological examination of P's capacity and condition.

(10) "NHS body" has the meaning given in section 148 of the Health and Social Care (Community Health and Standards) Act 2003 (c 43).

(11) "Requirement" means a requirement imposed under subsection (2) or (3).

NOTES

Initial Commencement
To be appointed: see s 68(1).

Appointment
Appointment: 1 October 2007: see SI 2007/1897, art 2(1)(b).

Subordinate Legislation
Court of Protection Rules 2007, SI 2007/1744 (made under sub-s (5)).

Practice and procedure

A1.59

50 Applications to the Court of Protection

(1) No permission is required for an application to the court for the exercise of any of its powers under this Act—

(a) by a person who lacks, or is alleged to lack, capacity,
(b) if such a person has not reached 18, by anyone with parental responsibility for him,
(c) by the donor or a donee of a lasting power of attorney to which the application relates,
(d) by a deputy appointed by the court for a person to whom the application relates, or
(e) by a person named in an existing order of the court, if the application relates to the order.

[(1A) Nor is permission required for an application to the court under section 21A by the relevant person's representative.]

(2) But, subject to Court of Protection Rules and to paragraph 20(2) of Schedule 3 (declarations relating to private international law), permission is required for any other application to the court.

(3) In deciding whether to grant permission the court must, in particular, have regard to—

(a) the applicant's connection with the person to whom the application relates,
(b) the reasons for the application,

(c) the benefit to the person to whom the application relates of a proposed order or directions, and
(d) whether the benefit can be achieved in any other way.

(4) "Parental responsibility" has the same meaning as in the Children Act 1989 (c 41).

NOTES

Initial Commencement
To be appointed: see s 68(1).

Appointment
Appointment: 1 October 2007: see SI 2007/1897, art 2(1)(b).

Amendment
Sub-s (1A): inserted by the Mental Health Act 2007, s 50(7), Sch 9, Pt 1, paras 1, 9. Date in force: to be appointed: see the Mental Health Act 2007, s 56(1).

Subordinate Legislation
Court of Protection Rules 2007, SI 2007/1744 (made under sub-s (2)).

A1.60

51 Court of Protection Rules

[(1) Rules of court with respect to the practice and procedure of the court (to be called "Court of Protection Rules") may be made in accordance with Part 1 of Schedule 1 to the Constitutional Reform Act 2005.]

(2) Court of Protection Rules may, in particular, make provision—

(a) as to the manner and form in which proceedings are to be commenced;
(b) as to the persons entitled to be notified of, and be made parties to, the proceedings;
(c) for the allocation, in such circumstances as may be specified, of any specified description of proceedings to a specified judge or to specified descriptions of judges;
(d) for the exercise of the jurisdiction of the court, in such circumstances as may be specified, by its officers or other staff;
(e) for enabling the court to appoint a suitable person (who may, with his consent, be the Official Solicitor) to act in the name of, or on behalf of, or to represent the person to whom the proceedings relate;
(f) for enabling an application to the court to be disposed of without a hearing;
(g) for enabling the court to proceed with, or with any part of, a hearing in the absence of the person to whom the proceedings relate;
(h) for enabling or requiring the proceedings or any part of them to be conducted in private and for enabling the court to determine who is to be admitted when the court sits in private and to exclude specified persons when it sits in public;
(i) as to what may be received as evidence (whether or not admissible apart from the rules) and the manner in which it is to be presented;
(j) for the enforcement of orders made and directions given in the proceedings.

(3) Court of Protection Rules may, instead of providing for any matter, refer to provision made or to be made about that matter by directions.

(4) Court of Protection Rules may make different provision for different areas.

NOTES

Initial Commencement
To be appointed: see s 68(1).

Appointment
Appointment: 1 October 2007: see SI 2007/1897, art 2(1)(b).

Amendment
Sub-s (1): substituted by SI 2006/1016, art 2, Sch 1, paras 30, 34. Date in force: 3 April 2006: see SI 2006/1016, art 1.

Subordinate Legislation
Court of Protection Rules 2007, SI 2007/1744.

A1.61

[52 Practice directions]

[(1) Directions as to the practice and procedure of the court may be given in accordance with Part 1 of Schedule 2 to the Constitutional Reform Act 2005.

(2) Practice directions given otherwise than under subsection (1) may not be given without the approval of—

(a) the Lord Chancellor, and
(b) the Lord Chief Justice.

(3) The Lord Chief Justice may nominate any of the following to exercise his functions under this section—

(a) the President of the Court of Protection;
(b) a judicial office holder (as defined in section 109(4) of the Constitutional Reform Act 2005).]

NOTES

Amendment
Substituted by SI 2006/1016, art 2, Sch 1, paras 30, 35. Date in force: 3 April 2006: see SI 2006/1016, art 1.

A1.62

53 Rights of appeal

(1) Subject to the provisions of this section, an appeal lies to the Court of Appeal from any decision of the court.

(2) Court of Protection Rules may provide that where a decision of the court is made by—

(a) a person exercising the jurisdiction of the court by virtue of rules made under section 51(2)(d),
(b) a district judge, or
(c) a circuit judge,

an appeal from that decision lies to a prescribed higher judge of the court and not to the Court of Appeal.

(3) For the purposes of this section the higher judges of the court are—

(a) in relation to a person mentioned in subsection (2)(a), a circuit judge or a district judge;
(b) in relation to a person mentioned in subsection (2)(b), a circuit judge;
(c) in relation to any person mentioned in subsection (2), one of the judges nominated by virtue of section 46(2)(a) to (c).

(4) Court of Protection Rules may make provision—

(a) that, in such cases as may be specified, an appeal from a decision of the court may not be made without permission;
(b) as to the person or persons entitled to grant permission to appeal;
(c) as to any requirements to be satisfied before permission is granted;
(d) that where a higher judge of the court makes a decision on an appeal, no appeal may be made to the Court of Appeal from that decision unless the Court of Appeal considers that—
  (i) the appeal would raise an important point of principle or practice, or
  (ii) there is some other compelling reason for the Court of Appeal to hear it;
(e) as to any considerations to be taken into account in relation to granting or refusing permission to appeal.

NOTES

Initial Commencement
To be appointed: see s 68(1).

Appointment
Appointment: 1 October 2007: see SI 2007/1897, art 2(1)(b).

Subordinate Legislation
Court of Protection Rules 2007, SI 2007/1744 (made under sub-ss (2), (4)).

Fees and costs

A1.63

54 Fees

(1) The Lord Chancellor may with the consent of the Treasury by order prescribe fees payable in respect of anything dealt with by the court.

(2) An order under this section may in particular contain provision as to—

- (a) scales or rates of fees;
- (b) exemptions from and reductions in fees;
- (c) remission of fees in whole or in part.

(3) Before making an order under this section, the Lord Chancellor must consult—

- (a) the President of the Court of Protection,
- (b) the Vice-President of the Court of Protection, and
- (c) the Senior Judge of the Court of Protection.

(4) The Lord Chancellor must take such steps as are reasonably practicable to bring information about fees to the attention of persons likely to have to pay them.

(5) Fees payable under this section are recoverable summarily as a civil debt.

NOTES

Initial Commencement
To be appointed: see s 68(1).

Appointment
Appointment: 1 October 2007: see SI 2007/1897, art 2(1)(b).

Subordinate Legislation
Court of Protection Fees Order 2007, SI 2007/1745 (made under sub-ss (1), (2)).

A1.64

55 Costs

(1) Subject to Court of Protection Rules, the costs of and incidental to all proceedings in the court are in its discretion.

(2) The rules may in particular make provision for regulating matters relating to the costs of those proceedings, including prescribing scales of costs to be paid to legal or other representatives.

(3) The court has full power to determine by whom and to what extent the costs are to be paid.

(4) The court may, in any proceedings—

- (a) disallow, or
- (b) order the legal or other representatives concerned to meet,

the whole of any wasted costs or such part of them as may be determined in accordance with the rules.

(5) "Legal or other representative", in relation to a party to proceedings, means any person exercising a right of audience or right to conduct litigation on his behalf.

(6) "Wasted costs" means any costs incurred by a party—

- (a) as a result of any improper, unreasonable or negligent act or omission on the part of any legal or other representative or any employee of such a representative, or
- (b) which, in the light of any such act or omission occurring after they were incurred, the court considers it is unreasonable to expect that party to pay.

NOTES

Initial Commencement
To be appointed: see s 68(1).

Appointment
Appointment: 1 October 2007: see SI 2007/1897, art 2(1)(b).

Subordinate Legislation
Court of Protection Rules 2007, SI 2007/1744.

A1.65

56 Fees and costs: supplementary

(1) Court of Protection Rules may make provision—

- (a) as to the way in which, and funds from which, fees and costs are to be paid;
- (b) for charging fees and costs upon the estate of the person to whom the proceedings relate;
- (c) for the payment of fees and costs within a specified time of the death of the person to whom the proceedings relate or the conclusion of the proceedings.

(2) A charge on the estate of a person created by virtue of subsection (1)(b) does not cause any interest of the person in any property to fail or determine or to be prevented from recommencing.

NOTES

Initial Commencement
To be appointed: see s 68(1).

Appointment
Appointment: 1 October 2007: see SI 2007/1897, art 2(1)(b).

Subordinate Legislation
Court of Protection Rules 2007, SI 2007/1744.

The Public Guardian

A1.66

57 The Public Guardian

(1) For the purposes of this Act, there is to be an officer, to be known as the Public Guardian.

(2) The Public Guardian is to be appointed by the Lord Chancellor.

(3) There is to be paid to the Public Guardian out of money provided by Parliament such salary as the Lord Chancellor may determine.

(4) The Lord Chancellor may, after consulting the Public Guardian—

- (a) provide him with such officers and staff, or
- (b) enter into such contracts with other persons for the provision (by them or their sub-contractors) of officers, staff or services,

as the Lord Chancellor thinks necessary for the proper discharge of the Public Guardian's functions.

(5) Any functions of the Public Guardian may, to the extent authorised by him, be performed by any of his officers.

NOTES

Initial Commencement
To be appointed: see s 68(1).

Appointment
Appointment: 1 October 2007: see SI 2007/1897, art 2(1)(b).

A1.67

58 Functions of the Public Guardian

(1) The Public Guardian has the following functions—

- (a) establishing and maintaining a register of lasting powers of attorney,
- (b) establishing and maintaining a register of orders appointing deputies,
- (c) supervising deputies appointed by the court,
- (d) directing a Court of Protection Visitor to visit—
  - (i) a donee of a lasting power of attorney,
  - (ii) a deputy appointed by the court, or
  - (iii) the person granting the power of attorney or for whom the deputy is appointed ("P"),

  and to make a report to the Public Guardian on such matters as he may direct,
- (e) receiving security which the court requires a person to give for the discharge of his functions,
- (f) receiving reports from donees of lasting powers of attorney and deputies appointed by the court,
- (g) reporting to the court on such matters relating to proceedings under this Act as the court requires,
- (h) dealing with representations (including complaints) about the way in which a donee of a lasting power of attorney or a deputy appointed by the court is exercising his powers,
- (i) publishing, in any manner the Public Guardian thinks appropriate, any information he thinks appropriate about the discharge of his functions.

(2) The functions conferred by subsection (1)(c) and (h) may be discharged in co-operation with any other person who has functions in relation to the care or treatment of P.

(3) The Lord Chancellor may by regulations make provision—

- (a) conferring on the Public Guardian other functions in connection with this Act;
- (b) in connection with the discharge by the Public Guardian of his functions.

(4) Regulations made under subsection (3)(b) may in particular make provision as to—

- (a) the giving of security by deputies appointed by the court and the enforcement and discharge of security so given;
- (b) the fees which may be charged by the Public Guardian;
- (c) the way in which, and funds from which, such fees are to be paid;
- (d) exemptions from and reductions in such fees;
- (e) remission of such fees in whole or in part;
- (f) the making of reports to the Public Guardian by deputies appointed by the court and others who are directed by the court to carry out any transaction for a person who lacks capacity.

(5) For the purpose of enabling him to carry out his functions, the Public Guardian may, at all reasonable times, examine and take copies of—

- (a) any health record,
- (b) any record of, or held by, a local authority and compiled in connection with a social services function, and
- (c) any record held by a person registered under Part 2 of the Care Standards Act 2000 (c 14),

so far as the record relates to P.

(6) The Public Guardian may also for that purpose interview P in private.

NOTES

Initial Commencement

To be appointed: see s 68(1).

Appointment

Appointment: 1 October 2007: see SI 2007/1897, art 2(1)(b).

Subordinate Legislation

Lasting Powers of Attorney, Enduring Powers of Attorney and Public Guardian Regulations 2007, SI 2007/1253 (made under sub-s (3)).

Public Guardian (Fees, etc) Regulations 2007, SI 2007/2051 (made under sub-ss (3), (4)).

Lasting Powers of Attorney, Enduring Powers of Attorney and Public Guardian (Amendment) Regulations 2007, SI 2007/2161 (made under sub-s (3)).

Public Guardian (Fees, etc) (Amendment) Regulations 2007, SI 2007/2616 (made under sub-ss (3), (4)).

A1.68

59 Public Guardian Board

(1) There is to be a body, to be known as the Public Guardian Board.

(2) The Board's duty is to scrutinise and review the way in which the Public Guardian discharges his functions and to make such recommendations to the Lord Chancellor about that matter as it thinks appropriate.

(3) The Lord Chancellor must, in discharging his functions under sections 57 and 58, give due consideration to recommendations made by the Board.

(4) ...

(5) The Board must have—

(a) at least one member who is a judge of the court, and
(b) at least four members who are persons appearing to the Lord Chancellor to have appropriate knowledge or experience of the work of the Public Guardian.

[(5A) Where a person to be appointed as a member of the Board is a judge of the court, the appointment is to be made by the Lord Chief Justice after consulting the Lord Chancellor.

(5B) In any other case, the appointment of a person as a member of the Board is to be made by the Lord Chancellor.]

(6) The Lord Chancellor may by regulations make provision as to—

(a) the appointment of members of the Board (and, in particular, the procedures to be followed in connection with appointments);
(b) the selection of one of the members to be the chairman;
(c) the term of office of the chairman and members;
(d) their resignation, suspension or removal;
(e) the procedure of the Board (including quorum);
(f) the validation of proceedings in the event of a vacancy among the members or a defect in the appointment of a member.

(7) Subject to any provision made in reliance on subsection (6)(c) or (d), a person is to hold and vacate office as a member of the Board in accordance with the terms of the instrument appointing him.

(8) The Lord Chancellor may make such payments to or in respect of members of the Board by way of reimbursement of expenses, allowances and remuneration as he may determine.

(9) The Board must make an annual report to the Lord Chancellor about the discharge of its functions.

[(10) The Lord Chief Justice may nominate any of the following to exercise his functions under this section—

(a) the President of the Court of Protection;
(b) a judicial office holder (as defined in section 109(4) of the Constitutional Reform Act 2005).]

NOTES

Initial Commencement
To be appointed: see s 68(1).

Appointment
Appointment: 1 October 2007: see SI 2007/1897, art 2(1)(b).

Amendment
Sub-s (4): repealed by SI 2006/1016, art 2, Sch 1, paras 30, 36(1), (2). Date in force: 3 April 2006: see SI 2006/1016, art 1.
Sub-ss (5A), (5B): inserted by SI 2006/1016, art 2, Sch 1, paras 30, 36(1), (3). Date in force: 3 April 2006: see SI 2006/1016, art 1.
Sub-s (10): inserted by SI 2006/1016, art 2, Sch 1, paras 30, 36(1), (4). Date in force: 3 April 2006: see SI 2006/1016, art 1.

Subordinate Legislation
Public Guardian Board Regulations 2007, SI 2007/1770 (made under sub-s (6)).

A1.69

60 Annual report

(1) The Public Guardian must make an annual report to the Lord Chancellor about the discharge of his functions.

(2) The Lord Chancellor must, within one month of receiving the report, lay a copy of it before Parliament.

NOTES

Initial Commencement
To be appointed: see s 68(1).

Appointment
Appointment: 1 October 2007: see SI 2007/1897, art 2(1)(b).

Court of Protection Visitors

A1.70

61 Court of Protection Visitors

(1) A Court of Protection Visitor is a person who is appointed by the Lord Chancellor to—

(a) a panel of Special Visitors, or
(b) a panel of General Visitors.

(2) A person is not qualified to be a Special Visitor unless he—

(a) is a registered medical practitioner or appears to the Lord Chancellor to have other suitable qualifications or training, and
(b) appears to the Lord Chancellor to have special knowledge of and experience in cases of impairment of or disturbance in the functioning of the mind or brain.

(3) A General Visitor need not have a medical qualification.

(4) A Court of Protection Visitor—

(a) may be appointed for such term and subject to such conditions, and
(b) may be paid such remuneration and allowances,

as the Lord Chancellor may determine.

(5) For the purpose of carrying out his functions under this Act in relation to a person who lacks capacity ("P"), a Court of Protection Visitor may, at all reasonable times, examine and take copies of—

(a) any health record,

(b) any record of, or held by, a local authority and compiled in connection with a social services function, and

(c) any record held by a person registered under Part 2 of the Care Standards Act 2000 (c 14),

so far as the record relates to P.

(6) A Court of Protection Visitor may also for that purpose interview P in private.

NOTES

Initial Commencement

To be appointed: see s 68(1).

Appointment

Appointment: 1 October 2007: see SI 2007/1897, art 2(1)(b).

PART 3
MISCELLANEOUS AND GENERAL

Declaratory provision

A1.71

62 Scope of the Act

For the avoidance of doubt, it is hereby declared that nothing in this Act is to be taken to affect the law relating to murder or manslaughter or the operation of section 2 of the Suicide Act 1961 (c 60) (assisting suicide).

NOTES

Initial Commencement

To be appointed: see s 68(1).

Appointment

Appointment: 1 October 2007: see SI 2007/1897, art 2(1)(b).

Private international law

A1.72

63 International protection of adults

Schedule 3—

(a) gives effect in England and Wales to the Convention on the International Protection of Adults signed at the Hague on 13th January 2000 (Cm 5881) (in so far as this Act does not otherwise do so), and

(b) makes related provision as to the private international law of England and Wales.

NOTES

Initial Commencement

To be appointed: see s 68(1).

Appointment

Appointment: 1 October 2007: see SI 2007/1897, art 2(1)(b).

General

A1.73

64 Interpretation

(1) In this Act—

"the 1985 Act" means the Enduring Powers of Attorney Act 1985 (c 29),
"advance decision" has the meaning given in section 24(1),
["authorisation under Schedule A1" means either—
  (a) a standard authorisation under that Schedule, or
  (b) an urgent authorisation under that Schedule;]
"the court" means the Court of Protection established by section 45,
"Court of Protection Rules" has the meaning given in section 51(1),
"Court of Protection Visitor" has the meaning given in section 61,
"deputy" has the meaning given in section 16(2)(b),
"enactment" includes a provision of subordinate legislation (within the meaning of the Interpretation Act 1978 (c 30)),
"health record" has the meaning given in section 68 of the Data Protection Act 1998 (c 29) (as read with section 69 of that Act),
"the Human Rights Convention" has the same meaning as "the Convention" in the Human Rights Act 1998 (c 42),
"independent mental capacity advocate" has the meaning given in section 35(1),
"lasting power of attorney" has the meaning given in section 9,
"life-sustaining treatment" has the meaning given in section 4(10),
"local authority"[, except in Schedule A1,] means—
  (a) the council of a county in England in which there are no district councils,
  (b) the council of a district in England,
  (c) the council of a county or county borough in Wales,
  (d) the council of a London borough,
  (e) the Common Council of the City of London, or
  (f) the Council of the Isles of Scilly,
"Mental Health Act" means the Mental Health Act 1983 (c 20),
"prescribed", in relation to regulations made under this Act, means prescribed by those regulations,
"property" includes any thing in action and any interest in real or personal property,
"public authority" has the same meaning as in the Human Rights Act 1998,
"Public Guardian" has the meaning given in section 57,
"purchaser" and "purchase" have the meaning given in section 205(1) of the Law of Property Act 1925 (c 20),
"social services function" has the meaning given in section 1A of the Local Authority Social Services Act 1970 (c 42),
"treatment" includes a diagnostic or other procedure,
"trust corporation" has the meaning given in section 68(1) of the Trustee Act 1925 (c 19), and
"will" includes codicil.

(2) In this Act, references to making decisions, in relation to a donee of a lasting power of attorney or a deputy appointed by the court, include, where appropriate, acting on decisions made.

(3) In this Act, references to the bankruptcy of an individual include a case where a bankruptcy restrictions order under the Insolvency Act 1986 (c 45) has effect in respect of him.

(4) "Bankruptcy restrictions order" includes an interim bankruptcy restrictions order.

[(5) In this Act, references to deprivation of a person's liberty have the same meaning as in Article 5(1) of the Human Rights Convention.

(6) For the purposes of such references, it does not matter whether a person is deprived of his liberty by a public authority or not.]

NOTES

Initial Commencement

To be appointed: see s 68(1).

Appointment

Appointment (for certain purposes): 1 April 2007: see SI 2007/563, art 2(4).
Appointment (for remaining purposes): 1 October 2007: see SI 2007/1897, art 2(2)(f).

Amendment

Sub-s (1): definition "authorisation under Schedule A1" inserted by the Mental Health Act 2007, s 50(7), Sch 9, Pt 1, paras 1, 10(1), (2). Date in force: 1 April 2008: see SI 2008/745, art 4(b).
Sub-s (1): in definition "local authority" words ", except in Schedule A1," in square brackets inserted by the Mental Health Act 2007, s 50(7), Sch 9, Pt 1, paras 1, 10(1), (3). Date in force: 1 April 2008: see SI 2008/745, art 4(b).
Sub-ss (5), (6): inserted by the Mental Health Act 2007, s 50(7), Sch 9, Pt 1, paras 1, 10(1), (4). Date in force: 1 April 2008: see SI 2008/745, art 4(b).

A1.74

65 Rules, regulations and orders

(1) Any power to make rules, regulations or orders under this Act[, other than the power in section 21]—

- (a) is exercisable by statutory instrument;
- (b) includes power to make supplementary, incidental, consequential, transitional or saving provision;
- (c) includes power to make different provision for different cases.

(2) Any statutory instrument containing rules, regulations or orders made by the Lord Chancellor or the Secretary of State under this Act, other than—

- (a) regulations under section 34 (loss of capacity during research project),
- (b) regulations under section 41 (adjusting role of independent mental capacity advocacy service),
- (c) regulations under paragraph 32(1)(b) of Schedule 3 (private international law relating to the protection of adults),
- (d) an order of the kind mentioned in section 67(6) (consequential amendments of primary legislation), or
- (e) an order under section 68 (commencement),

is subject to annulment in pursuance of a resolution of either House of Parliament.

(3) A statutory instrument containing an Order in Council under paragraph 31 of Schedule 3 (provision to give further effect to Hague Convention) is subject to annulment in pursuance of a resolution of either House of Parliament.

(4) A statutory instrument containing regulations made by the Secretary of State under section 34 or 41 or by the Lord Chancellor under paragraph 32(1)(b) of Schedule 3 may not be made unless a draft has been laid before and approved by resolution of each House of Parliament.

[(4A) Subsection (2) does not apply to a statutory instrument containing regulations made by the Secretary of State under Schedule A1.

(4B) If such a statutory instrument contains regulations under paragraph 42(2)(b), 129, 162 or 164 of Schedule A1 (whether or not it also contains other regulations), the instrument may not be made unless a draft has been laid before and approved by resolution of each House of Parliament.

(4C) Subject to that, such a statutory instrument is subject to annulment in pursuance of a resolution of either House of Parliament.]

[(5) An order under section 21—

- (a) may include supplementary, incidental, consequential, transitional or saving provision;
- (b) may make different provision for different cases;
- (c) is to be made in the form of a statutory instrument to which the Statutory Instruments Act 1946 applies as if the order were made by a Minister of the Crown; and
- (d) is subject to annulment in pursuance of a resolution of either House of Parliament.]

NOTES

Initial Commencement
To be appointed: see s 68(1).

Appointment
Appointment: 1 October 2007: see SI 2007/1897, art 2(1)(c).

Amendment
Sub-s (1): words ", other than the power in section 21" in square brackets inserted by SI 2006/1016, art 2, Sch 1, paras 30, 37(1), (2). Date in force: 3 April 2006: see SI 2006/1016, art 1.
Sub-ss (4A)–(4C): inserted by the Mental Health Act 2007, s 50(7), Sch 9, Pt 1, paras 1, 11. Date in force: 1 April 2008: see SI 2008/745, art 4(b).
Sub-s (5): inserted by SI 2006/1016, art 2, Sch 1, paras 30, 37(1), (3). Date in force: 3 April 2006: see SI 2006/1016, art 1.

A1.75

66 Existing receivers and enduring powers of attorney etc

(1) The following provisions cease to have effect—

(a) Part 7 of the Mental Health Act,
(b) the Enduring Powers of Attorney Act 1985 (c 29).

(2) No enduring power of attorney within the meaning of the 1985 Act is to be created after the commencement of subsection (1)(b).

(3) Schedule 4 has effect in place of the 1985 Act in relation to any enduring power of attorney created before the commencement of subsection (1)(b).

(4) Schedule 5 contains transitional provisions and savings in relation to Part 7 of the Mental Health Act and the 1985 Act.

Initial Commencement
To be appointed: see s 68(1).

Appointment
Appointment: 1 October 2007: see SI 2007/1897, art 2(1)(c).

A1.76

67 Minor and consequential amendments and repeals

(1) Schedule 6 contains minor and consequential amendments.

(2) Schedule 7 contains repeals.

(3) The Lord Chancellor may by order make supplementary, incidental, consequential, transitional or saving provision for the purposes of, in consequence of, or for giving full effect to a provision of this Act.

(4) An order under subsection (3) may, in particular—

(a) provide for a provision of this Act which comes into force before another provision of this Act has come into force to have effect, until the other provision has come into force, with specified modifications;
(b) amend, repeal or revoke an enactment, other than one contained in an Act or Measure passed in a Session after the one in which this Act is passed.

(5) The amendments that may be made under subsection (4)(b) are in addition to those made by or under any other provision of this Act.

(6) An order under subsection (3) which amends or repeals a provision of an Act or Measure may not be made unless a draft has been laid before and approved by resolution of each House of Parliament.

NOTES

Initial Commencement

To be appointed: see s 68(1).

Appointment

Appointment: 1 October 2007: see SI 2007/1897, art 2(1)(c).

Subordinate Legislation

Mental Capacity Act 2005 (Transitional and Consequential Provisions) Order 2007, SI 2007/1898 (made under sub-s (3)).

A1.77

68 Commencement and extent

(1) This Act, other than sections 30 to 41, comes into force in accordance with provision made by order by the Lord Chancellor.

(2) Sections 30 to 41 come into force in accordance with provision made by order by—

(a) the Secretary of State, in relation to England, and
(b) the National Assembly for Wales, in relation to Wales.

(3) An order under this section may appoint different days for different provisions and different purposes.

(4) Subject to subsections (5) and (6), this Act extends to England and Wales only.

(5) The following provisions extend to the United Kingdom—

(a) paragraph 16(1) of Schedule 1 (evidence of instruments and of registration of lasting powers of attorney),
(b) paragraph 15(3) of Schedule 4 (evidence of instruments and of registration of enduring powers of attorney).

(6) Subject to any provision made in Schedule 6, the amendments and repeals made by Schedules 6 and 7 have the same extent as the enactments to which they relate.

NOTES

Initial Commencement

Royal Assent

Royal Assent: 7 April 2005: (no specific commencement provision).

Subordinate Legislation

Mental Capacity Act 2005 (Commencement No 1) Order 2006, SI 2006/2814 (made under sub-ss (2)(a), (3)).
Mental Capacity Act 2005 (Commencement No 1) (Amendment) Order 2006, SI 2006/3473 (made under sub-s (2)(a), (3)).
Mental Capacity Act 2005 (Commencement No 1) (England and Wales) Order 2007, SI 2007/563 (made under sub-ss (1), (3)).
Mental Capacity Act 2005 (Commencement) (Wales) Order 2007, SI 2007/856 (made under sub-s (2)).
Mental Capacity Act 2005 (Commencement No 2) Order 2007, SI 2007/1897 (made under sub-ss (1), (3)).

A1.78

69 Short title

This Act may be cited as the Mental Capacity Act 2005.

NOTES

Initial Commencement

Royal Assent

Royal Assent: 7 April 2005: (no specific commencement provision).

[SCHEDULE A1
HOSPITAL AND CARE HOME RESIDENTS: DEPRIVATION OF LIBERTY]

NOTES

Amendment

Inserted by the Mental Health Act 2007, s 50(5), Sch 7. Date in force (for certain purposes): 1 April 2008: see SI 2008/745, art 4(a). Date in force (for remaining purposes): to be appointed: see the Mental Health Act 2007, s 56(1).

[PART 1
AUTHORISATION TO DEPRIVE RESIDENTS OF LIBERTY ETC]

NOTES

Amendment

Inserted by the Mental Health Act 2007, s 50(5), Sch 7. Date in force (for certain purposes): 1 April 2008: see SI 2008/745, art 4(a).Date in force (for remaining purposes): to be appointed: see the Mental Health Act 2007, s 56(1).

[Application of Part

A1.79

1 (1) This Part applies if the following conditions are met.

(2) The first condition is that a person ("P") is detained in a hospital or care home—for the purpose of being given care or treatment—in circumstances which amount to deprivation of the person's liberty.

(3) The second condition is that a standard or urgent authorisation is in force.

(4) The third condition is that the standard or urgent authorisation relates—

(a) to P, and
(b) to the hospital or care home in which P is detained.

Authorisation to deprive P of liberty

2 The managing authority of the hospital or care home may deprive P of his liberty by detaining him as mentioned in paragraph 1(2).

No liability for acts done for purpose of depriving P of liberty

3 (1) This paragraph applies to any act which a person ("D") does for the purpose of detaining P as mentioned in paragraph 1(2).

(2) D does not incur any liability in relation to the act that he would not have incurred if P—

(a) had had capacity to consent in relation to D's doing the act, and
(b) had consented to D's doing the act.

No protection for negligent acts etc

4 (1) Paragraphs 2 and 3 do not exclude a person's civil liability for loss or damage, or his criminal liability, resulting from his negligence in doing any thing.

(2) Paragraphs 2 and 3 do not authorise a person to do anything otherwise than for the purpose of the standard or urgent authorisation that is in force.

(3) In a case where a standard authorisation is in force, paragraphs 2 and 3 do not authorise a person to do anything which does not comply with the conditions (if any) included in the authorisation.]

NOTES

Amendment

Inserted by the Mental Health Act 2007, s 50(5), Sch 7. Date in force (for certain purposes): 1 April 2008: see SI 2008/745, art 4(a). Date in force (for remaining purposes): to be appointed: see the Mental Health Act 2007, s 56(1).

[PART 2
INTERPRETATION: MAIN TERMS]

NOTES

Amendment

Inserted by the Mental Health Act 2007, s 50(5), Sch 7. Date in force (for certain purposes): 1 April 2008: see SI 2008/745, art 4(a). Date in force (for remaining purposes): to be appointed: see the Mental Health Act 2007, s 56(1).

[Introduction

5 This Part applies for the purposes of this Schedule.

Detained resident

6 "Detained resident" means a person detained in a hospital or care home—for the purpose of being given care or treatment—in circumstances which amount to deprivation of the person's liberty.

Relevant person etc

7 In relation to a person who is, or is to be, a detained resident—

"relevant person" means the person in question;
"relevant hospital or care home" means the hospital or care home in question;
"relevant care or treatment" means the care or treatment in question.

Authorisations

8 "Standard authorisation" means an authorisation given under Part 4.

9 "Urgent authorisation" means an authorisation given under Part 5.

10 "Authorisation under this Schedule" means either of the following—

(a) a standard authorisation;
(b) an urgent authorisation.

11 (1) The purpose of a standard authorisation is the purpose which is stated in the authorisation in accordance with paragraph 55(1)(d).

(2) The purpose of an urgent authorisation is the purpose which is stated in the authorisation in accordance with paragraph 80(d).]

NOTES

Amendment

Inserted by the Mental Health Act 2007, s 50(5), Sch 7. Date in force (for certain purposes): 1 April 2008: see SI 2008/745, art 4(a). Date in force (for remaining purposes): to be appointed: see the Mental Health Act 2007, s 56(1).

[PART 3
THE QUALIFYING REQUIREMENTS]

NOTES

Amendment

Inserted by the Mental Health Act 2007, s 50(5), Sch 7. Date in force (for certain purposes): 1 April 2008: see SI 2008/745, art 4(a). Date in force (for remaining purposes): to be appointed: see the Mental Health Act 2007, s 56(1).

[The qualifying requirements

12 (1) These are the qualifying requirements referred to in this Schedule—

(a) the age requirement;
(b) the mental health requirement;
(c) the mental capacity requirement;
(d) the best interests requirement;
(e) the eligibility requirement;
(f) the no refusals requirement.

(2) Any question of whether a person who is, or is to be, a detained resident meets the qualifying requirements is to be determined in accordance with this Part.

(3) In a case where—

(a) the question of whether a person meets a particular qualifying requirement arises in relation to the giving of a standard authorisation, and
(b) any circumstances relevant to determining that question are expected to change between the time when the determination is made and the time when the authorisation is expected to come into force,

those circumstances are to be taken into account as they are expected to be at the later time.

The age requirement

13 The relevant person meets the age requirement if he has reached 18.

The mental health requirement

14 (1) The relevant person meets the mental health requirement if he is suffering from mental disorder (within the meaning of the Mental Health Act, but disregarding any exclusion for persons with learning disability).

(2) An exclusion for persons with learning disability is any provision of the Mental Health Act which provides for a person with learning disability not to be regarded as suffering from mental disorder for one or more purposes of that Act.

The mental capacity requirement

15 The relevant person meets the mental capacity requirement if he lacks capacity in relation to the question whether or not he should be accommodated in the relevant hospital or care home for the purpose of being given the relevant care or treatment.

The best interests requirement

16 (1) The relevant person meets the best interests requirement if all of the following conditions are met.

(2) The first condition is that the relevant person is, or is to be, a detained resident.

(3) The second condition is that it is in the best interests of the relevant person for him to be a detained resident.

(4) The third condition is that, in order to prevent harm to the relevant person, it is necessary for him to be a detained resident.

(5) The fourth condition is that it is a proportionate response to—

(a) the likelihood of the relevant person suffering harm, and
(b) the seriousness of that harm,

for him to be a detained resident.

The eligibility requirement

17 (1) The relevant person meets the eligibility requirement unless he is ineligible to be deprived of liberty by this Act.

(2) Schedule 1A applies for the purpose of determining whether or not P is ineligible to be deprived of liberty by this Act.

The no refusals requirement

18 The relevant person meets the no refusals requirement unless there is a refusal within the meaning of paragraph 19 or 20.

19 (1) There is a refusal if these conditions are met—

- (a) the relevant person has made an advance decision;
- (b) the advance decision is valid;
- (c) the advance decision is applicable to some or all of the relevant treatment.

(2) Expressions used in this paragraph and any of sections 24, 25 or 26 have the same meaning in this paragraph as in that section.

20 (1) There is a refusal if it would be in conflict with a valid decision of a donee or deputy for the relevant person to be accommodated in the relevant hospital or care home for the purpose of receiving some or all of the relevant care or treatment—

- (a) in circumstances which amount to deprivation of the person's liberty, or
- (b) at all.

(2) A donee is a donee of a lasting power of attorney granted by the relevant person.

(3) A decision of a donee or deputy is valid if it is made—

- (a) within the scope of his authority as donee or deputy, and
- (b) in accordance with Part 1 of this Act.]

NOTES

Amendment

Inserted by the Mental Health Act 2007, s 50(5), Sch 7. Date in force (for certain purposes): 1 April 2008: see SI 2008/745, art 4(a). Date in force (for remaining purposes): to be appointed: see the Mental Health Act 2007, s 56(1).

[PART 4
STANDARD AUTHORISATIONS]

NOTES

Amendment

Inserted by the Mental Health Act 2007, s 50(5), Sch 7. Date in force (for certain purposes): 1 April 2008: see SI 2008/745, art 4(a). Date in force (for remaining purposes): to be appointed: see the Mental Health Act 2007, s 56(1).

[Supervisory body to give authorisation

21 Only the supervisory body may give a standard authorisation.

22 The supervisory body may not give a standard authorisation unless—

- (a) the managing authority of the relevant hospital or care home have requested it, or
- (b) paragraph 71 applies (right of third party to require consideration of whether authorisation needed).

23 The managing authority may not make a request for a standard authorisation unless—

- (a) they are required to do so by paragraph 24 (as read with paragraphs 27 to 29),
- (b) they are required to do so by paragraph 25 (as read with paragraph 28), or
- (c) they are permitted to do so by paragraph 30.

Duty to request authorisation: basic cases

24 (1) The managing authority must request a standard authorisation in any of the following cases.

(2) The first case is where it appears to the managing authority that the relevant person—

(a) is not yet accommodated in the relevant hospital or care home,
(b) is likely—at some time within the next 28 days—to be a detained resident in the relevant hospital or care home, and
(c) is likely—
(i) at that time, or
(ii) at some later time within the next 28 days,
to meet all of the qualifying requirements.

(3) The second case is where it appears to the managing authority that the relevant person—

(a) is already accommodated in the relevant hospital or care home,
(b) is likely—at some time within the next 28 days—to be a detained resident in the relevant hospital or care home, and
(c) is likely—
(i) at that time, or
(ii) at some later time within the next 28 days,
to meet all of the qualifying requirements.

(4) The third case is where it appears to the managing authority that the relevant person—

(a) is a detained resident in the relevant hospital or care home, and
(b) meets all of the qualifying requirements, or is likely to do so at some time within the next 28 days.

(5) This paragraph is subject to paragraphs 27 to 29.

Duty to request authorisation: change in place of detention

25 (1) The relevant managing authority must request a standard authorisation if it appears to them that these conditions are met.

(2) The first condition is that a standard authorisation—

(a) has been given, and
(b) has not ceased to be in force.

(3) The second condition is that there is, or is to be, a change in the place of detention.

(4) This paragraph is subject to paragraph 28.

26 (1) This paragraph applies for the purposes of paragraph 25.

(2) There is a change in the place of detention if the relevant person—

(a) ceases to be a detained resident in the stated hospital or care home, and
(b) becomes a detained resident in a different hospital or care home ("the new hospital or care home").

(3) The stated hospital or care home is the hospital or care home to which the standard authorisation relates.

(4) The relevant managing authority are the managing authority of the new hospital or care home.

Other authority for detention: request for authorisation

27 (1) This paragraph applies if, by virtue of section 4A(3), a decision of the court authorises the relevant person to be a detained resident.

(2) Paragraph 24 does not require a request for a standard authorisation to be made in relation to that detention unless these conditions are met.

(3) The first condition is that the standard authorisation would be in force at a time immediately after the expiry of the other authority.

(4) The second condition is that the standard authorisation would not be in force at any time on or before the expiry of the other authority.

(5) The third condition is that it would, in the managing authority's view, be unreasonable to delay making the request until a time nearer the expiry of the other authority.

(6) In this paragraph—

(a) the other authority is—
 (i) the decision mentioned in sub-paragraph (1), or
 (ii) any further decision of the court which, by virtue of section 4A(3), authorises, or is expected to authorise, the relevant person to be a detained resident;
(b) the expiry of the other authority is the time when the other authority is expected to cease to authorise the relevant person to be a detained resident.

Request refused: no further request unless change of circumstances

28 (1) This paragraph applies if—

(a) a managing authority request a standard authorisation under paragraph 24 or 25, and
(b) the supervisory body are prohibited by paragraph 50(2) from giving the authorisation.

(2) Paragraph 24 or 25 does not require that managing authority to make a new request for a standard authorisation unless it appears to the managing authority that—

(a) there has been a change in the relevant person's case, and
(b) because of that change, the supervisory body are likely to give a standard authorisation if requested.

Authorisation given: request for further authorisation

29 (1) This paragraph applies if a standard authorisation—

(a) has been given in relation to the detention of the relevant person, and
(b) that authorisation ("the existing authorisation") has not ceased to be in force.

(2) Paragraph 24 does not require a new request for a standard authorisation ("the new authorisation") to be made unless these conditions are met.

(3) The first condition is that the new authorisation would be in force at a time immediately after the expiry of the existing authorisation.

(4) The second condition is that the new authorisation would not be in force at any time on or before the expiry of the existing authorisation.

(5) The third condition is that it would, in the managing authority's view, be unreasonable to delay making the request until a time nearer the expiry of the existing authorisation.

(6) The expiry of the existing authorisation is the time when it is expected to cease to be in force.

Power to request authorisation

30 (1) This paragraph applies if—

(a) a standard authorisation has been given in relation to the detention of the relevant person,
(b) that authorisation ("the existing authorisation") has not ceased to be in force,
(c) the requirement under paragraph 24 to make a request for a new standard authorisation does not apply, because of paragraph 29, and
(d) a review of the existing authorisation has been requested, or is being carried out, in accordance with Part 8.

(2) The managing authority may request a new standard authorisation which would be in force on or before the expiry of the existing authorisation; but only if it would also be in force immediately after that expiry.

(3) The expiry of the existing authorisation is the time when it is expected to cease to be in force.

(4) Further provision relating to cases where a request is made under this paragraph can be found in—

(a) paragraph 62 (effect of decision about request), and
(b) paragraph 124 (effect of request on Part 8 review).

Information included in request

31 A request for a standard authorisation must include the information (if any) required by regulations.

Records of requests

32 (1) The managing authority of a hospital or care home must keep a written record of—

(a) each request that they make for a standard authorisation, and
(b) the reasons for making each request.

(2) A supervisory body must keep a written record of each request for a standard authorisation that is made to them.

Relevant person must be assessed

33 (1) This paragraph applies if the supervisory body are requested to give a standard authorisation.

(2) The supervisory body must secure that all of these assessments are carried out in relation to the relevant person—

(a) an age assessment;
(b) a mental health assessment;
(c) a mental capacity assessment;
(d) a best interests assessment;
(e) an eligibility assessment;
(f) a no refusals assessment.

(3) The person who carries out any such assessment is referred to as the assessor.

(4) Regulations may be made about the period (or periods) within which assessors must carry out assessments.

(5) This paragraph is subject to paragraphs 49 and 133.

Age assessment

34 An age assessment is an assessment of whether the relevant person meets the age requirement.

Mental health assessment

35 A mental health assessment is an assessment of whether the relevant person meets the mental health requirement.

36 When carrying out a mental health assessment, the assessor must also—

(a) consider how (if at all) the relevant person's mental health is likely to be affected by his being a detained resident, and
(b) notify the best interests assessor of his conclusions.

Mental capacity assessment

37 A mental capacity assessment is an assessment of whether the relevant person meets the mental capacity requirement.

Best interests assessment

38 A best interests assessment is an assessment of whether the relevant person meets the best interests requirement.

39 (1) In carrying out a best interests assessment, the assessor must comply with the duties in sub-paragraphs (2) and (3).

(2) The assessor must consult the managing authority of the relevant hospital or care home.

(3) The assessor must have regard to all of the following—

(a) the conclusions which the mental health assessor has notified to the best interests assessor in accordance with paragraph 36(b);
(b) any relevant needs assessment;
(c) any relevant care plan.

(4) A relevant needs assessment is an assessment of the relevant person's needs which—

- (a) was carried out in connection with the relevant person being accommodated in the relevant hospital or care home, and
- (b) was carried out by or on behalf of—
  - (i) the managing authority of the relevant hospital or care home, or
  - (ii) the supervisory body.

(5) A relevant care plan is a care plan which—

- (a) sets out how the relevant person's needs are to be met whilst he is accommodated in the relevant hospital or care home, and
- (b) was drawn up by or on behalf of—
  - (i) the managing authority of the relevant hospital or care home, or
  - (ii) the supervisory body.

(6) The managing authority must give the assessor a copy of—

- (a) any relevant needs assessment carried out by them or on their behalf, or
- (b) any relevant care plan drawn up by them or on their behalf.

(7) The supervisory body must give the assessor a copy of—

- (a) any relevant needs assessment carried out by them or on their behalf, or
- (b) any relevant care plan drawn up by them or on their behalf.

(8) The duties in sub-paragraphs (2) and (3) do not affect any other duty to consult or to take the views of others into account.

40 (1) This paragraph applies whatever conclusion the best interests assessment comes to.

(2) The assessor must state in the best interests assessment the name and address of every interested person whom he has consulted in carrying out the assessment.

41 Paragraphs 42 and 43 apply if the best interests assessment comes to the conclusion that the relevant person meets the best interests requirement.

42 (1) The assessor must state in the assessment the maximum authorisation period.

(2) The maximum authorisation period is the shorter of these periods—

- (a) the period which, in the assessor's opinion, would be the appropriate maximum period for the relevant person to be a detained resident under the standard authorisation that has been requested;
- (b) 1 year, or such shorter period as may be prescribed in regulations.

(3) Regulations under sub-paragraph (2)(b)—

- (a) need not provide for a shorter period to apply in relation to all standard authorisations;
- (b) may provide for different periods to apply in relation to different kinds of standard authorisations.

(4) Before making regulations under sub-paragraph (2)(b) the Secretary of State must consult all of the following—

- (a) each body required by regulations under paragraph 162 to monitor and report on the operation of this Schedule in relation to England;
- (b) such other persons as the Secretary of State considers it appropriate to consult.

(5) Before making regulations under sub-paragraph (2)(b) the National Assembly for Wales must consult all of the following—

- (a) each person or body directed under paragraph 163(2) to carry out any function of the Assembly of monitoring and reporting on the operation of this Schedule in relation to Wales;
- (b) such other persons as the Assembly considers it appropriate to consult.

43 The assessor may include in the assessment recommendations about conditions to which the standard authorisation is, or is not, to be subject in accordance with paragraph 53.

44 (1) This paragraph applies if the best interests assessment comes to the conclusion that the relevant person does not meet the best interests requirement.

(2) If, on the basis of the information taken into account in carrying out the assessment, it appears to the assessor that there is an unauthorised deprivation of liberty, he must include a statement to that effect in the assessment.

(3) There is an unauthorised deprivation of liberty if the managing authority of the relevant hospital or care home are already depriving the relevant person of his liberty without authority of the kind mentioned in section 4A.

45 The duties with which the best interests assessor must comply are subject to the provision included in appointment regulations under Part 10 (in particular, provision made under paragraph 146).

Eligibility assessment

46 An eligibility assessment is an assessment of whether the relevant person meets the eligibility requirement.

47 (1) Regulations may—

(a) require an eligibility assessor to request a best interests assessor to provide relevant eligibility information, and
(b) require the best interests assessor, if such a request is made, to provide such relevant eligibility information as he may have.

(2) In this paragraph—

"best interests assessor" means any person who is carrying out, or has carried out, a best interests assessment in relation to the relevant person;
"eligibility assessor" means a person carrying out an eligibility assessment in relation to the relevant person;
"relevant eligibility information" is information relevant to assessing whether or not the relevant person is ineligible by virtue of paragraph 5 of Schedule 1A.

No refusals assessment

48 A no refusals assessment is an assessment of whether the relevant person meets the no refusals requirement.

Equivalent assessment already carried out

49 (1) The supervisory body are not required by paragraph 33 to secure that a particular kind of assessment ("the required assessment") is carried out in relation to the relevant person if the following conditions are met.

(2) The first condition is that the supervisory body have a written copy of an assessment of the relevant person ("the existing assessment") that has already been carried out.

(3) The second condition is that the existing assessment complies with all requirements under this Schedule with which the required assessment would have to comply (if it were carried out).

(4) The third condition is that the existing assessment was carried out within the previous 12 months; but this condition need not be met if the required assessment is an age assessment.

(5) The fourth condition is that the supervisory body are satisfied that there is no reason why the existing assessment may no longer be accurate.

(6) If the required assessment is a best interests assessment, in satisfying themselves as mentioned in sub-paragraph (5), the supervisory body must take into account any information given, or submissions made, by—

(a) the relevant person's representative,
(b) any section 39C IMCA, or
(c) any section 39D IMCA.

(7) It does not matter whether the existing assessment was carried out in connection with a request for a standard authorisation or for some other purpose.

(8) If, because of this paragraph, the supervisory body are not required by paragraph 33 to secure that the required assessment is carried out, the existing assessment is to be treated for the purposes of this Schedule—

(a) as an assessment of the same kind as the required assessment, and
(b) as having been carried out under paragraph 33 in connection with the request for the standard authorisation.

Duty to give authorisation

50 (1) The supervisory body must give a standard authorisation if—

(a) all assessments are positive, and
(b) the supervisory body have written copies of all those assessments.

(2) The supervisory body must not give a standard authorisation except in accordance with sub-paragraph (1).

(3) All assessments are positive if each assessment carried out under paragraph 33 has come to the conclusion that the relevant person meets the qualifying requirement to which the assessment relates.

Terms of authorisation

51 (1) If the supervisory body are required to give a standard authorisation, they must decide the period during which the authorisation is to be in force.

(2) That period must not exceed the maximum authorisation period stated in the best interests assessment.

52 A standard authorisation may provide for the authorisation to come into force at a time after it is given.

53 (1) A standard authorisation may be given subject to conditions.

(2) Before deciding whether to give the authorisation subject to conditions, the supervisory body must have regard to any recommendations in the best interests assessment about such conditions.

(3) The managing authority of the relevant hospital or care home must ensure that any conditions are complied with.

Form of authorisation

54 A standard authorisation must be in writing.

55 (1) A standard authorisation must state the following things—

(a) the name of the relevant person;
(b) the name of the relevant hospital or care home;
(c) the period during which the authorisation is to be in force;
(d) the purpose for which the authorisation is given;
(e) any conditions subject to which the authorisation is given;
(f) the reason why each qualifying requirement is met.

(2) The statement of the reason why the eligibility requirement is met must be framed by reference to the cases in the table in paragraph 2 of Schedule 1A.

56 (1) If the name of the relevant hospital or care home changes, the standard authorisation is to be read as if it stated the current name of the hospital or care home.

(2) But sub-paragraph (1) is subject to any provision relating to the change of name which is made in any enactment or in any instrument made under an enactment.

Duty to give information about decision

57 (1) This paragraph applies if—

(a) a request is made for a standard authorisation, and
(b) the supervisory body are required by paragraph 50(1) to give the standard authorisation.

(2) The supervisory body must give a copy of the authorisation to each of the following—

(a) the relevant person's representative;
(b) the managing authority of the relevant hospital or care home;
(c) the relevant person;
(d) any section 39A IMCA;
(e) every interested person consulted by the best interests assessor.

(3) The supervisory body must comply with this paragraph as soon as practicable after they give the standard authorisation.

58 (1) This paragraph applies if—

(a) a request is made for a standard authorisation, and
(b) the supervisory body are prohibited by paragraph 50(2) from giving the standard authorisation.

(2) The supervisory body must give notice, stating that they are prohibited from giving the authorisation, to each of the following—

(a) the managing authority of the relevant hospital or care home;
(b) the relevant person;
(c) any section 39A IMCA;
(d) every interested person consulted by the best interests assessor.

(3) The supervisory body must comply with this paragraph as soon as practicable after it becomes apparent to them that they are prohibited from giving the authorisation.

Duty to give information about effect of authorisation

59 (1) This paragraph applies if a standard authorisation is given.

(2) The managing authority of the relevant hospital or care home must take such steps as are practicable to ensure that the relevant person understands all of the following—

(a) the effect of the authorisation;
(b) the right to make an application to the court to exercise its jurisdiction under section 21A;
(c) the right under Part 8 to request a review;
(d) the right to have a section 39D IMCA appointed;
(e) how to have a section 39D IMCA appointed.

(3) Those steps must be taken as soon as is practicable after the authorisation is given.

(4) Those steps must include the giving of appropriate information both orally and in writing.

(5) Any written information given to the relevant person must also be given by the managing authority to the relevant person's representative.

(6) They must give the information to the representative as soon as is practicable after it is given to the relevant person.

(7) Sub-paragraph (8) applies if the managing authority is notified that a section 39D IMCA has been appointed.

(8) As soon as is practicable after being notified, the managing authority must give the section 39D IMCA a copy of the written information given in accordance with sub-paragraph (4).

Records of authorisations

60 A supervisory body must keep a written record of all of the following information—

(a) the standard authorisations that they have given;
(b) the requests for standard authorisations in response to which they have not given an authorisation;
(c) in relation to each standard authorisation given: the matters stated in the authorisation in accordance with paragraph 55.

Variation of an authorisation

61 (1) A standard authorisation may not be varied except in accordance with Part 7 or 8.

(2) This paragraph does not affect the powers of the Court of Protection or of any other court.

Effect of decision about request made under paragraph 25 or 30

62 (1) This paragraph applies where the managing authority request a new standard authorisation under either of the following—

(a) paragraph 25 (change in place of detention);
(b) paragraph 30 (existing authorisation subject to review).

(2) If the supervisory body are required by paragraph 50(1) to give the new authorisation, the existing authorisation terminates at the time when the new authorisation comes into force.

(3) If the supervisory body are prohibited by paragraph 50(2) from giving the new authorisation, there is no effect on the existing authorisation's continuation in force.

When an authorisation is in force

63 (1) A standard authorisation comes into force when it is given.

(2) But if the authorisation provides for it to come into force at a later time, it comes into force at that time.

64 (1) A standard authorisation ceases to be in force at the end of the period stated in the authorisation in accordance with paragraph 55(1)(c).

(2) But if the authorisation terminates before then in accordance with paragraph 62(2) or any other provision of this Schedule, it ceases to be in force when the termination takes effect.

(3) This paragraph does not affect the powers of the Court of Protection or of any other court.

65 (1) This paragraph applies if a standard authorisation ceases to be in force.

(2) The supervisory body must give notice that the authorisation has ceased to be in force.

(3) The supervisory body must give that notice to all of the following—

(a) the managing authority of the relevant hospital or care home;
(b) the relevant person;
(c) the relevant person's representative;
(d) every interested person consulted by the best interests assessor.

(4) The supervisory body must give that notice as soon as practicable after the authorisation ceases to be in force.

When a request for a standard authorisation is "disposed of"

66 A request for a standard authorisation is to be regarded for the purposes of this Schedule as disposed of if the supervisory body have given—

(a) a copy of the authorisation in accordance with paragraph 57, or
(b) notice in accordance with paragraph 58.

Right of third party to require consideration of whether authorisation needed

67 For the purposes of paragraphs 68 to 73 there is an unauthorised deprivation of liberty if—

(a) a person is already a detained resident in a hospital or care home, and
(b) the detention of the person is not authorised as mentioned in section 4A.

68 (1) If the following conditions are met, an eligible person may request the supervisory body to decide whether or not there is an unauthorised deprivation of liberty.

(2) The first condition is that the eligible person has notified the managing authority of the relevant hospital or care home that it appears to the eligible person that there is an unauthorised deprivation of liberty.

(3) The second condition is that the eligible person has asked the managing authority to request a standard authorisation in relation to the detention of the relevant person.

(4) The third condition is that the managing authority has not requested a standard authorisation within a reasonable period after the eligible person asks it to do so.

(5) In this paragraph "eligible person" means any person other than the managing authority of the relevant hospital or care home.

69 (1) This paragraph applies if an eligible person requests the supervisory body to decide whether or not there is an unauthorised deprivation of liberty.

(2) The supervisory body must select and appoint a person to carry out an assessment of whether or not the relevant person is a detained resident.

(3) But the supervisory body need not select and appoint a person to carry out such an assessment in either of these cases.

(4) The first case is where it appears to the supervisory body that the request by the eligible person is frivolous or vexatious.

(5) The second case is where it appears to the supervisory body that—

- (a) the question of whether or not there is an unauthorised deprivation of liberty has already been decided, and
- (b) since that decision, there has been no change of circumstances which would merit the question being decided again.

(6) The supervisory body must not select and appoint a person to carry out an assessment under this paragraph unless it appears to the supervisory body that the person would be—

- (a) suitable to carry out a best interests assessment (if one were obtained in connection with a request for a standard authorisation relating to the relevant person), and
- (b) eligible to carry out such a best interests assessment.

(7) The supervisory body must notify the persons specified in sub-paragraph (8)—

- (a) that the supervisory body have been requested to decide whether or not there is an unauthorised deprivation of liberty;
- (b) of their decision whether or not to select and appoint a person to carry out an assessment under this paragraph;
- (c) if their decision is to select and appoint a person, of the person appointed.

(8) The persons referred to in sub-paragraph (7) are—

- (a) the eligible person who made the request under paragraph 68;
- (b) the person to whom the request relates;
- (c) the managing authority of the relevant hospital or care home;
- (d) any section 39A IMCA.

70 (1) Regulations may be made about the period within which an assessment under paragraph 69 must be carried out.

(2) Regulations made under paragraph 129(3) apply in relation to the selection and appointment of a person under paragraph 69 as they apply to the selection of a person under paragraph 129 to carry out a best interests assessment.

(3) The following provisions apply to an assessment under paragraph 69 as they apply to an assessment carried out in connection with a request for a standard authorisation—

- (a) paragraph 131 (examination and copying of records);
- (b) paragraph 132 (representations);
- (c) paragraphs 134 and 135(1) and (2) (duty to keep records and give copies).

(4) The copies of the assessment which the supervisory body are required to give under paragraph 135(2) must be given as soon as practicable after the supervisory body are themselves given a copy of the assessment.

71 (1) This paragraph applies if—

- (a) the supervisory body obtain an assessment under paragraph 69,

(b) the assessment comes to the conclusion that the relevant person is a detained resident, and
(c) it appears to the supervisory body that the detention of the person is not authorised as mentioned in section 4A.

(2) This Schedule (including Part 5) applies as if the managing authority of the relevant hospital or care home had, in accordance with Part 4, requested the supervisory body to give a standard authorisation in relation to the relevant person.

(3) The managing authority of the relevant hospital or care home must supply the supervisory body with the information (if any) which the managing authority would, by virtue of paragraph 31, have had to include in a request for a standard authorisation.

(4) The supervisory body must notify the persons specified in paragraph 69(8)—

(a) of the outcome of the assessment obtained under paragraph 69, and
(b) that this Schedule applies as mentioned in sub-paragraph (2).

72 (1) This paragraph applies if—

(a) the supervisory body obtain an assessment under paragraph 69, and
(b) the assessment comes to the conclusion that the relevant person is not a detained resident.

(2) The supervisory body must notify the persons specified in paragraph 69(8) of the outcome of the assessment.

73 (1) This paragraph applies if—

(a) the supervisory body obtain an assessment under paragraph 69,
(b) the assessment comes to the conclusion that the relevant person is a detained resident, and
(c) it appears to the supervisory body that the detention of the person is authorised as mentioned in section 4A.

(2) The supervisory body must notify the persons specified in paragraph 69(8)—

(a) of the outcome of the assessment, and
(b) that it appears to the supervisory body that the detention is authorised.]

NOTES

Amendment

Inserted by the Mental Health Act 2007, s 50(5), Sch 7. Date in force (for certain purposes): 1 April 2008: see SI 2008/745, art 4(a). Date in force (for remaining purposes): to be appointed: see the Mental Health Act 2007, s 56(1).

[PART 5
URGENT AUTHORISATIONS]

NOTES

Amendment

Inserted by the Mental Health Act 2007, s 50(5), Sch 7. Date in force (for certain purposes): 1 April 2008: see SI 2008/745, art 4(a). Date in force (for remaining purposes): to be appointed: see the Mental Health Act 2007, s 56(1).

[Managing authority to give authorisation

74 Only the managing authority of the relevant hospital or care home may give an urgent authorisation.

75 The managing authority may give an urgent authorisation only if they are required to do so by paragraph 76 (as read with paragraph 77).

Duty to give authorisation

76 (1) The managing authority must give an urgent authorisation in either of the following cases.

(2) The first case is where—

(a) the managing authority are required to make a request under paragraph 24 or 25 for a standard authorisation, and
(b) they believe that the need for the relevant person to be a detained resident is so urgent that it is appropriate for the detention to begin before they make the request.

(3) The second case is where—

(a) the managing authority have made a request under paragraph 24 or 25 for a standard authorisation, and
(b) they believe that the need for the relevant person to be a detained resident is so urgent that it is appropriate for the detention to begin before the request is disposed of.

(4) References in this paragraph to the detention of the relevant person are references to the detention to which paragraph 24 or 25 relates.

(5) This paragraph is subject to paragraph 77.

77 (1) This paragraph applies where the managing authority have given an urgent authorisation ("the original authorisation") in connection with a case where a person is, or is to be, a detained resident ("the existing detention").

(2) No new urgent authorisation is to be given under paragraph 76 in connection with the existing detention.

(3) But the managing authority may request the supervisory body to extend the duration of the original authorisation.

(4) Only one request under sub-paragraph (3) may be made in relation to the original authorisation.

(5) Paragraphs 84 to 86 apply to any request made under sub-paragraph (3).

Terms of authorisation

78 (1) If the managing authority decide to give an urgent authorisation, they must decide the period during which the authorisation is to be in force.

(2) That period must not exceed 7 days.

Form of authorisation

79 An urgent authorisation must be in writing.

80 An urgent authorisation must state the following things—

(a) the name of the relevant person;
(b) the name of the relevant hospital or care home;
(c) the period during which the authorisation is to be in force;
(d) the purpose for which the authorisation is given.

81 (1) If the name of the relevant hospital or care home changes, the urgent authorisation is to be read as if it stated the current name of the hospital or care home.

(2) But sub-paragraph (1) is subject to any provision relating to the change of name which is made in any enactment or in any instrument made under an enactment.

Duty to keep records and give copies

82 (1) This paragraph applies if an urgent authorisation is given.

(2) The managing authority must keep a written record of why they have given the urgent authorisation.

(3) As soon as practicable after giving the authorisation, the managing authority must give a copy of the authorisation to all of the following—

(a) the relevant person;
(b) any section 39A IMCA.

Duty to give information about authorisation

83 (1) This paragraph applies if an urgent authorisation is given.

(2) The managing authority of the relevant hospital or care home must take such steps as are practicable to ensure that the relevant person understands all of the following—

(a) the effect of the authorisation;
(b) the right to make an application to the court to exercise its jurisdiction under section 21A.

(3) Those steps must be taken as soon as is practicable after the authorisation is given.

(4) Those steps must include the giving of appropriate information both orally and in writing.

Request for extension of duration

84 (1) This paragraph applies if the managing authority make a request under paragraph 77 for the supervisory body to extend the duration of the original authorisation.

(2) The managing authority must keep a written record of why they have made the request.

(3) The managing authority must give the relevant person notice that they have made the request.

(4) The supervisory body may extend the duration of the original authorisation if it appears to them that—

(a) the managing authority have made the required request for a standard authorisation,
(b) there are exceptional reasons why it has not yet been possible for that request to be disposed of, and
(c) it is essential for the existing detention to continue until the request is disposed of.

(5) The supervisory body must keep a written record that the request has been made to them.

(6) In this paragraph and paragraphs 85 and 86—

(a) "original authorisation" and "existing detention" have the same meaning as in paragraph 77;
(b) the required request for a standard authorisation is the request that is referred to in paragraph 76(2) or (3).

85 (1) This paragraph applies if, under paragraph 84, the supervisory body decide to extend the duration of the original authorisation.

(2) The supervisory body must decide the period of the extension.

(3) That period must not exceed 7 days.

(4) The supervisory body must give the managing authority notice stating the period of the extension.

(5) The managing authority must then vary the original authorisation so that it states the extended duration.

(6) Paragraphs 82(3) and 83 apply (with the necessary modifications) to the variation of the original authorisation as they apply to the giving of an urgent authorisation.

(7) The supervisory body must keep a written record of—

(a) the outcome of the request, and
(b) the period of the extension.

86 (1) This paragraph applies if, under paragraph 84, the supervisory body decide not to extend the duration of the original authorisation.

(2) The supervisory body must give the managing authority notice stating—

(a) the decision, and
(b) their reasons for making it.

(3) The managing authority must give a copy of that notice to all of the following—

(a) the relevant person;

(b) any section 39A IMCA.

(4) The supervisory body must keep a written record of the outcome of the request.

No variation

87 (1) An urgent authorisation may not be varied except in accordance with paragraph 85.

(2) This paragraph does not affect the powers of the Court of Protection or of any other court.

When an authorisation is in force

88 An urgent authorisation comes into force when it is given.

89 (1) An urgent authorisation ceases to be in force at the end of the period stated in the authorisation in accordance with paragraph 80(c) (subject to any variation in accordance with paragraph 85).

(2) But if the required request is disposed of before the end of that period, the urgent authorisation ceases to be in force as follows.

(3) If the supervisory body are required by paragraph 50(1) to give the requested authorisation, the urgent authorisation ceases to be in force when the requested authorisation comes into force.

(4) If the supervisory body are prohibited by paragraph 50(2) from giving the requested authorisation, the urgent authorisation ceases to be in force when the managing authority receive notice under paragraph 58.

(5) In this paragraph—

"required request" means the request referred to in paragraph 76(2) or (3);
"requested authorisation" means the standard authorisation to which the required request relates.

(6) This paragraph does not affect the powers of the Court of Protection or of any other court.

90 (1) This paragraph applies if an urgent authorisation ceases to be in force.

(2) The supervisory body must give notice that the authorisation has ceased to be in force.

(3) The supervisory body must give that notice to all of the following—

(a) the relevant person;
(b) any section 39A IMCA.

(4) The supervisory body must give that notice as soon as practicable after the authorisation ceases to be in force.]

NOTES

Amendment

Inserted by the Mental Health Act 2007, s 50(5), Sch 7. Date in force (for certain purposes): 1 April 2008: see SI 2008/745, art 4(a). Date in force (for remaining purposes): to be appointed: see the Mental Health Act 2007, s 56(1).

[PART 6
ELIGIBILITY REQUIREMENT NOT MET: SUSPENSION OF STANDARD AUTHORISATION]

NOTES

Amendment

Inserted by the Mental Health Act 2007, s 50(5), Sch 7. Date in force (for certain purposes): 1 April 2008: see SI 2008/745, art 4(a). Date in force (for remaining purposes): to be appointed: see the Mental Health Act 2007, s 56(1).

[91 (1) This Part applies if the following conditions are met.

(2) The first condition is that a standard authorisation—

(a) has been given, and
(b) has not ceased to be in force.

(3) The second condition is that the managing authority of the relevant hospital or care home are satisfied that the relevant person has ceased to meet the eligibility requirement.

(4) But this Part does not apply if the relevant person is ineligible by virtue of paragraph 5 of Schedule 1A (in which case see Part 8).

92 The managing authority of the relevant hospital or care home must give the supervisory body notice that the relevant person has ceased to meet the eligibility requirement.

93 (1) This paragraph applies if the managing authority give the supervisory body notice under paragraph 92.

(2) The standard authorisation is suspended from the time when the notice is given.

(3) The supervisory body must give notice that the standard authorisation has been suspended to the following persons—

- (a) the relevant person;
- (b) the relevant person's representative;
- (c) the managing authority of the relevant hospital or care home.

94 (1) This paragraph applies if, whilst the standard authorisation is suspended, the managing authority are satisfied that the relevant person meets the eligibility requirement again.

(2) The managing authority must give the supervisory body notice that the relevant person meets the eligibility requirement again.

95 (1) This paragraph applies if the managing authority give the supervisory body notice under paragraph 94.

(2) The standard authorisation ceases to be suspended from the time when the notice is given.

(3) The supervisory body must give notice that the standard authorisation has ceased to be suspended to the following persons—

- (a) the relevant person;
- (b) the relevant person's representative;
- (c) any section 39D IMCA;
- (d) the managing authority of the relevant hospital or care home.

(4) The supervisory body must give notice under this paragraph as soon as practicable after they are given notice under paragraph 94.

96 (1) This paragraph applies if no notice is given under paragraph 94 before the end of the relevant 28 day period.

(2) The standard authorisation ceases to have effect at the end of the relevant 28 day period.

(3) The relevant 28 day period is the period of 28 days beginning with the day on which the standard authorisation is suspended under paragraph 93.

97 The effect of suspending the standard authorisation is that Part 1 ceases to apply for as long as the authorisation is suspended.]

NOTES

Amendment

Inserted by the Mental Health Act 2007, s 50(5), Sch 7. Date in force (for certain purposes): 1 April 2008: see SI 2008/745, art 4(a). Date in force (for remaining purposes): to be appointed: see the Mental Health Act 2007, s 56(1).

[PART 7
STANDARD AUTHORISATIONS: CHANGE IN SUPERVISORY RESPONSIBILITY]

NOTES

Amendment

Inserted by the Mental Health Act 2007, s 50(5), Sch 7. Date in force (for certain purposes): 1 April 2008: see SI 2008/745, art 4(a). Date in force (for remaining purposes): to be appointed: see the Mental Health Act 2007, s 56(1).

[Application of this Part

98 (1) This Part applies if these conditions are met.

(2) The first condition is that a standard authorisation—

(a) has been given, and
(b) has not ceased to be in force.

(3) The second condition is that there is a change in supervisory responsibility.

(4) The third condition is that there is not a change in the place of detention (within the meaning of paragraph 25).

99 For the purposes of this Part there is a change in supervisory responsibility if—

(a) one body ("the old supervisory body") have ceased to be supervisory body in relation to the standard authorisation, and
(b) a different body ("the new supervisory body") have become supervisory body in relation to the standard authorisation.

Effect of change in supervisory responsibility

100 (1) The new supervisory body becomes the supervisory body in relation to the authorisation.

(2) Anything done by or in relation to the old supervisory body in connection with the authorisation has effect, so far as is necessary for continuing its effect after the change, as if done by or in relation to the new supervisory body.

(3) Anything which relates to the authorisation and which is in the process of being done by or in relation to the old supervisory body at the time of the change may be continued by or in relation to the new supervisory body.

(4) But—

(a) the old supervisory body do not, by virtue of this paragraph, cease to be liable for anything done by them in connection with the authorisation before the change; and
(b) the new supervisory body do not, by virtue of this paragraph, become liable for any such thing.]

NOTES

Amendment

Inserted by the Mental Health Act 2007, s 50(5), Sch 7. Date in force (for certain purposes): 1 April 2008: see SI 2008/745, art 4(a). Date in force (for remaining purposes): to be appointed: see the Mental Health Act 2007, s 56(1).

[PART 8
STANDARD AUTHORISATIONS: REVIEW]

NOTES

Amendment

Inserted by the Mental Health Act 2007, s 50(5), Sch 7. Date in force (for certain purposes): 1 April 2008: see SI 2008/745, art 4(a). Date in force (for remaining purposes): to be appointed: see the Mental Health Act 2007, s 56(1).

[Application of this Part

101 (1) This Part applies if a standard authorisation—

(a) has been given, and
(b) has not ceased to be in force.

(2) Paragraphs 102 to 122 are subject to paragraphs 123 to 125.

Review by supervisory body

102 (1) The supervisory body may at any time carry out a review of the standard authorisation in accordance with this Part.

(2) The supervisory body must carry out such a review if they are requested to do so by an eligible person.

(3) Each of the following is an eligible person—

(a) the relevant person;
(b) the relevant person's representative;
(c) the managing authority of the relevant hospital or care home.

Request for review

103 (1) An eligible person may, at any time, request the supervisory body to carry out a review of the standard authorisation in accordance with this Part.

(2) The managing authority of the relevant hospital or care home must make such a request if one or more of the qualifying requirements appear to them to be reviewable.

Grounds for review

104 (1) Paragraphs 105 to 107 set out the grounds on which the qualifying requirements are reviewable.

(2) A qualifying requirement is not reviewable on any other ground.

Non-qualification ground

105 (1) Any of the following qualifying requirements is reviewable on the ground that the relevant person does not meet the requirement—

(a) the age requirement;
(b) the mental health requirement;
(c) the mental capacity requirement;
(d) the best interests requirement;
(e) the no refusals requirement.

(2) The eligibility requirement is reviewable on the ground that the relevant person is ineligible by virtue of paragraph 5 of Schedule 1A.

(3) The ground in sub-paragraph (1) and the ground in sub-paragraph (2) are referred to as the non-qualification ground.

Change of reason ground

106 (1) Any of the following qualifying requirements is reviewable on the ground set out in sub-paragraph (2)—

(a) the mental health requirement;
(b) the mental capacity requirement;
(c) the best interests requirement;
(d) the eligibility requirement;
(e) the no refusals requirement.

(2) The ground is that the reason why the relevant person meets the requirement is not the reason stated in the standard authorisation.

(3) This ground is referred to as the change of reason ground.

Variation of conditions ground

107 (1) The best interests requirement is reviewable on the ground that—

(a) there has been a change in the relevant person's case, and
(b) because of that change, it would be appropriate to vary the conditions to which the standard authorisation is subject.

(2) This ground is referred to as the variation of conditions ground.

(3) A reference to varying the conditions to which the standard authorisation is subject is a reference to—

(a) amendment of an existing condition,
(b) omission of an existing condition, or
(c) inclusion of a new condition (whether or not there are already any existing conditions).

Notice that review to be carried out

108 (1) If the supervisory body are to carry out a review of the standard authorisation, they must give notice of the review to the following persons—

(a) the relevant person;
(b) the relevant person's representative;
(c) the managing authority of the relevant hospital or care home.

(2) The supervisory body must give the notice—

(a) before they begin the review, or
(b) if that is not practicable, as soon as practicable after they have begun it.

(3) This paragraph does not require the supervisory body to give notice to any person who has requested the review.

Starting a review

109 To start a review of the standard authorisation, the supervisory body must decide which, if any, of the qualifying requirements appear to be reviewable.

No reviewable qualifying requirements

110 (1) This paragraph applies if no qualifying requirements appear to be reviewable.

(2) This Part does not require the supervisory body to take any action in respect of the standard authorisation.

One or more reviewable qualifying requirements

111 (1) This paragraph applies if one or more qualifying requirements appear to be reviewable.

(2) The supervisory body must secure that a separate review assessment is carried out in relation to each qualifying requirement which appears to be reviewable.

(3) But sub-paragraph (2) does not require the supervisory body to secure that a best interests review assessment is carried out in a case where the best interests requirement appears to the supervisory body to be non-assessable.

(4) The best interests requirement is non-assessable if—

(a) the requirement is reviewable only on the variation of conditions ground, and
(b) the change in the relevant person's case is not significant.

(5) In making any decision whether the change in the relevant person's case is significant, regard must be had to—

(a) the nature of the change, and
(b) the period that the change is likely to last for.

Review assessments

112 (1) A review assessment is an assessment of whether the relevant person meets a qualifying requirement.

(2) In relation to a review assessment—

(a) a negative conclusion is a conclusion that the relevant person does not meet the qualifying requirement to which the assessment relates;

(b) a positive conclusion is a conclusion that the relevant person meets the qualifying requirement to which the assessment relates.

(3) An age review assessment is a review assessment carried out in relation to the age requirement.

(4) A mental health review assessment is a review assessment carried out in relation to the mental health requirement.

(5) A mental capacity review assessment is a review assessment carried out in relation to the mental capacity requirement.

(6) A best interests review assessment is a review assessment carried out in relation to the best interests requirement.

(7) An eligibility review assessment is a review assessment carried out in relation to the eligibility requirement.

(8) A no refusals review assessment is a review assessment carried out in relation to the no refusals requirement.

113 (1) In carrying out a review assessment, the assessor must comply with any duties which would be imposed upon him under Part 4 if the assessment were being carried out in connection with a request for a standard authorisation.

(2) But in the case of a best interests review assessment, paragraphs 43 and 44 do not apply.

(3) Instead of what is required by paragraph 43, the best interests review assessment must include recommendations about whether—and, if so, how—it would be appropriate to vary the conditions to which the standard authorisation is subject.

Best interests requirement reviewable but non-assessable

114 (1) This paragraph applies in a case where—

(a) the best interests requirement appears to be reviewable, but
(b) in accordance with paragraph 111(3), the supervisory body are not required to secure that a best interests review assessment is carried out.

(2) The supervisory body may vary the conditions to which the standard authorisation is subject in such ways (if any) as the supervisory body think are appropriate in the circumstances.

Best interests review assessment positive

115 (1) This paragraph applies in a case where—

(a) a best interests review assessment is carried out, and
(b) the assessment comes to a positive conclusion.

(2) The supervisory body must decide the following questions—

(a) whether or not the best interests requirement is reviewable on the change of reason ground;
(b) whether or not the best interests requirement is reviewable on the variation of conditions ground;
(c) if so, whether or not the change in the person's case is significant.

(3) If the supervisory body decide that the best interests requirement is reviewable on the change of reason ground, they must vary the standard authorisation so that it states the reason why the relevant person now meets that requirement.

(4) If the supervisory body decide that—

(a) the best interests requirement is reviewable on the variation of conditions ground, and
(b) the change in the relevant person's case is not significant,

they may vary the conditions to which the standard authorisation is subject in such ways (if any) as they think are appropriate in the circumstances.

(5) If the supervisory body decide that—

(a) the best interests requirement is reviewable on the variation of conditions ground, and

(b) the change in the relevant person's case is significant,

they must vary the conditions to which the standard authorisation is subject in such ways as they think are appropriate in the circumstances.

(6) If the supervisory body decide that the best interests requirement is not reviewable on—

(a) the change of reason ground, or
(b) the variation of conditions ground,

this Part does not require the supervisory body to take any action in respect of the standard authorisation so far as the best interests requirement relates to it.

Mental health, mental capacity, eligibility or no refusals review assessment positive

116 (1) This paragraph applies if the following conditions are met.

(2) The first condition is that one or more of the following are carried out—

(a) a mental health review assessment;
(b) a mental capacity review assessment;
(c) an eligibility review assessment;
(d) a no refusals review assessment.

(3) The second condition is that each assessment carried out comes to a positive conclusion.

(4) The supervisory body must decide whether or not each of the assessed qualifying requirements is reviewable on the change of reason ground.

(5) If the supervisory body decide that any of the assessed qualifying requirements is reviewable on the change of reason ground, they must vary the standard authorisation so that it states the reason why the relevant person now meets the requirement or requirements in question.

(6) If the supervisory body decide that none of the assessed qualifying requirements are reviewable on the change of reason ground, this Part does not require the supervisory body to take any action in respect of the standard authorisation so far as those requirements relate to it.

(7) An assessed qualifying requirement is a qualifying requirement in relation to which a review assessment is carried out.

One or more review assessments negative

117 (1) This paragraph applies if one or more of the review assessments carried out comes to a negative conclusion.

(2) The supervisory body must terminate the standard authorisation with immediate effect.

Completion of a review

118 (1) The review of the standard authorisation is complete in any of the following cases.

(2) The first case is where paragraph 110 applies.

(3) The second case is where—

(a) paragraph 111 applies, and
(b) paragraph 117 requires the supervisory body to terminate the standard authorisation.

(4) In such a case, the supervisory body need not comply with any of the other provisions of paragraphs 114 to 116 which would be applicable to the review (were it not for this sub-paragraph).

(5) The third case is where—

(a) paragraph 111 applies,
(b) paragraph 117 does not require the supervisory body to terminate the standard authorisation, and
(c) the supervisory body comply with all of the provisions of paragraphs 114 to 116 (so far as they are applicable to the review).

Variations under this Part

119 Any variation of the standard authorisation made under this Part must be in writing.

Notice of outcome of review

120 (1) When the review of the standard authorisation is complete, the supervisory body must give notice to all of the following—

(a) the managing authority of the relevant hospital or care home;
(b) the relevant person;
(c) the relevant person's representative;
(d) any section 39D IMCA.

(2) That notice must state—

(a) the outcome of the review, and
(b) what variation (if any) has been made to the authorisation under this Part.

Records

121 A supervisory body must keep a written record of the following information—

(a) each request for a review that is made to them;
(b) the outcome of each request;
(c) each review which they carry out;
(d) the outcome of each review which they carry out;
(e) any variation of an authorisation made in consequence of a review.

Relationship between review and suspension under Part 6

122 (1) This paragraph applies if a standard authorisation is suspended in accordance with Part 6.

(2) No review may be requested under this Part whilst the standard authorisation is suspended.

(3) If a review has already been requested, or is being carried out, when the standard authorisation is suspended, no steps are to be taken in connection with that review whilst the authorisation is suspended.

Relationship between review and request for new authorisation

123 (1) This paragraph applies if, in accordance with paragraph 24 (as read with paragraph 29), the managing authority of the relevant hospital or care home make a request for a new standard authorisation which would be in force after the expiry of the existing authorisation.

(2) No review may be requested under this Part until the request for the new standard authorisation has been disposed of.

(3) If a review has already been requested, or is being carried out, when the new standard authorisation is requested, no steps are to be taken in connection with that review until the request for the new standard authorisation has been disposed of.

124 (1) This paragraph applies if—

(a) a review under this Part has been requested, or is being carried out, and
(b) the managing authority of the relevant hospital or care home make a request under paragraph 30 for a new standard authorisation which would be in force on or before, and after, the expiry of the existing authorisation.

(2) No steps are to be taken in connection with the review under this Part until the request for the new standard authorisation has been disposed of.

125 In paragraphs 123 and 124—

(a) the existing authorisation is the authorisation referred to in paragraph 101;
(b) the expiry of the existing authorisation is the time when it is expected to cease to be in force.]

NOTES

Amendment

Inserted by the Mental Health Act 2007, s 50(5), Sch 7. Date in force (for certain purposes): 1 April 2008: see SI 2008/745, art 4(a). Date in force (for remaining purposes): to be appointed: see the Mental Health Act 2007, s 56(1).

[PART 9
ASSESSMENTS UNDER THIS SCHEDULE]

NOTES

Amendment

Inserted by the Mental Health Act 2007, s 50(5), Sch 7. Date in force (for certain purposes): 1 April 2008: see SI 2008/745, art 4(a). Date in force (for remaining purposes): to be appointed: see the Mental Health Act 2007, s 56(1).

[Introduction

126 This Part contains provision about assessments under this Schedule.

127 An assessment under this Schedule is either of the following—

(a) an assessment carried out in connection with a request for a standard authorisation under Part 4;
(b) a review assessment carried out in connection with a review of a standard authorisation under Part 8.

128 In this Part, in relation to an assessment under this Schedule—

"assessor" means the person carrying out the assessment;
"relevant procedure" means—
(a) the request for the standard authorisation, or
(b) the review of the standard authorisation;
"supervisory body" means the supervisory body responsible for securing that the assessment is carried out.

Supervisory body to select assessor

129 (1) It is for the supervisory body to select a person to carry out an assessment under this Schedule.

(2) The supervisory body must not select a person to carry out an assessment unless the person—

(a) appears to the supervisory body to be suitable to carry out the assessment (having regard, in particular, to the type of assessment and the person to be assessed), and
(b) is eligible to carry out the assessment.

(3) Regulations may make provision about the selection, and eligibility, of persons to carry out assessments under this Schedule.

(4) Sub-paragraphs (5) and (6) apply if two or more assessments are to be obtained for the purposes of the relevant procedure.

(5) In a case where the assessments to be obtained include a mental health assessment and a best interests assessment, the supervisory body must not select the same person to carry out both assessments.

(6) Except as prohibited by sub-paragraph (5), the supervisory body may select the same person to carry out any number of the assessments which the person appears to be suitable, and is eligible, to carry out.

130 (1) This paragraph applies to regulations under paragraph 129(3).

(2) The regulations may make provision relating to a person's—

(a) qualifications,
(b) skills,

(c) training,
(d) experience,
(e) relationship to, or connection with, the relevant person or any other person,
(f) involvement in the care or treatment of the relevant person,
(g) connection with the supervisory body, or
(h) connection with the relevant hospital or care home, or with any other establishment or undertaking.

(3) The provision that the regulations may make in relation to a person's training may provide for particular training to be specified by the appropriate authority otherwise than in the regulations.

(4) In sub-paragraph (3) the "appropriate authority" means—

(a) in relation to England: the Secretary of State;
(b) in relation to Wales: the National Assembly for Wales.

(5) The regulations may make provision requiring a person to be insured in respect of liabilities that may arise in connection with the carrying out of an assessment.

(6) In relation to cases where two or more assessments are to be obtained for the purposes of the relevant procedure, the regulations may limit the number, kind or combination of assessments which a particular person is eligible to carry out.

(7) Sub-paragraphs (2) to (6) do not limit the generality of the provision that may be made in the regulations.

Examination and copying of records

131 An assessor may, at all reasonable times, examine and take copies of—

(a) any health record,
(b) any record of, or held by, a local authority and compiled in accordance with a social services function, and
(c) any record held by a person registered under Part 2 of the Care Standards Act 2000,

which the assessor considers may be relevant to the assessment which is being carried out.

Representations

132 In carrying out an assessment under this Schedule, the assessor must take into account any information given, or submissions made, by any of the following—

(a) the relevant person's representative;
(b) any section 39A IMCA;
(c) any section 39C IMCA;
(d) any section 39D IMCA.

Assessments to stop if any comes to negative conclusion

133 (1) This paragraph applies if an assessment under this Schedule comes to the conclusion that the relevant person does not meet one of the qualifying requirements.

(2) This Schedule does not require the supervisory body to secure that any other assessments under this Schedule are carried out in relation to the relevant procedure.

(3) The supervisory body must give notice to any assessor who is carrying out another assessment in connection with the relevant procedure that they are to cease carrying out that assessment.

(4) If an assessor receives such notice, this Schedule does not require the assessor to continue carrying out that assessment.

Duty to keep records and give copies

134 (1) This paragraph applies if an assessor has carried out an assessment under this Schedule (whatever conclusions the assessment has come to).

(2) The assessor must keep a written record of the assessment.

(3) As soon as practicable after carrying out the assessment, the assessor must give copies of the assessment to the supervisory body.

135 (1) This paragraph applies to the supervisory body if they are given a copy of an assessment under this Schedule.

(2) The supervisory body must give copies of the assessment to all of the following—

- (a) the managing authority of the relevant hospital or care home;
- (b) the relevant person;
- (c) any section 39A IMCA;
- (d) the relevant person's representative.

(3) If—

- (a) the assessment is obtained in relation to a request for a standard authorisation, and
- (b) the supervisory body are required by paragraph 50(1) to give the standard authorisation,

the supervisory body must give the copies of the assessment when they give copies of the authorisation in accordance with paragraph 57.

(4) If—

- (a) the assessment is obtained in relation to a request for a standard authorisation, and
- (b) the supervisory body are prohibited by paragraph 50(2) from giving the standard authorisation,

the supervisory body must give the copies of the assessment when they give notice in accordance with paragraph 58.

(5) If the assessment is obtained in connection with the review of a standard authorisation, the supervisory body must give the copies of the assessment when they give notice in accordance with paragraph 120.

136 (1) This paragraph applies to the supervisory body if—

- (a) they are given a copy of a best interests assessment, and
- (b) the assessment includes, in accordance with paragraph 44(2), a statement that it appears to the assessor that there is an unauthorised deprivation of liberty.

(2) The supervisory body must notify all of the persons listed in sub-paragraph (3) that the assessment includes such a statement.

(3) Those persons are—

- (a) the managing authority of the relevant hospital or care home;
- (b) the relevant person;
- (c) any section 39A IMCA;
- (d) any interested person consulted by the best interests assessor.

(4) The supervisory body must comply with this paragraph when (or at some time before) they comply with paragraph 135.]

NOTES

Amendment

Inserted by the Mental Health Act 2007, s 50(5), Sch 7. Date in force (for certain purposes): 1 April 2008: see SI 2008/745, art 4(a). Date in force (for remaining purposes): to be appointed: see the Mental Health Act 2007, s 56(1).

[PART 10
RELEVANT PERSON'S REPRESENTATIVE]

NOTES

Amendment

Inserted by the Mental Health Act 2007, s 50(5), Sch 7. Date in force (for certain purposes): 1 April 2008: see SI 2008/745, art 4(a). Date in force (for remaining purposes): to be appointed: see the Mental Health Act 2007, s 56(1).

[The representative

137 In this Schedule the relevant person's representative is the person appointed as such in accordance with this Part.

138 (1) Regulations may make provision about the selection and appointment of representatives.

(2) In this Part such regulations are referred to as "appointment regulations".

Supervisory body to appoint representative

139 (1) The supervisory body must appoint a person to be the relevant person's representative as soon as practicable after a standard authorisation is given.

(2) The supervisory body must appoint a person to be the relevant person's representative if a vacancy arises whilst a standard authorisation is in force.

(3) Where a vacancy arises, the appointment under sub-paragraph (2) is to be made as soon as practicable after the supervisory body becomes aware of the vacancy.

140 (1) The selection of a person for appointment under paragraph 139 must not be made unless it appears to the person making the selection that the prospective representative would, if appointed—

- (a) maintain contact with the relevant person,
- (b) represent the relevant person in matters relating to or connected with this Schedule, and
- (c) support the relevant person in matters relating to or connected with this Schedule.

141 (1) Any appointment of a representative for a relevant person is in addition to, and does not affect, any appointment of a donee or deputy.

(2) The functions of any representative are in addition to, and do not affect—

- (a) the authority of any donee,
- (b) the powers of any deputy, or
- (c) any powers of the court.

Appointment regulations

142 Appointment regulations may provide that the procedure for appointing a representative may begin at any time after a request for a standard authorisation is made (including a time before the request has been disposed of).

143 (1) Appointment regulations may make provision about who is to select a person for appointment as a representative.

(2) But regulations under this paragraph may only provide for the following to make a selection—

- (a) the relevant person, if he has capacity in relation to the question of which person should be his representative;
- (b) a donee of a lasting power of attorney granted by the relevant person, if it is within the scope of his authority to select a person;
- (c) a deputy, if it is within the scope of his authority to select a person;
- (d) a best interests assessor;
- (e) the supervisory body.

(3) Regulations under this paragraph may provide that a selection by the relevant person, a donee or a deputy is subject to approval by a best interests assessor or the supervisory body.

(4) Regulations under this paragraph may provide that, if more than one selection is necessary in connection with the appointment of a particular representative—

- (a) the same person may make more than one selection;
- (b) different persons may make different selections.

(5) For the purposes of this paragraph a best interests assessor is a person carrying out a best interests assessment in connection with the standard authorisation in question (including the giving of that authorisation).

144 (1) Appointment regulations may make provision about who may, or may not, be—

(a) selected for appointment as a representative, or
(b) appointed as a representative.

(2) Regulations under this paragraph may relate to any of the following matters—

(a) a person's age;
(b) a person's suitability;
(c) a person's independence;
(d) a person's willingness;
(e) a person's qualifications.

145 Appointment regulations may make provision about the formalities of appointing a person as a representative.

146 In a case where a best interests assessor is to select a person to be appointed as a representative, appointment regulations may provide for the variation of the assessor's duties in relation to the assessment which he is carrying out.

Monitoring of representatives

147 Regulations may make provision requiring the managing authority of the relevant hospital or care home to—

(a) monitor, and
(b) report to the supervisory body on,

the extent to which a representative is maintaining contact with the relevant person.

Termination

148 Regulations may make provision about the circumstances in which the appointment of a person as the relevant person's representative ends or may be ended.

149 Regulations may make provision about the formalities of ending the appointment of a person as a representative.

Suspension of representative's functions

150 (1) Regulations may make provision about the circumstances in which functions exercisable by, or in relation to, the relevant person's representative (whether under this Schedule or not) may be—

(a) suspended, and
(b) if suspended, revived.

(2) The regulations may make provision about the formalities for giving effect to the suspension or revival of a function.

(3) The regulations may make provision about the effect of the suspension or revival of a function.

Payment of representative

151 Regulations may make provision for payments to be made to, or in relation to, persons exercising functions as the relevant person's representative.

Regulations under this Part

152 The provisions of this Part which specify provision that may be made in regulations under this Part do not affect the generality of the power to make such regulations.

Effect of appointment of section 39C IMCA

153 Paragraphs 159 and 160 make provision about the exercise of functions by, or towards, the relevant person's representative during periods when—

(a) no person is appointed as the relevant person's representative, but

(b) a person is appointed as a section 39C IMCA.]

NOTES

Amendment

Inserted by the Mental Health Act 2007, s 50(5), Sch 7. Date in force (for certain purposes): 1 April 2008: see SI 2008/745, art 4(a). Date in force (for remaining purposes): to be appointed: see the Mental Health Act 2007, s 56(1).

[PART 11
IMCAS]

NOTES

Amendment

Inserted by the Mental Health Act 2007, s 50(5), Sch 7. Date in force (for certain purposes): 1 April 2008: see SI 2008/745, art 4(a). Date in force (for remaining purposes): to be appointed: see the Mental Health Act 2007, s 56(1).

[Application of Part

154 This Part applies for the purposes of this Schedule.

The IMCAs

155 A section 39A IMCA is an independent mental capacity advocate appointed under section 39A.

156 A section 39C IMCA is an independent mental capacity advocate appointed under section 39C

157 A section 39D IMCA is an independent mental capacity advocate appointed under section 39D.

158 An IMCA is a section 39A IMCA or a section 39C IMCA or a section 39D IMCA.

Section 39C IMCA: functions

159 (1) This paragraph applies if, and for as long as, there is a section 39C IMCA.

(2) In the application of the relevant provisions, references to the relevant person's representative are to be read as references to the section 39C IMCA.

(3) But sub-paragraph (2) does not apply to any function under the relevant provisions for as long as the function is suspended in accordance with provision made under Part 10.

(4) In this paragraph and paragraph 160 the relevant provisions are—

(a) paragraph 102(3)(b) (request for review under Part 8);
(b) paragraph 108(1)(b) (notice of review under Part 8);
(c) paragraph 120(1)(c) (notice of outcome of review under Part 8).

160 (1) This paragraph applies if—

(a) a person is appointed as the relevant person's representative, and
(b) a person accordingly ceases to hold an appointment as a section 39C IMCA.

(2) Where a function under a relevant provision has been exercised by, or towards, the section 39C IMCA, there is no requirement for that function to be exercised again by, or towards, the relevant person's representative.

Section 39A IMCA: restriction of functions

161 (1) This paragraph applies if—

(a) there is a section 39A IMCA, and
(b) a person is appointed under Part 10 to be the relevant person's representative (whether or not that person, or any person subsequently appointed, is currently the relevant person's representative).

(2) The duties imposed on, and the powers exercisable by, the section 39A IMCA do not apply.

(3) The duties imposed on, and the powers exercisable by, any other person do not apply, so far as they fall to be performed or exercised towards the section 39A IMCA.

(4) But sub-paragraph (2) does not apply to any power of challenge exercisable by the section 39A IMCA.

(5) And sub-paragraph (3) does not apply to any duty or power of any other person so far as it relates to any power of challenge exercisable by the section 39A IMCA.

(6) Before exercising any power of challenge, the section 39A IMCA must take the views of the relevant person's representative into account.

(7) A power of challenge is a power to make an application to the court to exercise its jurisdiction under section 21A in connection with the giving of the standard authorisation.]

NOTES

Amendment

Inserted by the Mental Health Act 2007, s 50(5), Sch 7. Date in force (for certain purposes): 1 April 2008: see SI 2008/745, art 4(a). Date in force (for remaining purposes): to be appointed: see the Mental Health Act 2007, s 56(1).

[PART 12
MISCELLANEOUS]

NOTES

Amendment

Inserted by the Mental Health Act 2007, s 50(5), Sch 7. Date in force (for certain purposes): 1 April 2008: see SI 2008/745, art 4(a). Date in force (for remaining purposes): to be appointed: see the Mental Health Act 2007, s 56(1).

[Monitoring of operation of Schedule

162 (1) Regulations may make provision for, and in connection with, requiring one or more prescribed bodies to monitor, and report on, the operation of this Schedule in relation to England.

(2) The regulations may, in particular, give a prescribed body authority to do one or more of the following things—

- (a) to visit hospitals and care homes;
- (b) to visit and interview persons accommodated in hospitals and care homes;
- (c) to require the production of, and to inspect, records relating to the care or treatment of persons.

(3) "Prescribed" means prescribed in regulations under this paragraph.

163 (1) Regulations may make provision for, and in connection with, enabling the National Assembly for Wales to monitor, and report on, the operation of this Schedule in relation to Wales.

(2) The National Assembly may direct one or more persons or bodies to carry out the Assembly's functions under regulations under this paragraph.

Disclosure of information

164 (1) Regulations may require either or both of the following to disclose prescribed information to prescribed bodies—

- (a) supervisory bodies;
- (b) managing authorities of hospitals or care homes.

(2) "Prescribed" means prescribed in regulations under this paragraph.

(3) Regulations under this paragraph may only prescribe information relating to matters with which this Schedule is concerned.

Directions by National Assembly in relation to supervisory functions

165 (1) The National Assembly for Wales may direct a Local Health Board to exercise in relation to its area any supervisory functions which are specified in the direction.

(2) Directions under this paragraph must not preclude the National Assembly from exercising the functions specified in the directions.

(3) In this paragraph "supervisory functions" means functions which the National Assembly have as supervisory body, so far as they are exercisable in relation to hospitals (whether NHS or independent hospitals, and whether in Wales or England).

166 (1) This paragraph applies where, under paragraph 165, a Local Health Board ("the specified LHB") is directed to exercise supervisory functions ("delegated functions").

(2) The National Assembly for Wales may give directions to the specified LHB about the Board's exercise of delegated functions.

(3) The National Assembly may give directions for any delegated functions to be exercised, on behalf of the specified LHB, by a committee, sub-committee or officer of that Board.

(4) The National Assembly may give directions providing for any delegated functions to be exercised by the specified LHB jointly with one or more other Local Health Boards.

(5) Where, under sub-paragraph (4), delegated functions are exercisable jointly, the National Assembly may give directions providing for the functions to be exercised, on behalf of the Local Health Boards in question, by a joint committee or joint sub-committee.

167 (1) Directions under paragraph 165 must be given in regulations.

(2) Directions under paragraph 166 may be given—

(a) in regulations, or
(b) by instrument in writing.

168 The power under paragraph 165 or paragraph 166 to give directions includes power to vary or revoke directions given under that paragraph.

Notices

169 Any notice under this Schedule must be in writing.

Regulations

170 (1) This paragraph applies to all regulations under this Schedule, except regulations under paragraph 162, 163, 167 or 183.

(2) It is for the Secretary of State to make such regulations in relation to authorisations under this Schedule which relate to hospitals and care homes situated in England.

(3) It is for the National Assembly for Wales to make such regulations in relation to authorisations under this Schedule which relate to hospitals and care homes situated in Wales.

171 It is for the Secretary of State to make regulations under paragraph 162.

172 It is for the National Assembly for Wales to make regulations under paragraph 163 or 167.

173 (1) This paragraph applies to regulations under paragraph 183.

(2) It is for the Secretary of State to make such regulations in relation to cases where a question as to the ordinary residence of a person is to be determined by the Secretary of State.

(3) It is for the National Assembly for Wales to make such regulations in relation to cases where a question as to the ordinary residence of a person is to be determined by the National Assembly.]

NOTES

Amendment

Inserted by the Mental Health Act 2007, s 50(5), Sch 7. Date in force (for certain purposes): 1 April 2008: see SI 2008/745, art 4(a). Date in force (for remaining purposes): to be appointed: see the Mental Health Act 2007, s 56(1).

[PART 13
INTERPRETATION]

NOTES

Amendment

Inserted by the Mental Health Act 2007, s 50(5), Sch 7. Date in force (for certain purposes): 1 April 2008: see SI 2008/745, art 4(a). Date in force (for remaining purposes): to be appointed: see the Mental Health Act 2007, s 56(1).

[Introduction

174 This Part applies for the purposes of this Schedule.

Hospitals and their managing authorities

175 (1) "Hospital" means—

(a) an NHS hospital, or
(b) an independent hospital.

(2) "NHS hospital" means—

(a) a health service hospital as defined by section 275 of the National Health Service Act 2006 or section 206 of the National Health Service (Wales) Act 2006, or
(b) a hospital as defined by section 206 of the National Health Service (Wales) Act 2006 vested in a Local Health Board.

(3) "Independent hospital" means a hospital as defined by section 2 of the Care Standards Act 2000 which is not an NHS hospital.

176 (1) "Managing authority", in relation to an NHS hospital, means—

(a) if the hospital—
  (i) is vested in the appropriate national authority for the purposes of its functions under the National Health Service Act 2006 or of the National Health Service (Wales) Act 2006, or
  (ii) consists of any accommodation provided by a local authority and used as a hospital by or on behalf of the appropriate national authority under either of those Acts,

the Primary Care Trust, Strategic Health Authority, Local Health Board or Special Health Authority responsible for the administration of the hospital;
(b) if the hospital is vested in a Primary Care Trust, National Health Service trust or NHS foundation trust, that trust;
(c) if the hospital is vested in a Local Health Board, that Board.

(2) For this purpose the appropriate national authority is—

(a) in relation to England: the Secretary of State;
(b) in relation to Wales: the National Assembly for Wales;
(c) in relation to England and Wales: the Secretary of State and the National Assembly acting jointly.

177 "Managing authority", in relation to an independent hospital, means the person registered, or required to be registered, under Part 2 of the Care Standards Act 2000 in respect of the hospital.

Care homes and their managing authorities

178 "Care home" has the meaning given by section 3 of the Care Standards Act 2000.

179 "Managing authority", in relation to a care home, means the person registered, or required to be registered, under Part 2 of the Care Standards Act 2000 in respect of the care home.

Supervisory bodies: hospitals

180 (1) The identity of the supervisory body is determined under this paragraph in cases where the relevant hospital is situated in England.

(2) If a Primary Care Trust commissions the relevant care or treatment, that Trust is the supervisory body.

(3) If the National Assembly for Wales or a Local Health Board commission the relevant care or treatment, the National Assembly are the supervisory body.

(4) In any other case, the supervisory body are the Primary Care Trust for the area in which the relevant hospital is situated.

(5) If a hospital is situated in the areas of two (or more) Primary Care Trusts, it is to be regarded for the purposes of sub-paragraph (4) as situated in whichever of the areas the greater (or greatest) part of the hospital is situated.

181 (1) The identity of the supervisory body is determined under this paragraph in cases where the relevant hospital is situated in Wales.

(2) The National Assembly for Wales are the supervisory body.

(3) But if a Primary Care Trust commissions the relevant care or treatment, that Trust is the supervisory body.

Supervisory bodies: care homes

182 (1) The identity of the supervisory body is determined under this paragraph in cases where the relevant care home is situated in England or in Wales.

(2) The supervisory body are the local authority for the area in which the relevant person is ordinarily resident.

(3) But if the relevant person is not ordinarily resident in the area of a local authority, the supervisory body are the local authority for the area in which the care home is situated.

(4) In relation to England "local authority" means—

- (a) the council of a county;
- (b) the council of a district for which there is no county council;
- (c) the council of a London borough;
- (d) the Common Council of the City of London;
- (e) the Council of the Isles of Scilly.

(5) In relation to Wales "local authority" means the council of a county or county borough.

(6) If a care home is situated in the areas of two (or more) local authorities, it is to be regarded for the purposes of sub-paragraph (3) as situated in whichever of the areas the greater (or greatest) part of the care home is situated.

183 (1) Subsections (5) and (6) of section 24 of the National Assistance Act 1948 (deemed place of ordinary residence) apply to any determination of where a person is ordinarily resident for the purposes of paragraph 182 as those subsections apply to such a determination for the purposes specified in those subsections.

(2) In the application of section 24(6) of the 1948 Act by virtue of subsection (1), section 24(6) is to be read as if it referred to a hospital vested in a Local Health Board as well as to hospitals vested in the Secretary of State and the other bodies mentioned in section 24(6).

(3) Any question arising as to the ordinary residence of a person is to be determined by the Secretary of State or by the National Assembly for Wales.

(4) The Secretary of State and the National Assembly must make and publish arrangements for determining which cases are to be dealt with by the Secretary of State and which are to be dealt with by the National Assembly.

(5) Those arrangements may include provision for the Secretary of State and the National Assembly to agree, in relation to any question that has arisen, which of them is to deal with the case.

(6) Regulations may make provision about arrangements that are to have effect before, upon, or after the determination of any question as to the ordinary residence of a person.

(7) The regulations may, in particular, authorise or require a local authority to do any or all of the following things—

- (a) to act as supervisory body even though it may wish to dispute that it is the supervisory body;
- (b) to become the supervisory body in place of another local authority;
- (c) to recover from another local authority expenditure incurred in exercising functions as the supervisory body.

Same body managing authority and supervisory body

184 (1) This paragraph applies if, in connection with a particular person's detention as a resident in a hospital or care home, the same body are both—

- (a) the managing authority of the relevant hospital or care home, and
- (b) the supervisory body.

(2) The fact that a single body are acting in both capacities does not prevent the body from carrying out functions under this Schedule in each capacity.

(3) But, in such a case, this Schedule has effect subject to any modifications contained in regulations that may be made for this purpose.

Interested persons

185 Each of the following is an interested person—

- (a) the relevant person's spouse or civil partner;
- (b) where the relevant person and another person of the opposite sex are not married to each other but are living together as husband and wife: the other person;
- (c) where the relevant person and another person of the same sex are not civil partners of each other but are living together as if they were civil partners: the other person;
- (d) the relevant person's children and step-children;
- (e) the relevant person's parents and step-parents;
- (f) the relevant person's brothers and sisters, half-brothers and half-sisters, and stepbrothers and stepsisters;
- (g) the relevant person's grandparents;
- (h) a deputy appointed for the relevant person by the court;
- (i) a donee of a lasting power of attorney granted by the relevant person.

186 (1) An interested person consulted by the best interests assessor is any person whose name is stated in the relevant best interests assessment in accordance with paragraph 40 (interested persons whom the assessor consulted in carrying out the assessment).

(2) The relevant best interests assessment is the most recent best interests assessment carried out in connection with the standard authorisation in question (whether the assessment was carried out under Part 4 or Part 8).

187 Where this Schedule imposes on a person a duty towards an interested person, the duty does not apply if the person on whom the duty is imposed—

- (a) is not aware of the interested person's identity or of a way of contacting him, and
- (b) cannot reasonably ascertain it.

188 The following table contains an index of provisions defining or otherwise explaining expressions used in this Schedule—

age assessment	paragraph 34
age requirement	paragraph 13
age review assessment	paragraph 112(3)
appointment regulations	paragraph 138
assessment under this Schedule	paragraph 127
assessor (except in Part 8)	paragraph 33
assessor (in Part 8)	paragraphs 33 and 128

authorisation under this Schedule	paragraph 10
best interests (determination of)	section 4
best interests assessment	paragraph 38
best interests requirement	paragraph 16
best interests review assessment	paragraph 112(6)
care home	paragraph 178
change of reason ground	paragraph 106
complete (in relation to a review of a standard authorisation)	paragraph 118
deprivation of a person's liberty	section 64(5) and (6)
deputy	section 16(2)(b)
detained resident	paragraph 6
disposed of (in relation to a request for a standard authorisation)	paragraph 66
eligibility assessment	paragraph 46
eligibility requirement	paragraph 17
eligibility review assessment	paragraph 112(7)
eligible person (in relation to paragraphs 68 to 73)	paragraph 68
eligible person (in relation to Part 8)	paragraph 102(3)
expiry (in relation to an existing authorisation)	paragraph 125(b)
existing authorisation (in Part 8)	paragraph 125(a)
hospital	paragraph 175
IMCA	paragraph 158
in force (in relation to a standard authorisation)	paragraphs 63 and 64
in force (in relation to an urgent authorisation)	paragraphs 88 and 89
ineligible (in relation to the eligibility requirement)	Schedule 1A
interested person	paragraph 185
interested person consulted by the best interests assessor	paragraph 186
lack of capacity	section 2
lasting power of attorney	section 9
managing authority (in relation to a care home)	paragraph 179
managing authority (in relation to a hospital)	paragraph 176 or 177
maximum authorisation period	paragraph 42
mental capacity assessment	paragraph 37
mental capacity requirement	paragraph 15
mental capacity review assessment	paragraph 112(5)
mental health assessment	paragraph 35
mental health requirement	paragraph 14
mental health review assessment	paragraph 112(4)
negative conclusion	paragraph 112(2)(a)
new supervisory body	paragraph 99(b)
no refusals assessment	paragraph 48
no refusals requirement	paragraph 18
no refusals review assessment	paragraph 112(8)
non-qualification ground	paragraph 105
old supervisory body	paragraph 99(a)

positive conclusion	paragraph 112(2)(b)
purpose of a standard authorisation	paragraph 11(1)
purpose of an urgent authorisation	paragraph 11(2)
qualifying requirements	paragraph 12
refusal (for the purposes of the no refusals requirement)	paragraphs 19 and 20
relevant care or treatment	paragraph 7
relevant hospital or care home	paragraph 7
relevant managing authority	paragraph 26(4)
relevant person	paragraph 7
relevant person's representative	paragraph 137
relevant procedure	paragraph 128
review assessment	paragraph 112(1)
reviewable	paragraph 104
section 39A IMCA	paragraph 155
section 39C IMCA	paragraph 156
section 39D IMCA	paragraph 157
standard authorisation	paragraph 8
supervisory body (except in Part 8)	paragraph 180, 181 or 182
supervisory body (in Part 8)	paragraph 128 and paragraph 180, 181 or 182
unauthorised deprivation of liberty (in relation to paragraphs 68 to 73)	paragraph 67
urgent authorisation	paragraph 9
variation of conditions ground	paragraph 107]

NOTES

Amendment

Inserted by the Mental Health Act 2007, s 50(5), Sch 7. Date in force (for certain purposes): 1 April 2008: see SI 2008/745, art 4(a). Date in force (for remaining purposes): to be appointed: see the Mental Health Act 2007, s 56(1).

SCHEDULE 1
LASTING POWERS OF ATTORNEY: FORMALITIES

Section 9

PART 1
MAKING INSTRUMENTS

General requirements as to making instruments

A1.80

1 (1) An instrument is not made in accordance with this Schedule unless—

(a) it is in the prescribed form,
(b) it complies with paragraph 2, and
(c) any prescribed requirements in connection with its execution are satisfied.

(2) Regulations may make different provision according to whether—

(a) the instrument relates to personal welfare or to property and affairs (or to both);
(b) only one or more than one donee is to be appointed (and if more than one, whether jointly or jointly and severally).

(3) In this Schedule—

(a) "prescribed" means prescribed by regulations, and

(b) "regulations" means regulations made for the purposes of this Schedule by the Lord Chancellor.

Requirements as to content of instruments

2 (1) The instrument must include—

(a) the prescribed information about the purpose of the instrument and the effect of a lasting power of attorney,
(b) a statement by the donor to the effect that he—
  (i) has read the prescribed information or a prescribed part of it (or has had it read to him), and
  (ii) intends the authority conferred under the instrument to include authority to make decisions on his behalf in circumstances where he no longer has capacity,
(c) a statement by the donor—
  (i) naming a person or persons whom the donor wishes to be notified of any application for the registration of the instrument, or
  (ii) stating that there are no persons whom he wishes to be notified of any such application,
(d) a statement by the donee (or, if more than one, each of them) to the effect that he—
  (i) has read the prescribed information or a prescribed part of it (or has had it read to him), and
  (ii) understands the duties imposed on a donee of a lasting power of attorney under sections 1 (the principles) and 4 (best interests), and
(e) a certificate by a person of a prescribed description that, in his opinion, at the time when the donor executes the instrument—
  (i) the donor understands the purpose of the instrument and the scope of the authority conferred under it,
  (ii) no fraud or undue pressure is being used to induce the donor to create a lasting power of attorney, and
  (iii) there is nothing else which would prevent a lasting power of attorney from being created by the instrument.

(2) Regulations may—

(a) prescribe a maximum number of named persons;
(b) provide that, where the instrument includes a statement under sub-paragraph (1)(c)(ii), two persons of a prescribed description must each give a certificate under sub-paragraph (1)(e).

(3) The persons who may be named persons do not include a person who is appointed as donee under the instrument.

(4) In this Schedule, "named person" means a person named under sub-paragraph (1)(c).

(5) A certificate under sub-paragraph (1)(e)—

(a) must be made in the prescribed form, and
(b) must include any prescribed information.

(6) The certificate may not be given by a person appointed as donee under the instrument.

Failure to comply with prescribed form

3 (1) If an instrument differs in an immaterial respect in form or mode of expression from the prescribed form, it is to be treated by the Public Guardian as sufficient in point of form and expression.

(2) The court may declare that an instrument which is not in the prescribed form is to be treated as if it were, if it is satisfied that the persons executing the instrument intended it to create a lasting power of attorney.

NOTES

Initial Commencement

To be appointed: see s 68(1).

Appointment

Appointment: 1 October 2007: see SI 2007/1897, art 2(1)(d).

Subordinate Legislation

Lasting Powers of Attorney, Enduring Powers of Attorney and Public Guardian (Amendment) Regulations 2007, SI 2007/2161.

PART 2
REGISTRATION

Applications and procedure for registration

4 (1) An application to the Public Guardian for the registration of an instrument intended to create a lasting power of attorney—

(a) must be made in the prescribed form, and
(b) must include any prescribed information.

(2) The application may be made—

(a) by the donor,
(b) by the donee or donees, or
(c) if the instrument appoints two or more donees to act jointly and severally in respect of any matter, by any of the donees.

(3) The application must be accompanied by—

(a) the instrument, and
(b) any fee provided for under section 58(4)(b).

(4) A person who, in an application for registration, makes a statement which he knows to be false in a material particular is guilty of an offence and is liable—

(a) on summary conviction, to imprisonment for a term not exceeding 12 months or a fine not exceeding the statutory maximum or both;
(b) on conviction on indictment, to imprisonment for a term not exceeding 2 years or a fine or both.

5 Subject to paragraphs 11 to 14, the Public Guardian must register the instrument as a lasting power of attorney at the end of the prescribed period.

Notification requirements

6 (1) A donor about to make an application under paragraph 4(2)(a) must notify any named persons that he is about to do so.

(2) The donee (or donees) about to make an application under paragraph 4(2)(b) or (c) must notify any named persons that he is (or they are) about to do so.

7 As soon as is practicable after receiving an application by the donor under paragraph 4(2)(a), the Public Guardian must notify the donee (or donees) that the application has been received.

8 (1) As soon as is practicable after receiving an application by a donee (or donees) under paragraph 4(2)(b), the Public Guardian must notify the donor that the application has been received.

(2) As soon as is practicable after receiving an application by a donee under paragraph 4(2)(c), the Public Guardian must notify—

(a) the donor, and
(b) the donee or donees who did not join in making the application,

that the application has been received.

9 (1) A notice under paragraph 6 must be made in the prescribed form.

(2) A notice under paragraph 6, 7 or 8 must include such information, if any, as may be prescribed.

Power to dispense with notification requirements

10 The court may—

(a) on the application of the donor, dispense with the requirement to notify under paragraph 6(1), or
(b) on the application of the donee or donees concerned, dispense with the requirement to notify under paragraph 6(2),

if satisfied that no useful purpose would be served by giving the notice.

Instrument not made properly or containing ineffective provision

11 (1) If it appears to the Public Guardian that an instrument accompanying an application under paragraph 4 is not made in accordance with this Schedule, he must not register the instrument unless the court directs him to do so.

(2) Sub-paragraph (3) applies if it appears to the Public Guardian that the instrument contains a provision which—

(a) would be ineffective as part of a lasting power of attorney, or
(b) would prevent the instrument from operating as a valid lasting power of attorney.

(3) The Public Guardian—

(a) must apply to the court for it to determine the matter under section 23(1), and
(b) pending the determination by the court, must not register the instrument.

(4) Sub-paragraph (5) applies if the court determines under section 23(1) (whether or not on an application by the Public Guardian) that the instrument contains a provision which—

(a) would be ineffective as part of a lasting power of attorney, or
(b) would prevent the instrument from operating as a valid lasting power of attorney.

(5) The court must—

(a) notify the Public Guardian that it has severed the provision, or
(b) direct him not to register the instrument.

(6) Where the court notifies the Public Guardian that it has severed a provision, he must register the instrument with a note to that effect attached to it.

Deputy already appointed

12 (1) Sub-paragraph (2) applies if it appears to the Public Guardian that—

(a) there is a deputy appointed by the court for the donor, and
(b) the powers conferred on the deputy would, if the instrument were registered, to any extent conflict with the powers conferred on the attorney.

(2) The Public Guardian must not register the instrument unless the court directs him to do so.

Objection by donee or named person

13 (1) Sub-paragraph (2) applies if a donee or a named person—

(a) receives a notice under paragraph 6, 7 or 8 of an application for the registration of an instrument, and
(b) before the end of the prescribed period, gives notice to the Public Guardian of an objection to the registration on the ground that an event mentioned in section 13(3) or (6)(a) to (d) has occurred which has revoked the instrument.

(2) If the Public Guardian is satisfied that the ground for making the objection is established, he must not register the instrument unless the court, on the application of the person applying for the registration—

(a) is satisfied that the ground is not established, and
(b) directs the Public Guardian to register the instrument.

(3) Sub-paragraph (4) applies if a donee or a named person—

(a) receives a notice under paragraph 6, 7 or 8 of an application for the registration of an instrument, and
(b) before the end of the prescribed period—
 (i) makes an application to the court objecting to the registration on a prescribed ground, and
 (ii) notifies the Public Guardian of the application.

(4) The Public Guardian must not register the instrument unless the court directs him to do so.

Objection by donor

14 (1) This paragraph applies if the donor—

(a) receives a notice under paragraph 8 of an application for the registration of an instrument, and
(b) before the end of the prescribed period, gives notice to the Public Guardian of an objection to the registration.

(2) The Public Guardian must not register the instrument unless the court, on the application of the donee or, if more than one, any of them—

(a) is satisfied that the donor lacks capacity to object to the registration, and
(b) directs the Public Guardian to register the instrument.

Notification of registration

15 Where an instrument is registered under this Schedule, the Public Guardian must give notice of the fact in the prescribed form to—

(a) the donor, and
(b) the donee or, if more than one, each of them.

Evidence of registration

16 (1) A document purporting to be an office copy of an instrument registered under this Schedule is, in any part of the United Kingdom, evidence of—

(a) the contents of the instrument, and
(b) the fact that it has been registered.

(2) Sub-paragraph (1) is without prejudice to—

(a) section 3 of the Powers of Attorney Act 1971 (c 27) (proof by certified copy), and
(b) any other method of proof authorised by law.

NOTES

Initial Commencement
To be appointed: see s 68(1).

Appointment
Appointment: 1 October 2007: see SI 2007/1897, art 2(1)(d).

Subordinate Legislation
Lasting Powers of Attorney, Enduring Powers of Attorney and Public Guardian (Amendment) Regulations 2007, SI 2007/2161.

PART 3
CANCELLATION OF REGISTRATION AND NOTIFICATION OF SEVERANCE

17 (1) The Public Guardian must cancel the registration of an instrument as a lasting power of attorney on being satisfied that the power has been revoked—

(a) as a result of the donor's bankruptcy, or
(b) on the occurrence of an event mentioned in section 13(6)(a) to (d).

(2) If the Public Guardian cancels the registration of an instrument he must notify—

(a) the donor, and
(b) the donee or, if more than one, each of them.

18 The court must direct the Public Guardian to cancel the registration of an instrument as a lasting power of attorney if it—

(a) determines under section 22(2)(a) that a requirement for creating the power was not met,
(b) determines under section 22(2)(b) that the power has been revoked or has otherwise come to an end, or
(c) revokes the power under section 22(4)(b) (fraud etc).

19 (1) Sub-paragraph (2) applies if the court determines under section 23(1) that a lasting power of attorney contains a provision which—

(a) is ineffective as part of a lasting power of attorney, or
(b) prevents the instrument from operating as a valid lasting power of attorney.

(2) The court must—

(a) notify the Public Guardian that it has severed the provision, or
(b) direct him to cancel the registration of the instrument as a lasting power of attorney.

20 On the cancellation of the registration of an instrument, the instrument and any office copies of it must be delivered up to the Public Guardian to be cancelled.

NOTES

Initial Commencement
To be appointed: see s 68(1).

Appointment
Appointment: 1 October 2007: see SI 2007/1897, art 2(1)(d).

PART 4
RECORDS OF ALTERATIONS IN REGISTERED POWERS

Partial revocation or suspension of power as a result of bankruptcy

21 If in the case of a registered instrument it appears to the Public Guardian that under section 13 a lasting power of attorney is revoked, or suspended, in relation to the donor's property and affairs (but not in relation to other matters), the Public Guardian must attach to the instrument a note to that effect.

Termination of appointment of donee which does not revoke power

22 If in the case of a registered instrument it appears to the Public Guardian that an event has occurred—

(a) which has terminated the appointment of the donee, but
(b) which has not revoked the instrument,

the Public Guardian must attach to the instrument a note to that effect.

Replacement of donee

23 If in the case of a registered instrument it appears to the Public Guardian that the donee has been replaced under the terms of the instrument the Public Guardian must attach to the instrument a note to that effect.

Severance of ineffective provisions

24 If in the case of a registered instrument the court notifies the Public Guardian under paragraph 19(2)(a) that it has severed a provision of the instrument, the Public Guardian must attach to it a note to that effect.

Notification of alterations

25 If the Public Guardian attaches a note to an instrument under paragraph 21, 22, 23 or 24 he must give notice of the note to the donee or donees of the power (or, as the case may be, to the other donee or donees of the power).

NOTES

Initial Commencement
To be appointed: see s 68(1).

Appointment
Appointment: 1 October 2007: see SI 2007/1897, art 2(1)(d).

[SCHEDULE 1A
PERSONS INELIGIBLE TO BE DEPRIVED OF LIBERTY BY THIS ACT]

NOTES

Amendment
Inserted by the Mental Health Act 2007, s 50(6), Sch 8. Date in force: to be appointed: see the Mental Health Act 2007, s 56(1).

[PART 1
INELIGIBLE PERSONS]

NOTES

Amendment
Inserted by the Mental Health Act 2007, s 50(6), Sch 8. Date in force: to be appointed: see the Mental Health Act 2007, s 56(1).

[Application

A1.81

1 This Schedule applies for the purposes of—

(a) section 16A, and
(b) paragraph 17 of Schedule A1.

Determining ineligibility

2 A person ("P") is ineligible to be deprived of liberty by this Act ("ineligible") if—

(a) P falls within one of the cases set out in the second column of the following table, and
(b) the corresponding entry in the third column of the table—or the provision, or one of the provisions, referred to in that entry—provides that he is ineligible.

	Status of P	*Determination of ineligibility*
Case A	P is— (a)subject to the hospital treatment regime, and (b)detained in a hospital under that regime.	P is ineligible.
Case B	P is— (a)subject to the hospital treatment regime, but (b)not detained in a hospital under that regime.	See paragraphs 3 and 4.
Case C	P is subject to the community treatment regime.	See paragraphs 3 and 4.

Case D	P is subject to the guardianship regime.	See paragraphs 3 and 5.
Case E	P is— (a)within the scope of the Mental Health Act, but (b)not subject to any of the mental health regimes.	See paragraph 5.

Authorised course of action not in accordance with regime

3 (1) This paragraph applies in cases B, C and D in the table in paragraph 2.

(2) P is ineligible if the authorised course of action is not in accordance with a requirement which the relevant regime imposes.

(3) That includes any requirement as to where P is, or is not, to reside.

(4) The relevant regime is the mental health regime to which P is subject.

Treatment for mental disorder in a hospital

4 (1) This paragraph applies in cases B and C in the table in paragraph 2.

(2) P is ineligible if the relevant care or treatment consists in whole or in part of medical treatment for mental disorder in a hospital.

P objects to being a mental health patient etc

5 (1) This paragraph applies in cases D and E in the table in paragraph 2.

(2) P is ineligible if the following conditions are met.

(3) The first condition is that the relevant instrument authorises P to be a mental health patient.

(4) The second condition is that P objects—

(a) to being a mental health patient, or
(b) to being given some or all of the mental health treatment.

(5) The third condition is that a donee or deputy has not made a valid decision to consent to each matter to which P objects.

(6) In determining whether or not P objects to something, regard must be had to all the circumstances (so far as they are reasonably ascertainable), including the following—

(a) P's behaviour;
(b) P's wishes and feelings;
(c) P's views, beliefs and values.

(7) But regard is to be had to circumstances from the past only so far as it is still appropriate to have regard to them.]

NOTES

Amendment

Inserted by the Mental Health Act 2007, s 50(6), Sch 8. Date in force: to be appointed: see the Mental Health Act 2007, s 56(1).

[PART 2
INTERPRETATION]

NOTES

Amendment

Inserted by the Mental Health Act 2007, s 50(6), Sch 8. Date in force: to be appointed: see the Mental Health Act 2007, s 56(1).

[Application

6 This Part applies for the purposes of this Schedule.

Mental health regimes

7 The mental health regimes are—

(a) the hospital treatment regime,
(b) the community treatment regime, and
(c) the guardianship regime.

Hospital treatment regime

8 (1) P is subject to the hospital treatment regime if he is subject to—

(a) a hospital treatment obligation under the relevant enactment, or
(b) an obligation under another England and Wales enactment which has the same effect as a hospital treatment obligation.

(2) But where P is subject to any such obligation, he is to be regarded as not subject to the hospital treatment regime during any period when he is subject to the community treatment regime.

(3) A hospital treatment obligation is an application, order or direction of a kind listed in the first column of the following table.

(4) In relation to a hospital treatment obligation, the relevant enactment is the enactment in the Mental Health Act which is referred to in the corresponding entry in the second column of the following table.

Hospital treatment obligation	*Relevant enactment*
Application for admission for assessment	Section 2
Application for admission for assessment	Section 4
Application for admission for treatment	Section 3
Order for remand to hospital	Section 35
Order for remand to hospital	Section 36
Hospital order	Section 37
Interim hospital order	Section 38
Order for detention in hospital	Section 44
Hospital direction	Section 45A
Transfer direction	Section 47
Transfer direction	Section 48
Hospital order	Section 51

Community treatment regime

9 P is subject to the community treatment regime if he is subject to—

(a) a community treatment order under section 17A of the Mental Health Act, or
(b) an obligation under another England and Wales enactment which has the same effect as a community treatment order.

Guardianship regime

10 P is subject to the guardianship regime if he is subject to—

(a) a guardianship application under section 7 of the Mental Health Act,
(b) a guardianship order under section 37 of the Mental Health Act, or
(c) an obligation under another England and Wales enactment which has the same effect as a guardianship application or guardianship order.

England and Wales enactments

11 (1) An England and Wales enactment is an enactment which extends to England and Wales (whether or not it also extends elsewhere).

(2) It does not matter if the enactment is in the Mental Health Act or not.

P within scope of Mental Health Act

12 (1) P is within the scope of the Mental Health Act if—

(a) an application in respect of P could be made under section 2 or 3 of the Mental Health Act, and
(b) P could be detained in a hospital in pursuance of such an application, were one made.

(2) The following provisions of this paragraph apply when determining whether an application in respect of P could be made under section 2 or 3 of the Mental Health Act.

(3) If the grounds in section 2(2) of the Mental Health Act are met in P's case, it is to be assumed that the recommendations referred to in section 2(3) of that Act have been given.

(4) If the grounds in section 3(2) of the Mental Health Act are met in P's case, it is to be assumed that the recommendations referred to in section 3(3) of that Act have been given.

(5) In determining whether the ground in section 3(2)(c) of the Mental Health Act is met in P's case, it is to be assumed that the treatment referred to in section 3(2)(c) cannot be provided under this Act.

Authorised course of action, relevant care or treatment & relevant instrument

13 In a case where this Schedule applies for the purposes of section 16A—

"authorised course of action" means any course of action amounting to deprivation of liberty which the order under section 16(2)(a) authorises;
"relevant care or treatment" means any care or treatment which—
(a) comprises, or forms part of, the authorised course of action, or
(b) is to be given in connection with the authorised course of action;
"relevant instrument" means the order under section 16(2)(a).

14 In a case where this Schedule applies for the purposes of paragraph 17 of Schedule A1—

"authorised course of action" means the accommodation of the relevant person in the relevant hospital or care home for the purpose of being given the relevant care or treatment;
"relevant care or treatment" has the same meaning as in Schedule A1;
"relevant instrument" means the standard authorisation under Schedule A1.

15 (1) This paragraph applies where the question whether a person is ineligible to be deprived of liberty by this Act is relevant to either of these decisions—

(a) whether or not to include particular provision ("the proposed provision") in an order under section 16(2)(a);
(b) whether or not to give a standard authorisation under Schedule A1.

(2) A reference in this Schedule to the authorised course of action or the relevant care or treatment is to be read as a reference to that thing as it would be if—

(a) the proposed provision were included in the order, or
(b) the standard authorisation were given.

(3) A reference in this Schedule to the relevant instrument is to be read as follows—

(a) where the relevant instrument is an order under section 16(2)(a): as a reference to the order as it would be if the proposed provision were included in it;
(b) where the relevant instrument is a standard authorisation: as a reference to the standard authorisation as it would be if it were given.

Expressions used in paragraph 5

16 (1) These expressions have the meanings given—

"donee" means a donee of a lasting power of attorney granted by P;
"mental health patient" means a person accommodated in a hospital for the purpose of being given medical treatment for mental disorder;
"mental health treatment" means the medical treatment for mental disorder referred to in the definition of "mental health patient".

(2) A decision of a donee or deputy is valid if it is made—

(a) within the scope of his authority as donee or deputy, and
(b) in accordance with Part 1 of this Act.

Expressions with same meaning as in Mental Health Act

17 (1) "Hospital" has the same meaning as in Part 2 of the Mental Health Act.

(2) "Medical treatment" has the same meaning as in the Mental Health Act.

(3) "Mental disorder" has the same meaning as in Schedule A1 (see paragraph 14).]

NOTES

Amendment

Inserted by the Mental Health Act 2007, s 50(6), Sch 8. Date in force: to be appointed: see the Mental Health Act 2007, s 56(1).

SCHEDULE 2
PROPERTY AND AFFAIRS: SUPPLEMENTARY PROVISIONS

Section 18(4)

Wills: general

A1.82

1 Paragraphs 2 to 4 apply in relation to the execution of a will, by virtue of section 18, on behalf of P.

Provision that may be made in will

2 The will may make any provision (whether by disposing of property or exercising a power or otherwise) which could be made by a will executed by P if he had capacity to make it.

Wills: requirements relating to execution

3 (1) Sub-paragraph (2) applies if under section 16 the court makes an order or gives directions requiring or authorising a person ("the authorised person") to execute a will on behalf of P.

(2) Any will executed in pursuance of the order or direction—

(a) must state that it is signed by P acting by the authorised person,
(b) must be signed by the authorised person with the name of P and his own name, in the presence of two or more witnesses present at the same time,
(c) must be attested and subscribed by those witnesses in the presence of the authorised person, and
(d) must be sealed with the official seal of the court.

Wills: effect of execution

4 (1) This paragraph applies where a will is executed in accordance with paragraph 3.

(2) The Wills Act 1837 (c 26) has effect in relation to the will as if it were signed by P by his own hand, except that—

(a) section 9 of the 1837 Act (requirements as to signing and attestation) does not apply, and
(b) in the subsequent provisions of the 1837 Act any reference to execution in the manner required by the previous provisions is to be read as a reference to execution in accordance with paragraph 3.

(3) The will has the same effect for all purposes as if—

(a) P had had the capacity to make a valid will, and
(b) the will had been executed by him in the manner required by the 1837 Act.

(4) But sub-paragraph (3) does not have effect in relation to the will—

(a) in so far as it disposes of immovable property outside England and Wales, or
(b) in so far as it relates to any other property or matter if, when the will is executed—
(i) P is domiciled outside England and Wales, and
(ii) the condition in sub-paragraph (5) is met.

(5) The condition is that, under the law of P's domicile, any question of his testamentary capacity would fall to be determined in accordance with the law of a place outside England and Wales.

Vesting orders ancillary to settlement etc

5 (1) If provision is made by virtue of section 18 for—

(a) the settlement of any property of P, or
(b) the exercise of a power vested in him of appointing trustees or retiring from a trust,

the court may also make as respects the property settled or the trust property such consequential vesting or other orders as the case may require.

(2) The power under sub-paragraph (1) includes, in the case of the exercise of such a power, any order which could have been made in such a case under Part 4 of the Trustee Act 1925 (c 19).

Variation of settlements

6 (1) If a settlement has been made by virtue of section 18, the court may by order vary or revoke the settlement if—

(a) the settlement makes provision for its variation or revocation,
(b) the court is satisfied that a material fact was not disclosed when the settlement was made, or
(c) the court is satisfied that there has been a substantial change of circumstances.

(2) Any such order may give such consequential directions as the court thinks fit.

Vesting of stock in curator appointed outside England and Wales

7 (1) Sub-paragraph (2) applies if the court is satisfied—

(a) that under the law prevailing in a place outside England and Wales a person ("M") has been appointed to exercise powers in respect of the property or affairs of P on the ground (however formulated) that P lacks capacity to make decisions with respect to the management and administration of his property and affairs, and
(b) that, having regard to the nature of the appointment and to the circumstances of the case, it is expedient that the court should exercise its powers under this paragraph.

(2) The court may direct—

(a) any stocks standing in the name of P, or
(b) the right to receive dividends from the stocks,

to be transferred into M's name or otherwise dealt with as required by M, and may give such directions as the court thinks fit for dealing with accrued dividends from the stocks.

(3) "Stocks" includes—

(a) shares, and

(b) any funds, annuity or security transferable in the books kept by any body corporate or unincorporated company or society or by an instrument of transfer either alone or accompanied by other formalities,

and "dividends" is to be construed accordingly.

Preservation of interests in property disposed of on behalf of person lacking capacity

8 (1) Sub-paragraphs (2) and (3) apply if—

(a) P's property has been disposed of by virtue of section 18,
(b) under P's will or intestacy, or by a gift perfected or nomination taking effect on his death, any other person would have taken an interest in the property but for the disposal, and
(c) on P's death, any property belonging to P's estate represents the property disposed of.

(2) The person takes the same interest, if and so far as circumstances allow, in the property representing the property disposed of.

(3) If the property disposed of was real property, any property representing it is to be treated, so long as it remains part of P's estate, as if it were real property.

(4) The court may direct that, on a disposal of P's property—

(a) which is made by virtue of section 18, and
(b) which would apart from this paragraph result in the conversion of personal property into real property,

property representing the property disposed of is to be treated, so long as it remains P's property or forms part of P's estate, as if it were personal property.

(5) References in sub-paragraphs (1) to (4) to the disposal of property are to—

(a) the sale, exchange, charging of or other dealing (otherwise than by will) with property other than money;
(b) the removal of property from one place to another;
(c) the application of money in acquiring property;
(d) the transfer of money from one account to another;

and references to property representing property disposed of are to be construed accordingly and as including the result of successive disposals.

(6) The court may give such directions as appear to it necessary or expedient for the purpose of facilitating the operation of sub-paragraphs (1) to (3), including the carrying of money to a separate account and the transfer of property other than money.

9 (1) Sub-paragraph (2) applies if the court has ordered or directed the expenditure of money—

(a) for carrying out permanent improvements on any of P's property, or
(b) otherwise for the permanent benefit of any of P's property.

(2) The court may order that—

(a) the whole of the money expended or to be expended, or
(b) any part of it,

is to be a charge on the property either without interest or with interest at a specified rate.

(3) An order under sub-paragraph (2) may provide for excluding or restricting the operation of paragraph 8(1) to (3).

(4) A charge under sub-paragraph (2) may be made in favour of such person as may be just and, in particular, where the money charged is paid out of P's general estate, may be made in favour of a person as trustee for P.

(5) No charge under sub-paragraph (2) may confer any right of sale or foreclosure during P's lifetime.

Powers as patron of benefice

10 (1) Any functions which P has as patron of a benefice may be discharged only by a person ("R") appointed by the court.

(2) R must be an individual capable of appointment under section 8(1)(b) of the 1986 Measure (which provides for an individual able to make a declaration of communicant status, a clerk in Holy Orders, etc to be appointed to discharge a registered patron's functions).

(3) The 1986 Measure applies to R as it applies to an individual appointed by the registered patron of the benefice under section 8(1)(b) or (3) of that Measure to discharge his functions as patron.

(4) "The 1986 Measure" means the Patronage (Benefices) Measure 1986 (No 3).

NOTES

Initial Commencement

To be appointed: see s 68(1).

Appointment

Appointment: 1 October 2007: see SI 2007/1897, art 2(1)(d).

SCHEDULE 3
INTERNATIONAL PROTECTION OF ADULTS

Section 63

PART 1
PRELIMINARY

Introduction

A1.83

1 This Part applies for the purposes of this Schedule.

The Convention

2 (1) "Convention" means the Convention referred to in section 63.

(2) "Convention country" means a country in which the Convention is in force.

(3) A reference to an Article or Chapter is to an Article or Chapter of the Convention.

(4) An expression which appears in this Schedule and in the Convention is to be construed in accordance with the Convention.

Countries, territories and nationals

3 (1) "Country" includes a territory which has its own system of law.

(2) Where a country has more than one territory with its own system of law, a reference to the country, in relation to one of its nationals, is to the territory with which the national has the closer, or the closest, connection.

Adults with incapacity

4 "Adult" means a person who—

(a) as a result of an impairment or insufficiency of his personal faculties, cannot protect his interests, and
(b) has reached 16.

Protective measures

5 (1) "Protective measure" means a measure directed to the protection of the person or property of an adult; and it may deal in particular with any of the following—

(a) the determination of incapacity and the institution of a protective regime,
(b) placing the adult under the protection of an appropriate authority,
(c) guardianship, curatorship or any corresponding system,
(d) the designation and functions of a person having charge of the adult's person or property, or representing or otherwise helping him,
(e) placing the adult in a place where protection can be provided,
(f) administering, conserving or disposing of the adult's property,
(g) authorising a specific intervention for the protection of the person or property of the adult.

(2) Where a measure of like effect to a protective measure has been taken in relation to a person before he reaches 16, this Schedule applies to the measure in so far as it has effect in relation to him once he has reached 16.

Central Authority

6 (1) Any function under the Convention of a Central Authority is exercisable in England and Wales by the Lord Chancellor.

(2) A communication may be sent to the Central Authority in relation to England and Wales by sending it to the Lord Chancellor.

NOTES

Initial Commencement
To be appointed: see s 68(1).

Appointment
Appointment: 1 October 2007: see SI 2007/1897, art 2(1)(d).

PART 2
JURISDICTION OF COMPETENT AUTHORITY

Scope of jurisdiction

7 (1) The court may exercise its functions under this Act (in so far as it cannot otherwise do so) in relation to—

(a) an adult habitually resident in England and Wales,
(b) an adult's property in England and Wales,
(c) an adult present in England and Wales or who has property there, if the matter is urgent, or
(d) an adult present in England and Wales, if a protective measure which is temporary and limited in its effect to England and Wales is proposed in relation to him.

(2) An adult present in England and Wales is to be treated for the purposes of this paragraph as habitually resident there if—

(a) his habitual residence cannot be ascertained,
(b) he is a refugee, or
(c) he has been displaced as a result of disturbance in the country of his habitual residence.

8 (1) The court may also exercise its functions under this Act (in so far as it cannot otherwise do so) in relation to an adult if sub-paragraph (2) or (3) applies in relation to him.

(2) This sub-paragraph applies in relation to an adult if—

(a) he is a British citizen,
(b) he has a closer connection with England and Wales than with Scotland or Northern Ireland, and
(c) Article 7 has, in relation to the matter concerned, been complied with.

(3) This sub-paragraph applies in relation to an adult if the Lord Chancellor, having consulted such persons as he considers appropriate, agrees to a request under Article 8 in relation to the adult.

Exercise of jurisdiction

9 (1) This paragraph applies where jurisdiction is exercisable under this Schedule in connection with a matter which involves a Convention country other than England and Wales.

(2) Any Article on which the jurisdiction is based applies in relation to the matter in so far as it involves the other country (and the court must, accordingly, comply with any duty conferred on it as a result).

(3) Article 12 also applies, so far as its provisions allow, in relation to the matter in so far as it involves the other country.

10 A reference in this Schedule to the exercise of jurisdiction under this Schedule is to the exercise of functions under this Act as a result of this Part of this Schedule.

NOTES

Initial Commencement
To be appointed: see s 68(1).

Appointment
Appointment: 1 October 2007: see SI 2007/1897, art 2(1)(d).

PART 3
APPLICABLE LAW

Applicable law

11 In exercising jurisdiction under this Schedule, the court may, if it thinks that the matter has a substantial connection with a country other than England and Wales, apply the law of that other country.

12 Where a protective measure is taken in one country but implemented in another, the conditions of implementation are governed by the law of the other country.

Lasting powers of attorney, etc

13 (1) If the donor of a lasting power is habitually resident in England and Wales at the time of granting the power, the law applicable to the existence, extent, modification or extinction of the power is—

(a) the law of England and Wales, or
(b) if he specifies in writing the law of a connected country for the purpose, that law.

(2) If he is habitually resident in another country at that time, but England and Wales is a connected country, the law applicable in that respect is—

(a) the law of the other country, or
(b) if he specifies in writing the law of England and Wales for the purpose, that law.

(3) A country is connected, in relation to the donor, if it is a country—

(a) of which he is a national,
(b) in which he was habitually resident, or
(c) in which he has property.

(4) Where this paragraph applies as a result of sub-paragraph (3)(c), it applies only in relation to the property which the donor has in the connected country.

(5) The law applicable to the manner of the exercise of a lasting power is the law of the country where it is exercised.

(6) In this Part of this Schedule, "lasting power" means—

(a) a lasting power of attorney (see section 9),
(b) an enduring power of attorney within the meaning of Schedule 4, or
(c) any other power of like effect.

14 (1) Where a lasting power is not exercised in a manner sufficient to guarantee the protection of the person or property of the donor, the court, in exercising jurisdiction under this Schedule, may disapply or modify the power.

(2) Where, in accordance with this Part of this Schedule, the law applicable to the power is, in one or more respects, that of a country other than England and Wales, the court must, so far as possible, have regard to the law of the other country in that respect (or those respects).

15 Regulations may provide for Schedule 1 (lasting powers of attorney: formalities) to apply with modifications in relation to a lasting power which comes within paragraph 13(6)(c) above.

Protection of third parties

16 (1) This paragraph applies where a person (a "representative") in purported exercise of an authority to act on behalf of an adult enters into a transaction with a third party.

(2) The validity of the transaction may not be questioned in proceedings, nor may the third party be held liable, merely because—

- (a) where the representative and third party are in England and Wales when entering into the transaction, sub-paragraph (3) applies;
- (b) where they are in another country at that time, sub-paragraph (4) applies.

(3) This sub-paragraph applies if—

- (a) the law applicable to the authority in one or more respects is, as a result of this Schedule, the law of a country other than England and Wales, and
- (b) the representative is not entitled to exercise the authority in that respect (or those respects) under the law of that other country.

(4) This sub-paragraph applies if—

- (a) the law applicable to the authority in one or more respects is, as a result of this Part of this Schedule, the law of England and Wales, and
- (b) the representative is not entitled to exercise the authority in that respect (or those respects) under that law.

(5) This paragraph does not apply if the third party knew or ought to have known that the applicable law was—

- (a) in a case within sub-paragraph (3), the law of the other country;
- (b) in a case within sub-paragraph (4), the law of England and Wales.

Mandatory rules

17 Where the court is entitled to exercise jurisdiction under this Schedule, the mandatory provisions of the law of England and Wales apply, regardless of any system of law which would otherwise apply in relation to the matter.

Public policy

18 Nothing in this Part of this Schedule requires or enables the application in England and Wales of a provision of the law of another country if its application would be manifestly contrary to public policy.

NOTES

Initial Commencement

To be appointed: see s 68(1).

Appointment

Appointment: 1 October 2007: see SI 2007/1897, art 2(1)(d).

PART 4
RECOGNITION AND ENFORCEMENT

Recognition

19 (1) A protective measure taken in relation to an adult under the law of a country other than England and Wales is to be recognised in England and Wales if it was taken on the ground that the adult is habitually resident in the other country.

(2) A protective measure taken in relation to an adult under the law of a Convention country other than England and Wales is to be recognised in England and Wales if it was taken on a ground mentioned in Chapter 2 (jurisdiction).

(3) But the court may disapply this paragraph in relation to a measure if it thinks that—

(a) the case in which the measure was taken was not urgent,
(b) the adult was not given an opportunity to be heard, and
(c) that omission amounted to a breach of natural justice.

(4) It may also disapply this paragraph in relation to a measure if it thinks that—

(a) recognition of the measure would be manifestly contrary to public policy,
(b) the measure would be inconsistent with a mandatory provision of the law of England and Wales, or
(c) the measure is inconsistent with one subsequently taken, or recognised, in England and Wales in relation to the adult.

(5) And the court may disapply this paragraph in relation to a measure taken under the law of a Convention country in a matter to which Article 33 applies, if the court thinks that that Article has not been complied with in connection with that matter.

20 (1) An interested person may apply to the court for a declaration as to whether a protective measure taken under the law of a country other than England and Wales is to be recognised in England and Wales.

(2) No permission is required for an application to the court under this paragraph.

21 For the purposes of paragraphs 19 and 20, any finding of fact relied on when the measure was taken is conclusive.

Enforcement

22 (1) An interested person may apply to the court for a declaration as to whether a protective measure taken under the law of, and enforceable in, a country other than England and Wales is enforceable, or to be registered, in England and Wales in accordance with Court of Protection Rules.

(2) The court must make the declaration if—

(a) the measure comes within sub-paragraph (1) or (2) of paragraph 19, and
(b) the paragraph is not disapplied in relation to it as a result of sub-paragraph (3), (4) or (5).

(3) A measure to which a declaration under this paragraph relates is enforceable in England and Wales as if it were a measure of like effect taken by the court.

Measures taken in relation to those aged under 16

23 (1) This paragraph applies where—

(a) provision giving effect to, or otherwise deriving from, the Convention in a country other than England and Wales applies in relation to a person who has not reached 16, and
(b) a measure is taken in relation to that person in reliance on that provision.

(2) This Part of this Schedule applies in relation to that measure as it applies in relation to a protective measure taken in relation to an adult under the law of a Convention country other than England and Wales.

Supplementary

24 The court may not review the merits of a measure taken outside England and Wales except to establish whether the measure complies with this Schedule in so far as it is, as a result of this Schedule, required to do so.

25 Court of Protection Rules may make provision about an application under paragraph 20 or 22.

NOTES

Initial Commencement

To be appointed: see s 68(1).

Appointment

Appointment: 1 October 2007: see SI 2007/1897, art 2(1)(d).

PART 5
CO-OPERATION

Proposal for cross-border placement

26 (1) This paragraph applies where a public authority proposes to place an adult in an establishment in a Convention country other than England and Wales.

(2) The public authority must consult an appropriate authority in that other country about the proposed placement and, for that purpose, must send it—

(a) a report on the adult, and
(b) a statement of its reasons for the proposed placement.

(3) If the appropriate authority in the other country opposes the proposed placement within a reasonable time, the public authority may not proceed with it.

27 A proposal received by a public authority under Article 33 in relation to an adult is to proceed unless the authority opposes it within a reasonable time.

Adult in danger etc

28 (1) This paragraph applies if a public authority is told that an adult—

(a) who is in serious danger, and
(b) in relation to whom the public authority has taken, or is considering taking, protective measures,

is, or has become resident, in a Convention country other than England and Wales.

(2) The public authority must tell an appropriate authority in that other country about—

(a) the danger, and
(b) the measures taken or under consideration.

29 A public authority may not request from, or send to, an appropriate authority in a Convention country information in accordance with Chapter 5 (co-operation) in relation to an adult if it thinks that doing so—

(a) would be likely to endanger the adult or his property, or
(b) would amount to a serious threat to the liberty or life of a member of the adult's family.

NOTES

Initial Commencement

To be appointed: see s 68(1).

Appointment

Appointment: 1 October 2007: see SI 2007/1897, art 2(1)(d).

PART 6
GENERAL

Certificates

30 A certificate given under Article 38 by an authority in a Convention country other than England and Wales is, unless the contrary is shown, proof of the matters contained in it.

Powers to make further provision as to private international law

31 Her Majesty may by Order in Council confer on the Lord Chancellor, the court or another public authority functions for enabling the Convention to be given effect in England and Wales.

32 (1) Regulations may make provision—

- (a) giving further effect to the Convention, or
- (b) otherwise about the private international law of England and Wales in relation to the protection of adults.

(2) The regulations may—

- (a) confer functions on the court or another public authority;
- (b) amend this Schedule;
- (c) provide for this Schedule to apply with specified modifications;
- (d) make provision about countries other than Convention countries.

Exceptions

33 Nothing in this Schedule applies, and no provision made under paragraph 32 is to apply, to any matter to which the Convention, as a result of Article 4, does not apply.

Regulations and orders

34 A reference in this Schedule to regulations or an order (other than an Order in Council) is to regulations or an order made for the purposes of this Schedule by the Lord Chancellor.

Commencement

35 The following provisions of this Schedule have effect only if the Convention is in force in accordance with Article 57—

- (a) paragraph 8,
- (b) paragraph 9,
- (c) paragraph 19(2) and (5),
- (d) Part 5,
- (e) paragraph 30.

NOTES

Initial Commencement
To be appointed: see s 68(1).

Appointment
Appointment: 1 October 2007: see SI 2007/1897, art 2(1)(d).

SCHEDULE 4
PROVISIONS APPLYING TO EXISTING ENDURING POWERS OF ATTORNEY

Section 66(3)

PART 1
ENDURING POWERS OF ATTORNEY

Enduring power of attorney to survive mental incapacity of donor

A1.84

1 (1) Where an individual has created a power of attorney which is an enduring power within the meaning of this Schedule—

- (a) the power is not revoked by any subsequent mental incapacity of his,
- (b) upon such incapacity supervening, the donee of the power may not do anything under the authority of the power except as provided by sub-paragraph (2) unless or until the instrument creating the power is registered under paragraph 13, and
- (c) if and so long as paragraph (b) operates to suspend the donee's authority to act under the power, section 5 of the Powers of Attorney Act 1971 (c 27) (protection of donee and third persons), so far as applicable, applies as if the power had been revoked by the donor's mental incapacity,

and, accordingly, section 1 of this Act does not apply.

(2) Despite sub-paragraph (1)(b), where the attorney has made an application for registration of the instrument then, until it is registered, the attorney may take action under the power—

- (a) to maintain the donor or prevent loss to his estate, or
- (b) to maintain himself or other persons in so far as paragraph 3(2) permits him to do so.

(3) Where the attorney purports to act as provided by sub-paragraph (2) then, in favour of a person who deals with him without knowledge that the attorney is acting otherwise than in accordance with sub-paragraph (2)(a) or (b), the transaction between them is as valid as if the attorney were acting in accordance with sub-paragraph (2)(a) or (b).

Characteristics of an enduring power of attorney

2 (1) Subject to sub-paragraphs (5) and (6) and paragraph 20, a power of attorney is an enduring power within the meaning of this Schedule if the instrument which creates the power—

- (a) is in the prescribed form,
- (b) was executed in the prescribed manner by the donor and the attorney, and
- (c) incorporated at the time of execution by the donor the prescribed explanatory information.

(2) In this paragraph, "prescribed" means prescribed by such of the following regulations as applied when the instrument was executed—

- (a) the Enduring Powers of Attorney (Prescribed Form) Regulations 1986 (SI 1986/126),
- (b) the Enduring Powers of Attorney (Prescribed Form) Regulations 1987 (SI 1987/1612),
- (c) the Enduring Powers of Attorney (Prescribed Form) Regulations 1990 (SI 1990/1376),
- (d) the Enduring Powers of Attorney (Welsh Language Prescribed Form) Regulations 2000 (SI 2000/289).

(3) An instrument in the prescribed form purporting to have been executed in the prescribed manner is to be taken, in the absence of evidence to the contrary, to be a document which incorporated at the time of execution by the donor the prescribed explanatory information.

(4) If an instrument differs in an immaterial respect in form or mode of expression from the prescribed form it is to be treated as sufficient in point of form and expression.

(5) A power of attorney cannot be an enduring power unless, when he executes the instrument creating it, the attorney is—

- (a) an individual who has reached 18 and is not bankrupt, or
- (b) a trust corporation.

(6) A power of attorney which gives the attorney a right to appoint a substitute or successor cannot be an enduring power.

(7) An enduring power is revoked by the bankruptcy of the donor or attorney.

(8) But where the donor or attorney is bankrupt merely because an interim bankruptcy restrictions order has effect in respect of him, the power is suspended for so long as the order has effect.

(9) An enduring power is revoked if the court—

(a) exercises a power under sections 16 to 20 in relation to the donor, and
(b) directs that the enduring power is to be revoked.

(10) No disclaimer of an enduring power, whether by deed or otherwise, is valid unless and until the attorney gives notice of it to the donor or, where paragraph 4(6) or 15(1) applies, to the Public Guardian.

Scope of authority etc of attorney under enduring power

3 (1) If the instrument which creates an enduring power of attorney is expressed to confer general authority on the attorney, the instrument operates to confer, subject to—

(a) the restriction imposed by sub-paragraph (3), and
(b) any conditions or restrictions contained in the instrument,

authority to do on behalf of the donor anything which the donor could lawfully do by an attorney at the time when the donor executed the instrument.

(2) Subject to any conditions or restrictions contained in the instrument, an attorney under an enduring power, whether general or limited, may (without obtaining any consent) act under the power so as to benefit himself or other persons than the donor to the following extent but no further—

(a) he may so act in relation to himself or in relation to any other person if the donor might be expected to provide for his or that person's needs respectively, and
(b) he may do whatever the donor might be expected to do to meet those needs.

(3) Without prejudice to sub-paragraph (2) but subject to any conditions or restrictions contained in the instrument, an attorney under an enduring power, whether general or limited, may (without obtaining any consent) dispose of the property of the donor by way of gift to the following extent but no further—

(a) he may make gifts of a seasonal nature or at a time, or on an anniversary, of a birth, a marriage or the formation of a civil partnership, to persons (including himself) who are related to or connected with the donor, and
(b) he may make gifts to any charity to whom the donor made or might be expected to make gifts,

provided that the value of each such gift is not unreasonable having regard to all the circumstances and in particular the size of the donor's estate.

NOTES

Initial Commencement
To be appointed: see s 68(1).

Appointment
Appointment: 1 October 2007: see SI 2007/1897, art 2(1)(d).

PART 2
ACTION ON ACTUAL OR IMPENDING INCAPACITY OF DONOR

Duties of attorney in event of actual or impending incapacity of donor

4 (1) Sub-paragraphs (2) to (6) apply if the attorney under an enduring power has reason to believe that the donor is or is becoming mentally incapable.

(2) The attorney must, as soon as practicable, make an application to the Public Guardian for the registration of the instrument creating the power.

(3) Before making an application for registration the attorney must comply with the provisions as to notice set out in Part 3 of this Schedule.

(4) An application for registration—

(a) must be made in the prescribed form, and
(b) must contain such statements as may be prescribed.

(5) The attorney—

(a) may, before making an application for the registration of the instrument, refer to the court for its determination any question as to the validity of the power, and
(b) must comply with any direction given to him by the court on that determination.

(6) No disclaimer of the power is valid unless and until the attorney gives notice of it to the Public Guardian; and the Public Guardian must notify the donor if he receives a notice under this sub-paragraph.

(7) A person who, in an application for registration, makes a statement which he knows to be false in a material particular is guilty of an offence and is liable—

(a) on summary conviction, to imprisonment for a term not exceeding 12 months or a fine not exceeding the statutory maximum or both;
(b) on conviction on indictment, to imprisonment for a term not exceeding 2 years or a fine or both.

(8) In this paragraph, "prescribed" means prescribed by regulations made for the purposes of this Schedule by the Lord Chancellor.

NOTES

Initial Commencement
To be appointed: see s 68(1).

Appointment
Appointment: 1 October 2007: see SI 2007/1897, art 2(1)(d).

PART 3
NOTIFICATION PRIOR TO REGISTRATION

Duty to give notice to relatives

5 Subject to paragraph 7, before making an application for registration the attorney must give notice of his intention to do so to all those persons (if any) who are entitled to receive notice by virtue of paragraph 6.

6 (1) Subject to sub-paragraphs (2) to (4), persons of the following classes ("relatives") are entitled to receive notice under paragraph 5—

(a) the donor's spouse or civil partner,
(b) the donor's children,
(c) the donor's parents,
(d) the donor's brothers and sisters, whether of the whole or half blood,
(e) the widow, widower or surviving civil partner of a child of the donor,
(f) the donor's grandchildren,
(g) the children of the donor's brothers and sisters of the whole blood,
(h) the children of the donor's brothers and sisters of the half blood,
(i) the donor's uncles and aunts of the whole blood,
(j) the children of the donor's uncles and aunts of the whole blood.

(2) A person is not entitled to receive notice under paragraph 5 if—

(a) his name or address is not known to the attorney and cannot be reasonably ascertained by him, or
(b) the attorney has reason to believe that he has not reached 18 or is mentally incapable.

(3) Except where sub-paragraph (4) applies—

(a) no more than 3 persons are entitled to receive notice under paragraph 5, and
(b) in determining the persons who are so entitled, persons falling within the class in sub-paragraph (1)(a) are to be preferred to persons falling within the class in sub-paragraph (1)(b), those falling within the class in sub-paragraph (1)(b) are to be preferred to those falling within the class in sub-paragraph (1)(c), and so on.

(4) Despite the limit of 3 specified in sub-paragraph (3), where—

(a) there is more than one person falling within any of classes (a) to (j) of sub-paragraph (1), and
(b) at least one of those persons would be entitled to receive notice under paragraph 5,

then, subject to sub-paragraph (2), all the persons falling within that class are entitled to receive notice under paragraph 5.

7 (1) An attorney is not required to give notice under paragraph 5—

(a) to himself, or
(b) to any other attorney under the power who is joining in making the application,

even though he or, as the case may be, the other attorney is entitled to receive notice by virtue of paragraph 6.

(2) In the case of any person who is entitled to receive notice by virtue of paragraph 6, the attorney, before applying for registration, may make an application to the court to be dispensed from the requirement to give him notice; and the court must grant the application if it is satisfied—

(a) that it would be undesirable or impracticable for the attorney to give him notice, or
(b) that no useful purpose is likely to be served by giving him notice.

Duty to give notice to donor

8 (1) Subject to sub-paragraph (2), before making an application for registration the attorney must give notice of his intention to do so to the donor.

(2) Paragraph 7(2) applies in relation to the donor as it applies in relation to a person who is entitled to receive notice under paragraph 5.

Contents of notices

9 A notice to relatives under this Part of this Schedule must—

(a) be in the prescribed form,
(b) state that the attorney proposes to make an application to the Public Guardian for the registration of the instrument creating the enduring power in question,
(c) inform the person to whom it is given of his right to object to the registration under paragraph 13(4), and
(d) specify, as the grounds on which an objection to registration may be made, the grounds set out in paragraph 13(9).

10 A notice to the donor under this Part of this Schedule—

(a) must be in the prescribed form,
(b) must contain the statement mentioned in paragraph 9(b), and
(c) must inform the donor that, while the instrument remains registered, any revocation of the power by him will be ineffective unless and until the revocation is confirmed by the court.

Duty to give notice to other attorneys

11 (1) Subject to sub-paragraph (2), before making an application for registration an attorney under a joint and several power must give notice of his intention to do so to any other attorney under the power who is not joining in making the application; and paragraphs 7(2) and 9 apply in relation to attorneys entitled to receive notice by virtue of this paragraph as they apply in relation to persons entitled to receive notice by virtue of paragraph 6.

(2) An attorney is not entitled to receive notice by virtue of this paragraph if—

(a) his address is not known to the applying attorney and cannot reasonably be ascertained by him, or
(b) the applying attorney has reason to believe that he has not reached 18 or is mentally incapable.

Supplementary

12 Despite section 7 of the Interpretation Act 1978 (c 30) (construction of references to service by post), for the purposes of this Part of this Schedule a notice given by post is to be regarded as given on the date on which it was posted.

NOTES

Initial Commencement
To be appointed: see s 68(1).

Appointment
Appointment: 1 October 2007: see SI 2007/1897, art 2(1)(d).

PART 4
REGISTRATION

Registration of instrument creating power

13 (1) If an application is made in accordance with paragraph 4(3) and (4) the Public Guardian must, subject to the provisions of this paragraph, register the instrument to which the application relates.

(2) If it appears to the Public Guardian that—

(a) there is a deputy appointed for the donor of the power created by the instrument, and
(b) the powers conferred on the deputy would, if the instrument were registered, to any extent conflict with the powers conferred on the attorney,

the Public Guardian must not register the instrument except in accordance with the court's directions.

(3) The court may, on the application of the attorney, direct the Public Guardian to register an instrument even though notice has not been given as required by paragraph 4(3) and Part 3 of this Schedule to a person entitled to receive it, if the court is satisfied—

(a) that it was undesirable or impracticable for the attorney to give notice to that person, or
(b) that no useful purpose is likely to be served by giving him notice.

(4) Sub-paragraph (5) applies if, before the end of the period of 5 weeks beginning with the date (or the latest date) on which the attorney gave notice under paragraph 5 of an application for registration, the Public Guardian receives a valid notice of objection to the registration from a person entitled to notice of the application.

(5) The Public Guardian must not register the instrument except in accordance with the court's directions.

(6) Sub-paragraph (7) applies if, in the case of an application for registration—

(a) it appears from the application that there is no one to whom notice has been given under paragraph 5, or
(b) the Public Guardian has reason to believe that appropriate inquiries might bring to light evidence on which he could be satisfied that one of the grounds of objection set out in sub-paragraph (9) was established.

(7) The Public Guardian—

(a) must not register the instrument, and
(b) must undertake such inquiries as he thinks appropriate in all the circumstances.

(8) If, having complied with sub-paragraph (7)(b), the Public Guardian is satisfied that one of the grounds of objection set out in sub-paragraph (9) is established—

(a) the attorney may apply to the court for directions, and

(b) the Public Guardian must not register the instrument except in accordance with the court's directions.

(9) A notice of objection under this paragraph is valid if made on one or more of the following grounds—

(a) that the power purported to have been created by the instrument was not valid as an enduring power of attorney,
(b) that the power created by the instrument no longer subsists,
(c) that the application is premature because the donor is not yet becoming mentally incapable,
(d) that fraud or undue pressure was used to induce the donor to create the power,
(e) that, having regard to all the circumstances and in particular the attorney's relationship to or connection with the donor, the attorney is unsuitable to be the donor's attorney.

(10) If any of those grounds is established to the satisfaction of the court it must direct the Public Guardian not to register the instrument, but if not so satisfied it must direct its registration.

(11) If the court directs the Public Guardian not to register an instrument because it is satisfied that the ground in sub-paragraph (9)(d) or (e) is established, it must by order revoke the power created by the instrument.

(12) If the court directs the Public Guardian not to register an instrument because it is satisfied that any ground in sub-paragraph (9) except that in paragraph (c) is established, the instrument must be delivered up to be cancelled unless the court otherwise directs.

Register of enduring powers

14 The Public Guardian has the function of establishing and maintaining a register of enduring powers for the purposes of this Schedule.

NOTES

Initial Commencement

To be appointed: see s 68(1).

Appointment

Appointment: 1 October 2007: see SI 2007/1897, art 2(1)(d).

PART 5
LEGAL POSITION AFTER REGISTRATION

Effect and proof of registration

15 (1) The effect of the registration of an instrument under paragraph 13 is that—

(a) no revocation of the power by the donor is valid unless and until the court confirms the revocation under paragraph 16(3);
(b) no disclaimer of the power is valid unless and until the attorney gives notice of it to the Public Guardian;
(c) the donor may not extend or restrict the scope of the authority conferred by the instrument and no instruction or consent given by him after registration, in the case of a consent, confers any right and, in the case of an instruction, imposes or confers any obligation or right on or creates any liability of the attorney or other persons having notice of the instruction or consent.

(2) Sub-paragraph (1) applies for so long as the instrument is registered under paragraph 13 whether or not the donor is for the time being mentally incapable.

(3) A document purporting to be an office copy of an instrument registered under this Schedule is, in any part of the United Kingdom, evidence of—

(a) the contents of the instrument, and
(b) the fact that it has been so registered.

(4) Sub-paragraph (3) is without prejudice to section 3 of the Powers of Attorney Act 1971 (c 27) (proof by certified copies) and to any other method of proof authorised by law.

Functions of court with regard to registered power

16 (1) Where an instrument has been registered under paragraph 13, the court has the following functions with respect to the power and the donor of and the attorney appointed to act under the power.

(2) The court may—

- (a) determine any question as to the meaning or effect of the instrument;
- (b) give directions with respect to—
  - (i) the management or disposal by the attorney of the property and affairs of the donor;
  - (ii) the rendering of accounts by the attorney and the production of the records kept by him for the purpose;
  - (iii) the remuneration or expenses of the attorney whether or not in default of or in accordance with any provision made by the instrument, including directions for the repayment of excessive or the payment of additional remuneration;
- (c) require the attorney to supply information or produce documents or things in his possession as attorney;
- (d) give any consent or authorisation to act which the attorney would have to obtain from a mentally capable donor;
- (e) authorise the attorney to act so as to benefit himself or other persons than the donor otherwise than in accordance with paragraph 3(2) and (3) (but subject to any conditions or restrictions contained in the instrument);
- (f) relieve the attorney wholly or partly from any liability which he has or may have incurred on account of a breach of his duties as attorney.

(3) On application made for the purpose by or on behalf of the donor, the court must confirm the revocation of the power if satisfied that the donor—

- (a) has done whatever is necessary in law to effect an express revocation of the power, and
- (b) was mentally capable of revoking a power of attorney when he did so (whether or not he is so when the court considers the application).

(4) The court must direct the Public Guardian to cancel the registration of an instrument registered under paragraph 13 in any of the following circumstances—

- (a) on confirming the revocation of the power under sub-paragraph (3),
- (b) on directing under paragraph 2(9)(b) that the power is to be revoked,
- (c) on being satisfied that the donor is and is likely to remain mentally capable,
- (d) on being satisfied that the power has expired or has been revoked by the mental incapacity of the attorney,
- (e) on being satisfied that the power was not a valid and subsisting enduring power when registration was effected,
- (f) on being satisfied that fraud or undue pressure was used to induce the donor to create the power,
- (g) on being satisfied that, having regard to all the circumstances and in particular the attorney's relationship to or connection with the donor, the attorney is unsuitable to be the donor's attorney.

(5) If the court directs the Public Guardian to cancel the registration of an instrument on being satisfied of the matters specified in sub-paragraph (4)(f) or (g) it must by order revoke the power created by the instrument.

(6) If the court directs the cancellation of the registration of an instrument under sub-paragraph (4) except paragraph (c) the instrument must be delivered up to the Public Guardian to be cancelled, unless the court otherwise directs.

Cancellation of registration by Public Guardian

17 The Public Guardian must cancel the registration of an instrument creating an enduring power of attorney—

- (a) on receipt of a disclaimer signed by the attorney;
- (b) if satisfied that the power has been revoked by the death or bankruptcy of the donor or attorney or, if the attorney is a body corporate, by its winding up or dissolution;
- (c) on receipt of notification from the court that the court has revoked the power;

(d) on confirmation from the court that the donor has revoked the power.

NOTES

Initial Commencement

To be appointed: see s 68(1).

Appointment

Appointment: 1 October 2007: see SI 2007/1897, art 2(1)(d).

PART 6
PROTECTION OF ATTORNEY AND THIRD PARTIES

Protection of attorney and third persons where power is invalid or revoked

18 (1) Sub-paragraphs (2) and (3) apply where an instrument which did not create a valid power of attorney has been registered under paragraph 13 (whether or not the registration has been cancelled at the time of the act or transaction in question).

(2) An attorney who acts in pursuance of the power does not incur any liability (either to the donor or to any other person) because of the non-existence of the power unless at the time of acting he knows—

- (a) that the instrument did not create a valid enduring power,
- (b) that an event has occurred which, if the instrument had created a valid enduring power, would have had the effect of revoking the power, or
- (c) that, if the instrument had created a valid enduring power, the power would have expired before that time.

(3) Any transaction between the attorney and another person is, in favour of that person, as valid as if the power had then been in existence, unless at the time of the transaction that person has knowledge of any of the matters mentioned in sub-paragraph (2).

(4) If the interest of a purchaser depends on whether a transaction between the attorney and another person was valid by virtue of sub-paragraph (3), it is conclusively presumed in favour of the purchaser that the transaction was valid if—

- (a) the transaction between that person and the attorney was completed within 12 months of the date on which the instrument was registered, or
- (b) that person makes a statutory declaration, before or within 3 months after the completion of the purchase, that he had no reason at the time of the transaction to doubt that the attorney had authority to dispose of the property which was the subject of the transaction.

(5) For the purposes of section 5 of the Powers of Attorney Act 1971 (c 27) (protection where power is revoked) in its application to an enduring power the revocation of which by the donor is by virtue of paragraph 15 invalid unless and until confirmed by the court under paragraph 16—

- (a) knowledge of the confirmation of the revocation is knowledge of the revocation of the power, but
- (b) knowledge of the unconfirmed revocation is not.

Further protection of attorney and third persons

19 (1) If—

- (a) an instrument framed in a form prescribed as mentioned in paragraph 2(2) creates a power which is not a valid enduring power, and
- (b) the power is revoked by the mental incapacity of the donor,

sub-paragraphs (2) and (3) apply, whether or not the instrument has been registered.

(2) An attorney who acts in pursuance of the power does not, by reason of the revocation, incur any liability (either to the donor or to any other person) unless at the time of acting he knows—

- (a) that the instrument did not create a valid enduring power, and
- (b) that the donor has become mentally incapable.

(3) Any transaction between the attorney and another person is, in favour of that person, as valid as if the power had then been in existence, unless at the time of the transaction that person knows—

(a) that the instrument did not create a valid enduring power, and
(b) that the donor has become mentally incapable.

(4) Paragraph 18(4) applies for the purpose of determining whether a transaction was valid by virtue of sub-paragraph (3) as it applies for the purpose or determining whether a transaction was valid by virtue of paragraph 18(3).

NOTES

Initial Commencement
To be appointed: see s 68(1).

Appointment
Appointment: 1 October 2007: see SI 2007/1897, art 2(1)(d).

PART 7
JOINT AND JOINT AND SEVERAL ATTORNEYS

Application to joint and joint and several attorneys

20 (1) An instrument which appoints more than one person to be an attorney cannot create an enduring power unless the attorneys are appointed to act—

(a) jointly, or
(b) jointly and severally.

(2) This Schedule, in its application to joint attorneys, applies to them collectively as it applies to a single attorney but subject to the modifications specified in paragraph 21.

(3) This Schedule, in its application to joint and several attorneys, applies with the modifications specified in sub-paragraphs (4) to (7) and in paragraph 22.

(4) A failure, as respects any one attorney, to comply with the requirements for the creation of enduring powers—

(a) prevents the instrument from creating such a power in his case, but
(b) does not affect its efficacy for that purpose as respects the other or others or its efficacy in his case for the purpose of creating a power of attorney which is not an enduring power.

(5) If one or more but not both or all the attorneys makes or joins in making an application for registration of the instrument—

(a) an attorney who is not an applicant as well as one who is may act pending the registration of the instrument as provided in paragraph 1(2),
(b) notice of the application must also be given under Part 3 of this Schedule to the other attorney or attorneys, and
(c) objection may validly be taken to the registration on a ground relating to an attorney or to the power of an attorney who is not an applicant as well as to one or the power of one who is an applicant.

(6) The Public Guardian is not precluded by paragraph 13(5) or (8) from registering an instrument and the court must not direct him not to do so under paragraph 13(10) if an enduring power subsists as respects some attorney who is not affected by the ground or grounds of the objection in question; and where the Public Guardian registers an instrument in that case, he must make against the registration an entry in the prescribed form.

(7) Sub-paragraph (6) does not preclude the court from revoking a power in so far as it confers a power on any other attorney in respect of whom the ground in paragraph 13(9)(d) or (e) is established; and where any ground in paragraph 13(9) affecting any other attorney is established the court must direct the Public Guardian to make against the registration an entry in the prescribed form.

(8) In sub-paragraph (4), "the requirements for the creation of enduring powers" means the provisions of—

(a) paragraph 2 other than sub-paragraphs (8) and (9), and
(b) the regulations mentioned in paragraph 2.

Joint attorneys

21 (1) In paragraph 2(5), the reference to the time when the attorney executes the instrument is to be read as a reference to the time when the second or last attorney executes the instrument.

(2) In paragraph 2(6) to (8), the reference to the attorney is to be read as a reference to any attorney under the power.

(3) Paragraph 13 has effect as if the ground of objection to the registration of the instrument specified in sub-paragraph (9)(e) applied to any attorney under the power.

(4) In paragraph 16(2), references to the attorney are to be read as including references to any attorney under the power.

(5) In paragraph 16(4), references to the attorney are to be read as including references to any attorney under the power.

(6) In paragraph 17, references to the attorney are to be read as including references to any attorney under the power.

Joint and several attorneys

22 (1) In paragraph 2(7), the reference to the bankruptcy of the attorney is to be read as a reference to the bankruptcy of the last remaining attorney under the power; and the bankruptcy of any other attorney under the power causes that person to cease to be an attorney under the power.

(2) In paragraph 2(8), the reference to the suspension of the power is to be read as a reference to its suspension in so far as it relates to the attorney in respect of whom the interim bankruptcy restrictions order has effect.

(3) The restriction upon disclaimer imposed by paragraph 4(6) applies only to those attorneys who have reason to believe that the donor is or is becoming mentally incapable.

NOTES

Initial Commencement
To be appointed: see s 68(1).

Appointment
Appointment: 1 October 2007: see SI 2007/1897, art 2(1)(d).

PART 8
INTERPRETATION

23 (1) In this Schedule—

"enduring power" is to be construed in accordance with paragraph 2,
"mentally incapable" or "mental incapacity", except where it refers to revocation at common law, means in relation to any person, that he is incapable by reason of mental disorder (*within the meaning of the Mental Health Act*) of managing and administering his property and affairs and "mentally capable" and "mental capacity" are to be construed accordingly,
"notice" means notice in writing, and
"prescribed", except for the purposes of paragraph 2, means prescribed by regulations made for the purposes of this Schedule by the Lord Chancellor.

[(1A) In sub-paragraph (1), "mental disorder" has the same meaning as in the Mental Health Act but disregarding the amendments made to that Act by the Mental Health Act 2007.]

(2) Any question arising under or for the purposes of this Schedule as to what the donor of the power might at any time be expected to do is to be determined by assuming that he had full mental capacity at the time but otherwise by reference to the circumstances existing at that time.

NOTES

Initial Commencement
To be appointed: see s 68(1).

Appointment
Appointment: 1 October 2007: see SI 2007/1897, art 2(1)(d).

Amendment
Para 23: in sub-para (1) in definition ""mentally incapable" and "mental incapacity"" words "(within the meaning of the Mental Health Act)" in italics repealed by the Mental Health Act 2007, ss 1(4), 55, Sch 1, Pt 2, para 23(1), (2), Sch 11, Pt 1; for transitional provisions and savings see s 53, Sch 10, paras 1, 2(1)–(3), (4)(a), (g) thereto. Date in force: to be appointed: see the Mental Health Act 2007, s 56(1). Para 23: sub-para (1A) inserted by the Mental Health Act 2007, s 1(4), Sch 1, Pt 2, para 23(1), (3); for transitional provisions and savings see s 53, Sch 10, paras 1, 2(1)–(3), (4)(a) thereto. Date in force: to be appointed: see the Mental Health Act 2007, s 56(1).

SCHEDULE 5
TRANSITIONAL PROVISIONS AND SAVINGS

Section 66(4)

PART 1
REPEAL OF PART 7 OF THE MENTAL HEALTH ACT 1983

Existing receivers

A1.85

1 (1) This paragraph applies where, immediately before the commencement day, there is a receiver ("R") for a person ("P") appointed under section 99 of the Mental Health Act.

(2) On and after that day—

(a) this Act applies as if R were a deputy appointed for P by the court, but with the functions that R had as receiver immediately before that day, and
(b) a reference in any other enactment to a deputy appointed by the court includes a person appointed as a deputy as a result of paragraph (a).

(3) On any application to it by R, the court may end R's appointment as P's deputy.

(4) Where, as a result of section 20(1), R may not make a decision on behalf of P in relation to a relevant matter, R must apply to the court.

(5) If, on the application, the court is satisfied that P is capable of managing his property and affairs in relation to the relevant matter—

(a) it must make an order ending R's appointment as P's deputy in relation to that matter, but
(b) it may, in relation to any other matter, exercise in relation to P any of the powers which it has under sections 15 to 19.

(6) If it is not satisfied, the court may exercise in relation to P any of the powers which it has under sections 15 to 19.

(7) R's appointment as P's deputy ceases to have effect if P dies.

(8) "Relevant matter" means a matter in relation to which, immediately before the commencement day, R was authorised to act as P's receiver.

(9) In sub-paragraph (1), the reference to a receiver appointed under section 99 of the Mental Health Act includes a reference to a person who by virtue of Schedule 5 to that Act was deemed to be a receiver appointed under that section.

Orders, appointments etc

2 (1) Any order or appointment made, direction or authority given or other thing done which has, or by virtue of Schedule 5 to the Mental Health Act was deemed to have, effect under Part 7 of the Act immediately before the commencement day is to continue to have effect despite the repeal of Part 7.

(2) In so far as any such order, appointment, direction, authority or thing could have been made, given or done under sections 15 to 20 if those sections had then been in force—

(a) it is to be treated as made, given or done under those sections, and
(b) the powers of variation and discharge conferred by section 16(7) apply accordingly.

(3) Sub-paragraph (1)—

(a) does not apply to nominations under section 93(1) or (4) of the Mental Health Act, and
(b) as respects receivers, has effect subject to paragraph 1.

(4) This Act does not affect the operation of section 109 of the Mental Health Act (effect and proof of orders etc) in relation to orders made and directions given under Part 7 of that Act.

(5) This paragraph is without prejudice to section 16 of the Interpretation Act 1978 (c 30) (general savings on repeal).

Pending proceedings

3 (1) Any application for the exercise of a power under Part 7 of the Mental Health Act which is pending immediately before the commencement day is to be treated, in so far as a corresponding power is exercisable under sections 16 to 20, as an application for the exercise of that power.

(2) For the purposes of sub-paragraph (1) an application for the appointment of a receiver is to be treated as an application for the appointment of a deputy.

Appeals

4 (1) Part 7 of the Mental Health Act and the rules made under it are to continue to apply to any appeal brought by virtue of section 105 of that Act which has not been determined before the commencement day.

(2) If in the case of an appeal brought by virtue of section 105(1) (appeal to nominated judge) the judge nominated under section 93 of the Mental Health Act has begun to hear the appeal, he is to continue to do so but otherwise it is to be heard by a puisne judge of the High Court nominated under section 46.

Fees

5 All fees and other payments which, having become due, have not been paid to the former Court of Protection before the commencement day, are to be paid to the new Court of Protection.

Court records

6 (1) The records of the former Court of Protection are to be treated, on and after the commencement day, as records of the new Court of Protection and are to be dealt with accordingly under the Public Records Act 1958 (c 51).

(2) On and after the commencement day, the Public Guardian is, for the purpose of exercising any of his functions, to be given such access as he may require to such of the records mentioned in sub-paragraph (1) as relate to the appointment of receivers under section 99 of the Mental Health Act.

Existing charges

7 This Act does not affect the operation in relation to a charge created before the commencement day of—

(a) so much of section 101(6) of the Mental Health Act as precludes a charge created under section 101(5) from conferring a right of sale or foreclosure during the lifetime of the patient, or
(b) section 106(6) of the Mental Health Act (charge created by virtue of section 106(5) not to cause interest to fail etc).

Preservation of interests on disposal of property

8 Paragraph 8(1) of Schedule 2 applies in relation to any disposal of property (within the meaning of that provision) by a person living on 1st November 1960, being a disposal effected under the Lunacy Act 1890 (c 5) as it applies in relation to the disposal of property effected under sections 16 to 20.

Accounts

9 Court of Protection Rules may provide that, in a case where paragraph 1 applies, R is to have a duty to render accounts—

(a) while he is receiver;
(b) after he is discharged.

Interpretation

10 In this Part of this Schedule—

(a) "the commencement day" means the day on which section 66(1)(a) (repeal of Part 7 of the Mental Health Act) comes into force,
(b) "the former Court of Protection" means the office abolished by section 45, and
(c) "the new Court of Protection" means the court established by that section.

NOTES

Initial Commencement
To be appointed: see s 68(1).

Appointment
Appointment: 1 October 2007: see SI 2007/1897, art 2(1)(d).

PART 2
REPEAL OF THE ENDURING POWERS OF ATTORNEY ACT 1985

Orders, determinations, etc

11 (1) Any order or determination made, or other thing done, under the 1985 Act which has effect immediately before the commencement day continues to have effect despite the repeal of that Act.

(2) In so far as any such order, determination or thing could have been made or done under Schedule 4 if it had then been in force—

(a) it is to be treated as made or done under that Schedule, and
(b) the powers of variation and discharge exercisable by the court apply accordingly.

(3) Any instrument registered under the 1985 Act is to be treated as having been registered by the Public Guardian under Schedule 4.

(4) This paragraph is without prejudice to section 16 of the Interpretation Act 1978 (c 30) (general savings on repeal).

Pending proceedings

12 (1) An application for the exercise of a power under the 1985 Act which is pending immediately before the commencement day is to be treated, in so far as a corresponding power is exercisable under Schedule 4, as an application for the exercise of that power.

(2) For the purposes of sub-paragraph (1)—

(a) a pending application under section 4(2) of the 1985 Act for the registration of an instrument is to be treated as an application to the Public Guardian under paragraph 4 of Schedule 4 and any notice given in connection with that application under Schedule 1 to the 1985 Act is to be treated as given under Part 3 of Schedule 4,
(b) a notice of objection to the registration of an instrument is to be treated as a notice of objection under paragraph 13 of Schedule 4, and
(c) pending proceedings under section 5 of the 1985 Act are to be treated as proceedings on an application for the exercise by the court of a power which would become exercisable in relation to an instrument under paragraph 16(2) of Schedule 4 on its registration.

Appeals

13 (1) The 1985 Act and, so far as relevant, the provisions of Part 7 of the Mental Health Act and the rules made under it as applied by section 10 of the 1985 Act are to continue to have effect in relation to any appeal brought by virtue of section 10(1)(c) of the 1985 Act which has not been determined before the commencement day.

(2) If, in the case of an appeal brought by virtue of section 105(1) of the Mental Health Act as applied by section 10(1)(c) of the 1985 Act (appeal to nominated judge), the judge nominated under section 93 of the Mental Health Act has begun to hear the appeal, he is to continue to do so but otherwise the appeal is to be heard by a puisne judge of the High Court nominated under section 46.

Exercise of powers of donor as trustee

14 (1) Section 2(8) of the 1985 Act (which prevents a power of attorney under section 25 of the Trustee Act 1925 (c 19) as enacted from being an enduring power) is to continue to apply to any enduring power—

(a) created before 1st March 2000, and
(b) having effect immediately before the commencement day.

(2) Section 3(3) of the 1985 Act (which entitles the donee of an enduring power to exercise the donor's powers as trustee) is to continue to apply to any enduring power to which, as a result of the provision mentioned in sub-paragraph (3), it applies immediately before the commencement day.

(3) The provision is section 4(3)(a) of the Trustee Delegation Act 1999 (c 15) (which provides for section 3(3) of the 1985 Act to cease to apply to an enduring power when its registration is cancelled, if it was registered in response to an application made before 1st March 2001).

(4) Even though section 4 of the 1999 Act is repealed by this Act, that section is to continue to apply in relation to an enduring power—

(a) to which section 3(3) of the 1985 Act applies as a result of sub-paragraph (2), or
(b) to which, immediately before the repeal of section 4 of the 1999 Act, section 1 of that Act applies as a result of section 4 of it.

(5) The reference in section 1(9) of the 1999 Act to section 4(6) of that Act is to be read with sub-paragraphs (2) to (4).

Interpretation

15 In this Part of this Schedule, "the commencement day" means the day on which section 66(1)(b) (repeal of the 1985 Act) comes into force.

NOTES

Initial Commencement
To be appointed: see s 68(1).

Appointment
Appointment: 1 October 2007: see SI 2007/1897, art 2(1)(d).

SCHEDULE 6
MINOR AND CONSEQUENTIAL AMENDMENTS

Section 67(1)

Fines and Recoveries Act 1833 (c 74)

A1.86

1 (1) The Fines and Recoveries Act 1833 (c 74) is amended as follows.

(2) In section 33 (case where protector of settlement lacks capacity to act), for the words from "shall be incapable" to "is incapable as aforesaid" substitute "lacks capacity (within the meaning of the Mental Capacity Act 2005) to manage his property and affairs, the Court of Protection is to take his place as protector of the settlement while he lacks capacity".

(3) In sections 48 and 49 (mental health jurisdiction), for each reference to the judge having jurisdiction under Part 7 of the Mental Health Act substitute a reference to the Court of Protection.

Improvement of Land Act 1864 (c 114)

2 In section 68 of the Improvement of Land Act 1864 (c 114) (apportionment of rentcharges)—

(a) for ", curator, or receiver of" substitute "or curator of, or a deputy with powers in relation to property and affairs appointed by the Court of Protection for,", and
(b) for "or patient within the meaning of Part VII of the Mental Health Act 1983" substitute "person who lacks capacity (within the meaning of the Mental Capacity Act 2005) to receive the notice".

Trustee Act 1925 (c 19)

3 (1) The Trustee Act 1925 (c 19) is amended as follows.

(2) In section 36 (appointment of new trustee)—

(a) in subsection (6C), for the words from "a power of attorney" to the end, substitute "an enduring power of attorney or lasting power of attorney registered under the Mental Capacity Act 2005", and
(b) in subsection (9)—
  (i) for the words from "is incapable" to "exercising" substitute "lacks capacity to exercise", and
  (ii) for the words from "the authority" to the end substitute "the Court of Protection".

(3) In section 41(1) (power of court to appoint new trustee) for the words from "is incapable" to "exercising" substitute "lacks capacity to exercise".

(4) In section 54 (mental health jurisdiction)—

(a) for subsection (1) substitute—

"(1) Subject to subsection (2), the Court of Protection may not make an order, or give a direction or authority, in relation to a person who lacks capacity to exercise his functions as trustee, if the High Court may make an order to that effect under this Act.",

(b) in subsection (2)—
  (i) for the words from the beginning to "of a receiver" substitute "Where a person lacks capacity to exercise his functions as a trustee and a deputy is appointed for him by the Court of Protection or an application for the appointment of a deputy",
  (ii) for "the said authority", in each place, substitute "the Court of Protection", and
  (iii) for "the patient", in each place, substitute "the person concerned", and
(c) omit subsection (3).

(5) In section 55 (order made on particular allegation to be conclusive evidence of it)—

(a) for the words from "Part VII" to "Northern Ireland" substitute "sections 15 to 20 of the Mental Capacity Act 2005 or any corresponding provisions having effect in Northern Ireland", and
(b) for paragraph (a) substitute—
"(a) that a trustee or mortgagee lacks capacity in relation to the matter in question;".

(6) In section 68 (definitions), at the end add—

"(3) Any reference in this Act to a person who lacks capacity in relation to a matter is to a person—

(a) who lacks capacity within the meaning of the Mental Capacity Act 2005 in relation to that matter, or
(b) in respect of whom the powers conferred by section 48 of that Act are exercisable and have been exercised in relation to that matter.".

Law of Property Act 1925 (c 20)

4 (1) The Law of Property Act 1925 (c 20) is amended as follows.

(2) In section 22 (conveyances on behalf of persons who lack capacity)—

(a) in subsection (1)—
  (i) for the words from "in a person suffering" to "is acting" substitute ", either solely or jointly with any other person or persons, in a person lacking capacity (within the meaning of the Mental Capacity Act 2005) to convey or create a legal estate, a deputy appointed for him by the Court of Protection or (if no deputy is appointed", and
  (ii) for "the authority having jurisdiction under Part VII of the Mental Health Act 1983" substitute "the Court of Protection",
(b) in subsection (2), for "is incapable, by reason of mental disorder, of exercising" substitute "lacks capacity (within the meaning of that Act) to exercise", and
(c) in subsection (3), for the words from "an enduring power" to the end substitute "an enduring power of attorney or lasting power of attorney (within the meaning of the 2005 Act) is entitled to act for the trustee who lacks capacity in relation to the dealing.".

(3) In section 205(1) (interpretation), omit paragraph (xiii).

Administration of Estates Act 1925 (c 23)

5 (1) The Administration of Estates Act 1925 (c 23) is amended as follows.

(2) In section 41(1) (powers of personal representatives to appropriate), in the proviso—

(a) in paragraph (ii)—
  (i) for the words from "is incapable" to "the consent" substitute "lacks capacity (within the meaning of the Mental Capacity Act 2005) to give the consent, it", and
  (ii) for "or receiver" substitute "or a person appointed as deputy for him by the Court of Protection", and
(b) in paragraph (iv), for "no receiver is acting for a person suffering from mental disorder" substitute "no deputy is appointed for a person who lacks capacity to consent".

(3) Omit section 55(1)(viii) (definitions of "person of unsound mind" and "defective").

National Assistance Act 1948 (c 29)

6 In section 49 of the National Assistance Act 1948 (c 29) (expenses of council officers acting for persons who lack capacity)—

(a) for the words from "applies" to "affairs of a patient" substitute "applies for appointment by the Court of Protection as a deputy", and
(b) for "such functions" substitute "his functions as deputy".

USA Veterans' Pensions (Administration) Act 1949 (c 45)

7 In section 1 of the USA Veterans' Pensions (Administration) Act 1949 (c 45) (administration of pensions)—

(a) in subsection (4), omit the words from "or for whom" to "1983", and
(b) after subsection (4), insert—

"(4A) An agreement under subsection (1) is not to be made in relation to a person who lacks capacity (within the meaning of the Mental Capacity Act 2005) for the purposes of this Act if—

(a) there is a donee of an enduring power of attorney or lasting power of attorney (within the meaning of the 2005 Act), or a deputy appointed for the person by the Court of Protection, and
(b) the donee or deputy has power in relation to the person for the purposes of this Act.

(4B) The proviso at the end of subsection (4) also applies in relation to subsection (4A).".

Intestates' Estates Act 1952 (c 64)

8 In Schedule 2 to the Intestates' Estates Act 1952 (c 64) (rights of surviving spouse or civil partner in relation to home), for paragraph 6(1) substitute—

"(1) Where the surviving spouse or civil partner lacks capacity (within the meaning of the Mental Capacity Act 2005) to make a requirement or give a consent under this Schedule, the requirement or consent may be made or given by a deputy appointed by the Court of Protection with power in that respect or, if no deputy has that power, by that court.".

Variation of Trusts Act 1958 (c 53)

9 In section 1 of the Variation of Trusts Act 1958 (c 53) (jurisdiction of courts to vary trusts)—

(a) in subsection (3), for the words from "shall be determined" to the end substitute "who lacks capacity (within the meaning of the Mental Capacity Act 2005) to give his assent is to be determined by the Court of Protection", and
(b) in subsection (6), for the words from "the powers" to the end substitute "the powers of the Court of Protection".

Administration of Justice Act 1960 (c 65)

10 In section 12(1)(b) of the Administration of Justice Act 1960 (c 65) (contempt of court to publish information about proceedings in private relating to persons with incapacity) for the words from "under Part VIII" to "that Act" substitute "under the Mental Capacity Act 2005, or under any provision of the Mental Health Act 1983".

Industrial and Provident Societies Act 1965 (c 12)

11 In section 26 of the Industrial and Provident Societies Act 1965 (c 12) (payments for mentally incapable people), for subsection (2) substitute—

"(2) Subsection (1) does not apply where the member or person concerned lacks capacity (within the meaning of the Mental Capacity Act 2005) for the purposes of this Act and—

(a) there is a donee of an enduring power of attorney or lasting power of attorney (within the meaning of the 2005 Act), or a deputy appointed for the member or person by the Court of Protection, and
(b) the donee or deputy has power in relation to the member or person for the purposes of this Act.".

Compulsory Purchase Act 1965 (c 56)

12 In Schedule 1 to the Compulsory Purchase Act 1965 (c 56) (persons without power to sell their interests), for paragraph 1(2)(b) substitute—

"(b) do not have effect in relation to a person who lacks capacity (within the meaning of the Mental Capacity Act 2005) for the purposes of this Act if—

(i) there is a donee of an enduring power of attorney or lasting power of attorney (within the meaning of the 2005 Act), or a deputy appointed for the person by the Court of Protection, and

(ii) the donee or deputy has power in relation to the person for the purposes of this Act.".

Leasehold Reform Act 1967 (c 88)

13 (1) For section 26(2) of the Leasehold Reform Act 1967 (c 88) (landlord lacking capacity) substitute—

"(2) Where a landlord lacks capacity (within the meaning of the Mental Capacity Act 2005) to exercise his functions as a landlord, those functions are to be exercised—

(a) by a donee of an enduring power of attorney or lasting power of attorney (within the meaning of the 2005 Act), or a deputy appointed for him by the Court of Protection, with power to exercise those functions, or

(b) if no donee or deputy has that power, by a person authorised in that respect by that court.".

(2) That amendment does not affect any proceedings pending at the commencement of this paragraph in which a receiver or a person authorised under Part 7 of the Mental Health Act is acting on behalf of the landlord.

Medicines Act 1968 (c 67)

14 In section 72 of the Medicines Act 1968 (c 67) (pharmacist lacking capacity)—

(a) in subsection (1)(c), for the words from "a receiver" to "1959" substitute "he becomes a person who lacks capacity (within the meaning of the Mental Capacity Act 2005) to carry on the business",

(b) after subsection (1) insert—

"(1A) In subsection (1)(c), the reference to a person who lacks capacity to carry on the business is to a person—

(a) in respect of whom there is a donee of an enduring power of attorney or lasting power of attorney (within the meaning of the Mental Capacity Act 2005), or

(b) for whom a deputy is appointed by the Court of Protection,

and in relation to whom the donee or deputy has power for the purposes of this Act.",

(c) in subsection (3)(d)—

(i) for "receiver" substitute "deputy", and

(ii) after "guardian" insert "or from the date of registration of the instrument appointing the donee", and

(d) in subsection (4)(c), for "receiver" substitute "donee, deputy".

Family Law Reform Act 1969 (c 46)

15 For section 21(4) of the Family Law Reform Act 1969 (c 46) (consent required for taking of bodily sample from person lacking capacity), substitute—

"(4) A bodily sample may be taken from a person who lacks capacity (within the meaning of the Mental Capacity Act 2005) to give his consent, if consent is given by the court giving the direction under section 20 or by—

(a) a donee of an enduring power of attorney or lasting power of attorney (within the meaning of that Act), or

(b) a deputy appointed, or any other person authorised, by the Court of Protection,

with power in that respect.".

Local Authority Social Services Act 1970 (c 42)

16 (1) Schedule 1 to the Local Authority Social Services Act 1970 (c 42) (enactments conferring functions assigned to social services committee) is amended as follows.

(2) In the entry for section 49 of the National Assistance Act 1948 (expenses of local authority officer appointed for person who lacks capacity) for "receiver" substitute "deputy".

(3) At the end, insert—

"Mental Capacity Act 2005	
Section 39	Instructing independent mental capacity advocate before providing accommodation for person lacking capacity.
Section 49	Reports in proceedings.".

Courts Act 1971 (c 23)

17 In Part 1A of Schedule 2 to the Courts Act 1971 (c 23) (office-holders eligible for appointment as circuit judges), omit the reference to a Master of the Court of Protection.

Local Government Act 1972 (c 70)

18 (1) Omit section 118 of the Local Government Act 1972 (c 70) (payment of pension etc where recipient lacks capacity).

(2) Sub-paragraph (3) applies where, before the commencement of this paragraph, a local authority has, in respect of a person referred to in that section as "the patient", made payments under that section—

(a) to an institution or person having the care of the patient, or
(b) in accordance with subsection (1)(a) or (b) of that section.

(3) The local authority may, in respect of the patient, continue to make payments under that section to that institution or person, or in accordance with subsection (1)(a) or (b) of that section, despite the repeal made by sub-paragraph (1).

Matrimonial Causes Act 1973 (c 18)

19 In section 40 of the Matrimonial Causes Act 1973 (c 18) (payments to person who lacks capacity) (which becomes subsection (1))—

(a) for the words from "is incapable" to "affairs" substitute "("P") lacks capacity (within the meaning of the Mental Capacity Act 2005) in relation to the provisions of the order",
(b) for "that person under Part VIII of that Act" substitute "P under that Act",
(c) for the words from "such persons" to the end substitute "such person ("D") as it may direct", and
(d) at the end insert—

"(2) In carrying out any functions of his in relation to an order made under subsection (1), D must act in P's best interests (within the meaning of that Act).".

Juries Act 1974 (c 23)

20 In Schedule 1 to the Juries Act 1974 (c 23) (disqualification for jury service), for paragraph 3 substitute—

"**3** A person who lacks capacity, within the meaning of the Mental Capacity Act 2005, to serve as a juror.".

Consumer Credit Act 1974 (c 39)

21 For section 37(1)(c) of the Consumer Credit Act 1974 (c 39) (termination of consumer credit licence if holder lacks capacity) substitute—

"(c) becomes a person who lacks capacity (within the meaning of the Mental Capacity Act 2005) to carry on the activities covered by the licence.".

Solicitors Act 1974 (c 47)

22 (1) The Solicitors Act 1974 (c 47) is amended as follows.

(2) *For section 12(1)(j) (application for practising certificate by solicitor lacking capacity) substitute—*

> "*(j) while he lacks capacity (within the meaning of the Mental Capacity Act 2005) to act as a solicitor and powers under sections 15 to 20 or section 48 of that Act are exercisable in relation to him;".*

(3) In section 62(4) (contentious business agreements made by clients) for paragraphs (c) and (d) substitute—

> "(c) as a deputy for him appointed by the Court of Protection with powers in relation to his property and affairs, or
>
> (d) as another person authorised under that Act to act on his behalf.".

(4) In paragraph 1(1) of Schedule 1 (circumstances in which Law Society may intervene in solicitor's practice), for paragraph (f) substitute—

> "(f) a solicitor lacks capacity (within the meaning of the Mental Capacity Act 2005) to act as a solicitor and powers under sections 15 to 20 or section 48 of that Act are exercisable in relation to him;".

Local Government (Miscellaneous Provisions) Act 1976 (c 57)

23 In section 31 of the Local Government (Miscellaneous Provisions) Act 1976 (c 57) (the title to which becomes "Indemnities for local authority officers appointed as deputies or administrators"), for the words from "as a receiver" to "1959" substitute "as a deputy for a person by the Court of Protection".

Sale of Goods Act 1979 (c 54)

24 In section 3(2) of the Sale of Goods Act 1979 (c 54) (capacity to buy and sell) the words "mental incapacity or" cease to have effect in England and Wales.

Limitation Act 1980 (c 58)

25 In section 38 of the Limitation Act 1980 (c 58) (interpretation) substitute—

> (a) in subsection (2) for "of unsound mind" substitute "lacks capacity (within the meaning of the Mental Capacity Act 2005) to conduct legal proceedings", and
>
> (b) omit subsections (3) and (4).

Public Passenger Vehicles Act 1981 (c 14)

26 In section 57(2)(c) of the Public Passenger Vehicles Act 1981 (c 14) (termination of public service vehicle licence if holder lacks capacity) for the words from "becomes a patient" to "or" substitute "becomes a person who lacks capacity (within the meaning of the Mental Capacity Act 2005) to use a vehicle under the licence, or".

Judicial Pensions Act 1981 (c 20)

27 In Schedule 1 to the Judicial Pensions Act 1981 (c 20) (pensions of Supreme Court officers, etc), in paragraph 1, omit the reference to a Master of the Court of Protection except in the case of a person holding that office immediately before the commencement of this paragraph or who had previously retired from that office or died.

Supreme Court Act 1981 [Senior Courts Act 1981] (c 54)

28 In Schedule 2 to the *Supreme Court Act 1981* [Senior Courts Act 1981] (c 54) (qualifications for appointment to office in Supreme Court), omit paragraph 11 (Master of the Court of Protection).

Mental Health Act 1983 (c 20)

29 (1) The Mental Health Act is amended as follows.

(2) In section 134(3) (cases where correspondence of detained patients may not be withheld) for paragraph (b) substitute—

"(b) any judge or officer of the Court of Protection, any of the Court of Protection Visitors or any person asked by that Court for a report under section 49 of the Mental Capacity Act 2005 concerning the patient;".

(3) In section 139 (protection for acts done in pursuance of 1983 Act), in subsection (1), omit from "or in, or in pursuance" to "Part VII of this Act,".

(4) Section 142 (payment of pension etc where recipient lacks capacity) ceases to have effect in England and Wales.

(5) Sub-paragraph (6) applies where, before the commencement of sub-paragraph (4), an authority has, in respect of a person referred to in that section as "the patient", made payments under that section—

(a) to an institution or person having the care of the patient, or
(b) in accordance with subsection (2)(a) or (b) of that section.

(6) The authority may, in respect of the patient, continue to make payments under that section to that institution or person, or in accordance with subsection (2)(a) or (b) of that section, despite the amendment made by sub-paragraph (4).

(7) In section 145(1) (interpretation), in the definition of "patient", omit " (except in Part VII of this Act)".

(8) In section 146 (provisions having effect in Scotland), omit from "104(4)" to "section),".

(9) In section 147 (provisions having effect in Northern Ireland), omit from "104(4)" to "section),".

Administration of Justice Act 1985 (c 61)

30 In section 18(3) of the Administration of Justice Act 1985 (c 61) (licensed conveyancer who lacks capacity), for the words from "that person" to the end substitute "he becomes a person who lacks capacity (within the meaning of the Mental Capacity Act 2005) to practise as a licensed conveyancer.".

Insolvency Act 1986 (c 45)

31 (1) The Insolvency Act 1986 (c 45) is amended as follows.

(2) In section 389A (people not authorised to act as nominee or supervisor in voluntary arrangement), in subsection (3)—

(a) omit the "or" immediately after paragraph (b),
(b) in paragraph (c), omit "Part VII of the Mental Health Act 1983 or", and
(c) after that paragraph, insert
", or
(d) he lacks capacity (within the meaning of the Mental Capacity Act 2005) to act as nominee or supervisor".

(3) In section 390 (people not qualified to be insolvency practitioners), in subsection (4)—

(a) omit the "or" immediately after paragraph (b),
(b) in paragraph (c), omit "Part VII of the Mental Health Act 1983 or", and
(c) after that paragraph, insert
", or
(d) he lacks capacity (within the meaning of the Mental Capacity Act 2005) to act as an insolvency practitioner.".

Building Societies Act 1986 (c 53)

32 In section 102D(9) of the Building Societies Act 1986 (c 53) (references to a person holding an account on trust for another)—

(a) in paragraph (a), for "Part VII of the Mental Health Act 1983" substitute "the Mental Capacity Act 2005", and
(b) for paragraph (b) substitute—
"(b) to an attorney holding an account for another person under—
(i) an enduring power of attorney or lasting power of attorney registered under the Mental Capacity Act 2005, or
(ii) an enduring power registered under the Enduring Powers of Attorney (Northern Ireland) Order 1987;".

Public Trustee and Administration of Funds Act 1986 (c 57)

33 In section 3 of the Public Trustee and Administration of Funds Act 1986 (c 57) (functions of the Public Trustee)—

(a) for subsections (1) to (5) substitute—

"(1) The Public Trustee may exercise the functions of a deputy appointed by the Court of Protection.",

(b) in subsection (6), for "the 1906 Act" substitute "the Public Trustee Act 1906", and
(c) omit subsection (7).

Patronage (Benefices) Measure 1986 (No 3)

34 (1) The Patronage (Benefices) Measure 1986 (No 3) is amended as follows.

(2) In section 5 (rights of patronage exercisable otherwise than by registered patron), after subsection (3) insert—

"(3A) The reference in subsection (3) to a power of attorney does not include an enduring power of attorney or lasting power of attorney (within the meaning of the Mental Capacity Act 2005)."

(3) In section 9 (information to be sent to designated officer when benefice becomes vacant), after subsection (5) insert—

"(5A) Subsections (5B) and (5C) apply where the functions of a registered patron are, as a result of paragraph 10 of Schedule 2 to the Mental Capacity Act 2005 (patron's loss of capacity to discharge functions), to be discharged by an individual appointed by the Court of Protection.

(5B) If the individual is a clerk in Holy Orders, subsection (5) applies to him as it applies to the registered patron.

(5C) If the individual is not a clerk in Holy Orders, subsection (1) (other than paragraph (b)) applies to him as it applies to the registered patron."

Courts and Legal Services Act 1990 (c 41)

35 (1) The Courts and Legal Services Act 1990 (c 41) is amended as follows.

(2) In Schedule 11 (judges etc barred from legal practice), for the reference to a Master of the Court of Protection substitute a reference to each of the following—

(a) Senior Judge of the Court of Protection,
(b) President of the Court of Protection,
(c) Vice-President of the Court of Protection.

(3) In paragraph 5(3) of Schedule 14 (exercise of powers of intervention in registered foreign lawyer's practice), for paragraph (f) substitute—

"(f) he lacks capacity (within the meaning of the Mental Capacity Act 2005) to act as a registered foreign lawyer and powers under sections 15 to 20 or section 48 are exercisable in relation to him;".

Child Support Act 1991 (c 48)

36 In section 50 of the Child Support Act 1991 (c 48) (unauthorised disclosure of information)—

(a) in subsection (8)—

(i) immediately after paragraph (a), insert "or",
(ii) omit paragraphs (b) and (d) and the "or" immediately after paragraph (c), and
(iii) for ", receiver, custodian or appointee" substitute "or custodian", and

(b) after that subsection, insert—

"(9) Where the person to whom the information relates lacks capacity (within the meaning of the Mental Capacity Act 2005) to consent to its disclosure, the appropriate person is—

(a) a donee of an enduring power of attorney or lasting power of attorney (within the meaning of that Act), or
(b) a deputy appointed for him, or any other person authorised, by the Court of Protection,

with power in that respect.".

Social Security Administration Act 1992 (c 5)

37 In section 123 of the Social Security Administration Act 1992 (c 5) (unauthorised disclosure of information)—

(a) in subsection (10), omit—
(i) in paragraph (b), "a receiver appointed under section 99 of the Mental Health Act 1983 or",
(ii) in paragraph (d)(i), "sub-paragraph (a) of rule 41(1) of the Court of Protection Rules 1984 or",
(iii) in paragraph (d)(ii), "a receiver ad interim appointed under sub-paragraph (b) of the said rule 41(1) or", and
(iv) "receiver,", and

(b) after that subsection, insert—

"(11) Where the person to whom the information relates lacks capacity (within the meaning of the Mental Capacity Act 2005) to consent to its disclosure, the appropriate person is—

(a) a donee of an enduring power of attorney or lasting power of attorney (within the meaning of that Act), or
(b) a deputy appointed for him, or any other person authorised, by the Court of Protection,

with power in that respect.".

Judicial Pensions and Retirement Act 1993 (c 8)

38 (1) The Judicial Pensions and Retirement Act 1993 (c 8) is amended as follows.

(2) In Schedule 1 (qualifying judicial offices), in Part 2, under the cross-heading "Court officers", omit the reference to a Master of the Court of Protection except in the case of a person holding that office immediately before the commencement of this sub-paragraph or who had previously retired from that office or died.

(3) In Schedule 5 (retirement: the relevant offices), omit the entries relating to the Master and Deputy or temporary Master of the Court of Protection, except in the case of a person holding any of those offices immediately before the commencement of this sub-paragraph.

(4) In Schedule 7 (retirement: transitional provisions), omit paragraph 5(5)(i)(g) except in the case of a person holding office as a deputy or temporary Master of the Court of Protection immediately before the commencement of this sub-paragraph.

Leasehold Reform, Housing and Urban Development Act 1993 (c 28)

39 (1) For paragraph 4 of Schedule 2 to the Leasehold Reform, Housing and Urban Development Act 1993 (c 28) (landlord under a disability), substitute—

"**4** (1) This paragraph applies where a Chapter I or Chapter II landlord lacks capacity (within the meaning of the Mental Capacity Act 2005) to exercise his functions as a landlord.

(2) For the purposes of the Chapter concerned, the landlord's place is to be taken—

(a) by a donee of an enduring power of attorney or lasting power of attorney (within the meaning of the 2005 Act), or a deputy appointed for him by the Court of Protection, with power to exercise those functions, or

(b) if no deputy or donee has that power, by a person authorised in that respect by that court.".

(2) That amendment does not affect any proceedings pending at the commencement of this paragraph in which a receiver or a person authorised under Part 7 of the Mental Health Act 1983 (c 20) is acting on behalf of the landlord.

Goods Vehicles (Licensing of Operators) Act 1995 (c 23)

40 (1) The Goods Vehicles (Licensing of Operators) Act 1995 (c 23) is amended as follows.

(2) In section 16(5) (termination of licence), for "he becomes a patient within the meaning of Part VII of the Mental Health Act 1983" substitute "he becomes a person who lacks capacity (within the meaning of the Mental Capacity Act 2005) to use a vehicle under the licence".

(3) In section 48 (licence not to be transferable, etc)—

(a) in subsection (2)—
   (i) for "or become a patient within the meaning of Part VII of the Mental Health Act 1983" substitute ", or become a person who lacks capacity (within the meaning of the Mental Capacity Act 2005) to use a vehicle under the licence,", and
   (ii) in paragraph (a), for "became a patient" substitute "became a person who lacked capacity in that respect", and

(b) in subsection (5), for "a patient within the meaning of Part VII of the Mental Health Act 1983" substitute "a person lacking capacity".

Disability Discrimination Act 1995 (c 50)

41 In section 20(7) of the Disability Discrimination Act 1995 (c 50) (regulations to disapply provisions about incapacity), in paragraph (b), for "Part VII of the Mental Health Act 1983" substitute "the Mental Capacity Act 2005".

Trusts of Land and Appointment of Trustees Act 1996 (c 47)

42 (1) The Trusts of Land and Appointment of Trustees Act 1996 (c 47) is amended as follows.

(2) In section 9 (delegation by trustees), in subsection (6), for the words from "an enduring power" to the end substitute "an enduring power of attorney or lasting power of attorney within the meaning of the Mental Capacity Act 2005".

(3) In section 20 (the title to which becomes "Appointment of substitute for trustee who lacks capacity")—

(a) in subsection (1)(a), for "is incapable by reason of mental disorder of exercising" substitute "lacks capacity (within the meaning of the Mental Capacity Act 2005) to exercise", and

(b) in subsection (2)—
   (i) for paragraph (a) substitute—

"(a) a deputy appointed for the trustee by the Court of Protection,",
   (ii) in paragraph (b), for the words from "a power of attorney" to the end substitute "an enduring power of attorney or lasting power of attorney registered under the Mental Capacity Act 2005", and
   (iii) in paragraph (c), for the words from "the authority" to the end substitute "the Court of Protection".

Human Rights Act 1998 (c 42)

43 In section 4(5) of the Human Rights Act 1998 (c 42) (courts which may make declarations of incompatibility), after paragraph (e) insert—

"(f) the Court of Protection, in any matter being dealt with by the President of the Family Division, the Vice-Chancellor or a puisne judge of the High Court."

Access to Justice Act 1999 (c 22)

44 In paragraph 1 of Schedule 2 to the Access to Justice Act 1999 (c 22) (services excluded from the Community Legal Service), after paragraph (e) insert—

"(ea) the creation of lasting powers of attorney under the Mental Capacity Act 2005,
(eb) the making of advance decisions under that Act,".

Adoption and Children Act 2002 (c 38)

45 In section 52(1)(a) of the Adoption and Children Act 2002 (c 38) (parental consent to adoption), for "is incapable of giving consent" substitute "lacks capacity (within the meaning of the Mental Capacity Act 2005) to give consent".

Licensing Act 2003 (c 17)

46 (1) The Licensing Act 2003 (c 17) is amended as follows.

(2) In section 27(1) (lapse of premises licence), for paragraph (b) substitute—

"(b) becomes a person who lacks capacity (within the meaning of the Mental Capacity Act 2005) to hold the licence,".

(3) In section 47 (interim authority notice in relation to premises licence)—

(a) in subsection (5), for paragraph (b) substitute—
"(b) the former holder lacks capacity (within the meaning of the Mental Capacity Act 2005) to hold the licence and that person acts for him under an enduring power of attorney or lasting power of attorney registered under that Act,", and
(b) in subsection (10), omit the definition of "mentally incapable".

Courts Act 2003 (c 39)

47 (1) The Courts Act 2003 (c 39) is amended as follows.

(2) In section 1(1) (the courts in relation to which the Lord Chancellor must discharge his general duty), after paragraph (a) insert—

"(aa) the Court of Protection,".

(3) In section 64(2) (judicial titles which the Lord Chancellor may by order alter)—

(a) omit the reference to a Master of the Court of Protection, and
(b) at the appropriate place insert a reference to each of the following—
(i) Senior Judge of the Court of Protection,
(ii) President of the Court of Protection,
(iii) Vice-president of the Court of Protection.

NOTES

Initial Commencement
To be appointed: see s 68(1).

Appointment
Appointment: 1 October 2007: see SI 2007/1897, art 2(1)(d).

Amendment
Para 22: sub-para (2) repealed by the Legal Services Act 2007, s 210, Sch 23. Date in force: to be appointed: see the Legal Services Act 2007, s 211(2).
Para 28 heading: words "Supreme Court Act 1981" in italics repealed and subsequent words in square brackets substituted by the Constitutional Reform Act 2005, s 59(5), Sch 11, Pt 1, para 1(2). Date in force: to be appointed: see the Constitutional Reform Act 2005, s 148(1).
Para 28: words "Supreme Court Act 1981" in italics repealed and subsequent words in square brackets substituted by the Constitutional Reform Act 2005, s 59(5), Sch 11, Pt 1, para 1(2). Date in force: to be appointed: see the Constitutional Reform Act 2005, s 148(1).

SCHEDULE 7
REPEALS

Section 67(2)

A1.87

Short title and chapter	Extent of repeal
Trustee Act 1925 (c 19)	Section 54(3).
Law of Property Act 1925 (c 20)	Section 205(1)(xiii).
Administration of Estates Act 1925 (c 23)	Section 55(1)(viii)
USA Veterans' Pensions (Administration) Act 1949 (c 45)	In section 1(4), the words from "or for whom" to "1983".
Mental Health Act 1959 (c 72)	In Schedule 7, in Part 1, the entries relating to— section 33 of the Fines and Recoveries Act 1833, section 68 of the Improvement of Land Act 1864, section 55 of the Trustee Act 1925, section 205(1) of the Law of Property Act 1925, section 49 of the National Assistance Act 1948, and section 1 of the Variation of Trusts Act 1958.
Courts Act 1971 (c 23)	In Schedule 2, in Part 1A, the words "Master of the Court of Protection".
Local Government Act 1972 (c 70)	Section 118.
Limitation Act 1980 (c 58)	Section 38(3) and (4).
Supreme Court Act 1981 [Senior Courts Act 1981] (c 54)	In Schedule 2, in Part 2, paragraph 11.
Mental Health Act 1983 (c 20)	Part 7. In section 139(1) the words from "or in, or in pursuance" to "Part VII of this Act,". In section 145(1), in the definition of "patient" the words "(except in Part VII of this Act)". In sections 146 and 147 the words from "104(4)" to "section),". Schedule 3. In Schedule 4, paragraphs 1, 2, 4, 5, 7, 9, 14, 20, 22, 25, 32, 38, 55 and 56. In Schedule 5, paragraphs 26, 43, 44 and 45.

Enduring Powers of Attorney Act 1985 (c 29)	The whole Act.
Insolvency Act 1986 (c 45)	In section 389A(3)— the "or" immediately after paragraph (b), and in paragraph (c), the words "Part VII of the Mental Health Act 1983 or". In section 390(4)— the "or" immediately after paragraph (b), and in paragraph (c), the words "Part VII of the Mental Health Act 1983 or".
Public Trustee and Administration of Funds Act 1986 (c 57)	Section 2. Section 3(7).
Child Support Act 1991 (c 48)	In section 50(8)— paragraphs (b) and (d), and the "or" immediately after paragraph (c).
Social Security Administration Act 1992 (c 5)	In section 123(10)— in paragraph (b), "a receiver appointed under section 99 of the Mental Health Act 1983 or", in paragraph (d)(i), "sub-paragraph (a) of rule 41(1) of the Court of Protection Rules Act 1984 or", in paragraph (d)(ii), "a receiver ad interim appointed under sub-paragraph (b) of the said rule 41(1) or", and "receiver,".
Trustee Delegation Act 1999 (c 15)	Section 4. Section 6. In section 7(3), the words "in accordance with section 4 above".
Care Standards Act 2000 (c 14)	In Schedule 4, paragraph 8.
Licensing Act 2003 (c 17)	In section 47(10), the definition of "mentally incapable".
Courts Act 2003 (c 64)	In section 64(2), the words "Master of the Court of Protection".

NOTES

Initial Commencement
To be appointed: see s 68(1).

Appointment
Appointment: 1 October 2007: see SI 2007/1897, art 2(1)(d).

Amendment

In column 1 words "Supreme Court Act 1981" in italics repealed and subsequent words in square brackets substituted by the Constitutional Reform Act 2005, s 59(5), Sch 11, Pt 1, para 1(2). Date in force: to be appointed: see the Constitutional Reform Act 2005, s 148(1).

Appendix 2

ALL LEGISLATION AMENDED BY THE MENTAL CAPACITY ACT 2005

A2.1

Affected Acts	Amending/repealing provisions within the Mental Capacity Act 2005
Access to Justice Act 1999 c 22	Sch 6, para 44
Administration of Estates Act 1925 (15&16Geo5) c 23	Sch 6, para 5; Sch 7
Administration of Justice Act 1960 (8&9Eliz2) c 65	Sch 6, para 10
Administration of Justice Act 1985 c 61	Sch 6, para 30
Adoption and Children Act 2002 c 38	Sch 6, para 45
Building Societies Act 1986 c 53	Sch 6, para 32
Care Standards Act 2000 c 14	Sch 7
Child Support Act 1991 c 48	Sch 6, para 36; Sch 7
Compulsory Purchase Act 1965 c.66	Sch 6, para 12
Consumer Credit Act 1974 c.39	Sch 6, para 21
Courts Act 1971 c 23	Sch 6, para 17; Sch 7
Courts Act 2003 c 39	Sch 6, para 47; Sch 7
Courts and Legal Services Act 1990 c 41	Sch 6, para 35
Disability Discrimination Act 1995 c 50	Sch 6, para 41
Enduring Powers of Attorney Act 1985 c 29	s .66(1)(b); Sch 7
Family Law Reform Act 1969 c 46	Sch 6, para 15
Fines and Recoveries Act 1833 (3&4Will4) c 74	Sch 6, para 1
Goods Vehicles (Licensing of Operators) Act 1995 c 23	Sch 6, para 40
Human Rights Act 1998 c 42	Sch 6, para 43
Improvement of Land Act 1864 (27&28Vict) c 114	Sch 6, para 2
Industrial and Provident Societies Act 1960 (8&9Eliz2) c 65	Sch 6, para 11
Insolvency Act 1986 c 45	Sch 6, para 31; Sch 7

A2.1 *All legislation amended by the Mental Capacity Act 2005*

Affected Acts	Amending/repealing provisions within the Mental Capacity Act 2005
Intestates' Estates Act 1952 (15&16Geo5&1Eliz2) c 64	Sch 6, para 8
Judicial Pensions Act 1981 c 20	Sch 6, para 27
Judicial Pensions and Retirement Act 1993 c 8	Sch 6, para 38
Juries Act 1974 c 23	Sch 6, para 20
Law of Property Act 1925 (15&16Geo5) c 20	Sch 6, para 4; Sch 7
Leasehold Reform Act 1967 c 88	Sch 6, para 13
Leasehold Reform, Housing and Urban Development Act 1993 c 28	Sch 6, para 39(1)
Licensing Act 2003 c 17	Sch 6, para 46
Limitation Act 1980 c 58	Sch 6, para 25; Sch 7
Local Authority Social Services Act 1970 c 42	Sch 6, para 16
Local Government (Miscellaneous Provisions) Act 1976 c 57	Sch 6, para 23
Local Government Act 1972 c 70	Sch 6, para 18(1); Sch 7
Matrimonial Causes Act 1973 c 18	Sch 6, para 19
Medicines Act 1968 c 67	Sch 6, para 14
Mental Health Act 1959 (7&8Eliz2) c 72	Sch 7
Mental Health Act 1983 c 20	s 66(1)(a); Sch 6, para 29; Sch 7
National Assistance Act 1948 (11&12Geo6) c 29	Sch 6, para 6
Patronage (Benefices) Measure 1986 No 3	Sch 6, para 34
Powers of Attorney Act 1971 c 27	s.14(5), Sch 4; para1(1)(c)
Public Passenger Vehicles Act 1981 c 14	Sch 6, para 26
Public Trustee and Administration of Funds Act 1986 c 57	Sch 6, para 33; Sch 7
Sale of Goods Act 1979 c 54	Sch 6, para 24
Social Security Administration Act 1992 c 5	Sch 6, para 37; Sch 7
Solicitors Act 1974 c 47	Sch 6, para 22
Supreme Court Act 1981 c 54	Sch 6, para 28; Sch 7
Trustee Act a1925 (15&16Geo5) c 19	Sch 6, para 3; Sch 7
Trustee Delegation Act 1999 c 15	Sch 7
Trusts of Land and Appointment of Trustees Act 1996 c 47	Sch 6, para 42
U.S.A. Veterans' Pensions (Administration) Act 1949 (12,13&14Geo6) c 45	Sch 6, para 7; Sch 7
Variation of Trusts Act 1958 (6&7Eliz2) c 53	Sch 6, para 9
Wills Act 1837 (7Will4&1Vict) c 26	Sch 2, para 4(2)

Appendix 3

THE MENTAL CAPACITY ACT 2005 — CODE OF PRACTICE

Issued by the Lord Chancellor on 23 April 2007 in accordance with sections 42 and 43 of the Act

A3.1

FOREWORD BY LORD FALCONER

Foreword by Lord Falconer, Secretary of State for Constitutional Affairs and Lord Chancellor

The Mental Capacity Act 2005 is a vitally important piece of legislation, and one that will make a real difference to the lives of people who may lack mental capacity. It will empower people to make decisions for themselves wherever possible, and protect people who lack capacity by providing a flexible framework that places individuals at the very heart of the decision-making process. It will ensure that they participate as much as possible in any decisions made on their behalf, and that these are made in their best interests. It also allows people to plan ahead for a time in the future when they might lack the capacity, for any number of reasons, to make decisions for themselves.

The Act covers a wide range of decisions and circumstances, but legislation alone is not the whole story. We have always recognised that the Act needs to be supported by practical guidance, and the Code of Practice is a key part of this. It explains how the Act will operate on a day-to-day basis and offers examples of best practice to carers and practitioners.

Many individuals and organisations have read and commented upon earlier drafts of the Code of Practice and I am very grateful to all those who contributed to this process. This Code of Practice is a better document as a result of this input.

A number of people will be under a formal duty to have regard to the Code: professionals and paid carers for example, or people acting as attorneys or as deputies appointed by the Court of Protection. But for many people, the most important relationships will be with the wide range of less formal carers, the close family and friends who know the person best, some of whom will have been caring for them for many years. The Code is also here to provide help and guidance for them. It will be crucial to the Code's success that all those relying upon it have a document that is clear and that they can understand. I have been particularly keen that we do all we can to achieve this.

The Code of Practice will be important in shaping the way the Mental Capacity Act 2005 is put into practice and I strongly encourage you to take the time to read and digest it.

Lord Falconer of Thoroton

INTRODUCTION

The Mental Capacity Act 2005, covering England and Wales, provides a statutory framework for people who lack capacity to make decisions for themselves, or who have capacity and want to make preparations for a time when they may lack capacity in the future. It sets out who can take decisions, in which situations, and how they should go about this. The Act received Royal Assent on 7 April 2005 and will come into force during 2007.

The legal framework provided by the Mental Capacity Act 2005 is supported by this Code of Practice (the Code), which provides guidance and information about how the Act works in practice. Section 42 of the Act requires the Lord Chancellor to produce a Code of Practice for the guidance of a range of people with different duties and functions under the Act. Before the Code is prepared, section 43 requires that the Lord Chancellor must have consulted the National Assembly for Wales and such other persons as he considers appropriate. The Code is also subject to the approval of Parliament and must have been placed before both Houses of Parliament for a 40-day period without either House voting against it. This Code of Practice has been produced in accordance with these requirements.

The Code has statutory force, which means that certain categories of people have a legal duty to have regard to it when working with or caring for adults who may lack capacity to make decisions for themselves. These categories of people are listed below.

How should the Code of Practice be used?

The Code of Practice provides guidance to anyone who is working with and/ or caring for adults who may lack capacity to make particular decisions. It describes their responsibilities when acting or making decisions on behalf of individuals who lack the capacity to act or make these decisions for themselves. In particular, the Code of Practice focuses on those who have a duty of care to someone who lacks the capacity to agree to the care that is being provided.

Who is the Code of Practice for?

The Act does not impose a legal duty on anyone to 'comply' with the Code – it should be viewed as guidance rather than instruction. But if they have not followed relevant guidance contained in the Code then they will be expected to give good reasons why they have departed from it.

Certain categories of people are legally required to 'have regard to' relevant guidance in the Code of Practice. That means they must be aware of the Code of Practice when acting or making decisions on behalf of someone who lacks capacity to make a decision for themselves, and they should be able to explain how they have had regard to the Code when acting or making decisions.

The categories of people that are required to have regard to the Code of Practice include anyone who is:

- an attorney under a Lasting Power of Attorney (LPA) (see chapter 7)
- a deputy appointed by the new Court of Protection (see chapter 8)
- acting as an Independent Mental Capacity Advocate (see chapter 10)
- carrying out research approved in accordance with the Act (see chapter 11)
- acting in a professional capacity for, or in relation to, a person who lacks capacity working
- being paid for acts for or in relation to a person who lacks capacity.

The last two categories cover a wide range of people. People acting in a professional capacity may include:

- a variety of healthcare staff (doctors, dentists, nurses, therapists, radiologists, paramedics etc)

- social care staff (social workers, care managers, etc)
- others who may occasionally be involved in the care of people who lack capacity to make the decision in question, such as ambulance crew, housing workers, or police officers.

People who are being paid for acts for or in relation to a person who lacks capacity may include:

- care assistants in a care home
- care workers providing domiciliary care services, and
- others who have been contracted to provide a service to people who lack capacity to consent to that service.

However, the Act applies more generally to *everyone* who looks after, or cares for, someone who lacks capacity to make particular decisions for themselves. This includes family carers or other carers. Although these carers are not legally required to have regard to the Code of Practice, the guidance given in the Code will help them to understand the Act and apply it. They should follow the guidance in the Code as far as they are aware of it.

What does 'lacks capacity' mean?

One of the most important terms in the Code is 'a person who lacks capacity'.

Whenever the term 'a person who lacks capacity' is used, it **means a person who lacks capacity to make a particular decision or take a particular action for themselves at the time the decision or action needs to be taken.**

This reflects the fact that people may lack capacity to make some decisions for themselves, but will have capacity to make other decisions. For example, they may have capacity to make small decisions about everyday issues such as what to wear or what to eat, but lack capacity to make more complex decisions about financial matters.

It also reflects the fact that a person who lacks capacity to make a decision for themselves at a certain time may be able to make that decision at a later date. This may be because they have an illness or condition that means their capacity changes. Alternatively, it may be because at the time the decision needs to be made, they are unconscious or barely conscious whether due to an accident or being under anaesthetic or their ability to make a decision may be affected by the influence of alcohol or drugs.

Finally, it reflects the fact that while some people may always lack capacity to make some types of decisions – for example, due to a condition or severe learning disability that has affected them from birth – others may learn new skills that enable them to gain capacity and make decisions for themselves.

Chapter 4 provides a full definition of what is meant by 'lacks capacity'.

What does the Code of Practice actually cover?

The Code explains the Act and its key provisions.

- **Chapter 1** introduces the Mental Capacity Act 2005.
- **Chapter 2** sets out the five statutory principles behind the Act and the way they affect how it is put in practice.
- **Chapter 3** explains how the Act makes sure that people are given the right help and support to make their own decisions.

- **Chapter 4** explains how the Act defines 'a person who lacks capacity to make a decision' and sets out a single clear test for assessing whether a person lacks capacity to make a particular decision at a particular time.
- **Chapter 5** explains what the Act means by acting in the best interests of someone lacking capacity to make a decision for themselves, and describes the checklist set out in the Act for working out what is in someone's best interests.
- **Chapter 6** explains how the Act protects people providing care or treatment for someone who lacks the capacity to consent to the action being taken.
- **Chapter 7** shows how people who wish to plan ahead for the possibility that they might lack the capacity to make particular decisions for themselves in the future are able to grant Lasting Powers of Attorney (LPAs) to named individuals to make certain decisions on their behalf, and how attorneys appointed under an LPA should act.
- **Chapter 8** describes the role of the new Court of Protection, established under the Act, to make a decision or to appoint a decision-maker on someone's behalf in cases where there is no other way of resolving a matter affecting a person who lacks capacity to make the decision in question.
- **Chapter 9** explains the procedures that must be followed if someone wishes to make an advance decision to refuse medical treatment to come into effect when they lack capacity to refuse the specified treatment.
- **Chapter 10** describes the role of Independent Mental Capacity Advocates appointed under the Act to help and represent particularly vulnerable people who lack capacity to make certain significant decisions. It also sets out when they should be instructed.
- **Chapter 11** provides guidance on how the Act sets out specific safeguards and controls for research involving, or in relation to, people lacking capacity to consent to their participation.
- **Chapter 12** explains those parts of the Act which can apply to children and young people and how these relate to other laws affecting them.
- **Chapter 13** explains how the Act relates to the Mental Health Act 1983.
- **Chapter 14** sets out the role of the Public Guardian, a new public office established by the Act to oversee attorneys and deputies and to act as a single point of contact for referring allegations of abuse in relation to attorneys and deputies to other relevant agencies.
- **Chapter 15** examines the various ways that disputes over decisions made under the Act or otherwise affecting people lacking capacity to make relevant decisions can be resolved.
- **Chapter 16** summarises how the laws about data protection and freedom of information relate to the provisions of the Act.

What is the legal status of the Code

Where does it apply?

The Act and therefore this Code applies to everyone it concerns who is habitually resident or present in England and Wales. However, it will also be possible for the Court of Protection to consider cases which involve persons who have assets or property outside this jurisdiction, or who live abroad but have assets or property in England or Wales.

What happens if people don't comply with it?

There are no specific sanctions for failure to comply with the Code. But a failure to comply with the Code can be used in evidence before a court or tribunal in any civil or criminal proceedings, if the court or tribunal considers it to be relevant to those proceedings. For example, if a court or tribunal believes that anyone making decisions for someone who lacks capacity has not acted in the best interests of the person they care for, the court can use the person's failure to comply with the Code as evidence. That's why it's important that anyone working with or caring for a person who lacks capacity to make specific decisions should become familiar with the Code.

Where can I find out more?

The Code of Practice is not an exhaustive guide or complete statement of the law. Other materials have been produced by the Department for Constitutional Affairs, the Department of Health and the Office of the Public Guardian to help explain aspects of the Act from different perspectives and for people in different situations. These include guides for family carers and other carers and basic information of interest to the general public. Professional organisations may also produce specialist information and guidance for their members.

The Code also provides information on where to get more detailed guidance from other sources. A list of contact details is provided in Annex A and further information appears in the footnotes to each chapter. References made and any links provided to material or organisations do not form part of the Code and do not attract the same legal status. Signposts to further information are provided for assistance only and references made should not suggest that the Department for Constitutional Affairs endorses such material.

Using the code

References in the Code of Practice

Throughout the Code of Practice, the Mental Capacity Act 2005 is referred to as 'the Act' and any sections quoted refer to this Act unless otherwise stated. References are shown as follows: section 4(1). This refers to the section of the Act. The subsection number is in brackets.

Where reference is made to provisions from other legislation, the full title of the relevant Act will be set out, for example 'the Mental Health Act 1983', unless otherwise stated. (For example, in chapter 13, the Mental Health Act 1983 is referred to as MHA and the Mental Capacity Act as MCA.) The Code of Practice is sometimes referred to as the Code.

Scenarios used in the Code of Practice

The Code includes many boxes within the text in which there are scenarios, using imaginary characters and situations. These are intended to help illustrate what is meant in the main text. The scenarios should not in any way be taken as templates for decisions that need to be made in similar situations.

Alternative formats and further information

The Code is also available in Welsh and can be made available in other formats on request.

CONTENTS

What does the Act say about the Code of Practice?

2 What are the statutory principles and how should they be applied?

Quick summary
What is the role of the statutory principles?
How should the statutory principles be applied?
Principle 1: *'A person must be assumed to have capacity unless it is established that he lacks capacity.'* (*section1*(2))
Principle 2: *'A person is not to be treated as unable to make a decision unless all practicable steps to help him to do so have been taken without success.'* (*section1*(3))
Principle 3: *'A person is not to be treated as unable to make a decision merely because he makes an unwise decision.'* (*section 1*(4))
Principle 4: *'An act done, or decision made, under this Act for or on behalf of a person who lacks capacity must be done, or made, in his best interests.'* (*section 1*(5))
Principle 5: *'Before the act is done, or the decision is made, regard must be had to whether the purpose for which it is needed can be as effectively achieved in a way that is less restrictive of the person's rights and freedom of action.'* (*section 1*(6))

3 How should people be helped to make their own decisions?

Quick summary
How can someone be helped to make a decision?
What happens in emergency situations?
What information should be provided to people and how should it be provided?
What steps should be taken to put a person at ease?
What other ways are there to enable decision-making?

4 How does the Act define a person's capacity to make a decision and how should capacity be assessed

Quick summary
What is mental capacity?
What does the Act mean by 'lack of capacity'?
What safeguards does the Act provide around assessing someone's capacity?
What proof of lack of capacity does the Act require?
What is the test of capacity?
What does the Act mean by 'inability to make a decision'?
What other issues might affect capacity?
When should capacity be assessed?
Who should assess capacity?
What is 'reasonable belief' of lack of capacity?
What other factors might affect an assessment of capacity?
What practical steps should be taken when assessing capacity?
When should professionals be involved?
Are assessment processes confidential?
What if someone refuses to be assessed?
Who should keep a record of assessments?
How can someone challenge a finding of lack of capacity?

5 What does the Act mean when it talks about 'best interests'?

Quick summary
What is the best interests principle and who does it apply to?
What does the Act mean by best interests?
Who can be a decision-maker?
What must be taken into account when trying to work out someone's best interests?
What safeguards does the Act provide around working out someone's best interests?
How does a decision-maker work out what 'all relevant circumstances' are?

A3.1 *The Mental Capacity Act 2005 — Code of Practice*

Key words and phrases used in the Code

Annex A

1 WHAT IS THE MENTAL CAPACITY ACT 2005?

1.1 The Mental Capacity Act 2005 (the Act) provides the legal framework for acting and making decisions on behalf of individuals who lack the mental capacity to make particular decisions for themselves. Everyone working with and/or caring for an adult who may lack capacity to make specific decisions must comply with this Act when making decisions or acting for that person, when the person lacks the capacity to make a particular decision for themselves. The same rules apply whether the decisions are life-changing events or everyday matters.

1.2 The Act's starting point is to confirm in legislation that it should be assumed that an adult (aged 16 or over) has full legal capacity to make decisions for themselves (the right to autonomy) unless it can be shown that they lack capacity to make a decision for themselves at the time the decision needs to be made. This is known as the presumption of capacity. The Act also states that people must be given all appropriate help and support to enable them to make their own decisions or to maximise their participation in any decision-making process.

1.3 The underlying philosophy of the Act is to ensure that any decision made, or action taken, on behalf of someone who lacks the capacity to make the decision or act for themselves is made in their best interests.

1.4 The Act is intended to assist and support people who may lack capacity and to discourage anyone who is involved in caring for someone who lacks capacity from being overly restrictive or controlling. But the Act also aims to balance an individual's right to make decisions for themselves with their right to be protected from harm if they lack capacity to make decisions to protect themselves.

1.5 The Act sets out a legal framework of how to act and make decisions on behalf of people who lack capacity to make specific decisions for themselves. It sets out some core principles and methods for making decisions and carrying out actions in relation to personal welfare, healthcare and financial matters affecting people who may lack capacity to make specific decisions about these issues for themselves.

1.6 Many of the provisions in the Act are based upon existing common law principles (i.e. principles that have been established through decisions made by courts in individual cases). The Act clarifies and improves upon these principles and builds on current good practice which is based on the principles.

1.7 The Act introduces several new roles, bodies and powers, all of which will support the Act's provisions. These include:

- Attorneys appointed under Lasting Powers of Attorney (see chapter 7)
- The new Court of Protection, and court-appointed deputies (see chapter 8)
- Independent Mental Capacity Advocates (see chapter 10).

The roles, bodies and powers are all explained in more depth in the specific chapters of the Code highlighted above.

What decisions are covered by the Act, and what decisions are excluded?

1.8 The Act covers a wide range of decisions made, or actions taken, on behalf of people who may lack capacity to make specific decisions for themselves. These can be decisions about day-to-day matters – like what to wear, or what to buy when doing the weekly shopping – or decisions about major life-changing events, such as whether the person should move into a care home or undergo a major surgical operation.

1.9 There are certain decisions which can never be made on behalf of a person who lacks capacity to make those specific decisions. This is because they are either so personal to the individual concerned, or governed by other legislation.

1.10 Sections 27–29 and 62 of the Act set out the specific decisions which can never be made or actions which can never be carried out under the Act, whether by family members, carers, professionals, attorneys or the Court of Protection. These are summarised below.

Decisions concerning family relationships (section 27)

Nothing in the Act permits a decision to be made on someone else's behalf on any of the following matters:

- consenting to marriage or a civil partnership
- consenting to have sexual relations
- consenting to a decree of divorce on the basis of two years' separation
- consenting to the dissolution of a civil partnership
- consenting to a child being placed for adoption or the making of an adoption order
- discharging parental responsibility for a child in matters not relating to the child's property, or
- giving consent under the Human Fertilisation and Embryology Act 1990.

Mental Health Act matters (section 28)

Where a person who lacks capacity to consent is currently detained and being treated under Part 4 of the Mental Health Act 1983, nothing in the Act authorises anyone to:

- give the person treatment for mental disorder, or
- consent to the person being given treatment for mental disorder.

Further guidance is given in chapter 13 of the Code.

Voting rights (section 29)

Nothing in the Act permits a decision on voting, at an election for any public office or at a referendum, to be made on behalf of a person who lacks capacity to vote.

Unlawful killing or assisting suicide (section 62)

For the avoidance of doubt, nothing in the Act is to be taken to affect the law relating to murder, manslaughter or assisting suicide.

1.11 Although the Act does not allow anyone to make a decision about these matters on behalf of someone who lacks capacity to make such a decision for themselves (for example, consenting to have sexual relations), this does not prevent action being taken to protect a vulnerable person from abuse or exploitation.

How does the Act relate to other legislation?

1.12 The Mental Capacity Act 2005 will apply in conjunction with other legislation affecting people who may lack capacity in relation to specific matters. This means that healthcare and social care staff acting under the Act should also be aware of their obligations under other legislation, including (but not limited to) the:

- Care Standards Act 2000
- Data Protection Act 1998
- Disability Discrimination Act 1995
- Human Rights Act 1998
- Mental Health Act 1983
- National Health Service and Community Care Act 1990
- Human Tissue Act 2004.

What does the Act say about the Code of Practice?

1.13 Section 42 of the Act sets out the purpose of the Code of Practice, which is to provide guidance for specific people in specific circumstances. Section 43 explains the procedures that had to be followed in preparing the Code and consulting on its contents, and for its consideration by Parliament.

Section 42, subsections (4) and (5), set out the categories of people who are placed under a legal duty to 'have regard to' the Code and gives further information about the status of the Code. More details can be found in the Introduction, which explains the legal status of the Code.

2 WHAT ARE THE STATUTORY PRINCIPLES AND HOW SHOULD THEY BE APPLIED?

Section 1 of the Act sets out the five 'statutory principles' – the values that underpin the legal requirements in the Act. The Act is intended to be enabling and supportive of people who lack capacity, not restricting or controlling of their lives. It aims to protect people who lack capacity to make particular decisions, but also to maximise their ability to make decisions, or to participate in decision-making, as far as they are able to do so.

The five statutory principles are:

1. A person must be assumed to have capacity unless it is established that they lack capacity.
2. A person is not to be treated as unable to make a decision unless all practicable steps to help him to do so have been taken without success.
3. A person is not to be treated as unable to make a decision merely because he makes an unwise decision.
4. An act done, or decision made, under this Act for or on behalf of a person who lacks capacity must be done, or made, in his best interests.
5. Before the act is done, or the decision is made, regard must be had to whether the purpose for which it is needed can be as effectively achieved in a way that is less restrictive of the person's rights and freedom of action.

This chapter provides guidance on how people should interpret and apply the statutory principles when using the Act. Following the principles and applying them to the Act's framework for decision-making will help to ensure not only that appropriate action is taken in individual cases, but also to point the way to solutions in difficult or uncertain situations.

In this chapter, as throughout the Code, a person's capacity (or lack of capacity) refers specifically to their capacity to make a particular decision at the time it needs to be made.

Quick summary

- Every adult has the right to make their own decisions if they have the capacity to do so. Family carers and healthcare or social care staff must assume that a person has the capacity to make decisions, unless it can be established that the person does not have capacity.
- People should receive support to help them make their own decisions. Before concluding that individuals lack capacity to make a particular decision, it is important to take all possible steps to try to help them reach a decision themselves.
- People have the right to make decisions that others might think are unwise. A person who makes a decision that others think is unwise should not automatically be labelled as lacking the capacity to make a decision.
- Any act done for, or any decision made on behalf of, someone who lacks capacity must be in their best interests.
- Any act done for, or any decision made on behalf of, someone who lacks capacity should be an option that is less restrictive of their basic rights and freedoms – as long as it is still in their best interests.

What is the role of the statutory principles?

2.1 The statutory principles aim to:

- protect people who lack capacity and
- help them take part, as much as possible, in decisions that affect them.

They aim to assist and support people who may lack capacity to make particular decisions, not to restrict or control their lives.

2.2 The statutory principles apply to any act done or decision made under the Act. When followed and applied to the Act's decision-making framework, they will help people take appropriate action in individual cases. They will also help people find solutions in difficult or uncertain situations.

How should the statutory principles be applied?

Principle 1: *'A person must be assumed to have capacity unless it is established that he lacks capacity.'* (*section1*(2))

2.3 This principle states that every adult has the right to make their own decisions – unless there is proof that they lack the capacity to make a particular decision when it needs to be made. This has been a fundamental principle of the common law for many years and it is now set out in the Act.

2.4 It is important to balance people's right to make a decision with their right to safety and protection when they can't make decisions to protect themselves. But the starting assumption must always be that an individual has the capacity, until there is proof that they do not. Chapter 4 explains the Act's definition of 'lack of capacity' and the processes involved in assessing capacity.

Scenario: Assessing a person's capacity to make decisions

When planning for her retirement, Mrs Arnold made and registered a Lasting Power of Attorney (LPA) – a legal process that would allow her son to manage her property and financial affairs if she ever lacked capacity to manage them herself. She has now been diagnosed with dementia, and her son is worried that she is becoming confused about money.

Her son must assume that his mother has capacity to manage her affairs. Then he must consider each of Mrs Arnold's financial decisions as she makes them, giving her any help and support she needs to make these decisions herself.

Mrs Arnold's son goes shopping with her, and he sees she is quite capable of finding goods and making sure she gets the correct change. But when she needs to make decisions about her investments, Mrs Arnold gets confused – even though she has made such decisions in the past. She still doesn't understand after her son explains the different options.

Her son concludes that she has capacity to deal with everyday financial matters but not more difficult affairs at this time. Therefore, he is able to use the LPA for the difficult financial decisions his mother can't make. But Mrs Arnold can continue to deal with her other affairs for as long as she has capacity to do so.

2.5 Some people may need help to be able to make a decision or to communicate their decision. However, this does not necessarily mean that they cannot make that decision – unless there is proof that they do lack capacity to do so. Anyone who believes that a person lacks capacity should be able to prove their case. Chapter 4 explains the standard of proof required.

Principle 2: '*A person is not to be treated as unable to make a decision unless all practicable steps to help him to do so have been taken without success.*' (*section1*(*3*))

2.6 It is important to do everything practical (the Act uses the term 'practicable') to help a person make a decision for themselves before concluding that they lack capacity to do so. People with an illness or disability affecting their ability to make a decision should receive support to help them make as many decisions as they can. This principle aims to stop people being automatically labelled as lacking capacity to make particular decisions. Because it encourages individuals to play as big a role as possible in decision-making, it also helps prevent unnecessary interventions in their lives.

2.7 The kind of support people might need to help them make a decision varies. It depends on personal circumstances, the kind of decision that has to be made and the time available to make the decision. It might include:

- using a different form of communication (for example, non-verbal communication)
- providing information in a more accessible form (for example, photographs, drawings, or tapes)
- treating a medical condition which may be affecting the person's capacity or
- having a structured programme to improve a person's capacity to make particular decisions (for example, helping a person with learning disabilities to learn new skills).

Chapter 3 gives more information on ways to help people make decisions for themselves.

Scenario: Taking steps to help people make decisions for themselves

Mr Jackson is brought into hospital following a traffic accident. He is conscious but in shock. He cannot speak and is clearly in distress, making noises and gestures.

From his behaviour, hospital staff conclude that Mr Jackson currently lacks the capacity to make decisions about treatment for his injuries, and they give him urgent treatment. They hope that after he has recovered from the shock they can use an advocate to help explain things to him.

However, one of the nurses thinks she recognises some of his gestures as sign language, and tries signing to him. Mr Jackson immediately becomes calmer, and the doctors realise that he can communicate in sign language. He can also answer some written questions about his injuries.

The hospital brings in a qualified sign-language interpreter and concludes that Mr Jackson has the capacity to make decisions about any further treatment.

2.8 Anyone supporting a person who may lack capacity should not use excessive persuasion or 'undue pressure'.[1] This might include behaving in a manner which is overbearing or dominating, or seeking to influence the person's decision, and could push a person into making a decision they might not otherwise have made. However, it is important to provide appropriate advice and information.

1 Undue influence in relation to consent to medical treatment was considered in *Re T (Adult: Refusal of Treatment)* [1992] 4 All E R 649, 662 and in financial matters in *Royal Bank of Scotland v Etridge* [2001] UKHL 44.

Scenario: Giving appropriate advice and support

Sara, a young woman with severe depression, is getting treatment from mental health services. Her psychiatrist determines that she has capacity to make decisions about treatment, if she gets advice and support.

Her mother is trying to persuade Sara to agree to electro-convulsive therapy (ECT), which helped her mother when she had clinical depression in the past. However, a friend has told Sara that ECT is 'barbaric'.

The psychiatrist provides factual information about the different types of treatment available and explains their advantages and disadvantages. She also describes how different people experience different reactions or side effects. Sara is then able to consider what treatment is right for her, based on factual information rather than the personal opinions of her mother and friend.

2.9 In some situations treatment cannot be delayed while a person gets support to make a decision. This can happen in emergency situations or when an urgent decision is required (for example, immediate medical treatment). In these situations, the only practical and appropriate steps might be to keep a person informed of what is happening and why.

Principle 3: *'A person is not to be treated as unable to make a decision merely because he makes an unwise decision.' (section 1(4))*

2.10 Everybody has their own values, beliefs, preferences and attitudes. A person should not be assumed to lack the capacity to make a decision just because other people think their decision is unwise. This applies even if family members, friends or healthcare or social care staff are unhappy with a decision.

Scenario: Allowing people to make decisions that others think are unwise

Mr Garvey is a 40-year-old man with a history of mental health problems. He sees a Community Psychiatric Nurse (CPN) regularly. Mr Garvey decides to spend £2,000 of his savings on a camper van to travel around Scotland for six months. His CPN is concerned that it will be difficult to give Mr Garvey continuous support and treatment while travelling, and that his mental health might deteriorate as a result.

However, having talked it through with his CPN, it is clear that Mr Garvey is fully aware of these concerns and has the capacity to make this particular decision. He has decided he would like to have a break and thinks this will be good for him.

Just because, in the CPN's opinion, continuity of care might be a wiser option, it should not be assumed that Mr Garvey lacks the capacity to make this decision for himself.

2.11 There may be cause for concern if somebody:

- repeatedly makes unwise decisions that put them at significant risk of harm or exploitation or
- makes a particular unwise decision that is obviously irrational or out of character.

These things do not necessarily mean that somebody lacks capacity. But there might be need for further investigation, taking into account the person's past decisions and choices. For example, have they developed a medical condition or disorder that is affecting their capacity to make particular decisions? Are they easily influenced by undue pressure? Or do they need more information to help them understand the consequences of the decision they are making?

Scenario: Decisions that cause concern

Cyril, an elderly man with early signs of dementia, spends nearly £300 on fresh fish from a door-to-door salesman. He has always been fond of fish and has previously bought small amounts in this way. Before his dementia, Cyril was always very careful with his money and would never have spent so much on fish in one go.

This decision alone may not automatically mean Cyril now lacks capacity to manage all aspects of his property and affairs. But his daughter makes further enquiries and discovers Cyril has overpaid his cleaner on several occasions – something he has never done in the past. He has also made payments from his savings that he cannot account for.

His daughter decides it is time to use the registered Lasting Power of Attorney her father made in the past. This gives her the authority to manage Cyril's property and affairs whenever he lacks the capacity to manage them himself. She takes control of Cyril's chequebook to protect him from possible exploitation, but she can still ensure he has enough money to spend on his everyday needs.

Principle 4: *'An act done, or decision made, under this Act for or on behalf of a person who lacks capacity must be done, or made, in his best interests.'* (*section 1*(*5*))

2.12 The principle of acting or making a decision *in the best interests* of a person who lacks capacity to make the decision in question is a well-established principle in the common law.[2] This principle is now set out in the Act, so that a person's best interests must be the basis for all decisions made and actions carried out on their behalf in situations where they lack capacity to make those particular decisions for themselves. The only exceptions to this are around research (see chapter 11) and advance decisions to refuse treatment (see chapter 9) where other safeguards apply.

[2] See for example *Re MB (Medical Treatment)* [1997] 2 FLR 426, CA; *Re A (Male Sterilisation)* [2000] 1 FLR 549; *Re S (Sterilisation: Patient's Best Interests)* [2000] 2 FLR 389; *Re F (Adult Patient: Sterilisation)* [2001] Fam 15

2.13 It is impossible to give a single description of what 'best interests' are, because they depend on individual circumstances. However, section 4 of the Act sets out a checklist of steps to follow in order to determine what is in the best interests of a person who lacks capacity to make the decision in question each time someone acts or makes a decision on that person's behalf. See chapter 5 for detailed guidance and examples.

Principle 5: *'Before the act is done, or the decision is made, regard must be had to whether the purpose for which it is needed can be as effectively achieved in a way that is less restrictive of the person's rights and freedom of action.' (section 1(6))*

2.14 Before somebody makes a decision or acts on behalf of a person who lacks capacity to make that decision or consent to the act, they must always question if they can do something else that would interfere less with the person's basic rights and freedoms. This is called finding the 'less restrictive alternative'. It includes considering whether there is a need to act or make a decision at all.

2.15 Where there is more than one option, it is important to explore ways that would be less restrictive or allow the most freedom for a person who lacks capacity to make the decision in question. However, the final decision must always allow the original purpose of the decision or act to be achieved.

2.16 Any decision or action must still be in the best interests of the person who lacks capacity. So sometimes it may be necessary to choose an option that is not the least restrictive alternative if that option is in the person's best interests. In practice, the process of choosing a less restrictive option and deciding what is in the person's best interests will be combined. But both principles must be applied each time a decision or action may be taken on behalf of a person who lacks capacity to make the relevant decision.

Scenario: Finding a less restrictive option

Sunil, a young man with severe learning disabilities, also has a very severe and unpredictable form of epilepsy that is associated with drop attacks. These can result in serious injury. A neurologist has advised that, to limit the harm that might come from these attacks, Sunil should either be under constant close observation, or wear a protective helmet.

After assessment, it is decided that Sunil lacks capacity to decide on the most appropriate course of action for himself. But through his actions and behaviour, Sunil makes it clear he doesn't like to be too closely observed – even though he likes having company.

The staff of the home where he lives consider various options, such as providing a special room for him with soft furnishings, finding ways to keep him under close observation or getting him to wear a helmet. In discussion with Sunil's parents, they agree that the option that is in his best interests, and is less restrictive, will be the helmet – as it will enable him to go out, and prevent further harm.

3 HOW SHOULD PEOPLE BE HELPED TO MAKE THEIR OWN DECISIONS?

Before deciding that someone lacks capacity to make a particular decision, it is important to take all practical and appropriate steps to enable them to make that decision themselves (statutory principle 2, see chapter 2). In addition, as section 3(2) of the Act underlines, these steps (such as helping individuals to communicate) must be taken in a way which reflects the person's individual circumstances and meets their particular needs. This chapter provides practical guidance on how to support people to make decisions for themselves, or play as big a role as possible in decision-making.

In this chapter, as throughout the Code, a person's capacity (or lack of capacity) refers specifically to their capacity to make a particular decision at the time it needs to be made.

Quick summary

To help someone make a decision for themselves, check the following points:

PROVIDING RELEVANT INFORMATION

- Does the person have all the relevant information they need to make a particular decision?
- If they have a choice, have they been given information on all the alternatives?

COMMUNICATING IN AN APPROPRIATE WAY

- Could information be explained or presented in a way that is easier for the person to understand (for example, by using simple language or visual aids)?
- Have different methods of communication been explored if required, including non-verbal communication?
- Could anyone else help with communication (for example, a family member, support worker, interpreter, speech and language therapist or advocate)?

MAKING THE PERSON FEEL AT EASE

- Are there particular times of day when the person's understanding is better?
- Are there particular locations where they may feel more at ease?
- Could the decision be put off to see whether the person can make the decision at a later time when circumstances are right for them?

SUPPORTING THE PERSON

- Can anyone else help or support the person to make choices or express a view?

How can someone be helped to make a decision?

3.1 There are several ways in which people can be helped and supported to enable them to make a decision for themselves. These will vary depending on the decision to be made, the time-scale for making the decision and the individual circumstances of the person making it.

3.2 The Act applies to a wide range of people with different conditions that may affect their capacity to make particular decisions. So, the appropriate steps to take will depend on:

- a person's individual circumstances (for example, somebody with learning difficulties may need a different approach to somebody with dementia)
- the decision the person has to make and
- the length of time they have to make it.

3.3 Significant, one-off decisions (such as moving house) will require different considerations from day-to-day decisions about a person's care and welfare. However, the same general processes should apply to each decision.

3.4 In most cases, only some of the steps described in this chapter will be relevant or appropriate, and the list included here is not exhaustive. It is up to the people (whether family carers, paid carers, healthcare staff or anyone else) caring for or supporting an individual to consider what is possible and appropriate in individual cases. In all cases it is extremely important to find the most effective way of communicating with the person concerned. Good communication is essential for explaining relevant information in an appropriate way and for ensuring that the steps being taken meet an individual's needs.

3.5 Providing appropriate help with decision-making should form part of care planning processes for people receiving health or social care services. Examples include:

- Person Centred Planning for people with learning disabilities
- the Care Programme Approach for people with mental disorders
- the Single Assessment Process for older people in England, and
- the Unified Assessment Process in Wales.

What happens in emergency situations?

3.6 Clearly, in emergency medical situations (for example, where a person collapses with a heart attack or for some unknown reason and is brought unconscious into a hospital), urgent decisions will have to be made and immediate action taken in the person's best interests. In these situations, it may not be practical or appropriate to delay the treatment while trying to help the person make their own decisions, or to consult with any known attorneys or deputies. However, even in emergency situations, healthcare staff should try to communicate with the person and keep them informed of what is happening.

What information should be provided to people and how should it be provided?

3.7 Providing relevant information is essential in all decision-making. For example, to make a choice about what they want for breakfast, people need to know what food is available. If the decision concerns medical treatment, the doctor must explain the purpose and effect of the course of treatment and the likely consequences of accepting or refusing treatment.

3.8 All practical and appropriate steps must be taken to help people to make a decision for themselves. Information must be tailored to an individual's needs and abilities. It must also be in the easiest and most appropriate form of communication for the person concerned.

What information is relevant?

3.9 The Act cannot state exactly what information will be relevant in each case. Anyone helping someone to make a decision for themselves should therefore follow these steps.

- Take time to explain anything that might help the person make a decision. It is important that they have access to all the information they need to make an informed decision.
- Try not to give more detail than the person needs – this might confuse them. In some cases, a simple, broad explanation will be enough. But it must not miss out important information.
- What are the risks and benefits? Describe any foreseeable consequences of making the decision, and of not making any decision at all.
- Explain the effects the decision might have on the person and those close to them – including the people involved in their care.
- If they have a choice, give them the same information in a balanced way for all the options.
- For some types of decisions, it may be important to give access to advice from elsewhere. This may be independent or specialist advice (for example, from a medical practitioner or a financial or legal adviser). But it might simply be advice from trusted friends or relatives.

Communication – general guidance

3.10 To help someone make a decision for themselves, all possible and appropriate means of communication should be tried.

- Ask people who know the person well about the best form of communication (try speaking to family members, carers, day centre staff or support workers). They may also know somebody the person can communicate with easily, or the time when it is best to communicate with them.
- Use simple language. Where appropriate, use pictures, objects or illustrations to demonstrate ideas.
- Speak at the right volume and speed, with appropriate words and sentence structure. It may be helpful to pause to check understanding or show that a choice is available.
- Break down difficult information into smaller points that are easy to understand. Allow the person time to consider and understand each point before continuing.
- It may be necessary to repeat information or go back over a point several times.
- Is help available from people the person trusts (relatives, friends, GP, social worker, religious or community leaders)? If so, make sure the person's right to confidentiality is respected.
- Be aware of cultural, ethnic or religious factors that shape a person's way of thinking, behaviour or communication. For example, in some cultures it is important to involve the community in decision-making. Some religious beliefs (for example, those of Jehovah's Witnesses or Christian Scientists) may influence the person's approach to medical treatment and information about treatment decisions.
- If necessary, consider using a professional language interpreter. Even if a person communicated in English or Welsh in the past, they may have lost some verbal skills (for example, because of dementia). They may now prefer to communicate in their first language. It is often more appropriate to use a professional interpreter rather than to use family members.

- If using pictures to help communication, make sure they are relevant and the person can understand them easily. For example, a red bus may represent a form of transport to one person but a day trip to another.
- Would an advocate (someone who can support and represent the person) improve communication in the current situation? (See chapters 10 and 15 for more information about advocates.)

Scenario: Providing relevant information

Mrs Thomas has Alzheimer's disease and lives in a care home. She enjoys taking part in the activities provided at the home. Today there is a choice between going to a flower show, attending her usual pottery class or watching a DVD. Although she has the capacity to choose, having to decide is making her anxious.

The care assistant carefully explains the different options. She tells Mrs Thomas about the DVD she could watch, but Mrs Thomas doesn't like the sound of it. The care assistant shows her a leaflet about the flower show. She explains the plans for the day, where the show is being held and how long it will take to get there in the mini-van. She has to repeat this information several times, as Mrs Thomas keeps asking whether they will be back in time for supper. She also tells Mrs Thomas that one of her friends is going on the trip.

At first, Mrs Thomas is reluctant to disturb her usual routine. But the care assistant reassures her she will not lose her place at pottery if she misses a class. With this information, Mrs Thomas can therefore choose whether or not to go on the day trip.

Helping people with specific communication or cognitive problems

3.11 Where people have specific communication or cognitive problems, the following steps can help:

- Find out how the person is used to communicating. Do they use picture boards or Makaton (signs and symbols for people with communication or learning difficulties)? Or do they have a way of communicating that is only known to those close to them?
- If the person has hearing difficulties, use their preferred method of communication (for example, visual aids, written messages or sign language). Where possible, use a qualified interpreter.
- Are mechanical devices such as voice synthesisers, keyboards or other computer equipment available to help?
- If the person does not use verbal communication skills, allow more time to learn how to communicate effectively.
- For people who use non-verbal methods of communication, their behaviour (in particular, changes in behaviour) can provide indications of their feelings.
- Some people may prefer to use non-verbal means of communication and can communicate most effectively in written form using computers or other communication technologies. This is particularly true for those with autistic spectrum disorders.
- For people with specific communication difficulties, consider other types of professional help (for example, a speech and language therapist or an expert in clinical neuropsychology).

Scenario: Helping people with specific communication difficulties

David is a deafblind man with learning disabilities who has no formal communication. He lives in a specialist home. He begins to bang his head against the wall and repeats this behaviour throughout the day. He has not done this before.

The staff in the home are worried and discuss ways to reduce the risk of injury. They come up with a range of possible interventions, aimed at engaging him with activities and keeping him away from objects that could injure him. They assess these as less restrictive ways to ensure he is safe. But David lacks the capacity to make a decision about which would the best option.

The staff call in a specialist in challenging behaviour, who says that David's behaviour is communicative. After investigating this further, staff discover he is in pain because of tooth decay. They consult a dentist about how to resolve this, and the dentist decides it is in David's best interests to get treatment for the tooth decay. After treatment, David's head-banging stops.

What steps should be taken to put a person at ease?

3.12 To help put someone at ease and so improve their ability to make a decision, careful consideration should be given to both location and timing.

Location

3.13 In terms of location, consider the following:

- Where possible, choose a location where the person feels most at ease. For example, people are usually more comfortable in their own home than at a doctor's surgery.
- Would the person find it easier to make their decision in a relevant location? For example, could you help them decide about medical treatment by taking them to hospital to see what is involved?
- Choose a quiet location where the discussion can't be easily interrupted.
- Try to eliminate any background noise or distractions (for example, the television or radio, or people talking).
- Choose a location where the person's privacy and dignity can be properly respected.

Timing

3.14 In terms of timing, consider the following:

- Try to choose the time of day when the person is most alert – some people are better in the mornings, others are more lively in the afternoon or early evening. It may be necessary to try several times before a decision can be made.
- If the person's capacity is likely to improve in the foreseeable future, wait until it has done so – if practical and appropriate. For example, this might be the case after treatment for depression or a psychotic episode. Obviously, this may not be practical and appropriate if the decision is urgent.
- Some medication could affect a person's capacity (for example, medication which causes drowsiness or affects memory). Can the decision be delayed until side effects have subsided?
- Take one decision at a time – be careful to avoid making the person tired or confused.
- Don't rush – allow the person time to think things over or ask for clarification, where that is possible and appropriate.

- Avoid or challenge time limits that are unnecessary if the decision is not urgent. Delaying the decision may enable further steps to be taken to assist people to make the decision for themselves.

Scenario: Getting the location and timing right

Luke, a young man, was seriously injured in a road traffic accident and suffered permanent brain damage. He has been in hospital several months, and has made good progress, but he gets very frustrated at his inability to concentrate or do things for himself.

Luke now needs surgical treatment on his leg. During the early morning ward round, the surgeon tries to explain what is involved in the operation. She asks Luke to sign a consent form, but he gets angry and says he doesn't want to talk about it.

His key nurse knows that Luke becomes more alert and capable later in the day. After lunch, she asks him if he would like to discuss the operation again. She also knows that he responds better one-to-one than in a group. So she takes Luke into a private room and repeats the information that the surgeon gave him earlier. He understands why the treatment is needed, what is involved and the likely consequences. Therefore, Luke has the capacity to make a decision about the operation.

Support from other people

3.15 In some circumstances, individuals will be more comfortable making decisions when someone else is there to support them.

- Might the person benefit from having another person present? Sometimes having a relative or friend nearby can provide helpful support and reduce anxiety. However, some people might find this intrusive, and it could increase their anxiety or affect their ability to make a free choice. Find ways of getting the person's views on this, for example, by watching their behaviour towards other people.
- Always respect a person's right to confidentiality.

Scenario: Getting help from other people

Jane has a learning disability. She expresses herself using some words, facial expressions and body language. She has lived in her current community home all her life, but now needs to move to a new group home. She finds it difficult to discuss abstract ideas or things she hasn't experienced. Staff conclude that she lacks the capacity to decide for herself which new group home she should move to.

The staff involve an advocate to help Jane express her views. Jane's advocate spends time with her in different environments. The advocate uses pictures, symbols and Makaton to find out the things that are important to Jane, and speaks to people who know Jane to find out what they think she likes. She then supports Jane to show their work to her care manager, and checks that the new homes suggested for her are able to meet Jane's needs and preferences.

When the care manager has found some suitable places, Jane's advocate visits the homes with Jane. They take photos of the houses to help her distinguish between them. The advocate then uses the photos to help Jane work out which home she prefers. Jane's own feelings can now play an important part in deciding what is in her best interests – and so in the final decision about where she will live.

What other ways are there to enable decision-making?

3.16 There are other ways to help someone make a decision for themselves.

- Many people find it helpful to talk things over with people they trust – or people who have been in a similar situation or faced similar dilemmas. For example, people with learning difficulties may benefit from the help of a designated support worker or being part of a support network.
- If someone is very distressed (for example, following a death of someone close) or where there are long-standing problems that affect someone's ability to understand an issue, it may be possible to delay a decision so that the person can have psychological therapy, if needed.
- Some organisations have produced materials to help people who need support to make decisions and for those who support them. Some of this material is designed to help people with specific conditions, such as Alzheimer's disease or profound learning disability.
- It may be important to provide access to technology. For example, some people who appear not to communicate well verbally can do so very well using computers.

Scenario: Making the most of technology

Ms Patel has an autistic spectrum disorder. Her family and care staff find it difficult to communicate with her. She refuses to make eye contact, and gets very upset and angry when her carers try to encourage her to speak.

One member of staff notices that Ms Patel is interested in the computer equipment. He shows her how to use the keyboard, and they are able to have a conversation using the computer. An IT specialist works with her to make sure she can make the most of her computing skills to communicate her feelings and decisions.

4 HOW DOES THE ACT DEFINE A PERSON'S CAPACITY TO MAKE A DECISION AND HOW SHOULD CAPACITY BE ASSESSED?

This chapter explains what the Act means by 'capacity' and 'lack of capacity'. It provides guidance on how to assess whether someone has the capacity to make a decision, and suggests when professionals should be involved in the assessment.

In this chapter, as throughout the Code, a person's capacity (or lack of capacity) refers specifically to their capacity to make a particular decision at the time it needs to be made.

Quick summary

This checklist is a summary of points to consider when assessing a person's capacity to make a specific decision. Readers should also refer to the more detailed guidance in this chapter and chapters 2 and 3.

PRESUMING SOMEONE HAS CAPACITY

- The starting assumption must always be that a person has the capacity to make a decision, unless it can be established that they lack capacity.

UNDERSTANDING WHAT IS MEANT BY CAPACITY AND LACK OF CAPACITY

- A person's capacity must be assessed specifically in terms of their capacity to make a particular decision at the time it needs to be made.

TREATING EVERYONE EQUALLY

- A person's capacity must not be judged simply on the basis of their age, appearance, condition or an aspect of their behaviour.

SUPPORTING THE PERSON TO MAKE THE DECISION FOR THEMSELVES

- It is important to take all possible steps to try to help people make a decision for themselves (see chapter 2, principle 2, and chapter 3).

ASSESSING CAPACITY

Anyone assessing someone's capacity to make a decision for themselves should use the two-stage test of capacity.

- Does the person have an impairment of the mind or brain, or is there some sort of disturbance affecting the way their mind or brain works? (It doesn't matter whether the impairment or disturbance is temporary or permanent.)
- If so, does that impairment or disturbance mean that the person is unable to make the decision in question at the time it needs to be made?

ASSESSING ABILITY TO MAKE A DECISION

- Does the person have a general understanding of what decision they need to make and why they need to make it?
- Does the person have a general understanding of the likely consequences of making, or not making, this decision?
- Is the person able to understand, retain, use and weigh up the information relevant to this decision?
- Can the person communicate their decision (by talking, using sign language or any other means)? Would the services of a professional (such as a speech and language therapist) be helpful?

ASSESSING CAPACITY TO MAKE MORE COMPLEX OR SERIOUS DECISIONS

- Is there a need for a more thorough assessment (perhaps by involving a doctor or other professional expert)?

What is mental capacity?

4.1 Mental capacity is the ability to make a decision.

- This includes the ability to make a decision that affects daily life – such as when to get up, what to wear or whether to go to the doctor when feeling ill – as well as more serious or significant decisions.

- It also refers to a person's ability to make a decision that may have legal consequences – for them or others. Examples include agreeing to have medical treatment, buying goods or making a will.

4.2 The starting point must always be to assume that a person has the capacity to make a specific decision (see chapter 2, principle 1). Some people may need help to be able to make or communicate a decision (see chapter 3). But this does not necessarily mean that they lack capacity to do so. What matters is their ability to carry out the processes involved in making the decision – and not the outcome.

What does the Act mean by 'lack of capacity'?

4.3 Section 2(1) of the Act states:

> 'For the purposes of this Act, a person lacks capacity in relation to a matter if at the material time he is unable to make a decision for himself in relation to the matter because of an impairment of, or a disturbance in the functioning of, the mind or brain.'

This means that a person lacks capacity if:

- they have an impairment or disturbance (for example, a disability, condition or trauma) that affects the way their mind or brain works, and
- the impairment or disturbance means that they are unable to make a specific decision at the time it needs to be made.

4.4 An assessment of a person's capacity must be based on their ability to make a specific decision at the time it needs to be made, and not their ability to make decisions in general. Section 3 of the Act defines what it means to be unable to make a decision (this is explained in paragraph 4.14 below).

4.5 Section 2(2) states that the impairment or disturbance does not have to be permanent. A person can lack capacity to make a decision at the time it needs to be made even if:

- the loss of capacity is partial
- the loss of capacity is temporary
- their capacity changes over time.

A person may also lack capacity to make a decision about one issue but not about others.

4.6 The Act generally applies to people who are aged 16 or older. Chapter 12 explains how the Act affects children and young people – in particular those aged 16 and 17 years.

What safeguards does the Act provide around assessing someone's capacity?

4.7 An assessment that a person lacks capacity to make a decision must never be based simply on:

- their age
- their appearance
- assumptions about their condition, or
- any aspect of their behaviour. (section 2(3))

4.8 The Act deliberately uses the word 'appearance', because it covers all aspects of the way people look. So for example, it includes the physical characteristics of certain conditions (for example, scars, features linked to Down's syndrome or muscle spasms caused by cerebral palsy) as well as aspects of appearance like skin colour, tattoos and body piercings, or the way people dress (including religious dress).

4.9 The word 'condition' is also wide-ranging. It includes physical disabilities, learning difficulties and disabilities, illness related to age, and temporary conditions (for example, drunkenness or unconsciousness). Aspects of behaviour might include extrovert (for example, shouting or gesticulating) and withdrawn behaviour (for example, talking to yourself or avoiding eye contact).

Scenario: Treating everybody equally

Tom, a man with cerebral palsy, has slurred speech. Sometimes he also falls over for no obvious reason.

One day Tom falls in the supermarket. Staff call an ambulance, even though he says he is fine. They think he may need treatment after his fall.

When the ambulance comes, the ambulance crew know they must not make assumptions about Tom's capacity to decide about treatment, based simply on his condition and the effects of his disability. They talk to him and find that he is capable of making healthcare decisions for himself.

What proof of lack of capacity does the Act require?

4.10 Anybody who claims that an individual lacks capacity should be able to provide proof. They need to be able to show, *on the balance of probabilities*, that the individual lacks capacity to make a particular decision, at the time it needs to be made (section 2(4)). This means being able to show that it is more likely than not that the person lacks capacity to make the decision in question.

What is the test of capacity?

To help determine if a person lacks capacity to make particular decisions, the Act sets out a two-stage test of capacity.

Stage 1: Does the person have an impairment of, or a disturbance in the functioning of, their mind or brain?

4.11 Stage 1 requires proof that the person has an impairment of the mind or brain, or some sort of or disturbance that affects the way their mind or brain works. If a person does not have such an impairment or disturbance of the mind or brain, they will not lack capacity under the Act.

4.12 Examples of an impairment or disturbance in the functioning of the mind or brain may include the following:

- conditions associated with some forms of mental illness
- dementia

- significant learning disabilities
- the long-term effects of brain damage
- physical or medical conditions that cause confusion, drowsiness or loss of consciousness
- delirium
- concussion following a head injury, and
- the symptoms of alcohol or drug use.

Scenario: Assessing whether an impairment or disturbance is affecting someone's ability to make a decision

Mrs Collins is 82 and has had a stroke. This has weakened the left-hand side of her body. She is living in a house that has been the family home for years. Her son wants her to sell her house and live with him.

Mrs Collins likes the idea, but her daughter does not. She thinks her mother will lose independence and her condition will get worse. She talks to her mother's consultant to get information that will help stop the sale. But he says that although Mrs Collins is anxious about the physical effects the stroke has had on her body, it has not caused any mental impairment or affected her brain, so she still has capacity to make her own decision about selling her house.

Stage 2: Does the impairment or disturbance mean that the person is unable to make a specific decision when they need to?

4.13 For a person to lack capacity to make a decision, the Act says their impairment or disturbance must affect their ability to make the specific decision when they need to. But first people must be given all practical and appropriate support to help them make the decision for themselves (see chapter 2, principle 2). Stage 2 can only apply if all practical and appropriate support to help the person make the decision has failed. See chapter 3 for guidance on ways of helping people to make their own decisions.

What does the Act mean by 'inability to make a decision'?

4.14 A person is unable to make a decision if they cannot:

1. understand information about the decision to be made (the Act calls this 'relevant information')
2. retain that information in their mind
3. use or weigh that information as part of the decision-making process, or
4. communicate their decision (by talking, using sign language or any other means). See section 3(1).

4.15 These four points are explained in more detail below. The first three should be applied together. If a person cannot do any of these three things, they will be treated as unable to make the decision. The fourth only applies in situations where people cannot communicate their decision in any way.

Understanding information about the decision to be made

4.16 It is important not to assess someone's understanding before they have been given relevant information about a decision. Every effort must be made to provide information in a way that is most appropriate to help the person to understand. Quick or inadequate explanations are not acceptable unless the situation is urgent (see chapter 3 for some practical steps). Relevant information includes:

- the nature of the decision
- the reason why the decision is needed, and
- the likely effects of deciding one way or another, or making no decision at all.

4.17 Section 3(2) outlines the need to present information in a way that is appropriate to meet the individual's needs and circumstances. It also stresses the importance of explaining information using the most effective form of communication for that person (such as simple language, sign language, visual representations, computer support or any other means).

4.18 For example:

- a person with a learning disability may need somebody to read information to them. They might also need illustrations to help them to understand what is happening. Or they might stop the reader to ask what things mean. It might also be helpful for them to discuss information with an advocate.
- a person with anxiety or depression may find it difficult to reach a decision about treatment in a group meeting with professionals. They may prefer to read the relevant documents in private. This way they can come to a conclusion alone, and ask for help if necessary.
- someone who has a brain injury might need to be given information several times. It will be necessary to check that the person understands the information. If they have difficulty understanding, it might be useful to present information in a different way (for example, different forms of words, pictures or diagrams). Written information, audiotapes, videos and posters can help people remember important facts.

4.19 Relevant information must include what the likely consequences of a decision would be (the possible effects of deciding one way or another) – and also the likely consequences of making no decision at all (section 3(4)). In some cases, it may be enough to give a broad explanation using simple language. But a person might need more detailed information or access to advice, depending on the decision that needs to be made. If a decision could have serious or grave consequences, it is even more important that a person understands the information relevant to that decision.

Scenario: Providing relevant information in an appropriate format

Mr Leslie has learning disabilities and has developed an irregular heartbeat. He has been prescribed medication for this, but is anxious about having regular blood tests to check his medication levels. His doctor gives him a leaflet to explain:

- the reason for the tests
- what a blood test involves
- the risks in having or not having the tests, and
- that he has the right to decide whether or not to have the test.

The leaflet uses simple language and photographs to explain these things. Mr Leslie's carer helps him read the leaflet over the next few days, and checks that he understands it.

Mr Leslie goes back to tell the doctor that, even though he is scared of needles, he will agree to the blood tests so that he can get the right medication. He is able to pick out the equipment needed to do the blood test. So the doctor concludes that Mr Leslie can understand, retain and use the relevant information and therefore has the capacity to make the decision to have the test.

Retaining information

4.20 The person must be able to hold the information in their mind long enough to use it to make an effective decision. But section 3(3) states that people who can only retain information for a short while must not automatically be assumed to lack the capacity to decide – it depends on what is necessary for the decision in question. Items such as notebooks, photographs, posters, videos and voice recorders can help people record and retain information.

Scenario: Assessing a person's ability to retain information

Walter, an elderly man, is diagnosed with dementia and has problems remembering things in the short term. He can't always remember his great-grandchildren's names, but he recognises them when they come to visit. He can also pick them out on photographs.

Walter would like to buy premium bonds (a type of financial investment) for each of his great-grandchildren. He asks his solicitor to make the arrangements. After assessing his capacity to make financial decisions, the solicitor is satisfied that Walter has capacity to make this decision, despite his short-term memory problems.

Using or weighing information as part of the decision-making process

4.21 For someone to have capacity, they must have the ability to weigh up information and use it to arrive at a decision. Sometimes people can understand information but an impairment or disturbance stops them using it. In other cases, the impairment or disturbance leads to a person making a specific decision without understanding or using the information they have been given.[3]

[3] This issue has been considered in a number of court cases, including *Re MB* [1997] 2 FLR 426; *R v Collins and Ashworth Hospital Authority ex parte Brady* [2001] 58 BMLR 173.

4.22 For example, a person with the eating disorder anorexia nervosa may understand information about the consequences of not eating. But their compulsion not to eat might be too strong for them to ignore. Some people who have serious brain damage might make impulsive decisions regardless of information they have been given or their understanding of it.

Inability to communicate a decision in any way

4.23 Sometimes there is no way for a person to communicate. This will apply to very few people, but it does include:

- people who are unconscious or in a coma, or
- those with the very rare condition sometimes known as 'locked-in syndrome', who are conscious but cannot speak or move at all.

If a person cannot communicate their decision in any way at all, the Act says they should be treated as if they are unable to make that decision.

4.24 Before deciding that someone falls into this category, it is important to make all practical and appropriate efforts to help them communicate. This might call for the involvement of speech and language therapists, specialists in non-verbal communication or other professionals. Chapter 3 gives advice for communicating with people who have specific disabilities or cognitive problems.

4.25 Communication by simple muscle movements can show that somebody can communicate and may have capacity to make a decision.[4] For example, a person might blink an eye or squeeze a hand to say 'yes' or 'no'. In these cases, assessment must use the first three points listed in paragraph 4.14, which are explained in more depth in paragraphs 4.16–4.22.

[4] This was demonstrated in the case *Re AK (Adult Patient) (Medical Treatment: Consent)* [2001] 1 FLR 129

What other issues might affect capacity?

People with fluctuating or temporary capacity

4.26 Some people have fluctuating capacity – they have a problem or condition that gets worse occasionally and affects their ability to make decisions. For example, someone who has manic depression may have a temporary manic phase which causes them to lack capacity to make financial decisions, leading them to get into debt even though at other times they are perfectly able to manage their money. A person with a psychotic illness may have delusions that affect their capacity to make decisions at certain times but disappear at others. Temporary factors may also affect someone's ability to make decisions. Examples include acute illness, severe pain, the effect of medication, or distress after a death or shock. More guidance on how to support someone with fluctuating or temporary capacity to make a decision can be found in chapter 3, particularly paragraphs 3.12–3.16. More information about factors that may indicate that a person may regain or develop capacity in the future can be found at paragraph 5.28.

4.27 As in any other situation, an assessment must only examine a person's capacity to make a particular decision when it needs to be made. It may be possible to put off the decision until the person has the capacity to make it (see also guidance on best interests in chapter 5).

Ongoing conditions that may affect capacity

4.28 Generally, capacity assessments should be related to a specific decision. But there may be people with an ongoing condition that affects their ability to make certain decisions or that may affect other decisions in their life. One decision on its own may make sense, but may give cause for concern when considered alongside others.

4.29 Again, it is important to review capacity from time to time, as people can improve their decision-making capabilities. In particular, someone with an ongoing condition may become able to make some, if not all, decisions. Some people (for example, people with learning disabilities) will learn new skills throughout their life, improving their capacity to make certain decisions. So assessments should be reviewed from time to time. Capacity should always be reviewed:

- whenever a care plan is being developed or reviewed
- at other relevant stages of the care planning process, and
- as particular decisions need to be made.

4.30 It is important to acknowledge the difference between:

- unwise decisions, which a person has the right to make (chapter 2, principle 3), and
- decisions based on a lack of understanding of risks or inability to weigh up the information about a decision.

Information about decisions the person has made based on a lack of understanding of risks or inability to weigh up the information can form part of a capacity assessment – particularly if someone repeatedly makes decisions that put them at risk or result in harm to them or someone else.

Scenario: Ongoing conditions

Paul had an accident at work and suffered severe head injuries. He was awarded compensation to pay for care he will need throughout his life as a result of his head injury. An application was made to the Court of Protection to consider how the award of compensation should be managed, including whether to appoint a deputy to manage Paul's financial affairs. Paul objected as he believed he could manage his life and should be able to spend his money however he liked.

He wrote a list of what he intended to spend his money on. This included fully-staffed luxury properties and holiday villas, cars with chauffeurs, jewellery and various other items for himself and his family. But spending money on all these luxury items would not leave enough money to cover the costs of his care in future years.

The court judged that Paul had capacity to make day-to-day financial decisions, but he did not understand why he had received compensation and what the money was supposed to be used for. Nor did he understand how buying luxuries now could affect his future care. The court therefore decided Paul lacked capacity to manage large amounts of money and appointed a deputy to make ongoing financial decisions relating to his care. But it gave him access to enough funds to cover everyday needs and occasional treats.

What other legal tests of capacity are there?

4.31 The Act makes clear that the definition of 'lack of capacity' and the two-stage test for capacity set out in the Act are 'for the purposes of this Act'. This means that the definition and test are to be used in situations covered by this Act. Schedule 6 of the Act also amends existing laws to ensure that the definition and test are used in other areas of law not covered directly by this Act.

For example, Schedule 6, paragraph 20 allows a person to be disqualified from jury service if they lack the capacity (using this Act's definition) to carry out a juror's tasks.

4.32 There are several tests of capacity that have been produced following judgments in court cases (known as common law tests).[5] These cover:

- capacity to make a will[6]
- capacity to make a gift[7]
- capacity to enter into a contract[8]
- capacity to litigate (take part in legal cases),[9] and
- capacity to enter into marriage.[10]

[5] For details, see British Medical Association & Law Society, *Assessment of Mental Capacity: Guidance for Doctors and Lawyers* (Second edition) (London: BMJ Books, 2004)

6 *Banks v Goodfellow* (1870) LR 5 QB 549
7 *Re Beaney (deceased)* [1978] 2 All ER 595
8 *Boughton v Knight* (1873) LR 3 PD 64
9 *Masterman-Lister v Brutton & Co and Jewell & Home Counties Dairies* [2003] 3 All ER 162 (CA)
10 *Sheffield City Council v E & S* [2005] 1 FLR 965

4.33 The Act's new definition of capacity is in line with the existing common law tests, and the Act does not replace them. When cases come before the court on the above issues, judges can adopt the new definition if they think it is appropriate. The Act will apply to all other cases relating to financial, healthcare or welfare decisions.

When should capacity be assessed?

4.34 Assessing capacity correctly is vitally important to everyone affected by the Act. Someone who is assessed as lacking capacity may be denied their right to make a specific decision – particularly if others think that the decision would not be in their best interests or could cause harm. Also, if a person lacks capacity to make specific decisions, that person might make decisions they do not really understand. Again, this could cause harm or put the person at risk. So it is important to carry out an assessment when a person's capacity is in doubt. It is also important that the person who does an assessment can justify their conclusions. Many organisations will provide specific professional guidance for members of their profession.[11]

11 See for example, British Medical Association & Law Society, *Assessment of Mental Capacity: Guidance for Doctors and Lawyers* (Second edition) (London: BMJ Books, 2004); the Joint Royal Colleges Ambulance Service Liaison Committee Clinical Practice Guidelines (JRCALC, available online at www2.warwick.ac.uk/fac/med/research/hsri/ emergencycare/jrcalc_2006/clinical_guidelines_2006.pdf) and British Psychological Society, *Guidelines on assessing capacity* (BPS, 2006 available online at www.bps.org.uk)

4.35 There are a number of reasons why people may question a person's capacity to make a specific decision:

- the person's behaviour or circumstances cause doubt as to whether they have the capacity to make a decision
- somebody else says they are concerned about the person's capacity, or
- the person has previously been diagnosed with an impairment or disturbance that affects the way their mind or brain works (see paragraphs 4.11–4.12 above), and it has already been shown they lack capacity to make other decisions in their life.

4.36 The starting assumption must be that the person has the capacity to make the specific decision. If, however, anyone thinks a person lacks capacity, it is important to then ask the following questions:

- Does the person have all the relevant information they need to make the decision?
- If they are making a decision that involves choosing between alternatives, do they have information on all the different options?
- Would the person have a better understanding if information was explained or presented in another way?
- Are there times of day when the person's understanding is better?
- Are there locations where they may feel more at ease?
- Can the decision be put off until the circumstances are different and the person concerned may be able to make the decision?
- Can anyone else help the person to make choices or express a view (for example, a family member or carer, an advocate or someone to help with communication)?

4.37 Chapter 3 describes ways to deal with these questions and suggest steps which may help people make their own decisions. If all practical and appropriate steps fail, an assessment will then be needed of the person's capacity to make the decision that now needs to be made.

Who should assess capacity?

4.38 The person who assesses an individual's capacity to make a decision will usually be the person who is directly concerned with the individual at the time the decision needs to be made. This means that different people will be involved in assessing someone's capacity to make different decisions at different times.

For most day-to-day decisions, this will be the person caring for them at the time a decision must be made. For example, a care worker might need to assess if the person can agree to being bathed. Then a district nurse might assess if the person can consent to have a dressing changed.

4.39 For acts of care or treatment (see chapter 6), the assessor must have a 'reasonable belief' that the person lacks capacity to agree to the action or decision to be taken (see paragraphs 4.44–4.45 for a description of reasonable belief).

4.40 If a doctor or healthcare professional proposes treatment or an examination, they must assess the person's capacity to consent. In settings such as a hospital, this can involve the multi-disciplinary team (a team of people from different professional backgrounds who share responsibility for a patient). But ultimately, it is up to the professional responsible for the person's treatment to make sure that capacity has been assessed.

4.41 For a legal transaction (for example, making a will), a solicitor or legal practitioner must assess the client's capacity to instruct them. They must assess whether the client has the capacity to satisfy any relevant legal test. In cases of doubt, they should get an opinion from a doctor or other professional expert.

4.42 More complex decisions are likely to need more formal assessments (see paragraph 4.54 below). A professional opinion on the person's capacity might be necessary. This could be, for example, from a psychiatrist, psychologist, a speech and language therapist, occupational therapist or social worker. But the final decision about a person's capacity must be made by the person intending to make the decision or carry out the action on behalf of the person who lacks capacity – not the professional, who is there to advise.

4.43 Any assessor should have the skills and ability to communicate effectively with the person (see chapter 3). If necessary, they should get professional help to communicate with the person.

Scenario: Getting help with assessing capacity

Ms Dodd suffered brain damage in a road accident and is unable to speak. At first, her family thought she was not able to make decisions. But they soon discovered that she could choose by pointing at things, such as the clothes she wants to wear or the food she prefers. Her behaviour also indicates that she enjoys attending a day centre, but she refuses to go swimming. Her carers have assessed her as having capacity to make these decisions.

Ms Dodd needs hospital treatment but she gets distressed when away from home. Her mother feels that Ms Dodd is refusing treatment by her behaviour, but her father thinks she lacks capacity to say no to treatment that could improve her condition.

The clinician who is proposing the treatment will have to assess Ms Dodd's capacity to consent. He gets help from a member of staff at the day centre who knows Ms Dodd's communication well and also discusses things with her parents. Over several meetings the clinician explains the treatment options to Ms Dodd with the help of the staff member. The final decision about Ms Dodd's capacity rests with the clinician, but he will need to use information from the staff member and others who know Ms Dodd well to make this assessment.

What is 'reasonable belief' of lack of capacity?

4.44 Carers (whether family carers or other carers) and care workers do not have to be experts in assessing capacity. But to have protection from liability when providing care or treatment (see chapter 6), they must have a 'reasonable belief' that the person they care for lacks capacity to make relevant decisions about their care or treatment (section 5 (1)). To have this reasonable belief, they must have taken 'reasonable' steps to establish that that the person lacks capacity to make a decision or consent to an act at the time the decision or consent is needed. They must also establish that the act or decision is in the person's best interests (see chapter 5).

They do not usually need to follow formal processes, such as involving a professional to make an assessment. However, if somebody challenges their assessment (see paragraph 4.63 below), they must be able to describe the steps they have taken. They must also have objective reasons for believing the person lacks capacity to make the decision in question.

4.45 The steps that are accepted as 'reasonable' will depend on individual circumstances and the urgency of the decision. Professionals, who are qualified in their particular field, are normally expected to undertake a fuller assessment, reflecting their higher degree of knowledge and experience, than family members or other carers who have no formal qualifications. See paragraph 4.36 for a list of points to consider when assessing someone's capacity. The following may also be helpful:

- Start by assuming the person has capacity to make the specific decision. Is there anything to prove otherwise?
- Does the person have a previous diagnosis of disability or mental disorder? Does that condition now affect their capacity to make this decision? If there has been no previous diagnosis, it may be best to get a medical opinion.
- Make every effort to communicate with the person to explain what is happening.
- Make every effort to try to help the person make the decision in question.
- See if there is a way to explain or present information about the decision in a way that makes it easier to understand. If the person has a choice, do they have information about all the options?
- Can the decision be delayed to take time to help the person make the decision, or to give the person time to regain the capacity to make the decision for themselves?
- Does the person understand what decision they need to make and why they need to make it?
- Can they understand information about the decision? Can they retain it, use it and weigh it to make the decision?
- Be aware that the fact that a person agrees with you or assents to what is proposed does not necessarily mean that they have capacity to make the decision.

What other factors might affect an assessment of capacity?

4.46 It is important to assess people when they are in the best state to make the decision, if possible. Whether this is possible will depend on the nature and urgency of the decision to be made. Many of the practical steps suggested in chapter 3 will help to create the best environment for assessing capacity. The assessor must then carry out the two stages of the test of capacity (see paragraphs 4.11–4.25 above).

4.47 In many cases, it may be clear that the person has an impairment or disturbance in the functioning of their mind or brain which could affect their ability to make a decision. For example, there might be a past diagnosis of a disability or mental disorder, or there may be signs that an illness is returning. Old assumptions about an illness or condition should be reviewed. Sometimes an illness develops gradually (for example, dementia), and it is hard to know when it starts to affect capacity. Anyone assessing someone's capacity may need to ask for a medical opinion as to whether a person has an illness or condition that could affect their capacity to make a decision in this specific case.

Scenario: Getting a professional opinion

Mr Elliott is 87 years old and lives alone. He has poor short-term memory, and he often forgets to eat. He also sometimes neglects his personal hygiene. His daughter talks to him about the possibility of moving into residential care. She decides that he understands the reasons for her concerns as well as the risks of continuing to live alone and, having weighed these up, he has the capacity to decide to stay at home and accept the consequences.

Two months later, Mr Elliott has a fall and breaks his leg. While being treated in hospital, he becomes confused and depressed. He says he wants to go home, but the staff think that the deterioration in his mental health has affected his capacity to make this decision at this time. They think he cannot understand the consequences or weigh up the risks he faces if he goes home. They refer him to a specialist in old age psychiatry, who assesses whether his mental health is affecting his capacity to make this decision. The staff will then use the specialist's opinion to help their assessment of Mr Elliott's capacity.

4.48 Anyone assessing someone's capacity must not assume that a person lacks capacity simply because they have a particular diagnosis or condition. There must be proof that the diagnosed illness or condition affects the ability to make a decision when it needs to be made. The person assessing capacity should ask the following questions:

- Does the person have a general understanding of what decision they need to make and why they need to make it?
- Do they understand the likely consequences of making, or not making, this decision?
- Can they understand and process information about the decision? And can they use it to help them make a decision?

In borderline cases, or where there is doubt, the assessor must be able to show that it is more likely than not that the answer to these questions is 'no'.

What practical steps should be taken when assessing capacity?

4.49 Anyone assessing someone's capacity will need to decide which of these steps are relevant to their situation.

- They should make sure that they understand the nature and effect of the decision to be made themselves. They may need access to relevant documents and background information (for example, details of the person's finances if assessing capacity to manage affairs). See chapter 16 for details on access to information.
- They may need other relevant information to support the assessment (for example, healthcare records or the views of staff involved in the person's care).
- Family members and close friends may be able to provide valuable background information (for example, the person's past behaviour and abilities and the types of decisions they can currently make). But their personal views and wishes about what *they* would want for the person must not influence the assessment.
- They should again explain to the person all the information relevant to the decision. The explanation must be in the most appropriate and effective form of communication for that person.
- Check the person's understanding after a few minutes. The person should be able to give a rough explanation of the information that was explained. There are different methods for people who use non-verbal means of communication (for example, observing behaviour or their ability to recognise objects or pictures).
- Avoid questions that need only a 'yes' or 'no' answer (for example, did you understand what I just said?). They are not enough to assess the person's capacity to make a decision. But there may be no alternative in cases where there are major communication difficulties. In these cases, check the response by asking questions again in a different way.
- Skills and behaviour do not necessarily reflect the person's capacity to make specific decisions. The fact that someone has good social or language skills, polite behaviour or good manners doesn't necessarily mean they understand the information or are able to weigh it up.
- Repeating these steps can help confirm the result.

4.50 For certain kinds of complex decisions (for example, making a will), there are specific legal tests (see paragraph 4.32 above) in addition to the two-stage test for capacity. In some cases, medical or psychometric tests may also be helpful tools (for example, for assessing cognitive skills) in assessing a person's capacity to make particular decisions, but the relevant legal test of capacity must still be fulfilled.

When should professionals be involved?

4.51 Anyone assessing someone's capacity may need to get a professional opinion when assessing a person's capacity to make complex or major decisions. In some cases this will simply involve contacting the person's general practitioner (GP) or family doctor. If the person has a particular condition or disorder, it may be appropriate to contact a specialist (for example, consultant psychiatrist, psychologist or other professional with experience of caring for patients with that condition). A speech and language therapist might be able to help if there are communication difficulties. In some cases, a multi-disciplinary approach is best. This means combining the skills and expertise of different professionals.

4.52 Professionals should never express an opinion without carrying out a proper examination and assessment of the person's capacity to make the decision. They must apply the appropriate test of capacity. In some cases, they will need to meet the person more than once – particularly if the person has communication difficulties. Professionals can get background information from a person's family and carers. But the personal views of these people about what they want for the person who lacks capacity must not influence the outcome of that assessment.

4.53 Professional involvement might be needed if:

- the decision that needs to be made is complicated or has serious consequences
- an assessor concludes a person lacks capacity, and the person challenges the finding
- family members, carers and/or professionals disagree about a person's capacity
- there is a conflict of interest between the assessor and the person being assessed
- the person being assessed is expressing different views to different people – they may be trying to please everyone or telling people what they think they want to hear
- somebody might challenge the person's capacity to make the decision – either at the time of the decision or later (for example, a family member might challenge a will after a person has died on the basis that the person lacked capacity when they made the will)
- somebody has been accused of abusing a vulnerable adult who may lack capacity to make decisions that protect them
- a person repeatedly makes decisions that put them at risk or could result in suffering or damage.

Scenario: Involving professional opinion

Ms Ledger is a young woman with learning disabilities and some autistic spectrum disorders. Recently she began a sexual relationship with a much older man, who is trying to persuade her to move in with him and come off the pill. There are rumours that he has been violent towards her and has taken her bankbook.

Ms Ledger boasts about the relationship to her friends. But she has admitted to her key worker that she is sometimes afraid of the man. Staff at her sheltered accommodation decide to make a referral under the local adult protection procedures. They arrange for a clinical psychologist to assess Ms Ledger's understanding of the relationship and her capacity to consent to it.

4.54 In some cases, it may be a legal requirement, or good professional practice, to undertake a formal assessment of capacity. These cases include:

- where a person's capacity to sign a legal document (for example, a will), could later be challenged, in which case an expert should be asked for an opinion[12]
- to establish whether a person who might be involved in a legal case needs the assistance of the Official Solicitor or other litigation friend (somebody to represent their views to a court and give instructions to their legal representative) and there is doubt about the person's capacity to instruct a solicitor or take part in the case[13]
- whenever the Court of Protection has to decide if a person lacks capacity in a certain matter
- if the courts are required to make a decision about a person's capacity in other legal proceedings[14]
- if there may be legal consequences of a finding of capacity (for example, deciding on financial compensation following a claim for personal injury).

12 *Kenward v Adams*, The Times, 29 November 1975
13 Civil Procedure Rules 1998, r 21.1
14 *Masterman-Lister v Brutton & Co and Jewell & Home Counties Dairies* [2002] EWCA Civ 1889, CA at 54

Are assessment processes confidential?

4.55 People involved in assessing capacity will need to share information about a person's circumstances. But there are ethical codes and laws that require professionals to keep personal information confidential. As a general rule, professionals must ask their patients or clients if they can reveal information to somebody else – even close relatives. But sometimes information may be disclosed without the consent of the person who the information concerns (for example, to protect the person or prevent harm to other people).[15]

[15] For example, in the circumstances discussed in *W v Egdell and others* [1990] 1 All ER 835 at 848; *S v Plymouth City Council and C*, [2002] EWCA Civ 388) at 49

4.56 Anyone assessing someone's capacity needs accurate information concerning the person being assessed that is relevant to the decision the person has to make. So professionals should, where possible, make relevant information available. They should make every effort to get the person's permission to reveal relevant information. They should give a full explanation of why this is necessary, and they should tell the person about the risks and consequences of revealing, and not revealing information. If the person is unable to give permission, the professional might still be allowed to provide information that will help make an accurate assessment of the person's capacity to make the specific decision. Chapter 16 has more detail on how to access information.

What if someone refuses to be assessed?

4.57 There may be circumstances in which a person whose capacity is in doubt refuses to undergo an assessment of capacity or refuses to be examined by a doctor or other professional. In these circumstances, it might help to explain to someone refusing an assessment why it is needed and what the consequences of refusal are. But threats or attempts to force the person to agree to an assessment are not acceptable.

4.58 If the person lacks capacity to agree or refuse, the assessment can normally go ahead, as long as the person does not object to the assessment, and it is in their best interests (see chapter 5).

4.59 Nobody can be forced to undergo an assessment of capacity. If someone refuses to open the door to their home, it cannot be forced. If there are serious worries about the person's mental health, it may be possible to get a warrant to force entry and assess the person for treatment in hospital – but the situation must meet the requirements of the Mental Health Act 1983 (section 135). But simply refusing an assessment of capacity is in no way sufficient grounds for an assessment under the Mental Health Act 1983 (see chapter 13).

Who should keep a record of assessments?

4.60 Assessments of capacity to take day-to-day decisions or consent to care require no formal assessment procedures or recorded documentation. Paragraphs 4.44–4.45 above explain the steps to take to reach a 'reasonable belief' that someone lacks capacity to make a particular decision. It is good practice for paid care workers to keep a record of the steps they take when caring for the person concerned.

Professional records

4.61 It is good practice for professionals to carry out a proper assessment of a person's capacity to make particular decisions and to record the findings in the relevant professional records.

- A doctor or healthcare professional proposing treatment should carry out an assessment of the person's capacity to consent (with a multi-disciplinary team, if appropriate) and record it in the patient's clinical notes.

- Solicitors should assess a client's capacity to give instructions or carry out a legal transaction (obtaining a medical or other professional opinion, if necessary) and record it on the client's file.
- An assessment of a person's capacity to consent or agree to the provision of services will be part of the care planning processes for health and social care needs, and should be recorded in the relevant documentation. This includes:
- Person Centred Planning for people with learning disabilities
- the Care Programme Approach for people with mental illness
- the Single Assessment Process for older people in England, and
- the Unified Assessment Process in Wales.

Formal reports or certificates of capacity

4.62 In some cases, a more detailed report or certificate of capacity may be required, for example,

- for use in court or other legal processes
- as required by Regulations, Rules or Orders made under the Act.

How can someone challenge a finding of lack of capacity?

4.63 There are likely to be occasions when someone may wish to challenge the results of an assessment of capacity. The first step is to raise the matter with the person who carried out the assessment. If the challenge comes from the individual who is said to lack capacity, they might need support from family, friends or an advocate. Ask the assessor to:

- give reasons why they believe the person lacks capacity to make the decision, and
- provide objective evidence to support that belief.

4.64 The assessor must show they have applied the principles of the Mental Capacity Act (see chapter 2). Attorneys, deputies and professionals will need to show that they have also followed guidance in this chapter.

4.65 It might be possible to get a second opinion from an independent professional or another expert in assessing capacity. Chapter 15 has other suggestions for dealing with disagreements. But if a disagreement cannot be resolved, the person who is challenging the assessment may be able to apply to the Court of Protection. The Court of Protection can rule on whether a person has capacity to make the decision covered by the assessment (see chapter 8).

5 WHAT DOES THE ACT MEAN WHEN IT TALKS ABOUT 'BEST INTERESTS'?

One of the key principles of the Act is that any act done for, or any decision made on behalf of a person who lacks capacity must be done, or made, in that person's *best interests*. That is the same whether the person making the decision or acting is a family carer, a paid care worker, an attorney, a court-appointed deputy, or a healthcare professional, and whether the decision is a minor issue – like what to wear – or a major issue, like whether to provide particular healthcare.

As long as these acts or decisions are in the best interests of the person who lacks capacity to make the decision for themselves, or to consent to acts concerned with their care or treatment, then the decision-maker or carer will be protected from liability.

There are exceptions to this, including circumstances where a person has made an advance decision to refuse treatment (see chapter 9) and, in specific circumstances, the involvement of a person who lacks capacity in research (see chapter 11). But otherwise the underpinning principle of the Act is that all acts and decisions should be made in the best interests of the person without capacity.

Working out what is in someone else's best interests may be difficult, and the Act requires people to follow certain steps to help them work out whether a particular act or decision is in a person's best interests. In some cases, there may be disagreement about what someone's best interests really are. As long as the person who acts or makes the decision has followed the steps to establish whether a person has capacity, and done everything they reasonably can to work out what someone's best interests are, the law should protect them.

This chapter explains what the Act means by 'best interests' and what things should be considered when trying to work out what is in someone's best interests. It also highlights some of the difficulties that might come up in working out what the best interests of a person who lacks capacity to make the decision actually are.

In this chapter, as throughout the Code, a person's capacity (or lack of capacity) refers specifically to their capacity to make a particular decision at the time it needs to be made.

Quick summary

A person trying to work out the best interests of a person who lacks capacity to make a particular decision ('lacks capacity') should:

ENCOURAGE PARTICIPATION

- do whatever is possible to permit and encourage the person to take part, or to improve their ability to take part, in making the decision

IDENTIFY ALL RELEVANT CIRCUMSTANCES

- try to identify all the things that the person who lacks capacity would take into account if they were making the decision or acting for themselves

FIND OUT THE PERSON'S VIEWS

- try to find out the views of the person who lacks capacity, including:
  - the person's past and present wishes and feelings – these may have been expressed verbally, in writing or through behaviour or habits.
  - any beliefs and values (e.g. religious, cultural, moral or political) that would be likely to influence the decision in question.
  - any other factors the person themselves would be likely to consider if they were making the decision or acting for themselves.

AVOID DISCRIMINATION

- not make assumptions about someone's best interests simply on the basis of the person's age, appearance, condition or behaviour.

ASSESS WHETHER THE PERSON MIGHT REGAIN CAPACITY

- consider whether the person is likely to regain capacity (e.g. after receiving medical treatment). If so, can the decision wait until then?

IF THE DECISION CONCERNS LIFE-SUSTAINING TREATMENT

- not be motivated in any way by a desire to bring about the person's death. They should not make assumptions about the person's quality of life.

CONSULT OTHERS

- if it is practical and appropriate to do so, consult other people for their views about the person's best interests and to see if they have any information about the person's wishes and feelings, beliefs and values. In particular, try to consult:
  - anyone previously named by the person as someone to be consulted on either the decision in question or on similar issues
  - anyone engaged in caring for the person
  - close relatives, friends or others who take an interest in the person's welfare
  - any attorney appointed under a Lasting Power of Attorney or Enduring Power of Attorney made by the person
  - any deputy appointed by the Court of Protection to make decisions for the person.
- For decisions about major medical treatment or where the person should live and where there is no-one who fits into any of the above categories, an Independent Mental Capacity Advocate (IMCA) must be consulted. (See chapter 10 for more information about IMCAs.)
- When consulting, remember that the person who lacks the capacity to make the decision or act for themselves still has a right to keep their affairs private – so it would not be right to share every piece of information with everyone.

AVOID RESTRICTING THE PERSON'S RIGHTS

- see if there are other options that may be less restrictive of the person's rights.

TAKE ALL OF THIS INTO ACCOUNT

- weigh up all of these factors in order to work out what is in the person's best interests.

What is the best interests principle and who does it apply to?

5.1 The best interests principle underpins the Mental Capacity Act. It is set out in section 1(5) of the Act.

> 'An act done, or decision made, under this Act for or on behalf of a person who lacks capacity must be done, or made, in his best interests.'

The concept has been developed by the courts in cases relating to people who lack capacity to make specific decisions for themselves, mainly decisions concerned with the provision of medical treatment or social care.

5.2 This principle covers all aspects of financial, personal welfare and healthcare decision-making and actions. It applies to anyone making decisions or acting under the provisions of the Act, including:

- family carers, other carers and care workers
- healthcare and social care staff
- attorneys appointed under a Lasting Power of Attorney or registered Enduring Power of Attorney
- deputies appointed by the court to make decisions on behalf of someone who lacks capacity, and
- the Court of Protection.

5.3 However, as chapter 2 explained, the Act's first key principle is that people must be assumed to have capacity to make a decision or act for themselves unless it is established that they lack it. That means that working out a person's best interests is only relevant when that person has been assessed as lacking, or is reasonably believed to lack, capacity to make the decision in question or give consent to an act being done.

People with capacity are able to decide for themselves what they want to do. When they do this, they might choose an option that other people don't think is in their best interests. That is their choice and does not, in itself, mean that they lack capacity to make those decisions.

Exceptions to the best interests principle

5.4 There are two circumstances when the best interests principle will not apply. The first is where someone has previously made an advance decision to refuse medical treatment while they had the capacity to do so. Their advance decision should be respected when they lack capacity, even if others think that the decision to refuse treatment is not in their best interests (guidance on advance decisions is given in chapter 9).

The second concerns the involvement in research, in certain circumstances, of someone lacking capacity to consent (see chapter 11).

What does the Act mean by best interests?

5.5 The term 'best interests' is not actually defined in the Act. This is because so many different types of decisions and actions are covered by the Act, and so many different people and circumstances are affected by it.

5.6 Section 4 of the Act explains how to work out the best interests of a person who lacks capacity to make a decision at the time it needs to be made. This section sets out a checklist of common factors that must always be considered by anyone who needs to decide what is in the best interests of a person who lacks capacity in any particular situation. This checklist is only the starting point: in many cases, extra factors will need to be considered.

5.7 When working out what is in the best interests of the person who lacks capacity to make a decision or act for themselves, decision-makers must take into account all relevant factors that it would be reasonable to consider, not just those that they think are important. They must not act or make a decision based on what they would want to do if they were the person who lacked capacity.

Scenario: Whose best interests?

Pedro, a young man with a severe learning disability, lives in a care home. He has dental problems which cause him a lot of pain, but refuses to open his mouth for his teeth to be cleaned.

The staff suggest that it would be a good idea to give Pedro an occasional general anaesthetic so that a dentist can clean his teeth and fill any cavities. His mother is worried about the effects of an anaesthetic, but she hates to see him distressed and suggests instead that he should be given strong painkillers when needed.

While the views of Pedro's mother and carers are important in working out what course of action would be in his best interests, the decision must *not* be based on what would be less stressful for them. Instead, it must focus on Pedro's best interests.

Having talked to others, the dentist tries to find ways of involving Pedro in the decision, with the help of his key worker and an advocate, to try to find out the cause and location of the problem and to explain to him that they are trying to stop the pain. The dentist tries to find out if any other forms of dental care would be better, such as a mouthwash or dental gum.

The dentist concludes that it would be in Pedro's best interests for:

- a proper investigation to be carried out under anaesthetic so that immediate treatment can be provided
- options for his future dental care to be reviewed by the care team, involving Pedro as far as possible.

Who can be a decision-maker?

5.8 Under the Act, many different people may be required to make decisions or act on behalf of someone who lacks capacity to make decisions for themselves. The person making the decision is referred to throughout this chapter, and in other parts of the Code, as the 'decision-maker', and it is the decision-maker's responsibility to work out what would be in the best interests of the person who lacks capacity.

- For most day-to-day actions or decisions, the decision-maker will be the carer most directly involved with the person at the time.
- Where the decision involves the provision of medical treatment, the doctor or other member of healthcare staff responsible for carrying out the particular treatment or procedure is the decision-maker.
- Where nursing or paid care is provided, the nurse or paid carer will be the decision-maker.
- If a Lasting Power of Attorney (or Enduring Power of Attorney) has been made and registered, or a deputy has been appointed under a court order, the attorney or deputy will be the decision-maker, for decisions within the scope of their authority.

5.9 What this means is that a range of different decision-makers may be involved with a person who lacks capacity to make different decisions.

5.10 In some cases, the same person may make different types of decision for someone who lacks capacity to make decisions for themselves. For instance, a family carer may carry out certain acts in caring for the person on a day-to-day basis, but if they are also an attorney, appointed under a Lasting Power of Attorney (LPA), they may also make specific decisions concerning the person's property and affairs or their personal welfare (depending on what decisions the LPA has been set up to cover).

5.11 There are also times when a joint decision might be made by a number of people. For example, when a care plan for a person who lacks capacity to make relevant decisions is being put together, different healthcare or social care staff might be involved in making decisions or recommendations about the person's care package. Sometimes these decisions will be made by a team of healthcare or social care staff as a whole. At other times, the decision will be made by a specific individual within the team. A different member of the team may then implement that decision, based on what the team has worked out to be the person's best interests.

5.12 No matter who is making the decision, the most important thing is that the decision-maker tries to work out what would be in the best interests of the person who lacks capacity.

Scenario: Coming to a joint decision

Jack, a young man with a brain injury, lacks capacity to agree to a rehabilitation programme designed to improve his condition. But the healthcare and social care staff who are looking after him believe that he clearly needs the programme, and have obtained the necessary funding from the Primary Care Trust.

However, Jack's family want to take him home from hospital as they believe they can provide better care for him at home.

A 'best interests' case conference is held, involving Jack, his parents and other family members and the relevant professionals, in order to decide what course of action would be in the Jack's best interests.

A plan is developed to enable Jack to live at home, but attend the day hospital every weekday. Jack seems happy with the proposals and both the family carers and the healthcare and social care staff are satisfied that the plan is in his best interests.

What must be taken into account when trying to work out someone's best interests?

5.13 Because every case – and every decision – is different, the law can't set out all the factors that will need to be taken into account in working out someone's best interests. But section 4 of the Act sets out some common factors that must always be considered when trying to work out someone's best interests. These factors are summarised in the checklist here:

- Working out what is in someone's best interests cannot be based simply on someone's age, appearance, condition or behaviour. (see paragraphs 5.16–5.17).
- All relevant circumstances should be considered when working out someone's best interests (paragraphs 5.18–5.20).
- Every effort should be made to encourage and enable the person who lacks capacity to take part in making the decision (paragraphs 5.21–5.24).
- If there is a chance that the person will regain the capacity to make a particular decision, then it may be possible to put off the decision until later if it is not urgent (paragraphs 5.25–5.28).
- Special considerations apply to decisions about life-sustaining treatment (paragraphs 5.29–5.36).

- The person's past and present wishes and feelings, beliefs and values should be taken into account (paragraphs 5.37–5.48).
- The views of other people who are close to the person who lacks capacity should be considered, as well as the views of an attorney or deputy (paragraphs 5.49–5.55).

It's important not to take shortcuts in working out best interests, and a proper and objective assessment must be carried out on every occasion. If the decision is urgent, there may not be time to examine all possible factors, but the decision must still be made in the best interests of the person who lacks capacity. Not all the factors in the checklist will be relevant to all types of decisions or actions, and in many cases other factors will have to be considered as well, even though some of them may then not be found to be relevant.

5.14 What is in a person's best interests may well change over time. This means that even where similar actions need to be taken repeatedly in connection with the person's care or treatment, the person's best interests should be regularly reviewed.

5.15 Any staff involved in the care of a person who lacks capacity should make sure a record is kept of the process of working out the best interests of that person for each relevant decision, setting out:

- how the decision about the person's best interests was reached
- what the reasons for reaching the decision were
- who was consulted to help work out best interests, and
- what particular factors were taken into account.

This record should remain on the person's file.

For major decisions based on the best interests of a person who lacks capacity, it may also be useful for family and other carers to keep a similar kind of record.

What safeguards does the Act provide around working out someone's best interests?

5.16 Section 4(1) states that anyone working out someone's best interests must not make unjustified assumptions about what their best interests might be simply on the basis of the person's age, appearance, condition or any aspect of their behaviour. In this way, the Act ensures that people who lack capacity to make decisions for themselves are not subject to discrimination or treated any less favourably than anyone else.

5.17 'Appearance' is a broad term and refers to all aspects of physical appearance, including skin colour, mode of dress and any visible medical problems, disfiguring scars or other disabilities. A person's 'condition' also covers a range of factors including physical disabilities, learning difficulties or disabilities, age-related illness or temporary conditions (such as drunkenness or unconsciousness). 'Behaviour' refers to behaviour that might seem unusual to others, such as talking too loudly or laughing inappropriately.

Scenario: Following the checklist

Martina, an elderly woman with dementia, is beginning to neglect her appearance and personal hygiene and has several times been found wandering in the street unable to find her way home. Her care workers are concerned that Martina no longer has capacity to make appropriate decisions relating to her daily care. Her daughter is her personal welfare attorney and believes the time has come to act under the Lasting Power of Attorney (LPA).

She assumes it would be best for Martina to move into a care home, since the staff would be able to help her wash and dress smartly and prevent her from wandering.

However, it cannot be assumed *simply on the basis of her age, condition, appearance or behaviour* either that Martina lacks capacity to make such a decision or that such a move would be in her best interests.

Instead, steps must be taken to assess her capacity. If it is then agreed that Martina lacks the capacity to make this decision, all the relevant factors in the best interests' checklist must be considered to try to work out what her best interests would be.

Her daughter must therefore consider:

- Martina's past and present wishes and feelings
- the views of the people involved in her care
- any alternative ways of meeting her care needs effectively which might be less restrictive of Martina's rights and freedoms, such as increased provision of home care or attendance at a day centre.

By following this process, Martina's daughter can then take decisions on behalf of her mother and in her best interests, when her mother lacks the capacity to make them herself, on any matters that fall under the authority of the LPA.

How does a decision-maker work out what 'all relevant circumstances' are?

5.18 When trying to work out someone's best interests, the decision-maker should try to identify all the issues that would be most relevant to the individual who lacks capacity and to the particular decision, as well as those in the 'checklist'. Clearly, it is not always possible or practical to investigate in depth every issue which may have some relevance to the person who lacks capacity or the decision in question. So relevant circumstances are defined in section 4(11) of the Act as those:

'(a) of which the person making the determination is aware, and
(b) which it would be reasonable to regard as relevant.'

5.19 The relevant circumstances will of course vary from case to case. For example, when making a decision about major medical treatment, a doctor would need to consider the clinical needs of the patient, the potential benefits and burdens of the treatment on the person's health and life expectancy and any other factors relevant to making a professional judgement.[16] But it would not be reasonable to consider issues such as life expectancy when working out whether it would be in someone's best interests to be given medication for a minor problem.

[16] *An Hospital NHS Trust v S* [2003] EWHC 365 (Fam), paragraph 47

5.20 Financial decisions are another area where the relevant circumstances will vary. For example, if a person had received a substantial sum of money as compensation for an accident resulting in brain injury, the decision-maker would have to consider a wide range of circumstances when making decisions about how the money is spent or invested, such as:

- whether the person's condition is likely to change
- whether the person needs professional care, and

- whether the person needs to live somewhere else to make it easier for them.

These kinds of issues can only be decided on a case-by-case basis.

How should the person who lacks capacity be involved in working out their best interests?

5.21 Wherever possible, the person who lacks capacity to make a decision should still be involved in the decision-making process (section 4(4)).

5.22 Even if the person lacks capacity to make the decision, they may have views on matters affecting the decision, and on what outcome would be preferred. Their involvement can help work out what would be in their best interests.

5.23 The decision-maker should make sure that all practical means are used to enable and encourage the person to participate as fully as possible in the decision-making process and any action taken as a result, or to help the person improve their ability to participate.

5.24 Consulting the person who lacks capacity will involve taking time to explain what is happening and why a decision needs to be made. Chapter 3 includes a number of practical steps to assist and enable decision-making which may be also be helpful in encouraging greater participation. These include:

- using simple language and/or illustrations or photographs to help the person understand the options
- asking them about the decision at a time and location where the person feels most relaxed and at ease
- breaking the information down into easy-to-understand points
- using specialist interpreters or signers to communicate with the person.

This may mean that other people are required to communicate with the person to establish their views. For example, a trusted relative or friend, a full-time carer or an advocate may be able to help the person to express wishes or aspirations or to indicate a preference between different options.

More information on all of these steps can be found in chapter 3.

Scenario: Involving someone in working out their best interests

The parents of Amy, a young woman with learning difficulties, are going through a divorce and are arguing about who should continue to care for their daughter. Though she cannot understand what is happening, attempts are made to see if Amy can give some indication of where she would prefer to live.

An advocate is appointed to work with Amy to help her understand the situation and to find out her likes and dislikes and matters which are important to her. With the advocate's help, Amy is able to participate in decisions about her future care.

How do the chances of someone regaining and developing capacity affect working out what is in their best interests?

5.25 There are some situations where decisions may be deferred, if someone who currently lacks capacity may regain the capacity to make the decision for themselves. Section 4(3) of the Act requires the decision-maker to consider:

- whether the individual concerned is likely to regain the capacity to make that particular decision in the future, and
- if so, when that is likely to be.

It may then be possible to put off the decision until the person can make it for themselves.

5.26 In emergency situations – such as when urgent medical treatment is needed – it may *not* be possible to wait to see if the person may regain capacity so they can decide for themselves whether or not to have the urgent treatment.

5.27 Where a person currently lacks capacity to make a decision relating to their day-to-day care, the person may – over time and with the right support – be able to develop the skills to do so. Though others may need to make the decision on the person's behalf at the moment, all possible support should be given to that person to enable them to develop the skills so that they can make the decision for themselves in the future.

Scenario: Taking a short-term decision for someone who may regain capacity

Mr Fowler has suffered a stroke leaving him severely disabled and unable to speak. Within days, he has shown signs of improvement, so with intensive treatment there is hope he will recover over time. But at present both his wife and the hospital staff find it difficult to communicate with him and have been unable to find out his wishes.

He has always looked after the family finances, so Mrs Fowler suddenly discovers she has no access to his personal bank account to provide the family with money to live on or pay the bills. Because the decision can't be put off while efforts are made to find effective means of communicating with Mr Fowler, an application is made to the Court of Protection for an order that allows Mrs Fowler to access Mr Fowler's money.

The decision about longer-term arrangements, on the other hand, can be delayed until alternative methods of communication have been tried and the extent of Mr Fowler's recovery is known.

5.28 Some factors which may indicate that a person may regain or develop capacity in the future are:

- the cause of the lack of capacity can be treated, either by medication or some other form of treatment or therapy
- the lack of capacity is likely to decrease in time (for example, where it is caused by the effects of medication or alcohol, or following a sudden shock)
- a person with learning disabilities may learn new skills or be subject to new experiences which increase their understanding and ability to make certain decisions
- the person may have a condition which causes capacity to come and go at various times (such as some forms of mental illness) so it may be possible to arrange for the decision to be made during a time when they do have capacity

- a person previously unable to communicate may learn a new form of communication (see chapter 3).

How should someone's best interests be worked out when making decisions about life-sustaining treatment?

5.29 A special factor in the checklist applies to decisions about treatment which is necessary to keep the person alive ('life-sustaining treatment') and this is set out in section 4(5) of the Act. The fundamental rule is that anyone who is deciding whether or not life-sustaining treatment is in the best interests of someone who lacks capacity to consent to or refuse such treatment must not be motivated by a desire to bring about the person's death.

5.30 Whether a treatment is 'life-sustaining' depends not only on the type of treatment, but also on the particular circumstances in which it may be prescribed. For example, in some situations giving antibiotics may be life-sustaining, whereas in other circumstances antibiotics are used to treat a non-life-threatening condition. It is up to the doctor or healthcare professional providing treatment to assess whether the treatment is life-sustaining in each particular situation.

5.31 All reasonable steps which are in the person's best interests should be taken to prolong their life. There will be a limited number of cases where treatment is futile, overly burdensome to the patient or where there is no prospect of recovery. In circumstances such as these, it may be that an assessment of best interests leads to the conclusion that it would be in the best interests of the patient to withdraw or withhold life-sustaining treatment, even if this may result in the person's death. The decision-maker must make a decision based on the best interests of the person who lacks capacity. They must not be motivated by a desire to bring about the person's death for whatever reason, even if this is from a sense of compassion. Healthcare and social care staff should also refer to relevant professional guidance when making decisions regarding life-sustaining treatment.

5.32 As with all decisions, before deciding to withdraw or withhold life-sustaining treatment, the decision-maker must consider the range of treatment options available to work out what would be in the person's best interests. All the factors in the best interests checklist should be considered, and in particular, the decision-maker should consider any statements that the person has previously made about their wishes and feelings about life-sustaining treatment.

5.33 Importantly, section 4(5) cannot be interpreted to mean that doctors are under an obligation to provide, or to continue to provide, life-sustaining treatment where that treatment is not in the best interests of the person, even where the person's death is foreseen. Doctors must apply the best interests' checklist and use their professional skills to decide whether life-sustaining treatment is in the person's best interests. If the doctor's assessment is disputed, and there is no other way of resolving the dispute, ultimately the Court of Protection may be asked to decide what is in the person's best interests.

5.34 Where a person has made a written statement in advance that requests particular medical treatments, such as artificial nutrition and hydration (ANH), these requests should be taken into account by the treating doctor in the same way as requests made by a patient who has the capacity to make such decisions. Like anyone else involved in making this decision, the doctor must weigh written statements alongside all other relevant factors to decide whether it is in the best interests of the patient to provide or continue life-sustaining treatment.

5.35 If someone has made an advance decision to refuse life-sustaining treatment, specific rules apply. More information about these can be found in chapter 9 and in paragraph 5.45 below.

5.36 As mentioned in paragraph 5.33 above, where there is any doubt about the patient's best interests, an application should be made to the Court of Protection for a decision as to whether withholding or withdrawing life-sustaining treatment is in the patient's best interests.

How do a person's wishes and feelings, beliefs and values affect working out what is in their best interests?

5.37 Section 4(6) of the Act requires the decision-maker to consider, as far as they are 'reasonably ascertainable':

'(a) the person's past and present wishes and feelings (and in particular, any relevant written statements made by him when he had capacity),
(b) the beliefs and values that would be likely to influence his decision if he had capacity, and
(c) the other factors that he would be likely to consider if he were able to do so.'

Paragraphs 5.38–5.48 below give further guidance on each of these factors.

5.38 In setting out the requirements for working out a person's 'best interests', section 4 of the Act puts the person who lacks capacity at the centre of the decision to be made. Even if they cannot make the decision, their wishes and feelings, beliefs and values should be taken fully into account – whether expressed in the past or now. But their wishes and feelings, beliefs and values will not necessarily be the deciding factor in working out their best interests. Any such assessment must consider past and current wishes and feelings, beliefs and values alongside all other factors, but the final decision must be based entirely on what is in the person's best interests.

Scenario: Considering wishes and feelings as part of best interests

Andre, a young man with severe learning disabilities who does not use any formal system of communication, cuts his leg while outdoors. There is some earth in the wound. A doctor wants to give him a tetanus jab, but Andre appears scared of the needle and pushes it away. Assessments have shown that he is unable to understand the risk of infection following his injury, or the consequences of rejecting the injection.

The doctor decides that it is in the Andre's best interests to give the vaccination. She asks a nurse to comfort Andre, and if necessary, restrain him while she gives the injection. She has objective reasons for believing she is acting in Andre's best interests, and for believing that Andre lacks capacity to make the decision for himself. So she should be protected from liability under section 5 of the Act (see chapter 6).

What is 'reasonably ascertainable'?

5.39 How much someone can learn about a person's past and present views will depend on circumstances and the time available. 'Reasonably ascertainable' means considering all possible information in the time available. What is available in an emergency will be different to what is available in a non-emergency. But even in an emergency, there may still be an opportunity to try to communicate with the person or his friends, family or carers (see chapter 3 for guidance on helping communication).

What role do a person's past and present wishes and feelings play?

5.40 People who cannot express their current wishes and feelings in words may express themselves through their behaviour. Expressions of pleasure or distress and emotional responses will also be relevant in working out what is in their best interests. It is also important to be sure that other people have not influenced a person's views. An advocate could help the person make choices and express their views.

5.41 The person may have held strong views in the past which could have a bearing on the decision now to be made. All reasonable efforts must be made to find out whether the person has expressed views in the past that will shape the decision to be made. This could have been through verbal communication, writing, behaviour or habits, or recorded in any other way (for example, home videos or audiotapes).

5.42 Section 4(6)(a) places special emphasis on written statements the person might have made before losing capacity. These could provide a lot of information about a person's wishes. For example, these statements could include information about the type of medical treatment they would want in the case of future illness, where they would prefer to live, or how they wish to be cared for.

5.43 The decision-maker should consider written statements carefully. If their decision does not follow something a person has put in writing, they must record the reasons why. They should be able to justify their reasons if someone challenges their decision.

5.44 A doctor should take written statements made by a person before losing capacity which request specific treatments as seriously as those made by people who currently have capacity to make treatment decisions. But they would not have to follow a written request if they think the specific treatment would be clinically unnecessary or not appropriate for the person's condition, so not in the person's best interests.

5.45 It is important to note the distinction between a written statement expressing treatment preferences and a statement which constitutes an advance decision to refuse treatment. This is covered by section 24 of the Act, and it has a different status in law. Doctors cannot ignore a written statement that is a valid advance decision to refuse treatment. An advance decision to refuse treatment must be followed if it meets the Act's requirements and applies to the person's circumstances. In these cases, the treatment must not be given (see chapter 9 for more information). If there is not a valid and applicable advance decision, treatment should be provided based on the person's best interests.

What role do beliefs and values play?

5.46 Everybody's values and beliefs influence the decisions they make. They may become especially important for someone who lacks capacity to make a decision because of a progressive illness such as dementia, for example. Evidence of a person's beliefs and values can be found in things like their:

- cultural background
- religious beliefs
- political convictions, or
- past behaviour or habits.

Some people set out their values and beliefs in a written statement while they still have capacity.

Scenario: Considering beliefs and values

Anita, a young woman, suffers serious brain damage during a car accident. The court appoints her father as deputy to invest the compensation she received. As the decision-maker he must think about her wishes, beliefs and values before deciding how to invest the money.

Anita had worked for an overseas charity. Her father talks to her former colleagues. They tell him how Anita's political beliefs shaped her work and personal beliefs, so he decides not to invest in the bonds that a financial adviser had recommended, because they are from companies Anita would not have approved of. Instead, he employs an ethical investment adviser to choose appropriate companies in line with her beliefs.

What other factors should a decision-maker consider?

5.47 Section 4(6)(c) of the Act requires decision-makers to consider any other factors the person who lacks capacity would consider if they were able to do so. This might include the effect of the decision on other people, obligations to dependants or the duties of a responsible citizen.

5.48 The Act allows actions that benefit other people, as long as they are in the best interests of the person who lacks capacity to make the decision. For example, having considered all the circumstances of the particular case, a decision might be made to take a blood sample from a person who lacks capacity to consent, to check for a genetic link to cancer within the family, because this might benefit someone else in the family. But it might still be in the best interests of the person who lacks capacity. 'Best interests' goes beyond the person's medical interests.

For example, courts have previously ruled that possible wider benefits to a person who lacks capacity to consent, such as providing or gaining emotional support from close relationships, are important factors in working out the person's own best interests.[17] If it is likely that the person who lacks capacity would have considered these factors themselves, they can be seen as part of the person's best interests.

[17] See for example *Re Y (Mental Incapacity: Bone marrow transplant)* [1996] 2 FLR 787; *Re A (Male Sterilisation)* [2000] 1 FLR 549

Who should be consulted when working out someone's best interests?

5.49 The Act places a duty on the decision-maker to consult other people close to a person who lacks capacity, where practical and appropriate, on decisions affecting the person and what might be in the person's best interests. This also applies to those involved in caring for the person and interested in the person's welfare. Under section 4(7), the decision-maker has a duty to take into account the views of the following people, where it is practical and appropriate to do so:

- anyone the person has previously named as someone they want to be consulted
- anyone involved in caring for the person

- anyone interested in their welfare (for example, family carers, other close relatives, or an advocate already working with the person)
- an attorney appointed by the person under a Lasting Power of Attorney, and
- a deputy appointed for that person by the Court of Protection.

5.50 If there is no-one to speak to about the person's best interests, in some circumstances the person may qualify for an Independent Mental Capacity Advocate (IMCA). For more information on IMCAs, see chapter 10.

5.51 Decision-makers must show they have thought carefully about who to speak to. If it is practical and appropriate to speak to the above people, they must do so and must take their views into account. They must be able to explain why they did not speak to a particular person – it is good practice to have a clear record of their reasons. It is also good practice to give careful consideration to the views of family carers, if it is possible to do so.

5.52 It is also good practice for healthcare and social care staff to record at the end of the process why they think a specific decision is in the person's best interests. This is particularly important if healthcare and social care staff go against the views of somebody who has been consulted while working out the person's best interests.

5.53 The decision-maker should try to find out:

- what the people consulted think is in the person's best interests in this matter, and
- if they can give information on the person's wishes and feelings, beliefs and values.

5.54 This information may be available from somebody the person named before they lost capacity as someone they wish to be consulted. People who are close to the person who lacks capacity, such as close family members, are likely to know them best. They may also be able to help with communication or interpret signs that show the person's present wishes and feelings. Everybody's views are equally important – even if they do not agree with each other. They must be considered alongside the views of the person who lacks capacity and other factors. See paragraphs 5.62–5.69 below for guidance on dealing with conflicting views.

Scenario: Considering other people's views

Lucia, a young woman with severe brain damage, is cared for at home by her parents and attends a day centre a couple of days each week. The day centre staff would like to take some of the service users on holiday. They speak to Lucia's parents as part of the process of assessing whether the holiday would be in her best interests.

The parents think that the holiday would be good for her, but they are worried that Lucia gets very anxious if she is surrounded by strangers who don't know how to communicate with her. Having tried to seek Lucia's views and involve her in the decision, the staff and parents agree that a holiday would be in her best interests, as long as her care assistant can go with her to help with communication.

5.55 Where an attorney has been appointed under a Lasting Power of Attorney or Enduring Power of Attorney, or a deputy has been appointed by a court, they must make the decisions on any matters they have been appointed to deal with. Attorneys and deputies should also be consulted, if practical and appropriate, on other issues affecting the person who lacks capacity.

For instance, an attorney who is appointed only to look after the person's property and affairs may have information about the person's beliefs and values, wishes and feelings, that could help work out what would be in the person's best interests regarding healthcare or treatment decisions. (See chapters 7 and 8 for more information about the roles of attorneys and deputies.)

How can decision-makers respect confidentiality?

5.56 Decision-makers must balance the duty to consult other people with the right to confidentiality of the person who lacks capacity. So if confidential information is to be discussed, they should only seek the views of people who it is appropriate to consult, where their views are relevant to the decision to be made and the particular circumstances.

5.57 There may be occasions where it is in the person's best interests for personal information (for example, about their medical condition, if the decision concerns the provision of medical treatment) to be revealed to the people consulted as part of the process of working out their best interests (further guidance on this is given in chapter 16). Healthcare and social care staff who are trying to determine a person's best interests must follow their professional guidance, as well as other relevant guidance, about confidentiality.

When does the best interests principle apply?

5.58 Section 1(5) of the Act confirms that the principle applies to any act done, or any decision made, on behalf of someone where there is reasonable belief that the person lacks capacity under the Act. This covers informal day-to-day decisions and actions as well as decisions made by the courts.

Reasonable belief about a person's best interests

5.59 Section 4(9) confirms that if someone acts or makes a decision in the reasonable belief that what they are doing is in the best interests of the person who lacks capacity, then – provided they have followed the checklist in section 4 – they will have complied with the best interests principle set out in the Act. Coming to an incorrect conclusion about a person's capacity or best interests does not necessarily mean that the decision-maker would not get protection from liability (this is explained in chapter 6). But they must be able to show that it was reasonable for them to think that the person lacked capacity and that they were acting in the person's best interests at the time they made their decision or took action.

5.60 Where there is a need for a court decision, the court is likely to require formal evidence of what might be in the person's best interests. This will include evidence from relevant professionals (for example, psychiatrists or social workers). But in most day-to-day situations, there is no need for such formality. In emergency situations, it may not be practical or possible to gather formal evidence.

5.61 Where the court is not involved, people are still expected to have reasonable grounds for believing that they are acting in somebody's best interests. This does not mean that decision-makers can simply impose their own views. They must have objective reasons for their decisions – and they must be able to demonstrate them. They must be able to show they have considered all relevant circumstances and applied all elements of the best interests checklist.

Scenario: Demonstrating reasonable belief

Mrs Prior is mugged and knocked unconscious. She is brought to hospital without any means of identification. She has head injuries and a stab wound, and has lost a lot of blood. In casualty, a doctor arranges an urgent blood transfusion. Because this is necessary to save her life, the doctor believes this is in her best interests.

When her relatives are contacted, they say that Mrs Prior's beliefs meant that she would have refused all blood products. But since Mrs Prior's handbag had been stolen, the doctor had no idea who the woman was nor what her beliefs her. He needed to make an immediate decision and Mrs Prior lacked capacity to make the decision for herself. Therefore he had reasonable grounds for believing that his action was in his patient's best interests – and so was protected from liability.

Now that the doctor knows Mrs Prior's beliefs, he can take them into account in future decisions about her medical treatment if she lacks capacity to make them for herself. He can also consult her family, now that he knows where they are.

What problems could arise when working out someone's best interests?

5.62 It is important that the best interests principle and the statutory checklist are flexible. Without flexibility, it would be impossible to prioritise factors in different cases – and it would be difficult to ensure that the outcome is the best possible for the person who lacks capacity to make the particular decision. Some cases will be straightforward. Others will require decision-makers to balance the pros and cons of all relevant factors.[18] But this flexibility could lead to problems in reaching a conclusion about a person's best interests.

18 *Re A (Male Sterilisation)* [2000] 1 FLR 549

What happens when there are conflicting concerns?

5.63 A decision-maker may be faced with people who disagree about a person's best interests. Family members, partners and carers may disagree between themselves. Or they might have different memories about what views the person expressed in the past. Carers and family might disagree with a professional's view about the person's care or treatment needs.

5.64 The decision-maker will need to find a way of balancing these concerns or deciding between them. The first approach should be to review all elements of the best interests checklist with everyone involved. They should include the person who lacks capacity (as much as they are able to take part) and anyone who has been involved in earlier discussions. It may be possible to reach an agreement at a meeting to air everyone's concerns. But an agreement in itself might not be in the person's best interests. Ultimate responsibility for working out best interests lies with the decision-maker.

Scenario: Dealing with disagreement

Some time ago, Mr Graham made a Lasting Power of Attorney (LPA) appointing his son and daughter as joint attorneys to manage his finances and property. He now has Alzheimer's disease and has moved into private residential care. The son and daughter have to decide what to do with Mr Graham's house.

His son thinks it is in their father's best interests to sell it and invest the money for Mr Graham's future care. But his daughter thinks it is in Mr Graham's best interests to keep the property, because he enjoys visiting and spending time in his old home.

After making every effort to get Mr Graham's views, the family meets to discuss all the issues involved. After hearing other family views, the attorneys agree that it would be in their father's best interests to keep the property for so long as he is able to enjoy visiting it.

Family, partners and carers who are consulted

5.65 If disagreement continues, the decision-maker will need to weigh up the views of different parties. This will depend entirely upon the circumstances of each case, the people involved and their relationship with the person who lacks capacity. Sometimes the decision-maker will find that carers have an insight into how to interpret a person's wishes and feelings that can help them reach a decision.

5.66 At the same time, paid care workers and voluntary sector support workers may have specialist knowledge about up-to-date care options or treatments. Some may also have known the person for many years.

5.67 People with conflicting interests should not be cut out of the process (for example, those who stand to inherit from the person's will may still have a right to be consulted about the person's care or medical treatment). But decision-makers must always ensure that the interests of those consulted do not overly influence the process of working out a person's best interests. In weighing up different contributions, the decision-maker should consider:

- how long an individual has known the person who lacks capacity, and
- what their relationship is.

Scenario: Settling disagreements

Robert is 19 and has learning disabilities and autism. He is about to leave his residential special school. His parents want Robert to go to a specialist unit run by a charitable organisation, but he has been offered a place in a local supported living scheme. The parents don't think Robert will get appropriate care there.

The school sets up a 'best interests' meeting. People who attend include Robert, his parents, teachers from his school and professionals involved in preparing Robert's care plan. Robert's parents and teachers know him best. They set out their views and help Robert to communicate where he would like to live.

Social care staff identify some different placements within the county. Robert visits these with his parents. After further discussion, everyone agrees that a community placement near his family home would be in Robert's best interests.

Settling disputes about best interests

5.68 If someone wants to challenge a decision-maker's conclusions, there are several options:

- Involve an advocate to act on behalf of the person who lacks capacity to make the decision (see paragraph 5.69 below).
- Get a second opinion.
- Hold a formal or informal 'best interests' case conference.
- Attempt some form of mediation (see chapter 15).
- Pursue a complaint through the organisation's formal procedures.

Ultimately, if all other attempts to resolve the dispute have failed, the court might need to decide what is in the person's best interests. Chapter 8 provides more information about the Court of Protection.

Advocacy

5.69 An advocate might be useful in providing support for the person who lacks capacity to make a decision in the process of working out their best interests, if:

- the person who lacks capacity has no close family or friends to take an interest in their welfare, and they do not qualify for an Independent Mental Capacity Advocate (see chapter 10)
- family members disagree about the person's best interests
- family members and professionals disagree about the person's best interests
- there is a conflict of interest for people who have been consulted in the best interests assessment (for example, the sale of a family property where the person lives)
- the person who lacks capacity is already in contact with an advocate
- the proposed course of action may lead to the use of restraint or other restrictions on the person who lacks capacity
- there is a concern about the protection of a vulnerable adult.

6 WHAT PROTECTION DOES THE ACT OFFER FOR PEOPLE PROVIDING CARE OR TREATMENT?

Section 5 of the Act allows carers, healthcare and social care staff to carry out certain tasks without fear of liability. These tasks involve the personal care, healthcare or treatment of people who lack capacity to consent to them. The aim is to give legal backing for acts that need to be carried out in the best interests of the person who lacks capacity to consent.[19]

This chapter explains:

- how the Act provides protection from liability
- how that protection works in practice
- where protection is restricted or limited, and
- when a carer can use a person's money to buy goods or services without formal permission.

[19] The provisions of section 5 are based on the common law 'doctrine of necessity' as set out in *Re F (Mental Patient: Sterilisation)* [1990] 2 AC 1

In this chapter, as throughout the Code, a person's capacity (or lack of capacity) refers specifically to their capacity to make a particular decision at the time it needs to be made.

Quick summary

The following steps list all the things that people providing care or treatment should bear in mind to ensure they are protected by the Act.

ACTING IN CONNECTION WITH THE CARE OR TREATMENT OF SOMEONE WHO LACKS CAPACITY TO CONSENT

- Is the action to be carried out in connection with the care or treatment of a person who lacks capacity to give consent to that act?
- Does it involve major life changes for the person concerned? If so, it will need special consideration.
- Who is carrying out the action? Is it appropriate for that person to do so at the relevant time?

CHECKING WHETHER THE PERSON HAS CAPACITY TO CONSENT

- Have all possible steps been taken to try to help the person make a decision for themselves about the action?
- Has the two-stage test of capacity been applied?
- Are there reasonable grounds for believing the person lacks capacity to give permission?

ACTING IN THE PERSON'S BEST INTERESTS

- Has the best interests checklist been applied and all relevant circumstances considered?
- Is a less restrictive option available?
- Is it reasonable to believe that the proposed act is in the person's best interests?

UNDERSTANDING POSSIBLE LIMITATIONS ON PROTECTION FROM LIABILITY

- If restraint is being considered, is it necessary to prevent harm to the person who lacks capacity, and is it a proportionate response to the likelihood of the person suffering harm – and to the seriousness of that harm?
- Could the restraint be classed as a 'deprivation of the person's liberty'?
- Does the action conflict with a decision that has been made by an attorney or deputy under their powers?

PAYING FOR NECESSARY GOODS AND SERVICES

- If someone wishes to use the person's money to buy goods or pay for services for someone who lacks capacity to do so themselves, are those goods or services necessary and in the person's best interests?
- Is it necessary to take money from the person's bank or building society account or to sell the person's property to pay for goods or services? If so, formal authority will be required.

What protection do people have when caring for those who lack capacity to consent?

6.1 Every day, millions of acts are done to and for people who lack capacity either to:

- take decisions about their own care or treatment, or
- consent to someone else caring for them.

Such acts range from everyday tasks of caring (for example, helping someone to wash) to life-changing events (for example, serious medical treatment or arranging for someone to go into a care home).

In theory, many of these actions could be against the law. Legally, people have the right to stop others from interfering with their body or property unless they give permission. But what happens if someone lacks capacity to give permission? Carers who dress people who cannot dress themselves are potentially interfering with someone's body without their consent, so could theoretically be prosecuted for assault. A neighbour who enters and cleans the house of a person who lacks capacity could be trespassing on the person's property.

6.2 Section 5 of the Act provides 'protection from liability'. In other words, it protects people who carry out these actions. It stops them being prosecuted for acts that could otherwise be classed as civil wrongs or crimes. By protecting family and other carers from liability, the Act allows necessary caring acts or treatment to take place as if a person who lacks capacity to consent had consented to them. People providing care of this sort do not therefore need to get formal authority to act.

6.3 Importantly, section 5 does not give people caring for or treating someone the power to make any other decisions on behalf of those who lack capacity to make their own decisions. Instead, it offers protection from liability so that they can act in connection with the person's care or treatment. The power to make decisions on behalf of someone who lacks capacity can be granted through other parts of the Act (such as the powers granted to attorneys and deputies, which are explained in chapters 7 and 8).

What type of actions might have protection from liability?

6.4 Section 5(1) provides possible protection for actions carried out *in connection with care or treatment*. The action may be carried out on behalf of someone who is believed to lack capacity to give permission for the action, so long as it is in that person's best interests (see chapter 5). The Act does not define 'care' or 'treatment'. They should be given their normal meaning. However, section 64(1) makes clear that treatment includes diagnostic or other procedures.

6.5 Actions that might be covered by section 5 include:

6.4

PERSONAL CARE

- helping with washing, dressing or personal hygiene
- helping with eating and drinking
- helping with communication
- helping with mobility (moving around)
- helping someone take part in education, social or leisure activities
- going into a person's home to drop off shopping or to see if they are alright
- doing the shopping or buying necessary goods with the person's money
- arranging household services (for example, arranging repairs or maintenance for gas and electricity supplies)
- providing services that help around the home (such as homecare or meals on wheels)
- undertaking actions related to community care services (for example, day care, residential accommodation or nursing care) – but see also paragraphs 6.7–6.14 below
- helping someone to move home (including moving property and clearing the former home).

HEALTHCARE AND TREATMENT

- carrying out diagnostic examinations and tests (to identify an illness, condition or other problem)
- providing professional medical, dental and similar treatment
- giving medication
- taking someone to hospital for assessment or treatment
- providing nursing care (whether in hospital or in the community)
- carrying out any other necessary medical procedures (for example, taking a blood sample) or therapies (for example, physiotherapy or chiropody)
- providing care in an emergency.

6.6 These actions only receive protection from liability if the person is reasonably believed to lack capacity to give permission for the action. The action must also be in the person's best interests and follow the Act's principles (see paragraph 6.26 onwards).

6.7 Some acts in connection with care or treatment may cause major life changes with significant consequences for the person concerned. Those requiring particularly careful consideration include a change of residence, perhaps into a care home or nursing home, or major decisions about healthcare and medical treatment. These are described in the following paragraphs.

A change of residence

6.8 Sometimes a person cannot get sufficient or appropriate care in their own home, and they may have to move – perhaps to live with relatives or to go into a care home or nursing home. If the person lacks capacity to consent to a move, the decision-maker(s) must consider whether the move is in the person's best interests (by referring to the best interests checklist in chapter 5 and in particular the person's past and present wishes and feelings, as well as the views of other relevant people). The decision-maker(s) must also consider whether there is a less restrictive option (see chapter 2, principle 5).

This may involve speaking to:

- anyone currently involved in the person's care
- family carers and other family members close to the person and interested in their welfare
- others who have an interest in the person's welfare
- anyone the person has previously named as someone to be consulted, and
- an attorney or deputy who has been legally appointed to make particular decisions on their behalf.

6.9 Some cases will require an Independent Mental Capacity Advocate (IMCA). The IMCA represents and supports the person who lacks capacity and they will provide information to make sure the final decision is in the person's best interests (see chapter 10). An IMCA is needed when there is no-one close to the person who lacks capacity to give an opinion about what is best for them, and:

- an NHS body is proposing to provide serious medical treatment or
- an NHS body or local authority is proposing to arrange accommodation in hospital or a care home or other longer-term accommodation and
  - the person will stay in hospital longer than 28 days, or
  - they will stay in a care home for more than eight weeks.

There are also some circumstances where an IMCA may be appointed on a discretionary basis. More guidance is available in chapter 10.

6.10 Sometimes the final outcome may not be what the person who lacks capacity wanted. For example, they might want to stay at home, but those caring for them might decide a move is in their best interests. In all cases, those making the decision must first consider other options that might restrict the person's rights and freedom of action less (see chapter 2, principle 5).

6.11 In some cases, there may be no alternative but to move the person. Such a move would normally require the person's formal consent if they had capacity to give, or refuse, it. In cases where a person lacks capacity to consent, section 5 of the Act allows carers to carry out actions relating to the move – as long as the Act's principles and the requirements for working out best interests have been followed. This applies even if the person continues to object to the move.

However, section 6 places clear limits on the use of force or restraint by only permitting restraint to be used (for example, to transport the person to their new home) where this is necessary to protect the person from harm and is a proportionate response to the risk of harm (see paragraphs 6.40–6.53). Any action taken to move the person concerned or their property could incur liability unless protected under section 5.

6.12 If there is a serious disagreement about the need to move the person that cannot be settled in any other way, the Court of Protection can be asked to decide what the person's best interests are and where they should live. For example, this could happen if members of a family disagree over what is best for a relative who lacks capacity to give or deny permission for a move.

6.13 In some circumstances, being placed in a hospital or care home may deprive the person of their liberty (see paragraphs 6.49–6.53). If this is the case, there is no protection from liability – even if the placement was considered to be in the best interests of the person (section 6(5)). It is up to the decision-maker to first look at a range of alternative and less restrictive options to see if there is any way of avoiding taking away the person's liberty.

6.14 If there is no alternative way of caring for the person, specific authority will be required to keep the person in a situation which deprives them of their liberty. For instance, sometimes the Court of Protection might be prepared to grant an order of which a consequence is the deprivation of a person's liberty – if it is satisfied that this is in the person's best interests. In other cases, if the person needs treatment for a mental disorder and meets the criteria for detention under the Mental Health Act 1983, this may be used to admit or keep the person in hospital (see chapter 13).

Healthcare and treatment decisions

6.15 Section 5 also allows actions to be taken to ensure a person who lacks capacity to consent receives necessary medical treatment. This could involve taking the person to hospital for out-patient treatment or arranging for admission to hospital. Even if a person who lacks capacity to consent objects to the proposed treatment or admission to hospital, the action might still be allowed under section 5 (but see paragraphs 6.20 and 6.22 below). But there are limits about whether force or restraint can be used to impose treatment (see paragraphs 6.40–6.53).

6.16 Major healthcare and treatment decisions – for example, major surgery or a decision that no attempt is to be made to resuscitate the patient (known as 'DNR' decisions) – will also need special consideration. Unless there is a valid and applicable advance decision to refuse the specific treatment, healthcare staff must carefully work out what would be in the person's best interests (see chapter 5). As part of the process of working this out, they will need to consider (where practical and appropriate):

- the past and present wishes and feelings, beliefs and values of the person who lacks capacity to make the treatment decision, including any advance statement the person wrote setting out their wishes when they had capacity
- the views of anyone previously named by the person as someone to be consulted
- the views of anyone engaged in caring for the person
- the views of anyone interested in their welfare, and
- the views of any attorney or deputy appointed for the person.

In specific cases where there is no-one else available to consult about the person's best interests, an IMCA must be appointed to support and represent the person (see paragraph 6.9 above and chapter 10).

Healthcare staff must also consider whether there are alternative treatment options that might be less intrusive or restrictive (see chapter 2, principle 5). When deciding about the provision or withdrawal of life-sustaining treatment, anyone working out what is in the best interests of a person who lacks capacity must not be motivated by a desire to bring about the person's death (see chapter 5).

6.17 Multi-disciplinary meetings are often the best way to decide on a person's best interests. They bring together healthcare and social care staff with different skills to discuss the person's options and may involve those who are closest to the person concerned. But final responsibility for deciding what is in a person's best interest lies with the member of healthcare staff responsible for the person's treatment. They should record their decision, how they reached it and the reasons for it in the person's clinical notes. As long as they have recorded objective reasons to show that the decision is in the person's best interests, and the other requirements of section 5 of the Act are met, all healthcare staff taking actions in connection with the particular treatment will be protected from liability.

6.18 Some treatment decisions are so serious that the court has to make them – unless the person has previously made a Lasting Power of Attorney appointing an attorney to make such healthcare decisions for them (see chapter 7) or they have made a valid advance decision to refuse the proposed treatment (see chapter 9). The Court of Protection must be asked to make decisions relating to:[20]

- the proposed withholding or withdrawal of artificial nutrition and hydration (ANH) from a patient in a permanent vegetative state (PVS)
- cases where it is proposed that a person who lacks capacity to consent should donate an organ or bone marrow to another person
- the proposed non-therapeutic sterilisation of a person who lacks capacity to consent (for example, for contraceptive purposes)
- cases where there is a dispute about whether a particular treatment will be in a person's best interests.

See paragraphs 8.18–8.24 for more details on these types of cases.

[20] The procedures resulting from those court judgements are set out in a Practice Note from the Official Solicitor (available at www.officialsolicitor.gov.uk) and will be set out in a Practice Direction from the new Court of Protection.

6.19 This last category may include cases that introduce ethical dilemmas concerning untested or innovative treatments (for example, new treatments for variant Creutzfeldt-Jakob Disease (CDJ)) where it is not known if the treatment will be effective, or certain cases involving a termination of pregnancy. It may also include cases where there is conflict between professionals or between professionals and family members which cannot be resolved in any other way.

Where there is conflict, it is advisable for parties to get legal advice, though they may not necessarily be able to get legal aid to pay for this advice. Chapter 8 gives more information about the need to refer cases to court for a decision.

Who is protected from liability by section 5?

6.20 Section 5 of the Act is most likely to affect:

- family carers and other kinds of carers
- care workers
- healthcare and social care staff, and
- others who may occasionally be involved in the care or treatment of a person who lacks capacity to consent (for example, ambulance staff, housing workers, police officers and volunteer support workers).

6.21 At any time, it is likely that several people will be carrying out tasks that are covered by section 5 of the Act. Section 5 does not:

- give one person more rights than another to carry out tasks
- specify who has the authority to act in a specific instance
- allow somebody to make decisions relating to subjects other than the care or treatment of the person who lacks capacity, or
- allow somebody to give consent on behalf of a person who lacks capacity to do so.

6.22 To receive protection from liability under section 5, all actions must be related to the care or treatment of the person who lacks capacity to consent. Before taking action, carers must first reasonably believe that:

- the person lacks the capacity to make that particular decision at the time it needs to be made, and
- the action is in the person's best interests.

This is explained further in paragraphs 6.26–6.34 below.

Scenario: Protecting multiple carers

Mr Rose, an older man with dementia, gets help from several people. His sister sometimes cooks meals for him. A district nurse visits him to change the dressing on a pressure sore, and a friend often takes Mr Rose to the park, guiding him when they cross the road. Each of these individuals would be protected from liability under section 5 of the Act – but only if they take reasonable steps to check that he lacks capacity to consent to the actions they take and hold a reasonable belief that the actions are in Mr Rose's best interests.

6.23 Section 5 may also protect carers who need to use the person's money to pay for goods or services that the person needs but lacks the capacity to purchase for themselves. However, there are strict controls over who may have access to another person's money. See paragraphs 6.56–6.66 for more information.

6.24 Carers who provide personal care services must not carry out specialist procedures that are normally done by trained healthcare staff. If the action involves medical treatment, the doctor or other member of healthcare staff with responsibility for the patient will be the decision-maker who has to decide whether the proposed treatment is in the person's best interests (see chapter 5). A doctor can delegate responsibility for giving the treatment to other people in the clinical team who have the appropriate skills or expertise. People who do more than their experience or qualifications allow may not be protected from liability.

Care planning

6.25 Decisions about a person's care or treatment are often made by a multi-disciplinary team (a team of professionals with different skills that contribute to a person's care), by drawing up a care plan for the person. The preparation of a care plan should always include an assessment of the person's capacity to consent to the actions covered by the care plan, and confirm that those actions are agreed to be in the person's best interests. Healthcare and social care staff may then be able to assume that any actions they take under the care plan are in the person's best interests, and therefore receive protection from liability under section 5. But a person's capacity and best interests must still be reviewed regularly.

What steps should people take to be protected from liability?

6.26 As well as taking the following steps, somebody who wants to be protected from liability should bear in mind the statutory principles set out in section 1 of the Act (see chapter 2).

6.27 First, reasonable steps must be taken to find out whether a person has the capacity to make a decision about the proposed action (section 5(1)(a)). If the person has capacity, they must give their consent for anyone to take an action on their behalf, so that the person taking the action is protected from liability. For guidance on what is classed as 'reasonable steps', see paragraphs 6.29–6.34. But reasonable steps must always include:

- taking all practical and appropriate steps to help people to make a decision about an action themselves, and
- applying the two-stage test of capacity (see chapter 4).

The person who is going to take the action must have a 'reasonable belief' that the individual lacks capacity to give consent for the action at the time it needs to be taken.

6.28 Secondly, the person proposing to take action must have reasonable grounds for believing that the action is in the best interests of the person who lacks capacity. They should apply all elements of the best interests checklist (see chapter 5), and in particular

- consider whether the person is likely to regain capacity to make this decision in the future. Can the action wait until then?
- consider whether a less restrictive option is available (chapter 2, principle 5), and
- have objective reasons for thinking an action is in the best interests of the person who lacks capacity to consent to it.

What is 'reasonable'?

6.29 As explained in chapter 4, anyone assessing a person's capacity to make decisions for themselves or give consent must focus wholly on whether the person has capacity to make a specific decision at the time it needs to be made and not the person's capacity to make decisions generally. For example, a carer helping a person to dress can assess a person's capacity to agree to their help by explaining the different options (getting dressed or staying in nightclothes), and the consequences (being able to go out, or staying in all day).

6.30 Carers do not have to be experts in assessing capacity. But they must be able to show that they have taken *reasonable steps* to find out if the person has the capacity to make the specific decision. Only then will they have *reasonable grounds for believing* the person lacks capacity in relation to that particular matter. See paragraphs 4.44–4.45 for guidance on what is classed as 'reasonable' – although this will vary, depending on circumstances.

6.31 For the majority of decisions, formal assessment processes are unlikely to be required. But in some circumstances, professional practice requires some formal procedures to be carried out (for example, where consent to medical treatment is required, the doctor will need to assess – and record the person's capacity to consent). Under section 5, carers and professionals will be protected from liability as long as they are able to provide some objective reasons that explain why they believe that the person lacks capacity to consent to the action. If somebody challenges their belief, both carers and professionals will be protected from liability as long as they can show that they took steps to find out whether the person has capacity and that they have a reasonable belief that the person lacks capacity.

6.32 Similarly, carers, relatives and others involved in caring for someone who lacks capacity must have *reasonable grounds for believing* that their action is in the person's best interests. They must not simply impose their own views. They must be able to show that they considered all relevant circumstances and applied the best interests checklist. This includes showing that they have tried to involve the person who lacks capacity, and find out their wishes and feelings, beliefs and values. They must also have asked other people's opinions, where practical and appropriate. If somebody challenges their decision, they will be protected from liability if they can show that it was reasonable for them to believe that their action was in the person's best interests – in all the circumstances of that particular case.

6.33 If healthcare and social care staff are involved, their skills and knowledge will affect what is classed as 'reasonable'. For example, a doctor assessing somebody's capacity to consent to treatment must demonstrate more skill than someone without medical training. They should also record in the person's healthcare record the steps they took and the reasons for the finding. Healthcare and social care staff should apply normal clinical and professional standards when deciding what treatments to offer. They must then decide whether the proposed treatment is in the best interests of the person who lacks capacity to consent. This includes considering all relevant circumstances and applying the best interests checklist (see chapter 5).

6.34 Healthcare and social care staff can be said to have 'reasonable grounds for believing' that a person lacks capacity if:

- they are working to a person's care plan, and
- the care planning process involved an assessment of the person's capacity to make a decision about actions in the care plan.

It is also reasonable for them to assume that the care planning process assessed a person's best interests. But they should still make every effort to communicate with the person to find out if they still lack capacity and the action is still in their best interests.

Scenario: Working with a care plan

Margaret, an elderly woman, has serious mental health and physical problems. She lives in a nursing home and a care plan has been prepared by the multi-disciplinary team, in consultation with her relatives in deciding what course of action would be in Margaret's best interests. The care plan covers the medication she has been prescribed, the physiotherapy she needs, help with her personal care and other therapeutic activities such as art therapy.

Although attempts were made to involve Margaret in the care planning process, she has been assessed by the doctor responsible for her care as lacking capacity to consent to most aspects of her care plan. The care plan can be relied on by the nurse or care assistant who administers the medication, by the physiotherapist and art therapist, and also by the care assistant who helps with Margaret's personal care, providing them with reasonable grounds for believing that they are acting in her best interests.

However, as each act is performed, they must all take reasonable steps to communicate with Margaret to explain what they are doing and to ascertain whether she has the capacity to consent to the act in question. If they think she does, they must stop the treatment unless or until Margaret agrees that it should continue.

What happens in emergency situations?

6.35 Sometimes people who lack capacity to consent will require emergency medical treatment to save their life or prevent them from serious harm. In these situations, what steps are 'reasonable' will differ to those in non-urgent cases. In emergencies, it will almost always be in the person's best interests to give urgent treatment without delay. One exception to this is when the healthcare staff giving treatment are satisfied that an advance decision to refuse treatment exists (see paragraph 6.37).

What happens in cases of negligence?

6.36 Section 5 does not provide a defence in cases of negligence – either in carrying out a particular act or by failing to act where necessary. For example, a doctor may be protected against a claim of battery for carrying out an operation that is in a person's best interests. But if they perform the operation negligently, they are not protected from a charge of negligence. So the person who lacks capacity has the same rights in cases of negligence as someone who has consented to the operation.

What is the effect of an advance decision to refuse treatment?

6.37 Sometimes people will make an advance decision to refuse treatment while they still have capacity to do so and before they need that particular treatment. Healthcare staff must respect this decision if it is valid and applies to the proposed treatment.

6.38 If healthcare staff are satisfied that an advance decision is valid and applies to the proposed treatment, they are not protected from liability if they give any treatment that goes against it. But they are protected from liability if they did not know about an advance decision or they are not satisfied that the advance decision is valid and applies in the current circumstances (section 26(2)). See chapter 9 for further guidance.

What limits are there on protection from liability?

6.39 Section 6 imposes some important limitations on acts which can be carried out with protection from liability under section 5 (as described in the first part of this chapter). The key areas where acts might not be protected from liability are where there is inappropriate use of restraint or where a person who lacks capacity is deprived of their liberty.

Using restraint

6.40 Section 6(4) of the Act states that someone is using restraint if they:

- use force – or threaten to use force – to make someone do something that they are resisting, or
- restrict a person's freedom of movement, whether they are resisting or not.

6.41 Any action intended to restrain a person who lacks capacity will not attract protection from liability unless the following two conditions are met:

- the person taking action must reasonably believe that restraint is *necessary* to prevent *harm* to the person who lacks capacity, and
- the amount or type of restraint used and the amount of time it lasts must be a *proportionate response* to the likelihood and seriousness of harm.

See paragraphs 6.44–6.48 for more explanation of the terms *necessary, harm* and a *proportionate response.*

6.42 Healthcare and social care staff should also refer to:

- professional and other guidance on restraint or physical intervention, such as that issued by the Department of Health[21] or Welsh Assembly Government,[22] and
- limitations imposed by regulations and standards, such as the national minimum standards for care services (see chapter 14).

21 For guidance on using restraint with people with learning disabilities and autistic spectrum disorder, see *Guidance for restrictive physical interventions* (published by the Department of Health and Department for Education and Skills and available at www.dh.gov.uk/ assetRoot/04/06/84/61/04068461.pdf).

22 In Wales, the relevant guidance is the Welsh Assembly Government's *Framework for restrictive physical intervention policy and practice* (available at www.childrenfirst.wales. gov.uk/content/framework/phys-int-e.pdf).

6.43 In addition to the requirements of the Act, the common law imposes a duty of care on healthcare and social care staff in respect of all people to whom they provide services. Therefore if a person who lacks capacity to consent has challenging behaviour, or is in the acute stages of illness causing them to act in way which may cause harm to others, staff may, under the common law, take appropriate and necessary action to restrain or remove the person, in order to prevent harm, both to the person concerned and to anyone else.

However, within this context, the common law would not provide sufficient grounds for an action that would have the effect of depriving someone of their liberty (see paragraphs 6.49–6.53).

When might restraint be 'necessary'?

6.44 Anybody considering using restraint must have objective reasons to justify that restraint is necessary. They must be able to show that the person being cared for is likely to suffer harm unless proportionate restraint is used. A carer or professional must not use restraint just so that they can do something more easily. If restraint is necessary to prevent harm to the person who lacks capacity, it must be the minimum amount of force for the shortest time possible.

Scenario: Appropriate use of restraint

Derek, a man with learning disabilities, has begun to behave in a challenging way. Staff at his care home think he might have a medical condition that is causing him distress. They take him to the doctor, who thinks that Derek might have a hormone imbalance. But the doctor needs to take a blood test to confirm this, and when he tries to take the test Derek attempts to fight him off.

The results might be negative – so the test might not be necessary. But the doctor decides that a test is in Derek's best interests, because failing to treat a problem like a hormone imbalance might make it worse. It is therefore in Derek's best interests to restrain him to take the blood test. The temporary restraint is in proportion to the likely harm caused by failing to treat a possible medical condition.

What is 'harm'?

6.45 The Act does not define 'harm', because it will vary depending on the situation. For example,

- a person with learning disabilities might run into a busy road without warning, if they do not understand the dangers of cars
- a person with dementia may wander away from home and get lost, if they cannot remember where they live
- a person with manic depression might engage in excessive spending during a manic phase, causing them to get into debt
- a person may also be at risk of harm if they behave in a way that encourages others to assault or exploit them (for example, by behaving in a dangerously provocative way).

6.46 Common sense measures can often help remove the risk of harm (for example, by locking away poisonous chemicals or removing obstacles). Also, care planning should include risk assessments and set out appropriate actions to try to prevent possible risks. But it is impossible to remove all risk, and a proportionate response is needed when the risk of harm does arise.

What is a 'proportionate response'?

6.47 A 'proportionate response' means using the least intrusive type and minimum amount of restraint to achieve a specific outcome in the best interests of the person who lacks capacity. On occasions when the use of force may be necessary, carers and healthcare and social care staff should use the minimum amount of force for the shortest possible time.

For example, a carer may need to hold a person's arm while they cross the road, if the person does not understand the dangers of roads. But it would not be a proportionate response to stop the person going outdoors at all. It may be appropriate to have a secure lock on a door that faces a busy road, but it would not be a proportionate response to lock someone in a bedroom all the time to prevent them from attempting to cross the road.

6.48 Carers and healthcare and social care staff should consider less restrictive options before using restraint. Where possible, they should ask other people involved in the person's care what action they think is necessary to protect the person from harm. For example, it may be appropriate to get an advocate to work with the person to see if they can avoid or minimise the need for restraint to be used.

Scenario: Avoiding restraint

Oscar has learning disabilities. People at the college he attends sometimes cannot understand him, and he gets frustrated. Sometimes he hits the wall and hurts himself.

Staff don't want to take Oscar out of class, because he says he enjoys college and is learning new skills. They have allowed his support worker to sit with him, but he still gets upset. The support worker could try to hold Oscar back. But she thinks this is too forceful, even though it would stop him hurting himself.

Instead, she gets expert advice from members of the local community team. Observation helps them understand Oscar's behaviour better. They come up with a support strategy that reduces the risk of harmful behaviour and is less restrictive of his freedom.

When are acts seen as depriving a person of their liberty?

6.49 Although section 5 of the Act permits the use of restraint where it is necessary under the above conditions, section 6(5) confirms that there is no protection under the Act for actions that result in someone being deprived of their liberty (as defined by Article 5(1) of the European Convention on Human Rights). This applies not only to public authorities covered by the Human Rights Act 1998 but to everyone who might otherwise get protection under section 5 of the Act. It also applies to attorneys or deputies – they cannot give permission for an action that takes away a person's liberty.

6.50 Sometimes there is no alternative way to provide care or treatment other than depriving the person of their liberty. In this situation, some people may be detained in hospital under the Mental Health Act 1983 – but this only applies to people who require hospital treatment for a mental disorder (see chapter 13). Otherwise, actions that amount to a deprivation of liberty will not be lawful unless formal authorisation is obtained.

6.51 In some cases, the Court of Protection might grant an order that permits the deprivation of a person's liberty, if it is satisfied that this is in a person's best interests.

6.52 It is difficult to define the difference between actions that amount to a restriction of someone's liberty and those that result in a deprivation of liberty. In recent legal cases, the European Court of Human Rights said that the difference was 'one of degree or intensity, not one of nature or substance'.[23] There must therefore be particular factors in the specific situation of the person concerned which provide the 'degree' or 'intensity' to result in a deprivation of liberty. In practice, this can relate to:

- the type of care being provided
- how long the situation lasts
- its effects, or
- the way in a particular situation came about.[24]

23 *HL v The United Kingdom* (Application no, 45508/99). Judgement 5 October 2004, paragraph 89

24 In *HL v UK* (also known as the 'Bournewood' case), the European Court said that "the key factor in the present case [is] that the health care professionals treating and managing the applicant exercised complete and effective control over his care and movements". They found "the concrete situation was that the applicant was under continuous supervision and control and was not free to leave."

The European Court of Human Rights has identified the following as factors contributing to deprivation of liberty in its judgments on cases to date:

- restraint was used, including sedation, to admit a person who is resisting
- professionals exercised complete and effective control over care and movement for a significant period
- professionals exercised control over assessments, treatment, contacts and residence
- the person would be prevented from leaving if they made a meaningful attempt to do so
- a request by carers for the person to be discharged to their care was refused
- the person was unable to maintain social contacts because of restrictions placed on access to other people
- the person lost autonomy because they were under continuous supervision and control.[25]

25 These are listed in the Department of Health's draft illustrative Code of Practice guidance about the proposed safeguards. www.dh.gov.uk/assetRoot/04/14/17/64/04141764.pdf

6.53 The Government has announced that it intends to amend the Act to introduce new procedures and provisions for people who lack capacity to make relevant decisions but who need to be deprived of their liberty, in their best interests, otherwise than under the Mental Health Act 1983 (the so-called 'Bournewood provisions'). This chapter will be fully revised in due course to reflect those changes. Information about the Government's current proposals in respect of the Bournewood safeguards is available on the Department of Health website. This information includes draft illustrative Code of Practice guidance about the proposed safeguards. See paragraphs 13.52–13.55 for more details.

How does section 5 apply to attorneys and deputies?

6.54 Section 5 does not provide protection for actions that go against the decision of someone who has been authorised to make decisions for a person who lacks capacity to make such decision for themselves. For instance, if someone goes against the decision of an attorney acting under a Lasting Power of Attorney (LPA) (see chapter 7) or a deputy appointed by the Court of Protection (see chapter 8), they will not be protected under section 5.

6.55 Attorneys and deputies must only make decisions within the scope of the authority of the LPA or court order. Sometimes carers or healthcare and social care staff might feel that an attorney or deputy is making decisions they should not be making, or that are not in a person's best interests. If this is the case, and the disagreement cannot be settled any other way, either the carers, the staff or the attorney or deputy can apply to the Court of Protection. If the dispute concerns the provision of medical treatment, medical staff can still give life-sustaining treatment, or treatment which stops a person's condition getting seriously worse, while the court is coming to a decision (section 6(6)).

Who can pay for goods or services?

6.56 Carers may have to spend money on behalf of someone who lacks capacity to purchase necessary goods or services. For example, they may need to pay for a milk delivery or for a chiropodist to provide a service at the person's home. In some cases, they might have to pay for more costly arrangements such as house repairs or organising a holiday. Carers are likely to be protected from liability if their actions are properly taken under section 5, and in the best interests of the person who lacks capacity.

6.57 In general, a contract entered into by a person who lacks capacity to make the contract cannot be enforced if the other person knows, or must be taken to have known, of the lack of capacity. Section 7 of the Act modifies this rule and states that where the contract is for 'necessary' goods or services for a person who lacks capacity to make the arrangements for themselves, that person must pay a reasonable price for them.

What are necessary goods and services?

6.58 'Necessary' means something that is suitable to the person's condition in life (their place in society, rather than any mental or physical condition) and their actual requirements when the goods or services are provided (section 7(2)). The aim is to make sure that people can enjoy a similar standard of living and way of life to those they had before lacking capacity. For example, if a person who now lacks capacity previously chose to buy expensive designer clothes, these are still necessary goods – as long as they can still afford them. But they would not be necessary for a person who always wore cheap clothes, no matter how wealthy they were.

6.59 Goods are not necessary if the person already has a sufficient supply of them. For example, buying one or two new pairs of shoes for a person who lacks capacity could be necessary. But a dozen pairs would probably not be necessary.

How should payments be arranged?

6.60 If a person lacks capacity to arrange for payment for necessary goods and services, sections 5 and 8 allow a carer to arrange payment on their behalf.

6.61 The carer must first take reasonable steps to check whether a person can arrange for payment themselves, or has the capacity to consent to the carer doing it for them. If the person lacks the capacity to consent or pay themselves, the carer must decide what goods or services would be necessary for the person and in their best interests. The carer can then lawfully deal with payment for those goods and services in one of three ways:

- If neither the carer nor the person who lacks capacity can produce the necessary funds, the carer may promise that the person who lacks capacity will pay. A supplier may not be happy with this, or the carer may be worried that they will be held responsible for any debt. In such cases, the carer must follow the formal steps in paragraphs 6.62–6.66 below.

- If the person who lacks capacity has cash, the carer may use that money to pay for goods or services (for example, to pay the milkman or the hairdresser).
- The carer may choose to pay for the goods or services with their own money. The person who lacks capacity must pay them back. This may involve using cash in the person's possession or running up an IOU. (This is not appropriate for paid care workers, whose contracts might stop them handling their clients' money.) The carer must follow formal steps to get money held in a bank or building society account (see paragraphs 6.63–6.66 below).

6.62 Carers should keep bills, receipts and other proof of payment when paying for goods and services. They will need these documents when asking to get money back. Keeping appropriate financial records and documentation is a requirement of the national minimum standards for care homes or domiciliary care agencies.

Access to a person's assets

6.63 The Act does not give a carer or care worker access to a person's income or assets. Nor does it allow them to sell the person's property.

6.64 Anyone wanting access to money in a person's bank or building society will need formal legal authority. They will also need legal authority to sell a person's property. Such authority could be given in a Lasting Power of Attorney (LPA) appointing an attorney to deal with property and affairs, or in an order of the Court of Protection (either a single decision of the court or an order appointing a deputy to make financial decisions for the person who lacks capacity to make such decisions).

Scenario: Being granted access to a person's assets

A storm blew some tiles off the roof of a house owned by Gordon, a man with Alzheimer's disease. He lacks capacity to arrange for repairs and claim on his insurance. The repairs are likely to be costly.

Gordon's son decides to organise the repairs, and he agrees to pay because his father doesn't have enough cash available. The son could then apply to the Court of Protection for authority to claim insurance on his father's behalf and for him to be reimbursed from his father's bank account to cover the cost of the repairs once the insurance payment had been received.

6.65 Sometimes another person will already have legal control of the finances and property of a person who lacks capacity to manage their own affairs. This could be an attorney acting under a registered EPA or an appropriate LPA (see chapter 7) or a deputy appointed by the Court of Protection (see chapter 8). Or it could be someone (usually a carer) that has the right to act as an 'appointee' (under Social Security Regulations) and claim benefits for a person who lacks capacity to make their own claim and use the money on the person's behalf. But an appointee cannot deal with other assets or savings from sources other than benefits.

6.66 Section 6(6) makes clear that a family carer or other carer cannot make arrangements for goods or services to be supplied to a person who lacks capacity if this conflicts with a decision made by someone who has formal powers over the person's money and property, such as an attorney or deputy acting within the scope of their authority. Where there is no conflict and the carer has paid for necessary goods and services the carer may ask for money back from an attorney, a deputy or where relevant, an appointee.

7 WHAT DOES THE ACT SAY ABOUT LASTING POWERS OF ATTORNEY?

This chapter explains what Lasting Powers of Attorney (LPAs) are and how they should be used. It also sets out:

- how LPAs differ from Enduring Powers of Attorney (EPAs)
- the types of decisions that people can appoint attorneys to make (attorneys are also called 'donees' in the Act)
- situations in which an LPA can and cannot be used
- the duties and responsibilities of attorneys
- the standards required of attorneys, and
- measures for dealing with attorneys who don't meet appropriate standards.

This chapter also explains what should happen to EPAs that were made before the Act comes into force.

In this chapter, as throughout the Code, a person's capacity (or lack of capacity) refers specifically to their capacity to make a particular decision at the time it needs to be made.

Quick summary

ANYONE ASKED TO BE AN ATTORNEY SHOULD:

- consider whether they have the skills and ability to act as an attorney (especially if it is for a property and affairs LPA)
- ask themselves whether they actually want to be an attorney and take on the duties and responsibilities of the role.

BEFORE ACTING UNDER AN LPA, ATTORNEYS MUST:

- make sure the LPA has been registered with the Public Guardian
- take all practical and appropriate steps to help the donor make the particular decision for themselves.

WHEN ACTING UNDER AN LPA:

- make sure that the Act's statutory principles are followed
- check whether the person has the capacity to make that particular decision for themselves. If they do:
  - a personal welfare LPA cannot be used – the person must make the decision
  - a property and affairs LPA can be used even if the person has capacity to make the decision, unless they have stated in the LPA that they should make decisions for themselves when they have capacity to do so.

AT ALL TIMES, REMEMBER:

- anything done under the authority of the LPA must be in the person's best interests

- anyone acting as an attorney must have regard to guidance in this Code of Practice that is relevant to the decision that is to be made
- attorneys must fulfil their responsibilities and duties to the person who lacks capacity.

What is a Lasting Power of Attorney (LPA)?

7.1 Sometimes one person will want to give another person authority to make a decision on their behalf. A power of attorney is a legal document that allows them to do so. Under a power of attorney, the chosen person (the attorney or donee) can make decisions that are as valid as one made by the person (the donor).

7.2 Before the Enduring Powers of Attorney Act 1985, every power of attorney automatically became invalid as soon as the donor lacked the capacity to make their own decision. But that Act introduced the Enduring Power of Attorney (EPA). An EPA allows an attorney to make decisions about property and financial affairs even if the donor lacks capacity to manage their own affairs.

7.3 The Mental Capacity Act replaces the EPA with the Lasting Power of Attorney (LPA). It also increases the range of different types of decisions that people can authorise others to make on their behalf. As well as property and affairs (including financial matters), LPAs can also cover personal welfare (including healthcare and consent to medical treatment) for people who lack capacity to make such decisions for themselves.

7.4 The donor can choose one person or several to make different kinds of decisions. See paragraphs 7.21–7.31 for more information about personal welfare LPAs. See paragraphs 7.32–7.42 for more information about LPAs on property and affairs.

How do LPAs compare to EPAs?

7.5 There are a number of differences between LPAs and EPAs. These are summarised as follows:

- EPAs only cover property and affairs. LPAs can also cover personal welfare.
- Donors must use the relevant specific form (prescribed in regulations) to make EPAs and LPAs. There are different forms for EPAs, personal welfare LPAs and property and affairs LPAs.
- EPAs must be registered with the Public Guardian when the donor can no longer manage their own affairs (or when they start to lose capacity). But LPAs can be registered at any time before they are used – before or after the donor lacks capacity to make particular decisions that the LPA covers. If the LPA is not registered, it can't be used.
- EPAs can be used while the donor still has capacity to manage their own property and affairs, as can property and affairs LPAs, so long as the donor does not say otherwise in the LPA. But personal welfare LPAs can only be used once the donor lacks capacity to make the welfare decision in question.
- Once the Act comes into force, only LPAs can be made but existing EPAs will continue to be valid. There will be different laws and procedures for EPAs and LPAs.
- Attorneys making decisions under a registered EPA or LPA must follow the Act's principles and act in the best interests of the donor.
- The duties under the law of agency apply to attorneys of both EPAs and LPAs (see paragraphs 7.58–7.68 below).
- Decisions that the courts have made about EPAs may also affect how people use LPAs.

- Attorneys acting under an LPA have a legal duty to have regard to the guidance in this Code of Practice. EPA attorneys do not. But the Code's guidance will still be helpful to them.

How does a donor create an LPA?

7.6 The donor must also follow the right procedures for creating and registering an LPA, as set out below. Otherwise the LPA might not be valid. It is not always necessary to get legal advice. But it is a good idea for certain cases (for example, if the donor's circumstances are complicated).

7.7 Only adults aged 18 or over can make an LPA, and they can only make an LPA if they have the capacity to do so. For an LPA to be valid:

- the LPA must be a written document set out in the statutory form prescribed by regulations[26]
- the document must include prescribed information about the nature and effect of the LPA (as set out in the regulations)
- the donor must sign a statement saying that they have read the prescribed information (or somebody has read it to them) and that they want the LPA to apply when they no longer have capacity
- the document must name people (not any of the attorneys) who should be told about an application to register the LPA, or it should say that there is no-one they wish to be told
- the attorneys must sign a statement saying that they have read the prescribed information and that they understand their duties – in particular the duty to act in the donor's best interests
- the document must include a certificate completed by an independent third party,[27] confirming that:
  - in their opinion, the donor understands the LPA's purpose
  - nobody used fraud or undue pressure to trick or force the donor into making the LPA and
  - there is nothing to stop the LPA being created.

26 The prescribed forms will be available from the Office of the Public Guardian (OPG) or from legal stationers.

27 Details of who may and who may not be a certificate provider will be available in regulations. The OPG will produce guidance for certificate providers on their role.

Who can be an attorney?

7.8 A donor should think carefully before choosing someone to be their attorney. An attorney should be someone who is trustworthy, competent and reliable. They should have the skills and ability to carry out the necessary tasks.

7.9 Attorneys must be at least 18 years of age. For property and affairs LPAs, the attorney could be either:

- an individual (as long as they are not bankrupt at the time the LPA is made), or
- a trust corporation (often parts of banks or other financial institutions).

If an attorney nominated under a property and affairs LPA becomes bankrupt at any point, they will no longer be allowed to act as an attorney for property and affairs. People who are bankrupt can still act as an attorney for personal welfare LPAs.

7.10 The donor must name an individual rather than a job title in a company or organisation, (for example, 'The Director of Adult Services' or 'my solicitor' would not be sufficient). A paid care worker (such as a care home manager) should not agree to act as an attorney, apart from in unusual circumstances (for example, if they are the only close relative of the donor).

7.11 Section 10(4) of the Act allows the donor to appoint two or more attorneys and to specify whether they should act 'jointly', 'jointly and severally', or 'jointly in respect of some matters and jointly and severally in respect of others'.

- Joint attorneys must always act together. All attorneys must agree decisions and sign any relevant documents.
- Joint and several attorneys can act together but may also act independently if they wish. Any action taken by any attorney alone is as valid as if they were the only attorney.

7.12 The donor may want to appoint attorneys to act jointly in some matters but jointly and severally in others. For example, a donor could choose to appoint two or more financial attorneys jointly and severally. But they might say then when selling the donor's house, the attorneys must act jointly. The donor may appoint welfare attorneys to act jointly and severally but specify that they must act jointly in relation to giving consent to surgery. If a donor who has appointed two or more attorneys does not specify how they should act, they must always act jointly (section 10(5)).

7.13 Section 10(8) says that donors may choose to name replacement attorneys to take over the duties in certain circumstances (for example, in the event of an attorney's death). The donor may name a specific attorney to be replaced, or the replacements can take over from any attorney, if necessary. Donors cannot give their attorneys the right to appoint a substitute or successor.

How should somebody register and use an LPA?

7.14 An LPA must be registered with the Office of the Public Guardian (OPG) before it can be used. An unregistered LPA will not give the attorney any legal powers to make a decision for the donor. The donor can register the LPA while they are still capable, or the attorney can apply to register the LPA at any time.

7.15 There are advantages in registering the LPA soon after the donor makes it (for example, to ensure that there is no delay when the LPA needs to be used). But if this has not been done, an LPA can be registered after the donor lacks the capacity to make a decision covered by the LPA.

7.16 If an LPA is unregistered, attorneys must register it before making any decisions under the LPA. If the LPA has been registered but not used for some time, the attorney should tell the OPG when they begin to act under it – so that the attorney can be sent relevant, up-to-date information about the rules governing LPAs.

7.17 While they still have capacity, donors should let the OPG know of permanent changes of address for the donor or the attorney or any other changes in circumstances. If the donor no longer has capacity to do this, attorneys should report any such changes to the OPG. Examples include an attorney of a property and affairs LPA becoming bankrupt or the ending of a marriage between the donor and their attorney. This will help keep OPG records up to date, and will make sure that attorneys do not make decisions that they no longer have the authority to make.

What guidance should an attorney follow?

7.18 Section 9(4) states that attorneys must meet the requirements set out in the Act. Most importantly, they have to follow the statutory principles (section 1) and make decisions in the best interests of the person who lacks capacity (section 4). They must also respect any conditions or restrictions that the LPA document contains. See chapter 2 for guidance on how to apply the Act's principles.

7.19 Chapter 3 gives suggestions of ways to help people make their own decisions in accordance with the Act's second principle. Attorneys should also refer to the guidance in chapter 4 when assessing the donor's capacity to make particular decisions, and in particular, should follow the steps suggested for establishing a 'reasonable belief' that the donor lacks capacity (see paragraphs 4.44–4.45). Assessments of capacity or best interests must not be based merely on:

- a donor's age or appearance, or
- unjustified assumptions about any condition they might have or their behaviour.

7.20 When deciding what is in the donor's best interests, attorneys should refer to the guidance in chapter 5. In particular, they must consider the donor's past and present wishes and feelings, beliefs and values. Where practical and appropriate, they should consult with:

- anyone involved in caring for the donor
- close relatives and anyone else with an interest in their welfare
- other attorneys appointed by the donor.

See paragraphs 7.52–7.68 for a description of an attorney's duties.

Scenario: Making decisions in a donor's best interests

Mr Young has been a member of the Green Party for a long time. He has appointed his solicitor as his attorney under a property and affairs LPA. But Mr Young did not state in the LPA that investments made on his behalf must be ethical investments. When the attorney assesses his client's best interests, however, the attorney considers the donor's past wishes, values and beliefs. He makes sure that he only invests in companies that are socially and environmentally responsible.

What decisions can an LPA attorney make?

Personal welfare LPAs

7.21 LPAs can be used to appoint attorneys to make decisions about personal welfare, which can include healthcare and medical treatment decisions. Personal welfare LPAs might include decisions about:

- where the donor should live and who they should live with
- the donor's day-to-day care, including diet and dress
- who the donor may have contact with
- consenting to or refusing medical examination and treatment on the donor's behalf
- arrangements needed for the donor to be given medical, dental or optical treatment
- assessments for and provision of community care services
- whether the donor should take part in social activities, leisure activities, education or training

- the donor's personal correspondence and papers
- rights of access to personal information about the donor, or
- complaints about the donor's care or treatment.

7.22 The standard form for personal welfare LPAs allows attorneys to make decisions about anything that relates to the donor's personal welfare. But donors can add restrictions or conditions to areas where they would not wish the attorney to have the power to act. For example, a donor might only want an attorney to make decisions about their social care and not their healthcare. There are particular rules for LPAs authorising an attorney to make decisions about life-sustaining treatment (see paragraphs 7.30–7.31 below).

7.23 A general personal welfare LPA gives the attorney the right to make all of the decisions set out above although this is not a full list of the actions they can take or decisions they can make. However, a personal welfare LPA can only be used at a time when the donor lacks capacity to make a specific welfare decision.

Scenario: Denying attorneys the right to make certain decisions

Mrs Hutchison is in the early stages of Alzheimer's disease. She is anxious to get all her affairs in order while she still has capacity to do so. She makes a personal welfare LPA, appointing her daughter as attorney. But Mrs Hutchison knows that her daughter doesn't always get on with some members of the family – and she wouldn't want her daughter to stop those relatives from seeing her.

She states in the LPA that her attorney does not have the authority to decide who can contact her or visit her. If her daughter wants to prevent anyone having contact with Mrs Hutchison, she must ask the Court of Protection to decide.

7.24 Before making a decision under a personal welfare LPA, the attorney must be sure that:

- the LPA has been registered with the OPG
- the donor lacks the capacity to make the particular decision or the attorney reasonably believes that the donor lacks capacity to take the decisions covered by the LPA (having applied the Act's principles), and
- they are making the decision in the donor's best interests.

7.25 When healthcare or social care staff are involved in preparing a care plan for someone who has appointed a personal welfare attorney, they must first assess whether the donor has capacity to agree to the care plan or to parts of it. If the donor lacks capacity, professionals must then consult the attorney and get their agreement to the care plan. They will also need to consult the attorney when considering what action is in the person's best interests.

Personal welfare LPAs that authorise an attorney to make healthcare decisions

7.26 A personal welfare LPA allows attorneys to make decisions to accept or refuse healthcare or treatment unless the donor has stated clearly in the LPA that they do not want the attorney to make these decisions.

7.27 Even where the LPA includes healthcare decisions, attorneys do not have the right to consent to or refuse treatment in situations where:

- **the donor has capacity to make the particular healthcare decision** (section 11(7)(a))
  An attorney has no decision-making power if the donor can make their own treatment decisions.
- **the donor has made an advance decision to refuse the proposed treatment** (section 11(7)(b))
  An attorney cannot consent to treatment if the donor has made a valid and applicable advance decision to refuse a specific treatment (see chapter 9). But if the donor made an LPA after the advance decision, and gave the attorney the right to consent to or refuse the treatment, the attorney can choose not to follow the advance decision.
- **a decision relates to life-sustaining treatment** (section 11(7)(c))
  An attorney has no power to consent to or refuse life-sustaining treatment, unless the LPA document expressly authorises this (See paragraphs 7.30–7.31 below.)
- **the donor is detained under the Mental Health Act** (section 28)
  An attorney cannot consent to or refuse treatment for a mental disorder for a patient detained under the Mental Health Act 1983 (see also chapter 13).

7.28 LPAs cannot give attorneys the power to demand specific forms of medical treatment that healthcare staff do not believe are necessary or appropriate for the donor's particular condition.

7.29 Attorneys must always follow the Act's principles and make decisions in the donor's best interests. If healthcare staff disagree with the attorney's assessment of best interests, they should discuss the case with other medical experts and/or get a formal second opinion. Then they should discuss the matter further with the attorney. If they cannot settle the disagreement, they can apply to the Court of Protection (see paragraphs 7.45–7.49 below). While the court is coming to a decision, healthcare staff can give life-sustaining treatment to prolong the donor's life or stop their condition getting worse.

Personal welfare LPAs that authorise an attorney to make decisions about life-sustaining treatment

7.30 An attorney can only consent to or refuse life-sustaining treatment on behalf of the donor if, when making the LPA, the donor has specifically stated in the LPA document that they want the attorney to have this authority.

7.31 As with all decisions, an attorney must act in the donor's best interests when making decisions about such treatment. This will involve applying the best interests checklist (see chapter 5) and consulting with carers, family members and others interested in the donor's welfare. In particular, the attorney must not be motivated in any way by the desire to bring about the donor's death (see paragraphs 5.29–5.36). Anyone who doubts that the attorney is acting in the donor's best interests can apply to the Court of Protection for a decision.

Scenario: Making decisions about life-sustaining treatment

Mrs Joshi has never trusted doctors. She prefers to rely on alternative therapies. Because she saw her father suffer after invasive treatment for cancer, she is clear that she would refuse such treatment herself.

She is diagnosed with cancer and discusses her wishes with her husband. Mrs Joshi knows that he would respect her wishes if he ever had to make a decision about her treatment. She makes a personal welfare LPA appointing him as her attorney with authority to make all her welfare and healthcare decisions. She includes a specific statement authorising him to consent to or refuse life-sustaining treatment.

He will then be able to consider her views and make decisions about treatment in her best interests if she later lacks capacity to make those decisions herself.

Property and affairs LPAs

7.32 A donor can make an LPA giving an attorney the right to make decisions about property and affairs (including financial matters). Unless the donor states otherwise, once the LPA is registered, the attorney is allowed to make all decisions about the donor's property and affairs even if the donor still has capacity to make the decisions for themselves. In this situation, the LPA will continue to apply when the donor no longer has capacity.

7.33 Alternatively a donor can state in the LPA document that the LPA should only apply when they lack capacity to make a relevant decision. It is the donor's responsibility to decide how their capacity should then be assessed. For example, the donor may trust the attorney to carry out an assessment, or they may say that the LPA only applies if their GP or another doctor confirms in writing that they lack capacity to make specific decisions about property or finances. Financial institutions may wish to see the written confirmation before recognising the attorney's authority to act under the LPA.

7.34 The fact that someone has made a property and affairs LPA does not mean that they cannot continue to carry out financial transactions for themselves. The donor may have full capacity, but perhaps anticipates that they may lack capacity at some future time. Or they may have fluctuating or partial capacity and therefore be able to make some decisions (or at some times), but need an attorney to make others (or at other times). The attorney should allow and encourage the donor to do as much as possible, and should only act when the donor asks them to or to make those decisions the donor lacks capacity to make. However, in other cases, the donor may wish to hand over responsibility for all decisions to the attorney, even those they still have capacity to make.

7.35 If the donor restricts the decisions an attorney can make, banks may ask the attorney to sign a declaration that protects the bank from liability if the attorney misuses the account.[28]

[28] See British Banking Association's guidance for bank staff on *'Banking for mentally incapacitated and learning disabled customers'*.

7.36 If a donor does not restrict decisions the attorney can make, the attorney will be able to decide on any or all of the person's property and financial affairs. This might include:

- buying or selling property
- opening, closing or operating any bank, building society or other account
- giving access to the donor's financial information
- claiming, receiving and using (on the donor's behalf) all benefits, pensions, allowances and rebates (unless the Department for Work and Pensions has already appointed someone and everyone is happy for this to continue)
- receiving any income, inheritance or other entitlement on behalf of the donor
- dealing with the donor's tax affairs

- paying the donor's mortgage, rent and household expenses
- insuring, maintaining and repairing the donor's property
- investing the donor's savings
- making limited gifts on the donor's behalf (but see paragraphs 7.40–7.42 below)
- paying for private medical care and residential care or nursing home fees
- applying for any entitlement to funding for NHS care, social care or adaptations
- using the donor's money to buy a vehicle or any equipment or other help they need
- repaying interest and capital on any loan taken out by the donor.

7.37 A general property and affairs LPA will allow the attorney to carry out any or all of the actions above (although this is not a full list of the actions they can take). However, the donor may want to specify the types of powers they wish the attorney to have, or to exclude particular types of decisions. If the donor holds any assets as trustee, they should get legal advice about how the LPA may affect this.

7.38 The attorney must make these decisions personally and cannot generally give someone else authority to carry out their duties (see paragraphs 7.61–7.62 below). But if the donor wants the attorney to be able to give authority to a specialist to make specific decisions, they need to state this clearly in the LPA document (for example, appointing an investment manager to make particular investment decisions).

7.39 Donors may like to appoint someone (perhaps a family member or a professional) to go through their accounts with the attorney from time to time. This might help to reassure donors that somebody will check their financial affairs when they lack capacity to do so. It may also be helpful for attorneys to arrange a regular check that everything is being done properly. The donor should ensure that the person is willing to carry out this role and is prepared to ask for the accounts if the attorney does not provide them. They should include this arrangement in the signed LPA document. The LPA should also say whether the person can charge a fee for this service.

What gifts can an attorney make under a property and affairs LPA?

7.40 An attorney can only make gifts of the donor's money or belongings to people who are related to or connected with the donor (including the attorney) on specific occasions, including:

- births or birthdays
- weddings or wedding anniversaries
- civil partnership ceremonies or anniversaries, or
- any other occasion when families, friends or associates usually give presents (section 12(3)(b)).

7.41 If the donor previously made donations to any charity regularly or from time to time, the attorney can make donations from the person's funds. This also applies if the donor could have been expected to make such payments (section 12(2)(b)). But the value of any gift or donation must be reasonable and take into account the size of the donor's estate. For example, it would not be reasonable to buy expensive gifts at Christmas if the donor was living on modest means and had to do without essential items in order to pay for them.

7.42 The donor cannot use the LPA to make more extensive gifts than those allowed under section 12 of the Act. But they can impose stricter conditions or restrictions on the attorney's powers to make gifts. They should state these restrictions clearly in the LPA document when they are creating it. When deciding on appropriate gifts, the attorney should consider the donor's wishes and feelings to work out what would be in the donor's best interests. The attorney can apply to the Court of Protection for permission to make gifts that are not included in the LPA (for example, for tax planning purposes).

Are there any other restrictions on attorneys' powers?

7.43 Attorneys are not protected from liability if they do something that is intended to restrain the donor, unless:

- the attorney reasonably believes that the donor lacks capacity to make the decision in question, *and*
- the attorney reasonably believes that restraint is necessary to prevent harm to the donor, *and*
- the type of restraint used is in proportion to the likelihood and the seriousness of the harm.

If an attorney needs to make a decision or take action which may involve the use of restraint, they should take account of the guidance set out in chapter 6.

7.44 Attorneys have no authority to take actions that result in the donor being deprived of their liberty. Any deprivation of liberty will only be lawful if this has been properly authorised and there is other protection available for the person who lacks capacity. An example would be the protection around detention under the Mental Health Act 1983 (see chapter 13) or a court ruling. Chapter 6 gives more guidance on working out whether an action is restraint or a deprivation of liberty.

What powers does the Court of Protection have over LPAs?

7.45 The Court of Protection has a range of powers to:

- determine whether an LPA is valid
- give directions about using the LPA, and
- to remove an attorney (for example, if the attorney does not act in the best interests of the donor).

Chapter 8 gives more information about the Court of Protection's powers.

7.46 If somebody has doubts over whether an LPA is valid, they can ask the court to decide whether the LPA:

- meets the Act's requirements
- has been revoked (cancelled) by the donor, or
- has come to an end for any other reason.

7.47 The court can also stop somebody registering an LPA or rule that an LPA is invalid if:

- the donor made the LPA as a result of undue pressure or fraud, or
- the attorney behaves, has behaved or is planning to behave in a way that goes against their duties or is not in the donor's best interests.

7.48 The court can also clarify an LPA's meaning, if it is not clear, and it can tell attorneys how they should use an LPA. If an attorney thinks that an LPA does not give them enough powers, they can ask the court to extend their powers – if the donor no longer has capacity to authorise this. The court can also authorise an attorney to give a gift that the Act does not normally allow (section 12(2)), if it is in the donor's best interests.

7.49 All attorneys should keep records of their dealings with the donor's affairs (see also paragraph 7.67 below). The court can order attorneys to produce records (for example, financial accounts) and to provide specific reports, information or documentation. If somebody has concerns about an attorney's payment or expenses, the court could resolve the matter.

What responsibilities do attorneys have?

7.50 A donor cannot insist on somebody agreeing to become an attorney. It is down to the proposed attorney to decide whether to take on this responsibility. When an attorney accepts the role by signing the LPA document, this is confirmation that they are willing to act under the LPA once it is registered. An attorney can withdraw from the appointment if they ever become unable or unwilling to act, but if the LPA has been registered they must follow the correct procedures for withdrawing. (see paragraph 7.66 below).

7.51 Once the attorney starts to act under an LPA, they must meet certain standards. If they don't carry out the duties below, they could be removed from the role. In some circumstances they could face charges of fraud or negligence.

What duties does the Act impose?

7.52 Attorneys acting under an LPA have a duty to:

- follow the Act's statutory principles (see chapter 2)
- make decisions in the donor's best interests
- have regard to the guidance in the Code of Practice
- only make those decisions the LPA gives them authority to make.

Principles and best interests

7.53 Attorneys must act in accordance with the Act's statutory principles (section 1) and in the best interests of the donor (the steps for working out best interests are set out in section 4). In particular, attorneys must consider whether the donor has capacity to make the decision for themselves. If not, they should consider whether the donor is likely to regain capacity to make the decision in the future. If so, it may be possible to delay the decision until the donor can make it.

The Code of Practice

7.54 As well as this chapter, attorneys should pay special attention to the following guidance set out in the Code:

- chapter 2, which sets out how the Act's principles should be applied
- chapter 3, which describes the steps which can be taken to try to help the person make decisions for themselves

- chapter 4, which describes the Act's definition of lack of capacity and gives guidance on assessing capacity, and
- chapter 5, which gives guidance on working out the donor's best interests.

7.55 In some circumstances, attorneys might also find it useful to refer to guidance in:

- chapter 6, which explains when attorneys who have caring responsibilities may have protection from liability and gives guidance on the few circumstances when the Act allows restraint in connection with care and treatment
- chapter 8, which gives a summary of the Court of Protection's powers relating to LPAs
- chapter 9, which explains how LPAs may be affected if the donor has made an advance decision to refuse treatment, and
- chapter 15, which describes ways to settle disagreements.

Only making decisions covered by an LPA

7.56 A personal welfare attorney has no authority to make decisions about a donor's property and affairs (such as their finances). A property and affairs attorney has no authority in decisions about a donor's personal care. (But the same person could be appointed in separate LPAs to carry out both these roles.) Under any LPA, the attorney will have authority in a wide range of decisions. But if a donor includes restrictions in the LPA document, this will limit the attorney's authority (section 9(4)(b)). If the attorney thinks that they need greater powers, they can apply to the Court of Protection which may decide to give the attorney the authority required or alternatively to appoint the attorney as a deputy with the necessary powers (see chapter 8).

7.57 It is good practice for decision-makers to consult attorneys about any decision or action, whether or not it is covered by the LPA. This is because an attorney is likely to have known the donor for some time and may have important information about their wishes and feelings. Researchers can also consult attorneys if they are thinking about involving the donor in research (see chapter 11).

Scenario: Consulting attorneys

Mr Varadi makes a personal welfare LPA appointing his son and daughter as his joint attorneys. He also makes a property and affairs LPA, appointing his son and his solicitor to act jointly and severally. He registers the property and affairs LPA straight away, so his attorneys can help with financial decisions.

Two years later, Mr Varadi has a stroke, is unable to speak and has difficulty communicating his wishes. He also lacks the capacity to make decisions about treatment. The attorneys apply to register the personal welfare LPA. Both feel that they should delay decisions about Mr Varadi's future care, because he might regain capacity to make the decisions himself. But they agree that some decisions cannot wait.

Although the solicitor has no authority to make welfare decisions, the welfare attorneys consult him about their father's best interests. They speak to him about immediate treatment decisions and their suggestion to delay making decisions about his future care. Similarly, the property and affairs attorneys consult the daughter about the financial decisions that Mr Varadi does not have the capacity to make himself.

What are an attorney's other duties?

7.58 An attorney appointed under an LPA is acting as the chosen agent of the donor and therefore, under the law of agency, the attorney has certain duties towards the donor. An attorney takes on a role which carries a great deal of power, which they must use carefully and responsibly. They have a duty to:

- apply certain standards of care and skill (duty of care) when making decisions
- carry out the donor's instructions
- not take advantage of their position and not benefit themselves, but benefit the donor (fiduciary duty)
- not delegate decisions, unless authorised to do so
- act in good faith
- respect confidentiality
- comply with the directions of the Court of Protection
- not give up the role without telling the donor and the court.

In relation to property and affairs LPAs, they have a duty to:

- keep accounts
- keep the donor's money and property separate from their own.

Duty of care

7.59 'Duty of care' means applying a certain standard of care and skill – depending on whether the attorney is paid for their services or holds relevant professional qualifications.

- Attorneys who are not being paid must apply the same care, skill and diligence they would use to make decisions about their own life. An attorney who claims to have particular skills or qualifications must show greater skill in those particular areas than someone who does not make such claims.
- If attorneys are being paid for their services, they should demonstrate a higher degree of care and skill.
- Attorneys who undertake their duties in the course of their professional work (such as solicitors or corporate trustees) must display professional competence and follow their profession's rules and standards.

Fiduciary duty

7.60 A fiduciary duty means attorneys must not take advantage of their position. Nor should they put themselves in a position where their personal interests conflict with their duties. They also must not allow any other influences to affect the way in which they act as an attorney. Decisions should always benefit the donor, and not the attorney. Attorneys must not profit or get any personal benefit from their position, apart from receiving gifts where the Act allows it, whether or not it is at the donor's expense.

Duty not to delegate

7.61 Attorneys cannot usually delegate their authority to someone else. They must carry out their duties personally. The attorney may seek professional or expert advice (for example, investment advice from a financial adviser or advice on medical treatment from a doctor). But they cannot, as a general rule, allow someone else to make a decision that they have been appointed to make, unless this has been specifically authorised by the donor in the LPA.

7.62 In certain circumstances, attorneys may have limited powers to delegate (for example, through necessity or unforeseen circumstances, or for specific tasks which the donor would not have expected the attorney to attend to personally). But attorneys cannot usually delegate any decisions that rely on their discretion.

Duty of good faith

7.63 Acting in good faith means acting with honesty and integrity. For example, an attorney must try to make sure that their decisions do not go against a decision the donor made while they still had capacity (unless it would be in the donor's best interests to do so).

Duty of confidentiality

7.64 Attorneys have a duty to keep the donor's affairs confidential, unless:

- before they lost capacity to do so, the donor agreed that some personal or financial information may be revealed for a particular purpose (for example, they have named someone they want to check their financial accounts), or
- there is some other good reason to release it (for example, it is in the public interest or the best interests of the person who lacks capacity, or there is a risk of harm to the donor or others).

In the latter circumstances, it may be advisable for the attorney to get legal advice. Chapter 16 gives more information about confidentiality.

Duty to comply with the directions of the Court of Protection

7.65 Under sections 22 and 23 of the Act, the Court of Protection has wide-ranging powers to decide on issues relating to the operation or validity of an LPA. It can also:

- give extra authority to attorneys
- order them to produce records (for example, financial accounts), or
- order them to provide specific information or documentation to the court.

Attorneys must comply with any decision or order that the court makes.

Duty not to disclaim without notifying the donor and the OPG

7.66 Once someone becomes an attorney, they cannot give up that role without notifying the donor and the OPG. If they decide to give up their role, they must follow the relevant guidance available from the OPG.

Duty to keep accounts

7.67 Property and affairs attorneys must keep accounts of transactions carried out on the donor's behalf. Sometimes the Court of Protection will ask to see accounts. If the attorney is not a financial expert and the donor's affairs are relatively straightforward, a record of the donor's income and expenditure (for example, through bank statements) may be enough. The more complicated the donor's affairs, the more detailed the accounts may need to be.

Duty to keep the donor's money and property separate

7.68 Property and affairs attorneys should usually keep the donor's money and property separate from their own or anyone else's. There may be occasions where donors and attorneys have agreed in the past to keep their money in a joint bank account (for example, if a husband is acting as his wife's attorney). It might be possible to continue this under the LPA. But in most circumstances, attorneys must keep finances separate to avoid any possibility of mistakes or confusion.

How does the Act protect donors from abuse?

What should someone do if they think an attorney is abusing their position?

7.69 Attorneys are in a position of trust, so there is always a risk of them abusing their position. Donors can help prevent abuse by carefully choosing a suitable and trustworthy attorney. But others have a role to play in looking out for possible signs of abuse or exploitation, and reporting any concerns to the OPG. The OPG will then follow this up in co-operation with relevant agencies.

7.70 Signs that an attorney may be exploiting the donor (or failing to act in the donor's best interests) include:

- stopping relatives or friends contacting the donor – for example, the attorney may prevent contact or the donor may suddenly refuse visits or telephone calls from family and friends for no reason
- sudden unexplained changes in living arrangements (for example, someone moves in to care for a donor they've had little contact with)
- not allowing healthcare or social care staff to see the donor
- taking the donor out of hospital against medical advice, while the donor is having necessary medical treatment
- unpaid bills (for example, residential care or nursing home fees)
- an attorney opening a credit card account for the donor
- spending money on things that are not obviously related to the donor's needs
- the attorney spending money in an unusual or extravagant way
- transferring financial assets to another country.

7.71 Somebody who suspects abuse should contact the OPG immediately. The OPG may direct a Court of Protection Visitor to visit an attorney to investigate. In cases of suspected physical or sexual abuse, theft or serious fraud, the person should contact the police. They might also be able to refer the matter to the relevant local adult protection authorities.

7.72 In serious cases, the OPG will refer the matter to the Court of Protection. The court may revoke (cancel) the LPA or (through the OPG) prevent it being registered, if it decides that:

- the LPA does not meet the legal requirements for creating an LPA
- the LPA has been revoked or come to an end for any other reason
- somebody used fraud or undue pressure to get the donor to make the LPA
- the attorney has done something that they do not have authority to do, or
- the attorney has behaved or is planning to behave in a way that is not in the donor's best interests.

The court might then consider whether the authority previously given to an attorney can be managed by:

- the court making a single decision, or
- appointing a deputy.

What should an attorney do if they think someone else is abusing the donor?

7.73 An attorney who thinks someone else is abusing or exploiting the donor should report it to the OPG and ask for advice on what action they should take. They should contact the police if they suspect physical or sexual abuse, theft or serious fraud. They might also be able to refer the matter to local adult protection authorities.

7.74 Chapter 13 gives more information about protecting vulnerable people from abuse, ill treatment or neglect. It also discusses the duties and responsibilities of the various agencies involved, including the OPG and local authorities. In particular, it is a criminal offence (with a maximum penalty of five years' imprisonment, a fine, or both) for anyone (including attorneys) to wilfully neglect or ill-treat a person in their care who lacks capacity to make decisions for themselves (section 44).

What happens to existing EPAs once the Act comes into force?

7.75 Once the Act comes into force, it will not be possible to make new EPAs. Only LPAs can then be made.

7.76 Some donors will have created EPAs before the Act came into force with the expectation that their chosen attorneys will manage their property and affairs in the future, whether or not they have capacity to do so themselves.

7.77 If donors still have capacity after the Act comes into force, they can cancel the EPA and make an LPA covering their property and affairs. They should also notify attorneys and anyone else aware of the EPA (for example, a bank) that they have cancelled it.

7.78 Some donors will choose not to cancel their EPA or they may already lack the capacity to do so. In such cases, the Act allows existing EPAs, whether registered or not, to continue to be valid so that attorneys can meet the donor's expectations (Schedule 4). An EPA must be registered with the OPG when the attorney thinks the donor lacks capacity to manage their own affairs, or is beginning to lack capacity to do so.

7.79 EPA attorneys may find guidance in this chapter helpful. In particular, all attorneys must comply with the duties described in paragraphs 7.58–7.68 above. EPA attorneys can also be found liable under section 44 of the new Act, which sets out the new criminal offences of ill treatment and wilful neglect. The OPG has produced guidance on EPAs (see Annex A for details of publications and contact information).

8 WHAT IS THE ROLE OF THE COURT OF PROTECTION AND COURT-APPOINTED DEPUTIES?

This chapter describes the role of the Court of Protection and the role of court-appointed deputies. It explains the powers that the court has and how to make an application to the court. It also looks at how the court appoints a deputy to act and make decisions on behalf of someone who lacks capacity to make those decisions. In particular, it gives guidance on a deputy's duties and the consequences of not carrying them out responsibly.

The Office of the Public Guardian (OPG) produces detailed guidance for deputies. See the Annex for more details of the publications and how to get them. Further details on the court's procedures are given in the Court of Protection Rules and Practice Directions issued by the court.

In this chapter, as throughout the Code, a person's capacity (or lack of capacity) refers specifically to their capacity to make a particular decision at the time it needs to be made.

Quick summary

THE COURT OF PROTECTION HAS POWERS TO:

- decide whether a person has capacity to make a particular decision for themselves
- make declarations, decisions or orders on financial or welfare matters affecting people who lack capacity to make such decisions
- appoint deputies to make decisions for people lacking capacity to make those decisions
- decide whether an LPA or EPA is valid, and
- remove deputies or attorneys who fail to carry out their duties.

BEFORE ACCEPTING AN APPOINTMENT AS A DEPUTY, A PERSON THE COURT NOMINATES SHOULD CONSIDER WHETHER:

- they have the skills and ability to carry out a deputy's duties (especially in relation to property and affairs)
- they actually want to take on the duties and responsibilities.

ANYONE ACTING AS A DEPUTY MUST:

- make sure that they only make those decisions that they are authorised to make by the order of the court
- make sure that they follow the Act's statutory principles, including:
  - considering whether the person has capacity to make a particular decision for themselves. If they do, the deputy should allow them to do so unless the person agrees that the deputy should make the decision
  - taking all possible steps to try to help a person make the particular decision
- always make decisions in the person's best interests
- have regard to guidance in the Code of Practice that is relevant to the situation
- fulfil their duties towards the person concerned (in particular the duty of care and fiduciary duties to respect the degree of trust placed in them by the court).

What is the Court of Protection?

8.1 Section 45 of the Act sets up a specialist court, the Court of Protection, to deal with decision-making for adults (and children in a few cases) who may lack capacity to make specific decisions for themselves. The new Court of Protection replaces the old court of the same name, which only dealt with decisions about the property and financial affairs of people lacking capacity to manage their own affairs. As well as property and affairs, the new court also deals with serious decisions affecting healthcare and personal welfare matters. These were previously dealt with by the High Court under its inherent jurisdiction.

8.2 The new Court of Protection is a superior court of record and is able to establish precedent (it can set examples for future cases) and build up expertise in all issues related to lack of capacity. It has the same powers, rights, privileges and authority as the High Court. When reaching any decision, the court must apply all the statutory principles set out in section 1 of the Act. In particular, it must make a decision in the best interests of the person who lacks capacity to make the specific decision. There will usually be a fee for applications to the court.[29]

[29] Details of the fees charged by the court, and the circumstances in which the fees may be waived or remitted, are available from the Office of the Public Guardian (OPG).

How can somebody make an application to the Court of Protection?

8.3 In most cases concerning personal welfare matters, the core principles of the Act and the processes set out in chapters 5 and 6 will be enough to:

- help people take action or make decisions in the best interests of someone who lacks capacity to make decisions about their own care or treatment, or
- find ways of settling disagreements about such actions or decisions.

But an application to the Court of Protection may be necessary for:

- particularly difficult decisions
- disagreements that cannot be resolved in any other way (see chapter 15), or
- situations where ongoing decisions may need to be made about the personal welfare of a person who lacks capacity to make decisions for themselves.

8.4 An order of the court will usually be necessary for matters relating to the property and affairs (including financial matters) of people who lack capacity to make specific financial decisions for themselves, unless:

- their only income is state benefits (see paragraph 8.36 below), or
- they have previously made an Enduring Power of Attorney (EPA) or a Lasting Power of Attorney (LPA) to give somebody authority to manage their property and affairs (see chapter 7).

8.5 Receivers appointed by the court before the Act commences will be treated as deputies. But they will keep their existing powers and duties. They must meet the requirements set out in the Act and, in particular, follow the statutory principles and act in the best interests of the person for whom they have been appointed. They must also have regard to guidance in this chapter and other parts of the Code of Practice. Further guidance for receivers is available from the OPG.

Cases involving young people aged 16 or 17

8.6 Either a court dealing with family proceedings or the Court of Protection can hear cases involving people aged 16 or 17 who lack capacity. In some cases, the Court of Protection can hear cases involving people younger than 16 (for example, when somebody needs to be appointed to make longer-term decisions about their financial affairs). Under section 21 of the Mental Capacity Act, the Court of Protection can transfer cases concerning children to a court that has powers under the Children Act 1989. Such a court can also transfer cases to the Court of Protection, if necessary. Chapter 12 gives more detail on cases where this might apply.

Who should make the application?

8.7 The person making the application will vary, depending on the circumstances. For example, a person wishing to challenge a finding that they lack capacity may apply to the court, supported by others where necessary. Where there is a disagreement among family members, for example, a family member may wish to apply to the court to settle the disagreement – bearing in mind the need, in most cases, to get permission beforehand (see paragraphs 8.11–8.12 below).

8.8 For cases about serious or major decisions concerning medical treatment (see paragraphs 8.18–8.24 below), the NHS Trust or other organisation responsible for the patient's care will usually make the application. If social care staff are concerned about a decision that affects the welfare of a person who lacks capacity, the relevant local authority should make the application.

8.9 For decisions about the property and affairs of someone who lacks capacity to manage their own affairs, the applicant will usually be the person (for example, family carer) who needs specific authority from the court to deal with the individual's money or property.

8.10 If the applicant is the person who is alleged to lack capacity, they will always be a party to the court proceedings. In all other cases, the court will decide whether the person who lacks, or is alleged to lack, capacity should be involved as a party to the case. Where the person is a party to the case, the court may appoint the Official Solicitor to act for them.

Who must ask the court for permission to make an application?

8.11 As a general rule, potential applicants must get the permission of the Court of Protection before making an application (section 50). People who the Act says do not need to ask for permission include:

- a person who lacks, or is alleged to lack, capacity in relation to a specific decision or action (or anyone with parental responsibility, if the person is under 18 years)
- the donor of the LPA an application relates to – or their attorney
- a deputy who has been appointed by the court to act for the person concerned, and
- a person named in an existing court order relating to the application.

The Court of Protection Rules also set out specific types of cases where permission is not required.

8.12 When deciding whether to give permission for an application, the court must consider:

- the applicant's connection to the person the application is about
- the reasons for the application

- whether a proposed order or direction of the court will benefit the person the application is about, and
- whether it is possible to get that benefit another way.

Scenario: Considering whether to give permission for an application

Sunita, a young Asian woman, has always been close to her older brother, who has severe learning disabilities and lives in a care home. Two years ago, Sunita married a non-Asian man, and her family cut off contact with her. She still wants to visit her brother and to be consulted about his care and what is in his best interests. But the family is not letting her. The Court of Protection gives Sunita permission to apply to the court for an order allowing her contact with her brother.

What powers does the Court of Protection have?

8.13 The Court of Protection may:

- make declarations, decisions and orders on financial and welfare matters affecting people who lack, or are alleged to lack, capacity (the lack of capacity must relate to the particular issue being presented to the court)
- appoint deputies to make decisions for people who lack capacity to make those decisions
- remove deputies or attorneys who act inappropriately.

The Court can also hear cases about LPAs and EPAs. The court's powers concerning EPAs are set out in Schedule 4 of the Act.

8.14 The court must always follow the statutory principles set out in section 1 of the Act (see chapter 2) and make the decision in the best interests of the person concerned (see chapter 5).

What declarations can the court make?

8.15 Section 15 of the Act provides the court with powers to make a declaration (a ruling) on specific issues. For example, it can make a declaration as to whether a person has capacity to make a particular decision or give consent for or take a particular action. The court will require evidence of any assessment of the person's capacity and may wish to see relevant written evidence (for example, a diary, letters or other papers). If the court decides the person has capacity to make that decision, they will not take the case further. The person can now make the decision for themselves.

8.16 Applications concerning a person's capacity are likely to be rare – people can usually settle doubts and disagreements informally (see chapters 4 and 15). But an application may be relevant if:

- a person wants to challenge a decision that they lack capacity
- professionals disagree about a person's capacity to make a specific (usually serious) decision
- there is a dispute over whether the person has capacity (for example, between family members).

8.17 The court can also make a declaration as to whether a specific act relating to a person's care or treatment is lawful (either where somebody has carried out the action or is proposing to). Under section 15, this can include an omission or failure to provide care or treatment that the person needs.

This power to decide on the lawfulness of an act is particularly relevant for major medical treatment cases where there is doubt or disagreement over whether the treatment would be in the person's best interests. Healthcare staff can still give life-sustaining treatment, or treatment which stops a person's condition getting seriously worse, while the court is coming to a decision.

Serious healthcare and treatment decisions

8.18 Prior to the Act coming into force, the courts decided that some decisions relating to the provision of medical treatment were so serious that in each case, an application should be made to the court for a declaration that the proposed action was lawful before that action was taken. Cases involving any of the following decisions should therefore be brought before a court:

- decisions about the proposed withholding or withdrawal of artificial nutrition and hydration (ANH) from patients in a permanent vegetative state (PVS)
- cases involving organ or bone marrow donation by a person who lacks capacity to consent
- cases involving the proposed non-therapeutic sterilisation of a person who lacks capacity to consent to this (e.g. for contraceptive purposes) and
- all other cases where there is a doubt or dispute about whether a particular treatment will be in a person's best interests.

8.19 The case law requirement to seek a declaration in cases involving the withholding or withdrawing of artificial nutrition and hydration to people in a permanent vegetative state is unaffected by the Act[30] and as a matter of practice, these cases should be put to the Court of Protection for approval.

30 *Airedale NHS Trust v Bland* [1993] AC 789

8.20 Cases involving organ or bone marrow donation by a person who lacks capacity to consent should also be referred to the Court of Protection. Such cases involve medical procedures being performed on a person who lacks capacity to consent but which would benefit a third party (though would not necessarily directly or physically benefit the person who lacks capacity). However, sometimes such procedures may be in the person's overall best interests (see chapter 5). For example, the person might receive emotional, social and psychological benefits as a result of the help they have given, and in some cases the person may experience only minimal physical discomfort.

8.21 A prime example of this is the case of *Re Y*[31] where it was found to be in Y's best interests for her to donate bone marrow to her sister. The court decided that it was in Y's best interests to continue to receive strong emotional support from her mother, which might be diminished if her sister's health were to deteriorate further, or she were to die. Further details on this area are available in Department of Health or Welsh Assembly guidance.[32]

31 *Re Y (Mental incapacity: Bone marrow transplant)* [1996] 2 FLR 787

32 Reference Guide to Consent for Examination or Treatment, Department of Health, March 2001 www.dh.gov.uk/PublicationsAndStatistics/Publications/PublicationsPolicyAndGuidance/PublicationsPolicyAndGuidanceArticle/fs/en?CONTENT_ID=4006757&chk=snmdw8

8.22 Non-therapeutic sterilisation is the sterilisation for contraceptive purposes of a person who cannot consent. Such cases will require a careful assessment of whether such sterilisation would be in the best interests of the person who lacks capacity and such cases should continue to be referred to the court.[33] The court has also given guidance on when certain termination of pregnancy cases should be brought before the court.[34]

[33] See e.g. *Re A (medical treatment: male sterilisation)* (1999) 53 BMLR 66 where a mother applied for a declaration that a vasectomy was in the best interests of A, her son, (who had Down's syndrome and was borderline between significant and severe impairment of intelligence), in the absence of his consent. After balancing the burdens and benefits of the proposed vasectomy to A, the Court of Appeal held that the vasectomy would not be in A's best interests.

[34] *D v An NHS Trust (Medical Treatment: Consent: Termination)* [2004] 1 FLR 1110

8.23 Other cases likely to be referred to the court include those involving ethical dilemmas in untested areas (such as innovative treatments for variant CJD), or where there are otherwise irresolvable conflicts between healthcare staff, or between staff and family members.

8.24 There are also a few types of cases that should generally be dealt with by the court, since other dispute resolution methods are unlikely to be appropriate (see chapter 15). This includes, for example, cases where it is unclear whether proposed serious and/or invasive medical treatment is likely to be in the best interests of the person who lacks capacity to consent.

What powers does the court have to make decisions and appoint deputies?

8.25 In cases of serious dispute, where there is no other way of finding a solution or when the authority of the court is needed in order to make a particular decision or take a particular action, the court can be asked to make a decision to settle the matter using its powers under section 16.

However, if there is a need for ongoing decision-making powers and there is no relevant EPA or LPA, the court may appoint a deputy to make future decisions. It will also state what decisions the deputy has the authority to make on the person's behalf.

8.26 In deciding what type of order to make, the court must apply the Act's principles and the best interests checklist. In addition, it must follow two further principles, intended to make any intervention as limited as possible:

- Where possible, the court should make the decision itself in preference to appointing a deputy.
- If a deputy needs to be appointed, their appointment should be as limited in scope and for as short a time as possible.

What decisions can the court make?

8.27 In some cases, the court must make a decision, because someone needs specific authority to act and there is no other route for getting it. These include cases where:

- there is no EPA or property and affairs LPA in place and someone needs to make a financial decision for a person who lacks capacity to make that decision (for example, the decision to terminate a tenancy agreement), or
- it is necessary to make a will, or to amend an existing will, on behalf of a person who lacks capacity to do so.

8.28 Examples of other types of cases where a court decision might be appropriate include cases where:

- there is genuine doubt or disagreement about the existence, validity or applicability of an advance decision to refuse treatment (see chapter 9)
- there is a major disagreement regarding a serious decision (for example, about where a person who lacks capacity to decide for themselves should live)
- a family carer or a solicitor asks for personal information about someone who lacks capacity to consent to that information being revealed (for example, where there have been allegations of abuse of a person living in a care home)
- someone suspects that a person who lacks capacity to make decisions to protect themselves is at risk of harm or abuse from a named individual (the court could stop that individual contacting the person who lacks capacity).

8.29 Anyone carrying out actions under a decision or order of the court must still also follow the Act's principles.

Scenario: Making a decision to settle disagreements

Mrs Worrell has Alzheimer's disease. Her son and daughter argue over which care home their mother should move to. Although Mrs Worrell lacks the capacity to make this decision herself, she has enough money to pay the fees of a care home.

Her solicitor acts as attorney in relation to her financial affairs under a registered EPA. But he has no power to get involved in this family dispute – nor does he want to get involved.

The Court of Protection makes a decision in Mrs Worrell's best interests, and decides which care home can best meet her needs. Once this matter is resolved, there is no need to appoint a deputy.

What powers does the court have in relation to LPAs?

8.30 The Court of Protection can determine the validity of an LPA or EPA and can give directions as to how an attorney should use their powers under an LPA (see chapter 7). In particular, the court can cancel an LPA and end the attorney's appointment. The court might do this if the attorney was not carrying out their duties properly or acting in the best interests of the donor. The court must then decide whether it is necessary to appoint a deputy to take over the attorney's role.

What are the rules for appointing deputies?

8.31 Sometimes it is not practical or appropriate for the court to make a single declaration or decision. In such cases, if the court thinks that somebody needs to make future or ongoing decisions for someone whose condition makes it likely they will lack capacity to make some further decisions in the future, it can appoint a deputy to act for and make decisions for that person. A deputy's authority should be as limited in scope and duration as possible (see paragraphs 8.35–8.39 below).

How does the court appoint deputies?

8.32 It is for the court to decide who to appoint as a deputy. Different skills may be required depending on whether the deputy's decisions will be about a person's welfare (including healthcare), their finances or both. The court will decide whether the proposed deputy is reliable and trustworthy and has an appropriate level of skill and competence to carry out the necessary tasks.

8.33 In the majority of cases, the deputy is likely to be a family member or someone who knows the person well. But in some cases the court may decide to appoint a deputy who is independent of the family (for example, where the person's affairs or care needs are particularly complicated). This could be, for example, the Director of Adult Services in the relevant local authority (but see paragraph 8.60 below) or a professional deputy. The OPG has a panel of professional deputies (mainly solicitors who specialise in this area of law) who may be appointed to deal with property and affairs if the court decides that would be in the person's best interests.

When might a deputy need to be appointed?

8.34 Whether a person who lacks capacity to make specific decisions needs a deputy will depend on:

- the individual circumstances of the person concerned
- whether future or ongoing decisions are likely to be necessary, and
- whether the appointment is for decisions about property and affairs or personal welfare.

Property and affairs

8.35 The court will appoint a deputy to manage a person's property and affairs (including financial matters) in similar circumstances to those in which they would have appointed a receiver in the past. If a person who lacks capacity to make decisions about property and affairs has not made an EPA or LPA, applications to the court are necessary:

- for dealing with cash assets over a specified amount that remain after any debts have been paid
- for selling a person's property, or
- where the person has a level of income or capital that the court thinks a deputy needs to manage.

8.36 If the only income of a person who lacks capacity is social security benefits and they have no property or savings, there will usually be no need for a deputy to be appointed. This is because the person's benefits can be managed by an *appointee*, appointed by the Department for Work and Pensions to receive and deal with the benefits of a person who lacks capacity to do this for themselves. Although appointees are not covered by the Act, they will be expected to act in the person's best interests and must do so if they are involved in caring for the person. If the court does appoint a property and affairs deputy for someone who has an appointee, it is likely that the deputy would take over the appointee's role.

8.37 Anybody considered for appointment as a property and affairs deputy will need to sign a declaration giving details of their circumstances and ability to manage financial affairs. The declaration will include details of the tasks and duties the deputy must carry out. The deputy must assure the court that they have the skills, knowledge and commitment to carry them out.

Personal welfare (including healthcare)

8.38 Deputies for personal welfare decisions will only be required in the most difficult cases where:

- important and necessary actions cannot be carried out without the court's authority, or
- there is no other way of settling the matter in the best interests of the person who lacks capacity to make particular welfare decisions.

8.39 Examples include when:

- someone needs to make a series of linked welfare decisions over time and it would not be beneficial or appropriate to require all of those decisions to be made by the court. For example, someone (such as a family carer) who is close to a person with profound and multiple learning disabilities might apply to be appointed as a deputy with authority to make such decisions
- the most appropriate way to act in the person's best interests is to have a deputy, who will consult relevant people but have the final authority to make decisions
- there is a history of serious family disputes that could have a detrimental effect on the person's future care unless a deputy is appointed to make necessary decisions
- the person who lacks capacity is felt to be at risk of serious harm if left in the care of family members. In these rare cases, welfare decisions may need to be made by someone independent of the family, such as a local authority officer. There may even be a need for an additional court order prohibiting those family members from having contact with the person.

Who can be a deputy?

8.40 Section 19(1) states that deputies must be at least 18 years of age. Deputies with responsibility for property and affairs can be either an individual or a trust corporation (often parts of banks or other financial institutions). No-one can be appointed as a deputy without their consent.

8.41 Paid care workers (for example, care home managers) should not agree to act as a deputy because of the possible conflict of interest – unless there are exceptional circumstances (for example, if the care worker is the only close relative of the person who lacks capacity). But the court can appoint someone who is an office-holder or in a specified position (for example, the Director of Adult Services of the relevant local authority). In this situation, the court will need to be satisfied that there is no conflict of interest before making such an appointment (see paragraphs 8.58–8.60).

8.42 The court can appoint two or more deputies and state whether they should act 'jointly', 'jointly and severally' or 'jointly in respect of some matters and jointly and severally in respect of others' (section 19 (4)(c)).

- Joint deputies must always act together. They must all agree decisions or actions, and all sign any relevant documents.
- Joint and several deputies can act together, but they may also act independently if they wish. Any action taken by any deputy alone is as valid as if that person were the only deputy.

8.43 Deputies may be appointed jointly for some issues and jointly and severally for others. For example, two deputies could be appointed jointly and severally for most decisions, but the court might rule that they act jointly when selling property.

Scenario: Acting jointly and severally

Toby had a road accident and suffered brain damage and other disabilities. He gets financial compensation but lacks capacity to manage this amount of money or make decisions about his future care. His divorced parents are arguing about where their son should live and how his compensation money should be used. Toby has always been close to his sister, who is keen to be involved but is anxious about dealing with such a large amount of money.

The court decides where Toby will live. It also appoints his sister and a solicitor as joint and several deputies to manage his property and affairs. His sister can deal with any day-to-day decisions that Toby lacks capacity to make, and the solicitor can deal with more complicated matters.

What happens if a deputy can no longer carry out their duties?

8.44 When appointing a deputy, the court can also appoint someone to be a successor deputy (someone who can take over the deputy's duties in certain situations). The court will state the circumstances under which this could occur. In some cases it will also state a period of time in which the successor deputy can act. Appointment of a successor deputy might be useful if the person appointed as deputy is already elderly and wants to be sure that somebody will take over their duties in the future, if necessary.

Scenario: Appointing a successor deputy

Neil, a man with Down's syndrome, inherits a lot of money and property. His parents were already retired when the court appointed them as joint deputies to manage Neil's property and affairs. They are worried about what will happen to Neil when they cannot carry out their duties as deputies any more. The court agrees to appoint other relatives as successor deputies. They will then be able to take over as deputies after the parents' death or if his parents are no longer able to carry out the deputy's role.

Can the court protect people lacking capacity from financial loss?

8.45 Under section 19(9)(a) of the Act the court can ask a property and affairs deputy to provide some form of security (for example, a guarantee bond) to the Public Guardian to cover any loss as a result of the deputy's behaviour in carrying out their role. The court can also ask a deputy to provide reports and accounts to the Public Guardian, as it sees fit.

Are there any restrictions on a deputy's powers?

8.46 Section 20 sets out some specific restrictions on a deputy's powers. In particular, a deputy has no authority to make decisions or take action:

- if they do something that is intended to restrain the person who lacks capacity – apart from under certain circumstances (guidance on the circumstances when restraint might be permitted is given in chapter 6)[35]
- if they think that the person concerned has capacity to make the particular decision for themselves
- if their decision goes against a decision made by an attorney acting under a Lasting Power of Attorney granted by the person before they lost capacity, or
- to refuse the provision or continuation of life-sustaining treatment for a person who lacks capacity to consent – such decisions must be taken by the court.

If a deputy thinks their powers are not enough for them to carry out their duties effectively, they can apply to the court to change their powers. See paragraph 8.54 below.

[35] It is worth noting that there is a drafting error in section 20 of the Act. The word 'or' in section 20(11)(a) should have been 'and' in order to be consistent with sections 6(3)(a) and 11(4)(a). The Government will make the necessary amendment to correct this error at the earliest available legislative opportunity.

What responsibilities do deputies have?

8.47 Once a deputy has been appointed by the court, the order of appointment will set out their specific powers and the scope of their authority. On taking up the appointment, the deputy will assume a number of duties and responsibilities and will be required to act in accordance with certain standards. Failure to comply with the duties set out below could result in the Court of Protection revoking the order appointing the deputy and, in some circumstances, the deputy could be personally liable to claims for negligence or criminal charges of fraud.

8.48 Deputies should always inform any third party they are dealing with that the court has appointed them as deputy. The court will give the deputy official documents to prove their appointment and the extent of their authority.

8.49 A deputy must act whenever a decision or action is needed and it falls within their duties as set out in the court order appointing them. A deputy who fails to act at all in such situations could be in breach of duty.

What duties does the Act impose?

8.50 Deputies must:

- follow the Act's statutory principles (see chapter 2)
- make decisions or act in the best interests of the person who lacks capacity
- have regard to the guidance in this Code of Practice
- only make decisions the Court has given them authority to make.

Principles and best interests

8.51 Deputies must act in accordance with the Act's statutory principles (section 1) and in particular the best interests of the person who lacks capacity (the steps for working out best interests are set out in section 4). In particular, deputies must consider whether the person has capacity to make the decision for themselves. If not, they should consider whether the person is likely to regain capacity to make the decision in the future. If so, it may be possible to delay the decision until the person can make it.

The Code of Practice

8.52 As well as this chapter, deputies should pay special attention to the following guidance set out in the Code:

- chapter 2, which sets out how the Act's principles should be applied
- chapter 3, which describes the steps which can be taken to try to help the person make decisions for themselves
- chapter 4, which describes the Act's definition of lack of capacity and gives guidance on assessing capacity, and
- chapter 5, which gives guidance on working out someone's best interests.

8.53 In some situations, deputies might also find it useful to refer to guidance in:

- chapter 6, which explains when deputies who have caring responsibilities may have protection from liability and gives guidance on the few circumstances when the Act allows restraint in connection with care and treatment, and
- chapter 15, which describes ways to settle disagreements.

Only making decisions the court authorises a deputy to make

8.54 A deputy has a duty to act only within the scope of the actual powers given by the court, which are set out in the order of appointment. It is possible that a deputy will think their powers are not enough for them to carry out their duties effectively. In this situation, they must apply to the court either to:

- ask the court to make the decision in question, or
- ask the court to change the deputy's powers.

What are a deputy's other duties?

8.55 Section 19(6) states that a deputy is to be treated as 'the agent' of the person who lacks capacity when they act on their behalf. Being an agent means that the deputy has legal duties (under the law of agency) to the person they are representing. It also means that when they carry out tasks within their powers, they are not personally liable to third parties.

8.56 Deputies must carry out their duties carefully and responsibly. They have a duty to:

- act with due care and skill (duty of care)
- not take advantage of their situation (fiduciary duty)
- indemnify the person against liability to third parties caused by the deputy's negligence
- not delegate duties unless authorised to do so
- act in good faith
- respect the person's confidentiality, and
- comply with the directions of the Court of Protection.

Property and affairs deputies also have a duty to:

- keep accounts, and
- keep the person's money and property separate from own finances.

Duty of care

8.57 'Duty of care' means applying a certain standard of care and skill – depending on whether the deputy is paid for their services or holds relevant professional qualifications.

- Deputies who are not being paid must use the same care, skill and diligence they would use when making decisions for themselves or managing their own affairs. If they do not, they could be held liable for acting negligently. A deputy who claims to have particular skills or qualifications must show greater skill in those particular areas than a person who does not make such claims.
- If deputies are being paid for their services, they are expected to demonstrate a higher degree of care or skill when carrying out their duties.
- Deputies whose duties form part of their professional work (for example, solicitors or accountants) must display normal professional competence and follow their profession's rules and standards.

Fiduciary duty

8.58 A fiduciary duty means deputies must not take advantage of their position. Nor should they put themselves in a position where their personal interests conflict with their duties. For example, deputies should not buy property that they are selling for the person they have been appointed to represent. They should also not accept a third party commission in any transactions. Deputies must not allow anything else to influence their duties. They cannot use their position for any personal benefit, whether or not it is at the person's expense.

8.59 In many cases, the deputy will be a family member. In rare situations, this could lead to potential conflicts of interests. When making decisions, deputies should follow the Act's statutory principles and apply the best interests checklist and not allow their own personal interests to influence the decision.

8.60 Sometimes the court will consider appointing the Director of Adult Services in England or Director of Social Services in Wales of the relevant local authority as a deputy. The court will need to be satisfied that the authority has arrangements to avoid possible conflicts of interest. For example where the person for whom a financial deputy is required receives community care services from the local authority, the court will wish to be satisfied that decisions about the person's finances will be made in the best interests of that person, regardless of any implications for the services provided.

Duty not to delegate

8.61 A deputy may seek professional or expert advice (for example, investment advice from a financial adviser or a second medical opinion from a doctor). But they cannot give their decision-making responsibilities to someone else. In certain circumstances, the court will authorise the delegation of specific tasks (for example, appointing a discretionary investment manager for the conduct of investment business).

8.62 In certain circumstances, deputies may have limited powers to delegate (for example, through necessity or unforeseen circumstances, or for specific tasks which the court would not have expected the deputy to attend to personally). But deputies cannot usually delegate any decisions that rely on their discretion. If the deputy is the Director of Adult Services in England or Director of Social Services in Wales, or a solicitor, they can delegate specific tasks to other staff. But the deputy is still responsible for any actions or decisions taken, and can therefore be held accountable for any errors that are made.

Duty of good faith

8.63 Acting in good faith means acting with honesty and integrity. For example, a deputy must try to make sure that their decisions do not go against a decision the person made while they still had capacity (unless it would be in the person's best interests to do so).

Duty of confidentiality

8.64 Deputies have a duty to keep the person's affairs confidential, unless:

- before they lost capacity to do so, the person agreed that information could be revealed where necessary
- there is some other good reason to release information (for example, it is in the public interest or in the best interests of the person who lacks capacity, or where there is a risk of harm to the person concerned or to other people).

In the latter circumstances, it is advisable for the deputy to contact the OPG for guidance or get legal advice. See chapter 16 for more information about revealing personal information.

Duty to comply with the directions of the Court of Protection

8.65 The Court of Protection may give specific directions to deputies about how they should use their powers. It can also order deputies to provide reports (for example, financial accounts or reports on the welfare of the person who lacks capacity) to the Public Guardian at any time or at such intervals as the court directs. Deputies must comply with any direction of the court or request from the Public Guardian.

Duty to keep accounts

8.66 A deputy appointed to manage property and affairs is expected to keep, and periodically submit to the Public Guardian, correct accounts of all their dealings and transactions on the person's behalf.

Duty to keep the person's money and property separate

8.67 Property and affairs deputies should usually keep the person's money and property separate from their own or anyone else's. This is to avoid any possibility of mistakes or confusion in handling the person's affairs. Sometimes there may be good reason not to do so (for example, a husband might be his wife's deputy and they might have had a joint account for many years).

Changes of contact details

8.68 A deputy should inform the OPG of any changes of contact details or circumstances (for the deputy or the person they are acting for). This will help make sure that the OPG has up-to-date records. It will also allow the court to discharge people who are no longer eligible to act as deputies.

Who is responsible for supervising deputies?

8.69 Deputies are accountable to the Court of Protection. The court can cancel a deputy's appointment at any time if it decides the appointment is no longer in the best interests of the person who lacks capacity.

8.70 The OPG is responsible for supervising and supporting deputies. But it must also protect people lacking capacity from possible abuse or exploitation. Anybody who suspects that a deputy is abusing their position should contact the OPG immediately. The OPG may instruct a Court of Protection Visitor to visit a deputy to investigate any matter of concern. It can also apply to the court to cancel a deputy's appointment.

8.71 The OPG will consider carefully any concerns or complaints against deputies. But if somebody suspects physical or sexual abuse or serious fraud, they should contact the police and/or social services immediately, as well as informing the OPG. Chapter 14 gives more information about the role of the OPG. It also discusses the protection of vulnerable people from abuse, ill treatment or wilful neglect and the responsibilities of various relevant agencies.

9 WHAT DOES THE ACT SAY ABOUT ADVANCE DECISIONS TO REFUSE TREATMENT?

This chapter explains what to do when somebody has made an advance decision to refuse treatment. It sets out:

- what the Act means by an 'advance decision'
- guidance on making, updating and cancelling advance decisions
- how to check whether an advance decision exists
- how to check that an advance decision is valid and that it applies to current circumstances
- the responsibilities of healthcare professionals when an advance decision exists
- how to handle disagreements about advance decisions.

In this chapter, as throughout the Code, a person's capacity (or lack of capacity) refers specifically to their capacity to make a particular decision at the time it needs to be made.

Quick summary

- An advance decision enables someone aged 18 and over, while still capable, to refuse specified medical treatment for a time in the future when they may lack the capacity to consent to or refuse that treatment.
- An advance decision to refuse treatment must be valid and applicable to current circumstances. If it is, it has the same effect as a decision that is made by a person with capacity: healthcare professionals must follow the decision.
- Healthcare professionals will be protected from liability if they:

  - stop or withhold treatment because they reasonably believe that an advance decision exists, and that it is valid and applicable
  - treat a person because, having taken all practical and appropriate steps to find out if the person has made an advance decision to refuse treatment, they do not know or are not satisfied that a valid and applicable advance decision exists.
- People can only make an advance decision under the Act if they are 18 or over and have the capacity to make the decision. They must say what treatment they want to refuse, and they can cancel their decision – or part of it – at any time.
- If the advance decision refuses life-sustaining treatment, it must:
  - be in writing (it can be written by a someone else or recorded in healthcare notes)
  - be signed and witnessed, and
  - state clearly that the decision applies even if life is at risk.
- To establish whether an advance decision is valid and applicable, healthcare professionals must try to find out if the person:
  - has done anything that clearly goes against their advance decision
  - has withdrawn their decision
  - has subsequently conferred the power to make that decision on an attorney, or
  - would have changed their decision if they had known more about the current circumstances.
- Sometimes healthcare professionals will conclude that an advance decision does not exist, is not valid and/or applicable – but that it is an expression of the person's wishes. The healthcare professional must then consider what is set out in the advance decision as an expression of previous wishes when working out the person's best interests (see chapter 5).
- Some healthcare professionals may disagree in principle with patients' decisions to refuse life-sustaining treatment. They do not have to act against their beliefs. But they must not simply abandon patients or act in a way that that affects their care.
- Advance decisions to refuse treatment for mental disorder may not apply if the person who made the advance decision is or is liable to be detained under the Mental Health Act 1983.

How can someone make an advance decision to refuse treatment?

What is an advance decision to refuse treatment?

9.1 It is a general principle of law and medical practice that people have a right to consent to or refuse treatment. The courts have recognised that adults have the right to say in advance that they want to refuse treatment if they lose capacity in the future – even if this results in their death. A valid and applicable advance decision to refuse treatment has the same force as a contemporaneous decision. This has been a fundamental principle of the common law for many years and it is now set out in the Act. Sections 24–26 of the Act set out the when a person can make an advance decision to refuse treatment. This applies if:

- the person is 18 or older, and
- they have the capacity to make an advance decision about treatment.

Information on advance decisions to refuse treatment made by young people (under the age of 18) will be available at www.dh.gov.uk/consent

9.2 Healthcare professionals must follow an advance decision if it is valid and applies to the particular circumstances. If they do not, they could face criminal prosecution (they could be charged for committing a crime) or civil liability (somebody could sue them).

9.3 Advance decisions can have serious consequences for the people who make them. They can also have an important impact on family and friends, and professionals involved in their care. Before healthcare professionals can apply an advance decision, there must be proof that the decision:

- exists
- is valid, and
- is applicable in the current circumstances.

These tests are legal requirements under section 25(1). Paragraphs 9.38–9.44 explain the standard of proof the Act requires.

Who can make an advance decision to refuse treatment?

9.4 It is up to individuals to decide whether they want to refuse treatment in advance. They are entitled to do so if they want, but there is no obligation to do so. Some people choose to make advance decisions while they are still healthy, even if there is no prospect of illness. This might be because they want to keep some control over what might happen to them in the future. Others may think of an advance decision as part of their preparations for growing older (similar to making a will). Or they might make an advance decision after they have been told they have a specific disease or condition.

Many people prefer not to make an advance decision, and instead leave healthcare professionals to make decisions in their best interests at the time a decision needs to be made. Another option is to make a Lasting Power of Attorney. This allows a trusted family member or friend to make personal welfare decisions, such as those around treatment, on someone's behalf, and in their best interests if they ever lose capacity to make those decisions themselves (see paragraph 9.33 below and chapter 7).

9.5 People can only make advance decisions to *refuse* treatment. Nobody has the legal right to demand specific treatment, either at the time or in advance. So no-one can insist (either at the time or in advance) on being given treatments that healthcare professionals consider to be clinically unnecessary, futile or inappropriate. But people can make a request or state their wishes and preferences in advance. Healthcare professionals should then consider the request when deciding what is in a patient's best interests (see chapter 5) if the patient lacks capacity.

9.6 Nobody can ask for and receive procedures that are against the law (for example, help with committing suicide). As section 62 sets out, the Act does not change any of the laws relating to murder, manslaughter or helping someone to commit suicide.

Capacity to make an advance decision

9.7 For most people, there will be no doubt about their capacity to make an advance decision. Even those who lack capacity to make some decisions may have the capacity to make an advance decision. In some cases it may be helpful to get evidence of a person's capacity to make the advance decision (for example, if there is a possibility that the advance decision may be challenged in the future). It is also important to remember that capacity can change over time, and a person who lacks capacity to make a decision now might be able to make it in the future.

Chapter 3 explains how to assess a person's capacity to make a decision.

Scenario: Respecting capacity to make an advance decision

Mrs Long's family has a history of polycystic ovary syndrome. She has made a written advance decision refusing any treatment or procedures that might affect her fertility. The document states that her ovaries and uterus must not be removed. She is having surgery to treat a blocked fallopian tube and, during the consent process, she told her doctor about her advance decision.

During surgery the doctor discovers a solid mass that he thinks might be cancerous. In his clinical judgement, he thinks it would be in Mrs Long's best interests for him to remove the ovary. But he knows that Mrs Long had capacity when she made her valid and applicable advance decision, so he must respect her rights and follow her decision. After surgery, he can discuss the matter with Mrs Long and advise her about treatment options.

9.8 In line with principle 1 of the Act, that 'a person must be assumed to have capacity unless it is established that he lacks capacity', healthcare professionals should always start from the assumption that a person who has made an advance decision had capacity to make it, *unless* they are aware of reasonable grounds to doubt the person had the capacity to make the advance decision at the time they made it. If a healthcare professional is not satisfied that the person had capacity at the time they made the advance decision, or if there are doubts about its existence, validity or applicability, they can treat the person without fear of liability. It is good practice to record their decisions and the reasons for them. The Act does not require them to record their assessment of the person's capacity at the time the decision was made, but it would be good practice to do so.

9.9 Healthcare professionals may have particular concerns about the capacity of someone with a history of suicide attempts or suicidal thoughts who has made an advance decision. It is important to remember that making an advance decision which, if followed, may result in death does not necessarily mean a person is or feels suicidal. Nor does it necessarily mean the person lacks capacity to make

the advance decision. If the person is clearly suicidal, this may raise questions about their capacity to make an advance decision at the time they made it.

What should people include in an advance decision?

9.10 There are no particular formalities about the format of an advance decision. It can be written or verbal, unless it deals with life-sustaining treatment, in which case it must be written and specific rules apply (see paragraphs 9.24–9.28 below).

9.11 An advance decision to refuse treatment:

- must state precisely what treatment is to be refused – a statement giving a general desire not to be treated is not enough
- may set out the circumstances when the refusal should apply – it is helpful to include as much detail as possible
- will only apply at a time when the person lacks capacity to consent to or refuse the specific treatment.

Specific rules apply to life-sustaining treatment.

9.12 People can use medical language or everyday language in their advance decision. But they must make clear what their wishes are and what treatment they would like to refuse.

9.13 An advance decision refusing all treatment in any situation (for example, where a person explains that their decision is based on their religion or personal beliefs) may be valid and applicable.

9.14 It is recommended that people who are thinking about making an advance decision get advice from:

- healthcare professionals (for example, their GP or the person most closely involved with current healthcare or treatment), or
- an organisation that can provide advice on specific conditions or situations (they might have their own format for recording an advance decision).

But it is up to the person whether they want to do this or not. Healthcare professionals should record details of any discussion on healthcare records.

9.15 Some people may also want to get legal advice. This will help them make sure that they express their decision clearly and accurately. It will also help to make sure that people understand their advance decision in the future.

9.16 It is a good idea to try to include possible future circumstances in the advance decision. For example, a woman may want to state in the advance decision whether or not it should still apply if she later becomes pregnant. If the document does not anticipate a change in circumstance, healthcare professionals may decide that it is not applicable if those particular circumstances arise.

9.17 If an advance decision is recorded on a patient's healthcare records, it is confidential. Some patients will tell others about their advance decision (for example, they might tell healthcare professionals, friends or family). Others will not. People who do not ask for their advance decision to be recorded on their healthcare record will need to think about where it should be kept and how they are going to let people know about their decision.

Written advance decisions

9.18 A written document can be evidence of an advance decision. It is helpful to tell others that the document exists and where it is. A person may want to carry it with them in case of emergency, or carry a card, bracelet or other indication that they have made an advance decision and explaining where it is kept.

9.19 There is no set form for written advance decisions, because contents will vary depending on a person's wishes and situation. But it is helpful to include the following information:

- full details of the person making the advance decision, including date of birth, home address and any distinguishing features (in case healthcare professionals need to identify an unconscious person, for example)
- the name and address of the person's GP and whether they have a copy of the document
- a statement that the document should be used if the person ever lacks capacity to make treatment decisions

- a clear statement of the decision, the treatment to be refused and the circumstances in which the decision will apply
- the date the document was written (or reviewed)
- the person's signature (or the signature of someone the person has asked to sign on their behalf and in their presence)
- the signature of the person witnessing the signature, if there is one (or a statement directing somebody to sign on the person's behalf).

See paragraphs 9.24–9.28 below if the advance decision deals with life-sustaining treatment.

9.20 Witnessing the person's signature is not essential, except in cases where the person is making an advance decision to refuse life-sustaining treatment. But if there is a witness, they are witnessing the signature and the fact that it confirms the wishes set out in the advance decision. It may be helpful to give a description of the relationship between the witness and person making the advance decision. The role of the witness is to witness the person's signature, it is not to certify that the person has the capacity to make the advance decision – even if the witness is a healthcare professional or knows the person.

9.21 It is possible that a professional acting as a witness will also be the person who assesses the person's capacity. If so, the professional should also make a record of the assessment, because acting as a witness does not prove that there has been an assessment.

Verbal advance decisions

9.22 There is no set format for verbal advance decisions. This is because they will vary depending on a person's wishes and situation. Healthcare professionals will need to consider whether a verbal advance decision exists and whether it is valid and applicable (see paragraphs 9.38– 9.44).

9.23 Where possible, healthcare professionals should record a verbal advance decision to refuse treatment in a person's healthcare record. This will produce a written record that could prevent confusion about the decision in the future. The record should include:

- a note that the decision should apply if the person lacks capacity to make treatment decisions in the future
- a clear note of the decision, the treatment to be refused and the circumstances in which the decision will apply
- details of someone who was present when the oral advance decision was recorded and the role in which they were present (for example, healthcare professional or family member), and
- whether they heard the decision, took part in it or are just aware that it exists.

What rules apply to advance decisions to refuse life-sustaining treatment?

9.24 The Act imposes particular legal requirements and safeguards on the making of advance decisions to refuse life-sustaining treatment. Advance decisions to refuse life-sustaining treatment *must* meet specific requirements:

- They must be put in writing. If the person is unable to write, someone else should write it down for them. For example, a family member can write down the decision on their behalf, or a healthcare professional can record it in the person's healthcare notes.

- The person must sign the advance decision. If they are unable to sign, they can direct someone to sign on their behalf in their presence.
- The person making the decision must sign in the presence of a witness to the signature. The witness must then sign the document in the presence of the person making the advance decision. If the person making the advance decision is unable to sign, the witness can witness them directing someone else to sign on their behalf. The witness must then sign to indicate that they have witnessed the nominated person signing the document in front of the person making the advance decision.
- The advance decision must include a clear, specific written statement from the person making the advance decision that the advance decision is to apply to the specific treatment even if life is at risk.
- If this statement is made at a different time or in a separate document to the advance decision, the person making the advance decision (or someone they have directed to sign) must sign it in the presence of a witness, who must also sign it.

9.25 Section 4(10) states that life-sustaining treatment is treatment which a healthcare professional who is providing care to the person regards as necessary to sustain life. This decision will not just depend on the type of treatment. It will also depend on the circumstances in which the healthcare professional is giving it. For example, in some situations antibiotics may be life-sustaining, but in others they can be used to treat conditions that do not threaten life.

9.26 Artificial nutrition and hydration (ANH) has been recognised as a form of medical treatment. ANH involves using tubes to provide nutrition and fluids to someone who cannot take them by mouth. It bypasses the natural mechanisms that control hunger and thirst and requires clinical monitoring. An advance decision can refuse ANH. Refusing ANH in an advance decision is likely to result in the person's death, if the advance decision is followed.

9.27 It is very important to discuss advance decisions to refuse life-sustaining treatment with a healthcare professional. But it is not compulsory. A healthcare professional will be able to explain:

- what types of treatment may be life-sustaining treatment, and in what circumstances
- the implications and consequences of refusing such treatment (see also paragraph 9.14).

9.28 An advance decision cannot refuse actions that are needed to keep a person comfortable (sometimes called basic or essential care). Examples include warmth, shelter, actions to keep a person clean and the offer of food and water by mouth. Section 5 of the Act allows healthcare professionals to carry out these actions in the best interests of a person who lacks capacity to consent (see chapter 6). An advance decision can refuse artificial nutrition and hydration.

When should someone review or update an advance decision?

9.29 Anyone who has made an advance decision is advised to regularly review and update it as necessary. Decisions made a long time in advance are not automatically invalid or inapplicable, but they may raise doubts when deciding whether they are valid and applicable. A written decision that is regularly reviewed is more likely to be valid and applicable to current circumstances – particularly for progressive illnesses. This is because it is more likely to have taken on board changes that have occurred in a person's life since they made their decision.

9.30 Views and circumstances may change over time. A new stage in a person's illness, the development of new treatments or a major change in personal circumstances may be appropriate times to review and update an advance decision.

How can someone withdraw an advance decision?

9.31 Section 24(3) allows people to cancel or alter an advance decision at any time while they still have capacity to do so. There are no formal processes to follow. People can cancel their decision verbally or in writing, and they can destroy any original written document. Where possible, the person who made the advance decision should tell anybody who knew about their advance decision that it has been cancelled. They can do this at any time. For example, they can do this on their way to the operating theatre or immediately before being given an anaesthetic. Healthcare professionals should record a verbal cancellation in healthcare records. This then forms a written record for future reference.

How can someone make changes to an advance decision?

9.32 People can makes changes to an advance decision verbally or in writing (section 24(3)) whether or not the advance decision was made in writing. It is good practice for healthcare professionals to record a change of decision in the person's healthcare notes. But if the person wants to change an advance decision to include a refusal of life-sustaining treatment, they must follow the procedures described in paragraphs 9.24–9.28.

How do advance decisions relate to other rules about decision-making?

9.33 A valid and applicable advance decision to refuse treatment is as effective as a refusal made when a person has capacity. Therefore, an advance decision overrules:

- the decision of any personal welfare Lasting Power of Attorney (LPA) made before the advance decision was made. So an attorney cannot give consent to treatment that has been refused in an advance decision made after the LPA was signed
- the decision of any court-appointed deputy (so a deputy cannot give consent to treatment that has been refused in an advance decision which is valid and applicable)
- the provisions of section 5 of the Act, which would otherwise allow healthcare professionals to give treatment that they believe is in a person's best interests.

9.34 An LPA made after an advance decision will make the advance decision invalid, if the LPA gives the attorney the authority to make decisions about the same treatment (see paragraph 9.40).

9.35 The Court of Protection may make declarations as to the existence, validity and applicability of an advance decision, but it has no power to overrule a valid and applicable advance decision to refuse treatment.

9.36 Where an advance decision is being followed, the best interests principle (see chapter 5) does not apply. This is because an advance decision reflects the decision of an adult with capacity who has made the decision for themselves. Healthcare professionals must follow a valid and applicable advance decision, even if they think it goes against a person's best interests.

Advance decisions regarding treatment for mental disorder

9.37 Advance decisions can refuse any kind of treatment, whether for a physical or mental disorder. But generally an advance decision to refuse treatment for mental disorder can be overruled if the person is detained in hospital under the Mental Health Act 1983, when treatment could be given compulsorily under Part 4 of that Act. Advance decisions to refuse treatment for other illnesses or conditions are not affected by the fact that the person is detained in hospital under the Mental Health Act. For further information see chapter 13.

How can somebody decide on the existence, validity and applicability of advance decisions?

Deciding whether an advance decision exists

9.38 It is the responsibility of the person making the advance decision to make sure their decision will be drawn to the attention of healthcare professionals when it is needed. Some people will want their decision to be recorded on their healthcare records. Those who do not will need to find other ways of alerting people that they have made an advance decision and where somebody will find any written document and supporting evidence. Some people carry a card or wear a bracelet. It is also useful to share this information with family and friends, who may alert healthcare professionals to the existence of an advance decision. But it is not compulsory. Providing their GP with a copy of the written document will allow them to record the decision in the person's healthcare records.

9.39 It is important to be able to establish that the person making the advance decision was 18 or over when they made their decision, and that they had the capacity to make that decision when they made it, in line with the two-stage test for capacity set out in chapter 3. But as explained in paragraphs 9.7–9.9 above, healthcare professionals should always start from the assumption that the person had the capacity to make the advance decision.

Deciding whether an advance decision is valid

9.40 An existing advance decision must still be valid at the time it needs to be put into effect. Healthcare professionals must consider the factors in section 25 of the Act before concluding that an advance decision is valid. Events that would make an advance decision invalid include those where:

- the person withdrew the decision while they still had capacity to do so
- after making the advance decision, the person made a Lasting Power of Attorney (LPA) giving an attorney authority to make treatment decisions that are the same as those covered by the advance decision (see also paragraph 9.33)
- the person has done something that clearly goes against the advance decision which suggests that they have changed their mind.

Scenario: Assessing whether an advance decision is valid

A young man, Angus, sees a friend die after prolonged hospital treatment. Angus makes a signed and witnessed advance decision to refuse treatment to keep him alive if he is ever injured in this way. The advance decision includes a statement that this will apply even if his life is at risk.

A few years later, Angus is seriously injured in a road traffic accident. He is paralysed from the neck down and cannot breathe without the help of a machine. At first he stays conscious and gives permission to be treated. He takes part in a rehabilitation programme. Some months later he loses consciousness.

At this point somebody finds his written advance decision, even though Angus has not mentioned it during his treatment. His actions before his lack of capacity obviously go against the advance decision. Anyone assessing the advance decision needs to consider very carefully the doubt this has created about the validity of the advance decision, and whether the advance decision is valid and applicable as a result.

Deciding whether an advance decision is applicable

9.41 To be applicable, an advance decision must apply to the situation in question and in the current circumstances. Healthcare professionals must first determine if the person still has capacity to accept or refuse treatment at the relevant time (section 25(3)). If the person has capacity, they can refuse treatment there and then. Or they can change their decision and accept treatment. The advance decision is not applicable in such situations.

9.42 The advance decision must also apply to the proposed treatment. It is not applicable to the treatment in question if (section 25(4)):

- the proposed treatment is not the treatment specified in the advance decision
- the circumstances are different from those that may have been set out in the advance decision, or
- there are reasonable grounds for believing that there have been changes in circumstance, which would have affected the decision if the person had known about them at the time they made the advance decision.

9.43 So when deciding whether an advance decision applies to the proposed treatment, healthcare professionals must consider:

- how long ago the advance decision was made, and
- whether there have been changes in the patient's personal life (for example, the person is pregnant, and this was not anticipated when they made the advance decision) that might affect the validity of the advance decision, and
- whether there have been developments in medical treatment that the person did not foresee (for example, new medications, treatment or therapies).

9.44 For an advance decision to apply to life-sustaining treatment, it must meet the requirements set out in paragraphs 9.24–9.28.

Scenario: Assessing if an advance decision is applicable

Mr Moss is HIV positive. Several years ago he began to have AIDS-related symptoms. He has accepted general treatment, but made an advance decision to refuse specific retro-viral treatments, saying he didn't want to be a 'guinea pig' for the medical profession. Five years later, he is admitted to hospital seriously ill and keeps falling unconscious.

The doctors treating Mr Moss examine his advance decision. They are aware that there have been major developments in retro-viral treatment recently. They discuss this with Mr Moss's partner and both agree that there are reasonable grounds to believe that Mr Moss may have changed his advance decision if he had known about newer treatment options. So the doctors decide the advance decision does not apply to the new retro-virals and give him treatment.

If Mr Moss regains his capacity, he can change his advance decision and accept or refuse future treatment.

What should healthcare professionals do if an advance decision is not valid or applicable?

9.45 If an advance decision is not valid or applicable to current circumstances:

- healthcare professionals must consider the advance decision as part of their assessment of the person's best interests (see chapter 5) if they have reasonable grounds to think it is a true expression of the person's wishes, and
- they must not assume that because an advance decision is either invalid or not applicable, they should always provide the specified treatment (including life-sustaining treatment) – they must base this decision on what is in the person's best interests.

What happens to decisions made before the Act comes into force?

9.46 Advance decisions made before the Act comes into force may still be valid and applicable. Healthcare professionals should apply the rules in the Act to advance decisions made before the Act comes into force, subject to the transitional protections that will apply to advance decisions that refuse life-sustaining treatment. Further guidance will be available at www.dh.gov.uk/consent.

What implications do advance decisions have for healthcare professionals?

What are healthcare professionals' responsibilities?

9.47 Healthcare professionals should be aware that:

- a patient they propose to treat may have refused treatment in advance, and
- valid and applicable advance decisions to refuse treatment have the same legal status as decisions made by people with capacity at the time of treatment.

9.48 Where appropriate, when discussing treatment options with people who have capacity, healthcare professionals should ask if there are any specific types of treatment they do not wish to receive if they ever lack capacity to consent in the future.

9.49 If somebody tells a healthcare professional that an advance decision exists for a patient who now lacks capacity to consent, they should make reasonable efforts to find out what the decision is. Reasonable efforts might include having discussions with relatives of the patient, looking in the patient's clinical notes held in the hospital or contacting the patient's GP.

9.50 Once they know a verbal or written advance decision exists, healthcare professionals must determine whether:

- it is valid (see paragraph 9.40), and
- it is applicable to the proposed treatment (see paragraphs 9.41–9.44).

9.51 When establishing whether an advance decision applies to current circumstances, healthcare professionals should take special care if the decision does not seem to have been reviewed or updated for some time. If the person's current circumstances are significantly different from those when the decision was made, the advance decision may not be applicable. People close to the person concerned, or anyone named in the advance decision, may be able to help explain the person's prior wishes.

9.52 If healthcare professionals are satisfied that an advance decision to refuse treatment exists, is valid and is applicable, they must follow it and not provide the treatment refused in the advance decision.

9.53 If healthcare professionals are not satisfied that an advance decision exists that is both valid and applicable, they can treat the person without fear of liability. But treatment must be in the person's best interests (see chapter 5). They should make clear notes explaining why they have not followed an advance decision which they consider to be invalid or not applicable.

9.54 Sometimes professionals can give or continue treatment while they resolve doubts over an advance decision. It may be useful to get information from someone who can provide information about the person's capacity when they made the advance decision. The Court of Protection can settle disagreements about the existence, validity or applicability of an advance decision. Section 26 of the Act allows healthcare professionals to give necessary treatment, including life-sustaining treatment, to stop a person's condition getting seriously worse while the court decides.

Do advance decisions apply in emergencies?

9.55 A healthcare professional must provide treatment in the patient's best interests, unless they are satisfied that there is a advance decision that is:

- valid, and
- applicable in the circumstances.

9.56 Healthcare professionals should not delay emergency treatment to look for an advance decision if there is no clear indication that one exists. But if it is clear that a person has made an advance decision that is likely to be relevant, healthcare professionals should assess its validity and applicability as soon as possible. Sometimes the urgency of treatment decisions will make this difficult.

When can healthcare professionals be found liable?

9.57 Healthcare professionals must follow an advance decision if they are satisfied that it exists, is valid and is applicable to their circumstances. Failure to follow an advance decision in this situation could lead to a claim for damages for battery or a criminal charge of assault.

9.58 But they are protected from liability if they are not:

- aware of an advance decision, or
- satisfied that an advance decision exists, is valid and is applicable to the particular treatment and the current circumstances (section 26(2)).

If healthcare professionals have genuine doubts, and are therefore not 'satisfied', about the existence, validity or applicability of the advance decision, treatment can be provided without incurring liability.

9.59 Healthcare professionals will be protected from liability for failing to provide treatment if they 'reasonably believe' that a valid and applicable advance decision to refuse that treatment exists. But they must be able to demonstrate that their belief was reasonable (section 26(3)) and point to reasonable grounds showing why they believe this. Healthcare professionals can only base their decision on the evidence that is available at the time they need consider an advance decision.

9.60 Some situations might be enough in themselves to raise concern about the existence, validity or applicability of an advance decision to refuse treatment. These could include situations when:

- a disagreement between relatives and healthcare professionals about whether verbal comments were really an advance decision
- evidence about the person's state of mind raises questions about their capacity at the time they made the decision (see paragraphs 9.7–9.9)
- evidence of important changes in the person's behaviour before they lost capacity that might suggest a change of mind.

In cases where serious doubt remains and cannot be resolved in any other way, it will be possible to seek a declaration from the court.

What if a healthcare professional has a conscientious objection to stopping or providing life-sustaining treatment?

9.61 Some healthcare professionals may disagree in principle with patients' rights to refuse life-sustaining treatment. The Act does not change the current legal situation. They do not have to do something that goes against their beliefs. But they must not simply abandon patients or cause their care to suffer.

9.62 Healthcare professionals should make their views clear to the patient and the healthcare team as soon as someone raises the subject of withholding, stopping or providing life-sustaining treatment. Patients who still have capacity should then have the option of transferring their care to another healthcare professional, if it is possible to do this without affecting their care.

9.63 In cases where the patient now lacks capacity but has made a valid and applicable advance decision to refuse treatment which a doctor or health professional cannot, for reasons of conscience, comply with, arrangements should be made for the management of the patient's care to be transferred to another healthcare professional.[36] Where a transfer cannot be agreed, the Court of Protection can direct those responsible for the person's healthcare (for example, a Trust, doctor or other health professional) to make arrangements to take over responsibility for the person's healthcare (section 17(1)(e)).

[36] *Re B (Adult: Refusal of Medical Treatment)* [2002] EWHC 429 (Fam) at paragraph 100(viii)

What happens if there is a disagreement about an advance decision?

9.64 It is ultimately the responsibility of the healthcare professional who is in charge of the person's care when the treatment is required to decide whether there is an advance decision which is valid and applicable in the circumstances. In the event of disagreement about an advance decision between healthcare professionals, or between healthcare professionals and family members or others close to the person, the senior clinician must consider all the available evidence. This is likely to be a hospital consultant or the GP where the person is being treated in the community.

9.65 The senior clinician may need to consult with relevant colleagues and others who are close to or familiar with the patient. All staff involved in the person's care should be given the opportunity to express their views. If the person is in hospital, their GP may also have relevant information.

9.66 The point of such discussions should not be to try to overrule the person's advance decision but rather to seek evidence concerning its validity and to confirm its scope and its applicability to the current circumstances. Details of these discussions should be recorded in the person's healthcare records. Where the senior clinician has a reasonable belief that an advance decision to refuse medical treatment is both valid and applicable, the person's advance decision should be complied with.

When can somebody apply to the Court of Protection?

9.67 The Court of Protection can make a decision where there is genuine doubt or disagreement about an advance decision's existence, validity or applicability. But the court does not have the power to overturn a valid and applicable advance decision.

9.68 The court has a range of powers (sections 16–17) to resolve disputes concerning the personal care and medical treatment of a person who lacks capacity (see chapter 8). It can decide whether:

- a person has capacity to accept or refuse treatment at the time it is proposed
- an advance decision to refuse treatment is valid
- an advance decision is applicable to the proposed treatment in the current circumstances.

9.69 While the court decides, healthcare professionals can provide life-sustaining treatment or treatment to stop a serious deterioration in their condition. The court has emergency procedures which operate 24 hours a day to deal with urgent cases quickly. See chapter 8 for guidance on applying to the court.

10 WHAT IS THE NEW INDEPENDENT MENTAL CAPACITY ADVOCATE SERVICE AND HOW DOES IT WORK?

This chapter describes the new Independent Mental Capacity Advocate (IMCA) service created under the Act. The purpose of the IMCA service is to help particularly vulnerable people who lack the capacity to make important decisions about serious medical treatment and changes of accommodation, and who have no family or friends that it would be appropriate to consult about those decisions. IMCAs will work with and support people who lack capacity, and represent their views to those who are working out their best interests.

The chapter provides guidance both for IMCAs and for everyone who may need to instruct an IMCA. It explains how IMCAs should be appointed. It also explains the IMCA's duties and the situations when an IMCA should be instructed. Both IMCAs and decision-makers are required to have regard to the Code of Practice.

In this chapter, as throughout the Code, a person's capacity (or lack of capacity) refers specifically to their capacity to make a particular decision at the time it needs to be made.

Quick summary

Understanding the role of the IMCA service

- The aim of the IMCA service is to provide independent safeguards for people who lack capacity to make certain important decisions and, at the time such decisions need to be made, have no-one else (other than paid staff) to support or represent them or be consulted.
- IMCAs must be independent.

Instructing and consulting an IMCA

- An IMCA *must* be instructed, and then consulted, for people lacking capacity who have no-one else to support them (other than paid staff), whenever:
  - an NHS body is proposing to provide serious medical treatment, or
  - an NHS body or local authority is proposing to arrange accommodation (or a change of accommodation) in hospital or a care home, and
  - the person will stay in hospital longer than 28 days, or
  - they will stay in the care home for more than eight weeks.
- An IMCA *may* be instructed to support someone who lacks capacity to make decisions concerning:
  - care reviews, where no-one else is available to be consulted
  - adult protection cases, whether or not family, friends or others are involved

Ensuring an IMCA's views are taken into consideration

- The IMCA's role is to support and represent the person who lacks capacity. Because of this, IMCAs have the right to see relevant healthcare and social care records.
- Any information or reports provided by an IMCA must be taken into account as part of the process of working out whether a proposed decision is in the person's best interests.

What is the IMCA service?

10.1 Sections 35–41 of the Act set up a new IMCA service that provides safeguards for people who:

- lack capacity to make a specified decision at the time it needs to be made
- are facing a decision on a long-term move or about serious medical treatment and
- have nobody else who is willing and able to represent them or be consulted in the process of working out their best interests.

10.2 Regulations made under the Act also state that IMCAs may be involved in other decisions, concerning:

- a care review, or
- an adult protection case.

In adult protection cases, an IMCA may be appointed even where family members or others are available to be consulted.

10.3 Most people who lack capacity to make a specific decision will have people to support them (for example, family members or friends who take an interest in their welfare). Anybody working out a person's best interests must consult these people, where possible, and take their views into account (see chapter 5). But if a person who lacks capacity has nobody to represent them or no-one who it is appropriate to consult, an IMCA must be instructed in prescribed circumstances. The prescribed circumstances are:

- providing, withholding or stopping serious medical treatment
- moving a person into long-term care in hospital or a care home (see 10.11 for definition), or
- moving the person to a different hospital or care home.

The only exception to this can be in situations where an urgent decision is needed. Further details on the situations where there is a duty to instruct an IMCA are given in paragraphs 10.40–10.58.

In other circumstances, an IMCA *may* be appointed for the person (see paragraphs 10.59–10.68). These include:

- care reviews or
- adult protection cases.

10.4 The IMCA will:

- be independent of the person making the decision
- provide support for the person who lacks capacity
- represent the person without capacity in discussions to work out whether the proposed decision is in the person's best interests
- provide information to help work out what is in the person's best interests (see chapter 5), and
- raise questions or challenge decisions which appear not to be in the best interests of the person.

The information the IMCA provides must be taken into account by decision-makers whenever they are working out what is in a person's best interests. See paragraphs 10.20–10.39 for more information on an IMCA's role. For more information on who is a decision-maker, see chapter 5.

10.5 The IMCA service will build on good practice in the independent advocacy sector. But IMCAs have a different role from many other advocates. They:

- provide statutory advocacy
- are instructed to support and represent people who lack capacity to make decisions on specific issues
- have a right to meet in private the person they are supporting
- are allowed access to relevant healthcare records and social care records
- provide support and representation specifically while the decision is being made, and
- act quickly so their report can form part of decision-making.

Who is responsible for delivering the service?

10.6 The IMCA service is available in England and Wales. Both countries have regulations for setting up and managing the service.

- England's regulations[37] are available at www.opsi.gov.uk/si/ si200618.htm and www.opsi.gov.uk/si/dsis2006.htm.
- The regulations for Wales[38] are available at www.new.wales.gov.uk/consultations/closed/healandsoccarecloscons/.

Guidance has been issued to local health boards and local authorities involved in commissioning IMCA services for their area.

[37] *The Mental Capacity Act 2005 (Independent Mental Capacity Advocate) (General) Regulations 2006 SI: 2006 /No 1832*. The 'General Regulations'. These regulations set out the details on how the IMCA will be appointed, the functions of the IMCA, including their role in challenging the decision-maker and include definitions of 'serious medical treatment' and 'NHS body'.
The Mental Capacity Act 2005 (Independent Mental Capacity Advocate) (Expansion of Role) Regulations 2006 SI: 2883. The 'Expansion Regulations'. These regulations specify the circumstances in which local authorities and NHS bodies may provide the IMCA service on a discretionary basis. These include involving the IMCA in a care review and in adult protection cases.

[38] *The Mental Capacity Act 2005 (Independent Mental Capacity Advocate) (Wales) Regulations 2007 SI: /No* (W.). These regulations will remain in draft form until they are made by the National Assembly for Wales. The target coming into force date is 1 October 2007. Unlike the two sets of English regulations there will be one set only for Wales. Although the Welsh regulations will remain in draft form until the coming into force date, these have been drafted to give effect to similar and corresponding provisions to the regulations in England.

10.7 In England the Secretary of State for Health delivers the service through local authorities, who work in partnership with NHS organisations. Local authorities have financial responsibility for the service. In Wales the National Assembly for Wales delivers the service through local health boards, who have financial responsibility for the service and work in partnership with local authority social services departments and other NHS organisations. The service is commissioned from independent organisations, usually advocacy organisations.

10.8 Local authorities or NHS organisations are responsible for instructing an IMCA to represent a person who lacks capacity. In these circumstances they are called the 'responsible body'.

10.9 For decisions about serious medical treatment, the responsible body will be the NHS organisation providing the person's healthcare or treatment. But if the person is in an independent or voluntary sector hospital, the responsible body will be the NHS organisation arranging and funding the person's care, which should have arrangements in place with the independent or voluntary sector hospital to ensure an IMCA is appointed promptly.

10.10 For decisions about admission to accommodation in hospital for 28 days or more, the responsible body will be the NHS body that manages the hospital. For admission to an independent or voluntary sector hospital for 28 days or more, the responsible body will be the NHS organisation arranging and funding the person's care. The independent or voluntary hospital must have arrangements in place with the NHS organisation to ensure that an IMCA can be appointed without delay.

10.11 For decisions about moves into long-term accommodation[39] (for eight weeks or longer), or about a change of accommodation, the responsible body will be either:

- the NHS body that proposes the move or change of accommodation (e.g. a nursing home), or
- the local authority that has carried out an assessment of the person under the NHS and Community Care Act 1990 and decided the move may be necessary.

[39] This may be accommodation in a care home, nursing home, ordinary and sheltered housing, housing association or other registered social housing or in private sector housing provided by a local authority or in hostel accommodation.

10.12 Sometimes NHS organisations and local authorities will make decisions together about moving a person into long-term care. In these cases, the organisation that must instruct the IMCA is the one that is ultimately responsible for the decision to move the person. The IMCA to be instructed is the one who works wherever the person is at the time that the person needs support and representation.

What are the responsible body's duties?

10.13 The responsible body:

- *must* instruct an IMCA to support and represent a person in the situations set out in paragraphs 10.40–10.58
- *may* decide to instruct an IMCA in situations described in paragraphs 10.59–10.68
- *must*, in all circumstances when an IMCA is instructed, take properly into account the information that the IMCA provides when working out whether the particular decision (such as giving, withholding or stopping treatment, changing a person's accommodation, or carrying out a recommendation following a care review or an allegation requiring adult protection) is in the best interests of the person who lacks capacity.

10.14 The responsible body should also have procedures, training and awareness programmes to make sure that:

- all relevant staff know when they need to instruct an IMCA and are able to do so promptly
- all relevant staff know how to get in touch with the IMCA service and know the procedure for instructing an IMCA
- they record an IMCA's involvement in a case and any information the IMCA provides to help decision-making
- they also record how a decision-maker has taken into account the IMCA's report and information as part of the process of working out the person's best interests (this should include reasons for disagreeing with that advice, if relevant)
- they give access to relevant records when requested by an IMCA under section 35(6)(b) of the Act
- the IMCA gets information about changes that may affect the support and representation the IMCA provides
- decision-makers let all relevant people know when an IMCA is working on a person's case, and
- decision-makers inform the IMCA of the final decision taken and the reason for it.

10.15 Sometimes an IMCA and staff working for the responsible body might disagree. If this happens, they should try to settle the disagreement through discussion and negotiation as soon as possible. If they cannot do this, they should then follow the responsible body's formal procedures for settling disputes or complaints (see paragraphs 10.34 to 10.39 below).

10.16 In some situations the IMCA may challenge a responsible body's decision, or they may help somebody who is challenging a decision. The General Regulations in England and the Regulations in Wales set out when this may happen (see also chapter 15). If there is no other way of resolving the disagreement, the decision may be challenged in the Court of Protection.

Who can be an IMCA?

10.17 In England, a person can only be an IMCA if the local authority approves their appointment. In Wales, the local health board will provide approval. Qualified employees of an approved organisation can act as IMCAs. Local authorities and health boards will usually commission independent advocacy organisations to provide the IMCA service. These organisations will work to appropriate organisational standards set through the contracting/commissioning process.

10.18 Individual IMCAs must:

- have specific experience
- have IMCA training
- have integrity and a good character, and
- be able to act independently.

All IMCAs must complete the IMCA training in order that they can work as an independent mental capacity advocate. A national advocacy qualification is also being developed, which will include the IMCA training.

Before a local authority or health board appoints an IMCA, they must carry out checks with the Criminal Records Bureau (CRB) to get a criminal record certificate or enhanced criminal record certificate for that individual.[40]

40 IMCAs were named as a group that is subject to mandatory checking under the new vetting and barring system in the Safeguarding Vulnerable Groups Act 2006. Roll-out of the bulk of the scheme will take place in 2008.

10.19 IMCAs must be independent. People cannot act as IMCAs if they:

- care for or treat (in a paid or professional capacity) the person they will be representing (this does not apply if they are an existing advocate acting for that person), or
- have links to the person instructing them, to the decision-maker or to other individuals involved in the person's care or treatment that may affect their independence.

What is an IMCA's role?

10.20 An IMCA must decide how best to represent and support the person who lacks capacity that they are helping. They:

- must confirm that the person instructing them has the authority to do so
- should interview or meet in private the person who lacks capacity, if possible
- must act in accordance with the principles of the Act (as set out in section 1 of the Act and chapter 2 of the Code) and take account of relevant guidance in the Code

- may examine any relevant records that section 35(6) of the Act gives them access to
- should get the views of professionals and paid workers providing care or treatment for the person who lacks capacity
- should get the views of anybody else who can give information about the wishes and feelings, beliefs or values of the person who lacks capacity
- should get hold of any other information they think will be necessary
- must find out what support a person who lacks capacity has had to help them make the specific decision
- must try to find out what the person's wishes and feelings, beliefs and values would be likely to be if the person had capacity
- should find out what alternative options there are
- should consider whether getting another medical opinion would help the person who lacks capacity, and
- must write a report on their findings for the local authority or NHS body.

10.21 Where possible, decision-makers should make decisions based on a full understanding of a person's past and present wishes. The IMCA should provide the decision-maker with as much of this information as possible – and anything else they think is relevant. The report they give the decision-maker may include questions about the proposed action or may include suggested alternatives, if they think that these would be better suited to the person's wishes and feelings.

10.22 Another important part of the IMCA's role is communicating their findings. Decision-makers should find the most effective way to enable them to do this. In some of the IMCA pilot areas,[41] hospital discharge teams added a 'Need to instruct an IMCA?' question on their patient or service user forms. This allowed staff to identify the need for an IMCA as early as possible, and to discuss the timetable for the decision to be made. Some decisions need a very quick IMCA response, others will allow more time. In the pilot areas, IMCA involvement led to better informed discharge planning, with a clearer focus on the best interests of a person who lacked capacity. It did not cause additional delays in the hospital discharge.

[41] For further information see www.dh.gov.uk/imca

Representing and supporting the person who lacks capacity

10.23 IMCAs should take account of the guidance in chapter 5.

- IMCAs should find out whether the decision-maker has given all practical and appropriate support to help the person who lacks capacity to be involved as much as possible in decision-making. If the person has communication difficulties, the IMCA should also find out if the decision-maker has obtained any specialist help (for example, from a speech and language therapist).
- Sometimes an IMCA may find information to suggest a person might regain capacity in the future, either so they can make the decision themselves or be more involved in decision-making. In such a situation, the IMCA can ask the decision-maker to delay the decision, if it is not urgent.
- The IMCA will need to get as much information as possible about the person's wishes, feelings, beliefs and values – both past and present. They should also consider the person's religion and any cultural factors that may influence the decision.

10.24 Sometimes a responsible body will not have time to instruct an IMCA (for example in an emergency or if a decision is urgent). If this is the case, this should be recorded, with the reason an IMCA has not been instructed. Where the decision concerns a move of accommodation, the local authority must appoint an IMCA as soon as possible afterwards. Sometimes the IMCA will not have time to carry out full investigations. In these situations, the IMCA must make a judgement about what they can achieve in the time available to support and represent the person who lacks capacity.

10.25 Sometimes an IMCA might not be able to get a good picture of what the person might want. They should still try to make sure the decision-maker considers all relevant information by:

- raising relevant issues and questions, and
- providing additional, relevant information to help the final decision.

Finding and evaluating information

10.26 Section 35(6) provides IMCAs with certain powers to enable them to carry out their duties. These include:

- the right to have an interview in private with the person who lacks capacity, and
- the right to examine, and take copies of, any records that the person holding the record thinks are relevant to the investigation (for example, clinical records, care plans, social care assessment documents or care home records).

10.27 The IMCA may also need to meet professionals or paid carers providing care or treatment for the person who lacks capacity. These people can help assess the information in case records or other sources. They can also comment on possible alternative courses of action. Ultimately, it is the decision-maker's responsibility to decide whether a proposed course of action is in the person's best interests. However, the Act requires the decision-maker to take account of the reports made and information given by the IMCA. In most cases a decision on the person's best interests will be made through discussion involving all the relevant people who are providing care or treatment, as well as the IMCA.

Finding out the person's wishes and feelings, beliefs and values

10.28 The IMCA needs to try and find out what the person's wishes and feelings might be, and what their underlying beliefs and values might also be. The IMCA should try to communicate both verbally and non-verbally with the person who may lack capacity, as appropriate. For example, this might mean using pictures or photographs. But there will be cases where the person cannot communicate at all (for example, if they are unconscious). The IMCA may also talk to other professionals or paid carers directly involved in providing present or past care or treatment. The IMCA might also need to examine health and social care records and any written statements of preferences the person may have made while they still had capacity to do so.

Chapter 5 contains further guidance on finding out the views of people who lack capacity. Chapter 3 contains further guidance on helping someone to make their own decision.

Considering alternative courses of action

10.29 The IMCA will need to check whether the decision-maker has considered all possible options. They should also ask whether the proposed option is less restrictive of the person's rights or future choices or would allow them more freedom (chapter 2, principle 5).

10.30 The IMCA may wish to discuss possible options with other professionals or paid carers directly involved in providing care or treatment for the person. But they must respect the confidentiality of the person they are representing.

Scenario: Using an IMCA

Mrs Nolan has dementia. She is being discharged from hospital. She has no close family or friends. She also lacks the capacity to decide whether she should return home or move to a care home. The local authority instructs an IMCA.

Mrs Nolan tells the IMCA that she wants to go back to her own home, which she can remember and describe. But the hospital care team thinks she needs additional support, which can only be provided in a care home.

The IMCA reviewed all the assessments of Mrs Nolan's needs, spoke to people involved in her care and wrote a report stating that Mrs Nolan had strong and clear wishes. The IMCA also suggested that a care package could be provided to support Mrs Nolan if she were allowed to return home. The care manager now has to decide what is in Mrs Nolan's best interests. He must consider the views of the hospital care team and the IMCA's report.

Getting a second medical opinion

10.31 For decisions about serious medical treatment, the IMCA may consider seeking a second medical opinion from a doctor with appropriate expertise. This puts a person who lacks the capacity to make a specific decision in the same position as a person who has capacity, who has the right to request a second opinion.

What happens if the IMCA disagrees with the decision-maker?

10.32 The IMCA's role is to support and represent their client. They may do this through asking questions, raising issues, offering information and writing a report. They will often take part in a meeting involving different healthcare and social care staff to work out what is in the person's best interests. There may sometimes be cases when an IMCA thinks that a decision-maker has not paid enough attention to their report and other relevant information and is particularly concerned about the decision made. They may then need to challenge the decision.

10.33 An IMCA has the same rights to challenge a decision as any other person caring for the person or interested in his welfare. The right of challenge applies both to decisions about lack of capacity and a person's best interests.

10.34 Chapter 15 sets out how disagreements can be settled. The approach will vary, depending on the type and urgency of the disagreement. It could be a formal or informal approach.

Disagreements about health care or treatment

- Consult the Patient Advice and Liaison Service (England)
- Consult the Community Health Council (Wales)
- Use the NHS Complaints Procedure
- Refer the matter to the local continuing care review panel

- Engage the services of the Independent Complaints Advocacy Service (England) or another advocate.

Disagreements about social care

- Use the care home's complaints procedure (if the person is in a care home)
- Use the local authority complaints procedure.

10.35 Before using these formal methods, the IMCA and the decision-maker should discuss the areas they disagree about – particularly those that might have a serious impact on the person the IMCA is representing. The IMCA and decision-maker should make time to listen to each other's views and to understand the reason for the differences. Sometimes these discussions can help settle a disagreement.

10.36 Sometimes an IMCA service will have a steering group, with representatives from the local NHS organisations and the local authority. These representatives can sometimes negotiate between two differing views. Or they can clarify policy on a certain issue. They should also be involved if an IMCA believes they have discovered poor practice on an important issue.

10.37 IMCAs may use complaints procedures as necessary to try to settle a disagreement – and they can pursue a complaint as far as the relevant ombudsman if needed. In particularly serious or urgent cases, an IMCA may seek permission to refer a case to the Court of Protection for a decision. The Court will make a decision in the best interests of the person who lacks capacity.

10.38 The first step in making a formal challenge is to approach the Official Solicitor (OS) with the facts of the case. The OS can decide to apply to the court as a litigation friend (acting on behalf of the person the IMCA is representing). If the OS decides not to apply himself, the IMCA can ask for permission to apply to the Court of Protection. The OS can still be asked to act as a litigation friend for the person who lacks capacity.

10.39 In extremely serious cases, the IMCA might want to consider an application for judicial review in the High Court. This might happen if the IMCA thinks there are very serious consequences to a decision that has been made by a public authority. There are time limits for making an application, and the IMCA would have to instruct solicitors – and may be liable for the costs of the case going to court. So IMCAs should get legal advice before choosing this approach. The IMCA can also ask the OS to consider making the claim.

What decisions require an IMCA?

10.40 There are three types of decisions which require an IMCA to be instructed for people who lack capacity. These are:

- decisions about providing, withholding or stopping serious medical treatment
- decisions about whether to place people into accommodation (for example a care home or a long stay hospital), and
- decisions about whether to move people to different long stay accommodation.

For these decisions all local authorities and all health bodies must refer the same kinds of decisions to an IMCA for anyone who lacks capacity and qualifies for the IMCA service.

10.41 There are two further types of decisions where the responsible body has the power to instruct an IMCA for a person who lacks capacity. These are decisions relating to:

- care reviews and
- adult protection cases.

In such cases, the relevant local authority or NHS body must decide in each individual case whether it would be of particular benefit to the person who lacks capacity to have an IMCA to support them. The factors which should be considered are explained in paragraphs 10.59–10.68.[42]

[42] See chapter 11 for information about the role of 'consultees' when research is proposed involving a person who lacks capacity to make a decision about whether to agree to take part in research. In certain situations IMCAs may be involved as consultees for research purposes.

Decisions about serious medical treatment

10.42 Where a serious medical treatment decision is being considered for a person who lacks the capacity to consent, and who qualifies for additional safeguards, section 37 of the Act imposes a duty on the NHS body to instruct an IMCA. NHS bodies must instruct an IMCA whenever they are proposing to take a decision about 'serious medical treatment', or proposing that another organisation (such as a private hospital) carry out the treatment on their behalf, if:

- the person concerned does not have the capacity to make a decision about the treatment, and
- there is no-one appropriate to consult about whether the decision is in the person's best interests, other than paid care staff.

10.43 Regulations for England and Wales set out the definition of 'serious medical treatment' for decisions that require an IMCA. It includes treatments for both mental and physical conditions.

Serious medical treatment is defined as treatment which involves giving new treatment, stopping treatment that has already started or withholding treatment that could be offered in circumstances where:

- if a single treatment is proposed there is a fine balance between the likely benefits and the burdens to the patient and the risks involved
- a decision between a choice of treatments is finely balanced, or
- what is proposed is likely to have serious consequences for the patient.

10.44 'Serious consequences' are those which could have a serious impact on the patient, either from the effects of the treatment itself or its wider implications. This may include treatments which:

- cause serious and prolonged pain, distress or side effects
- have potentially major consequences for the patient (for example, stopping life-sustaining treatment or having major surgery such as heart surgery), or
- have a serious impact on the patient's future life choices (for example, interventions for ovarian cancer).

10.45 It is impossible to set out all types of procedures that may amount to 'serious medical treatment', although some examples of medical treatments that might be considered serious include:

- chemotherapy and surgery for cancer
- electro-convulsive therapy
- therapeutic sterilisation
- major surgery (such as open-heart surgery or brain/neuro-surgery)
- major amputations (for example, loss of an arm or leg)
- treatments which will result in permanent loss of hearing or sight
- withholding or stopping artificial nutrition and hydration, and
- termination of pregnancy.

These are illustrative examples only, and whether these or other procedures are considered serious medical treatment in any given case, will depend on the circumstances and the consequences for the patient. There are also many more treatments which will be defined as serious medical treatments under the Act's regulations. Decision-makers who are not sure whether they need to instruct an IMCA should consult their colleagues.

10.46 The only situation in which the duty to instruct an IMCA need not be followed, is when an urgent decision is needed (for example, to save the person's life). This decision must be recorded with the reason for the non-referral. Responsible bodies will however still need to instruct an IMCA for any serious treatment that follows the emergency treatment.

10.47 While a decision-maker is waiting for the IMCA's report, they must still act in the person's best interests (for example, to give treatment that stops the person's condition getting worse).

Scenario: Using an IMCA for serious medical treatment

Mr Jones had a fall and suffered serious head injuries. Hospital staff could not find any family or friends. He needed urgent surgery, but afterwards still lacked capacity to accept or refuse medical treatment.

The hospital did not involve an IMCA in the decision to operate, because it needed to make an emergency decision. But it did instruct an IMCA when it needed to carry out further serious medical treatment.

The IMCA met with Mr Jones looked at his case notes and reviewed the options with the consultant. The decision-maker then made the clinical decision about Mr Jones' best interests taking into account the IMCA's report.

10.48 Some decisions about medical treatment are so serious that the courts need to make them (see chapter 8). But responsible bodies should still instruct an IMCA in these cases. The OS may be involved as a litigation friend of the person who lacks capacity.

10.49 Responsible bodies do not have to instruct an IMCA for patients detained under the Mental Health Act 1983, if:

- the treatment is for mental disorder, and
- they can give it without the patient's consent under that Act.

10.50 If serious medical treatment proposed for the detained patient is not for their mental disorder, the patient then has a right to an IMCA – as long as they meet the Mental Capacity Act's requirements. So a detained patient without capacity to consent to cancer treatment, for example, should qualify for an IMCA if there are no family or friends whom it would be appropriate to consult.

Decisions about accommodation or changes of residence

10.51 The Act imposes similar duties on NHS bodies and local authorities who are responsible for long-term accommodation decisions for a person who lacks the capacity to agree to the placement and who qualifies for the additional safeguard of an IMCA. The right to an IMCA applies to decisions about long-term accommodation in a hospital or care home if it is:

- provided or arranged by the NHS, or
- residential care that is provided or arranged by the local authority or provided under section 117 of the Mental Health Act 1983, or
- a move between such accommodation.

10.52 Responsible bodies have a duty to instruct an IMCA if:

- an NHS organisation proposes to place a person who lacks capacity in a hospital – or to move them to another hospital – for longer than 28 days, or
- an NHS organisation proposes to place a person who lacks capacity in a care home – or to move them to a different care home – for what is likely to be longer than eight weeks.

In either situation the other qualifying conditions apply. So, if the accommodation is for less than 28 days in a hospital or less than 8 weeks in a care home, then an IMCA need not be appointed.

10.53 The duty also applies if a local authority carries out an assessment under section 47 of the NHS and Community Care Act 1990, and it decides to:

- provide care services for a person who lacks capacity in the form of residential accommodation in a care home or its equivalent (see paragraph 10.11) which is likely to be longer than eight weeks, or
- move a person who lacks capacity to another care home or its equivalent for a period likely to exceed eight weeks.

10.54 In some cases, a care home may decide to de-register so that they can provide accommodation and care in a different way. If a local authority makes the new arrangements, then an IMCA should still be instructed if a patient lacks capacity and meets the other qualifying conditions.

10.55 Sometimes a person's placement will be longer than expected. The responsible body should involve an IMCA as soon as they realise the stay will be longer than 28 days or eight weeks, as appropriate.

10.56 People who fund themselves in long-term accommodation have the same rights to an IMCA as others, if the local authority:

- carries out an assessment under section 47 of the NHS and Community Care Act 1990, and
- decides it has a duty to the person (under either section 21 or 29 of the National Assistance Act 1947 or section 117 of the Mental Health Act 1983).

10.57 Responsible bodies can only put aside the duty to involve an IMCA if the placement or move is urgent (for example, an emergency admission to hospital or possible homelessness). The decision-maker must involve an IMCA as soon as possible after making an emergency decision, if:

- the person is likely to stay in hospital for longer than 28 days, or
- they will stay in other accommodation for longer than eight weeks.

10.58 Responsible bodies do not have to involve IMCAs if the person in question is going to be required to stay in the accommodation under the Mental Health Act 1983. But if a person is discharged from detention, they have a right to an IMCA in future accommodation decisions (if they meet the usual conditions set out in the Act).

When can a local authority or NHS body decide to instruct an IMCA?

10.59 The Expansion Regulations have given local authorities and NHS bodies the power to apply the IMCA role to two further types of decisions:

- a care review, and
- adult protection cases that involve vulnerable people.

10.60 In these situations, the responsible body must consider in each individual case whether to instruct an IMCA. Where an IMCA is instructed:

- the decision-maker must be satisfied that having an IMCA will be of particular benefit to the person who lacks capacity
- the decision-maker must also follow the best interests checklist, including getting the views of anyone engaged in caring for a person when assessing their best interests, and
- the decision-maker must consider the IMCA's report and related information when making a decision.

10.61 Responsible bodies are expected to take a strategic approach in deciding when they will use IMCAs in these two additional situations. They should establish a policy locally for determining these decisions, setting out the criteria for appointing an IMCA including the issues to be taken into account when deciding if an IMCA will be of particular benefit to the person concerned. However, decision-makers will need to consider each case separately to see if the criteria are met. Local authorities or NHS bodies may want to publish their approach for ease of access, setting out the ways they intend to use these additional powers and review it periodically.

Involving an IMCA in care reviews

10.62 A responsible body can instruct an IMCA to support and represent a person who lacks capacity when:

- they have arranged accommodation for that person
- they aim to review the arrangements (as part of a care plan or otherwise), and
- there are no family or friends who it would be appropriate to consult.

10.63 Section 7 of the Local Authority Social Services Act 1970 sets out current requirements for care reviews. It states that there should be a review 'within three months of help being provided or major changes made to services'. There should then be a review every year – or more often, if needed.

10.64 Reviews should relate to decisions about accommodation:

- for someone who lacks capacity to make a decision about accommodation
- that will be provided for a continuous period of more than 12 weeks
- that are not the result of an obligation under the Mental Health Act 1983, and
- that do not relate to circumstances where sections 37 to 39 of the Act would apply.

10.65 Where the person is to be detained or required to live in accommodation under the Mental Health Act 1983, an IMCA will not be needed since the safeguards available under that Act will apply.

Involving IMCAs in adult protection cases

10.66 Responsible bodies have powers to instruct an IMCA to support and represent a person who lacks capacity where it is alleged that:

- the person is or has been abused or neglected by another person, or
- the person is abusing or has abused another person.

The responsible bodies can only instruct an IMCA if they propose to take, or have already taken, protective measures. This is in accordance with adult protection procedures set up under statutory guidance.[43]

[43] Published guidance: *No secrets: Guidance on developing and implementing multi-agency policies and procedures to protect vulnerable adults from abuse* for England (on the Department of Health website) and *In safe hands* in Wales.
No secrets applies to adults aged 18 or over. The Children Act 1989 applies to 16 and 17 year olds who may be facing abuse. Part V of the Act covers the Protection of Children, which includes at section 47 the duty to investigate by a local authority in order to decide whether they should take any action to safeguard or promote a child's welfare where he or she requires protection or may suffer harm. See also chapter 12 of this Code.

10.67 In adult protection cases (and no other cases), access to IMCAs is not restricted to people who have no-one else to support or represent them. People who lack capacity who have family and friends can still have an IMCA to support them in the adult protection procedures.

10.68 In some situations, a case may start out as an adult protection case where a local authority may consider whether or not to involve an IMCA under the criteria they have set – but may then become a case where the allegations or evidence give rise to the question of whether the person should be moved in their best interests. In these situations the case has become one where an IMCA must be involved if there is no-one else appropriate to support and represent the person in this decision.

Who qualifies for an IMCA?

10.69 Apart from the adult protection cases discussed above, IMCAs are only available to people who:

- lack capacity to make a specific decision about serious medical treatment or long-term accommodation, *and*
- have no family or friends who are available and appropriate to support or represent them apart from professionals or paid workers providing care or treatment, *and*
- have not previously named someone who could help with a decision, *and*

- have not made a Lasting Power of Attorney or Enduring Power of Attorney (see paragraph 10.70 below).

10.70 The Act says that IMCAs cannot be instructed if:

- a person who now lacks capacity previously named a person that should be consulted about decisions that affect them, and that person is available and willing to help
- the person who lacks capacity has appointed an attorney, either under a Lasting Power of Attorney or an Enduring Power of Attorney, and the attorney continues to manage the person's affairs
- the Court of Protection has appointed a deputy, who continues to act on the person's behalf.

10.71 However, where a person has no family or friends to represent them, but does have an attorney or deputy who has been appointed solely to deal with their property and affairs, they should not be denied access to an IMCA. The Government is seeking to amend the Act at the earliest opportunity to ensure that, in such circumstances, an IMCA should always be appointed to represent the person's views when they lack the capacity to make decisions relating to serious medical treatment or long-term accommodation moves.

10.72 A responsible body can still instruct an IMCA if the Court of Protection is deciding on a deputy, but none is in place when a decision needs to be made.

Scenario: Qualifying for an IMCA

Ms Lewis, a woman with a history of mental health problems has lived in a care home for several years. Her home will soon close, and she has no-one who could help her. She has become very anxious and now lacks capacity to make a decision about future accommodation. The local authority instructs an IMCA to support her. The IMCA visits Ms Lewis, talks to staff who have been involved in her care and reviews her case notes.

In his report, the IMCA includes the information that Ms Lewis is very close to another client in the care home. The IMCA notes that they could move together – if it is also in the interests of the other client. The local authority now has to decide on the best interests of the client, considering the information that the IMCA has provided.

Will IMCAs be available to people in prisons?

10.73 IMCAs should be available to people who are in prison and lack capacity to make decisions about serious medical treatment or long-term accommodation.

Who is it 'appropriate to consult'?

10.74 The IMCA is a safeguard for those people who lack capacity, who have no-one close to them who 'it would be appropriate to consult'. (This is apart from adult protection cases where this criterion does not apply.) The safeguard is intended to apply to those people who have little or no network of support, such as close family or friends, who take an interest in their welfare or no-one willing or able to be formally consulted in decision-making processes.

10.75 The Act does not define those 'whom it would be appropriate to consult' and the evaluation of the IMCA pilots reported that decision-makers in the local authority and in the NHS, whose decision it is to determine this, sometimes found it difficult to establish when an IMCA was required.[44] Section 4(7) provides that consultation about a person's best interests shall include among others, anyone:

- named by the person as someone to be consulted on a relevant decision
- engaged in caring for them, or
- interested in their welfare (see chapter 4).

[44] see www.dh.gov.uk/PolicyAndGuidance/HealthAndSocialCareTopics/SocialCare/IMCA/fs/en

10.76 The decision-maker must determine if it is possible and practical to speak to these people, and those described in paragraph 10.70 when working out whether the proposed decision is in the person's best interests. If it is not possible, practical and appropriate to consult anyone, an IMCA should be instructed.

10.77 There may be situations where a person who lacks capacity has family or friends, but it is not practical or appropriate to consult them. For example, an elderly person with dementia may have an adult child who now lives in Australia, or an older person may have relatives who very rarely visit. Or, a family member may simply refuse to be consulted. In such cases, decision-makers must instruct an IMCA – for serious medical treatment and care moves and record the reason for the decision.

10.78 The person who lacks capacity may have friends or neighbours who know their wishes and feelings but are not willing or able to help with the specific decision to be made. They may think it is too much of a responsibility. If they are elderly and frail themselves, it may be too difficult for them to attend case conferences and participate formally. In this situation, the responsible body should instruct an IMCA, and the IMCA may visit them and enable them to be involved more informally.

10.79 If a family disagrees with a decision-maker's proposed action, this is not grounds for concluding that there is nobody whose views are relevant to the decision.

10.80 A person who lacks capacity and already has an advocate may still be entitled to an IMCA. The IMCA would consult with the advocate. Where that advocate meets the appointment criteria for the IMCA service, they may be appointed to fulfil the IMCA role for this person in addition to their other duties.

11 HOW DOES THE ACT AFFECT RESEARCH PROJECTS INVOLVING A PERSON WHO LACKS CAPACITY?

It is important that research involving people who lack capacity can be carried out, and that is carried out properly. Without it, we would not improve our knowledge of what causes a person to lack or lose capacity, and the diagnosis, treatment, care and needs of people who lack capacity.

This chapter gives guidance on involving people who lack capacity to consent to take part in research. It sets out:

- what the Act means by 'research'
- the requirements that people must meet if their research project involves somebody who lacks capacity

- the specific responsibilities of researchers, and
- how the Act applies to research that started before the Act came into force.

This chapter only deals with research in relation to adults. Further guidance will be provided on how the Act applies in relation to research involving those under the age of 18.

In this chapter, as throughout the Code, a person's capacity (or lack of capacity) refers specifically to their capacity to make a particular decision at the time it needs to be made.

Quick summary

The Act's rules for research that includes people who lack capacity to consent to their involvement cover:

- when research can be carried out
- the ethical approval process
- respecting the wishes and feelings of people who lack capacity
- other safeguards to protect people who lack capacity
- how to engage with a person who lacks capacity
- how to engage with carers and other relevant people.

This chapter also explains:

- the specific rules that apply to research involving human tissue and
- what to do if research projects have already been given the go-ahead.

The Act applies to all research that is intrusive. 'Intrusive' means research that would be unlawful if it involved a person who had capacity but had not consented to take part. The Act does not apply to research involving clinical trials (testing new drugs).

Why does the Act cover research?

11.1 Because the Act is intended to assist and support people who may lack capacity, the Act protects people who take part in research projects but lack capacity to make decisions about their involvement. It makes sure that researchers respect their wishes and feelings. The Act does not apply to research that involves clinical trials of medicines – because these are covered by other rules.[45]

[45] The Medicines for Human Use (Clinical Trials) Regulations 2004.

How can research involving people who lack capacity help?

A high percentage of patients with Down's syndrome lack capacity to agree or refuse to take part in research. Research involving patients with Down's syndrome has shown that they are more likely than other people to get pre-senile dementia. Research has also shown that when this happens the pathological changes that occur in a person with Down's syndrome (changes affecting their body and brain) are similar to those that occur in someone with Alzheimer's disease. This means that we now know that treatment similar to that used for memory disorders in patients with Alzheimer's is appropriate to treat dementia in those with Down's syndrome.

What is 'research'?

11.2 The Act does not have a specific definition for 'research'. The Department of Health and National Assembly for Wales publications *Research governance framework for health and social care* both state:

> 'research can be defined as the attempt to derive generalisable new knowledge by addressing clearly defined questions with systematic and rigorous methods.'[46]

Research may:

- provide information that can be applied generally to an illness, disorder or condition
- demonstrate how effective and safe a new treatment is
- add to evidence that one form of treatment works better than another
- add to evidence that one form of treatment is safer than another, or
- examine wider issues (for example, the factors that affect someone's capacity to make a decision).

46 www.dh.gov.uk/PublicationsAndStatistics/Publications/PublicationsPolicyAndGuidance/PublicationsPolicyAndGuidanceArticle/fs/en?CONTENT_ID=4008777&chk=dMRd/5 and www.word.wales.gov.uk/content/governance/governance-e.htm

11.3 Researchers must state clearly if an activity is part of someone's care and not part of the research. Sometimes experimental medicine or treatment may be performed for the person's benefit and be the best option for their care. But in these cases, it may be difficult to decide whether treatment is research or care. Where there is doubt, the researcher should seek legal advice.

What assumptions can a researcher make about capacity?

11.4 Researchers should assume that a person has capacity, unless there is proof that they lack capacity to make a specific decision (see chapter 3). The person must also receive support to try to help them make their own decision (see chapter 2). The person whose capacity is in question has the right to make decisions that others might not agree with, and they have the right not to take part in research.

What research does the Act cover?

11.5 It is expected that most of the researchers who ask for their research to be approved under the Act will be medical or social care researchers. However, the Act can cover more than just medical and social care research. Intrusive research which does not meet the requirements of the Act cannot be carried out lawfully in relation to people who lack capacity.

11.6 The Act applies to research that:

- is 'intrusive' (if a person taking part had capacity, the researcher would need to get their consent to involve them)
- involves people who have an impairment of, or a disturbance in the functioning of, their mind or brain which makes them unable to decide whether or not to agree to take part in the research (i.e. they lack capacity to consent), and
- is not a clinical trial covered under the Medicines for Human Use (Clinical Trials) Regulations 2004.

11.7 There are circumstances where no consent is needed to lawfully involve a person in research. These apply to all persons, whether they have capacity or not:

- Sometimes research only involves data that has been anonymised (it cannot be traced back to individuals). Confidentiality and data protection laws do not apply in this case.
- Under the Human Tissue Act 2004, research that deals only with human tissue that has been anonymised does not require consent (see paragraphs 11.37–11.40). This applies to both those who have capacity and those who do not. But the research must have ethical approval, and the tissue must come from a living person.[47]
- If researchers collected human tissue samples before 31 August 2006, they do not need a person's consent to work on them. But they will normally have to get ethical approval.
- Regulations[48] made under section 251 of the NHS Act 2006 (formerly known as section 60 of the Health and Social Care Act 2001[49]) allow people to use confidential patient information without breaking the law on confidentiality by applying to the Patient Information Advisory Group for approval on behalf of the Secretary of State.[50]

47 Human Tissue Act 2004 section 1(9).

48 Health Service (Control of Patient Information) Regulations 2002 Section I. 2002/1438.

49 Section 60 of the Health and Social Care Act 2001 was included in the NHS Act 2006 which consolidated all the previous health legislation still in force.

50 The Patient Information Advisory Group considers applications on behalf of the Secretary of State to allow the common law duty of confidentiality to be aside. It was established under section 61of the Health and Social Care Act 2006 (now known as section 252 of the NHS Act 2006). Further information can be found at www.advisorybodies.doh.gov.uk/PIAG.

Who is responsible for making sure research meets the Act's requirements?

11.8 Responsibility for meeting the Act's requirements lies with:

- the 'appropriate body', as defined in regulations made by the Secretary of State (for regulations applying in England) or the National Assembly for Wales (for regulations applying in Wales) (see paragraph 11.10), and
- the researchers carrying out the research (see paragraphs 11.20–11.40).

How can research get approval?

11.9 Research covered by the Act cannot include people who lack capacity to consent to the research unless:

- it has the approval of 'the appropriate body', and
- it follows other requirements in the Act to:
  - consider the views of carers and other relevant people
  - treat the person's interests as more important than those of science and society, and
  - respect any objections a person who lacks capacity makes during research.

11.10 An 'appropriate body' is an organisation that can approve research projects. In England, the 'appropriate body' must be a research ethics committee recognised by the Secretary of State.[51] In Wales, the 'appropriate body' must be a research ethics committee recognised by the Welsh Assembly Government.

51 Mental Capacity Act 2005 (Appropriate Body) (England) Regulations 2006

11.11 The appropriate body can only approve a research project if the research is linked to:

- an impairing condition that affects the person who lacks capacity, or
- the treatment of that condition (see paragraph 11.17)

and:

- there are reasonable grounds for believing that the research would be less effective if only people with capacity are involved, and
- the research project has made arrangements to consult carers and to follow the other requirements of the Act.

11.12 Research must also meet one of two requirements:

1. The research must have some chance of benefiting the person who lacks capacity, as set out in paragraph 11.14 below. The benefit must be in proportion to any burden caused by taking part, or
2. The aim of the research must be to provide knowledge about the cause of, or treatment or care of people with, the same impairing condition – or a similar condition.

If researchers are relying on the second requirement, the Act sets out further requirements that must be met:

- the risk to the person who lacks capacity must be negligible
- there must be no significant interference with the freedom of action or privacy of the person who lacks capacity, and
- nothing must be done to or in relation to the person who lacks capacity which is unduly invasive or restrictive (see paragraphs 11.16–11.19 below).

11.13 An impairing condition:

- is caused by (or may be caused by) an impairment of, or disturbance in the functioning of, the person's mind or brain
- causes (or may cause) an impairment or disturbance of the mind or brain, or
- contributes to (or may contribute to) an impairment or disturbance of the mind or brain.

Balancing the benefit and burden of research

11.14 Potential benefits of research for a person who lacks capacity could include:

- developing more effective ways of treating a person or managing their condition
- improving the quality of healthcare, social care or other services that they have access to
- discovering the cause of their condition, if they would benefit from that knowledge, or
- reducing the risk of the person being harmed, excluded or disadvantaged.

11.15 Benefits may be direct or indirect (for example, the person might benefit at a later date if policies or care packages affecting them are changed because of the research). It might be that participation in the research itself will be of benefit to the person in particular circumstances. For example, if the research involves interviews and the person has the opportunity to express their views, this could be considered of real benefit to a particular individual.

Providing knowledge about causes, treatment or care of people with the same impairing condition or a similar condition

11.16 It is possible for research to be carried out which doesn't actually benefit the person taking part, as long as it aims to provide knowledge about the causes, treatment or care of people with the same impairing condition, or a similar condition. *'Care'* and *'treatment' are* not limited to medical care and treatment. For example, research could examine how day-to-day life in prison affects prisoners with mental health conditions.

11.17 It is the person's actual condition that must be the same or similar in research, not the underlying cause. A *'similar condition'* may therefore have a different cause to that suffered by the participant. For example, research into ways of supporting people with learning disabilities to live more independently might involve a person with a learning disability caused by a head trauma. But its findings might help people with similar learning disabilities that have different causes.

Scenario: Research that helps find a cause or treatment

Mr Neal has Down's syndrome. For many years he has lived in supported housing and worked in a local supermarket. But several months ago, he became aggressive, forgetful and he started to make mistakes at work. His consultant believes that this may indicate the start of Alzheimer's disease.

Mr Neal's condition is now so bad that he does not have capacity to consent to treatment or make other decisions about his care. A research team is researching the cause of dementia in people with Down's syndrome. They would like to involve Mr Neal. The research satisfies the Act's requirement that it is intended to provide knowledge of the causes or treatment of that condition, even though it may not directly benefit Mr Neal. So the approving body might give permission – if the research meets other requirements.

11.18 Any risk to people involved in this category of research must be 'negligible' (minimal). This means that a person should suffer no harm or distress by taking part. Researchers must consider risks to psychological wellbeing as well as physical wellbeing. This is particularly relevant for research related to observations or interviews.

11.19 Research in this category also must not affect a person's freedom of action or privacy in a significant way, and it should not be unduly invasive or restrictive. What will be considered as unduly invasive will be different for different people and different types of research. For example, in psychological research some people may think a specific question is intrusive, but others would not. Actions will not usually be classed as unduly invasive if they do not go beyond the experience of daily life, a routine medical examination or a psychological examination.

Scenario: Assessing the risk to research participants

A research project is studying:

- how well people with a learning disability make financial decisions, and
- communication techniques that may improve their decision-making capacity.

Some of the participants lack capacity to agree to take part. The Research Ethics Committee is satisfied that some of these participants may benefit from the study because their capacity to make financial decisions may be improved. For those who will not gain any personal benefit, the Committee is satisfied that:

- the research meets the other conditions of the Act
- the research methods (psychological testing and different communication techniques) involve no risk to participants, and

- the research could not have been carried out as effectively with people who have capacity.

What responsibilities do researchers have?

11.20 Before starting the research, the research team must make arrangements to:

- obtain approval for the research from the 'appropriate body'
- get the views of any carers and other relevant people before involving a person who lacks capacity in research (see paragraphs 11.22–11.28). There is an exception to this consultation requirement in situations where urgent treatment needs to be given or is about to be given
- respect the objections, wishes and feelings of the person, and
- place more importance on the person's interests than on those of science and society.

11.21 The research proposal must give enough information about what the team will do if a person who lacks capacity needs urgent treatment during research and it is not possible to speak to the person's carer or someone else who acts or makes decisions on behalf of the person (see paragraphs 11.32–11.36).

Consulting carers

11.22 Once it has been established that a person lacks capacity to agree to participate, then before they are included in research the researcher must consult with specified people in accordance with section 32 of the Act to determine whether the person should be included in the research.

Who can researchers consult?

11.23 The researcher should as a matter of good practice take reasonable steps to identify someone to consult. That person (the consultee) must be involved in the person's care, interested in their welfare and must be willing to help. They must not be a professional or paid care worker. They will probably be a family member, but could be another person.

11.24 The researcher must take into account previous wishes and feelings that the person might have expressed about who they would, or would not, like involved in future decisions.

11.25 A person is not prevented from being consulted if they are an attorney authorised under a registered Lasting Power of Attorney or are a deputy appointed by the Court of Protection. But that person must not be acting in a professional or paid capacity (for example, person's solicitor).

11.26 Where there is no-one who meets the conditions mentioned at paragraphs 11.23 and 11.25, the researcher must nominate a person to be the consulted. In this situation, they must follow guidance from the Secretary of State for Health in England or the National Assembly for Wales (the guidance will be available from mid-2007). The person who is nominated must have no connection with the research project.

11.27 The researcher must provide the consultee with information about the research project and ask them:

- for advice about whether the person who lacks capacity should take part in the project, and
- what they think the person's feelings and wishes would be, if they had capacity to decide whether to take part.

11.28 Sometimes the consultee will say that the person would probably not take part in the project or that they would ask to be withdrawn. In this situation, the researcher must not include the person in the project, or they should withdraw them from it. But if the project has started, and the person is getting treatment as part of the research, the researcher may decide that the person should not be withdrawn if the researcher reasonably believes that this would cause a significant risk to the person's health. The researcher may decide that the person should continue with the research while the risk exists. But they should stop any parts of the study that are not related to the risk to the person's health.

What other safeguards does the Act require?

11.29 Even when a consultee agrees that a person can take part in research, the researcher must still consider the person's wishes and feelings.

11.30 Researchers must not do anything the person who lacks capacity objects to. They must not do anything to go against any advance decision to refuse treatment or other statement the person has previously made expressing preferences about their care or treatment. They must assume that the person's interests in this matter are more important than those of science and society.

11.31 A researcher must withdraw someone from a project if:

- they indicate in any way that they want to be withdrawn from the project (for example, if they become upset or distressed), or
- any of the Act's requirements are no longer met.

What happens if urgent decisions are required during the research project?

11.32 Anyone responsible for caring for a person must give them urgent treatment if they need it. In some circumstances, it may not be possible to separate the research from the urgent treatment.

11.33 A research proposal should explain to the appropriate body how researchers will deal with urgent decisions which may occur during the project, when there may not be time to carry out the consultations required under the Act. For example, after a patient has arrived in intensive care, the doctor may want to chart the course of an injury by taking samples or measurements immediately and then taking further samples after some type of treatment to compare with the first set.

11.34 Special rules apply where a person who lacks capacity is getting, or about to get, urgent treatment and researchers want to include them in a research project. If in these circumstances a researcher thinks that it is necessary to take urgent action for the purposes of the research, and they think it is not practical to consult someone about it, the researcher can take that action if:

- they get agreement from a registered medical practitioner not involved with the research, or
- they follow a procedure that the appropriate body agreed to at approval stage.

11.35 The medical practitioner may have a connection to the person who lacks capacity (for example, they might be their doctor). But they must not be involved in the research project in any way. This is to avoid conflicts of interest.

11.36 This exception to the duty to consult only applies:

- for as long as the person needs urgent treatment, and
- when the researcher needs to take action urgently for research to be valid.

It is likely to be limited to research into procedures or treatments used in emergencies. It does not apply where the researcher simply wants to act quickly.

What happens for research involving human tissue?

11.37 A person with capacity has to give their permission for someone to remove tissue from their body (for example, taking a biopsy (a sample) for diagnosis or removal of tissue in surgery). The Act allows the removal of tissue from the body of a person who lacks capacity, if it is in their best interests (see chapter 5).

11.38 People with capacity must also give permission for the storage or use of tissue for certain purposes, set out in the Human Tissue Act 2004, (for example, transplants and research). But there are situations in which permission is not required by law:

- research where the samples are anonymised and the research has ethical approval[52]
- clinical audit
- education or training relating to human health
- performance assessment
- public health monitoring, and
- quality assurance.

[52] Section 1(9) of the Human Tissue Act 2004

11.39 If an adult lacks capacity to consent, the Human Tissue Act 2004 says that tissue can be stored or used without seeking permission if the storage or use is:

- to get information relevant to the health of another individual (for example, before conducting a transplant), as long as the researcher or healthcare professional storing or using the human tissue believes they are doing it in the best interests of the person who lacks capacity to consent
- for a clinical trial approved and carried out under the Medicines for Human Use (Clinical Trials) Regulations 2004, or
- for intrusive research:
  - after the Mental Capacity Act comes into force
  - that meets the Act's requirements, and
  - that has ethical approval.

11.40 Tissue samples that were obtained before 31 August 2006 are existing holdings under the Human Tissue Act. Researchers can work with these tissues without seeking permission. But they will still need to get ethical approval. Guidance is available in the Human Tissue Authority Code of Practice on consent.[53]

[53] www.hta.gov.uk

What should happen to research that started before the Act came into force?

What if a person has capacity when research starts but loses capacity?

11.41 Some people with capacity will agree to take part in research but may then lose capacity before the end of the project. In this situation, researchers will be able to continue research as long as they comply with the conditions set out in the Mental Capacity Act 2005 (Loss of Capacity During Research Project) (England) Regulations 2007 or equivalent Welsh regulations.

The regulations only apply to tissue and data collected before the loss of capacity from a person who gave consent before 31 March 2008 to join a project that starts before 1 October 2007.

11.42 The regulations do not cover research involving direct intervention (for example, taking of further blood pressure readings) or the taking of further tissue after loss of capacity. Such research must comply with sections 30 to 33 of the Act to be lawful.

11.43 Where the regulations do apply, research can only continue if the project already has procedures to deal with people who lose capacity during the project. An appropriate body must have approved the procedures. The researcher must follow the procedures that have been approved.

11.44 The researcher must also:

- seek out the views of someone involved in the person's care or interested in their welfare and if a carer can't be found they must nominate a consultee (see paragraphs 11.22–11.28)
- respect advance decisions and expressed preferences, wishes or objections that the person has made in the past, and
- treat the person's interests as more important than those of science and society.

The appropriate body must be satisfied that the research project has reasonable arrangements to meet these requirements.

11.45 If at any time the researcher believes that procedures are no longer in place or the appropriate body no longer approves the research, they must stop research on the person immediately.

11.46 Where regulations do apply, research does not have to:

- be linked to an impairing condition of the person
- have the potential to benefit that person, or
- aim to provide knowledge relevant to others with the same or a similar condition.

What happens to existing projects that a person never had capacity to agree to?

11.47 There are no regulations for projects that:

- started before the Act comes into force, and
- a person never had the capacity to agree to.

Projects that already have ethical approval will need to obtain approval from an appropriate body under sections 30 and 31 of the Mental Capacity Act and to comply with the requirements of sections 32 and 33 of that Act by 1 October 2008. Research that does not have ethical approval must get approval from an appropriate body by 1 October 2007 to continue lawfully. This is the case in England and it is expected that similar arrangements will apply in Wales.

12 HOW DOES THE ACT APPLY TO CHILDREN AND YOUNG PEOPLE?

This chapter looks at the few parts of the Act that may affect children under 16 years of age. It also explains the position of young people aged 16 and 17 years and the overlapping laws that affect them.

This chapter does not deal with research. Further guidance will be provided on how the Act applies in relation to research involving those under the age of 18.

Within this Code of Practice, 'children' refers to people aged below 16. 'Young people' refers to people aged 16–17. This differs from the Children Act 1989 and the law more generally, where the term 'child' is used to refer to people aged under 18.

In this chapter, as throughout the Code, a person's capacity (or lack of capacity) refers specifically to their capacity to make a particular decision at the time it needs to be made.

Quick summary

CHILDREN UNDER 16

- The Act does not generally apply to people under the age of 16.
- There are two exceptions:
  - The Court of Protection can make decisions about a child's property or finances (or appoint a deputy to make these decisions) if the child lacks capacity to make such decisions within section 2(1) of the Act and is likely to still lack capacity to make financial decisions when they reach the age of 18 (section 18(3)).
  - Offences of ill treatment or wilful neglect of a person who lacks capacity within section 2(1) can also apply to victims younger than 16 (section 44).

YOUNG PEOPLE AGED 16–17 YEARS

- Most of the Act applies to young people aged 16–17 years, who may lack capacity within section 2(1) to make specific decisions.
- There are three exceptions:
  - Only people aged 18 and over can make a Lasting Power of Attorney (LPA).
  - Only people aged 18 and over can make an advance decision to refuse medical treatment.
  - The Court of Protection may only make a statutory will for a person aged 18 and over.

CARE OR TREATMENT FOR YOUNG PEOPLE AGED 16–17

- People carrying out acts in connection with the care or treatment of a young person aged 16–17 who lacks capacity to consent within section 2(1) will generally have protection from liability (section 5), as long as the person carrying out the act:
  - has taken reasonable steps to establish that the young person lacks capacity
  - reasonably believes that the young person lacks capacity and that the act is in the young person's best interests, and
  - follows the Act's principles.
- When assessing the young person's best interests (see chapter 5), the person providing care or treatment must consult those involved in the young person's care and anyone interested in their welfare – if it is practical and appropriate to do so. This may include the young person's parents. Care should be taken not to unlawfully breach the young person's right to confidentiality (see chapter 16).
- Nothing in section 5 excludes a person's civil liability for loss or damage, or his criminal liability, resulting from his negligence in carrying out the act.

LEGAL PROCEEDINGS INVOLVING YOUNG PEOPLE AGED 16–17

- Sometimes there will be disagreements about the care, treatment or welfare of a young person aged 16 or 17 who lacks capacity to make relevant decisions. Depending on the circumstances, the case may be heard in the family courts or the Court of Protection.
- The Court of Protection may transfer a case to the family courts, and vice versa.

Does the Act apply to children?

12.1 Section 2(5) of the Act states that, with the exception of section 2(6), as explained below, no powers under the Act may be exercised in relation to a child under 16.

12.2 Care and treatment of children under the age of 16 is generally governed by common law principles. Further information is provide at www.dh.gov.uk/consent.

Can the Act help with decisions about a child's property or finances?

12.3 Section 2(6) makes an exception for some decisions about a child's property and financial affairs. The Court of Protection can make decisions about property and affairs of those under 16 in cases where the person is likely to still lack capacity to make financial decisions after reaching the age of 18. The court's ruling will still apply when the person reaches the age of 18, which means there will not be a need for further court proceedings once the person reaches the age of 18.

12.4 The Court of Protection can:

- make an order (for example, concerning the investment of an award of compensation for the child), and/or
- appoint a deputy to manage the child's property and affairs and to make ongoing financial decisions on the child's behalf.

In making a decision, the court must follow the Act's principles and decide in the child's best interests as set out in chapter 5 of the Code.

Scenario: Applying the Act to children

Tom was nine when a drunk driver knocked him off his bicycle. He suffered severe head injuries and permanent brain damage. He received a large amount of money in compensation. He is unlikely to recover enough to be able to make financial decisions when he is 18. So the Court of Protection appoints Tom's father as deputy to manage his financial affairs in order to pay for the care Tom will need in the future.

What if somebody mistreats or neglects a child who lacks capacity?

12.5 Section 44 covers the offences of ill treatment or wilful neglect of a person who lacks capacity to make relevant decisions (see chapter 14). This section also applies to children under 16 and young people aged 16 or 17. But it only applies if the child's lack of capacity to make a decision for themselves is caused by an impairment or disturbance that affects how their mind or brain works (see chapter 4). If the lack of capacity is solely the result of the child's youth or immaturity, then the ill treatment or wilful neglect would be dealt with under the separate offences of child cruelty or neglect.

Does the Act apply to young people aged 16–17?

12.6 Most of the Act applies to people aged 16 years and over. There is an overlap with the Children Act 1989. For the Act to apply to a young person, they must lack capacity to make a particular decision (in line with the Act's definition of lack of capacity described in chapter 4). In such situations either this Act or the Children Act 1989 may apply, depending upon the particular circumstances.

However, there may also be situations where neither of these Acts provides an appropriate solution. In such cases, it may be necessary to look to the powers available under the Mental Health Act 1983 or the High Court's inherent powers to deal with cases involving young people.

12.7 There are currently no specific rules for deciding when to use either the Children Act 1989 or the Mental Capacity Act 2005 or when to apply to the High Court. But, the examples below show circumstances where this Act may be the most appropriate (see also paragraphs 12.21–12.23 below).

- In unusual circumstances it might be in a young person's best interests for the Court of Protection to make an order and/or appoint a property and affairs deputy. For example, this might occur when a young person receives financial compensation and the court appoints a parent or a solicitor as a property and affairs deputy.
- It may be appropriate for the Court of Protection to make a welfare decision concerning a young person who lacks capacity to decide for themselves (for example, about where the young person should live) if the court decides that the parents are not acting in the young person's best interests.
- It might be appropriate to refer a case to the Court of Protection where there is disagreement between a person interested in the care and welfare of a young person and the young person's medical team about the young person's best interests or capacity.

Do any parts of the Act not apply to young people aged 16 or 17?

LPAs

12.8 Only people aged 18 or over can make a Lasting Power of Attorney (LPA) (section 9(2)(c)).

Advance decisions to refuse treatment

12.9 Information on decisions to refuse treatment made in advance by young people under the age of 18 will be available at www.dh.gov.uk/consent.

Making a will

12.10 The law generally does not allow anyone below the age of 18 to make a will. So section 18(2) confirms that the Court of Protection can only make a statutory will on behalf of those aged 18 and over.

What does the Act say about care or treatment of young people aged 16 or 17?

Background information concerning competent young people

12.11 The Family Law Reform Act 1969 presumes that young people have the legal capacity to agree to surgical, medical or dental treatment.[54] This also applies to any associated procedures (for example, investigations, anaesthesia or nursing care).

[54] Family Law Reform Act 1969, section 8(1)

12.12 It does not apply to some rarer types of procedure (for example, organ donation or other procedures which are not therapeutic for the young person) or research. In those cases, anyone under 18 is presumed to lack legal capacity, subject to the test of 'Gillick competence' (testing whether they are mature and intelligent enough to understand a proposed treatment or procedure).[55]

[55] In the case of *Gillick v West Norfolk and Wisbech Area Health Authority* [1986] 1 AC 112 the court found that a child below 16 years of age will be competent to consent to medical treatment if they have sufficient intelligence and understanding to understand what is proposed. This test applies in relation to all people under 18 where there is no presumption of competence in relation to the procedure – for example where the procedure is not one referred to in section 8 of the Family Law Reform Act 1969, e.g. organ donation.

12.13 Even where a young person is presumed to have legal capacity to consent to treatment, they may not necessarily be able to make the relevant decision. As with adults, decision-makers should assess the young person's capacity to consent to the proposed care or treatment (see chapter 4). If a young person lacks capacity to consent within section 2(1) of the Act because of an impairment of, or a disturbance in the functioning of, the mind or brain then the Mental Capacity Act will apply in the same way as it does to those who are 18 and over. If however they are unable to make the decision for some other reason, for example because they are overwhelmed by the implications of the decision, the Act will not apply to them and the legality of any treatment should be assessed under common law principles.

12.14 If a young person has capacity to agree to treatment, their decision to consent must be respected. Difficult issues can arise if a young person has legal and mental capacity and refuses consent – especially if a person with parental responsibility wishes to give consent on the young person's behalf. The Family Division of the High Court can hear cases where there is disagreement. The Court of Protection has no power to settle a dispute about a young person who is said to have the mental capacity to make the specific decision.

12.15 It may be unclear whether a young person lacks capacity within section 2(1) of the Act. In those circumstances, it would be prudent for the person providing care or treatment for the young person to seek a declaration from the court.

If the young person lacks capacity to make care or treatment decisions

12.16 Under the common law, a person with parental responsibility for a young person is generally able to consent to the young person receiving care or medical treatment where they lack capacity under section 2(1) of the Act. They should act in the young person's best interests.

12.17 However if a young person lacks the mental capacity to make a specific care or treatment decision within section 2(1) of the Act, healthcare staff providing treatment, or a person providing care to the young person, can carry out treatment or care with protection from liability (section 5) whether or not a person with parental responsibility consents.[56] They must follow the Act's principles and make sure that the actions they carry out are in the young person's best interests. They must make every effort to work out and consider the young person's wishes, feelings, beliefs and values – both past and present – and consider all other factors in the best interests checklist (see chapter 5).

[56] Nothing in section 5 excludes a person's civil liability for loss or damage, or his criminal liability, resulting from his negligence in doing the Act.

12.18 When assessing a young person's best interests, healthcare staff must take into account the views of anyone involved in caring for the young person and anyone interested in their welfare, where it is practical and appropriate to do so. This may include the young person's parents and others with parental responsibility for the young person. Care should be taken not to unlawfully breach the young person's right to confidentiality (see chapter 16).

12.19 If a young person has said they do not want their parents to be consulted, it may not be appropriate to involve them (for example, where there have been allegations of abuse).

12.20 If there is a disagreement about whether the proposed care or treatment is in the best interests of a young person, or there is disagreement about whether the young person lacks capacity and there is no other way of resolving the matter, it would be prudent for those in disagreement to seek a declaration or other order from the appropriate court (see paragraphs 12.23–12.25 below).

Scenario: Working out a young person's best interests

Mary is 16 and has Down's syndrome. Her mother wants Mary to have dental treatment that will improve her appearance but is not otherwise necessary.

To be protected under section 5 of the Act, the dentist must consider whether Mary has capacity to agree to the treatment and what would be in her best interests. He decides that she is unable to understand what is involved or the possible consequences of the proposed treatment and so lacks capacity to make the decision.

But Mary seems to want the treatment, so he takes her views into account in deciding whether the treatment is in her best interests. He also consults with both her parents and with her teacher and GP to see if there are other relevant factors to take into account.

He decides that the treatment is likely to improve Mary's confidence and self-esteem and is in her best interests.

12.21 There may be particular difficulties where young people with mental health problems require in-patient psychiatric treatment, and are treated informally rather than detained under the Mental Health Act 1983. The Mental Capacity Act and its principles apply to decisions related to the care and treatment of young people who lack mental capacity to consent, including treatment for mental disorder. As with any other form of treatment, somebody assessing a young person's best interests should consult anyone involved in caring for the young person or anyone interested in their welfare, as far as is practical and appropriate. This may include the young person's parents or those with parental responsibility for the young person.

But the Act does not allow any actions that result in a young person being deprived of their liberty (see chapter 6). In such circumstances, detention under the Mental Health Act 1983 and the safeguards provided under that Act might be appropriate (see also chapter 13).

12.22 People may disagree about a young person's capacity to make the specific decision or about their best interests, or it may not be clear whether they lack capacity within section 2(1) or for some other reason. In this situation, legal proceedings may be necessary if there is no other way of settling the disagreement (see chapters 8 and 15). If those involved in caring for the young person or who are interested in the young person's welfare do not agree with the proposed treatment, it may be necessary for an interested party to make an application to the appropriate court.

What powers do the courts have in cases involving young people?

12.23 A case involving a young person who lacks mental capacity to make a specific decision could be heard in the family courts (probably in the Family Division of the High Court) or in the Court of Protection.

12.24 If a case might require an ongoing order (because the young person is likely to still lack capacity when they are 18), it may be more appropriate for the Court of Protection to hear the case. For one-off cases not involving property or finances, the Family Division may be more appropriate.

12.25 So that the appropriate court hears a case, the Court of Protection can transfer cases to the family courts, and vice versa (section 21).

Scenario: Hearing cases in the appropriate court

Shola is 17. She has serious learning disabilities and lacks the capacity to decide where she should live. Her parents are involved in a bitter divorce. They cannot agree on several issues concerning Shola's care – including where she should live. Her mother wants to continue to look after Shola at home. But her father wants Shola to move into a care home.

In this case, it may be more appropriate for the Court of Protection to deal with the case. This is because an order made in the Court of Protection could continue into Shola's adulthood. However an order made by the family court under the Children Act 1989 would end on Shola's eighteenth birthday.

13 WHAT IS THE RELATIONSHIP BETWEEN THE MENTAL CAPACITY ACT AND THE MENTAL HEALTH ACT 1983?

This chapter explains the relationship between the Mental Capacity Act 2005 (MCA) and the Mental Health Act 1983 (MHA). It:

- sets out when it may be appropriate to detain someone under the MHA rather than to rely on the MCA
- describes how the MCA affects people lacking capacity who are also subject to the MHA
- explains when doctors cannot give certain treatments for a mental disorder (in particular, psychosurgery) to someone who lacks capacity to consent to it, and
- sets out changes that the Government is planning to make to both Acts.

It does not provide a full description of the MHA. The MHA has its own Memorandum to explain the Act and its own Code of Practice to guide people about how to use it.[57]

[57] Department of Health & Welsh Office, *Mental Health Act 1983 Code of Practice* (TSO, 1999), www.dh.gov.uk/assetRoot/04/07/49/61/04074961.pdf

In this chapter, as throughout the Code, a person's capacity (or lack of capacity) refers specifically to their capacity to make a particular decision at the time it needs to be made.

Quick summary

- Professionals may need to think about using the MHA to detain and treat somebody who lacks capacity to consent to treatment (rather than use the MCA), if:
  - it is not possible to give the person the care or treatment they need without doing something that might deprive them of their liberty
  - the person needs treatment that cannot be given under the MCA (for example, because the person has made a valid and applicable advance decision to refuse an essential part of treatment)
  - the person may need to be restrained in a way that is not allowed under the MCA
  - it is not possible to assess or treat the person safely or effectively without treatment being compulsory (perhaps because the person is expected to regain capacity to consent, but might then refuse to give consent)
  - the person lacks capacity to decide on some elements of the treatment but has capacity to refuse a vital part of it – and they have done so, or
  - there is some other reason why the person might not get treatment, and they or somebody else might suffer harm as a result.
- Before making an application under the MHA, decision-makers should consider whether they could achieve their aims safely and effectively by using the MCA instead.
- Compulsory treatment under the MHA is not an option if:

  - the patient's mental disorder does not justify detention in hospital, or
  - the patient needs treatment only for a physical illness or disability.
- The MCA applies to people subject to the MHA in the same way as it applies to anyone else, with four exceptions:
  - if someone is detained under the MHA, decision-makers cannot normally rely on the MCA to give treatment for mental disorder or make decisions about that treatment on that person's behalf
  - if somebody can be treated for their mental disorder without their consent because they are detained under the MHA, healthcare staff can treat them even if it goes against an advance decision to refuse that treatment
  - if a person is subject to guardianship, the guardian has the exclusive right to take certain decisions, including where the person is to live, and
  - Independent Mental Capacity Advocates do not have to be involved in decisions about serious medical treatment or accommodation, if those decisions are made under the MHA.
- Healthcare staff cannot give psychosurgery (i.e. neurosurgery for mental disorder) to a person who lacks capacity to agree to it. This applies whether or not the person is otherwise subject to the MHA.

Who does the MHA apply to?

13.1 The MHA provides ways of assessing, treating and caring for people who have a serious mental disorder that puts them or other people at risk. It sets out when:

- people with mental disorders can be detained in hospital for assessment or treatment
- people who are detained can be given treatment for their mental disorder without their consent (it also sets out the safeguards people must get in this situation), and
- people with mental disorders can be made subject to guardianship or after-care under supervision to protect them or other people.

13.2 Most of the MHA does not distinguish between people who have the capacity to make decisions and those who do not. Many people covered by the MHA have the capacity to make decisions for themselves. Most people who lack capacity to make decisions about their treatment will never be affected by the MHA, even if they need treatment for a mental disorder.

13.3 But there are cases where decision-makers will need to decide whether to use the MHA or MCA, or both, to meet the needs of people with mental health problems who lack capacity to make decisions about their own treatment.

What are the MCA's limits?

13.4 Section 5 of the MCA provides legal protection for people who care for or treat someone who lacks capacity (see chapter 6). But they must follow the Act's principles and may only take action that is in a person's best interests (see chapter 5). This applies to care or treatment for physical and mental conditions. So it can apply to treatment for people with mental disorders, however serious those disorders are.

13.5 But section 5 does have its limits. For example, somebody using restraint only has protection if the restraint is:

- necessary to protect the person who lacks capacity from harm, and

- in proportion to the likelihood and seriousness of that harm.

13.6 There is no protection under section 5 for actions that deprive a person of their liberty (see chapter 6 for guidance). Similarly, the MCA does not allow giving treatment that goes against a valid and applicable advance decision to refuse treatment (see chapter 9).

13.7 None of these restrictions apply to treatment for mental disorder given under the MHA – but other restrictions do.

When can a person be detained under the MHA?

13.8 A person may be taken into hospital and detained for assessment under section 2 of the MHA for up to 28 days if:

- they have a mental disorder that is serious enough for them to be detained in a hospital for assessment (or for assessment followed by treatment) for at least a limited period, and
- they need to be detained to protect their health or safety, or to protect others.

13.9 A patient may be admitted to hospital and detained for treatment under section 3 of the MHA if:

- they have a mental illness, severe mental impairment, psychopathic disorder or mental impairment (the MHA sets out definitions for these last three terms)
- their mental disorder is serious enough to need treatment in hospital
- treatment is needed for the person's health or safety, or for the protection of other people – and it cannot be provided without detention under this section, and
- (if the person has a mental impairment or psychopathic disorder) treatment is likely to improve their condition or stop it getting worse.

13.10 Decision-makers should consider using the MHA if, in their professional judgment, they are not sure it will be possible, or sufficient, to rely on the MCA. They do not have to ask the Court of Protection to rule that the MCA does not apply before using the MHA.

13.11 If a clinician believes that they can safely assess or treat a person under the MCA, they do not need to consider using the MHA. In this situation, it would be difficult to meet the requirements of the MHA anyway.

13.12 It might be necessary to consider using the MHA rather than the MCA if:

- it is not possible to give the person the care or treatment they need without carrying out an action that might deprive them of their liberty
- the person needs treatment that cannot be given under the MCA (for example, because the person has made a valid and applicable advance decision to refuse all or part of that treatment)
- the person may need to be restrained in a way that is not allowed under the MCA
- it is not possible to assess or treat the person safely or effectively without treatment being compulsory (perhaps because the person is expected to regain capacity to consent, but might then refuse to give consent)
- the person lacks capacity to decide on some elements of the treatment but has capacity to refuse a vital part of it – and they have done so, or

- there is some other reason why the person might not get the treatment they need, and they or somebody else might suffer harm as a result.

13.13 But it is important to remember that a person cannot be treated under the MHA unless they meet the relevant criteria for being detained. Unless they are sent to hospital under Part 3 of the MHA in connection with a criminal offence, people can only be detained where:

- the conditions summarised in paragraph 13.8 or 13.9 are met
- the relevant people agree that an application is necessary (normally two doctors and an approved social worker), and
- (in the case of section 3) the patient's nearest relative has not objected to the application.

'Nearest relative' is defined in section 26 of the MHA. It is usually, but not always, a family member.

Scenario: Using the MHA

Mr Oliver has a learning disability. For the last four years, he has had depression from time to time, and has twice had treatment for it at a psychiatric hospital. He is now seriously depressed and his care workers are worried about him.

Mr Oliver's consultant has given him medication and is considering electro-convulsive therapy. The consultant thinks this care plan will only work if Mr Oliver is detained in hospital. This will allow close observation and Mr Oliver will be stopped if he tries to leave. The consultant thinks an application should be made under section 3 of the MHA.

The consultant also speaks to Mr Oliver's nearest relative, his mother. She asks why Mr Oliver needs to be detained when he has not needed to be in the past. But after she hears the consultant's reasons, she does not object to the application. An approved social worker makes the application and obtains a second medical recommendation. Mr Oliver is then detained and taken to hospital for his treatment for depression to begin.

13.14 Compulsory treatment under the MHA is not an option if:

- the patient's mental disorder does not justify detention in hospital, or
- the patient needs treatment only for a physical illness or disability.

13.15 There will be some cases where a person who lacks capacity cannot be treated either under the MHA or the MCA – even if the treatment is for mental disorder.

Scenario: Deciding whether to use the MHA or MCA

Mrs Carter is in her 80s and has dementia. Somebody finds her wandering in the street, very confused and angry. A neighbour takes her home and calls her doctor. At home, it looks like she has been deliberately smashing things. There are cuts on her hands and arms, but she won't let the doctor touch them, and she hasn't been taking her medication.

Her doctor wants to admit her to hospital for assessment. Mrs Carter gets angry and says that they'll never keep her in hospital. So the doctor thinks that it might be necessary to use the MHA. He arranges for an approved social worker to visit. The social worker discovers that Mrs Carter was expecting her son this morning, but he has not turned up. They find out that he has been delayed, but could not call because Mrs Carter's telephone has become unplugged.

When she is told that her son is on his way, Mrs Carter brightens up. She lets the doctor treat her cuts – which the doctor thinks it is in her best interests to do as soon as possible. When Mrs Carter's son arrives, the social worker explains the doctor is very worried, especially that Mrs Carter is not taking her medication. The son explains that he will help his mother take it in future. It is agreed that the MCA will allow him to do that. The social worker arranges to return a week later and calls the doctor to say that she thinks Mrs Carter can get the care she needs without being detained under the MHA. The doctor agrees.

How does the MCA apply to a patient subject to guardianship under the MHA?

13.16 Guardianship gives someone (usually a local authority social services department) the exclusive right to decide where a person should live – but in doing this they cannot deprive the person of their liberty. The guardian can also require the person to attend for treatment, work, training or education at specific times and places, and they can demand that a doctor, approved social worker or another relevant person have access to the person wherever they live. Guardianship can apply whether or not the person has the capacity to make decisions about care and treatment. It does not give anyone the right to treat the person without their permission or to consent to treatment on their behalf.

13.17 An application can be made for a person who has a mental disorder to be received into guardianship under section 7 of the MHA when:

- the situation meets the conditions summarised in paragraph 13.18
- the relevant people agree an application for guardianship should be made (normally two doctors and an approved social worker), and
- the person's nearest relative does not object.

13.18 An application can be made in relation to any person who is 16 years or over if:

- they have a mental illness, severe mental impairment, psychopathic disorder or mental impairment that is serious enough to justify guardianship (see paragraph 13.20 below), and
- guardianship is necessary in the interests of the welfare of the patient or to protect other people.

13.19 Applicants (usually approved social workers) and doctors supporting the application will need to determine whether they could achieve their aims without guardianship. For patients who lack capacity, the obvious alternative will be action under the MCA.

13.20 But the fact that the person lacks capacity to make relevant decision is not the only factor that applicants need to consider. They need to consider all the circumstances of the case. They may conclude that guardianship is the best option for a person with a mental disorder who lacks capacity to make those decisions if, for example:

- they think it is important that one person or authority should be in charge of making decisions about where the person should live (for example, where there have been long-running or difficult disagreements about where the person should live)

- they think the person will probably respond well to the authority and attention of a guardian, and so be more prepared to accept treatment for the mental disorder (whether they are able to consent to it or it is being provided for them under the MCA), or
- they need authority to return the person to the place they are to live (for example, a care home) if they were to go absent.

Decision-makers must never consider guardianship as a way to avoid applying the MCA.

13.21 A guardian has the exclusive right to decide where a person lives, so nobody else can use the MCA to arrange for the person to live elsewhere. Somebody who knowingly helps a person leave the place a guardian requires them to stay may be committing a criminal offence under the MHA. A guardian also has the exclusive power to require the person to attend set times and places for treatment, occupation, education or training. This does not stop other people using the MCA to make similar arrangements or to treat the person in their best interests. But people cannot use the MCA in any way that conflicts with decisions which a guardian has a legal right to make under the MHA. See paragraph 13.16 above for general information about a guardian's powers.

How does the MCA apply to a patient subject to after-care under supervision under the MHA?

13.22 When people are discharged from detention for medical treatment under the MHA, their responsible medical officer may decide to place them on after-care under supervision. The responsible medical officer is usually the person's consultant psychiatrist. Another doctor and an approved social worker must support their application.

13.23 After-care under supervision means:

- the person can be required to live at a specified place (where they can be taken to and returned, if necessary)
- the person can be required to attend for treatment, occupation, education or training at a specific time and place (where they can be taken, if necessary), and
- their supervisor, any doctor or approved social worker or any other relevant person must be given access to them wherever they live.

13.24 Responsible medical officers can apply for after-care under supervision under section 25A of the MHA if:

- the person is 16 or older and is liable to be detained in a hospital for treatment under section 3 (and certain other sections) of the MHA
- the person has a mental illness, severe mental impairment, psychopathic disorder or mental impairment
- without after-care under supervision the person's health or safety would be at risk of serious harm, they would be at risk of serious exploitation, or other people's safety would be at risk of serious harm, and
- after-care under supervision is likely to help make sure the person gets the after-care services they need.

'Liable to be detained' means that a hospital is allowed to detain them. Patients who are liable to be detained are not always actually in hospital, because they may have been given permission to leave hospital for a time.

13.25 After-care under supervision can be used whether or not the person lacks capacity to make relevant decisions. But if a person lacks capacity, decision-makers will need to decide whether action under the MCA could achieve their aims before making an application. The kinds of cases in which after-care under supervision might be considered for patients who lack capacity to take decisions about their own care and treatment are similar to those for guardianship.

How does the Mental Capacity Act affect people covered by the Mental Health Act?

13.26 There is no reason to assume a person lacks capacity to make their own decisions just because they are subject (under the MHA) to:

- detention
- guardianship, or
- after-care under supervision.

13.27 People who lack capacity to make specific decisions are still protected by the MCA even if they are subject to the MHA (this includes people who are subject to the MHA as a result of court proceedings). But there are four important exceptions:

- if someone is liable to be detained under the MHA, decision-makers cannot normally rely on the MCA to give mental health treatment or make decisions about that treatment on someone's behalf
- if somebody can be given mental health treatment without their consent because they are liable to be detained under the MHA, they can also be given mental health treatment that goes against an advance decision to refuse treatment
- if a person is subject to guardianship, the guardian has the exclusive right to take certain decisions, including where the person is to live, and
- Independent Mental Capacity Advocates do not have to be involved in decisions about serious medical treatment or accommodation, if those decisions are made under the MHA.

What are the implications for people who need treatment for a mental disorder?

13.28 Subject to certain conditions, Part 4 of the MHA allows doctors to give patients who are liable to be detained treatment for mental disorders without their consent – whether or not they have the capacity to give that consent. Paragraph 13.31 below lists a few important exceptions.

13.29 Where Part 4 of the MHA applies, the MCA cannot be used to give medical treatment for a mental disorder to patients who lack capacity to consent. Nor can anyone else, like an attorney or a deputy, use the MCA to give consent for that treatment. This is because Part 4 of the MHA already allows clinicians, if they comply with the relevant rules, to give patients medical treatment for mental disorder even though they lack the capacity to consent. In this context, medical treatment includes nursing and care, habilitation and rehabilitation under medical supervision.

13.30 But clinicians treating people for mental disorder under the MHA cannot simply ignore a person's capacity to consent to treatment. As a matter of good practice (and in some cases in order to comply with the MHA) they will always need to assess and record:

- whether patients have capacity to consent to treatment, and
- if so, whether they have consented to or refused that treatment.

For more information, see the MHA Code of Practice.

13.31 Part 4 of the MHA does not apply to patients:

- admitted in an emergency under section 4(4)(a) of the MHA, following a single medical recommendation and awaiting a second recommendation
- temporarily detained (held in hospital) under section 5 of the MHA while awaiting an application for detention under section 2 or section 3
- remanded by a court to hospital for a report on their medical condition under section 35 of the MHA
- detained under section 37(4), 135 or 136 of the MHA in a place of safety, or
- who have been conditionally discharged by the Mental Health Review Tribunal (and not recalled to hospital).

13.32 Since the MHA does not allow treatment for these patients without their consent, the MCA applies in the normal way, even if the treatment is for mental disorder.

13.33 Even when the MHA allows patients to be treated for mental disorders, the MCA applies in the normal way to treatment for physical disorders. But sometimes healthcare staff may decide to focus first on treating a detained patient's mental disorder in the hope that they will get back the capacity to make a decision about treatment for the physical disorder.

13.34 Where people are subject to guardianship or after-care under supervision under the MHA, the MCA applies as normal to all treatment. Guardianship and after-care under supervision do not give people the right to treat patients without consent.

Scenario: Using the MCA to treat a patient who is detained underthe MHA

Mr Peters is detained in hospital under section 3 of the MHA and is receiving treatment under Part 4 of the MHA. Mr Peters has paranoid schizophrenia, delusions, hallucinations and thought disorder. He refuses all medical treatment. Mr Peters has recently developed blood in his urine and staff persuaded him to have an ultrasound scan. The scan revealed suspected renal carcinoma.

His consultant believes that he needs a CT scan and treatment for the carcinoma. But Mr Peters refuses a general anaesthetic and other medical procedures. The consultant assesses Mr Peters as lacking capacity to consent to treatment under the MCA's test of capacity. The MHA is not relevant here, because the CT scan is not part of Mr Peters' treatment for mental disorder.

Under section 5 of the MCA, doctors can provide treatment without consent. But they must follow the principles of the Act and believe that treatment is in Mr Peters' best interests.

How does the Mental Health Act affect advance decisions to refuse treatment?

13.35 The MHA does not affect a person's advance decision to refuse treatment, unless Part 4 of the MHA means the person can be treated for mental disorder without their consent. In this situation healthcare staff can treat patients for their mental disorder, even if they have made an advance decision to refuse such treatment.

13.36 But even then healthcare staff must treat a valid and applicable advance decision as they would a decision made by a person with capacity at the time they are asked to consent to treatment. For example, they should consider whether they could use a different type of treatment which the patient has not refused in advance. If healthcare staff do not follow an advance decision, they should record in the patient's notes why they have chosen not to follow it.

13.37 Even if a patient is being treated without their consent under Part 4 of the MHA, an advance decision to refuse other forms of treatment is still valid. Being subject to guardianship or after-care under supervision does not affect an advance decision in any way. See chapter 9 for further guidance on advance decisions to refuse treatment.

Scenario: Deciding on whether to follow an advance decision to refuse treatment

Miss Khan gets depression from time to time and has old physical injuries that cause her pain. She does not like the side effects of medication, and manages her health through diet and exercise. She knows that healthcare staff might doubt her decision-making capacity when she is depressed. So she makes an advance decision to refuse all medication for her physical pain and depression.

A year later, she gets major depression and is detained under the MHA. Her GP (family doctor) tells her responsible medical officer (RMO) at the hospital about her advance decision. But Miss Khan's condition gets so bad that she will not discuss treatment. So the RMO decides to prescribe medication for her depression, despite her advance decision. This is possible because Miss Khan is detained under the MHA.

The RMO also believes that Miss Khan now lacks capacity to consent to medication for her physical pain. He assesses the validity of the advance decision to refuse medication for the physical pain. Her GP says that Miss Khan seemed perfectly well when she made the decision and seemed to understand what it meant. In the GP's view, Miss Khan had the capacity to make the advance decision. The RMO decides that the advance decision is valid and applicable, and does not prescribe medication for Miss Khan's pain – even though he thinks it would be in her best interests. When Miss Khan's condition improves, the consultant will be able to discuss whether she would like to change her mind about treatment for her physical pain.

Does the MHA affect the duties of attorneys and deputies?

13.38 In general, the MHA does not affect the powers of attorneys and deputies. But there are two exceptions:

- they will not be able to give consent on a patient's behalf for treatment under Part 4 of the MHA, where the patient is liable to be detained under the MHA (see 13.28–13.34 above), and
- they will not be able to take decisions:
  - about where a person subject to guardianship should live, or
  - that conflict with decisions that a guardian has a legal right to make.

13.39 Being subject to the MHA does not stop patients creating new Lasting Powers of Attorney (if they have the capacity to do so). Nor does it stop the Court of Protection from appointing a deputy for them.

13.40 In certain cases, people subject to the MHA may be required to meet specific conditions relating to:

- leave of absence from hospital
- after-care under supervision, or
- conditional discharge.

Conditions vary from case to case, but could include a requirement to:

- live in a particular place
- maintain contact with health services, or
- avoid a particular area.

13.41 If an attorney or deputy takes a decision that goes against one of these conditions, the patient will be taken to have gone against the condition. The MHA sets out the actions that could be taken in such circumstances. In the case of leave of absence or conditional discharge, this might involve the patient being recalled to hospital.

13.42 Attorneys and deputies are able to exercise patients' rights under the MHA on their behalf, if they have the relevant authority. In particular, some personal welfare attorneys and deputies may be able to apply to the Mental Health Review Tribunal (MHRT) for the patient's discharge from detention, guardianship or after-care under supervision.

13.43 The MHA also gives various rights to a patient's nearest relative. These include the right to:

- insist that a local authority social services department instructs an approved social worker to consider whether the patient should be made subject to the MHA
- apply for the patient to be admitted to hospital or guardianship
- object to an application for admission for treatment
- order the patient's discharge from hospital (subject to certain conditions) and
- order the patient's discharge from guardianship.

13.44 Attorneys and deputies may not exercise these rights, unless they are themselves the nearest relative If the nearest relative and an attorney or deputy disagree, it may be helpful for them to discuss the issue, perhaps with the assistance of the patient's clinicians or social worker. But ultimately they have different roles and both must act as they think best. An attorney or deputy must act in the patient's best interests.

13.45 It is good practice for clinicians and others involved in the assessment or treatment of patients under the MHA to try to find out if the person has an attorney or deputy. But this may not always be possible. So attorneys and deputies should contact either:

- the healthcare professional responsible for the patient's treatment (generally known as the patient's RMO)
- the managers of the hospital where the patient is detained
- the person's guardian (normally the local authority social services department), or
- the person's supervisor (if the patient is subject to after-care under supervision).

Hospitals that treat detained patients normally have a Mental Health Act Administrator's office, which may be a useful first point of contact.

Does the MHA affect when Independent Mental Capacity Advocates must be instructed?

13.46 As explained in chapter 10, there is no duty to instruct an Independent Mental Capacity Advocate (IMCA) for decisions about serious medical treatment which is to be given under Part 4 of the MHA. Nor is there a duty to do so in respect of a move into accommodation, or a change of accommodation, if the person in question is to be required to live in it because of an obligation under the MHA. That obligation might be a condition of leave of absence or conditional discharge from hospital or a requirement imposed by a guardian or a supervisor.

13.47 However, the rules for instructing an IMCA for patients subject to the MHA who might undergo serious medical treatment not related to their mental disorder are the same as for any other patient.

13.48 The duty to instruct an IMCA would also apply as normal if accommodation is being planned as part of the after-care under section 117 of the MHA following the person's discharge from detention (and the person is not going to be required to live in it as a condition of after-care under supervision). This is because the person does not have to accept that accommodation.

What is the effect of section 57 of the Mental Health Act on the MCA?

13.49 Section 57 of the MHA states that psychosurgery (neurosurgery for mental disorder) requires:

- the consent of the patient, and
- the approval of an independent doctor and two other people appointed by the Mental Health Act Commission.

Psychosurgery is any surgical operation that destroys brain tissue or the function of brain tissue.

13.50 The same rules apply to other treatments specified in regulations under section 57. Currently, the only treatment included in regulations is the surgical implantation of hormones to reduce a man's sex drive.

13.51 The combined effect of section 57 of the MHA and section 28 of the MCA is, effectively, that a person who lacks the capacity to consent to one of these treatments for mental disorder may never be given it. Healthcare staff cannot use the MCA as an alternative way of giving these kinds of treatment. Nor can an attorney or deputy give permission for them on a person's behalf.

What changes does the Government plan to make to the MHA and the MCA?

13.52 The Government has introduced a Mental Health Bill into Parliament in order to modernise the MHA. Among the changes it proposes to make are:

- some amendments to the criteria for detention, including a new requirement that appropriate medical treatment be available for patients before they can be detained for treatment
- the introduction of supervised treatment in the community for suitable patients following a period of detention and treatment in hospital. This will help make sure that patients get the treatment they need and help stop them relapsing and returning to hospital

- the replacement of the approved social worker with the approved mental health professional. This will open up the possibility of approved mental healthcare professionals being drawn from other disciplines as well as social work. Other changes will open up the possibility of clinicians who are not doctors being approved to take on the role of the responsible medical officer. This role will be renamed the responsible clinician.
- provisions to make it possible for patients to apply to the county court for an unsuitable nearest relative to be replaced, and
- the abolition of after-care under supervision.

13.53 The Bill will also amend the MCA to introduce new procedures and provisions to make relevant decisions but who need to be deprived of their liberty, in their best interests, otherwise than under the Mental Health Act 1983 (the so-called 'Bournewood provisions').[58]

[58] This refers to the European Court of Human Rights judgement (5 October 2004) in the case of *HL v The United Kingdom* (Application no, 45508/99).

13.54 This chapter, as well as chapter 6, will be fully revised in due course to reflect those changes. Information about the Government's current proposals in respect of the Bournewood safeguards is available on the Department of Health website. This information includes draft illustrative Code of Practice guidance about the proposed safeguards.[59]

[59] See www.dh.gov.uk/PublicationsAndStatistics/Publications/PublicationsPolicyAndGuidance/PublicationsPolicyAndGuidanceArticle/fs/en?CONTENT_ID=4141656&chk=jlw07L

13.55 In the meantime, people taking decisions under both the MCA and the MHA must base those decisions on the Acts as they stand now.

14 WHAT MEANS OF PROTECTION EXIST FOR PEOPLE WHO LACK CAPACITY TO MAKE DECISIONS FOR THEMSELVES?

This chapter describes the different agencies that exist to help make sure that adults who lack capacity to make decisions for themselves are protected from abuse. It also explains the services those agencies provide and how they supervise people who provide care for or make decisions on behalf of people who lack capacity. Finally, it explains what somebody should do if they suspect that somebody is abusing a vulnerable adult who lacks capacity.

In this chapter, as throughout the Code, a person's capacity (or lack of capacity) refers specifically to their capacity to make a particular decision at the time it needs to be made.

Quick summary

- Always report suspicions of abuse of a person who lacks capacity to the relevant agency.

CONCERNS ABOUT AN APPOINTEE

- When someone is concerned about the collection or use of social security benefits by an appointee on behalf a person who lacks capacity, they should contact the local Jobcentre Plus. If the appointee is for someone who is over the age of 60, contact The Pension Service.

CONCERNS ABOUT AN ATTORNEY OR DEPUTY

- If someone is concerned about the actions of an attorney or deputy, they should contact the Office of the Public Guardian.

CONCERNS ABOUT A POSSIBLE CRIMINAL OFFENCE

- If there is a good reason to suspect that someone has committed a crime against a vulnerable person, such as theft or physical or sexual assault, contact the police.
- In addition, social services should also be contacted, so that they can support the vulnerable person during the investigation.

CONCERNS ABOUT POSSIBLE ILL-TREATMENT OR WILFUL NEGLECT

- The Act introduces new criminal offences of ill treatment or wilful neglect of a person who lacks capacity to make relevant decisions (section 44).
- If someone is not being looked after properly, contact social services.
- In serious cases, contact the police.

CONCERNS ABOUT CARE STANDARDS

- In cases of concern about the standard of care in a care home or an adult placement scheme, or about the care provided by a home care worker, contact social services.
- It may also be appropriate to contact the Commission for Social Care Inspection (in England) or the Care and Social Services Inspectorate for Wales.

CONCERNS ABOUT HEALTHCARE OR TREATMENT

- If someone is concerned about the care or treatment given to the person in any NHS setting (such as an NHS hospital or clinic) contact the managers of the service.
- It may also be appropriate to make a formal complaint through the NHS complaints procedure (see chapter 15).

What is abuse?

14.1 The word 'abuse' covers a wide range of actions. In some cases, abuse is clearly deliberate and intentionally unkind. But sometimes abuse happens because somebody does not know how to act correctly – or they haven't got appropriate help and support. It is important to prevent abuse, wherever possible. If somebody is abused, it is important to investigate the abuse and take steps to stop it happening.

14.2 Abuse is anything that goes against a person's human and civil rights. This includes sexual, physical, verbal, financial and emotional abuse. Abuse can be:

- a single act
- a series of repeated acts
- a failure to provide necessary care, or
- neglect.

Abuse can take place anywhere (for example, in a person's own home, a care home or a hospital).

14.3 The main types of abuse are:

Type of abuse	Examples
Financial	• theft • fraud • undue pressure • misuse of property, possessions or benefits • dishonest gain of property, possessions or benefits.
Physical	• slapping, pushing, kicking or other forms of violence • misuse of medication (for example, increasing dosage to make someone drowsy) • inappropriate punishments (for example, not giving someone a meal because they have been 'bad').
Sexual	• rape • sexual assault • sexual acts without consent (this includes if a person is not able to give consent or the abuser used pressure).
Psychological	• emotional abuse • threats of harm, restraint or abandonment • refusing contact with other people • intimidation • threats to restrict someone's liberty.
Neglect and acts of omission	• ignoring the person's medical or physical care needs • failing to get healthcare or social care • withholding medication, food or heating.

14.4 The Department of Health and the National Assembly for Wales have produced separate guidance on protecting vulnerable adults from abuse. *No secrets*[60] (England) and *In safe hands*[61] (Wales) both define vulnerable adults as people aged 18 and over who:

- need community care services due to a mental disability, other disability, age or illness, and
- may be unable to take care of themselves or protect themselves against serious harm or exploitation.

This description applies to many people who lack capacity to make decisions for themselves.

[60] Department of Health and Home Office, *No secrets: Guidance on developing and implementing multi-agency policies and procedures to protect vulnerable adults from abuse*, (2000) www.dh.gov.uk/assetRoot/04/07/45/40/04074540.pdf

[61] National Assembly for Wales, *In safe hands: Implementing adult protection procedures in Wales* (2000), http://new.wales.gov.uk.about.departments/dhss/publications/social_services_publications/reports/insafehands?lang=en

14.5 Anyone who thinks that someone might be abusing a vulnerable adult who lacks capacity should:

- contact the local social services (see paragraphs 14.27–14.28 below)
- contact the Office of the Public Guardian (see paragraph 14.8 below), or
- seek advice from a relevant telephone helpline[62] or through the Community Legal Service.[63]

Full contact details are provided in Annex A.

62 For example, the Action on Elder Abuse (0808 808 8141), Age Concern (0800 009966) or CarersLine (0808 808 7777)

63 Community Legal Service Direct www.clsdirect.org.uk

14.6 In most cases, local adult protection procedures will say who should take action (see paragraphs 14.28–14.29 below). But some abuse will be a criminal offence, such as physical assault, sexual assault or rape, theft, fraud and some other forms of financial exploitation. In these cases, the person who suspects abuse should contact the police urgently. The criminal investigation may take priority over all other forms of investigation. So all agencies will have to work together to plan the best way to investigate possible abuse.

14.7 The Fraud Act 2006 (due to come into force in 2007) creates a new offence of 'fraud by abuse of position'. This new offence may apply to a range of people, including:

- attorneys under a Lasting Power of Attorney (LPA) or an Enduring Power of Attorney (EPA), or
- deputies appointed by the Court of Protection to make financial decisions on behalf of a person who lacks capacity.

Attorneys and deputies may be guilty of fraud if they dishonestly abuse their position, intend to benefit themselves or others, and cause loss or expose a person to the risk of loss. People who suspect fraud should report the case to the police.

How does the Act protect people from abuse?

The Office of the Public Guardian

14.8 Section 57 of the Act creates a new Public Guardian, supported by staff of the Office of the Public Guardian (OPG). The Public Guardian helps protect people who lack capacity by:

- setting up and managing a register of LPAs
- setting up and managing a register of EPAs
- setting up and managing a register of court orders that appoint deputies
- supervising deputies, working with other relevant organisations (for example, social services, if the person who lacks capacity is receiving social care)
- sending Court of Protection Visitors to visit people who may lack capacity to make particular decisions and those who have formal powers to act on their behalf (see paragraphs 14.10–14.11 below)
- receiving reports from attorneys acting under LPAs and from deputies
- providing reports to the Court of Protection, as requested, and
- dealing with representations (including complaints) about the way in which attorneys or deputies carry out their duties.

14.9 Section 59 of the Act creates a Public Guardian Board to oversee and review how the Public Guardian carries out these duties.

Court of Protection Visitors

14.10 The role of a Court of Protection Visitor is to provide independent advice to the court and the Public Guardian. They advise on how anyone given power under the Act should be, and is, carrying out their duties and responsibilities. There are two types of visitor: General Visitors and Special Visitors. Special visitors are registered medical practitioners with relevant expertise. The court or Public Guardian can send whichever type of visitor is most appropriate to visit and interview a person who may lack capacity. Visitors can also interview attorneys or deputies and inspect any relevant healthcare or social care records. Attorneys and deputies must co-operate with the visitors and provide them with all relevant information. If attorneys or deputies do not co-operate, the court can cancel their appointment, where it thinks that they have not acted in the person's best interests.

Scenario: Using a General Visitor

Mrs Quinn made an LPA appointing her nephew, Ian, as her financial attorney. She recently lost capacity to make her own financial decisions, and Ian has registered the LPA. He has taken control of Mrs Quinn's financial affairs.

But Mrs Quinn's niece suspects that Ian is using Mrs Quinn's money to pay off his own debts. She contacts the OPG, which sends a General Visitor to visit Mrs Quinn and Ian. The visitor's report will assess the facts. It might suggest the case go to court to consider whether Ian has behaved in a way which:

- goes against his authority under the LPA, or
- is not in Mrs Quinn's best interests.

The Public Guardian will decide whether the court should be involved in the matter. The court will then decide if it requires further evidence. If it thinks that Ian is abusing his position, the court may cancel the LPA.

14.11 Court of Protection Visitors have an important part to play in investigating possible abuse. But their role is much wider than this. They can also check on the general wellbeing of the person who lacks capacity, and they can give support to attorneys and deputies who need help to carry out their duties.

How does the Public Guardian oversee LPAs?

14.12 An LPA is a private arrangement between the donor and the attorney (see chapter 7). Donors should only choose attorneys that they can trust. The OPG provides information to help potential donors understand:

- the impact of making an LPA
- what they can give an attorney authority to do
- what to consider when choosing an attorney.

14.13 The Public Guardian must make sure that an LPA meets the Act's requirements. Before registering an LPA, the OPG will check documentation. For property and affairs LPAs, it will check whether an attorney appointed under the LPA is bankrupt since this would revoke the authority.

14.14 The Public Guardian will not usually get involved once somebody has registered an LPA – unless someone is worried about how an attorney is carrying out their duties. If concerns are raised about an attorney, the OPG works closely with organisations such as local authorities and NHS Trusts to carry out investigations.

How does the Public Guardian supervise deputies?

14.15 Individuals do not choose who will act as a deputy for them. The court will make the decision. There are measures to make sure that the court appoints an appropriate deputy. The OPG will then supervise deputies and support them in carrying out their duties, while also making sure they do not abuse their position.

14.16 When a case comes before the Court of Protection, the Act states that the court should make a decision to settle the matter rather than appoint a deputy, if possible. Deputies are most likely to be needed for financial matters where someone needs continued authority to make decisions about the person's money or other assets. It will be easier for the courts to make decisions in cases where a one-off decision is needed about a person's welfare, so there are likely to be fewer personal welfare deputies. But there will be occasions where ongoing decisions about a person's welfare will be required, and so the court will appoint a personal welfare deputy (see chapter 8).

Scenario: Appointing deputies

Peter was in a motorbike accident that left him permanently and seriously brain-damaged. He has minimal awareness of his surroundings and an assessment has shown that he lacks capacity to make most decisions for himself.

Somebody needs to make several decisions about what treatment Peter needs and where he should be treated. His parents feel that healthcare staff do not always consider their views in decisions about what treatment is in Peter's best interests. So they make an application to the court to be appointed as joint personal welfare deputies.

There will be many care or treatment decisions for Peter in the future. The court decides it would not be practical to make a separate decision on each of them. It also thinks Peter needs some continuity in decision-making. So it appoints Peter's parents as joint personal welfare deputies.

14.17 The OPG may run checks on potential deputies if requested to by the court. It will carry out a risk assessment to determine what kind of supervision a deputy will need once they are appointed.

14.18 Deputies are accountable to the court. The OPG supervises the deputy's actions on the court's behalf, and the court may want the deputy to provide financial accounts or other reports to the OPG. The Public Guardian deals with complaints about the way deputies carry out their duties. It works with other relevant agencies to investigate them. Chapter 8 gives detailed information about the responsibilities of deputies.

What happens if someone says they are worried about an attorney or deputy?

14.19 Many people who lack capacity are likely to get care or support from a range of agencies. Even when an attorney or deputy is acting on behalf of a person who lacks capacity, the other carers still have a responsibility to the person to provide care and act in the person's best interests. Anybody who is caring for a person who lacks capacity, whether in a paid or unpaid role, who is worried about how attorneys or deputies carry out their duties should contact the Public Guardian.

14.20 The OPG will not always be the most appropriate organisation to investigate all complaints. It may investigate a case jointly with:

- healthcare or social care professionals
- social services
- NHS bodies
- the Commission for Social Care Inspection in England or the Care and Social Services Inspectorate for Wales (CSSIW)[64]
- the Healthcare Commission in England or the Healthcare Inspectorate for Wales, and
- in some cases, the police.

[64] In April 2007, the Care Standards Inspectorate for Wales (CSIW) and the Social Services Inspectorate for Wales (SSIW) came together to form the Care and Social Services Inspectorate for Wales.

14.21 The OPG will usually refer concerns about personal welfare LPAs or personal welfare deputies to the relevant agency. In certain circumstances it will alert the police about a case. When it makes a referral, the OPG will make sure that the relevant agency keeps it informed of the action it takes. It will also make sure that the court has all the information it needs to take possible action against the attorney or deputy.

14.22 Examples of situations in which a referral might be necessary include where:

- someone has complained that a welfare attorney is physically abusing a donor – the OPG would refer this case to the relevant local authority adult protection procedures and possibly the police
- the OPG has found that a solicitor appointed as a financial deputy for an elderly woman has defrauded her estate – the OPG would refer this case to the police and the Law Society Consumer Complaints Service.

How does the Act deal with ill treatment and wilful neglect?

14.23 The Act introduces two new criminal offences: ill treatment and wilful neglect of a person who lacks capacity to make relevant decisions (section 44). The offences may apply to:

- anyone caring for a person who lacks capacity – this includes family carers, healthcare and social care staff in hospital or care homes and those providing care in a person's home
- an attorney appointed under an LPA or an EPA, or
- a deputy appointed for the person by the court.

14.24 These people may be guilty of an offence if they ill-treat or wilfully neglect the person they care for or represent. Penalties will range from a fine to a sentence of imprisonment of up to five years – or both.

14.25 Ill treatment and neglect are separate offences.[65] For a person to be found guilty of ill treatment, they must either:

- have deliberately ill-treated the person, or
- be reckless in the way they were ill-treating the person or not.

It does not matter whether the behaviour was likely to cause, or actually caused, harm or damage to the victim's health.

[65] *R v Newington* (1990) 91 Cr App R 247, CA

14.26 The meaning of 'wilful neglect' varies depending on the circumstances. But it usually means that a person has deliberately failed to carry out an act they knew they had a duty to do.

Scenario: Reporting abuse

Norma is 95 and has Alzheimer's disease. Her son, Brendan, is her personal welfare attorney under an LPA. A district nurse has noticed that Norma has bruises and other injuries. She suspects Brendan may be assaulting his mother when he is drunk. She alerts the police and the local Adult Protection Committee.

Following a criminal investigation, Brendan is charged with ill-treating his mother. The Public Guardian applies to the court to cancel the LPA. Social services start to make alternative arrangements for Norma's care.

What other measures protect people from abuse?

14.27 Local agencies have procedures that allow them to work together (called multi-agency working) to protect vulnerable adults – in care settings and elsewhere. Most areas have Adult Protection Committees. These committees:

- create policy (including reporting procedures)
- oversee investigations and other activity between agencies
- carry out joint training, and
- monitor and review progress.

Other local authorities have developed multi-agency Adult Protection Procedures, which are managed by a dedicated Adult Protection Co-ordinator.

14.28 Adult Protection Committees and Procedures (APCP) involve representatives from the NHS, social services, housing, the police and other relevant agencies. In England, they are essential points of contact for anyone who suspects abuse or ill treatment of a vulnerable adult. They can also give advice to the OPG if it is uncertain whether an intervention is necessary in a case of suspected abuse. In Wales, APCPs are not necessarily points of contact themselves, but they publish details of points of contact.

Who should check that staff are safe to work with vulnerable adults?

14.29 Under the Safeguarding Vulnerable Groups Act 2006, criminal record checks are now compulsory for staff who:

- have contact with service users in registered care homes
- provide personal care services in someone's home, and
- are involved in providing adult placement schemes.

14.30 Potential employers must carry out a pre-employment criminal record check with the Criminal Records Bureau (CRB) for all potential new healthcare and social care staff. This includes nursing agency staff and home care agency staff.

See Annex A for sources of more detailed information.

14.31 The Protection of Vulnerable Adults (POVA) list has the names of people who have been barred from working with vulnerable adults (in England and Wales). Employers providing care in a residential setting or a person's own home must check whether potential employees are on the list.[66] If they are on the list, they must:

- refuse to employ them, or
- employ them in a position that does not give them regular contact with vulnerable adults.

It is an offence for anyone on the list to apply for a care position. In such cases, the employer should report the person making the application.

[66] www.dh.gov.uk/PublicationsAndStatistics/Publications/PublicationsPolicyAndGuidance/PublicationsPolicyAndGuidanceArticle/fs/en?CONTENT_ID=4085855&chk=p0kQeS

Who is responsible for monitoring the standard of care providers?

14.32 All care providers covered by the Care Standards Act 2000 must register with the Commission for Social Care Inspection in England (CSCI) or the Care and Social Services Inspectorate for Wales (CSSIW).[67] These agencies make sure that care providers meet certain standards. They require care providers to have procedures to protect people from harm or abuse. These agencies can take action if they discover dangerous or unsafe practices that could place people at risk.

[67] See note 64 above regarding the merger of the Care Standards Inspectorate for Wales and the Social Services Inspectorate for Wales.

14.33 Care providers must also have effective complaints procedures. If providers cannot settle complaints, CSCI or CSSIW can look into them.

14.34 CSCI or CSSIW assesses the effectiveness of local adult protection procedures. They will also monitor the arrangements local councils make in response to the Care Standards Act.

What is an appointee, and who monitors them?

14.35 The Department for Work and Pensions (DWP) can appoint someone (an appointee) to claim and spend benefits on a person's behalf[68] if that person:

- gets social security benefits or pensions
- lacks the capacity to act for themselves
- has not made a property and affairs LPA or an EPA, and

- the court has not appointed a property and affairs deputy.

68 www.dwp.gov.uk/publications/dwp/2005/gl21_apr.pdf

14.36 The DWP checks that an appointee is trustworthy. It also investigates any allegations that an appointee is not acting appropriately or in the person's interests. It can remove an appointee who abuses their position. Concerns about appointees should be raised with the relevant DWP agency (the local Jobcentre Plus, or if the person is aged 60 or over, The Pension Service).

Are there any other means of protection that people should be aware of?

14.37 There are a number of additional means that exist to protect people who lack capacity to make decisions for themselves. Healthcare and social care staff, attorneys and deputies should be aware of:

- National Minimum Standards (for example, for healthcare, care homes, and home care agencies) which apply to both England and Wales (see paragraph 14.38)
- National Service Frameworks, which set out national standards for specific health and care services for particular groups (for example, for mental health services[69] or services for older people[70])
- complaints procedures for all NHS bodies and local councils (see chapter 15)
- Stop Now Orders (also known as Enforcement Orders) that allow consumer protection bodies to apply for court orders to stop poor trading practices (for example, unfair door-step selling or rogue traders).[71]
- The Public Interest Disclosure Act 1998, which encourages people to report malpractice in the workplace and protects people who report malpractice from being sacked or victimised.

69 www.dh.gov.uk/assetRoot/04/07/72/09/04077209.pdf and www.wales.nhs.uk/sites3/page.cfm?orgid=438&pid=11071

70 www.dh.gov.uk/assetRoot/04/07/12/83/04071283.pdf and www.wales.nhs.uk/sites3/home.cfm?orgid=439&redirect=yes&CFID=298511&CFTOKEN=6985382

71 www.oft.gov.uk/Business/Legal/Stop+Now+Regulations.htm

14.38 Information about all national minimum standards are available on the CSCI[72] and Healthcare Commission websites[73] and the Welsh Assembly Government website. Chapter 15 gives guidance on complaints procedures. Individual local authorities will have their own complaints system in place.

72 www.csci.org.uk/information_for_service_providers/national_minimum_standards/default.htm

73 www.healthcarecommission.org.uk/_db/_documents/The_annual_health_check_in_2006_2007_assessing_and_rating_the_NHS_200609225143.pdf

15 WHAT ARE THE BEST WAYS TO SETTLE DISAGREEMENTS AND DISPUTES ABOUT ISSUES COVERED IN THE ACT?

Sometimes people will disagree about:

- a person's capacity to make a decision
- their best interests
- a decision someone is making on their behalf, or
- an action someone is taking on their behalf.

It is in everybody's interests to settle disagreements and disputes quickly and effectively, with minimal stress and cost. This chapter sets out the different options available for settling disagreements. It also suggests ways to avoid letting a disagreement become a serious dispute. Finally, it sets out when it might be necessary to apply to the Court of Protection and when somebody can get legal funding.

In this chapter, as throughout the Code, a person's capacity (or lack of capacity) refers specifically to their capacity to make a particular decision at the time it needs to be made.

Quick summary

- When disagreements occur about issues that are covered in the Act, it is usually best to try and settle them before they become serious.
- Advocates can help someone who finds it difficult to communicate their point of view. (This may be someone who has been assessed as lacking capacity.)
- Some disagreements can be effectively resolved by mediation.
- Where there is a concern about healthcare or social care provided to a person who lacks capacity, there are formal and informal ways of complaining about the care or treatment.
- The Health Service Ombudsman or the Local Government Ombudsman (in England) or the Public Services Ombudsman (in Wales) can be asked to investigate some problems that have not been resolved through formal complaints procedures.
- Disputes about the finances of a person who lacks capacity should usually be referred to the Office of the Public Guardian (OPG).
- When other methods of resolving disagreements are not appropriate, the matter can be referred to the Court of Protection.
- There are some decisions that are so serious that the Court of Protection should always make them.

What options are there for settling disagreements?

15.1 Disagreements about healthcare, social or other welfare services may be between:

- people who have assessed a person as lacking capacity to make a decision and the person they have assessed (see chapter 4 for how to challenge an assessment of lack of capacity)
- family members or other people concerned with the care and welfare of a person who lacks capacity
- family members and healthcare or social care staff involved in providing care or treatment
- healthcare and social care staff who have different views about what is in the best interests of a person who lacks capacity.

15.2 In general, disagreements can be resolved by either formal or informal procedures, and there is more information on both in this chapter. However, there are some disagreements and some subjects that are so serious they can only be resolved by the Court of Protection.

15.3 It is usually best to try and settle disagreements before they become serious disputes. Many people settle them by communicating effectively and taking the time to listen and to address worries. Disagreements between family members are often best settled informally, or sometimes through mediation. When professionals are in disagreement with a person's family, it is a good idea to start by:

- setting out the different options in a way that is easy to understand
- inviting a colleague to talk to the family and offer a second opinion
- offering to get independent expert advice

- using an advocate to support and represent the person who lacks capacity
- arranging a case conference or meeting to discuss matters in detail
- listening to, acknowledging and addressing worries, and
- where the situation is not urgent, allowing the family time to think it over.

Further guidance on how to deal with problems without going to court may also be found in the Community Legal Services Information Leaflet 'Alternatives to Court'.[74]

[74] CLS (Community Legal Services) Direct Information Leaflet Number 23, www.clsdirect.org.uk/legalhelp/leaflet23.jsp?lang=en

When is an advocate useful?

15.4 An advocate helps communicate the feelings and views of someone who has communication difficulties. The definition of advocacy set out in the Advocacy Charter adopted by most advocacy schemes is as follows: 'Advocacy is taking action to help people say what they want, secure their rights, represent their interests and obtain services they need. Advocates and advocacy schemes work in partnership with the people they support and take their side. Advocacy promotes social inclusion, equality and social justice.'[75]

An advocate may be able to help settle a disagreement simply by presenting a person's feelings to their family, carers or professionals. Most advocacy services are provided by the voluntary sector and are arranged at a local level. They have no link to any agency involved with the person.

[75] Advocacy across London, *Advocacy Charter* (2002)

15.5 Using advocates can help people who find it difficult to communicate (including those who have been assessed as lacking capacity) to:

- say what they want
- claim their rights
- represent their interests, and
- get the services they need.

15.6 Advocates may also be involved in supporting the person during mediation (see paragraphs 15.7–15.13 below) or helping with complaints procedures. Sometimes people who lack capacity or have been assessed as lacking capacity have a legal right to an advocate, for example:

- when making a formal complaint against the NHS (see paragraph 15.18), and
- where the Act requires the involvement of an Independent Mental Capacity Advocate (IMCA) (see chapter 10).

When is mediation useful?

15.7 A mediator helps people to come to an agreement that is acceptable to all parties. Mediation can help solve a problem at an early stage. It offers a wider range of solutions than the court can – and it may be less stressful for all parties, more cost-effective and quicker. People who come to an agreement through mediation are more likely to keep to it, because they have taken part in decision-making.

15.8 Mediators are independent. They have no personal interest in the outcome of a case. They do not make decisions or impose solutions. The mediator will decide whether the case is suitable for mediation. They will consider the likely chances of success and the need to protect the interests of the person who lacks capacity.

15.9 Any case that can be settled through negotiation is likely to benefit from mediation. It is most suitable when people are not communicating well or not understanding each other's point of view. It can improve relationships and stop future disputes, so it is a good option when it is in the person's interests for people to have a good relationship in the future.

Scenario: Using mediation

Mrs Roberts has dementia and lacks capacity to decide where she should live. She currently lives with her son. But her daughter has found a care home where she thinks her mother will get better care. Her brother disagrees.

Mrs Roberts is upset by this family dispute, and so her son and daughter decide to try mediation. The mediator believes that Mrs Roberts is able to communicate her feelings and agrees to take on the case. During the sessions, the mediator helps them to focus on their mother's best interests rather than imposing their own views. In the end, everybody agrees that Mrs Roberts should continue to live with her son. But they agree to review the situation again in six months to see if the care home might then be better for her.

15.10 In mediation, everybody needs to take part as equally as possible so that a mediator can help everyone involved to focus on the person's best interests. It might also be appropriate to involve an advocate to help communicate the wishes of the person who lacks capacity.

15.11 The National Mediation Helpline[76] helps callers to identify an effective means of resolving their difficulty without going to court. It will arrange an appointment with a trained and accredited mediator. The Family Mediation Helpline[77] can provide information on family mediation and referrals to local family mediation services. Family mediators are trained to deal with the emotional, practical and financial needs of those going through relationship breakdown.

[76] National Mediation Helpline, Tel: 0845 60 30 809, www.nationalmediationhelpline.com
[77] Family Mediation Helpline, Tel: 0845 60 26 627, www.familymediationhelpline.co.uk

15.12 Healthcare and social care staff may also take part in mediation processes. But it may be more appropriate to follow the relevant healthcare or social care complaints procedures (see paragraphs 15.14–15.32).

15.13 In certain situations (mainly family mediation), legal aid may be available to fund mediation for people who meet the qualifying criteria (see paragraphs 15.38–15.44).

How can someone complain about healthcare?

15.14 There are formal and informal ways of complaining about a patient's healthcare or treatment. Healthcare staff and others need to know which methods are suitable in which situations.

15.15 In England, the Patient Advice and Liaison Service (PALS) provides an informal way of dealing with problems before they reach the complaints stage. PALS operate in every NHS and Primary Care Trust in England. They provide advice and information to patients (or their relatives or carers) to try to solve problems quickly. They can direct people to specialist support services (for example, advocates, mental health support teams, social services or interpreting services). PALS do not investigate complaints. Their role is to explain complaints procedures and direct people to the formal NHS complaints process, if necessary. NHS complaints procedures deal with complaints about something that happened in the past that requires an apology or explanation. A court cannot help in this situation, but court proceedings may be necessary in some clinical negligence cases (see paragraph 15.22).

15.16 In Wales, complaints advocates based at Community Health Councils provide advice and support to anyone with concerns about treatment they have had.

Disagreements about proposed treatments

15.17 If a case is not urgent, the supportive atmosphere of the PALS may help settle it. In Wales, the local Community Health Council may be able to help. But urgent cases about proposed serious treatment may need to go to the Court of Protection (see paragraphs 15.35–15.36).

Scenario: Disagreeing about treatment or an assessment

Mrs Thompson has Alzheimer's and does not want a flu jab. Her daughter thinks she should have the injection. The doctor does not want to go against the wishes of his patient, because he believes she has capacity to refuse treatment.

Mrs Thompson's daughter goes to PALS. A member of staff gives her information and advice about what is meant by capacity to consent to or refuse treatment, and tells her how to find out about the flu jab. The PALS staff speak to the doctor, and then they explain his clinical assessment to Mrs Thompson's daughter.

The daughter is still unhappy. PALS staff advise her that the Independent Complaints Advocacy Service can help if she wishes to make a formal complaint.

The formal NHS complaints procedure

15.18 The formal NHS complaints procedure deals with complaints about NHS services provided by NHS organisations or primary care practitioners. As a first step, people should try to settle a disagreement through an informal discussion between:

- the healthcare staff involved
- the person who may lack capacity to make the decision in question (with support if necessary)
- their carers, and
- any appropriate relatives.

If the person who is complaining is not satisfied, the Independent Complaints Advocacy Service (ICAS) may help. In Wales, the complaints advocates based at Community Health Councils will support and advise anyone who wants to make a complaint.

15.19 In England, if the person is still unhappy after a local investigation, they can ask for an independent review by the Healthcare Commission. If the patient involved in the complaint was or is detained under the Mental Health Act 1983, the Mental Health Act Commission can be asked to look into the complaint. If people are still unhappy after this stage, they can go to the Health Service Ombudsman. More information on how to make a complaint in England is available from the Department of Health.

15.20 In Wales, if patients are still unhappy after a local investigation, they can ask for an independent review of their complaint by independent lay reviewers. After this, they can take their case to the Public Services Ombudsman for Wales. People can take their complaint direct to the Ombudsman if:

- the complaint is about care or treatment that took place after 1 April 2006, and
- they have tried to settle the problem locally first.

The Mental Health Act Commission may also investigate complaints about the care or treatment of detained patients in Wales, if attempts have been made to settle the complaint locally without success.

15.21 Regulations about first trying to settle complaints locally do not apply to NHS Foundation Trusts. But these Trusts are covered by the independent review stage operated by the Healthcare Commission and by the Health Service Ombudsman. People who have a complaint about an NHS Foundation Trust should contact the Trust for advice on how to make a complaint.

Cases of clinical negligence

15.22 The NHS Litigation Authority oversees all clinical negligence cases brought against the NHS in England. It actively encourages people to try other forms of settling complaints before going to court. The National Assembly for Wales also encourages people to try other forms of settling complaints before going to court.

How can somebody complain about social care?

15.23 The social services complaints procedure has been reformed. The reformed procedure came into effect on 1 September 2006 in England and on 1 April 2006 in Wales.

15.24 A service provider's own complaints procedure should deal with complaints about:

- the way in which care services are delivered
- the type of services provided, or
- a failure to provide services.

15.25 Care agencies contracted by local authorities or registered with the Commission for Social Care Inspection (CSCI) in England or Care and Social Services Inspectorate for Wales (CSSIW) are legally obliged to have their own written complaints procedures. This includes residential homes, agencies providing care in people's homes, nursing agencies and adult placement schemes. The procedures should set out how to make a complaint and what to do with a complaint that cannot be settled locally.

Local authority complaints procedures

15.26 For services contracted by a local authority, it may be more appropriate to use the local authority's complaints procedure. A simple example would be a situation where a local authority places a person in a care home and the person's family are not happy with the placement. If their complaint is not about the services the home provides (for example, it might be about the local authority's assessment of the person's needs), it might be more appropriate to use the local authority's complaints procedure.

15.27 As a first step, people should try to settle a disagreement through an informal discussion, involving:

- the professionals involved
- the person who may lack capacity to make the decision in question (with support if necessary)
- their carers, and
- any appropriate relatives.

15.28 If the person making the complaint is not satisfied, the local authority will carry out a formal investigation using its complaints procedure. In England, after this stage, a social service Complaints Review Panel can hear the case. In Wales complaints can be referred to the National Assembly for Wales for hearing by an independent panel.

Other complaints about social care

15.29 People can take their complaint to the CSCI in England or the CSSIW in Wales, if:

- the complaint is about regulations or national minimum standards not being met, and
- the complainants are not happy with the provider's own complaints procedure or the response to their complaint.

15.30 If a complaint is about a local authority's administration, it may be referred to the Commission for Local Administration in England (the Local Government Ombudsman) or the Public Services Ombudsman for Wales.

What if a complaint covers healthcare and social care?

15.31 Taking a complaint through NHS or local authority complaints procedures can be a complicated process – especially if the complaint covers a number of service providers or both healthcare and social care. In such situations, local authorities and the NHS must work together and agree which organisation will lead in handling the complaint. If a person is not happy with the outcome, they can take their case to the Health Service Ombudsman or to the Local Government Ombudsman (in England). There is guidance which sets out how organisations should work together to handle complaints that cover healthcare and social care (in England *Learning from Complaints* and in Wales *Listening and learning*). The Public Services Ombudsman for Wales handles complaints that cover both healthcare and social care.

Who can handle complaints about other welfare issues?

15.32 The Independent Housing Ombudsman deals with complaints about registered social landlords in England. This applies mostly to housing associations. But it also applies to many landlords who manage homes that were formerly run by local authorities and some private landlords. In Wales, the Public Services Ombudsman for Wales deals with complaints about registered social landlords. Complaints about local authorities may be referred to the Local Government Ombudsman in England or the Public Services Ombudsman for Wales. They look at complaints about decisions on council housing, social services, Housing Benefit and planning applications. More information about complaints to an Ombudsman is available on the relevant websites (see Annex A).

What is the best way to handle disagreement about a person's finances?

15.33 Some examples of disagreements about a person's finances are:

- disputes over the amount of money a person who lacks capacity should pay their carer
- disputes over whether a person who lacks capacity should sell their house
- somebody questioning the actions of a carer, who may be using the money of a person who lacks capacity inappropriately or without proper authority
- somebody questioning the actions of an attorney appointed under a Lasting Power of Attorney or an Enduring Power of Attorney or a deputy appointed by the court.

15.34 In all of the above circumstances, the most appropriate action would usually be to contact the Office of the Public Guardian (OPG) for guidance and advice. See chapter 14 for further details on the role of the OPG.

How can the Court of Protection help?

15.35 The Court of Protection deals with all areas of decision-making for adults who lack capacity to make particular decisions for themselves (see chapter 8 for more information about its roles and responsibilities). But the court is not always the right place to settle problems involving people who lack capacity. Other forms of settling disagreements may be more appropriate and less distressing.

15.36 There are some decisions that are so serious that the court should always make them. There are also other types of cases that the court should deal with when another method would generally not be suitable. See chapter 8 for more information about both kinds of cases.

Right of Appeal

15.37 Section 53 of the Act describes the rights of appeal against any decision taken by the Court of Protection. There are further details in the Court of Protection Rules. It may be advisable for anyone who wishes to appeal a decision made by the court to seek legal advice.

Will public legal funding be available?

15.38 Depending on their financial situation, once the Act comes into force people may be entitled to:

- publicly funded legal advice from accredited solicitors or advice agencies
- legal representation before the new Court of Protection (in the most serious cases).

Information about solicitors and organisations who give advice on different areas of law is available from Community Legal Services Direct (CLS Direct).[78] Further information about legal aid and public funding can be obtained from the Legal Services Commission.[79] See Annex A for full contact details.

15.39 People who lack capacity to instruct a solicitor or conduct their own case will need a litigation friend. This person could be a relative, friend, attorney or the Official Solicitor (when no-one else is available). The litigation friend is able to instruct the solicitor and conduct the case on behalf of a person who lacks capacity to give instructions. If the person qualifies for public legal funding, the litigation friend can claim funding on their behalf.

[78] CLS Direct, Tel: 0845 345 4 345, www.clsdirect.org.uk
[79] www.legalservices.gov.uk

When can someone get legal help?

15.40 Legal help is a type of legal aid (public funding) that pays for advice and assistance on legal issues, including those affecting a person who lacks capacity. But it does not provide representation for a full court hearing, although there is a related form of funding called 'help at court' under which a legal representative can speak in court on a client's behalf on an informal basis. To qualify for legal help, applicants must show that:

- they get specific social security benefits, or they earn less than a specific amount and do not have savings or other financial assets in excess of a specific amount
- they would benefit sufficiently from legal advice to justify the amount it costs, and
- they cannot get another form of funding.

15.41 Legal help can include:

- help from a solicitor or other representative in writing letters
- in exceptional circumstances, getting a barrister's opinion, and
- assistance in preparing for Court of Protection hearings.

15.42 People cannot get legal help for making a Lasting Power of Attorney or an advance decision to refuse treatment. But they can get general help and information from the OPG. The OPG cannot give legal or specialist advice. For example, they will not be able to advise someone on what powers they should delegate to their attorney under an LPA.

When can someone get legal representation?

15.43 Public funding for legal representation in the Court of Protection will be available from solicitors with a relevant contract – but only for the most serious cases. To qualify, applicants will normally face the same test as for legal help to qualify financially (paragraph 15.40). They will generally have to satisfy more detailed criteria than applicants for legal help, relating, for instance, to their prospects of being successful, to whether legal representation is necessary and to the cost benefit of being represented. They will also have to establish that the case could not be brought or funded in another way and that there are not alternatives to court proceedings that should be explored first.

15.44 Serious personal welfare cases that were previously heard by the High Court will continue to have public funding for legal representation when they are transferred to the Court of

Protection. These cases will normally be related to personal liberty, serious welfare decisions or medical treatment for a person who lacks capacity. But legal representation may also be available in other types of cases, depending on the particular circumstances.

16 WHAT RULES GOVERN ACCESS TO INFORMATION ABOUT A PERSON WHO LACKS CAPACITY?

This chapter gives guidance on:

- what personal information about someone who lacks capacity people involved in their care have the right to see, and
- how they can get hold of that information.

This chapter is only a general guide. It does not give detailed information about the law. Nor does it replace professional guidance or the guidance of the Information Commissioner's Office on the Data Protection Act 1998 (this guidance is available on its website, see Annex A). Where necessary, people should take legal advice.

This chapter is mainly for people such as family carers and other carers, deputies and attorneys, who care for or represent someone who lacks capacity to make specific decisions and in particular, lacks capacity to allow information about them to be disclosed. Professionals have their own codes of conduct, and they may have the support of experts in their organisations.

In this chapter, as throughout the Code, a person's capacity (or lack of capacity) refers specifically to their capacity to make a particular decision at the time it needs to be made.

Quick summary

QUESTIONS TO ASK WHEN REQUESTING PERSONAL INFORMATION ABOUT SOMEONE WHO MAY LACK CAPACITY

- Am I acting under a Lasting Power of Attorney or as a deputy with specific authority?
- Does the person have capacity to agree that information can be disclosed? Have they previously agreed to disclose the information?
- What information do I need?
- Why do I need it?
- Who has the information?
- Can I show that:
  - I need the information to make a decision that is in the best interests of the person I am acting for, and
  - the person does not have the capacity to act for themselves?
- Do I need to share the information with anyone else to make a decision that is in the best interests of the person who lacks capacity?
- Should I keep a record of my decision or action?
- How long should I keep the information for?
- Do I have the right to request the information under section 7 of the Data Protection Act 1998?

QUESTIONS TO ASK WHEN CONSIDERING WHETHER TO DISCLOSE INFORMATION

- Is the request covered by section 7 of the Data Protection Act 1998? Is the request being made by a formally authorised representative?

If not:

- Is the disclosure legal?
- Is the disclosure justified, having balanced the person's best interests and the public interest against the person's right to privacy?

QUESTIONS TO ASK TO DECIDE WHETHER THE DISCLOSURE IS LEGAL OR JUSTIFIED

- Do I (or does my organisation) have the information?
- Am I satisfied that the person concerned lacks capacity to agree to disclosure?
- Does the person requesting the information have any formal authority to act on behalf of the person who lacks capacity?
- Am I satisfied that the person making the request:
  - is acting in the best interests of the person concerned?
  - needs the information to act properly?
  - will respect confidentiality?
  - will keep the information for no longer than necessary?
- Should I get written confirmation of these things?

What laws and regulations affect access to information?

16.1 People caring for, or managing the finances of, someone who lacks capacity may need information to:

- assess the person's capacity to make a specific decision
- determine the person's best interests, and
- make appropriate decisions on the person's behalf.

16.2 The information they need varies depending on the circumstances. For example:

- a daughter providing full-time care for an elderly parent will make decisions based on her own experience and knowledge of her parent
- a deputy may need information from other people. For instance, if they were deciding whether a person needs to move into a care home or whether they should sell the person's home, they might need information from family members, the family doctor, the person's bank and their solicitor to make sure they are making the decision in the person's best interests.

16.3 Much of the information needed to make decisions under the Act is sensitive or confidential. It is regulated by:

- the Data Protection Act 1998
- the common law duty of confidentiality
- professional codes of conduct on confidentiality, and
- the Human Rights Act 1998 and European Convention on Human Rights, in particular Article 8 (the right to respect for private and family life), which means that it is only lawful to reveal someone's personal information if:
  - there is a legitimate aim in doing so
  - a democratic society would think it necessary to do so, and
  - the kind and amount of information disclosed is in relation to the need.

What information do people generally have a right to see?

16.4 Section 7 of the Data Protection Act 1998 gives everyone the right to see personal information that an organisation holds about them. They may also authorise someone else to access their information on their behalf. The person holding the information has a legal duty to release it. So, where possible, it is important to try to get a person's consent before requesting to see information about them.

16.5 A person may have the capacity to agree to someone seeing their personal information, even if they do not have the capacity to make other decisions. In some situations, a person may have previously given consent (while they still had capacity) for someone to see their personal information in the future.

16.6 Doctors and lawyers cannot share information about their clients, or that clients have given them, without the client's consent. Sometimes it is fair to assume that a doctor or lawyer already has someone's consent (for example, patients do not usually expect healthcare staff or legal professionals to get consent every time they share information with a colleague – but staff may choose to get clients' consent in writing when they begin treating or acting for that person). But in other circumstances, doctors and lawyers must get specific consent to 'disclose' information (share it with someone else).

16.7 If someone's capacity changes from time to time, the person needing the information may want to wait until that person can give their consent. Or they may decide that it is not necessary to get access to information at all, if the person will be able to make a decision on their own in the future.

16.8 If someone lacks the capacity to give consent, someone else might still be able to see their personal information. This will depend on:

- whether the person requesting the information is acting as an agent (a representative recognised by the law, such as a deputy or attorney) for the person who lacks capacity
- whether disclosure is in the best interests of the person who lacks capacity, and
- what type of information has been requested.

When can attorneys and deputies ask to see personal information?

16.9 An attorney acting under a valid LPA or EPA (and sometimes a deputy) can ask to see information concerning the person they are representing, as long as the information applies to decisions the attorney has the legal right to make.

16.10 In practice, an attorney or deputy may only require limited information and may not need to make a formal request. In such circumstances, they can approach the information holder informally. Once satisfied that the request comes from an attorney or deputy (having seen appropriate authority), the person holding information should be able to release it. The attorney or deputy can still make a formal request for information in the future.

16.11 The attorney or deputy must treat the information confidentially. They should be extremely careful to protect it. If they fail to do so, the court can cancel the LPA or deputyship.

16.12 Before the Act came into effect, only a few receivers were appointed with the general authority to manage a person's property and affairs. So they needed specific authority from the Court of Protection to ask for access to the person's personal information. Similarly, a deputy who only has authority to act in specific areas only has the right to ask for information relating to decisions in those specific areas. For information relating to other areas, the deputy will need to apply to the Court of Protection.

16.13 Requests for personal information must be in writing, and there might be a fee. Information holders should release it promptly (always within 40 calendar days). Fees may be particularly high for getting copies of healthcare records – particularly where information may be in unusual formats (for example, x-rays). The maximum fee is currently £50. Complaints about a failure to comply with the Data Protection Act 1998 should be directed to the Information Commissioner's Office (see Annex A for contact details).

What limitations are there?

16.14 Attorneys and deputies should only ask for information that will help them make a decision they need to make on behalf of the person who lacks capacity. For example, if the attorney needs to know when the person should take medication, they should not ask to see the entire healthcare record. The person who releases information must make sure that an attorney or deputy has official authority (they may ask for proof of identity and appointment). When asking to see personal information, attorneys and deputies should bear in mind that their decision must always be in the best interests of the person who lacks capacity to make that decision.

16.15 The attorney or deputy may not know the kind of information that someone holds about the person they are representing. So sometimes it might be difficult for them to make a specific request. They might even need to see all the information to make a decision. But again, the 'best interests' principle applies.

Scenario: Giving attorneys access to personal information

Mr Yapp is in the later stages of Alzheimer's disease. His son is responsible for Mr Yapp's personal welfare under a Lasting Power of Attorney. Mr Yapp has been in residential care for a number of years. But his son does not think that the home is able to meet his father's current needs as his condition has recently deteriorated.

The son asks to see his father's records. He wants specific information about his father's care, so that he can make a decision about his father's best interests. But the manager of the care home refuses, saying that the Data Protection Act stops him releasing personal information.

Mr Yapp's son points out that he can see his father's records, because he is his personal welfare attorney and needs the information to make a decision. The Data Protection Act 1998 requires the care home manager to provide access to personal data held on Mr Yapp.

16.16 The deputy or attorney may find that some information is held back (for example, when this contains references to people other than the person who lacks capacity). This might be to protect another person's privacy, if that person is mentioned in the records. It is unlikely that information relating to another person would help an attorney make a decision on behalf of the person who lacks capacity. The information holder might also be obliged to keep information about the other person confidential. There might be another reason why the person does not want information about them to be released. Under these circumstances, the attorney does not have the right to see that information.

16.17 An information holder should not release information if doing so would cause serious physical or mental harm to anyone – including the person the information is about. This applies to information on health, social care and education records.

16.18 The Information Commissioner's Office can give further details on:

- how to request personal information
- restrictions on accessing information, and
- how to appeal against a decision not to release information.

When can someone see information about healthcare or social care?

16.19 Healthcare and social care staff may disclose information about somebody who lacks capacity only when it is in the best interests of the person concerned to do so, or when there is some other, lawful reason for them to do so.

16.20 The Act's requirement to consult relevant people when working out the best interests of a person who lacks capacity will encourage people to share the information that makes a consultation meaningful. But people who release information should be sure that they are acting lawfully and that they can justify releasing the information. They need to balance the person's right to privacy with what is in their best interests or the wider public interest (see paragraphs 16.24–16.25 below).

16.21 Sometimes it will be fairly obvious that staff should disclose information. For example, a doctor would need to tell a new care worker about what drugs a person needs or what allergies the person has. This is clearly in the person's best interests.

16.22 Other information may need to be disclosed as part of the process of working out someone's best interests. A social worker might decide to reveal information about someone's past when discussing their best interests with a close family member. But staff should always bear in mind that the Act requires them to consider the wishes and feelings of the person who lacks capacity.

16.23 In both these cases, staff should only disclose as much information as is relevant to the decision to be made.

Scenario: Sharing appropriate information

Mr Jeremy has learning disabilities. His care home is about to close down. His care team carries out a careful assessment of his needs. They involve him as much as possible, and use the support of an Independent Mental Capacity Advocate. Following the assessment, he is placed with carers under an adult placement scheme.

The carers ask to see Mr Jeremy's case file, so that they can provide him with appropriate care in his best interests. The care manager seeks Mr Jeremy's consent to disclosure of his notes, but believes that Mr Jeremy lacks capacity to make this decision. She recognises that it is appropriate to provide the carers with sufficient information to enable them to act in Mr Jeremy's best interests. But it is not appropriate for them to see all the information on the case file. Much of it is not relevant to his current care needs. The care manager therefore only passes on relevant information from the file.

16.24 Sometimes a person's right to confidentiality will conflict with broader public concerns. Information can be released if it is in the public interest, even if it is not in the best interests of the person who lacks capacity. It can be difficult to decide in these cases, and information holders should consider each case on its merits. The NHS Code on Confidentiality gives examples of when disclosure is in the public interest. These include situations where disclosing information could prevent, or aid investigation of, serious crimes, or to prevent serious harm, such as spread of an infectious disease. It is then necessary to judge whether the public good that would be achieved by the disclosure outweighs *both* the obligation of confidentiality to the individual concerned *and* the broader public interest in the provision of a confidential service.

16.25 For disclosure to be in the public interest, it must be proportionate and limited to the relevant details. Healthcare or social care staff faced with this decision should seek advice from their legal advisers. It is not just things for 'the public's benefit' that are in the public interest -disclosure for the benefit of the person who lacks capacity can also be in the public interest (for example, to stop a person who lacks capacity suffering physical or mental harm).

What financial information can carers ask to see?

16.26 It is often more difficult to get financial information than it is to get information on a person's welfare. A bank manager, for example, is less likely to:

- know the individual concerned
- be able to make an assessment of the person's capacity to consent to disclosure, and
- be aware of the carer's relationship to the person.

So they are less likely than a doctor or social worker to be able to judge what is in a person's best interests and are bound by duties to keep clients' affairs confidential. It is likely that someone wanting financial information will need to apply to the Court of Protection for access to that information. This clearly does not apply to an attorney or a deputy appointed to manage the person's property and affairs, who will generally have the authority (because of their appointment) to obtain all relevant information about the person's property and affairs.

Is information still confidential after someone shares it?

16.27 Whenever a carer gets information, they should treat the information in confidence, and they should not share it with anyone else (unless there is a lawful basis for doing so). In some circumstances, the information holder might ask the carer to give a formal confirmation that they will keep information confidential.

16.28 Where the information is in written form, carers should store it carefully and not keep it for longer than necessary. In many cases, the need to keep the information will be temporary. So the carer should be able to reassure the information holder that they will not keep a permanent record of the information.

What is the best way to settle a disagreement about personal information?

16.29 A carer should always start by trying to get consent from the person whose information they are trying to access. If the person lacks capacity to consent, the carer should ask the information holder for the relevant information and explain why they need it. They may need to remind the information holder that they have to make a decision in the person's best interests and cannot do so without the relevant information.

16.30 This can be a sensitive area and disputes will inevitably arise. Healthcare and social care staff have a difficult judgement to make. They might feel strongly that disclosing the information would not be in the best interests of the person who lacks capacity and would amount to an invasion of their privacy. This may be upsetting for the carer who will probably have good motives for wanting the information. In all cases, an assessment of the interests and needs of the person who lacks capacity should determine whether staff should disclose information.

16.31 If a discussion fails to settle the matter, and the carer still is not happy, there are other ways to settle the disagreement (see chapter 15). The carer may need to use the appropriate complaints procedure. Since the complaint involves elements of data protection and confidentiality, as well as best interests, relevant experts should help deal with the complaint.

16.32 In cases where carers and staff cannot settle their disagreement, the carer can apply to the Court of Protection for the right to access to the specific information. The court would then need to decide if this was in the best interests of the person who lacks capacity to consent. In urgent cases, it might be necessary for the carer to apply directly to the court without going through the earlier stages.

KEY WORDS AND PHRASES USED IN THE CODE

The table below is not a full index or glossary. Instead, it is a list of key terms used in the Code or the Act, and the main references to them. References in bold indicate particularly valuable content for that term.

Acts in connection with care or treatment	Tasks carried out by carers, healthcare or social care staff which involve the personal care, healthcare or medical treatment of people who lack capacity to consent to them – referred to in the Act as 'section 5 acts'.	**Chapter 6** 2.13–2.14, 4.39 Best interests and _ 5.10, 5,39 Deprivation of liberty and _ 6.39. 6.49–6.52

Advance decision to refuse treatment	A decision to refuse specified treatment made in advance by a person who has capacity to do so. This decision will then apply at a future time when that person lacks capacity to consent to, or refuse, the specified treatment. This is set out in Section 24(1) of the Act. Specific rules apply to advance decisions to refuse life-sustaining treatment.	**Chapter 9** (**all**) Best interests and _ 5.5, 5.35, 5.45 Protection from liability and _ 6.37–6.38 LPAs and _ 7.55 Deputies and _ 8.28 Research and _ 11.30 Young people and _ 12.9 Mental Health Act 13.35–13.37
Adult protection procedures	Procedures devised by local authorities, in conjunction with other relevant agencies, to investigate and deal with allegations of abuse or ill treatment of vulnerable adults, and to put in place safeguards to provide protection from abuse.	**Chapter 14** 14.6, 14.22, 14.27–28, 14.34 IMCAs and _ 10.66–10.67
After-care under supervision	Arrangements for supervision in the community following discharge from hospital of certain patients previously detained under the Mental Health Act 1983.	**Chapter 13** **13.22–13.25**, 13.34, 13.37, 13.40, 13.42, 13.45, 13.48, 13.52
Agent	A person authorised to act on behalf of another person under the law of agency. Attorneys appointed under an LPA or EPA are agents and court-appointed deputies are deemed to be agents and must undertake certain duties as agents.	LPAs and _ 7.58–7.68 Deputies and _ 8.55–8.68
Appointee	Someone appointed under Social Security Regulations to claim and collect social security benefits or pensions on behalf of a person who lacks capacity to manage their own benefits. An appointee is permitted to use the money claimed to meet the person's needs.	Role of _ 6:65–6.66 Deputies and _ 8.56 Concerns about _ 14:35–14.36
Appropriate body	A committee which is established to advise on, or on matters which include, the ethics of intrusive research in relation to people who lack capacity to consent to it, and is recognised for those purposes by the Secretary of State (in England) or the National Assembly for Wales (in Wales).	**Chapter 11** 11.8–11.11, 11.20, 11.33–11.34, 11.43–11.47.
Approved Social Worker (ASW)	A specially trained social worker with responsibility for assessing a person's needs for care and treatment under the Mental Health Act 1983. In particular, an ASW assesses whether the person should be admitted to hospital for assessment and/or treatment.	**Chapter 13** 13.16, 13.22–13.23, 13.43, 13.52

Artificial Nutrition and Hydration (ANH)	Artificial nutrition and hydration (ANH) has been recognised as a form of medical treatment. ANH involves using tubes to provide nutrition and fluids to someone who cannot take them by mouth. It bypasses the natural mechanisms that control hunger and thirst and requires clinical monitoring.	**9.26** 5.34 6.18 8.18
Attorney	Someone appointed under either a Lasting Power of Attorney (LPA) or an Enduring Power of Attorney (EPA), who has the legal right to make decisions within the scope of their authority on behalf of the person (the donor) who made the Power of Attorney.	**Chapter 7** Best interests principle and _ 5.2, 5.13, 5.49, 5.55 Protection from liability as _ 6.54–6.55 Court of Protection and _ 8.30 Advance decisions and _ 9.33 Mental Health Act and _ 13.38–13.45 Public Guardian and _ 14.7–14.14 Legal help and _ 15.39–15.42 Accessing personal information as _ 16.9–16.16
Best interests	Any decisions made, or anything done for a person who lacks capacity to make specific decisions, must be in the person's best interests. There are standard minimum steps to follow when working out someone's best interests. These are set out in section 4 of the Act, and in the non-exhaustive checklist in 5.13.	**Chapter 2 (Principle 4) Chapter 5** Protection from liability and _ 6.4–6.18 Reasonable belief and _ 6.32–6.36 Deprivation of liberty and _ 6.51–6.53 Acting as an attorney and _ 7.19–7.20, 7.29, 7.53 Court of Protection and _ 8.14–8.26 Acting as a deputy and _ 8.50–8.52 Advance decisions and _ 9.4–9.5
Bournewood provisions	A name given to some proposed new procedures and safeguards for people who lack capacity to make relevant decisions but who need to be deprived of their liberty, in their best interests, otherwise than under the Mental Health Act 1983. The name refers to a case which was eventually decided by the European Court of Human Rights.	6.53–6.54 13.53–13.54

Capacity	The ability to make a decision about a particular matter at the time the decision needs to be made. The legal definition of a person who lacks capacity is set out in section 2 of the Act.	**Chapter 4**
Carer	Someone who provides *unpaid* care by looking after a friend or neighbour who needs support because of sickness, age or disability. In this document, the role of the carer is different from the role of a professional care worker.	**Acting as decision-maker 5.8–5.10 Protection from liability 6.20–6.24** Assessing capacity as _ 4.44–4.45 Acting with reasonable belief 6.29–6.34 Paying for goods and services 6.56–6.66 Accessing information 16.26–16.32
Care worker	Someone employed to provide personal care for people who need help because of sickness, age or disability. They could be employed by the person themselves, by someone acting on the person's behalf or by a care agency.	Assessing capacity as _4.38, 4.44–4.45 Protection from liability 6.20 Paying for goods and services 6.56–6.66 Acting as an attorney 7.10 Acting as a deputy 8.41
Children Act 1989	A law relating to children and those with parental responsibility for children.	**Chapter 12**
Complaints Review Panel	A panel of people set up to review and reconsider complaints about health or social care services which have not been resolved under the first stage of the relevant complaints procedure.	15.28
Consultee	A person who is consulted, for example about the involvement in a research project of a person who lacks capacity to consent to their participation in the research.	11.23, 11.28–29, 11.44

Court of Protection	The specialist Court for all issues relating to people who lack capacity to make specific decisions. The Court of Protection is established under section 45 of the Act.	**Chapter 8** _ must always make decisions about these issues 6.18 Decisions about life-sustaining treatment 5.33–5.36 LPAs and _ 7.45–7.49 Advance decisions and _ 9.35, 9.54, 9.67–9.69 Decisions regarding children and young people 12.3–12.4, 12.7, 12.10, 12.23–12.25 Access to legal help 15.40–15.44
Court of Protection Visitor	Someone who is appointed to report to the Court of Protection on how attorneys or deputies are carrying out their duties. Court of Protection Visitors are established under section 61 of the Act. They can also be directed by the Public Guardian to visit donors, attorney and deputies under section 58 (1) (d).	**14.10–14.11** Attorneys and _ 7.71 Deputies and _ 8.71
Criminal Records Bureau (CRB)	An Executive Agency of the Home Office which provides access to criminal record information. Organisations in the public, private and voluntary sectors can ask for the CRB to check candidates for jobs to see if they have any criminal records which would make them unsuitable for certain work, especially that involves children or vulnerable adults. For some jobs, a CRB check is mandatory.	Checking healthcare and social care staff 14.29–14.30 Checking IMCAs 10.18
Data Protection Act 1998	A law controlling the handling of, and access to, personal information, such as medical records, files held by public bodies and financial information held by credit reference agencies.	**Chapter 16**
Decision-maker	Under the Act, many different people may be required to make decisions or act on behalf of someone who lacks capacity to make decisions for themselves. The person making the decision is referred to throughout the Code, as the 'decision-maker', and it is the decision-maker's responsibility to work out what would be in the best interests of the person who lacks capacity.	**Chapter 5** Working with IMCAs 10.4, 10.21–10.29 Applying the MHA 13.3, 13.10, 13.27

Declaration	A kind of order made by the Court of Protection. For example, a declaration could say whether a person has or lacks capacity to make a particular decision, or declaring that a particular act would or would not be lawful. The Court's power to make declarations is set out in section 15 of the Act.	**8.13–8.19** Advance decisions and _ 9.35
Deprivation of liberty	Deprivation of liberty is a term used in the European Convention on Human Rights about circumstances when a person's freedom is taken away. Its meaning in practice is being defined through case law.	**6.49–6.54** Protection from liability 6.13–6.14 Attorneys and _ 7.44 Mental Health Act and _ 13.12, 13.16
Deputy	Someone appointed by the Court of Protection with ongoing legal authority as prescribed by the Court to make decisions on behalf of a person who lacks capacity to make particular decisions as set out in Section 16(2) of the Act.	**Chapter 8** Best interests principle and _ 5.2, 5.13, 5.49, 5.55 Protection from liability as _ 6.54–6.55 Attorneys becoming _ 7.56 Advance decisions and _ 9.33 IMCAs and _ 10.70–72 Acting for children and young people 12.4, 12.7 Public Guardian and _ 14.15–14.18 Complaints about 14.19–14.25 Accessing personal information as _ 16.9–16.16
Donor	A person who makes a Lasting Power of Attorney or Enduring Power of Attorney.	**Chapter 7**
Enduring Power of Attorney (EPA)	A Power of Attorney created under the Enduring Powers of Attorney Act 1985 appointing an attorney to deal with the donor's property and financial affairs. Existing EPAs will continue to operate under Schedule 4 of the Act, which replaces the EPA Act 1985.	**Chapter 7** See also LPA
Family carer	A family member who looks after a relative who needs support because of sickness, age or disability. It does not mean a professional care-worker employed by a disabled person or a care assistant in a nursing home, for example.	See carer

Family Division of the High Court	The Division of the High Court that has the jurisdiction to deal with all matrimonial and civil partnership matters, family disputes, matters relating to children and some disputes about medical treatment.	12.14, 12.23
Fiduciary duty	Anyone acting under the law of agency will have this duty. In essence, it means that any decision taken or act done as an agent (such as an attorney or deputy) must not benefit themselves, but must benefit the person for whom they are acting.	_ for attorneys 7.58 _ for deputies 8.58
Guardianship	Arrangements, made under the Mental Health Act 1983, for a guardian to be appointed for a person with mental disorder to help ensure that the person gets the care they need in the community.	**13.16–13.21** 13.1, 13.25–13.27, 13.54
Health Service Ombudsman	An independent person whose organisation investigates complaints about National Health Service (NHS) care or treatment in England which have not been resolved through the NHS complaints procedure.	15.19, 15.21, 15.31
Human Rights Act 1998	A law largely incorporating into UK law the substantive rights set out in the European Convention on Human Rights.	6.49 16.3
Human Tissue Act 2004	A law to regulate issues relating to whole body donation and the taking, storage and use of human organs and tissue.	11.7 11.38–11.39
Ill treatment	Section 44 of the Act introduces a new offence of ill treatment of a person who lacks capacity by someone who is caring for them, or acting as a deputy or attorney for them. That person can be guilty of ill treatment if they have deliberately ill-treated a person who lacks capacity, or been reckless as to whether they were ill-treating the person or not. It does not matter whether the behaviour was likely to cause, or actually caused, harm or damage to the victim's health.	14.23–14.26
Independent Complaints Advocacy Service (ICAS)	In England, a service to support patients and their carers who wish to pursue a complaint about their NHS treatment or care.	15.18
Independent Mental Capacity Advocate (IMCA)	Someone who provides support and representation for a person who lacks capacity to make specific decisions, where the person has no-one else to support them. The IMCA service is established under section 35 of the Act and the functions of IMCAs are set out in section 36. It is not the same as an ordinary advocacy service.	**Chapter 10** Consulting to work out best interests 5.51 Involvement in changes of residence 6.9 Involvement in serious medical decisions 6.16 MHA and _ 13.46–13.48

Information Commissioner's Office	An independent authority set up to promote access to official information and to protect personal information. It has powers to ensure that the laws about information, such as the Data Protection Act 1998, are followed.	16.13 16.18
Lasting Power of Attorney (LPA)	A Power of Attorney created under the Act (see Section 9(1)) appointing an attorney (or attorneys) to make decisions about the donor's personal welfare (including healthcare) and/or deal with the donor's property and affairs.	**Chapter 7** Best interests principle and _ 5.2, 5.13, 5.49, 5.55 Protection from liability as _ 6.54–6.55 Court of Protection and _ 8.30 Advance decisions and _ 9.33 Mental Health Act and _ 13.38–13.45 Public Guardian and _ 14.7–14.14 Legal help and _ 15.39–15.42 Accessing personal information as _ 16.9–16.16
Life-sustaining treatment	Treatment that, in the view of the person providing healthcare, is necessary to keep a person alive See Section 4(10) of the Act.	**Providing or stopping _ in best interests 5.29–5.36** **Advance decisions to refuse _ 9.10–9.11, 9.19–9.20, 9.24–9.28** Protection from liability when providing _ 6.16, 6.55 Attorneys and _ 7.22, 7.27, 7.29–7.30 Deputies and _ 8.17, 8.46 Conscientious objection to stopping _ 9.61–9.63 IMCAs and _ 10.44
Litigation friend	A person appointed by the court to conduct legal proceedings on behalf of, and in the name of, someone who lacks capacity to conduct the litigation or to instruct a lawyer themselves.	4.54 10.38 15.39
Local Government Ombudsman	In England, an independent organisation that investigates complaints about councils and local authorities on most council matters including housing, planning, education and social services.	15.30–15.32

Makaton	A language programme using signs and symbols, for the teaching of communication, language and literacy skills for people with communication and learning difficulties.	3.11
Mediation	A process for resolving disagreements in which an impartial third party (the mediator) helps people in dispute to find a mutually acceptable resolution.	15.7–15.13
Mental capacity	See capacity	
Mental Health Act 1983	A law mainly about the compulsory care and treatment of patients with mental health problems. In particular, it covers detention in hospital for mental health treatment.	**Chapter 13** Deprivation of liberty other than in line with _ 6.50–6.53, 7.44 Attorneys and _ 7.27 Advance decisions and _9.37 IMCAs and 10.44, 10.51, 10.56–10.58 Children and young people and _ 12.6, 12.21 Complaints regarding _ 15.19
Mental Health Review Tribunal	An independent judicial body with powers to direct the discharge of patients who are detained under the Mental Health Act 1983.	13.31 13.42
NHS Litigation Authority	A Special Health Authority (part of the NHS), responsible for handling negligence claims made against NHS bodies in England.	15.22
Office of the Public Guardian (OPG)	The Public Guardian is an officer established under Section 57 of the Act. The Public Guardian will be supported by the Office of the Public Guardian, which will supervise deputies, keep a register of deputies, Lasting Powers of Attorney and Enduring Powers of Attorney, check on what attorneys are doing, and investigate any complaints about attorneys or deputies. The OPG replaces the Public Guardianship Office (PGO) that has been in existence for many years.	**14.8–14.22** Registering LPAs with _ 7.14–7.17 Supervision of attorneys by _ 7.69–7.74 Registering EPAs with _ 7.78 Guidance for EPAs _ 7.79 Guidance for receivers_ 8.5 Panel of deputies of _ 8.35 Supervision of deputies by _ 8.69–8.77

Official Solicitor	Provides legal services for vulnerable persons, or in the interests of achieving justice. The Official Solicitor represents adults who lack capacity to conduct litigation in county court or High Court proceedings in England and Wales, and in the Court of Protection.	Helping with formal assessment of capacity 4.54 Acting in applications to the Court of Protection 8.10 Acting as litigation friend 10.38, 15.39
Patient Advice and Liaison Service (PALS)	In England, a service providing information, advice and support to help NHS patients, their families and carers. PALS act on behalf of service users when handling patient and family concerns and can liaise with staff, managers and, where appropriate, other relevant organisations, to find solutions.	15.15–15.17
Permanent vegetative state (PVS)	A condition caused by catastrophic brain damage whereby patients in PVS have a permanent and irreversible lack of awareness of their surroundings and no ability to interact at any level with those around them.	6.18 8.18
Personal welfare	Personal welfare decisions are any decisions about person's healthcare, where they live, what clothes they wear, what they eat and anything needed for their general care and well-being. Attorneys and deputies can be appointed to make decisions about personal welfare on behalf of a person who lacks capacity. Many acts of care are to do with personal welfare.	**_ LPAs 7.21–7.31** **_ deputies 8.38–8.39** Advance decisions about _ 9.4, 9.35 Role of High Court in decisions about _ 15.44
Property and affairs	Any possessions owned by a person (such as a house or fat, jewellery or other possessions), the money they have in income, savings or investments and any expenditure. Attorneys and deputies can be appointed to make decisions about property and affairs on behalf of a person who lacks capacity.	**_ LPAs 7.32–7.42** **_ deputies 8.34–8.37** Restrictions on _ LPA 7.56 Duties of _ attorney 7.58, 7.67–7.68 _ EPAs 7.76–7.77 OPG panel of _ deputies 8.35 Duties of _ deputy 8.56, 8.67–8.68 _ of children and young people 12.3–12.4, 12.7
Protection from liability	Legal protection, granted to anyone who has acted or made decisions in line with the Act's principles.	**Chapter 6**
Protection of Vulnerable Adults (POVA) list	A register of individuals who have abused, neglected or otherwise harmed vulnerable adults in their care or placed vulnerable adults at risk of harm. Providers of care must not offer such individuals employment in care positions.	14.31

Public Services Ombudsman for Wales	An independent body that investigates complaints about local government and NHS organisations in Wales, and the National Assembly for Wales, concerning matters such as housing, planning, education, social services and health services.	15.20 15.30–15.32
Receiver	Someone appointed by the former Court of Protection to manage the property and affairs of a person lacking capacity to manage their own affairs. Existing receivers continue as deputies with legal authority to deal with the person's property and affairs.	8.5 8.35
Restraint	See Section 6(4) of the Act. The use or threat of force to help do an act which the person resists, or the restriction of the person's liberty of movement, whether or not they resist. Restraint may only be used where it is necessary to protect the person from harm and is proportionate to the risk of harm.	**6.39–6.44, 6.47–53** Use of _ in moves between accommodation 6.11 Use of _ in healthcare and treatment decisions 6.15 Attorneys and _ 7.43–7.44 Deputies and _ 8.46 MHA and _ 13.5
Statutory principles	The five key principles are set out in Section 1 of the Act. They are designed to emphasise the fundamental concepts and core values of the Act and to provide a benchmark to guide decision-makers, professionals and carers acting under the Act's provisions. The principles generally apply to all actions and decisions taken under the Act.	**Chapter 2**
Two-stage test of capacity	Using sections 2 and 3 of the Act to assess whether or not a person has capacity to make a decision for themselves at that time.	**4.10–4.13** Protection from liability 6.27 Applying _ to advance decisions 9.39
Wilful neglect	An intentional or deliberate omission or failure to carry out an act of care by someone who has care of a person who lacks (or whom the person reasonably believes lacks) capacity to care for themselves. Section 44 introduces a new offence of wilful neglect of a person who lacks capacity.	14.23–14.26

Written statements of wishes and feelings	Written statements the person might have made before losing capacity about their wishes and feelings regarding issues such as the type of medical treatment they would want in the case of future illness, where they would prefer to live, or how they wish to be cared for. They should be used to help find out what someone's wishes and feelings might be, as part of working out their best interests. They are not the same as advance decisions to refuse treatment and are not binding.	5.34 5.37 5.42–5.44

ANNEX A

The following list provides contact details for some organisations that provide information, guidance or materials related to the Code of Practice and the Mental Capacity Act. The list is not exhaustive: many other organisations may also produce their own materials.

British Banking Association

Provides guidance for bank staff on *'Banking for mentally incapacitated and learning disabled customers'*.

Available from www.bba.org.uk/bba/jsp/polopoly.jsp?d=146&a=5757, price £10 (members) /£12 (non-members). Not inclusive of VAT.
web: www.bba.org.uk
telephone: 020 7216 8800

British Medical Association

Co-authors (with the Law Society) of *Assessment of Mental Capacity: Guidance for Doctors and Lawyers* (Second edition) (London: BMJ Books, 2004). www.bma.org.uk/ap.nsf/Content/Assessmentmental?OpenDocument& Highlight=2,mental,capacity

Available from BMJ Books (www.bmjbookshop.com), price £20.99
web: www.bma.org.uk
telephone: 020 7387 4499

British Psychological Society

Publishers of *Guidelines on assessing capacity*-professional guidance available online to members.
web: www.bps.org.uk
telephone: (0)116 254 9568

Commission for Social Care Inspection

The Commission for Social Care Inspection (CSCI) registers, inspects and reports on social care services in England.
web: www.csci.org.uk
telephone: 0845 015 0120 / 0191 233 3323
textphone: 0845 015 2255 / 0191 233 3588

Community Legal Services Direct

Provides free legal information to people living in England and Wales to help them deal with legal problems.
web: www.clsdirect.org.uk
telephone (helpline): 0845 345 4 345

Criminal Records Bureau (CRB)

The CRB runs criminal records checks on people who apply for jobs working with children and vulnerable adults.
web: www.crb.org.uk
telephone: 0870 90 90 811

Department for Constitutional Affairs

The government department with responsibility for the Mental Capacity Act and the Code of Practice. Also publishes guidance for specific audiences www.dca.gov.uk/legal-policy/mental-capacity/guidance.htm

Department of Health

Publishes guidance for healthcare and social care staff in England. Key publications referenced in the Code include:

- on using restraint with people with learning disabilities and autistic spectrum disorder, see *Guidance for restrictive physical interventions* www.dh.gov.uk/assetRoot/04/06/84/61/04068461.pdf
- on adult protection procedures, see *No secrets: Guidance on developing and implementing multi-agency policies and procedures to protect vulnerable adults from abuse* www.dh.gov.uk/assetRoot/04/07/45/44/04074544.pdf
- on consent to examination and treatment, including advance decisions to refuse treatment www.dh/gov.uk/consent
- on the proposed Bournewood safeguards, a draft illustrative Code of Practice www.dh.gov.uk/assetRoot/04/14/17/64/04141764.pdf
- on IMCAs and the IMCA pilots www.dh.gov.uk/imca

DH also is responsible for the *Mental Health Act 1983 Code of Practice* (TSO 1999) www.dh.gov.uk/assetRoot/04/07/49/61/04074961.pdf

Family Mediation Helpline

Provides general information on family mediation and contact details for mediation services in your local area.
web: www.familymediationhelpline.co.uk
telephone: 0845 60 26 627

Healthcare Commission

The health watchdog in England, undertaking reviews and investigations into the provision of NHS and private healthcare services.
web: www.healthcarecommission.org.uk
telephone helpline: 0845 601 3012
switchboard: 020 7448 9200

Healthcare Inspectorate for Wales

Undertakes reviews and investigations into the provision of NHS funded care, either by or for Welsh NHS organisations.
web: www.hiw.org.uk
email: hiw@wales.gsi.gov.uk
telephone: 029 2092 8850

Housing Ombudsman Service

The Housing Ombudsman Service considers complaints against member organisations, and deals with other housing disputes.
web: www.ihos.org.uk
email: info@housing-ombudsman.org.uk
telephone: 020 7421 3800

Information Commissioner's Office

The Information Commissioner's Office is the UK's independent authority set up to promote access to official information and to protect personal information.
web: www.ico.gov.uk
telephone helpline: 08456 30 60 60

Legal Services Commission

Looks after legal aid in England and Wales, and provides information, advice and legal representation.
web: www.legalservices.gov.uk

See also Community Legal Services Direct.

Local Government Ombudsman

The Local Government Ombudsmen investigate complaints about councils and certain other bodies.
web: www.lgo.org.uk
telephone: 0845 602 1983

National Mediation Helpline

Provides access to a simple, low cost method of resolving a wide range of disputes.

The National Mediation Helpline is operated on behalf of the Department for Constitutional Affairs (DCA) in conjunction with the Civil Mediation Council (CMC).
web: www.nationalmediationhelpline.com
telephone: 0845 60 30 809

Office of the Public Guardian

The new Public Guardian is established under the Act and will be supported by the Office of the Public Guardian, which will replace the current Public Guardianship Office (PGO). The OPG will be an executive agency of the Department for Constitutional Affairs. Amongst its other roles, it provides forms for LPAs and EPAs.
web: From October 2007, a new website will be created at www.publicguardian.gov.uk

Official Solicitor

Provides legal services for vulnerable people and is able to represent people who lack capacity and act as a litigation friend.
web: www.officialsolicitor.gov.uk
telephone: 020 7911 7127

Patient Advice and Liaison Service (PALS)

Provides information about the NHS and help resolve concerns or problems with the NHS, including support when making complaints.
web: www.pals.nhs.uk

The site includes contact details for local PALS offices around the country.

Patient Information Advisory Group

Considers applications on behalf of the Secretary of State to allow the common law duty of confidentiality to be aside.
web: www.advisorybodies.doh.gov.uk/PIAG

Public Service Ombudsman for Wales

Investigates complaints about local authorities and NHS organisations in Wales, and about the National Assembly Government for Wales.
web: www.ombudsman-wales.org.uk
telephone: 01656 641 150

Welsh Assembly Government

Produces key pieces of guidance for healthcare and social care staff, including:

- *In safe hands-Implementing Adult Protection Procedures in Wales* (July 2000) http://new.wales.gov.uk/about/departments/dhss/publications/ social_services_publications/reports/ insafehands?lang=en
- *Framework for restrictive physical intervention policy and practice* (available at www.childrenfirst.wales.gov.uk/content/framework/ phys-int-e.pdf)

Copies of this publication can be downloaded from www.guardianship.gsi.gov.uk

Hard copies of this publication are available from TSO

For more information on the Mental Capacity Act contact the Public Guardianship Office:

9am – 5pm, Mon – Fri
Telephone: 0845 330 2900 (local call rate)
or +44 207 664 7000 (for callers outside UK)
Text Phone: 020 7664 7755
Fax: 0870 739 5780 (UK callers)
Email: custserv@guardianship.gsi.gov.uk
Website: www.guardianship.gsi.gov.uk

Post:

Public Guardianship Office
Archway Tower
2 Junction Road
London
N19 5SZ

Appendix 4

STATUTORY INSTRUMENTS

MENTAL CAPACITY ACT 2005 (INDEPENDENT MENTAL CAPACITY ADVOCATES) (GENERAL) REGULATIONS 2006

(SI 2006/1832)

Made . . . . *7th July 2006*

Laid before Parliament . . . . *13th July 2006*

Coming into force in accordance with regulation 1(2)

The Secretary of State makes these Regulations in exercise of the powers conferred on her by sections 35(2) and (3), 36, 37(6) and (7), 38(8), 64(1) and 65(1) of the Mental Capacity Act 2005.

A4.1

1 Citation, commencement and extent

(1) These Regulations may be cited as the Mental Capacity Act 2005 (Independent Mental Capacity Advocates) (General) Regulations 2006.

(2) These Regulations shall come into force—

- (a) for the purpose of enabling the Secretary of State to make arrangements under section 35 of the Act, and for the purpose of enabling local authorities to approve IMCAs, on 1st November 2006, and
- (b) for all other purposes, on 1st April 2007.

(3) These Regulations apply in relation to England only.

A4.2

2 Interpretation

(1) In these Regulations—

"the Act" means the Mental Capacity Act 2005; and
"IMCA" means an independent mental capacity advocate.

(2) In these Regulations, references to instructions given to a person to act as an IMCA are to instructions given under sections 37 to 39 of the Act or under regulations made by virtue of section 41 of the Act.

A4.3

3 Meaning of NHS Body

(1) For the purposes of sections 37 and 38 of the Act, "NHS body" means a body in England which is—

- (a) a Strategic Health Authority;

(b) an NHS foundation trust;
(c) a Primary Care Trust;
(d) an NHS Trust; or
(e) a Care Trust.

(2) In this regulation—

"Care Trust" means a body designated as a Care Trust under section 45 of the Health and Social Care Act 2001;
"NHS foundation trust" has the meaning given in section 1 of the Health and Social Care (Community Health and Standards) Act 2003;
"NHS trust" means a body established under section 5 of the National Health Service and Community Care Act 1990;
"Primary Care Trust" means a body established under section 16A of the National Health Service Act 1977; and
"Strategic Health Authority" means a Strategic Health Authority established under section 8 of the National Health Service Act 1977.

A4.4

4 Meaning of serious medical treatment

(1) This regulation defines serious medical treatment for the purposes of section 37 of the Act.

(2) Serious medical treatment is treatment which involves providing, withdrawing or withholding treatment in circumstances where—

(a) in a case where a single treatment is being proposed, there is a fine balance between its benefits to the patient and the burdens and risks it is likely to entail for him,
(b) in a case where there is a choice of treatments, a decision as to which one to use is finely balanced, or
(c) what is proposed would be likely to involve serious consequences for the patient.

A4.5

5 Appointment of independent mental capacity advocates

(1) No person may be appointed to act as an IMCA for the purposes of sections 37 to 39 of the Act, or regulations made by virtue of section 41 of the Act, unless—

(a) he is for the time being approved by a local authority on the grounds that he satisfies the appointment requirements, or
(b) he belongs to a class of persons which is for the time being approved by a local authority on the grounds that all persons in that class satisfy the appointment requirements.

(2) The appointment requirements, in relation to a person appointed to act as an IMCA, are that—

(a) he has appropriate experience or training or an appropriate combination of experience and training;
(b) he is a person of integrity and good character; and
(c) he is able to act independently of any person who instructs him.

(3) Before a determination is made in relation to any person for the purposes of paragraph (2)(b), there must be obtained in respect of that person—

(a) an enhanced criminal record certificate issued pursuant to section 113B of the Police Act 1997; or
(b) if the purpose for which the certificate is required is not one prescribed under subsection (2) of that section, a criminal record certificate issued pursuant to section 113A of that Act.

A4.6

6 Functions of an independent mental capacity advocate

(1) This regulation applies where an IMCA has been instructed by an authorised person to represent a person ("P").

(2) "Authorised person" means a person who is required or enabled to instruct an IMCA under sections 37 to 39 of the Act or under regulations made by virtue of section 41of the Act.

(3) The IMCA must determine in all the circumstances how best to represent and support P.

(4) In particular, the IMCA must—

- (a) verify that the instructions were issued by an authorised person;
- (b) to the extent that it is practicable and appropriate to do so—
  - (i) interview P, and
  - (ii) examine the records relevant to P to which the IMCA has access under section 35(6) of the Act;
- (c) to the extent that it is practicable and appropriate to do so, consult—
  - (i) persons engaged in providing care or treatment for P in a professional capacity or for remuneration, and
  - (ii) other persons who may be in a position to comment on P's wishes, feelings, beliefs or values; and
- (d) take all practicable steps to obtain such other information about P, or the act or decision that is proposed in relation to P, as the IMCA considers necessary.

(5) The IMCA must evaluate all the information he has obtained for the purpose of—

- (a) ascertaining the extent of the support provided to P to enable him to participate in making any decision about the matter in relation to which the IMCA has been instructed;
- (b) ascertaining what P's wishes and feelings would be likely to be, and the beliefs and values that would be likely to influence P, if he had capacity in relation to the proposed act or decision;
- (c) ascertaining what alternative courses of action are available in relation to P;
- (d) where medical treatment is proposed for P, ascertaining whether he would be likely to benefit from a further medical opinion.

(6) The IMCA must prepare a report for the authorised person who instructed him.

(7) The IMCA may include in the report such submissions as he considers appropriate in relation to P and the act or decision which is proposed in relation to him.

A4.7

7 Challenges to decisions affecting persons who lack capacity

(1) This regulation applies where—

- (a) an IMCA has been instructed to represent a person ("P") in relation to any matter, and
- (b) a decision affecting P (including a decision as to his capacity) is made in that matter.

(2) The IMCA has the same rights to challenge the decision as he would have if he were a person (other than an IMCA) engaged in caring for P or interested in his welfare.

MENTAL CAPACITY ACT 2005 (INDEPENDENT MENTAL CAPACITY ADVOCATES) (EXPANSION OF ROLE) REGULATIONS 2006

(SI 2006/2883)

Made . . . . 30th October 2006

Coming into force in accordance with regulation 1(2)

The Secretary of State makes these Regulations in exercise of the powers conferred on her by sections 41(1) and (2), 64(1) and 65(1) of the Mental Capacity Act 2005.

A draft of this instrument has been laid before Parliament in accordance with section 65(4) of the Mental Capacity Act 2005 and approved by resolution of each House of Parliament.

A4.8

1 Citation, commencement, extent and interpretation

(1) These Regulations may be cited as the Mental Capacity Act 2005 (Independent Mental Capacity Advocates) (Expansion of Role) Regulations 2006.

(2) These Regulations shall come into force—

- (a) for the purpose of enabling the Secretary of State to make arrangements by virtue of regulation 2, on 1st November 2006, and
- (b) for all other purposes, on 1st April 2007.

(3) These Regulations apply in relation to England only.

(4) In these Regulations—

"the Act" means the Mental Capacity Act 2005;
"IMCA" means an independent mental capacity advocate; and
"NHS body" means a body in England which is—
- (a) a Strategic Health Authority;
- (b) an NHS foundation trust;
- (c) a Primary Care Trust;
- (d) an NHS Trust; or
- (e) a Care Trust.

(5) In the definition of "NHS body" in paragraph (4)—

"Care Trust" means a body designated as a Care Trust under section 45 of the Health and Social Care Act 2001;
"NHS foundation trust" has the meaning given in section 1 of the Health and Social Care (Community Health and Standards) Act 2003;
"NHS trust" means a body established under section 5 of the National Health Service and Community Care Act 1990;
"Primary Care Trust" means a body established under section 16A of the National Health Service Act 1977; and
"Strategic Health Authority" means a Strategic Health Authority established under section 8 of the National Health Service Act 1977.

A4.9

2 Adjustment of the obligation to make arrangements imposed by section 35 of the Act

Arrangements made by the Secretary of State under section 35 of the Act may include such provision as she considers reasonable for the purpose of enabling IMCAs to be available to represent and support persons in the circumstances specified in regulation 3 or 4.

A4.10

3 Review of arrangements as to accommodation

(1) The circumstances specified in this regulation are where—

(a) qualifying arrangements have been made by an NHS body or local authority as to the accommodation of a person ("P") who lacks capacity to agree to the arrangements;
(b) a review of the arrangements is proposed or in progress (whether under a care plan or otherwise);
(c) the NHS body is satisfied, or the local authority are satisfied, that there is no person, other than a person engaged in providing care or treatment for P in a professional capacity or for remuneration, whom it would be appropriate to consult in determining what would be in P's best interests;
(d) none of the following exist—
  (i) a person nominated by P (in whatever manner) as a person to be consulted in matters affecting his interests,
  (ii) a donee of a lasting power of attorney created by P,
  (iii) a deputy appointed by the Court of Protection for P, or
  (iv) a donee of an enduring power of attorney (within the meaning of Schedule 4 to the Act) created by P; and
(e) sections 37, 38 and 39 of the Act do not apply.

(2) In this regulation—

"accommodation" means—
  (a) accommodation in a care home or hospital, or
  (b) residential accommodation provided in accordance with—
    (i) section 21 or 29 of the National Assistance Act 1948, or
    (ii) section 117 of the Mental Health Act 1983,
  as the result of a decision taken by a local authority under section 47 of the National Health Service and Community Care Act 1990;

"care home" and "hospital" have the same meaning as in section 38 of the Act; and
"qualifying arrangements" means arrangements—
  (a) under which accommodation has been provided for P for a continuous period of 12 weeks or more, and
  (b) which are not made as a result of an obligation imposed on P under the Mental Health Act 1983.

A4.11

4 Adult protection cases

(1) The circumstances specified in this regulation are where—

(a) an NHS body proposes to take or has taken, or a local authority propose to take or have taken, protective measures in relation to a person ("P") who lacks capacity to agree to one or more of the measures;
(b) the proposal is made or the measures have been taken—
  (i) following the receipt of an allegation or evidence that P is being, or has been, abused or neglected by another person or that P is abusing, or has abused, another person, and
  (ii) in accordance with arrangements relating to the protection of vulnerable adults from abuse which are made pursuant to guidance issued under section 7 of the Local Authority Social Services Act 1970; and
(c) none of the following provisions apply—
  (i) section 37, 38 or 39 of the Act, or
  (ii) regulation 3 of these Regulations.

(2) The reference to protective measures in relation to P includes measures to minimise the risk that any abuse or neglect of P, or abuse by P, will continue.

A4.12

5 Instructing an IMCA

(1) In the circumstances specified in regulation 3 or 4, an NHS body or local authority may instruct an IMCA to represent P if the NHS body is satisfied, or the local authority are satisfied, that it would be of particular benefit to P to be so represented.

(2) An NHS body which instructs, or a local authority which instruct, an IMCA under paragraph (1) must—

(a) in making any decision resulting from a review of arrangements as to P's accommodation, or

(b) in making any decision, or further decision, about protective measures in relation to P,

take into account any information given, or submissions made, by the IMCA.

LASTING POWERS OF ATTORNEY, ENDURING POWERS OF ATTORNEY AND PUBLIC GUARDIAN REGULATIONS 2007

(SI 2007/1253)

Made . . . . *16th April 2007*

Laid before Parliament . . . . *17th April 2007*

Coming into force . . . . *1st October 2007*

The Lord Chancellor makes the following Regulations in exercise of the powers conferred by sections 13(6)(a), 58(3) and 64(1) of, and Schedules 1 and 4 to, the Mental Capacity Act 2005.

PART 1
PRELIMINARY

A4.13

1 Citation and commencement

(1) These Regulations may be cited as the Lasting Powers of Attorney, Enduring Powers of Attorney and Public Guardian Regulations 2007.

(2) These Regulations shall come into force on 1 October 2007.

A4.14

2 Interpretation

(1) In these Regulations—

"the Act" means the Mental Capacity Act 2005;

"court" means the Court of Protection;

"LPA certificate", in relation to an instrument made with a view to creating a lasting power of attorney, means the certificate which is required to be included in the instrument by virtue of paragraph 2(1)(e) of Schedule 1 to the Act;

"named person", in relation to an instrument made with a view to creating a lasting power of attorney, means a person who is named in the instrument as being a person to be notified of any application for the registration of the instrument;

"prescribed information", in relation to any instrument intended to create a lasting power of attorney, means the information contained in the form used for the instrument which appears under the heading "prescribed information".

A4.15

3 Minimal differences from forms prescribed in these Regulations

(1) In these Regulations, any reference to a form—

- (a) in the case of a form set out in Schedules 1 to 7 to these Regulations, is to be regarded as including a Welsh version of that form; and
- (b) in the case of a form set out in Schedules 2 to 7 to these Regulations, is to be regarded as also including—
  - (i) a form to the same effect but which differs in an immaterial respect in form or mode of expression;
  - (ii) a form to the same effect but with such variations as the circumstances may require or the court or the Public Guardian may approve; or
  - (iii) a Welsh version of a form within (i) or (ii).

A4.16

4 Computation of time

(1) This regulation shows how to calculate any period of time which is specified in these Regulations.

(2) A period of time expressed as a number of days must be computed as clear days.

(3) Where the specified period is 7 days or less, and would include a day which is not a business day, that day does not count.

(4) When the specified period for doing any act at the office of the Public Guardian ends on a day on which the office is closed, that act will be done in time if done on the next day on which the office is open.

(5) In this regulation—

"business day" means a day other than—
- (a) a Saturday, Sunday, Christmas Day or Good Friday; or
- (b) a bank holiday under the Banking and Financial Dealings Act 1971, in England and Wales; and

"clear days" means that in computing the number of days—
- (a) the day on which the period begins, and
- (b) if the end of the period is defined by reference to an event, the day on which that event occurs,

are not included.

PART 2
LASTING POWERS OF ATTORNEY

Instruments intended to create a lasting power of attorney

A4.17

5 Forms for lasting powers of attorney

The forms set out in Parts 1 and 2 of Schedule 1 to these Regulations are the forms which, in the circumstances to which they apply, are to be used for instruments intended to create a lasting power of attorney.

A4.18

6 Maximum number of named persons

The maximum number of named persons that the donor of a lasting power of attorney may specify in the instrument intended to create the power is 5.

A4.19

7 Requirement for two LPA certificates where instrument has no named persons

Where an instrument intended to create a lasting power of attorney includes a statement by the donor that there are no persons whom he wishes to be notified of any application for the registration of the instrument—

(a) the instrument must include two LPA certificates; and
(b) each certificate must be completed and signed by a different person.

A4.20

8 Persons who may provide an LPA certificate

(1) Subject to paragraph (3), the following persons may give an LPA certificate—

(a) a person chosen by the donor as being someone who has known him personally for the period of at least two years which ends immediately before the date on which that person signs the LPA certificate;
(b) a person chosen by the donor who, on account of his professional skills and expertise, reasonably considers that he is competent to make the judgments necessary to certify the matters set out in paragraph (2)(1)(e) of Schedule 1 to the Act.

(2) The following are examples of persons within paragraph (1)(b)—

(a) a registered health care professional;
(b) a barrister, solicitor or advocate called or admitted in any part of the United Kingdom;
(c) a registered social worker; or
(d) an independent mental capacity advocate.

(3) A person is disqualified from giving an LPA certificate in respect of any instrument intended to create a lasting power of attorney if that person is—

(a) a family member of the donor;
(b) a donee of that power;
(c) a donee of—
 (i) any other lasting power of attorney, or
 (ii) an enduring power of attorney,
which has been executed by the donor (whether or not it has been revoked);
(d) a family member of a donee within sub-paragraph (b);
(e) a director or employee of a trust corporation acting as a donee within sub-paragraph (b);
(f) a business partner or employee of—
 (i) the donor, or
 (ii) a donee within sub-paragraph (b);
(g) an owner, director, manager or employee of any care home in which the donor is living when the instrument is executed; or
(h) a family member of a person within sub-paragraph (g).

(4) In this regulation—

"care home" has the meaning given in section 3 of the Care Standards Act 2000;
"registered health care professional" means a person who is a member of a profession regulated by a body mentioned in section 25(3) of the National Health Service Reform and Health Care Professions Act 2002; and

"registered social worker" means a person registered as a social worker in a register maintained by—
- (a) the General Social Care Council;
- (b) the Care Council for Wales;
- (c) the Scottish Social Services Council; or
- (d) the Northern Ireland Social Care Council.

A4.21

9 Execution of instrument

(1) An instrument intended to create a lasting power of attorney must be executed in accordance with this regulation.

(2) The donor must read (or have read to him) all the prescribed information.

(3) As soon as reasonably practicable after the steps required by paragraph (2) have been taken, the donor must—

- (a) complete the provisions of Part A of the instrument that apply to him (or direct another person to do so); and
- (b) subject to paragraph (7), sign Part A of the instrument in the presence of a witness.

(4) As soon as reasonably practicable after the steps required by paragraph (3) have been taken—

- (a) the person giving an LPA certificate, or
- (b) if regulation 7 applies (two LPA certificates required), each of the persons giving a certificate,

must complete the LPA certificate at Part B of the instrument and sign it.

(5) As soon as reasonably practicable after the steps required by paragraph (4) have been taken—

- (a) the donee, or
- (b) if more than one, each of the donees,

must read (or have read to him) all the prescribed information.

(6) As soon as reasonably practicable after the steps required by paragraph (5) have been taken, the donee or, if more than one, each of them—

- (a) must complete the provisions of Part C of the instrument that apply to him (or direct another person to do so); and
- (b) subject to paragraph (7), must sign Part C of the instrument in the presence of a witness.

(7) If the instrument is to be signed by any person at the direction of the donor, or at the direction of any donee, the signature must be done in the presence of two witnesses.

(8) For the purposes of this regulation—

- (a) the donor may not witness any signature required for the power;
- (b) a donee may not witness any signature required for the power apart from that of another donee.

(9) A person witnessing a signature must—

- (a) sign the instrument; and
- (b) give his full name and address.

(10) Any reference in this regulation to a person signing an instrument (however expressed) includes his signing it by means of a mark made on the instrument at the appropriate place.

Registering the instrument

A4.22

10 Notice to be given by a person about to apply for registration of lasting power of attorney

Schedule 2 to these Regulations sets out the form of notice ("LPA 001") which must be given by a donor or donee who is about to make an application for the registration of an instrument intended to create a lasting power of attorney.

A4.23

11 Application for registration

(1) Schedule 3 to these Regulations sets out the form ("LPA 002") which must be used for making an application to the Public Guardian for the registration of an instrument intended to create a lasting power of attorney.

(2) Where the instrument to be registered which is sent with the application is neither—

(a) the original instrument intended to create the power, nor
(b) a certified copy of it,

the Public Guardian must not register the instrument unless the court directs him to do so.

(3) In paragraph (2) "a certified copy" means a photographic or other facsimile copy which is certified as an accurate copy by—

(a) the donor; or
(b) a solicitor or notary.

A4.24

12 Period to elapse before registration in cases not involving objection or defect

The period at the end of which the Public Guardian must register an instrument in accordance with paragraph 5 of Schedule 1 to the Act is the period of 6 weeks beginning with—

(a) the date on which the Public Guardian gave the notice or notices under paragraph 7 or 8 of Schedule 1 to the Act of receipt of an application for registration; or
(b) if notices were given on more than one date, the latest of those dates.

A4.25

13 Notice of receipt of application for registration

(1) Part 1 of Schedule 4 to these Regulations sets out the form of notice ("LPA 003A") which the Public Guardian must give to the donee (or donees) when the Public Guardian receives an application for the registration of a lasting power of attorney.

(2) Part 2 of Schedule 4 sets out the form of notice ("LPA 003B") which the Public Guardian must give to the donor when the Public Guardian receives such an application.

(3) Where it appears to the Public Guardian that there is good reason to do so, the Public Guardian must also provide (or arrange for the provision of) an explanation to the donor of—

(a) the notice referred to in paragraph (2) and what the effect of it is; and
(b) why it is being brought to his attention.

(4) Any information provided under paragraph (3) must be provided—

(a) to the donor personally; and
(b) in a way that is appropriate to the donor's circumstances (for example using simple language, visual aids or other appropriate means).

A4.26

14 Objection to registration: notice to Public Guardian [to be given by the donee of the power or a named person]

(1) This regulation deals with any objection to the registration of an instrument as a lasting power of attorney which is to be made to the Public Guardian [by the donee of the power or a named person].

(2) Where [the donee of the power or a named person]—

- (a) is entitled to receive notice under paragraph 6, 7 or 8 of Schedule 1 to the Act of an application for the registration of the instrument, and
- (b) wishes to object to registration on a ground set out in paragraph 13(1) of Schedule 1 to the Act,

he must do so before the end of the period of 5 weeks beginning with the date on which the notice is given.

(3) A notice of objection must be given in writing, setting out—

- (a) the name and address of the objector;
- (b) ... the name and address of the donor of the power;
- (c) if known, the name and address of the donee (or donees); and
- (d) the ground for making the objection.

(4) The Public Guardian must notify the objector as to whether he is satisfied that the ground of the objection is established.

(5) At any time after receiving the notice of objection and before giving the notice required by paragraph (4), the Public Guardian may require the objector to provide such further information, or produce such documents, as the Public Guardian reasonably considers necessary to enable him to determine whether the ground for making the objection is established.

(6) Where—

- (a) the Public Guardian is satisfied that the ground of the objection is established, but
- (b) by virtue of section 13(7) of the Act, the instrument is not revoked,

the notice under paragraph (4) must contain a statement to that effect.

(7) Nothing in this regulation prevents an objector from making a further objection under paragraph 13 of Schedule 1 to the Act where—

- (a) the notice under paragraph (4) indicates that the Public Guardian is not satisfied that the particular ground of objection to which that notice relates is established; and
- (b) the period specified in paragraph (2) has not expired.

NOTES

Provision heading: words "to be given by the donee of the power or a named person" in square brackets inserted by SI 2007/2161, regs 2, 3(1). Date in force: 1 October 2007: see SI 2007/2161, reg 1.

Para (1): words "by the donee of the power or a named person" in square brackets inserted by SI 2007/2161, regs 2, 3(2). Date in force: 1 October 2007: see SI 2007/2161, reg 1.

Para (2): words "the donee of the power or a named person" in square brackets substituted by SI 2007/2161, regs 2, 3(3). Date in force: 1 October 2007: see SI 2007/2161, reg 1.

Para (3): in sub-para (b) words omitted revoked by SI 2007/2161, regs 2, 3(4). Date in force: 1 October 2007: see SI 2007/2161, reg 1.

A4.27

[14A Objection to registration: notice to Public Guardian to be given by the donor]

[(1) This regulation deals with any objection to the registration of an instrument as a lasting power of attorney which is to be made to the Public Guardian by the donor of the power.

(2) Where the donor of the power—

(a) is entitled to receive notice under paragraph 8 of Schedule 1 to the Act of an application for the registration of the instrument, and
(b) wishes to object to the registration,

he must do so before the end of the period of 5 weeks beginning with the date on which the notice is given.

(3) The donor of the power must give notice of his objection in writing to the Public Guardian, setting out—

(a) the name and address of the donor of the power;
(b) if known, the name and address of the donee (or donees); and
(c) the ground for making the objection.]

NOTES

Inserted by SI 2007/2161, regs 2, 4. Date in force: 1 October 2007: see SI 2007/2161, reg 1.

A4.28

15 Objection to registration: application to the court

(1) This regulation deals with any objection to the registration of an instrument as a lasting power of attorney which is to be made to the court.

(2) The grounds for making an application to the court are—

(a) that one or more of the requirements for the creation of a lasting power of attorney have not been met;
(b) that the power has been revoked, or has otherwise come to an end, on a ground other than the grounds set out in paragraph 13(1) of Schedule 1 to the Act;
(c) any of the grounds set out in paragraph (a) or (b) of section 22(3) of the Act.

(3) Where any person—

(a) is entitled to receive notice under paragraph 6, 7 or 8 of Schedule 1 to the Act of an application for the registration of the instrument, and
(b) wishes to object to registration on one or more of the grounds set out in paragraph (2),

he must make an application to the court before the end of the period of 5 weeks beginning with the date on which the notice is given.

(4) The notice of an application to the court, which a person making an objection to the court is required to give to the Public Guardian under paragraph 13(3)(b)(ii) of Schedule 1 to the Act, must be in writing.

A4.29

16 Notifying applicants of non-registration of lasting power of attorney

Where the Public Guardian is prevented from registering an instrument as a lasting power of attorney by virtue of—

(a) paragraph 11(1) of Schedule 1 to the Act (instrument not made in accordance with Schedule),
(b) paragraph 12(2) of that Schedule (deputy already appointed),
(c) paragraph 13(2) of that Schedule (objection by donee or named person on grounds of bankruptcy, disclaimer, death etc),
(d) paragraph 14(2) of that Schedule (objection by donor), or
(e) regulation 11(2) of these Regulations (application for registration not accompanied by original instrument or certified copy),

he must notify the person (or persons) who applied for registration of that fact.

A4.30

17 Notice to be given on registration of lasting power of attorney

(1) Where the Public Guardian registers an instrument as a lasting power of attorney, he must—

(a) retain a copy of the instrument; and
(b) return to the person (or persons) who applied for registration the original instrument, or the certified copy of it, which accompanied the application for registration.

(2) Schedule 5 to these Regulations sets out the form of notice ("LPA 004") which the Public Guardian must give to the donor and donee (or donees) when the Public Guardian registers an instrument.

(3) Where it appears to the Public Guardian that there is good reason to do so, the Public Guardian must also provide (or arrange for the provision of) an explanation to the donor of—

(a) the notice referred to in paragraph (2) and what the effect of it is; and
(b) why it is being brought to his attention.

(4) Any information provided under paragraph (3) must be provided—

(a) to the donor personally; and
(b) in a way that is appropriate to the donor's circumstances (for example using simple language, visual aids or other appropriate means).

(5) "Certified copy" is to be construed in accordance with regulation 11(3).

Post-registration

A4.31

18 Changes to instrument registered as lasting power of attorney

(1) This regulation applies in any case where any of paragraphs 21 to 24 of Schedule 1 to the Act requires the Public Guardian to attach a note to an instrument registered as a lasting power of attorney.

(2) The Public Guardian must give a notice to the donor and the donee (or, if more than one, each of them) requiring him to deliver to the Public Guardian—

(a) the original of instrument which was sent to the Public Guardian for registration;
(b) any office copy of that registered instrument; and
(c) any certified copy of that registered instrument.

(3) On receipt of the document, the Public Guardian must—

(a) attach the required note; and
(b) return the document to the person from whom it was obtained.

A4.32

19 Loss or destruction of instrument registered as lasting power of attorney

(1) This regulation applies where—

(a) a person is required by or under the Act to deliver up to the Public Guardian any of the following documents—
  (i) an instrument registered as a lasting power of attorney;
  (ii) an office copy of that registered instrument;
  (iii) a certified copy of that registered instrument; and
(b) the document has been lost or destroyed.

(2) The person required to deliver up the document must provide to the Public Guardian in writing—

(a) if known, the date of the loss or destruction and the circumstances in which it occurred;
(b) otherwise, a statement of when he last had the document in his possession.

A4.33

20 Disclaimer of appointment by a donee of lasting power of attorney

(1) Schedule 6 to these Regulations sets out the form ("LPA 005") which a donee of an instrument registered as a lasting power of attorney must use to disclaim his appointment as donee.

(2) The donee must send—

- (a) the completed form to the donor; and
- (b) a copy of it to—
  - (i) the Public Guardian; and
  - (ii) any other donee who, for the time being, is appointed under the power.

A4.34

21 Revocation by donor of lasting power of attorney

(1) A donor who revokes a lasting power to attorney must—

- (a) notify the Public Guardian that he has done so; and
- (b) notify the donee (or, if more than one, each of them) of the revocation.

(2) Where the Public Guardian receives a notice under paragraph (1)(a), he must cancel the registration of the instrument creating the power if he is satisfied that the donor has taken such steps as are necessary in law to revoke it.

(3) The Public Guardian may require the donor to provide such further information, or produce such documents, as the Public Guardian reasonably considers necessary to enable him to determine whether the steps necessary for revocation have been taken.

(4) Where the Public Guardian cancels the registration of the instrument he must notify—

- (a) the donor; and
- (b) the donee or, if more than one, each of them.

22 Revocation of a lasting power of attorney on death of donor

(1) The Public Guardian must cancel the registration of an instrument as a lasting power of attorney if he is satisfied that the power has been revoked as a result of the donor's death.

(2) Where the Public Guardian cancels the registration of an instrument he must notify the donee or, if more than one, each of them.

PART 3
ENDURING POWERS OF ATTORNEY

A4.35

23 Notice of intention to apply for registration of enduring power of attorney

(1) Schedule 7 to these Regulations sets out the form of notice ("EP1PG") which an attorney (or attorneys) under an enduring power of attorney must give of his intention to make an application for the registration of the instrument creating the power.

(2) In the case of the notice to be given to the donor, the attorney must also provide (or arrange for the provision of) an explanation to the donor of—

- (a) the notice and what the effect of it is; and
- (b) why it is being brought to his attention.

(3) The information provided under paragraph (2) must be provided—

- (a) to the donor personally; and
- (b) in a way that is appropriate to the donor's circumstances (for example using simple language, visual aids or other appropriate means).

A4.36

24 Application for registration

(1) Schedule 8 to these Regulations sets out the form ("EP2PG") which must be used for making an application to the Public Guardian for the registration of an instrument creating an enduring power of attorney.

(2) Where the instrument to be registered which is sent with the application is neither—

- (a) the original instrument creating the power, nor
- (b) a certified copy of it,

the Public Guardian must not register the instrument unless the court directs him to do so.

(3) "Certified copy", in relation to an enduring power of attorney, means a copy certified in accordance with section 3 of the Powers of Attorney Act 1971.

A4.37

25 Notice of objection to registration

(1) This regulation deals with any objection to the registration of an instrument creating an enduring power of attorney which is to be made to the Public Guardian under paragraph 13(4) of Schedule 4 to the Act.

(2) A notice of objection must be given in writing, setting out—

- (a) the name and address of the objector;
- (b) if different, the name and address of the donor of the power;
- (c) if known, the name and address of the attorney (or attorneys); and
- (d) the ground for making the objection.

A4.38

26 Notifying applicants of non-registration of enduring power of attorney

Where the Public Guardian is prevented from registering an instrument creating an enduring power of attorney by virtue of—

- (a) paragraph 13(2) of Schedule 4 to the Act (deputy already appointed),
- (b) paragraph 13(5) of that Schedule (receipt by Public Guardian of valid notice of objection from person entitled to notice of application to register),
- (c) paragraph 13(7) of that Schedule (Public Guardian required to undertake appropriate enquiries in certain circumstances), or
- (d) regulation 24(2) of these Regulations (application for registration not accompanied by original instrument or certified copy),

he must notify the person (or persons) who applied for registration of that fact.

A4.39

27 Registration of instrument creating an enduring power of attorney

(1) Where the Public Guardian registers an instrument creating an enduring power of attorney, he must—

- (a) retain a copy of the instrument; and
- (b) return to the person (or persons) who applied for registration the original instrument, or the certified copy of it, which accompanied the application.

(2) "Certified copy" has the same meaning as in regulation 24(3).

A4.40

28 Objection or revocation not applying to all joint and several attorneys

In a case within paragraph 20(6) or (7) of Schedule 4 to the Act, the form of the entry to be made in the register in respect of an instrument creating the enduring power of attorney is a stamp bearing the following words (inserting the information indicated, as appropriate)—

"THE REGISTRATION OF THIS ENDURING POWER OF ATTORNEY IS QUALIFIED AND EXTENDS TO THE APPOINTMENT OF .... (insert name of attorney(s) not affected by ground(s) of objection or revocation) ONLY AS THE ATTORNEY(S) OF .... (insert name of donor)".

A4.41

29 Loss or destruction of instrument registered as enduring power of attorney

(1) This regulation applies where—

- (a) a person is required by or under the Act to deliver up to the Public Guardian any of the following documents—
  - (i) an instrument registered as an enduring power of attorney;
  - (ii) an office copy of that registered instrument; or
  - (iii) a certified copy of that registered instrument; and
- (b) the document has been lost or destroyed.

(2) The person who is required to deliver up the document must provide to the Public Guardian in writing—

- (a) if known, the date of the loss or destruction and the circumstances in which it occurred;
- (b) otherwise, a statement of when he last had the document in his possession.

PART 4
FUNCTIONS OF THE PUBLIC GUARDIAN

The registers

A4.42

30 Establishing and maintaining the registers

(1) In this Part "the registers" means—

- (a) the register of lasting powers of attorney,
- (b) the register of enduring powers of attorney, and
- (c) the register of court orders appointing deputies,

which the Public Guardian must establish and maintain.

(2) On each register the Public Guardian may include—

- (a) such descriptions of information about a registered instrument or a registered order as the Public Guardian considers appropriate; and
- (b) entries which relate to an instrument or order for which registration has been cancelled.

A4.43

31 Disclosure of information on a register: search by the Public Guardian

(1) Any person may, by an application made under paragraph (2), request the Public Guardian to carry out a search of one or more of the registers.

(2) An application must—

- (a) state—

(i) the register or registers to be searched;
(ii) the name of the person to whom the application relates; and
(iii) such other details about that person as the Public Guardian may require for the purpose of carrying out the search; and

(b) be accompanied by any fee provided for under section 58(4)(b) of the Act.

(3) The Public Guardian may require the applicant to provide such further information, or produce such documents, as the Public Guardian reasonably considers necessary to enable him to carry out the search.

(4) As soon as reasonably practicable after receiving the application—

(a) the Public Guardian must notify the applicant of the result of the search; and
(b) in the event that it reveals one or more entries on the register, the Public Guardian must disclose to the applicant all the information appearing on the register in respect of each entry.

A4.44

32 Disclosure of additional information held by the Public Guardian

(1) This regulation applies in any case where, as a result of a search made under regulation 31, a person has obtained information relating to a registered instrument or a registered order which confers authority to make decisions about matters concerning a person ("P").

(2) On receipt of an application made in accordance with paragraph (4), the Public Guardian may, if he considers that there is good reason to do so, disclose to the applicant such additional information as he considers appropriate.

(3) "Additional information" means any information relating to P—

(a) which the Public Guardian has obtained in exercising the functions conferred on him under the Act; but
(b) which does not appear on the register.

(4) An application must state—

(a) the name of P;
(b) the reasons for making the application; and
(c) what steps, if any, the applicant has taken to obtain the information from P.

(5) The Public Guardian may require the applicant to provide such further information, or produce such documents, as the Public Guardian reasonably considers necessary to enable him to determine the application.

(6) In determining whether to disclose any additional information to P, the Public Guardian must, in particular, have regard to—

(a) the connection between P and the applicant;
(b) the reasons for requesting the information (in particular, why the information cannot or should not be obtained directly from P);
(c) the benefit to P, or any detriment he may suffer, if a disclosure is made; and
(d) any detriment that another person may suffer if a disclosure is made.

Security for discharge of functions

A4.45

33 Persons required to give security for the discharge of their functions

(1) This regulation applies in any case where the court orders a person ("S") to give to the Public Guardian security for the discharge of his functions.

(2) The security must be given by S—

(a) by means of a bond which is entered into in accordance with regulation 34; or
(b) in such other manner as the court may direct.

(3) For the purposes of paragraph (2)(a), S complies with the requirement to give the security only if—

(a) the endorsement required by regulation 34(2) has been provided; and
(b) the person who provided it has notified the Public Guardian of that fact.

(4) For the purposes of paragraph (2)(b), S complies with the requirement to give the security—

(a) in any case where the court directs that any other endorsement must be provided, only if—
  (i) that endorsement has been provided; and
  (ii) the person who provided it has notified the Public Guardian of that fact;
(b) in any case where the court directs that any other requirements must be met in relation to the giving of the security, only if the Public Guardian is satisfied that those other requirements have been met.

A4.46

34 Security given under regulation 33(2)(a): requirement for endorsement

(1) This regulation has effect for the purposes of regulation 33(2)(a).

(2) A bond is entered into in accordance with this regulation only if it is endorsed by—

(a) an authorised insurance company; or
(b) an authorised deposit-taker.

(3) A person may enter into the bond under—

(a) arrangements made by the Public Guardian; or
(b) other arrangements which are made by the person entering into the bond or on his behalf.

(4) The Public Guardian may make arrangements with any person specified in paragraph (2) with a view to facilitating the provision by them of bonds which persons required to give security to the Public Guardian may enter into.

(5) In this regulation—

"authorised insurance company" means—
  (a) a person who has permission under Part 4 of the Financial Services and Markets Act 2000 to effect or carry out contracts of insurance;
  (b) an EEA firm of the kind mentioned in paragraph 5(d) of Schedule 3 to that Act, which has permission under paragraph 15 of that Schedule to effect or carry out contracts of insurance;
  (c) a person who carries on insurance market activity (within the meaning given in section 316(3) of that Act); and

"authorised deposit-taker" means—
  (a) a person who has permission under Part 4 of the Financial Services and Markets Act 2000 to accept deposits;
  (b) an EEA firm of the kind mentioned in paragraph 5(d) of Schedule 3 to that Act, which has permission under paragraph 15 of that Schedule to accept deposits.

(6) The definitions of "authorised insurance company" and "authorised deposit-taker" must be read with—

(a) section 22 of the Financial Services and Markets Act 2000;
(b) any relevant order under that section; and
(c) Schedule 2 to that Act.

A4.47

35 Security given under regulation 33(2)(a): maintenance or replacement

(1) This regulation applies to any security given under regulation 33(2)(a).

(2) At such times or at such intervals as the Public Guardian may direct by notice in writing, any person ("S") who has given the security must satisfy the Public Guardian that any premiums payable in respect of it have been paid.

(3) Where S proposes to replace a security already given by him, the new security is not to be regarded as having been given until the Public Guardian is satisfied that—

(a) the requirements set out in sub-paragraphs (a) and (b) of regulation 33(3) have been met in relation to it; and
(b) no payment is due from S in connection with the discharge of his functions.

A4.48

36 Enforcement following court order of any endorsed security

(1) This regulation applies to any security given to the Public Guardian in respect of which an endorsement has been provided.

(2) Where the court orders the enforcement of the security, the Public Guardian must—

(a) notify any person who endorsed the security of the contents of the order; and
(b) notify the court when payment has been made of the amount secured.

A4.49

37 Discharge of any endorsed security

(1) This regulation applies to any security given by a person ("S") to the Public Guardian in respect of which an endorsement has been provided.

(2) The security may be discharged if the court makes an order discharging it.

(3) In any other case, the security may not be discharged until the end of the period of 7 years commencing with whichever of the following dates first occurs—

(a) if the person on whose behalf S was appointed to act dies, the date of his death;
(b) if S dies, the date of his death;
(c) if the court makes an order which discharges S but which does not also discharge the security under paragraph (2), the date of the order;
(d) the date when S otherwise ceases to be under a duty to discharge the functions in respect of which he was ordered to give security.

(4) For the purposes of paragraph (3), if a person takes any step with a view to discharging the security before the end of the period specified in that paragraph, the security is to be treated for all purposes as if it were still in place.

Deputies

A4.50

38 Application for additional time to submit a report

(1) This regulation applies where the court requires a deputy to submit a report to the Public Guardian and specifies a time or interval for it to be submitted.

(2) A deputy may apply to the Public Guardian requesting more time for submitting a particular report.

(3) An application must—

(a) state the reason for requesting more time; and
(b) contain or be accompanied by such information as the Public Guardian may reasonably require to determine the application.

(4) In response to an application, the Public Guardian may, if he considers it appropriate to do so, undertake that he will not take steps to secure performance of the deputy's duty to submit the report at the relevant time on the condition that the report is submitted on or before such later date as he may specify.

A4.51

39 Content of reports

(1) Any report which the court requires a deputy to submit to the Public Guardian must include such material as the court may direct.

(2) The report must also contain or be accompanied by—

(a) specified information or information of a specified description; or
(b) specified documents or documents of a specified description.

(3) But paragraph (2)—

(a) extends only to information or documents which are reasonably required in connection with the exercise by the Public Guardian of functions conferred on him under the Act; and
(b) is subject to paragraph (1) and to any other directions given by the court.

(4) Where powers as respects a person's property and affairs are conferred on a deputy under section 16 of the Act, the information specified by the Public Guardian under paragraph (2) may include accounts which—

(a) deal with specified matters; and
(b) are provided in a specified form.

(5) The Public Guardian may require—

(a) any information provided to be verified in such manner, or
(b) any document produced to be authenticated in such manner,

as he may reasonably require.

(6) "Specified" means specified in a notice in writing given to the deputy by the Public Guardian.

A4.52

40 Power to require final report on termination of appointment

(1) This regulation applies where—

(a) the person on whose behalf a deputy was appointed to act has died;
(b) the deputy has died;
(c) the court has made an order discharging the deputy; or
(d) the deputy otherwise ceases to be under a duty to discharge the functions to which his appointment relates.

(2) The Public Guardian may require the deputy (or, in the case of the deputy's death, his personal representatives) to submit a final report on the discharge of his functions.

(3) A final report must be submitted—

(a) before the end of such reasonable period as may be specified; and
(b) at such place as may be specified.

(4) The Public Guardian must consider the final report, together with any other information that he may have relating to the discharge by the deputy of his functions.

(5) Where the Public Guardian is dissatisfied with any aspect of the final report he may apply to the court for an appropriate remedy (including enforcement of security given by the deputy).

(6) "Specified" means specified in a notice in writing given to the deputy or his personal representatives by the Public Guardian.

A4.53

41 Power to require information from deputies

(1) This regulation applies in any case where—

- (a) the Public Guardian has received representations (including complaints) about—
  - (i) the way in which a deputy is exercising his powers; or
  - (ii) any failure to exercise them; or
- (b) it appears to the Public Guardian that there are other circumstances which—
  - (i) give rise to concerns about, or dissatisfaction with, the conduct of the deputy (including any failure to act); or
  - (ii) otherwise constitute good reason to seek information about the deputy's discharge of his functions.

(2) The Public Guardian may require the deputy—

- (a) to provide specified information or information of a specified description; or
- (b) to produce specified documents or documents of a specified description.

(3) The information or documents must be provided or produced—

- (a) before the end of such reasonable period as may be specified; and
- (b) at such place as may be specified.

(4) The Public Guardian may require—

- (a) any information provided to be verified in such manner, or
- (b) any document produced to be authenticated in such manner,

as he may reasonably require.

(5) "Specified" means specified in a notice in writing given to the deputy by the Public Guardian.

A4.54

42 Right of deputy to require review of decisions made by the Public Guardian

(1) A deputy may require the Public Guardian to reconsider any decision he has made in relation to the deputy.

(2) The right under paragraph (1) is exercisable by giving notice of exercise of the right to the Public Guardian before the end of the period of 14 days beginning with the date on which notice of the decision is given to the deputy.

(3) The notice of exercise of the right must—

- (a) state the grounds on which reconsideration is required; and
- (b) contain or be accompanied by any relevant information or documents.

(4) At any time after receiving the notice and before reconsidering the decision to which it relates, the Public Guardian may require the deputy to provide him with such further information, or to produce such documents, as he reasonably considers necessary to enable him to reconsider the matter.

(5) The Public Guardian must give to the deputy—

- (a) written notice of his decision on reconsideration, and
- (b) if he upholds the previous decision, a statement of his reasons.

Miscellaneous functions

A4.55

43 Applications to the Court of Protection

The Public Guardian has the function of making applications to the court in connection with his functions under the Act in such circumstances as he considers it necessary or appropriate to do so.

A4.56

44 Visits by the Public Guardian or by Court of Protection Visitors at his direction

(1) This regulation applies where the Public Guardian visits, or directs a Court of Protection Visitor to visit, any person under any provision of the Act or these Regulations.

(2) The Public Guardian must notify (or make arrangements to notify) the person to be visited of—

- (a) the date or dates on which it is proposed that the visit will take place;
- (b) to the extent that it is practicable to do so, any specific matters likely to be covered in the course of the visit; and
- (c) any proposal to inform any other person that the visit is to take place.

(3) Where the visit is to be carried out by a Court of Protection Visitor—

- (a) the Public Guardian may—
  - (i) give such directions to the Visitor, and
  - (ii) provide him with such information concerning the person to be visited,

  as the Public Guardian considers necessary for the purposes of enabling the visit to take place and the Visitor to prepare any report the Public Guardian may require; and
- (b) the Visitor must seek to carry out the visit and take all reasonable steps to obtain such other information as he considers necessary for the purpose of preparing a report.

(4) A Court of Protection Visitor must submit any report requested by the Public Guardian in accordance with any timetable specified by the Public Guardian.

(5) If he considers it appropriate to do so, the Public Guardian may, in relation to any person interviewed in the course of preparing a report—

- (a) disclose the report to him; and
- (b) invite him to comment on it.

A4.57

45 Functions in relation to persons carrying out specific transactions

(1) This regulation applies where, in accordance with an order made under section 16(2)(a) of the Act, a person ("T") has been authorised to carry out any transaction for a person who lacks capacity.

(2) The Public Guardian has the functions of—

- (a) receiving any reports from T which the court may require;
- (b) dealing with representations (including complaints) about—
  - (i) the way in which the transaction has been or is being carried out; or
  - (ii) any failure to carry it out.

(3) Regulations 38 to 41 have effect in relation to T as they have effect in relation a deputy.

A4.58

46 Power to require information from donees of lasting power of attorney

(1) This regulation applies where it appears to the Public Guardian that there are circumstances suggesting that the donee of a lasting power of attorney may—

- (a) have behaved, or may be behaving, in a way that contravenes his authority or is not in the best interests of the donor of the power,
- (b) be proposing to behave in a way that would contravene that authority or would not be in the donor's best interests, or
- (c) have failed to comply with the requirements of an order made, or directions given, by the court.

(2) The Public Guardian may require the donee—

(a) to provide specified information or information of a specified description; or
(b) to produce specified documents or documents of a specified description.

(3) The information or documents must be provided or produced—

(a) before the end of such reasonable period as may be specified; and
(b) at such place as may be specified.

(4) The Public Guardian may require—

(a) any information provided to be verified in such manner, or
(b) any document produced to be authenticated in such manner,

as he may reasonably require.

(5) "Specified" means specified in a notice in writing given to the donee by the Public Guardian.

A4.59

47 Power to require information from attorneys under enduring power of attorney

(1) This regulation applies where it appears to the Public Guardian that there are circumstances suggesting that, having regard to all the circumstances (and in particular the attorney's relationship to or connection with the donor) the attorney under a registered enduring power of attorney may be unsuitable to be the donor's attorney.

(2) The Public Guardian may require the attorney—

(a) to provide specified information or information of a specified description; or
(b) to produce specified documents or documents of a specified description.

(3) The information or documents must be provided or produced—

(a) before the end of such reasonable period as may be specified; and
(b) at such place as may be specified.

(4) The Public Guardian may require—

(a) any information provided to be verified in such manner, or
(b) any document produced to be authenticated in such manner,

as he may reasonably require.

(5) "Specified" means specified in a notice in writing given to the attorney by the Public Guardian.

A4.60

48 Other functions in relation to enduring powers of attorney

The Public Guardian has the following functions—

(a) directing a Court of Protection Visitor—
  (i) to visit an attorney under a registered enduring power of attorney, or
  (ii) to visit the donor of a registered enduring power of attorney,
and to make a report to the Public Guardian on such matters as he may direct;
(b) dealing with representations (including complaints) about the way in which an attorney under a registered enduring power of attorney is exercising his powers.

SCHEDULES 1–8

A4.61

For the text of these forms conatined in these Schedules, please see http://www.publicguardian.gov.uk/forms/forms.htm, noting that the form at Schedule 7 has been amended by reg 12 of the Public Guardian (Fees etc) Regulations 2007, SI 2007/2051.

COURT OF PROTECTION RULES 2007

(SI 2007/1744)

The President of the Family Division of the High Court (the judicial office holder nominated by the Lord Chief Justice) with the agreement of the Lord Chancellor, makes the following Rules in exercise of the powers conferred by sections 49(5), 50(2), 51, 53(2) and (4), 55, 56 and 65(1) of the Mental Capacity Act 2005, and in accordance with Part 1 of Schedule 1 to the Constitutional Reform Act 2005.

PART 1
PRELIMINARY

A4.62

1 Title and commencement

These Rules may be cited as the Court of Protection Rules 2007 and come into force on 1 October 2007.

A4.63

2 Revocations

The following rules are revoked—

- (a) the Court of Protection Rules 2001; and
- (b) the Court of Protection (Enduring Powers of Attorney) Rules 2001.

PART 2
THE OVERRIDING OBJECTIVE

A4.64

3 The overriding objective

(1) These Rules have the overriding objective of enabling the court to deal with a case justly, having regard to the principles contained in the Act.

(2) The court will seek to give effect to the overriding objective when it—

- (a) exercises any power under these Rules; or
- (b) interprets any rule or practice direction.

(3) Dealing with a case justly includes, so far as is practicable—

- (a) ensuring that it is dealt with expeditiously and fairly;
- (b) ensuring that P's interests and position are properly considered;
- (c) dealing with the case in ways which are proportionate to the nature, importance and complexity of the issues;
- (d) ensuring that the parties are on an equal footing;
- (e) saving expense; and
- (f) allotting to it an appropriate share of the court's resources, while taking account of the need to allot resources to other cases.

A4.65

4 The duty of the parties

The parties are required to help the court to further the overriding objective.

A4.66

5 Court's duty to manage cases

(1) The court will further the overriding objective by actively managing cases.

(2) Active case management includes—

- (a) encouraging the parties to co-operate with each other in the conduct of the proceedings;
- (b) identifying at an early stage—
  - (i) the issues; and
  - (ii) who should be a party to the proceedings;
- (c) deciding promptly—
  - (i) which issues need a full investigation and hearing and which do not; and
  - (ii) the procedure to be followed in the case;
- (d) deciding the order in which issues are to be resolved;
- (e) encouraging the parties to use an alternative dispute resolution procedure if the court considers that appropriate;
- (f) fixing timetables or otherwise controlling the progress of the case;
- (g) considering whether the likely benefits of taking a particular step justify the cost of taking it;
- (h) dealing with as many aspects of the case as the court can on the same occasion;
- (i) dealing with the case without the parties needing to attend at court;
- (j) making use of technology; and
- (k) giving directions to ensure that the case proceeds quickly and efficiently.

PART 3
INTERPRETATION AND GENERAL PROVISIONS

A4.67

6 Interpretation

In these Rules—

"the Act" means the Mental Capacity Act 2005;

"applicant" means a person who makes, or who seeks permission to make, an application to the court;

"application form" means the document that is to be used to begin proceedings in accordance with Part 9 of these Rules or any other provision of these Rules or the practice directions which requires the use of an application form;

"application notice" means the document that is to be used to make an application in accordance with Part 10 of these Rules or any other provision of these Rules or the practice directions which requires the use of an application notice;

"attorney" means the person appointed as such by an enduring power of attorney created, or purporting to have been created, in accordance with the regulations mentioned in paragraph 2 of Schedule 4 to the Act;

"business day" means a day other than—

- (a) a Saturday, Sunday, Christmas Day or Good Friday; or
- (b) a bank holiday in England and Wales, under the Banking and Financial Dealings Act 1971;

"child" means a person under 18;

"court" means the Court of Protection;

"deputy" means a deputy appointed under the Act;

"donee" means the donee of a lasting power of attorney;

"donor" means the donor of a lasting power of attorney, except where this expression is used in rule 68 or 201(5) (where it means the donor of an enduring power of attorney);

"enduring power of attorney" means an instrument created in accordance with such of the regulations mentioned in paragraph 2 of Schedule 4 to the Act as applied when it was executed;

"filing" in relation to a document means delivering it, by post or otherwise, to the court office;

"judge" means a judge nominated to be a judge of the court under the Act;

"lasting power of attorney" has the meaning given in section 9 of the Act;

"legal representative" means a barrister or a solicitor, solicitor's employee or other authorised litigator (as defined in the Courts and Legal Services Act 1990) who has been instructed to act for a party in relation to any application;

"LSC funded client" means an individual who receives services funded by the Legal Services Commission as part of the Community Legal Service within the meaning of Part I of the Access to Justice Act 1999;

"order" includes a declaration made by the court;

"P" means any person (other than a protected party) who lacks or, so far as consistent with the context, is alleged to lack capacity to make a decision or decisions in relation to any matter that is the subject of an application to the court and references to a person who lacks capacity are to be construed in accordance with the Act;

"party" is to be construed in accordance with rule 73;

"permission form" means the form that is to be used to make an application for permission to begin proceedings in accordance with Part 8 of these Rules;

"personal welfare" is to be construed in accordance with section 17 of the Act;

"President" and "Vice-President" refer to those judges appointed as such under section 46(3)(a) and (b) of the Act;

"property and affairs" is to be construed in accordance with section 18 of the Act;

"protected party" means a party or an intended party (other than P or a child) who lacks capacity to conduct the proceedings;

"respondent" means a person who is named as a respondent in the application form or notice, as the case may be;

"Senior Judge" means the judge who has been nominated to be Senior Judge under section 46(4) of the Act, and references in these Rules to a circuit judge include the Senior Judge;

"Visitor" means a person appointed as such by the Lord Chancellor under section 61 of the Act.

A4.68

7 Court officers

(1) Where these Rules permit or require the court to perform an act of a purely formal or administrative character, that act may be performed by a court officer.

(2) A requirement that a court officer carry out any act at the request of any person is subject to the payment of any fee required by a fees order for the carrying out of that act.

A4.69

8 Computation of time

(1) This rule shows how to calculate any period of time which is specified—

- (a) by these Rules;
- (b) by a practice direction; or
- (c) in an order or direction of the court.

(2) A period of time expressed as a number of days must be computed as clear days.

(3) In this rule "clear days" means that in computing the number of days—

- (a) the day on which the period begins; and
- (b) if the end of the period is defined by reference to an event, the day on which that event occurs,

are not included.

(4) Where the specified period is 7 days or less, and would include a day which is not a business day, that day does not count.

(5) When the specified period for doing any act at the court office ends on a day on which the office is closed, that act will be done in time if done on the next day on which the court office is open.

A4.70

9 Application of the Civil Procedure Rules

In any case not expressly provided for by these Rules or the practice directions made under them, the Civil Procedure Rules 1998 (including any practice directions made under them) may be applied with any necessary modifications, insofar as is necessary to further the overriding objective.

PART 4
COURT DOCUMENTS

A4.71

10 Documents used in court proceedings

(1) The court will seal or otherwise authenticate with the stamp of the court the following documents on issue—

- (a) a permission form;
- (b) an application form;
- (c) an application notice;
- (d) an order; and
- (e) any other document which a rule or practice direction requires to be sealed or stamped.

(2) Where these Rules or any practice direction require a document to be signed, that requirement is satisfied if the signature is printed by computer or other mechanical means.

(3) A practice direction may make provision for documents to be filed or sent to the court by—

- (a) facsimile; or
- (b) other means.

A4.72

11 Documents required to be verified by a statement of truth

(1) The following documents must be verified by a statement of truth—

- (a) a permission form, an application form or an application notice, where the applicant seeks to rely upon matters set out in the document as evidence;
- (b) a witness statement;
- (c) a certificate of—
  - (i) service or non-service; or
  - (ii) notification or non-notification;
- (d) a deputy's declaration; and
- (e) any other document required by a rule or practice direction to be so verified.

(2) Subject to paragraph (3), a statement of truth is a statement that—

- (a) the party putting forward the document;
- (b) in the case of a witness statement, the maker of the witness statement; or
- (c) in the case of a certificate referred to in paragraph (1)(c), the person who signs the certificate,

believes that the facts stated in the document being verified are true.

(3) If a party is conducting proceedings with a litigation friend, the statement of truth in—

- (a) a permission form;
- (b) an application form; or

(c) an application notice,

is a statement that the litigation friend believes the facts stated in the document being verified are true.

(4) The statement of truth must be signed—

(a) in the case of a permission form, an application form or an application notice—
(i) by the party or litigation friend; or
(ii) by the legal representative on behalf of the party or litigation friend; and
(b) in the case of a witness statement, by the maker of the statement.

(5) A statement of truth which is not contained in the document which it verifies must clearly identify that document.

(6) A statement of truth in a permission form, an application form or an application notice may be made by—

(a) a person who is not a party; or
(b) two or more parties jointly,

where this is permitted by a relevant practice direction.

A4.73

12 Failure to verify a document

If a permission form, application form or application notice is not verified by a statement of truth, the applicant may not rely upon the document as evidence of any of the matters set out in it unless the court permits.

A4.74

13 Failure to verify a witness statement

If a witness statement is not verified by a statement of truth, it shall not be admissible in evidence unless the court permits.

A4.75

14 False statements

(1) Proceedings for contempt of court may be brought against a person if he makes, or causes to be made, a false statement in a document verified by a statement of truth without an honest belief in its truth.

(2) Proceedings under this rule may be brought only—

(a) by the Attorney General; or
(b) with the permission of the court.

A4.76

15 Personal details

(1) Where a party does not wish to reveal—

(a) his home address or telephone number;
(b) P's home address or telephone number;
(c) the name of the person with whom P is living (if that person is not the applicant); or
(d) the address or telephone number of his place of business, or the place of business of any of the persons mentioned in sub-paragraphs (b) or (c),

he must provide those particulars to the court.

(2) Where paragraph (1) applies, the particulars given will not be revealed to any person unless the court so directs.

(3) Where a party changes his home address during the course of the proceedings, he must give notice of the change to the court.

(4) Where a party does not reveal his home address, he must nonetheless provide an address for service which must be within the jurisdiction of the court.

A4.77

16 Supply of documents to a party from court records

Unless the court orders otherwise, a party to proceedings may inspect or obtain from the records of the court a copy of—

(a) any document filed by a party to the proceedings; or
(b) any communication in the proceedings between the court and—
  (i) a party to the proceedings; or
  (ii) another person.

A4.78

17 Supply of documents to a non-party from court records

(1) Subject to rules 20 and 92(2), a person who is not a party to proceedings may inspect or obtain from the court records a copy of any judgment or order given or made in public.

(2) The court may, on an application made to it, authorise a person who is not a party to proceedings to—

(a) inspect any other documents in the court records; or
(b) obtain a copy of any such documents, or extracts from such documents.

(3) A person making an application for an authorisation under paragraph (2) must do so in accordance with Part 10.

(4) Before giving an authorisation under paragraph (2), the court will consider whether any document is to be provided on an edited basis.

A4.79

18 Subsequent use of court documents

(1) Where a document has been filed or disclosed, a party to whom it was provided may use the document only for the purpose of the proceedings in which it was filed or disclosed, except where—

(a) the document has been read to or by the court or referred to at a public hearing; or
(b) the court otherwise permits.

(2) Paragraph (1)(a) is subject to any order of the court made under rule 92(2).

A4.80

19 Editing information in court documents

(1) A party may apply to the court for an order that a specified part of a document is to be edited prior to the document's service or disclosure.

(2) An order under paragraph (1) may be made at any time.

(3) Where the court makes an order under this rule any subsequent use of that document in the proceedings shall be of the document as edited, unless the court directs otherwise.

(4) An application under this rule must be made in accordance with Part 10.

A4.81

20 Public Guardian to be supplied with court documents relevant to supervision of deputies

(1) This rule applies in any case where the court makes an order—

(a) appointing a person to act as a deputy; or
(b) varying an order under which a deputy has been appointed.

(2) Subject to paragraphs (3) and (6), the Public Guardian is entitled to be supplied with a copy of qualifying documents if he reasonably considers that it is necessary for him to have regard to them in connection with the discharge of his functions under section 58 of the Act in relation to the supervision of deputies.

(3) The court may direct that the right to be supplied with documents under paragraph (2) does not apply in relation to such one or more documents, or descriptions of documents, as the court may specify.

(4) A direction under paragraph (3) or (6) may be given—

(a) either on the court's own initiative or on an application made to it; and
(b) either—
   (i) at the same time as the court makes the order which appoints the deputy, or which varies it; or
   (ii) subsequently.

(5) "Qualifying documents" means documents which—

(a) are filed in court in connection with the proceedings in which the court makes the order referred to in paragraph (1); and
(b) are relevant to—
   (i) the decision to appoint the deputy;
   (ii) any powers conferred on him;
   (iii) any duties imposed on him; or
   (iv) any other terms applying to those powers and duties which are contained in the order.

(6) The court may direct that any document is to be provided to the Public Guardian on an edited basis.

A4.82

21 Provision of court order to Public Guardian

Any order of the court requiring the Public Guardian to do something, or not to do something, will be served by the court on the Public Guardian as soon as practicable and in any event not later than 7 days after the order was made.

A4.83

22 Amendment of application

(1) The court may allow or direct an applicant, at any stage of the proceedings, to amend his application form or notice.

(2) The amendment may be effected by making in writing the necessary alterations to the application form or notice, but if the amendments are so numerous or of such a nature or length that written alteration would make it difficult or inconvenient to read, a fresh document amended as allowed or directed may be issued.

A4.84

23 Clerical mistakes or slips

The court may at any time correct any clerical mistakes in an order or direction or any error arising in an order or direction from any accidental slip or omission.

A4.85

24 Endorsement of amendment

Where an application form or notice, order or direction has been amended under this Part, a note shall be placed on it showing the date on which it was amended and the alteration shall be sealed.

PART 5
GENERAL CASE MANAGEMENT POWERS

A4.86

25 The court's general powers of case management

(1) The list of powers in this rule is in addition to any powers given to the court by any other rule or practice direction or by any other enactment or any powers it may otherwise have.

(2) The court may—

- (a) extend or shorten the time for compliance with any rule, practice direction, or court order or direction (even if an application for extension is made after the time for compliance has expired);
- (b) adjourn or bring forward a hearing;
- (c) require P, a party, a party's legal representative or litigation friend, to attend court;
- (d) hold a hearing and receive evidence by telephone or any other method of direct oral communication;
- (e) stay the whole or part of any proceedings or judgment either generally or until a specified date or event;
- (f) consolidate proceedings;
- (g) hear two or more applications on the same occasion;
- (h) direct a separate hearing of any issue;
- (i) decide the order in which issues are to be heard;
- (j) exclude an issue from consideration;
- (k) dismiss or give judgment on an application after a decision is made on a preliminary basis;
- (l) direct any party to file and serve an estimate of costs; and
- (m) take any step or give any direction for the purpose of managing the case and furthering the overriding objective.

(3) A judge to whom a matter is allocated may, if he considers that the matter is one which ought properly to be dealt with by another judge, transfer the matter to such a judge.

(4) Where the court gives directions it may take into account whether or not a party has complied with any rule or practice direction.

(5) The court may make any order it considers appropriate even if a party has not sought that order.

(6) A power of the court under these Rules to make an order includes a power to vary or revoke the order;

(7) Rules 25.12 to 25.15 of the Civil Procedure Rules 1998 (which make provision about security for costs) apply in proceedings to which these Rules apply as if the references in those Rules to "defendant" and "claimant" were to "respondent" and "applicant" respectively.

A4.87

26 Court's power to dispense with requirement of any rule

In addition to its general powers and the powers listed in rule 25, the court may dispense with the requirement of any rule.

A4.88

27 Exercise of powers on the court's own initiative

(1) Except where these Rules or some other enactment make different provision, the court may exercise its powers on its own initiative.

(2) The court may make an order on its own initiative without hearing the parties or giving them the opportunity to make representations.

(3) Where the court proposes to make an order on its own initiative it may give the parties and any person it thinks fit an opportunity to make representations and, where it does so, it will specify the time by which, and the manner in which, the representations must be made.

(4) Where the court proposes—

(a) to make an order on its own initiative; and
(b) to hold a hearing to decide whether to make the order,

it will give the parties and may give any other person it thinks likely to be affected by the order at least 3 days' notice of the hearing.

A4.89

28 General power of the court to rectify matters where there has been an error of procedure

Where there has been an error of procedure, such as a failure to comply with a rule or practice direction—

(a) the error does not invalidate any step taken in the proceedings unless the court so orders; and
(b) the court may waive the error or require it to be remedied or may make such other order as appears to the court to be just.

PART 6
SERVICE OF DOCUMENTS

Service generally

A4.90

29 Scope

(1) Subject to paragraph (2), the rules in this Part apply to—

(a) the service of documents; and
(b) to the requirement under rule 70 for a person to be notified of the issue of an application form,

and references to "serve", "service", "notice" and "notify", and kindred expressions shall be construed accordingly.

(2) The rules in this Part do not apply where—

(a) any other enactment, a rule in another Part or a practice direction makes different provision; or
(b) the court directs otherwise.

A4.91

30 Who is to serve

(1) The general rule is that the following documents will be served by the court—

- (a) an order or judgment of the court;
- (b) an acknowledgment of service or notification; and
- (c) except where the application is for an order for committal, a notice of hearing.

(2) Any other document is to be served by the party seeking to rely upon it, except where—

- (a) a rule or practice direction provides otherwise; or
- (b) the court directs otherwise.

(3) Where the court is to serve a document—

- (a) it is for the court to decide which of the methods of service specified in rule 31 is to be used; and
- (b) if the document is being served on behalf of a party, that party must provide sufficient copies.

A4.92

31 Methods of service

(1) A document may be served by any of the methods specified in this rule.

(2) Where it is not known whether a solicitor is acting on behalf of a person, the document may be served by—

- (a) delivering it to the person personally;
- (b) delivering it at his home address or last known home address; or
- (c) sending it to that address, or last known address, by first class post (or by an alternative method of service which provides for delivery on the next working day).

(3) Where a solicitor—

- (a) is authorised to accept service on behalf of a person; and
- (b) has informed the person serving the document in writing that he is so authorised,

the document must be served on the solicitor, unless personal service is required by an enactment, rule, practice direction or court order.

(4) Where it appears to the court that there is a good reason to authorise service by a method other than those specified in paragraphs (2) or (3), the court may direct that service is effected by that method.

(5) A direction that service is effected by an alternative method must specify—

- (a) the method of service; and
- (b) the date when the document will be deemed to be served.

(6) A practice direction may set out how documents are to be served by document exchange, electronic communication or other means.

A4.93

32 Service of documents on children and protected parties

(1) The following table shows the person on whom a document must be served if it is a document which would otherwise be served on—

- (a) a child; or
- (b) a protected party.

Type of document	Nature of party	Person to be served

Application form	Child	—A person who has parental responsibility for the child within the meaning of the Children Act 1989; or —if there is no such person, a person with whom the child resides or in whose care the child is.
Application form	Protected party	—The person who is authorised to conduct the proceedings in the protected party's name or on his behalf; or —a person who is a duly appointed attorney, donee or deputy of the protected party; or —if there is no such person, a person with whom the protected party lives or in whose care the latter is.
Application for an order appointing a litigation friend, where a child or protected party has no litigation friend	Child or protected party	—See rule 145 (appointment of litigation friend by court order—supplementary).
Any other document	Child or protected party	—The litigation friend or other duly authorised person who is conducting the proceedings on behalf of the child or protected party.

(2) The court may make an order for service on a child or a protected party by permitting the document to be served on some person other than the person specified in the table set out in paragraph (1) above (which may include service on the child or the protected party).

(3) An application for an order under paragraph (2) may be made without notice.

(4) The court may order that, although a document has been served on someone other than the person specified in the table, the document is to be treated as if it had been properly served.

(5) This rule does not apply in relation to the service of documents upon a child in any case where the court has made an order under rule 141(4) permitting the child to conduct proceedings without a litigation friend.

A4.94

33 Service of documents on P if he becomes a party

(1) If P becomes a party to the proceedings, all documents to be served on him must be served on his litigation friend or other person duly authorised to conduct proceedings on P's behalf.

(2) The court may make an order for service on P by permitting the document to be served on some person other than the person specified in paragraph (1) above (which may include service on P).

(3) An application for an order under paragraph (2) may be made without notice.

(4) The court may order that, although a document has been served on someone other than a person specified in paragraph (1), the document is to be treated as if it had been properly served.

(5) This rule does not apply in relation to the service of documents upon P in any case where the court has made an order under rule 147(2) (procedure where appointment of a litigation friend comes to an end—for P).

A4.95

34 Substituted service

Where it appears to the court that it is impracticable for any reason to serve a document in accordance with any of the methods provided under rule 31, the court may make an order for substituted service of the document by taking such steps as the court may direct to bring it to the notice of the person to be served.

A4.96

35 Deemed service

(1) A document which is served in accordance with these Rules or any relevant practice direction shall be deemed to be served on the day shown in the following table—

Method of service	*Deemed day of service*
First class post (or other service for next-day delivery)	The second day after it was posted.
Document exchange	The second day after it was left at the document exchange.
Delivering the document to a permitted address	The day after it was delivered to that address.
Fax	If it is transmitted on a business day before 4pm, on that day; or in any other case, on the business day after the day on which it is transmitted
Other electronic means	The second day after the day on which it is transmitted.

(2) If a document is served personally—

(a) after 5pm, on a business day; or
(b) at any time on a Saturday, Sunday or a Bank Holiday,

it will be treated as being served on the next business day.

A4.97

36 Certificate of service

(1) Where a rule, practice direction or court order requires a certificate of service for the document, the certificate must state the details set out in the following table—

Method of service	*Details to be certified*
First class post (or any other service for next-day delivery)	Date of posting
Personal service	Date of personal service
Document exchange	Date when the document was left at the document exchange.

Delivery of document to permitted address	Date when the document was delivered to that address.
Fax	Date of transmission.
Other electronic means	Date of transmission and the means used.
Alternative method permitted by the court	As required by the court.

(2) The certificate must be filed within 7 days after service of the document to which it relates.

A4.98

37 Certificate of non-service

(1) Where an applicant or other person is unable to serve any document under these Rules or as directed by the court, he must file a certificate of non-service stating the reasons why service has not been effected.

(2) The certificate of non-service must be filed within 7 days of the latest date on which service should have been effected.

A4.99

38 Power of court to dispense with service

(1) The court may dispense with any requirement to serve a document.

(2) An application for an order to dispense with service may be made without notice.

Service out of the jurisdiction

A4.100

39 Application of Family Procedure (Adoption) Rules 2005

(1) The rules in Section 2 of Part 6 of the Family Procedure (Adoption) Rules 2005 ("the 2005 Rules") apply, with the modifications set out in this rule, to the service of documents out of the jurisdiction.

(2) References in the 2005 Rules to the Hague Convention shall be read in these Rules as references to the Convention on the International Protection of Adults signed at the Hague on 13th January 2000 (Cm 5881).

(3) References in the 2005 Rules to the Senior Master of the Queen's Bench Division shall be read in these Rules as references to the Senior Judge.

PART 7
NOTIFYING P

General requirement to notify P

A4.101

40 General

(1) Subject to paragraphs (2) and (3), the rules in this Part apply where P is to be given notice of any matter or document, or is to be provided with any document, either under the Rules or in accordance with an order or direction of the court.

(2) If P becomes a party, the rules in this Part do not apply and service is to be effected in accordance with Part 6 or as directed by the court.

(3) In any case the court may, either on its own initiative or on application, direct that P must not be notified of any matter or document, or provided with any document, whether in accordance with this Part or at all.

A4.102

41 Who is to notify P

(1) Where P is to be notified under this Part, notification must be effected by—

(a) the applicant;
(b) the appellant (where the matter relates to an appeal);
(c) an agent duly appointed by the applicant or the appellant; or
(d) such other person as the court may direct.

(2) The person within paragraph (1) is referred to in this Part as "the person effecting notification".

Circumstances in which P must be notified

A4.103

42 Application forms

(1) P must be notified—

(a) that an application form has been issued by the court;
(b) that an application form has been withdrawn; and
(c) of the date on which a hearing is to be held in relation to the matter, where that hearing is for disposing of the application.

(2) Where P is to be notified that an application form has been issued, the person effecting notification must explain to P—

(a) who the applicant is;
(b) that the application raises the question of whether P lacks capacity in relation to a matter or matters, and what that means;
(c) what will happen if the court makes the order or direction that has been applied for; and
(d) where the application contains a proposal for the appointment of a person to make decisions on P's behalf in relation to the matter to which the application relates, details of who that person is.

(3) Where P is to be notified that an application form has been withdrawn, the person effecting notification must explain to P—

(a) that the application form has been withdrawn; and
(b) the consequences of that withdrawal.

(4) The person effecting notification must also inform P that he may seek advice and assistance in relation to any matter of which he is notified.

A4.104

43 Appeals

(1) P must be notified—

(a) that an appellant's notice has been issued by the court;
(b) that an appellant's notice has been withdrawn; and
(c) of the date on which a hearing is to be held in relation to the matter, where that hearing is for disposing of the appellant's notice.

(2) Where P is to be notified that an appellant's notice has been issued, the person effecting notification must explain to P—

(a) who the appellant is;
(b) the issues raised by the appeal; and
(c) what will happen if the court makes the order or direction that has been applied for.

(3) Where P is to be notified that an appellant's notice has been withdrawn, the person effecting notification must explain to P—

(a) that the appellant's notice has been withdrawn; and
(b) the consequences of that withdrawal.

(4) The person effecting notification must also inform P that he may seek advice and assistance in relation to any matter of which he is notified.

A4.105

44 Final orders

(1) P must be notified of a final order of the court.

(2) Where P is notified in accordance with this rule, the person effecting notification must explain to P the effect of the order.

(3) The person effecting notification must also inform P that he may seek advice and assistance in relation to any matter of which he is notified.

A4.106

45 Other matters

(1) This rule applies where the court directs that P is to be notified of any other matter.

(2) The person effecting notification must explain to P such matters as may be directed by the court.

(3) The person effecting notification must also inform P that he may seek advice and assistance in relation to any matter of which he is notified.

Manner of notification, and accompanying documents

A4.107

46 Manner of notification

(1) Where P is to be notified under this Part, the person effecting notification must provide P with the information specified in rules 42 to 45 in a way that is appropriate to P's circumstances (for example, using simple language, visual aids or any other appropriate means).

(2) The information referred to in paragraph (1) must be provided to P personally.

(3) P must be provided with the information mentioned in paragraph (1) as soon as practicable and in any event within 21 days of the date on which—

(a) the application form or appellant's notice was issued or withdrawn;
(b) the order was made; or
(c) the person effecting notification received the notice of hearing from the court and in any event no later than 14 days before the date specified in the notice of the hearing,

as the case may be.

A4.108

47 Acknowledgment of notification

When P is notified that an application form or an appellant's notice has been issued, he must also be provided with a form for acknowledging notification.

A4.109

48 Certificate of notification

The person effecting notification must, within 7 days beginning with the date on which notification in accordance with this Part was given, file a certificate of notification which certifies—

(a) the date on which P was notified; and
(b) that he was notified in accordance with this Part.

A4.110

49 Dispensing with requirement to notify, etc

(1) The applicant, the appellant or other person directed by the court to effect notification may apply to the court seeking an order—

(a) dispensing with the requirement to comply with the provisions in this Part; or
(b) requiring some other person to comply with the provisions in this Part.

(2) An application under this rule must be made in accordance with Part 10.

PART 8
PERMISSION

A4.111

50 General

Subject to these Rules and to section 50(1) of, and paragraph 20 of Schedule 3 to, the Act, the applicant must apply for permission to start proceedings under the Act.

(Section 50(1) of the Act specifies persons who do not need to apply for permission. Paragraph 20 of Schedule 3 to the Act specifies an application for which permission is not needed.)

A4.112

51 Where the court's permission is not required

The permission of the court is not required—

(1) where an application is made by—

(a) the Official Solicitor; or
(b) the Public Guardian;

(2) where the application concerns—

(a) P's property and affairs, unless the application is of a kind specified in rule 52;
(b) a lasting power of attorney which is, or purports to be, created under the Act; or
(c) an instrument which is, or purports to be, an enduring power of attorney;

(3) where an application is made in accordance with Part 10; or

(4) where a person files an acknowledgment of service or notification in accordance with this Part or Part 9, for any order proposed that is different from that sought by the applicant.

A4.113

52 Exceptions to rule 51(2)(a)

(1) For the purposes of rule 51(2)(a), the permission of the court is required to make any of the applications specified in this rule.

(2) An application for the exercise of the jurisdiction of the court under section 54(2) of the Trustee Act 1925, where the application is made by a person other than—

- (a) a person who has made an application for the appointment of a deputy;
- (b) a continuing trustee; or
- (c) any other person who, according to the practice of the Chancery Division, would have been entitled to make the application if it had been made in the High Court.

(3) An application under section 36(9) of the Trustee Act 1925 for leave to appoint a new trustee in place of P, where the application is made by a person other than—

- (a) a co-trustee; or
- (b) another person with the power to appoint a new trustee.

(4) An application seeking the exercise of the court's jurisdiction under section 18(1)(b) (where the application relates to making a gift of P's property), (h) or (i) of the Act, where the application is made by a person other than—

- (a) a person who has made an application for the appointment of a deputy;
- (b) a person who, under any known will of P or under his intestacy, may become entitled to any property of P or any interest in it;
- (c) a person who is an attorney appointed under an enduring power of attorney which has been registered in accordance with the Act or the regulations referred to in Schedule 4 to the Act;
- (d) a person who is a donee of a lasting power of attorney which has been registered in accordance with the Act; or
- (e) a person for whom P might be expected to provide if he had capacity to do so.

(5) An application under section 20 of the Trusts of Land and Appointment of Trustees Act 1996, where the application is made by a person other than a beneficiary under the trust or, if there is more than one, by both or all of them.

A4.114

53 Permission—supplementary

(1) The provisions of rule 52(2) apply with such modifications as may be necessary to an application under section 18(1)(j) of the Act for an order for the exercise of any power vested in P of appointing trustees or retiring from a trust.

(2) Where part of the application concerns a matter which requires permission, and part of it does not, permission need only be sought for that part of it which requires permission.

A4.115

54 Application for permission

The applicant must apply for permission by filing a permission form and must file with it—

- (a) any information or documents specified in the relevant practice direction;
- (b) a draft of the application form which he seeks permission to have issued; and
- (c) an assessment of capacity form, where this is required by the relevant practice direction.

A4.116

55 What the court will do when an application for permission to start proceedings is filed

Within 14 days of a permission form being filed, the court will issue it and—

- (a) grant the application in whole or in part, or subject to conditions, without a hearing and may give directions in connection with the issue of the application form;
- (b) refuse the application without a hearing; or
- (c) fix a date for the hearing of the application.

A4.117

56 Persons to be notified of the hearing of an application for permission

(1) Where the court fixes a date for a hearing under rule 55(c), it will notify the applicant and such other persons as it thinks fit, and provide them with—

(a) subject to paragraph (2), the documents mentioned in rule 54; and
(b) a form for acknowledging notification.

(2) The court may direct that any document is to be provided on an edited basis.

A4.118

57 Acknowledgment of notification of permission application

(1) Any person who is notified of an application for permission and who wishes to take part in the permission hearing must file an acknowledgment of notification in accordance with the following provisions of this rule.

(2) The acknowledgment of notification must be filed not more than 21 days after notice of the application was given.

(3) The court will serve the acknowledgment of notification on the applicant and on any other person who has filed such an acknowledgment.

(4) The acknowledgment of notification must—

(a) state whether the person acknowledging notification consents to the application for permission;
(b) state whether he opposes the application for permission, and if so, set out the grounds for doing so;
(c) state whether he proposes that permission should be granted to make an application for a different order, and if so, set out what that order is;
(d) provide an address for service, which must be within the jurisdiction of the court; and
(e) be signed by him or his legal representative.

(5) The acknowledgment of notification may include or be accompanied by an application for directions.

(6) Subject to rules 120 and 123 (restrictions on filing an expert's report and court's power to restrict expert evidence), where a person opposes the application for permission or proposes that permission is granted for a different order, the acknowledgment of notification must be accompanied by a witness statement containing any evidence upon which that person intends to rely.

A4.119

58 Failure to file acknowledgment of notification

Where a person notified of the application for permission has not filed an acknowledgment of notification in accordance with rule 57, he may not take part in a hearing to decide whether permission should be given unless the court permits him to do so.

A4.120

59 Service of an order giving or refusing permission

The court will serve—

(a) the order granting or refusing permission;
(b) if refusing permission without a hearing, the reasons for its decision in summary form; and
(c) any directions,

on the applicant and on any other person notified of the application who filed an acknowledgment of notification.

A4.121

60 Appeal against a permission decision following a hearing

Where the court grants or refuses permission following a hearing, any appeal against the permission decision shall be dealt with in accordance with Part 20 (appeals).

PART 9
HOW TO START PROCEEDINGS

Initial steps

A4.122

61 General

(1) Applications to the court to start proceedings shall be made in accordance with this Part and, as applicable, Part 8 and the relevant practice directions.

(2) The appropriate forms must be used in the cases to which they apply, with such variations as the case requires, but not so as to omit any information or guidance which any form gives to the intended recipient.

(3) If permission to make an application is required, the court shall not issue the application form until permission is granted.

A4.123

62 When proceedings are started

(1) The general rule is that proceedings are started when the court issues an application form at the request of the applicant.

(2) An application form is issued on the date entered on the application form by the court.

A4.124

63 Contents of the application form

The application form must—

- (a) state the matter which the applicant wants the court to decide;
- (b) state the order which the applicant is seeking;
- (c) name—
  - (i) the applicant;
  - (ii) P;
  - (iii) as a respondent, any person (other than P) whom the applicant reasonably believes to have an interest which means that he ought to be heard in relation to the application (as opposed to being notified of it in accordance with rule 70); and
  - (iv) any person whom the applicant intends to notify in accordance with rule 70; and
- (d) if the applicant is applying in a representative capacity, state what that capacity is.

A4.125

64 Documents to be filed with the application form

When an applicant files his application form with the court, he must also file—

(a) in accordance with the relevant practice direction, any evidence upon which he intends to rely;
(b) if permission was required to make the application, a copy of the court's order granting permission;
(c) an assessment of capacity form, where this is required by the relevant practice direction;
(d) any other documents referred to in the application form; and
(e) such other information and material as may be set out in a practice direction.

A4.126

65 What the court will do when an application form is filed

As soon as practicable after an application form is filed the court will issue the application form in any case where permission—

(a) is not required; or
(b) has been granted by the court; and

do anything else that may be set out in a practice direction.

Steps following issue of application form

A4.127

66 Applicant to serve the application form on named respondents

(1) As soon as practicable and in any event within 21 days of the date on which the application form was issued, the applicant must serve a copy of the application form on any person who is named as a respondent in the application form, together with copies of any documents filed in accordance with rule 64 and a form for acknowledging service.

(2) The applicant must file a certificate of service within 7 days beginning with the date on which the documents were served.

A4.128

67 Applications relating to lasting powers of attorney

(1) Where the application concerns the powers of the court under section 22 or 23 of the Act (powers of the court in relation to the validity and operation of lasting powers of attorney) the applicant must serve a copy of the application form, together with copies of any documents filed in accordance with rule 64 and a form for acknowledging service—

(a) unless the applicant is the donor or donee of the lasting power of attorney ("the power"), on the donor and every donee of the power;
(b) if he is the donor, on every donee of the power; and
(c) if he is a donee, on the donor and any other donee of the power,

but only if the above-mentioned persons have not been served or notified under any other rule.

(2) Where the application is solely in respect of an objection to the registration of a power, the requirements of rules 66 and 70 do not apply to an application made under this rule by—

(a) a donee of the power; or
(b) a person named in a statement made by the donor of the power in accordance with paragraph 2(1)(c)(i) of Schedule 1 to the Act.

(3) The applicant must comply with paragraph (1) as soon as practicable and in any event within 21 days of date on which the application form was issued.

(4) The applicant must file a certificate of service within 7 days beginning with the date on which the documents were served.

(5) Where the applicant knows or has reasonable grounds to believe that the donor of the power lacks capacity to make a decision in relation to any matter that is the subject of the application, he must notify the donor in accordance with Part 7.

A4.129

68 Applications relating to enduring powers of attorney

(1) Where the application concerns the powers of the court under paragraphs 2(9), 4(5)(a) and (b), 7(2), 10(c), 13, or 16(2), (3), (4) and (6) of Schedule 4 to the Act, the applicant must serve a copy of the application form, together with copies of any documents filed in accordance with rule 64 and a form for acknowledging service—

- (a) unless the applicant is the donor or attorney under the enduring power of attorney ("the power"), on the donor and every attorney of the power;
- (b) if he is the donor, on every attorney under the power; or
- (c) if he is an attorney, on the donor and any other attorney under the power,

but only if the above-mentioned persons have not been served or notified under any other rule.

(2) Where the application is solely in respect of an objection to the registration of a power, the requirements of rules 66 and 70 do not apply to an application made under this rule by—

- (a) an attorney under the power; or
- (b) a person listed in paragraph 6(1) of Schedule 4 to the Act.

(3) The applicant must comply with paragraph (1) as soon as practicable and in any event within 21 days of the date on which the application form was issued.

(4) The applicant must file a certificate of service within 7 days beginning with the date on which the documents were served.

(5) Where the applicant knows or has reasonable grounds to believe that the donor of the power lacks capacity to make a decision in relation to any matter that is the subject of the application, he must notify the donor in accordance with Part 7.

A4.130

69 Applicant to notify P of an application

P must be notified in accordance with Part 7 that an application form has been issued, unless the requirement to do so has been dispensed with under rule 49.

A4.131

70 Applicant to notify other persons of an application

(1) As soon as practicable and in any event within 21 days of the date on which the application form was issued, the applicant must notify the persons specified in the relevant practice direction—

- (a) that an application form has been issued;
- (b) whether it relates to the exercise of the court's jurisdiction in relation to P's property and affairs, or his personal welfare, or to both; and
- (c) of the order or orders sought.

(2) Notification of the issue of the application form must be accompanied by a form for acknowledging notification.

(3) The applicant must file a certificate of notification within 7 days beginning with the date on which notification was given.

A4.132

71 Requirements for certain applications

A practice direction may make additional or different provision in relation to specified applications.

Responding to an application

A4.133

72 Responding to an application

(1) A person who is served with or notified of an application form and who wishes to take part in proceedings must file an acknowledgment of service or notification in accordance with this rule.

(2) The acknowledgment of service or notification must be filed not more than 21 days after the application form was served or notification of the application was given.

(3) The court will serve the acknowledgment of service or notification on the applicant and on any other person who has filed such an acknowledgment.

(4) The acknowledgment of service or notification must—

- (a) state whether the person acknowledging service or notification consents to the application;
- (b) state whether he opposes the application and, if so, set out the grounds for doing so;
- (c) state whether he seeks a different order from that set out in the application form and, if so, set out what that order is;
- (d) provide an address for service, which must be within the jurisdiction of the court; and
- (e) be signed by him or his legal representative.

(5) Subject to rules 120 and 123 (restriction on filing an expert's report and court's power to restrict expert evidence), where a person who has been served in accordance with rule 66, 67 or 68 opposes the application or seeks a different order, the acknowledgment of service must be accompanied by a witness statement containing any evidence upon which that person intends to rely.

(6) In addition to complying with the other requirements of this rule, an acknowledgment of notification filed by a person notified of the application in accordance with rule 67(5), 68(5), 69 or 70 must—

- (a) indicate whether the person wishes to be joined as a party to the proceedings; and
- (b) state the person's interest in the proceedings.

(7) Subject to rules 120 and 123 (restriction on filing an expert's report and court's power to restrict expert evidence), where a person has been notified in accordance with rule 67(5), 68(5), 69, 70, the acknowledgment of notification must be accompanied by a witness statement containing any evidence of his interest in the proceedings and, if he opposes the application or seeks a different order, any evidence upon which he intends to rely.

(8) The court will consider whether to join a person mentioned in paragraph (6) as a party to the proceedings and, if it decides to do so, will make an order to that effect.

(9) Where a person who is notified in accordance with rule 67(5), 68(5), 69 or 70 complies with the requirements of this rule, he need not comply with the requirements of rule 75 (application to be joined as a party).

(10) Where a person has filed an acknowledgment of notification in accordance with rule 57 (acknowledgment of notification of permission application) he must still acknowledge service or notification of an issued application form in accordance with this rule.

(11) A practice direction may make provision about responding to applications.

The parties to the proceedings

A4.134

73 Parties to the proceedings

(1) Unless the court otherwise directs, the parties to any proceedings are—

(a) the applicant; and
(b) any person who is named as a respondent in the application form and who files an acknowledgment of service in respect of the application form.

(2) The court may order a person to be joined as a party if it considers that it is desirable to do so for the purpose of dealing with the application.

(3) The court may at any time direct that any person who is a party to the proceedings is to be removed as a party.

(4) Unless the court orders otherwise, P shall not be named as a respondent to any proceedings.

(5) A party to the proceedings is bound by any order or direction of the court made in the course of those proceedings.

A4.135

74 Persons to be bound as if parties

(1) The persons mentioned in paragraph (2) shall be bound by any order made or directions given by the court in the same way that a party to the proceedings is so bound.

(2) The persons referred to in paragraph (1) are—

(a) P; and
(b) any person who has been served with or notified of an application form in accordance with these Rules.

A4.136

75 Application to be joined as a party

(1) Any person with sufficient interest may apply to the court to be joined as a party to the proceedings.

(2) An application to be joined as a party must be made by filing an application notice in accordance with Part 10 which must—

(a) state the full name and address of the person seeking to be joined as a party to the proceedings;
(b) state his interest in the proceedings;
(c) state whether he consents to the application;
(d) state whether he opposes the application and, if so, set out the grounds for doing so;
(e) state whether he proposes that an order different from that set out in the application form should be made and, if so, set out what that order is;
(f) provide an address for service, which must be within the jurisdiction of the court; and
(g) be signed by him or his legal representative.

(3) Subject to rules 120 and 123 (restriction on filing an expert's report and court's power to restrict expert evidence), an application to be joined must be accompanied by—

(a) a witness statement containing evidence of his interest in the proceedings and, if he proposes that an order different from that set out in the application form should be made, the evidence on which he intends to rely; and
(b) a sufficient number of copies of the application notice to enable service of the application on every other party to the proceedings.

(4) The court will serve the application notice and any accompanying documents on all parties to the proceedings.

(5) The court will consider whether to join a person applying under this rule as a party to the proceedings and, if it decides to do so, will make an order to that effect.

A4.137

76 Applications for removal as a party to proceedings

A person who wishes to be removed as a party to the proceedings must apply to the court for an order to that effect in accordance with Part 10.

PART 10
APPLICATIONS WITHIN PROCEEDINGS

A4.138

77 Types of applications for which the Part 10 procedure may be used

(1) The Part 10 procedure is the procedure set out in this Part.

(2) The Part 10 procedure may be used if the application is made by any person—

- (a) in the course of existing proceedings; or
- (b) as provided for in a rule or practice direction.

(3) The court may grant an interim remedy before an application form has been issued only if—

- (a) the matter is urgent; or
- (b) it is otherwise necessary to do so in the interests of justice.

(4) An application made during the course of existing proceedings includes an application made during appeal proceedings.

A4.139

78 Application notice to be filed

(1) Subject to paragraph (5), the applicant must file an application notice to make an application under this Part.

(2) The applicant must, when he files the application notice, file the evidence upon which he relies (unless such evidence has already been filed).

(3) The court will issue the application notice and, if there is to be a hearing, give notice of the date on which the matter is to be heard by the court.

(4) Notice under paragraph (3) must be given to—

- (a) the applicant;
- (b) anyone who is named as a respondent in the application notice (if not otherwise a party to the proceedings);
- (c) every party to the proceedings; and
- (d) any other person, as the court may direct.

(5) An applicant may make an application under this Part without filing an application notice if—

- (a) this is permitted by any rule or practice direction; or
- (b) the court dispenses with the requirement for an application notice.

(6) If the applicant makes an application without giving notice, the evidence in support of the application must state why notice has not been given.

A4.140

79 What an application notice must include

An application notice must state—

(a) what order or direction the applicant is seeking;
(b) briefly, the grounds on which the applicant is seeking the order or direction; and
(c) such other information as may be required by any rule or a practice direction.

A4.141

80 Service of an application notice

(1) Subject to paragraphs (4) and (5), the applicant must serve a copy of the application notice on—

(a) anyone who is named as a respondent in the application notice (if not otherwise a party to the proceedings);
(b) every party to the proceedings; and
(c) any other person, as the court may direct,

as soon as practicable and in any event within 21 days of the date on which it was issued.

(2) The application notice must be accompanied by a copy of the evidence filed in support.

(3) The applicant must file a certificate of service within 7 days beginning with the date on which the documents were served.

(4) This rule does not require a copy of evidence to be served on a person upon whom it has already been served, but the applicant must in such a case give to that person notice of the evidence upon which he intends to rely.

(5) An application may be made without serving a copy of the application notice if this is permitted by—

(a) a rule;
(b) a practice direction; or
(c) the court.

A4.142

81 Applications without notice

(1) This rule applies where the court has dealt with an application which was made without notice having been given to any person.

(2) Where the court makes an order, whether granting or dismissing the application, the applicant must, as soon as practicable or within such period as the court may direct, serve the documents mentioned in paragraph (3) on—

(a) anyone named as a respondent in the application notice (if not otherwise a party to the proceedings);
(b) every party to the proceedings; and
(c) any other person, as the court may direct.

(3) The documents referred to in paragraph (2) are—

(a) a copy of the application notice;
(b) the court's order; and
(c) any evidence filed in support of the application.

(Rule 89 provides for reconsideration of orders made without a hearing or without notice to a person.)

Interim remedies

A4.143

82 Orders for interim remedies

(1) The court may grant the following interim remedies—

- (a) an interim injunction;
- (b) an interim declaration; or
- (c) any other interim order it considers appropriate.

(2) Unless the court orders otherwise, a person on whom an application form is served under Part 9, or who is given notice of such an application, may not apply for an interim remedy before he has filed an acknowledgment of service or notification in accordance with Part 9.

(3) This rule does not limit any other power of the court to grant interim relief.

PART 11
HUMAN RIGHTS

A4.144

83 General

(1) A party who seeks to rely upon any provision of or right arising under the Human Rights Act 1998 ("the 1998 Act") or who seeks a remedy available under that Act must inform the court in the manner set out in the relevant practice direction specifying—

- (a) the Convention right (within the meaning of the 1998 Act) which it is alleged has been infringed and details of the alleged infringement; and
- (b) the remedy sought and whether this includes a declaration of incompatibility under section 4 of the 1998 Act.

(2) The court may not make a declaration of incompatibility unless 21 days' notice, or such other period of notice as the court directs, has been given to the Crown.

(3) Where notice has been given to the Crown, a Minister or other person permitted by the 1998 Act will be joined as a party on filing an application in accordance with rule 75 (application to be joined as a party).

PART 12
DEALING WITH APPLICATIONS

A4.145

84 Dealing with the application

(1) As soon as practicable after any application has been issued the court shall consider how to deal with it.

(2) The court may deal with an application or any part of an application at a hearing or without a hearing.

(3) In considering whether it is necessary to hold a hearing, the court shall, as appropriate, have regard to—

- (a) the nature of the proceedings and the orders sought;
- (b) whether the application is opposed by a person who appears to the court to have an interest in matters relating to P's best interests;
- (c) whether the application involves a substantial dispute of fact;
- (d) the complexity of the facts and the law;
- (e) any wider public interest in the proceedings;
- (f) the circumstances of P and of any party, in particular as to whether their rights would be adequately protected if a hearing were not held;

(g) whether the parties agree that the court should dispose of the application without a hearing; and
(h) any other matter specified in the relevant practice direction.

(4) Where the court considers that a hearing is necessary, it will—

(a) give notice of the hearing date to the parties and to any other person it directs; and
(b) state whether the hearing is for disposing of the matter or for directions.

(5) Where the court decides that it can deal with the matter without a hearing it will do so and serve a copy of its order on the parties and on any other person it directs.

A4.146

85 Directions

(1) The court may—

(a) give directions in writing; or
(b) set a date for a directions hearing; and
(c) do anything else that may be set out in a practice direction.

(2) When giving directions, the court may do any of the following—

(a) require a report under section 49 of the Act and give directions as to any such report;
(b) give directions as to any requirements contained in these Rules or a practice direction for the giving of notification to any person or for that person to do anything in response to a notification;
(c) if the court considers that P should be a party to the proceedings, give directions joining him as a party;
(d) if P is joined as a party to proceedings, give directions as to the appointment of a litigation friend;
(e) if the court considers that any other person or persons should be a party to the proceedings, give directions joining them as a party;
(f) if the court considers that any party to the proceedings should not be a party, give directions for that person's removal as a party;
(g) give directions for the management of the case and set a timetable for the steps to be taken between the giving of directions and the hearing;
(h) subject to rule 86, give directions as to the type of judge who is to hear the case;
(i) give directions as to whether the proceedings or any part of them are to be heard in public, or as to whether any particular person should be permitted to attend the hearing, or as to whether any publication of the proceedings is to be permitted;
(j) give directions as to the disclosure of documents, service of witness statements and any expert evidence;
(k) give directions as to the attendance of witnesses and as to whether, and the extent to which, cross-examination will be permitted at any hearing; and
(l) give such other directions as the court thinks fit.

(3) The court may give directions at any time—

(a) on its own initiative; or
(b) on the application of a party.

(4) Subject to paragraphs (5) and (6) and unless these Rules or a practice direction provide otherwise or the court directs otherwise, the time specified by a rule or by the court for a person to do any act may be varied by the written agreement of the parties.

(5) A party must apply to the court if he wishes to vary —

(a) the date the court has fixed for the final hearing; or
(b) the period within which the final hearing is to take place.

(6) The time specified by a rule or practice direction or by the court may not be varied by the parties if the variation would make it necessary to vary the date the court has fixed for any hearing or the period within which the final hearing is to take place.

Allocation of proceedings

A4.147

86 Court's jurisdiction in certain kinds of case to be exercised by certain judges

(1) The court will consider whether the application is of a type specified in the relevant practice direction as being one which must be dealt with by—

(a) the President;
(b) the Vice-President; or
(c) one of the other judges nominated by virtue of section 46(2)(a) to (c) of the Act.

(2) The practice direction made under this rule shall specify the categories of case which must be dealt with by a judge mentioned in paragraph (1).

(3) Applications in any matter other than those specified in the relevant practice direction may be dealt with by any judge.

Disputing the jurisdiction of the court

A4.148

87 Procedure for disputing the court's jurisdiction

(1) A person who wishes to—

(a) dispute the court's jurisdiction to hear an application; or
(b) argue that the court should not exercise its jurisdiction,

may apply to the court at any time for an order declaring that it has no such jurisdiction or should not exercise any jurisdiction that it may have.

(2) An application under this rule must be—

(a) made by using the form specified in the relevant practice direction; and
(b) supported by evidence.

(3) An order containing a declaration that the court has no jurisdiction or will not exercise its jurisdiction may also make further provision, including—

(a) setting aside the application;
(b) discharging any order made; and
(c) staying the proceedings.

Participation in hearings

A4.149

88 Participation in hearings

(1) The court may hear P on the question of whether or not an order should be made, whether or not he is a party to the proceedings.

(2) The court may proceed with a hearing in the absence of P if it considers that it would be appropriate to do so.

(3) A person other than P who is served with or notified of the application may only take part in a hearing if—

(a) he files an acknowledgment in accordance with the Rules and is made a party to the proceedings; or
(b) the court permits.

Reconsideration of court orders

A4.150

89 Orders made without a hearing or without notice to any person

(1) This rule applies where the court makes an order—

(a) without a hearing; or
(b) without notice to any person who is affected by it.

(2) Where this rule applies—

(a) P;
(b) any party to the proceedings; or
(c) any other person affected by the order,

may apply to the court for reconsideration of the order made.

(3) An application under paragraph (2) must be made—

(a) within 21 days of the order being served or such other period as the court may direct; and
(b) in accordance with Part 10.

(4) The court will—

(a) reconsider the order without directing a hearing; or
(b) fix a date for the matter to be heard, and notify all parties to the proceedings and such other persons as the court may direct, of that date.

(5) Where an application is made in accordance with this rule, the court may affirm, set aside or vary any order made.

(6) Reconsideration may be by any judge of the court—

(a) including the judge who made the decision in respect of which the reconsideration is sought; but
(b) may not be by a judge who is not a prescribed higher judge within the meaning of section 53(3) of the Act in relation to the first-mentioned judge.

(7) No application may be made seeking a reconsideration of a decision that has been made under paragraph (5).

(8) An appeal against a decision made under paragraph (5) may be made in accordance with Part 20 (appeals).

(9) Any order made without a hearing or without notice to any person, other than one made under paragraph (5), must contain a statement of the right to apply for a reconsideration of the decision in accordance with this rule.

(10) An application made under this rule may include a request that the court reconsider the matter at a hearing.

PART 13
HEARINGS

Private hearings

A4.151

90 General rule—hearing to be in private

(1) The general rule is that a hearing is to be held in private.

(2) A private hearing is a hearing which only the following persons are entitled to attend—

(a) the parties;
(b) P (whether or not a party);
(c) any person acting in the proceedings as a litigation friend;

(d) any legal representative of a person specified in any of sub-paragraphs (a) to (c); and
(e) any court officer.

(3) In relation to a private hearing, the court may make an order—

(a) authorising any person, or class of persons, to attend the hearing or a part of it; or
(b) excluding any person, or class of persons, from attending the hearing or a part of it.

A4.152

91 Court's general power to authorise publication of information about proceedings

(1) For the purposes of the law relating to contempt of court, information relating to proceedings held in private may be published where the court makes an order under paragraph (2).

(2) The court may make an order authorising—

(a) the publication of such information relating to the proceedings as it may specify; or
(b) the publication of the text or a summary of the whole or part of a judgment or order made by the court.

(3) Where the court makes an order under paragraph (2) it may do so on such terms as it thinks fit, and in particular may—

(a) impose restrictions on the publication of the identity of—
  (i) any party;
  (ii) P (whether or not a party);
  (iii) any witness; or
  (iv) any other person;
(b) prohibit the publication of any information that may lead to any such person being identified;
(c) prohibit the further publication of any information relating to the proceedings from such date as the court may specify; or
(d) impose such other restrictions on the publication of information relating to the proceedings as the court may specify.

Power to order a public hearing

A4.153

92 Court's power to order that a hearing be held in public

(1) The court may make an order—

(a) for a hearing to be held in public;
(b) for a part of a hearing to be held in public; or
(c) excluding any person, or class of persons, from attending a public hearing or a part of it.

(2) Where the court makes an order under paragraph (1), it may in the same order or by a subsequent order—

(a) impose restrictions on the publication of the identity of—
  (i) any party;
  (ii) P (whether or not a party);
  (iii) any witness; or
  (iv) any other person;
(b) prohibit the publication of any information that may lead to any such person being identified;
(c) prohibit the further publication of any information relating to the proceedings from such date as the court may specify; or
(d) impose such other restrictions on the publication of information relating to the proceedings as the court may specify.

Supplementary

A4.154

93 Supplementary provisions relating to public or private hearings

(1) An order under rule 90, 91 or 92 may be made—

(a) only where it appears to the court that there is good reason for making the order;
(b) at any time; and
(c) either on the court's own initiative or on an application made by any person in accordance with Part 10.

(2) A practice direction may make further provision in connection with—

(a) private hearings;
(b) public hearings; or
(c) the publication of information about any proceedings.

PART 14
ADMISSIONS, EVIDENCE AND DEPOSITIONS

Admissions

A4.155

94 Making an admission

(1) Without prejudice to the ability to make an admission in any other way, a party may admit the truth of the whole or part of another party's case by giving notice in writing.

(2) The court may allow a party to amend or withdraw an admission.

Evidence

A4.156

95 Power of court to control evidence

The court may—

(a) control the evidence by giving directions as to—
  (i) the issues on which it requires evidence;
  (ii) the nature of the evidence which it requires to decide those issues; and
  (iii) the way in which the evidence is to be placed before the court;
(b) use its power under this rule to exclude evidence that would otherwise be admissible;
(c) allow or limit cross-examination; and
(d) admit such evidence, whether written or oral, as it thinks fit.

A4.157

96 Evidence of witnesses—general rule

(1) The general rule is that any fact which needs to be proved by evidence of a witness is to be proved—

(a) where there is a final hearing, by their oral evidence; or
(b) at any other hearing, or if there is no hearing, by their evidence in writing.

(2) Where a witness is called to give oral evidence under paragraph (1)(a), his witness statement shall stand as his evidence in chief unless the court directs otherwise.

(3) A witness giving oral evidence at the final hearing may, if the court permits—

(a) amplify his witness statement; and

(b) give evidence in relation to new matters which have arisen since the witness statement was made.

(4) The court may so permit only if it considers that there is good reason not to confine the evidence of the witness to the contents of his witness statement.

(5) This rule is subject to—

(a) any provision to the contrary in these Rules or elsewhere; or
(b) any order or direction of the court.

A4.158

97 Written evidence—general rule

A party may not rely upon written evidence unless—

(a) it has been filed in accordance with these Rules or a practice direction;
(b) it is expressly permitted by these Rules or a practice direction; or
(c) the court gives permission.

A4.159

98 Evidence by video link or other means

The court may allow a witness to give evidence through a video link or by other communication technology.

A4.160

99 Service of witness statements for use at final hearing

(1) A witness statement is a written statement which contains the evidence which that person would be allowed to give orally.

(2) The court will give directions about the service of any witness statement that a party intends to rely upon at the final hearing.

(3) The court may give directions as to the order in which witness statements are to be served.

(Rules 11 and 100 require witness statements to be verified by a statement of truth.)

A4.161

100 Form of witness statement

A witness statement must contain a statement of truth and comply with the requirements set out in the relevant practice direction.

A4.162

101 Witness summaries

(1) A party who wishes to file a witness statement for use at final hearing, but is unable to do so, may apply, without notice, to be permitted to file a witness summary instead.

(2) A witness summary is a summary of—

(a) the evidence, if known, which would otherwise be included in a witness statement; or
(b) if the evidence is not known, the matters about which the party filing the witness summary proposes to question the witness.

(3) Unless the court directs otherwise, a witness summary must include the name and address of the intended witness.

(4) Unless the court directs otherwise, a witness summary must be filed within the period in which a witness statement would have had to be filed.

(5) Where a party files a witness summary, so far as practicable, rules 96(3)(a) (amplifying witness statements) and 99 (service of witness statements for use at a final hearing) shall apply to the summary.

A4.163

102 Affidavit evidence

Evidence must be given by affidavit instead of or in addition to a witness statement if this is required by the court, a provision contained in any rule, a practice direction or any other enactment.

A4.164

103 Form of affidavit

An affidavit must comply with the requirements set out in the relevant practice direction.

A4.165

104 Affidavit made outside the jurisdiction

A person may make an affidavit outside the jurisdiction in accordance with—

- (a) this Part; or
- (b) the law of the place where he makes the affidavit.

A4.166

105 Notarial acts and instruments

A notarial act or instrument may, without further proof, be received in evidence as duly authenticated in accordance with the requirements of law unless the contrary is proved.

A4.167

106 Summoning of witnesses

(1) The court may allow or direct any party to issue a witness summons requiring the person named in it to attend before the court and give oral evidence or produce any document to the court.

(2) An application by a party for the issue of a witness summons may be made by filing an application notice which includes—

- (a) the name and address of the applicant and of his solicitor, if any;
- (b) the name, address and occupation of the proposed witness;
- (c) particulars of any document which the proposed witness is to be required to produce; and
- (d) the grounds on which the application is made.

(3) The general rule is that a witness summons is binding if it is served at least 7 days before the date on which the witness is required to attend before the court, and the requirements of paragraph (6) have been complied with.

(4) The court may direct that a witness summons shall be binding although it will be served less than 7 days before the date on which the witness is required to attend before the court.

(5) Unless the court directs otherwise, a witness summons is to be served by the person making the application.

(6) At the time of service the witness must be offered or paid—

- (a) a sum reasonably sufficient to cover his expenses in travelling to and from the court; and
- (b) such sum by way of compensation for loss of time as may be specified in the relevant practice direction.

(7) The court may order that the witness is to be paid such general costs as it considers appropriate.

A4.168

107 Power of court to direct a party to provide information

(1) Where a party has access to information which is not reasonably available to the other party, the court may direct that party to prepare and file a document recording the information.

(2) The court will give directions about serving a copy of that document on the other parties.

Depositions

A4.169

108 Evidence by deposition

(1) A party may apply for an order for a person to be examined before the hearing takes place.

(2) A person from whom evidence is to be obtained following an order under this rule is referred to as a "deponent" and the evidence is referred to as a "deposition".

(3) An order under this rule shall be for a deponent to be examined on oath before—

- (a) a circuit judge or a district judge, whether or not nominated as a judge of the court;
- (b) an examiner of the court; or
- (c) such other person as the court appoints.

(4) The order may require the production of any document which the court considers is necessary for the purposes of the examination.

(5) The order will state the date, time and place of the examination.

(6) At the time of service of the order, the deponent must be offered or paid—

- (a) a sum reasonably sufficient to cover his expenses in travelling to and from the place of examination; and
- (b) such sum by way of compensation for loss of time as may be specified in the relevant practice direction.

(7) Where the court makes an order for a deposition to be taken, it may also order the party who obtained the order to file a witness statement or witness summary in relation to the evidence to be given by the person to be examined.

A4.170

109 Conduct of examination

(1) Subject to any directions contained in the order for examination, the examination must be conducted in the same way as if the witness were giving evidence at a final hearing.

(2) If all the parties are present, the examiner may conduct the examination of a person not named in the order for examination if all the parties and the person to be examined consent.

(3) The examiner must ensure that the evidence given by the witness is recorded in full.

(4) The examiner must send a copy of the deposition—

- (a) to the person who obtained the order for the examination of the witness; and
- (b) to the court.

(5) The court will give directions as to the service of a copy of the deposition on the other parties.

A4.171

110 Fees and expenses of examiners of the court

(1) An examiner of the court may charge a fee for the examination and he need not send the deposition to the court until the fee is paid, unless the court directs otherwise.

(2) The examiner's fees and expenses must be paid by the party who obtained the order for examination.

(3) If the fees and expenses due to an examiner are not paid within a reasonable time, he may report that fact to the court.

(4) The court may order the party who obtained the order for examination to deposit in the court office a specified sum in respect of the examiner's fees and, where it does so, the examiner will not be asked to act until the sum has been deposited.

(5) An order under this rule does not affect any decision as to the person who is ultimately to bear the costs of the examination.

A4.172

111 Examiners of the court

(1) The Lord Chancellor shall appoint persons to be examiners of the court.

(2) The persons appointed shall be barristers or solicitor-advocates who have been practising for a period of not less than 3 years.

(3) The Lord Chancellor may revoke an appointment at any time.

(4) In addition to appointing persons in accordance with this rule, examiners appointed under rule 34.15 of the Civil Procedure Rules 1998 may act as examiners in the court.

A4.173

112 Enforcing attendance of a witness

(1) If a person served with an order to attend before an examiner—

- (a) fails to attend; or
- (b) refuses to be sworn for the purpose of the examination or to answer any lawful question or produce any document at the examination,

a certificate of his failure or refusal, signed by the examiner, must be filed by the party requiring the deposition.

(2) On the certificate being filed, the party requiring the deposition may apply to the court for an order requiring that person to attend or to be sworn or to answer any question or produce any document, as the case may be.

(3) An application for an order under this rule may be made without notice.

(4) The court may order the person against whom an order is sought or made under this rule to pay any costs resulting from his failure or refusal.

A4.174

113 Use of deposition at a hearing

(1) A deposition ordered under rule 108, 115 or 116 may be put in evidence at a hearing unless the court orders otherwise.

(2) A party intending to put a deposition in evidence at a hearing must file notice of his intention to do so on the court and serve the notice on every other party.

(3) Unless the court directs otherwise, he must file the notice at least 14 days before the day fixed for the hearing.

(4) The court may require a deponent to attend the hearing and give evidence orally.

Taking evidence outside the jurisdiction

A4.175

114 Interpretation

In this Section—

- (a) "Regulation State" has the same meaning as "Member State" in the Taking of Evidence Regulation, that is all Member States except Denmark; and
- (b) "the Taking of Evidence Regulation" means Council Regulation (EC) No 1206/2001 of 28 May 2001 on co-operation between the courts of Member States in the taking of evidence in civil and commercial matters.

A4.176

115 Where a person to be examined is in another Regulation State

(1) This rule applies where a party wishes to take a deposition from a person who is—

- (a) outside the jurisdiction; and
- (b) in a Regulation State.

(2) The court may order the issue of the request to a designated court ("the requested court") in the Regulation State in which the proposed deponent is.

(3) If the court makes an order for the issue of a request, the party who sought the order must file—

- (a) a draft Form A as set out in the annex to the Taking of Evidence Regulation (request for the taking of evidence);
- (b) except where paragraph (4) applies, a translation of the form;
- (c) an undertaking to be responsible for the costs sought by the requested court in relation to—
  - (i) fees paid to experts and interpreters; and
  - (ii) where requested by that party, the use of special procedure or communications technology; and
- (d) an undertaking to be responsible for the court's expenses.

(4) There is no need to file a translation if—

- (a) English is one of the official languages of the Regulation State where the examination is to take place; or
- (b) the Regulation State has indicated, in accordance with the Taking of Evidence Regulation, that English is a language which it will accept.

(5) Where article 17 of the Taking of Evidence Regulation (direct taking of evidence by the requested court) allows evidence to be taken directly in another Regulation State, the court may make an order for the submission of a request in accordance with that article.

(6) If the court makes an order for the submission of a request under paragraph (5), the party who sought the order must file—

(a) draft Form I as set out in the annex to the Taking of Evidence Regulation (request for direct taking of evidence);
(b) except where paragraph (4) applies, a translation of the form; and
(c) an undertaking to be responsible for the requested court's expenses.

A4.177

116 Where a person to be examined is out of the jurisdiction—letter of request

(1) This rule applies where a party wishes to take a deposition from a person who is—

(a) out of the jurisdiction; and
(b) not in a Regulation State within the meaning of rule 114.

(2) The court may order the issue of a letter of request to the judicial authorities of the country in which the proposed deponent is.

(3) A letter of request is a request to a judicial authority to take the evidence of that person, or arrange for it to be taken.

(4) If the government of a country permits a person appointed by the court to examine a person in that country, the court may make an order appointing a special examiner for that purpose.

(5) A person may be examined under this rule on oath or affirmation in accordance with any procedure permitted in the country in which the examination is to take place.

(6) If the court makes an order for the issue of a letter of request, the party who sought the order must file—

(a) the following documents and, except where paragraph (7) applies, a translation of them—
  (i) a draft letter of request;
  (ii) a statement of the issues relevant to the proceedings; and
  (iii) a list of questions or the subject matter of questions to be put to the person to be examined; and
(b) an undertaking to be responsible for the Secretary of State's expenses.

(7) There is no need to file a translation if—

(a) English is one of the official languages of the country where the examination is to take place; or
(b) a practice direction has specified that country is a country where no translation is necessary.

Section 49 reports

A4.178

117 Reports under section 49 of the Act

(1) This rule applies where the court requires a report to be made to it under section 49 of the Act.

(2) It is the duty of the person who is required to make the report to help the court on the matters within his expertise.

(3) Unless the court directs otherwise, the person making the report must—

(a) contact or seek to interview such persons as he thinks appropriate or as the court directs
(b) to the extent that it is practicable and appropriate to do so, ascertain what P's wishes and feelings are, and the beliefs and values that would be likely to influence P if he had the capacity to make a decision in relation to the matter to which the application relates;
(c) describe P's circumstances; and
(d) address such other matters as are required in a practice direction or as the court may direct.

(4) The court will send a copy of the report to the parties and to such persons as the court may direct.

(5) Subject to paragraphs (6) and (7), the person who is required to make the report may examine and take copies of any document in the court records.

(6) The court may direct that the right to inspect documents under this rule does not apply in relation to such documents, or descriptions of documents, as the court may specify.

(7) The court may direct that any information is to be provided to the maker of the report on an edited basis.

A4.179

118 Written questions to person making a report under section 49

(1) Where a report is made under section 49 the court may, on the application of any party, permit written questions relevant to the issues before the court to be put to the person by whom the report was made.

(2) The questions sought to be put to the maker of the report shall be submitted to the court, and the court may put them to the maker of the report with such amendments (if any) as it thinks fit and the maker of the report shall give his replies in writing to the questions so put.

(3) The court will send a copy of the replies given by the maker of the report under this rule to the parties and to such other persons as the court may direct.

PART 15
EXPERTS

A4.180

119 References to expert

A reference to an expert in this Part—

- (a) is to an expert who has been instructed to give or prepare evidence for the purpose of court proceedings; but
- (b) does not include any person instructed to make a report under section 49 of the Act.

A4.181

120 Restriction on filing an expert's report

(1) No person may file expert evidence unless the court or a practice direction permits, or if it is filed with the permission form or application form and is evidence—

- (a) that P is a person who lacks capacity to make a decision or decisions in relation to the matter or matters to which the application relates;
- (b) as to P's best interests; or
- (c) that is required by any rule or practice direction to be filed with the permission form or application form.

(2) An applicant may only rely upon any expert evidence so filed in support of the permission form or application form to the extent and for the purposes that the court allows.

(Rule 64(a) requires the applicant to file any evidence upon which he wishes to rely with the application form and rule 54 requires certain documents to be filed with the application for permission form.)

A4.182

121 Duty to restrict expert evidence

Expert evidence shall be restricted to that which is reasonably required to resolve the proceedings.

A4.183

122 Experts—overriding duty to the court

It is the duty of the expert to help the court on the matters within his expertise.

A4.184

123 Court's power to restrict expert evidence

(1) Subject to rule 120, no party may file or adduce expert evidence unless the court or a practice direction permits.

(2) When a party applies for a direction under this rule he must—

- (a) identify the field in respect of which he wishes to rely upon expert evidence;
- (b) where practicable, identify the expert in that field upon whose evidence he wishes to rely;
- (c) provide any other material information about the expert; and
- (d) provide a draft letter of instruction to the expert.

(3) Where a direction is given under this rule, the court shall specify the field or fields in respect of which the expert evidence is to be provided.

(4) The court may specify the person who is to provide the evidence referred to in paragraph (3).

(5) Where a direction is given under this rule for a party to call an expert or put in evidence an expert's report, the court shall give directions for the service of the report on the parties and on such other persons as the court may direct.

(6) The court may limit the amount of the expert's fees and expenses that the party who wishes to rely upon the expert may recover from any other party.

A4.185

124 General requirement for expert evidence to be given in a written report

Expert evidence is to be given in a written report unless the court directs otherwise.

A4.186

125 Written questions to experts

(1) A party may put written questions to—

- (a) an expert instructed by another party; or
- (b) a single joint expert appointed under rule 130,

about a report prepared by such person.

(2) Written questions under paragraph (1)—

- (a) may be put once only;
- (b) must be put within 28 days beginning with the date on which the expert's report was served; and
- (c) must be for the purpose only of clarification of the report.

(3) Paragraph (2) does not apply in any case where—

(a) the court permits it to be done on a further occasion;
(b) the other party or parties agree; or
(c) any practice direction provides otherwise.

(4) An expert's answers to questions put in accordance with paragraph (1) shall be treated as part of the expert's report.

(5) Paragraph (6) applies where—

(a) a party has put a written question to an expert instructed by another party in accordance with this rule; and
(b) the expert does not answer that question.

(6) The court may make one or both of the following orders in relation to the party who instructed the expert—

(a) that the party may not rely upon the evidence of that expert; or
(b) that the party may not recover the fees and expenses of that expert, or part of them, from any other party.

(7) Unless the court otherwise directs, and subject to any final costs order that may be made, the instructing party is responsible for the payment of the expert's fees and expenses, including the expert's costs of answering questions put by any other party.

A4.187

126 Contents of expert's report

(1) The court may give directions as to the matters to be covered in an expert's report.

(2) An expert's report must comply with the requirements set out in the relevant practice direction.

(3) At the end of an expert's report there must be a statement that—

(a) the expert understands his duty to the court; and
(b) he has complied with that duty.

(4) The expert's report must state the substance of all material instructions, whether written or oral, on the basis of which the report was written.

(5) The instructions to the expert shall not be privileged against disclosure.

A4.188

127 Use by one party of expert's report disclosed by another

Where a party has disclosed an expert's report, any party may use that expert's report as evidence at any hearing in the proceedings.

A4.189

128 Discussions between experts

(1) The court may, at any stage, direct a discussion between experts for the purpose of requiring the experts to—

(a) identify and discuss the expert issues in the proceedings; and
(b) where possible, reach an agreed opinion on those issues.

(2) The court may specify the issues which the experts must discuss.

(3) The court may direct that following a discussion between the experts they must prepare a statement for the court showing—

(a) those issues on which they agree; and
(b) those issues on which they disagree and a summary of their reasons for disagreeing.

(4) Unless the court otherwise directs, the content of the discussions between experts may be referred to at any hearing or at any stage in the proceedings.

A4.190

129 Expert's right to ask court for directions

(1) An expert may file a written request for directions to assist him in carrying out his function as an expert.

(2) An expert must, unless the court directs otherwise, provide a copy of any proposed request for directions under paragraph (1)—

(a) to the party instructing him, at least 7 days before he files the request; and
(b) to all other parties, at least 4 days before he files it.

(3) The court, when it gives directions, may also direct that a party be served with a copy of the directions.

A4.191

130 Court's power to direct that evidence is to be given by a single joint expert

(1) Where two or more parties wish to submit expert evidence on a particular issue, the court may direct that the evidence on that issue is to be given by one expert only.

(2) The parties wishing to submit the expert evidence are called "the instructing parties".

(3) Where the instructing parties cannot agree who should be the expert, the court may—

(a) select the expert from a list prepared or identified by the instructing parties; or
(b) direct the manner by which the expert is to be selected.

A4.192

131 Instructions to a single joint expert

(1) Where the court gives a direction under rule 130 for a single joint expert to be used, each party may give instructions to the expert.

(2) Unless the court otherwise directs, when an instructing party gives instructions to the expert he must, at the same time, send a copy of the instructions to the other instructing parties.

(3) The court may give directions about—

(a) the payment of the expert's fees and expenses; and
(b) any inspection, examination or experiments which the expert wishes to carry out.

(4) The court may, before an expert is instructed, limit the amount that can be paid by way of fees and expenses to the expert.

(5) Unless the court otherwise directs, and subject to any final costs order that may be made, the instructing parties are jointly and severally liable for the payment of the expert's fees and expenses.

PART 16
DISCLOSURE

A4.193

132 Meaning of disclosure

A party discloses a document by stating that the document exists or has existed.

A4.194

133 General or specific disclosure

(1) The court may either on its own initiative or on the application of a party make an order to give general or specific disclosure.

(2) General disclosure requires a party to disclose—

- (a) the documents on which he relies; and
- (b) the documents which—
  - (i) adversely affect his own case;
  - (ii) adversely affect another party's case; or
  - (iii) support another party's case.

(3) An order for specific disclosure is an order that a party must do one or more of the following things—

- (a) disclose documents or classes of documents specified in the order;
- (b) carry out a search to the extent stated in the order; or
- (c) disclose any document located as a result of that search.

(4) A party's duty to disclose documents is limited to documents which are or have been in his control.

(5) For the purpose of paragraph (4) a party has or has had a document in his control if—

- (a) it is or was in his physical possession;
- (b) he has or has had possession of it; or
- (c) he has or has had a right to inspect or take copies of it.

A4.195

134 Procedure for general or specific disclosure

(1) This rule applies where the court makes an order under rule 133 to give general or specific disclosure.

(2) Each party must make, and serve on every other party, a list of documents to be disclosed.

(3) A copy of each list must be filed within 7 days of the date on which it is served.

(4) The list must identify the documents in a convenient order and manner and as concisely as possible.

(5) The list must indicate—

- (a) the documents in respect of which the party claims a right or duty to withhold inspection (see rule 138); and
- (b) the documents that are no longer in his control, stating what has happened to them.

A4.196

135 Ongoing duty of disclosure

(1) Where the court makes an order to give general or specific disclosure under rule 133, any party to whom the order applies is under a continuing duty to provide such disclosure as is required by the order until the proceedings are concluded.

(2) If a document to which the duty of disclosure imposed by paragraph (1) extends comes to a party's notice at any time during the proceedings, he must immediately notify every other party.

A4.197

136 Right to inspect documents

(1) A party to whom a document has been disclosed has a right to inspect any document disclosed to him except where—

(a) the document is no longer in the control of the party who disclosed it; or
(b) the party disclosing the document has a right or duty to withhold inspection of it.

(2) The right to inspect disclosed documents extends to any document mentioned in—

(a) a document filed or served in the course of the proceedings by any other party; or
(b) correspondence sent by any other party.

A4.198

137 Inspection and copying of documents

(1) Where a party has a right to inspect a document, he—

(a) must give the party who disclosed the document written notice of his wish to inspect it; and
(b) may request a copy of the document.

(2) Not more than 14 days after the date on which the party who disclosed the document received the notice under paragraph (1)(a), he must permit inspection of the document at a convenient place and time.

(3) Where a party has requested a copy of the document, the party who disclosed the document must supply him with a copy not more than 14 days after the date on which he received the request.

(4) For the purposes of paragraph (2), the party who disclosed the document must give reasonable notice of the time and place for inspection.

(5) For the purposes of paragraph (3), the party requesting a copy of the document is responsible for the payment of reasonable copying costs, subject to any final costs order that may be made.

A4.199

138 Claim to withhold inspection or disclosure of document

(1) A party who wishes to claim that he has a right or duty to withhold inspection of a document, or part of a document, must state in writing—

(a) that he has such a right or duty; and
(b) the grounds on which he claims that right or duty.

(2) The statement must be made in the list in which the document is disclosed (see rule 134(2)).

(3) A party may, by filing an application notice in accordance with Part 10, apply to the court to decide whether the claim made under paragraph (1) should be upheld.

A4.200

139 Consequence of failure to disclose documents or permit inspection

A party may not rely upon any document which he fails to disclose or in respect of which he fails to permit inspection unless the court permits.

PART 17
LITIGATION FRIEND

A4.201

140 Who may act as a litigation friend

(1) A person may act as a litigation friend on behalf of a person mentioned in paragraph (2) if he—

(a) can fairly and competently conduct proceedings on behalf of that person; and
(b) has no interests adverse to those of that person.

(2) The persons for whom a litigation friend may act are—

(a) P;
(b) a child; or
(c) a protected party.

A4.202

141 Requirement for a litigation friend

(1) Subject to rule 147, P (if a party to proceedings) must have a litigation friend.

(2) A protected party (if a party to the proceedings) must have a litigation friend.

(3) A child (if a party to proceedings) must have a litigation friend to conduct those proceedings on his behalf unless the court makes an order under paragraph (4).

(4) The court may make an order permitting the child to conduct proceedings without a litigation friend.

(5) An application for an order under paragraph (4)—

(a) may be made by the child;
(b) if the child already has a litigation friend, must be made on notice to the litigation friend; and
(c) if the child has no litigation friend, may be made without notice.

(6) Where—

(a) the court has made an order under paragraph (4); and
(b) it subsequently appears to the court that it is desirable for a litigation friend to conduct the proceedings on behalf of the child,

the court may appoint a person to be the child's litigation friend.

A4.203

142 Litigation friend without a court order

(1) This rule does not apply—

(a) in relation to P;
(b) where the court has appointed a person under rule 143 or 144; or
(c) where the Official Solicitor is to act as litigation friend.

(2) A deputy with the power to conduct legal proceedings in the name of the protected party or on the protected party's behalf is entitled to be a litigation friend of the protected party in any proceedings to which his power relates.

(3) If no one has been appointed by the court, or in the case of a protected party, there is no deputy with the power to conduct proceedings, a person who wishes to act as a litigation friend must—

(a) file a certificate of suitability stating that he satisfies the conditions specified in rule 140(1); and
(b) serve the certificate of suitability on—
  (i) the person on whom an application form is to be served in accordance with rule 32 (service on children and protected parties); and
  (ii) every other person who is a party to the proceedings.

(4) If the person referred to in paragraph (2) wishes to act as a litigation friend for the protected party, he must file and serve a copy of the court order which appointed him on those persons mentioned in paragraph (3)(b).

A4.204

143 Litigation friend by court order

(1) The court may make an order appointing—

(a) the Official Solicitor; or
(b) some other person,

to act as a litigation friend.

(2) The court may act under paragraph (1)—

(a) either on its own initiative or on the application of any person; but
(b) only with the consent of the person to be appointed.

(3) An application for an order under paragraph (1) must be supported by evidence.

(4) The court may not appoint a litigation friend under this rule unless it is satisfied that the person to be appointed satisfies the conditions specified in rule 140(1).

(5) The court may at any stage of the proceedings give directions as to the appointment of a litigation friend.

A4.205

144 Court's power to prevent a person from acting as litigation friend or to order change

(1) The court may either on its own initiative or on the application of any person—

(a) direct that a person may not act as a litigation friend;
(b) terminate a litigation friend's appointment; or
(c) appoint a new litigation friend in place of an existing one.

(2) An application for an order under paragraph (1) must be supported by evidence.

(3) The court may not appoint a litigation friend under this rule unless it is satisfied that the person to be appointed satisfies the conditions specified in rule 140(1).

A4.206

145 Appointment of litigation friend by court order—supplementary

The applicant must serve a copy of an application for an order under rule 143 or 144 on—

(a) the person on whom an application form is to be served in accordance with rule 32 (service on children and protected parties);
(b) every other person who is a party to the proceedings;
(c) any person who is the litigation friend, or who is purporting to act as the litigation friend, when the application is made; and
(d) unless he is the applicant, the person who it is proposed should be the litigation friend,

as soon as practicable and in any event within 21 days of the date on which it was issued.

A4.207

146 Procedure where appointment of litigation friend comes to an end—for a child or protected party

(1) This rule applies—

(a) when a child reaches 18, provided he is neither—
  (i) P; nor
  (ii) a protected party; and
(b) where a protected party ceases to be a person who lacks capacity to conduct the proceedings himself.

(2) Where paragraph (1)(a) applies, the litigation friend's appointment ends.

(3) Where paragraph (1)(b) applies, the litigation friend's appointment continues until it is brought to an end by a court order

(4) An application for an order under paragraph (3) may be made by—

(a) the former protected party;
(b) his litigation friend; or
(c) any other person who is a party to the proceedings.

(5) The applicant must serve a copy of the application notice seeking an order under this rule on all parties to the proceedings as soon as practicable and in any event within 21 days of the date on which it was issued.

(6) Where paragraph (2) applies the child must serve notice on every other party—

(a) stating that he has reached full age;
(b) stating that the appointment of the litigation friend has ended; and
(c) providing his address for service.

(7) Where paragraph (3) applies, the former protected party must provide his address for service to all other parties to the proceedings.

A4.208

147 Procedure where appointment of litigation friend comes to an end—for P

(1) This rule applies where P ceases to be a person who lacks capacity to conduct the proceedings himself but continues to lack capacity in relation to the matter or matters to which the application relates.

(2) The litigation friend's appointment continues until it is brought to an end by a court order.

(3) An application for an order under paragraph (2) may be made by—

(a) P;
(b) his litigation friend; or
(c) any other person who is a party to the proceedings.

(4) The applicant must serve a copy of the application notice seeking an order under this rule on all other parties to the proceedings as soon as practicable and in any event within 21 days of the date on which it was issued.

(5) Where the court makes an order under this rule, P must provide his address for service to all other parties to the proceedings.

A4.209

148 Procedure where P ceases to lack capacity

(1) This rule applies where P ceases to lack capacity both to conduct the proceedings himself and in relation to the matter or matters to which the application relates.

(2) The litigation friend's appointment continues until it is brought to an end by a court order.

(3) An application may be made by—

(a) P;
(b) his litigation friend; or
(c) any other person who is a party to the proceedings,

for the proceedings to come to an end.

(4) The applicant must serve a copy of the application notice seeking an order under this rule on all parties to the proceedings as soon as practicable and in any event within 21 days of the date on which it was issued.

A4.210

149 Practice direction in relation to litigation friends

A practice direction may make additional or different provision in relation to litigation friends.

PART 18
CHANGE OF SOLICITOR

A4.211

150 Change of solicitor

(1) This rule applies where a party to proceedings—

(a) for whom a solicitor is acting wants to change his solicitor or act in person; or
(b) after having conducted the proceedings in person, appoints a solicitor to act on his behalf (except where the solicitor is appointed only to act as an advocate for a hearing).

(2) The party proposing the change must—

(a) file a notice of the change with the court; and
(b) serve the notice of the change on every other party to the proceedings and, if there is one, on the solicitor who will cease to act.

(3) The notice must state the party's address for service.

(4) The notice filed at court must state that it has been served as required by paragraph (2)(b).

(5) Where there is a solicitor who will cease to act, he will continue to be considered the party's solicitor unless and until—

(a) the notice is filed and served in accordance with paragraphs (2), (3) and (4); or
(b) the court makes an order under rule 152 and the order is served in accordance with that rule.

A4.212

151 LSC funded clients

(1) Where the certificate of any person ("A") who is an LSC funded client is revoked or discharged—

(a) the solicitor who acted for A will cease to be the solicitor acting in the case as soon as his retainer is determined under regulation 4 of the Community Legal Services (Costs) Regulations 2000; and
(b) if A wishes to continue and appoints a solicitor to act on his behalf, rule 150(2), (3) and (4) will apply as if A had previously conducted the application in person.

(2) In this rule, "certificate" means a certificate issued under the Funding Code (approved under section 9 of the Access to Justice Act 1999).

A4.213

152 Order that a solicitor has ceased to act

(1) A solicitor may apply for an order declaring that he has ceased to be the solicitor acting for a party.

(2) Where an application is made under this rule—

(a) the solicitor must serve the application notice on the party for whom the solicitor is acting, unless the court directs otherwise; and
(b) the application must be supported by evidence.

(3) Where the court makes an order that a solicitor has ceased to act, the solicitor must—

(a) serve a copy of the order on every other party to the proceedings; and
(b) file a certificate of service.

A4.214

153 Removal of solicitor who has ceased to act on application of another party

(1) Where—

(a) a solicitor who has acted for a party—
  (i) has died;
  (ii) has become bankrupt;
  (iii) has ceased to practice; or
  (iv) cannot be found; and
(b) the party has not served a notice of a change of solicitor or notice of intention to act in person as required by rule 150,

any other party may apply for an order declaring that the solicitor has ceased to be the solicitor acting for the other party in the case.

(2) Where an application is made under this rule, the applicant must serve the application on the party to whose solicitor the application relates, unless the court directs otherwise.

(3) Where the court makes an order under this rule—

(a) the court will give directions about serving a copy of the order on every other party to the proceedings; and
(b) where the order is served by a party, that party must file a certificate of service.

A4.215

154 Practice direction relating to change of solicitor

A practice direction may make additional or different provision in relation to change of solicitor.

PART 19
COSTS

A4.216

155 Interpretation

(1) In this Part—

(a) "additional liability" means the percentage increase, the insurance premium, or the additional amount in respect of provision made by a membership organisation, as the case may be;
(b) "authorised court officer" means any officer of the Supreme Court Costs Office, whom the Lord Chancellor has authorised to assess costs;

(c) "costs" include fees, charges, disbursements, expenses, reimbursement permitted to a litigant in person, any additional liability incurred under a funding arrangement and any fee or reward charged by a lay representative for acting on behalf of a party in proceedings;
(d) "costs judge" means a taxing Master of the Supreme Court;
(e) "costs officer" means a costs judge or an authorised court officer;
(f) "detailed assessment" means the procedure by which the amount of costs or remuneration is decided by a costs officer in accordance with Part 47 of the Civil Procedure Rules 1998 (which are applied to proceedings under these Rules, with modifications, by rule 160);
(g) "fixed costs" are to be construed in accordance with the relevant practice direction;
(h) "fund" includes any estate or property held for the benefit of any person or class of persons and any fund to which a trustee or personal representative is entitled in his capacity as such;
(i) "funding arrangement" means an arrangement where a person has—
   (i) entered into a conditional fee agreement or a collective conditional fee agreement which provides for a success fee within the meaning of section 58(2) of the Courts and Legal Services Act 1990;
   (ii) taken out an insurance policy to which section 29 of the Access to Justice Act 1999 (recovery of insurance premiums by way of costs) applies; or
   (iii) made an agreement with a membership organisation to meet his legal costs;
(j) "insurance premium" means a sum of money paid or payable for insurance against the risk of incurring a costs liability in the proceedings, taken out after the event that is the subject matter of the claim;
(k) "membership organisation" means a body prescribed for the purposes of section 30 of the Access to Justice Act 1999 (recovery where body undertakes to meet costs liabilities);
(l) "paying party" means a party liable to pay costs;
(m) "percentage increase" means the percentage by which the amount of a legal representative's fee can be increased in accordance with a conditional fee agreement which provides for a success fee;
(n) "receiving party" means a party entitled to be paid costs;
(o) "summary assessment" means the procedure by which the court, when making an order about costs, orders payment of a sum of money instead of fixed costs or "detailed assessment".

(2) The costs to which the rules in this Part apply include—

(a) where the costs may be assessed by the court, costs payable by a client to his solicitor; and
(b) costs which are payable by one party to another party under the terms of a contract, where the court makes an order for an assessment of those costs.

(3) Where advocacy or litigation services are provided to a client under a conditional fee agreement, costs are recoverable under this Part notwithstanding that the client is liable to pay his legal representative's fees and expenses only to the extent that sums are recovered in respect of the proceedings, whether by way of costs or otherwise.

(4) In paragraph (3), the reference to a conditional fee agreement is to an agreement which satisfies all the conditions applicable to it by virtue of section 58 of the Courts and Legal Services Act 1990.

A4.217

156 Property and affairs—the general rule

Where the proceedings concern P's property and affairs the general rule is that the costs of the proceedings or of that part of the proceedings that concerns P's property and affairs, shall be paid by P or charged to his estate.

A4.218

157 Personal welfare—the general rule

Where the proceedings concern P's personal welfare the general rule is that there will be no order as to the costs of the proceedings or of that part of the proceedings that concerns P's personal welfare.

A4.219

158 Apportioning costs—the general rule

Where the proceedings concern both property and affairs and personal welfare the court, insofar as practicable, will apportion the costs as between the respective issues.

A4.220

159 Departing from the general rule

(1) The court may depart from rules 156 to 158 if the circumstances so justify, and in deciding whether departure is justified the court will have regard to all the circumstances, including—

- (a) the conduct of the parties;
- (b) whether a party has succeeded on part of his case, even if he has not been wholly successful; and
- (c) the role of any public body involved in the proceedings.

(2) The conduct of the parties includes—

- (a) conduct before, as well as during, the proceedings;
- (b) whether it was reasonable for a party to raise, pursue or contest a particular issue;
- (c) the manner in which a party has made or responded to an application or a particular issue; and
- (d) whether a party who has succeeded in his application or response to an application, in whole or in part, exaggerated any matter contained in his application or response.

(3) Without prejudice to rules 156 to 158 and the foregoing provisions of this rule, the court may permit a party to recover their fixed costs in accordance with the relevant practice direction.

A4.221

160 Rules about costs in the Civil Procedure Rules to apply

(1) Subject to the provisions of these Rules, Parts 44, 47 and 48 of the Civil Procedure Rules 1998 ("the 1998 Rules") shall apply with the modifications in this rule and such other modifications as may be appropriate, to costs incurred in relation to proceedings under these Rules as they apply to costs incurred in relation to proceedings in the High Court.

(2) The provisions of Part 47 of the 1998 Rules shall apply with the modifications in this rule and such other modifications as may be appropriate, to a detailed assessment of the remuneration of a deputy under these Rules as they apply to a detailed assessment of costs in proceedings to which the 1998 Rules apply.

(3) Where the definitions in Part 43 (referred to in Parts 44, 47 and 48) of the 1998 Rules are different from the definitions in rule 155 of these Rules, the latter shall prevail.

(4) Rules 44.1, 44.3(1) to (5), 44.6, 44.7, 44.9, 44.10, 44.11. 44.12 and 44.12A of the 1998 Rules do not apply.

(5) In rule 44.17 of the 1998 Rules, the references to Parts 45 and 46 do not apply.

(6) In rule 47.3(1)(c) of the 1998 Rules, the words "unless the costs are being assessed under rule 48.5 (costs where money is payable to a child or a patient)" are removed.

(7) In rule 47.3(2) of the 1998 Rules, the words "or a district judge" are removed.

(8) Rule 47.4(3) and (4) of the 1998 Rules do not apply.

(9) Rules 47.9(4), 47.10 and 47.11 of the 1998 Rules do not apply where the costs are to be paid by P or charged to his estate.

(10) Rules 48.2, 48.3, 48.6A, and 48.10 of the 1998 Rules do not apply.

(11) Rule 48.1(1) of the 1998 Rules is removed and is replaced by the following: "This paragraph applies where a person applies for an order for specific disclosure before the commencement of proceedings".

A4.222

161 Detailed assessment of costs

(1) Where the court orders costs to be assessed by way of detailed assessment, the detailed assessment proceedings shall take place in the High Court.

(2) A fee is payable in respect of the detailed assessment of costs and on an appeal against a decision made in a detailed assessment of costs.

(3) Where a detailed assessment of costs has taken place, the amount payable by P is the amount which the court certifies as payable.

A4.223

162 Employment of a solicitor by two or more persons

Where two or more persons having the same interest in relation to a matter act in relation to the proceedings by separate legal representatives, they shall not be permitted more than one set of costs of the representation unless and to the extent that the court certifies that the circumstances justify separate representation.

A4.224

163 Costs of the Official Solicitor

Any costs incurred by the Official Solicitor in relation to proceedings under these Rules or in carrying out any directions given by the court and not provided for by remuneration under rule 167 shall be paid by such persons or out of such funds as the court may direct.

A4.225

164 Procedure for assessing costs

Where the court orders a party, or P, to pay costs to another party it may either—

(a) make a summary assessment of the costs; or
(b) order a detailed assessment of the costs by a costs officer,

unless any rule, practice direction or other enactment provides otherwise.

A4.226

165 Costs following P's death

An order or direction that costs incurred during P's lifetime be paid out of or charged on his estate may be made within 6 years after P's death.

A4.227

166 Costs orders in favour of or against non-parties

(1) Where the court is considering whether to make a costs order in favour of or against a person who is not a party to proceedings—

- (a) that person must be added as a party to the proceedings for the purposes of costs only; and
- (b) he must be given a reasonable opportunity to attend a hearing at which the court will consider the matter further.

(2) This rule does not apply where the court is considering whether to make an order against the Legal Services Commission.

A4.228

167 Remuneration of a deputy, donee or attorney

(1) Where the court orders that a deputy, donee or attorney is entitled to remuneration out of P's estate for discharging his functions as such, the court may make such order as it thinks fit, including an order that—

- (a) he be paid a fixed amount;
- (b) he be paid at a specified rate; or
- (c) the amount of the remuneration shall be determined in accordance with the schedule of fees set out in the relevant practice direction.

(2) Any amount permitted by the court under paragraph (1) shall constitute a debt due from P's estate.

(3) The court may order a detailed assessment of the remuneration by a costs officer, in accordance with rule 164(b).

A4.229

168 Practice direction as to costs

A practice direction may make further provision in respect of costs in proceedings.

PART 20
APPEALS

A4.230

169 Scope of this Part

This Part applies to an appeal against any decision of the court except where, in relation to those cases that are to be dealt with in accordance with Part 22 (transitory and transitional provisions), Part 22 makes different provision.

A4.231

170 Interpretation

(1) In the following provisions of this Part—

- (a) "appeal judge" means a judge of the court to whom an appeal is made;
- (b) "first instance judge" means the judge of the court from whose decision an appeal is brought;
- (c) "appellant" means the person who brings or seeks to bring an appeal;
- (d) "respondent" means—

(i) a person other than the appellant who was a party to the proceedings before the first instance judge and who is affected by the appeal; or
(ii) a person who is permitted or directed by the first instance judge or the appeal judge to be a party to the appeal.

(2) In this Part, where the expression "permission" is used it means "permission to appeal" unless otherwise stated.

A4.232

171 Dealing with appeals

(1) The court may deal with an appeal or any part of an appeal at a hearing or without a hearing.

(2) In considering whether it is necessary to hold a hearing, the court shall have regard to the matters set out in rule 84(3).

(Rule 89 provides for reconsideration of orders made without a hearing or without notice to a person.)

A4.233

172 Permission to appeal

(1) Subject to paragraph (8), an appeal against a decision of the court may not be made without permission.

(2) Any person bound by an order of the court by virtue of rule 74 (persons to be bound as if parties) may seek permission to appeal under this Part.

(3) Permission is to be granted or refused in accordance with this Part.

(4) An application for permission to appeal may be made to the first instance judge or the appeal judge.

(5) Where an application for permission is refused by the first instance judge, a further application for permission may be made in accordance with paragraphs (6) and (7).

(6) Where the decision sought to be appealed is a decision of a district judge, permission may be granted or refused by—

(a) the President;
(b) the Vice-President;
(c) one of the other judges nominated by virtue of section 46(2)(a) to (c) of the Act; or
(d) a circuit judge.

(7) Where the decision sought to be appealed is a decision of a circuit judge, permission may only be granted or refused by one of the judges mentioned in paragraph (6)(a) to (c).

(8) Permission is not required to appeal against an order for committal to prison.

A4.234

173 Matters to be taken into account when considering an application for permission

(1) Permission to appeal shall be granted only where—

(a) the court considers that the appeal would have a real prospect of success; or
(b) there is some other compelling reason why the appeal should be heard.

(2) An order giving permission may—

(a) limit the issues to be heard; and
(b) be made subject to conditions.

A4.235

174 Parties to comply with the practice direction

All parties to an appeal must comply with any relevant practice direction.

A4.236

175 Appellant's notice

(1) Where the appellant seeks permission from the appeal judge, it must be requested in the appellant's notice.

(2) The appellant must file an appellant's notice at the court within—

- (a) such period as may be directed or specified in the order of the first instance judge; or
- (b) where that judge makes no such direction or order, 21 days after the date of the decision being appealed.

(3) The court will issue the appellant's notice and unless it orders otherwise, the appellant must serve the appellant's notice on each respondent and on such other persons as the court may direct, as soon as practicable and in any event within 21 days of the date on which it was issued.

(4) The appellant must file a certificate of service within 7 days beginning with the date on which he served the appellant's notice.

A4.237

176 Respondent's notice

(1) A respondent who—

- (a) is seeking permission from the appeal judge to appeal; or
- (b) wishes to ask the appeal judge to uphold the order of the first instance judge for reasons different from or additional to those given by the first instance judge,

must file a respondent's notice.

(2) Where the respondent seeks permission from the appeal judge, permission must be requested in the respondent's notice.

(3) A respondent's notice must be filed within—

- (a) such period as may be directed by the first instance judge; or
- (b) where the first instance judge makes no such direction, 21 days beginning with the date referred to in paragraph (4).

(4) The date is the soonest of—

- (a) the date on which the respondent is served with the appellant's notice where—
  - (i) permission to appeal was given by the first instance judge; or
  - (ii) permission to appeal is not required;
- (b) the date on which the respondent is served with notification that the appeal judge has given the appellant permission to appeal; or
- (c) the date on which the respondent is served with the notification that the application for permission to appeal and the appeal itself are to be heard together.

(5) The court will issue a respondent's notice and, unless it orders otherwise, the respondent must serve the respondent's notice on the appellant, any other respondent and on such other parties as the court may direct, as soon as practicable and in any event within 21 days of the date on which it was issued.

(6) The respondent must file a certificate of service within 7 days beginning with the date on which the copy of the respondent's notice was served.

A4.238

177 Variation of time

(1) An application to vary the time limit for filing an appellant's or respondent's notice must be made to the appeal judge.

(2) The parties may not agree to extend any date or time limit for or in respect of an appeal set by—

- (a) these Rules;
- (b) the relevant practice direction; or
- (c) an order of the appeal judge or the first instance judge.

A4.239

178 Power of appeal judge on appeal

(1) In relation to an appeal, an appeal judge has all the powers of the first instance judge whose decision is being appealed.

(2) In particular, the appeal judge has the power to—

- (a) affirm, set aside or vary any order made by the first instance judge;
- (b) refer any claim or issue to that judge for determination;
- (c) order a new hearing;
- (d) make a costs order.

(3) The appeal judge may exercise his powers in relation to the whole or part of an order made by the first instance judge.

A4.240

179 Determination of appeals

(1) An appeal will be limited to a review of the decision of the first instance judge unless—

- (a) a practice direction makes different provision for a particular category of appeal; or
- (b) the appeal judge considers that in the circumstances of the appeal it would be in the interests of justice to hold a re-hearing.

(2) Unless he orders otherwise, the appeal judge will not receive—

- (a) oral evidence; or
- (b) evidence that was not before the first instance judge.

(3) The appeal judge will allow an appeal where the decision of the first instance judge was—

- (a) wrong; or
- (b) unjust, because of a serious procedural or other irregularity in the proceedings before the first instance judge.

(4) The appeal judge may draw any inference of fact that he considers justified on the evidence.

(5) At the hearing of the appeal a party may not rely upon a matter not contained in his appellant's or respondent's notice unless the appeal judge gives permission.

A4.241

180 Allocation

Except in accordance with the relevant practice direction—

- (a) an appeal from a first instance decision of a circuit judge shall be heard by a judge of the court nominated by virtue of section 46(2)(a) to (c) of the Act; and
- (b) an appeal from a decision of a district judge shall be heard by a circuit judge.

Appeals to the Court of Appeal

A4.242

181 Appeals against decision of a puisne judge of the High Court, etc

(1) Where the decision sought to be appealed is a decision of a judge nominated by virtue of section 46(2)(a) to (c) of the Act, an appeal will lie only to the Court of Appeal.

(2) The judge nominated by virtue of section 46(2)(a) to (c) of the Act may grant permission to appeal to the Court of Appeal in accordance with this Part, where the decision sought to be appealed was a decision made by a judge so nominated as a first instance judge.

A4.243

182 Second appeals

(1) A decision of a judge of the court which was itself made on appeal from a judge of the court may only be appealed further to the Court of Appeal.

(2) Permission is required from the Court of Appeal for such an appeal.

(3) The Court of Appeal will not give permission unless it considers that—

(a) the appeal would raise an important point of principle or practice; or
(b) there is some other compelling reason for the Court of Appeal to hear it.

(4) Nothing in this rule or in rule 181 applies to a second appeal from a decision of a nominated officer.

PART 21
ENFORCEMENT

A4.244

183 Enforcement methods—general

(1) The rules in this Part make provision for the enforcement of judgments and orders.

(2) The relevant practice direction may set out methods of enforcing judgments or orders.

(3) An application for an order for enforcement may be made on application by any person in accordance with Part 10.

A4.245

184 Application of the Civil Procedure Rules 1998 and RSC Orders

The following provisions apply, as far as they are relevant and with such modifications as may be necessary, to the enforcement of orders made in proceedings under these Rules—

(a) Parts 70 (General Rules about Enforcement of Judgments and Orders), 71 (Orders to Obtain Information from Judgment Debtors), 72 (Third Party Debt Orders) and 73 (Charging Orders, Stop Orders and Stop Notices) of the Civil Procedure Rules 1998; and
(b) Orders 45 (Enforcement of Judgments and Orders: General), 46 (Writs of Execution: General) and 47 (Writs of Fieri Facias) of the Rules of the Supreme Court.

Orders for committal

A4.246

185 Contempt of court—generally

An application relating to the committal of a person for contempt of court shall be made to a judge and the power to punish for contempt may be exercised by an order of committal.

A4.247

186 Application for order of committal

(1) An application for an order of committal must be made by filing an application notice, stating the grounds of the application, and must be supported by an affidavit made in accordance with the relevant practice direction.

(2) Subject to paragraph (3), the application notice, a copy of the affidavit in support thereof and notice of the date of the hearing of the application must be served personally on the person sought to be committed.

(3) Without prejudice to its powers under Part 6, the court may dispense with service under this rule if it thinks it just to do so.

A4.248

187 Oral evidence

If on the hearing of the application the person sought to be committed expresses a wish to give oral evidence on his own behalf, he shall be entitled to do so.

A4.249

188 Hearing for committal order

(1) Except where the court permits, no grounds shall be relied upon at the hearing except the grounds set out in the application notice.

(2) Notwithstanding rule 90(1) (general rule—hearing to be in private), when determining an application for committal the court will hold the hearing in public unless it directs otherwise.

(3) If the court hearing an application in private decides that a person has committed a contempt of court, it shall state publicly—

(a) the name of that person;
(b) in general terms the nature of the contempt in respect of which the order of committal is being made; and
(c) any punishment imposed.

(4) If the person sought to be committed does not attend the hearing, the court may fix a date and time for the person to be brought before the court.

A4.250

189 Power to suspend execution of committal order

(1) A judge who has made an order of committal may direct that the execution of the order of committal shall be suspended for such period or on such terms and conditions as may be specified.

(2) Where an order is suspended under paragraph (1), the applicant for the order of committal must, unless the court otherwise directs, serve on the person against whom it was made a notice informing him of the making and terms of the direction under that paragraph.

A4.251

190 Warrant for arrest

A warrant for the arrest of a person against whom an order of committal has been made shall not, without further order of the court, be enforced more than 2 years after the date on which the warrant is issued.

A4.252

191 Discharge of person committed

(1) The court may, on the application of any person committed to prison for contempt of court, discharge him.

(2) Where a person has been committed for failing to comply with a judgment or order requiring him to deliver any thing to some other person or to deposit it in court or elsewhere, and a writ of sequestration has also been issued to enforce that judgment or order, then, if the thing is in the custody or power of the person committed, the commissioners appointed by the writ of sequestration may take possession of it as if it were the property of that person and, without prejudice to the generality of paragraph (1), the court may discharge the person committed and may give such directions for dealing with the thing taken by the commissioners as it thinks fit.

A4.253

192 Penal notices

(1) The court may direct that a penal notice is to be attached to any order warning the person on whom the copy of the order is served that disobeying the order would be a contempt of court punishable by imprisonment or a fine.

(2) Unless the court gives a direction under paragraph (1), a penal notice may not be attached to any order.

(3) A penal notice is to be in the following terms: "You must obey this order. If you do not, you may be sent to prison for contempt of court.".

A4.254

193 Saving for other powers

The rules in this Part do not limit the power of the court to make an order requiring a person guilty of contempt to pay a fine or give security for his good behaviour and those rules, so far as applicable, shall apply in relation to an application for such an order as they apply in relation to an application for an order of committal.

A4.255

194 Power of court to commit on its own initiative

The preceding provisions of these Rules shall not be taken as affecting the power of the court to make an order for committal on its own initiative against a person guilty of contempt of court.

PART 22
TRANSITORY AND TRANSITIONAL PROVISIONS

A4.256

195 Transitory provision: applications by former receivers

(1) This rule and rule 196—

- (a) apply in any case where a person becomes a deputy by virtue of paragraph 1(2) of Schedule 5 to the Act; but
- (b) shall cease to have effect at the end of the period specified in the relevant practice direction.

(2) The deputy may make an application to the court in connection with—

- (a) any decision in connection with the day-to-day management of P's property and affairs; or
- (b) any supplementary decision which is necessary to give full effect to any order made, or directions given, before 1st October 2007 under Part 7 of the Mental Health Act 1983.

(3) Decisions within paragraph (2) include those that may be specified in the relevant practice direction.

(4) An application—

- (a) may relate only to a particular decision or decisions to be made on P's behalf;
- (b) must specify details of the decision or decisions to be made; and
- (c) must be made using the application form set out in the relevant practice direction.

A4.257

196 Transitory provision: dealing with applications under rule 195

(1) The court may, in determining an application under rule 195, treat the application as if it were an application to vary the functions of the deputy which is made in accordance with the relevant practice direction made under rule 71, and dispose of it accordingly.

(2) In any other case, an application under rule 195 may be determined by an order made or directions given by—

- (a) the court; or
- (b) a person nominated under paragraph (3).

(3) The Senior Judge or the President may nominate an officer or officers of the court for the purpose of determining applications under rule 195.

(4) Where an officer has been nominated under paragraph (3) to determine an application, he may refer to a judge any proceedings or any question arising in any proceedings which ought, in the officer's opinion, to be considered by a judge.

A4.258

197 Appeal against a decision of a nominated officer

(1) This rule applies in relation to decisions made under rules 195 and 196 by a nominated officer.

(2) An appeal from a decision to which this rule applies lies to a judge of the court nominated by virtue of section 46(2)(e) of the Act.

(3) No permission is required for an appeal under paragraph (2).

(4) A judge determining an appeal under paragraph (2) has all the powers that an appeal judge on appeal has by virtue of rule 178.

(5) An appeal from a decision made under paragraph (2) ("a second appeal") lies to a judge of the court nominated by virtue of section 46(2)(d) of the Act.

(6) A second appeal may be made from a decision of a nominated officer, and a judge to whom such an appeal is made may, if he considers the matter is one which ought to be heard by a judge of the court nominated by virtue of section 46(2)(a) to (c), transfer the matter to such a judge.

(7) An appeal from a decision made on a second appeal lies to the Court of Appeal.

A4.259

198 Application of Rules to proceedings within paragraphs 3 and 12 of Schedule 5 to the Act

(1) In this rule, "pending proceedings" means proceedings on an application within paragraph 3 or 12 of Schedule 5 to the Act.

(2) A practice direction shall make provision for the extent to which these Rules shall apply to pending proceedings.

A4.260

199 Practice direction

A practice direction may make additional or different provision in relation to transitory and transitional matters.

PART 23
MISCELLANEOUS

A4.261

200 Order or directions requiring a person to give security for discharge of functions

(1) This rule applies where the court makes an order or gives a direction—

(a) conferring functions on any person (whether as deputy or otherwise); and
(b) requiring him to give security for the discharge of those functions.

(2) The person on whom functions are conferred must give the security before he undertakes to discharge his functions, unless the court permits it to be given subsequently.

(3) Paragraphs (4) to (6) apply where the security is required to be given before any action can be taken.

(4) Subject to paragraph (5), the security must be given in accordance with the requirements of regulation 33(2)(a) of the Public Guardian Regulations (which makes provision about the giving of security by means of a bond that is endorsed by an authorised insurance company or deposit-taker).

(5) The court may impose such other requirements in relation to the giving of the security as it considers appropriate (whether in addition to, or instead of, those specified in paragraph (4)).

(6) In specifying the date from which the order or directions referred to in paragraph (1) are to take effect, the court will have regard to the need to postpone that date for such reasonable period as would enable the Public Guardian to be satisfied that—

(a) if paragraph (4) applies, the requirements of regulation 34 of the Public Guardian Regulations have been met in relation to the security; and
(b) any other requirements imposed by the court under paragraph (5) have been met.

(7) "The Public Guardian Regulations" means the Lasting Powers of Attorney, Enduring Powers of Attorney and Public Guardian Regulations 2007.

A4.262

201 Objections to registration of an enduring power of attorney: request for directions

(1) This rule applies in any case where—

(a) the Public Guardian (having received a notice of objection to the registration of an instrument creating an enduring power of attorney) is prevented by paragraph 13(5) of Schedule 4 to the Act from registering the instrument except in accordance with the court's directions; and
(b) on or before the relevant day, no application for the court to give such directions has been made under Part 9 (how to start proceedings).

(2) In paragraph (1)(b) the relevant day is the later of—

(a) the final day of the period specified in paragraph 13(4) of Schedule 4 to the Act; or
(b) the final day of the period of 14 days beginning with the date on which the Public Guardian receives the notice of objection.

(3) The Public Guardian may seek the court's directions about registering the instrument by filing a request in accordance with the relevant practice direction.

(4) As soon as practicable and in any event within 21 days of the date on which the request was made, the court will notify—

(a) the person (or persons) who gave the notice of objection; and
(b) the attorney or, if more than one, each of them.

(5) As soon as practicable and in any event within 21 days of the date on which the request is filed, the Public Guardian must notify the donor of the power that the request has been so filed.

(6) The notice under paragraph (4) must—

(a) state that the Public Guardian has requested the court's directions about registration;
(b) state that the court will give directions in response to the request unless an application under Part 9 is made to it before the end of the period of 21 days commencing with the date on which the notice is issued; and
(c) set out the steps required to make such an application.

(7) "Notice of objection" means a notice of objection which is made in accordance with paragraph 13(4) of Schedule 4 to the Act.

A4.263

A4.264

202 Disposal of property where P ceases to lack capacity

(1) This rule applies where P ceases to lack capacity.

(2) In this rule, "relevant property" means any property belonging to P and forming part of his estate, and which—

(a) remains under the control of anyone appointed by order of the court; or
(b) is held under the direction of the court.

(3) The court may at any time make an order for any relevant property to be transferred to P, or at P's direction, provided that it is satisfied that P has the capacity to make decisions in relation to that property.

(4) An application for an order under this rule is to be made in accordance with Part 10.

COURT OF PROTECTION FEES ORDER 2007

(SI 2007/1745)

Made . . . . *16th July 2007*
Laid before Parliament . . . . *19th July 2007*
Coming into force . . . . *1st October 2007*

The Lord Chancellor makes this Order in exercise of the powers conferred by section 54(1) and (2) and 65(1) of the Mental Capacity Act 2005, with the consent of the Treasury and after consulting in accordance with section 54(3) of that Act:

A4.265

1 Citation and commencement

This Order may be cited as the Court of Protection Fees Order 2007 and comes into force on 1 October 2007.

A4.266

2 Interpretation

In this Order—

"the Act" means the Mental Capacity Act 2005;
"appellant" means the person who brings or seeks to bring an appeal;
"court" means the Court of Protection;
"P" means any person (other than a protected party) who lacks or, so far as consistent with the context, is alleged to lack capacity to make a decision or decisions in relation to any matter that is the subject of an application to the court and references to a person who lacks capacity are to be construed in accordance with the Act;
"protected party" means a party or an intended party (other than P or a child) who lacks capacity to conduct the proceedings;
"the Regulations" means the Lasting Powers of Attorney, Enduring Powers of Attorney and Public Guardian Regulations 2007; and
"the Rules" means the Court of Protection Rules 2007.

A4.267

3 Schedule of fees

The fees set out in the Schedule to this Order shall apply in accordance with the following provisions of this Order.

A4.268

4 Application fee

(1) An application fee shall be payable by the applicant on making an application under Part 9 of the Rules (how to start proceedings) in accordance with the following provisions of this article.

(2) Where permission to start proceedings is required under Part 8 of the Rules (permission), the fee prescribed by paragraph (1) shall be payable on making an application for permission.

(3) The fee prescribed by paragraph (1) shall not be payable where the application is made under—

(a) rule 67 of the Rules (applications relating to lasting powers of attorney) by—

(i) the donee of a lasting power of attorney, or
(ii) a person named in a statement made by the donor of a lasting power of attorney in accordance with paragraph 2(1)(c)(i) of Part 1 of Schedule 1 to the Act,

and is solely in respect of an objection to the registration of a lasting power of attorney; or

(b) rule 68 of the Rules (applications relating to enduring powers of attorney) by—
(i) a donor of an enduring power of attorney,
(ii) an attorney under an enduring power of attorney, or
(iii) a person listed in paragraph 6(1) of Part 3 of Schedule 4 to the Act,

and is solely in respect of an objection to the registration of an enduring power of attorney.

(4) The fee prescribed by paragraph (1) shall not be payable where the application is made by the Public Guardian.

(5) Where a fee has been paid under paragraph (1) it shall be refunded where P dies within five days of the application being filed.

A4.269

5 Appeal fee

(1) An appeal fee shall be payable by the appellant on the filing of an appellant's notice under Part 20 of the Rules (appeals) in accordance with the following provisions of this article.

(2) The fee prescribed by paragraph (1) shall not be payable where the appeal is—

(a) brought by the Public Guardian; or
(b) an appeal against a decision of a nominated officer made under rule 197 of the Rules (appeal against a decision of a nominated officer).

(3) The fee prescribed by paragraph (1) shall be refunded where P dies within five days of the appellant's notice being filed.

A4.270

6 Hearing fees

(1) A hearing fee shall be payable by the applicant where the court has—

(a) held a hearing in order to determine the case; and
(b) made a final order, declaration or decision.

(2) A hearing fee shall be payable by the appellant in relation to an appeal where the court has—

(a) held a hearing in order to determine the appeal; and
(b) made a final order, declaration or decision in relation to the appeal.

(3) The fees prescribed by paragraphs (1) and (2) shall not be payable where the hearing is in respect of an application or appeal brought by the Public Guardian.

(4) The fee prescribed by paragraph (2) shall not be payable where the hearing is in respect of an appeal against a decision of a nominated officer made under rule 197 of the Rules (appeal against a decision of a nominated officer).

(5) The fee prescribed by paragraph (1) shall not be payable where the applicant was not required to pay an application fee under Article 4(1) by virtue of Article 4(3).

(6) The fees prescribed by paragraphs (1) and (2) shall be payable by the applicant or appellant as the case may be within 30 days of the date of the invoice for the fee.

A4.271

7 Fee for request for copy of court document

(1) A fee for a copy of a court document shall be payable by the person requesting the copy of the document.

(2) A fee for a certified copy of a court document shall be payable by the person requesting the certified copy of the document.

(3) The fees prescribed by paragraphs (1) and (2) shall be payable at the time the request for the copy is made to the court.

A4.272

8 Exemptions

(1) Subject to paragraph (2) no fee shall be payable under this Order by a person who, at the time when a fee would otherwise become payable, is in receipt of any qualifying benefit.

(2) Paragraph (1) does not apply to a person who has an award of damages in excess of £16,000 which has been disregarded for the purposes of determining eligibility for that benefit.

(3) The following are qualifying benefits for the purposes of paragraph 1 above—

- (a) income support under the Social Security Contributions and Benefits Act 1992;
- (b) working tax credit, provided that—
  - (i) child tax credit is being paid to the person, or to a couple (as defined in section 3(5)(A) of the Tax Credits Act 2002) which includes the person; or
  - (ii) there is a disability element or severe disability element (or both) to the tax credit received by the person;
- (c) income-based jobseeker's allowance under the Jobseekers Act 1995;
- (d) guarantee credit under the State Pensions Credit Act 2002;
- (e) council tax benefit under the Social Security Contributions and Benefits Act 1992; and
- (f) housing benefit under the Social Security Contributions and Benefits Act 1992.

A4.273

9 Reductions and remissions in exceptional circumstances

Where it appears to the Lord Chancellor that the payment of any fee prescribed by this Order would, owing to the exceptional circumstances of the particular case, involve undue hardship, he may reduce or remit the fee in that case.

A4.274

10 Transitional provision

(1) In this article "Court of Protection" means the office of the Supreme Court called the Court of Protection which ceases to exist under section 45(6) of the Act.

(2) Where a hearing that takes place on or after 1 October 2007 was listed by the Court of Protection before 1 October 2007, no hearing fee shall be payable under Article 6.

SCHEDULE
Fees to be Taken

Article 3

A4.275

Column 1	Column 2
Application fee (Article 4)	£400.00
Appeal fee (Article 5)	£400.00

Hearing fees (Article 6)	£500.00
Copy of a document fee (Article 7(1))	£5.00
Certified copy of a document fee (Article 7(2))	£25.00

MENTAL CAPACITY ACT 2005 (TRANSITIONAL AND CONSEQUENTIAL PROVISIONS) ORDER 2007

(SI 2007/1898)

Made . . . . 22nd June 2007

Laid before Parliament . . . . 4th July 2007

Coming into force . . . . 1st October 2007

The Lord Chancellor makes the following Order, in exercise of the powers conferred upon him by section 67(3) of the Mental Capacity Act 2005.

A4.276

1 Citation and commencement

This Order may be cited as the Mental Capacity Act 2005 (Transitional and Consequential Provisions) Order 2007, and comes into force on 1 October 2007.

A4.277

2 Interpretation

In this Order—

(a) "the Act" means the Mental Capacity Act 2005; and
(b) "Court of Protection" refers—
 (i) the first time the expression appears in article 4, to the office of the Supreme Court called the Court of Protection mentioned in section 45(6) of the Act, and
 (ii) where the expression appears in articles 3, 4(a) and (b), to the superior court of record established by section 45(1) of the Act.

A4.278

3 Proceedings begun in the High Court before 1 October 2007

(1) This article applies to any proceedings about P's personal welfare begun in the High Court before 1 October 2007 in respect of which the Court of Protection would, but for this article, have jurisdiction on and after that date under section 16 of the Act.

(2) The proceedings may continue to be dealt with, until they are finally decided, in accordance with the arrangements existing immediately before 1 October 2007.

(3) For the purposes of paragraph (2), an application is finally decided when it is determined and there is no possibility of the determination being reversed or varied on an appeal.

(4) In dealing with proceedings under this article, the High Court retains all the powers and jurisdiction in relation to any matter that is the subject of the proceedings that it had immediately before the commencement of the Act.

(5) In this article—

- (a) "P" means any person (other than a protected party) who lacks, or so far as consistent with the context is alleged to lack, capacity to make a decision or decisions in relation to any matter that is the subject of an application to the court and references to a person who lacks capacity are to be construed in accordance with the Act;
- (b) "personal welfare" is to be construed in accordance with section 17 of the Act; and
- (c) "protected party" means a party, or an intended party (other than P or a child), who lacks capacity to conduct the proceedings.

A4.279

4 Senior Judge of the Court of Protection

The person who, immediately before the commencement of Part 2 of the Act, holds the office of Master of the Court of Protection, shall be treated as—

- (a) being a circuit judge nominated under section 46(1) of the Act to exercise the jurisdiction of the Court of Protection; and
- (b) having been appointed the Senior Judge of the Court of Protection under section 46(4) of the Act.

A4.280

5 Advance decisions to refuse life-sustaining treatment

(1) An advance decision refusing life-sustaining treatment shall be treated as valid and applicable to a treatment and does not have to satisfy the requirements mentioned in paragraph (3) if the conditions in paragraph (2) are met.

(2) The conditions that must be met are that—

- (a) a person providing health care for a person ("P") reasonably believes that—
  - (i) P has made the advance decision refusing life-sustaining treatment before 1 October 2007, and
  - (ii) P has lacked the capacity to comply with the provisions mentioned in paragraph (3) since 1 October 2007;
- (b) the advance decision is in writing;
- (c) P has not—
  - (i) withdrawn the decision at a time when he had capacity to do so, or
  - (ii) done anything else clearly inconsistent with the advance decision remaining his fixed decision;
- (d) P does not have the capacity to give or refuse consent to the treatment in question at the material time;
- (e) the treatment in question is the treatment specified in the advance decision;
- (f) any circumstances specified in the advance decision are present; and
- (g) there are no reasonable grounds for believing that circumstances exist which P did not anticipate at the time of the advance decision and which would have affected his decision had he anticipated them.

(3) The requirements that do not have to be satisfied are as follows—

- (a) the requirement for the decision to be verified by a statement by P to the effect that the advance decision is to apply to that treatment even if life is at risk (section 25(5)(a) of the Act); and
- (b) the requirement for a signed and witnessed advance decision (section 25(6)(b) to (d) of the Act).

(4) In this article, "advance decision" has the meaning given in section 24(1) of the Act.

A4.281

6 Minor and consequential amendments

Schedule 1 contains minor and consequential amendments.

SCHEDULE 1
MINOR AND CONSEQUENTIAL AMENDMENTS

Article 6

Trustee Savings Bank Life Annuity Regulations 1930

A4.282

1 In regulation 16(2) of the Trustee Savings Bank Life Annuity Regulations 1930—

(a) for the words "a person who is incapable, by reason of mental disorder within the meaning of the Mental Health Act 1959, of managing and administering his property and affairs" substitute "a person who lacks mental capacity within the meaning of the Mental Capacity Act 2005 (c 9) to administer and manage his property and affairs"; and
(b) for the word "receiver" substitute "deputy".

Savings Contract Regulations 1969

2 (1) The Savings Contract Regulations 1969 are amended in accordance with this paragraph.

(2) In regulation 2(1) (interpretation), omit the entries for "mentally disordered person" and "receiver" and, in the appropriate alphabetical position, insert—

(a) ""deputy" in the application of these Regulations to England and Wales, means, in relation to any decision made for a person who lacks capacity, a deputy appointed by the Court of Protection for that person with power to make decisions in relation to the matters in question;"; and
(b) ""person who lacks capacity" means a person who lacks capacity within the meaning of the Mental Capacity Act 2005 (c 9);".

(3) In regulation 7 (payment in case of mentally disordered persons)—

(a) in the title, for "mentally disordered persons" substitute "persons who lack capacity"; and
(b) in paragraphs (1) and (2) in each place—
  (i) for "mentally disordered person" substitute "person who lacks capacity", and
  (ii) for "receiver" substitute "deputy".

(4) In regulation 12 (persons under disability)—

(a) for "mentally disordered person" substitute "person who lacks capacity"; and
(b) for "receiver" substitute "deputy".

(5) In regulation 27 (application to Scotland)—

(a) in paragraph (a), for "mentally disordered person" substitute "person who lacks capacity"; and
(b) in paragraph (b), for "receiver in relation to a mentally disordered person" substitute "deputy in relation to a person who lacks capacity".

(6) In regulation 28(2) (application to Northern Ireland)—

(a) in sub-paragraph (a), for "mentally disordered person" substitute "person who lacks capacity"; and
(b) in sub-paragraph (b), for "receiver in relation to a mentally disordered person" substitute "deputy in relation to a person who lacks capacity".

(7) In regulation 29(2)(a) (application to the Isle of Man), for "receiver in relation to a mentally disordered person" substitute "deputy in relation to a person who lacks capacity".

(8) In regulation 30 (application to the Channel Islands)—

(a) in paragraphs (2)(a) and (3)(a), for "mentally disordered person" substitute "person who lacks capacity"; and

(b) in paragraphs (2)(b) and (3)(b), for "receiver in relation to a mentally disordered person" substitute "deputy in relation to a person who lacks capacity".

Pensions Increase (Judicial Pensions) Regulations 1972

3 In paragraph 9 of the Schedule to the Pensions Increase (Judicial Pensions) Regulations 1972, omit the reference to a Master of the Court of Protection except in the case of a person holding that office immediately before the commencement of this paragraph or who had previously retired from that office or died.

National Savings Bank Regulations 1972

4 (1) The National Savings Bank Regulations 1972 are amended in accordance with this paragraph.

(2) In regulation 2(1) (interpretation), omit the entries for "mentally disordered person" and "receiver" and, in the appropriate alphabetical position, insert—

(a) ""deputy" in the application of these Regulations to England and Wales, means, in relation to any decision made for a person who lacks capacity, a deputy appointed by the Court of Protection for that person with power to make decisions in relation to the matters in question;"; and

(b) ""person who lacks capacity" means a person who lacks capacity within the meaning of the Mental Capacity Act 2005 (c 9);".

(3) In regulation 7 (mentally disordered persons)—

(a) in the title, for "Mentally disordered persons" substitute "Persons who lack capacity";

(b) in paragraph (1), for "mentally disordered person, by his receiver" substitute "person who lacks capacity, by his deputy";

(c) in paragraphs (2), (3) and (4) in each place—

(i) for "mentally disordered person" substitute "person who lacks capacity", and

(ii) for "receiver" substitute "deputy";

(4) In regulation 8(4)(c) (joint accounts)—

(a) for "mentally disordered person" substitute "person who lacks capacity"; and

(b) for "receiver" substitute "deputy".

(5) In regulation 9(4) (trust accounts)—

(a) for both references to "mentally disordered person" substitute "person who lacks capacity"; and

(b) for "receiver" substitute "deputy".

(6) In regulation 37(1)(b) (payment under nomination)—

(a) for "mentally disordered person" substitute "person who lacks capacity"; and

(b) for "receiver" substitute "deputy".

(7) In regulation 45 (persons under disability)—

(a) for "mentally disordered person" substitute "person who lacks capacity"; and

(b) for "receiver" substitute "deputy".

(8) In regulation 57(2)(a) (application to the Isle of Man), for "receiver in relation to a mentally disordered person" substitute "deputy in relation to a person who lacks capacity".

(9) In regulation 58 (application to the Channel Islands)—

(a) in paragraphs (2)(a) and (3)(a), for "mentally disordered person" substitute "person who lacks capacity"; and

(b) in paragraphs (2)(b) and (3)(b), for "receiver in relation to a mentally disordered person" substitute "deputy in relation to a person who lacks capacity".

Premium Savings Bond Regulations 1972

5 (1) The Premium Savings Bond Regulations 1972 are amended in accordance with this paragraph.

(2) In regulation 2(1) (interpretation), omit the entries for "mentally disordered person" and "receiver" and, in the appropriate alphabetical position, insert—

- (a) ""deputy" in the application of these Regulations to England and Wales, means, in relation to any decision made for a person who lacks capacity, a deputy appointed by the Court of Protection for that person with power to make decisions in relation to the matters in question;"; and
- (b) ""person who lacks capacity" means a person who lacks capacity within the meaning of the Mental Capacity Act 2005 (c 9);".

(3) In regulation 4 (persons entitled to purchase and hold bonds)—

- (a) in paragraph (3)(b), for "mentally disordered person, by his receiver" substitute "a person who lacks capacity, by his deputy"; and
- (b) in paragraph (5)(b), for "mentally disordered person" substitute "person who lacks capacity".

(4) In regulation 10 (payment in case of mentally disordered persons)—

- (a) in the title, for "Mentally disordered persons" substitute "Persons who lack capacity";
- (b) in paragraph (1)—
  - (i) for "mentally disordered person" substitute "person who lacks capacity", and
  - (ii) for "receiver" substitute "deputy"; and
- (c) in paragraph (2), for "mentally disordered person for whose estate no receiver" substitute "person who lacks capacity for whom no deputy has been appointed in relation to his property and affairs".

(5) In regulation 16 (persons under disability)—

- (a) for "mentally disordered person" substitute "person who lacks capacity"; and
- (b) for "receiver" substitute "deputy".

(6) In regulation 31 (application to Scotland)—

- (a) in paragraph (a), for "mentally disordered person" substitute "person who lacks capacity"; and
- (b) in paragraph (b), for "receiver in relation to a mentally disordered person" substitute "deputy in relation to a person who lacks capacity".

(7) In regulation 32(2) (application to Northern Ireland)—

- (a) in paragraph (a), for "mentally disordered person" substitute "person who lacks capacity"; and
- (b) in paragraph (b), for "receiver in relation to a mentally disordered person" substitute "deputy in relation to a person who lacks capacity".

(8) In regulation 33(2)(a) (application to the Isle of Man), for "receiver in relation to a mentally disordered person" substitute "deputy in relation to a person who lacks capacity".

(9) In regulation 34 (application to the Channel Islands)—

- (a) in paragraphs (2)(a) and (3)(a), for "mentally disordered person" substitute "person who lacks capacity"; and
- (b) in paragraphs (2)(b) and (3)(b), for "receiver in relation to a mentally disordered person" substitute "deputy in relation to a person who lacks capacity".

National Savings Stock Register Regulations 1976

6 (1) The National Savings Stock Register Regulations 1976 are amended in accordance with this paragraph.

(2) In regulation 2(1) (interpretation), omit the entries for "mentally disordered person" and "receiver" and, in the appropriate alphabetical position, insert—

(a) ""deputy" in the application of these Regulations to England and Wales, means, in relation to any decision made for a person who lacks capacity, a deputy appointed by the Court of Protection for that person with power to make decisions in relation to the matters in question;"; and

(b) ""person who lacks capacity" means a person who lacks capacity within the meaning of the Mental Capacity Act 2005 (c 9);".

(3) In regulation 31 (persons under disability)—

(a) in paragraphs (1) and (2) in each place—
   (i) for "mentally disordered person" substitute "person who lacks capacity"; and
   (ii) for "receiver" substitute "deputy"; and

(b) in paragraphs (3) and (4), for "mentally disordered person" substitute "person who lacks capacity".

(4) In regulation 59 (application to Scotland)—

(a) in paragraph (a), for "mentally disordered person" substitute "person who lacks capacity"; and

(b) in paragraph (b), for "receiver in relation to a mentally disordered person" substitute "deputy in relation to a person who lacks capacity".

(5) In regulation 60(2) (application to Northern Ireland)—

(a) in paragraph (a), for "mentally disordered person" substitute "person who lacks capacity"; and

(b) in paragraph (b), for "receiver in relation to a mentally disordered person" substitute "deputy in relation to a person who lacks capacity".

(6) In regulation 61(2)(a) (application to the Isle of Man), for "receiver in relation to a mentally disordered person" substitute "deputy in relation to a person who lacks capacity".

(7) In regulation 62 (application to the Channel Islands)—

(a) in paragraphs (2)(a) and (3)(a), for "mentally disordered person" substitute "person who lacks capacity"; and

(b) in paragraphs (2)(b) and (3)(b), for "receiver in relation to a mentally disordered person" substitute "deputy in relation to a person who lacks capacity".

Motor Vehicles (Tests) Regulations 1981

7 In regulation 9(1)(c) (cessations: general) of the Motor Vehicles (Tests) Regulations 1981, for the words from "patient" to "Mental Health Act 1983" substitute "person who lacks capacity (within the meaning of the Mental Capacity Act 2005 (c 9)) to carry on the activities covered by the authorisation".

The Mental Health Review Tribunal Rules 1983

8 For rule 7(c) (notice to other persons interested) of the Mental Health Review Tribunal Rules 1983, substitute—

"(c) where there is an extant order of either—
   (i) the office of the Supreme Court called the Court of Protection mentioned in section 45(6) of the Mental Capacity Act 2005 (c 9), or
   (ii) the superior court of record established by section 45(1) of the Mental Capacity Act 2005,

to the court referred to in sub-paragraph (ii) of this rule;"

Savings Certificates (Yearly Plan) Regulations 1984

9 (1) The Savings Certificates (Yearly Plan) Regulations 1984 are amended in accordance with this paragraph.

(2) In regulation 2 (interpretation), omit the entries for "mentally disordered person" and "receiver" and, in the appropriate alphabetical position, insert—

(a) ""deputy" in the application of these Regulations to England and Wales, means, in relation to any decision made for a person who lacks capacity, a deputy appointed by the Court of Protection for that person with power to make decisions in relation to the matters in question;"; and
(b) ""person who lacks capacity" means a person who lacks capacity within the meaning of the Mental Capacity Act 2005 (c 9);".

(3) In regulation 4(2)(b) (persons entitled to enter into agreements and to hold certificates), for "mentally disordered person, by his receiver" substitute "person who lacks capacity, by his deputy".

(4) In regulation 5(2) (maximum payments), for "mentally disordered person" substitute "person who lacks capacity".

(5) In regulation 8 (repayment in case of persons under 7 years of age and mentally disordered persons)—

(a) in the title, for "mentally disordered persons" substitute "persons who lack capacity";
(b) in paragraph (2), for "mentally disordered person, by his receiver" substitute "person who lacks capacity, by his deputy"; and
(c) in paragraph (3), for "mentally disordered person for whose estate no receiver" substitute "person who lacks capacity for whom no deputy".

(6) In regulation 9(1)(a) (repayment in case of joint trustees)—

(a) for "mentally disordered person" substitute "person who lacks capacity"; and
(b) for "receiver" substitute "deputy".

(7) In regulation 10(1)(a) (repayment in case of certificate held by person jointly)—

(a) for "mentally disordered person" substitute "person who lacks capacity"; and
(b) for "receiver" substitute "deputy".

(8) In regulation 18 (persons under disability)—

(a) for "mentally disordered person" substitute "person who lacks capacity"; and
(b) for "receiver" substitute "deputy".

(9) In regulation 33 (application to Scotland)—

(a) in paragraph (a), for "mentally disordered person" substitute "person who lacks capacity"; and
(b) in paragraph (b), for "receiver in relation to a mentally disordered person" substitute "deputy in relation to a person who lacks capacity".

(10) In regulation 34(2) (application to Northern Ireland)—

(a) in paragraph (a), for "mentally disordered person" substitute "person who lacks capacity"; and
(b) in paragraph (b), for "receiver in relation to a mentally disordered person" substitute "deputy in relation to a person who lacks capacity".

(11) In regulation 35(2)(a) (application to the Isle of Man), for "receiver in relation to a mentally disordered person" substitute "deputy in relation to a person who lacks capacity".

(12) In regulation 36 (application to the Channel Islands)—

(a) in paragraphs (2)(a) and (3)(a), for "mentally disordered person" substitute "person who lacks capacity"; and
(b) in paragraphs (2)(b) and (3)(b), for "receiver in relation to a mentally disordered person" substitute "deputy in relation to a person who lacks capacity".

Road Vehicles (Construction and Use) Regulations 1986

10 In paragraph 5(1)(c) of Part 1 of Schedule 3B (authorised sealers) to the Road Vehicles (Construction and Use) Regulations 1986, for the words from "patient" to "Mental Health Act 1983", substitute "person who lacks capacity (within the meaning of the Mental Capacity Act 2005 (c 9)) to carry on the activities covered by the authorisation".

Operation of Public Service Vehicles (Partnership) Regulations 1986

11 On the entry as to section 57(2) of the Public Passenger Vehicles Act 1981, in column 2 of Part 1 of the Schedule to the Operation of Public Service Vehicles (Partnership) Regulations 1986, for the words from "patient" to "Mental Health Act 1983", substitute "person who lacks capacity (within the meaning of the Mental Capacity Act 2005 (c 9)) to carry on the activities covered by the licence".

Insolvency Rules 1986

12 (1) The Insolvency Rules 1986 are amended in accordance with this paragraph.

(2) In rule 4.214 (witness unfit for examination)—

- (a) in paragraph (1)—
  - (i) omit the words "mental disorder or", and
  - (ii) before "is suffering" insert "is a person who lacks capacity within the meaning of the Mental Capacity Act 2005 (c 9) or", and
- (b) in paragraph (3)(a), for the words "patient within the meaning of the Mental Health Act 1983" substitute "person who lacks capacity within the meaning of the Mental Capacity Act 2005".

(3) In rule 6.174 (bankrupt unfit for examination)—

- (a) in paragraph (1)—
  - (i) omit the words "mental disorder or", and
  - (ii) before "is suffering" insert "is a person who lacks capacity within the meaning of the Mental Capacity Act 2005 or", and
- (b) in paragraph (3)(a), for the words "patient within the meaning of the Mental Health Act 1983", substitute "person who lacks capacity within the meaning of the Mental Capacity Act 2005".

(4) In the heading to Part 7 of Chapter 7, for "Persons Incapable of Managing their Affairs", substitute "Persons who Lack Capacity to Manage their Affairs".

(5) In rule 7.43 (introductory)—

- (a) in paragraph (1), for "is incapable of managing and administering his property and affairs", substitute "lacks capacity within the meaning of the Mental Capacity Act 2005 to manage and administer his property and affairs"; and
- (b) in paragraph (1)(a), for "mental disorder within the meaning of the Mental Health Act 1983", substitute "lacking capacity within the meaning of the Mental Capacity Act 2005".

(6) In paragraph 4.64 of Part 4 of Schedule 4, Forms Index (companies winding up)—

- (a) after the words "person who", insert "lacks capacity to manage and administer his property and affairs or"; and
- (b) for the words "mental disorder or", substitute "a".

(7) In paragraph 6.57 of Part 6 of Schedule 4, Forms Index (bankruptcy)—

- (a) after the words "bankrupt who", insert "lacks capacity to manage and administer his property and affairs or"; and
- (b) for the words "mental disorder or", substitute "a".

(8) For form 4.64 in Schedule 4 (forms), substitute the form in Schedule 2 (Part 1).

(9) For form 6.57 in Schedule 4 (forms), substitute the form in Schedule 2 (Part 2).

Non-contentious Probate Rules 1987

13 (1) Rule 31 (grant to attorneys) and 35 (grants in case of mental incapacity) of the Non-contentious Probate Rules 1987 are amended in accordance with this paragraph.

(2) For rule 31(3) substitute—

"(3) Where the donor referred to in paragraph (1) above lacks capacity within the meaning of the Mental Capacity Act 2005 (c 9) and the attorney is acting under an enduring power of attorney or lasting power of attorney, the application shall be made in accordance with rule 35."

(3) For rule 35, in the title, for the words "mental incapacity" substitute "lack of mental capacity".

(4) In rule 35(1), for the words "incapable person" substitute "person who lacks capacity within the meaning of the Mental Capacity Act 2005".

(5) In rule 35(2)—

- (a) for the words "is by reason of mental incapacity incapable of managing", substitute "lacks capacity within the meaning of the Mental Capacity Act 2005 to manage";
- (b) for each reference to an incapable person substitute a reference to a person who lacks capacity within the meaning of the Mental Capacity Act 2005; and
- (c) at the end of sub-paragraph (b), insert "or lasting power of attorney".

(6) In rule 35(4), for the words "incapable person", substitute "person who lacks capacity within the meaning of the Mental Capacity Act 2005".

Judicial Pension (Preservation of Benefits) Order 1988

14 In Schedule 2 to the Judicial Pension (Preservation of Benefits) Order 1988, omit the reference to a Master of the Court of Protection except in the case of a person holding that office immediately before the commencement of this paragraph or who had previously retired from that office or died.

Judicial Pensions (Requisite Benefits) Order 1988

15 In Schedule 2 (office) to the Judicial Pensions (Requisite Benefits) Order 1988, omit the reference to a Master of the Court of Protection except in the case of a person holding that office immediately before the commencement of this paragraph or who had previously retired from that office or died.

Church of England Pensions Regulations 1988

16 (1) Regulation 30 (payment of pensions in respect of persons suffering from mental disorder) of the Church of England Pensions Regulations 1988 is amended in accordance with this paragraph.

(2) In paragraph (1)—

- (a) for the words "is incapable by reason of mental disorder within the meaning of the Mental Health Act, 1983, of managing and administering", substitute "lacks capacity (within the meaning of the Mental Capacity Act 2005 (c 9)) to manage and administer"; and
- (b) in sub-paragraph (a), for the words "suffering from mental disorder", substitute "a person lacking capacity (within the meaning of the Mental Capacity Act 2005) to manage and administer his property and affairs".

(3) In paragraph (2)—

- (a) for the words "authority having jurisdiction under Part VII of the Mental Health Act, 1983", substitute "Court of Protection"; and
- (b) for each reference to "that authority" substitute a reference to "the Court of Protection".

(4) In paragraph (3)—

- (a) for the words "the authority having jurisdiction under Part VII of the Mental Health Act, 1983 give", substitute "the Court of Protection gives"; and
- (b) for the words "that authority", substitute "the Court of Protection".

Savings Certificates Regulations 1991

17 (1) The Savings Certificates Regulations 1991 are amended in accordance with this paragraph.

(2) In regulation 2(1) (interpretation), omit the entries for "mentally disordered person" and "receiver" and in the appropriate alphabetical position, insert—

(a) ""deputy" in the application of these Regulations to England and Wales, means, in relation to any decision made for a person who lacks capacity, a deputy appointed by the Court of Protection for that person with power to make decisions in relation to the matters in question;"; and
(b) ""person who lacks capacity" means a person who lacks capacity within the meaning of the Mental Capacity Act 2005 (c 9);".

(3) In regulation 4(2)(c) (persons entitled to purchase and hold certificates), for "mentally disordered person, by his receiver" substitute "person who lacks capacity, by his deputy".

(4) In regulation 9 (repayment in case of persons under 7 years of age and mentally disordered persons)—

(a) in the title, for "mentally disordered persons" substitute "persons who lack capacity";
(b) in paragraph (2), for "mentally disordered person shall be made by his receiver" substitute "person who lacks capacity shall be made by his deputy"; and
(c) in paragraph (4), for the words from "mentally disordered person for" to "of the mentally disordered person" substitute "person who lacks capacity in respect of whom no deputy has been appointed, the Director of Savings may, if he thinks fit, pay the whole or any part of the amount repayable in respect of the certificate to any person who satisfies him that he will apply the payment for the maintenance or otherwise for the benefit of the person who lacks capacity".

(5) In regulation 10(1)(a) (repayment in case of certificate held by persons jointly)—

(a) for "mentally disordered person" substitute "person who lacks capacity"; and
(b) for "receiver" substitute "person who lacks capacity".

(6) In regulation 18 (persons under disability)—

(a) for "mentally disordered person" substitute "person who lacks capacity"; and
(b) for "receiver" substitute "deputy".

(7) In regulation 33 (application to Scotland)—

(a) in paragraph (a), for "mentally disordered person" substitute "person who lacks capacity"; and
(b) in paragraph (b), for "receiver in relation to a mentally disordered person" substitute "deputy in relation to a person who lacks capacity".

(8) In regulation 34 (application to Northern Ireland)—

(a) in paragraph (b), for "mentally disordered person" substitute "person who lacks capacity"; and
(b) in paragraph (c), for "receiver in relation to a mentally disordered person" substitute "deputy in relation to a person who lacks capacity".

(9) In regulation 35(2) (application to the Isle of Man)—

(a) in paragraph (a), for "mentally disordered person" substitute "person who lacks capacity"; and
(b) in paragraph (b), for "receiver in relation to any act or thing done in respect of a mentally disordered person shall be construed as a reference to a receiver" substitute "deputy in relation to any decision made for a person who lacks capacity shall be construed as a reference to a deputy".

(10) In regulation 36 (application to the Channel Islands)—

(a) in paragraphs (2)(a) and (3)(a), for "mentally disordered person" substitute "person who lacks capacity"; and
(b) in paragraphs (2)(b) and (3)(b), for "receiver in relation to a mentally disordered person" substitute "deputy in relation to a person who lacks capacity".

(11) In paragraph 2 of Part 1 of Schedule 1 (persons entitled to hold index-linked certificates to be purchased before 7th September 1981), for "receiver on behalf of and in the name of a mentally disordered person" substitute "deputy on behalf of and in the name of a person who lacks capacity".

Savings Certificates (Children's Bonus Bonds) Regulations 1991

18 (1) The Savings Certificates (Children's Bonus Bonds) Regulations 1991 are amended in accordance with this paragraph.

(2) In regulation 2(1) (interpretation), omit the entries for "mentally disordered person" and "receiver" and, in the appropriate alphabetical position, insert—

(a) ""deputy" in the application of these Regulations to England and Wales, means, in relation to any decision made for a person who lacks capacity, a deputy appointed by the Court of Protection for that person with power to make decisions in relation to the matters in question;"; and

(b) ""person who lacks capacity" means a person who lacks capacity within the meaning of the Mental Capacity Act 2005 (c 9);".

(3) In regulation 8(2) (repayment in case of persons under 16 years of age), for "mentally disordered person" substitute "person who lacks capacity".

(4) In regulation 9 (repayment in case of mentally disordered persons)—

(a) in the title, for "mentally disordered persons" substitute "persons who lack capacity";

(b) in paragraph (1), for "mentally disordered person shall be made by his receiver" substitute "person who lacks capacity shall be made by his deputy"; and

(c) in paragraph (2), for "mentally disordered person for whose estate no receiver" substitute "person who lacks capacity for whom no deputy".

(5) In regulation 15 (persons under disability)—

(a) for "mentally disordered person" substitute "person who lacks capacity"; and

(b) for "receiver" substitute "deputy".

(6) In regulation 29 (application to Scotland)—

(a) in paragraph (a), for "mentally disordered person" substitute "person who lacks capacity"; and

(b) in paragraph (b), for "receiver in relation to a mentally disordered person" substitute "deputy in relation to a person who lacks capacity".

(7) In regulation 30 (application to Northern Ireland)—

(a) in paragraph (a), for "mentally disordered person" substitute "person who lacks capacity"; and

(b) in paragraph (b), for "receiver in relation to a mentally disordered person" substitute "deputy in relation to a person who lacks capacity".

(8) In regulation 31(2) (application to the Isle of Man)—

(a) in paragraph (a), for "mentally disordered person" substitute "person who lacks capacity"; and

(b) in paragraph (b), for "receiver in relation to any act or thing done in respect of a mentally disordered person shall be construed as a reference to a receiver" substitute "deputy in relation to any decision made for a person who lacks capacity shall be construed as a reference to a deputy".

(9) In regulation 32 (application to the Channel Islands)—

(a) in paragraphs (2)(a) and (3)(a), for "mentally disordered person" substitute "person who lacks capacity"; and

(b) in paragraphs (2)(b) and (3)(b), for "receiver in relation to a mentally disordered person" substitute "deputy in relation to a person who lacks capacity".

Judicial Pensions (Transfer Between Judicial Pension Schemes) Regulations 1995

19 In Schedule 2 (existing judicial scheme judicial offices included in each arrangement) to the Judicial Pensions (Transfer Between Judicial Pension Schemes) Regulations 1995, under the cross-heading "District Judiciary Scheme", omit the reference to a Master of the Court of Protection except in the case of a person holding that office immediately before the commencement of this paragraph or who had previously retired from that office or died.

Judicial Pensions (Additional Voluntary Contributions) Regulations 1995

20 In Schedule 4 (existing judicial scheme judicial offices included in each arrangement) to the Judicial Pensions (Additional Voluntary Contributions) Regulations 1995, under the cross-heading "District Judiciary Scheme", omit the reference to a Master of the Court of Protection except in the case of a person holding that office immediately before the commencement of this paragraph or who had previously retired from that office or died.

Goods Vehicles (Licensing of Operators) Regulations 1995

21 (1) Regulations 29 (partnerships) and 31 (continuance of licence on death, bankruptcy etc) of the Goods Vehicles (Licensing of Operators) Regulations 1995 are amended in accordance with this paragraph.

(2) In regulation 29(11)(b), for the words from "patient" to "Mental Health Act 1983", substitute "person who lacks capacity (within the meaning of the Mental Capacity Act 2005 (c 9)) to carry on the activities covered by the licence".

(3) In regulation 31—

- (a) in paragraph (2), for the words from "patient" to "Mental Health Act 1983", substitute "person who lacks capacity (within the meaning of the Mental Capacity Act 2005) to carry on the activities covered by the licence"; and
- (b) in paragraph (3), for the words from "patient" to "Mental Health Act 1983", substitute "person who lacks capacity (within the meaning of the Mental Capacity Act 2005) to carry on the activities covered by the licence".

Landfill Tax Regulations 1996

22 For regulation 33(1C)(a) (bodies eligible for approval) of the Landfill Tax Regulations 1996, substitute—

"(a) in England and Wales, the person lacks capacity within the meaning of the Mental Capacity Act 2005 (c 9) to administer and manage his property and affairs;".

Family Law Act 1996 (Allocation of Proceedings) Order 1997

23 In article 8(2)(b) (transfer from family proceedings court to county court) of the Family Law Act 1996 (Allocation of Proceedings) Order 1997, for the words "a person who, by reason of mental disorder within the meaning of the Mental Health Act 1983, is incapable of managing and administering his property and affairs" substitute "a person lacking capacity within the meaning of the Mental Capacity Act 2005 (c 9) to conduct the proceedings".

General Chiropractic Council (Constitution and Procedure) Rules Order 1999

24 In rule 2 (grounds of removal) of the General Chiropractic Council (Constitution and Procedure) Rules Order of Council 1999, in paragraph (1)(d) for "or is otherwise incapable, by reason of mental disorder, of properly managing his property or affairs", substitute "or lacks capacity within the meaning of the Mental Capacity Act 2005 (c 9), to properly manage his property or affairs".

Health Service Medicines (Price Control Appeals) Regulations 2000

25 In regulation 7 (appointment of tribunal) of the Health Service Medicines (Price Control Appeals) Regulations 2000, in paragraph (3)(b), for "incapacity" substitute "lack of capacity (within the meaning of the Mental Capacity Act 2005 (c 9))".

Ionising Radiation (Medical Exposure) Regulations 2000

26 In regulation 7 (optimisation) of the Ionising Radiation (Medical Exposure) Regulations 2000—

- (a) in paragraph (5)(b), after "capacity" insert "(within the meaning of the Mental Capacity Act 2005 (c 9) in the case of a child aged sixteen or seventeen)"; and
- (b) in paragraph (5)(c), after "capacity" insert "(within the meaning of the Mental Capacity Act 2005)".

Carers (Services) and Direct Payments (Amendment) (England) Regulations 2001

27 For regulation 2(2) (services of an intimate nature and prescribed circumstances) of the Carers (Services) and Direct Payments (Amendment) (England) Regulations 2001, substitute—

"(2) Where a service (A) is being delivered to the person cared for, a service of an intimate nature may be provided if—

(a) during the delivery of service A, the person cared for asks the person delivering that service to provide a service of an intimate nature;
(b) the person lacks capacity (within the meaning of the Mental Capacity Act 2005 (c 9)) to consent to the provision of a service of an intimate nature and it is provided in accordance with the principles of that Act; or
(c) except where sub-paragraph (b) applies, the person cared for is in a situation in which he is likely to suffer serious personal harm unless a service of an intimate nature is provided to him and the person providing service A reasonably believes that it is necessary to provide a service of an intimate nature because the likelihood of serious personal harm to the person cared for is imminent.".

Care Homes Regulations 2001

28 (1) The Care Homes Regulations 2001 are amended in accordance with this paragraph.

(2) In regulation 2 (interpretation), in paragraph (1), in the appropriate alphabetical position, insert—

(a) ""the 2005 Act" means the Mental Capacity Act 2005 (c 9);" and
(b) ""lacks capacity" means lacks capacity within the meaning of the 2005 Act;".

(3) In regulation 13 (further requirements as to health and welfare), for paragraph (7) substitute—

"(7) The registered person shall ensure that no service user is subject to physical restraint unless—

(a) restraint of the kind employed is the only practicable means of securing the welfare of that or any other service user and there are exceptional circumstances; or
(b) in the case of a person who lacks capacity in relation to the matter in question, the act meets the conditions of section 6 of the 2005 Act.".

Private and Voluntary Health Care (England) Regulations 2001

29 (1) The Private and Voluntary Health Care (England) Regulations 2001 are amended in accordance with this paragraph.

(2) In regulation 2 (interpretation)—

(a) in paragraph (1), at the beginning insert—

""the 2005 Act" means the Mental Capacity Act 2005 (c 9);"; and

(b) at the end, add—

"(4) For the purpose of any decision required to be made under these Regulations as to a person's capacity, lack of capacity shall be interpreted in accordance with the 2005 Act and any reference to a person who lacks capacity shall be construed accordingly.".

(3) In regulation 9 (policies and procedures), in paragraph (3)—

(a) in sub-paragraph (a), for "competence" substitute "capacity";
(b) in sub-paragraph (b), for "competent patient" substitute "patient who has capacity"; and
(c) for sub-paragraph (c), substitute—
"(c) in the case of patient who lacks capacity the requirements of the 2005 Act are complied with before any treatment proposed for him is administered; and".

(4) In regulation 16 (care and welfare of patients), in paragraphs (1) and (3), after "so far as practicable," insert "(and, where the person lacks capacity, in accordance with the principles of the 2005 Act)".

(5) In regulation 35 (resuscitation), in paragraph (2)—

(a) in sub-paragraph (a), for "are competent" substitute "have the capacity"; and
(b) after sub-paragraph (a), insert—
"(aa) take proper account of valid and applicable advance decisions made by patients under the 2005 Act;".

(6) In regulation 37 (surgical procedures)—

(a) in paragraph (2), after "a patient" insert "who has the capacity to do so";
(b) in paragraph (3), for "is not competent" substitute "lacks the capacity"; and
(c) after paragraph (3), insert—

"(4) In the case of a patient who lacks capacity to consent to surgery, the registered person shall take proper account of any valid and applicable advance decisions made by the patient under the 2005 Act.".

Domiciliary Care Agencies Regulations 2002

30 (1) The Domiciliary Care Agencies Regulations 2002 are amended in accordance with this paragraph.

(2) In regulation 2 (interpretation), in paragraph (1), in the appropriate alphabetical position, insert—

""the 2005 Act" means the Mental Capacity Act 2005 (c 9);
"lacks capacity" means lacks capacity within the meaning of the 2005 Act;".

(3) In regulation 14 (arrangements for the provision of personal care), for paragraph (10) substitute—

"(10) The registered person shall ensure that no service user is subject to physical restraint unless—

(a) restraint of the kind employed is the only practicable means of securing the welfare of that or any other service user and there are exceptional circumstances; or
(b) in the case of a person who lacks capacity in relation to the matter in question, the act meets the conditions of section 6 of the 2005 Act.".

Land Registration Rules 2003

31 (1) Rule 61 (documents executed by attorney) of, and Schedule 3 (forms referred to in rule 206) to, the Land Registration Rules 2003 are amended in accordance with this paragraph.

(2) In rule 61—

(a) for paragraph (1)(c) substitute—
"(c) a document which under section 4 of the Evidence and Powers of Attorney Act 1940, paragraph 16 of Part 2 of Schedule 1, or paragraph 15(3) of Part 5 of Schedule 4 to the Mental Capacity Act 2005 (c 9) is sufficient evidence of the contents of the power, or"; and
(b) for paragraph (2) substitute—

"(2) If an order or direction under section 22 or 23 of, or paragraph 16 of Part 5 of Schedule 4 to, the Mental Capacity Act 2005 has been made with respect to a power or the donor of the power or the attorney appointed under it, the order or direction must be produced to the registrar.".

(3) In Schedule 3—

(a) in Form 1 (certificate as to execution of power of attorney (rule 61))—
(i) for the first bullet point substitute—

"the power of attorney ("the power") is in existence [and is made and, where required, has been registered under (*state statutory provisions under which the power is made and, where required, has been registered, if applicable*)],", and
(ii) in the fourth bullet point, for the words "or section 7(3) of the Enduring Powers of Attorney Act 1985", substitute—

", paragraph 16 of Part 2 of Schedule 1, or paragraph 15(3) of Part 5 of Schedule 4 to the Mental Capacity Act 2005"; and

(b) in Form 2 (statutory declaration/certificate as to non-revocation for powers more than 12 months old at the date of the disposition for which they are used (rule 62)—
   (i) in the third bullet point, for the words "valid enduring power", substitute "valid lasting or enduring power of attorney",
   (ii) after the third bullet point, insert—

"Where the power is in the form prescribed for a lasting power of attorney—

—that a lasting power of attorney was not created, or
—of circumstances which, if the lasting power of attorney had been created, would have terminated the attorney's authority to act as an attorney, or", and
   (iii) in the heading immediately before the fourth bullet point, after the words "enduring power", insert "of attorney".

National Health Service (Travel Expenses and Remission of Charges) Regulations 2003

32 In regulation 7 (claims to entitlement) of the National Health Service (Travel Expenses and Remission of Charges) Regulations 2003, for paragraph (3), substitute—

"(3) A claim may be made on behalf of another person where that person—

(a) is unable by reason of physical incapacity; or
(b) lacks capacity within the meaning of the Mental Capacity Act 2005 (c 9),

to make the claim himself.".

Child Trust Funds Regulations 2004

33 In regulation 33A(2) (the official solicitor or accountant of court to be the person who has the authority to manage an account) of the Child Trust Funds Regulations 2004, in Condition 4—

(a) in sub-paragraph (a), for the word "receiver" substitute "deputy";
(b) for sub-paragraph (b), substitute "(b) determined that such a person lacks capacity within the meaning of the Mental Capacity Act 2005 (c 9) to manage the child's property and affairs"; and
(c) in the modifications of condition 4 for Scotland—
   (i) in sub-paragraph (b), for the word "receiver" substitute "deputy"; and
   (ii) in sub-paragraph (c), for the word "patient" substitute "person lacking capacity".

National Health Service (Complaints) Regulations 2004

34 In regulation 8 (person who may make complaints) of the National Health Service (Complaints) Regulations 2004—

(a) in paragraph (2)(c), omit "or mental" and "or";
(b) after paragraph(2)(c), insert—
"(cc) is unable because he lacks capacity within the meaning of the Mental Capacity Act 2005 (c 9) to make the complaint himself; or";
(c) in paragraph (3), after "who is" insert "physically"; and
(d) after paragraph (3) insert—

"(3A) In the case of a patient or person affected who lacks capacity within the meaning of the Mental Capacity Act 2005 the representative must be either a person appointed or authorised to act on his behalf under the 2005 Act or another person who, in the opinion of the complaints manager, had or has a sufficient interest in his welfare and is a suitable person to act as representative".

Commonhold Regulations 2004

35 (1) In the table of contents in Schedule 2 (articles of association) to the Commonhold Regulations 2004, under the heading "Votes of Members", for the words "Entitlement to vote—Mental Capacity" substitute "Entitlement to vote—lack of mental capacity".

(2) In the title to article 29 of Schedule 2 (articles of association) to the Commonhold Regulations 2004, for the words "mental incapacity" substitute "lack of mental capacity".

(3) In article 29 of Schedule 2 (articles of association) to the Commonhold Regulations 2004, for each reference to "receiver" substitute a reference to "deputy".

Adult Placement Schemes (England) Regulations 2004

36 (1) The Adult Placement Schemes (England) Regulations 2004 are amended in accordance with this paragraph.

(2) In regulation 2 (interpretation), in the appropriate alphabetical position, insert—

(a) ""the 2005 Act" means the Mental Capacity Act 2005 (c 9);"; and
(b) ""lacks capacity" means lacks capacity within the meaning of the 2005 Act;".

(3) In regulation 17 (carer agreements), for paragraph (2)(e) substitute—

"(e) specifies that a service user is not to be subject to physical restraint unless—
(i) restraint of the kind employed is the only practicable means of securing the welfare of that, or another, service user; or
(ii) in the case of a person who lacks capacity in relation to the matter in question, the act meets the conditions of section 6 of the 2005 Act;'

(4) In regulation 19 (adult placement carer handbook), for paragraph (3)(c) substitute—

"(c) specifies that a service user is not to be subject to physical restraint unless—
(i) restraint of the kind employed is the only practicable means of securing the welfare of that, or another, service user, or
(ii) in the case of a person who lacks capacity in relation to the matter in question, the act meets the conditions of section 6 of the 2005 Act;".

Damages (Variation of Periodical Payments) Order 2005

37 For article 3(d) (defendant's financial resources) of the Damages (Variation of Periodical Payments) Order 2005, substitute—

"(d) the order is made by consent and the claimant is neither a child, nor a person who lacks capacity within the meaning of the Mental Capacity Act 2005 (c 9) to administer and manage his property and affairs nor a patient within the meaning of Part VII of the Mental Health (Northern Ireland) Order 1986,".

Disability Discrimination (Service Providers and Public Authorities Carrying Out Functions) Regulations 2005

38 In regulation 3(b) (circumstances in which mental incapacity justification does not apply) of the Disability Discrimination (Service Providers and Public Authorities Carrying Out Functions) Regulations 2005, for the words "functions conferred by or under Part 7 of the Mental Health Act 1983", substitute "being a deputy appointed by the Court of Protection".

Disability Discrimination (Private Clubs etc) Regulations 2005

39 (1) In regulation 3(b) (circumstances in which mental incapacity justification does not apply) of the Disability Discrimination (Private Clubs etc) Regulations 2005, for the words "functions conferred by or under Part 7 of the Mental Health Act 1983", substitute "being a deputy appointed by the Court of Protection".

(2) In regulation 13(3)(b) (duty of associations to make adjustments: justification) of these regulations, for the words "functions conferred by or under Part 7 of the Mental Health Act 1983", substitute "being a deputy appointed by the Court of Protection".

Disability Discrimination (Premises) Regulations 2006

40 In regulation 2(b) (circumstances in which mental incapacity justification does not apply) of the Disability Discrimination (Premises) Regulations 2006 , for the words "functions conferred by or under Part 7 of the Mental Health Act 1983", substitute "being a deputy appointed by the Court of Protection".

SCHEDULE 2
AMENDMENTS TO FORMS IN SCHEDULE 4 (FORMS) OF THE INSOLVENCY RULES 1986: FORM 4.64 AND FORM 6.57

PART 1
NEW FORM 4.64

A4.283

Rule 4.214 **Form 4.64**

Order as to Examination of Person who Lacks Capacity to Manage and Administer his Property and Affairs or is Suffering from Physical Affliction or Disability

(TITLE)

Mr Registrar in chambers

(a) "The official receiver" or insert name and address of applicant and the capacity in which he makes the application

Upon the application of (a)

And upon hearing

And upon reading the evidence

(b) Insert name of examinee

And the court being satisfied that (b) lacks capacity within the meaning of the Mental Capacity Act 2005 to manage and administer his property and affairs or is suffering from physical affliction or disability and [is unfit to undergo a public examination.

It is ordered that the order dated be stayed]

[is unfit to attend the public examination fixed by the order dated

It is ordered that the said order be varied as follows]

Dated ____________________

(c) Delete warning where the order for public examination is stayed

Warning to person to be examined (c)

If you fail without reasonable excuse to attend your public examination at the time and place set out in the order above you will be liable to be arrested without further notice (section 134(2) of the Insolvency Act 1986).

You will also be guilty of contempt of court (section 134(1) of the Insolvency Act 1986) and liable to be committed to prison or fined.

PART 2
NEW FORM 6.57

A4.284

Rule 4.214	**Form 4.64** **Order as to Examination of Person who Lacks Capacity to Manage and Administer his Property and Affairs or is Suffering from Physical Affliction or Disability**
	(TITLE) Mr Registrar in chambers
(a) "The official receiver" or insert name and address of applicant and the capacity in which he makes the application	Upon the application of (a)
	And upon hearing And upon reading the evidence
(b) Insert name of examinee	And the court being satisfied that (b) lacks capacity within the meaning of the Mental Capacity Act 2005 to manage and administer his property and affairs or is suffering from physical affliction or disability and [is unfit to undergo a public examination. It is ordered that the order dated be stayed] [is unfit to attend the public examination fixed by the order dated It is ordered that the said order be varied as follows] Dated ____________________________
(c) Delete warning where the order for public examination is stayed	Warning to person to be examined (c)
	If you fail without reasonable excuse to attend your public examination at the time and place set out in the order above you will be liable to be arrested without further notice (section 134(2) of the Insolvency Act 1986). You will also be guilty of contempt of court (section 134(1) of the Insolvency Act 1986) and liable to be committed to prison or fined.

Appendix 5

TABLE OF FORMS FOR LPAS AND EPAS

A5.1

FORMS FOR LPAs AND EPAs

The Lasting Powers of Attorney, Enduring Powers of Attorney and Public Guardian Regulations 2007 (SI 2007/1253) Schedules 1–8								
Schedule	*1*	2	3	*4*	5	6	*7*[1]	*8*
Form no	LPA PA LPA PW	LPA 001	LPA 002	LPA 003A LPA 003B	LPA 004	LPA 005		
Regulation	Reg 5	Reg 10	Reg 11	Reg 13	Reg 17	Reg 20	Reg 23	Reg 24
Instrument or notice	Part 1: Creating property and affairs LPA Part 2: Creating personal welfare LPA	Notice of intention to register LPA	Application to register LPA	Part 1: Notice to attorney of application to register. Objections on LPA 7. Part 2: Notice to donor of application to register. Objections on LPA 6.	Notice of registration of LPA.	Disclaimer by donee of LPA	Notice of intention to apply to register EPA.	Application to register EPA.

1 As amended by reg 12 of the Public Guardian (Fees etc) Regulations 2007, SI 2007/2051.

Index

[all references are to paragraph number]